# LONGMAN

# GRAMMAR OF SPOKEN AND WRITTEN ENGLISH

# LONGMAN

# GRAMMAR

# OF SPOKEN

# AND WRITTEN

# ENGLISH

Douglas Biber
Stig Johansson
Geoffrey Leech
Susan Conrad
Edward Finegan

FOREWORD BY
Randolph Quirk

Pearson Education Limited
*Edinburgh Gate*
*Harlow*
*Essex CM20 2JE*
*England*
*and Associated Companies throughout the World.*

Visit our website: http://www.longman.com

First published 1999
Ninth impression 2011

Words that the editors have reason to believe constitute trademarks have been
described as such. However, neither the presence nor the absence of such a
description should be regarded as affecting the legal status of any trademark.

ISBN 978-0-582-23725-4

Library of Congress Cataloging-in-Publication Data
Longman grammar of spoken and written English / Douglas Biber . . . [et al.];
foreword by Randolph Quirk.
    p.     cm.
    Includes bibliographical references and index.
    ISBN 0–582–23725–4 (hardcover)
    1. English language—Grammar.    I. Biber, Douglas.
PE1112.L66  1999
428.2—dc21                          99–29033
                                           CIP

British Library Cataloguing-in-Publication Data
A catalogue record for this book is available from
the British Library.

Designed by First Edition, London
Set in Minion and Helvetica by MFK Mendip,
Frome, Somerset
Printed in China
SWTC/09

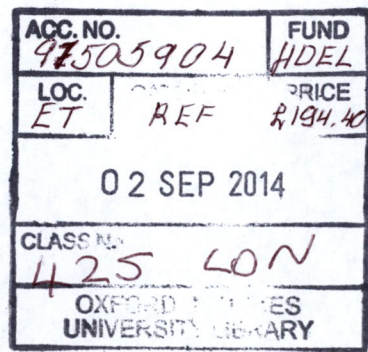

# Foreword

Douglas Biber and his numerous colleagues are to be congratulated on a book so replete with interesting and innovative features, not least by way of frequency data. For anyone planning corpus-based grammatical study, of any language on earth, the *LGSWE* will rapidly establish itself as indispensable. And since any such study must inevitably involve collaborative teamwork, some examination of Biber's management skills in organizing this huge enterprise will not come amiss either, given the size and diversity of the American and British corpora analysed and the need to coordinate the activity at centres many thousands of kilometres apart.

The co-authors were lucky in being led by a man of such determination, vision, energy, and fine track record in corpus theory and computational practice. But Biber was lucky in his co-authors, too. There was his Arizona colleague, Susan Conrad, who, in addition to a major contribution to the actual writing, invested much time and energy in the relevant research from the earliest stages of the project. There was also, far away in Scandinavia, the highly experienced grammarian, Stig Johansson, who played a key role in the research, planning, and writing. And Biber was especially lucky in having as his partner in the massive task, both of general design and of implementing detailed insights, a scholar of Geoffrey Leech's stature in the fields of semantics, pragmatics, grammatology, and computational linguistics.

**Randolph Quirk**
University College London
March 1999

# Abbreviations and symbols

| | |
|---|---|
| ACAD | academic prose |
| AmE | American English |
| A | adverbial |
| $A_c$ | circumstance adverbial |
| $A_l$ | linking adverbial |
| $A_s$ | stance adverbial |
| BrE | British English |
| *CGEL* | R. Quirk et al., *A Comprehensive Grammar of the English Language* |
| CONV | conversation |
| FICT | fiction writing |
| *LDOCE* | *Longman Dictionary of Contemporary English* |
| LSWE Corpus | Longman Spoken and Written English Corpus |
| NEWS | news writing |
| O | object |
| $O_d$ | direct object |
| $O_i$ | indirect object |
| $O_p$ | prepositional object |
| P | predicative |
| $P_o$ | object predicative |
| $P_s$ | subject predicative |
| S | subject |
| v. | versus (*i.e.* contrasted with) |
| V | verb (phrase) |
| ( ) | parentheses ( ) enclose an optional part of an example or a formula |
| <...> | an omitted section of a corpus example |
| <–> | the location of ellipsis (in an example) |
| <sic> | (in an example) confirmation that the example is accurately reproduced: e.g. *Dicken's* <sic> *famous novel* |
| < > | an editorial comment on an example: e.g. <unclear> |
| [ ] | brackets *[ ]* in an example enclose either: (a) a grammatically defined constituent, such as a phrase or a clause, or (b) a part of an example highlighted for attention. Primary highlighting is signalled by **bold face** and secondary highlighting by *[ ]*. |
| – | in transcribed speech, a dash at the end of a word signals that it is incomplete, i.e. is a word fragment: e.g. *thi–, this* |
| – | in transcribed speech, a dash signals a pause |
| * | unacceptable: e.g. *\*They needed not leave.* |
| ? | marginally acceptable: e.g. *?a most promising pupil of hers* |
| ?* | on the boundary of unacceptability: e.g. *?\*excuse me a little* |
| † | truncated example |

# Preface

Since its planning first began in 1992, this book has gone through a complex process of gestation involving many kinds of collaborative work—computational, editorial, and authorial. The research-based work required for this project has been on a scale probably unmatched in the writing of any previous grammar of the English language. As authors, we ourselves have individually played somewhat varied roles in the research project and the writing of the book. Further, we were aided from the start by the dedicated efforts of several research assistants, and at various points along the way helped by the expertise of academic reviewers and advisers, as well as editors and publishers. In this Preface we briefly explain our own individual roles in the work, and pay tribute to the many friends and associates to whom we owe a great deal for their valued aid and support.

As for our contributions as authors, it should be explained that, although each author took on individual responsibility for the initial drafting of specific chapters, the chapter drafts subsequently went through a number of stages of redrafting and editing. The result is that the volume as it stands is the joint responsibility of all authors. For the record, however, we identify here the author or authors principally associated with each chapter: Chapter 1: DB; Chapters 2, 3, and 4: SJ; Chapters 5 and 6: DB; Chapter 7: EF (first draft), DB, and SC; Chapters 8 and 9: DB; Chapter 10: SC; Chapter 11: SJ; Chapters 12 and 13: DB; Chapter 14: EF (first draft), GL; Appendix: DB. In later stages, GL and DB assumed primary editorial responsibility for the whole book, while DB worked with Meg Davies on the conceptual index and with Jenia Walter and Victoria Clark on the lexical index.

The initial three or four years of the project were largely taken up with planning and research. Authorial/editorial meetings took place at Cambridge, London, Feusisberg (Switzerland), Flagstaff (Arizona), and Lancaster. DB, as lead author, took on the principal role of organizing and directing the corpus investigations at Northern Arizona University, Flagstaff, on which most of the quantitative information in this grammar is based. At the same time, other authors had access to the LSWE Corpus at their own universities, and were able to undertake their own corpus-based research at their home site. Although the authors were widely separated in geographical terms, they kept in close and detailed contact throughout the project by electronic mail and other means. The work of the international team was thus well balanced and integrated in terms of the spread of effort between North America and Europe.

One curious minor dilemma which the team faced, in trying to produce a book giving equal weight to American and British English, was in the choice of spelling standard: should we adopt British or American spelling conventions? Either choice would appear to contravene the ideal of an objectively international view of the English language. In the end we resorted to a chapter-by-chapter solution to this dilemma: each chapter was printed in accordance with the spelling conventions adopted by its main author or authors.

At Northern Arizona University, in addition to the growing contribution of Susan Conrad (who began as a research assistant but became a co-author during the course of the book's composition), very important contributions to the research project were made by Marie Helt and Erika Konrad, who became key members of the Arizona project team. In addition, Marie's PhD research on discourse markers provided a significant intellectual input to Chapter 14. Other contributions were made by Susan Carkin, Sarah

Rilling, Jennifer Rey, and Jena Burges. Also at NAU, Jenia Walter and Victoria Clark helped with the compilation of the lexical index.

At an early stage in the preparation of the book, the authors benefited from the comments of distinguished academics who reviewed the plan, and read one or two 'trial' chapters: Florent Aarts, Paul Bruthiaux, Paul J. Hopper, Yoshihiko Ikegami, Graeme Kennedy, Christian Mair, Keith Mitchell, Randolph Quirk (Lord Quirk), Jan Svartvik, and Michael Stubbs. We also received valuable comments from Bengt Altenberg and Gunnel Tottie, who read draft versions of individual chapters. (Bengt's online *ICAME* Bibliography also provided us with an extremely useful starting point for our own Bibliography.) At a later stage, pre-final draft chapters were presented to the Longman Linglex Advisory Committee, where again a strong impetus to improve the book's content and presentation was provided by valuable and (often) trenchant critiques from a group of leading British linguists, under the chairmanship of Lord Quirk: Rod Bolitho, Gillian Brown, David Crystal, Philip Scholfield, Katie Wales, John Wells, and Yorick Wilks. Alan Tonkyn offered useful advice and information on C-units (Chapter 14).

Our indebtedness to Lord Quirk goes further: we acknowledge our debt to *A Comprehensive Grammar of the English Language*, by Randolph Quirk, Sidney Greenbaum, Geoffrey Leech, and Jan Svartvik (Longman, 1985), as a previous large-scale grammar of English from which we have taken inspiration for a project of similar scope. From *CGEL* we have also borrowed, with few exceptions, the grammatical framework of concepts and terminology which has provided the present book with its descriptive apparatus. While advances in corpus technology have allowed us to go beyond *CGEL* in important ways—particularly in the exemplification and quantitative investigation of grammar across different language varieties, spoken and written— *CGEL's* attention to detail and comprehensive coverage is something to which this grammar does not attempt to aspire. In many ways, the two grammars complement rather than compete with each other.

To one member of the Linglex advisory committee we owe a special debt—Philip Scholfield, who, when the book was being assembled for publication, went through it with a fine-tooth comb in his capacity as editor for style and presentation. This reference to 'style and presentation' does not adequately represent Philip's contribution, which led to much redrafting in the interests of consistency of style, terminology, layout, and level of detail. We also owe a special debt to Meg Davies for assuming primary responsibility for the conceptual index and compiling the index under very strict time constraints.

Finally we take the opportunity of this Preface to pay tribute to members of the Longman staff and editorial team who have steered this project from its inception to the final stages of publication. Sheila Dallas, although she came late to the project, played a crucial role in seeing the book from final draft stage through several proofs into print: she dedicated herself to the success of the project, working beyond the call of duty to get chapters edited to strict deadlines. Adam Gadsby, the publisher in charge of this book project from beginning to end, was a dependable and supportive colleague, motivating us through thick and thin in the progress of the book. He not only kept us on track organizationally, but also contributed a great deal to the conceptual development of the grammar. Last but far from least, we express our gratitude to Della Summers, the Director of Longman Dictionaries, as prime mover of this project who, at a time when the idea was as strange to us as to the rest of the world, inspired us to plan a truly corpus-based grammar, and persuaded us to turn that vision into a reality.

DB  SJ  GL  SC  EF

# Contents summary

# Contents in detail

# 5 Verbs 357

**9 The form and function of complement clauses** 657

# Symbols and notational conventions

## 1 Reference to corpus examples

By far the majority of examples and text extracts given in this book are of authentic discourse taken from the texts and transcriptions in our Corpus (see sections 1.1, 1.4 of Chapter 1). These examples are marked as coming from one of the four main subdivisions of the corpus:

| | |
|---|---|
| (CONV) | *conversation transcription* |
| (FICT) | *fiction text* |
| (NEWS) | *newspaper text* |
| (ACAD) | *academic text* |

Some examples are truncated to save space. These are marked with an icon (†) occurring after one of the above abbreviations:

| | |
|---|---|
| (CONV†), (FICT†), (NEWS†), (ACAD†) | *truncated examples* |

Truncated examples, showing an incomplete sentence or conversational turn, are used only when the omitted parts are judged to have no bearing on the grammatical point being illustrated, and where overly long examples might distract rather than help the reader. For example:

a   *Every atom **has** a dense nucleus.* (ACAD†)
b   *Every atom **has** a dense nucleus that contains practically all of the mass of the atom.* (ACAD)

Example *a* is a truncated version of the complete sentence in example *b*. Note that even with truncation, dispensable material is almost always omitted from the beginning or end of an example, not from the middle. In this sense, virtually every example quoted is a continuous 'slice of linguistic reality'. Occasional cases of medial omission are marked by the insertion of <...> at the point where the omission occurs: an example can be seen in Text sample 1, 1.2.1.

| | |
|---|---|
| <...> | signals *a part of an example where words have been omitted* |

Other abbreviations used to label examples (and also used in running text) are:

| | | |
|---|---|---|
| AmE | *American English* | These abbreviations are also used more generally, in referring to American and British varieties of English, as represented in the American and British parts of our Corpus. |
| BrE | *British English* | |

## 2 Reference to invented examples

In a few cases, invented examples which are not from the Corpus are used to show a contrast between two variant sentences, one of which is authentic and the other reconstructed to act as a comparison. These invented examples are signalled negatively, by the fact that they are not followed by a bracketed label such as (CONV). The following warning symbols are sometimes attached to invented examples:

| * [preceding] | *an example which is unacceptable in English* |
| ? [preceding] | *an example which is marginally acceptable* |
| ?* [preceding] | *an example which is on the boundary of unacceptability* |

e.g.: *They needed not have.*
*?a most promising pupil of hers*
*?*excuse me a little*

## 3 Symbols and conventions used within examples

| **bold face** | marks | *the main item highlighted for attention in an example*. |
| *[ ]* | marks | 1. (where needed) *a second element highlighted for attention.* |
| | or | 2. the boundaries of *grammatical units* (phrases, clauses, etc.). |

e.g.: 1. *Watch out! [Here] **comes Amanda!*** (CONV)
2. *I hope [[you][can talk][to me][about it]]* (CONV†)

| <–> | marks a point in the text where an *ellipsis* occurs (see 3.7) |
| < > | 1. occasionally marks *ellipted words* in examples (given in *italics*) |
| | 2. otherwise marks a *comment* relating to an example, e.g. |
| <sic> | (in an example) confirms that the example is accurately reproduced, in spite of appearances. |

e.g. *Dicken's <sic> famous novel*

## 4 Symbols and conventions used in transcriptions of speech

| *A:* | Where spoken examples contain contributions from *different speakers*, these are indicated by different capital letters (*A* = first speaker, *B* = second speaker, etc.) |
| *B:* | |
| etc. | |
| – | 1. A dash at the end of a word signals that it is *incomplete.* |
| | 2. Where the dash is surrounded by spaces, it indicates a *pause.* |

e.g. 1. *thi–, this*
2. *What is the name – or?*

| { } | In Chapter 14, { } are used to mark the beginning and end of *overlap* between speakers (i.e. simultaneous speech) |
| / | Also in Chapter 14, / is used to indicate the location of speaker *overlap*, where the exact beginning and end of the overlap is unimportant for the purpose of the example. |

Other punctuation in the transcriptions (. , ? !) follows conventional orthographic practice, and has no fixed prosodic or linguistic significance.

## 5 Grammatical symbols

( )  signals *optional elements* (in formulae and occasionally in examples)

*Elements of clause structure* are represented by the following symbols:

| | |
|---|---|
| A | adverbial |
| $A_c$ | circumstance adverbial |
| $A_l$ | linking adverbial |
| $A_s$ | stance adverbial |
| O | object |
| $O_d$ | direct object |
| $O_i$ | indirect object |
| $O_p$ | prepositional object |
| P | predicative |
| $P_o$ | object predicative |
| $P_s$ | subject predicative |
| S | subject |
| V | verb, verb phrase (V is also sometimes used for verb as a *word class*) |

*Clause structures* are represented by a combination of the above symbols; e.g.:

| | |
|---|---|
| SV | subject + verb |
| SVA | subject + verb + adverbial |
| $SVO_iO_d$ | subject + verb + indirect object + direct object |
| $SVP_s$ | subject + verb + subject predicative |

*Phrase types*:

| | |
|---|---|
| NP | noun phrase (see 2.7.1) |
| VP | verb phrase (see 2.7.2) |

## 6 Other abbreviations or symbols

| | |
|---|---|
| CGEL | R. Quirk et al., *A Comprehensive Grammar of the English Language* |
| LDOCE | *Longman Dictionary of Contemporary English* |
| LSWE | Longman Spoken and Written English (Corpus) |

# SECTION A

# Introductory

# 1

# Introduction: a corpus-based approach to English grammar

*See page xiii for contents in detail*

## 1.1 Introduction

Every time that we write or speak, we are faced with a myriad of choices: not only choices in what we say but in how we say it. The vocabulary and grammar that we use to communicate are influenced by a number of factors, such as the reason for the communication, the context, the people with whom we are communicating, and whether we are speaking or writing. Taken together, these choices give rise to systematic patterns of use in English.

Traditionally, such patterns have not been included under the umbrella of grammar. Most grammars have focused on structural considerations: cataloguing and describing the form and meaning of grammatical constructions rather than how they are actually used in spoken and written discourse. In part, the restrictive emphasis of past descriptions has existed simply because grammar has been defined as the study of structures. But the disregard of use has also been due to our lack of adequate information about the actual patterns of language features in real-world contexts.

The *Longman Grammar of Spoken and Written English* (*LGSWE*) describes the actual use of grammatical features in different varieties of English: mainly conversation, fiction, newspaper language, and academic prose. Each of these varieties is termed a **register**, and each extended sample of language from a register constitutes a **text**. Many texts exist in the written medium: for example, an academic journal article, a newspaper report, a history textbook, or a novel. Other texts have their origin in speech: for example, a face-to-face conversation or a lecture—although spoken texts obviously have to be transcribed before being subjected to linguistic analysis. Under natural circumstances, texts occur and are understood in their **discourse** settings, which comprise all of the linguistic, situational, social, psychological, and pragmatic factors that influence the interpretation of any instance of language in actual use. A collection of spoken and written texts, organized by register and coded for other discourse considerations, comprises a **corpus**.

The *LGSWE* adopts a **corpus-based** approach, which means that the grammatical descriptions are based on the patterns of structure and use found in a large collection of spoken and written texts, stored electronically, and searchable by computer. In all, the Corpus used for *LGSWE* contains over 40 million words of text representing six major register categories. Sections 1.4 and 1.5 describe the design and composition of this Corpus in detail.

This book complements previous grammatical descriptions by investigating the linguistic patterns actually used by speakers and writers in the late twentieth century. Its descriptions show that structure and use are not independent aspects of the English language; analysis of both is required to understand how English grammar really functions in the day-to-day communicative activities of speakers and writers. Although the grammar is primarily organized along structural lines, the descriptions emphasize not only their formal properties but also the use of these structures.

Our focus on use constitutes an entire extra dimension for grammatical description, one that is as important to real language communication as the structural catalogue of elements and constructions. By adopting a corpus-based approach, the *LGSWE* investigates the patterns of use in data-intensive ways that until recently have not been feasible.

This chapter describes the distinctive goals of the *LGSWE*, along with the textual resources and analytical techniques used to achieve those goals. Section 1.1.1 provides a detailed discussion of the major goals. Section 1.2 explains the interplay between structure and use that forms the basis of the *LGSWE*. Section 1.3 introduces a major factor related to use—dialect and register distinctions in English—and discusses the unique emphasis on register variation in the *LGSWE*. Section 1.4 discusses the representation of those varieties in the Corpus we have used: the **Longman Spoken and Written English Corpus** (the LSWE Corpus). Section 1.5 provides a detailed description of the major register categories in the Corpus.

The remaining major sections, 1.6–8, explain the methodology of large-scale corpus analysis, including: the techniques used for grammatical investigation of the LSWE Corpus (1.6); the presentation and interpretation of quantitative findings about use (1.7); and the discussion and functional interpretation of those findings (1.8). Finally, 1.9 presents an overview of the major sections and chapters, while 1.10 identifies the intended groups of readers together with a sample of the potential uses of the *LGSWE*.

## 1.1.1 Major goals of the *LGSWE*

This grammar offers a new kind of descriptive and explanatory account of English grammar: it uses up-to-date technology to chart new domains, with new high-resolution detail. At the same time, it offers an overall picture in relation to the whole communicative system of the English language.

The *LGSWE* describes not only the range of grammatical features in English, but also the actual use of each major feature. We consider the ways in which a feature is used, the extent of its use, and its variability in relation to other features. We also consider the factors that favor or disfavor each variant.

We use the term **grammatical feature** as a general cover for anything that recurs in texts that can be given a linguistic description. Features include: word classes, such as 'noun' and 'preposition'; structural patterns, such as subject-verb-object; phrasal and clausal categories, such as verb phrases and adverbial clauses of time; and other structural distinctions, such as progressive aspect or indefinite-ness. Morphological, lexical, and semantically oriented categories are also included, as are quantitatively defined features such as type-token ratio (2.2.1). The aim of the book is to study the various ways in which grammatical features occur and recur in actual use.

Our studies show that much of the variation among features is highly systematic: speakers of a language make choices in morphology, lexicon, and grammar depending on a number of linguistic and non-linguistic contextual factors. Important components of the situational context include the purpose of communication, the physical mode (spoken or written), the production circumstances, and various demographic characteristics of the speaker/writer. The patterns of variation associated with these factors can be analyzed with respect to two main language 'varieties': **dialects**, or varieties associated with different groups of speakers, and **registers**, or situationally defined varieties.

The *LGSWE* sets out to provide full descriptions of both the structure and the use of grammatical features in English. Thus, for most grammatical features and structural variants of any significance, we have undertaken empirical research to understand better how the feature is used and why one feature is chosen over other related ones. More specifically, *LGSWE* includes:

**Structural description:**

- all major grammatical units and constructions in English, including discussion of their internal structures, external roles in higher structures, and meanings
- the range of **variants** for each structure (i.e. the range of choices that can be made with roughly the same communicative effect; see 1.2.3 for examples)
- the comparison of structural features that are related paradigmatically in their grammatical role (e.g. different types of complement clauses, of noun modifiers, of adverbials).

**Description of patterns of use:**

- what speakers and writers typically do v. what they rarely do; i.e. the **frequency** of different features
- the distribution of grammatical features across registers (1.2.1)
- the distribution of grammatical features in relation to other features:
  - (a) the association of grammatical features with particular sets of lexical words (1.2.2)
  - (b) the preferred use of grammatical variants in particular discourse contexts (1.2.3)
  - (c) dialect differences (between AmE and BrE; 1.3.2).

The essential resource for achieving these goals is a large electronic database of naturally occurring language: a corpus of texts. In fact, we have found corpus analysis to be indispensable for our descriptions of both structure and use. In 1.2, we provide a fuller discussion of the aspects of use addressed in the *LGSWE*, while sections 1.6–8 cover methodological issues relating to corpus-based analyses.

## 1.2 Structure and use in English grammar

Grammar can be studied from several different perspectives. One basic difference lies in whether the primary goal is **theoretical** or **descriptive**. Studies with a theoretical orientation focus on discovering abstract underlying principles in relation to a model of linguistic competence, typically analyzing relatively few grammatical constructions in depth. In contrast, descriptive studies (such as ours) attempt to provide a more comprehensive characterization of grammatical phenomena in an individual language like English.

Among grammars with a descriptive orientation, there are further differences. One of these is the scope of coverage and the level of detail; few grammars attempt a truly exhaustive description of English grammar. A related distinction concerns the domain of the term 'grammar'. While some studies describe only syntactic constructions, others also include morphology and the interface between grammar and other levels of the language, such as phonology, the lexicon, and semantics.

In *LGSWE* our approach is descriptive and, beyond that, also empirical. We have aimed to be as comprehensive as possible, while recognizing that even in a book of this size, coverage of all details is impossible. To avoid allocating too much space to justifying a descriptive framework, we have relied on previous descriptions of English. We are obviously much indebted to many English grammarians past and present.

In particular, the descriptive framework and terminology of *LGSWE* closely follows Quirk et al., *A Comprehensive Grammar of the English Language* (*CGEL*) (Longman, 1985). *CGEL* is probably the most detailed grammar of present-day English yet written, and its grammatical system has gained a broad currency through its use in other grammars, textbooks, and academic publications. In the few areas where we have departed from *CGEL*, it has been for a specific reason. For example, the term 'complement' (3.11.1, Chapter 9) is used in *LGSWE* in a broad sense that is well-entrenched in American tradition, and roughly equivalent to 'complementation' in *CGEL*. To avoid confusion, we have adopted 'complement' in this American sense, and have replaced the terms 'subject complement' and 'object complement' in *CGEL* with 'subject predicative' and 'object predicative' in *LGSWE*.

The overriding goal has been to use categories and terms that are familiar and unobjectionable to the widest range of grammar users. Since *CGEL* is terminologically conservative, generally following informed tradition in its choice of grammatical terms and categories, we have rarely departed from its overall framework.

Another important difference among descriptive grammars concerns the extent to which they deal with the communicative function and use of particular structures. In this grammar, we have tried to give equal emphasis to descriptions of both structure and use. We have applied empirical corpus-based methods to investigate aspects of grammar in both of these domains.

Through study of authentic texts, corpus-based analysis of grammatical structure can uncover characteristics that were previously unsuspected. For example, we have found that speakers in conversation use a number of relatively complex and sophisticated grammatical constructions, contradicting the widely held belief that conversation is grammatically simple. One example of this type is the conversational use of complex relative clause constructions with a deeply embedded 'gap' (8.7.2.1):

> *There's so many things [that I want to learn <...>].* (CONV)
>
> *That's the bit [that we don't tend to know so much about <...>].* (CONV)

The gap, where a noun phrase would normally occur, is marked <...>. In both examples, it is separated from the beginning of the relative clause by a complex structure including two verbs. (Note that our general practice is to mark clause and other constituent boundaries with [], where they need to be pointed out.)

Conversely, supposedly colloquial, inexplicit grammatical features sometimes turn out to be common in formal academic writing. For example, when using a relative clause with the head noun *way*, academic writers might be expected to use a combination of preposition + relative pronoun—*in which*—since this form explicitly marks how *way* integrates with the relative clause, as in:

> 1 **The way [in which this happens]** *gives important information on the inner organization.* (ACAD)

However, by searching a corpus we find that writers of formal or technical texts commonly leave out both the relative pronoun and the preposition, resulting in simplified constructions (8.7.4.2):

> 2 *Silicates are classified and named according to* **the way [the tetrahedra are linked].** (ACAD)

instead of the more explicit variant:

> **3** *Silicates are classified and named according to* **the way [in which the tetrahedra are linked]**.

As these examples show, corpus-based analysis provides fresh perspectives and exemplification of traditional structural descriptions. However, corpus-based methods are even more important for analyses of language use.

For example, the most interesting findings relating to the two structures described above are probably their patterns of use rather than their structural properties. That is, what seems particularly noteworthy is that a complex type of relative clause occurs primarily in conversation, while being rare in expository writing (8.7.2.1). It is equally surprising that a type of reduced and simplified relative clause construction would be common in expository prose (8.7.4.2). Similarly unexpected patterns of use exist for many of the core grammatical features of English.

As already mentioned, one of the most important uses of corpus-based investigation is to provide information about frequency of use. Teachers, students, materials writers, and those with a purely academic interest will all find it useful to know which grammatical patterns are common and which are rare. Hitherto this information has been based on native-speaker intuition. However, native speakers rarely have accurate perceptions of these differences: a large representative corpus, such as the LSWE Corpus, is the only reliable source of frequency information.

When it comes to describing differences across registers, native-speaker intuition is even less reliable. Although we are generally aware that a few features are typical of certain registers (such as the use of the passive in technical academic prose) most native speakers are not aware of the more pervasive differences in the use of core grammatical features. Yet most grammatical features are in fact distributed in strikingly different ways across registers.

For example, many single-word and phrasal verbs (such as *think, know, come on,* and *get in*) are much more common in conversation than in written registers such as news reportage or academic prose. Perhaps more surprisingly, several modal verbs (e.g. *can, will, would*) are also much more common in conversation than in most written registers. These same kinds of differences hold for clausal constructions. For example, for those used to thinking of spoken language as structurally simpler than written language, it is surprising to learn that *that-*complement clause constructions (as in *I think [Stuart's gone a bit mad]!*) are much more common in conversation than in written expository registers (usually with the introductory word *that* omitted in speech; see also 1.2.1).

In the *LGSWE*, grammatical features are examined in the light of three interrelated aspects of use: (1) **register distribution**, (2) **lexico-grammatical patterns**, and (3) **grammatical/discourse factors**. These three aspects of use are introduced and illustrated in the following subsections.

## 1.2.1    Register distribution

The *LGSWE* is innovative in its focus on the grammatical characteristics of particular kinds of text—what we refer to as **registers**. As already noted, the four major registers considered are conversation, fiction, newspaper language, and academic prose. Even a casual inspection of texts from different registers reveals extensive linguistic differences. A comparison of the two text samples below, one from a newspaper story and one from a conversation in an art gallery, illustrates such differences.

Newspaper language and conversation are among the most familiar kinds of writing and speech. Probably most speakers of English read newspapers (occasionally at least), and all engage in conversation. In other respects, though, these two registers are opposites. Newspaper stories are written, and the language used is carefully edited and revised. They have a relatively focused purpose: to convey and evaluate information about recent events and newsworthy people. They claim a relatively objective presentation of information, often adopting an institutional voice. These situational characteristics typically result in carefully crafted texts with little overt evidence of personal opinions, as illustrated in Text sample 1:

Text sample 1: NEWSPAPER REPORT

<an extract from the British newspaper *The Independent*, October 1989; from an article describing the historical background of the Rivonia treason trial in South Africa, which began in 1963>

*In a recent book on the trial <...>, Hilda Bernstein, the wife of one of those on trial, wrote: "The Rivonia trial was a confrontation in which the opposing forces in South Africa appeared face to face <...>"*

*The defendants tried to prove that Umkhonto we Sizwe was not part of the ANC. They denied that they had adopted a plan for guerrilla warfare and denied that the ANC was communist.*

*The state's case was based mainly on accusations of sabotage and planned sabotage, a case well supported by the evidence found at Rivonia. Detailed plans for Operation Mayibuye, an outline for guerrilla warfare and foreign intervention, were revealed. Mr Sisulu said that it was just a draft plan, which had not been adopted.* (NEWS)

The situational characteristics of conversations are quite different. For one thing, conversations are spoken rather than written, and they are produced online (14.1.2.6), with the words and grammatical organization being composed on the spot, as the conversation itself unfolds. There is little time to plan ahead, or to edit afterwards. Although it is possible to repair an utterance, by saying it a second time the way that we really wanted to say it, we cannot erase an utterance and replace it with an edited version. Conversations also differ from newspaper texts in that they are personal and directly interactive. Conversational partners are involved with one another's personal attitudes and opinions, and interact with one another to build a discourse jointly.

The situational characteristics of conversation make it difficult to collect and analyze. To collect texts from news, the analyst merely needs to buy a newspaper. Furthermore, there is no doubt concerning the words and structures used in the text. In contrast, a conversational text must be captured by a tape recorder at the very moment that it is uttered; once that opportunity is past, the conversation is irretrievably lost. Further, a tape-recorded conversation is still inadequate for grammatical analysis—it must be transcribed to render the spoken sounds into written words and structures.

Transcription is not at all a mechanical process. In some cases, an utterance can have more than one interpretation. In other cases, it is simply impossible to determine what was said, due to factors such as background noise, speakers talking at the same time, or a speaker simply talking too fast. These unintelligible stretches of speech are marked as <unclear> in the transcriptions here. Speakers are marked at the beginning of each utterance, as *A:*, *B:*, etc. A dash (–) is used to indicate a pause. When necessary, background or non-verbal information is indicated in angle brackets.

Text sample 2: FACE-TO-FACE CONVERSATION

> <a service encounter in a picture gallery/framing shop in the USA; speaker *A* is a middle-aged woman working in the shop; speakers *B* and *C* are customers>
>
> *A: Okay, so we have two separate ones, or do you want that on one?*
> *B: No, two, I'll, I'll, how much are those? Eighteen, well here's a twenty –*
>   *twenty-one, plus tax – so put that towards her bill.*
> *A: Okay.*
> *C: Ooh, that's a neat picture.*
> *A: And do we have you on our customer list yet?*
> *B: Yes.*
> *A: What is the name – or? Aha! Hey, we like to see those –*
> *C:* <whispering> *I want this too.*
> *B: You do?*
> *C: Yes I do.*
> *?:* <unclear; giggle>
>
> <later in the same conversation:>
>
> *A: Okay, so we need to put – I'm confused now.* <laugh>
> *B: They can all go in the same sack.*
> *A: That's – can it all go on the thing too, or?*
> *B: Yeah – I tell you what, just ring it all up together.*
> *A: Okay.* (CONV)

As illustrated by these two text extracts, there are striking linguistic differences between news texts and conversations. One obvious difference is in the overall sentence structure. In the newspaper article, all sentences are completed, and many sentences are long and structurally complex. In contrast, the very notion of a sentence in conversation is problematic. If we use the sentence-final punctuation – full stop (.), question mark (?), or exclamation mark (!) – in Text sample 2 as a guide, then many sentence units are brief. They include simple responses (*yeah, okay*) as well as utterances that are left incomplete as a speaker changes thoughts during an utterance (e.g. *No, two, I'll, I'll, how much are those? Okay, so we need to put – I'm confused now*).

We argue in 14.1 that the 'sentence' is a notion that is not applicable to spoken language. It is true that the transcriptions contain orthographic sentences, defined as units beginning with a capital letter and ending with a period or other sentence-final punctuation mark. However, punctuation in the spoken texts must be treated with caution; the corpus transcribers marked punctuation to reflect spoken prosody, but there are no hard and fast rules to follow when punctuating natural conversation.

The conversation also has numerous contracted forms, such as *I'll, here's, I'm, that's,* whereas all forms are fully spelled out in the newspaper text. In addition, many of the referents in the conversation are not explicitly identified, so that hearers must rely on the context for understanding (e.g. *do you want that on one? That's – can it all go on the thing too, or?*).

Other linguistic differences between these text samples are less obvious. Because of the interactive nature of the conversation, there are frequent references to *you* (the addressee). Similarly, there are frequent direct questions (e.g. *do you want that on one? how much are those? do we have you on our customer list yet? what is the name? you do?*) and imperatives (e.g. *put that towards her bill; just ring it all up together*). These constructions would not be appropriate without a specific addressee (*you*). The fact that news reports are not addressed to any individual reader accounts for the absence of second person pronouns, direct questions, and imperatives in Text sample 1.

Further, speakers in the conversation make frequent reference to themselves (*I, we*), describing their own personal thoughts, feelings, past and present activities, etc. (e.g. *Hey, we like to see those, I want this too, Yes I do, Okay, so we need to put—I'm confused now*). In contrast, the news report adopts an impersonal tone with no acknowledged individual author, and thus it has no first person pronouns at all.

Finally, because its overriding purpose is to report past events, almost all the verbs in the news report are in the past tense. In the conversation, present tense and verb phrases with modals are predominant, reflecting the emphasis on the participants' immediate interaction and activities (*here's a twenty, they can all go*) or the expression of their current attitudes and feelings (*we like, I want*). Once they are pointed out, such differences are clear and might seem obvious; but many of them escape notice on casual inspection and as a result are overlooked in the teaching and study of English grammar.

In fact, many important linguistic differences among registers cannot be discerned from a simple inspection of individual texts; they emerge very clearly, however, from analysis of a corpus. Such analyses show that linguistic features are not uniformly distributed across registers. Rather, there are systematic differences, which correspond to the situational differences among registers (with respect to interactiveness, production circumstances, purpose, etc.).

Indeed, Chapter 2 (2.3.5, 2.4.14) shows that even basic word classes—such as nouns, adjectives, verbs, and adverbs—are far from evenly distributed across registers. Nouns and prepositional phrases are much more common in news than in conversation, whereas verbs and adverbs are much more common in conversation. These distributional patterns reflect differing functional priorities. For example, news texts have an informational focus, frequently using nouns to refer to people and things in the world; further, there is a premium on space-saving presentation of information, making it desirable to pack nouns, adjectives, and prepositional phrases densely into every news story. In contrast, the interpersonal focus of conversation results in frequent use of verbs to narrate events and to present personal attitudes, while the online production and context-dependent circumstances of conversation make it more appropriate to use pronouns instead of nouns.

Even when a construction occurs with comparable frequency across registers, there are often important structural and functional differences in its use. *That*-clauses, which are relatively common in both newspaper texts and conversations, provide a good example of this type. For news, Text sample 1 illustrates the typical pattern, with *that*-clauses used to report the speech of others (cf. 1.2.2); **1** and **2** below are taken from Text sample 1:

1 *They denied **that they had adopted a plan for guerrilla warfare.*** (NEWS)

2 *Mr Sisulu said **that it was just a draft plan**.* (NEWS)

Conversation also has frequent *that*-clauses (although the initial *that* is often omitted):

3 *I think **you need a good old pair of scissors**.* (CONV)

4 *I think **it's political more than anything at the moment**.* (CONV)

5 *I know **I've let it go a bit this time**.* (CONV)

6 *I know **she was there**.* (CONV)

7 *I realise **that there's been something on your mind recently** <...> and I hope **you can talk to me about it**.* (CONV)

As illustrated by these examples, the kind of *that*-clauses typically found in conversations differ from those used in newspaper reports in at least three major respects:

- Verbs that take *that*-clauses in conversation usually convey personal thoughts, attitudes, or feelings (such as *think, mean, know, realise, believe, feel*), with *think* being by far the most common (accounting for about 75 percent of all verbs taking a *that*-clause). In contrast, verbs of speaking account for over half of all verbs taking a *that*-clause in news. (See 1.2.2 and the detailed discussion in 9.2.2.)

- In conversation, the subject of the main clause in constructions with *that*-clauses is frequently *I*, referring to the speaker (in the LSWE Corpus, this pattern occurs 65 percent of the time). In contrast, the norm in news reports is for subject noun phrases to refer to third person entities, usually humans (e.g. *she, he, Mr Sisulu*)—this happens about 80 percent of the time in the LSWE Corpus.

- In conversation, *that* is typically omitted (85 percent of the time in the Corpus); in news reports, *that* is rarely omitted (only about 25 percent of the time in the Corpus; 9.2.8).

These linguistic differences fit the differing communicative purposes of news reports and conversations. News reports purport to provide a factual, objective reportage of recent events. By consistently using a third person perspective, these reports give the impression of an unbiased presentation of the news. Using first person pronouns, or verbs conveying personal thoughts or feelings, would run directly counter to these underlying purposes. Conversation is the opposite of news writing in these respects: people who converse directly with one another expect to hear about each other's personal thoughts and feelings.

Similar patterns exist for most other linguistic features discussed in this book: there are often important linguistic differences among registers, and, in most cases, they can be explained by reference to the situational differences among registers.

## 1.2.2 Lexico-grammatical patterns

Syntax and lexicon are often treated as independent components of English. Analysis of real texts shows, however, that most syntactic structures tend to have an associated set of words or phrases that are frequently used with them.

For example, consider the following sentences from newspaper articles:

*She said **that as long as there is a demand for drugs, dealers and producers will find ways to meet that demand**.* (NEWS)

*French Defense Minister Charles Hernu said Sunday in Cairo **that France will sell Egypt 20 Mirage 2000 jets**.* (NEWS)

*Wright said **that he would serve as Speaker until the Democratic Caucus chooses his successor at a session Tuesday**.* (NEWS)

*The ayatollah's aides said **that on his orders they telephoned Teheran yesterday afternoon**.* (NEWS)

*He declared that **she had researched projects, studied stocks and visited drilling sites to guide the firm's investments**.* (NEWS)

*He recalled **that his last but one predecessor, Pope Paul VI, had been invited to Poland in 1966**.* (NEWS)

*McCartor noted **that there are limits to U.S. authority with sovereign nations**.* (NEWS)

These sentences further illustrate some of the trends introduced in 1.2.1. In news articles, there is a restricted set of main-clause verbs that commonly occur with *that*-clauses. These are all verbs from one **semantic domain**, used to introduce reported speech (*say, declare, recall, note, warn*), with the verb *say* occurring by far the most frequently. The subject of these verbs is normally a particular human being, and so there is a strong tendency for the words filling the subject slot to be either third person pronouns (*he, she, they*) or proper nouns (*Charles Hernu, Wright, Mcartor*).

Consideration of the entire LSWE Corpus shows that *that*-clauses occur with a relatively restricted set of main-clause verbs, but that a few of these verbs are especially common. In particular, the verbs *say, think,* and *know* are much more common than any other verbs in combination with a *that*-clause. In contrast, *to*-infinitive clauses occur with a wider range of main-clause verbs, but only the verb *want* is particularly common with this construction. Overall, *that*-clauses and *to*-clauses occur with roughly the same high frequency in the Corpus, but they have very different lexical associations: *to*-clauses occur with a large number of different main-clause verbs from several different semantic domains, while *that*-clauses occur with a much more restricted set of main-clause verbs but a few very high-frequency items (9.2.2, 9.4.2).

Many other aspects of English grammar have similar systematic associations with lexical classes. Findings such as these are based on empirical investigation of the lexico-grammatical associations that actually occur in a large corpus of texts. These patterns are not merely arbitrary associations; rather, particular grammatical structures often occur with restricted lexical classes because both the structures and the lexical classes serve the same underlying communicative tasks or functions.

In many cases, however, the lexico-grammatical associations differ markedly from register to register. Thus the lexico-grammatical associations found in newspaper articles are quite different from those found in conversation, because, as already shown, speakers in a conversation typically have quite different communicative purposes from the writers of newspaper reports.

Corpus analysis across registers is essential for a full understanding of both the grammatical patterns and the lexico-grammatical patterns of the language.

## 1.2.3 Grammatical/discourse factors

Many grammatical constructions in English have two or more formal alternatives which can be considered optional variants, in the sense that they are nearly equivalent in meaning. For example, 1.2.1 illustrated how *that*-clauses can occur with or without the complementizer *that*. Similarly, relative clauses have several variants: with a *wh*-relative pronoun (*the Next empire [which he founded]*), with *that* as the relative pronoun (*taboo subjects [that people don't talk about]*), or with no relative pronoun at all (*a book [I've got]*).

There are also many English constructions that have variants with different word orders. For example, adverbs can occur at many different places in a clause (10.2.6, 10.3.4); in the following sentence, the adverb *actually* could be placed in at least four different slots with little semantic difference:

> **Actually** I'm surprised to find myself in the academic world again. (FICT)
> cf. I'm **actually** surprised to find myself in the academic world again.
> cf. I'm surprised **actually** to find myself in the academic world again.
> cf. I'm surprised to find myself in the academic world again, **actually**.

Similarly, elements that can occur as indirect objects immediately after the verb can also often occur as prepositional objects after the direct object (11.2.4.1). Compare the following pair of sentences:

> He gave **Robert** half his wages.
> v. He gave half his wages **to Robert**. (FICT †)

In other cases, English has a system of several related variants rather than a simple choice between two variants. For example, referring expressions can be expressed as pronouns, simple noun phrases, or various kinds of complex noun phrases. In the following text passage, *the Oxford Tories* are subsequently referred to in three different ways: as *men from Magdalen and Christ Church whose fair hair flopped over their foreheads and who talked of horses*; *they*; and *the gents*:

> **The Oxford Tories** consisted in the main of **men from Magdalen and Christ Church whose fair hair flopped over their foreheads and who talked of horses**. **They** were **the gents** and we were the players. (FICT)

While many grammars point out the structural similarities among variants, they usually offer little explanation of when and why the different forms are used. In contrast, the *LGSWE* is concerned with the grammatical and discourse factors that relate to the choice among structurally and semantically related variants (4.1).

For example, there are several grammatical/discourse factors that relate to the omission of the complementizer *that*. One is register (1.2.1). Another is lexical (1.2.2): *that* is more likely to be omitted after very common verbs, such as *say* and *think*. However, these do not exhaust the discourse factors that may be relevant. Other factors that favor omission are: the use of a personal pronoun (rather than a full noun phrase) as the subject of the main clause; the use of a main-clause subject that is co-referential with the subject of the *that*-clause (for example *I think I ...*); and the use of an active voice main-clause verb (v. passive voice). A sentence illustrating all these factors is:

> *Hey I think I saw her the other day.* (CONV)
>
> (See 9.2.8 for a full discussion.)

The analyses in the *LGSWE* show that similar kinds of discourse factors influence structural choices throughout English grammar.

## 1.3 Varieties of English

Most of the descriptions of grammatical use in the *LGSWE* are framed relative to occurrence in different **varieties**: that is, **registers** (varieties relating to different circumstances and purposes) and, to a lesser extent, **dialects** (varieties associated with different groups of speakers). In this section, we introduce these distinctions and discuss the relative importance of register and dialect for our analyses.

### 1.3.1 Registers of English

Register distinctions are defined in non-linguistic terms, with respect to situational characteristics such as mode, interactiveness, domain, communicative purpose, and topic. For example, newspaper editorials are distinguished as being (a) written, (b) published in a newspaper, and (c) primarily intended to express an informed opinion on matters already in the news. Editorials are not directly interactive (often there is no acknowledged author of the editorial), and they can be written about almost any topic.

In many cases, registers are institutionalized varieties or text types within a culture, such as novels, letters, editorials, sermons, and debates. However, registers can be defined at almost any level of generality. Thus, novels are a sub-register of the broader text-variety of fiction. At the same time, novels themselves can be broken down into more detailed categories such as detective novels or historical novels.

The situational characteristics that define registers have direct functional correlates, and, as a result, there are usually important differences in the use of grammatical features among registers. To take an easy example (as we saw in 1.2.1), face-to-face conversation is directly interactive, with participants talking a lot about themselves and each other. As a result, conversation is characterized grammatically by a frequent use of the first person pronouns *I* and *we* (referring directly to the speaker) and the second person pronoun *you* (referring directly to the listener). In contrast, newspaper articles are not directly interactive, are not directed to any individual reader, and often have no acknowledged author. Since there is no specific author or reader to refer to, newspaper texts use first person or second person pronouns comparatively rarely. However, since newspaper articles are intended to provide current information about important people and events, they commonly use proper nouns referring to known people, places, or institutions.

Since it would be too difficult and time-consuming to analyze all varieties grammatically, we describe grammatical use with respect to just four major registers: conversation (CONV), fiction (FICT), news (NEWS), and academic prose (ACAD). These registers have the virtue of being (a) important, highly productive varieties of the language, and (b) different enough from one another to represent a wide range of variation. In general terms, these four registers represent different combinations of situational characteristics, as summarized in Table 1.1.

Table 1.1  **Summary of the major situational differences among the four primary registers used in this grammar**

|  | CONV | FICT | NEWS | ACAD |
|---|---|---|---|---|
| mode | spoken | written (+ written dialogue) | written | written |
| interactiveness and online production | yes | (restricted to fictional dialogue) | no | no |
| shared immediate situation | yes | no | no | no |
| main communicative purpose/content | personal communication | pleasure reading | information/ evaluation | information/ argumentation/ explanation |
| audience | individual | wide-public | wide-public | specialist |
| dialect domain | local | global | regional/ national | global |

Conversation differs from the other three registers in being spoken, directly interactive, and arguably the most basic form of human communication. Although conversational partners can have a range of communicative purposes, these usually involve a focus on the lives and interests of the interlocutors themselves. In addition, the interlocutors share the same physical and temporal context, and often share extensive personal background knowledge.

All three written registers differ from conversation in many of these respects: they are written, not directly interactive, lack specific addressees, and have communicative purposes not focused on the personal concerns of the writer/ reader. Fiction is intermediate in that it includes the conversational dialogue of fictional characters. Fiction has purposes associated with pleasure reading, while news and academic prose have a more informational focus. Fiction and news are similar in usually being written for a diverse, wide-public audience, in contrast to academic prose texts, which are written for more specialist audiences.

In addition to these situational differences, the four registers differ in their general dialect characteristics. Conversation and news can both be considered 'local' or 'regional', in that they reflect dialectal as well as register differences. In conversation, speakers often share the same regional as well as social dialect. Similarly, newspapers tend to be written for, and read in, a single region or nation, and thus they provide one of the best reflections of American English v. British English dialect differences in writing. In contrast, academic prose, and to a lesser extent fiction, can be regarded as 'global', in that they are typically written for an international audience with relatively little influence from the national dialect of the author.

In Table 1.1, the four registers are ordered (from left to right) according to the extent of their situational differences. Although conversation is distinguished from all the written registers, it has more in common with fiction than with news and academic prose. In their informational purposes, news and academic prose are more remote from conversation, with academic prose being the most distant, given its global and specialist nature. We use this order to display corpus findings throughout the book; in many cases (but, interestingly, far from all) the frequencies of grammatical features rise or fall consistently from left to right across these four registers, reflecting the influence of these situational characteristics.

Finally, it is important to emphasize that there are major sub-registers within each of these four register categories, and thus there is a considerable amount of linguistic variation within each category. For example, newspaper writing includes not only news reportage, but also editorials, reviews, etc. Further, newspaper texts have been collected from different kinds of newspapers (e.g. the *Wall Street Journal* v. the *Daily Mirror*). Similarly, academic prose texts have been collected from several major disciplines, and fiction texts include a wide range of sub-registers (e.g. adventure fiction, romance fiction, and modern-day classics).

The four registers described throughout the *LGSWE* are important benchmarks, spanning much of the range of register variation in English. Future investigations of the sub-varieties within each register will produce further important findings.

## 1.3.2  Dialect distinctions

Two main kinds of dialects are commonly distinguished: geographic or **regional dialects,** associated with speakers living in a particular location; and **social dialects**, associated with a given demographic group (e.g. women v. men, older v. younger speakers, or members of different social classes).

Regional dialects, like registers, can be considered at many different levels of specificity. At the highest level, we can distinguish among national varieties of English: in particular, for the purposes of this grammar, between American English (AmE) and British English (BrE)—see also the discussion in section 1.4.

Although the varieties of English spoken in most countries tend to be relatively similar to either AmE or BrE (or both), they can of course be considered as distinct national varieties in their own right. National varieties can be recognized in countries such as Australia, Canada, India, Ireland, New Zealand, Scotland, Singapore, South Africa, Wales, and the West Indies. It should be noted, however, that dialect distinctions do not correspond neatly to national or regional boundaries. There are major regional dialects within most countries, and these regional dialects sometimes extend across national boundaries (e.g. Canada and the USA). For example, the New England, midland, and southern dialects can be distinguished in the United States; the southern and northern English dialects in Great Britain. At a more specific level, many major cities, such as Boston or Liverpool, can be said to have their own distinct dialect.

Within these regional dialects, there is additional variation associated with social distinctions, such as ethnicity, social class, gender, and education. Over recent decades, sociolinguists have used a comparative approach to study these social dialects, describing the linguistic patterns of variation across social groups in major urban centers such as New York City, Norwich, Belfast, and Montreal.

In terms of their linguistic characteristics, dialects are distinguished primarily by pronunciation differences, and to a lesser extent by lexical and grammatical differences—which is one reason why we give dialect differences less attention than register differences in this work. Regional dialects can sometimes be distinguished by categorical differences; for example, speakers of some dialects distinguish the pronunciation of *saw* and *sore*, while others do not, in effect dropping the [r] sound. Social dialects, on the other hand, tend to be distinguished in terms of relative frequency of use, for example, by the extent to which different social groups prefer one pronunciation over another.

## 1.3.3 Standard and non-standard English

There is no official government-sponsored academy that regulates usage for the English language, but there is still a widely recognized **standard English**: the dialectal variety that has been codified in dictionaries, grammars, and usage handbooks. This same variety has been adopted by most major publishers internationally, resulting in a very high degree of uniformity among published English texts around the world. The differences between the American and British standards for written English, for example, are restricted mostly to a small set of spelling and lexical variants, such as *theater* v. *theatre*, *favor* v. *favour*, *elevator* v. *lift* (see below).

For the most part, the notion of 'standard' English does not play a large role in the descriptions offered in the present grammar. For written registers, we adopt an implicit, descriptive approach to characterize 'standard' English, in that we describe the grammatical forms and patterns actually used in published texts (as opposed to prescribing explicitly the forms that should be used in 'standard English').

Although it is more difficult to apply the notion of a standard to spoken English, a similar approach can be used: we define standard spoken English as including grammatical characteristics shared widely across dialects, excluding those variants restricted to local or limited social/regional varieties. This approach recognizes that conversation has special grammatical characteristics not typically found in writing, and so we do not impose a written standard on our analyses of conversation. Further, we recognize that there are somewhat different spoken standards for AmE and BrE, and we include discussion of those differences where relevant (particularly in Chapter 14). However, it is not our purpose here to survey the range of regional and social dialect variants in spoken English.

### 1.3.3.1 Variation within standard English

It would also be wrong to assume that standard English is fixed, with little or no variability. In fact, one of the major goals of the *LGSWE* is to describe the patterns of variation that exist within standard English, and to account for those patterns in terms of contextual factors. For example, standard English uses two relative pronouns with inanimate head nouns—*that* and *which*:

> *I could give you figures* **that** *would shock you.* (FICT)
>
> *This chapter is devoted to a discussion of various flow processes* **which** *occur in open systems.* (ACAD)

In most sentences, either of these two forms would be grammatical, although there are a number of contextual factors that favor the use of one or the other (8.7.1.5). Thus, the existence of a standard variety has not levelled out variability of this type. In particular, the notion that the standard insists on 'uniformity'— allowing just one variant of each grammatical feature—is a serious fallacy, arising from a misleading application to language of the notion of 'standard' and 'standardization' taken from other walks of life.

In most cases, variation within the standard does not attract attention from ordinary speakers. However, speakers of English do tend to be aware of selected grammatical features and sometimes have strong opinions about what forms are 'correct'. Thus, while the choice between *that* and *which* has a relatively low profile, the choice between *who* and *whom* has attracted more attention; purists claim that only *whom* is the proper choice when the pronoun refers to a human and functions logically as an object. In contrast, speakers of English regularly prefer the pronoun *who*, as in:

> There's a girl **who** I work with who's pregnant. (CONV) <relative clause>
>
> He reckoned the copy of Memories he's got is sung by **who**? (CONV) <direct question>
>
> Shall I tell you **who** Sally fancies? (CONV) <indirect question>

(In fact, the use of *who* in such contexts dates back at least to Shakespeare.)

In the *LGSWE*, we do not argue that any one alternative is the correct choice in such cases. Rather, we focus on describing the actual patterns of use and the possible reasons for those patterns. It turns out that speakers often use other strategies to circumvent controversial choices between grammatical variants; for example, in relative clauses speakers prefer *that* or the zero relativizer over either *who* or *whom* (8.7.1.4).

Throughout the *LGSWE*, we discuss in passing several traditional usage controversies; in addition to the *who–whom* choice, these include dangling participles, stranded prepositions, and the case of pronouns following *be*. However, our primary goal is to describe the patterns of use across the breadth of English grammar, rather than focusing on a handful of usage issues.

There is a basic difference between the variability found within standard English and that found among non-standard dialects: the patterns of variation within standard English are widely shared across dialects, while the variants associated with non-standard English are usually restricted to particular social/regional dialects (14.4.5).

Examples of variability within standard English can be found at most linguistic levels. With respect to pronunciation, there is a wide range of differences accepted as standard. For the other linguistic levels, much of the variability is due to the existence of somewhat different national standards for AmE and BrE. The most widely known differences relate to spelling (e.g. *behaviour* v. *behavior*; *centre* v. *center*) and word choice (e.g. *petrol* v. *gas(oline)*; *boot* v. *trunk*).

There are fewer grammatical differences between AmE and BrE. For example, AmE has two participle forms for the verb *get*—*got* and *gotten*—while BrE uses only the form *got*:

> Angie I think we've **got** a leak. (BrE CONV)
>
> v. They've **got** money. (AmE CONV)
>
> And we still haven't **gotten** a damn pumpkin. (AmE CONV)

Another difference between the two standards concerns subject-verb agreement with singular collective nouns (such as *government, committee, corporation*). In BrE, these nouns can occur with either singular or plural verbs, while in AmE they occur only with singular verbs (cf. 3.9.2.3):

*They're limiting the numbers, the **government are limiting** the numbers.* (BrE CONV)

*And of course local **government is** the most wonderful procrastinator in the world.* (BrE CONV)

v. *The Indian **government was** still **doing** one hour a week of modern news in Sanskrit.* (AmE CONV)

In contrast to these dialect differences, which are largely conventional, most linguistic variation is functionally motivated (influenced by discourse or register factors) and shared by both standard AmE and BrE. As already noted in 1.2, variation of this type is one of the central focuses of the present grammar.

### 1.3.3.2 Variation within non-standard English

The kinds of features associated with non-standard English are similar to those above, except that these forms are stigmatized and restricted to particular social/ regional dialects. For example, the relative pronoun *what* can be used as an alternant to *which* and *that* in some dialects of BrE, as in:

*They were by the pub **what** we stayed in.* (CONV)

In some social dialects of English, it is also possible to use the verb inflection *-s* for all persons in the present tense; this is especially found with the verb *say* (see 3.9.4) and with *go* meaning 'say' and introducing direct speech quotations (14.4.4.3), as in:

*I **goes** don't you dare, you little cat.* (CONV)

*So I **goes** you must be a pervert too.* (CONV)

Variants such as these are considered non-standard in that they are restricted to particular social dialects (usually non-prestige dialects) and often restricted regionally as well. Such non-standard variants are largely outside the scope of the present grammar, which focuses instead on the variants shared generally across regional and social dialects. The primary exceptions to this general focus are the major differences between standard BrE and AmE (considered in various chapters, particularly Chapter 14), and a brief survey of non-standard features in 14.4.5. Further, the distinction between standard and non-standard English in conversation is sometimes unclear. Since our purpose in every chapter, and especially in Chapter 14, includes describing the patterns of use characteristic of conversation, we have not excluded examples containing features that some readers might regard as non-standard.

## 1.3.4 The relative importance of register and dialect differences

Native speakers of English are generally more aware of dialect differences than register differences. The reason for this is simple: we distinguish among people in dialectal terms, commonly making judgments about social class, education, ethnicity, and region based on a speaker's use of dialect features.

In fact, dialect differences are not as pervasive as we might imagine. Pronunciation differences are the most studied and apparently the most important perceptually; when speakers complain that they cannot understand another dialect, they are often reacting to pronunciation differences. Word choice also varies to some extent across dialects. However, the core grammatical structures are relatively uniform across dialects, which explains how (after adjustments have been made at the level of phonological perception) we can usually talk to one another with little difficulty.

Although native speakers are less consciously aware of register distinctions, it turns out that grammatical differences across registers are more extensive than those across dialects. When speakers switch between registers, they are doing different things with language, using language for different purposes, and producing language under different circumstances. Many language choices—especially between grammatical variants—are functionally motivated, related to these differing purposes and production circumstances. As a result, there are often extensive linguistic differences among registers.

Regardless of any dialect differences, speakers using the same register are doing similar communicative tasks; therefore, in most basic respects the characteristic grammatical features of a register are relatively constant across speakers and dialects. To illustrate, consider the following four conversational extracts. Apart from differences in topic and a few characteristic words, there is almost nothing in these transcriptions to indicate the regional and social dialects of the speakers.

Text sample 3 <watching television>

>A: *Oh, could you put it back to the Tony, I want to see who wins, is it Glenn Close?*
>B: *Sure*
>A: *Sorry.*
>B: *No, it's okay*
>A: *Yes, she did win, I knew she would*
>B: *Sorry about that –*
>A: *No, you don't have to turn it up*
>B: *Uh – that's cool*
>A: *Who wins?*
>B: *Pardon?*
>A: *Who wins?*
>B: *I don't know*
>A: *Oh, you don't know?*
>B: *No, I wouldn't watch it if I knew that*
>A: *Oh.* (CONV)

Text sample 4 <in the living room>

>A: *Well can't I leave all this stuff here?*
>B: *Well if you pile it up in some nice fashion.*
>C: *You might find it in the trash in the morning though if you don't pick it up.*
>B: *Guy is bugging Amanda nutso because he doesn't pick up after himself.*
>D: *Only when you're out of town cos –*
>C: *Yeah Guy I really don't like walking in the bathroom and seeing your underwear hanging off the mirror.*
>B: *That's enough.*

C: *It's kind of disgusting – how do you get them to stick there by the way?*
A: *Velcro.* (CONV)

Text sample 5 <in the kitchen>

C: *You thinking of a special occasion?*
A: *Yes my birthday Rufus –*
C: *Right, what do you want, spritzer or –*
A: *No I'll have an orange that erm, straight from the bottle.*
C: *Paul what do you want to drink?*
B: *Er –*
C: *There's not enough room to <unclear>*
B: *Can I have a coke please?*
C: *Some of those dishes need to go up here.*
A: *Up where?*
C: *Pass them to me I'll do it now, some of those fruit dishes, there's not enough room there for the glasses.* (CONV)

Text sample 6 <playing a video game>

A: *What?*
C: *Well I'm going to be*
B: *Reckon I should – Oh aye! You shoot, you shoot from the ground.*
A: *Did you buy a remote?*
C: *Francis, I'll show you how to make them shoot.*
  *You don't even have to – hit them off the ground. It's like these <unclear>. You stay in the <unclear> for*
B: *Right. You hate that.*
A: *That goes on disk two.*
B: *What?*
A: *There.*
B: *This one?*
A: *This tape goes in, into to it.*
C: *One goes in the <unclear>.*
A: *That's alright. Leave it.* (CONV)

There are few obvious social/regional dialect features differentiating these conversations, even in terms of lexical choice. Readers might have noted the use of *that's cool* in Text sample 3, *bugging* and *nutso* in Text sample 4, and *reckon* and *aye* in Text sample 6. These words and expressions are most likely to be used by particular groups of English speakers, although it is not always obvious what those groups are. In addition, there are some differences in topic which might be linked to different social groups.

At the level of grammar, however, there are few (if any) obvious differences across these extracts. For example, all four rely on simple declarative and interrogative sentence structures, frequent contracted forms, frequent use of pronominal forms, relatively simple noun phrase structures, relatively frequent use of modal verbs, and reliance on the active rather than passive voice.

Based on the transcripts themselves, it would be possible to imagine that all four extracts could have been spoken by the same speakers—say a family interacting in four different situations. In fact, the speakers in these conversations come from strikingly different backgrounds: Text sample 3 is from a conversation between two male Black American adults (early 30s) living in a suburb of Los Angeles; they both have some college education and professional occupations (e.g. Speaker B works in computers/accounting). Text sample 4 is from a conversation among young adults (ages 18–23) living in the Rocky Mountain West of the USA (in Montana); most of these speakers have a high-school education and working-class occupations (e.g. as a stock clerk). Text sample 5 is from a conversation between a middle-aged married couple living in a suburb of London; they are both college educated and have professional occupations (as a teacher and draftsman). Speaker B is their school-aged child. Finally, Text sample 6 is from a conversation in a working-class family living in Northern Ireland. The conversation is between a father and his children; the adult is middle-aged, with a high-school education, employed as a baker.

This impression of 'sameness' at the level of grammar reflects the fact that conversations all take place in similar circumstances. Situationally, conversations are very similar in their production circumstances, primary purposes, and interactiveness. For example, all conversations are spoken (rather than written), and produced spontaneously, with the words and grammatical organization being assembled on the spot as the conversation unfolds. In addition, most conversations are personal, private, and directly interactive. Speakers express their own personal attitudes, feelings, and concerns, and they interact with one another to build a shared discourse jointly. In conversing, a speaker's use of grammatical features is strongly influenced by situational characteristics of this type.

In contrast to the similarities among texts within a register (even when they come from different dialects), a comparison of texts from different registers shows striking linguistic differences. To illustrate, compare the conversational Text samples 3–6 with the following extract from an academic science book:

Text sample 7

> There is also some evidence that increased mortality may occur in eggs which are exposed to relatively low temperatures shortly after they are laid, and which consequently attain little embryonic growth (Pickford 1966b). For example, eggs laid after freeze-up revealed a general increase in mortality as oviposition extended later into the autumn when temperatures were declining. That this egg mortality was not due to parental ageing was indicated by the similar trends taking place in pods laid by old or young adults. (ACAD)

The contextual characteristics of this science text are strikingly different from those of the conversational texts. It is written, carefully planned, edited, and revised. It is produced by an author who does not overtly refer to himself in the text. The production is not interactive: the text is addressed to a large audience of readers who are scientists, but these addressees are never directly referred to, and don't 'talk back' in the text. The primary purpose of the text is to present detailed and precise information, explanations, and arguments about the biology of grasshoppers, as opposed to the (inter)personal purposes of conversational participants in Text samples 3–6.

Due to the influence of these contextual factors, the linguistic characteristics of the science text are dramatically different from those of the conversational texts. The three sentences of the science text sample are grammatically complete, as well as relatively long and grammatically complex. None of the reduced or interactive linguistic characteristics common in conversation occur in this text. On the other hand, science texts contain numerous linguistic characteristics rarely found in conversation. In Text sample 7, these characteristics include morphologically complex vocabulary items (e.g. *mortality, embryonic, oviposition*), complex noun phrase constructions (e.g. *eggs which are exposed to relatively low temperatures shortly after they are laid, the similar trends taking place in pods laid by old or young adults*), and frequent passive constructions (e.g. *are exposed, are laid, was indicated*).

The extensive linguistic differences between the conversational extracts and this science extract reflect the fundamental influence of register on grammatical choice. When speakers switch between registers, they are doing very different things with language. The present grammar therefore places a great deal of emphasis on register differences. In most cases, it is simply inaccurate or misleading to speak of a general pattern of use for English; instead, each register has distinctive patterns, associated with its particular communicative priorities and circumstances. Consequently, most of the corpus findings reported in the following chapters are presented as comparative descriptions based on the distinctive frequency patterns in each register (rather than overall patterns of use).

Apart from register differences, we also describe dialect differences between AmE and BrE. However, the grammar pays considerably less attention to dialect variation than it does to register variation, dealing with dialect differences only where they are of particular significance.

## 1.4   Representation of varieties in the LSWE Corpus

A corpus is a large, systematic collection of texts stored on computer. The Corpus used in the present project—the **Longman Spoken and Written English Corpus** (the LSWE Corpus)—contains over 40 million words of text, providing a sound basis for reliable analyses of grammatical patterns.

The LSWE Corpus is constructed to provide a systematic representation of different registers, particularly focusing on the four registers of conversation, fiction, news, and academic prose. One of the most important general findings of this project is that many overall descriptions of general English are incomplete and can be even misleading or inaccurate. Descriptions of general English, based on an averaging of patterns across texts and registers, often obscure important differences and usually do not, in fact, represent the patterns of any register consistently. It is thus essential to represent and analyze each register in the Corpus separately.

### 1.4.1   Register distinctions in the LSWE Corpus

We have constructed a core Corpus of four main registers: conversation, fiction, newspaper language, and academic prose, as displayed in Table 1.2 below. In our choice of these four registers, we have attempted to balance breadth of coverage with economy of analysis and presentation. The four core registers cover much of the range of variation in English, while being restricted to a manageable number of distinctions. Obviously, there are many other registers that could have been included, such as government documents, junk mail, personal letters, and so on. Two additional registers included in our Corpus as supplementary categories are non-conversational speech (e.g. lectures, public meetings) and general written non-fiction prose. However, most analyses in the grammar are based on the core Corpus of four registers.

These four registers are major categories that span much of the range of situational and linguistic variation in English (1.3.1). At one extreme, conversation is the one register that virtually all native speakers control. At the other extreme, academic prose is highly specialized; most native speakers do not read academic prose on a regular basis, and even fewer produce it. In between these two poles, fiction and news represent written registers that are relatively popular rather than specialized; most native speakers read both fiction and newspapers, at least occasionally. The main differences between these two registers relate to purpose and content: fiction depicting imaginary narrative events for aesthetic and recreational purposes; news having a more informational focus.

Practical considerations forbid any attempt to cover the complete range of register variation in English. Each grammatical feature must be analyzed separately in each register, so that every additional register greatly increases the analytical work required for the grammar. Moreover, we have found that presenting results from an extended range of registers makes it difficult for readers to appreciate the overall picture. The four 'core' registers used for most analyses balance these two considerations: they include a manageable number of distinctions while covering much of the range of variation in English.

The composition of the complete LSWE Corpus is presented in Table 1.2. In addition to the four core registers, the full Corpus includes supplementary samples for two additional registers (non-conversational speech and general prose). The subcorpora for non-conversational speech and general prose are used for two types of analysis: for overall findings from the complete Corpus, and for a few analyses that specifically target one or the other of these registers.

**Table 1.2**  **Overall composition of the LSWE Corpus**

|  | number of texts | number of words |
|---|---|---|
| **core registers** | | |
| conversation (BrE) | 3,436 | 3,929,500 |
| fiction (AmE & BrE) | 139 | 4,980,000 |
| news (BrE) | 20,395 | 5,432,800 |
| academic prose (AmE & BrE) | 408 | 5,331,800 |
| **AmE texts for dialect comparisons** | | |
| conversation (AmE) | 329 | 2,480,800 |
| news (AmE) | 11,602 | 5,246,500 |
| **supplementary registers** | | |
| non-conversational speech (BrE) | 751 | 5,719,500 |
| general prose (AmE & BrE) | 184 | 6,904,800 |
| **total Corpus** | 37,244 | 40,025,700 |

The LSWE Corpus was designed to include about five million words of text in each register. However, there is no need to use subcorpora with exactly the same number of words, because all frequency counts are normed to a common basis (occurrences per million words of text; 1.7).

For the most part, the Corpus represents contemporary English, with the vast majority of texts being produced after 1980. The only exception to this is a relatively small number of fiction texts which are 'classics' from the first half of the twentieth century (see the explanation in 1.5.2).

## 1.4.2 Dialect distinctions in the LSWE Corpus

The subcorpora for AmE conversation and news are used for AmE v. BrE dialect comparisons. Since, for most grammatical features, differences across registers are more important than those across dialects (1.3.4), we focus primarily on register patterns of use based on analysis of the four core registers. However, where there was evidence that a given feature is used quite differently across the dialects, we investigated and compared the patterns for AmE and BrE.

For most of these dialect comparisons, we concentrated on the registers of conversation and news, since these are the 'local/regional' registers most likely to reflect AmE v. BrE differences (1.3). In contrast, fiction and academic prose can be considered largely 'global' registers, the language being influenced by authors, editors, and publishing houses often located on different continents, with an eye to an international readership. For this reason, AmE v. BrE differences have mostly been levelled in fiction and academic prose, while they are more apparent in conversation and news.

We should emphasize that the present grammar does not attempt an overall treatment of dialect differences in English. A comprehensive survey of dialect differences would be extremely rewarding, and similar corpus-based techniques could be profitably used to investigate dialect features.[1] However, such an investigation is beyond the scope of the present grammar.

## 1.4.3 Size of the LSWE Corpus

As Table 1.2 shows, the complete LSWE Corpus contains 37,244 texts and about 40,026,000 words. Texts in the Corpus vary considerably in their length, depending on the register. At one extreme, newspaper texts tend to be quite short, only about 250 words in an average text in the BrE subcorpus and about 450 words per article in the AmE subcorpus. At the other extreme, fiction and academic prose texts tend to be very long, with an average of about 35,000 words per text in fiction and 13,000 words per text in academic prose. In fact, these subcorpora include a number of complete books, plus other texts that represent multiple chapters from a book. The specific composition of each register subcorpus is discussed further in 1.5 below.

For a better understanding of the amount of text represented in the LSWE Corpus, it is useful to have some concrete benchmarks for comparison. For example, in both academic books and fiction novels, an average page contains between 300 and 400 words, depending on the size of the page and the print. Thus, most complete books contain between 30,000 and 200,000 words.

Based on a typical 300-page book that contains around 100,000 words, nine or ten complete books would constitute a one-million word sample (albeit one with little diversity across authors).

In conversation, speech rate can fluctuate considerably, depending on the level of involvement and the influence of other activities occurring at the same time (such as playing a game, watching TV, or eating). However, on average speakers produce around 7,000 words per hour in the conversational texts of the LSWE Corpus, or a little under 120 words per minute. Based on this speech rate, a one-million word corpus corresponds to 140–150 hours of conversational interaction.

## 1.4.4 Representativeness and accuracy of the LSWE Corpus

No corpus provides a perfect representation of a language, and the LSWE Corpus is no exception to this rule. There are a number of competing factors to be considered when compiling a corpus, including:

- How are text samples selected?
- How many text samples should be included?
- How long should text samples be?
- How large should the entire corpus be?
- Should the corpus distinguish among registers? If so, what registers should it include?
- Should the corpus include both spoken and written registers?
- What time and resources are available for corpus construction?
- How much attention should be given to proofreading and editing the corpus?

Corpus compilers have usually emphasized some of these factors over others. At one extreme, many corpora have been designed to include texts from multiple registers, with considerable attention given to a random selection of texts within each register, to relative length of text samples, and to careful proofreading and editing of texts once they have been entered into a computer. These corpora are usually relatively small (say, between 50,000 and two million words), but they are labor-intensive, often requiring many years to complete. These corpora are sometimes referred to as **balanced**, because they aim to represent different registers by appropriately balanced amounts of text, while covering the widest possible range of variation within their sample frame. The British National Corpus (see Burnard 1995) is exceptional in that it is fairly 'balanced' yet very large—100 million words.

At the other extreme are corpora that have been designed primarily to be very large (over 100 million words). Such corpora usually do not represent registers in a systematic way and give little or no attention to the random selection of texts; they are based on the assumption that all important patterns will be represented if the corpus is large enough. As a result, such corpora are mostly made up of texts that can be captured opportunistically, such as news articles from selected newspapers that are available in electronic form, or books from large publishing companies. Corpora of this type can be compiled relatively efficiently and quickly. Further, little effort is given to proofreading and editing of texts, again based on the assumption that overall patterns in a large corpus will be little influenced by a sprinkling of minor typographical errors, repetitions, or other problems with scanning and transmission.

The designers and compilers of the LSWE Corpus have tried to achieve a middle ground, taking all of these factors into consideration. With over 40 million words, the LSWE Corpus is much larger than earlier 'balanced' corpora (such as the Brown and LOB, which each contained one million words). At the same time, the Corpus includes a representative sampling of texts across multiple registers.

The subcorpus for conversation is probably the most representative sampling of this register compiled to date. It is many times larger than most previous conversational corpora, and it has been collected in genuinely natural settings (where most previous conversational corpora have typically been collected in restricted or artificial settings).

The BrE subcorpus of conversation is a part of the British National Corpus, which was collected by Longman. The British Market Research Bureau was subcontracted to collect natural, everyday conversation from a representative sample of the British population. For the AmE subcorpus, Longman contracted Professor Jack Du Bois and his team at the University of California, Santa Barbara, to collect conversations from a representative sample of the US population along similar lines.

The fiction subcorpus includes samples from many novels representing all the major types of contemporary fiction. News texts have been collected from several different newspapers, which differ in both political orientation and distribution. In addition, individual articles have been sampled from across the range of sections and subject areas.

Finally, the academic prose subcorpus includes samples from books and research articles across a wide range of academic disciplines. (The composition of the subcorpus for each register is discussed in detail in 1.5.1–4.)

The LSWE Corpus has been edited to correct major problems (such as duplicate articles in news, or repeated passages due to scanning errors), and our working with the Corpus on a daily basis over several years has convinced us that typographical and word-level scanning errors are generally rare and not systematic.

A few orthographic variations have been introduced in the spoken corpora by transcribers; for example, the semi-modals are sometimes transcribed as two words and sometimes as a single contracted form, as in:

*going to* v. *gonna*

*got to* v. *gotta*

*want to* v. *wanna*

There are also some variations in the spelling of words not typically found in writing, such as *OK* v. *okay*, and *cause* v. *cos*. Most transcription differences are a low-level variation and are dealt with in a similar way to the spelling differences found across written dialects. In fact, a transcriber's choice in writing, say, *gotta* rather than *got to*, is likely to be significant in reflecting pronunciation (14.1.2.1).

Any variation in transcriptions was dealt with in a controlled manner during the automatic and interactive computational analyses (1.6), ensuring that the corpus findings are reliable.

## 1.5 Description of the register categories in the LSWE Corpus

The subcorpus for each of the four main register categories is described in detail in the following sections.

### 1.5.1 Conversation

The sampling for the conversation subcorpus was carried out along demographic lines: a set of informants was identified to represent the range of English speakers in the country (UK or USA) across age, sex, social group, and regional spread. Then, these informants tape-recorded all their conversational interactions over a period of a week, using a high-quality tape recorder. All conversations were subsequently transcribed orthographically, for use in lexicographic and grammatical research.

Tables 1.3 and 1.4 present the approximate breakdown of speakers by age and sex for the BrE and AmE conversational corpora. The numbers are approximate, because it is difficult to track all interlocutors participating in conversations. The subcorpus was constructed around selected target participants, who controlled the tape recorder and kept records of the other interlocutors. However, it is often difficult to determine whether interlocutors across two conversations are the same or different.[2]

Table 1.3 **Approximate number of speakers in the BrE conversation subcorpus, by age and sex**

| age bracket (in years) | female speakers | male speakers | total |
|---|---|---|---|
| less than 10 | 30 | 25 | 55 |
| 11–19 | 35 | 45 | 80 |
| 20–29 | 40 | 40 | 80 |
| 30–39 | 35 | 25 | 60 |
| 40–49 | 40 | 30 | 70 |
| 50–59 | 30 | 25 | 55 |
| 60 + | 45 | 30 | 75 |
| unknown | 15 | 5 | 20 |
| total | 270 | 225 | 495 |

### 1.5.2 Fiction

The fiction subcorpus is composed of texts from several national varieties, although the majority of these texts are from BrE (79 out of 139 texts). A large number of the remaining fiction texts are from AmE (41 texts), while 19 texts are from other varieties. The breakdown for fiction texts by national dialect is given in Table 1.5.

Fiction texts from 'other' national dialects were collected from five major regions: Australian (2 texts), Canadian (1 text), Caribbean (11 texts), Irish (2

Table 1.4    **Number of speakers in the AmE conversation subcorpus, by age and sex**

| age bracket (in years) | female speakers | male speakers | total |
|---|---|---|---|
| less than 20 | 65 | 47 | 112 |
| 21–30 | 66 | 48 | 114 |
| 31–40 | 44 | 50 | 94 |
| 41–50 | 57 | 25 | 82 |
| 51–60 | 36 | 15 | 51 |
| 61+ | 24 | 14 | 38 |
| total | 292 | 199 | 491 |

Table 1.5    **Distribution of fiction texts across national varieties**

| national variety | number of texts | number of words |
|---|---|---|
| American | 41 | 1,095,200 |
| British | 79 | 3,347,100 |
| other | 19 | 537,700 |

texts), and West African (1 text). (The national variety is uncertain for 2 texts in the subcorpus.)

All the texts in the BrE and AmE samples, and most of the texts from other dialects, are excerpts from novels. (A few of the texts from other national dialects are short stories.) The large majority of these texts were published after 1950: 112 texts after 1950; 27 texts before 1950. Some examples of pre-1950 texts are:

- Graham Greene, *The Power and the Glory* (1940)
- James Joyce, *Ulysses* (1922)
- W. Somerset Maugham, *Of Human Bondage* (1915)
- D. H. Lawrence, *Sons and Lovers* (1913)

Fiction tends to have a long shelf-life, particularly when the books become classics. Such works are still widely read and upheld as examples of the English language at the end of the twentieth century. As a result, these older texts have a role in defining the receptive grammatical usage up to the present day. However, it should be emphasized that such texts make up less than 1 percent of the total number of texts in the LSWE Corpus.

Further, the large majority of the texts in the fiction subcorpus were written for an adult audience. In AmE and BrE fiction, out of a total of 139 texts, 125 (4,529,800 words) were written for adults and 14 (450,200 words) for teens and older children.

The following are some examples of novels for teenagers and older children:

post-1950:
- Adele Geras, *The Green Behind the Glass* (1982)
- Graham Greene, *Doctor Fischer of Geneva* (1980)
- Penelope Lively, *The Ghost of Thomas Kempe* (1973)

pre-1950:
- Jack London, *The Call of the Wild* (1903)
- Kenneth Grahame, *The Wind in the Willows* (1908)

Target audience is not always clear-cut, since some of the earlier novels written for adults have become 'classics' read mostly by older children (such as *The Call of the Wild*).

Overall this subcorpus was designed to include texts from many different kinds of fiction. For example, it includes mystery fiction (e.g. *'C' is for Corpse* by Sue Grafton), romance fiction (e.g. *Jerusalem the Golden* by Margaret Drabble), historical fiction (e.g. *Shogun* by James Clavell), adventure fiction (e.g. *Airport* by Arthur Hailey), and science fiction (e.g. *Dune* by Frank Herbert). Roughly half the texts in the subcorpus can be classified as 'general' fiction. These include modern classics like *Mr. Sammler's Planet* by Saul Bellow, and *Catch 22* by Joseph Heller, as well as most of the pre-1950 novels listed above.

## 1.5.3    News

Unless otherwise stated, the register analyses of news in the grammar are based on a subcorpus of BrE news texts sampled from ten different newspapers, representing a range of political and regional differences. The AmE news subcorpus is used for a number of AmE/BrE comparisons and text examples. The following British newspapers contributed to the core corpus:

**national newspapers:** *The Independent, The Guardian, Daily Mirror, Sunday People*, and *Today*; **regional newspapers:** *Liverpool Echo, The Belfast Telegraph, The East Anglian Daily Times, The Northern Echo, The Scotsman*.

The national newspapers, mostly published in London, represent different readership levels which are important in the British press: *The Guardian* and *The Independent* represent 'highbrow', broadsheet newspapers; the *Daily Mirror* and the *Sunday People* represent popular, tabloid newspapers; and *Today* represents an in-between category.

Texts are also sampled from across the various topics found in most newspapers. (Many of these subject areas are allotted a separate section in newspapers.) The majority of the news texts in the subcorpus are from three major subject areas: domestic/local/city news, foreign/world news, and sports news. Other major categories are business news (including commerce, economics, and finance articles); arts (including cinema, television, fine arts, and the media in general, and also some articles on entertainment personalities); and social news (covering everything from reports about society people and events to results of polls concerning social issues). The complete list of subject areas covered in the BrE news subcorpus is given in Table 1.6.

The subcorpus for AmE news is taken from three major sources: the Associated Press news service, the *San Jose Mercury*, and the *Wall Street Journal*. Samples are split fairly evenly between these three sources (1.6–1.8 million words from each). The approximate breakdown of the AmE news subcorpus by topic is given in Table 1.7.[3] Many of the major categories in the AmE subcorpus are similar to those in the BrE subcorpus: arts/entertainment, business/economics, domestic/local/city news, foreign/world news, and sports. There are also some differences, though: in the AmE subcorpus, social news is not a major category, while international trade, politics, and law all receive more attention.

Table 1.6    **Breakdown of the BrE news subcorpus by topic**

| topic or section | number of words | topic or section | number of words |
|---|---|---|---|
| **major categories** | | | |
| arts | 418,400 | foreign/world news | 1,156,100 |
| business | 542,800 | social news | 501,300 |
| domestic/local/city news | 1,233,900 | sports | 1,218,700 |
| **minor categories** | | | |
| architecture | 6,400 | living | 8,300 |
| auto | 1,400 | nature | 5,500 |
| editorial | 68,900 | real estate | 3,500 |
| education | 3,900 | religion | 10,300 |
| fashion | 5,400 | royalty | 31,500 |
| food | 14,100 | science and technology | 16,600 |
| gardening | 2,100 | title page | 21,600 |
| health | 28,100 | travel | 93,700 |
| law | 39,900 | | |

Table 1.7    **Approximate breakdown of the AmE news subcorpus by topic**

| topic or section | number of words | topic or section | number of words |
|---|---|---|---|
| **major categories** | | | |
| arts/entertainment | 325,000 | international trade | 260,000 |
| business/economics | 1,545,000 | politics | 350,000 |
| domestic/local/city news | 995,000 | law | 260,000 |
| foreign/world news | 680,000 | sports | 260,000 |
| **minor categories** | | | |
| advertising/marketing | 15,000 | housing/consumer advice | 25,000 |
| editorials/letters to the editor | 105,000 | labor/workplace | 35,000 |
| education | 90,000 | military | 50,000 |
| food/wine | 50,000 | religion | 50,000 |
| health | 35,000 | science/medicine/technology | 95,000 |
| history | 30,000 | weather | 35,000 |

## 1.5.4    Academic prose

The academic prose subcorpus includes both book extracts and research articles. There are fewer book extracts, but they are much longer on average than the research articles, with most extracts including several chapters.

For the 75 book extracts, the total number of words is 2,655,000 and the average text length is 35,400 words. For the 333 research articles, the total number of words is 2,676,800 and the average text length is 8,050 words.

Most of the books included in the academic subcorpus are trade books written for an audience with technical background knowledge (59 out of 75 book extracts). Only 16 of the book extracts are written for a lay audience, including student textbooks.

Table 1.8 shows that the book extracts are taken from a wide range of academic disciplines, including sciences, social sciences, and humanities. The research articles included in the academic prose subcorpus are either journal articles or papers published in an edited collection (such as conference proceedings). Nearly all of these texts are complete articles, written for a technical audience. These articles are taken from a wide range of academic disciplines, similar to those for the book extracts (see Table 1.9).

**Table 1.8** **Breakdown of academic book extracts across disciplines**

| subject | number of texts | number of words |
|---|---|---|
| agriculture | 4 | 179,000 |
| biology/ecology | 6 | 190,200 |
| chemistry | 4 | 158,200 |
| computing | 8 | 269,300 |
| education | 7 | 225,700 |
| engineering/technology | 7 | 185,700 |
| geology/geography | 4 | 152,200 |
| law/history | 5 | 184,700 |
| linguistics/literature | 5 | 149,600 |
| mathematics | 6 | 216,600 |
| medicine | 6 | 201,200 |
| psychology | 3 | 118,400 |
| sociology | 10 | 424,200 |
| **total** | **75** | **2,655,000** |

## 1.5.5 Supplementary registers

Two supplementary registers are included in the LSWE Corpus. The first is **non-conversational speech**, which complements the conversation corpus in that it includes a range of more formal speech events found in specific situational contexts. The texts in this subcorpus were collected by Longman as part of the British National Corpus. Some of these speech events are monologues, such as sermons, TV newsreading/reporting, some types of sports broadcasting, and many of the lectures and speeches. However, roughly one third of the lectures and speeches involve some question/answer interaction or other forms of discussion, and thus include a dialogue element. The remaining speech events are typically dialogic, involving at least two speakers, although they are more task-oriented and more informational than a typical face-to-face conversation.

Speech events represented in the subcorpus of context-governed speech:

- lectures (classroom and public)
- teaching (school, tutorials, religious instruction, hands-on types of teaching, such as photography or drawing instruction)
- planned speeches
- sermons

Table 1.9    **Breakdown of academic research articles across disciplines**

| subject | number of texts | number of words |
|---|---|---|
| agriculture | 2 | 78,700 |
| anthropology/archeology | 9 | 152,100 |
| biology/entomology | 19 | 369,100 |
| chemistry/physics | 2 | 31,700 |
| computing | 1 | 29,700 |
| ecology | 4 | 13,100 |
| education | 11 | 410,600 |
| geology | 1 | 39,400 |
| law/history/politics | 5 | 189,200 |
| linguistics | 2 | 58,800 |
| mathematics | 6 | 33,100 |
| medicine | 257 | 752,000 |
| nursing | 2 | 75,200 |
| psychology | 3 | 124,100 |
| sociology | 9 | 320,000 |
| **total** | 333 | 2,676,800 |

- ceremonial discourse (religious ceremonies, such as baptisms and confirmations, as well as public ceremonies, such as grand openings)
- courtroom discourse
- debates
- auctions
- public meetings
- committee meetings (faculty, staff, and board meetings)
- club meetings
- private meetings
- interviews
- medical consultations
- radio broadcasting (phone-in talk shows)
- sports broadcasting
- TV broadcasting (with interviews, reporting, phone-ins, etc.)
- TV newsreading, reporting
- TV documentaries (narration and interviews)

The other major supplementary register is a **general prose** (non-fiction) category. This consists of excerpts from non-fiction books written for a general lay readership. As Table 1.10 shows, these books cover a wide range of subject areas of general interest to readers.

Table 1.10    **Breakdown of general prose texts across subjects (AmE and BrE)**

| subject | number of texts |
|---|:---:|
| biography (and autobiography) | 31 |
| business<br>(employment, personnel management,<br>finance, marketing, administration,<br>commerce, development, and planning) | 21 |
| economics | 8 |
| education | 1 |
| fine arts | 13 |
| food and wine | 10 |
| history/civilization | 25 |
| hobbies | 3 |
| literary essays | 2 |
| literature/literary criticism | 9 |
| linguistics/sociolinguistics | 3 |
| maths/science | 3 |
| mythology | 2 |
| philosophy | 5 |
| politics/government | 21 |
| religion | 22 |
| sports | 2 |
| travel | 3 |
| **total** | **184** |

# 1.6    Grammatical analysis of the LSWE Corpus

The grammatical investigations were carried out using a variety of computational, interactive, and detailed 'manual' textual analyses, mainly by a team led by Doug Biber, including Susan Conrad, Marie Helt, and Erika Konrad. In all cases, the overarching concern was to achieve an accurate description of the distributional patterns of the target feature (i.e. the linguistic form or construction being investigated).

Beyond this concern, the choice of analytical technique was determined by three major considerations: (1) the need to base each investigation on a representative sample of English texts: that is, analyzing a large corpus from multiple registers; (2) the extent to which automatic or semi-automatic computational techniques were reliable in analyzing the target feature; and (3) the need to complete individual analyses in an efficient and timely manner, so that no single investigation became a book in itself.

As a preliminary step to the grammatical analyses, we **tagged** the entire LSWE Corpus; that is, using an automatic tagging program, we assigned to each running word in the Corpus a grammatical label such as 'plural common noun' or 'past tense lexical verb'. The 'tagger' (developed by Biber) used online dictionaries, probabilistic information, and grammatical rules to analyze the grammatical characteristics of every word in the Corpus. With a relatively complex set of tags, the tagger attained accuracy of 90–95 percent. The automatic tagging provided the basis for recognizing many core grammatical categories (such as nouns, verbs, adjectives) and more complex features (such as complement clauses). However, the actual grammatical analyses for the book were based on a number of additional procedures, described below.

The first step for most grammatical analyses was to develop automatic computer programs to investigate the distribution of target features (such as modal auxiliaries, passives, etc.). For this purpose, programs were developed to use the pre-assigned grammatical tags, together with more detailed lexical and grammatical information, to identify occurrences of target features and to analyze contextual variants. Some of these programs also created large online databases, for example frequency lists of all verbs or adjectives found in the Corpus. The main advantage of developing accurate computer programs is that they allow efficient analysis of the entire Corpus. Further, they provide kinds of information that could not reasonably be obtained otherwise, such as identifying the 50 most common verbs in a register.

However, the description of many grammatical features involves meaning distinctions (e.g. the distinction between animate and inanimate noun phrases, or the various verb valency patterns). These characteristics cannot be accurately analyzed using only automatic techniques; instead they require a human analyst.

In addition, most grammatical categories include at least a few highly ambiguous lexical items, which raise serious problems for automatic analyses. To take a simple example, the phrases *kind of* and *sort of* are two common expressions used for hedging (7.14.2.6), as in:

> Or if you can **sort of** wedge it in there. (CONV)

> And I **kind of** brushed it off. (CONV)

A blind count of these forms would incorrectly show that these hedges are common in academic prose as well as conversation. This is because these same expressions are almost always used as part of a noun phrase, rather than a hedge, in academic prose; for example:

> This is **the sort of** case in which judges must exercise discretionary power. (ACAD†)

> It has become fashionable to say that **this kind of** equality is unimportant. (ACAD)

In fact, our analysis shows that conversation also commonly uses these expressions as parts of noun phrases rather than hedges, as in:

> What **sort of** ideas have you come up with? (CONV)

> I mean, do we want these **kind of** people in our team? (CONV)

Problems of this type, where particular words or phrases can perform quite different grammatical tasks, arise in the analysis of almost every grammatical feature. Further, it is often the most common words that serve the greatest range of functions. For example, the words *get, go,* and *see* are some of the most common verbs in English, but these same words can function as a transitive or intransitive verb, as a copular verb (e.g. *go bad*), as part of common fixed discourse phrases (*I see, you see*), or as part of semi-modal verbs (*have got to, be going to*). The word *like*, also very common as a verb, is even more flexible in the range of other functions it serves (including preposition, conjunction, and adverbial hedge).

Because of difficulties of this type, we used a number of other analytical techniques to complement the automatic analyses. First, **KWIC** (Key Word In Context) **concordance** files were generated for every analysis, and these files were checked by hand to determine if non-target features were inadvertently being included in the analysis. For example, we searched for all sequences of noun + relative adverb (e.g. *where, when, why*) to identify the most common head nouns taking relative clauses with adverbial gaps. However, as the following concordance lines illustrate, some of these sequences were in fact adverbial clauses (as in **1**) rather than noun postmodifier clauses (as in **2**):

(1)

Noun + Rel = way + when

File = 00002.FCT

not interfere in case she might become saddled with the

responsibility . She was thus pleased in a vindictive

way *when* the old man came to stay and , for

the time being anyway , so attracted the child 's

(2)

Noun + Rel = day + when

File = 00002.FCT

she found the kitchen the most comforting part of the

house . Her father and his wife arrived one

day *when* she was at school . When she got home

, she was too shy to go in , and

At the same time, texts were checked by hand to ensure that the automatic analysis was not disregarding occurrences of the target feature.

Depending on the extent and nature of the problems uncovered during these checks, one of several corrective techniques was used. First of all, for many analyses KWIC files were coded by hand. Many of these KWIC files were produced by computer programs, which utilized various grammatical and lexical characteristics of the target feature and context. In other cases, we used a concordancing package—Corpus.Bench (a proprietary tool developed by TEXTware A/S, Copenhagen)—to do rapid, online searches in the Corpus. Corpus.Bench was especially helpful when a target feature could be identified using selected lexical items. Once a concordance listing was generated, we typically analyzed a random sample of tokens (usually between 500 and 2,000 occurrences) of the target feature for each register. In some cases, quantitative findings are based on these hand-coded files, while in other cases it was possible to adjust the automated counts based on these hand analyses.

Interactive grammar-checker programs (developed by the research team under Biber at Northern Arizona University) were required to analyze the characteristics of some other features. These programs work in a similar way to a spell-checker in a word processor: automatic techniques are used to provide a 'best guess', which is often correct, but all codes are checked and corrected (if needed) by a human analyst. For example, automatic computational tools cannot provide reliable analyses of the informational characteristics of noun phrases (e.g. 'given' v. 'new' information; 'anaphoric' or 'exophoric' reference; and the distance from a previous co-referent if anaphoric). In this case, an interactive grammar-checking program is used to code each noun phrase. The program cycles through a text, stopping when it reaches each noun or pronoun. It then prompts the user to select the correct codes for that noun phrase.

As with a spell-checker, there are several advantages to using an interactive grammar-checking tool for analyses of this type. First, continuing with the above example, the tool identifies noun phrases automatically (so the analyst does not have to read through the text trying to spot noun phrases). Second, the tool provides an initial analysis of the informational characteristics of the noun phrase—when the initial analysis is correct, the user simply accepts that code. Finally, the interactive tool provides a list of other possible correct analyses to choose from, so that the user just selects the number corresponding to the correct analysis (if the initial analysis is not correct). By using such interactive 'grammar-checking' tools, we were able to analyze relatively large samples of text for a range of more complex linguistic characteristics.

A final analytical issue relates to the treatment of surface inconsistencies, due either to spelling variability (such as *analyze* v. *analyse*) or variability among transcription practices (such as *OK* v. *okay*). Although this kind of variation causes minor irritations for analysts, it poses no special problems. Rather, the analytic techniques described above can be used by merely extending the search to include all spelling/transcription variants.

Once the grammatical analyses were completed, additional computer programs were used to compile frequency counts, and to analyze the distributional and co-occurrence patterns. All counts were normalized to a common basis of frequency per million words. (Section 1.7 discusses these quantitative findings further.)

The quantitative findings were then interpreted in functional terms, based on further examination of concordance files and complete texts (1.8). Thus, the human analysis of text extracts was central at every stage: despite the use of sophisticated computational and quantitative techniques, all stages of the analysis have been shaped and guided by human observation of grammatical features in natural discourse contexts.

As a result of the considerations discussed above, different analytical techniques and corpus samples were used for particular grammatical investigations. The 'analysis notes' at the end of the book give specific methodological information for each of these analyses.

## 1.7 Quantitative findings in the grammar

All **frequency counts** reported in the grammar are **normalized** to a common basis, per million words of text (based on 'orthographic words', separated by spaces; 2.2.2). This allows a direct comparison of results for different features. Some features are extremely common; for example, the pronoun *I* occurs almost 40,000 times per million words in conversation (i.e. one *I* every 25 words on average). Other features are much less common; for example, the most common phrasal verb in academic prose—*carry out*—occurs less than 200 times per million words.

In most cases, frequency counts are based on the full sample of texts from each register. Normalizing the counts thus also allows for a direct comparison across registers. For example, a feature that occurs 780 times in the BrE conversation subcorpus (with 3.9 million words) is equivalent to a feature that occurs 1,080 times in the BrE news subcorpus (with 5.4 million words), since both of these translate to normalized frequencies of 200 per million words. That is:

- Conversation: 780 tokens ÷ 3.9 million words = 200 tokens per million words
- News: 1,080 tokens ÷ 5.4 million words = 200 tokens per million words

Analyses using interactive grammar-checking programs were based on much smaller samples, usually between 100,000 and 500,000 words per register. However, frequency counts from these analyses were also normalized to the standard basis per million words. (The coded files from these analyses were also used to produce proportional data reporting percentages—see below.) Slightly different procedures were adopted in parts of Chapter 14, 'The Grammar of Conversation'; they are discussed in the analysis notes to that chapter.

Normalized frequency counts can be translated into terms that are more familiar to most readers, using minutes of speech or book pages as the basis. Thus Table 1.11 provides the equivalences for several common **frequency benchmarks** used throughout the grammar. These translations are computed using an average speech rate of 120 words per minute and an average of 400 words per page for the written registers.

**Table 1.11** **Spoken and written equivalencies for common frequency benchmarks**

| occurrences per million words | speech—occurs once every: | writing—occurs once every: |
|---|---|---|
| 1000 | 8.5 minutes | 2.5 pages |
| 200 | 42.5 minutes | 12 pages |
| 100 | 85 minutes | 25 pages |
| 40 | 200 minutes | 60 pages |
| 20 | 400 minutes | 125 pages |
| 10 | 800 minutes | 250 pages |

Several factors can cause minor fluctuations in the frequency counts computed for lexico-grammatical features. Counts will vary somewhat from one corpus to another, even when the corpora are similar in their design. More importantly, most counts reflect underlying decisions about the forms to include in a feature class. For example, should words like *well*, *right*, and *okay*, at the beginning of a spoken utterance, be counted as adverbs, discourse markers, or neither? Should -*ing* forms as complements (such as *running* in *she loves running*) be counted as verb participles, nouns, or something else? Although we have tried hard to be consistent, decisions of this type can sometimes result in relatively large frequency differences for a feature class. Finally, when working with large corpus files, there will always be some variability due to error, depending on occasional human mistakes or inaccuracy of methodological tools.

Because of the influence of such factors, we report frequencies at a level of precision that we judge to be replicable, rather than reporting the exact frequency obtained in our analysis. These rounded frequencies accurately measure the relative use of features—across registers and relative to other features—without suggesting the sometimes spurious accuracy of an exact count. We report rounded frequencies in two ways: first, in many cases we present quantitative findings in graphs and figures; and second, we often report frequencies in terms of benchmarks (e.g. more than 100 occurrences per million words). Because of this rounding, the sum of individual counts is sometimes slightly different from a single cumulative count for the same feature class.

Frequencies at this level of precision are replicable across different sub-samples from the LSWE Corpus, and we feel confident that they could be replicated in other comparably representative corpora as well. It should be emphasized that the influence of register is significant in any attempt to replicate quantitative findings. For example, we would *not* expect that the frequencies reported here could be replicated through analysis of a corpus consisting of texts from a single register.

In addition to frequency counts, quantitative findings in the grammar are sometimes reported as **percentages**. For example, the verbs *tell* and *promise* can both occur with intransitive, transitive, and ditransitive valency patterns (5.2.4). However, our corpus analysis shows that they have very different associations with these valencies (e.g. *promise* occurs a high proportion of the time with a simple transitive pattern, while *tell* occurs most of the time with a ditransitive pattern). Associations of this type are reported through percentages. For example, about 55 percent of the tokens of *promise* analyzed in fiction take a monotransitive pattern, while about 70 percent of the tokens of *tell* analyzed in that register take a ditransitive pattern. (Similar to frequency counts, we have also rounded percentages to a level of precision that we can replicate.) Findings reported as percentages provide no information about overall frequency. For example, the fact that the verb *tell* is over ten times more common in fiction than the verb *promise* is not reflected at all in the proportional findings given above. Thus, findings reported as percentages are intended to answer research questions relating to proportional use, rather than questions concerning how common a feature is in absolute terms.

In a few cases, we have also used **mutual information** scores to assess the strength of collocational associations. The mutual information index is based on the probability of observing two words together compared to the probability of observing each word independently. A score of about one shows that there is little or no relationship between the words: their actual frequency of co-occurrence is much the same as that which would be expected from their combined separate rates of occurrence, assuming no special tendency to co-occur. A score much greater than one shows that the words tend to co-occur at a rate much greater than chance.

Finally, it should be noted that we do not report inferential statistics (testing statistical significance) in the grammar. However, we focus only on those patterns that are clearly important in addition to being statistically significant. Given the size of the LSWE Corpus and the extremely large number of observations included in most of our analyses, it is easy to achieve statistical significance; indeed, with a large sample size, quite small differences are often 'statistically significant' (i.e. likely not to be due to chance). Such differences are often not important or interesting, though. On the other hand, corpus analysis of most linguistic features uncovers many findings that show large differences across registers and across comparable forms: findings that are clearly important in addition to being statistically significant. These latter findings are the focus of our discussion in the *LGSWE*.

# 1.8 Functional interpretation of quantitative findings

Functional interpretation of the quantitative findings plays a pervasive role in our grammatical descriptions (illustrated in 1.2.1–3 above). This role is formalized in a standard sequencing of expository subsections throughout the chapters: first an introduction (presenting the basic structural description of the grammatical feature in question), then 'Corpus Findings' (presenting the distributional patterns for the grammatical feature), followed by 'Discussion of Findings'. In the 'Discussion' subsections, we illustrate the discourse patterns described quantitatively in the 'Findings' subsections, and attempt to account for those patterns in functional terms. This means that we leave behind the rigor of quantitative methods, and indulge in a more interpretive approach.

In addition, functional considerations played an important but less obvious role in shaping the corpus analyses themselves. That is, our corpus analyses began with decisions concerning the factors to investigate: i.e. those factors most likely to be important in describing the use of the target grammatical feature. The identification of these potentially important contextual factors is guided by functional considerations, based on a prior understanding of register and discourse characteristics in relation to the communicative functions served by the target feature. Thus, although we do not present them formally, our investigations of use have been guided by hypotheses derived from our collective prior experience in the realm of English grammar. The empirical corpus analyses validate some of these prior hypotheses, while disconfirming others, and the 'Discussion' subsections are the main place where these conclusions are described.

There are three major types of functional association described in the *LGSWE*: (1) the **work that a feature performs** in discourse; (2) the **processing constraints** that it reflects; and (3) the **situational** or **social distinctions** that it conventionally indexes. Throughout the *LGSWE*, these functional notions are used to interpret the observed patterns of use.

## 1.8.1 Function as the performance of tasks

In the first type of functional association, linguistic features can be said to actually perform particular tasks in discourse. For example, first person pronouns 'function' to refer to the speaker/writer; relative clauses 'function' to elaborate and make explicit referential identities; passives 'function' to give informational prominence to the noun phrase occurring before the main clause verb; *that*-clauses together with main-clause verbs of speaking 'function' to provide indirect reports of speech.

It is useful to distinguish among six major kinds of tasks or functions performed by linguistic features in discourse: ideational, textual, personal, interpersonal, contextual, and aesthetic. **Ideational** tasks—using linguistic structures to identify referents or to convey propositional information about those referents—have sometimes been regarded as the primary function of language. Simple declarative clauses have a basic ideational function, presenting a proposition about some referent(s). Constructions such as relative clauses or some kinds of prepositional phrases also serve important ideational tasks by specifying or elaborating the identity of the referents in a construction. Not surprisingly, structures functioning to perform ideational tasks are prominent in the expository written registers, which have informational purposes. However, ideational tasks are only one of the major functions served by linguistic features.

Linguistic features are being used to perform **textual** tasks when they contribute to the formation of a coherent text (rather than a string of unrelated structures). Textual tasks are of two major types: marking **information structure** and marking **cohesion.**

Information structure refers to the way in which referential information is packaged or presented within clauses, as well as the way in which clauses are packaged or presented within texts (11.1.1). Speakers and writers often make choices about the ordering of structural components, to mark specific components as being more prominent or presenting new information. Examples of grammatical constructions used for informational packaging include passive constructions, extraposed clauses, and clefts.

**Passive construction** (11.3):
>    *This book was written for beginning students.*
v.    *We wrote this book for beginning students.*

**Extraposed construction** (9.2.7, 9.4.7):
>    *It's nice to hear the wind.*
v.    *To hear the wind is nice.*

**Cleft construction** (11.6):
>    *It is for this reason that we have deliberately emphasized a broad view.*
v.    *We have deliberately emphasized a broad view for this reason.*

**Cohesion** refers to the integration which is achieved between different parts of a text by various types of semantic and referential linkages. For example, 'chains of reference' are a common phenomenon of both spoken and written discourse, whereby clauses in sequence are referentially linked. The components of the chain are different kinds of referring expressions (e.g. pronouns, proper nouns, repeated noun phrases, synonyms) referring to the same real-world entities (4.1.2–4).

When linguistic features are used for **personal** tasks, they express the individual attitudes, thoughts, and feelings of the speaker (see especially Chapter 12 on **stance**). For example, first person pronouns together with verbs of thinking (e.g. *think, know*), desire (e.g. *want*), or other emotional state (e.g. *hope, worry*) often serve personal functions (9.2.2, 9.4.2). Similarly, stance adverbs such as *unfortunately* and *hopefully* often serve to present the personal attitudes of the speaker towards some proposition (10.3). These tasks are important in many spoken registers (e.g. conversation, interviews) as well as in written registers such as personal letters and newspaper editorials.

**Interpersonal** tasks differ from personal tasks in that they depend on and determine some aspect of the relationship among participants. For example, in conversation, the choice of various types of interrogative and imperative clauses governs, and is governed by, the interactive relation between the speaker and addressee (3.13.2, 3.13.4, 14.4.2–3). Similarly, the choice of different address terms (or vocatives) reflects the status of the addressee in relation to that of the speaker (see, for example, 14.4.1 on the choice between first name and surname address).

Grammatical structures serve **contextual** tasks when they make reference to (or depend on) some aspect of the situation shared by speaker and listeners.

Features serving these tasks can refer to either a physical or spatial situation (e.g. *here, there, that tree over there, the book on the table*), a temporal situation (e.g. *yesterday, last year*), or to some imaginatively or emotively evoked situation (e.g. when a joke begins with *there was this guy* <...>, 4.4.3E).

Finally, **aesthetic** functions are uppermost when grammatical forms are selected according to conventions of 'good style' or 'proper grammar'. Examples of these considerations include the use of a varied vocabulary, using synonyms instead of repetition, and the avoidance of dispreferred structures such as 'dangling' participles and non-standard forms (see, for example, 14.4.5).

## 1.8.2 Function as a reflection of processing constraints

A second kind of functional association relates to the processing constraints that a linguistic variant is typically associated with. That is, the patterns of use associated with a grammatical feature are often strongly influenced by differing production and comprehension circumstances. For example, speakers use more contracted forms under the pressures of online production. Generalized content words, such as hedges (*kind of, sort of*) or general nouns (e.g. *thing*), also reflect the difficulty of more precise lexical expression under real-time production circumstances (although they can also be used deliberately to be vague or imprecise). Conversely, writers who have the time to revise and polish their output can use a wider range of words and more complex grammatical structures (such as heavy embedding in noun phrases; 8.1). Other processing considerations, such as the preference for placing longer constituents at the end of the clause (**end weight**, 11.1.3), apply to both spoken and written registers.

These functional considerations are psycholinguistic; this type of variation is often not consciously controlled by the speaker. In contrast, the speaker/writer's role is more active in manipulating grammatical features to perform discourse tasks. Some features can be functional in both senses, however. For example, a high type/token ratio (i.e. a high degree of lexical diversity in a text; 2.2.1) serves to increase the semantic precision and informational density of a written text, and thus it can be required to perform a challenging ideational task; at the same time, it is a functional reflection of considerable opportunity for careful production, as in many writing situations, as opposed to the real-time production constraints characterizing most speaking situations.

## 1.8.3 Function as social or situational indexing

Finally, the third major kind of functional association relates to the way that grammatical forms can conventionally **index** particular situations or social groups. That is, people sometimes choose to use particular grammatical features simply for the conventional associations that they have with some situation or type of speaker.

For example, the use of **jargon** ('in-group' vocabulary) reinforces the status of speakers as members of particular groups, such as sororities, professions, or gender groups. Expletives (14.3.3.9) and vocatives (14.4.1) can also be used for this purpose. A speaker or writer can also use this kind of association to suggest a formal or informal air. For example, reduced pronunciations (14.1.2.6), situational ellipsis (3.7.5, 14.3.5.1), or contraction (Appendix), which are all typical of conversation, can be used to signal a degree of informality in writing.

'Function' in this sense refers to a **conventional** association of particular features with particular situations or social groups. That is, both speakers and writers must be aware of these associations to exploit them effectively.

Many grammatical features are functional in both of the last two senses; that is, they conventionally index a situation, and they reflect the processing circumstances of the situation. For example, hedges (*kind of, sort of*; 7.14.2.6) are particularly common in conversation, and thus they can be used to index informality. In contrast, the class of downtoners (e.g. *barely, mildly, partially*) have a similar meaning, but they occur most commonly in academic prose; as a result, these forms can be used to index a more formal presentation. However, the latter set of words is more specific in meaning than the former, indicating particular kinds or degrees of uncertainty (whereas hedges mark a more generalized uncertainty). Thus, the register distribution of these forms is a functional reflection of the greater opportunity for careful word choice in writing situations, in addition to conventionally indexing those situations (cf. 7.14.2.4 and 7.14.2.6).

## 1.8.4 Other explanatory considerations

In addition to the above considerations, **diachronic change** is sometimes invoked to account for the observed patterns of use. For example, semi-modal verbs (such as *have got to* and *be going to*) are more common in conversation than the other registers (6.6.2); this distribution can be explained in part by the fact that these are relatively recent developments in English, and conversation is typically the register where innovations first take hold. Although the reasons for diachronic change itself are beyond the scope of this work, it is useful to draw attention to those patterns of use where a historical perspective is relevant.

## 1.9 Overview of the grammar

For the most part, this book is organized along fairly traditional, structural lines, working 'upward' from smaller units to larger and more complex ones. **Section B** presents an overview of the word classes (Chapter 2) and grammatical constructions (Chapter 3) found in English; **Section C** provides more detailed descriptions of the major word classes and their phrases (Chapter 4 on the basic noun phrase; Chapters 5 and 6 on verbs and the verb phrase; Chapter 7 on adjectives, adverbs, and their phrases). **Section D** tackles more complex structures (Chapter 8 on the complex noun phrase; Chapter 9 on verb and adjective complementation; Chapter 10 on adverbials).

However, despite the conventional labels, the actual content of these chapters departs radically from previous grammars. In particular, this can be regarded as the first **empirical corpus-based** grammar of English, in that quantitative, empirical investigations of language use are found throughout every chapter. This characteristic of the grammar is less striking in Section B (Chapters 2 and 3), since the primary purpose of those chapters is to provide a basic descriptive framework of English word classes and grammatical structures, laying the foundation for following chapters. However, even these two chapters present numerous discussions of the overall distributional patterns found in English. Discussions of this type are given even more prominence in Sections C and D, where we have attempted to give equal attention to structure and use in our detailed descriptions of grammatical features.

In **Section E**, 'Grammar in a wider perspective', we have included discussion of a number of important specialized topics which look 'outward' from grammar to other aspects of language study in the widest sense: word order and related syntactic choices in Chapter 11; grammar and stance in Chapter 12; grammar and lexical expressions in Chapter 13; and the special grammar of conversation in Chapter 14. These last chapters explore the interface between grammar and discourse analysis, lexis, and pragmatics; in this way, they further show how a corpus-based approach can be adopted to present grammar in a radically new and revealing perspective.

## 1.10   Potential users and uses of the *LGSWE*

Given the innovative nature of this grammar, it can be used for a wider range of purposes than most conventional grammars. English language students and researchers will benefit from the new perspectives offered here: a thorough description of English grammar, which is illustrated throughout with real corpus examples, and which gives equal attention to the ways that speakers and writers actually use these linguistic resources. The information presented here will obviously be important for future research studies of English grammar. However, the special characteristics of the *LGSWE* should also make it an important resource for investigating research questions in a wide range of other sub-disciplines; for example:

- **functional linguistics:** What factors influence the choice among *who*, *whom*, *that*, and zero as relative pronoun?
- **stylistics:** What is distinctive about the kinds and numbers of adverbials used commonly in fiction?
- **dialectology:** How often do Americans really use *gotten* rather than *got*, and in what meanings of the verb?
- **sociolinguistics:** How prevalent in actual use are structures condemned by purists, such as *none* with plural concord?
- **psycholinguistics:** How do the constraints of real-time processing influence the use of grammatical features in conversation?
- **lexicology:** What are the most common and most productive types of verb derivation in English?
- **discourse analysis and text linguistics:** How do factors of cohesion and informational prominence influence word order choices in English?
- **conversation analysis:** How much repetition is there really in conversation? What kinds of expressions tend to be repeated?
- **pragmatics:** How does shared knowledge between the speaker/writer and listener/reader influence the use of the short passive in English?
- **historical linguistics:** How far advanced are verbs like *burn* and *learn* towards becoming fully regular in their written past tense/past participle forms (i.e. occurring as *burned, learned* v. *burnt, learnt*)?
- **register variation:** What are the linguistic characteristics of news reportage; how does this register differ from other registers?

- and, of course, **corpus linguistics:** What new kinds of information about the English language can be discovered using corpus-based analysis?

In addition, the *LGSWE* is equally important as a resource for English language teaching, especially English as a second/foreign language. In particular, the detailed descriptions of language use should provide key information for materials writers—from the author of an entire coursebook to the teacher constructing a single exercise or test for a class. The frequency information should prove to be especially useful, including frequencies of the most common grammatical variants, the most common words in a grammatical class, and the most common words occurring with each grammatical construction. In addition, the *LGSWE* is organized to support the development of materials for English for Specific Purposes/English for Academic Purposes (ESP/EAP), in that it describes the distinctive patterns of use in each of four major registers.

In many respects, the patterns of use described in the *LGSWE* will be surprising to materials writers, since they run directly counter to the patterns often found in ESL/EFL coursebooks. For example, progressive aspect verbs are the norm in most books that teach English conversation, in marked contrast to the language produced by speakers in actual conversation, where simple aspect verbs are more than 20 times more common than progressive aspect verbs. Similarly, most ESP/EAP instructors will be surprised to learn that modal verbs are much more common in conversation than in academic prose; in fact, only the modal *may* is used much more commonly in academic prose.

The *LGSWE* is packed with answers to numerous other basic questions of this type, such as: What are the most common verbs in English? Are the most common verbs in conversation different from the common verbs in newspaper language or academic prose? Are phrasal verbs really all that common in conversation? Which individual phrasal verbs are especially common, and in which registers? What is the most popular order of adjectives before a noun? When passives are used, is the long passive (with a *by*-phrase) the norm or the short passive (without a *by*-phrase)? What verbs usually occur in the passive voice? What verbs usually occur with *that*-clauses or *to*-clauses? Which **lexical bundles** (or lexical phrases) are most common in conversation and in academic prose? And so on.

An additional major use of this book is for natural language processing, i.e. the automatic processing of human language by computer, where highly detailed models of English grammar are increasingly being embodied in computer systems for such tasks as speech synthesis and recognition, machine-aided translation, and information extraction from electronic resources. Such systems are often probabilistic, and dependent on accurate quantitative information about the language. For example, it will be important to 'know' how the frequencies of grammatical structures in spoken language differ from those in various kinds of written language, if systems are to be successfully adapted to the processing of speech as well as writing.

In sum, our goal has been to produce a reference book that is equally useful to students, academic researchers, and pedagogically oriented teachers and materials developers. By focusing on the language actually produced by speakers and writers in different contexts, we offer an important complementary perspective to more traditional descriptions of English grammar.

# Basic grammar: description and distribution

# 2

# Word and phrase grammar

*See page xiii for contents in detail*

## 2.1  The nature of grammatical units

Speech is a continuous stream of sound without a clear division into units, but it can be analysed into meaningful elements which recur and combine according to rules. In writing, such an analysis is expressed through the division into words and sentences. Far more distinctions are needed, however, for a proper grammatical description.

Our primary task in Chapters 2 and 3 is to introduce, define, and illustrate the grammatical terms and categories used to talk about these units throughout this book. At the same time, however, we will present new information about the general distributional patterns of the major grammatical categories.

The essence of **grammatical units** is that they are meaningful and combine with each other in systematic ways. We may distinguish a **hierarchy of units** as shown below:

**discourse**

| (sentence) | If I wash up all this stuff somebody else can dry it |
| clause | If I wash up all this stuff \| somebody else can dry it |
| phrase | If \| I \| wash up \| all this stuff \| somebody \| else \| can dry \| it |
| word | If \| I \| wash \| up \| all \| this \| stuff \| somebody \| else \| can \| dry \| it |
| morpheme | If \| I \| wash \| up \| all \| this \| stuff \| some \| body \| else \| can \| dry \| it |

**phoneme/grapheme**

Most typically, a unit consists of one or more elements on the level below, i.e. a **clause** consists of one or more phrases, a **phrase** consists of one or more words, a **word** of one or more **morphemes**, etc. (See 2.2.5 on morphemes; 2.2–5 on words; 2.6–10 on phrases; and Chapter 3 on clauses.)

The grammatical units, from morpheme to sentence, form a system connecting sound/writing and **discourse**. If we were to describe discourse in terms of phonemes or graphemes alone, there would be a countless number of sound/sign—meaning pairings, and the language would be impossible to describe (and learn). The intervening levels make it possible to describe language in terms of a limited number of units and rules determining their combinations. Using language means making infinite use of these finite resources (to echo the famous words of Wilhelm von Humboldt).

The focus of the description in Chapters 2 and 3 will be on words, phrases, and clauses. Morphemes will only be briefly touched on in describing the structure of words. **Sentences** will not be separately described, as it is debatable whether this notion is applicable to speech (3.13).

In general, this book differs from a conventional grammar in paying more attention to the use of grammatical elements in discourse. The ultimate aim is to show how different types of discourse may be characterized by a different selection of grammatical elements, and, in turn, to examine what usage in discourse may reveal about the nature of grammatical elements.

At each level, grammatical units can be characterized in four main ways.

### A  Structure

Units can be characterized in terms of their **internal structure**, e.g. words in terms of bases and affixes (2.2.5), phrases in terms of head and modifiers (2.7.1–4), and clauses in terms of clause elements (3.2).

B **Syntactic role**

Units can be described in terms of their **syntactic role**, i.e. their role in building up larger syntactic units. There is no one-to-one correspondence between structure and syntactic role. Note, in particular, that each phrase type characteristically has a number of different syntactic roles (2.6.2).

C **Meaning**

Units can be described in terms of meaning. Although it is often possible to establish broad correspondences, there is no simple relationship between structure and meaning, or between syntactic role and meaning. Note, in particular, that elements of the clause may correspond to a range of **semantic roles** (3.2.1.1; 3.2.4.1) and that independent clauses may have different **speech act functions** (3.13).

D **Distribution and discourse function**

In this grammar, grammatical units are further characterized with respect to their **distribution**. A great deal of emphasis is placed on patterns of selection and use, especially in different registers, and on the interpretation of distributional differences in terms of **discourse function**.

## 2.2 Words and their characteristics

To the ordinary language user, words are the basic elements of language. They are clearly shown in writing; they are the units which dictionaries are organized around. Yet the definition of 'word' is far from straightforward.

Provisionally, we may say that words are characterized by some degree of internal stability and external independence. Insertions can only be made between words, not within words (points of insertion are shown by the words added within parentheses):

*This (new) washing-machine (here) is (very) efficient.*

not:

*... wash(-clothes-)ing-(handy-)machine ... .*

The independence of words is shown phonologically by the fact that they may be preceded and followed by pauses; orthographically by their separation by means of spaces or punctuation marks; syntactically by the fact that they may be used alone as a single utterance; and semantically by the possibility of assigning to them one or more dictionary meanings. The applicability of these criteria differs, however, depending upon the type of word; see also 2.2.3. It has also been said that words are prefabricated units (though this claim may also be made for lexical bundles—see Chapter 13): they are typically learned and used as wholes.

## 2.2.1 Word types and word tokens

### 2.2.1.1 Use of words in text examples

To examine the notion of the word further, let us first compare two brief passages:

Text sample 1: NEWS REPORT

*Mr Ladislav Adamec, the Czechoslovak Prime Minister, threatened to quit last night, as hard bargaining continued for a second day with the opposition over the shape of the new government.*

*Mr Adamec had talks with the opposition leader, Mr Vaclav Havel, on the cabinet lineup. He later went on national television to state that he would stand down unless his new government gained public backing.*

. . .

*The opposition Civic Forum, which rejected the Communist-dominated cabinet unveiled by Mr Adamec at the weekend, is demanding a more representative government staffed mainly by experts.*

*Mr Adamec said that he was having trouble recruiting such experts into the cabinet. The Prime Minister's threat appeared to seek a weakening of the opposition demands, but may also have been directed at hardline elements in the Communist Party reluctant to yield any further to the opposition.*

Text sample 2: CONVERSATION IN A BARBER SHOP

*A1: I will put, I won't smile. – Tell me what would you like now?*

*B1: Erm – shortened up please Pete – erm – shaved a little bit at the back and sides – and then just sort of brushed back on the top a bit.*

*A2: Right, and when you say shaved a little bit*

*B2: Yeah yo– – you sort of just – got your thing and zazoom!*

*A3: Yeah but – is it that short really?*

*B3: Yeah to–, yeah and I*

*A4: <unclear> you want a number four?*

*B4: Yeah I think so.*

. . .

<later in the same conversation>

*A5: So yeah, I was well pleased, cos you remember the time before I said I wasn't perfect.*

*B5: <unclear>*

*A6: That's right yeah – yeah – I mean I'm being honest.*

*B6: Yeah – mm.*

*A7: But I was well pleased with this one.*

*B7: Yeah.*

*A8: I was – I thought it looked good – and I thought, I was quite confident that it would stay in very well, you know? –*

*B8: Mm.*

These passages contain 139 and 140 running words, respectively, if we just go by the number of forms separated by spaces (ignoring speaker identifications, transcriber comments, and incomplete words in the second passage). Notice that the spoken text contains forms which we would not normally recognize as words: *erm* (B1), *zazoom* (B2). There is also the spoken variant *cos* for *because* (A5).

We notice further that some of the words recur, e.g. *government* in the first passage (paragraphs 1, 2, and 3) and *shaved* in the second (B1 and A2). If we count the number of different word forms, we get lower figures: 105 for the first and 80 for the second passage. The relationship between the number of different word forms, or **types**, and the number of running words, or **tokens**, is called the type-token ratio (or **TTR**). Specifically TTR as a percentage = (types/tokens)×100. The figures for the two sample passages are given in Table 2.1.

**Table 2.1** **Type-token ratios in two text samples**

|  | CONV | NEWS |
|---|---|---|
| running words (tokens) | 140 | 139 |
| different word forms (types) | 80 | 105 |
| type-token ratio (%) | 57 | 75 |

As Table 2.1 shows, there is a much lower type-token ratio in the conversation passage. It means that there is far more repetition in this text. There are also striking differences in the word forms repeated. The forms most frequently repeated in Text sample 1 are: *the* (10), *Mr* (5); in Text sample 2: *I* (13), *yeah* (10).

## 2.2.1.2 TTR across the registers

**CORPUS FINDINGS** [5]

➤ The type-token ratio (TTR) varies with the length of the text: longer texts have many more repeated words and therefore a much lower TTR.
  ➤ The same relationship between TTR and text length is found in all registers.
➤ The TTR is lower in the conversation texts than in all the written registers.
➤ Surprisingly, the TTR in academic prose is somewhat lower than in fiction and news.

**DISCUSSION OF FINDINGS**

In longer texts, there is a greater chance that words which have already been used will be repeated. This is true both of the most frequent words which recur in all kinds of texts (*the, of, and*, etc.) and of the words which are connected with the topic of a particular text.

TTR is low in conversation because it is less concerned with the trans- mission of information than writing. Moreover, conversation is spon- taneously produced, with little time for planning and varying the choice of words. Repetition is characteristic of spoken language. It may be used for emphasis, to help the planning of the speaker, or to make sure that the message gets across to the hearer. The repetition can be quite extreme:

> *This, I had this letter come, right, and it said – now they've got this duck and they didn't know what to call it and so Gemma said well I think – erm Eileen, auntie Eileen*

**Figure 2.1**

**Mean TTR for samples of different length**

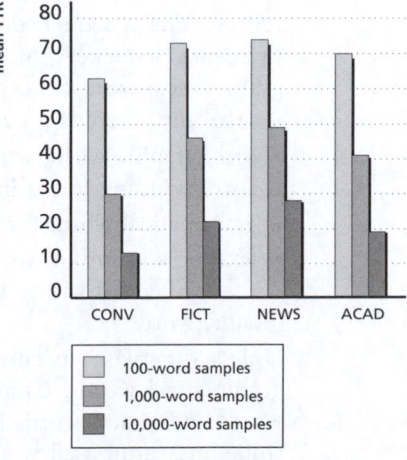

| 100-word samples |
| 1,000-word samples |
| 10,000-word samples |

*ought to name it so – I, I was asked to name this duck. So I said well I think Drusilla's a nice name for a duck.* (CONV)

*I I I me– I appreci– I understand women saying, wait a minute, you know, just cuz I'm a woman I shouldn't have to pay more if I have short hair, and I agree with that, I do agree with that, I I do agree with that, that's er th– that's obvious, but very few women, very few women, have hair that's that short, and I, an– an– I an– I mean I think it's a shame that there should have to be a lawsuit over it.* (AmE CONV)

The repetitive nature of conversation is discussed further in Chapters 13 and 14.

The TTR differences among the written registers are more surprising. We naturally expect a somewhat higher TTR for fiction, where the focus is more on form and elegance of expression. The high TTR in news reflects the extremely high density of nominal elements in that register, used to refer to a diverse range of people, places, objects, events, etc. At the other extreme, academic prose has the second lowest TTR, reflecting the fact that a great deal of academic writing has a restricted technical vocabulary and is therefore less variable than fiction and news reportage.

## 2.2.2 Orthographic words, grammatical words, and lexemes

The TTR is a crude measure which defines word tokens from the spaces in written text (including transcribed speech) and identifies types usually just by sameness of spelling. This does not take into account the meaning and grammatical status of words. In particular, many such **orthographic words** (including in this term their spoken counterparts) can be grouped together to form one **lexeme**: a group of related forms which share the same meaning and belong to the same word class (part of speech). For example, *is* and *was* in the first passage above belong to a single lexeme, as do *think* and *thought* in the second passage.

On the other hand, there are cases where one form must be regarded as representing different **grammatical words** in different contexts. For example, the orthographic word *that* can be a demonstrative pronoun (e.g. *that's right*; 4.14) or a complementizer (e.g. *I was quite confident that it would stay ...*; 9.2). In the spoken text we also find single orthographic words that must be analysed as representing a sequence of two grammatical words: *that's*, *wasn't*, etc. Finally, there are sequences of orthographic words that function together as single grammatical words, e.g. *sort of* in the conversation text.

In sum, there is a need to distinguish the following:

- orthographic word: word forms separated by spaces in written text, and the corresponding forms in speech
- grammatical word: the basic sense of 'word' for grammatical purposes
- lexeme: a group of word forms that share the same basic meaning (apart from that associated with the inflections that distinguish them) and belong to the same word class.

Unless otherwise specified, the general term 'word' will be used to refer to grammatical words. Grammatical word as here defined includes both function words and lexical words (2.2.3) and is not identified only with the former (as is sometimes done): all words are regarded as having grammatical properties and status.

## 2.2.3     The three major word classes

Words can be broadly grouped into three classes according to their main functions and their grammatical behaviour: **lexical words**, **function words**, and **inserts**.

### 2.2.3.1     Lexical words

Lexical words are the main carriers of meaning in a text. In speech they are generally stressed. They are characteristically the words that remain in the information-dense language of telegrams, lecture notes, headlines, etc.:

> *Arriving tomorrow* (telegram)
> *Family killed in fire* (newspaper headline)

Lexical words are numerous and are members of open classes (2.2.4). They often have a complex internal structure (2.2.5), and they can be the heads of phrases (2.7). There are four main classes of lexical words: nouns, verbs, adjectives, and adverbs. (See also the survey of lexical words in 2.3.)

### 2.2.3.2     Function words

While lexical words are the main building blocks of texts, function words provide the mortar which binds the text together. Function words often have a wide range of meanings and serve two major roles: indicating relationships between lexical words or larger units, or indicating the way in which a lexical word or larger unit is to be interpreted.

Function words are members of closed systems (2.2.4). They are characteristically short and lack internal structure (2.2.5). In speech they are generally unstressed. They are frequent and tend to occur in any text, whereas the occurrence of individual nouns, verbs, adjectives, and adverbs varies greatly in frequency and is bound to the topic of the text. As we shall see later, however, there is also a great deal of variation in the frequency of function words depending upon the type of text. The most important differences between function words and lexical words are summarized in Table 2.2.

**Table 2.2     Typical differences between lexical words and function words**

| features | lexical words | function words |
|---|---|---|
| frequency | low | high |
| head of phrase | yes | no |
| length | long | short |
| lexical meaning | yes | no |
| morphology | variable | invariable |
| openness | open | closed |
| number | large | small |
| stress | strong | weak |

Function words can be grouped into a number of classes, which will be surveyed in 2.4 below.

### 2.2.3.3 Inserts

Inserts are a relatively newly recognized category of word. They do not form an integral part of a syntactic structure, but are inserted rather freely in the text. They are often marked off by intonation, pauses, or by punctuation marks in writing. They characteristically carry emotional and interactional meanings and are especially frequent in spoken texts. Some examples are (see also the analysis of the sample passage in 2.2.8):

> **Hm hm**, *very good*. (CONV)     **Yeah**, *I will*. **Bye**. (CONV†)
> **Cheers** *man*. (CONV)

Inserts are generally simple in form, though they often have a deviant phonological structure (e.g. *hm, uhhuh, ugh, yeah*).

Inserts are more marginal than lexical words and function words. It can indeed be debated whether some of the forms in our conversation passage should be recognized as words at all. But there is no doubt that they play an important role in communication. If we are to describe spoken language adequately, we need to pay more attention to them than has traditionally been done (see Chapter 14).

Traditionally, interjections are the only type of insert that has been described in most grammars. Inspection of the examples in our conversation texts shows, however, that there is a variety of forms and that the traditional term 'interjection' (*LDOCE*: 'a phrase, word, or set of sounds used as a sudden remark usu. expressing feeling') is inappropriate, except perhaps in the etymological sense of 'something thrown in between'. Hence, the new term 'insert'.

Inserts can be grouped into a number of classes, which will be surveyed in 2.5 below.

## 2.2.4 Closed systems v. open classes

A **closed system** contains a limited number of members, and new members cannot easily be added. The principal closed systems in English are the groups of function words, such as auxiliaries, conjunctions, and prepositions. With **open classes**, membership is indefinite and unlimited. Nouns, verbs, adjectives, and adverbs, i.e. the groups of lexical words, form open classes and easily admit new members. For example, we can easily form new nouns with the suffix *-ee*, adjectives with *-ish*, verbs with *-ize*, and adverbs with *-wise*:

- *gossipee, franchisee, internee, retiree,* etc.
- *birdish, broadish, coquettish, heathenish,* etc.
- *bureaucratize, mythologize, periodize, solubilize,* etc.
- *crabwise, fanwise, frogwise, starwise,* etc.

The distinction between closed systems and open classes is not completely clearcut, however. Thus we may find that new prepositions develop out of verb forms (e.g. *regarding*) and sequences of orthographic words (e.g. *on account of*), and auxiliaries (e.g. *can* and *will*) have developed out of lexical verbs. But while the development of new function words is a very slow process which may take centuries, the creation of new lexical words may be instantaneous using the regular word formation processes of the language.

Inserts contain some subgroups which are more or less closed, e.g. greetings and the response words *yes* and *no* (with variants such as *yeah, yep,* and *nope*). Other types of inserts can be created rather freely, e.g. *zazoom* in our sample conversation passage. Inserts therefore straddle the closed system v. open class distinction.

Another group of words which cannot be easily classified as closed or open is the traditional class of numerals. On the one hand, there is a limited number of simple forms (*one, two, three*, etc.); on the other hand, these can be used to build up a virtually unlimited number of more complex forms.

## 2.2.5    The structure of words: morphology

Function words are generally invariable, apart from minor phonological or orthographic variations. They regularly have a very simple structure and cannot be decomposed into smaller meaning-carrying elements. In most cases they consist of a single **morpheme**, which is the smallest meaning-carrying unit. Note, however, that some pronouns can be broken down into more than one morpheme (such as *someone* and *herself*; 2.4.2), and that the primary auxiliaries take inflections of the same kind as lexical verbs (2.4.3).

As with function words, inserts are generally invariable. They may consist of a single morpheme (*yes, no, please*, etc.) or of an invariable lexicalized sequence (*you know, I mean, excuse me*, etc.; 2.5).

Lexical words may consist of a single morpheme, but they are often more complex in structure. Complex word forms result from three main processes: **inflection**, **derivation**, and **compounding** (described in the following three subsections).

### 2.2.5.1    Inflection

Lexical words may take **inflectional suffixes** to signal meaningful relationships similar to those expressed by function words (compare: *the girl's mother* v. *the mother of the girl, commoner* v. *more common*). The role of inflection is limited in English compared with many other languages; relationships are more commonly expressed by function words or by word order. However, the following categories are marked by inflection.

- nouns: base (*boy*); plural (*boys*); genitive (*boy's, boys'*)
- verbs: base (*live, write*); third person singular present indicative (*lives, writes*); past tense (*lived, wrote*); past participle (*lived, written*); *ing*-participle (*living, writing*)
- adjectives: base (*dark*); comparative (*darker*); superlative (*darkest*)
- adverbs: base (*soon*); comparative (*sooner*); superlative (*soonest*)

In accordance with grammatical tradition, the genitive suffix is here treated as an inflection of nouns. However, the genitive suffix differs from inflectional suffixes in that it is attached to a phrase rather than to a single word. This is the reasoning behind our recognition of genitive phrases (2.7.6).

### 2.2.5.2    Derivation

While inflection does not change the identity of a word (i.e. the word remains the same lexeme), derivation is used to form new lexemes, either by adding **derivational prefixes** or **suffixes**. In general, derivation changes either the meaning or the word class.

- prefixes: ***ex**-president, **re**read, **un**known*
- suffixes: *boy**hood**, **central**ize, green**ish**, deriv**ation***

Words can be built up using a number of prefixes and suffixes, and may become very complex, e.g.: *pre-industr-ial, industr-ial-ize, industr-ial-iz-ation*. Derivational suffixes may be followed by inflectional suffixes (but not the other way around), as in *organiz-ation+s, central-ize+s*.

### 2.2.5.3  Compounding

Inflection and derivation result in complex forms, consisting of a **base** plus one or more **affixes** (prefixes or suffixes). In compounding, we find independently existing bases combined to form new lexemes. There is a wide range of compound types in English, including:

- noun + noun: *chairman, girlfriend, shopkeeper, textbook*
- adjective + noun: *bluebird, Englishman, flatfish, nobleman*
- verb + noun: *cry-baby, guesswork, playboy, washing-machine*
- noun + adjective: *care-free, colour-fast, sky-blue, user-friendly*

The unity of compounds is shown by their tendency to be pronounced with **unity stress** (i.e. stress on the first element) and written as one word or with a hyphen; there is a great deal of variation, however, both in phonological and orthographic patterns. In addition, compounds frequently have a meaning which is not predictable from the individual parts. For example, the compound *bluebird* (with primary stress on *blue*) is not the same as the phrase *a blue bird* (with primary stress on *bird*). The former refers to a particular kind of bird; the latter is a description of the colour of a bird (which is not necessarily a bluebird).

Syntactically, compounds show limited possibilities of substitution compared with phrases. For example, in a phrase such as *blue birds* either element can be replaced by a wide range of other words. In contrast, such substitution is far more restricted in compounds. Compare:

| free substitution in phrases: (stress on the 2nd element) | | restricted substitution in compounds: (stress on the 1st element) | |
|---|---|---|---|
| blue birds | blue birds | bluebirds | bluebirds |
| black  " | "  flowers | blackbirds | *blueflowers |
| rare  " | "  lights | *rarebirds | *bluelights |
| small  " | "  noses | *smallbirds | bluenoses |
| young " | "  walls | *youngbirds | *bluewalls |

Note also that when substitution is possible with compounds, the meaning change may be more than the individual words suggest. Thus, blackbirds and bluebirds are different kinds of birds, not just birds that differ in colour. Bluenoses are either inhabitants in Nova Scotia or strict puritans (AmE). (See 4.8.2 and 8.3 for further discussion of noun-noun compounds.)

### 2.2.5.4  Multi-word lexical units

A **multi-word lexical unit** is a sequence of word forms which functions as a single grammatical unit. The sequence has become **lexicalized**. A typical example is *look into*, which is used in much the same way as the verb *investigate*. Another example is the adverb *sort of*.

Multi-word lexical units differ from free combinations of words in the same way as compounds differ from phrases, i.e. they show limited possibilities of substitution (cf. 2.2.5.3). Compounds can indeed be regarded as a type of multi-word unit which tends to be written as a single word (cf. 8.3). As with compounds, multi-word units tend to acquire meanings which are not predictable from the individual parts (in which case they are often described as **idioms**; 13.3).

Some important groups of multi-word units are phrasal and prepositional verbs (5.3), complex prepositions (2.4.5.2), correlative coordinators (2.4.7.1), and complex subordinators (2.4.8.1). In addition, many inserts consist of lexicalized sequences of word forms (2.5).

Multi-word lexical units should be distinguished from **collocations**, which consist of independent words that tend to co-occur. For example, the adjectives *broad* and *wide* are found in different collocations, though they are broadly synonymous.

- *broad:* accent, agreement, daylight, grin, mind, outline, shoulders, smile, support, etc.
- *wide:* appeal, area, distribution, experience, interests, margin, selection, variety, etc.

This grammar also uses the notion **lexical bundle** for sequences of words that tend to co-occur, irrespective of their idiomaticity and whether or not the sequence of words constitutes a grammatical unit. See the detailed account in Chapter 13.

## 2.2.6   Core v. peripheral members of word classes

The categories we operate with in the real world are not homogeneous (e.g. birds include ostriches as well as sparrows), and word classes are no exception. For example, nouns can be more or less 'nouny'. A typical noun has singular, plural, and genitive forms; it can be preceded by the definite or the indefinite article; and it typically refers to a person or thing, or some other entity (see also 2.3.1). Such nouns are *boy, car,* etc. Yet in the class of nouns we regularly include words which only have some of the features characteristic of nouns, e.g. *information* (which is invariable and cannot be preceded by the indefinite article), and *Sarah* (which does not normally occur in the plural or combine with articles).

Just as the characteristics of the members of a class may vary, there may be unclear borderlines between the characteristics of one class and another. For a discussion of some cases of this kind, see 2.4.5.3 (preposition v. conjunction, preposition v. infinitive marker), 2.4.6.2 (adverbial particles v. prepositions), 2.4.7.2 (coordinator v. adverb), and 2.3.6 (words ending in *-ing*).

We set up grammatical classes, as well as semantic classes and syntactic roles, because we note that elements show similarities in their behaviour. But the flexibility and complexity of language defy our neat classification systems. The famous American linguist Edward Sapir once said that 'all grammars leak'. The openness that is characteristic of language must be reflected in our grammatical description. We must be prepared to look for similarities in terms of more-or-less rather than either-or.

## 2.2.7   Multiple class membership

Fuzzy borderlines are not the only type of overlap between classes. **Homonymy** is also common in English, where a single form belongs to more than one word class. A form such as *right* can be a lexical word (noun, verb, adjective, or adverb) or an insert (see A2 in Text sample 2). *Like* can be a lexical word (noun, verb, adjective, or adverb) or a function word (preposition or subordinator). A number of forms can belong to more than one function word class, e.g. *to* (preposition and infinitive marker), *for* (preposition and subordinator). For more examples, see Table 2.3.

**Table 2.3**   **Words in more than one word class**

N = noun    V = verb    Adj. = adjective    Adv. = adverb    Prep. = preposition
Sub. = subordinator

| form | N | V | Adj. | Adv. | Prep. | Sub. | examples |
|---|---|---|---|---|---|---|---|
| before | | | | ● | | | She had never asked him that **before**. |
| | | | | | ● | | He was there **before** her. |
| | | | | | | ● | They'd started leaving **before** I arrived. |
| early | | | ● | | | | Steele kicked an **early** penalty goal. |
| | | | | ● | | | He had also kicked a penalty goal **early** in the match |
| fight | ● | | | | | | There was a hell of a **fight**. |
| | | ● | | | | | They're too big to **fight**. |
| narrow | | ● | | | | | He plans to **narrow** his focus to certain markets. |
| | | | ● | | | | Current review programs are too **narrow**. |
| red | ● | | | | | | Her hair was a lovely shade of dark **red**. |
| | | | ● | | | | Her face was bright **red** with excitement. |
| round | ● | | | | | | I think he deserves a **round** of applause. |
| | | ● | | | | | I can **round** up Dave and Peter. |
| | | | ● | | | | Just give me an idea in **round** figures. |
| | | | | ● | | | It takes a long time to turn them **round**. |
| | | | | | ● | | That's just **round** the corner. |
| weekly | ● | | | | | | The elderly woman from the local **weekly** looked up at the platform. |
| | | | ● | | | | **Weekly** rents will now vary widely. |
| | | | | ● | | | My caravan is being cleaned **weekly**. |

Homonymy exists for both written forms (**homographs**) and spoken forms (**homophones**). Some of the most frequent words in the language are homophones, as in common pronunciations of *an/and*, *have/of*, and *to/too/two*. Moreover, if we consider that the main inflections (the plural and genitive of nouns, the third person singular present indicative of verbs; the past tense and past participle forms of verbs) are also homophonous, it becomes apparent that the degree of homophony in English is quite extensive. This appears to reflect a principle of economy, making the most of a limited number of forms, which is kept in check by the need to provide a clear and/or varied form of expression.

## 2.2.8 Use of lexical words, function words, and inserts

In the following two passages, taken from the text samples used earlier in the chapter, the three major classes of words are distinguished typographically by the use of small capitals (lexical words), lower-case (function words), and bold (inserts); multi-word units are hyphenated:

Text sample 1: NEWS REPORT

> MR LADISLAV ADAMEC, the CZECHOSLOVAK PRIME MINISTER, THREATENED to QUIT LAST NIGHT, as HARD BARGAINING CONTINUED for a second DAY with the OPPOSITION over the SHAPE of the NEW GOVERNMENT.
>
> MR ADAMEC HAD TALKS with the OPPOSITION LEADER, MR VACLAV HAVEL, on the CABINET LINEUP. He LATER WENT on NATIONAL TELEVISION to STATE that he would STAND-DOWN unless his NEW GOVERNMENT GAINED PUBLIC BACKING.

Text sample 2: CONVERSATION IN A BARBER SHOP

> A1: i will PUT, i won't SMILE. – TELL me what would you LIKE NOW?
>
> B1: **erm** – SHORTENED-UP **please** PETE – **erm** – SHAVED A-LITTLE-BIT at the BACK and SIDES – and THEN JUST SORT-OF BRUSHED-BACK on the TOP A-BIT.
>
> A2: **right**, and when you SAY SHAVED A-LITTLE-BIT
>
> B2: **yeah** yo– – you SORT-OF JUST – GOT your THING and **zazoom**!
>
> A3: **yeah** but – is it that SHORT REALLY?
>
> B3: **yeah** to–, **yeah** and i
>
> A4: <unclear> you WANT a NUMBER four?
>
> B4: **yeah** i THINK so.

Although there are some problems of classification here, it is obvious that there are wide differences between the texts in the distribution of the three types; see Table 2.4.

Table 2.4 **The distribution of lexical words, function words, and inserts in two text samples**

|                | CONV       | NEWS      |
|----------------|------------|-----------|
| lexical words  | 29 (41%)   | 40 (63%)  |
| function words | 31 (44%)   | 24 (37%)  |
| inserts        | 10 (15%)   | –         |
| **total**      | 70         | 64        |

While lexical words are predominant in the news text, the distribution of lexical words and function words is more equal in the conversational passage, which also includes a fair number of inserts. The distribution shown in our short passages is typical of these two registers (2.2.9). News texts are written to provide information; hence there is a preponderance of lexical words. In conversation, on the other hand, the informational aspect is less pronounced, and the use of inserts reflects the need for expressing emotional and interactional meanings.

The distribution of lexical words, function words, and inserts will be dealt with further in the detailed account of individual grammatical topics.

## 2.2.9     Lexical density

The **lexical density** of a text is the proportion of the text made up of lexical word tokens (nouns, lexical verbs, adjectives, and adverbs). The comparison in the preceding reveals that there are wide differences between our two text samples in the proportion of lexical words: we now look at this more broadly across registers.

**CORPUS FINDINGS [1,8]**

➤ Lexical words account for almost half of the words in the LSWE Corpus, but there is considerable variation among registers (see Figure 2.2 in 2.3.5):
  ➤ Conversation has by far the lowest lexical density.
  ➤ News has the highest lexical density.

**DISCUSSION OF FINDINGS**

Since lexical words are the main carriers of meaning, we may expect differences in lexical density to reflect differences in information load. As pointed out in the preceding section, the informative aspect is less pronounced in conversation than in news texts. The fact that information is less tightly packed simplifies the tasks of both speaker and listener in online processing.

    Since a written text is planned and offers the possibility of re-reading, it can tolerate a much higher information load than conversation. The main purpose of news reportage is to convey information, and preferably as concisely as possible; it is thus no surprise that it has the highest score for lexical density. The lowest score among the written registers is found in fiction, presumably partly due to the dialogue passages and partly to the complex purposes of fictional writing (where the informational aspect is combined with aesthetic concerns). The score for academic prose is intermediate, reflecting the purposes of this register (where the framing of information, including argumentation and evaluation, are also important).

## 2.3     Survey of lexical words

There are four main classes of lexical words: nouns, verbs, adjectives, and adverbs. Each class is characterized by a combination of morphological, syntactic, and semantic features. However, the classes are not homogeneous, and class membership is to some extent a matter of degree (cf. 2.2.6).

## 2.3.1     Nouns

Words such as *book, girl, gold, information* are **common nouns**. Words such as *Sarah* and *Oslo* are **proper nouns**. Nouns have the following characteristics:

**A    Morphological characteristics**
Nouns are inflected for **number** (4.5) and **case** (4.6): *one book, two books, Sarah's book*. Many nouns, however, are uncountable and do not inflect for number (e.g. *gold, information*). Case inflection is severely restricted in present-day English.

Nouns often have a complex morphological structure. Examples of compound and derived nouns: *bombshell, bridgehead, clothes-line; bomber, brightness, friendship.* (See also 4.8.2 and 8.3.)

**B  Syntactic characteristics**

Nouns can occur as the **head** of **noun phrases**: *the new **book** about Wittgenstein, new **information** I found.* The possibilities of modification are severely restricted with some nouns, particularly proper nouns (e.g. *Sarah*).

Noun phrases have a wide range of syntactic roles: subject, direct object, indirect object, etc. (2.7.1.1).

**C  Semantic characteristics**

Nouns commonly refer to concrete entities, such as people and things in the external world (e.g. *book, girl*), but they may also denote qualities and states (e.g. *freedom, friendship*).

In clauses, nouns and noun phrases are typically associated with semantic roles such as agent, affected, and recipient. See examples in 3.2.1.1, 3.2.4.1, and 3.2.5.

For a detailed account of nouns and their characteristics, see 4.2–8 and Chapter 8.

## 2.3.2  Lexical verbs

Words such as *admit, build, choose, write* are lexical verbs. The **primary verbs** *have, be,* and *do* behave both like lexical verbs and auxiliaries (2.4.3). Lexical verbs have the following characteristics:

**A  Morphological characteristics**

Lexical verbs vary for **tense**, **aspect**, and **voice**:

> He ***writes*** *page after page about tiny details.* (FICT)
>
> *They **wrote** about Venus being a jungle paradise.* (FICT)
>
> *He had **written** to an old journalist friend.* (FICT†)
>
> *I wonder if you are **writing** any more songs?* (FICT)
>
> *The article was **written** with penetrating vehemence.* (FICT†)

Many verbs are, however, restricted with respect to variation in aspect and voice (6.3–4).

Verbs often have a complex morphological structure. Examples of multi-word and derived verbs: *bring up, rely on, look forward to; hyphenate, itemize, soften.* (See also 5.2.7 and 5.3.)

**B  Syntactic characteristics**

Lexical verbs occur as the head or **main verb** of **verb phrases**: *has **written**, will be **writing*** (2.7.2). Verb phrases serve as the centre of clauses (2.7.2.1 and 3.2.2).

**C  Semantic characteristics**

Lexical verbs denote actions, processes, or states and serve to establish the relationship between the participants in an action, process, or state.

For a detailed account of verbs and their characteristics, see Chapters 5, 6, and 9.

## 2.3.3    Adjectives

Words such as *dark, heavy, eager, guilty* are adjectives. Adjectives have the following characteristics:

### A    Morphological characteristics

Many adjectives can be inflected for **comparison**: *dark, darker, darkest.* Inflectional comparison is restricted, however.

Adjectives are often complex. Examples of compound and derived adjectives: *colour-blind, home-made, ice-cold; acceptable, forgetful, influential.* Many adjectives are derived from *ed*-participles and *ing*-participles: *surprised, interesting,* etc.

### B    Syntactic characteristics

Adjectives can occur as the **head** in **adjective phrases**: *very **dark**, **eager** to help, **guilty** of a serious crime.* Adjective phrases are typically used as **premodifiers** in noun phrases and as **predicatives** in clauses (2.7.3.1).

Under special circumstances, adjectives can function as head of a noun phrase:

> *Of course he was rich, but **the rich** were usually mean.* (FICT)

> *"Show me how **the impossible** can be possible!"* (FICT)

### C    Semantic characteristics

Most typically, adjectives describe qualities of people, things, and states of affairs: *a **heavy** box, he is **guilty**, the situation is **serious**.* Such descriptive adjectives are normally **gradable**, i.e. they allow comparison, whether inflectional or not, and degree modification: *darker, **very** heavy, **extremely** serious.*

Many adjectives serve as **classifiers**: ***criminal** law, **medical** student, **urban** district.* Other adjectives have an identifying or intensifying meaning: *the **identical** car, **utter** nonsense.* Classifying, identifying, and intensifying adjectives are normally non-gradable and non-predicating (i.e. they do not occur as predicatives in clauses).

For a detailed account of adjectives and their characteristics, see 7.2–10.

## 2.3.4    Adverbs

Words such as *clearly, eagerly, however, now* are adverbs. Adverbs have the following characteristics:

### A    Morphological characteristics

Many adverbs are formed from adjectives by means of the ending *-ly*: *clearly, eagerly.* Others have no such ending: *however, now.* A few adverbs admit comparison of the same type as adjectives: *soon, sooner, soonest.*

### B    Syntactic characteristics

Adverbs occur as the **head** of **adverb phrases**: *very **clearly**, more **eagerly** than I had expected* (2.7.4). Adverb phrases are most typically used as **modifiers** in adjective and adverb phrases, and as **adverbials** in the clause (2.7.4.1).

**C  Semantic characteristics**

As modifiers, adverbs most typically express **degree** with respect to the following adjective or adverb: *totally wrong, just outside*. As adverbials (clause elements), they have three main types of meaning:

- They specify the circumstances under which an action, process, or state takes place, as in: *she writes **well**; they leave **tomorrow***.
- They convey the speaker's or writer's attitude towards the information contained in the rest of the clause: ***surely** you don't believe this, it is **apparently** wrong*.
- They express the connection between clauses: ***nevertheless** it wasn't true, I'm not sure **though***.

The three types are termed **circumstance adverbials**, **stance adverbials**, and **linking adverbials**.

Adverbs are more heterogeneous than the other lexical word classes. Individual members may differ greatly both in form and meaning. The borderline between adverbs and other word classes is also unclear. As clause elements, they border on inserts. The borderline between adverb and adjective is described further in 7.12.2.

For a detailed account of adverbs and their characteristics, see 7.11–15 and Chapter 10.

## 2.3.5  Lexical word classes

**CORPUS FINDINGS** [1]

➤ The lexical word classes vary greatly in overall frequency:
  ➤ Nouns are by far the most frequent lexical word class; on average every fourth word is a noun.
  ➤ Verbs are less frequent (on average every tenth word is a verb), followed by adjectives and adverbs.
➤ The lexical word classes also vary greatly across registers:
  ➤ Nouns are most common in news (and to a lesser extent in academic prose); they are by far least common in conversation.
  ➤ Adjectives are most common in academic prose; they are least common in conversation.
  ➤ Verbs and adverbs are most common in conversation and fiction.
➤ The proportion of the lexical word classes varies with register:
  ➤ In conversation, nouns and verbs are about equally frequent.
  ➤ In news reportage and academic prose, there are three to four nouns per lexical verb.
➤ The registers with the highest frequency of nouns, i.e. news reportage and academic prose, have the highest frequency of adjectives.

**Figure 2.2**

**Distribution of lexical word classes across registers**

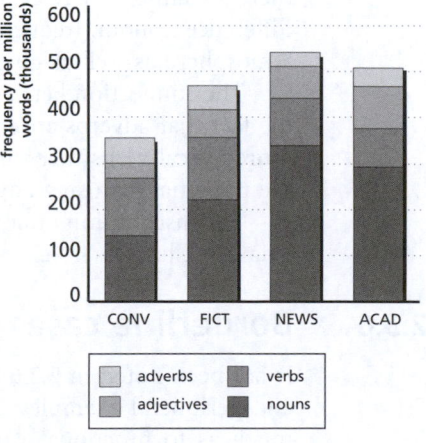

➤ The registers with the highest frequency of verbs, i.e. conversation and fiction, have the highest frequency of adverbs.

**DISCUSSION OF FINDINGS**

The striking prominence of nouns and verbs follows from the fact that these word classes—or, rather, the corresponding phrase types—are necessary elements in a clause (see Chapter 3). Adjectives and adverbs are elements which can more easily be dispensed with.

The low frequency of nouns in conversation is connected with the lower density of information (2.2.1, 2.2.9) and the high frequency of pronouns (2.4.14). In news and academic prose, the focus is on the transmission of information, where nouns are crucial. The somewhat lower frequency of nouns in fiction is due in part to the dialogue passages.

Lexical verbs are very frequent in conversation, where clauses are characteristically short (3.1.1) and thus more numerous. Since a verb is required in each clause, there will consequently also be more verbs. Moreover, there are certain meanings commonly needing to be expressed in conversation that are best conveyed by verbs (see also 5.1.1). The high frequency of verbs in fiction is partly due to the dialogue passages and the related use of reporting clauses (3.11.5). Additionally, verbs are a crucial means of narration, which is arguably the most important language use in fiction.

Altogether, the relative proportion of nouns v. lexical verbs reflects the density of information packaging and the complexity of phrases and clauses in the registers. A high ratio of nouns to verbs corresponds to longer clauses and more complex phrases embedded in clauses.

The connection between the frequencies of nouns and adjectives is not surprising, as one of the main uses of adjectives is to modify nouns. The fact that there are almost twice as many adjectives in fiction as in conversation reflects the difference in noun frequency and the need to use adjectives in fiction to evoke an atmosphere as well as give a physical description.

The connection between the frequencies of lexical verbs and adverbs is due to the fact that adverbs are most typically used as adverbials (clause elements). The more lexical verbs there are, the higher is the number of clauses and the greater the potential for using adverbials.

The distribution of nouns, verbs, adjectives, and adverbs is dealt with in more detail in Chapters 4–7.

## 2.3.6 Borderline cases of lexical word class membership

It has been noted in 2.2.6 that word classes are not homogeneous, but have core and peripheral examples. This applies to the four major lexical word classes, as much as to functional word classes, and leads to the problem of dealing with borderline cases: word tokens of unclear status, which could be categorized in one word class or another, depending on how the criteria for membership of classes are employed. As illustrated in 2.3.1–4 above, the criteria for assigning word tokens to one class or another can be **morphological, syntactic,** or **semantic**. Moreover, they can be either **actual** or **potential**. That is, the criteria can either be applied directly to the form and context of the word as it appears in a text, or they can be applied indirectly, by testing out various changes to the text and seeing whether they result in changes of acceptability or meaning. Since such criteria can conflict with one another, the dilemma of whether to favour one classification or another can sometimes be resolved only by arbitrary decision.

It would take too long at this point to attempt a general survey of such borderline phenomena. Instead, to illustrate the general principle, we will look at the case of words ending in *-ing*: a particularly ambiguous ending in English grammar. In this section, we discuss *-ing* words as borderline cases with reference to A nouns v. verbs, B nouns v. adjectives, and C verbs v. adjectives.

## A    Nouns v. verbs

The *ing*-participle form of the verb is easily confused with the base form of many nouns ending in *-ing* (such as *painting, writing, dancing*). The verb participle is easy to recognize in certain circumstances: (1) when it is followed by a verb complement such as an object, or (2) when it is qualified by an adverbial such as *quickly* or *in winter*.

  1  **scoring** *the first goal* (NEWS†)

  2  **becoming** *misty overnight* (NEWS†)

The noun form, on the other hand, is easy to recognize when it fills the typical nominal slot of the head of a noun phrase (e.g. preceded by determiners or adjectives; followed by an *of*-phrase or relative clause):

  3  *the* **banning** *of some chemicals* (NEWS†)

  4  *some enthusiastic* **bidding** *from Bloomfields* (NEWS†)

  5  *her* **dancing***, which was bad beyond measure* (FICT†)

The noun status of a word is particularly obvious when it takes a plural: *meeting/ meetings*. Moreover, core nouns such as *painting(s)* and *building(s)* reveal their noun status clearly through their concrete meaning, in referring to objects.

One particular area of difficulty is the **mixed construction**, as in *There is no denying it* (FICT†), where the determiner *no* suggests that *denying* is a noun, while the following object *it* suggests that it is a verb. On balance, since the verb category is the one which applies most generally to *-ing* words, the *-ing* form should be considered a verb in such cases.

The biggest problem in distinguishing nouns from verbs, however, is that of the naked *-ing* form, where a word ending in *-ing* could be either a noun or a verb, and occurs without any of the clear noun criteria or verb criteria in its context. This commonly happens where the *-ing* word fills the slot of subject, object, or prepositional complement alone:

  *I find that* **writing** *is like* **drinking***. A man must learn to control it.* (FICT)

Note that one of these slots could be filled either with a noun phrase (in which case the word is a noun head) or with an *ing*-clause (3.12.2), in which case it is a verb. For example, *the matter needed checking* (NEWS†) could be expanded either as … *careful checking* or as *checking carefully*. Again, on balance, as the more general category of *-ing* words, the verb should be regarded as the default classification here.

## B    Nouns v. adjectives

Alongside nouns in *-ing* discussed above, there are many *-ing* **participial adjectives** such as *interesting* and *lasting*. Difficulties arise particularly when an *-ing* word occurs before the head of a noun phrase, as a premodifier. Not only adjectives, but nouns can occur in this position: e.g. *security* in *His security police* (NEWS†), alongside *Local* in *Local police* (NEWS†).

One way to resolve unclear cases is to see whether the *-ing* word in question could occur (1) in the most typical positions for nouns or (2) in the most typical positions for adjectives. For (1), we consider it as head of a noun phrase, with accompanying determiners or modifiers if needed – see **3–5** above; for (2) we consider it as head of an adjective phrase – typically after the verb *be*, with degree adverb modifiers (e.g. *very, too*) if needed:

6 *it was **very** confusing* (CONV†)

7 *he was **so** interesting* (CONV†)

8 *Jenny's heart was **too** loving and forgiving.* (FICT)

Another, more meaning-oriented test, is whether the *-ing* form as modifier can be paraphrased by a relative clause of the form '*who/which be* + verb-*ing*' or '*who/which* verb(*s/ed*)'. For example, *the travelling public* is 'the public which is travelling', or (more likely) 'the public which travels'. This meaning identifies the word as an adjective. The modifying noun, on the other hand, is often paraphrasable by the nominal use of the *-ing* form: *a travelling rug* means 'a rug for *travelling* (with)'. Other interesting cases of ambiguity are:

| noun | adjective |
| --- | --- |
| *finishing school* | *finishing touches* |
| *living standards* | *living creatures* |
| *the sitting room* | *sitting tenants* |
| *dancing classes* | *the dancing children* |
| *working conditions* | *a working mother* |

It can be seen from these examples that noun modifiers often have a purposive meaning (e.g. *living arrangements* = 'arrangements for living'), in contrast to the more descriptive adjectival meaning. However, this test cannot resolve all borderline noun/adjective *-ing* words: *warning shots*, for example, is ambiguous between the purposive and descriptive interpretations: it could be paraphrased either 'shots intended as a warning' or 'shots which warn'.

Coordination can occasionally provide useful evidence for word-class assignment, on the grounds that words will coordinate with words of the same class. Thus *teaching and project work* (where *teaching* is a noun) contrasts with *living and dead roots* (where *living* is an adjective). As with most criteria, however, this is not conclusive, since elsewhere adjectives can sometimes be coordinated with nouns: e.g. *classical and quantum objects*.

## C   Verbs v. adjectives

The *ing*-participle of the verb is often difficult to distinguish from a participial adjective. For example, the progressive form of the verb (*be* + verb-*ing*), as in *is working*, is superficially identical in form to the copula followed by a predicative adjective (e.g. *is surprising*). However, if the *-ing* word is followed by a verb complement (such as an object), it is clearly a verb: *... is eating lunch.* On the other hand, if it is preceded by a degree adverb such as *very, so,* and *too*, it is just as clearly an adjective: *... was too tempting.*

Where neither of these expansions are possible, the 'naked *-ing*' form can be difficult to classify: e.g. *one man was missing.* Being able to transpose the word to the adjectival premodifying position (as in *the missing man*) does not define it as an adjective necessarily, as many verbs in *-ing* can be transposed into that slot: e.g. *The mother is nursing (her child)* → *a nursing mother*. However, in this and similar cases (e.g. *is daring/binding/promising*) adjective status is indicated by the impossibility of using a non-progressive form of the verb (X *is promising* → *\*X promises*) unless a complement is added (X *promises a great deal*). Another useful criterion relates to the aspectual meaning of the *-ing* form: if it is a verb, it will have a progressive (dynamic) meaning, whereas if it is an adjective, its meaning will be stative. Compare *His voice was irritating me* (progressive) with *His voice was (very) irritating* (stative): the former sentence denotes something temporarily in progress at a past time, whereas the latter denotes a general past state of affairs. Yet a further commonly used test is the substitution of *seem* or some other copular verb for the verb *be*: *It seems surprising* (where *surprising* is a predicative adjective) contrasts with *\*She seems working (hard)*.

Two other morphological criteria for adjective status are also sometimes useful. First, an *-ing* word is signalled as an adjective if it begins with the negative prefix *un-*. Thus *unyielding* is an adjective because the prefix *un-* negates the whole of the rest of the word: *un-* + *yielding*; on the other hand, it cannot be a verb, as there is no verb *\*unyield*. (Note, incidentally, that there are verbs such as *unwind/unwinding*, where the *un-* is a different prefix: it is reversative rather than negative in meaning.) Second, an *-ing* word is an adjective if it can be converted into an adverb by the addition of an *-ly*, as in *surprisingly*, *appallingly*.

## 2.4 Survey of function words

Function words can be broadly grouped as follows according to the units they are most closely related to:

| grammatical unit | function word class |
| --- | --- |
| noun phrase | determiners, pronouns, numerals, prepositions |
| verb phrase | primary auxiliaries, modal auxiliaries, adverbial particles |
| phrase/clause | coordinators |
| clause | subordinators, *wh*-words, the negator *not*, existential *there*, the infinitive marker *to* |

There is a good deal of overlap between the function word classes; see especially 2.4.2.1, 2.4.5.3, 2.4.6.1–2, 2.4.7.2, and 2.4.8.3. The relevance of the admittedly simplified grouping above will be partially confirmed by distributional patterns presented later in the chapter (2.4.14). A more detailed description of the distribution of the individual classes is deferred until later chapters, except in the case of coordinators (2.4.7.3–5) and numerals (2.4.13.3).

## 2.4.1 Determiners

**Determiners** are used to narrow down the reference of a noun. The most important are:

- the **definite article** (*the* book), which specifies that the referent is assumed to be known to the speaker and the addressee;

- the **indefinite article** (*a book*), which narrows down the reference to a single member of a class;
- **demonstrative determiners** (*this* book, *that* book, etc.), which establish the reference by proximity to the speaker and the addressee;
- **possessive determiners** (*my* book, *your* book, *her* book, etc.), which establish a connection with the participants in the speech situation or some other entity and thereby limit the reference of the noun;
- **quantifiers** (*some* book, *many* books, etc.), which specify the number or amount of the entities referred to.

In addition, there are determiner uses of **wh-words** (2.4.9) and **numerals** (2.4.13). The uses of determiners are dealt with in detail in 4.4.

## 2.4.2 Pronouns

**Pronouns** are used instead of full noun phrases in two situations: (1) when the entities referred to are identifiable through the speech situation or the surrounding text; and (2) when the reference is unknown or general. Pronouns can be viewed as economy devices. Rather than giving a detailed specification, they serve as pointers, requiring the listener or reader to find the exact meaning in the surrounding (usually preceding) text or in the speech situation.

There are several major classes of pronouns:

- **Personal pronouns** refer to the speaker, the addressee, or other entities: *I must tell* **you** *about* **it**.
- **Demonstrative pronouns** refer to entities which are proximate v. distant in the speech situation: *Look at* **this!** *Have you seen* **those?**
- **Reflexive pronouns** mark identity with a preceding noun phrase, usually in subject position: *I hurt* **myself**. *She came to* **herself** *after a few minutes*.
- **Reciprocal pronouns** mark identity with a preceding noun phrase used as subject and referring to more than one entity. They indicate that there is a mutual relationship between the entities referred to: *They clung to* **each other** (i.e. he clung to her and she clung to him).
- **Possessive pronouns** are equivalent to a possessive determiner + a noun which is recoverable from the context: *I brought my camera. Did you bring* **yours?**
- **Indefinite pronouns** were historically noun phrases consisting of a quantifier + a noun with a general meaning. They refer to entities which the speaker cannot, or does not want to, specify more exactly: **Everything** *in here is old. I suppose* **somebody** *got hurt*.

Other indefinite pronouns are similar in form to quantifiers: *some, any, both, none*, etc.

Two additional groups which are normally described as pronouns are:

- **Relative pronouns**, which mark identity with a preceding noun phrase, termed the **antecedent**: [My sister], **whom** *you met yesterday, owns* [a house] **which** *was built in the eighteenth century*.
- **Interrogative pronouns**, which refer to unknown entities that the speaker wants the addressee to specify: **Who** *wrote this letter?*

Interrogative pronouns are in a way the opposite of relative pronouns, since they point forward to a following noun phrase (provided that the addressee is able and willing to give the desired specification). Interestingly, the two groups overlap in form, as they are both expressed by **wh-words** (2.4.9).

Most pronouns differ from nouns in that they are rarely used to build up phrases. Compare: *the red-haired man – he*. Further, some pronouns (unlike nouns) allow a distinction between **nominative** and **accusative case**: *I – me, he – him*, etc. Compare:

> **The woman** *wore a fashionable wrap.* (FICT)
> v.  **She** *wore a fashionable wrap.*

> *He approached* **the young woman**. (FICT)
> v.  *He approached* **her**.

The nominative case of pronouns is used in subject position, the accusative case elsewhere. Nouns have a **common case**, which is used regardless of syntactic position. In addition, both nouns and some pronouns have a **genitive case**. See the detailed account of case and case variation in 4.6 and 4.10.6.

The uses of pronouns are described in detail in 4.9–16; the conditions favouring the use of full noun phrases v. pronouns are described in 4.1.2–4.

## 2.4.2.1   Overlap of pronoun, determiner, and adverb classes

Pronouns and determiners are closely related: they overlap in form and are both connected with the specification of reference. Often there are alternative forms, using either a determiner + noun or a pronoun. For example, many quantifiers can be used both as determiners and as pronouns, some also as adverbs. Compare:

Quantifiers used as determiners:

> *He kept whistling at* **all** *the girls.* (CONV†)
> **Each** *novelist aims to make a single novel of the material he has been given.* (ACAD†)
> *I have* **a little** *money in my room.* (FICT)
> *The Trust deserves as* **much** *help as possible.* (NEWS)

Quantifiers used as pronouns:

> *Is that* **all** *I've got dad?* (CONV)
> **Each** *has the job of writing his chapter to make the novel being constructed the best it can be.* (ACAD†)
> *"Water?" – "Just* **a little**, *and a lot of ice."* (FICT)
> *We haven't had to spend* **much** *in the past two or three years.* (NEWS)

*None* is the pronoun form corresponding to *no*:

> *Several other types of position transducer have been proposed, but* **none** *have been successful commercially.* (ACAD†)

Quantifiers used as adverbs:

> *Don't get* **all** *mucky.* (CONV)
> *The UVF and UFF claimed responsibility for two murders* **each**. (NEWS)
> *It was* **a little** *hard for him to understand.* (FICT†)
> *UK consumers have a* **much** *smaller appetite for cheese than their continental neighbours.* (NEWS)

*Either* and *neither* may be determiners, pronouns, part of correlative coordinators (2.4.7.1), or adverbs. Compare (see also 4.4.4):

*Either/neither* used as determiners:

> **Either** *extreme is possible.* (ACAD†)
>
> **Neither** *man got drunk.* (FICT)

*Either/neither* used as pronouns:

> *He might deny that* **either** *is superior to the other in political morality.* (ACAD†)
>
> **Neither** *spoke Hebrew.* (FICT)

*Either/neither* used as part of correlative coordinators:

> **Either** *we can know the position exactly, in which case we sacrifice all specification of momentum, or we can make the converse choice.* (ACAD)
>
> *She was* **neither** *shocked nor surprised.* (FICT†)

*Either/neither* used as adverbs:

> *A: It's not my fault.*
>
> *B: It's not mine* **either**. (CONV)
>
> *I'm not old and* **neither** *is Chambers.* (FICT)

## 2.4.2.2 Other pro-forms

In addition to pronouns, there are some other function words which recapitulate a neighbouring expression, with the effect of reducing grammatical complexity. The following are the most important.

The **pro-form** *so*, which replaces clauses or verb complements:

> *"D'you think they're going to attack?" "I expect* **so**.*"* (FICT) <so = that they're going to attack>
>
> *Despite the excesses of some tabloids, freedom of the press is sacrosanct and should remain* **so**. (NEWS) <so = sacrosanct>

The **pro-predicates** *do* and *do so*:

> *I don't like this any more than you* **do**. (FICT) <do = like this>
>
> *Health workers cannot use the proper techniques unless they are trained to* **do so**. (ACAD) <do so = use the proper techniques>

There are also adverbial pro-forms:

| | |
|---|---|
| *now* 'at this time' | *here* 'in this place' |
| *then* 'at that time' | *there* 'in that place' |
| *therefore* 'for that reason' | *hence* 'as a result of this' |
| *thus* 'in this way; as a result of this' | *so* 'in this way; as a result of this' |

Note also the adverbial counterparts of interrogative pronouns and relative pronouns (2.4.9).

## 2.4.3 Primary auxiliaries

**Primary auxiliaries** and **modal auxiliaries** are used to build up complex verb phrases and cannot occur alone unless a lexical verb is recoverable from the context. They reject *do*-insertion when used with *not* or in questions.

There are three primary auxiliaries: *be, have,* and *do.* They have inflections like lexical verbs, but are regularly unstressed and often appear in writing as **contracted forms** such as *'re, 've.* (As regards the contracted forms and their distribution, see 3.8.2.5 and the Appendix.)

The primary auxiliaries specify the way in which the lexical verb of the clause, or the clause as a whole, is to be interpreted. The auxiliary *have* is used to form the **perfective aspect** (as in *winter **had** come*). The auxiliary *be* is used to build the **progressive aspect** (as in *I **was** coming out of my favorite cafe*) and the **passive voice** (as in *he **was** invited to stay on*). See also the detailed description of aspect and voice in 6.3 and 6.4.

The auxiliary *do* is used as **operator** (3.2.9) in negative and independent interrogative clauses which lack another auxiliary. This use, normally referred to as ***do*-support** or ***do*-insertion**, gives English clauses a very regular structure, with the subject regularly preceding the lexical verb and the negator *not* regularly appearing between an auxiliary and a lexical verb.

*Be, have,* and *do* can all also be used as main verbs (2.7.2): *be* as a **copula** (e.g. *Miss Foley **was** at the door, she **was** angry with Mrs Ramsay*), *have* and *do* as **transitive verbs** (as in *he **had** a small face, Katheryn **did** her share of griping*). *Be* differs from other main verbs in that it is not used with the auxiliary *do*, except in imperative clauses (3.13.4.1). With lexical *have* there is some variation in the use of the auxiliary *do* (3.8.2.1, 3.13.2.8). The use of the auxiliary *do* is completely regular in combination with *do* as a lexical verb:

> *Why **did** he **do** that?*     *We **didn't** do anything.*

The verbs *be, have,* and *do* considered as both auxiliaries and main verbs together are referred to by the overall term **primary verb** (5.1 and 5.4).

## 2.4.4 Modal auxiliaries

As with auxiliaries in general, the modals reject *do*-insertion. They are used to build up complex verb phrases and cannot occur alone unless a lexical verb is recoverable from the context. There are nine central modal auxiliaries: *can, could, may, might, must, shall, should, will, would.* They differ from other verbs, both lexical verbs and primary auxiliaries, in that they have no non-finite forms. Some modals have contracted forms, like the primary auxiliaries, such as *'d* for *would.* (As regards the contracted forms and their distribution, see 3.8.2.5 and the Appendix.)

The modal auxiliaries express a wide range of meanings, having to do with concepts such as ability, permission, necessity, and obligation. Although they can convey meanings that relate to time differences (e.g. *can* v. *could*), the differences among them relate primarily to modality rather than tense.

The verbs *dare (to), need (to), ought to,* and *used to* are on the borderline between auxiliaries and lexical verbs, and can be regarded as **marginal auxiliaries**. They vary with respect to *do*-insertion (3.8.2.3–4, 3.13.2.8).

In addition, there are multi-word verbs which are related in meaning to the modal auxiliaries, such as: *have to, (had) better, (have) got to, be supposed to, be going to.* These expressions, together with the marginal auxiliaries, can be referred to as **semi-modals** (6.6). As most of these expressions are formally more flexible than the modal auxiliaries, they are important resources for the expression of modal meanings. Apart from with *have to*, generally, no *do*-insertion is used.

As regards the uses and meanings of modal expressions, see also 6.6.

## 2.4.5 Prepositions

**Prepositions** are links which introduce **prepositional phrases**. As the most typical complement in a prepositional phrase is a noun phrase, they can be regarded as a device which connects noun phrases with other structures. Many prepositions in English correspond to case inflections in other languages (note also the connection between the genitive inflection and *of*-phrases in English; 2.7.6).

Most common prepositions are short, invariable forms: *about, after, around, as, at, by, down, for, from, in, into, like, of, off, on, round, since, than, to, towards, with, without,* etc.

### 2.4.5.1 Free v. bound prepositions

An important distinction can be drawn between **free** v. **bound** prepositions. Free prepositions have an independent meaning; the choice of preposition is not dependent upon any specific words in the context. In contrast, bound prepositions often have little independent meaning, and the choice of the preposition depends upon some other word (often the preceding verb). The same prepositional form can function as a free or a bound preposition:

Free prepositions:

> But the only other thing perhaps, he'll go **with** one of the kids, that's a possibility. (CONV)

> Late one morning **in** June, **in** the thirty-first year of his life, a message was brought to Michael K as he raked leaves **in** De Waal Park. (FICT)

> A modest, smiling, bespectacled figure was suddenly seen **on** the stairs. **On** the wall, a brilliant sunrise appeared, then a vivid blue sky. (NEWS†)

Bound prepositions:

> They've got to be willing to part **with** that bit of money. (CONV)

> She confided **in** him above all others. (FICT)

> The calculations generally rely **on** an after-tax rate of return of 8% annually. (NEWS†)

Verb + preposition combinations such as *confide in, rely on,* and *part with* are usually regarded as forming a multi-word unit and are called **prepositional verbs** (5.3.3).

Although some prepositions can be both free and bound (as in the examples above), many prepositions are always, or almost always, free: *above, across, against, along, among(st), before, behind, below, beside, besides, between, beyond, considering, despite, during, following, inside, like, near, opposite, outside, past, regarding, since, through, throughout, till, toward(s), under, unlike, until, within, without.*

In addition, **complex prepositions** are normally free; see the next section. Finally it should be noted that some grammars refer to bound prepositions, especially as part of prepositional verbs, as 'particles'. This grammar, however, reserves the term 'particle' for adverbial particles—see 2.4.6.

**2.4.5.2** **Complex prepositions**

Some multi-word sequences function semantically and syntactically as single prepositions. Two-word prepositions generally end in a common simple preposition. Ending in:

| | |
|---|---|
| *as:* | *such as* |
| *for:* | *as for, but for, except for, save for* |
| *from:* | *apart from, aside from, as from, away from* |
| *of:* | *ahead of, as of, because of, devoid of, exclusive of, inside of, instead of, irrespective of, out of, outside of, regardless of, upwards of, void of* |
| *on:* | *depending on* |
| *to:* | *according to, as to, close to, contrary to, due to, next to, on to, opposite to, owing to, preliminary to, preparatory to, previous to, prior to, relative to, subsequent to, thanks to, up to* |
| *with:* | *along with, together with.* |

Others: *as against, as per, as regards, rather than.*

Three-word prepositions most commonly consist of a simple preposition + noun + another simple preposition. Ending in:

| | |
|---|---|
| *as:* | *as far as, as well as* |
| *for:* | *in exchange for, in return for* |
| *from:* | *as distinct from* |
| *of:* | *by means of, by virtue of, by way of, for lack of, for want of, in aid of, in back of, in case of, in charge of, in consequence of, in favour of, in front of, in lieu of, in light of, in need of, in place of, in respect of, in search of, in spite of, in terms of, in view of, on account of, on behalf of, on grounds of, on top of* |
| *to:* | *as opposed to, by reference to, in addition to, in contrast to, in reference to, in regard to, in relation to, with regard to, with reference to, with respect to* |
| *with:* | *at variance with, in accordance with, in comparison with, in compliance with, in conformity with, in contact with, in line with.* |

There are also four-word prepositions. These are similar to three-word prepositions, except that they include the definite or the indefinite article and usually end in *of*:

*as a result of, at the expense of, for the sake of, in the case of, in the event of, in the light of, on the ground(s) of, on the part of, with the exception of.*

Other sequences, such as *at the back of* and *in the middle of*, can be considered free combinations. The distinction between complex prepositions and free combinations is a matter of degree. At one extreme, many complex prepositions have close parallels in form and/or meaning with simple prepositions. Compare:

| | | | |
|---|---|---|---|
| *as well as* | v. *besides* | *on top of* | v. *over* |
| *by means of* | v. *with* | *opposite to* | v. *opposite* |
| *in addition to* | v. *besides* | *prior to* | v. *before* |
| *in front of* | v. *before* | *subsequent to* | v. *after* |
| *in spite of* | v. *despite* | *with regard to* | v. *regarding* |
| *on to, up to* | v. *into* | | |

At the other extreme, four-word free combinations allow considerable variability and are transparent in their meanings:

| | | |
|---|---|---|
| *across* | *the front* | *of the green* |
| *against* | *the back* | *of his neck* |
| *at* | *the back* | *of the stage* |
| *at* | *the centre* | *of the system* |
| *in* | *the back* | *of the vehicle* |
| *in* | *the side* | *of the neck* |
| *on* | *the far side* | *of the track* |
| *outside* | *the front* | *of the house* |
| *to* | *the front* | *of the court* |
| *through* | *the middle* | *of nesting terns* |

As variability is a matter of degree, it is impossible to establish a clear borderline between free combinations and complex prepositions.

## 2.4.5.3 Overlap between prepositions and other word classes

Many of the same orthographic words can function as prepositions, subordinators, adverbs, and occasionally even verbs and adjectives; for examples, see Table 2.5 (cf. Table 2.7 in 2.4.8.3).

Table 2.5 **Overlap between prepositions and other word classes**

V = verb   Adj. = adjective   Adv. = adverb   Prep. = preposition
Sub. = subordinator

| form | Prep. | Sub. | Adv. | Adj. | V | examples |
|---|---|---|---|---|---|---|
| *as* | ● | | | | | This was the beginning of his life **as a** cultivator. |
| | | ● | | | | **As** they watched, a flash of fire appeared. |
| *before* | ● | | | | | It's long **before** that. |
| | | ● | | | | He sort of skidded **before** he got there. |
| | | | ● | | | Whatever he did **before** at home I'm not sure. |
| *following* | ● | | | | | **Following** heavy rain the meeting is in danger. |
| | | | | | ● | He said someone was **following** him. |
| *opposite* | ● | | | | | She sat **opposite** him. |
| | | | | ● | | She saw him coming in the **opposite** direction. |
| *outside* | ● | | | | | It's sitting **outside** your house. |
| | | | ● | | | He's gone **outside**. |
| | | | | ● | | You can open the **outside** window. |
| *than* | ● | | | | | No one knows more **than** me how much I owe to this country. |
| | | ● | | | | Malcolm spoke more abruptly **than** he meant. |

It is difficult to draw a clear borderline between the prepositional and subordinator use of *as* and *than* (see the discussion in 4.10.6.2 of case variation after these words). The borderline is also blurred before *ing*-participles:

1 ***By*** *doing such a mass balance at the level of the individual process steps, the greatest 'leaks' in the process leading to environmental pollution become visible.* (ACAD)

2 ***While*** *declining to say what his views were on proportional representation, he promised to continue Labour's debate on electoral reform now being considered by an internal committee.* (NEWS)

3 *He said Noriega had called two or three times **since** turning himself over to U.S. forces.* (NEWS)

Both prepositions and subordinators can precede *ing*-clauses: *by* is a clear case of a preposition and *while* is just as clearly a subordinator; neither has the opposite use. However, forms such as *since*, *before*, and *after* occur as both prepositions and subordinators, making it hard to determine their use in examples such as **3**.

The distinction between the preposition *to* and the infinitive marker (2.4.12) is generally clear.

Preposition *to*:

*"Oh, how good you are **to** me!" Yes, I am, she told herself, though she stoutly denied it **to** his face.* (FICT)

*We shall look forward **to** seeing your report.* (NEWS†)

Infinitive marker *to*:

*He really needs **to** get it sorted out this year.* (CONV†)

*But most shoppers were delighted **to** see him.* (NEWS)

The preposition is followed by a noun phrase or an *-ing* form, the infinitive marker by an infinitive clause.

The borderline is blurred with some adjectives and verbs which can be followed by either a prepositional phrase with an *-ing* form as complement or by an infinitive.

Preposition *to*:

4 *It is most kind of you to consent **to** seeing me at such short notice.* (FICT)
   *cf. It is most kind of you to consent to it.*

5 *She was accustomed **to** hanging up her coat.* (FICT)
   *cf. She was accustomed to it.*

Infinitive marker *to*:

6 *He did consent **to** take a couple of aspirin; he even dozed off for a while.* (FICT)

7 *The muscles round his mouth and the cleft pad of his chin briefly compress the flesh into dimpled bloodlessness in one of those tics developed by men accustomed **to** conceal their irritation with subordinates.* (FICT)

Usage in these cases varies with the individual word. In **7** *accustomed to concealing* would be more expected. Other verbs are more restricted in their variability. For example, only *to*-infinitives were found with *agree to*, while only *-ing* forms were found with *contribute to*.

There is also a great deal of overlap between prepositions and adverbial particles (2.4.6.2).

## 2.4.6 Adverbial particles

**Adverbial particles** are a small group of short invariable forms with a core meaning of motion and result. The most important are: *about, across, along, around, aside, away, back, by, down, forth, home, in, off, on, out, over, past, round, through, under, up.*

While prepositions have a special relationship to nouns, adverbial particles are closely linked to verbs: most typically, prepositions precede noun phrases, and adverbial particles are added to verbs. Adverbial particles are used in two main ways: to build **multi-word verbs** (5.3): *bring **up**, look **down** on, take **in***, etc.; to build **extended prepositional phrases** (2.7.5.1): e.g. ***back** to the roots, **down** in the middle, **up** in the mountains.* This use has led to the development of complex prepositions such as *on to*, and *up to* (cf. 2.4.5.2).

The relationship between the two uses can be seen in examples such as:

> I'm taking it **down** to him tomorrow. (CONV)

> We were going **back** to the hotel when it happened. (NEWS)

In examples of this kind, the particle faces both ways. On the one hand, it is closely related to the verb (*go back, take down*). On the other hand, it serves as a specification of the following prepositional phrase (*back to ...*, *down to ...*).

Adverbial particles should be distinguished from adverbs (2.4.6.1) and from prepositions (2.4.6.2).

### 2.4.6.1 Adverbial particles v. adverbs

Adverbial particles differ from adverbs in a number of ways. They are shorter and less complex than most adverbs. Their core meaning is quite restricted, while the meanings of adverbs may vary widely (7.14). Above all, they have particular characteristics of distribution:

> Bring **in** the stool from the bathroom. (FICT)
> cf. *\*Bring **here** the stool from the bathroom.*
> It swallowed **up** the two men. (FICT)
> cf. *\*It swallowed **completely** the two men.*

The adverbial particles in these examples, but not the adverbs *here* and *completely*, may precede a simple definite noun phrase as direct object. This is evidence of the close connection between the two parts of the complex verb. (Regarding the placement of adverbial particles, see also 11.2.4.4.)

### 2.4.6.2 Adverbial particles v. prepositions

The forms which are used as adverbial particles can also be used as prepositions, with a few exceptions: *aside, away, back, forth, home, out.* Note, however, that these forms can be part of complex prepositions or extended prepositional phrases: *aside from, (go) away from, (come) back to/from, (go) forth to, (come) home to/from, out of*, etc.

The close connection between adverbial particles and prepositions is shown in examples such as:

> They staggered **up** the last steep of the mountain. (FICT †)
> cf. *They staggered **up**.*

*He walked slowly **up** the steps on to the platform.* (FICT†)
*cf. He walked slowly **up**.*

These pairs contain closely analogous examples, one with a preposition and the other with an adverbial particle. By these means, we can choose between specifying direction only or direction + path/goal.

Adverbial particles and prepositions further overlap before *here, there, now,* and *then*. Adverbial particles in this context have the meaning and distribution of adverbs; they can be glossed as 'in/to this/that place', 'at this/that moment/time', and they can be omitted without seriously injuring the meaning:

*That lady I worked for in Kentucky gave them to me when I got married.*
*What they called married **back** there and **back** then.* (FICT)

In contrast, prepositions in the same context are obligatory elements:

***From** there they were resettled within Japan or in a third country.* (NEWS)

Many forms can function as either an adverbial particle or a preposition in this context:

**1** *I knew that there was a man **in** there.* (NEWS†)
**2** ***In** there I feel skinnier than ever.* (FICT)

In **1**, *in* can be omitted with little change in meaning. In other words, it is used much like an adverbial particle in an extended prepositional phrase. In **2**, though, *in* is less freely omissible and therefore behaves more like a preposition (cf. 2.7.5).

Regarding the borderline between adverbial particles and prepositions, see also the account of phrasal and prepositional verbs in 5.3.

## 2.4.7 Coordinators

**Coordinators**, or **coordinating conjunctions**, are used to build coordinate structures, both phrases and clauses. Unlike prepositions (2.4.5) and subordinators (2.4.8), which both mark the following structure as subordinate, they link elements which have the same syntactic role. The main coordinators are *and, but,* and *or*, with a core meaning of addition, contrast, and alternative, respectively:

*At the end of the day it's just greed **and** profit to gain.* (CONV)

*Just read up on it **and** let us know.* (CONV)

*It would damage those tentative, **but** increasing signs of recovery.* (NEWS†)

*I don't want to speak too soon, **but** I think I have been fairly consistent this season.* (NEWS)

*Is this necessarily good **or** bad?* (ACAD)

*They may imply the same sequence of uplift, erosion, and subsidence, **or** they may reflect a fall and rise of global sea level.* (ACAD)

*But* has a more limited distribution than *and* and *or*, and chiefly connects clauses. *Or* has a negative counterpart, *nor*, which is used after negative clauses:

*The donkeys did not come back, **nor** did the eleven men, **nor** did the helicopter.* (FICT)

*His clothes were lying at his side; he hadn't bothered to seek the shelter of the rushes. **Nor** did he know.* (FICT)

If it is expanded by *neither, nor* can also connect clause elements; see 2.4.7.1.

### 2.4.7.1    Correlative coordinators

Corresponding to each simple coordinator there is a more complex form:

> The couple were **both** shoved **and** jostled. (CONV)

> It's yes or no, isn't it? **Either** you agree with it **or** you don't agree with it. (NEWS)

> Everyone was testy as a result, and **neither** Zack **nor** Jane had slept that night, but they looked happy anyway. (FICT)

> We use **not only** the colors reflected from mineral surfaces **but also** the colors transmitted through minerals in microscopic thin sections. (ACAD†)

These **correlative coordinators** stress the meaning of addition, alternative, or contrast. At the same time, they also single out each of the coordinated elements.

### 2.4.7.2    Coordinators v. other word classes

Coordinators are closely related to adverbs occurring as linking adverbials (3.2.8.3), but, unlike the latter, their position is fixed at the clause boundary. Compare the flexibility of the adverbial *nevertheless* with the coordinator *but* in the following examples:

> **Nevertheless**, they carved out a 5.7 per cent share of the overall vote. (NEWS)
> cf. **But** they carved out a 5.7 per cent share of the overall vote.

> They **nevertheless** carved out a 5.7 per cent share of the overall vote.
> cf. *They **but** carved out a 5.7 per cent share of the overall vote.

> They carved out a 5.7 per cent share of the overall vote **nevertheless**.
> cf. *They carved out a 5.7 per cent share of the overall vote **but**.

While coordinators are mutually exclusive, linking adverbials may be preceded by coordinators:

> And **nevertheless**, they carved out a 5.7 per cent share of the overall vote.
> cf. *And **but** they carved out a 5.7 per cent share of the overall vote.

A further difference is that linking adverbials, but not coordinators, are often marked off by commas in writing, or by slight pauses in speech.

The borderline between coordinators and linking adverbials is blurred with *so*, *yet*, and *neither*:

> I can't say I'm looking forward to it, but it's essential, **so** it has to be done. (NEWS)

> At least we still get promoted, **so** our season's not been completely lost. (NEWS)

> He didn't signal or wave. **Neither** did I. (FICT)

> He doesn't know how to react to it. And **neither** will anyone else, unless you show them. (FICT)

*So*, *yet*, and *neither* are like coordinators in that they are fixed at the clause boundary (in the uses illustrated above), but they are like linking adverbials in that they easily combine with coordinators (*and so, and yet, but neither*). Note also that *so* is closely related to the complex subordinator *so that* (2.4.8.1).

There is a close relationship between *neither* and *nor* in clause-initial position, but while a coordinator is often found before *neither*, similar examples are rare with *nor*:

> Martha will not like it and **nor** shall I. (FICT)

> *These are not moments of thirst …; but **nor** are they causes of drunkenness.* (NEWS †)

Apart from being used as a coordinator, *but* can also be a preposition, an adverb, and part of a complex subordinator:

as a preposition:

> *Nobody knew that **but** me and nobody had her milk **but** me.* (FICT)

as an adverb:

> *Important as sterling is domestically, it is **but** one arena in the global battle to contain the dollar.* (NEWS)

as part of a complex subordinator:

> *There was no question **but that** the army, the Lebanese Forces militia, and a whole wave of volunteers would have put up a desperate resistance.* (NEWS)

In all these uses *but* is heavily restricted contextually.

## 2.4.7.3 Simple coordinators: distribution

There are marked differences between the registers in the distribution of the coordinators.

**CORPUS FINDINGS 2**

➤ *And* is by far the most common coordinator in all the registers (Figure 2.3).
  ➤ *And* is considerably more frequent in fiction and academic prose than in conversation and news.
➤ *But* is most frequent in conversation and fiction, and least frequent in academic prose.
➤ *Or* is far more common in academic prose than in the other registers.
➤ *Nor* is so rare in all registers that it does not show up in Figure 2.3.
➤ *And* serves very different grammatical roles across the registers (Figure 2.4):[4]
  ➤ In conversation, and to a lesser extent fiction, *and* is generally used as a clause-level connector.
  ➤ In academic prose, *and* is more typically used as a phrase-level connector.

**Figure 2.3**
**Distribution of coordinators across registers**

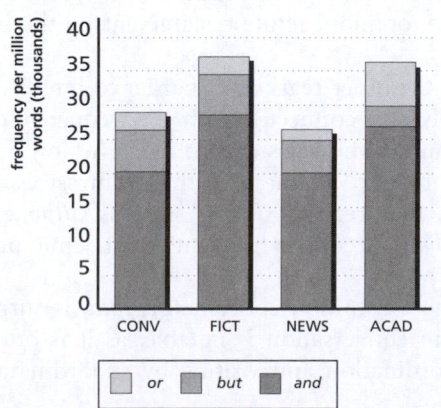

**Figure 2.4**
**Percentage use of *and* as phrase-level v. clause-level connector**

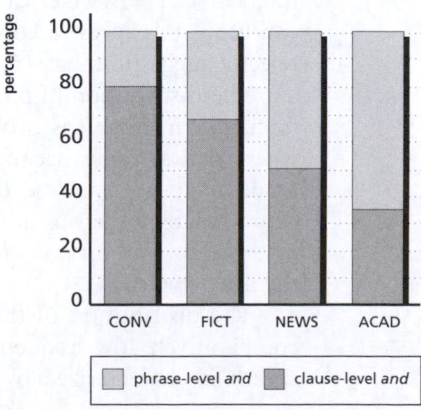

### DISCUSSION OF FINDINGS

*Nor* is far less common than all the other coordinators, presumably because negation is less frequent overall than positive forms. However, *nor* is somewhat more common in fiction than conversation. We can see this as a reflection of a general difference in negation patterns, viz. the preference for negation by *not* in conversation and the more common use of other negative forms in fiction (3.8.4.2).

In contrast, the positive alternative coordinator *or* is particularly frequent in academic prose:

1 *Such movements may come from local **or** regional deformation of the land **or** from a global rise **or** fall of sea level.* (ACAD)

2 *According to Chamberlain and Moulton, these broke into small chunks, **or** planetesimals, which went flying as cold bodies into orbits around the Sun in the plane of the passing start.* (ACAD)

3 *We have unraveled the kinematics, **or** motions, of the process, but the dynamics, **or** forces, that are responsible have yet to be understood.* (ACAD†)

Academic discourse invites a consideration of alternative modes of explanation (see **1**). Additionally, there is a frequent need to explain particular terms and concepts, moving from everyday to technical **2** or the reverse **3**. As regards other factors that might explain the high frequency of *or* in scientific prose, see also the comments below on *and*.

*But* is the only coordinator which is more frequent in conversation than in all the other registers:

4 *I think he will have salad **but** he doesn't like tomatoes.* (CONV†)

5 A: *The golden rule is if you're reversing you must look behind you!*
 B: *Yeah, **but** she said she did.* (CONV)

6 A: *If perhaps you were to spread erm – a wire netting over the pond Mollie?*
 B: *Well yes I know, **but** I'm not having that! **But** erm – what I am going to do **but** I can't do it until – the spring.* (CONV)

The high frequency of *but* should be seen in conjunction with the high frequency of negatives in conversation (3.8.1). Negation and contrast are closely related concepts. The high frequency in both cases is due to the fact that conversation is interactive. The speaker can use *but* to modify a statement (**4**), and the addressee can use it to express a contrary opinion, refute a statement by the interlocutor, reject a suggestion, etc. (**5**, **6**).

The distribution of *but* in the other registers is harder to interpret. The high frequency in fiction is probably also connected with the frequency of negation, where fiction ranks second among the registers (3.8.1). The low frequency in academic prose may be due in part to the fact that contrast is more often expressed by other means in that register: forms such as *although*, *however*, *nevertheless*, and *on the other hand* are more frequent in academic prose than in the other registers.

The distribution of the most common coordinator, *and*, is surprising. The comparatively low frequency in conversation is notable, as it is often said that speech is characterized by coordination and writing by subordination. In fact, with the exception of *but*, the frequency of all coordinators is relatively low in conversation, while subordinators are more frequent in conversation than in news and academic prose (2.4.14). This distribution is probably connected with the high frequency of verbs in conversation (2.3.5), which in its turn means that clauses are more numerous. The more clauses there are, the greater the need for clause-level connectors (such as *but* and the subordinators).

In contrast, *and* can be used as a phrase-level connector as well as a clause-level connector. The low degree of coordination at the phrase level in conversation, which is consistent with the general simplicity of phrases in this register (2.10), accounts for the unexpectedly low frequency of *and* in conversation.

On the other hand, the high degree of phrase-level coordination is responsible for the high overall frequency of *and* in academic prose:

> *A distinction is needed between elements, which include nitrogen, phosphorus* **and** *potassium, which are mobile in the phloem* **and** *those which are comparatively immobile, for example, calcium, boron* **and** *iron,* **and** *are transferred only slowly to the developing organ.*
>
> *An example of the uptake* **and** *transfer of nitrogen* **and** *phosphorus during the period of grain filling of winter wheat is given in Table 2.5.*
> (ACAD)

Of the six instances of *and* in this passage, only one (the fourth) is a clause-level coordinator. The high frequency of *or* in academic prose is probably also to a great extent a reflection of coordination at the phrase level.

It remains something of a mystery why news reportage should deviate from the other written registers in having a much lower frequency of both *and* and *or*; in fact, even lower than in conversation. There is, however, a connection with the high lexical density in news reportage (2.2.9) and the fact that colons and semi-colons are almost twice as frequent as in the other written registers. The following example illustrates the way newspaper text often juxtaposes sentences without overt connectors, omits the *and* before the last item in a list (*drawings*) where it would be normal in other registers, and prefers a semi-colon to a connector (in the last sentence).

> *This year, new work by 20 artists includes sculptures, paintings, installations, drawings. No restrictions were made on entries, but positive encouragement was given to artists "working in new ways". The final selection was made after studio visits. Artists include Louise and Jane Wilson, who comment on their relationship as twins through a photographic-sculptural work; their identical degree show at Dundee and Newcastle.* (NEWS)

See 2.9.1 for further discussion of clause-level and phrase-level coordination.

## 2.4.7.4    Sentence/turn-initial coordinators

There is a well-known prescriptive reaction against beginning an orthographic sentence with a coordinator. Nevertheless, in actual texts we quite frequently find coordinators in this position.

**CORPUS FINDINGS** [3,6]

➤ Proportionally, turn-initial coordinators are considerably more common in conversation than sentence-initial coordinators in the written registers.

➤ Sentence-initial coordinators are least common in academic prose.

➤ *But* and *nor* are much more likely to occur in sentence/turn-initial position than *and* or *or*.

### DISCUSSION OF FINDINGS

The prescription against initial coordinators seems most influential in academic prose. The higher frequencies in fiction and news reportage probably reflect the fact that these registers often include more spontaneous discourse, including fiction dialogue and quoted speech in news, evidencing the lack of attention to prescriptive rules of ordinary speech. It further turns out that sentence-initial coordinators often occur at paragraph boundaries, where they create a marked effect:

**Figure 2.5**
**Percentage use of coordinators in sentence/turn-initial position**

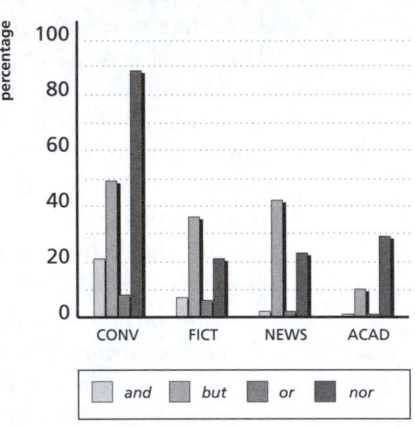

> He seemed so full of life that time.
>    ***And*** then what could it have been, six weeks after we started coming in here, eight at the outside, off he goes. (FICT)
>
> No indeed, poems were not made out of intentions.
>    ***But*** perhaps they could come from hope. (FICT)
>
> Had Norwich not defeated Notts County in the fifth round that afternoon, it could well have been Mr Stringer's first and last address to the nation's footballing public.
>    ***But*** win Norwich did and they have since gone on to preserve their First Division lives and reach the FA Cup semi-finals. (NEWS)

The frequency with which coordinators occur in sentence/turn-initial position, and even at paragraph boundaries, suggests that the traditional analysis of coordination may not always be the best one, i.e. where the coordinator connects equal elements and is related in the same way to each of these elements. Rather, in these cases, the coordinator is more closely connected with the element which it introduces, and there is good reason to regard it as an initiator of the following phrase or clause on a par with prepositions and subordinators (except that it does not mark the following structure as subordinate).

**Table 2.6**    **Distribution of correlative coordinators across registers; occurrences per million words**

each ● marks 100

|  | CONV | FICT | NEWS | ACAD |
|---|---|---|---|---|
| *both–and* | ● ● | ● ● ● ● | ● ● ● ● ● ● | ● ● ● ● ● ● ● ● ● ● ● ● |
| *either–or* | ● ● | ● ● | ● | ● ● ● ● ● |
| *neither–nor* | – | ● | – | ● |

### 2.4.7.5 Correlative coordinators: distribution

➤ The correlative coordinators are generally more frequent in the written registers, especially academic prose (see Table 2.6).

➤ The order of frequency of the three types follows that for *and*, *or*, and *nor* separately (2.4.7.3)

**DISCUSSION OF FINDINGS**

Correlative coordinators are especially common in academic prose, because they explicitly spell out the exact specification and elaboration that this register requires:

> *We can think of the electron < ... > as following paths* **both** *direct* **and** *indirect, moving* **both** *rapidly* **and** *slowly.* (ACAD†)

> *Symptoms may appear first in* **either** *younger* **or** *older leaves.* (ACAD)

## 2.4.8 Subordinators

**Subordinators**, or **subordinating conjunctions**, are words which introduce (mainly finite) dependent clauses. Grammatically, subordinators have a purely syntactic role, and this distinguishes them from other clause initiators (such as *wh*-words), which can also have a role as subject, object, adverbial, etc.

Subordinators fall into three major subclasses:

(1) The great majority of subordinators introduce **adverbial clauses**: *after*, *as*, *because*, *if*, *since*, *(al)though*, *whether*, *while*, etc. See the account of adverbial clauses in 3.11.2, and Chapter 10 (especially 10.2.8).

(2) Three subordinators introduce **degree clauses**: *as*, *than*, *that* (3.11.4 and 7.8).

(3) Three subordinators introduce **complement clauses** (or **nominal clauses**): *if*, *that*, *whether*. See the account of complement clauses in 3.11.1, and Chapter 9.

The subordinators in (1) and (2) indicate the meaning relationship between the dependent clause and the superordinate structure: time, reason, condition, comparison, etc. The subordinators in (3) have little meaning apart from marking structural dependency and are often classified as **complementizers**, i.e. words which introduce complement clauses. Among complementizers are also included *wh*-words when introducing complement clauses (2.4.9) and the infinitive marker *to* (2.4.12).

### 2.4.8.1 Complex subordinators

A number of subordinators introducing adverbial clauses are multi-word units. Most of them end in *as* or *that* (which is often optional).

Ending in:

| | |
|---|---|
| *as*: | *according as, as far as, as long as, as soon as* |
| *that*: | *given (that), granted/granting (that), on condition (that), provided/ providing (that), seeing (that), supposing (that); directly (that), immediately (that), now (that), the moment (that); but that, except (that), in that, in order that, so (that), such that* |

Others: *as if, as though, even if, even though, in case, no matter (+ wh-word)*

For illustrations, see 10.2.8.

### 2.4.8.2 Correlative subordinators

A few subordinators have a special relationship to a form in the superordinate structure. The subordinator and the form it correlates with cooperate to express the relationship between the clauses:

1 ***If** we had moved in [then] we'd have to spend fifty thousand pound to get it up to scratch.* (CONV)

2 *And El-ahrairah knew then that **although** he would not be mocked, [yet] Frith was his friend.* (FICT)

3 ***As** the castle was frozen, [so] were they; **as** the castle was slowly crumbling but they stayed in their stasis, [so] their hopes, their chances decayed.* (FICT†)

These are not complex subordinators: the subordinators (*if, although,* and *as*) are simple, but the semantic relationship is reinforced by an adverb in the matrix clause (*then, yet, so*). The adverb can generally be omitted in these cases (except in the type with inversion of the subject and the verb in **3**).

Another kind of correlative subordination is found in clauses following a degree element in the superordinate structure: *as/so ... as, more/-er/less ... than, so/such ... that.*

4 *You are not **as** dumb **as** you look are you?* (CONV)

5 *I was confused by all these solicitous questions, and found myself telling **more** lies **than** I had to.* (FICT)

6 *Confidence is **so** fragile at this stage **that** if recovery were to falter, interest rates would have to be reduced further.* (NEWS)

A special type of comparative structure contains *the ... the ...* expressing proportion, either connecting clauses **7** or verbless structures **8**:

7 ***The** more systematically we analyse the problem or idea to be communicated, **the** clearer it becomes.* (ACAD)

8 ***The** more rapid the cooling, **the** finer the grain size and **the** poorer the crystallinity.* (ACAD)

See the account of degree clauses in 3.11.4 and 7.8.

### 2.4.8.3 Overlap between subordinators and other word classes

There is a good deal of overlap between subordinators and other word classes. For examples, see Table 2.7 (see also 2.4.5.3 and Table 2.5).

The most extreme case of overlap is found with *that*, which can introduce degree clauses **1**, adverbial clauses (as part of a complex subordinator in **2**), and complement clauses **3**:

1 *The way you two do the work it looks so fine **that** I didn't think I could see it properly.* (CONV)

2 *But police do not think the arson attack was a deliberate attempt to put out lights in the town **so that** looting could take place.* (NEWS)

3 *We assume **that** the store is randomly accessible.* (ACAD†)

**Table 2.7** **Overlap between subordinators and other word classes**

Sub. = subordinator   Prep. = preposition   Adv. = adverb

| form | Sub. | Prep. | Adv. | examples |
|------|------|-------|------|----------|
| *for* | ● | | | *I concede the point,* **for** *I have stated it many times in the past.* |
| | | ● | | *Oh we're quite happy to rent* **for** *a while.* |
| *like* | ● | | | *Here today and gone today,* **like** *I said.* |
| | | ● | | **Like** *many marine painters he had never been at sea.* |
| *since* | ● | | | *But this day is something I've dreamed of* **since** *I was a kid.* |
| | | ● | | **Since** *Christmas, sales have moved ahead.* |
| | | | ● | *She had not heard one word from him* **since**. |
| *though* | ● | | | *She had never heard of him,* **though** *she did not say so.* |
| | | | ● | *That's nice* **though** *isn't it?* |

In addition, *that* is used as a degree adverb (as in *that good*), as a relativizer (2.4.9), and as a demonstrative determiner or pronoun (2.4.1–2).

## 2.4.9   *Wh*-words

As with subordinators, *wh*-words introduce clauses. With two exceptions (*how* and *that*), *wh*-words begin with *wh* and are used in two ways:

as **interrogative clause markers**:

> **What** *do they want?* (FICT)     **Which** *one do you mean?* (FICT)
>
> **When** *are you leaving?* (FICT)

Interrogative clause markers are used as pronouns (*who, whom, what, which*), determiners (*what, which, whose*), or adverbs (*how, when, where, why*). As adverbs, *wh*-words nevertheless have a linking role and thus straddle the divide between function words and lexical words (2.2.3.1–2). (See also the account of *wh*-questions in 3.13.2.1.)

as **relativizers** (introducing a **relative clause**):

> *the kind of person* **who** *needs emotional space* (NEWS†)
>
> *the car* **which** *she had abandoned* (FICT†)
>
> *a small place* **where** *everyone knows everyone else* (NEWS†)

Relativizers are used as pronouns (*who, whom, which, that*), determiners (*which, whose*), or adverbs (*when, where, why*). See also the account of relative clauses in 3.11.3 and 8.7.

Although relativizers and subordinators are alike in that they introduce dependent clauses, there is an important difference: in addition to the linking role, relativizers have a syntactic role as clause element or part of a clause element. Moreover, the relativizer normally has a close relationship with a preceding noun phrase: the clause it introduces is generally a postmodifier in a noun phrase and the choice of relativizer is to a large extent dependent upon the head of this noun phrase (e.g. the choice of *who* v. *which* in the examples above (8.7.1.3). There is no such relation between noun phrases and subordinators.

Two further uses of *wh*-words are:

as **complementizers** (introducing a complement clause):

> *I don't know **what** I would have done without her.* (NEWS)
>
> *I give them **whatever** I have in my pocket.* (NEWS)
>
> *Vada wonders **where** she stands in her father's affections.* (NEWS)

Complement clauses introduced by *wh*-words are either **dependent interrogative clauses** or **nominal relative clauses** (3.11.1 and 9.3).

as **adverbial clause links**:

> *They could not improve upon that, **whatever** they might say.* (FICT)
>
> ***However** they vary, each formation comprises a distinctive set of rock layers.* (ACAD)

Adverbial clauses introduced by *wh*-words express temporal, locative, or concessive relationships.

In the last two uses, *wh*-words are often combined with *-ever*, which gives the form the meaning 'no matter what/when/where ...'. Such forms are the rule in concessive *wh*-clauses.

## 2.4.10 Existential *there*

**Existential** *there* has a unique syntactic role; there is no other word in English which behaves in the same way. It is often described as an anticipatory subject:

> ***There** were people on the floor. **There** was one bloke with a piece of glass sticking out of his head. Then **there** were 20 to 30 people standing there shocked and bewildered.* (NEWS)

See the account of existential *there* in 3.6.3 and 11.4.

Existential *there* should be distinguished from **locative** *there*, which is used as an adverb. The two types frequently co-occur in the same clause, as in the following examples (existential *there* in bold; locative *there* marked by *[]*):

> *"But it's empty, **there**'s no one [there]," the child said.* (FICT)
>
> *"**There** is real value [there]," says Cant.* (NEWS)

## 2.4.11 The negator *not*

*Not* is in many ways like an adverb, but it has special characteristics which make it natural to single it out as a unique member of a class by itself. The main use of *not* (and its reduced form *n't*) is to negate a clause; see the account of *not*-negation in 3.8.2. Clausal negation can, however, be expressed by other means, in particular by pronouns and determiners; see the account of *no*-negation in 3.8.3.

Apart from negating clauses, *not* can be used to restrict the scope of quantifying expressions or to negate adjective or adverb phrases (see also the comments on local negation in 3.8.5):

> *Have you noticed that by and large, **not all** the time of course but – I should say that eighty percent of the time birds face that way?* (CONV)
>
> *On the other side of the world, the Freedom League had inspired a **not-very-original** headline.* (FICT)

> *Robertson, **not unexpectedly**, claimed afterwards that his strike should have been recognised.* (NEWS)

*Not* is also part of a number of common multi-word lexical units, e.g. the correlative coordinator *not only … but* (2.4.7.1) and the insert *not at all*.

## 2.4.12 The infinitive marker *to*

The **infinitive marker** *to* is another unique word which does not easily fit into any of the other classes. Its chief use is as a complementizer preceding the infinitive form of verbs (cf. 9.4):

> *What do you want **to** drink?* (CONV)
>
> *I'm just happy **to** be here right now.* (CONV)

In addition, *to* occurs as part of two complex infinitive markers, *in order to* and *so as to*, both introducing adverbial clauses expressing purpose:

> *You don't have to live under the same laws as a foreigner **in order to** trade with him.* (NEWS)
>
> *Each has the job of writing his chapter **so as to** make the novel being constructed the best it can be.* (ACAD)

On its own, *to* can also be used to introduce such adverbial clauses (3.12.1, 10.1.2):

> *She called me **to** say a lawyer was starting divorce proceedings* (FICT)

The infinitive marker *to* also occurs as part of other multi-word lexical units, including *ought to, used to,* and *have to* (2.4.4). The infinitive marker *to* should be distinguished from the preposition *to* (2.4.5.3).

## 2.4.13 Numerals

**Numerals** are a closed set of simple forms which can be used to build up an indefinite number of more complex forms. They are most commonly used as heads or determiners in noun phrases. There are two distinct sets of numerals, which differ both in form and meaning: **cardinals** (2.4.13.1) and **ordinals** (2.4.13.2). (See 2.7.7.1 for some remarks on more complex numeral phrases.)

### 2.4.13.1 Cardinals

Cardinal numerals answer the question 'How many?' and specify entities by quantity. They are most commonly used as determiners:

> ***Four** people were arrested.* (NEWS)

However, cardinal numerals also occur as heads in noun phrases:

> ***Four** of the yen traders have pleaded guilty.* (NEWS†)

In examples such as the following, cardinals are inflected like nouns:

> *Cops in **twos** and **threes** huddle, lightly tap their thighs with night sticks and smile at me with benevolence.* (FICT)
>
> *They're at most in their middle **twenties** or so.* (FICT†)
>
> *"I can see **sixes** and **sevens** just as easily I can visualise birdies," he said.* (NEWS)
>
> *Damage is estimated at **hundreds** of **millions** of pounds.* (NEWS)

There are different words for '0', chiefly *nil, nought, o,* and *zero*:

> A: *What's Ray's telephone number?*
> B: *Eight four five **o** eight.* (CONV)
> *When they came home and found that Woking had won five **nil** they thought they'd chosen the wrong one.* (CONV)
> *It's **nought** point five.* (CONV)
> *This is United 284. Roger; **zero** six **zero**.* (FICT)
> *It also gives the outside temperature, which in our case rarely exceeded **zero**.* (NEWS)

### 2.4.13.2    Ordinals

Ordinal numerals answer the question 'Which?' and serve to place entities in order or in a series. They are used as determiners or heads of noun phrases and are normally preceded by a determiner (usually the definite article or a possessive determiner).

Ordinals as determiners:

> *I was doing my **third** week as a young crime reporter and had just about finished my **second** and last story of the day when the phone rang.* (FICT)

Ordinals as noun phrase heads:

> *Three men will appear before Belfast magistrates today on charges of intimidation. A **fourth** will be charged with having information likely to be of use to terrorists. The **fifth**, a woman, was remanded on the same charge yesterday.* (NEWS)

In examples such as the following, ordinals are treated like regular nouns:

> *In addition, he owned a **fifth** of the new Holiday Inn out on Route 54.* (FICT†)
> *Which is the largest, two **thirds** or three **sevenths**?* (FICT)
> *The pupil can identify the place value of a column or a digit for values of **tenths**, **hundredths**, and **thousandths**.* (ACAD†)

Ordinals can also be used adverbially:

> 1 *Young men and boys in single file, each carrying a pot of wine, came **first**.* (FICT)
> 2 ***First** I'll deal with my dispatches, then we'll talk.* (FICT)
> 3 *Michael Schumacher was **fifth** fastest in his Camel Benetton Ford.* (NEWS†)

In **1** the ordinal is a circumstance adverbial (3.2.8.1), in **2** a linking adverbial (3.2.8.3), and in **3** the ordinal is a modifier in an adjective phrase (2.7.3).

### 2.4.13.3    Numerals: distribution

Numerals can be given in either alphabetic or digit form:

|  | alphabetic forms | digit forms |
|---|---|---|
| cardinal numerals | zero, one, two | 0, 1, 2 |
|  | ten, eleven, twelve | 10, 11, 12 |
| ordinal numerals | first, second, third | 1st, 2nd, 3rd |
|  | tenth, eleventh, twelfth | 10th, 11th, 12th |

In actual use, though, one or the other form is normally preferred.

**CORPUS FINDINGS [3]**

➤ The frequency of cardinal numerals decreases with increasing numbers.
  ➤ Exceptions are forms for round numbers (10, 20, etc.), which have higher frequencies than the neighbouring forms.
➤ Ordinals are less frequent than the corresponding cardinals.
➤ The frequency of alphabetic forms generally decreases with increasing numbers, both among cardinals and ordinals.
  ➤ Alphabetic forms are considerably more common than digit forms for numerals lower than ten. This preference for alphabetic forms is more pronounced for ordinals than for cardinals.
  ➤ In contrast, digit forms are more common than alphabetic forms for numerals between 10 and 19.
  ➤ Alphabetic and digit forms of cardinals are about equally common in the case of round numbers. Alphabetic forms of cardinals are predominant with *hundred*, *thousand*, and *million*.
  ➤ *Zero* is by far the most common alphabetical form referring to 0.

**DISCUSSION OF FINDINGS**

The frequency of the numerals overall presumably reflects real life needs of communication, and that for many purposes people find it easier to process round figures than precise ones where numbers are larger. The preference for some numbers to be written alphabetically reflects a common stylistic prescription, and to some extent is related to the length of the written form. Those most often written alphabetically tend to be those that, when so written, have relatively short written forms. Numbers such as *nineteen*, *thirty-five*, or *seven hundred and eighty-two* require more effort to write than *six* or *forty*, and a principle of psychological ease favours the digit versions.

The distribution of the numerals in the registers and in relation to other kinds of determiners is discussed further in 4.4.5.1.

## 2.4.14  Major function word classes: distribution

Although it is often said that function words, as opposed to individual lexical words, are frequent in any text, there are wide differences among registers in the distribution both of individual function words and of the function word classes.

**CORPUS FINDINGS [1]**

➤ Pronouns in conversation are by far the most frequent class of function word.
  ➤ In contrast, pronouns are relatively rare in news and academic prose.
➤ Prepositions are the most frequent function word class in news and academic prose; they are much less common in conversation.
  ➤ Similarly, determiners are much less common in conversation than in the written registers.
➤ Auxiliaries, both primary and modal, and adverbial particles are more common in conversation and fiction than in the other registers.
➤ Coordinators and subordinators vary to a lesser extent across registers than the other function word classes.

**Figure 2.6**
**Distribution of function word classes—conversation**

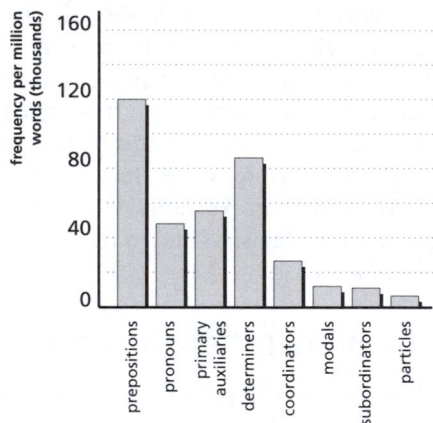

**Figure 2.7**
**Distribution of function word classes—fiction**

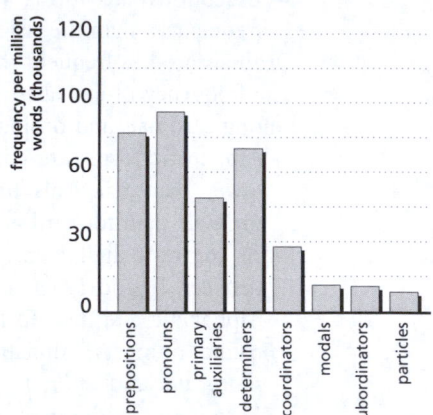

**Figure 2.8**
**Distribution of function word classes—news**

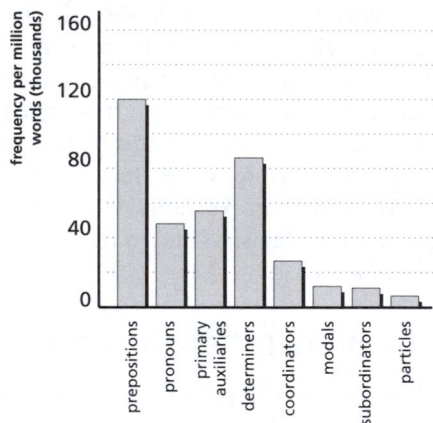

**Figure 2.9**
**Distribution of function word classes—academic prose**

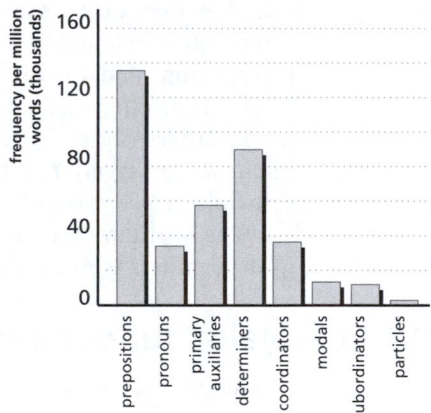

**DISCUSSION OF FINDINGS**

The distribution of function words is closely connected with the distribution of the lexical word classes (2.3.5). The low frequency of nouns in conversation is compensated for by the high pronoun density. Conversely, a high frequency of nouns in news and academic prose corresponds to a low density of pronouns (see also 4.1.2).

Function words associated with verbs vary in frequency with the density of lexical verbs. Conversation and fiction have the highest frequency of lexical verbs and also the highest frequency of auxiliaries and adverbial particles, which specify or extend lexical verbs.

Similarly, function words associated with nouns vary in frequency with the density of nouns. Academic prose and news reportage have the highest frequency of nouns and also the highest frequency of prepositions and determiners, which serve as extensions or specifications of nouns.

With respect to all these features, fiction takes up an intermediate position between conversation and the other registers, reflecting the overall distribution of lexical words (2.3.5).

It is somewhat surprising that subordinators are relatively rare in all registers, but somewhat more common in conversation and fiction than in academic prose and news reportage. This distribution reflects the fact that complexity in expository writing resides at the phrase level rather than at the level of clause combinations (thus the high frequency of prepositions; see also 2.10 and Chapter 8). In contrast, conversation and fiction have a high frequency of verbs, hence also of clauses and clause combinations.

As differences are less marked with coordinators and subordinators than with the function words that operate specifically at the phrase level, it seems justified to conclude that register differences are more connected with the build-up of phrases than with the connection of clauses.

## 2.5    Survey of inserts

There is a wide variety of **inserts** in conversation. The following survey gives some typical examples. See also the detailed account of conversation in Chapter 14.

- Interjections

    *Tt oh! **Ouch** my neck hurts.* (CONV)

    ***Oh dear!** What's that?* (CONV)

- Greetings, farewells

    ***Hi** Shirl. Alright?* (CONV)

    ***Good morning**, Gary Jones speaking, can I help you?* (CONV)

    A: ***Goodbye**.*

    B: ***Bye bye.*** (CONV)

- Discourse markers

    *Oh this'll be a good idea! **Right**, we can do this.* (CONV)

    *Yeah, **well** it's just different.* (CONV)

- Attention signals

    ***Hey look** – that's the way to do it.* (CONV)

    ***Hey hey hey hey** what's the problem – what's the problem?* (CONV)

- Response elicitors

    *Look, you can serve out for once. I'm sta–, tired! You do it **alright**?* (CONV†)

    *Pat, come over here in about twenty-five minutes, **okay**?* (CONV)

- Responses

    A: *Actually, I'm going to need more milk then, if we're going to have chocolate cake.*

    B: ***Yeah. Alright. Yeah**, we got a lot of milk.* (CONV)

- Hesitators

    *What about that **erm**, what about that other place that **er** timber place on the way to Kilkern, **erm** we went there, you, oh you went in to ask about some walnut, do you remember when **er** –* (CONV†)

- Thanks

    *Here's your pen,* **thanks**. (CONV)

    *Can I have another two Diet Cokes please?* **Thank you**. (CONV)

- The politeness marker *please*

    *A: Can I have a bit* **please**?

    *B: Ask nicely.*

    *A:* **Please** *can I have a bit of Kit Kat?* (CONV)

- Apologies

    *Er,* **excuse me**! *Ooh!* **Pardon me**. (CONV)

    *A: I said – said no eating!*

    *B:* **Sorry** *miss. I'll spit it out straight away.* (CONV)

- Expletives

    **Oh Jesus**, *I didn't know it was that cold.* (AmE CONV)

## 2.6    **Phrases and their characteristics**

### 2.6.1    **Constituency**

Language forms do not just consist of sequences of words put together like beads on a string. They can can be broken down into units (or **constituents**), which can again be analysed hierarchically into successively smaller units (2.1). The following example contains three major **phrases**, as indicated by bracketing:

> 1 *[The opposition] [is demanding] [a more representative government].*
> (NEWS†)

A phrase may consist of a single word or of a group of words. The identity of phrases can be shown by substitution; a multi-word phrase can often be replaced by a single word without destroying the overall meaning. Thus compare **1a** with **1** above:

> **1a** *It <i.e. the opposition> demands something <i.e. a more representative government>.*

The identity of phrases can also be shown by movement tests; a phrase can be moved as a unit (phrases can, however, also be split up under certain circumstances; 2.7). Compare **1b** with **1** above:

> **1b** *A more representative government is demanded by the opposition.*

Phrases can be **embedded** at different **levels**, and in some cases a given structure can have more than one interpretation. Thus consider the following example (adapted from Text sample 1; cf. 2.6.3):

> **2** *Mr Adamec threatened to quit last night.* (NEWS†)

Notice that there are two possible meanings, corresponding to different groupings of the words (or different **phrase structures**):

> **2a** *[Mr Adamec] [threatened] [to quit] [last night].*
>
> **2b** *[Mr Adamec] [threatened] [to quit [last night]].*

**2a** corresponds to the meaning 'Mr Adamec expressed the threat last night' (this meaning is the more likely one in the context). In **2b** *to quit* and *last night* form a larger constituent and the meaning is 'Mr Adamec threatened that he would resign last night'. Only the first meaning can be paraphrased by:

> **2c** *Last night Mr Adamec threatened to quit.*

Notice that the phrase *last night* is more deeply embedded in **2b**. We shall come back to the embedding of phrases later (2.8).

The basic points on phrase constituency can be summarized as follows:

- Words make up phrases, which behave like units.
- Phrases can be identified by substitution and movement tests.
- Differences in phrase structure correlate with differences in meaning.
- Phrases can be embedded at different levels.

## 2.6.2 Form v. syntactic role of phrases

Phrase types differ both in their internal **phrase structure** and in their **syntactic roles**, i.e. their relations to larger structures. The syntactic roles are crucial for the interpretation of the phrases. To take a simple example, it is these relations which determine the difference in meaning between *I could beat him on my bicycle* and *He could beat me*, where the noun phrases in subject and object position are interchanged.

It is important to notice that a phrase type characteristically has a number of different syntactic roles. Noun phrases are particularly flexible in this respect. In the account below of the syntactic roles of the phrase types, references are frequently made to concepts introduced in Chapter 3, in particular to the elements of the clause (3.2).

## 2.6.3 Phrases in text samples

The distribution of phrases in discourse can be illustrated by comparing the two text passages discussed earlier in 2.2.1.1. The words in these passages have been grouped into phrases (shown by brackets; *would ... like* in Text sample 2 comprises a **discontinuous phrase**). Only multi-word phrases have been marked, and phrases embedded within phrases have not been marked. Sequences which have been regarded as multi-word lexical units (2.2.5.4) are not identified as phrases. Cohesive units above the level of the phrase, i.e. clauses, are also not marked (3.1).

Text sample 1: NEWS REPORT

> *[Mr Ladislav Adamec, the Czechoslovak Prime Minister,] threatened [to quit] [last night], as [hard bargaining] continued [for a second day] [with the opposition] [over the shape of the new government].*
>
> *[Mr Adamec] had talks [with the opposition leader, Mr Vaclav Havel,] [on the cabinet lineup]. He later went [on national television] [to state] that he [would stand down] unless [his new government] gained [public backing].*
>
> *...*
>
> *[The opposition Civic Forum, which rejected the Communist-dominated cabinet unveiled by Mr Adamec at the weekend,] [is demanding] [a more representative government staffed mainly by experts].*

Text sample 2: CONVERSATION IN A BARBER SHOP

> *A: I [will put], I [won't smile]. – Tell me what [would) you (like] now?*
> *B: Erm – shortened up please Pete – erm – shaved a little bit [at the back and sides] – and then just sort of brushed back [on the top] a bit.*

> A: *Right, and when you say shaved a little bit*
> B: *Yeah yo— — you sort of just – got [your thing] and zazoom!*
> A: *Yeah but – is it [that short] really?*
> B: *Yeah to–, yeah and I*
> A: *<unclear> you want [a number four]?*
> B: *Yeah I think so.*

The composition of the two passages in terms of phrases is summarized in Table 2.8.

**Table 2.8** **The distribution of phrases of varying length in two text samples**

| phrases | CONV | NEWS |
|---|---|---|
| 1 word | 51 | 12 |
| 2 words | 5 | 8 |
| 3 words | 2 | 4 |
| 4+ words | 1 | 6 |

The news text contains longer phrases as well as a larger number of multi-word phrases. Only a very small number of the words in the news text do not form part of multiword phrases (approximately 13 per cent out of the total number of word forms), as against a very high frequency of single words in the conversational passage (approximately 70 per cent out of the total number of word forms).

Our comparison is incomplete in that it does not include phrases within phrases. These occur particularly in the news text. This example (from the first paragraph) can be broken down as follows:

*[over [the shape [of [the new government]]]]*

        prepositional phrase
        noun phrase
        prepositional phrase
        noun phrase

Noun phrases and prepositional phrases, in particular, frequently have a very complex structure, containing several layers of embedded phrases (see also 2.8 and Chapter 8, especially 8.3.7).

Though the comparison above is limited, it shows that there are wide differences between texts from different registers. There is far more structural integration in the news text than in the conversation passage. The same type of difference will be found when the texts are analysed on the clause level (3.1.1).

## 2.7 Types of phrase

Corresponding to each type of lexical word, there is a major phrase type with the lexical word as head and a number of accompanying elements: **noun phrases** (2.7.1), **verb phrases** (2.7.2), **adjective phrases** (2.7.3), and **adverb phrases** (2.7.4). Each phrase type can consist of the head only.

A fifth major category is the **prepositional phrase** (2.7.5). In addition, there are some more marginal phrase types, in particular **genitive phrases** (2.7.6) and **numeral phrases** (2.7.7).

## 2.7.1 Noun phrases

A noun phrase in the strict sense consists of a noun (2.3.1) as **head**, either alone or accompanied by **determiners** (which specify the reference of the noun; 2.4.1) and **modifiers** (which describe or classify the entity denoted by the head noun). The head is in bold in the following examples (head nouns in embedded noun phrases are not highlighted):

| | |
|---|---|
| a **house** | these **houses** |
| the **house** | some **houses** |
| their **house** | many **houses** |
| his bristly short **hair** | her below-the-knee **skirt** |
| her gold **watch** | the **city** proper |
| the then **president** | the **journey** back |
| the little **girl** next door | any printed **material** discovered |
| heavy **rain** driven by gales | which might be construed as |
| predicted for last night | dissent |

The head noun can also be followed by **complements**, which complete the meaning of the noun and typically take the form of *that*-clauses or infinitive clauses (8.5):

1 *[The popular **assumption** that language simply serves to communicate "thoughts" or "ideas"] is too simplistic.* (ACAD)

2 *He feels awkward about [her **refusal** to show any sign of emotion].* (NEWS†)

Head nouns followed by complements are typically abstract nouns derived from verbs or adjectives (cf. *it is assumed that ..., she refuses to ...*).

Besides common nouns, noun phrases may be headed by proper nouns **3**, pronouns (**4–8**), and nominalized adjectives (**9, 10**):

3 ***Dawn** lives in **Wembley**.* (FICT)

4 ***They** said **they**'d got **it**.* (CONV)

5 *"**Anybody** can see **that**."* (FICT)

6 *"There's [**nothing** special] about **us**."* (FICT)

7 *Do **you** want [**anything** else]?* (CONV)

8 *"Have **you** got [**everything** you need]?"* (FICT)

9 *Of course he was rich, but [the **rich**] were usually mean.* (FICT)

10 *"Show me how [the **impossible**] can be possible!"* (FICT)

These other noun phrases are like noun phrases with common noun heads both with respect to their syntactic roles and as regards some aspects of structure (e.g. the use of determiners with nominalized adjectives and postmodifiers with some pronouns). Note that the term 'noun phrase' or 'NP' is frequently used more widely for any unit which appears in the positions characteristic of noun-headed structures (including clauses). If needed, noun phrases in this broad sense may be singled out as **nominals** (a term which can also apply to nominal clauses; 3.11.1).

Noun phrases can be very complex, and frequently we find several layers of embedding (see also 2.8 and 8.1). The structure and uses of noun phrases are dealt with in detail in Chapters 4 and 8.

## 2.7.1.1 The syntactic roles of noun phrases

Noun phrases may have a wide range of syntactic roles. A to E are the most typical nominal roles.

**A** Subject (cf. 3.2.1)

> *Two women* *had come in and* *she* *asked them to wait, giving them magazines to look at.* (FICT)

**B** Direct object (cf. 3.2.4)

> *The pilot saw* *a field* *ahead.* (FICT†)

**C** Indirect object (3.2.5)

> *At primary school he had been allowed to make* *her* *a birthday card.* (FICT†)

In the following example, subjects are given in bold, direct objects are marked by *[]*, and indirect objects are marked by *{}*:

> *Louisiana officials* *argue that* *the U.S. Supreme Court decision last spring, upholding Missouri's abortion restrictions, gave {the states} [enough flexibility] to make [abortion] illegal, except when necessary to save [the mother's life].* (NEWS)

**D** Prepositional object (cf. 3.2.6)

> *I don't know whether my brain can cope with* *all this.* (CONV)
>
> *Both methods rely on* *the accurate determination of the temperature and pressure of the gas.* (ACAD)

**E** Complement of preposition (cf. 2.7.5)

> *He worked in* *a shop* *– probably at* *that time.* (CONV)
>
> *The economic growth figures have already been marginally trimmed in* *the last month* *and may be revised further in* *a review that will be carried out just before [the publication of [the World Economic Outlook]].* (NEWS†)

**F** Subject predicative (cf. 3.2.3)

> *Well, his son Charlie was* *a great mate of our Rob's.* (CONV)
>
> *He retired after three minor heart attacks at the age of 36, giving up his number seven world ranking, and became* *captain of the US Davis Cup team.* (NEWS)

**G** Object predicative (cf. 3.2.7)

> *No, I know but they'll probably christen her* *Victoria.* (CONV)
>
> *The world championship is the ultimate; any top player to lose at the Crucible can consider it* *a failure.* (NEWS)

**H** Adverbial (cf. 3.2.8)

> *K walked* *all day* *and slept* *the night* *in a eucalyptus grove with the wind roaring in the branches high overhead.* (FICT)
>
> *Mr Thesiger, who will be eighty* *next summer, arrived in London* *last week.* (NEWS)

**I** Premodifier of noun (cf. 8.2)

*He was also chairman of Labour's **home policy** committee.* (NEWS)

*The **economic growth** figures have already been marginally trimmed in the last month.* (NEWS†)

**J** Apposition (cf. 8.10)

*He and the club's solicitor and director, **Maurice Watkins**, sat either side of Edwards while on the flanks were placed two more lawyers, one representing Knighton's take-over firm, **MK Trafford Holdings**, and the other, United's merchant bank, **Ansbacher**.* (NEWS)

**K** Premodifier in adjective or adverb phrase (cf. 2.7.3–4)

*He spent the next few days among the sequoias on Mount Tamalpais, running a dozen miles every morning among trees **two hundred and fifty feet** tall and **twenty-two centuries** old.* (FICT)

*The story broke all right, but **two weeks** earlier than planned.* (NEWS†)

In addition, noun phrases can be used as peripheral elements in the clause: detached predicative (3.4.1), parenthetical (3.4.2), preface (3.4.3), tag (3.4.4), and vocative (3.4.6). Finally, they may occur independently of any clause structure (3.15).

## 2.7.1.2 Discontinuous noun phrases

Complex noun phrases may be split up under certain circumstances, as in the following examples:

*A **rumour** spread through the camp **that a relieving force from Dinapur had been cut to pieces on the way to Krishnapur**.* (FICT)

*The **time** was coming **for me to leave Frisco** or I would go crazy.* (FICT)

*In this chapter **a description** will be given **of the food assistance programs that address the needs of the family**.* (ACAD†)

This arrangement is in agreement with general principles for the ordering of elements within the clause (11.1.1 and 11.1.3).

## 2.7.2 Verb phrases

Verb phrases contain a lexical verb (2.3.2) or primary verb (2.4.3) as head or **main verb**, either alone or accompanied by one or more auxiliaries (2.4.3–4). The auxiliaries specify the way in which the action, state, or process denoted by the main verb is to be interpreted. In addition, the first auxiliary has the special role of **operator** (3.2.9). The main verb is in bold in the following examples:

*was **walking**     had been **making***
*can **see**     should have **said***

These verb phrases are all **finite** (literally 'limited'), i.e. specified for tense or modality. In addition, finite verb phrases may be marked for aspect and voice. See the detailed description in Chapter 6.

Note that the term 'verb phrase' or 'VP' is sometimes used in other grammars to refer to the main verb plus accompanying elements, including objects and predicatives. This use corresponds to **predicate** (3.2) in our treatment.

**Non-finite** verb phrases do not contain any specification of tense and modality, and therefore have fewer possibilities of variation:

> *having **gone***    *to be **caught***
> *to have **gone***    *being **caught***

Thus compare the following non-finite verb phrase with the fuller expression that would be required by a finite verb phrase:

> *In view of your comments, I think we can safely tell the hotel what [to **do**] with their bed.* (NEWS)
> *cf. ... tell the hotel what they [should **do**] with their bed.*

Regarding non-finite constructions, see also 3.12.

Both finite and non-finite verb phrases may be marked for the perfective aspect (*has gone, to have gone*, etc.). Both also have passive forms (*was being thanked, to be killed*, etc.). The passive auxiliary does not specify the verb in the same sense as markers of tense, aspect, and modality. The passive is rather connected with the way the participants in a situation are presented (3.6.2).

### 2.7.2.1    The syntactic role of verb phrases

The only syntactic role of finite verb phrases is to serve as a central clause element (3.2.2). Non-finite verb phrases have the same role in non-finite clauses (marked by brackets in the following examples):

> *I hate [**travelling** by myself].* (FICT)

> *Already they have stopped [**voting** on racial lines].* (NEWS)

With non-finite verb forms, it is important to distinguish between their role as verb phrase in the non-finite clause and the role which the non-finite clause as a whole has in the larger structure. It may be difficult to uphold a clear distinction where the non-finite clause consists only of the non-finite form:

> *Stop **talking**.* (FICT)

Here, strictly, *talking* may be analysed as the central element in a minimal clause that is the object of *stop*.

Many verb forms may have roles characteristic of nouns and adjectives. Such uses are limited to participle forms (ending in *-ed* or *-ing*), originally so called because they participate in more than one word class. In these cases, verb forms tend to acquire the characteristics of nouns and adjectives. Compare: *building* and *house* (nouns), *exciting* and *dramatic* (adjectives), *tired* and *weary* (adjectives); see 2.3.6.

### 2.7.2.2    Discontinuous verb phrases

Unlike the other phrase types, verb phrases are often **discontinuous**. This frequently occurs in clauses with **subject-operator inversion** (3.6.1.1 and 11.2.3.2) and *not*-negation (3.8.2). In addition, adverbials are frequently placed between the elements of the verb phrase:

> *You know the English **will** always **have** gardens wherever they find themselves.* (FICT)

> *The current year **has** definitely **started** well.* (NEWS)

As regards the placement of adverbials with complex verb phrases, see 10.1.3.

Quite a different type of split-verb phrase is found where verbs are fronted for the purposes of contrast or cohesion (11.2.3–4).

### 2.7.2.3 Auxiliary-only verb phrases

Under certain circumstances, the verb phrase consists only of an auxiliary:

> *She realized that she would never leave. She* **couldn't**. (FICT)
>
> *Oh they're going round the bay* **are** *they?* (CONV)
>
> *It looks terrible it* **does**, *I would have it one way or the other.* (CONV)

See the sections on ellipsis (3.7), question tags (3.13.2.4), imperative tags (3.13.4.1), and declarative tags (3.4.4C).

## 2.7.3 Adjective phrases

Adjective phrases contain an adjective (2.3.3) as **head**, optionally accompanied by **modifiers** in the form of single words, phrases, and clauses. The adjective head is in bold in the following examples:

> *so* **lucky**                              *good* **enough**
>
> *desperately* **poor**                      **guilty** *of a serious crime*
>
> **slow** *to respond*                       **subject** *to approval by . . .*
>
> *so* **obnoxious** *that she had to be*      *more* **blatant** *than anything they had*
> *expelled*                                   *done in the past*

The accompanying elements in an adjective phrase characteristically indicate the degree of the quality denoted by the adjective (e.g. 'How lucky/poor?') or describe the respect in which the quality is to be interpreted (e.g. 'Guilty/slow in what respect?'). In the latter case, the accompanying elements serve to complete the meaning of the adjective and are generally called **complements**. Complements generally take the form of prepositional phrases or clauses.

The structure and uses of adjective phrases are described in detail in Chapter 7. As regards the complementation of adjectives, see also 9.2.5, 9.4.5, and 9.5.3.

### 2.7.3.1 The syntactic roles of adjective phrases

Adjective phrases may have the following syntactic roles. A and B are the most typical roles.

**A** Premodifier of noun (cf. 2.7.1 and 7.4)

> *That* **tough brave little old** *fellow Wells had had prophetic visions after all.* (FICT)
>
> *He writes* **catchy** *tunes with* **lavish** *pop hooks and* **huge** *slices of melody.* (NEWS)

**B** Subject predicative (cf. 3.2.3 and 7.5)

> *He's* **totally crazy**. (CONV)
>
> *Everything became* **bitingly clear** *to me.* (FICT†)

**C** Postmodifier of noun (cf. 2.7.1 and 7.6)

> *Diana was ready to tell the other three people* **present**. (NEWS†)

**D** Object predicative (cf. 3.2.7 and 7.5)

> *He considered it* **more dangerous than any horse he had ever ridden**. (NEWS†)

> *The individual can then select the most suitable for any task, which we hope will make her **more adaptable and able to deal with unfamiliar situations**.* (ACAD†)

Adjective phrases can also be used as detached predicatives (3.4.1 and 7.6.5), as clause links (7.6.3), and independently of any clause structure (3.15 and 7.6.4). Adjectives may further take on nominal roles (7.6.2).

### 2.7.3.2 Discontinuous adjective phrases

Adjective phrases modifying nouns can be split into a combined pre- and postmodifier:

> *You couldn't have a **better** name **than that**.* (FICT)

> *When he plays his best, he's a **really tough** player **to beat**.* (NEWS†)

This arrangement is in agreement with general principles for the ordering of elements within the clause (11.1.1 and 11.1.3).

## 2.7.4 Adverb phrases

Adverb phrases contain an adverb (2.3.4) as **head**, optionally accompanied by **modifiers** in the form of single words, phrases, and clauses. The head is in bold in the following examples:

| | |
|---|---|
| *hardly **ever*** | ***fortunately** enough* |
| *quite **melodiously*** | *very **quickly*** |
| *so **quickly** you don't even enjoy it* | *much more **quickly** than envisaged* |

Adverb phrases are similar in structure to adjective phrases. Modifiers of adverbs are chiefly expressions of degree.

Adverb phrases should be distinguished from **adverbials**, which are clause elements that can be realized in a variety of ways (e.g. by adverb phrases, prepositional phrases, clauses; see 3.2.8 and Chapter 10, especially 10.1.2).

### 2.7.4.1 The syntactic roles of adverb phrases

Adverb phrases may have the following syntactic roles (A and B are the most typical):

**A** Modifier in adjective or adverb phrase (cf. 2.7.3–4 and 7.13.1–2)

> *I thought it was **utterly** disgraceful.* (CONV)

> *For all that he was an attractive little creature with a **sweetly** expressive face.* (FICT)

> *Whoever took it acted **totally** inhumanely.* (NEWS†)

**B** Adverbials on the clause level (cf. 3.2.8 and 7.13.5)

> *She smiled **sweetly**.* (FICT†)

> *They sang **boomingly well**.* (FICT)

The borderline between between modifiers and adverbials is not always clear:

> **1a** *This is a really surprising development.*
> **1b** *Really this is a surprising development.*
> **1c** *This development is really surprising.*

While *really* in **1a** is unambiguously a modifier of the following adjective and in **1b** an adverbial, **1c** is structurally ambiguous. However, the ambiguity is more structural than semantic, because the overriding meaning in all the examples is an expression of the speaker's attitude to the message.

**C** Pre- and postmodifier in noun phrase (cf. 2.7.1 and 7.13.3)

> The investigation found no evidence that the **then** Democratic candidate had been involved in illegal activities. (NEWS†)

> The long journey **home** was a nightmare. (FICT†)

**D** Complement of preposition (cf. 2.7.5 and 7.13.4)

> She had only just got back from **abroad**. (FICT†)

> There had been no complaints until **recently**. (NEWS†)

**E** Premodifier in prepositional phrase (cf. 2.7.5.1 and 7.13.3)

> I stopped **just** outside the circle of light. (FICT†)

> Every night he drove to work in his '35 Ford, punched the clock **exactly** on time, and sat down at the rolltop desk. (FICT)

See also the detailed description of adverb phrases in 7.11–15 and the detailed account of adverbials in Chapter 10.

## 2.7.5 Prepositional phrases

Prepositional phrases consist of a preposition (2.4.5) and a **complement**, most typically in the form of a noun phrase. The typical prepositional phrase may indeed be viewed as a noun phrase extended by a link showing its relationship to surrounding structures. The complement is in bold in the following examples:

> to **town**      in **the morning**
> to **him**       on **the night** [of the first day]
> to **Sue**       in **a street** [with no name]

Note that prepositional phrases are often embedded within larger phrases, as in the last two examples; see also 2.8.

Prepositions also take nominal clauses as complements, but normally only *wh*-clauses **1** and *ing*-clauses **2**:

> **1** Component drawings carry instructions [on **where they are used and from what they are made**]. (ACAD)

> **2** By that time the strain of the cruise was telling on them; they talked little among themselves till they surfaced three days [after **leaving Darwin**]. (FICT)

The prepositions *but* **3**, *except* **4**, and *save* **5** may, however, be followed by infinitive clauses:

> **3** Governments, whatever their own inclinations, will have no choice [but **to fashion childcare policies**]. (NEWS)

> **4** I have nothing new to say, [except **to say that when I do have something to say I will say it**]. (NEWS)

> **5** What was there to say? What I did say served no purpose [save **to spoil his temper**]. (FICT)

Additionally, the complement may be an adverb **6**, **7**, or another prepositional phrase **8**:

> **6** *So you're sitting [in **here**] at the moment are you Stanley?* (CONV)
> **7** *Allow yourself time for home thoughts [from **abroad**].* (NEWS)
> **8** *[From **behind the wire fencing**], a uniformed guard eyes us with binoculars.* (NEWS)

Prepositional phrases as complements of prepositions are chiefly found in expressions of direction.

## 2.7.5.1 Extended prepositional phrases

Prepositional phrases can be preceded by adverbial particles (2.4.6) and other modifying elements. The modifier may be a specification of the relationship expressed by the preposition or an expression of degree:

> **back** *to the fifties*      *exactly at noon*
> **down** *in the south*      *considerably to the right*
> **nearly** *till eleven*

Notice that modification of this type may lead to the development of complex prepositions (2.4.5.2).

## 2.7.5.2 The syntactic roles of prepositional phrases

Prepositional phrases vary with respect to how closely they are connected with surrounding structures (cf. the comments on free v. bound prepositions in 2.4.5.1).

**A** Adverbial on the clause level (cf. 3.2.8 and Chapter 10)

> *He worked **in a shop** – probably **at that time**.* (CONV †)
> *He retired [**after three minor heart attacks**] [**at the age of 36**].* (NEWS †)

**B** Postmodifier and complement of noun (2.7.1 and Chapter 8)

> *What about that erm, what about that other place that er timber place [**on the way [to Kilkern]**]?* (CONV †)
> *He was a poet, a teacher **of philosophy**, and a man **with a terrible recent history**.* (NEWS)
> *Or at least that is the ambition [**of the industrial development commission [of a small Pennsylvania steel town]**].* (NEWS)

It may be difficult to decide whether a prepositional phrase following a noun is a postmodifier of the noun or an adverbial in the clause:

> *Ten tourists were injured yesterday when they jumped off a chair lift to escape a brush fire **on Mount Solaro in the Mediterranean island of Capri**.* (NEWS)

In this case, the prepositional phrase *on Mount Solaro* ... could be analysed as either an adverbial (specifying the location of the accident) or a postmodifier of the head *fire*. The following two examples illustrate how the same prepositional phrase can have different roles:

> *The seal had been fired at by a man **with a rifle**.* (FICT †)
> *AM, 37, is alleged to have shot Robert **with a rifle**.* (NEWS †)

The *with*-phrase in the first example is a postmodifier of a noun, in the second an adverbial.

**C** Premodifier of nouns (2.7.1)

> *It probably fell out of the sky after an **in-flight** explosion.* (ACAD†)
>
> *He was nabbed by a new British Rail patrol waging war on fare-dodgers and he had to fork out an **on-the-spot** £10 fine.* (NEWS)

**D** Complement of adjectives (2.7.3)

> *I'm not afraid **of anything**.* (CONV)
>
> *The plant is equally susceptible **to drought** during this period.* (ACAD)

Prepositional phrases are further used in connection with prepositional verbs and other types of complex verbs (5.3).

## 2.7.5.3 Stranded prepositions

A preposition is said to be **stranded** if it is not followed by its complement or, where the preposition is bound to a preceding verb, by the prepositional object:

> 1 *As soon as Unoka understood [what] his friend was driving **at**, he burst out laughing.* (FICT)
>
> 2 *[What more] could a child ask **for**?* (NEWS)
>
> 3 *"Without the money to pay for your promises, your manifesto is not worth [the paper] it is written **on**," said Mr Lamont.* (NEWS)
>
> 4 *If [you] get sat **on** it is because you allow [yourself] to be sat **on**.* (NEWS)
>
> 5 *I didn't know that one had gone, usually it's the bulb over there that had gone, but I find [it] so difficult to get **at**, you change it.* (CONV)
>
> 6 *[The whites] didn't bear speaking **on**.* (FICT)

In such cases, the prepositional complement/object is identified with a previous noun phrase, enclosed in *[]* in the examples above. Stranded prepositions are chiefly found in interrogative clauses (**1**, **2**), relative clauses **3**, passive constructions **4**, infinitival complement clauses **5**, and *ing*-clauses **6**. In the last three types, the preposition cannot be placed before its complement, but this is often possible with interrogative pronouns and relative pronouns as prepositional complement. However, stranded prepositions are the preferred choice in interrogative clauses (2.7.5.4) and they are also common in relative clauses (8.7.1.4, 8.7.4).

## 2.7.5.4 Stranded prepositions in independent *wh*-questions

Prescriptive grammarians have often claimed that stranded prepositions are unacceptable and should be avoided. Nevertheless, in many uses there is no alternative (as explained in 2.7.5.3). Moreover, where there is an alternative, speakers and writers often prefer the structure with a stranded preposition. We will examine one such case. The following structures will be distinguished (cf. 3.13.2.1):

Preposition + *wh*-word, full VS clause:

> ***In** [which sport, apart from rowing,] could you do that?* (NEWS)

Preposition + *wh*-word, full SV clause:

> *You can't drink it **with** [what]?* (CONV)

Preposition + *wh*-word, fragment:

> *Was she really going to clear everything out of here?* **For** *[what]?* **For** *[whom]?*
> (FICT)

Stranded preposition, full clause:

> *[What age group] are you applying to work* **with**? (CONV)

Stranded preposition, fragment:

> *A: I wish daddy was back.*
> *B: [What]* **for**? (CONV)

---

### CORPUS FINDINGS [9]

➤ Prepositions vary in their potential for stranding:
  ➤ Forms commonly used as stranded prepositions: *about, after, at, by, for, from, in, like, of, on, to, with.*
  ➤ Forms attested as stranded prepositions (1 to 5 instances in the material examined): *against, around, into, near, off, through, under, up.*

➤ The potential for stranding broadly correlates with the distinction between free and bound prepositions (2.4.5.1). Forms which are typically used as stranded prepositions are those which are closely linked to a preceding word, i.e. they are bound prepositions (e.g. part of a prepositional verb).

➤ Full *wh*-questions with a preceding preposition chiefly occur in academic prose and news. They are rare in fiction and virtually non-existent in conversation.

➤ Fragments consisting of preposition plus *wh*-word are found in all the registers, but are proportionally more common in the written registers than in conversation.

➤ Structures with a stranded preposition are the most common type, except in academic prose.

➤ Fragments with a stranded preposition are found in conversation and fiction. They were unattested in the material from news and academic prose.

➤ The two types of fragment are about equally common in conversation, but preposition plus *wh*-word is the predominant choice in the written registers.

**Table 2.9**  **Preference for question structures with *wh*-word and preposition, expressed as a percentage of occurrences within each register**

each ■ represents 5%  □ represents less than 2.5%

| | CONV | FICT | NEWS | ACAD |
|---|---|---|---|---|
| **preposition + *wh*-word** | | | | |
| VS-clause | □ | ■ | ■■■ | ■■■■■■■ ■■ |
| SV-clause | ■ | □ | ■ | □ |
| fragment | ■■■ | ■■■■■ | ■■■■■ | ■■■■■■ |
| **stranded preposition** | | | | |
| clause | ■■■■■■■ ■■■■■■■ | ■■■■■■■ ■■■■ | ■■■■■■■ ■■■■ | ■■■■ |
| fragment | ■■■ | ■■ | □ | □ |

**DISCUSSION OF FINDINGS**

The study confirms the general view among descriptive grammarians that preposition + *wh*-word is a choice associated with careful public writing. Except in academic prose, it is clearly a minority choice. Where this structure does occur, the prepositional phrase is generally an adverbial which is fairly independent in relation to the verb:

> *For what reason had she introduced them then? he asked.* (FICT)
>
> *In which county is Weymouth?* (NEWS)
>
> *At what age should I start discussing periods with my daughter?* (NEWS)

In many of these cases, there is no alternative to a stranded preposition:

> *By what strange chance had she missed the real person?* (FICT)
> *cf. *What strange chance had she missed the real person by?*
>
> *To what extent can the wastage be reduced?* (ACAD)
> *cf. *What extent can the wastage be reduced to?*
>
> *In what circumstances has natural justice been excluded?* (ACAD)
> *cf. *What circumstances has natural justice been excluded in?*

More rarely, we find examples with prepositional verbs:

> *And to what are you assenting?* (FICT†)
>
> *For what, or for whom, will most of us be voting?* (NEWS)
>
> *To what semantic fields do words belong?* (ACAD)

The bond between the verb and the preposition (*assent to, vote for, belong to*) here makes it less natural to have the preposition in front position.

Stranded prepositions are normal where there is a close relation between the preposition and the preceding word:

> *Who are you looking for?* (CONV)
>
> *Who do you hang around with?* (CONV)
>
> *What else can we depend on?* (FICT)
>
> *What are you so afraid of?* (FICT)
>
> *What were you referring to?* (NEWS)
>
> *So how many more Beatles songs can Jim and Mike possibly listen to?* (NEWS)

We also find, particularly in conversation, a stranded preposition where it is not tied to a preceding word and the combination of *wh*-word plus preposition functions as an adverbial:

> *What time are you making them at?* (CONV)
>
> *Who do you have morning coffee with?* (CONV)
>
> *Which half do you want the marmalade on?* (CONV)
>
> *Which order shall we go in?* (FICT)
>
> *Which ocean are the Maldives in?* (NEWS)

Though the two structures overlap and a stranded preposition can often be placed before the *wh*-word (with a change in stylistic effect), there are many cases where there is no alternative to the structure with a stranded preposition. Questions of this kind are common in conversation:

*When does it close at?* (CONV)

*cf. *At when does it close?*

*Where's dad at?* (CONV)

*cf. *At where is dad?*

*What does she sleep there for?* (CONV)

*cf. *For what does she sleep there?*

*Why are you two arguing for?* (CONV)

*cf. *For why are you two arguing?*

The type *what ... for* (in the sense of 'why') is particularly common.

From the above, we see that there is no simple relationship between full interrogative clauses with a stranded preposition and those where the preposition precedes its complement. Further complexities are found if we study question fragments. Fragments with preposition plus *wh*-word are quite common in conversation, although full clauses with preposition plus *wh*-word are extremely rare (the ratio is approximately 16 to 1 in the material examined for Table 2.9). In other words, these fragments cannot just be regarded as reduced forms of full interrogative clauses.

The two types of fragment are not necessarily equivalent:

**1** *A: Did you use it?*

  *B: Yes.*

  *A: For what?*

  *B: Well I tried to fix them on the door and they wouldn't stay.* (CONV)

**2** *A: Ask her then!*

  *B: Ask her for what?* (CONV)

**3** *A: Come here!*

  *B: What for?* (CONV)

**4** *A: You owe her one pound sixty now.*

  *B: What for?*

  *A: For er, those er – pads.* (CONV)

In the sequence *for what* the preposition has its ordinary meaning; **1** is a question about purpose. With this type, the question often repeats part of a preceding sentence, as in **2**. On the other hand, *what for* often asks for a reason **3**, though it may also be used in questions where *for* has its ordinary meaning **4**.

To conclude, the choice between questions with stranded prepositions and related structures is a complex matter, where grammar, lexicon, and register all play an important role.

## 2.7.6   Genitive phrases

**Genitive phrases** are structured like noun phrases, except for the addition of a **genitive suffix**:

  **the Queen's** *press secretary*

  **the President's** *dramatic decision*

  *in* **a month or two's** *time*

The suffix marks a relation between two noun phrases in much the same way as a preposition. Compare:

*the car's* performance

*the performance* **of the car**

Genitive phrases are regularly used in pre-nominal position (as in the examples above), but they can also be found in nominal positions. See the detailed description of the genitive in 4.6.

## 2.7.7    Numeral phrases

Combinations of numerals (2.4.13) generally conform to the structure of noun phrases, but they also have special characteristics which make it natural to treat them separately. For example, they may be spoken and written in quite different ways:

| | |
|---|---|
| 225 | two hundred and twenty-five |
| 2 + 2 | two plus two |
| $25 | twenty-five dollars |
| 22.08 | twenty-two point zero eight |
| 1966 | nineteen sixty-six (the year) |
| 10 a.m. | ten o'clock (in the morning) |
| 2.15 p.m. | two fifteen, a quarter past two (in the afternoon) |

The conventions vary with the type of numerical expression (2.7.7.2). Numeral phrases have similar syntactic roles to those of noun phrases and determiners.

### 2.7.7.1    Complex numbers

Complex cardinal numbers are built up by juxtaposition of simple numerals (2.4.13), except that *and* is regularly inserted between *hundred/thousand/million* and numbers below 100. The following are examples of complex numbers from conversation (digit forms are given within < >):

1 **A hundred and seventy-two** <172> *that's quite high isn't it?* (CONV†)

2 *That would be* **three thousand six hundred** <3600>. (CONV†)

3 *Cost* **two thousand, nine hundred and ninety-five** <2975> *pounds.* (CONV†)

Before *hundred*, *thousand*, and *million*, the determiner *a* is usually used instead of *one* (as in **1** above).

### 2.7.7.2    Types of numerical expressions

There are several special types of **numerical expression**. The following examples are all taken from conversation (with a numerical translation given in brackets).

**A    Clock time**

Hours are often specified, as in all the examples below, without using the 24-hour clock or indicating overtly a.m. or p.m. The context and shared knowledge of the speaker and hearer normally make it obvious what is meant. For parts of whole hours the number of minutes is specified, using *past*, *to*, or neither of these. However, the word *minutes* is often omitted. There are alternative expressions also used for the 15, 30, and 45 minute points (examples **1, 2, 3, 5**).

1  *It's **a quarter past – fifteen minutes past six** <6.15>.* (CONV†)
2  *So you put it in at what? **Quarter to one** <12.45>? **Ten to one** <12.50>?* (CONV)
3  *A: What time are we leaving, Brenda?*
   *B: **Half past nine** <9.30>* (CONV)
4  *Then I pick him up at **three thirty**. <3.30>* (CONV)
5  *My boys were in bed at **half nine** <9.30> at fourteen.* (BrE CONV)
6  *This finishes at **six fifty** <6.50>. So you're gonna have to remember the oven goes out at **six fifteen** <6.15>.* (CONV)

## B  Dates

The word *day* is not normally included with the ordinal number identifying it, and the specification of the date is generally as exact as is required in the context. Hence, no year is mentioned in **1**, and the century is unspecified in **4**.

1  *Any time between June and **July the ninth** <9 July> then.* (CONV)
2  *On **the fourth of July two thousand and nineteen** <4 July, 2019>* (CONV)
3  *In **nineteen seventy-nine** <1979> an unusual – phenomenon happened.* (CONV)
4  *A: You er deserted in October didn't you?*
   *B: **October thirty-two** <i.e. 1932>.* (CONV)

## C  Currency

Often the words for the currency units (*pounds, pence/p; dollars, cents*) are omitted as predictable. This is especially so when sums of money involving two sizes of unit are being specified: both are absent in **2**, **4**, and one in **1**. Contrast example **3**.

1  *You can have one player and it costs **forty-four pound ninety-nine** <£44.99>.* (BrE CONV†)
2  *A: It's **three ten** <£3.10> isn't it, didn't you say?*
   *B: **Three fifty** <£3.50>.* (BrE CONV)
3  *And they can be yours for just **one hundred and forty nine dollars**. <$149.00>* (AmE CONV)
4  *I told him I wanted **five fifty** <$5.50> an hour.* (AmE CONV)

The singular form *pound* in **1** is colloquial; *pounds* would normally be considered standard. Compare also the expression in example **3** in E below.

## D  Temperature

Again the words for units and scales of temperature may be absent, when the speaker feels this information is shared already with the hearer—wholly in example **1**, partly in **2**.

1  *The erm wind chill factor is **twenty-two** <22°> below.* (CONV†)
2  *It's **ten degrees – ten above zero** <10°>.* (CONV†)
3  *The Three Hundred Club is for people who have a, done a South Pole Streak from sauna, **two thousand, oh two hundred degrees fahrenheit** <2000 ... 200° F> to outdoors **minus one hundred degrees fahrenheit** <−100° F>.* (CONV†)
4  *So it's **twenty-five degrees celsius** <25° C> in January?* (CONV)

## E Decimals, percentages, fractions

Decimals after the point are spoken as a sequence of digits, not a whole number. For example, one will not typically hear *four point thirty*—cf. **4** and examples in F. Example **3** is special in that the reference is to a sum of money.

1 *Point five* <.5> *of a quart is a pint.* (CONV†)

2 *It's* **nought point five** <0.5>. (CONV)

3 *He's got this other stuff in there, some promotional special offer* **one point seventy-nine** <£1.79> *for a litre.* (CONV†)

4 **Four point three O** <4.30>, *okay.* (CONV)

5 *David Jones the chief economist of Nat West Bank expects output to rise by only* **point six percent** <.6%> *this year.* (CONV)

6 *Then it's going down another* <...> **three quarters of a percent** <¾ %>. (CONV†)

## F Mathematical expressions

These may include words for arithmetic operations such as *and/plus/add* for addition, *minus/take away/subtract* for subtraction, *times/multiplied by* for multiplication, *over/divided by* for division and *is/makes/equals* for equation.

*Twenty-two point two eight plus twenty point four eight minus forty-seven point six eight* $<22.28 + 20.48 - 47.68>$. (CONV†)

*Fifteen add fifteen is thirty add one is thirty-one* $<15 + 15 = 30; 30 + 1 = 31>$. (BrE CONV†)

*Mine's twelve plus tip, so I'm going to put in fourteen.* $<\$12 + \$2\ tip = \$14>$ (AmE CONV)

*Two point nine eight times four to the power of two* $<(2.98 \times 4^2)\ or\ (2.98 \times 4)^2>$. (CONV†)

*V equals point two five eight cubed* $<V = .258^3>$. (CONV)

## 2.7.7.3 Approximate numbers

Where it is not possible to specify an exact number, an alternative is to use a round number, such as 10, 30, 500 (note the higher frequency of round numbers, 2.4.13.3). Other options are provided by quantifying nouns (4.3.6) and determiners (4.4.4). In addition, there are various ways of qualifying exact numbers.

## A The derivational suffix *-ish*

1 *A: Phone later on ah, Ron, later, later on.*
   *B: About* **elevenish**. (CONV)

2 *And say he's round about the* **fortyish** – *age.* (CONV†)

3 *A plump,* **fiftyish** *woman, she was already efficiently turned out in her white uniform.* (FICT)

4 *I suppose they'll come about three and we must send for them* **sixish** *as usual?* (FICT)

The suffix *-ish* in such examples means 'approximately'.

**B   Combinations with *odd***

The expression number + *odd* refers to a relatively small amount over that specified; e.g. *300 odd* means 'slightly over 300':

> *A **hundred and fifty odd** meals a day.* (CONV)
>
> *Is it only a **thirty odd** hour week?* (CONV)
>
> *You could have gotten **a hundred and some odd** dollars for it.* (FICT†)
>
> *I drove the **twenty-odd** miles back to town and ate lunch.* (FICT)
>
> *We've got **60-odd** officers going out tonight.* (NEWS)

**C   Approximating adverbs**

Approximating adverbs include *about, around, some,* and *approximately, roughly,* and *circa.*

> *Every time I got to them they had **about twenty odd** teachers there.* (CONV†)
>
> *I spent **about two** hours in the bar.* (FICT†)
>
> *The radial shields are **about 1.5–2** times as long as broad.* (ACAD†)
>
> ***Approximately 60%** of the community are of Polish and Russian ancestry, and **approximately 40%** are blacks who were born and raised in this midwestern community.* (ACAD)

**D   Coordination tags**

The tag *(and) something* means 'a little more than the number stated', while *or something/or so* mean 'a little more or a little less'.

> *We've paid **four thousand seven hundred and something**.* (CONV†)
>
> *Oh I think they were **hundred and something** each maybe more.* (CONV)
>
> *I think they paid him out – **thirty thousand or something like that**.* (CONV)
>
> A: *How many were in?*
> B: ***Four hundred or so**.* (CONV)
>
> *In his opinion, only **2,000 or so**, or about 30 percent, of the 6,800 "modern standard characters" needed to write contemporary Chinese are free words.* (ACAD†)
>
> *That must have been in **1964 or so** whatever the last year was for the New York World's Fair.* (FICT)
>
> *Some, including Portland, Oregon, charge **$1 or so** to recycle a tree.* (NEWS)

## 2.7.7.4   Approximating numeral expressions

**CORPUS FINDINGS 2**

➤ Overall, with the exception of some forms (*circa, approximately, around, roughly, some, or so*), approximating expressions are found much more often in conversation than in the other registers. The frequency of approximating expressions is not proportional to the number of numerals (4.4.5.1). If it were, we would have expected fewer approximating expressions in conversation than in academic prose and news reportage.

➤ Occurrences with *-ish* are infrequent and almost exclusively restricted to conversation and fiction.

➤ Those containing *odd* are moderately common in conversation (over 40 per million words), but they also occur occasionally in the written registers (especially in direct speech).

➤ *About* is the most common approximating adverb, in all registers; *approximately* is used primarily in academic prose.

➤ While the tag *and something* is relatively rare and virtually restricted to conversation, expressions with *or so* are more common and are found in all registers (cf. 2.9.2.1).

**DISCUSSION OF FINDINGS**

Approximating expressions fit in with the communicative purposes of conversation, where complete explicitness may not be necessary, and some degree of vagueness may actually be desirable. See also Chapter 14. We even see such expressions cluster together:

    *Fish is normally **about one twenty odd**.* (CONV †)

    *Your total was – **about four thir– about four fifty roughly**.* (CONV)

    *A: How much did that cost you to do that?*

    *B: **About six pound or something**.* (CONV)

See also 2.7.7.3A examples **1** and **2**.

## 2.8    Embedding of phrases

Noun phrases and prepositional phrases frequently have a very complex structure and can contain several layers of embedding:

1 *[the direct result [of [the continuing loss [of [yet another typical feature [of [the English countryside]]]]]]]* (NEWS)

2 *[at [the expense [of [a brief excursion [into [the mathematical realm [of [complex numbers]]]]]]]]* (ACAD)

The structure of these phrases can be seen in Figures 2.10 and 2.11.

    As phrases can also contain clauses (e.g. relative clauses modifying noun phrases and degree clauses modifying adjective phrases), and as clauses are in their turn built up of phrases, the complexity can be very great indeed (cf. 3.11.3–4 and Chapter 9). In addition, phrases can be expanded by **coordination** (2.9).

## 2.9    Coordination of phrases

Phrases can be linked by means of **coordinating conjunctions** (2.4.7).

- noun phrases: *my brother and his friends; friends or family or neighbours*
- verb phrases: *fight and argue; make or break*
- adjective phrases: *black and white; pale yellow or very pale greenish-yellow*
- adverb phrases: *deliberately and defiantly; now or never*

Parts of phrases can also be coordinated. Both heads and modifiers can be coordinated in noun phrases, verb phrases, adjective phrases, and adverb phrases. The coordinated elements are in bold in the examples below.

- noun phrases: **red and blue** *dresses; red **dresses and skirts***

Figure 2.10 **The structure of a complex noun phrase**
(NP = noun phrase, Prep. = preposition, PP = prepositional phrase)

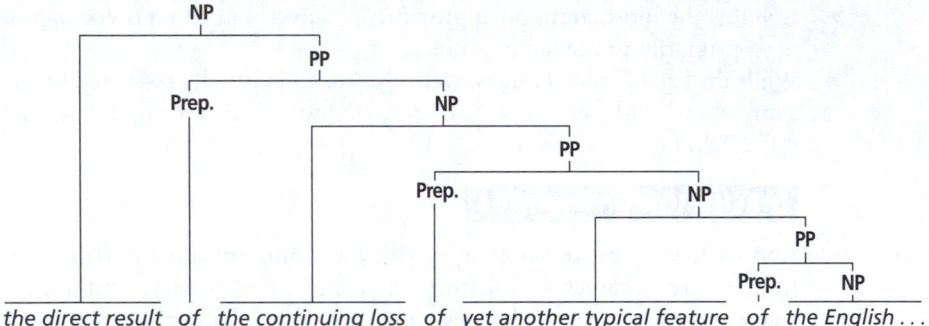

Figure 2.11 **The structure of a complex prepositional phrase**
(NP = noun phrase, Prep. = preposition, PP = prepositional phrase)

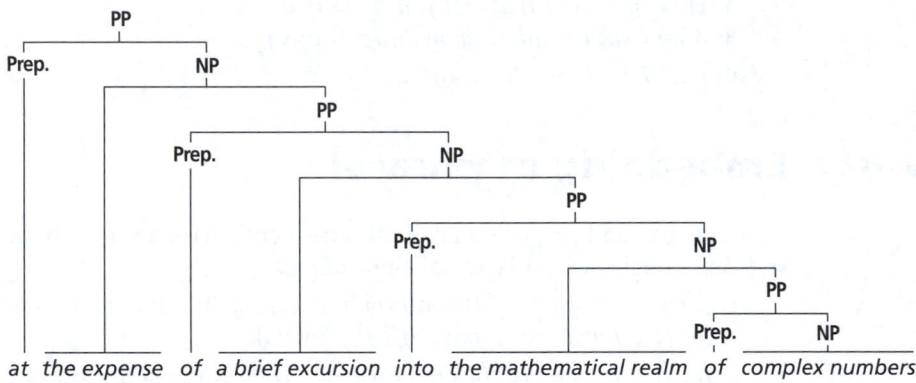

- verb phrases: ***can and will*** *win; can **read and write***
- adjective phrases: ***absolutely and unquestionably*** *wrong; absolutely **wrong and unacceptable***
- adverb phrases: ***obviously and glaringly*** *often; very **clearly and beautifully***

In prepositional phrases, the preposition and, more typically, the complement can be coordinated. The coordinated elements are in bold in the following examples:

> ***in and around*** *the city*
>
> ***with or without*** *your help*
>
> *in **North America and western Europe***
>
> *with **no parents and no support***

Coordinated phrases may be ambiguous. An adjective may modify only the closest noun or two coordinated nouns:

1 *The regulations also apply to **new** buildings and alterations and extensions of existing buildings.* (NEWS)

2 *There was much talk of **new** investment and jobs following in the wake of the announcement.* (NEWS†)

3 *We are always anxious to encourage **new** developments and **new** jobs in Cleveland.* (NEWS†)

In **1** *new* clearly modifies only the nearest noun, while in **2** *new* modifies both of the coordinated nouns. In **3**, all doubt is removed by the repetition of *new*.

## 2.9.1 Phrasal v. clausal coordination

Coordinators can connect both phrases and clauses (2.4.7). Phrasal and clausal coordination overlap, in that many instances of **phrasal coordination** can be analysed as **clausal coordination**:

1 *Mother and I saw it.* (FICT)

2 *The money will be used to buy video equipment and a new painting.* (NEWS†)

3 *He found a couple of oranges. One he gave to the woman and one to the child.* (FICT†)

4 *In one hand he held his Bible, and in the other a piece of wood which he had broken from his stool.* (FICT)

All these examples could be analysed as containing clausal coordination, with ellipsis of the common elements in one of the clauses:

**1b** *Mother <saw it> and I saw it.*

**2b** *The money will be used to buy video equipment and <it will be used to buy> a new painting.*

**3b** *One he gave to the woman and one <he gave> to the child.*

**4b** *In one hand he held his Bible, and in the other <he held> a piece of wood which he had broken from his stool.*

However, in **1** and **2**, the coordinated elements are an expansion of a simple noun phrase, and thus these are best considered as phrasal coordination. In contrast, the coordinated elements in **3** and **4** cannot be analysed as expansions of a simple phrase type, and thus it is more natural to choose an analysis in terms of clausal coordination.

## 2.9.2 Coordination tags

Coordinated elements are characteristically related both in form and meaning. This is presumably why it makes sense to choose a structure of coordination. The elements have a connection with each other, and they have the same relationship to surrounding structures. Yet this does not always apply.

In conversation, and sometimes in fictional dialogue, we find coordination tags which are best regarded as some kind of vagueness markers or hedges (see also 2.7.7.3D):

*Did you get that bit erm, when I was speaking to you about how everybody hates you **and stuff**?* (CONV)

*They're all sitting down **and stuff**.* (CONV)

*He has a lot of contacts **and things**.* (CONV†)

*She's made some good friends at school. She's had two or three of them home to stay **and things**.* (CONV†)

*There wasn't a rule saying don't smoke and then you get busted **and all that**.* (CONV†)

*Oh I have fun with men all the time, chasing them **and that**.* (CONV)

*Oh Emma, I know you've just been criticising Robin, calling him a fat bastard **and everything**.* (CONV)

*She uses a food processor **or something**.* (CONV)

*Are they going out for dinner **or something**?* (CONV)

The element following the conjunction in these structures is an unstressed noun or pronoun with a general meaning. It cannot be reordered and placed before the conjunction (which is often the case with other types of coordination), and it is added after clauses as well as after noun phrases. Semantically, these elements are clearly subordinate; they do not have independent reference, but rather serve to indicate that the expression preceding the conjunction is not to be taken as precise or exhaustive.

## 2.9.2.1 Distribution of coordination tags

**CORPUS FINDINGS** [2]

➤ Most coordination tags are particularly frequent in conversation (see Table 2.10).

Table 2.10 **Frequency of common coordination tags in conversation; occurrences per million words**

each ● represents 25

| | |
|---|---|
| or something | ●●●●●●●●●●●●●●●● |
| and everything | ●●●●●● |
| and things (like that) | ●●●● |
| and stuff (like that) | ●● |

➤ The coordination tags *or so*, *and so on*, and *etc.* are exceptional in that they are more common in the written registers (see Table 2.11).

Table 2.11 **Frequency of other coordination tags across registers; occurrences per million words**

each ■ represents 10   ☐ represents less than 5 words

| | CONV | FICT | NEWS | ACAD |
|---|---|---|---|---|
| or so | ■ | ■■■■■ | ■■ | ■■ |
| and so on | ☐ | ■■■■■ | ☐ | ■■■■■■■■■■ |
| etc. | ☐ | ☐ | ■ | ■■■■■■■■■■■■■■■■■■■■ |

**DISCUSSION OF FINDINGS**

As with numerical approximating expressions (2.7.7.3), coordination tags fit in with the communicative purposes of conversation, emphasizing the interpersonal involvement rather than complete explicitness (cf. 14.1.2.3).

The coordination tag *or so* is uncharacteristic in that it is more common in the written registers than in conversation:

*She's been away for the last week **or so**.* (CONV)

*I doubt if I had the necessary day **or so** to spare.* (FICT)

*I waited for a day **or so**.* (NEWS†)

*We lived with her for several years **or so**.* (FICT†)

These examples are not too dissimilar to those with numbers in 2.7.7.3D.

Another coordination tag which is common in writing, and particularly in academic prose, is *and so on* together with the related abbreviation *etc.* These are often needed to signal that a list is incomplete. The requirements for explicitness in this register mean that where writers wish to be brief, or perhaps are not sure of the full list, they will often cover themselves by the use of a partial list plus such a tag.

*It includes information about the file such as its size, history, **and so on**.* (ACAD)

*The Libertas catalogue menu offered a choice of six search modes (author and title, title, subject, **etc**.).* (ACAD)

## 2.10   Simple v. complex phrases

As illustrated in 2.6.3, simple v. complex phrases are distributed quite differently across registers.

**CORPUS FINDINGS** [7]

➤ There are far more one-word phrases in conversation than in the other registers.

➤ The proportion of complex phrases (with four or more words) is much higher in academic prose and news reportage than in the other registers.

**DISCUSSION OF FINDINGS**

The complexity of phrases in academic prose and news reportage reflects the higher lexical density in these registers (2.2.9), which is associated with a greater potential for the formation of complex phrases (usually built up around lexical words; 2.7). Complex phrases and a high lexical density are well-adapted to serve academic prose and news reportage, which typically deal with complex subject matter and have a high information load.

Information is much less-tightly packed in conversation, which simplifies both the planning of the speaker and the decoding of the hearer. Fiction takes up an intermediate position for the reasons mentioned earlier (2.2.9, 2.3.5).

The complexity of phrases has important consequences for the make-up of clauses in the four registers. Clauses in conversation tend to be shorter and less complex than in the other registers (3.1.1).

# 3

# Clause grammar

*See page xiii for contents in detail*

## 3.1    Clause v. non-clausal material

A clause is a unit structured around a verb phrase. The lexical verb in the verb phrase characteristically denotes an action (*drive, run, shout,* etc.) or a state (*know, seem, resemble,* etc.). For a full account see 5.2.

The verb phrase is accompanied by one or more elements which denote the participants involved in the action, state, etc. (agent, affected, recipient, etc.), the attendant circumstances (time, place, manner, etc.), the attitude of the speaker/ writer to the message, the relationship of the clause to the surrounding structures, etc. Together with the verb phrase, these are the **clause elements**. The clause elements are realized by phrases or by embedded clauses.

## 3.1.1    Use of clauses v. non-clausal material in text samples

To illustrate the distribution of clauses in discourse, we can reconsider the two sample texts used in 2.2.1.1. The verb phrases are given in bold below, and the elements of the same clause are enclosed within brackets. Note that there may be several layers of embedding (cf. 3.10).

Text sample 1: NEWS REPORT

> [Mr Ladislav Adamec, the Czechoslovak Prime Minister, **threatened** [to **quit**] last night, [as hard bargaining **continued** for a second day with the opposition over the shape of the new government.]]
>
> [Mr Adamec **had** talks with the opposition leader, Mr Vaclav Havel, on the cabinet lineup.] [He later **went** on national television [to **state** [that he **would stand down** [unless his new government **gained** public backing.]]]]
>
> . . .
>
> [The opposition Civic Forum, [which **rejected** the Communist-dominated cabinet [**unveiled** by Mr Adamec at the weekend,]] **is demanding** a more representative government [**staffed** mainly by experts.]]
>
> [Mr Adamec **said** [that he **was having** trouble [**recruiting** such experts into the cabinet.]]] [The Prime Minister's threat **appeared** [to **seek** a weakening of the opposition demands,]] [but **may** also **have been directed** at hardline elements in the Communist Party reluctant [to **yield** any further to the opposition.]]

Text sample 2: CONVERSATION IN A BARBER SHOP

> A: [I **will put**,] [I **won't smile**.] – [Tell me [what **would** you **like** now?]]
> B: Erm – [**shortened up** please Pete] – erm – [**shaved** a little bit at the back and sides] – [and then just sort of **brushed back** on the top a bit.]
> A: Right, and [when you **say** [**shaved** a little bit]]
> B: Yeah yo– – [you sort of just – **got** your thing] and zazoom!
> A: Yeah [but – **is** it that short really?]
> B: Yeah to–, yeah and I
> A: <unclear> [you **want** a number four?]
> B: Yeah [I **think** so.]
>
> . . .

A: *So yeah, [I **was** well pleased,] [cos you **remember** [the time before I **said** [I **wasn't** perfect.]]]*

B: <unclear>

A: *[That's right] yeah – yeah – [[I **mean**] I'm **being** honest.]*

B: *Yeah – mm.*

A: *[But I **was** well pleased with this one.]*

B. *Yeah.*

A: *[I **was**] – [I **thought** [it **looked** good]] – [and I **thought**,] [I **was** quite confident [that it **would stay** in very well,] [you **know**?]] –*

B: *Mm.*

There are some issues of analysis here: comment clauses have been attached to the clause they are related to (3.11.6), and coordinated clauses treated as independent. However, the differences between the two samples are striking. We notice, first of all, that the conversation text contains a good deal of **non-clausal material**, while all the words and phrases in the news text belong to clausal units. Second, there are more single-clause units in the conversation text, which is also characterized by shorter clauses and a lower degree of embedding. See Tables 3.1 and 3.2.

**Table 3.1** **Distribution of clausal units and non-clausal material in two text samples**

| form | CONV | NEWS |
|---|---|---|
| non-clausal word forms | 21 | 0 |
| single-clause units | 15 | 1 |
| two-clause units | 3 | 2 |
| three-clause units | 2 | 2 |
| four-clause units | 0 | 2 |

**Table 3.2** **Number of clauses in two text samples grouped by the level of embedding; the mean clause length, measured in word forms, is given in parentheses**

| embedding level | CONV | NEWS |
|---|---|---|
| top level | 20 (6) | 7 (20) |
| embedding level 1 | 6 (4.5) | 8 (9.5) |
| embedding level 2 | 1 (3) | 3 (8) |
| embedding level 3 | 0 | 1 (7) |

The differences shown in the tables can be summed up by saying that there is less structural integration in the conversation text, where clauses also tend to be shorter than in the newspaper text. In addition, there are great differences in the way clauses are constructed and combined. We shall examine some of these differences in the detailed account of clause structure.

## 3.2    Major clause elements

The core of the clause can be divided into two main parts: the **subject** and what is traditionally called the **predicate**. Structurally, these correspond broadly to a nominal part and a part with a verbal nucleus; semantically, to a **topic** and a **comment**. Together they express a **proposition**. The predicate can be broken down into a **verb phrase** proper and a number of **complements** (**objects**, **predicatives**, obligatory **adverbials**). Note that 'predicate' is used here in the traditional grammatical sense, while later (in Chapter 9) the term is used in a logical sense (predicate v. argument(s)).

The main **structural realizations** of clause elements are summarized in Table 3.3. We notice that noun phrases and finite clauses are the most varied in the clause elements they realize, while adverbial elements are the most heterogeneous in terms of how they are realized (they are very heterogeneous elements in other respects as well, as we shall see in 3.2.8 below). Adjective phrases, adverb phrases, and prepositional phrases are associated quite specifically with particular clause elements. Finally, there is one-to-one correspondence between phrase type and clause element with verb phrases, which is why the same term can be used for both.

**Table 3.3    Typical realizations of the major clause elements**

adj. = adjective   prep. = preposition   inf. = infinitive

| clause element | noun phrase | verb phrase | adj. phrase | adv. phrase | prep. phrase | finite clause | *ing-* clause | inf. clause | *ed-* clause |
|---|---|---|---|---|---|---|---|---|---|
| | | | | | | structural realization | | | |
| subject | ● | | | | | ● | ● | ● | |
| verb phrase | | ● | | | | | | | |
| subject predicative | ● | | ● | | ● | ● | ● | ● | |
| direct object | ● | | | | | ● | ● | ● | ● |
| indirect object | ● | | | | | ● | | | |
| prepositional object | ● | | | | | ● | ● | | |
| object predicative | ● | | ● | | | ● | | ● | |
| adverbial | ● | | | ● | ● | ● | ● | ● | ● |

The structure of the clause can be represented in the form of a tree diagram. See the examples in Figures 3.1 and 3.2.

The clause is well suited to some purposes for which we need to use language: to predicate something of a person, thing, or state of affairs. Where the discourse

**Figure 3.1    Clause with direct object**

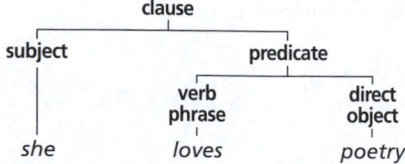

she    loves    poetry

Figure 3.2     **Clause with adverbial**

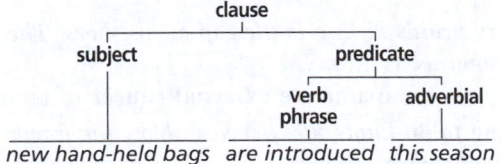

new hand-held bags   are introduced   this season

function is predominantly informative and the discourse has been carefully produced (as in the news text above), texts can normally be broken down exhaustively into clauses. Spontaneous interaction, however, tends to produce texts with a great deal of non-clausal material and with a less transparent clause structure (as in Text sample 2).

The elements which make up the core of the clause are introduced in the following subsections.

## 3.2.1     Subject (S)

All finite clauses (except imperative clauses; 3.13.4) regularly contain a **subject**. The subject is characterized by the following formal features. It:

- occurs with all types of verbs (3.5.1–9)
- is characteristically a noun phrase, but may also be a nominal clause (3.11.1, 3.12.1, 3.12.2, and 9.1.3)
- is in the nominative case of pronouns (in finite clauses; cf. 3.2.1.3)
- characteristically precedes the verb phrase, but is obligatorily placed after the operator (3.2.9) in independent interrogative clauses, except when the subject is a *wh*-word (3.13.2.1)
- determines the form of the verb phrase in the present tense and in the past tense of the verb *be* (3.9)
- may correspond to a *by*-phrase in passive paraphrases (3.6.2).

The following are examples of different forms of realization for subjects; *[]* indicate clause boundaries:

> Oh [**they**'re digging up the road], what a surprise. [**They** always dig up the road though]. (CONV)
>
> [**This** was such a tight fit [that **putting it back** was always a tense moment;]] [**bending his knees and moving them in and out** seemed to help.] (FICT)
>
> [**A poll at the weekend** showed [that **seven out of 10 Protestants** would want the Ulster Unionists to side with the Tories [if **no party** wins an overall majority.]]] (NEWS)

The referent of the subject is frequently given in the linguistic or situational context; hence, it is very often realized by a personal pronoun or a definite noun phrase (4.1.2).

## 3.2.1.1     Semantic roles of subjects

With transitive action verbs, the subject often denotes an **agent**, i.e. the wilful initiator of the action:

*Well why didn't **he** say that yesterday then? Or is **he** twisting what **she** says?* (CONV)

***A little girl with wiry braids*** *kicks a bottle cap at his shoes.* ***The pigeons*** *wheel and scuttle around us.* (FICT)

The subject may also express the inanimate **external causer** of an event:

***A biting wind gusting to 30 knots*** *threatened to blow the fragile, 15-ft fibreglass hydroplane off course.* (NEWS)

In other cases, the subject identifies the **instrument** or means used by an agent to perform an action:

***Tactics*** *can win you these games, but more often than not it is whether the players have the experience and the bottle.* (NEWS)

Although the subject is often associated with agency, it may express a number of non-agentive roles. With many stative verbs (denoting relationship and mental states of perception, cognition, and emotion), we find a **recipient** subject, used for an animate being who is the non-volitional receiver or experiencer involved in an action or state:

***I*** *heard it over the weekend.* (CONV)

***He*** *owns a house in Hartford, and two income properties in Newark.* (NEWS)

*"**I** don't know what is wrong but **I** don't feel right," he said.* (NEWS)

Some verbs may combine either with a recipient or an agent subject. In the following group of examples, the subject denotes the recipient **1**, the agent **2**, and the source **3** of the smell:

   **1** ***She*** *could smell the oil and petrol.* (FICT)

   **2** ***The soldier*** *took a pinch and smelled it cautiously.* (FICT)

   **3** *I don't want you near me.* ***You*** *smell.* (FICT)

Verbs denoting position in space combine with a **positioner** subject. The positioner role is particularly common with intransitive verbs:

*Unable to stand **Anna K** sat against a wall with her legs before her.* (FICT)

Many English intransitive verbs combine with an **affected** subject, i.e. a role typically found with direct objects (3.2.4.1):

   **4** *But N's mother dropped her pot of soup the other day and **it** broke on the floor.* (FICT)

   **5** *He has swum across although he knows that **more than a dozen escapers** have drowned there in recent weeks.* (NEWS)

Affected subjects are normal in passive constructions (3.6.2). Very often identical verbs, or related pairs of verbs, are used both intransitively with an affected subject and transitively with an agent subject and an affected object. Compare these examples with **4** and **5** above:

   **6** ***They*** *broke four legs off a bed making it unrepairable.* (NEWS)

   **7** *He carried it to the sink and then **he** drowned it.* (FICT)

Included among affected subjects are often the **identified** or **characterized** participants in clauses with copular verbs (3.5.3).

Other, less common, semantic roles are expressed by **local** (**8**, **9**), **temporal** (**10**, **11**, **12**), and **eventive 13** subjects:

   **8** ***The first floor*** *contains paper sculptures.* (NEWS)

   **9** ***My left arm*** *ached and **my legs** felt like wood.* (FICT)

10 *Thursday's about the worst day isn't it?* (CONV)

11 *A: I know you've got to come.*
*B: Tomorrow is great.* (CONV†)

12 *Coming to Belfast this month are The Breeders and Levellers, while* **next month** *sees Jethro Tull in town.* (NEWS) <the reference is to music performers>

13 *A post-mortem examination will take place today in Vancouver to confirm identification from dental records.* (NEWS)

Local and temporal roles are generally expressed by adverbials (3.2.8.1) rather than the subject. Eventive subjects typically contain nouns derived from verbs.

### 3.2.1.2 Dummy subjects

Frequently *it* is used as a **semantically empty** (or non-referential) subject, particularly in speaking about the weather **1**, about time **2**, or about distance **3**:

1 *It was not as cold as on the previous night.* (FICT)

2 *By the time you get back it's nine o'clock.* (CONV)

3 *It was seven miles to the nearest town and I had to bus or walk everywhere.* (FICT)

The predicates here do not suggest any participant involved semantically, but *it* is obligatorily inserted simply to complete the structure of the clause grammatically.

Special types of dummy subjects are found in existential clauses (3.6.3), with extraposition (3.6.4), and with clefting (3.6.5).

### 3.2.1.3 Subjects in non-finite clauses

In non-finite clauses, there is often no subject, and the relevant participant must be supplied from the surrounding text. Where the subject is expressed in non-finite clauses, it is a noun phrase (i.e. it cannot be a clause) and always precedes the verb phrase. It is in the accusative case of pronouns and the common case of nouns:

*Do you want [**us**] to put them back in?* (CONV)

*I asked [**Mother**] to put his crib in the garage.* (CONV)

With *ing*-clauses, however, the subject may also be a genitive form of a noun or possessive determiner. Compare accusative in **1** and common case in **3** with the genitive in **2** and **4**:

1 *Can you bear it, the thought of **him** going away?* (FICT)

2 *So it ended up by **his** going off with her.* (FICT†)

3 *The retail trade is making optimistic noises about **shoppers** coming back to the High Street.* (NEWS†)

4 *He spoke about **Sir Michael's** coming to the area.* (NEWS†)

There is no agreement in form between the subject and the verb phrase in non-finite clauses. See also 3.12.

## 3.2.2 Verb phrase (V)

With the **verb phrase**, there is a direct relationship between clause element and phrase type; see 2.7.2 and Table 3.3. The verb phrase is central in the clause both in the sense that it is regularly found in medial position and in the sense that the **valency** potential of the lexical verb determines the occurrence of the other major clause elements (excepting, in general, subjects and adverbials; 3.5 and 5.2.4).

The characteristic meanings of verbs were briefly mentioned at the beginning of 3.1. See also the detailed account of verb phrases in Chapters 5 and 6.

## 3.2.3    Subject predicative ($P_s$)

The **subject predicative** has the following formal features. It:

- is found with copular verbs only (3.5.3)
- is realized by a noun phrase or an adjective phrase, but may also be a finite or non-finite nominal clause or even a prepositional phrase (3.11.1, 3.12.1, 3.12.2, 5.5.2, 9.1.3)
- is in the nominative or accusative case of pronouns (4.10.6.1)
- typically follows immediately after the verb phrase.

Examples of different forms of realization are (*[]* indicate clause boundaries):

1   *[His skin was **very pink**] [and felt **warm to touch**] [and he complained of ["feeling **hot and sweaty**".]]* (ACAD)
2   *[The tall fellow with grey hair is **Dr. Fraker**.]* (FICT)
3   *[But he also recognises [that part of his role is [**to accept criticism.**]]]* (NEWS)
4   *[The first news of his condition was [**that he was bruised and in shock.**]]* (NEWS†)
5   *[I don't feel **in a mood for fireworks**.]* (FICT)

The subject predicative either **characterizes** the referent of the subject as in **1**, or **identifies** the subject referent as in **2**. In some grammars it is called 'subject complement'. The semantic role associated with subject predicatives may be called **attribute**; see also 3.5.3.

## 3.2.4    Direct object ($O_d$)

The **direct object** has the following formal characteristics. It:

- is found with transitive verbs only (3.5.4, 3.5.6–9)
- is characteristically a noun phrase, but may also be a nominal clause (3.11.1, 3.12.1, 3.12.2, and Chapter 9)
- is in the accusative case of pronouns
- typically follows immediately after the verb phrase, but there may be an intervening indirect object
- corresponds to the subject in passive paraphrases; with ditransitive verbs, the direct object may be retained or correspond to the passive subject (3.6.2).

Examples of different forms of realization are (*[]* indicate clause boundaries):

*[We want [to go and see **Cinderella**.]]* (CONV)
*[[Bending **his knees**] [and moving **them** in and out] seemed to help.]* (FICT†)
*[I really don't know [**what I'm gonna do**.]]* (CONV)

*[She said [that she probably had stomach ache [because she was happy.]]]*
(CONV)

*[After an hour the rain stopped,] [the birds began **singing**,] [a rainbow appeared in the west.]* (FICT)

As compared with the subject, the referent of the direct object is more characteristically new than given (4.1.2).

### 3.2.4.1 Semantic roles of direct objects

The direct object typically denotes an animate or inanimate participant **affected** by an action, or directly involved in an action (without being an agent or a recipient):

1 *This suggests that he is worried that those who can might rather walk the dog or paint **the house** than work for minimal benefit.* (NEWS)

In other cases, we find a **resultant** object, where the referent is a result of the action denoted by the verb:

2 *But then to be fair, I cannot recall any colleague who could paint **a self-portrait** with absolute honesty.* (FICT)

Some verbs may take either an affected or a resultant object, e.g. *paint* in 1 and 2 above.

Less typically, we find **locative** (3, 4) and **instrumental** (5) objects, expressing roles which are otherwise associated with adverbials (cf. 3.2.8.1):

3 *Desperately thirsting for black blood, without which it could not live, the dragon swam **the Ohio** at will.* (FICT)
   cf. *swam **across** the Ohio*

4 *The Finances of the most powerful country in the world will jump **the rails** this weekend.* (NEWS)
   cf. *jump **off** the rails* <likening an economy to a run-away train>

5 *He took a walk about the streets, kicking **his feet** in the sea of dry leaves on the pavement.* (FICT)
   cf. *kicking **with** his feet*

Note that the verbs combining with locative and instrumental objects can normally also take prepositional phrases as adverbials.

It is arguable whether locative and instrumental objects should really be analysed as direct objects. The same is true of the objects of **measure** in examples such as the following (the verb is marked in *[ ]*):

*This bomber and its cargo probably [weighs] **over a hundred tons**.* (FICT)

*The troupe currently performs in a converted dairy that [seats] **211**.* (NEWS†)

*A computer word [holds] **a fixed number of bits**, in a range from about 2 to 64.* (ACAD†)

Superficially these clauses look like structures with a direct object. However, they differ from clauses with ordinary direct objects in that they do not allow a passive paraphrase, and they answer questions of the type 'How much, how many?' in preference to 'What?'.

In some cases the direct object does not really express a participant role, but rather a verbal notion. This is true of **cognate** objects, which most typically repeat the meaning of the preceding verb (the verb is given in *[ ]*):

> *And she [laughed]* **her laugh, that shocking laugh which turned heads and caused her to blush and put a hand over her naked mouth.** (FICT)
> *cf. And she laughed in that shocking way which . . .*
> *And Ghani, who stood blindly beside the sheet for three long years, smiling and smiling and smiling, began once again to [smile]* **his secret smile, which was mirrored in the lips of the wrestlers.** (FICT)
> *cf. . . . to smile in his secret way, which . . .*

Verbs combining with cognate objects are normally intransitive and do not otherwise take a direct object. The object typically contains a noun derived from the same verb. The noun generally has some sort of modification, which carries the main new information, somewhat like an adverbial, as in the examples above.

Deverbal nouns are also characteristic of **eventive** objects. But unlike constructions with cognate objects, where the verb and the object reinforce each other, the eventive object combines with a semantically light verb (usually *do*, *give*, *have*, *make*, or *take*) and the verbal meaning is carried mainly by the object (see also 13.3.2):

> *Yeah, that's a point. I must have* **a look** *in Martin's fridge.* (CONV)
> *Go and have* **a sleep***!* (CONV)
> *Take* **a walk** *down some of these tracks down here.* (CONV)

### 3.2.4.2   Dummy objects

*It* may be used as a **semantically empty** or **dummy** object:

> *He squashed her with a look, exchanging eye signals with Bobby that it was time to beat* **it***.* (FICT)
> *In no time at all the herd was legging* **it** *back to the high land in a wild stampede.* (FICT†)
> *<. . .> or will he decide to tough* **it** *out and attempt to form a minority administration?* (NEWS†)

In these examples, *it* is incorporated into verbal idioms: *beat it* = 'get away', *leg it* = 'walk, run', *tough it out* = 'persevere'.

Dummy object *it* can also be used as an anticipatory element in the same way as the dummy subject *it* (3.6.4). Note also reflexive empty objects as in *avail oneself of*, *behave oneself* (4.12D).

## 3.2.5   Indirect object (O$_i$)

The **indirect object** has the following formal characteristics. It:

- is found with ditransitive verbs only (3.5.6)
- is characteristically a noun phrase, but may occasionally be a finite nominal clause (*wh*-clauses only; 3.11.1)
- is in the accusative case of pronouns
- is normally placed between the verb phrase and the direct object
- may be retained as object, or correspond to the subject, in passive paraphrases (3.6.2)
- often allows a paraphrase with a prepositional object (3.2.6 and 3.5.7).

Examples of different forms of realization are (*[ ]* indicate clause boundaries):

1 *[What gives **the hundreds of rocks and minerals** the properties [that make them so useful and beautiful?]]* (ACAD)

2 *[Tactics can win **you** these games,] [but more often than not it is [whether the players have the experience and the bottle.]]* (NEWS)

3 *[A Belgian cycling union official confirmed [that an unnamed rider had tested positive]] [and said [that [if it were Yates,] he would receive a 10-minute penalty [that would lose **him** the race.]]]* (NEWS)

The participant roles characteristic of the indirect object are **recipient** (corresponding to a paraphrase with *to*; see example **1** above) and **benefactive** (corresponding to a paraphrase with *for*; see example **2**). The action denoted by the verb is generally favourable from the point of view of the referent of the indirect object, but this is not necessarily so, as shown in example **3**.

**Affected** indirect objects occur with the semantically light verb *give* and an eventive direct object, corresponding to the direct object of a simple verb:

Give **it** a good shake though. (CONV)
cf. Shake it well though

You are supposed to give **it** a good bees waxing once a year. (CONV)
cf. – wax it well with bees wax –

I am sure there are a lot of farmers who want to give **it** a try. (NEWS)
<i.e. ... farmers who want to try it>

See also 3.2.4.1 for discussion of similar constructions with direct objects.

## 3.2.6 Prepositional object (O_p)

**Prepositional objects** have the following formal characteristics. They:

- occur with prepositional verbs (2.4.5.1, 3.5.5, 3.5.7, and 5.3.3)
- are realized by noun phrases or nominal clauses (*ing*-clauses and *wh*-clauses only; 3.11.1 and 3.12.2)
- are in the accusative case of pronouns
- are normally placed after the verb phrase
- have a complement of the preposition that may correspond to the subject in equivalent passive constructions (though there is considerable variability depending upon the individual verb); in this case, the preposition is stranded after the verb (3.6.2).

Examples of different forms of realization are ( *[ ]* indicate clause boundaries):

*[Perhaps, [he thought,] it was better [when one did not have to rely on **other people**.]]* (FICT) <prepositional V: *rely on*>

*[On the drive back to Moscow we talked about [**what was going to happen**.]]* (NEWS) <prepositional V: *talked about*>

*[The plan provides for [**integrating and coordinating their efforts and contributions with those of the national plan**.]]* (ACAD) <prepositional V: *provides for*>

The preposition faces in two directions, both to the verb and the object. This is why it makes sense to talk both about **prepositional verbs** and prepositional objects.

Prepositional objects and indirect objects are alike in that they require a mediating element (a preposition or a direct object). The correspondence is particularly close with indirect objects and corresponding prepositional constructions:

Indirect object

>   He *[gave]* **Carrie** *a ring.* (FICT)

Prepositional object

>   *Mr Evans [gave] it [to]* **me**. (FICT)

To stress the correspondence, it may be convenient to use the term **oblique object**.

Prepositional objects express many of the same semantic roles as direct and indirect objects; the main difference is that there is a relational marker, which sometimes makes the meaning relationship more explicit. Prepositional objects may be difficult to distinguish from prepositional phrases as adverbials (3.5.5) and in particular *to*-phrases corresponding to indirect objects may be alternatively analysed as **recipient adverbials** (10.2.1G).

## 3.2.7 Object predicative (P$_o$)

The **object predicative** (in some grammars called 'object complement') has the following formal characteristics. It:

- occurs with complex transitive verbs (3.5.8)
- is characteristically a noun phrase or an adjective phrase, but may occasionally be a finite nominal clause (*wh*-clauses only; 3.11.1)
- is normally placed immediately after the direct object
- is retained as a predicative in passive constructions (and is then to be analysed as a subject predicative).

Examples of different forms of realization (*[]* indicate clause boundaries):

>   *No, [I know,] [but they'll probably christen her* **Victoria**.*]* (CONV)
>   *[He did not find her* **amusing**] *[and she found him* **quite disastrously dull**.*]* (FICT)

The object predicative is preceded by *as*, or occasionally *for*, with some verbs (the verbs are marked by *[]*):

>   *They [regard] that [as]* **an excuse**. (CONV†)
>   *Police are [treating] the incident [as]* **murder**. (NEWS)
>   *You know sometimes I would almost [take] you [for]* **a bloody Welshman?** (FICT)

The relationship between the direct object and the object predicative is much the same as that between a subject and a subject predicative. The semantic role it expresses may be termed **attribute**. See also 3.5.8.

## 3.2.8 Adverbials (A)

**Adverbials** have the following formal characteristics:

- they can generally be added more or less independently of the type of verb (3.5)
- they are generally optional in the clause structure (but see 3.5.2 and 3.5.9)

- they are characteristically realized by adverb phrases, prepositional phrases, or clauses (3.11.2 and 3.12.1–3)
- they are more mobile than the other clause elements, often occupying a variety of positions in the clause (10.1.3, 10.2.6, 10.2.8.6, 10.3.4, 10.4.4)
- their positions are determined to a larger extent by textual and pragmatic factors than the positions of other clause elements, which are more determined by syntax (11.2.1)
- unlike the other clause elements, more than one adverbial may co-occur in the same clause (3.5).

Adverbials are more heterogeneous than the other clause elements. They are realized by a wide range of forms (cf. Table 3.3) and express a wide range of meanings. There are three main types: **circumstance adverbials**, **stance adverbials**, and **linking adverbials**. These differ both in meaning and with respect to the applicability of the criteria listed above. Stance adverbials and linking adverbials are alike in being more peripheral in the clause than circumstance adverbials. The three types will be briefly introduced below; for more detail, see Chapter 10.

### 3.2.8.1 Circumstance adverbials (A$_c$)

**Circumstance adverbials** typically describe the circumstances or conditions of an action or state. They answer questions like: 'Where? When? How? Why? To what extent?' These differ from the questions eliciting subjects, objects, and predicatives: 'Who? What? Which?'

> Examples of circumstance adverbials are (indicated by bold and *[]*):
>
> *It's going to be tough [**for a week or so**] but they've got to get used to staying [**on the floor,**] I'm not having them [**on the furniture**] [**all the time**] [**because they [just about] ruin it.**]* (CONV)
>
> *[**Tomorrow,**] [**on the last shopping day before Christmas,**] one of London's sporting institutions will close its doors [**forever**].* (NEWS)

See also the section on adverbial clauses (3.11.2).

> Prepositional phrases as circumstance adverbials may be difficult to distinguish from constructions with prepositional objects (3.5.5). Though adverbials can normally be left out without injuring the clause structure, there are obligatory circumstance adverbials in some cases (3.5.2 and 3.5.9).
>
> Circumstance adverbials may express a wide range of semantic roles: place (position, source, goal), time (position, frequency, duration), manner, instrument, etc. See the detailed account in 10.2.1.

### 3.2.8.2 Stance adverbials (A$_s$)

**Stance adverbials** typically express the attitude of the speaker/writer towards the form or content of the message:

> *And then **of course** the Air Force, they'd be one up again **I suppose**.* (CONV)
>
> ***Sadly**, it was impossible to keep up with the friends I had made in London.* (FICT)
>
> *It would be unfortunate, **to put it mildly**, if now or at some later stage he should collapse when so much depended upon him.* (FICT)

> *Fortunately, over the past few years there have been attempts by social services and local authorities to review the value of care for young people.* (NEWS)

Stance adverbials can be paraphrased by a range of expressions of stance; see Chapter 12. Most comment clauses (3.11.6) can also be included under stance adverbials.

Stance adverbials are more loosely attached to the clause than circumstance adverbials: they are more mobile and are more often prosodically or orthographically separated from the rest of the clause. Unlike circumstance adverbials, they are not part of the predicate. See Figures 3.3 and 3.4.

**Figure 3.3**  **Clause with circumstance adverbial**
**(*naturally* = 'in a natural manner')**

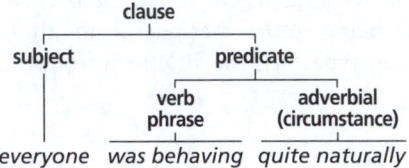

**Figure 3.4**  **Clause with stance adverbial**
**(*naturally* = 'of course')**

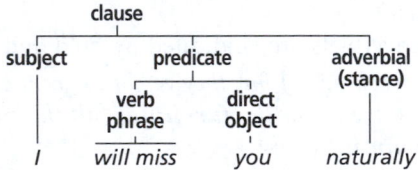

Note that the same form may be used as a circumstance adverbial or a stance adverbial, especially if it is a single-word *-ly* adverb. (See also the examples in Figures 3.3 and 3.4.)

Adverbs used as head of a circumstance adverbial:

1 *She spoke **frankly** about herself now and then.* (FICT)

2 *I doubt whether I could have indicated it more **clearly** than by the importance I placed on foreign affairs in the last year.* (NEWS)

Adverbs used as stance adverbial:

3 ***Frankly**, Kris didn't want to know.* (FICT)

4 ***Clearly** there is integration between the private and public sectors.* (ACAD)

Stance adverbials are characteristically placed in clause-initial position, while circumstance adverbials are just as typically placed after the verb. Note, however, that the stance adverbials in **3** and **4** can easily be moved to another position without affecting the meaning of the clause. The circumstance adverbials in **1** and **2** can hardly take up any other position. Compare:

1a *\***Frankly** she spoke about herself now and then.*
    *\*She **frankly** spoke about herself now and then.*

> **3a** Kris, **frankly**, didn't want to know.
> Kris didn't want to know, **frankly**.

Another difference is that circumstance adverbials, but not stance adverbials, can be elicited by a question form of the type 'How did S V?'

We can sum up the differences by saying that circumstance adverbials are more like central clause elements such as subjects and objects, while stance adverbials resemble the peripheral elements dealt with below (3.4).

### 3.2.8.3 Linking adverbials (A$_l$)

**Linking adverbials** express the type of connection between clauses. They are more peripheral in clause structure than circumstance adverbials and are not part of the predicate. Like stance adverbials, they are mobile and often prosodically and orthographically separated from the rest of the clause, and they cannot be elicited by question forms (cf. 3.2.8.2):

> You've got to go to Merseyside **though** for that. (CONV)
>
> The Conservatives, fighting in Ulster for the first time in 70 years, failed to win any seats. **Nevertheless**, they carved out a 5.7 per cent share of the overall vote. (NEWS)

The same form can sometimes be used as a circumstance adverbial:

> I bet I walked **further** than you did today. (CONV)
>
> The quantitative relationship between the volume and pressure of a gas was **first** stated by Robert Boyle in 1662. (ACAD)

and as a linking adverbial:

> **Further**, these atoms interact with each other and with their environment in unknown ways. (ACAD)
>
> How can (new) environmental requirements be met through the treatment of waste streams? <...> **First** there must be good insight into the materials as part of the company. (ACAD†)

Linking adverbials should be distinguished from coordinators (2.4.7.2, 3.3).

Linking adverbials can be particularly dense in academic prose, as in the following passage (10.4.1.8):

> A number of different considerations guided our examination of the different models. **Firstly**, in a manner similar to AAM, the models we investigated distinguish different model components. **Thus** it is of interest to determine whether a mapping exists between these components and the Amigo Components. The mapping is carried out, as far as possible, during the respective model descriptions. **On one hand**, this offers the possibility of a uniform and comparable representation of the models. **On the other**, it can be determined whether the individual models consider components which go beyond the AAM. (ACAD)

## 3.2.9 The operator

In addition to the clause elements dealt with above, it is convenient to recognize the special role of the **operator**. The operator is found in finite clauses only. It is required in special structures, particularly in independent interrogative clauses and clauses negated by *not*. The operator role is realized thus (operator in bold, verb phrase elements in *[]*):

**A** the first auxiliary in the verb phrase:

> *You['re joking]!* (CONV)
>
> *[Are] you [joking]?* (CONV)
>
> *You [are]n't [gonna get] them!* (CONV)
>
> *We [can give] these to Reg.* (CONV)
>
> *[Can] we [give] you a cheque?* (CONV)
>
> *We [can]'t [use] these.* (CONV †)

**B** insertion of the auxiliary *do*:

> *She [lives] in a hole in the ground.* (CONV)
>
> *Where [does] she [live]?* (CONV)
>
> *Well he [does]n't [live] down there now.* (CONV)

**C** the copular verb *be* and, less commonly, transitive *have*:

> *You['re] mad.* (CONV)
>
> *[Are] you serious?* (CONV)
>
> *You['re] not pretty.* (CONV)
>
> *I [have] a lot of feeling – right?* (CONV)
>
> *[Have] you any money?* (BrE CONV)
>
> *I [have]n't any money.* (BrE CONV)

For details on the formation of interrogative and negative clauses, see 3.8.2–3 and 3.13.2. As regards variation in the use of the auxiliary *do* with certain verbs, see 3.8.2.1–4 and 3.13.2.8.

The operator is also used to underline the truth of a positive statement (5.4.3.4–5). Where there is a form that can serve as operator, this is stressed. If not, the auxiliary *do* is inserted. Compare:

> *I [think] they're both nice.* (CONV)
>
> *I [do think] they have rather gone over the top.* (CONV)

The operator is also used in declarative tags (3.4.4), question tags (3.13.2.4), and declarative clauses with subject-operator inversion (11.2.3.2).

## 3.3 Clause links

Clauses can be linked to each other in a variety of ways, as will be shown in detail later in this book (see especially Chapters 8–10). The principal types of structural links are **coordinators** (2.4.7), **subordinators** (2.4.8), and **wh-words** (2.4.9).

- Coordinator

> ***And*** *I went down there* ***and*** *they had no idea what it was* ***and****, uh, the doctor was exhausted and tired and overworked* ***and*** *he just said, psshh, I've never seen anything like it.* (CONV)

- Subordinator

> *He was screaming* ***because*** *he had to go home.* (CONV)

- *Wh*-word

  *The two people **who** found it are expected to receive the value of the brooch.* (CONV)

- No link

  *I know. I saw it this morning. It's really smart isn't it?* (CONV)

Coordinators are similar to linking adverbials, but differ from these in that their position is fixed at the clause boundary (see 2.4.7.2). Coordinated clauses may be represented in a tree diagram as shown in Figure 3.5. Explicit clause links may be omitted in series of coordinate structures. Coordination is often combined with ellipsis (3.7.1).

Dependent finite clauses are generally introduced by a subordinator (see Figure 3.6). Subordinators such as *that*, whose principal role is to introduce a clause as complement (see Chapter 9), are termed **complementizers**. The complementizer *that* is frequently omitted (9.2.8). Conditional clauses may be marked by subject-operator inversion rather than by a subordinator (11.2.3.5D).

**Figure 3.5**    **Coordinated clauses**

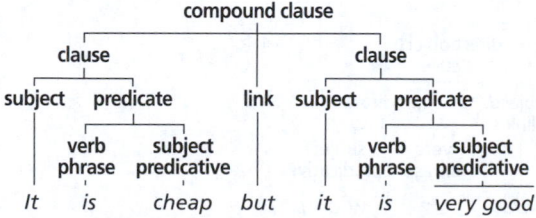

**Figure 3.6**    **Main clause with embedded adverbial clause**

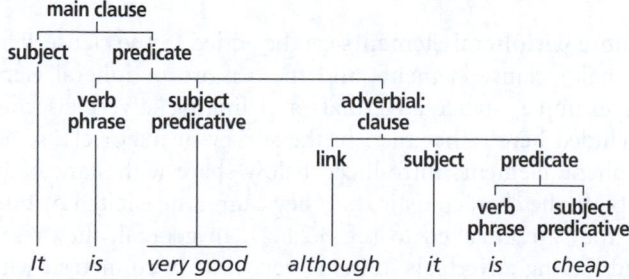

*Wh*-words differ from coordinators and subordinators in that, besides their linking function, they have a structural role within the embedded clause (as clause element or part of a clause element); see Figures 3.7 and 3.8. The clause link is frequently omitted in relative clauses (8.7.1.9).

Apart from the cases mentioned above, the lack of a clause link is normal with non-finite clauses (3.12) and the following types of finite dependent clauses: reporting clauses (3.11.5), comment clauses (3.11.6), declarative tags (3.4.4C), and question tags (3.4.4B; 3.13.2.4).

Figure 3.7    Main clause with embedded relative clause
(where it is relevant, the form of realization is given after a colon)

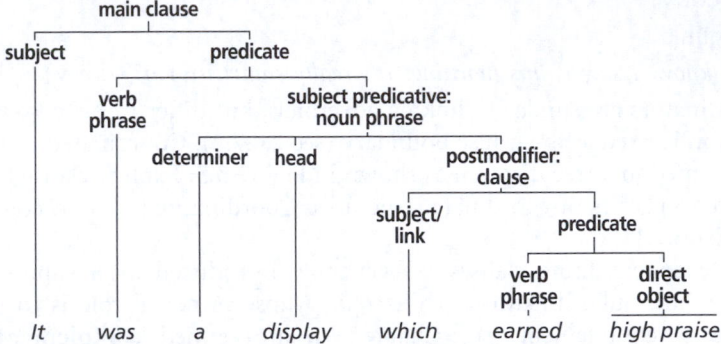

Figure 3.8    Main clause with embedded nominal *wh*-clause
(where it is relevant, the form of realization is given after a colon)

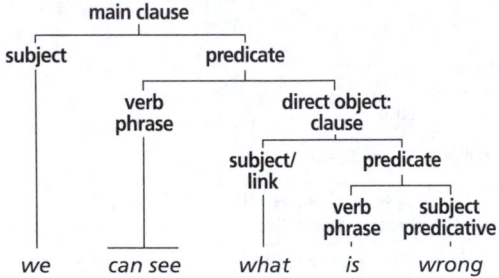

# 3.4    Peripheral elements

A variety of more **peripheral elements** can be added to the clause. The borderline between the major clause elements and these more peripheral elements is not absolute. For example, stance adverbials and linking adverbials could arguably have been included here rather than in the survey of major clause elements.

The peripheral elements introduced below share with stance adverbials and linking adverbials, the characteristic that they cannot be elicited by question forms of the clause they are attached to (cf. 3.2.8.2). In general, they resemble stance adverbials and linking adverbials in being very loosely connected with the clause and outside the predicate. Compare comment clauses (3.11.6).

## 3.4.1    Detached predicatives and related forms

**Detached predicatives** are similar to subject predicatives (3.2.3) both in form and meaning, but unlike the latter, they can be used independently of the type of verb. They are loosely attached to the core of the clause, usually at the beginning or the end, and characteristically take the form of a noun phrase or an adjective phrase which describes the subject referent:

1 ***A 5ft 9in guard out of Oral Roberts University in Tulsa,*** *Johnson played for the Lancaster Lightnings in the Continental Basketball Association before moving to this country to join Newcastle.* (NEWS)

2 ***Unable to stand,*** *Anna K sat against the wall with her legs before her like a beggarwoman.* (FICT†)

3 ***A republican,*** *he recognized the authority of Victor Emmanuel.* (FICT)

4 *Dreadnought nodded,* ***glad to have been understood so easily.*** (FICT)

Detached predicatives are characteristic of descriptive writing. By adding a detached predicative, it is possible to express a great deal of information very concisely and place part of the message in the shade as background (initial position) or supplementary information (end position). As regards adjective phrases as detached predicatives, see also 7.6.5.

Detached predicatives are often described as abbreviated or verbless clauses, with omission of the verb *be* and with a subject recoverable from that of the main clause, and are often similar in meaning to non-restrictive relative clauses. Such elements would often be interpreted as implying a reason, not just giving a description. Example **2** may be understood as 'Because she was unable to stand'.

In some cases, called **absolute constructions**, the detached element can be paraphrased as a clause with its own subject:

*"Oh, but I do!" Miss Tish exclaimed,* ***face in a veil of truth.*** (FICT)
*cf. . . . exclaimed. Her face was in a veil of truth.*

Such constructions are often introduced by the preposition *with*:

*As Dandelion ended, Acorn, who was on the windward side of the little group, suddenly started and sat back,* ***with ears up and nostrils twitching.*** (FICT)

***With the golden share intact,*** *the company is under no immediate pressure to negotiate with the likes of GM and Ford and is likely to press for the most advantageous terms available.* (NEWS)

Again the last example is less of a description of the referent of *the company*, and has more the force of an adverbial 'Since the golden share is intact . . .'.

Syntactically and semantically, detached predicatives are similar to supplementive clauses (3.12.4).

## 3.4.2 Parentheticals

**Parenthetical elements** are used particularly in writing to give additional information which is related to, but not part of, the main message of the clause. They are marked off typographically by parentheses, dashes, or some other typographic device. Very often they take the form of noun phrases or numeral phrases. A typical instance is the use of cross-references within parentheses (as in this book).

*Contrary to Labour's claims, the report said the proportion of national income spent on education is almost the same now* ***(5.1 per cent)*** *as it was when the Conservatives came to power in 1979* ***(5.2 per cent).*** (NEWS)

*At precisely 11.07* ***(Earth time),*** *a message flashed up on the ITN screen.* (NEWS)

*As the chart* ***(right)*** *shows <. . .>* (NEWS†)

> *The first thing we notice about the rocks of the Grand Canyon is a pronounced layering, or stratification (**Figure 2-6**).* (ACAD)

Parentheticals may also consist of complete independent clauses:

> *He probably believes this, underestimating the overbearing effect on his underlings of his great height, his formidable courage in overcoming a physical handicap (**he lost a leg in the war**) and his high connections.* (NEWS)

> *One of the first to make it in modern times (**some Greeks had known it long before**) was Leonardi da Vinci.* (ACAD)

The term 'parenthetical' can potentially be applied very widely to include stance adverbials (3.2.8.2), detached predicatives (3.4.1), discourse markers (3.4.5), etc. The term is used here for elements which cannot be assigned to a more specific category.

## 3.4.3 Prefaces

If detached predicatives and parentheticals are especially associated with writing, the next few categories are typical of speech. **Preface** is the term used here for what is often called 'left dislocation'. It consists of a noun phrase, with a co-referent pronoun (marked here with *[]*) following in the core of the clause:

> ***Poor old Doctor Jones**, [he] said you'll never wear your heart out.* (CONV)

> *Well you see **somebody like PC Jones**, being an older person, [he] does it properly I suppose.* (CONV)

> *And actually you know **this Time Chemicals**, [they], [they] deliver you know, [they] come here with the stuff.* (CONV)

> ***This woman**, [she]'s ninety odd.* (CONV)

> ***Mark** – will [he] be first to finish?* (CONV)

> *But **Anna-Luise** what could have attracted [her] to a man in his fifties?* (FICT)

Prefaces differ from initial noun phrases as detached predicatives (3.4.1) in that they are restrictive in meaning. They define rather than give additional information and can replace the co-referent pronoun: cf. *Poor old Doctor Jones said* . . . .

The preface is used to establish a topic first and then attach a proposition. It aids the planning of the speaker as well as the decoding of the hearer, because it breaks up a complex task into parts. By this arrangement the speaker can check that the hearer has clearly identified the main referent before going on to the main point. The hearer's response may be verbal (*yes*, *mm*, and the like) or non-verbal (nodding, eye-contact). See also the more detailed account of prefaces in 11.5.1.

In writing, a preface can take the form of a noun phrase introduced by *as to* or *as for*, and the co-reference with pronouns may be less clear:

> ***As for problem kids**, the association feels [this] is a matter for discussion with [their] parents.* (NEWS)

Arguably *this* relates to something like 'the issue of problem kids' while *their* refers more directly to *problem kids*.

> ***As to all the rest**, I am well pleased <with [it]>, and no further talk <about [it]> is needed.* (FICT)

Arguably the elements containing the co-referent pronouns in this last example are ellipted (here supplied in <>).

## 3.4.4    Tags

**Tags** are short structures which can be added at the end of the clause in conversation or in written representations of speech. They take either the form of a noun phrase or of an interrogative or declarative clause.

### A    Noun phrase tags

**Noun phrase tags** are usually described as involving 'right dislocation':

> *Oh [he] was a, [he] was a lovely man, wasn't [he],* **Doctor Jones?** (CONV)
>
> *I think their kid's got a bloody new organ – and I heard [it] all before I got out of bed* **this bloody organ.** (CONV)
>
> *[It] makes you wonder, you know,* **all this unemployment.** (CONV)
>
> *[It] was a good book* **this.** (CONV)
>
> *No, I think [it]'s about nine hundred* **that one.** (CONV)
>
> *A: And I mean the way he did that table <...>*
> *B: [It]'s nice* **that table** *anyway.* (CONV)
>
> *"[It]'s beautiful—" Letitia murmured, watching her, "***your hair***".* (FICT)

Noun phrase tags are formally like prefaces in that there is a detached noun phrase and a co-referent pronoun inside the core of the clause. Their function is to clarify or underline the reference of the noun phrase (11.5.2–3).

### B    Question tags

**Interrogative tags**, or **question tags**, consist of an auxiliary plus a personal pronoun:

> *Oh yes, if they want to come it doesn't matter if it's convenient to you or not* **does it?** (CONV)
>
> *Well I don't see the point, I mean we're staying in every bloody daft day* **aren't we?** *You know?* (CONV)
>
> *Well you wouldn't be ninety-five if you were weakling* **would you** *Stanley?* (CONV)

Noun phrase tags and question tags frequently combine:

> *It looks lovely though* **that one, doesn't it?** (CONV)
>
> *It's much better* **that** *though* **isn't it?** (CONV)
>
> *It looks good* **that doesn't it?** (CONV)
>
> *That's marvellous* **that, isn't it** *yes?* (CONV)

The function of question tags is to appeal to the addressee for agreement. They are generally found after declarative clauses, but can also be tagged on to interrogative and imperative clauses (3.13.2.4 and 3.13.4.1).

### C    Declarative tags

**Declarative tags** are similar to question tags, but they are far less frequent and their function is quite different, in that they emphasize the speech-act function of the main clause:

> *It looks terrible* **it does,** *I would have it one way or the other.* (CONV)

> *Yeah I thoroughly enjoyed it **I did**.* (CONV)
>
> *He's alright **he is**.* (CONV)
>
> *But I don't like veg **I don't**.* (CONV)

Alternative expressions with a similar function are stance adverbs like *really* and *certainly*:

> *It **really** is a total mess.* (FICT)
>
> *He **certainly** groaned a lot.* (FICT)

## 3.4.5 Discourse markers

**Discourse markers** are particularly characteristic of spoken dialogue. They are words and expressions which are loosely attached to the clause and facilitate the ongoing interaction. Centrally, they include inserts (2.5), such as interjections to express an emotional reaction of the speaker, *please* to appeal to the listener, or *well* to express hesitation, or qualified agreement:

> ***Please**, Dad, I know you're busy and that, but I must know.* (FICT)
>
> *"One moment, **please**, sir."* (FICT)
>
> ***Well** that's true, yes, yes, I mean that's the Lakes, it's lovely up there isn't it?* (CONV)
>
> *Oh **well**, he would have to sell some stock. General Dynamics, probably.* (FICT)

Some multi-word expressions can also be included:

> ***Good grief** what's that I wonder?* (CONV)

Lexically, discourse markers are undecomposable, although they may have grammatical structure (e.g. *good grief* has the structure of a noun phrase). They do not affect the propositional meaning of the clause, instead having a purely pragmatic function.

It is uncertain whether we should regard discourse markers as part of the clause or as extra-clausal units (as applies also to parentheticals in writing). It is probably correct to say that there are degrees of integration, as expressed by prosody and the type of orthographic marker. Where there is clear prosodic or orthographic separation, they are best treated as independent nonclausal units.

Discourse markers are closely related to stance adverbials (3.2.8.2), comment clauses (3.11.6), and question tags (3.13.2.4). See also the account of conversation in Chapter 14.

## 3.4.6 Vocatives

**Vocatives**, in the form of noun phrases (very often proper names), can be freely added to the clause. Vocatives are used to single out the addressee of a message:

> *Are you singing **mate**?* (CONV)
>
> ***Mum**, I'm making such a big sandwich.* (CONV)
>
> *Oh, **Madonna, God, and Lord Jesus**, for the love of God, come to earth again and change this world where sometimes we dare not even trust priests.* (FICT)

As with discourse markers, the degree of integration in the clause may vary. Vocatives are especially important in imperative clauses (3.13.4). (See also 14.4.1.)

## 3.5 Major clause patterns

Combinations of the major clause elements conform to a limited number of patterns. All of these contain a subject and a verb phrase (though the former is not visible in imperatives and some dependent clauses). The occurrence of other major clause elements is determined by the potential of the individual verb, often referred to as its **valency**, a term originally used in chemistry for the combinatory potential of atoms. Hence the treatment of major clause patterns involves us also in an outline of the major grammatical classes of verb. We may distinguish between **one-place** verbs (combining with a subject only), **two-place** verbs (combining with a subject and another element), and **three-place** verbs (combining with a subject and two other elements). However, many verbs allow more than one pattern, so we should perhaps more correctly speak of verbs being 'used with' particular valencies. Tables 3.4 and 3.5 give examples of verbs occurring in the main patterns outlined in 3.5.1–9 (see also 5.2.5).

This approach may be related to the older grammmatical classification of verbs (or verb uses) into **intransitive**, **transitive** and **copular**, which we also make use of. Essentially verbs used in the one-place SV pattern are intransitive, those occurring in the two-place SVP$_s$ pattern are copulas. We also regard those in the SVA pattern as copulas, though some grammars would call them intransitive. Verbs in two- and three-place patterns with an O$_d$ are transitive, with more elaborated names also employed for use in more specific patterns (see later). Those in the SVO$_p$ pattern are, again with some room for debate, treated as transitive.

Clauses assigned to the same pattern may differ with respect to the realization of particular elements, such as the use of a particular type of clause as direct object. If such details are taken into account, the total number of patterns is much larger.

One or more adverbials can be freely added to all the patterns. By contrast, the other elements are normally required (but cf. 3.7), and only one of each is allowed in each clause. There may also be clause links (3.3) and peripheral elements of the types described above (3.4).

Each pattern is especially adapted for the expression of some characteristic meaning(s). But as the semantic roles of the clause elements may vary (see the survey in 3.2), so do the meanings of the clause patterns. If the same few clause patterns are to be used to encode a virtually unlimited range of experience, we cannot expect a one-to-one correspondence between form and meaning.

The following subsections briefly introduce each of the major clause patterns.

## 3.5.1 Subject—verb phrase

The SV clause pattern expresses propositions answering the question 'What does/did X do?' and is seen in the three clauses containing an intransitive verb in this example (relevant clause boundaries are indicated by brackets):

> We stayed [*sitting* in the driveway] [then **went** to the police station in Yateley [until their relatives **arrived**.]] (NEWS)
> <the S *we* is recoverable in the first two SV clauses>

As can be seen in two of these SV clauses, the pattern often has an optional adverbial added. For more examples of verbs appearing with this pattern, see

Table 3.4    **Examples of verbs combining with different clause patterns: one- and two-place verbs**

(Items which can also be used as three-place verbs are in bold. More marginal uses are indicated by parentheses.)

| SV | SVP$_s$ | SVA | SVO$_d$ | SVO$_p$ |
|---|---|---|---|---|
| appear | appear | | | |
| | | | ask | ask for |
| (be) | be | be | | |
| | become | | | |
| | | | believe | believe in |
| | | | blame | |
| break | | | break | |
| burn | | | burn | |
| (call) | | | call | call for/on |
| | | | christen | |
| come | (come) | | | |
| (consider) | | | consider | |
| | | | declare | |
| die | | | | |
| drink | | | drink | |
| drive | | | drive | |
| eat | | | eat | |
| | | | elect | |
| fall | (fall) | | | |
| | feel | | feel | |
| | | | forgive | |
| | get | get | get | get at/over |
| (give) | | | give | |
| go | (go) | | | |
| grow | grow | | grow | grow into |
| (happen) | | happen | | happen to |
| hear | | | hear | hear about |
| increase | | | increase | |
| keep | (keep) | keep | keep | |
| kiss | | | kiss | |
| (last) | | last | | |
| leave | | | leave | |
| | lie | lie | lay | |
| (look) | look | look | | look after/at/for/into |
| | (make) | | make | |
| meet | | | meet | meet with |
| move | | | move | |

**Table 3.4**    **continued**

| SV | SVP$_s$ | SVA | SVO$_d$ | SVO$_p$ |
|---|---|---|---|---|
| *(occur)* | | *occur* | | *occur to* |
| | | | *offer* | |
| *open* | | | *open* | |
| *pay* | | | *pay* | *pay for* |
| | *prove* | | *prove* | |
| *read* | | | *read* | |
| *(remain)* | *remain* | *remain* | | |
| *rise* | | | *raise* | |
| *see* | | | *see* | |
| | *seem* | | | |
| *stop* | | | *stop* | |
| | | | *suggest* | |
| *talk* | | | *talk* | *talk to/about* |
| *think* | | | | *think* |
| *turn* | *(turn)* | | *turn* | *turn into/to* |
| *vary* | | | *vary* | |
| *wait* | | | | *wait for* |
| | | | *warn* | *warn of* |
| *wash* | | | *wash* | |
| | | | *wish* | *wish for* |

Table 3.4. As shown in the table, intransitive verbs typically have other uses as well (3.5.4).

## 3.5.2   Subject—verb phrase—obligatory adverbial

Some verbs require an adverbial without which the proposition is incomplete. Clauses conforming to this pattern typically answer questions like 'When is/was X?', 'Where is/was X?':

> *Three bomb victims **were** still in St Bartholomew's Hospital last night.* (NEWS)
>
> *The baby was **lying** on his back.* (FICT†)
>
> *It'll take us thirty days [to **get** there].* (FICT)
>
> *The pleasant summer **lasted** well into March.* (FICT)

For more examples of verbs used with this pattern, see Table 3.4.

The adverbial in constructions of this type is less mobile than other time and place adverbials and cannot usually be dispensed with. However, the adverbial can sometimes be left out, provided that there is enough contextual support. The missing adverbial is supplied in < > in the examples below:

> *Two other patients were also released from Guy's yesterday afternoon. [One **remained** <in hospital> for an exploratory operation on a shoulder injury].* (NEWS)

Table 3.5 **Examples of three-place verbs combining with different clause patterns**

(Items which can also be used as one- or two-place verbs are in bold, see Table 3.4)

| SVO$_i$O$_d$ | SVO$_d$O$_p$ | SVO$_d$P$_o$ | SVO$_d$A |
|---|---|---|---|
| ask | ask something *of* somebody<br>ask somebody *about* something | | |
| | | believe | |
| | blame something *on* somebody<br>blame somebody *for* something | | |
| call | call something *for* somebody | call | call somebody *somewhere* |
| | | christen | |
| | | consider | |
| | | declare | |
| | | drive | drive somebody *somewhere* |
| | | elect | |
| find | find something *for* somebody | find | |
| forgive | forgive somebody *for*<br>something | | |
| get | get something *for* somebody | get | get somebody *somewhere* |
| give | give something *to* somebody | | |
| | | keep | keep something *somewhere* |
| | | lay | lay something *somewhere* |
| leave | leave something *to* somebody<br>leave something *for* somebody | | |
| make | make something *for* somebody/<br>*into* something | make | |
| offer | offer something *to* somebody | | |
| pay | pay somebody *for* something | | |
| | | | place something *somewhere* |
| | prove something *to* somebody | prove | |
| | put something *to* somebody | | put something *somewhere* |
| read | read something *to* somebody | | |
| | remind somebody *of* something | | |
| | | | see somebody *somewhere* |
| send | send something *to* somebody | | send something *somewhere* |
| show | show something *to* somebody | (show) | show somebody *somewhere* |
| | | | stand something *somewhere* |
| | suggest something *to* somebody | | |
| | suspect somebody *of* something | | |
| take | take something *to* somebody | | take somebody *somewhere* |
| | talk somebody *into* something | | |
| tell | tell something *to* somebody<br>tell somebody *about* something | | |
| | turn something *into* something | (turn) | |
| | warn somebody *of* something | | |
| (wash) | wash something *for* somebody | (wash) | wash something *somewhere* |
| wish | | (wish) | |

> *"Why have I been sent here?"* he wanted to say. *"[How long do I have to* **stay** <here>?*]"* (FICT)

In addition, verbs which normally require an adverbial may have special uses without an adverbial:

> *But it is not expected to* **last**. (NEWS)

Thus, it is often not possible to draw a clear distinction between the SVA pattern and the SV pattern with an optional adverbial.

## 3.5.3 Subject—verb phrase—subject predicative

There are two main varieties of this pattern, both containing a copular verb and a subject predicative (expressing the semantic role of attribute). We may call the two varieties the **characterizing pattern** and the **identifying pattern**.

### 3.5.3.1 The characterizing pattern

Clauses with the characterizing pattern have a characterized participant as subject and answer the question 'What is/was X like?' or 'How did X change/How has X changed?':

> *[I've* **been** *a skinhead for eight years.] [Now I* **am** *a Klansman and a politician.]* (NEWS)
>
> *He's American.* (CONV)
>
> *I had intended [to* **become** *an Anglican priest] but I saw more dark than light.* (NEWS)
>
> *[He* **remained** *anxious about the surgery and its outcome] but felt that he understood what was happening to him.* (ACAD)

In this clause type, a property is ascribed to the referent of the subject. The property may be expressed by a noun phrase or an adjective phrase. The verbs in the first two examples are **current copular** verbs, which describe a state and do not occur in the progressive aspect. The third example contains a **resulting copular** verb, which denotes a change of state. For more examples of copular verbs, see Table 3.4.

Copular verbs differ widely in collocational patterns. Some admit a very wide range of forms in predicative position (e.g. *be, become, get*), while others are severely restricted (e.g. *come, fall, go, turn: come true, fall ill, go mad, turn traitor*, etc). See also 5.5.

Some verbs of perception can be used both as current copulas and as transitive verbs. Compare verbs used as current copulas:

> *Yeah, Peter, Peter oh dear mummy* **feels** *pretty rough this morning.* (CONV)
>
> *But gas cooking is nice. It* **tastes** *different. It's nice.* (CONV)
>
> *He set about arranging the room, bringing out the gin and vermouth bottles from his liquor cabinet and on second thought the pernod because it* **smelled** *so much stronger.* (FICT)

with verbs used transitively:

> *Smelling the food, he* **felt** *the saliva seep in his mouth.* (FICT)
>
> *Then he* **tasted** *the brandy: it was rough but he needed it.* (FICT)
>
> *The soldier took a pinch and* **smelled** *it cautiously.* (FICT)

In general there is a close connection between copulas and intransitive verbs; many verbs are found both with the SV and the SVP$_s$ pattern (cf. Table 3.4). Note also the connection between the SVP$_s$ pattern (**1, 3**) with non-progressive verbs such as *be* and the SV pattern (**2, 4**):

1 *He **was a gambler**. It is one of the family faults.* (FICT)
2 *This one **gambled**, got into debt and disposed of the pearls to a money-lender.* (FICT†)
3 *He employed five in midfield, where Burns **was a prodigious worker**.* (NEWS)
4 *Mind you, they've **worked** hard.* (CONV†)

The meaning expressed is much the same, but the SV pattern primarily describes an action, while the SVP$_s$ characterizes the subject referent with respect to this action.

The SVP$_s$ pattern is superficially similar to other patterns when it contains forms ending in *-ed* and *-ing* in predicative position.

Clauses with passive **5** or progressive (**6, 7**) verb phrases:

5 *The lake **was closed** by the British Waterways Board.* (NEWS)
6 *Then when he **was entertaining** one of his friends he couldn't get his stove to burn right.* (FICT†)
7 *All that we **are writing** about are ideas, but ideas which can transform us into different people, if acted upon.* (ACAD)

Clauses with copular *be* + subject predicative:

8 *The store was **closed** by the time we got there.* (FICT)
9 *Perhaps it's **entertaining** for those like you to discount the concerns of environmentalists.* (NEWS†)
10 *One can return to them time and time again in memory, or use them as a fund upon which to build the part of one's life which is **writing**.* (FICT)

In examples **5–7**, the *-ed* and *-ing* forms are part of the verb phrase. In **8–10**, on the other hand, we find a copula and a subject predicative. There is a clear difference in meaning: action in the first group, description in the second. We can recognize the subject predicative by the fact that it is less verb-like. For example, in **8** *closed* contrasts with a clear adjective such as *open*; in **9**, *entertaining* can be preceded by the degree adverb *very* (which cannot modify clear verb forms); and in **10**, *writing* can be paraphrased by a noun phrase: *the activity of writing*.

## 3.5.3.2    The identifying pattern

Clauses following the identifying pattern answer the question 'Which one is/was X?' The copular verb is invariably *be*. The subject predicative is a definite noun phrase (not an adjective phrase or indefinite noun phrase, as is usually the case with the characterizing pattern):

*My headmistress **was** the president of the Shakespeare League.* (CONV)
*The only reliable source of work **is** the water industry.* (NEWS)
*Meredith **is** the leader in providing multimedia packages.* (NEWS)
*Delaware Park **is** the city's showpiece.* (NEWS†)

This pattern expresses identity between the subject and the subject predicative. Note that the order can usually be reversed, whereas this is far less common with the characterizing pattern.

## 3.5.4   Subject—verb phrase—direct object

This pattern contains a subject, a two-place **monotransitive** verb, and a direct object. The direct object most typically expresses the participant or entity which is affected by the action denoted by the verb:

> And it was Mary who finished – up in casualty [after Carssier **kicked** her three times in the stomach.] (CONV†)

> Energy must be absorbed [to **break** a bond.] (ACAD)

For more examples of verbs with this pattern, see Table 3.4. It is striking that a lot of English verbs have both transitive and intransitive uses. They fall into a number of types with differences in relationship between the transitive and intransitive counterpart.

### A   Ergative verbs

With **ergative** verbs, the relationship between the object and the verb in the SVO$_d$ pattern is the same as that between the subject and the verb in the SV pattern.

Ergative verbs in SVO$_d$ pattern:

> I tried to **roll** boulders into the river to make stepping-stones, but it's too deep, they disappeared. (FICT)

> In Manila and New Delhi, demonstrators **burned** effigies of Uncle Sam and President Bush. (NEWS†)

Ergative verbs in SV pattern:

> Under the seat where it could not **roll** and break, a bottle of Chablis wine knocked back and forth. (FICT†)

> Pulverized coal **burns** approximately like oil or gas. (ACAD†)

Ergative verbs include: *break, change, increase, move, open* (see Table 3.4). Occasionally there is a pair of cognate verbs, one intransitive and the other transitive: *rise* v. *raise, lie* v. *lay*.

### B   Object-deleting verbs

With **object-deleting** verbs, the relationship between the subject and the verb is the same in both patterns.

Object-deleting verbs in SVO$_d$ pattern:

> They've **painted** that haven't they? (CONV)

> He **wrote** his PhD on the climate. (NEWS†)

Object-deleting verbs in SV pattern:

> He always **writes** in capital letters doesn't he? (CONV)

> This facility receives "green" Falcon 10 and 20 aircraft direct from France, and installs interiors and avionics, and also **paints** and delivers direct to the corporate customer. (ACAD)

Object-deleting verbs include:

> drive, drink, eat, read.

### C  Pseudo-intransitive verbs

Many transitive verbs have a special intransitive use:

> *It's true that my CV **reads** like that of a Conservative.* (NEWS†)
>
> *Many of the better-quality junk issues will **sell** easily, traders said.* (NEWS)
>
> *Carbol fuchsin is especially useful for autoradiography as it will not interfere with emulsion and will not **wash out** in developer.* (ACAD)

As with ergative verbs, the subject in the SV pattern corresponds to the direct object in the SVO$_d$ pattern. The difference is that the **pseudo-intransitive** type normally requires an adverbial, very often *easily* or *well*, or the negator *not*. Arguably this type could be included under the SVA pattern (3.5.2); nevertheless, as we find examples without adverbials, the SV analysis seems preferable:

> *If they <= football fans> think they are being ripped off, the new strips <= football shirts/shorts> won't **sell**.* (NEWS)

### D  Reflexive verbs

Some verbs may have much the same **reflexive** meaning whether used intransitively or with a reflexive object.

Verbs used intransitively:

> *In the morning I shaved again and **dressed** and drove downtown in the usual way and parked in the usual place.* (FICT†)
>
> *His head was indistinct in the cloud, but when he came out Brigg saw it was the one who never **washed**.* (FICT)

Verbs used with a reflexive object:

> *There, since it would be in some sense an official visit, I **dressed** myself with care so as to make a proper impression on the captain.* (FICT)
>
> *So he had risen in the bitter cold of four-fifteen, **washed** himself in the prescribed fashion, dressed and put on his father's astrakhan cap.* (FICT†)

As the above examples show, there may be a slight difference in meaning in the SVO$_d$ pattern, suggesting that the action is done with deliberate care. Contrast a verb such as *shoot* which has no such reflexive meaning when used intransitively.

### E  Reciprocal verbs

Some verbs expressing a **reciprocal** relationship have both transitive and intransitive uses. Whereas in D above the understood object is a reflexive form such as *herself*, with reciprocal verbs the understood object is *one another* or *each other*.

Reciprocal verbs used intransitively:

> *The two women **kissed**.* (FICT)
>
> *The two men **met** yesterday.* (NEWS†)

Reciprocal verbs used transitively:

> *Gabrielle **kissed** her parents goodnight.* (FICT)
>
> *That's where I **met** my wife.* (CONV)

The intransitive uses in A–E above can be described as reductions of the transitive patterns (eliminating the agent role or the affected role). Other cases of overlap between transitive and intransitive patterns should rather be described as expansions of the SV pattern, e.g. structures with cognate and eventive objects (3.2.4.1).

The SVO$_d$ pattern is also closely associated with more extended transitive patterns, as will be shown in 3.5.6, 3.5.8, and 3.5.9.

## 3.5.5 Subject—verb phrase—prepositional object

This pattern contains a subject, a two-place **prepositional verb**, and a prepositional object:

> He's got to go [and **deal with** the children], take them to and from work, then run a business. (CONV)

> Perhaps, he thought, it was better [when one did not have to **rely on** other people]. (FICT)

> Mr Baker said many of the 45,000 people [who **applied for** refugee status in Britain last year] were bogus. (NEWS)

For more examples of verbs with this pattern, see 5.3.3.

Clauses with this pattern may be difficult to distinguish from clauses with prepositional phrases as adverbials (3.5.1). The following are some distinguishing characteristics:

### A Lexicalization

With a prepositional object, the verb and the preposition form one lexical unit and can frequently be replaced by a single word; for example, *look into* could be replaced by *examine* in **1**:

> 1 Meanwhile, a joint economic commission will **look into** the ways of economic and industrial co-operation. (NEWS)

In contrast, the lexical verb retains its literal meaning when it is used as an intransitive verb with an adverbial:

> 2 I **looked into** the alleyway and saw the dogs going mad. (NEWS)

Notice also that in **1**, the preposition *into* cannot be replaced by any other preposition without injuring the meaning of the verb. In **2**, however, *look* can combine with a range of prepositions, such as *across*, *down*, *out of*, etc.

A single-word near-synonym can be found for many prepositional verbs. Compare *deal with*: *handle*; *apply for*: *seek*; *look like*: *resemble*; *stand for*: *tolerate*; *think about*: *consider*. Some, such as *rely on*, are not amenable to this, however.

### B Passive paraphrase

The prepositional object frequently admits a passive paraphrase, while this is rare with prepositional phrases as adverbials. Compare:

> 1a The ways of economic and industrial co-operation will be **looked into** by a joint economic commission.
>
> v. 2a *The alleyway was **looked into** ...

### C Question type

The prepositional object can be elicited by a question with 'Who?' or 'What?', while the adverbial prepositional phrase is more compatible with an adverbial-type question. Compare:

> 1b What will the commission **look into**?
>
> v. 2b Where did you **look**?

**D    Omissibility**

The preposition plus prepositional object cannot be omitted without injuring the structure and meaning of the clause. Compare:

    **1c** *Meanwhile, a joint economic commission will **look**.*

v.  **2c** *I **looked** and saw the dogs going mad.*

In all these respects, there is a clear parallel between prepositional objects and direct objects, and between adverbial prepositional phrases and adverbials in general. But, in practice, it is often difficult to separate the two types, and we should think of them more in terms of degree than as sharply delimited categories. In particular one aspect of their behaviour argues more for an SVA analysis: the fact that it is usually possible to insert an adverbial between the verb and the preposition (see also 5.3):

    *We need not **look** further **into** the views.* (ACAD†)

    *I never **thought** much **about** it.* (FICT)

## 3.5.6    Subject—verb phrase—indirect object—direct object

This pattern contains a **ditransitive** verb. It can be described as the SVO$_d$ pattern expanded by a recipient or benefactive role (3.2.5):

    *Well that **tells** you the voltage of the battery.* (CONV)

    *No [you **left** him a note] didn't you?* (CONV)

    *Jacobus' wife **brought** him a mug of tea.* (FICT)

    *His own airport commissioners **voted** him a handsome raise.* (FICT)

    *But I can do an ad for a few thousand, [then **show** them the sales figures].* (NEWS)

For more examples of verbs following this pattern, see Table 3.5. Notice that most ditransitive verbs also have ditransitive prepositional uses: compare the first example in this section with the last in 3.5.7.

Although the SVO$_i$O$_d$ pattern normally expresses an additional semantic role compared with the SVO$_d$ pattern, there is one type where the structurally more complex pattern expresses much the same meaning as the simpler one, viz. in clauses with ditransitive light verb *give* followed by an affected indirect object (3.2.5).

## 3.5.7    Subject—verb phrase—direct object—prepositional object

This pattern is characterized by the use of a **three-place prepositional** verb:

    *You **accuse** her **of** encouraging him?* (FICT)

    *Teachers were asked [to **read** each question **to** pupils twice.]* (ACAD)

For more examples of verbs following this pattern, see Table 3.5.

Notice that there is often, though not always, an alternative construction without a preposition. Notice also that there are sometimes alternative prepositional constructions available. Compare:

*Yeah, I was really quite, quite upset about it. Well I don't **blame** you **for** it.* (CONV)

v. *Some business analysts **blame** the problem **on** tough competition in the insurance market.* (NEWS)

*Don't you **tell** me **about** war.* (FICT)

v. *He only **told** his name **to** an Italian painter named Carlino.* (FICT†)

The alternative constructions provide good means of adjusting the form of the message according to the requirements of context (11.2.4.1).

## 3.5.8 Subject—verb phrase—direct object—object predicative

The pattern contains a **complex transitive** verb. There are different subtypes which differ distinctly in meaning:

1 *Yeah I always wanted [to **paint** that a different colour.]* (CONV)

2 *The agent pulled out a gun [and **shot** him dead.]* (NEWS)

3 *Dave **considered** it accurate.* (FICT)

4 *Well she **found** it cold here.* (CONV)

5 *We approached them as we would any other group of women. [We did not **call** them prostitutes.]* (ACAD)

6 *The Airport Operators Council **re-elected** him president.* (FICT)

In all the subtypes there is an attributive relationship between the direct object and the object predicative; cf. the relationship between the subject and the subject predicative (3.5.3). The relationship can be either **current** or **resulting**, corresponding to the difference of meaning between 'be' and 'become' (cf. 5.5).

In **1** and **2** above, there is a reference to an action that causes the referent of the direct object to change, i.e. these express a resulting relationship. In **3** and **4**, there is a 'be' relationship, as can be brought out by a paraphrase with a clause: *considered/found that it was*. Finally, **5** and **6** illustrate the use of the $SVO_dP_o$ pattern with verbs of naming, electing, and the like.

Verbs conforming to this pattern are generally also compatible with the simpler $SVO_d$ pattern. See Table 3.4.

## 3.5.9 Subject—verb phrase—direct object—obligatory adverbial

As with the other more complex transitive patterns, this clause pattern can be described as an elaboration of the simpler $SVO_d$ pattern, with the addition of a further semantic role:

*She **placed** the baby on a blanket in the living room.* (FICT†)

***Put** a note on my door.* (CONV)

*[You could **take** it to the kitchen] [and **put** it under the grill of the electric cooker [in order to get it hot]], without knowing why it should be hot.* (FICT)

For more examples of verbs compatible with this pattern, see Table 3.5.

Apart from *place* and *put*, all these verbs can also appear with a simpler pattern, usually $SVO_d$. Sometimes, however, the $SVO_dA$ pattern appears to be an elaboration of the SV pattern:

> **Stand** *the syringe upright for 1 min to allow larger pieces of debris to settle into the tip.* (ACAD)

The adverbial in the $SVO_dA$ pattern most typically expresses location. Unlike adverbials in general, it cannot normally be moved or be dispensed with (without making the proposition incomplete). It differs from ordinary locative adverbials in that it does not specify the circumstances of the 'placing', 'putting', etc., but rather describes where the referent of the direct object ends up.

Just as the $SVO_dP_o$ pattern exhibits an attributive relationship analogous to that found between subject and subject predicative (3.5.8), the $SVO_dA$ pattern expresses a locative relationship between the direct object and the adverbial similar to that between a subject and an obligatory adverbial (3.5.2).

The $SVO_dA$ pattern is clearly related to the $SVO_dO_p$ pattern; notice that a number of verbs can appear with both patterns (see Table 3.5). The main difference is that there is an idiomatic link between the verb and the preposition in the prepositional object construction, while the adverbial pattern is less constrained (e.g. *accuse of* v. *put in/on/under*). Moreover, the adverbial can be realized by an adverb as well as by a prepositional phrase. Finally, there is a difference in the types of questions the patterns answer ('Who/What?' v. 'Where?') and in the semantic roles associated with the two patterns.

## 3.5.10  More complex patterns

In addition to the patterns dealt with above, there are more complex patterns, e.g. with a direct object followed by a finite or non-finite clause. See 5.2.4 and Chapter 9.

# 3.6  Variations on clause patterns

In addition to the basic clause patterns (presented in 3.5 in their most typical form), there are variations depending upon a range of structural, semantic, pragmatic, and textual factors. The present section illustrates these other patterns.

## 3.6.1  Order variations

The principal types of order variations are: **inversion** of the subject and (the first part of) the verb phrase; **fronting** of objects and other elements which are normally in post-verbal position; and **postponement** of objects and of adverbial particles of phrasal verbs (5.3.2). In addition, there is of course great variability in the placement of adverbials; 10.1.3.

Order changes frequently combine with other structural changes, as will be shown in 3.6.2–5.

### 3.6.1.1  Inversion

There are two main types of inversion: **subject-operator inversion** and **subject-verb inversion**. These differ both in structure and in their conditions of use.

Subject-operator inversion chiefly occurs in independent interrogative clauses, where it is completely regular (3.13.2); less commonly, it is found in declarative clauses (11.2.3.2).

Subject-verb inversion is chiefly found in independent declarative clauses in examples such as the following, where the SVA pattern becomes AVS (inverted subject in bold):

> There was a dip, a grass ravine, by the road, and some mist was crouching in the deepest part. Across it hung **a wooden bridge leading to the office blocks and the other buildings on the far bank**. At the root of the road were **the little mountains that were the roofs of the Chinese village**. (FICT)

This type of inversion is connected with the distribution of information in the text and is far less common than subject-initial placement (see the detailed description in 11.2.3.1). Note that the first sentence in the example is of a different kind; it has existential *there* as subject (3.6.3) and so has no inversion.

### 3.6.1.2 Fronting

**Fronting** of objects, predicatives, and other elements which are normally in post-verbal position is structurally conditioned and completely regular where they contain *wh*-words, that is, in independent interrogative clauses, exclamative clauses, nominal *wh*-clauses, and relative clauses:

> Oh, [**what a memory** I have.] (FICT) <fronted O$_d$>
>
> Don't you know [**what** a camp is?] (FICT) <fronted P$_s$>
>
> By murdering 11 men and injuring many others these people have polluted yet more the very cause [**which** they claim [to be serving.]] (NEWS) <fronted O$_d$ of *serving* in dependent clause>

See also the description of interrogative and exclamative clauses in 3.13.2–3, of nominal *wh*-clauses in 3.11.1, and of relative clauses in 3.11.3 and 8.7.

Fronting is also found in independent declarative clauses in examples of the following kind:

> People choose who they want. [**This** they had tried [to instill in her in their unobtrusive way.]] (FICT)
>
> Instead he says: ["The team is good enough [to stay up]] [but [**whether we will do**] I don't know."] (NEWS)

In the first example, there is fronting of the direct object of *instill*; in the second, the object of *know* (a nominal clause) is fronted.

Fronting in independent declarative clauses is often combined with subject-verb inversion (for an example, see 3.6.1.1). Both order variations are motivated by textual factors; see also the detailed account in 11.2.2.

### 3.6.1.3 Postponement

A direct object which is heavy and contains more information than the object predicative may be **postponed**, i.e. placed after the object predicative:

> Mr Major has repeatedly made clear **his strong opposition to changing the voting system**. (NEWS)

More typically, the object predicative *clear* would occur at the end of the clause:

> Mr Major has made this <O$_d$> clear <P$_o$>.

Another kind of postponement is found where adverbial particles of phrasal verbs are placed after the direct object:

*I'll help you take your bags **up**.* (FICT)
*cf. I'll help you take up your bags.*

Where the direct object is an unstressed pronoun, the particle is obligatorily placed after it:

*I'll help you take them **up**.*

Elsewhere, postponement, like fronting and subject-verb inversion in independent declarative clauses, is connected with the distribution of information in the text. See the detailed account in 11.2.4.3–4.

## 3.6.2    The passive

Corresponding to the basic patterns containing an object (of any of the three types), we find a **passive** counterpart, as illustrated below:

*Suddenly, armed soldiers broke the shop windows.* (NEWS)
*cf. The shop windows were broken (by armed soldiers).*

*Together these elements account for more than 99 per cent of the mass of the Earth.* (ACAD)
*cf. More than 99 per cent of the mass of the Earth is accounted for (by these elements).*

The passive is much more than an order variation with an SVA pattern. It involves a structural reorganization of the clause, and can be described as a systematic means of choosing a participant other than the agent as the starting-point for a message, without departing from the normal subject-initial word order.

The passive takes two principal forms, which we may call the **short passive** (without an expressed agent phrase) and the **long passive** (with an expressed agent phrase). The former, which is by far the more common, involves condensation as well as structural reorganization.

Passive and active constructions are by no means equivalent, and their use varies widely depending upon the type of text. See the detailed account of the passive in 6.4 and 11.3.

## 3.6.3    Existential *there*

Clauses with *be* (and some other verbs chiefly denoting existence, appearance, or motion) often have an anticipatory subject, the so-called **existential** *there*, in the ordinary subject position. This construction serves to introduce new information, usually in the form of an indefinite noun phrase later in the clause:

***There**'s a mark on this chair.* (CONV)

***There**'s always one that you don't like when you're working in a big group.* (CONV†)

See also the long example in 3.6.1.1, which illustrates both the use of existential *there* and subject-verb inversion.

By using existential *there* rather than the ordinary SV pattern, it is possible to postpone (and thus prepare the addressee for) new information, without departing from the normal SV order. Both syntactic and textual requirements are then fulfilled. See the detailed description of existential clauses in 11.4.

### 3.6.4 Extraposition

The dummy subject *it* is frequently used in the ordinary subject position, anticipating a finite or non-finite clause in **extraposition** ( *[]* identify the extraposed clause):

> *It was hard to believe [that he had become this savage with the bare knife.]* (FICT)
>
> *cf. [That he had become this savage with the bare knife] was hard to believe.*
>
> *It really hurts me [to be going away.]* (NEWS)
>
> *cf. [To be going away] really hurts me.*

Dummy subject *it* may also be used to anticipate a following object clause where there is an intervening obligatory clause element. In this case there is no alternative to extraposition:

> *He found it hard [to believe that he had spent a day chasing after them like a madman with a knife.]* (FICT)
>
> *We leave it to the reader [to appreciate what this will mean in due course.]* (ACAD)

As with existential *there*, anticipatory *it* allows an organization where both syntactic and textual requirements are fulfilled. See the detailed treatment of extraposition in Chapter 9.

### 3.6.5 Clefting

A clause can be **clefted**, i.e. divided into two parts, each with its own verb. There are two main types.

- *it*-cleft:

> *It was a fibre tip refill that I was trying to get, but I didn't buy a fibre tip refill.* (CONV)
>
> *cf. I was trying to get a fibre tip refill.*

- *wh*-cleft:

> *What I want is a country of real opportunity where everyone is free to choose.* (NEWS)
>
> *cf. I want a country of real opportunity.*

Both types of clefts are used to bring particular elements of the structure into focus, but they are by no means equivalent. See the detailed description in 11.6.

### 3.6.6 Condensation

Most of the variations taken up above involve a structural rearrangement in comparison with one of the basic clause patterns, frequently including the addition of extra words. In addition, elements of the clause can be omitted. For example, there is regularly no subject in imperative clauses (3.13.4).

The short passive (3.6.2) can be viewed as a form of **condensation**. Here also belongs the condensation which is typical of non-finite clauses (3.12). The principal type of condensation is ellipsis, which is dealt with in 3.7.

## 3.7    Ellipsis

Ellipsis is the omission of elements which are precisely recoverable from the linguistic or situational context. In the following examples, ellipted material is restored in <>.

> 1  *He squeezed her hand but <he> met with no response.* (FICT)
>
> 2  *He and his mate both jumped out, he* <jumped out> *to go to the women, his mate* <jumped out> *to stop other traffic on the bridge.* (FICT)
>
> 3  *Perhaps, as the review gathers steam, this can now change. It needs to* <change>. (NEWS)

Notice that the elements within angle brackets, which were not part of the original text, can be added without changing the meaning of the clause and without producing an ungrammatical structure. These are the hallmarks of ellipsis.

Depending upon the location in the clause, we can distinguish between **initial ellipsis** (**1** above; there may be a preceding coordinator), **medial ellipsis** as in **2**, and **final ellipsis** as in **3**.

Omission of elements which are recoverable from the linguistic context may be called **textual ellipsis**. This occurs in coordinated clauses (3.7.1), comparative clauses (3.7.2), question-answer sequences (3.7.3), and other contexts where adjacent clauses are related in form and meaning (3.7.4). Particularly in conversation, we also find omission of function words and **situational ellipsis** (3.7.5), where the omission and interpretation are dependent upon the situational context.

## 3.7.1    Ellipsis in coordinated clauses

Ellipsis is commonly found in coordinated clauses that share elements with a preceding clause. The clauses may be explicitly marked by a coordinator or joined without a link. In the following examples, ellipted material has been restored:

> *This gay guy who came into the pub completely fell in love with Ben and* <he> *was like declaring his undying love.* (CONV)
>
> *I thought they were on the – seat but they're not* <on the seat>. (CONV)
>
> *The morning was clear, not yet hot, the sky* <was> *as blank as a canvas being prepared for paint.* (FICT)
>
> *You've become part of me, and I* <have become part>, *of you.* (FICT)
>
> *The pattern of sex differences was that girls generally scored better than the boys on the money and number pattern items and boys* <scored better> *on the measures.* (ACAD)

Ellipsis in coordinated clauses is common both in spoken and written registers.

## 3.7.2    Ellipsis in comparative clauses

Comparative clauses characteristically mirror the structure of a preceding clause. Elements which are shared are normally left out in the comparative clause (or replaced by a pro-form). Examples with ellipted material added are:

> *She looks older than my mother* <does>. (CONV)

*One result was that older people made greater head movements than younger people <did>.* (ACAD)

Ellipsis is normal in comparative clauses in both spoken and written registers. (See also 3.11.4 and 7.8 on comparative clauses.)

### 3.7.3 Ellipsis in question-answer sequences

Ellipsis is the rule in question-answer sequences. For obvious reasons, such sequences are virtually restricted to conversation and fictional dialogue.

> 1 *A: Have you got an exam on Monday?*
> *B: <I've got> two exams <on Monday>.*
> *A: What exams <have you got>?*
> *B: <I've got>German, reading and French oral, French oral's a doddle.*
> *A: Is it <a doddle>?* (CONV)
>
> 2 *A: When's he coming back?*
> *B: <He's coming back> Next Friday.*
> *A: <He's coming back> Next Friday, oh right.* (CONV)

In the give-and-take of conversation, the speaker and the addressee leave out what is easily recoverable from the linguistic or situational context. Notice that *next Friday* is repeated in the last interchange, although it is strictly speaking unnecessary. By repeating, the speaker acknowledges that he/she has understood and accepts the answer.

In conversation, a minimum amount of form is put to maximum use. See also the account of question-answer sequences in 14.3.4.1–2.

### 3.7.4 Other types of textual ellipsis

A full interrogative clause is sometimes followed by a more specific question which is elliptic in form (spoken by the same person):

> *What was the mileage when we got there? <Was it> A hundred and eleven?* (CONV)
>
> *What time <are> they supposed to be back? <Are they supposed to be back> Early?* (CONV)
>
> *What would you like to drink? <Would you like> Scotch, bourbon?* (FICT)

In the same way we find full declarative clauses followed by elliptic statements:

> *"I don't want money,"* he said, *"just something to do. Sweep the floor or something like that. Clean the garden."* (FICT)
>
> *Maybe Henry would realize she was not as nice as she pretended to be. Maybe not, though.* (FICT)

Textual ellipsis of the types illustrated in this section is characteristic of conversation and of dialogue or the representation of thought in fiction.

### 3.7.5 Omission of function words and situational ellipsis

Unstressed function words are frequently left out in conversation. For example, subject pronouns which are recoverable from the linguistic or situational context are commonly omitted:

*Do you know the woman at the end of our road, right?* <She> *Takes me to –
school every day – She's got a D reg Sierra* (CONV)

<I> *Saw Susan and her boyfriend in Alder weeks ago.* (CONV)

<I> *Suppose I ought to tell you that shouldn't I?* (CONV)

A: *What did he say?*
B: <He> *Said he was ill, he looked ill though.* (CONV)
A: *He's a really sweet guy.*
B: *But erm*
A: <He> *Just thinks too much and smokes too much.* (CONV)

Unstressed auxiliaries are also frequently left out, both in declarative and interrogative sentences. Ellipsis is common with *have got* and *had better*:

*What* <are> *you going to do?* <Are> *You going to do her a postcard?* (CONV)

*You*<'d> *better get yourself a lawyer, man, a damned good one.* (FICT)

A: *I've got a spider in here.*
B: *You*<'ve got> *what?*
A: *I*<'ve> *got a spider in here.* (CONV)

A number of these examples would be regarded by purists as incorrect English despite their frequency in real conversation of educated speakers.

Both subject and auxiliary may be ellipted:

<We're> *Too old to change aren't we?* (CONV)

*So* <it's> *no wonder that people had begun to watch him rather uneasily.* (FICT)

<He's> *A very strong fellow your father.* (FICT)

Other structures are clausally incomplete, although it is not transparent what exactly has been omitted. In the following examples, apparent gaps are marked by <–>:

*And we got our furniture – in this place and there's a story in this one – So we* <–> *to the hardware shop and we bought some mats and – dishes and – God knows what!* (CONV)

A: *I don't think pepper's a very useful deterrent –*
B: <–> *One shower of rain and you've lost it anyway.* (CONV)

*Gillespie made his examination. "*<–> *Middle-aged man," he said, "*<–> *anywhere between forty-five and sixty, more probably in middle or late fifties.* <–> *Body seems in fair condition,* <–> *own hair,* <–> *not thinning. Ah, yes—*<–> *depressed fracture of skull. He's been in the water for some time,* <–> *clothing* <–> *utterly soaked,* <–> *whole body* <–> *chilled."* (FICT)

Although in most cases we can quite easily fill in the gaps left by ellipsis, on pragmatic as much as grammatical evidence, we are reaching a point in these latter examples where ellipsis merges with non-clausal material (3.15). Compare block language 4.4.1.2H. On ellipsis in conversation, see further 14.3.5.

# 3.8   Negation

Clausal negation is used to deny or reject a proposition. Clauses are negated by the insertion of the negator *not* or by some other negative word (*no, nothing,* etc.).

The two types may be called *not*-**negation** and *no*-**negation**. After an initial overview we will look at these separately in 3.8.2 and 3.8.3 and confront them in 3.8.4.

## 3.8.1 Overall frequency of negation

**CORPUS FINDINGS** [1]

➤ Negative forms are many times more common in conversation than in writing.

**Table 3.6** **Distribution of *not/n't* v. other negative forms; occurrences per million words**

each ● represents 500

| | *not/n't* | other negative forms |
|---|---|---|
| CONV | ●●●●●●●●●●●●●●●●●●●●●●●●●● ●●●●●●●●●●●●●●●●●●●●●●●● | ●●●●● |
| FICT | ●●●●●●●●●●●●●●●●●●●●●●● | ●●●●●●●●● |
| NEWS | ●●●●●●●●●● | ●●●● |
| ACAD | ●●●●●●●● | ●●● |

**DISCUSSION OF FINDINGS**

A number of factors contribute to the very high frequency of negative forms in spoken discourse:

• Verbs are more numerous in conversation than in the other registers (cf. 2.3.5). As negation is most often tied to the verb, we naturally expect a higher proportion of negative forms as well.

• Clauses are shorter and more numerous overall than in the other registers (cf. 3.1), which in its turn means that we can expect a higher proportion of negative clauses. Because of the close association between clauses and verbs, we cannot really distinguish between these two points.

• There is a great deal of repetition in conversation (cf. 2.2.1), including repetition of negative forms.

• Certain structures which include negative forms are characteristic of spoken discourse: multiple negation (3.8.7.1) and question tags (3.13.2.4).

• A number of verbs which collocate strongly with the negator *not* are particularly frequent in conversation. Notably, these include mental verbs like: *forget, know, mind, remember, think, want, worry*. See also 3.8.4.4.

• Finally, and perhaps most important, conversation is interactive and invites both agreement and disagreement, while writing generally presents the perspective of a single author or author group. This is reflected both in the far higher frequency of the response word *no* in conversation (not included in the frequencies above) and in the much higher overall frequency of other negative forms.

The higher frequency of negative forms in fiction than in the other written registers is probably due mainly to the dialogue passages.

There are also great differences between the registers in the use of individual negative forms. These matters will be taken up in the sections below.

## 3.8.2 *Not*-negation

The negator *not* is inserted after the operator (3.2.9) in the verb phrase. If there is no other auxiliary, *do* is obligatorily inserted as operator:

> You **can** do this but you **can't** do that. (CONV)
>
> I **didn't study** the label. (CONV)
>
> cf. I **studied** the label.

All uses of *be* behave like auxiliaries and require no *do*-insertion:

> It just **wasn't** worth our while. (CONV)
>
> They **are not** that little. (NEWS†)

The exception to this rule is negative imperatives:

> **Don't be** silly! (CONV)
>
> **Don't be** so hard on yourself. (FICT)

The use of the auxiliary *do* varies with the transitive verb *have*, and with *have to* and the marginal modal auxiliaries *dare*, *need*, *ought to*, and with *used to* (3.8.2.1–4).

The negator *not* is usually attached as an **enclitic** to the preceding operator and appears in informal writing as the contracted form *n't*. In speech and informal written English the auxiliary may alternatively be contracted with a preceding word, leaving a full form of *not* (3.8.2.5–6).

## 3.8.2.1 The auxiliary *do* in negative clauses with transitive *have (got)*

The transitive verb *have (got)* has a bewildering number of possible negative forms. There are five main types:

- *Not*-negation, lexical verb construction (with *do*)

> She **doesn't have** a dime. (FICT)
>
> We simply **do not have** enough money. (NEWS)

- *Not*-negation, auxiliary-like construction (without *do*)

> I **haven't** a clue what her name was! (CONV)
>
> I **haven't** any spirit to argue. (NEWS)

- *Not*-negation, *have got*

> We **haven't got** any cheesecake. (CONV)
>
> I **haven't got** a mother. (FICT†)

- *No*-negation, *have*

> He **had no** clue that I liked him. (CONV)
>
> He liked the fact that Venice **had no** cars. (FICT)
>
> Such rocks **have no** fossils. (ACAD†)

- *No*-negation, *(have) got*

> According to you I've **got no** friends. (CONV)
>
> I said to him, "I've **got no** work now, what can I afford?" (FICT)

In a non-standard variant of the last type, *got* is used alone (without *have*) with *no*-negation (cf. 3.7.5):

> She **got no** light on her bike. (CONV)

> You **got nothing** to worry about. (FICT†)

The distribution of the five main types of negation with the lexical verb *have* is shown in Table 3.7. (The findings reported in this table are limited to object noun phrases opening with particular determiners; they do not include all definite and indefinite objects. If all objects are taken into account, the difference in the frequency of *do*-insertion between BrE and AmE becomes sharper.)

**CORPUS FINDINGS** [3,5]

➤ With an indefinite object, *no*-negation with *have* is the majority form in all registers except British conversation.

➤ With a definite object, *not*-negation with *do* is the majority choice, except in BrE conversation and BrE fiction.

➤ Preferences differ in BrE and AmE:
  ➤ *Do*-insertion is more common in AmE in clauses with a definite object.
  ➤ *Got*-forms are frequent in BrE, but rare in AmE.

➤ *Not*-negation with *have* is rare in all the registers, except in British fiction.

**Table 3.7** **Negation of lexical *have*, expressed as a percentage within each register**

DO = all forms of *do*   NOT = *not* or the contracted form *n't*   HAVE = all forms of *have*   A = *a, an*   ANY = *any, anybody, anyone, anything*   NO = *no, nobody, none, nothing*

each ■ represents 10%   □ represents less than 5%   – marks alternatives that are unattested in the LSWE Corpus

Followed by the indefinite article or an *any*-form:

| | AmE CONV | BrE CONV | AmE FICT | BrE FICT | NEWS | ACAD |
|---|---|---|---|---|---|---|
| DO NOT *have* A/ANY | ■ | ■■ | ■■ | □ | ■ | ■ |
| HAVE NOT A/ANY | – | □ | □ | ■ | □ | □ |
| HAVE NOT *got* A/ANY | – | ■■■ | – | □ | □ | □ |
| HAVE NO | ■■■■ ■■■ ■ | ■■ | ■■■■ ■■■■ | ■■■■ ■■■■ | ■■■■ ■■■■ | ■■■■ ■■■■ |
| HAVE *got* NO | – | ■■ | – | □ | □ | – |

Followed by the definite article:

| | AmE CONV | BrE CONV | AmE FICT | BrE FICT | NEWS | ACAD |
|---|---|---|---|---|---|---|
| DO NOT *have the* | ■■■■ ■■■ ■ | ■■■ | ■■■■ ■■ | ■■ | ■■■■ ■■■■ | ■■■■ ■■■■ ■ |
| HAVE NOT *the* | – | ■ | ■■■ | ■■■■ ■■ | ■ | ■ |
| HAVE NOT *got the* | ■ ■■ | ■■■■ ■■ | ■ | ■■ | ■ | □ |

**DISCUSSION OF FINDINGS**

The difference in negative form depending upon whether the object is a definite or an indefinite noun phrase reflects the fact that *no*-negation is only a possible option in the latter case. As regards the high frequency of *no*-negation with *have*, see also 3.8.4.3B.

*Do*-insertion and the *have got* constructions represent two ways of regularizing the negation of transitive *have* to the pattern of lexical verbs generally. Different forms of regularization have been chosen in BrE and AmE. The choice of *do*-insertion in American English agrees with the greater preference for this option in general in AmE (see below and 3.13.2.8). The high frequency of the *have got* construction in conversation, at least in BrE, is consistent with an explanation of register differences against the background of linguistic change in that *have got* represents a more recent development in the history of the language.

The greater variability in BrE conversation, in comparison to AmE conversation, may reflect a greater tendency for American forms to be adopted in BrE than the reverse. The same tendency is found in questions and negative clauses (3.13.2.8A).

The use of *have* without *do*-insertion in British fiction probably reflects a conservative choice. It appears to occur particularly in collocations, such as *haven't a clue, haven't (the) time, haven't the heart/nerve/right/sense to, haven't the faintest/foggiest/slightest idea.*

### 3.8.2.2   The auxiliary *do* in negative clauses with the semi-modal *have to*

The semi-modal *have to* has three options in negative clauses:
- Lexical verb construction (with *do*)

    You **don't have to** have a conscience. (CONV)

    You **don't have to** help me. (FICT)

    It **does not have to** be Friday. (NEWS†)
- Auxiliary construction (without *do*)

    Oh I wish I **hadn't to** go out tonight. (CONV)

    Oh well er I asked Joyce and she said erm, he **hasn't to** go in, he's not bad enough. (CONV)
- Have got to

    So she said oh she **hasn't got to** wear them as much now. (CONV†)

    We don't have to, **ain't got to** take really too much muck. (CONV)

**CORPUS FINDINGS** [1,3]

In actual use, *do*-insertion is virtually the only choice for negation with *have to*, except in BrE conversation.

**DISCUSSION OF FINDINGS**

The use of *have got* in British conversation agrees with the tendency found for the transitive verb *have*, though the frequency is far lower. The pattern of use here

**Table 3.8**  **Percentage of each variant for *have to* in negative clauses**

DO = all forms of *do*   HAVE = all forms of *have*   NOT = *not* or the contracted form *n't*

each ■ represents 10%   □ represents less than 5%   – marks alternatives that are unattested in the LSWE Corpus

| | AmE CONV | BrE CONV | FICT | NEWS | ACAD |
|---|---|---|---|---|---|
| DO NOT *have to* | ■■■■■ ■■■■■ | ■■■■■ ■■ | ■■■■■ ■■■■■ | ■■■■■ ■■■■■ | ■■■■■ ■■■■■ |
| HAVE NOT *to* | – | □ | – | – | – |
| HAVE NOT *got to* | – | ■■■ | □ | – | – |

shows consistency for the verb *have* which is not differentiated in line with its quite different function as a semi-modal.

### 3.8.2.3   The auxiliary *do* in negative clauses with *dare* and *need*

The verbs *dare* and *need* have two primary options in negative clauses:

* Lexical verb construction (with *do*)

    *I **didn't dare** swing round.* (CONV†)

    *They **don't dare** do a thing.* (FICT)

    *I **didn't dare to** mention Hella.* (FICT)

    *You **don't need to** crawl any more Charlotte.* (CONV)

    *She **doesn't need to** work, or think.* (FICT)

    *They **do not need to** belong to the same phase.* (ACAD)

With *dare* we find instances both with and without a following infinitive marker.

* Auxiliary construction (without *do*)

    *No, I **daren't** tell her.* (CONV)

    *But they **dared not** complain openly.* (FICT)

    *Supervision **need not** be so intense.* (NEWS)

    *The details **need not** concern us here.* (ACAD†)

When there is no *do*-insertion, *dare* and *need* lack an infinitive marker, i.e. they behave like modal auxiliaries.

**CORPUS FINDINGS** [1,3]

➤ *Dare* and *need* show different tendencies with respect to *do*-insertion.
  ➤ Preferences also vary with tense.
➤ *Dare* is considerably less frequent than *need*; it is found chiefly in fiction and BrE conversation.
  ➤ The auxiliary construction is the predominant choice for negation with *dare* in BrE.
  ➤ *Do*-insertion is the predominant choice for negation with *dare* in AmE fiction.
➤ *Need* is commonly used in the present tense.
  ➤ The auxiliary construction is the predominant choice for negation with *need* in the written registers.
  ➤ *Do*-insertion is the more common type in conversation.
  ➤ *Do*-insertion is the only option instanced in American conversation.

**Table 3.9** **Frequencies of each variant for *dare* and *need* in negative clauses; occurrences per million words**

DO = all forms of *do*   DARE = all forms of *dare*   NEED = all forms of *need*

each ■ represents 5   □ represents fewer than 3   – marks alternatives that are unattested in the LSWE Corpus

|  | AmE CONV | BrE CONV | AmE FICT | BrE FICT | NEWS | ACAD |
|---|---|---|---|---|---|---|
| ***dare*** | | | | | | |
| present −DO | – | ■■ | □ | ■■ | □ | – |
| present +DO | □ | □ | □ | □ | □ | – |
| past −DO | – | – | □ | ■■ | □ | – |
| past +DO | – | □ | ■■ | ■ | □ | □ |
| ***need*** | | | | | | |
| present −DO | – | ■■ | ■■ | ■■■■■ ■■ | ■■ | ■■■■■ ■■■■ |
| present +DO | ■■■■■ ■■ | ■■■■■ ■ | □ | ■ | ■ | ■■ |
| past −DO | – | – | – | – | – | – |
| past +DO | □ | □ | □ | ■ | □ | □ |

---

**DISCUSSION OF FINDINGS**

The auxiliary construction of *dare* and *need* is virtually restricted to the present tense. The past tense form *dared not*, which is chiefly found in British fiction, is presumably a conservative choice. *Need* without *do* behaves like a modal auxiliary and has no past tense form: *\*They needed not leave.*

The results further indicate that *dare* and *need* are probably obsolescent as modal auxiliaries, at least in AmE. This pattern corresponds to a general trend towards less frequent use of certain auxiliaries in AmE (6.6). The exclusive use of *do*-insertion in American conversation agrees with the more common use of *do*-insertion in general in AmE (see above and 3.13.2.8).

### 3.8.2.4 The auxiliary *do* in negative clauses with *ought to* and *used to*

*Ought to* and *used to* have two primary options in negative clauses:
- Auxiliary construction (without *do*)
    *So I think I **oughtn't to** spend more.* (CONV†)
    *One **ought not to** complain.* (FICT)
    *Gentlemen **used not to** have any traffic <= dealings> with him.* (FICT†)
    *Because it **used not to** understand markets, it cannot conceivably have rectified this gap in its political intelligence.* (NEWS)
- Lexical verb construction (with *do*)
    *He **didn't ought to** be doing that sort of job.* (CONV†)
    *You **didn't ought to** have let that fire out.* (FICT)
    *We **didn't used to** see much of it.* (CONV)

She **didn't used to** be like this, Renata. (FICT)

She **didn't used to** do that. (FICT)

Note that it is the past tense form of *do* that is chosen both with *ought to* and *used to*.

➤ Negative forms of *used to* and *ought to* are rare in all registers, in both AmE and BrE.
  ➤ The only moderately common form is the auxiliary construction *ought NOT to* in BrE fiction (occurring c. ten times per million words).

**DISCUSSION OF FINDINGS**

Negative constructions are generally avoided with *used to* and *ought to*. To some extent, alternative forms are used instead:

I **don't think you ought to** say that. (CONV)

"I **don't think they ought to** be there." (FICT)

I **never used to** say that. (CONV)

By the use of a superordinate clause with *think*, the speaker is able to avoid using a negative form of *ought to* (cf. also 3.13.2.8D). Similarly, *never used to* is used more frequently in conversation than either *used not to* or *didn't used to*. Further, the use of *do* here, especially with *ought to*, is somewhat stigmatized.

## 3.8.2.5 Full form v. operator contraction v. *not*-contraction

Function words in English frequently have reduced forms. Here the focus is on contracted forms in negative constructions. There are three possible ways of realizing an operator followed by the negator *not*, though the two contracted ways are not equally available for all operators:

- Full forms

  I hope you **are not** a "Van Gogh". (FICT)

  It **is not** a sterilizing agent. (ACAD†)

- *Not*-contraction

  You're alright **aren't** you? (CONV)

  This **isn't** a bad sort of place at all. (FICT)

  He **can't** do anything else. (NEWS)

Note that there are special *not*-contracted forms of *shall* and *will* + *not*: *shan't*, *won't*:

  But it **won't** be good for the party. (NEWS)

- Operator contraction

  **It's not** a secret. (FICT)

  I hope **we're not** a contrary indicator. (NEWS)

This is only available, at least as a written variant, for *am/is/are*, *have/has/had* and modals *will* and *would*.

**CORPUS FINDINGS [1,3]**

The occurrence of these contraction types varies with register and with the choice of operator (see Appendix):

➤ Full forms are virtually the only choice in academic prose. Contraction is most common in conversation, followed by fiction and news.

➤ Operator contraction is common with the present tense forms of *be* (*you're not*, *it's not*, etc.).
  ➤ *Am* has only operator contraction (*I'm not*; but see 3.8.2.6).
  ➤ Operator-contracted forms such as *we'll not*, *she'd not* are rare.

➤ Apart from the present tense forms of *be*, *not*-contraction is the most common type of reduced form (*can't*, *couldn't*, *don't*, etc.).

➤ Some operators are regularly or predominantly used with full forms in all the registers: *may not*, *might not*. The *not*-contraction with *may* is obsolescent.

The choice of the two types of contraction was examined in detail with *is* and *are*:

➤ Most occurrences of *not*-contraction with *is* and *are* are found in clause-initial position (chiefly in interrogative clauses, where operator contraction is not available).

➤ Most occurrences of operator contraction are found with pronouns.
  ➤ Operator contraction is less common with preceding nouns than is *not*-contraction.

➤ Operator contraction is somewhat more common in clause-final position than *not*-contraction:
  ➤ c. 10% of the tokens of *'s not* and *'re not* occur in clause-final position;
  ➤ less than 5% of the tokens of *isn't* and *aren't* occur in clause-final position.

**Table 3.10** **Percentage grammatical distribution of contraction variants for *is* + *not* and *are* + *not*** [6]

each ■ represents 5%    □ represents less than 2.5    – marks alternatives that are unattested in the LSWE Corpus

| preceding form | contracted variant | | | |
| --- | --- | --- | --- | --- |
| | *'s not* | *isn't* | *'re not* | *aren't* |
| clause-initial | – | ■■■■■ ■■■■■ ■ | – | ■■■■■ ■■■■■ ■■ |
| personal pronoun | ■■■■■ ■■■■■ ■■ | ■■■■ | ■■■■■ ■■■■■ ■■■■■ ■■ | ■■■ |
| noun | ■ | ■■ | – | ■■■ |
| *that* | ■■■ | □ | – | – |
| *there* | ■■ | ■ | – | ■ |
| *other* | □ | ■■ | □ | □ |

**DISCUSSION OF FINDINGS**

The patterns of reduction are dependent upon how frequently the associated forms co-occur. For example, in a sequence consisting of *it* + *is* + *not* there are two very frequent pairs: *it's* and *isn't*. On the other hand, the combination of a particular noun + *is* + *not* produces only one very frequent pattern: *isn't*. Forms which frequently co-occur tend to be treated as single units in speech processing (cf. the observations on *there's* in 3.9.1.5).

There are indications that operator contraction may be felt as the more emphatic alternative in clause-final position, and perhaps more generally. Operator contraction involving forms of *be*, with *not* unreduced, frequently co-occurs with the response word *no*, with an exclamation mark at the end of the clause, or where there is a marked contrast with the immediate context:

> *No I'm not, don't rewind it. It's not.* (CONV)
>
> *It's not fair!* (CONV)
>
> *No, they're not!* (CONV)
>
> *"I'm almost finished."—"No, you're not. You're about to begin."* (FICT)

There are almost certainly other factors which influence the distribution of the two reduction patterns with *is* and *are*. For example, phonological factors are obviously at work in the absence of *this's* and *there're*.

### 3.8.2.6 *Aren't I* and *ain't*

There is considerable variability among the present tense forms of *be* used for negative interrogative clauses with a first person singular subject (*I*). The form preferred by many prescriptive grammarians—*am I not* (or *amn't I*)—is rarely attested in natural conversation. Instead, *aren't I* is the predominant form (occurring about five times per million words):

> *I'm naughty **aren't I**?* (CONV)
>
> ***Aren't I** allowed to have a bit?* (CONV)
>
> *"I'm right **aren't I**?" Rick said.* (FICT)
>
> ***Aren't I** supposed to understand?* (FICT)

*Ain't* is widely regarded as non-standard but is relatively widespread in use. *Ain't* applies to all persons and may correspond both to *be* and *have*:

- *Ain't* corresponding to *be*

  > *There **ain't** a tape in there.* (CONV)
  >
  > *If the show **ain't** a killer, they're gone.* (FICT)
  >
  > *There **ain't** nothing we can do.* (FICT)
  >
  > *I'm whispering now, **ain't** I?* (FICT)

- *Ain't* corresponding to *have*

  > *I **ain't** done nothing.* (CONV)
  >
  > *You still got to move stuff around **ain't** you?* (CONV)
  >
  > *I said no, I **ain't** had no motors in of your type.* (CONV)
  >
  > ***Ain't** you got any consideration?* (FICT)

*Ain't* is the paradigm case of a frequent though unacceptable form. It often combines with another stigmatized form, viz. dependent multiple negation (3.8.7.1). As the examples above show, *ain't* may correspond to negative forms of both *be* and *have* (the latter in auxiliary uses only). In fiction, four out of five occurrences correspond to *be*; in conversation, the distribution is more evenly divided between forms corresponding to *be* and *have*.

*Ain't* is lacking in the academic texts and occurs a few times only in quoted speech in the news texts. In conversation, it is very common (c. 400 occurrences per million words), and it is also relatively common in fiction (c. 40 occurrences per million words). However, compared with the normal negative forms of *be* and *have*, it is very infrequent. The lack of the form outside conversation, quoted speech, and dialogue in fiction testifies to the continued stigmatization of the form.

### 3.8.3    *No*-negation

Clauses can be negated by other negative forms than *not*:

*They had **no** sympathy for him.* (FICT)
cf. *They did**n't** have **any** sympathy for him.*

*There was **nobody** in the hut and the fireplace was cold.* (FICT)
cf. *There was**n't anybody** in the hut.*

*Now, West Ham have **no one** with the wit to surmount such obstacles.* (NEWS)
cf. *West Ham do **not** have **anyone** ...*

*It's **no** good pretending you've any aptitude for art when it's quite clear you've **none** at all.* (FICT)
cf. *It's **not any** good pretending ... when you have**n't any** at all.*

*Say **nothing**!* (CONV)
cf. ***Don't** say **anything**.*

*There's **nowhere** to stand.* (FICT†)
cf. *There is**n't anywhere** to stand.*

*I'll **never** be able to tell her.* (FICT†)
cf. *I wo**n't ever** be able to tell her.*

*Walter shared **neither** view.* (FICT)
cf. *Walter did**n't** share **either** view.*

*I did not like the Gelong snake, **nor** did I trust it.* (FICT)
cf. *... **and** I did**n't** trust it (**either**).*

In other words, the correspondences are:

| | |
|---|---|
| *no—not any* | *nowhere—not anywhere* |
| *nobody—not anybody* | *never—not ever* |
| *no one—not anyone* | *neither—not either* |
| *none—not any* | *nor—and not* |
| *nothing—not anything* | |

Where *no*-negation and *not*-negation are both possible, there is sometimes a slight difference in meaning. This is true of clauses containing *not a* v. *no*:

*She's **not a** dictatorial person.* (FICT)
*He is ten years old, he is **not a** baby.* (FICT)
*But he is **not a** thrilling speaker.* (NEWS)
*He was**n't a** union member.* (NEWS†)

v.    *He was **no** fool.* (FICT)
*She was **no** great beauty.* (FICT†)
*He is **no** quitter.* (NEWS†)
*He is **no** great orator.* (NEWS†)

*Not*-negation is the more neutral choice in such constructions. It can be used both to give a neutral characterization and to express a judgement. The latter is characteristic of *no*-negation. Compare also:

    **1** *He's **a** teacher, like you.* (FICT)

v.    *He's **not a** teacher.*

    **2** *He's **some** mensch.* (FICT)

v.    *He's **no** mensch.*

    *He's **not much of a** mensch.*

In **1** there is a neutral description of category membership. However, the forms in **2** are all evaluative. Similarly, *He's no teacher* would be much more likely than **1** to be evaluative and refer to a person's pedagogical abilities rather than his actual objective profession. We note that a quantifier may be used to highlight an evaluation both in positive and negative contexts.

    Although it is hard to pin down differences in communicative effect between the two negation types, it seems that *no*-negation may be more emphatic. It is probably significant that *no*-words normally receive some stress, while *not* is characteristically reduced and appended to the preceding auxiliary. *No*-negation is decidedly emphatic where it occurs repeatedly in the same context:

> *And we will keep on winning with **no** wheeling, **no** dealing, **no** horse-trading and **no** electoral pacts.* (NEWS)

> *In the drunk tank it is not so good. **No** bunk, **no** chair, **no** blankets, **no** nothing.* (FICT)

A paraphrase using *without any/not any* would be far less expressive.

## 3.8.4   Occurrence of *not*-negation v. *no*-negation

We now examine in some detail the competition between the two major forms of negation.

### 3.8.4.1   Variability of *not*-negation and *no*-negation

The alternative forms of negation are often not available.

**CORPUS FINDINGS [7]**

➤ A *no*-negated form can usually be replaced with *not*-negation (c. 80% of the time), while *not*-negation can be formally replaced by *no*-negation only about 30% of the time.

**DISCUSSION OF FINDINGS**

For a *not*-negated structure to be restated in terms of *no*-negation, *not* must co-occur with some other form which can incorporate the negative element (most typically an *any*-form). The main correspondences are listed in 3.8.3. The negative element can also be incorporated in an indefinite noun phrase without *any*:

> *She doesn't have a car yet.* (FICT)
> cf. *She has no car yet.*

Contrast *She doesn't have the car yet* where a *no*-negated form is impossible.

There are contexts where *no*-negation cannot be re-expressed with *not*-negation. First, a *no*-form is not replaceable by *not* plus an *any*-form in pre-verbal position. This is the most important restriction on the variability of *no*-negation:

> *"**Nobody** stole it?" said James.* (FICT)
>
> ***Nothing** can happen to you, and **nothing** can get you.* (FICT)
>
> ***No one** was certain whether or not this would have the desired effect.* (NEWS†)

Examples of other cases where a simple replacement with *not*-negation is unlikely are:

1. *She had affection in her and **nowhere** to spend it.* (FICT†)
2. *Following the share sale, it will be in an extremely strong financial position, with **no** borrowings.* (NEWS)
3. *Only 50 per cent of authorities would classify as vulnerable a young homeless person with **no** parents and **no** support.* (NEWS)

The coordination in **1** makes a simple *not anywhere* substitution awkward, though *not*-negation is perfectly acceptable with a slight re-wording: *... and didn't have anywhere to spend it*. Although **2** and **3** do not accept a simple *not any* replacement, we can easily formulate a paraphrase using *without* plus an *any*-form, e.g. *without any borrowings*. Here the negative element is incorporated in the preposition.

## 3.8.4.2 Relative frequency of *not*-negation v. *no*-negation

There are great differences in the relative use of *not*-negation v. *no*-negation.

### CORPUS FINDINGS [7]

➤ In the written registers, about three out of ten negative forms are of the *no*-type; the corresponding figure for conversation is only about one in ten.

**Table 3.11 Proportional distribution of *not*-negation v. *no*-negation**

each ● represents 5% of the occurrences of negation

| | *not*-negation | *no*-negation |
|---|---|---|
| CONV | ● ● ● ● ● ● ● ● ● ● ● ● ● ● ● ● ● ● | ● ● |
| FICT | ● ● ● ● ● ● ● ● ● ● ● ● ● ● ● | ● ● ● ● ● |
| NEWS | ● ● ● ● ● ● ● ● ● ● ● ● ● | ● ● ● ● ● ● ● |
| ACAD | ● ● ● ● ● ● ● ● ● ● ● ● ● ● ● | ● ● ● ● ● |

### DISCUSSION OF FINDINGS

Although there is some register variation, it is quite clear that *no*-negation is the minority choice overall. We can thus regard *not*-negation as the default choice. Apart from the overall difference, we also find great differences in the use of individual *no*-forms. Notably, *no one, none, neither,* and *nor* are relatively infrequent in conversation.

It is striking that fiction and conversation, which are the registers with the highest number of negative forms overall, are quite different as regards the frequency of *no*-forms. All the forms are very frequent in the fiction texts, while only a few of the *no*-forms are more common in conversation than in the corpus as a whole (and, with the exception of *never*, the difference is slight). How do we account for the difference? One factor is perhaps that *no*-negation is historically the older form. It seems reasonable that older forms should be better preserved in writing than in conversation, which is at the forefront of linguistic change.

We now look more closely at factors related to the choice between the two types of negation.

## 3.8.4.3 Choice of *no*-negation v. *not*-negation

### A Syntax

In some positions *no*-negation is the only possible choice, notably where a *no*-form precedes the verb phrase (3.8.4.1). In addition, the use of *no*-negation v. *not*-negation varies somewhat with the type of clause.

Table 3.12 **Distribution of *not*-negation v. *no*-negation by clause type**

each ● represents 5% of the occurrences of negation

| clause type | *not*-negation | *no*-negation |
|---|---|---|
| independent declarative | ● ● ● ● ● ● ● ● ● ● ● ● ● ● ● ● | ● ● ● ● |
| imperative | ● ● ● ● ● ● ● ● ● ● ● ● ● ● ● ● ● ● | ● ● |
| interrogative | ● ● ● ● ● ● ● ● ● ● ● ● ● ● ● ● ● ● ● | ● |
| embedded | ● ● ● ● ● ● ● ● ● ● ● ● ● ● | ● ● ● ● ● ● |

**CORPUS FINDINGS [7]**

➤ *No*-negation is proportionally more common in embedded clauses and, to a lesser extent, in independent declarative clauses.

**DISCUSSION OF FINDINGS**

These differences are probably mainly a reflection of the distribution of clause types in the registers, as embedded clauses are more common in the written registers (where *no*-negation is more favoured), and imperative and interrogative clauses are far more frequent in conversation (where *no*-negation is infrequent overall).

### B Verb

**CORPUS FINDINGS [7]**

➤ There is some variation in the use of *not*-negation v. *no*-negation depending upon the choice of operator (Table 3.13).

➤ The distribution of the two negation types varies a great deal depending upon the lexical verb (Table 3.14):

   ➤ *No*-negation is extremely common with existential *be* and also more common with lexical *have* than with other lexical verbs.

Table 3.13 **Distribution of *not*-negation v. *no*-negation by operator**

BE = all forms of *be*   HAVE = all forms of *have*

each • represents 5% of the occurrences of negation

| operator | *not*-negation | *no*-negation |
|---|---|---|
| BE | •••••••••••••••••• | •• |
| HAVE | •••••••••••••• | ••••••• |
| Modal | ••••••••••••••••• | •••• |
| DO/None | •••••••••••••• | ••••• |

Table 3.14 **Distribution of *not*-negation v. *no*-negation by main verb**

BE = all forms of *be*   HAVE = all forms of *have*

each • represents 5% of the occurrences of negation

| main verb | *not*-negation | *no*-negation |
|---|---|---|
| existential *there* BE | • | •••••••••• •••••••••• |
| copula BE | •••••••••••••••••• | •••• |
| HAVE | •••••••••••••• | •••••••• |
| other lexical verb | •••••••••••••••••• | •••• |

### DISCUSSION OF FINDINGS

The sharp difference in use between existential *be* and copular *be* simply reflects the fact that the former is characteristically followed by an indefinite noun phrase which can incorporate the negative element:

> **There's no** *doubt about that.* (CONV)

> *But* **there was no** *laughter.* (FICT)

The high frequency of *no*-negation with lexical *have* is discussed further in 3.8.2.1 above, which focuses on contexts where there is potential variation between the two negation patterns. If we turn to copular *be* in contexts where there is potential variation between the two negation patterns, we find that *no*-negation is used in approximately 70–80 per cent of the examples in all the registers. In other words, *no*-negation is very frequent indeed with both *have* and *be*.

## C   Collocations

A study of the examples of *no*-negation with *be* and *have* reveals that there are a great many frequent word combinations.

### CORPUS FINDINGS [1]

➤ The most common collocations with *be* and *have* are:
  ➤ Existential *there* + *be* + \_\_\_\_
     Occurring c. twice per million words:
     *no chance, no evidence, no reason*

Occurring c. five times per million words:

*no doubt, no need, no point, no sign, no way*

➤ *have +* _____

Occurring from two to five times per million words:

*no choice, no desire, no effect, no intention, no reason*

Occurring c. ten times per million words:

*no idea.*

➤ Recurrent combinations of this kind are far less conspicuous with *not*-negation, but see also 3.8.4.4.

**DISCUSSION OF FINDINGS**

As already pointed out, *no*-negation, which is historically the older form, is much more common in the written registers than in the conversation texts. It is significant that when *no*-negation does occur in conversation, it commonly occurs with frequent verbs or specific collocations. The evidence indicates that speech overwhelmingly prefers *not*-negation; but that the older type is preserved particularly with elements which may be stored and processed as chunks rather than as combinations of independent units.

## 3.8.4.4 *Not*-negation collocations

We have already seen that in many ways *not*-negation is the default choice in any case. However, we further find that, although collocations appear to be more marked with *no*-negation than with *not*-negation, there are also words which co-occur with *not* far more frequently than would be predicted by chance.

Tables 3.15–17 give lists of forms which characteristically precede or follow *not* (both the full and the contracted form), as measured by the mutual information index (see 1.7). Note that the measures apply to individual word forms, not lexemes, considering only the immediately preceding and following word forms. To be included in the tables, the minimum number of co-occurrences was set to 20.

Table 3.15 **Word forms preceding *not* (*not* or *n't*), grouped by the measure of mutual information**

| mutual information | operators | adverbs | other |
|---|---|---|---|
| 50– | *do, does, did* | | |
| 20–25 | *can, could, 'm* | | |
| 15–19 | *should, will/won't, would, 're, dare* | | |
| 10–14 | *shall/shan't, am* | *certainly* | |
| 5–9 | *is, are, was, were, has, have, had, may, might, need* | | *why, decided* |
| 2–4 | *must, 's* | *maybe, probably, perhaps, of course, still, therefore* | *but, or, better, though, although* |

**Table 3.16** **Word forms following *not* (*not* or *n't*), grouped by the measure of mutual information**

| mutual information | adjectives | adverbs | lexical verbs |
|---|---|---|---|
| 70 – | | *necessarily* | *bother* |
| 50 – 69 | | | *exceed* |
| 40 – 49 | | | *intend, realize, worry* |
| 30 – 39 | *surprising* | | *afford, belong, bothered, dare, know, seem* |
| 20 – 29 | | | *affect, believe, blame, care, exist, forget, knowing, realize, recognize, remember, understand, want* |
| 15 – 19 | *fit, interested, sure* | *even, really, yet* | *appear, depend, eat, expect, hurt, imagine, involve, matter, mention, mind, notice, speak, think, touch* |
| 10 – 14 | *easy, fair, worth* | *exactly, fully, merely, possibly, quite* | *agree, allowed, apply, ask, bear, contain, cry, count, feel, get, going, hear, help, kill, need, occur, require, stand, stop, supposed, tell, wait, wake, wish* |

**Table 3.17** **Word forms following *n't*, grouped by the measure of mutual information**

| mutual information | word forms |
|---|---|
| 100 – | *bother* |
| 80 – 99 | *worry* |
| 60 – 79 | *realize, afford* |
| 40 – 59 | *know, want, seem, deserve* |
| 33 – 39 | *blame, forget, belong, remember, think* |

**CORPUS FINDINGS [2]**

➤ The operators and some adverbs used as stance adverbials or linking adverbials commonly co-occur with a following *not*.

➤ There is a wider range of forms which commonly co-occur with a preceding *not*, chiefly mental verbs.

➤ The association with mental verbs is especially strong with contracted *n't*.

**DISCUSSION OF FINDINGS**

Among forms which characteristically precede *not*, the operators are the most conspicuous. This is not surprising, as an operator is required in finite clauses with *not*-negation. It is nevertheless worth noting how closely related forms tend to cluster. *Do*-forms are naturally at the top, as they do not form an independent choice but are obligatorily inserted if there is no other operator (3.2.9).

In the position following *not* we find a far greater number of forms with a high co-occurrence score, chiefly lexical verbs, as is to be expected. There is a preponderance of mental verbs, and this is even more striking if the comparison is restricted to forms following contracted *n't* (as in Table 3.17), which for the most part represent the patterns of co-occurrence in conversation. The co-occurrence of negation and mental verbs appears to be an important factor contributing to the very high frequency of negative forms in spoken discourse.

## 3.8.5 The scope of negation

The **scope** of negation is that part of a clause that is affected by the negative form. The scope may be restricted to a single word or phrase. Examples of such **local negation** are:

1 *You've abducted a **not unknown** holder of government office, a member of the House of Representatives.* (FICT)
2 *One rabbit can finish off a few hundred young trees **in no time**.* (FICT)
3 ***Not surprisingly**, two GOP Assembly incumbents were defeated for re-election in California that November.* (NEWS†)
4 *Robertson, **not unexpectedly**, claimed afterwards that his strike should have been recognised.* (NEWS)
5 ***Not infrequently** two or more adjacent cells may become confluent owing to the atrophy of the vein or veins separating them.* (ACAD)

In **1** the negative effect is located within a noun phrase. In the other examples, it is limited to time adverbials or stance adverbials. In all these cases, there is no doubt that the propositions expressed in the clause as a whole are positive.

A special type of local negation is found with *nowhere* and *nobody*:

6 *It's in the middle of **nowhere**, isn't it?* (CONV†)
7 *Cats appear from **nowhere**.* (FICT†)
8 *"You murdered Schopee, and he's not **a nobody**." – "Nobody's a **nobody**."* (FICT)

*Nowhere* in **6** and **7** means 'an unknown or little known place' and cannot be paraphrased by *not … anywhere*. In **8** *nobody* is used as a noun meaning 'a person of no importance' (note the indefinite article) and does not allow a paraphrase with *not … anybody*. This use freely combines with other negative forms.

With **clausal negation**, the entire proposition is denied or rejected, and the negative scope extends from the negative form until the end of the clause. Placement of the adverbial before or after *not* may correlate with a difference in meaning:

9 *"Our investigations indicate that this substance was **not deliberately** administered."* (FICT)
10 *Alexander looked at Wilkie who **deliberately did not** see him.* (FICT)
11 ***Don't just** see the world, see how it works, do some work yourself.* (NEWS)
12 *You're not being serious. I **just can't** believe you.* (FICT)

Thus, in **9** and **11** the adverbial is inside the scope of negation, while in **10** and **12** the adverbial is outside the scope of negation.

## 3.8.6   Assertive and non-assertive forms

There are forms which are restricted to either **assertive** or **non-assertive** contexts. The most important are:

|  | assertive | non-assertive |
|---|---|---|
| **adverbs** | already | yet |
|  | sometimes | ever |
|  | somewhat | at all |
|  | somewhere | anywhere |
|  | still | any more |
|  | too | either |
| **determiners/pronouns** | some | any |
|  | somebody | anybody |
|  | someone | anyone |
|  | something | anything |

Non-assertive forms are used in negative clauses following the negative form (including subordinate clauses, as in examples **4–6**):

    1   *There **aren't any** crisps.* (CONV)

    2   *"But he **doesn't** have to do **anything** at all," she had said slowly.* (FICT)

    3   *I **won't** belong to **anything, ever** again.* (FICT)

    4   *I **don't** think [we had **any** cheese] did we?* (CONV)

    5   *I **don't** suppose [it's there **any** more].* (CONV)

    6   *I **haven't** noticed [I've lost **any** weight].* (CONV†)

Although non-assertive forms are particularly associated with negation, their use extends far beyond clauses with *not*-negation and *no*-negation:

Interrogative clauses:

    7   *Does **anyone ever** ring the bell Carrie?* (CONV)

    8   *Do you need **any** more, **anybody**?* (CONV)

    9   *Wonder if Tamsin had **any** luck selling her house.* (CONV)

Conditional clauses:

    10   *If they **haven't** got **any** scampi get an extra fishcake and an extra spring roll.* (CONV)

    11   *If there are **any** problems in performance-related pay, we can iron these out.* (NEWS)

Temporal clauses introduced by *before*:

    12   *I was with him before **anyone** else was.* (FICT)

    13   *He opened his mouth but before he could get **any** words out, Matthew said, "I don't want to sell my share either."* (FICT)

After implicitly negative verbs (**14, 15**), adjectives **16**, adverbs **17**, and the preposition *without* (**18, 19**):

    14   *After being charged, McIntyre had [denied] being a member of **any** party* (NEWS)

    15   *Most scientists, however, [refuse] to pay **any** heed or give **any** credence to Psychical Research.* (ACAD†)

16 *On the first occasion Mr Reynolds met the stoma care nurse he was very quiet and seemed [reluctant] to discuss **anything**.* (ACAD)

17 *But I very [rarely] fry **anything** anyway.* (CONV)

18 *Ten minutes had gone by [without] **anybody**'s coming to see if they were hit or not, to finish them off.* (FICT)

19 *Jane requires you to guess at and check a set of mathematical functions [without] **ever** giving you the answers.* (ACAD)

In certain constructions expressing comparison (**20–22**) and degree (**23, 24**):

20 *The company can mend its ways and make cars as reliable as **any** of its competitors'.* (NEWS)

21 *I can trust you, Babes, more than **anybody**.* (FICT)

22 *This area produces more aquarium plants than **any** other area.* (ACAD†)

23 *I'm too old for **any** of that.* (CONV)

24 *At this level, eight games are too few to allow **any** margin for error.* (NEWS†)

Assertive forms are used in a clause before the negative form (**25–27**):

25 *For **some** reason it did not surprise him.* (FICT†)

26 *They are kind of fun to hear. **Some** of them I haven't heard since I was his age.* (FICT)

27 *The particles of **some** solids do not possess sufficient order to define a regular crystalline structure.* (ACAD)

Assertive forms may also occur after the negative form, in which case they are outside the scope of negation (**28–30**):

28 *I don't mind talking, not to **some** people.* (CONV)

29 *Underwriter Salomon Brothers Inc. indicated it couldn't find sufficient buyers for **some** of the bonds.* (NEWS)

30 *They don't come here any more, for **some** reason or other.* (FICT†)

Assertive forms commonly occur in interrogative clauses which function as requests or offers, as well as in negative interrogative clauses:

31 *Could I have **some** cheese and onion please?* (CONV)

32 *Would you like **some** juice or anything?* (CONV)

33 *Didn't I have **some** bloody funny hands?* (CONV) <speaking of playing cards>

The use of the assertive forms in **31** and **32** reflects the fact that it is polite to assume that the request or offer will be accepted. In negative interrogative clauses, as in **33**, there is often an underlying positive assumption; cf. *I had some bloody funny hands didn't I?* Contrast these examples with the interrogative clauses in **7** to **9** above, where there is no positive bias of this kind. See also 14.4.2.2.

## 3.8.7  Multiple negation

Sometimes two or more negative forms co-occur in the same clause. There are two basically different types of **multiple negation**, one—**dependent**—in which the negative forms co-occur in the same clause to express a single negative meaning (3.8.7.1), and one in which the negative forms have **independent** negative force (3.8.7.2).

### 3.8.7.1 Dependent multiple negation

Two or more negative forms may co-occur within the same clause to express a single negative meaning. This represents a very old pattern which is found in casual speech, although it is socially stigmatized:

> You've **never** seen **nothing** like it. (CONV)
> cf. You've never seen anything like it.
>
> I told her **not** to say **nothing** to **nobody**. (CONV†)
> cf. ... not to say anything to anybody.
>
> Besides, I **never** said **nothing** about fishing. (FICT)
> cf. I never said anything about fishing.
>
> There **ain't nothing** we can do. (FICT)
> cf. There isn't anything we can do.
>
> There **ain't no** elm trees on the North Moors. (FICT†)
> cf. There aren't any elm trees ...

In examples such as these, negative forms are used where non-assertive forms would occur in writing and careful speech.

Because of the repetition of the negative forms, this type of negation appears to have a strengthening effect. This is no doubt true of:

> And now they just don't know what to do, there's no jobs, there's **no nothing**. (CONV)
>
> But without that heater they've no hot water, **no nothing**! (CONV)

Here *no nothing* equals *not anything*.

Multiple negation of this kind is relatively rare and is generally restricted to conversation and fictional dialogue. Interestingly this distribution does not fit the picture seen earlier for *no*-negation. As with *no*-negation, this type of multiple negation is very old, so it ought to be better represented in the written registers. This is apparently a case where prescriptive traditions have been particularly influential, resulting in the present-day distribution of this form.

A special type of dependent multiple negation, which is not of the stigmatized kind, is found with repetition of *not*:

> 1 A: *Did Jill say what time Caroline's appointment was?*
>   B: *No. Er – **not** to me she did**n't**.* (CONV)
>
> 2 A: *The fact you get the films or – recent films.*
>   B: ***Not** all of them they're **not**.* (CONV)
>
> 3 *"Can I speak to Peter Holmes?"—"**Not** here, you can't."* (FICT)

These examples exploit the two most prominent positions in the clause, i.e. the beginning and the end. One element (usually an adverbial) is fronted for emphasis, and the preceding *not* makes it clear that it is included within the scope of negation while at the same time strengthening the negation. A less emphatic form would be (cf. **1**): *She didn't, not to me*; this would be a case of independent multiple negation.

### 3.8.7.2 Independent multiple negation

Negative forms may naturally co-occur in cases of repetition or reformulation (see also the examples of repeated *no*-negation at the end of 3.8.3). In these cases, the negative forms are not integrated within the same clause:

> *Won't eat any veggies you know, **none**.* (CONV)

> ***No, not** tomorrow, she said.* (FICT)

> *Rising, working, there is **no** reason any more, **no** reason for anything, **no** reason why not, **nothing** to breathe but a sour gas bottled in empty churches, **nothing** to rise by.* (FICT†)

> *There's **no one** to blame **not** really.* (FICT†)

In these examples, the negative forms are independent, since none of them can be replaced by non-assertive forms (without also adding *not*).

Repeated occurrences of *not* within the same clause, each with its own negative force, are also found. Here two negatives can make a positive meaning:

> *Oh well you sleep on sherry though – it makes you sleepy, you **can't not** sleep.* (CONV) <meaning that you just have to sleep>

> *Of the many directives gummed to the glass partition, one took the trouble to thank me for not smoking. I hate that. I mean, it's a bit previous, isn't it, don't you think? I have**n't not** smoked yet.*
> *As it did turn out, I **never** did **not** smoke in the end. I lit a cigarette and kept them coming. The frizzy-rugged beaner at the wheel shouted something and threw himself around for a while, but I kept on **not not** smoking quietly in the back, and nothing happened.* (FICT)

Other cases of independent multiple negation are illustrated in:

> 1  A: *Well at a price yeah. I mean – they do**n't** do **nothing** for **nothing**.*
>    B: *No of course not. They're are out to get money, aren't they?* (CONV)

> 2  ***Not** a house in the country ai**n't** packed to its rafters.* (FICT†)

> 3  *It was **not** for **nothing** that he was chosen as Mr Squeaky Clean after the sexual and financial aberrations of his two predecessors.* (NEWS)

> 4  ***Do we not** in fact have **no** decent idea of a set of things if we have no settled rule as to counting them, whether or not we are able to act effectively on the rule?* (ACAD)

While dependent multiple negation is characteristic of, and virtually restricted to, conversation (and dialogue in fiction), independent multiple negation is a complex choice which requires deliberate planning. It is not stigmatized and is found particularly in writing. We do, however, also find colloquial examples. In **2** the two negatives cancel each other, and the result is a positive statement 'Every house in the country is packed to its rafters.' Example **1** is of particular interest in that it illustrates how dependent and independent multiple negation may combine. The first occurrence of *nothing* corresponds to a non-assertive form, the second carries independent negative force. The meaning is presumably 'They don't do anything for nothing.'

## 3.9    Subject-verb concord

The subject and the verb phrase agree in number and person, as shown in Table 3.18. With the exception of the verb *be*, this subject-verb **concord** is limited to the present tense. The basic grammatical rule is that the *s*-form of lexical verbs and the primary auxiliaries (2.3.2) is used with a third person singular subject in the present tense indicative.

**Table 3.18    Subject-verb concord**

| present tense | | | | past tense |
| --- | --- | --- | --- | --- |
| lexical verb | DO | HAVE | BE | BE |
| I walk | do | have | am | was |
| you walk | do | have | are | were |
| he/she/it walks | does | has | is | was |
| we/you/they walk | do | have | are | were |

There is no subject-verb concord with the modal auxiliaries (which lack *s*-forms; 2.4.4), verb forms in non-finite clauses (which are not marked for tense; 3.12), or imperative clauses (3.13.4). Similarly, subjunctive forms, which are possible in certain finite dependent clauses, do not show subject-verb concord:

1 *I told her she could stay with me until she found a place, but she insisted that she **pay** her own way.* (FICT)

2 *The way in which we work, whether it **be** in an office or on the factory floor, has undergone a major transformation in the past decade.* (NEWS)

3 *My head felt as if it **were** split open.* (FICT†)

The base form of the verb is used in the present subjunctive (as in **1** and **2**), and the form *were* in the past subjunctive (as in **3**).

In practice, concord patterns are not always straightforward. There are complications connected with the form of the subject (3.9.1), the meaning of the subject (3.9.2), and the distance between the head of the subject noun phrase and the verb phrase (3.9.3). Moreover, there is a great deal of social and dialectal variation in concord patterns (3.9.4).

### 3.9.1    Complications with concord patterns

Sometimes the number of the subject may be in doubt, either because it is not clearly marked or because the number of the subject noun phrase is variable. Some pronouns combine either with singular or plural verb forms, e.g. the *wh*-words *who/which* and the forms *former/latter* when used pronominally. Concord is then dependent upon whether reference is made to one or more entities.

Concord patterns with *which*:

*He is beside a rock face which **is** like the loose side of a gigantic mule.* (FICT†)

*These are the moments which **are** calculable, and cannot be assessed in words.* (FICT†)

Concord patterns with *former/latter*:

> There are still professional watermen in the Tideway and still Phelpses on the river, but the former **are** a dying breed and the latter **are** amateur competitors. (NEWS)

> Its signal should prompt the operator to switch off the hexamine supply and to discharge the contents of the reactor into the emergency tank. The latter **is** filled with water. (ACAD)

See also concord patterns with quantifying expressions in subject position; 3.9.1.4.

Overall, where the subject is not a pronoun or a noun-headed phrase, the tendency is to use singular verb forms, e.g. with clausal subjects (3.9.1.6). Note also the tendency towards singular concord with existential *there* (3.9.1.5). In general, we may say that singular concord is used unless there are clear reasons for using the plural.

### 3.9.1.1 Concord with plural forms not ending in *-s*

Apparent exceptions to the concord rule are countable nouns lacking an overt plural inflection (*sheep, people, series*, etc.; cf. 4.5.4). Compare:

> The [sheep] **is** infected by ingesting the mollusc. (ACAD†)
> In its grassy centre the dark-wooled [sheep] **were** grazing. (FICT†)
> "The [series] **is** based around a failed football star." (NEWS†)
> The faunal and stratigraphic [series] **have** have the same order. (ACAD†)

See also the plural concord with the nouns *people* and *police*; 4.5.5C.

Some foreign plurals (cf. 4.5.3) are variously treated as singular or plural, however.

With *data*, singular and plural concord are about equally common; with *media*, plural concord is the majority choice:

> The [data] **is** a red flag, but lacking the financial data you can't make a case that discrimination is widespread. (NEWS)
> Conventionally this [data] **has** only been available from a separate source/data base. (ACAD)
> These [data] **are** valuable when planning monitoring programmes. (ACAD†)
> To anyone in Western Europe or the USA, what the [media] alarmingly **describes** as a "tidal wave" looks like a tiny splash. (NEWS)
> The [media], all too often criticized for helping to spread inaccurate news, **are** constantly faced with the risk that the information they collect may be less than reliable. (NEWS)

*Criteria* (with the odd exception) and *phenomena* are regularly used with plural concord. They stand out from the nouns considered above in having a singular form (*criterion* and *phenomenon*) which differs in meaning from their plural counterparts in a regular manner.

### 3.9.1.2 Concord with singular forms ending in *-s*

Another apparent exception to the concord rule is found with nouns ending in *-s* which behave like singular forms (*billiards, darts, measles*, etc.; cf. 4.5.5E). Invariable nouns ending in *-ics* are variously treated as singular or plural:

> *Reagan, who claimed that air pollution is caused by trees, is the man you should be quoting to back up your position that [economics] **is** more important than the Earth.* (NEWS)
>
> *"With costs being significantly less than they were several years ago, the [economics] **are** pretty good," says George Kadane, head of the company.* (NEWS)
>
> *You are at ease in USA and yet your [ethics] **are** rooted in Indian tradition.* (FICT)
>
> *In particular, the professional [ethics] **arises** from the requirement that analysis be unbiased.* (ACAD†)
>
> *The [mathematics] **are** quite complex. Clinton needs 2,145 delegates to win outright <...>* (NEWS†)
>
> *The Cockcroft Report pointed out that traditionally [mathematics] in school **has** rarely been about anything. [Mathematics] which **challenges** pupils <...> is more likely to involve practical, oral and mental activities than writing.* (ACAD†)
>
> *[Politics] **wishes** to change reality, it **requires** power, and thus it **is** primarily in the service of power.* (NEWS)
>
> *The oppositionist [politics] of the 1970s and early 1980s **are** over.* (NEWS)

Where plural concord is found, the meaning tends to be different from the sense of 'discipline, field of study', which is characteristic of *-ics* nouns. Note the tendency of examples of plural concord to contain a definite article or a possessive pronoun (*the economics, your ethics,* etc.) and refer to specific instances of economic facts, ethical views etc.

Some other *-ics* nouns are attested in the LSWE Corpus only with plural concord:

> *The [acoustics] at the Anglican Cathedral **have** often given rise to speculation about its suitability for Philharmonic concerts.* (NEWS)
>
> *Detailed [statistics] **are** not available for the inner city itself.* (NEWS†)
>
> *His [tactics] **have** been ridiculed, principally on grounds of inflexibility.* (NEWS)

*Statistics* and *tactics* have corresponding singular forms (e.g. *a startling statistic, a delaying tactic*), and they therefore behave in the same way as regular nouns such as *eccentric-eccentrics, epileptic-epileptics. Statistics* can, however, also be used with singular concord to refer to an academic discipline, like the invariable noun *acoustics.*

### 3.9.1.3  Concord with coordinated subjects

Subjects realized by noun phrases coordinated by *and* take plural concord:

> *[Peters and Waterman] **state** that an effective leader must be the master of two ends of the spectrum.* (ACAD†)
>
> *[Tolerance and openness] **have** been made excuses for much which is in fact lubricious (and usually commercial) exploitation of them.* (ACAD)

There are occasional exceptions to the general rule:

> 1  *Although [the room and the whole house] **was** full of really good stuff made or renovated by Dadda, secretly he valued nothing more than this bust.* (FICT)
>
> 2  *[This bomber and its cargo] probably **weighs** over a hundred tons.* (FICT)

3 *In addition, [lack of good, affordable pre-school and out-of-school childcare, and responsibility for the care of elderly relatives and household chores]* **means** *that part-time work seems the only practical option.* (NEWS)

4 *[The very large number of neurons (around a million in the brain of Apis according to Witthoft, 1967), and the multiplicity of possible connections among them]* **means** *that the nervous pathways between and within the ganglia are extremely complicated.* (ACAD)

Where singular concord is found, the reference is usually to something which can be viewed as a single entity or concept. In **1** the room is part of the house. In **2** something is predicated of two entities viewed as a unit. The circumstances referred to in the subject noun phrases in **3** and **4** are collectively said to have particular consequences. It is significant that both examples contain the verb *mean*; an equivalence is set up between the coordinated noun phrases and the following *that*-clause.

Subject noun phrases coordinated by *or* generally take singular concord if the coordinated noun phrases are singular:

*[Welch, or his son, or Johns]* **was** *about to take a bath.* (FICT)

*Check that [no food or drink]* **has** *been consumed.* (ACAD)

However, examples with plural concord also occur occasionally:

*I'll wait until [my sister or mother]* **come** *down, and I'll eat with them.* (FICT)

Where one of the noun phrases coordinated by *or* is plural, plural concord is the rule:

*In fact, it is likely to prove "immeasurably worse" than [either Conservatives or Labour]* **have** *realised.* (NEWS)

*Whether [interest rates or intervention]* **were** *the chosen instrument, and in what combination, was probably a secondary question.* (NEWS)

Plural concord is also regular where both of the noun phrases coordinated by *or* are plural.

Coordination with *neither-nor* produces singular concord where both the coordinated noun phrases are singular, and plural concord where both are plural (that is, the pattern is the same as with *or*):

*[Neither geologic evidence nor physical theory]* **supports** *this conclusion.* (ACAD)

*But [neither the pilots nor the machinists]* **appear** *interested.* (NEWS)

As with *or*, we find occasional examples of plural concord with coordinated noun phrases in the singular:

*[Neither Hugh Dundas, his wife (who is my sister), nor their American partner Don Tafner]* **were** *at all keen to run in the first place.* (NEWS)

In the few instances where one of the coordinated noun phrases is plural and the other singular we find plural concord (again, the same pattern as with *or*):

*[Neither Lorillard nor the researchers who studied the workers]* **were** *aware of any research on smokers of the Kent cigarettes.* (ACAD)

Coordination of different grammatical persons is straightforward with *and*: a plural verb form is used (in agreement with the general rule). Where *or, either-or,* and *neither-nor* coordinate different grammatical persons, the verb tends to agree with the closest noun phrase:

> *Not one leaf is to go out of the garden until [either I or my chief taster]* **gives** *the order.* (FICT)

> *In many years of service [neither Phillips nor I]* **have** *seen anything like it.* (FICT)

The pattern here is in agreement with the principle of proximity (3.9.3).

### 3.9.1.4  Concord with indefinite pronouns and quantifying expressions

The indefinite pronouns *anybody/anyone, everybody/everyone, nobody/no one,* and *somebody/someone* combine with singular verb forms, even though co-referent pronouns and determiners may be plural forms (see also 3.9.5):

> *[Somebody]'s got an eyeball in* **their** *food.* (CONV)

> *[Everybody]'s doing what* **they** *think* **they**'re *supposed to do.* (FICT)

> *[Nobody]* **has their** *fridges repaired any more,* **they** *can't afford it.* (FICT)

Quantifiers followed by uncountable nouns or singular pronouns take singular concord. This pattern is found not only when the quantifier precedes the noun immediately, but also when there is an intervening *of* and when the noun must be supplied from the context (and the determiner thus functions pronominally):

> *[Some] of it* **is** *genuine, some of it all a smoke-screen.* (NEWS)

> *For Ghofar's owners, [most] of the "motivation"* **has** *come from the horse's trainer David Elsworth.* (NEWS)

> *[A lot] of hacking* **goes** *on inside companies by employees trying to find easier ways of doing their jobs.* (NEWS)

The most important quantifiers which pattern in this way are: *all, any, none, some, little/less/least, much/more/most, a great deal, a little, a lot, lots, plenty.*

Concord patterns vary with quantifiers followed by *of* and a plural countable noun or pronoun. Plural concord is the rule with *all, some, few/fewer/fewest, many/more/most, a few, a great many, a lot, lots, plenty, both* (and numerals except *one*):

> *You know [lots] of other people in big business* **have** *given money.* (CONV)

> *[Most] of the copies* **are** *seized in raids.* (NEWS)

Singular concord is the rule with *each* and the numeral *one,* but both singular and plural forms are found with *either* and *neither*:

> *He has talked to the press far more than [either] of us* **believes** *is appropriate.* (FICT†)

> *I don't give a damn what [either] of you whores* **think** *of me.* (FICT)

> *[Neither] of these words* **is** *much help.* (FICT)

> *[Neither] of us* **believe** *in useless symbols.* (FICT)

Concord patterns also vary with *any* and *none,* which combine with both singular and plural verb forms. Usage is fairly evenly divided between singular and plural concord with *none of*:

> *[None] of us* **has** *been aboard except Vinck.* (FICT)

> *[None] of us really* **believe** *it's ever going to happen not to us, she said at last.* (FICT)

However, *none* alone shows a distinct preference for singular concord:

> [None] **describes** *him/herself as such in the party's official literature.* (NEWS)

Plural concord is the norm in conversation, while in the written registers there is an overall preference for singular concord.

Similar patterns are found for expressions containing nouns which specify a quantity or an amount with respect to a following noun (such as *per cent, a third, two thirds, a/the majority, the bulk, the rest*). As with quantifiers, singular concord is used with reference to uncountable nouns and singular pronouns, while plural concord is used with reference to plural nouns and pronouns:

> *As to foreign trade in Eastern Europe,* [two thirds] *of it* **is** *within the Comecon area.* (NEWS)
>
> [Half] *the group's sales* **are** *now outside Britain. About* [a third] *of products* **are** *manufactured overseas.* (NEWS)
>
> [The bulk] *of the proceeds* **are** *to be used to cut its borrowings.* (NEWS)
> [The bulk] *of the crop* **is** *dried.* (ACAD†)
>
> [The rest] *of it* **is** *no secret.* (FICT)
>
> *"Are you running a motel or what?"* [The rest] *of the aliens* **look** *at me,* **look** *at each other,* **look** *down at their food.* (FICT)

Plural verb forms are regularly found with *a number of* and *a bunch of* + plural nouns:

> *So what if* [a bunch of] *men* **talk** *in loud voices and drink the night?* (FICT)
>
> [A number of] *Arab countries* **have** *condemned the UN resolution.* (NEWS†)

Plural verb forms are also sometimes found with *a group of* and *a series of* + plural noun:

> *Under a nearby tree,* [a group of] *children* **were** *having their school lunch.* (NEWS†)
>
> [A series of] *profit downgradings* **were** *shrugged off.* (NEWS)

However, where the message focus is on the unit rather than on the individuals (as with *the number*), we regularly find singular verb forms:

> [The number] *of instances* **was** *surprisingly large.* (FICT)
>
> [The second group] *of books* **is** *those written by botanists.* (ACAD†)

The same type of distinction is found with collective nouns (3.9.2.3). But whereas the plural is the more frequent option with quantifying nouns, it is a far less frequent choice with collective nouns. There is, however, no hard and fast borderline between the two groups.

Plural concord is predominant with expressions of the type *one in / out of* + numeral, though singular verb forms are also found:

> [One in] *five* **were** *scared of other prisoners.* (NEWS)
>
> [One in] *five pairs of socks sold in Britain* **is** *made by Sherwood.* (NEWS†)

In these expressions the reference is to a group. Singular concord is presumably sometimes chosen because of the strong pull of *one* in the direction of the singular (cf. the *one of* constructions taken up in 3.9.3).

### 3.9.1.5  Concord with existential *there*

While singular concord is the rule with the dummy subject *it* (3.2.1.2), the verb phrase combining with existential *there* takes its number from the **notional**

**subject** (cf. 3.9.2). A plural form is generally used with plural noun phrases; a singular form otherwise:

> *[There]* **is** *virtually no place on Earth that is not moving vertically and horizontally, however slowly.* (ACAD)

> *[There]* **was** *candlelight, and [there]* **were** *bunks with quilts heaped on top.* (FICT)

This pattern is regularly found in written English.

In conversation, however, we frequently find a singular form of *be* followed by plural noun phrases. The verb is regularly contracted and attached to the preceding *there*:

> **There's** *so many police forces that don't even have computers yet so they can't link in with stuff.* (CONV)

> *Gary,* **there's** *apples if you want one.* (CONV)

In fact, such examples are somewhat more common in conversation than the standard constructions with plural verb plus plural noun phrase.

Preferences in conversation differ depending upon the tense form of the verb. In particular, singular past-tense verb forms are more rarely followed by plural noun phrases:

> *Well if he would have come down here that night, or that day – when [there]* **was** *three cars in – in the drive –* (CONV)

There is a simple explanation for the special behaviour of *there's*: because of the contraction, *there's* tends to behave as a single invariable unit for the purposes of speech processing. The connection is far less close with *there was*, which is not reduced to a single syllable in speech and is not contracted in writing.

The special behaviour of *there's* is matched by a similar tendency for *here's*, *where's*, and *how's*:

> **Here's** *your shoes.* (CONV)

> *Oh* **here's** *some better prices.* (CONV)

> **Where's** *your tapes?* (CONV)

> **Where's** *the Ingeles now, Father?* (FICT)

> **How's** *mum and dad?* (CONV†)

> *A:* **How's** *things?*
> *B: Not too bad.* (CONV)

Such forms are limited to conversation (and the occasional example in fictional dialogue).

A singular form of *be* is often followed by coordinated noun phrases in the written registers:

> *[There]* **was** *a huge cake in the dining room, and a band playing outside.* (FICT)

> *When he left an hour later [there]* **was** *no shrug and not much of a smile.* (NEWS)

Where a singular noun phrase follows immediately after *be*, singular concord is the more frequent choice in both speech and writing. This is no doubt a proximity effect (cf. 3.9.3).

**3.9.1.6    Concord with clausal subjects**

Singular concord is the regular pattern when the subject is a finite or non-finite clause:

> *Many times he had told her that [carrying cases, boxes, parcels, or packages]* **was** *a task only for servants.* (FICT)
>
> *[To accept a US mediation plan]* **means** *that an Israeli-Palestinian meeting is now likely in the New Year.* (NEWS)

This behaviour with respect to subject-verb concord is matched by the use of singular pronouns co-referent with clauses: *It was a task ...,* **This** *means that ....*

Nominal relative clauses (3.11.1) stand out from other clausal subjects. Here we find plural as well as singular concord:

Singular concord:

> *[What we have just described]* **is** *the general pattern of the internal heat engine's work output as we can see it today.* (ACAD)
>
> *I think [what we do know]* **is** *this.* (NEWS)

Plural concord:

> *Television captures brilliantly the beauty, colour and class of Augusta. [What it does not convey]* **are** *the undulations <...>* (NEWS†)
>
> *[What is needed]* **are** *effective regulators.* (NEWS)

In these cases, the number of the verb is influenced by the number of the following subject predicative.

**3.9.2    Notional concord**

The choice of verb form may be determined by the meaning rather than the form of the subject. Consider:

> *King prawns cooked in chili salt and pepper* **was** *very much better, a simple dish succulently executed.* (NEWS)

In this example, a singular verb form is chosen to agree with the dish being referred to, rather than the individual prawns specified in the subject noun phrase.

The following sections describe some of the major types of **notional concord** (see also 3.9.1.2 and 3.9.1.3)

**3.9.2.1    Concord with names, titles, and quotations**

Plural names, titles, and quotations take singular concord, if the reference is to a single entity (a country, a newspaper, a slogan, etc.):

> *This country can ill afford an operation that would permit others to argue that [the United States]* **does** *not respect international law.* (NEWS)
>
> *[The New York Times]* **was**, *as usual, dryly factual.* (FICT†)

Co-referent pronouns are in the singular: *It does not respect ...,* *It was dryly factual,* etc.

**3.9.2.2    Concord with measure expressions**

Plural measure expressions take singular verb forms, if the reference is to a single measure (amount, weight, length, time, etc.):

> A: <. . .> *when you're bigger, and you've got a real lot to lose, and [two pounds] is nothing.*
> B: *Yeah, [two pounds] is nothing, yes that's true.*
> C: *[Two pounds] is actually quite lot.* (CONV †)
>
> *[Eighteen years] is a long time in the life of a motor car.* (NEWS)

Co-referent pronouns are in the singular: **This** *is nothing*, **This** *is a long time.*

## 3.9.2.3  Concord with collective nouns

Singular collective nouns allow either singular or plural concord (at least in BrE), depending upon whether the focus is on the group as a whole or on the individuals making up the group. Compare:

> *It is alleged that the [flock] is infected with Salmonella Typhimurium.* (NEWS)
>
> *The Catholic [flock] – who constitute one third of Malawi's population – are tired of dividing their loyalties.* (NEWS)

In actual use, though, singular concord is the preferred pattern.

**CORPUS FINDINGS** [2]

> ➤ Most common collective nouns prefer singular concord, although a few collective nouns commonly take plural concord:
> > ➤ Occurring over 80% of the time with singular concord: *audience, board, committee, government, jury, public.*
> > ➤ Occurring over 80% of the time with plural concord: *staff.*
> > ➤ Occurring commonly with both singular and plural concord: *crew, family.*

**DISCUSSION OF FINDINGS**

Most collective nouns, such as *committee* and *government*, typically take singular concord:

> *Writing in the Harvard International Review, he says that his [committee] approves covert operations only when there's a consensus.* (NEWS)
>
> *The [Government] has indicated it will make provision in the Bill for such an amendment.* (NEWS)

In contrast, a few collective nouns such as *family* and *crew* regularly take both singular and plural concord in BrE, although singular concord is preferred in AmE:

> *Her own [family] has suffered the anguish of repossession.* (NEWS)
> *The [family] are absolutely devastated. They are coping as well as possible, but they are desperately upset.* (NEWS)
> *She was nice to everyone in the cast, even the actors no one else knew, and the [crew] was crazy about her.* (FICT)
> *The aircraft was substantially damaged and the three [crew] were injured.* (NEWS)

In fact, nearly all collective nouns occasionally occur with plural concord in BrE:

> *The [Government] have decreed that we will have to rebid for our betting licence in 1992.* (NEWS)

Note that examples with plural verb forms frequently contain plural personal pronouns and possessive determiners co-referent with the collective noun:

> *The [committee]* **were** *in there, [they] had all [their] special seats there,*
> *[their] drinks ready right, and [they] said right girls, you ready to start?*
> (CONV)

The use of the relative pronoun *who* with a collective noun as antecedent also tends to combine with plural verb forms. However, there is no complete agreement between the choice of verb forms and co-referent pronouns/ determiners (3.9.5).

For plural concord to be available, the meaning of the verb must clearly be applicable to individual members of the group. Thus singular concord only is found in cases such as: *The committee comprises/consists of/has eight members.* But singular concord extends far beyond such examples and is the predominant choice with a wide range of verbs. Sometimes there is variation in the same context:

> *Most of those seasons have involved a struggle against relegation and, while*
> *they have been lucky to survive some, this [team]* **are** *good enough to stay up.*
> *<...> Indeed, he says: "This [team]* **is** *good enough to stay up but whether we*
> *will I don't know."* (NEWS†)

Here the same statement is reproduced exactly, once with plural concord and once with singular concord.

The word *staff* is exceptional in that plural concord is by far the more frequent option:

> *The [staff]* **carry** *messages from guest to guest.* (FICT)
> *When [staff]* **are** *absent, a class is split between other teachers.* (NEWS)

*Staff* differs from other collective nouns in combining with numerals and quantifiers such as *all* and *some*, and in being able to occur without determiners. We may conclude that *staff* behaves very much like s-less plurals of the type *police* and *people* (cf. 4.5.5C).

Another special case is the use of plural concord with singular proper names where they denote sports teams:

> *Reg, see where [Tottenham]* **are** *in the league?* (CONV)
> *[England]* **have** *been here almost a week, practising every day in sauna-bath*
> *temperatures for their opening match against Sri Lanka on Sunday.* (NEWS)

This pattern is regularly found in BrE news but does not occur in AmE (unless the name of the sports team is in the plural, e.g. *the New York Giants*).

## 3.9.3 Concord and proximity

The regular pattern of grammatical concord may be disturbed by **proximity**, i.e. the tendency for the verb to agree with a noun which is closer to the verb (typically in a postmodifier) but which is not the head of the subject noun phrase:

> *I don't water mine very often. I wait till the, [one] of the [leaves]* **start** *to go*
> *a bit yellow and then.* (CONV)
> *[One] of the [girls]* **have** *got bronchitis.* (CONV†)
> *It had been a long day, and [not one] of the [people] who'd auditioned* **were**
> *up to par.* (FICT)

Such clear deviations from grammatical concord are mostly found in speech, where they are explicable from the psycholinguistic constraints of a limited short-term memory and the pressure of online construction of linguistic output. They are rare in writing though we do find proximity effects in special cases. A singular verb form may be chosen in agreement with the closest of a sequence of coordinated noun phrases (3.9.1.3 and 3.9.1.5). In the following example with subject-verb inversion, the verb agrees with the first of a series of coordinated noun phrases:

> Among the Toads **was** [[an alcoholic film actor called Richard Deane,] [a Divisionaire – a very high rank in the Swiss army, which only has a general in time of war – called Krueger,] [an international lawyer named Kips,] [a tax advisor, Monsieur Belmont,] [and an American woman with blue hair called Mrs Montgomery]]. (FICT)

The proximity principle often operates together with notional concord. For example, it may reinforce the use of plural concord with quantifying expressions containing *of* plus a plural noun phrase (3.9.1.4). A related case is the occasional use of plural concord with species nouns (*kind of, form of, type of*):

> All [kind of] people **were** waiting for buses or just standing around. (FICT)

> It remains to be seen what precise [form of] words **are** agreed by the 12 heads of government. (NEWS†)

Plural concord in these cases is probably due partly to proximity, and partly to the fact that expressions with species nouns behave in some respects like determiners (4.3.7 and 4.3.8).

Proximity also plays a role where the subject is followed by *as well as* + a plural noun. Compare:

> 1  But General Noriega's capacity to inspire personal loyalty, [as well as the power of his purse], **is** well known to US intelligence. (NEWS)

> 2  An old man [as well as several women] **were** at home. (FICT†)

Note the use of singular concord in **1**, where the noun following *as well as* is singular, v. the use of plural concord in **2**, which contains a plural noun phrase immediately preceding the verb. Again proximity operates together with notional concord, as the meaning approaches that of coordination (cf. 3.9.1.3).

In one particular pattern there is a deviation from grammatical concord which seems to work against the principle of proximity, viz. in relative clauses with an antecedent noun phrase consisting of *one of* + a plural noun phrase. Compare:

> 3  I realize I am [one of the very few Americans] who **knows** the sound of rocks cutting through flesh and striking bone. (FICT)

> 4  Mr Devaty is [one of the few dissidents] who **do** not come from a Prague-based intellectual background. (NEWS)

Logically, the relative clause defines the group from which an individual is singled out, and plural concord would seem to be the natural choice (as in **4**). It is also the more frequent choice. The cases of singular concord (as in **3**) should probably be ascribed to the pull of the numeral *one* towards the singular (cf. 3.9.1.4), combined with the fact that the main clause makes reference to a single person.

## 3.9.4  Non-standard concord in conversation

The complexity of concord patterns is increased by the variability of verb forms in speech. Conversation and, less frequently, dialogue in fiction produce many examples which do not follow the ordinary rules of grammatical concord. Some examples of non-standard forms are (see also 14.4.5.3):

> Are you in agreement with her, I **says**. (CONV)
>
> Times **is** hard. (CONV)
>
> Well he **don't** go down the street so much. (CONV)
>
> A: Yes, I was a nurse.
>
> B: **Was** you?
>
> A: Mm! Wonderful life! (CONV)

In some cases, different verb forms are used in the main clause and a following question tag (see also 3.13.2.4).

> And that**'s** the first marriage they had in there for twenty five years **weren't** it? (CONV)
>
> There **was** no problem **were** there Paul? (CONV)

### CORPUS FINDINGS [1]

➤ Apart from a few special cases, non-standard verb forms are relatively infrequent in the LSWE Corpus, even in conversation (see Table 3.19).

Table 3.19 **Percentage use of non-standard forms in conversation**

(clear examples of the subjunctive have been excluded for *I were* and *she were*)

| standard form | non-standard form | % use of non-standard form |
| --- | --- | --- |
| *I was* | *I were* | c. 5% |
| *you were* | *you was* | c. 10% |
| *she was* | *she were* | c. 10% |
| *they were* | *they was* | c. 5% |
| *I say* | *I says* | c. 50% |
| *you say* | *you says* | less than 2% |
| *he doesn't* | *he don't* | c. 40% |
| *they don't* | *they doesn't* | less than 2% |

### DISCUSSION OF FINDINGS

The frequency of non-standard forms varies with the particular sequence. High numbers are notable in two cases: *he don't* and particularly *I says*, which speakers use in reporting their own speech:

> No she ain't got the Family Allowance, she says oh I was gonna leave that cos **I says** to her **I says** – have you drawn your Family Allowance? She says er no then she – afterwards **I says** well don't forget to get Kath's money <...> (CONV†)

This pattern provides a window on speech processing, since the verb forms appear to be part of chunks where the individual elements are not independently chosen (e.g. *that's* and *weren't it*). The same mechanism accounts for the apparent discord with *there's*, *where's*, and *how's* (3.9.1.5). Another instance of chunking is the use of *aren't I*, which is the majority choice in interrogative clauses (3.8.2.6);

except for this use, the forms *I* and *are* never combine. As regards the fixed combination *says I*, see 11.2.3.6B.

### 3.9.5 Subject-verb concord and pronominal reference

There is normally agreement between subject-verb concord and pronominal reference, i.e. between the number of the verb form followed by the subject and the number of pronouns and determiners co-referent with the subject. Discrepancies occur, however, with indefinite pronouns as subject **1** and with collective nouns **2**:

1 *Everybody's doing what **they** think **they**'re supposed to do.* (FICT)
2 *Her own family **has** suffered the anguish of repossession, and her personal story of how her local Liberal Democrat-controlled council helped **them** made her the winner in the school's mock election.* (NEWS)

Where discrepancies occur, there are several relevant factors: there is more 'discord' with co-referent pronouns and determiners than with verb forms; discord typically occurs where there is considerable distance between the co-referent noun phrases; discord is generally motivated by notional considerations, i.e. the tendency towards agreement with the meaning, rather than the form, of the subject noun phrase.

See also the account of pronominal reference in Chapter 4 (4.7.2B, 4.10.3).

## 3.10 Types of dependent clauses

A clause may be embedded in a larger structure, either as a clause element or as part of a phrase which realizes a clause element (see Figures 3.6, 3.7, and 3.8 in 3.3). There are very often several layers of **embedding**; see Text sample 1 in 3.1, where embedded clauses are identified by bracketing.

An embedded clause is called a **dependent clause**. The superordinate clause, in which it is embedded, is termed the **main clause**. In the following examples, the clause elements of the main clause are shown in *[]*:

*[Maya] [is drinking] [her first bourbon] [tonight] [because Vern left today for San Francisco State].* (FICT)

The main clause is: *Maya is drinking her first bourbon tonight* + $A_c$. $A_c =$ Dependent clause: *because Vern left today for San Francisco State*.

Here the main clause has the structure $SVO_dA_cA_c$ with the last of these clause elements being realized by a dependent clause. Frequently it is necessary to refer to elements in the part of the main clause other than the dependent material, e.g. its subject or verb phrase (*Maya* and *is drinking* in the above example). We call these the **main clause subject**, **main clause verb**, etc. Note that the latter is not, as in many grammars, called the 'main verb', as this term is reserved for the head verb in a verb phrase, whatever clause it is in (2.7.2). There are two main verbs in the above example: *drinking* and *left*.

Embedded clauses may be finite (3.11) or non-finite (3.12), depending upon the structure of their verb phrase. Occasionally we find clauses with the structure of dependent clauses which are not embedded in any higher clause: these we call unembedded dependent clauses (3.14). Main clauses which are not part of any larger syntactic structure are referred to as **independent clauses** (3.13).

## 3.11 Finite dependent clauses

A **finite** dependent clause contains a verb phrase which is marked for tense or modality. There is regularly a subject except under conditions of ellipsis (3.7). Finite dependent clauses are regularly marked by a clause link, either a subordinator or a *wh*-word (3.3).

The grammatical roles of finite dependent clauses are many and varied (cf. Table 3.3 in 3.2). It is not always clear to what extent clauses should be regarded as independent or as part of other structures. There are degrees of integration, ranging from clear subordination to loosely attached structures. The clearly subordinate types are described first (3.11.1–4), followed by a survey of more peripheral types (3.11.5–7).

### 3.11.1 Nominal clauses

**Nominal clauses** are used as subject, subject predicative, or direct object in the main clause. Finite nominal clauses are introduced by the (omissible) subordinator *that* or by a *wh*-word. Subject clauses are usually extraposed (3.6.4, 9.2.7, and 9.4.7), though the following examples illustrate them in their basic clause element positions.

*That*-clauses (9.2):

> **That this was a tactical decision** <S> *quickly became apparent.* (NEWS)
>
> *They believe* **that the minimum wage could threaten their jobs** <O$_d$>. (NEWS)
>
> *The important point, he said, was* **that his party had voted with the Government more often in the last decade than in the previous one** <P$_s$>. (NEWS)

*Wh*-clauses (9.3):

> *"***What I don't understand,***"* <S> *she said, "is* **why they don't let me know anything.***"* <P$_s$> (FICT)
>
> *Understanding* **how a planet generates and gets rid of heat** <O$_d$> *is essential if we are to understand* **how that planet works** <O$_d$>. (ACAD)

*Wh*-clauses may also appear as other clause elements:

> *Any reciprocal learning will depend mainly on* **what Japanese companies choose to make available** <O$_p$>. (NEWS†)
>
> *Give* **whoever has it** <O$_i$> *your old Cub.* (FICT†)
>
> *Perhaps it is us who made them* **what they are**? <P$_o$> (FICT)

Nominal *wh*-clauses are often divided into two types: **dependent interrogative clauses** (or **indirect questions**) and **nominal relative clauses**. Compare:

> 1 *I forgot to ask you* **what was in the caravans***, the sleeping arrangement.* (CONV)
>
> 2 *I mean basically we can go up the Top Shop and buy* **what we like** *can't we?* (CONV)

Example **1** contains a dependent interrogative clause; notice that we might paraphrase it as 'I forgot to ask you this question, about what ...'. In the nominal relative clause **2**, the *wh*-word can be paraphrased by *that which* or *anything* *which*, i.e. with an antecedent and a relativizer as in ordinary relative clauses (cf. 3.11.3).

*That*-clauses are further used as complements in adjective phrases **3** and noun phrases **4**:

> 3   He was unaware **that a Garda Inquiry was being conducted into the allegation**, he stated. (NEWS)

> 4   There is a fear **that such rules will be over-bureaucratic**. (NEWS†)

*Wh*-clauses, characteristically more versatile than *that*-clauses, may appear as complements in adjective phrases **5**, noun phrases **6**, and prepositional phrases **7**:

> 5   Be very careful **what you tell me**. (FICT)

> 6   If he were in a hurry it opens up the interesting question **why he should be in a hurry**. (FICT†)

> 7   She was afraid of **what might happen if Chielo suddenly turned round and saw her**. (FICT)

For a detailed account of nominal clauses as complements in noun phrases and as verb and adjective complements, see 8.12–13 and Chapter 9.

A nominal clause is closely integrated with the main clause in which it is embedded. It cannot normally be left out without injuring the structure of the main clause. Its freedom of movement is limited (apart from extraposition; 3.6.4).

Clauses containing **direct speech** are often analysed as nominal clauses, embedded within the clause containing the reporting verb:

> Veronica said, **"Take them both up to their room, Nanny."** (FICT)

However, the relationship between the clauses is looser in such structures than is normally the case with nominal clauses. Where the clause containing the reporting verb is short and mobile, it is indeed best regarded as a dependent peripheral element (3.11.5). There is, however, no clear line of demarcation, and alternative analyses are often equally justified.

Because nominal clauses are normally selected or **controlled** by a preceding verb, adjective, noun or preposition, they are frequently referred to as **complement clauses**, the term used in discussing their complement role in 8.5 and in Chapter 9.

## 3.11.2   Adverbial clauses

**Adverbial clauses** are used as adverbials in the main clause, generally as circumstance adverbials (cf. 3.2.8.1). As with adverbials in general, they are optional and have some freedom of positioning; both initial and final placement are common. Adverbial clauses are regularly marked by a subordinator indicating the relationship to the main clause.

> **If we were having a caravan like that**, I would be too frightened to let it. (CONV)

> There's a term and a half left **before he moves on**. (CONV)

> **When the houses were ready**, prices of up to £51,000 were quoted. (NEWS)

> Most ions are colourless, **although some have distinct colours**. (ACAD)

Adverbial *wh*-clauses (**1** below) should be distinguished from nominal *wh*-clauses (as in **2**):

1 *The rain had just about stopped* **when Kramer started walking to the subway**. (FICT)
  *cf. The rain had stopped at that time.*

2 *We don't know* **when he called you up**. (FICT)
  *cf. We don't know this.*

Note the different types of substitution (i.e., an adverbial phrase in **1** v. a noun phrase in **2**). See also the detailed account of adverbial clauses in Chapter 10.

## 3.11.3 Relative clauses

A **relative clause** (also called 'adjectival clause' in some grammars) is characteristically a postmodifier in a noun phrase. It is introduced by a *wh*-word, which has a grammatical role in the relative clause in addition to its linking function (cf. 3.3). The **relativizer** points back to the head of the noun phrase, which is generally referred to as the **antecedent**. Relative clauses may be either **restrictive** or **non-restrictive**.

Restrictive relative clauses are used to establish the reference of the antecedent, while non-restrictive relatives give additional information which is not required for identification. Compare:

1 *We have 30 men* **who are working from 6am to 11pm** *and most of the extra payments we would expect to receive may go on overtime.* (NEWS)

2 *He warned the public not to approach the men,* **who are armed and dangerous**. (NEWS)

The restrictive clause in **1** identifies a group of men who are working long hours. The non-restrictive clause in **2** gives information about some particular men whose identity is already known.

Restrictive and non-restrictive clauses clauses differ in a number of respects: the choice of relativizer, the type of antecedent, etc. See the detailed account of relative clauses in 8.7.

Some types of relative clauses are not used as postmodifiers of nouns. This is true of nominal relative clauses, where the *wh*-word can be regarded as representing both the antecedent and the relativizer (3.11.1). It also applies to so-called **sentential relative clauses** or **sentence relatives**, introduced by *which*:

*All you told me was that Miss White was retiring but I hadn't to tell anyone,* **which I haven't done, which I don't intend do**. (CONV)

*The waves are transverse,* **which means that the direction of oscillation has to be perpendicular to the direction of the motion of the wave**. (ACAD)

A sentential relative clause can be paraphrased by expressions such as *something which* (where the *which*-clause is actually a postmodifier in a noun phrase) or *and that* (with a coordinate clause). Sentential relative clauses are always non-restrictive. See also 10.3.2.2.

## 3.11.4 Comparative clauses and other degree clauses

Comparative expressions, such as comparative forms of adjectives and adverbs (*bigger, more carefully*, etc.), require a basis of comparison. This basis of comparison may be clear from the situational context or the preceding text, but it is often given in the form of a following **comparative clause** introduced by *as* or *than*:

> *Maybe Henry would realize she was not **as** nice **as she pretended to be**.* (FICT)
>
> *She fled these Sunday afternoons earlier **than she should have**, and was punished by guilty dreams because of it.* (FICT)

Ellipsis is frequent in the comparative clause, which usually mirrors the structure of the main clause (3.7.2).

A related type of clause expresses **result** or consequences in relation to a preceding degree expression:

*so/such* + *that*-clause:

> *He awoke **so** cold **that he could barely straighten his legs**.* (FICT)

The syntactic role of the degree expression varies; most typically it is a modifier of an adjective or adverb. See also 7.8 for a more detailed discussion of comparative clauses.

## 3.11.5   Reporting clauses

A **reporting clause** accompanies direct reports of somebody's speech or thought. It specifies the speaker/thinker, the addressee (sometimes), the type of act (*ask*, *say*, *think*, etc.), and frequently also the mode of the act (*abruptly*, *apologetically*, *bitterly*, etc.). The reporting clause may be placed in initial, medial, or final position:

> ***They said**, "Yes, sir," and saluted.* (FICT)
>
> *"Yes," **thought Fleury**, "she's going at it hammer and tongs for his benefit."* (FICT)
>
> *"Please come too," **she begged**. – "I'll be back when I feel like it," **he said (to her) without emotion**. – "I'm sorry," **she whimpered**.* (FICT †)
>
> *Can we do some singing? **he asks**.* (FICT)
>
> *"Of course, dear. Please do come over," **she invited**.* (FICT †)
>
> *Madonna, forgive me, **he prayed**, forgive me for doubting the Holy Father.* (FICT)

Note that the choice of verb varies from straightforward verbs of saying to verbs describing the form or function of the speech act. As shown in the first of these examples, the reporting clause may be coordinated with narrative text.

As there is no link specifying the type of connection, the syntactic role of the reporting clause is indeterminate. The clause containing the reporting verb is often described as the main clause, with the direct speech in object position. This analysis is obviously excluded where the verb in the reporting clause does not normally take a direct object (verbs such as *whimper*, *exult*, *smile*). Note also the clear difference between indirect and direct speech:

> 1  *And she said that everything was mouldy.* (CONV)
>
> 2  ***She said**, "Everything is mouldy." / "Everything," **she said**, "is mouldy" / "Everything is mouldy," **she said**.*

In **1** there is indirect speech, with a subordinator introducing a regular nominal clause (3.11.1); the connection between the two clauses is close. In **2**, this structure is paraphrased using direct speech. Note that the connection is much looser, as shown by the comma and the mobility of the reporting clause. The order of the subject and the verb phrase of reporting clauses may vary depending upon its position and internal structure (11.2.3.6–7).

## 3.11.6 Comment clauses

**Comment clauses** are similar in structure to reporting clauses: they are loosely connected to the main clause, they normally lack an explicit link, and they are usually short and can appear in a variety of positions. They differ from reporting clauses by being more formulaic, and in the frequency counts later in the book we therefore choose to regard some of them (notably *you know* and *I mean*) as inserts (2.5). They are also usually in the present rather than past tense, first or second rather than third person, and comment on a thought rather than the delivery of a wording.

> *It's a good tip **you know**, isn't it?* (CONV)
>
> *It's a nice approach **I think**.* (CONV)
>
> ***You know** it makes you wonder, **you know**, **you see** all this unemployment.* (CONV)
>
> ***I mean** it's, it's general **I suppose I mean** if it would be better to switch it on and off which you can do and er, **you know**, **I mean** we can't sit here continually talking.* (CONV)
>
> ***Mind you**, he was probably still as sound as a bell.* (FICT)
>
> *The following exchange was overheard (**I swear**), by a reader from Quainton, Bucks, in his local pub.* (NEWS)
>
> *The conclusion, **it seems**, is intolerable.* (ACAD)

Many comment clauses directly express the speaker's or writer's attitude to the message and can therefore be grouped among stance adverbials (3.2.8.2, 10.3.2).

The syntactic role of comment clauses is indeterminate in much the same way as with reporting clauses. In medial and final position they are best described as peripheral elements. In initial position they may look superficially like main clauses with an embedded nominal clause. Compare:

> ***You know**, there's no money to be made out of ri–, recycling.* (CONV)
>
> v. *You know (that) there's no money to be made out of recycling.*

In the first example, the speaker tells the addressee something the latter perhaps does not know; the function of *you know* is to underline the truth of the statement. This is clearly a comment clause. The second example is ambiguous: it either means 'you are aware that …' or it is identical in meaning to the first example. The first interpretation corresponds to a structure with an embedded nominal clause (*that* can be inserted), the second to a structure with a comment clause (*that* cannot be used).

Comment clauses are very characteristic of speech; see the detailed account in 10.3.2, 12.2, and 12.5.

## 3.11.7 Other peripheral clauses

In addition to reporting clauses and comment clauses, we find two further types of loosely attached dependent clauses. They are typical of conversation, and take their name from their position in relation to the main clause: **question tags** (3.4.4B, 3.13.2.4) and **declarative tags** (3.4.4C).

## 3.12 Non-finite clauses

**Non-finite clauses** are regularly **dependent**. They are more compact and less explicit than finite clauses: they are not marked for tense and modality, and they frequently lack an explicit subject and subordinator. Compare the following examples to paraphrases using finite clauses:

> **1a** *I don't know **what to write about**.* (CONV)
>
> **1b** *I don't know **what I should write about**.*
>
> **2a** ***Crossing**, he lifted the rolled umbrella high and pointed to show cars, buses, speeding trucks, and cabs.* (FICT†)
>
> **2b** ***As he was crossing**, he lifted the rolled umbrella high and pointed to show cars, buses, speeding trucks, and cabs.*
>
> **3a** ***Style being a relational concept**, the aim of literary stylistics is to be relational in a more interesting sense than that **already mentioned**.* (ACAD†)
>
> **3b** ***Since style is a relational concept**, the aim of literary stylistics is to be relational in a more interesting sense than that **which has already been mentioned**.*

To interpret a non-finite clause, it is necessary to use clues from the main clause and often also from the wider context.

There are three main types of non-finite clause, each containing a different type of verb phrase: **infinitive clauses** (3.12.1), *ing*-**clauses** (3.12.2), and *ed*-**clauses** (3.12.3). The three types differ considerably with respect to the grammatical roles they can play. Infinitive clauses and *ing*-clauses are the most versatile grammatically (cf. Table 3.3 in 3.2 above). Non-finite clauses are often loosely integrated into the main clause (3.12.4) and may even lack a verb altogether (3.12.5). For details on the use of non-finite clauses, see Chapters 8 and 9.

## 3.12.1 Infinitive clauses

**Infinitive clauses** can have a range of syntactic roles:

**A** Subject

> *Artificial pearls before real swine were cast by these jet-set preachers. **To have thought this** made him more cheerful.* (FICT)
>
> *"I believe that homosexuality is a gift from God. **To deny that gift** is to deny God's will, saying His way isn't good enough."* (NEWS)

**B** Extraposed subject

> *It's difficult **to maintain a friendship**.* (CONV†)
>
> *It is a mistake **to take sides**.* (NEWS)

**C** Subject predicative

> *"My goal now is **to look to the future**."* (NEWS)

*The only way out of the dilemma is* **to suppose that sometimes the photon gets through and sometimes it does not.** (ACAD)

**D** Direct object

*Do you want* **me to send them today?** (CONV)

*He upset you very much, and I hate* **to see that.** (FICT)

**E** Object predicative

*Some of these issues dropped out of Marx's later works because he considered them* **to have been satisfactorily dealt with.** (ACAD†)

*Feare (1970a) thought it* **to be at least 90% during the first winter.** (ACAD)

**F** Adverbial

*A little group of people had gathered by Mrs. Millings* **to watch the police activities on the foreshore.** (FICT)

**To succeed again** *they will have to improve their fitness and concentration.* (NEWS†)

**G** Part of noun phrase

*He is the third man* **to be murdered on the corner of the Donegal Road and the Falls Road in the past two years.** (NEWS)

*They say that failure* **to take precautions against injuring others** *is negligent.* (ACAD)

In the first example, the infinitive clause is a postmodifier comparable with a relative clause, in the second a noun complement.

**H** Part of adjective phrase

*They're too big* **to fight,** *that's the trouble isn't it?* (CONV)

*I think the old man's a bit afraid* **to go into hospital.** (CONV†)

In all these roles except A and F (and the first type illustrated in G), *to*-infinitive clauses act as complement clauses (9.4).

## 3.12.2   *Ing*-clauses

*Ing*-clauses can have a range of syntactic roles:

**A** Subject

**Having a fever** *is pleasant, vacant.* (FICT)

**Understanding how a planet generates and gets rid of its heat** *is essential if we are to understand how that planet works.* (ACAD)

**B** Extraposed subject

*Anyway I says to Alice it's not fair* **getting in somebody's car feeling the way I feel I says – and puking in car.** (CONV)

*"There is only around five tonnes of newsprint left and it's very difficult* **getting supplies into Sarajevo."** (NEWS)

**C** Subject predicative

*Erm what I'm thinking of is* **disconnecting the pipe there, and running it through – that way.** (CONV)

*The real problem is* **getting something done about the cheap imports.** (NEWS)

**D** Direct object

*I started **thinking about Christmas.*** (CONV†)

*"It's as if the guy never stops **thinking about the issue.**"* (NEWS)

**E** Prepositional object

*No-one could rely on **his going to bed early** last night.* (FICT†)

**F** Adverbial

*I didn't come out of it **looking particularly well,** I know.* (FICT)

***Having established the direction of the line,** we now wish to find some point on the line.* (ACAD)

**G** Part of noun phrase

*I think he smashed two cars **coming down the road.*** (CONV)

*The man **making the bogus collections** was described as middle aged.* (NEWS)

**H** Part of adjective phrase

*It might be worth **giving him a bell to let him know what's happening.*** (CONV†)

*The town is busy **taking advantage of its first City Challenge victory by implementing plans aimed at revitalising East Middlesbrough.*** (NEWS)

**I** Complement of preposition

*Jordan said he would get tough with the homeless by **running identification checks on them.*** (NEWS†)

*The art of **expanding limited recall by asking leading, open-ended questions** is a subtle one.* (ACAD)

### 3.12.3  *Ed*-clauses

***Ed*-clauses** are less versatile than the other types of non-finite clauses. They can have the following roles:

**A** Direct object

*God you've gone mad with the sugar in yours. Do you want **it topped up?*** (CONV)

*Two-year-old Constantin will have **his cleft palate repaired.*** (NEWS†)

**B** Adverbial

***When told by police how badly injured his victims were** he said: "Good, I hope they die."* (NEWS)

***Taken in the order shown** they provide propulsive jets increasing mass flow and increasing jet velocity.* (ACAD†)

**C** Part of noun phrase

*There wasn't a scrap of evidence to link him with the body **found on the Thames foreshore at low tide.*** (FICT†)

*This, as we have seen, is the course **chosen by a large minority of households.*** (ACAD†)

## 3.12.4 Supplementive clauses

In the examples given above, the non-finite clauses have been clearly integrated within the main clause as clause elements or parts of phrases. Loosely integrated clauses, marked off by a comma in writing, are found in initial, medial, or final position:

> **Directed by Benjamin Twist, who, incidentally, is one of the names being mentioned as a possible successor to Nowozielski,** *the production is a delightfully theatrical retelling of Dicken's <sic> famous novel.* (NEWS)

> *The celebrated bust,* **looking like two dunces' caps applied to her chest***, was encased in a puce halter-necked sweater which left all but essentials bare.* (FICT)

> *He walked with a lilting gait,* **his left Achilles tendon apparently shortened, pulling his left heel up***. (FICT)

> *She gazed down at the floor,* **biting her lip, face clouded***. (FICT)

The relationship between the non-finite clause and the main clause is very loose in these examples, both syntactically and semantically (cf. 3.12.2F and the account of detached predicatives in 3.4.1). By using a **supplementive clause**, the speaker marks the information given in the clause as subordinate: as background (initial position), parenthetical (medial position), or supplementary (final position). See also 10.2.1.9.

## 3.12.5 Verbless clauses

Among non-finite clauses we may also include verbless clauses such as:

> 1 *She had also been taught,* **when in difficulty***, to think of a good life to imitate.* (FICT)

> 2 **Although not a classic***, this 90-minute video is worth watching.* (NEWS†)

> 3 *He does not believe celibacy should be demanded of priests* **whether gay or straight***.* (NEWS)

> 4 *Every day,* **if possible***, allot time at your desk to sorting and filing everything you have collected since the previous day by way of either elicited or spontaneous data.* (ACAD)

Such clauses can usually be related to finite clauses with the verb *be* and, apart from formulaic expressions such as *if possible* (in **4**), *if so* and *if necessary*, have the same subject as the main clause. Compare with **1** *when she was in difficulty* and with **2** *Although it is not a classic*. Although there is no overt verb phrase, these clauses can be analysed in terms of clause elements: subordinator + $A_c$ or $P_s$. Sometimes they can be closely paraphrased by a detached predicative structure (3.4.1) simply by omitting the subordinator: compare with **2** *Not a classic, this 90-minute video is worth watching*. As with supplementive clauses, their role is usually adverbial.

Verbless clauses in the written registers typically mark information as communicatively less important, while in conversation they are usually limited to the formulaic expressions. See also 10.1.2 and 10.2.8.4.

## 3.13   Major types of independent clauses

An **independent clause** is not part of any larger structure, but it may contain embedded clauses or be coordinated with clauses on the same level:

- **Simple** independent clause (single clause)

     *You can give me a cheque.* (CONV)

- **Complex** independent clause (with one or more dependent clauses)

     *If we pay too much they'll give us the money back.* (CONV†)

- **Compound** independent clause (coordinated independent clauses)

     *He was crying and so I gave him back his jacket.* (CONV†)

Independent clauses are finite, that is, they contain a verb form which specifies their tense or modality.

Independent clauses correspond to what is generally defined as sentences in other grammars. This term is preferred, as it is difficult to give a good linguistic definition of a sentence which applies equally well to writing and spontaneous speech (see also the discussion of clausal and non-clausal units in speech in 14.3.3–4).

Independent clauses are used to perform **speech-act functions**. There is a broad correspondence between four basic speech-act functions and four principal structural types of independent clauses, marked by the order of the subject and verb phrase, and/or by the use of a *wh*-word:

| speech-act function | structure | example |
|---|---|---|
| inform | SV structure | *It's strong.* |
| elicit | VS structure | *Is it strong?* |
| | *wh*-word, VS structure | *How good is she?* |
| | *wh*-word | *Who was there?* |
| direct | V structure | *Be strong!* |
| express | *wh*-word, SV structure | *How good she is!* |

The first type gives information and expects no specific response from the addressee. The second asks for information and expects a linguistic response. The third is used to give orders or requests and expects some action from the addressee. The fourth type expresses the feelings of the speaker/writer and, like the first, invites no specific type of response.

As structure and speech-act function often do not agree, it is useful to distinguish between a structural and a functional classification:

| structural types | functional types |
|---|---|
| declarative clause | statement |
| interrogative clause | question |
| imperative clause | command, request |
| exclamative clause | exclamation |

In practice, many grammars use the functional terms interchangeably with the structural ones, and we will follow this tradition when speaking for example of *wh*-questions as a type of interrogative clause.

The four structural types will be briefly described below (3.13.1–4), with regard to their form and the relationship between form and speech-act function.

## 3.13.1  Declarative clauses

**Declarative clauses** are marked by SV structure and typically express statements. They are the predominant type of independent clause in news and academic prose:

> Police yesterday disarmed a parcel bomb at a black human rights office in Florida, the latest in a rash of mail bombings in the South that have killed a judge and a civil rights lawyer. The FBI said white supremacists might be behind the attacks. (NEWS)

Under special circumstances, declarative clauses may have VS order (11.2.3 and 3.6.1.1).

In conversation and fictional dialogue, declarative clauses can be used (with appropriate intonation in speech) to express questions:

1   A: **So he's left her?**
    B: She left him – (CONV)
2   A: **You felt alright when you left?**
    B: Yes. (CONV)
3   A: She's gonna go back tonight.
    B: Does, **she lives in Hitchin?** (CONV)
4   **"You weren't happy together?"** – "No," I said. (FICT†)

In these examples, the speaker asks for confirmation rather than for information. Note the use of *so* in **1**, signalling that this is a conclusion drawn by the speaker. In **3** speaker B clearly starts out with a regular *yes/no*-question, but changes tack and opts for a declarative clause.

The effect of using a declarative question is somewhat different in:

5   A: Have I got bad breath?
    B: Yep!
    C: Yes.
    A: **I have?** (CONV)
6   A: Do you understand?
    B: No.
    A: **You don't understand?** Why don't you understand? (CONV)
7   **"You don't know where I could get something to eat?"** asked K. "I haven't eaten anything since yesterday." (FICT)

In **5** and **6**, the first speaker starts out with a regular interrogative structure asking for information. After hearing the response, the speaker repeats the question in the form of a declarative clause expressing surprise or disbelief. The question in **7** has a tentative ring; it is as if, by seeming to assume a negative answer, the speaker does not want to impose on the addressee.

## 3.13.2  Interrogative clauses

Naturally enough, **interrogative clauses** tend to occur in dialogue situations. As the account below will show, they are frequent only in conversation and (to a lesser extent) in fiction.

There are three main types of independent interrogative clauses: **wh-questions** (3.13.2.1), **yes/no-questions** (3.13.2.2), and **alternative questions** (3.13.2.3). Their basic uses are to supply missing information (*wh*-questions), to invite the addressee to indicate whether a proposition is true or not (*yes/no*-questions), and to select among alternatives presented (alternative questions). In addition, there is a special type of interrogative clause which has the same clause structure but differs sharply from other interrogative clauses both in form and use: this is the **question tag** (3.13.2.4).

## 3.13.2.1 *Wh*-questions

*Wh*-questions open with a *wh*-word which indicates an element to be specified by the addressee. The rest is taken to be already known. The element to be specified could be a clause element (subject, object, predicative, adverbial) or part of a phrase. *What + do* is used to ask for specification of the verb phrase:

>  ***Who****'s calling?* <S> (CONV)
>  ***What*** *d'you mean?* <O$_d$> (CONV)
>  ***Who*** *are you talking about?* <O$_p$> (CONV †)
>  ***Who*** *is it for?* <complement of a preposition> (CONV)
>  ***How*** *was your trip, Nick?* <P$_s$> (CONV)
>  ***What*** *are they doing?* <V> (CONV)
>  ***Which*** *photos are we going to look at?* <part of noun phrase> (CONV)
>  ***Whose*** *turn is it tonight?* <part of noun phrase> (CONV)
>  ***When*** *did you see Mark?* <A$_c$> (CONV)
>  ***Where*** *does she live?* <A$_c$> (CONV)
>  ***Why*** *did you buy that?* <A$_c$> (CONV)
>  ***How*** *old's Wendy?* <part of adjective phrase> (CONV)

Note the SV order when the *wh*-word is the subject.

In informal language *how come* followed by SV order is found as an alternative to *why*:

>  ***How come*** *the garage sells it cheaper?* (CONV)
>  ***How come*** *you're here?* (FICT †)

*How come* is rare compared with *why* and is used mostly in conversation.

In informal language the *wh*-word may be reinforced by a following expletive:

>  ***What the heck*** *has happened?* (CONV)
>  ***Who the fuck*** *did that?* (CONV)
>  ***What the devil****'s this?* (CONV)
>  "***What the hell****'s the matter with you?*" (FICT)
>  "***What the deuce*** *have you got there?*" (FICT)
>  "***Where on earth*** *have you been, Gordon?*" (FICT)

These structures signal a strong emotional involvement on the part of the speaker.

When the speaker asks for specification of two pieces of information, there can be more than one *wh*-word in the same clause. Only one of these can then be placed in initial position:

*Who's getting **what**?* (CONV)

***Who** is bringing in **what**?* (FICT)

The most natural answer to a *wh*-question supplies the missing information, by itself or, more rarely, in the context of a whole clause:

A: ***Who** told you that?*

B: *My mate Sue.* (CONV)

A: ***Who** sent it?*

B: *Guy sent it.* (CONV†)

In spontaneous conversation the relationship between question and answer is frequently far more complex. Very often the speaker asking the question also suggests an answer, in the form of an elliptic *yes/no*-question or alternative question:

1  A: ***Who** drove, **Karen**?*

   B: *No she can't drive. It was our mum.* (CONV)

2  A: ***When**'s that, **in the afternoon**?*

   B: *Yeah.* (CONV)

3  A: ***Who** had my monitor, **Gary or – Dave**?*

   B: *Er Gary.* (CONV)

4  *"**What** would you like to drink? **Scotch, bourbon? A Martini?** I'm an awful drink mixer."* (FICT)

These sequences combine *wh*-questions and *yes/no*-questions (**1, 2**) or *wh*-questions and alternative questions (**3, 4**).

Particularly in spontaneous conversation *wh*-questions are frequently elliptic and may consist of a *wh*-word only:

5  A: *Do you know Jasons down there?*

   B: ***Who**?*

   A: *Jasons.* (CONV) <*Jasons* seems to be the name of a shop>

6  A: *I think he's a real so and so.*

   B: ***Who**, the father?* (CONV)

7  A: *Oh it's six o'clock isn't it?*

   B: ***What**?* (CONV)

8  A: *No, they're in hospital, badly injured.*

   B: ***What**? **What**? Broken limbs?* (CONV)

*What* is frequently used to ask for repetition **7** or to introduce a more specific question **8**.

The *wh*-word sometimes stays in the regular position for the relevant phrase or clause element, especially in echoing what has been said by the previous speaker:

A: *And I think she's stealing stuff as well.*

B: *She's **what**?* (CONV)

A: *How how fast can you pick it up?*

B: *How fast can **what**?*

A: *How fast can you pick it up?* (CONV)

Such **echo questions** may express surprise or disbelief and ask for confirmation rather than information.

Although *wh*-questions most typically ask for information, they may have other speech-act functions. Consider the following examples:

   **9** *A: Andrew and Fergie split.*
      *B: No wonder.*
      *A:* **Who** *cares?* (CONV)

  **10** **Who** *cares? It doesn't matter.* (FICT)

  **11** **Who** *needs sitcoms?* (NEWS)

  **12** **How** *dare you speak to me like that?* **Who** *do you think you are?*
      (CONV†)

  **13** **Why** *don't you come with us for an hour or so? Mum'll be there after*
      *bingo at half past nine.* (CONV)

  **14** **Why** *don't we go next week?* (CONV)

Examples **9** to **11** contain **rhetorical questions** expressing an opinion rather than asking a question. By choosing an interrogative form, the speaker appears to let the addressee be the judge, but no overt response is expected. This is therefore a type of question that can just as well occur in monologue as in dialogue. The interrogative structures in **12** express a strong rebuke and certainly do not ask for information. *Wh*-questions opening with *why don't you/we* are frequently used to express invitations **13** or suggestions **14**, in which case they do not ask for an explanation. Contrast the real information question in **15**, where the *wh*-question has a third person subject and is combined with a *yes/no*-question:

  **15** **Why** *didn't he come, was he ill?* (CONV)

The point in this last example is to find out why an event in the past did not occur, rather than to suggest a future action.

## 3.13.2.2 *Yes/no*-questions

*Yes/no*-questions open with the operator (3.2.9) followed by the subject. All the elements are taken to be already specified, and the addressee is expected to supply a truth value, by answering *yes* or *no*. Needless to say, there are other possible answers indicating various degrees of certainty (*definitely, certainly, perhaps*, etc.). The addressee may also supply additional information.

  **1** *A: Is it Thursday today?*
      *B: No, Friday.* (CONV)

  **2** *A: Do you think he'll be any better?*
      *B: Maybe. Yeah.* (CONV)

  **3** *A: Could I have green eyes?*
      *B: Yeah.*
      *A: If you had blue and dad had brown.*
      *B: Well greeny tinge I suppose, yeah.* (CONV)

  **4** *A: Have you got a busy week now Michael?*
      *B: Well Tuesday is my busiest day.* (CONV)

*Yes/no*-questions are frequently elliptic:

  **5** *You alright?* (CONV) <*are* omitted>

  **6** *A: You got the other one?* <*have* omitted>
      *B: What, the adaptor?* (CONV)

  **7** *Got what you want?* (CONV) <*have you* omitted>

> 8 *Alright? Anything else?* (CONV)
>
> 9 *A: There's more gravy here.* **Anybody?**
>    *B: Mm. Just a little. Mm.* (CONV)

In **5** and **6** the operator is missing, and in **7** both the operator and the subject are omitted (cf. *Have you got what you want?*). In **8** and **9** the questions are expressed by a phrase rather than a clause, and it is impossible to reconstruct a non-elliptical version of the interrogative clause with any certainty. Note also B's questioning response in **6**, with an elliptic *wh*-question followed by an elliptic *yes/no*-question.

Yes/no questions are often used for purposes other than asking for information:

> 10 *A: Isn't that lovely!*
>    *B: Oh that's lovely.* (CONV)
>
> 11 *A: Isn't that, that terrible!*
>    *B: I couldn't believe it when I saw it.* (CONV)
>
> 12 *A: Will you give me your money woman!*
>    *B: Shut up!* (CONV)
>
> 13 *Will you behave!* (CONV)
>
> 14 *Could I have two pounds please?* (CONV)
>
> 15 *Can we turn that light off please?* (CONV)
>
> 16 *Morning Alf! Erm – Can I ask you to pick up Doreen on Tuesday morning?* (CONV)

The interrogative structures in **10** and **11** express exclamations, in **12** and **13** commands, and in **14** to **16** requests. Note the use of *please* in **14** and **15**; in contrast, *please* cannot be added to simple *yes/no* questions (as in **1–4** above) without altering the speech-act function.

Especially in conversation, *yes/no*-questions frequently have a minimal form, consisting only of the operator and a pronoun:

> *A: She's a teacher.*
> *B: Oh is she?* (CONV)
>
> *A: He's got our books actually.*
> *B: Has he?* (CONV)

These **comment questions** do not really ask for information, but are used to provide feedback and keep the conversation going.

### 3.13.2.3 Alternative questions

An **alternative question** is structurally similar to a *yes/no*-question in opening with the operator followed by the subject, but rather than expecting an answer in terms of *yes* or *no* it presents alternatives for the addressee to choose between:

> 1 *A: Do you want one or two?*
>    *B: Two.* (CONV)
>
> 2 *A: So do you like my haircut or not?*
>    *B: It's alright.* (CONV)

While **1** presents a choice between alternatives within the clause, the alternatives in **2** affect the whole clause. This type could be regarded as a more explicit way of asking a *yes/no*-question; note that *or not* could be left out without causing any drastic change of meaning.

Conversation frequently contains interrogative structures ending in *or anything/something*:

*Did Jones's grandma die **or something**?* (CONV)

*Do you want a drink of water **or anything**?* (CONV)

Although these structures are superficially similar to alternative questions, they are really *yes/no*-questions. The purpose of the coordination tags (2.9.2) is to make the questions less precise; see also the account of hedges in 10.3, 12.2, and 12.5.

Alternative questions proper are related in function to *wh*-questions. Both types of interrogative clauses ask for specification of an unknown element, in one case represented by a *wh*-word and and in the other by listed alternatives. Both types may combine in the same context:

*Which one should I use, the blue or the pink?* (CONV)

Here the *wh*-question is followed by an elliptic alternative question. The alternative question narrows down the range of possible answers offered by the *wh*-question.

## 3.13.2.4 Question tags

Although **question tags** are not strictly independent clauses (cf. 3.11.7), it is convenient to deal with them here. Question tags consist of an operator and a personal pronoun. The former is identical to the operator of the clause to which it is appended (if there is no form that can serve as operator, a form of *do* is inserted), and the latter is co-referent with the subject of the preceding clause.

Question tags are most often added to declarative clauses:

1 *She's so generous, **isn't she**?* (CONV)

2 *She's not a lesbian, **is she**?* (CONV)

3 *She doesn't like things that blow up, **does she**?* (CONV)

4 *If you talk nice and polite, people listen to you. If you shout, this is no good, **is it**?* (CONV)

5 *It seems a shame to break it up, **doesn't it**, when it's so good.* (CONV)

6 *Say money isn't everything, **is it**, at the end of the day.* (CONV)

Note that the tag does not necessarily have to be placed at the very end of the clause (**5, 6**), though it cannot precede the verb phrase of the main clause.

The main clause and the tag are generally opposite in **polarity**: negative tags (**1, 5**) are added to positive declarative clauses, while positive tags are added to negative declarative clauses (**2, 3, 6**). A clause with *no*-negation counts as a negative clause and is followed by a positive tag **4**. The main function of the tags is to elicit confirmation or agreement (thus involving the addressee in the conversation) rather than to elicit information.

Tags appended to declarative clauses can also be identical in polarity to the main clause:

7 *A: She likes her granddad, **does she**?*
  *B: Yeah.* (CONV)

8 *A: It's my ball.*
  *B: It's your ball **is it**?* (CONV)

   **9** A: *That's the airing cupboard through there. But it*
   B: *This is the airing cupboard in here* **is it**?
   A: *doesn't air. I'll be honest with you, it doesn't air.* (CONV)

   **10** *So he's been beating Tracey with mum's shoes,* **has he**? (CONV)

Such structures, which frequently echo a previous statement or draw a conclusion from something the previous speaker has said, are similar to the comment questions taken up at the end of 3.13.2.2.

Tags are often added to a phrase or an incomplete clause. Note the various uses illustrated in:

   **11** *Nice kitchen* **isn't it**? (CONV)

   **12** A: *She scalded all her back.*
   B: *Oh badly burnt* **was it**? (CONV)

   **13** A: *<...> round the back of Allard Avenue – Sherwood* **is it**?
   B: *Sherwood, yeah Sherwood Avenue.* (CONV†)

   **14** *What's up, cold* **is it**? (CONV)

   **15** A: *When does he go to school?*
   B: *Next June* **is it**?
   C: *Next September* **isn't it**?
   D: *No this September.* (CONV)

Example **11** appeals to the addressee in the same way as **1** to **6** above, while **12** expresses a comment as do **7** to **10**. The tags in **13** and **14**, however, are more like regular *yes/no*-questions eliciting information (cf. *Is it Sherwood? Is it cold?*), so they could be considered ordinary *yes/no*-questions with fronting of the subject predicative (cf. 11.2.2.2). In **15** B's positive tag asks for information, while C appeals to the addressee for confirmation.

There are additional complications connected with the form of question tags and the contexts in which they are used.

**A   Change of subject or auxiliary**

Tags are not always strictly modelled on the main clause, due to changes in the course of speaking:

   **16** *He's a right little misery when he wakes up,* **ain't you** *boy?* (CONV)

   **17** *I'm not talking dirty <laugh>,* **are we**? (CONV)

   **18** *You only had these two bags,* **didn't we**? (CONV)

   **19** *I don't think she'll be very pleased,* **would she**? (CONV)

Examples **16** to **18** are cases where the speaker has shifted the assignment of conversational roles during the course of speaking. In **16** the tag is addressed to the boy who is referred to in the third person in the main clause, which was directed to another addressee; in addition, the speaker opts for the colloquial negative form *ain't* rather than a standard form of *be*. In **17** there is also a change of subject (and verb); while the main clause refers to the speaker only, the tag includes the addressee. Example **18** is similar, but in this case the reference is extended from the addressee to include both the speaker and the addressee. A change in the auxiliary is illustrated in **19**, from the neutral future-referring *'ll* to the hypothetical *would*. Note also that the tag in **19** is based on a subordinate clause rather than on the main clause; this is found with main clause verbs of opinion such as *believe, doubt, think*.

**B   Alternatives to question tags modelled on the main clause**

There is a range of other expressions which can be tagged on to a clause, with much the same effect as a question tag; these include: *right? yeah? eh? OK? don't you think?* (See 14.3.3.5.)

A particularly interesting case is the use of *innit* which is derived from a regular question tag (= *isn't it*) and commonly occurs in BrE conversation.

   **20**  *Bit old, this programme, innit?* (CONV)

   **21**  *No one could speak French on that French trip, not even the teachers. That's so stupid, innit?* (CONV)

   **22**  *I'm gonna cut a load and go pick David up I suppose innit?* (CONV)

   **23**  A: *And all of the Indians in Slough say innit? Innit? It's every second word.*
          B: *Hello, innit!*
          A: *They say that, hello, innit. Seventy p please, innit?* (CONV)

In **20** and **21** it would be possible to insert the regular question tag *isn't it*. In **22**, on the other hand, *innit* is independent of the structure of the main clause. As **23** indicates, this usage is often stigmatized.

**C   Question tags added to interrogative clauses**

Although question tags are generally added to declarative clauses, they may also be appended to interrogative clauses:

   **24**  *Do you want this do you, anywhere?* (CONV)

   **25**  A: *Oh that Earnest film's on tonight.*
          B: *Oh is it tonight is it?*
          A: *Yeah.* (CONV)

This use is parallel to the use of declarative tags (3.4.4C). In both cases the tag underlines the speech-act function of the main clause.

**D   Question tags added to imperative clauses**

Question tags may also be added to imperative clauses, in which case they generally take the form *will you*:

   **26**  *Oh, Clare, turn it up will you please?* (CONV)

   **27**  *Give them a message from me will you?* (CONV)

Other possible forms of tags added to imperative clauses are *can't you, won't you, would you* and *shall we*:

   **28**  *Go and see the ladies now can't you? That's it!* (CONV)

   **29**  *"Listen, keep this quiet, won't you?"* (FICT)

   **30**  *Ah, you fix that up for me Sean would you?* (CONV)

   **31**  *Let's try that shall we?* (CONV)

   **32**  *Get one for Ricky shall we?* (CONV)

*Would you* is less forceful than *will you*, but much less common.

*Shall we* occurs especially in suggestions opening with *let's* as in **31** (see also 14.4.3). The type illustrated in **32** can be regarded as either an ellipted form of an imperative with *let's*, or a variant of an ordinary interrogative clause: *Shall we get one for Ricky?*

## 3.13.2.5 Interrogatives in general: distribution

**CORPUS FINDINGS** [1]

➤ Questions are many times more common in conversation than in writing.
➤ Expressed in another way, there is on average one question per every 40 words in conversation. (In fact the frequency for conversation is under-represented; it is based on question marks and these are sometimes left out by transcribers when dealing with question tags, declarative structures used as questions, and comment questions.)

Table 3.20 **Distribution of questions (based on the frequency of question marks)**

each ● represents 500 occurrences per million words

| | |
|---|---|
| CONV | ● ● ● ● ● ● ● ● ● ● ● ● ● ● ● ● ● ● ● ● ● ● ● ● ● ● ● ● ● ● ● ● ● ● ● ● ● ● ● ● ● ● ● ● ● ● ● ● ● ● ● ● ● ● ● ● ● |
| | ● ● ● ● ● ● ● ● ● |
| FICT | ● ● ● ● ● ● ● ● ● ● ● ● ● ● ● ● |
| NEWS | ● |
| ACAD | ● |

**DISCUSSION OF FINDINGS**

The high frequency of questions in conversation is natural, considering that the situation is interactive, with a constant give-and-take among participants. Similarly, the presence of dialogue accounts for the relatively high frequency in fiction. News and academic prose, on the other hand, are non-interactive and naturally make less use of questions.

## 3.13.2.6 Question types: distribution

**CORPUS FINDINGS** [8]

➤ There are wide differences in the forms that questions normally take (see Table 3.21).
➤ Questions are most typically expressed by full independent clauses in the written registers.
　➤ In particular, *wh*-questions are proportionally more common in news and academic prose.
➤ Questions expressed by declarative clauses are found particularly in conversation and fiction.
➤ Nearly half the questions in conversation consist of fragments or tags.
　➤ Questions without clause structure are found in all registers.
　➤ About every fourth question in conversation is a question tag; the most common type of question tag is negative.

**DISCUSSION OF FINDINGS**

The preferred question types in conversation reflect its interactive nature. Because of the shared context, questions can easily take the form of fragments. Further, question tags are a frequent means of seeking agreement and keeping the conversation going. The tags are most often added to a positive statement, as positive clauses are in general more common than negative clauses. *Yes/no-*

Table 3.21   **Preference for question type, expressed as a percentage**

each ■ represents 5%   □ represents less than 2.5%

| | CONV | FICT | NEWS | ACAD |
|---|---|---|---|---|
| **independent clause** | | | | |
| *wh*-question | ■■■■ | ■■■■■■■ | ■■■■■■■<br>■■ | ■■■■■■■<br>■■■ |
| *yes/no*-question | ■■■■■ | ■■■■■■ | ■■■■■■■ | ■■■■■■■ |
| alternative question | □ | □ | □ | □ |
| declarative question | ■■ | ■ | □ | □ |
| **fragments** | | | | |
| *wh*-question | ■ | ■■ | ■■ | ■ |
| other | ■■■ | ■■■ | ■ | ■ |
| **tag** | | | | |
| positive | ■ | □ | □ | □ |
| negative | ■■■■ | ■ | □ | □ |

questions are predominant among independent clauses in conversation, chiefly because they are often used as comment questions (cf. 3.13.2.2). Questions in declarative form are also relatively common, as the speech-act function can be made clear by intonation and/or contextual clues. The relatively low percentage of *wh*-questions (in comparison with the written registers) indicates that questions in conversation are used less to seek information than to maintain and reinforce the common ground among the participants. However, because the overall frequency of questions is so much higher in conversation (3.13.2.5), *wh*-questions are also by far more frequent in conversation than in news or academic prose.

The distribution of question forms in fiction is similar to that in conversation, because fictional dialogue is modelled on conversation. The most notable difference is the much lower proportion of question tags; this agrees with the lower frequency of discourse markers (14.3.3.3) in fiction as compared with conversation. The focus is more on content, as shown by the higher frequency of *wh*-questions.

The focus on content is strongest in news and academic prose, where *wh*-questions make up about half of all questions. Tags are very rare and fragments less common than in the other registers. The great majority of questions take the form of full independent clauses, as there is less contextual support. News is somewhat closer to conversation than academic prose, no doubt because of the occurrence of quoted speech.

It is actually somewhat surprising that questions are used at all in academic prose, which would seem to be consistently monologic:

1 *It is important to observe the patient's skin for signs of circulatory failure. Are the hands, nail beds and feet pink and warm? Do the patient's lips and tongue appear blue? Pulse and blood pressure are also important indicators of circulatory status.* (ACAD)

2 *Are there any important differences in the social origins of the younger and older clerks? The following table shows the social origins of male clerks in three different age groups.* (ACAD)

3 *Does the fixity on a particular occasion set in as a purely mental act of knowledge? At a transition from small to large physical systems? At the interface of matter and mind that we call consciousness? In one of the many subsequent worlds into which the universe has divided itself?* (ACAD)

4 *How then, do we balance these two factors? The answer lies in a thermodynamic state function known as free energy or the Gibbs function, G.* (ACAD)

5 *How far will the magnetic flux penetrate? Is there a simple way of describing the decay of the magnetic flux mathematically? There is. We can use the following one-dimensional model.* (ACAD)

6 *Given the conception we have, are mental events as we have conceived them excluded from being physical? They are not.*

In **1** the writer suggests questions which medical students should ask themselves in examining a patient. The questions in **2** to **4** announce a research theme, or focus the attention on particular aspects of the phenomena discussed (note also how *wh*-fragments can be used for this purpose: *how about . . . ?*, *what about . . . ?*). In **5** and **6** the question-answer technique is used to express a forceful statement. The common ground here is the didactic strategy typical of academic textbooks, of explaining by posing a question and then providing an answer.

The use of questions in news also goes far beyond quoted speech. Examples **7** to **11** below resemble rhetorical questions:

7 *Does it really matter what a few politicians or academics say? Probably not.* (NEWS)

8 *How many fathers would drive their daughter 120 miles through mountainous terrain so that she could attend weekly ballet and singing lessons? Not many, probably; but then Leo Brennan is exceptional by most standards.* (NEWS)

9 *How is it possible, in a legal democracy, for a sheriff to give a court order without evidence from both parties? Is there not some obligation on the part of the pursuer to justify his claim?* (NEWS)

10 *Traditionally, Canada was said to be bound by the Canadian Pacific's ribbon of steel. And what else is there? The monarchy? Excuse me. A shared culture? A third of the country speaks French. Ice hockey? Maybe. A shared distrust of the United States? Most likely.* (NEWS)

11 *Sign up for the green team. Do you want to know what's happening to our countryside, forests, seas and seashores at home and across the world? Do you want to know how easy it is to affect the environment of the world by planting trees or buying eco-friendly products? If so, read this feature every week.* (NEWS)

In these examples, the writer attempts to involve the reader in a dialogue, illustrating how all language use is potentially dialogic, whether the addressee is present or not.

### 3.13.2.7  Choice between interrogative *who* and *whom*

In questions, the nominative form *who* is encroaching upon the traditional territory of the accusative form *whom*.

**CORPUS FINDINGS** [1,10]

➤ Interrogative *who* is much more common than the accusative form *whom* (see Table 3.22).
  ➤ This difference is most marked in conversation, where interrogative *whom* is virtually non-existent.

Table 3.22  **Distribution of interrogative *who* v. *whom*; occurrences per million words**

each ■ represents 50   ☐ represents less than 25   – represents options not attested in the LSWE Corpus

| | interrogative *who* | interrogative *whom* |
|---|---|---|
| CONV | ■■■■■■■■■■■■■■■■■■■■■■■■■ | – |
| FICT | ■■■■■■■ | ☐ |
| NEWS | ■■■ | ☐ |
| ACAD | ■ | ☐ |

**DISCUSSION OF FINDINGS**

The distribution of interrogative *who* v. *whom* across registers—with a lower frequency of *whom* in conversation than in the written registers—reflects a pattern often found in linguistic change, with the most advanced stage in conversation and a more conservative usage being preserved in literary language.

Further, the distribution of *who* v. *whom* varies with the context of use.

**A   After prepositions**

In the written registers interrogative *whom* is consistently used when it is the complement of a preceding preposition:

> For **whom** would I be working? (FICT)
>
> It did not say how or by **whom**. (NEWS)
>
> To what or **whom** do we attribute style? (ACAD†)

However, written language where the writer is not trying to distance the text so much from conversational style prefers structures with a **stranded preposition** (see B below).

In conversation, *who* is consistently used in this context:

> He reckoned the copy of Memories he's got is sung by **who**? (CONV)
>
> The most interesting thing about going, coming back to it is trying to work out who's got married to **who** and – who's divorcing who and what baby belongs to which person. (CONV)
>
> A: Obliged to make polite conversation all the time oh!
> B: With **who**? (CONV)

However, it is even more common in conversation to use an alternative structure with a stranded preposition (see B below).

**B    Other positions**

When the preposition is stranded at the end of the clause (cf. 2.7.5.4), we find *who* as the regular choice in conversation:

> *Amanda, **who** are you going out with?* (CONV)
>
> *I hope she knows **who** he's talking to!* (CONV)

In this context, *who* is also normally used in the written registers:

> *She didn't need two guesses to figure out **who** the car belonged to.* (FICT)
>
> *Please help, I just don't know **who** to turn to.* (NEWS)

*Who* is also typically used in object position:

> ***Who** can I trust?* (CONV†)
>
> ***Who** you playing today?* (CONV)
>
> *"**Who** are you calling creep?"* (FICT)
>
> *And **who** do we have here?* (NEWS)

Less frequently, *whom* is found in these positions in the written registers:

> *"I know **whom** she belongs to."* (FICT†)
>
> *"**Whom** do you favour?"* (FICT)
>
> *"What's on trial as much as GAF is whether federal prosecutors in the Wall Street cases know **whom** to prosecute, with **whom** to plea bargain, and **whom** to leave alone."* (NEWS)

### 3.13.2.8    Auxiliary *do* in independent interrogative clauses

As in negative clauses (3.8.2), independent interrogative clauses with certain verbs show variation in the presence or absence of the auxiliary *do*. The relevant verbs are *have* as a transitive verb, and the semi-modal *have to*, together with the marginal auxiliaries *dare* and *need*, *ought to*, and *used to* (see also 6.6). As questions are rare in news and academic prose, the account below focuses on conversation and fiction.

**A    Transitive *have***

The transitive verb *have (got)* has several possible question forms. There are three main types:

- Lexical verb construction (with *do*)

> ***Did** you **have** a good walk?* (CONV)
>
> *"**Do** you **have** a long way to go?"* (FICT)

- Auxiliary construction (without *do*)

> ***Have** you any comments on this Mick?* (CONV)
>
> ***Have** you any idea what you've done, what you're involved in?* (FICT)

- ***Have got***

> ***Have** you **got** a busy week now Michael?* (CONV)
>
> ***Have** you **got** a cigarette, Jim?* (FICT)

**CORPUS FINDINGS** [4]

The distribution of the three types of interrogative clause structure with the lexical verb *have* is shown in Table 3.23.

**Table 3.23** **Interrogative clauses with lexical *have*, expressed as a percentage within each register (conversation and fiction) and dialect (AmE and BrE)**

DO = all forms of *do*   HAVE = all forms of *have*   pronoun = any personal pronoun
A = *a, an*   ANY = *any, anybody, anyone, anything*

each ■ represents 10%   □ represents less than 5%   – marks alternatives that are unattested in the LSWE Corpus

| | AmE CONV | BrE CONV | AmE FICT | BrE FICT |
|---|---|---|---|---|
| DO pronoun *have* A/ANY | ■■■■■ ■■■■■ | ■■ | ■■■■■ ■■■ | ■■ |
| HAVE pronoun A/ANY | – | ■ | ■ | ■■■■■ ■ |
| HAVE pronoun GOT A/ANY | □ | ■■■■■ ■■ | ■ | ■■ |

➤ *Do*-insertion is strongly preferred in AmE; in contrast, *have got* is preferred in BrE conversation, and *have* without *do*-insertion in BrE fiction.

**DISCUSSION OF FINDINGS**

The tendencies with respect to *do*-insertion in questions are the same as in negative clauses (cf. 3.8.2.1). The high frequency of *do*-insertion in AmE questions agrees with the more frequent use of *do*-insertion in AmE in general. Similarly, the high frequency of *have got* in BrE questions is in agreement with common use of *have got* in BrE in general. The preference for *have* without *do*-insertion in BrE fiction probably reflects conservative usage.

The fact that BrE uses *do*-insertion to some extent (i.e. the AmE norm), whereas AmE very rarely uses *have* without *do*-insertion (i.e. the BrE norm), may reflect a greater tendency for American forms to be adopted in BrE than vice versa. Note that the same tendency is found both in questions and negative clauses.

## B   The semi-modal *have to*

The semi-modal *have to* has three main question types:

- Lexical verb construction (with *do*)

    Look, **do** I **have to** tell you everything? (CONV)

    "Why **do** we **have to** row?" he said quietly. (FICT)

- Auxiliary construction (without *do*)

    **Have** they **to** pay for her to be there? (CONV)

    How many more different strokes **have** you **to** do for your map? (CONV)

- *Have got to*

    **Have** you **got to** peel some of the stuff off? (CONV)

    **Has** it **got to** be on the ferry has it? (CONV)

**CORPUS FINDINGS** [4]

➤ *Do*-insertion is the only choice in AmE conversation and fiction, and it is predominant also in the BrE material.

Table 3.24    **Interrogative clauses with semi-modal *have to*, expressed as a percentage within each register**

DO = all forms of *do*   HAVE = all forms of *have*   pronoun = any personal pronoun

each ■ represents 10%   □ represents less than 5%   – marks alternatives that are unattested in the sample

|  | AmE CONV | BrE CONV | AmE FICT | BrE FICT |
|---|---|---|---|---|
| DO pronoun HAVE *to* | ■■■■■<br>■■■■■ | ■■■■■<br>■■ | ■■■■■<br>■■■■■ | ■■■■■<br>■■■ |
| HAVE pronoun *to* | – | ■ | – | – |
| HAVE pronoun *got to* | – | ■■ | – | ■■ |

**DISCUSSION OF FINDINGS**

The tendencies are the same as in negative clauses (cf. 3.8.2.2). The pattern is similar to that for transitive *have*, but with a more marked general preference for the form with *do* insertion.

C   ***Dare* and need**

The verbs *dare* and *need* have two primary options in questions:

• Lexical verb construction (with *do*)

> *Do* you **dare to** help those who robbed us? (FICT)
>
> *Do* we **dare** leave the guitar, should we put it behind the screen? (CONV)
>
> *Do* you **need to** go somewhere? (CONV)

With *dare* we find instances both with and without a following infinitive marker.

• Auxiliary construction (without *do*)

> Gwendoline, go out of the room. How **dare** you squeal like that. (CONV)
>
> For children of all ages this is a fascinating display and one, **dare** I say it, which reaches new heights. (NEWS)
>
> Well, position has been frozen. **Need** we say more? (CONV)
>
> You needn't do anything violent, **need you**? (FICT)

When there is no *do*-insertion, *dare* and *need* lack an infinitive marker, i.e. they behave like modal auxiliaries.

**CORPUS FINDINGS** [4]

➤ *Dare* and *need* have different preferences with respect to *do*-insertion in questions.
> ➤ The auxiliary construction (without *do*) is preferred with *dare*, being used c. 90% of the time in the LSWE Corpus.
> ➤ The lexical verb construction (with *do*) is preferred with *need*, being used c. 90% of the time in the LSWE Corpus.

**DISCUSSION OF FINDINGS**

The auxiliary constructions in both of these cases are limited to special formulaic usages, where *do*-insertion would not be an alternative. *Dare* generally occurs in interrogative clauses of the types *how dare you* and *dare I say* (cf. the examples above). These are not information-seeking questions; the former type expresses a rebuke, the latter a speaker comment. *Need* is used in speaker comments of the type *need we say more* and in question tags (see examples above).

The auxiliary uses of the two verbs in interrogative clauses thus seem to be becoming fossilized forms. In conversation, *need* is used productively with *do*-insertion, like any other verb with a *to*-infinitive complement. *Dare*, on the other hand, seems to be on the wane and is chiefly found in a small number of collocations without *do*-insertion.

Both the auxiliary and the lexical verb constructions are commonly used with *dare* and *need* in negative clauses (cf. 3.8.2.3) though *dare* is overall less frequent. It is possible that the contracted forms *daren't* and *needn't* have contributed to the preservation of the auxiliary construction in negative clauses.

### D   *Ought to* and *used to*

The marginal auxiliaries *ought to* and *used to* have two main options in questions:

- Lexical verb construction (with *do*)

    **Did** you **used to** play tennis? (CONV)

    **Did** you **used to** have long hair? (FICT)

- Auxiliary construction (without *do*)

    "**Ought** I **to** take it?" (FICT)

    "**Ought** it **to** have been a palace?" (FICT)

---

**CORPUS FINDINGS** [4]

➤ Both *ought to* and *used to* are rare in interrogative clauses.
  ➤ *Ought to* in interrogative clauses is found only in BrE fiction and only without *do*-insertion.
  ➤ In AmE and BrE conversation, *used to* occurs only with *do*-insertion.

---

**DISCUSSION OF FINDINGS**

It is worth noting that these two verbs are infrequent both in interrogative clauses and negative clauses (cf. 3.8.2.4), perhaps because they are felt to be anomalous. Where they do occur, preferences with respect to *do*-insertion are the same in both types of clauses: the auxiliary construction with *ought to* and the lexical verb construction with *used to*. Examples such as the following illustrate ways in which interrogative forms of *ought to* can be avoided:

1  *He ought to sit down,* **shouldn't he**? (CONV)

2  *It's turning cold.* **Don't you think you ought to** *put a jacket on?* (CONV)
    cf. *Oughtn't you to put a jacket on?*

3  **Do you think I ought to** *go then?* (CONV)
    cf. *Ought I to go then?*

4  *I said he's he was jumping on the chair,* **should he ought to**? (CONV)

In **1**, *should* replaces *ought to* in the question tag. In **2** and **3** the speaker avoids forming an interrogative structure with *ought to* by opting for a superordinate clause with *think* (cf. similar examples quoted in 3.8.2.4). Possibly the unfamiliarity with *ought to* may result in the speaker using deviant combinations, as shown in **4**, where it co-occurs with a modal just as a regular lexical verb such as *wish to* could.

In view of the considerable attention given to these marginal auxiliaries in grammatical descriptions of English and English language teaching materials, it is worth noting how rare they are, particularly in negative and interrogative auxiliary constructions.

## 3.13.3 Exclamative clauses

Exclamations can be expressed in a range of structures, both clausal and non-clausal:

1 *What a good dad he is!* (CONV)
2 *What a cheek!* (CONV)
3 *Isn't that infuriating though!* (CONV)
4 *Fancy being married ten times by the time you're thirty-seven!* (CONV)
5 *Look at that! Incredible!* (CONV)
6 *He's a hooligan!* (CONV)
7 *Oh, that's a shame!* (CONV)
8 *Oh great! Oh great!* (CONV)

Examples **1** and **2** illustrate special exclamative structures, one in the form of a full exclamative clause, the other in the form of a phrase. In the other examples, the exclamations are expressed by other clause types or structures: an interrogative clause **3**, imperative clauses (**4**, **5**), declarative clauses (**6**, **7**), and non-clausal forms **8**. Needless to say, exclamations occur chiefly in conversation and in fictional dialogue.

## 3.13.4 Imperative clauses

Formally, **imperative clauses** are characterized by the lack of a subject, use of the base form of the verb, and the absence of modals as well as tense and aspect markers.

***Get off** the table.* (CONV)
***Don't forget** about the deposit.* (CONV)
***Hold on**, are we late?* (CONV)

Imperatives are typically used in contexts where the addressee is apparent; the subject is usually omitted but understood to refer to the addressee. Imperatives typically urge the addressee to do something (or not to do something) after the moment of speaking; hence there is no need for tense, aspect, or modal specification.

A special type of imperative clause is found with the verb *let* used with a first person plural pronoun (*us*, usually contracted to *'s*) to express a suggestion involving both the speaker and the addressee:

***Let**'s catch up with Louise.* (CONV)

### 3.13.4.1 The realization of imperative clauses

The addressee in imperative clauses is sometimes specified in the form of a subject or, more commonly, as a vocative (see also 14.4.1):

1 ***You** go home and go to sleep.* (CONV)
2 *Don't **you** dare talk to me like that **Clare**, I've had enough.* (CONV)
3 ***Melissa**, take those things away.* (CONV†)

4 *Go away* **you scalliwag you.** (CONV)

5 *Listen* **you big shit.** (CONV)

6 **Everyone** *ask Leon.* (CONV†)

7 *Right,* **troops** *forward march.* (CONV)

A second-person pronoun is generally placed before the verb in positive clauses (as in **1**) and after the verb *do* in negative clauses (as in **2**). When the position of *you* is fixed in relation to the verb, it is best analysed as subject. *Clare* **2** and *Melissa* **3**, on the other hand, are vocatives and can be freely placed either at the beginning or the end of the clause. In **4** and **5** the pronoun *you* is included in a vocative. The analysis of **6** and **7** is more uncertain: *everyone* and *troops*, identifying the addressees, could be analysed either as subject or as vocative.

The effect of adding a subject or a vocative may be to soften or sharpen the command (compare **4** and **5** above), or just to single out the addressee. The type illustrated in **2** has a sharp and threatening quality. Imperatives can also be modified by the addition of the tag *will you* (3.13.2.4D), less commonly *would you*, the politeness marker *please*, the auxiliary *do*, or the adverb *just*:

8 *Pick your plates up from down there* **will you?** (CONV)

9 *Pass me his drink* **please.** (CONV†)

10 *Oh, Clare, turn it up* **will you please?** (CONV)

11 **Do** *ring Cathy if you feel like it.* (CONV†)

12 *"***Please do** *come over," she invited.* (FICT)

13 **Just** *dump it at the door there.* (CONV)

In spite of the interrogative form, *will you* does not soften the command (**8**, **10**), but rather makes it more precise and insistent; it can hardly be used in speaking to a superior. *Please*, on the other hand, generally has a softening effect; in **9** it gives the imperative the force of a request, in **10** and **12** it expresses a polite appeal to the addressee. The auxiliary *do* makes a positive imperative more urgent, or it can (as in **11** and **12**) be used to add a politely persuasive force to an offer, suggestion or invitation. *Just* (as in **13**) makes the imperative seem less demanding and easier to comply with.

Apart from expressing commands and requests, imperative clauses can be used for a wide range of purposes, e.g. to express suggestions **11** and invitations **12**. There is invariably an appeal of some kind to the addressee, with the possible exception of coordinate structures such as those in **14** and **15**:

14 **Touch them** <tuning knobs> *and the telly goes wrong.* (CONV†)

15 **Go to the Third Eye Centre** *tomorrow, and you'll find bed mattresses bolted to the wall, tarred and feathered, and covered in discarded clothes.* (NEWS)

In **14** and **15** the coordinate clauses express a conditional relationship: 'if you touch them, the telly goes wrong', 'if you go to ..., you'll find ...'. However, the imperative force is retained if we rephrase the examples more freely: 'don't touch them ...', 'if you want to see ..., go to the ...'.

Just as imperative clauses can be used for purposes other than expressing commands, so commands can be expressed by means other than imperative clauses:

16 *Will you be quiet for goodness' sake! I can't hear myself think.* (CONV)

17 *Out of the way, get out of the way, come on!* (CONV)

**18** *Oh quickly, there's a car coming!* (CONV)

**19** *Slowly Bern!* (CONV)

In **16** a command is expressed by an interrogative clause opening with the modal auxiliary *will*. In **17** *out of the way* is used by itself in the same way as the following imperative clause. Although there is no imperative clause in **18** and **19**, the speaker clearly gives a command to the addressee ('hurry up' and 'take it easy', respectively).

## 3.13.4.2 Imperative clauses: distribution

**CORPUS FINDINGS** [9]

➤ Imperatives are many times more common in conversation than in writing (see Table 3.25).

   ➤ There are far fewer imperatives than questions in conversation and fiction, while there is a tendency in the opposite direction for news and academic prose (see also Table 3.20).

Table 3.25 **Distribution of imperatives; occurrences per million words**

each ● represents 500 occurrences per million words

| | |
|---|---|
| CONV | ●●●●●●●●●●●●●●●●●●●●●●● |
| FICT | ●●●● |
| NEWS | ●● |
| ACAD | ●● |

➤ Specification of the addressee and the use of softening devices are generally rare with imperatives: less than 20% of all imperatives in conversation and fiction have such features.

   ➤ The most common modifications are an overt second-person subject (*you*) and a final vocative.

   ➤ Surprisingly, modifications are slightly more common in fiction than in conversation (c. every sixth imperative clause in conversation v. every fourth imperative clause in fiction).

**DISCUSSION OF FINDINGS**

The frequent use of imperatives in conversation is due to the fact that the situation is interactive, with participants often involved in some sort of non-linguistic activity at the moment of speaking. In such situations, it is natural to use language for the purposes of monitoring the actions of the addressee or expressing suggestions involving both the speaker and the addressee (*let's* ...). Imperative clauses are, however, not only used to monitor actions, but also to regulate the conversational interchange, as in these examples:

   **Wait a minute**, *did you have a good day at work?* (CONV)

   *"***Hold on!***" continued Jennings, quieting the dissenters.* (FICT)

Other examples are *look* used as an attention getter, *hear hear* used to express agreement, *say* introducing an idea, and *mind you* expressing a comment. Some expressions of this kind are lexicalized and are best regarded as inserts (2.5).

The lower frequency of imperative clauses in fiction follows from the simple fact that imperatives are virtually restricted to dialogue passages.

Imperative clauses, like questions, are rare in news and academic prose, as these registers are non-interactive. Nevertheless, imperative clauses do occur in both registers and are actually somewhat more common than questions. Many of the imperatives in news are used to give instructions on how to perform certain actions (**1** below). In news we also find imperatives in quoted speech and where the journalist addresses the reader directly; the purpose may be to plan the text **2**, to acknowledge something **3**, or to give instructions on how to obtain information **4**.

> **1** *Try to push and lift at the same time—go on, try to get the back wheels off the ground as you go along!* (NEWS)
> <tongue-in-cheek instructions for supermarket trolley exercises>
>
> **2** *Let's take the Irish Cricket Annual first.* (NEWS)
>
> **3** *Let's face it, the whole sport has become more professional off the field.* (NEWS†)
>
> **4** *For full details of performances, talks, workshops, contact the Third Eye Centre.* (NEWS†)

Imperative clauses in academic prose are chiefly used as a means of guiding the reader in interpreting the text. The imperative clause in **5** is like **2** in announcing what the following text passage will be about. The types illustrated in **6** to **8** are commonly used for incidental points of guidance, such as referring the reader to other texts or other parts of the same text. Examples **9** and **10** illustrate another common type, where the premises are set up for a scientific argument.

> **5** *In looking for the answers, let us begin with those citizens who have been around for the longest time, the elderly and those in later middle age.* (ACAD)
>
> **6** *Note that x may occur free and bound in P.* (ACAD)
>
> **7** *See also Section 5.2.* (ACAD)
>
> **8** *For detailed discussions of the definition of a system, the meaning of feedback, and other issues we have glossed over, consult the control-theory literature.* (ACAD)
>
> **9** *Let <mathematical formula> be the breeding population of blowflies at time t and let <mathematical formula> be the number of eggs produced.* (ACAD)
>
> **10** *Suppose we believe that the snow is what is muffling the sound of the traffic <...>* (ACAD†)

The registers also differ with respect to the specification of the addressee and the use of softening devices. Such modifications are rare in news and academic prose, where the imperative is typically directed to the general reader and does not demand any favours. These modifications are also relatively rare in conversation and fiction. The lower proportion of modification in conversation is probably due to the informal situations and the intimate relationship between many of the participants. Question tags, *please*, and *do* are rare both in conversation and fiction. One notable difference between the two registers is the higher frequency of *just* in conversation.

# 3.14 Unembedded dependent clauses

Just as phrases can be used without being attached to a larger structure (3.15), so can dependent clauses. The following examples illustrate such **unembedded dependent clauses**: a nominal relative clause **1**, a sentential relative clause **2**, and *ing*-clauses (**3, 4**):

1 *A: Where's that?*
  *B: It's er*
  *C: Mayes.* **What used to be Mayes the food shop**. (CONV)

2 *The scientists can only wait and hope.*
  <new paragraph> **Which is what I shall be doing for the next three months**. (NEWS)

3 *He suspected the criminal was aware that a tall old white man (passing as blind?) had observed, had seen the minutest details of his crimes.* **Staring down. As if watching own-heart surgery**. (FICT)

4 **Renorming super-reflexive Banach spaces** <chapter title> (ACAD)

Unembedded dependent clauses are especially common in conversation. Two important types are clauses of reason introduced by *because/cos* (cf. 10.2.6.5) and relative clauses introduced by *which*. Apart from conversation, unembedded dependent clauses are sometimes found in dialogue in fiction and very informal news texts. It is notable that *which* clauses of this kind are far more common in conversation than in the written registers, although the relativizer *which* is relatively rare overall in conversation (8.7.1.2). Some typical examples are:

*because / cos:*

*A: You will be careful with that, won't you?*
*B: Yeah!*
*A:* **Cos it costs a lot of money**. (CONV)

*A: Go and pick your dice up.*
*B: I'll get it.*
*A:* **Cos you'll need another go won't you?** (CONV)

*I've been told that men don't like women, period. Oh yeah? Who does then?* **Because women don't like women**. (FICT)

*which:*

*A: Well – the good news for the environmentalists is the bike runs on unleaded.*
*B: Mhm.*
*A:* **Which is good news**. *Cos like that's – not so expensive.* (CONV)

*A: I know, you said before you hardly miss a lunch.*
*B: Never –* **Which is crazy**! *I mean, I really do resent it sometimes.* (CONV)

*Sneaky, insincere? Depends how it's done.* **Which brings us onto those Americans**. *"Have a nice day." How exaggerated, how American, we Brits recoil.* (NEWS)

Unembedded dependent clauses are connected with the evolving nature of conversation. Clauses of reason, which are particularly common, allow the speaker to add some words of explanation or justification without planning an argument in advance. *Which*-clauses are typically sentence relatives (cf. 10.3.2.2), which allow the speaker to express a comment on something that has just been said. These constructions commonly open with expressions such as:

> *Which is what/why/where ...*
> *Which means/explains ...*
> *Which brings me to ...*

The special advantage of the relative link is that it signals a close connection to the immediately preceding text.

# 3.15 Non-clausal material

Conversation contains a great deal of material that is not integrated in clauses, as shown in the comparison of two text samples early in this chapter (3.1.1). However, **non-clausal** material is found in writing as well as speech and extends far beyond ellipsis (3.7), where missing elements can be precisely recovered from the context.

Non-clausal material may consist of single words or of syntactic non-clausal units. There are thus two defining characteristics of non-clausal material: (a) internally it cannot be analysed in terms of clause structure, and (b) it is not analysable as part of any neighbouring clause. (See also 14.3.1.3–4.)

## 3.15.1 Non-clausal material in writing

Non-clausal material is regularly found in contexts such as public notices, telegrams, newspaper headlines, book titles, figure captions, tables, and lists. More interestingly, we find non-clausal material in running written text, often referred to as **sentence fragments**. Following are some examples of non-clausal material in news:

1 *Council jobs reform pledge.* (NEWS) <headline>
2 *Elderly care crisis warning.* (NEWS) <headline>
3 *Image crisis for Clinton over haircut.* (NEWS) <headline>
4 *Safari jackets are still favourites with more mature male travellers. Often worn with pale, open-necked sports shirts and dodgy cravats. Very Alan Whicker. Velcro.* (NEWS)
5 *And now for something completely different: cheap and cheerful claret.* (NEWS)

In newspaper headlines (as in examples **1** to **3**), the non-clausal syntax provides an economical way of summarizing the main points of information given in the article. The effect of the non-clausal syntax in parts of **4** is to focus on different aspects of the jackets described, without adding unnecessary information (which the reader can easily deduce). The fragment in **5** announces a new topic to be developed later in the text; the same effect could have been produced by a new headline.

Non-clausal material is also found occasionally in academic prose, especially in textbooks:

6 *Now there is no bar to having more than one particle in each state. Quite the contrary.* (ACAD)

7 *But what is that? Is it a number? Well ... yes. It can't be a real number since its square is negative. Of course.* (ACAD)

In **6** the fragment *quite the contrary* underlines the point expressed in an effective manner. In **7** the writer adopts an informal style and enters into a dialogue with the reader. Apart from examples of this kind, non-clausal material is commonly used in academic prose in headings and lists of various kinds.

In fiction, non-clausal syntax is a means often employed to mirror the stream of thought of a fictional character:

*He wondered if Ajayi had finished the game yet. Probably not. Prevaricating woman.* (FICT)

*Strange memories on this nervous night in Las Vegas. Five years later? Six? It seems like a lifetime, or at least a Main Era the kind of peak that never comes again.* (FICT)

Non-clausal material is of course also common in fictional dialogue, though not to the same extent as in real conversation:

"*Well, Father, how is it going?*"
"*What is going?*"
"*The work. H. G. Wells?*"
"*As usual.*" (FICT)

## 3.15.2 Non-clausal material in conversation

Non-clausal material is far more common in conversation than in the written registers. This is partly because of the online production circumstances and partly because conversation develops out of cooperation between the participants. Moreover, the participants share the same context and often know each other very well. As a result, far more can be left unexpressed for the listener to infer; should misunderstandings arise, they can be cleared up by appealing to the speaker.

There is a wide range of non-clausal material in conversation, expressing a variety of speech functions (statement, question, command, exclamation, etc.). One important type consists of inserts (2.5), such as response words, interjections, greetings, apologies, and thanks. In addition, conversation frequently uses ordinary words and phrases which are not integrated in clauses (14.3.3). The following passage shows how a conversation develops in cooperation between the participants, through a sequence of questions and answers using full clauses as well as non-clausal material:

A: *Where do you go for that, Bath Travel for that then Neil?*
B: *Where?*
A: *For that brochure.*
B: *Bath Travel, where's that?*
A: *No, where do you get the – thing from then?*
B: *What?*
A: *Butlins?*
B: *Well – I got it from that travel agent's.*
A: *Oh.*
B: *er the one*
A: *In the precinct?*
B: *by, yeah, by Boots.*
A: *Oh yeah.* (CONV)

Although the syntax looks chaotic, the last part would have been pretty much a regular independent clause, if said all in one go by one speaker: *I got it from that travel agent's, the one in the precinct by Boots.* This illustrates the underlying similarity between the grammar of conversation and of other registers (see also 14.1).

# Key word classes and their phrases

# 4

# Nouns, pronouns, and the simple noun phrase

## 4.1 Overview of nominals in discourse

**Noun phrases** vary greatly both in structure and complexity, and they can have a wide range of syntactic roles (2.7.1.1). In this chapter we are particularly concerned with the characteristics of the word classes which make up the heads of typical noun phrases, i.e. nouns and pronouns. We also consider here the characteristics of **simple noun phrases**, consisting of determiner plus head or of a single noun or pronoun. More complex noun phrases are dealt with in Chapter 8.

### 4.1.1 Use of nominals in discourse

By way of placing noun phrases in a wider perspective, we will begin by looking more broadly at how **nominals** (2.7.1) are used. Nominal elements include not only phrases headed by a noun or pronoun, but all constituents which appear in positions characteristic of noun-headed structures including, for example, phrases with adjectives used as noun phrase heads (7.6.2) and complement clauses (3.11.1). Later, for the main part of this chapter, we concentrate on noun phrases in the narrow sense.

#### 4.1.1.1 Density and types of nominal elements

We have bracketed all nominal elements in the four passages below. Note that there may be several layers of embedding, with nominal elements occurring as constituents in higher-level noun phrases.

Text sample 1: FACE-TO-FACE CONVERSATION

> A: Well [I] thought [you] were going to talk to [me] about [Christmas presents].
> B: [I] have spoken to [you] about [Christmas presents]. [I]'ve told [you] [about all [I] can tell [you]]. Why don't [you], why don't [you] sit down and tell [me] [what [you] want for [Christmas]]. [I] mean [that] would be useful.
> A: Oh [darling]. Tut. [Nothing [I] particularly want for [Christmas]].
> B: <unclear>
> A: Well [you] bought [me] [the new vacuum cleaner].

Text sample 2: FICTION

> [It] was [a beautiful January day] and [the Japan Current] brought [enough warm sea air] ashore to create [a near-summer atmosphere], even though [a small family of [icebergs]] huddled in [the channel], so [they] rode with [the carriage windows] open. At [the glacier, [whose former cave] had been long obliterated by [ice crashing down from [the face above]]], [they] walked for [some time] along [the front], touching [the monstrous snout] from [time] to [time] and even leaning against [it] when [they] stopped to talk.
> "[Missy] told [me] [the other day], [Nancy], [that [I] was in [love] with [you]]."
> "[I]'ve always been in [love] with [you], [Tom]. [You] know [that]. Since [that first day in there]," and [she] pointed to [where [the blue-roofed cave] had been]."

Text sample 3: NEWS REPORTAGE

> [[AUSTRALIA's best-known businessman and yachtsman], [Alan Bond]], had [little time] to savour [his victory in [[Australia's premier yacht race], [the Sydney to Hobart]]].
>
> [The first [Mr Bond] knew of [the successful move by [the National Australia Bank] to put [his brewery businesses] into [receivership]]], was through [a radio news bulletin] aboard [[his $3.5million maxi-yacht], [Drumbeat]].
>
> On [his arrival in [Hobart]], [Mr Bond] told [journalists] [[he] was not finished yet]. "[I] have just got [it] confirmed, but [these things] take [time], and there's [a long way to go] yet."
>
> But [Mr Bond] was vague on [details], because [the rules of [the race]] are [that once [a boat] has started, [it] may not make [contact] except with [officials] until [the event] is over].

Text sample 4: ACADEMIC PROSE

> [Nonlinear systems theory] is of [great importance] to [anyone interested in [feedback systems]]. [It] is also true [that [the theory of [feedback systems]] has made [important contributions to [nonlinear systems theory]]]. [This chapter] discusses [some chaotic feedback systems, drawn from [electronic circuit theory] and elsewhere], and shows [how [they] may be analysed]. So far, [most of the techniques required] have been taken directly from [the usual differential and difference equation theory], but [some results with [a more control system-theoretic flavour]] are now available.

If we examine the four passages, we find great differences in the distribution of nominal elements. In the news report, nominal elements make up about 80 per cent of the text (measured in terms of the number of words). The corresponding figures for the other Text samples are approximately: academic prose 75 per cent, fiction 70 per cent, and conversation 55 per cent. In other words, nominal elements make up between a half and four-fifths of these texts.

The difference in the coverage of nominal elements can be related to their types. Single pronouns abound in the conversation text, while longer and more complex structures are predominant in the written registers. It is this difference in the complexity of nominal elements which is the main difference among registers, not the frequency of nominal elements.

## 4.1.1.2 The role of nominal elements in discourse

To examine the role of nominal elements, it may be instructive to see what a text looks like with nominals only and with the nominals eliminated. Compare the following passages with Text samples 1 and 3; a dash has been inserted in all cases where material has been left out; all brackets have been left in the text.

Text sample 1A: CONVERSATION EXTRACT WITH NOMINAL ELEMENTS ONLY

> A: – [I] – [you] – [me] – [Christmas presents].
> B: [I] – [you] – [Christmas presents]. [I] – [you] – [about all [I] can tell [you]]. – [you], – [you] – [me] [what [you] want for [Christmas]]. [I] – [that] –.
> A: – [darling]. – . [Nothing [I] particularly want for [Christmas]].
> B: <unclear>
> A: – [you] – [me] [the new vacuum cleaner].

Text sample 1B: CONVERSATION EXTRACT WITHOUT NOMINAL ELEMENTS

A: *Well [ – ] thought [ – ] were going to talk to [ – ] about [ – ].*
B: *[ – ] have spoken to [ – ] about [ – ]. [ – ]'ve told [ – ] [ – [ – ]]. Why
    don't [ – ], why don't [ – ] sit down and tell [ – ] [ – [ – ] – [ – ]]. [ – ]
    mean [ – ] would be useful.*
A: *Oh [ – ]. Tut. [ – [ – ] – [ – ]].*
B: <unclear>
A: *Well [ – ] bought [ – ] [ – ].*

Text sample 3A: NEWS EXTRACT WITH NOMINAL ELEMENTS ONLY

*[[AUSTRALIA's best-known businessman and yachtsman], [Alan Bond]], –
[little time] – [his victory in [Australia's premier yacht race], [the Sydney to
Hobart]].*

   *[The first [Mr Bond] knew of [the successful move by [the National
Australia Bank] to put [his brewery businesses] into [receivership]]], – [a
radio news bulletin] – [[his $3.5million maxi-yacht], [Drumbeat]].*

   *– [his arrival in [Hobart]], [Mr Bond] – [journalists] [[he] was not
finished yet]. "[I] – [it] – [these things] – [time], – [a long way to go] –." –
[Mr Bond] – [details], – [the rules of [the race]] – [that once [a boat] has
started, [it] may not make [contact] except with [officials] until [the event] is
over].*

Text sample 3B: NEWS EXTRACT WITHOUT NOMINAL ELEMENTS

*[[ – ], [ – ]], had [ – ] to savour [ – [[ – ], [ – ]]]. [ – [ – ] – [ – [ – ] –
[ – ] – [ – ]]], was through [ – ] aboard [[ – ], [ – ]].*

   *On [ – [ – ]], [ – ] told [ – ] [[ – ] – ]. "[ – ] have just got [ – ]
confirmed, but [ – ] take [ – ], and there's [ – ] yet."*

   *But [ – ] was vague on [ – ], because [ – [ – ]] are [ – [ – ] – [ – ] –
[ – ] – [ -] – [ – ] – ].*

Although neither the A nor the B versions make complete sense, there is quite a
striking difference. The versions without nominal elements (the B versions) give
very few clues as to what the text is about. The versions with only nominal
elements (the A versions), on the other hand, are far more informative because of
the **referential specification** given by the nominal elements. That is, the
nominals, which normally play key roles as clause elements (2.7.1.1), specify who
and what the text is about.

## 4.1.1.3 Establishing reference

Establishing reference requires both lexical and grammatical means. Nouns are
the main lexical means of referential specification. There are different types of
nouns, with characteristic differences in meaning and grammatical behaviour
(4.3). With the exception of proper nouns (4.3.3), they normally require
determiners (4.4), and they are also often accompanied by premodifiers and
postmodifiers. These make up noun phrases (4.2). Text sample 3 contains a wide
variety of noun phrases.

   The referential specification in Text sample 1 is rather different. It contains a
great many pronouns (4.9). These do not normally combine with determiners,
though pronouns with very general reference may be accompanied by modifiers
(as in: *about **all** I can tell you*; **nothing** *I particularly want for Christmas*; cf.

8.1.2). Pronouns have a very important role in establishing **chains of reference** (4.1.1.4).

In conversation, establishing reference requires a great deal of cooperation between the speaker and the addressee. Speakers tend to use the minimum description that they think will achieve successful reference from the hearer's point of view, but sometimes get caught out by overdoing this brevity:

1  A: *Who gave you **that**?*
   B: *Who gave me **what**?*
   A: ***That**.*
   B: ***What**?* (CONV)

2  A: *How's **the box** going?*
   B: *Which **box**?*
   A: ***The new one**.*
   B: *Oh **that one** –* (CONV)

In these examples A overestimated the obviousness of the reference, and this required hearer-initiated **repair**. The clarification was provided by the two characteristic means available. In example **1** it was attempted by direct reference to something in the non-linguistic situation of utterance, using the **deictic** word *that*, which might well be accompanied by pointing. In example **2** the more successful clarification is achieved by providing a richer linguistic description of the intended referent.

In the following exchange, there is also a repair sequence, but for a different reason (a simple mishearing of *I*). In addition, this exchange illustrates how speakers can further elaborate the descriptions of previously introduced referents:

   A: ***Sue and I** go to **this cafe**, I told you, at Newtown, didn't I?*
   B: ***Sue and who**?*
   A: ***Sue and I**.*
   B: *Oh.*
   A: *Yeah, and there's just **a little tea room** and **the staff**, lunches dinner time and teas in the afternoon, right opposite Bradgate's Park.*
   B: *Oh **that one**.*
   A: *Yeah and **the girls that serve in there**, there's three girls that serve in there, one works in the kitchen actually helping with the food, but the other two serve at the tables, **they**'ve all got A levels but **they** can't get jobs.* (CONV)

Speaker A begins talking about *a little tea room* and *the staff*, but realizes that the description may not be enough for the hearer (perhaps because of an indication of incomprehension, e.g. by facial expression), and so adds more information. Though the information on the place is not syntactically integrated, the hearer's reply indicates that it was sufficient. After providing more information on the staff, speaker A can then get to the main point: *they've all got A levels but they can't get jobs*. Sequences of this kind are characteristic of conversation. For more examples, see 4.4.1.3 and 4.10.1.

Another characteristic of referential specification in conversation is that the description used to characterize a referent may be rather vague. In many cases, it may not be necessary to agree on an exact description; on the contrary, some degree of imprecision may be desirable:

*That's why I said, it looks like it's from a bank. It's in a white envelope wi–*
*you know where you've got that plastic* **thingy** *– and it's got your name and*
*address? Well, it's one of them.* (CONV)

*It's a full door which is er when you open it it stays open and it's got er* **what**
**do you call it?** **Handle or a knob or whatever you call it** *with all the*
*proper kind of things on it.* (CONV†)

A: *You know you get all the little erm – they bring you around all you–, the*
   *little chutneys* **and things**. *You know, like like pickle*
B: *Oh I see.*
A: **and stuff.** *And erm*
B: *Oh that's great.*
A: *onions* **and other stuff like that.** *It's really nice.* (CONV)

Though the above descriptions are approximate, they are apparently successful in
identifying the referents to the hearer. For more examples of approximate
references in conversation, see 2.9.2, 4.3.6, and 4.3.7.

In the examples given so far, we have been concerned with **specific** reference.
As will become clear later, noun phrases are not always devoted to referential
specification in this straightforward way. There are also **generic** and **classifying**
uses of noun phrases (4.4.1.1, 4.4.1.4, 4.10.2).

## 4.1.1.4    Chains of reference

Text sample 3 illustrates how reference is established and maintained in news. It
also illustrates **chains of reference**, i.e. sequences of noun phrases all referring to
the same thing. This constitutes an important aspect of textual cohesion, which
makes a text more than just a series of sentences. Three chains of reference are:

1 *Australia's best-known businessman and yachtsman, Alan Bond—his*
  *victory—Mr Bond—his brewery businesses—his $3.5million maxi-*
  *yacht—his arrival—Mr Bond—he ...*

2 *Australia's premier yacht race, the Sydney to Hobart—the race—the*
  *event*

3 *a boat—it*

Reference is initially established in the first two cases through a detailed **definite**
**description** (*Australia's best-known businessman ...; Australia's premier yacht*
*race ...*). In **3**, reference is initially established through an indefinite noun phrase.
Reference is maintained in **1** by the repetition of the name (a proper noun) and
the use of possessive determiners and the pronoun *he*. In **2** reference is
maintained by definite noun phrases, and in **3** by the personal pronoun *it*. The
noun phrases in each chain are in a relation of **co-reference**. Subsequent
mentions of a referent are called **anaphoric expressions**.

Co-reference may take different forms depending on the degree of shared
knowledge among participants and the communicative purposes of the text.
There are also important differences between the first mention of a referent and
subsequent anaphoric expressions referring to the same thing. The main devices
used for co-reference (cf. 4.1.3) are:

first mention:

    definite description

    indefinite noun phrase

proper noun

1st or 2nd person pronoun

demonstrative pronoun with situational reference

subsequent (anaphoric) mention:

repeated noun or synonym

noun phrase with a definite article or demonstrative determiner

3rd person pronoun

demonstrative pronoun referring to linguistic context.

Detailed descriptions of the various ways of establishing anaphoric reference are given in following sections: noun phrases with the definite article in 4.4.1.3; noun phrases with a demonstrative determiner in 4.4.3; personal pronouns in 4.10; and demonstrative pronouns in 4.14. With full noun phrases, a distinction can also be made between repetition of the same noun v. the use of a synonym (used in a broad sense for a semantically related noun with identical reference in the particular text, e.g. *Mercedes – car – vehicle*). The distribution of anaphoric expressions across registers is discussed in 4.1.3.

Continuity of reference may also be achieved through ellipsis (3.7), which signals the closest type of connection in the referential chain. Other devices typically vary depending on the distance to the previous mention (4.1.4).

## 4.1.2   Pronouns v. full noun phrases

The distribution of nouns and pronouns varies greatly depending upon register (2.3.5, 2.4.14). It further turns out that the use of pronouns v. full noun phrases varies in relation to syntactic role.

**CORPUS FINDINGS** [3,16]

➤ Pronouns are slightly more common than nouns in conversation.

➤ At the other extreme, nouns are many times more common than pronouns in news and academic prose.

➤ The noun-pronoun ratio varies greatly depending upon syntactic role.

➤ The relative frequency of nouns is much higher in object position and as a complement or object of a preposition than in subject position.

**DISCUSSION OF FINDINGS**

Figure 4.1

**Distribution of nouns v. pronouns across registers**

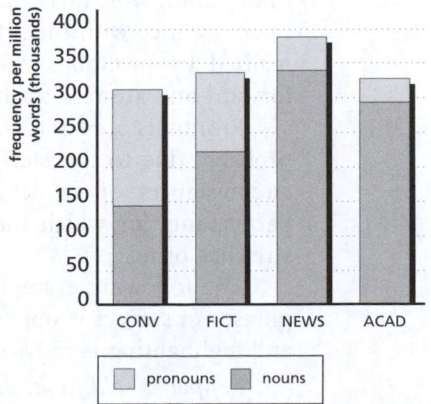

As illustrated in 4.1.1, there are important differences in the reliance on nouns v. pronouns across registers. In conversation, the shared situation and personal involvement of the participants result in a dense use of pronouns. In contrast, the informational purposes of news and academic prose result in a much more frequent use of nouns, and proportionally many fewer pronouns. (See also 2.3.5, 2.4.14.)

**Table 4.1**  **Proportional use of nouns v. pronouns in different syntactic roles (written registers only); percentage of the total nouns + pronouns in that syntactic role**

each ■ represents 5%    □ represents less than 2.5% (note: prepositional objects are included with prepositional complements in the count)

| | % use of nouns | % use of pronouns |
|---|---|---|
| **FICT** | | |
| subject | ■■■■■■■ | ■■■■■■■■■■ ■■■ |
| object | ■■■■■■■■■■ ■■■■ | ■■■■■■ |
| prepositional complement | ■■■■■■■■■■ ■■■■■■ | ■■■ |
| **NEWS** | | |
| subject | ■■■■■■■■■■ ■■■■■ | ■■■■■ |
| object | ■■■■■■■■■■ ■■■■■■■■■ | ■ |
| prepositional complement | ■■■■■■■■■■ ■■■■■■■■■■ | □ |
| **ACAD** | | |
| subject | ■■■■■■■■■■ ■■■■■ | ■■■■ |
| object | ■■■■■■■■■■ ■■■■■■■■■ | ■ |
| prepositional complement | ■■■■■■■■■■ ■■■■■■■■■■ | □ |

The differences associated with syntactic role relate to the typical distribution of information within clauses. Subjects are more likely than objects to express information which has already been introduced or which is given in the context, in accordance with the information principle (11.1.1). Hence, subjects are often realized by pronouns, while objects more typically carry the communication forward and are realized by full noun phrases.

Pronouns are least likely to be used as complements of prepositions. This is probably due to the fact that prepositional phrases more typically refer to the circumstances of an action, while subjects and objects are used for central participants for which there is a greater need for repeated reference in longer stretches of text.

The following examples illustrate the distribution of pronouns v. full noun phrases in subject v. object position. Subjects are in bold, objects are given in [], and highlighting is restricted to subjects and objects at top levels:

*Pepper is sold fresh, dried or powdered. **It** has [the highest average nutritional value (anv)] (see Table 2.2).*

*Since **it** can be dried and stored **it** has [the advantage of maintaining a more or less uniform price level irrespective of season]. (ACAD)*

*Although **Her Majesty's Railway Inspectorate** has expressed [concern over drivers' behaviour at automatic barriers], **it** believes **they** offer [the best blend of safety and cost efficiency].*

*This* has not satisfied [*Essex County Council*], *which* has produced [*statistics showing fatal accidents are four times more likely to happen at automatic gates*]. (NEWS)

## 4.1.3 The forms of anaphoric expressions

As discussed in 4.1.1, different types of nominal expressions are used for anaphoric reference. Corresponding to the overall distribution of nouns v. pronouns, there are also striking differences in the distribution of anaphoric expressions across registers.

**CORPUS FINDINGS** [5,6]

➤ Personal pronouns and definite noun phrases are the main anaphoric devices.
  ➤ Personal pronouns are the predominant type of anaphoric expression in conversation and fiction.
  ➤ Definite noun phrases are predominant in news and academic prose.
➤ Demonstrative pronouns are comparatively rare.
➤ Noun phrases with demonstrative determiners are generally rare, except in academic prose.

Table 4.2 **Use of different types of anaphoric expressions; as a percentage of the total anaphoric expressions within each register**

each ■ represents 5%     □ represents less than 2.5%

| | CONV | FICT | NEWS | ACAD |
|---|---|---|---|---|
| personal pronoun | ■■■■■ ■■■■■ ■■■■■ ■■ | ■■■■■ ■■■■■ ■■■■■ | ■■■■■ ■■■ | ■■■■■ |
| demonstrative pronoun | ■ | □ | □ | □ |
| definite article + repeated noun | ■ | ■■ | ■■■■■ ■■ | ■■■■■ ■■■ |
| definite article + synonym | □ | ■■ | ■■■■ | ■■ |
| demonstrative determiner + repeated noun | □ | □ | □ | ■■ |
| demonstrative determiner + synonym | □ | □ | □ | ■■ |

**DISCUSSION OF FINDINGS**

From the following examples we can see just how the uses of anaphoric devices differ between conversation and academic prose (all anaphoric noun phrases are in bold):

1 ***They****'ve got so much money. **They their** house is full of, **it**'s worth two hundred and fifty thousand. **Their** house in Suffolk got to be worth about two hundred thousand. **They**'re buying a house this year in France. My cousin works at Jones <unclear> does designs. **She**'s a designer, **she**'s very famous. **She** designs a lot of clothes for Lord Browning. **Her** best friend is Princess Margaret. (CONV)*

> 2 *Four carefully chosen plants in the centre row of the maintenance plot are placed under muslin bags to prevent cross-pollination. When flowering is over* **the bags** *are removed and* **the plants** *allowed to ripen normally.* **These four plants** *are the insurance against accidental loss of the pure line.* (ACAD)

The overwhelming majority of anaphoric expressions in conversation are pronouns. Because of the lower overall frequency of nouns in conversation, there is less competition between potential referents and a pronoun will be sufficient for identification. Moreover, if there is uncertainty, the addressee can ask for clarification:

> *A: So there's no father?*
> *B: Which I think is a blessing cos I think* **he**'*s a real so and so.*
> *A:* **Who, the father?**
> *B: Mm,* **he** *was an actor in Emmerdale Farm.* (CONV)

The high frequency of pronouns in fiction is partly to do with the colloquial nature of fictional dialogue. In addition, fiction characteristically focuses on a small number of main characters and typically maintains one topic throughout a sustained narrative.

In academic prose and news, there is a dense use of nouns (4.1.2) and hence a great deal of potential competition among referents. These registers therefore require more specific anaphoric devices. The use of a definite noun phrase rather than a pronoun also makes it possible to include additional information (see e.g. *these four plants* in **2**). Use of a repeated noun is most common in academic prose, presumably because it allows a more exact form of reference (e.g. *feedback systems* in 4.1.1.1, Text sample 4).

The comparatively low frequency of demonstratives is connected with the fact that they are more precise anaphoric devices. In addition to specifying identity, they are deictic—they signal a connection with the immediate linguistic or non-linguistic context (see also 4.1.4). Demonstrative pronouns are more frequent in conversation, which is heavily situation-dependent and relies on implicit rather than explicit links and references. On the other hand, academic prose has a relatively high frequency of noun phrases with demonstrative determiners, as these provide a precise form of reference (used with a noun to refer to the immediate linguistic context).

Synonyms provide a less unambiguous reference than repeated nouns and are therefore less common. They are, however, relatively common in the written registers. A probable reason is that lexical variation is valued in these genres. In addition, the use of a synonym or an alternative definite description makes it possible to draw attention to different aspects of a referent:

> *For years those of us who have played a cat and mouse game with cagey manager Billy Bingham over team selections could always be sure that* **Donaghy**'*s name would be the first one down on the sheet. Now, for the first time in over a decade there is uncertainty over* **the Chelsea veteran**'*s inclusion. Recently* **the 35-year old Belfast man** *has been playing the Irish "sweeper" role, in front of the back four.* (NEWS)

> **Kylie Minogue**$_1$ *has blasted* **Madonna**$_2$ *for ripping off other people's styles.*
> <subscripts indicate co-referential noun phrases>

> **The Aussie singer**$_1$, *who has herself been accused of copying Madonna, has hit out at* **the American superstar**$_2$. (NEWS)

By the choice of these anaphoric expressions the writer produces a more varied and informative text, but may require the reader to do a little more pragmatic work to figure out which noun phrases actually co-refer.

## 4.1.4 Forms of anaphoric expression in relation to distance

Another factor influencing the choice among the various types of anaphoric expressions is the distance to the nearest previous mention.

**CORPUS FINDINGS** [5,6]

➤ In all registers, anaphoric distance varies with the type of anaphoric expression.
➤ Going from lower to higher mean distances, the anaphoric distance generally increases as follows:

**lowest mean distance**

↑ demonstrative pronoun

personal pronoun

demonstrative with synonym

demonstrative with repeated noun

*the* with synonym

↓ *the* with repeated noun

**highest mean distance**

Table 4.3 **Average number of intervening words between mentions for different types of anaphoric expressions**

each ● represents 5

|  | CONV | FICT | NEWS | ACAD |
|---|---|---|---|---|
| demonstrative pronoun | ● ● ● | ● | ● ● ● | ● ● |
| personal pronoun | ● ● ● | ● ● ● ● | ● ● ● ● | ● ● ● ● |
| demonstrative determiner + synonym | ● ● ● ● | ● ● ● ● ● | ● ● ● ● | ● ● ● |
| demonstrative determiner + repeated noun | ● ● ● | ● ● ● ● ● ● ● | ● ● ● ● | ● ● ● ● ● |
| definite article + synonym | ● ● ● ● ● ● ● ● | ● ● ● ● ● ● ● | ● ● ● ● ● ● ● | ● ● ● ● ● ● ● |
| definite article + repeated noun | ● ● ● ● ● ● ● | ● ● ● ● ● ● ● ● ● | ● ● ● ● ● ● ● ● | ● ● ● ● ● ● ● |

**DISCUSSION OF FINDINGS**

The following two samples illustrate anaphoric expressions with typical differences in anaphoric distance; the use of definite noun phrases alternating with pronouns is illustrated in **1**, while noun phrases alternating with demonstrative determiners are illustrated in **2**:

1 *A **school girl** yesterday dropped a legal bid to divorce her parents after **she** made up with her mother.*

> *The 14-year-old* had asked the High Court to rule that **she** could live with her boyfriend's family.
>
> The deal was struck after talks between lawyers and Official Solicitor David Venables.
>
> But it is not yet known whether **the teenager** is returning to her mother or remaining with her 18-year-old boyfriend's family. (NEWS)

2  In 1882 H. Weber gave **a set of postulates for abstract groups of finite order**$_1$. **These postulates**$_1$ are essentially those in use today.

> Two other directions taken in the 19th century by the theory of groups should perhaps be mentioned. One is Dyck's concentration on **systems of generators for a group**$_2$ and on relations satisfied by **these generators**$_2$. (ACAD) <subscripts indicate co-referential noun phrases>

A comparison of the use of personal pronouns and *the*-marked noun phrases shows a clear relationship between explicitness and anaphoric distance. Full noun phrases are more explicit than personal pronouns and are characteristically used with a larger anaphoric distance. A repeated noun is in its turn a more explicit marker than a synonym and therefore allows a somewhat larger span in relation to the previous mention.

The short anaphoric distance of demonstrative pronouns is connected with their basic meaning (4.14); they mark entities as known with reference to the immediate context, either the situational context or the immediate co-text. Noun phrases with demonstrative determiners are more specific than demonstrative pronouns and thus have a larger anaphoric distance. The difference between repeated nouns and synonyms is in the same direction as for *the*-marked noun phrases.

The clearer differentiation between anaphoric devices in the written registers is probably due to the fact that there is more time to plan in composing a written text. The writer can therefore make a more considered use of the language resources.

## 4.2  The basic structure of noun-headed phrases

Phrases with nouns as heads are structured as shown in Table 4.4 (with examples taken from 4.1.1.1: Text sample 3). Just a quick glance at the table reveals a fundamental difference between **head** and **determiner**, on the one hand, and **premodifiers** and **postmodifiers**, on the other.

Premodifiers and postmodifiers are frequently lacking; where they occur, they can usually be omitted without injuring the structure and basic meaning of the phrase. Compare:

> *his $3.5 million maxi-yacht* v. *his maxi-yacht*
>
> *his arrival in Hobart* v. *his arrival*

If the various possibilities of adding pre- and postmodifiers are used, noun phrases can be very complex. See the detailed account in Chapter 8.

Both head and determiner are normally required, and neither can be omitted without destroying the identity of the noun phrase (e.g. *a boat* v. *\*a* and *\*boat*, *the event* v. *\*the* and *\*event*). This is presumably because both elements carry

Table 4.4 **The basic structure of noun-headed phrases**

| determiner | premodifier | head | postmodifier |
|---|---|---|---|
| a | | boat | |
| the | | race | |
| | | Alan Bond | |
| | | officials | |
| his | $3.5 million | maxi-yacht | |
| Australia's | best-known | businessman and yachtsman | |
| the | | rules | of the race |
| his | | arrival | in Hobart |
| a | long | way | to go |

meanings which are indispensable for the interpretation of the noun phrase. The head noun makes it clear what sort of entity is being referred to (*boat, car, plane*, etc.). The determiner specifies the instance we are talking about (*a boat, this boat, his boat*, etc.).

While the description above gives the basic structure of the noun phrase, it needs to be refined and extended in a number of ways. This will become clear in the following survey of nouns and determiners.

# 4.3 Types of nouns

Nouns can be broadly grouped into a small number of classes which differ in meaning and grammatical behaviour. There is an important distinction between **common** and **proper** nouns. Common nouns can be **countable** or **uncountable**.

Countable nouns refer to entities which can be counted; they have both singular and plural forms (*a cow, two cows*, etc.). Both in the singular and the plural there is a contrast between **definite** and **indefinite** forms (*a cow* v. *the cow, cows* v. *the cows*).

Uncountable nouns refer to entities which cannot be counted and do not vary for number. Though they do not combine with the indefinite article, they allow a contrast between an indefinite and a definite form (e.g. *milk* v. *the milk*). The most typical uncountable nouns are singular, but we also find plural nouns which do not vary for number and do not combine with numerals (4.3.2.2).

Proper nouns lack both the contrast in number and definiteness (e.g. *Sue*, but not normally *a Sue, the Sue, Sues*). The overwhelming majority of proper nouns are both definite and singular.

The differences among the major noun types are summarized in Table 4.5.

Table 4.5 **Main types of nouns**

| | common countable | | common uncountable | | proper |
|---|---|---|---|---|---|
| | **indefinite** | **definite** | **indefinite** | **definite** | |
| singular | a cow | the cow | milk | the milk | Sue |
| plural | cows | the cows | – | – | – |

The contrast between the types of nouns is not a simple reflection of reality, but rather reflects how we choose to conceptualize the entities which we want to talk about. This is particularly clear with nouns which can be either countable or uncountable.

1 *Well we've got **an oak** out the front.* (CONV)
2 *The daughter had to bring in logs of **oak** and pine.* (FICT†)
3 *On May 29, a window was broken by **a stone**.* (NEWS)
4 *In this flat landscape of scrub and **stone** there was nowhere one could hide.* (FICT)

Examples **1** and **3** refer to an individual specimen, while in **2** and **4** the reference is to oak and stone as material or an undifferentiated mass (cf. 4.3.2.1).

Proper nouns need no specification of number and definiteness, because they only name instances and do not denote classes (compare *Sue* v. *a girl*). They are used in situations where the speaker and the addressee know which individual is referred to without any further specification.

Nevertheless, the borderline between proper nouns and common nouns is not clearcut. For example, proper nouns can occur with non-restrictive modifiers (cf. 3.11.3):

*The court heard that **little** Harry's death could have been prevented if social workers had not overruled detectives.* (NEWS)

***Beautiful** Di is not so perfect.* (NEWS) <headline>

In these examples the modifier does not serve to distinguish Harry or Di from others of that name, but rather additionally to characterize a person already uniquely identified.

Further, proper nouns are sometimes used with possessive determiners:

*I'm gonna have to – phone **our** Sue.* (CONV)

*Oh did I tell you o– – **our** Joanie's coming over.* (CONV)

In some cases, proper nouns can be used as common nouns (e.g. *a Ford*); 4.3.3.3.

In going through the characteristics of some important noun classes, we will repeatedly come back to the remarkable flexibility of nouns.

## 4.3.1  Use of countable nouns in Text samples

If we inspect Text samples 1–4 again (4.1.1.1), we find large numbers of countable nouns. They denote, for example:

| | |
|---|---|
| persons | *businessman, journalist, yachtsman* |
| concrete objects | *boat, present, vacuum cleaner* |
| actions/events | *event, move, race* |
| other abstractions | *contribution, result, rule* |

It needs to be stressed again that countability is not a simple reflection of things observed in the external world. For example, even a countable noun such as *thing* is used not only with reference to discrete concrete objects, but also to abstractions which do not so obviously or naturally come as distinct entities; see the use of *these things* in the following example:

*I have just got it confirmed, but these things take time.* (CONV)

Countable nouns outnumber uncountables by far in our Text samples, and it is likely that this relationship holds for English texts generally. This pattern reflects a tendency of English to view things—whether concrete or abstract—as separate countable entities.

The most obvious grammatical feature of countable nouns is the variation in number (4.5). Countability is also reflected in co-occurrence patterns with determiners (4.4).

## 4.3.2    Use of uncountable nouns in Text samples

The uncountable nouns in Text samples 1–4 (in 4.1.1.1) are so few that they can all be enumerated:

| | |
|---|---|
| Sample 1 | – |
| Sample 2 | *ice, love, air, time* |
| Sample 3 | *arrival, contact, news, receivership, time* |
| Sample 4 | *feedback, importance, theory* |

The examples give an idea of the types of meanings which are common with uncountable nouns: substances (*air, ice*), emotional and other states (*love, receivership*), qualities (*importance*), events (*arrival*), relations (*contact*), and abstract concepts (*feedback, news, theory, time*).

Grammatically, uncountable nouns are marked by the lack of number variation. Further, they do not combine with determiners that presuppose a notion of countability (4.4).

Many nouns which are basically uncountable also have countable uses with a difference in meaning. Examples from above include: *contact* (denoting a social connection, a person one knows who is in a position to help, or an electrical part), *time* (denoting a particular occasion or a period in history), *ice* (denoting a serving of ice cream, in BrE), *love* (denoting an object of love or a person who is loved), *air* (denoting a tune or a type of appearance/manner). The next few sections will focus on the complex relationship between countable and uncountable nouns.

### 4.3.2.1    Countable and uncountable uses of nouns

The use of a noun as countable or uncountable is lexically restricted, and the difference in meaning varies to a large extent with the individual noun. Following are some examples illustrating countable and uncountable uses of the same noun.

The countable use <C> is for separate things or individual instances, while the uncountable use <U> is for something viewed as substance or material. Many nouns which are countable in their basic meaning have uncountable uses:

> *The rattling carriage was full of rucksacks and hikers, and black-dressed Greek ladies with* **chickens**. <C> (FICT)
> *Would you like some* **chicken** *for dinner?* <U> (CONV)
> *Tests on naturally contaminated* **eggs** *show multiplication cannot occur in an intact* **egg**, *not even in the yolk.* <C> (NEWS†)
> *She cooked me* **egg** *and chips and sat by me while I ate.* <U> (FICT)
> *There is no way to tell how old* **a rock** *is merely by looking at its minerals.* <C> (ACAD†)
> **Rock** *is defined as the inorganic mineral material covering the earth's surface.* <U> (ACAD†)

In addition, many basically uncountable nouns have countable uses:

1 *Plant beverages include **tea**, coffee, wine, alcoholic drinks, intoxicants, and sweet beverages.* <U> (ACAD)
2 *Six **teas** please.* <C> (CONV)
3 *We learned to eat brown rice and yogurt and to tolerate kasha and odd-tasting **teas**.* <C> (FICT)
4 *It was in fact impossible to be strenuously diligent after one of Mrs Sutton's **teas**.* <C> (FICT †)
5 *I think I would like some **wine** though.* <U> (CONV)
6 *That was only one forty nine a bottle. Which is cheap cos a lot of non-alcoholic **wines** are expensive.* <C> (CONV)

The countable instances of *tea* are used in the senses 'a cup of tea' **2**, 'a type of tea' **3**, and 'a small meal usually served in the afternoon with a cup of tea' **4**. The uses illustrated in **2** and **3** are often found with other basically uncountable nouns.

Abstract nouns, which tend to be basically uncountable, also have countable uses:

*It pulls together a series of wide-ranging recommendations for business, transport and **education**.* <U> (NEWS)
*Although she was a girl she wanted an **education**.* <C> (NEWS†)
*I don't think her parents gave her much – very much **freedom**.* (CONV)
*These are tiny **freedoms**, and if a woman enjoys being part of a couple, they should count for nothing.* <C> (NEWS)
*They had received **kindness**, thoughts and good wishes from total strangers.* <U> (NEWS†)
*It would be a "cruel **kindness**" to uphold the county court order.* <C> (NEWS)

In these examples, the uncountable use refers to the general phenomenon, while the countable use refers to individual instances or types.

Instead of using the same form as an uncountable and a countable noun, it is also possible to resort to a combination with a unit noun (4.3.5), a quantifying noun (4.3.6), or a species noun (4.3.7). Given the right context, here a preceding unit noun, we find uncountable uses of what would appear to be typical concrete countable nouns, like *floor* and *road*:

*Stooping swiftly with a sudden angry movement, she wrenched back the piece of **floor**.* (FICT †)
*The testing grounds were selected to permit both signs and dummies to be erected along the same stretch of **road**.* (ACAD)

In the second example, *road*, normally countable, is treated as uncountable to combine with *stretch*. However, the combination *stretch of road* is countable again, but in a different sense.

### 4.3.2.2 Plural uncountables

Although it may seem to be a contradiction, there are plural uncountables. These are morphologically plural nouns which do not vary for number and do not combine with numerals:

*She wears those jigsaw-type **clothes**, **trousers** usually.* (CONV)

He was a grey-haired man with a plausible voice and careful **manners**.
(FICT) <*manners* means 'social behaviour' and is not just the plural of
*manner*.>

She reached for the **scissors**. (FICT)

Letters of **thanks** have been flooding into our offices. (NEWS)

Countable reference can be achieved in some cases through a combination with
the noun *pair* (4.3.5): *a pair of trousers, a pair of scissors*. See also the survey of
plural-only nouns (4.5.5).

## 4.3.3 Proper nouns

Text samples 1–4 (in 4.1.1.1) provide illustrations of some important categories of
proper nouns:

| | |
|---|---|
| Personal names | *Alan Bond, Nancy, Tom* |
| Geographical names | *Australia, Hobart, the Japan Current* |
| Name of object | *Drumbeat* <a boat> |
| Institution | *the National Australia Bank* |

The most typical proper nouns (e.g. *Tom, Hobart*) are arbitrary designations
which have no lexical meaning. There are no defining characteristics for those
who carry the name *Tom*, except that they are male. Grammatically, these nouns
have the characteristic that they are used without determiners and do not vary in
number. Orthographically, they are marked by an initial capital letter. Yet these
characteristics of proper nouns do not apply without qualification.

Many proper nouns are made up of ordinary lexical words. *Drumbeat* does
have a lexical meaning, which does not, however, describe the object to which it
refers. *The Japan Current* and *the National Australia Bank* are indeed noun
phrases which describe the phenomena they refer to. But grammatically these
noun phrases are like proper nouns, in that they do not vary for number and
definiteness. The same applies to a host of more familiar examples: *the Indian
Ocean, the Sahara (Desert), the Library of Congress*, etc.

### 4.3.3.1 Initial capitals

The use of initial capitals of words is more widespread in English than in many
other languages and extends beyond proper nouns. Uses for which capitalization
is conventional:

- personal names (e.g. *Sam, Jones*)
- geographical names (e.g. *Canada, Tokyo*)
- objects and commercial products (e.g. *Voyager, Chevrolet, Kleenex*)
- holidays, months, and days of the week (e.g. *Christmas, January, Tuesday*)
- religions, followers of particular religions, and some religious concepts (e.g.
  *Buddhism, a Buddhist, God, the Devil, Heaven, Hell*)
- family member address terms (e.g. *Father, Mother, Uncle*; capitalization is
  optional in such examples)
- persons or bodies with a unique public function (e.g. *the Queen, the President,
  Congress, Parliament, the Commonwealth*)
- public buildings, institutions, laws, etc. (e.g. *the Library of Congress, the British
  Library, the University of Essex, the Fire Precautions Act*)

- political parties and members of political parties (e.g. *the Labour Party*, *a Republican*, *the Democrats*)
- languages and nationalities (e.g. *English*, *an American*, *a Swede*, *the Australians*)
- adjectives, and common nouns, themselves derived from proper nouns (e.g. *(a) Marxist*, *Marxism*, *Victorian*, *the Victorians*, *a New Yorker*, *Londoners*).

Capitalized nouns range from clear proper nouns to clear common nouns. Some of the types illustrated above vary for number and definiteness, and thus behave like ordinary countable nouns:

*a Buddhist—Buddhists*

*a/the Republican—(the) Republicans*

*a/the Swede—(the) Swedes*

Others are invariable like clear proper nouns, although they may be obligatorily accompanied by the definite article (4.3.3.2): *the Devil*, *the British Library*, etc.

We may conclude that the relationship between proper nouns and common nouns is complex. On the one hand, proper nouns may derive from ordinary descriptive phrases. On the other, they may give rise to derivatives which behave like common nouns, or they may themselves acquire uses as common nouns (4.3.3.3).

### 4.3.3.2   Proper nouns regularly occurring with the definite article

Many proper nouns are regularly preceded by the definite article; these are most typically those derived from descriptive noun phrases. Some important groups are:

A Plural geographical names (e.g. *the Cayman Islands*, *the Bahamas*):

> They crossed **the Great Smoky Mountains** in midwinter. (FICT)

B Other geographical names, such as rivers, seas, and canals (e.g. *the Potomac*, *the Panama Canal*):

> The liaison officer studied the chart of **the Pacific**. (FICT)

C Public institutions, such as hotels, restaurants, theatres, museums, libraries, etc. (e.g. *the Ritz*, *the Metropolitan Museum*):

> **The Library of Congress** – America's largest – has more than 400 miles of bookshelves. (NEWS)

Some categories are quite fluid regarding the presence or absence of the definite article:

D Names of ships, particularly those well-known in history, take the definite article (e.g. *The Titanic*, *the Bos Esperanca*, v. *Salader 3*, *Saratoga*):

> They left in separate car convoys for the docks in Leith where **the Britannia** is berthed. (NEWS)

But compare:

> **Britannia** left her home port of Portsmouth only six times last year cruising for just 31 days. (NEWS)

E Many newspapers and some periodicals take the definite article (e.g. *The Times*, *The Guardian*, v. *Time*, *Newsweek*):

> Yeah we saw that in **the Radio Times**. (CONV)

But compare:

> *We did the one in* **Radio Times** *didn't we?* (CONV†)

### 4.3.3.3 Proper nouns functioning as common nouns

In some cases, proper nouns can function as common nouns. Following are some typical uses:

A  Person or family called X

> *I haven't been in touch with* **the Joneses** *for ages.* (CONV)
>
> *The last bridegroom to be married in Crathie church was also* **a Tim**. (NEWS)

B  Person like X

> *I'm well aware that I have neither the imagination nor the intellectual capacities of* **a Jefferson**. (FICT†)
>
> *But a man who takes control of a state whether it be for good or ill,* **a Napoleon** *or* **a Genghis Khan**, **a Caesar** *or* **a Charlemagne**, *these are remembered and remembered as great.* (ACAD)

C  Product of X

> *I got* **a Bentley**, *two* **Cadillacs**, *a Chrysler station wagon, and* **an MG** *for my boy.* (FICT)
>
> *Sarah Davis's room was next door to the gallery, but her walls were covered with inexpensive Gauguin reproductions,* **a Rubens** *("The Head of a Negro"),* **a Modigliani** *and* **a Picasso**. (FICT)

In the following example, the reference is to an action associated with the person carrying the name:

> *You could do* **an Arnold Schwarzenegger**, *just go* – <unclear> *break the door.* (CONV)

## 4.3.4 Collective nouns

**Collective nouns** refer to groups of single entities. Typical examples are: *army, audience, board, committee, crew, family, jury, staff, team.* All these nouns behave like ordinary countable nouns, i.e. they vary in number and definiteness:

> *They elected a leader and* **a committee** *to represent the three urban communities where they lived.* (ACAD†)
>
> *The constitution and composition of this* **committee** *vary from school to school.* (ACAD†)
>
> *Specifically the* **committees** *have the following functions.* (ACAD†)

Although collective nouns normally behave like ordinary countable nouns, they are marked by special patterns with respect to subject-verb concord (3.9.2.3) and co-referent pronouns (4.10.3). Note the special behaviour of *staff*, which appears to be on the borderline between collective nouns and plural-only nouns (3.9.2.3).

Among collective nouns we find large numbers of proper nouns denoting official bodies and organizations, e.g. *the Air Force, the BBC, the Senate, the United Nations, British Rail, NBC, Congress, Parliament.* As with proper nouns in general, these collective nouns allow no contrast in number and definiteness:

> *The administration is an adept player and so is **Congress**.* (NEWS)
>
> *It is vital that **the United Nations** should now act on that groundwork and drive the peacemaking process forward.* (NEWS)
>
> *The traditional view is that **Parliament** has no power to bind its successors.* (ACAD)

Here also belong names of firms and names of countries or cities when used to refer to the population or to a subset representing the population (e.g. a sports team):

> *Last night **Ford** declined to comment on the long-awaited Jaguar/GM statement.* (NEWS)
>
> ***Liverpool** stayed on long without kicking a ball.* (NEWS)

Some collective expressions, apart from proper nouns, also do not generally exhibit any contrast in number and definiteness. These include singular noun phrases with the definite article, such as *the aristocracy* and *the press*. The reference here is to a class in its entirety:

> ***The Aristocracy** never fails to fascinate.* (NEWS)
>
> *To me it is not freedom of **the press** if **the press** speaks only on one side.* (ACAD)

Note also the collective reference of nominalized adjectives with the definite article: *the blind, the poor*, etc. (cf. 7.6.2).

Many collective nouns are fairly general in meaning (*batch, crowd, flock, group, herd*, etc.) and combine normally, or at least very frequently, with a following *of*-phrase specifying the type of entity making up the group, expressed by a plural countable noun. They may be termed **quantifying collectives**:

> ***Two little groups of people** stood at a respectable distance beyond the stools.* (FICT)
>
> *Mr Johnson told me they were **a particularly fine batch of sausages** today.* (FICT)
>
> *There was **a small crowd of people** around.* (NEWS)
>
> *The aircraft flew into **a large flock of seagulls** just after take-off, and sustained multiple birdstrikes.* (ACAD)

Note the similarity with forms such as *a number of* and *a couple of* which are treated as quantifying determiners (4.3.8 and 4.4.4.1).

## 4.3.4.1 Collocations of quantifying collectives

There are wide differences in collocational patterns between individual collective nouns.

**CORPUS FINDINGS [1]**

➤ Collective nouns differ in their productivity in combining with collocates, both in terms of the number of collocates and in terms of the range of entities making up the group.

➤ *Bunch of, group of*, and *set of* are by far the most productive, each combining with over 100 different collocates.

| Collective noun | Selected collocates |
|---|---|
| *batch of* | cakes, cards, blood tests, messages, pigs |
| *bunch of* | amateurs, idiots, perverts, thieves; daffodils, roses; bananas, grapes |
| *clump of* | azalea, dandelions, elms, trees |
| *crowd of* | demonstrators, fans, spectators, shoppers |
| *flock of* | birds, doves, geese, sheep, children |
| *gang of* | bandits, drunken youths, hecklers, thugs |
| *group of* | adults, friends, girls; animals, insects; atoms, buildings, chemicals, diseases, things |
| *herd of* | cows, deer, elephants |
| *host of* | advisors, angels, stars; facts, possibilities |
| *pack of* | dogs, rogues, lies |
| *series of* | accidents, assertions, events, tests |
| *set of* | assumptions, characteristics, conditions; books, brakes, drawers, glasses, friends |
| *shoal of* | fish, mackerel |
| *swarm of* | bees, hornets; panicked men, possibilities |
| *troop of* | British tommies, inspectors |

### DISCUSSION OF FINDINGS

Most collective nouns are associated with a particular type of entity: people (e.g. *crowd* and *gang*), animals (e.g. *flock*, *herd*, *shoal*, and *swarm*), plants (e.g. *bouquet* and *clump*), or inanimate objects or entities (e.g. *batch* and *set*). However, the most productive collective nouns—*bunch*, *group*, and *set*—are very flexible with respect to the type of entity they refer to. In most cases the nouns are used for neutral descriptions, but *bunch*, *gang*, and *pack* frequently have negative connotations. As the word suggests, *series* relates to things or events placed or occurring in sequence.

The choice of collocation may be used to suggest how a group of entities is viewed:

1 *When Anna entered **a group of young men** were talking eagerly round the table.* (FICT†)

2 *Then we could pretend that **a bunch of drunken men** watched a bit of group sex.* (FICT†)

3 *A **swarm of panicked men**, most with rifles, approached the blinding, erupting generator, shielding their eyes and shouting at one another.* (FICT†)

In **3** the choice of noun suggests a large number of men moving about and sounding like a swarm of bees.

The same type of metaphor is found with other collective nouns:

4 *There's probably **a flock of messages** on my desk.* (FICT)

5 *With the end of the ballgame, we disperse in pairs toward **the herd of station wagons** corraled in the gravel parking lot.* (FICT)

6 *Immediately upon their entrance, they were watched by **a shoal of white faces** gazing at them from behind cold masks.* (FICT)

In **4** the messages are seen to resemble a flock of birds, in **5** the station wagons seem like a herd of cattle (note also the choice of the word *corraled*), while the white faces in **6** are like a shoal of fish. Not unexpectedly, such examples of metaphoric use are particularly common in fiction.

Modifiers can be inserted either before the collective noun or as part of the following noun phrase. Compare the following:

Before the collective noun:

> *a fine bunch of men; a distant clump of trees; a large flock of sheep; a moving, surging swarm of people*

After *of*:

> *the bunch of shaggy chrysanthemums, the clumps of white flox, a flock of small shepherds, a swarm of unseen atoms*

In both positions:

> *great bunches of dried herbs, England's last wild herd of red deer, a little swarm of minute birds*

The modifiers may thus qualify the group (e.g. *large flock*) or entities making up the group (e.g. *red deer*). The collective noun may be preceded by evaluative adjectives (e.g. *fine, grand, great*) which qualify the whole of the complex noun phrase rather than the collective noun alone. For example, the adjective in *a fine bunch of men* applies both to the bunch and the men.

## 4.3.5 Unit nouns

**Unit nouns** are in a way the opposite of collective nouns: rather than providing a collective reference for separate entities, they make it possible to split up an undifferentiated mass and refer to separate instances of a phenomenon. Both types of noun provide alternative ways of viewing and referring, collective nouns with respect to countables and unit nouns with respect to uncountables.

Unit nouns are characteristically general in meaning (*bit, piece, slice*, etc.), and they are followed by an *of*-phrase specifying the type of matter or phenomenon referred to. Grammatically, they behave like ordinary countable nouns.

> *I watched **a bit of television news**.* (CONV†)
>
> *They offered him **a slice of soft white bread**.* (FICT)
>
> *Eric Robinson has **two pieces of advice** for worried customers.* (NEWS†)

### 4.3.5.1 Collocations of unit nouns

**CORPUS FINDINGS [1]**

➤ As with collective nouns, unit nouns tend to have marked collocational patterns.

➤ *Bit of* and *piece of* are the most productive, each combining with well over 100 different collocates.

| Unit noun | Selected collocates |
|---|---|
| *act of* | *adultery, aggression, courage, defiance, folly, kindness* |
| *bit of* | *beef, cake, cheese, sugar; cloth, paper, grass, wood; conversation, excitement, fun, luck* |
| *chip of* | *glass, ice, paint, stone* |

| | |
|---|---|
| *chunk of* | *chocolate, meat; concrete, gold, rock; data, text, time* |
| *game of* | *cards, chess, golf, tennis* |
| *grain of* | *corn, dust, salt, sand; doubt, sense* |
| *item of* | *clothing, equipment; information, news* |
| *loaf of* | *bread* |
| *lump of* | *clay, coal, plutonium, soil; butter, cheese, fat, meat* |
| *piece of* | *cake, chicken, toast; chalk, land, wood; advice, evidence* |
| *pair of* | *clippers, glasses, pants, pliers, pyjamas, tweezers* |
| *rasher of* | *bacon* |
| *scrap of* | *material, paper; hope, information* |
| *sheet of* | *cardboard, iron, paper, plastic; flame, water* |
| *slice of* | *bread, ham, pie* |
| *sliver of* | *glass, light* |
| *speck of* | *dirt, paint; trouble* |
| *sprinkling of* | *sugar, sunshine* |
| *strip of* | *bacon, cloth, land, tissue* |
| *trace of* | *blood, lipstick, poison; anxiety, remorse, vanity* |
| *whit of* | *concern* |

### DISCUSSION OF FINDINGS

Some unit nouns have a precise meaning and a very narrow field of use (e.g. *loaf, rasher, sliver, whit*), while other unit nouns are more general in meaning and combine with a wide variety of nouns (notably *bit* and *piece*). A few unit nouns are used only or very frequently in negative contexts: *not a speck of, no trace of, not a whit of*.

*Pair* is a special case in that it is often used for countable reference with plural uncountables referring to objects consisting of two equal parts (4.5.5; see also 4.3.6.2):

> With **a good pair of binoculars**, *badgers can be watched in comfort from the roadside*. (NEWS†)

> *She quickly picked up* **a pair of scissors** *and snipped off a piece of her long blond hair.* (FICT)

Many uncountable nouns can combine with a variety of unit nouns. For example, *paper* can combine with any of the following unit nouns:

> *ball, bit, flake, fragment, heap, length, mound, pad, piece, pile, reel, roll, scrap, sheaf, sheet, slip, sliver, square, strip, twist, wad*

By the choice of unit noun, it is possible to bring out different aspects of the entity (size, shape, etc.).

Modifiers can be inserted either before the unit noun or as part of the following noun phrase. Compare the following:

Before the unit noun:

> *a valuable piece of advice, an astonishing piece of news, a nice piece of work, furry pieces of animal hide, a huge piece of paper*

After *of*:

> *a piece of legal advice, a few words of useless advice, a bit of good news, many pieces of investigative journalism*

In both positions:

> *solid old pieces of English furniture, a thick piece of broken glass, no specific item of bad news.*

The modifiers may thus qualify the unit (e.g. *thick piece*) or the undifferentiated mass (e.g. *broken glass*). The unit noun may be preceded by evaluative adjectives (e.g. *astonishing, nice, valuable*) which qualify the whole of the complex noun phrase rather than the unit noun alone. For example, *a valuable piece of advice* means more or less the same as *a piece of valuable advice*.

## 4.3.6　Quantifying nouns

**Quantifying nouns** are used to refer to quantities of both masses and entities, which are specified in a following *of*-phrase by uncountable nouns and plural countables. Quantifying collectives (4.3.4.1) and unit nouns (4.3.5) are special cases of quantifying nouns used with countable and uncountable nouns, respectively. Quantifying nouns vary in number like ordinary countable nouns (but note the special behaviour of *foot* and *pound*; 4.5.4B). As regards the relationship between quantifying nouns and determiners, see 4.3.8.

There is a wide range of quantifying nouns. The survey below illustrates the major categories.

### 4.3.6.1　Collocations of types of quantifying nouns

#### A　Nouns denoting type of container

| Noun | Selected collocates |
| --- | --- |
| *barrel of* | *apples, brandy, fish, powder* |
| *basket of* | *eggs, flowers, bread, fruit, toiletries* |
| *box of* | *books, chocolates, cigars, matches, soap, tissues* |
| *crate of* | *champagne, explosives, fruit* |
| *cup of* | *coffee, soup, tea* |
| *keg of* | *beer, stout* |
| *pack of* | *cards, cigarettes, notes, peanuts* |
| *packet of* | *biscuits, candles, chips, cocaine, envelopes* |
| *sack of* | *coal, grain, mail, potatoes, rice, rubbish* |

Some of these nouns can be used more generally, and metaphorically, as quantifying nouns:

> *That was when Fernandez was hired from Miami for $195,000 a year and **a basket of pension plans** that would excite a baseball player.* (NEWS)
>
> *He knows he's **a sack of scum**.* (NEWS†)
>
> ***Packets of data** are multiplexed together.* (ACAD†)

*Pack* can also be used as a collective noun, without any suggestion of a container (4.3.4.1).

As regards the use of words for containers, see also F below.

#### B　Nouns denoting shape

| Noun | Selected collocates |
| --- | --- |
| *heap of* | *ashes, blankets, bones, leaves, rubble* |
| *pile of* | *bills, bodies, bricks, cushions, rocks, rubbish, wood* |
| *stick of* | *celery, driftwood, incense* |
| *wedge of* | *bronze, ice* |

*Heap* and *pile* are also used more generally, typically expressing exaggeration or a very large amount:

> *Oh god, I've got **heaps of things** to do.* (CONV†)
>
> *She said she had **heaps of common sense** and they'd be able to cope.* (NEWS)
>
> *They must have cost **a pile of money**.* (FICT)
>
> *Levellers play music which has vitality, a sense of adventure and **piles of gusto**.* (NEWS)

### C   Standardized measure terms

| Noun | Selected collocates |
|---|---|
| pint, gallon, quart, litre | of beer, blood, gas, gin, milk, oil, petrol, water, whisky, wine |
| foot, inch, yard, metre | of cloth, concrete, earth, fabric, material, sediment, wire |
| ounce, pound, gram, kilo(gram) | of butter, cheese, cocaine, flour, gold, heroin, margarine, meat, opium, potatoes, sugar |
| ton, tonne | of aluminium, bricks, explosives, ore, sewage |

Different measures apply to different products or types of material. Occasionally, measure terms are used more generally, especially *ounce* and *ton*:

> *He ain't **an ounce of trouble**, not a bloody ounce that man.* (CONV)
>
> *I didn't seem to have **an ounce of grown-up character** to draw on.* (FICT)
>
> *I wish you and yours every joy in life, old chap, and **tons of money**, and may you never die till I shoot you.* (FICT†)
>
> *"Sweet Freedom" is perhaps his best known ditty in these climes even though he has released **tons of songs** for the consumption of the masses* (NEWS†)

Combinations of this kind normally express exaggeration, indicating a very small amount (*ounce*) or large amount (*ton*).

### D   Plural numerals

Numerals are used either as determiners or as heads of noun phrases (2.4.13, 4.4.5). However, plural forms of round numbers are used with a following *of*-phrase and a plural countable noun to express approximate numbers: *tens of thousands, hundreds of applicants, thousands of accidents, billions of dollars*, etc.

The following nouns are also used to express approximate numbers:

| Nouns | Selected collocates |
|---|---|
| dozens, scores | of animals, books, drivers, people, women |

Expressions with plural numerals may be used very loosely as vague expressions for large numbers:

> *Oh goodness, darling, you've seen it **hundreds of times**.* (FICT)
>
> *It's only a lot of wood-pigeons cooing! A sound you must have heard **thousands of times**.* (FICT)

Though restricted to occurrence with plural countable nouns, the plural numerals differ from the quantifying collectives of 4.3.4.1 in taking unambiguous plural concord and not admitting premodifiers in the same way.

**E   Nouns denoting large quantities**

| Noun | Selected collocates |
|---|---|
| *a load of* | *batteries, cars, fuel, junk, money, stuff; bullshit, crap, garbage, nonsense, rubbish* |
| *loads of* | *books, cakes, friends, girls, money, things, work* |
| *a mass of* | *blood, bodies, detail, flames, material, stuff* |
| *masses of* | *abstentions, homework, money, neurons, people* |

The nouns *load* and *mass* are distributed quite differently across the registers: *load/loads* is much more common in conversation than in the written registers, while *mass* is used primarily in the written registers. Other examples of nouns for large quantities are *heap* and *pile* (see B above), *tons* (see C above), numerals (see D above), and *host* (see 4.3.4.1).

**F   Nouns ending in *-ful***

The suffix *-ful* can be added to almost any noun denoting some kind of container to form a quantifying noun, resulting in nouns such as:

*basketful, bellyful, bowlful, earful, eyeful, forkful, houseful, kettleful, planetful, plateful, pocketful, roomful, shovelful, tankful, teaspoonful, thimbleful.*

Many of these have marked collocational patterns. *Handful of* is the most common, occurring over ten times per million words.

| Noun | Selected collocates |
|---|---|
| *armful of* | *straw, grass, magazines, pots and pans, red roses* |
| *fistful of* | *cash, dollars, matches, money* |
| *handful of* | *gravel, peanuts, pencils, salt, sand; boys, enthusiasts, people; cases, films, occasions, sites* |
| *mouthful of* | *coffee, cereal, dirt, food, ice cream, teeth* |
| *spoonful of* | *broth, cream, custard, sprouts, stuffing, sugar, tea* |

In addition to being the most common form of this type, *handful* stands out by appearing in the majority of cases where the reference is to a small amount rather than literally to what can be contained in a hand. Apart from *handful*, nouns ending in *-ful* are regularly used in a literal meaning.

### 4.3.6.2   *Pair* v. *couple*

| Noun | Selected collocates |
|---|---|
| *pair of* | *arms, eyes, glasses, gloves, hands, pants, shoes, socks* |
| *couple of* | *days, feet <denoting measurement>, hours; babies, balloons, boys, examples, kids* |

As the small selection of examples shows, *pair* and *couple* have quite different collocational patterns. *Pair of* is used with reference to entities that occur in groups of two, either generally or in a specific context. Often these are expressed by plural uncountables, with respect to which it behaves as a unit noun (4.3.5.1) which can itself be modified, though ordinary plural countables (e.g. *eyes*, *socks*) also occur with it. *Couple of*, on the other hand, applies only to plural countables and only takes the form *a couple of*: it is treated later as a quantifying determiner (4.4.4.1). Furthermore, while both the singular form *a pair of* and the plural form *pairs of* are used for an exact specification of number, *couple* usually indicates a small approximate number rather than just two and does not indicate two items that belong together as a set. Not surprisingly, the two forms are quite differently distributed across registers:

➤ A *pair of* occurs in all registers while *a couple of* is notably absent in academic prose.

Table 4.6 **Distribution of *pair of* v. *couple of*; occurrences per million words**

each ■ represents 20      □ represents less than 10

|  | CONV | FICT | NEWS | ACAD |
|---|---|---|---|---|
| *a pair of* | ■■■ | ■■■ | ■ | ■■■ |
| *pairs of* | □ | □ | □ | ■ |
| *a couple of* | ■■■■■■■■■■ | ■■■■■ | ■■■■ | □ |

**DISCUSSION OF FINDINGS**

The difference in the frequency of *a couple of* between academic prose and conversation agrees with the distribution of some other quantifying expressions which are also predominantly associated with particular registers (4.4.4.1). The difference of meaning accords with this pattern, since we have seen (e.g. 4.1.1.3) how conversation often thrives on imprecision.

## 4.3.7  Species nouns

**Species nouns** are found in patterns which are superficially like those of quantifying nouns. However, they are used to refer not to the amount but to the type of entity or mass expressed by a following *of*-phrase. They behave grammatically like ordinary countable nouns. Common species nouns are: *class, kind, make, sort, species, type*:

> A: *What do you normally have with that then?*
> B: *Just erm, some **sort** of pilau rice or something.* (CONV)
> *I think she's impervious to that **kind** of thing.* (NEWS)
> *The scheme covers any **make** of machine.* (NEWS†)
> *Limestones, one **class** of sedimentary rock, are made up of calcium carbonate.* (ACAD†)
> *There are two **types** of bond energy.* (ACAD†)
> *Under these conditions certain **species** of bacteria break down the waste to form methane gas.* (ACAD)

Species nouns combine with countable as well as uncountable nouns. With countable nouns there tends to be agreement in number between the species noun and the following noun (e.g. *that kind of thing* v. *all kinds of things*). But we also find singular species nouns combining with a following plural noun and plural species nouns combining with a following singular noun:

Singular species noun + plural noun:

> *I don't know **what kind of dinosaurs** they all are.* (CONV)
> *I mean, do we want **these kind of people** in our team?* (CONV)
> ***What sort of things** are effects?* (ACAD)

Plural species noun + singular noun:

> *Thieves tended to target **certain types of car** he said.* (NEWS)

> *For **these kinds of question** it is necessary that the marked cell populations differ in the expression of the gene.* (ACAD†)

There is a close relationship between species nouns and determiners. Singular countable nouns appear to behave like uncountables in these expressions. The determiner preceding the species noun occasionally agrees with the noun in the *of*-phrase rather than with the species noun (as in *these kind of people*). See also 4.3.8.

## 4.3.7.1 Species nouns: distribution

**CORPUS FINDINGS [2]**

➤ Species nouns are distributed quite differently across registers.
> ➤ With the exception of *sort(s)* and the singular form *kind*, species nouns are far more common in academic prose than in the other registers.

**Table 4.7** **Distribution of species nouns; occurrences per million words**

each ■ represents 20     □ represents less than 10

| | CONV | FICT | NEWS | ACAD |
|---|---|---|---|---|
| *sort* | ■■■■■■■■ ■■■■■■■ | ■■■■■■■■■■ | ■■■■ | ■■■ |
| *sorts* | ■ | ■ | □ | □ |
| *kind* | ■■■ | ■■■■■■■■■■ | ■■■ | ■■■■■■■ |
| *kinds* | □ | ■ | □ | ■■■■ |
| *type* | ■ | ■ | ■■ | ■■■■■■■■■■ |
| *types* | □ | □ | □ | ■■■■■■■■■■ |
| *species* | □ | □ | □ | ■■ |

**DISCUSSION OF FINDINGS**

The higher frequency of species nouns in academic prose occurs because classification is an important aspect of academic procedure and discourse.

*Sort of* and *kind of* in conversation and fiction have somewhat different functions from those in academic prose. They may be part of a question designed to establish the precise type of something being referred to:

> ***What sort of little silver thing** is it?* (CONV)

But very often, rather than serving the purposes of exact definition, these forms introduce greater vagueness (cf. 4.1.1.3):

> *It's **a very difficult sort of situation**.* (CONV†)

> *There's **a kind of mystery** here, wasn't there?* (CONV)

> *She loves doing **this kind of thing**, doesn't she?* (CONV†)

> ***A silly sort of drink** really.* (FICT)

> *Goodness knows **what sort of state** his feet were in.* (FICT†)

*There must be something, **some kind of hint or memory**.* (FICT)

*His eyes had **a kind of icy brilliance** about them.* (FICT)

The singular forms *sort of* and *kind of* are also used more generally as vagueness markers, or **hedges**:

*I **kind of** danced into work.* (CONV†)

*Yes, yes, it's **sort of** all a bit naked isn't it?* (CONV)

Examples of this kind are not included in the frequency counts above, as they do not behave as species nouns (see 10.3 for a detailed account of hedges).

The association of the vagueness marker *sort of* with conversation fits in with the general focus on personal involvement rather than informational precision (14.1.2.3). The association is so strong that the species noun *sort* tends to be avoided in academic prose, where species expressions are generally very common. News reportage, which lacks the specific needs which lead to a high frequency of species nouns in academic prose, has a relatively low frequency of species expressions.

## 4.3.8 Noun v. determiner

It is not always easy to identify the head of a noun phrase, particularly with quantifying nouns and species nouns. Compare:

1 *We drank our bottle of champagne.* (FICT†)
   cf. *How much champagne did we drink?*

2 *He uncorked the bottle of Chablis.* (FICT)
   cf. *What did he uncork?*

In **1** it could be argued that the head is *champagne*, in **2** *bottle*. In other words, *a bottle of X* could be interpreted either way depending upon circumstances.

Combinations of quantifying nouns plus *of* specify the reference of a following noun in much the same way as quantifying determiners (4.4.4). Compare these examples with quantifying nouns:

*We knew **masses of** people.* (CONV†)

***Loads of** people go out there.* (CONV†)

and these which we treat as involving determiners:

*There's so **many** people in that place.* (CONV†)

*There were **lots of** people going through the tills.* (CONV)

***A number of** people said to me how much they enjoyed yesterday's service.* (CONV)

It is not possible to draw a clear borderline between determiner and noun in these cases. Variation in form, such as the use of an adjective modifier, may be an indication that we have a noun rather than a determiner, as in *a great mass of* or *a large mass of*. But even combinations which are generally analysed as determiners have possibilities of expansion, as in *a mere few, a select few, a very few*; or *a fair lot of, a great lot of, a whole lot of*.

On the other hand, the high frequency of *load(s) of* in conversation (4.3.6.1E) is an indication that it is coming to be used like a determiner. Note that *loads of* behaves in the same way as *a lot of / lots of* with regard to concord (3.9.1.4), i.e. concord is determined by the noun following *of*: *There was loads of traffic on the road.*

Species nouns narrow down the reference of a noun in the same way as the semi-determiner *such* (4.4.6D). Compare:

> To some degree **such** differences of definition may be a function of the extension of the tongue. (ACAD)

> Differences **of this kind** are both substantial and early to appear. (ACAD†)

> **These kinds of** questions cannot be transformed into hypothesis form. (ACAD)

As with the quantifying expressions, it is not clear how these structures should be analysed. There are indications that species nouns may be felt to be subordinate in much the same way as a determiner. In the following examples, the demonstrative determiner agrees with the noun following *of*. Note also that it is the noun following *of* which controls subject-verb concord in the last example:

> I hate **these sort of things**. (CONV)

> It does not in any way cause **these sort of problems**. (NEWS†)

> When Giggs gets going he's a handful, particularly when he gets in **those type of crosses**. (NEWS)

> **These kind of decisions** are normally made by the teacher alone. (ACAD†)

Constructions such as *these kind of decisions* are generally rare. The construction *these sort of Xs* occurs about 5 times per million words in conversation, but such constructions with *kind* or *type* are rarely used. The superficially more grammatical construction *these kinds of* is even less common and chiefly restricted to academic prose.

# 4.4 Determiners

**Determiners** are function words which are used to specify the reference of a noun (2.4.1). Co-occurrence patterns differ depending upon the type of noun; Table 4.8. Additionally, it is possible to recognize positional subgroups among the determiners themselves. Broadly three groups may be identified:

- **Predeterminers**: *all*, *both*, *half* and multipliers like *double*, *once* and *twice*.
- **Central determiners**: articles, demonstrative determiners, and possessive determiners.
- **Postdeterminers**, with two subgroups: (1) ordinal numerals and the semi-determiners *same*, *other*, *former*, *latter*, *last*, and *next*; (2) cardinal numerals and quantifying determiners.

Table 4.9 exemplifies the more common combinations. Note however that in indefinite noun phrases, *other* follows cardinal numbers and quantifying determiners: e.g. *two other projects*, *many other people*. On the co-occurrence patterns of the quantifiers (which are different when followed by *of*) see also 4.4.4; on semi-determiners see also 4.4.6.

In addition to the determiners taken up in the tables, there are central determiner functions of *wh*-words (4.4.7). Specifying genitives also occupy the central determiner slot (4.6.3).

**Table 4.8**     **Co-occurrence patterns of some major classes of determiners and nouns**

| determiner type | countable nouns | | uncountable nouns |
|---|---|---|---|
| | singular | plural | |
| article | – | books | money |
| | a book | – | – |
| | the book | the books | the money |
| possessive | my/your ... book | my/your ... books | my/your ... money |
| demonstrative | this book | these books | this milk |
| | that book | those books | that milk |
| quantifier | every book | – | – |
| | each book | – | – |
| | – | all (of) the books | all (of) the milk |
| | – | many (of the) books | much (of the) milk |
| | – | a great many books | a great deal of milk |
| | – | a lot of books | a lot of milk |
| | – | lots of books | lots of milk |
| | – | plenty of books | plenty of milk |
| | – | some (of the) books | some (of the) milk |
| | – | (a) few books | (a) little milk |
| | – | several books | – |
| | – | a couple of books | – |
| | – | enough books | enough milk |
| | either book | both books | – |
| | neither book | – | – |
| | any book | any (of the) books | any (of the) milk |
| | no book | no books | no milk |
| | – | none of the books | none of the milk |
| numeral | one book | two/three ... (of the) books | – |

**Table 4.9**     **Positional groups of determiners**

| predeterminer | central determiner | postdeterminer | | head |
|---|---|---|---|---|
| | | (1) | (2) | |
| all | the | | four | races |
| all | those | other | | guys |
| both | these | | | problems |
| half | a | | | cup |
| half | the | | | size |
| twice/double | the | | | size |
| | the | | many/few | occasions |
| | her | first | | marriage |
| | the | last | two | years |
| | the/those | other | two | fellows |

## 4.4.1 The articles

The **definite** and the **indefinite article** are the most common and most basic of the determiners. Both articles take a different spoken form when the following word begins with a vowel:

| | | | |
|---|---|---|---|
| /ə/ | *a house* | /ən/ | *an hour* |
| | *a Member of Parliament* | | *an MP* |
| /ðə/ | *the house* | /ðɪ/ | *the hour* |
| | *the Member of Parliament* | | *the MP* |

In some cases, the written form can be misleading. Thus *a* is used before words like *union* and *university*, which are pronounced with an initial /j/, while *an* is found before words with initial silent *h*, such as *heir, honest, honour(able), hour*.

There is variation in the form of the indefinite article before some words spelled with an initial *h* in an unstressed syllable. For example, in the LSWE Corpus the word *history* is always used with *a*, but *historical* takes *a* and *an* with about equal frequency.

The occurrence of the articles varies depending upon the type of noun (4.4). In addition to the definite and the indefinite article, it is customary to recognize a **zero article** (4.4.1.2).

### 4.4.1.1 The indefinite article

The **indefinite article** is used with singular countable nouns. It narrows down the reference of the following noun to a single member of a class and is often used to introduce a new **specific** entity in discourse. Subsequent references generally take the form of definite noun phrases or personal pronouns, as shown in the following example:

> 1 **A cat₁** was the victim of a cruel attack when **she₁** was shot in the neck by **a pellet₂**. **The tortoiseshell cat₁** was found wounded and frightened in Grangetown, Middlesbrough, and brought to an animal sanctuary. **The pellet₂** went right through **the cat₁**'s neck and came out the other side, leaving a gaping wound. (NEWS) <subscripts indicate co-referential noun phrases>

The indefinite article can also be used in contexts where the noun phrase does not refer to any specific individual. Compare:

> 2 *I'm looking for **a millionaire**, she says, but I don't see many around –* (CONV)
>
> 3 *"I feel terrible. I need **a friend**." * (FICT)
>
> 4 *Police are looking for **a scruffy man aged 17 to 21**. * (NEWS)

In **2** and **3** the reference is to a **non-specific** new entity, while **4** refers to a particular newly introduced entity (cf. the use of *certain*; 4.4.6D).

The indefinite article can also serve, as in **5**, to **classify** an entity (3.5.3.1), or it can be used **generically 6** to express what is typical of any member of a class (see also 4.4.1.4).

> 5 *My husband is **a doctor**. * (FICT)
>
> 6 **A doctor** *is not better than his patient. * (FICT†)

## 4.4.1.2  The zero article

Corresponding to the indefinite article with singular countable nouns, we find the **zero article** with uncountables **1** and with plural countable nouns (**2** and **3**):

> 1  *We have **wine** on the table girls, drink it.* (CONV †)
> 2  *Two of his cousins are **teachers**, his sister's a teacher.* (CONV)
> 3  *Inside the house Mr Summers found a family of **cats** shut in the bathroom.* (NEWS)

The reference in such constructions is to an indefinite number or amount (often equivalent to *some*). Note the classifying use of plural indefinite noun phrases (as in **2**), which is parallel to the classifying use of the indefinite article (4.4.1.1).

Zero-article noun phrases commonly express non-specific or generic reference (4.4.1.4). Some special uses of zero-article noun phrases are treated below. Arguably some of these cases should be analysed as involving neutralization of article distinctions, rather than as cases of zero article. What is important to note is that these structures involve nouns which in other contexts behave as ordinary countable nouns.

### A  Meals

> *Are they going out for **dinner** or something?* (CONV)
> *She tried to recall the sight of them standing in the hall after **lunch**.* (FICT)

Here the reference is to the meal as an institution. In contrast, the definite article is used if a special meal is singled out:

> *Bye bye, dear, thanks for **the lunch**.* (CONV)
> ***The dinner** was excellent, exquisite.* (FICT)

### B  Institutions

The zero article is used where the focus is on the type of institution rather than on a specific entity:

> *They're in **hospital**, badly injured.* (BrE CONV)
> *The ceremony took place in **church**.* (FICT †)
> *We were at **university** together.* (FICT)
> *They are prepared to go to **jail** for their cause.* (NEWS)

but compare:

> *It's the diamond jubilee of **the hospital**.* (CONV †)
> ***The church** serves a population of 18,000.* (NEWS)
> ***The university** has increased the number of students compared with previous years.* (NEWS)
> *Jane turned around to look at Gabby in the back seat of the Rolls, which they had left parked outside **the jail**.* (FICT)

### C  Predicatives with unique reference

English normally requires an article with singular countable nouns in predicative position:

> *He is **a director of the Eastern Ravens Trust**, which helps disabled people in the area.* (ACAD)
> *The Lord Chancellor is **a member of all three organs of government**.* (NEWS)

*He was made **an honorary member of the club**.* (NEWS†)

However, when the predicative noun phrase names a unique role or position, the zero article alternates with the definite article:

*Lukman was re-elected **OPEC president** in November.* (NEWS†)

*Jez Zan is **managing director of Argonaut Software**.* (NEWS†)

*Simon Burns is **[the] chairman of the appeal fund**.* (NEWS†)

In the LSWE Corpus, the pattern with the zero article outnumbers the pattern with the definite article by about 5 to 1 (based on a study of all occurrences of *is* + *chairman/director*[1]).

### D   Means of transport and communication

This type is restricted to prepositional phrases opening with *by*, but affects nouns that are elsewhere uncountable as well as countable:

*go by **bus/car/coach/plane/sea/taxi/train***

*travel by **air/car/horse/rail***

*contact by **radio/telephone***

*send by **mail/post/satellite link***

but compare:

*She took **the train** to the campus.* (FICT)

*He saw me off on **the bus**.* (FICT)

*You remind me of a birthday present somebody's sent through **the mail**.* (FICT)

### E   Times of the day

The zero article is used especially with some prepositional phrases:

*Tomorrow at **dawn** we'll begin our journey.* (FICT†)

*It's not safe to walk the streets at **night**.* (NEWS)

but compare:

*She sat and waited for **the dawn**.* (FICT†)

*He woke up again in the middle of **the night**.* (CONV†)

### F   Days, months, and seasons

The definite article is used when there is postmodification (as in **4** and **5**), and the reference is clearly specific. There is considerable variation with words for the seasons.

**1** *It was on the radio on **Sunday**.* (CONV)

**2** *The UN team spent three weeks visiting the camps in **September**.* (NEWS)

**3** *When **winter** comes in 12 weeks, they will freeze.* (NEWS)

but compare:

**4** *That was **the Sunday** before we moved.* (CONV†)

**5** *The needle and syringe exchange scheme began in **the summer** of 1984.* (ACAD)

**6** *Most of **the winter** I never see daylight.* (NEWS)

### G   Parallel structures

The zero article is sometimes found in combinations of identical or semantically related nouns in structures of the type: X + preposition/coordinator + Y:

*He travelled from **country** to **country**.* (FICT)

*She has had to make the difficult transition from **child** to **adult star**.* (NEWS†)

*Thankfully, it has turned out all right for **mother** and **baby**.* (NEWS)

*This broadly relates to communications between **lawyer** and **client**.* (ACAD†)

As these nouns are countable, we would normally expect an article. Examples of this kind are often frozen idiomatic expressions, as in *from start to finish, from time to time, eye to eye, face to face*; there is a great deal of variation depending upon the individual collocation.

## H   Block language

The zero article is normal with noun phrases in **block language**, which is to be found in newspaper headlines, labels, notices, etc., where communicative needs strip language of all but the most information-bearing forms. Compare:

**Fire** *kills **teenager** after **hoax*** <headline> (NEWS)

with:

*A **teenager** died in **a blaze** at his home after firemen were diverted by a call that turned out to be **a student prank**.* (NEWS)

Note the contrast between: *fire—a blaze, teenager—a teenager, hoax—a student prank*. The headline retains forms representing all the essential clause elements, but the noun phrases have no overt articles. The exact interpretation of block language is highly dependent upon the context, in this case the following newspaper text.

## I   Vocatives

Normally countable nouns lack overt determiners when used as forms of address (3.4.6):

*I'll see you later, **mate**.* (CONV)

**Teacher! Teacher! Teacher!** (CONV)

*No hard feelings, **Doctor**.* (FICT)

*Do you want that, **baby**?* (FICT)

## 4.4.1.3   The definite article

The **definite article** combines with both countable and uncountable nouns. It specifies that the referent of the noun phrase is assumed to be known to the speaker and the addressee. The knowledge could be based on the preceding text, in which case we speak of **anaphoric reference** (see also example **1** in 4.4.1.1):

1   *A **doctor** was allowed to carry on working after telling fellow general practitioners **he** had contracted Aids, health officials revealed yesterday. <...> **The doctor**, who died last summer, broke health service guidelines <...>* (NEWS†)

In many cases, though, the connection is inferred rather than signalled by repetition, and we speak of **indirect anaphoric reference**:

2   **The Mercedes** *took a hard bounce from a pothole. "Christ," said Sherman, "I didn't even see that." He leaned forward over **the steering wheel**. **The headlights** shot across the concrete columns in a delirium.* (FICT)

> 3  *He found **her blue Ford Escort** in the car park. **The vehicle** was locked and **the lights** were off.* (FICT)

In both **2** and **3**, once a car has been introduced, it is possible to refer to things connected with cars as contextually given (e.g. *the steering wheel, the lights*). In other words, the use of the definite article is dependent partly upon the preceding text and partly upon general pragmatic knowledge. Example **3** also shows how a subsequent reference to the same entity may take the form of a semantically related word with definite reference (*the vehicle*).

Reference may also be established through something following later in the text, e.g. a restrictive relative clause or some other modifier of the noun:

> 4  *Another potential voter starts to tell him about **the car that went through his garden wall**.* (NEWS)

> 5  ***The patterns of industrial development in the United States** are too varied to be categorized easily.* (ACAD)

This is called **cataphoric** reference.

The use of the definite article may also reflect the shared situational context of the speaker and hearer. Examples of such **situational** reference are:

> 6  *I think there's somebody at **the door** now.* (CONV)

> 7  *A: He's a farmer.*
> *B: But how can he make money like that?*
> *A: Cos they get money off **the government** don't they, farmers?* (CONV)

Situational reference ranges from reliance on the immediate speech situation (as in **6**) to dependence upon the larger shared context (as in **7**).

If there is a mismatch between the speaker's and the hearer's perception of the situation, we may get a problem of interpretation:

> 8  *A: Could you get me from **the shelf** the black felt pen?*
> *B: **Which shelf**?*
> *A: **The big one with all the** <unclear> **on top**.* (CONV)

> 9  *A: When is the, **the sale** in <unclear>? Is it next Saturday?*
> *B: **Which sale**?*
> *A: Well **the big sale**, you know, **with the furniture and everything**.*
> (CONV)

In such cases, the problem is usually put right later in the exchange (cf. 4.1.1.3).

The interpretation of definite noun phrases often requires extensive pragmatic inferencing on the part of the addressee. Some more complex examples are:

> 10  ***Ampofo** was being outboxed, but then amazingly put his opponent down in the third and fifth rounds. **The new champion**, who lost the title to Regan a year ago, said: <...>* (NEWS†)

> 11  *A woman and a child had a narrow escape yesterday when their car left the road. **The accident** happened at about 9.25am at Marks Tey, near Colchester.* (NEWS†)

> 12  ***The lovers** parked **the car** in **the darkest place they could find**, on **the edge of a bank**. And they were so carried away, they forgot to put on **the handbrake**. **The car** rolled 20 yards into **the river**, then **the man** kicked out **the wind-screen** and they swam to safety.* (NEWS)

In **10** the reader must infer that Ampofo is the new champion, in **11** that the events of the first sentence constitute an accident. Example **12**, which tells a little anecdote, contains straightforward cases of anaphoric reference (the second occurrence of *the car*), indirect anaphoric reference (*the handbrake, the windscreen*), and cataphoric reference (*the darkest place they could find, the edge of a bank*). More work is required to interpret *the river* (inferrable from the preceding *bank*) and *the man* (inferrable from the preceding *the lovers*). Finally, *the lovers* and *the car* are used without any introduction, and the reader must imagine a situation with a specific couple and a specific car.

People, things, and events are, particularly in fiction, frequently presented to the reader as if familiar, though they have had no previous introduction:

> 13  *All this happened more or less.* **The war parts** *anyway, are pretty much*
>     *true.* (FICT) <opening of novel>

This device is a way of quickly involving the reader in the story, inviting their active cooperation in building up a mental picture of the fictional world (cf. the similar use of personal pronouns; 4.10.1.3).

## 4.4.1.4  Generic reference

Reference is **generic** when a noun phrase refers to a whole class rather than to an individual person or thing. Compare the following:

Indefinite specific reference:

> *Inside the house Mr Summers found a family of* **cats** *shut in the bathroom.*
> (NEWS)

> *If there is* **wine** *on the table then have a drink.* (ACAD)

Generic reference:

> *They're very nice* **cats** *are.* (CONV)

> **Beer** *is, quite rightly, Britain's favourite Friday night drink.* (NEWS)

With uncountables (such as *beer* and *wine*), the rule is to use the zero article to express generic reference.

Note that the reference can be perceived as generic even when there is premodification.

> *In Ghana* **coconut wine** *is not as popular and common as* **palm wine**.
> (ACAD†)

> *Newland Archer prided himself on his knowledge of* **Italian art**. (FICT)

With countable nouns there is a variety of ways of expressing generic reference. The most flexible type uses the zero article with plural countable nouns (such as *cats* and *dogs*):

> **Roses** *are red,* **violets** *are blue, I'm writing to tell you I'm in love with you.*
> (CONV)

> **Horses** *are intelligent animals.* (CONV)

> **Girls** *can be tough, stuck up or cheap, mousy or boy-crazy; or they can be*
> *brains and sucks and brown-nosers, like* **boys**, *if they are thought to study too*
> *much.* (FICT)

Less commonly we find a singular countable noun preceded by an indefinite article or a definite article:

> **A doctor** *is not better than his patient.* (FICT†)

> *The horse is less to the Arab than clay is to the Bursley man.* (FICT)

Note the variation in:

> *Trees are alive but not alive as animals are. What is the difference? First, the tree is more accessible.* (FICT)

Both definite and indefinite plurals can be used with nationality words:

> *The Americans are so jealous because they haven't got a Royal Family of their own.* (NEWS)

> *"It's wrong," Jill goes on to say, "when you say Americans are exploiters, to forget that the first things they exploit are themselves."* (FICT)

The definite article is regularly used to express generic reference with nominalized adjectives (7.2.5.2).

## 4.4.1.5 Reference patterns of definite noun phrases

Although anaphoric reference may intuitively seem to be the most basic use of the definite article, other uses are in fact equally or more common.

Table 4.10 **Percentage use of different types of reference patterns for definite noun phrases in each register**

each ■ represents 5%     □ represents less than 2.5%

| | CONV | FICT | NEWS | ACAD |
|---|---|---|---|---|
| situational | ■■■■■■■■■■■ | ■■ | ■■ | ■■ |
| anaphoric | ■■■■ | ■■■■■■ | ■■■■■■ | ■■■■ |
| cataphoric | ■ | ■■■ | ■■■■■■ | ■■■■■■■■ |
| indirect | ■ | ■■ | ■■■ | ■■■ |
| generic | □ | □ | ■ | ■ |
| idiom | □ | □ | □ | □ |
| uncertain | ■■ | ■■■■■ | ■ | ■ |

### CORPUS FINDINGS [8]

➤ There are marked differences across registers in the reference patterns of noun phrases with the definite article.

➤ Surprisingly, anaphoric reference accounts for less than a third of the definite noun phrases in all the registers.

➤ Situational reference is found in more than 50% of the cases in conversation, but accounts for only c. 10% of the examples in the written registers.

➤ Cataphoric reference represents 30–40% of the definite noun phrases in news and academic prose.

➤ The figures for generic reference are generally low.

➤ There is a high proportion of uncertain examples in fiction.

### DISCUSSION OF FINDINGS

Despite the perception that definite noun phrases are usually used for anaphoric reference, they are more commonly used for other purposes. At the same time, anaphoric reference is marked by pronouns and a range of other devices (4.1.3). The special advantage of definite noun phrases as compared with pronouns is that they are more precise and allow expansion in addition to a specification of identity.

The high frequency of cataphoric reference in academic prose and news reportage is connected with the complexity of noun phrases in these registers. The cataphoric use of the definite article provides a succinct textual way of specifying reference. Generic reference is slightly more common in these registers than in fiction and conversation, presumably because the latter are more concerned with the lives and activities of specific individuals.

In conversation cataphoric reference is rare, reflecting the simplicity of noun phrases in this register (cf. Chapter 8). In contrast, situational reference is predominant, as in the following example:

> *You know last week my aunty she put her down in* **the** *kitchen and* **the** *telephone rang. And* **the** *telephone's on* **the** *wall in* **the** *kitchen.* <unclear> *picked it up. All of a sudden she turns round, just sees my little cousin screaming* <unclear>. *My little cousin's pulled* **the** *kettle of boiling water down her, all down her back.* (CONV)

The reliance on situational reference is due to the fact that conversation is embedded in a situation which is shared by the speaker and hearer. Moreover, conversational partners are usually closely related as family members or friends, and can thus rely on a great deal of shared knowledge.

## 4.4.1.6 Definite and indefinite articles: distribution

**CORPUS FINDINGS** [2]

➤ Articles are generally least common in conversation and most common in academic prose.

➤ The distribution of the indefinite article is relatively similar across registers: approximately 20,000 per million words in the written registers, and about 13,000 per million words in conversation.

  ➤ The form *an* of the indefinite article is much less frequent than *a*, although it is slightly more common in news and academic prose.

➤ There are much greater differences across registers in the distribution of the definite article than of the indefinite article:

  ➤ The definite article is more than twice as common as the indefinite article in the written registers.

  ➤ In conversation, the frequencies of the indefinite and the definite article are more similar.

Figure 4.2

**Distribution of definite and indefinite articles across registers**

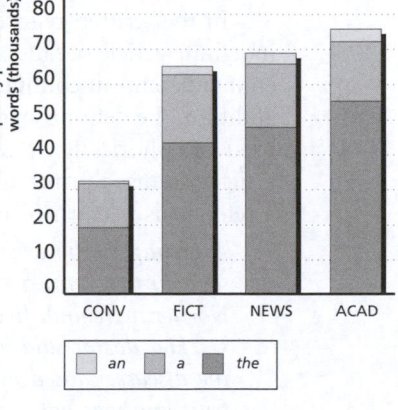

**DISCUSSION OF FINDINGS**

There is clearly a relationship between the frequency of articles and of nouns (2.3.5). For example, the frequency of nouns is much lower in conversation than in the other registers, resulting in a much lower frequency of articles (which also corresponds to a high frequency of personal pronouns).

Given that nouns are most common in news, we might also have expected that articles would be most frequent in that register. However, the overall frequency of articles is in fact highest in academic prose. There are various reasons for the less dense use of articles in news. First, proper nouns, which are typically used without determiners (4.3.3), are especially common in news. Second, possessive determiners are quite common in news; these are used instead of a definite article (4.4.2.1). Third, genitives are especially common in news (4.6.11). Specifying genitives (like possessive determiners) are mutually exclusive with the articles (4.6.3). Finally, complex premodifying structures are especially character-istic of news (Chapter 8). Determiners in such structures specify the whole of the noun phrase, rather than the individual nouns.

Because all registers have a similar need to introduce new entities in discourse (cf. 4.4.1.1), the indefinite article occurs with similar frequencies across registers. However, conversation makes somewhat less use of the indefinite article, presumably because this register is more repetitive (cf. 2.2.1) and because it deals with familiar topics. In addition, conversation sometimes makes use of the demonstrative determiners *this/these* in introducing new entities (4.4.3).

The relatively equal distribution of the definite and indefinite articles in conversation can be attributed to two factors. First, there is a high frequency of singular nouns in relation to plural nouns in conversation (4.5.6), resulting in more indefinite articles than otherwise expected. Second, pronouns are preferred over noun phrases as anaphoric expressions in conversation (4.1.3), resulting in fewer definite articles.

The slightly higher frequency of *an* in news and academic prose reflects the vocabulary of those registers, where *an* is required more commonly with Latinate vocabulary (which has many words beginning with *ab-*, *ad-*, *ex-*, *in-*, *ob-*, etc.).

In the written registers, the definite article is much more common than the indefinite article because it has a greater range of uses. First, it combines with both countable and uncountable nouns, as well as both singular and plural nouns. In addition, the definite article is used commonly for subsequent mention, and when used cataphorically, it can also introduce new referents. In contrast, indefinite articles are used primarily to introduce a new referent. While the introduction of a referent is performed once, subsequent mention is often repeated:

> **A teenager** *who existed on a junk food diet developed scurvy, the bane of seamen two centuries ago, it was revealed yesterday.* **The 14-year-old**, *from Northern Ireland, lived on cola, chocolate, hamburgers and crisps.*
>
> *Her doctor said he had heard of only four or five western teenagers with the disease, caused by a deficiency in vitamin C.* **The girl** *did not eat much fruit and was not keen on vegetables, said Dr Kevin McKenna.* (NEWS)

## 4.4.1.7 Definite and indefinite articles in relation to syntactic role

Similar to the distribution of nouns and pronouns (4.1.2), definite and indefinite noun phrases vary in important ways in relation to syntactic role.

**CORPUS FINDINGS** [3,16]

➤ The proportional use of definite and indefinite articles varies greatly depending upon syntactic role.
  ➤ The relative frequency of definite articles is much higher in subject position and as a complement/object of a preposition than in object position.

Table 4.11 **Proportional use of definite and indefinite articles in different syntactic roles (written registers only)**

each ● represents 5%

| | % use of definite articles | % use of indefinite articles |
|---|---|---|
| **FICT** | | |
| subject | ● ● ● ● ● ● ● ● ● ● ● ● ● ● ● ● ● ● ● ● | ● ● ● ● |
| object | ● ● ● ● ● ● ● ● ● ● ● | ● ● ● ● ● ● ● ● ● ● |
| prepositional complement | ● ● ● ● ● ● ● ● ● ● ● ● ● ● ● ● ● ● | ● ● ● ● |
| **NEWS** | | |
| subject | ● ● ● ● ● ● ● ● ● ● ● ● ● ● ● ● ● ● ● | ● ● ● |
| object | ● ● ● ● ● ● ● ● ● ● ● ● | ● ● ● ● ● ● ● ● ● ● |
| prepositional complement | ● ● ● ● ● ● ● ● ● ● ● ● ● ● | ● ● ● ● ● ● ● |
| **ACAD** | | |
| subject | ● ● ● ● ● ● ● ● ● ● ● ● ● ● ● ● ● ● ● ● | ● ● ● |
| object | ● ● ● ● ● ● ● ● ● ● ● ● | ● ● ● ● ● ● ● ● ● ● |
| prepositional complement | ● ● ● ● ● ● ● ● ● ● ● ● ● ● ● | ● ● ● ● ● ● |

**DISCUSSION OF FINDINGS**

There is a preferred distribution of information in the clause, corresponding to a gradual rise in information load. This may be called the information principle (11.1.1). In English, the subject is regularly placed early in the clause. By using a definite noun phrase for the subject, the speaker/writer can provide both a link with the preceding text and a starting-point for the message to come.

Indefinite subjects are much less common but by no means rare. When new information is introduced in subject position, it is marked as thematically important and will often be referred to later in the text by definite noun phrases (see example 1 in 4.4.1.1).

The object belongs to the part of the clause that is characteristically associated with new information. Hence there is a higher proportion of indefinite noun phrases in that position.

The slightly greater difference between subject and object position in academic prose and news could perhaps be taken to mean that clauses in these registers conform more consistently to the information principle. This would agree with the purposes of these registers.

## 4.4.1.8 Definite determiners: distribution

Definite noun phrases can be marked using three different sets of forms: the definite article (*the*), possessive determiners (e.g. *his*, *her*; 4.4.2), and demonstrative determiners (*this*, *these*, *that*, *those*; 4.4.3). However, these sets are used to differing extents in the different registers.

**CORPUS FINDINGS** [2]

➤ The definite article is far more frequent than other definite determiners.

➤ There are large differences among registers in the use of all definite determiners.

➤ Possessive determiners are far less frequent than the definite article.

➤ Possessive determiners are notably common in fiction.

  ➤ Conversation and news rely on possessive determiners to a greater extent than academic prose.

➤ Demonstrative determiners are far less frequent than the definite article.

➤ Demonstrative determiners are most frequent in academic prose.

  ➤ However, demonstrative determiners are proportionally most common in conversation (comprising c. 15% of all definite determiners)

**Figure 4.3**

**Distribution of definite determiners across registers**

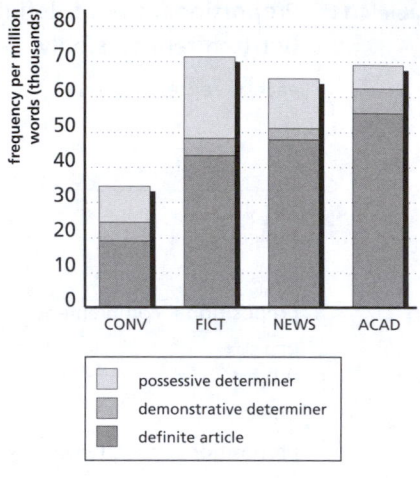

Legend:
- possessive determiner
- demonstrative determiner
- definite article

**DISCUSSION OF FINDINGS**

The definite article is a more neutral determiner than the possessive forms, in that it marks an entity as known without specifying how it is related to other entities. Therefore it has a wider distribution in all the registers than the possessive determiners.

Possessive determiners are particularly associated with human beings, and they characteristically serve to identify entities by their relationships to human beings. Hence they are very common in fiction, which is overwhelmingly concerned with humans and their relationships. For the same reason, possessive determiners are also relatively common in conversation, in spite of the low frequency of nouns in that register (2.3.5). They are also common in news, where human-centred topics are abundant. The density of possessive determiners is low in academic prose, which deals with entities of all kinds and focuses less commonly on human beings.

Conversation has a proportionally higher use of demonstrative determiners in relation to the definite article, presumably because it is embedded in a situation where both participants are present and it is more natural to make situational references in terms of proximity. (See also 4.1.3 and 4.1.4.)

The relationship between the definite article and the other definite determiners is discussed in more detail in 4.4.2 and 4.4.3 below.

## 4.4.2 Possessive determiners

**Possessive determiners** specify a noun phrase by relating it to the speaker/writer (*my*, *our*), the addressee (*your*) or other entities mentioned in the text or given in the speech situation (*his, her, its, their*). This series of possessive determiners corresponds to the series of personal pronouns (4.10). Closely related to the possessive determiners are genitive phrases consisting of a noun phrase and a genitive suffix (4.6.3).

Possessive determiners make noun phrases definite. They combine with countable as well as uncountable nouns and occasionally also with proper nouns:

> She didn't want to spoil **her** shoes. (FICT†)

> Oh did I tell you o– – **our** Joanie's coming over. (CONV)

The additional determiner *own* may be added to stress that something is related to a particular entity, in contrast to some other entity:

> We want industry to cut down on **its own** waste, and make better use of other people's. (NEWS)

The relationships expressed by possessive determiners extend far beyond possession (cf. the account of the semantic relationships between head and genitive phrase in 4.6.12.3).

## 4.4.2.1   Possessive determiners: distribution

**CORPUS FINDINGS 2**

➤ Individual possessive determiners have quite different distributions across registers (see Table 4.12):

Table 4.12   **Distribution of possessive determiners; occurrences per million words**

each ■ represents 500     □ represents less than 250

| | CONV | FICT | NEWS | ACAD |
|---|---|---|---|---|
| *my* | ■■■■■ | ■■■■■■■ | ■■ | ■ |
| *our* | ■ | ■■ | ■■ | ■■ |
| *your* | ■■■■■ | ■■■ | ■ | □ |
| *his* | ■■■ | ■■■■■■■■■■■■ ■■■■■■■ | ■■■■■■■■■■■■ ■ | ■■ |
| *her* | ■■ | ■■■■■■■■■■ | ■■■■ | ■ |
| *its* | ■ | ■■ | ■■■ | ■■■ |
| *their* | ■ | ■■■■ | ■■■■■■ | ■■■■■ |

➤ With the exception of *our*, forms which refer to the speaker and the addressee are by far most common in conversation and fiction: *our* is more frequent in the written registers (including academic prose) than in conversation.

➤ Forms with third person human reference (*his, her*) are very common in fiction and relatively common in news: *his* is more common than *her* in all the registers.

➤ Forms with non-human reference (*its* and in many cases *their*) are most common in news and academic prose.

➤ Possessive determiners are rarely accompanied by *own*.

  ➤ This combination is slightly more common in academic prose, where c. 5% of all possessive determiners are accompanied by *own*.

**DISCUSSION OF FINDINGS**

The distribution of individual possessive determiners reflects differences in the speech situation and in the typical topics of the texts (compare the distribution of personal pronouns; 4.10.5). Determiners referring to the speaker and the addressee are naturally common in conversation, where both participants are in immediate contact and tend to talk about matters of immediate concern to themselves. The same is true of the speech situations represented in fictional dialogue.

The general concern in fiction with individuals and their thoughts and actions is reflected in the high frequency of third-person determiners with predominantly human reference (*his, her*). The relatively infrequent use of third person possessive determiners in conversation is related to the low noun density in that register (2.3.5). The skewing in the distribution of *his* v. *her* indicates that traditional sex-role biases continue to be a powerful factor influencing language use.

In spite of the generally dense use of nouns, most possessive determiners are relatively rare in academic prose. Reflecting the non-personal subject matter of many texts in academic prose, the two most common forms can both be used for non-human reference (exclusively so in the case of *its*). The relatively high frequency of *our* in academic prose has to do with the use of the first person plural in referring to the author or jointly to the author and the reader (see also 4.10.1.1); for example, *our findings, our next task*, etc.

The slightly greater proportion of possessive determiners accompanied by *own* in academic prose probably reflects the value attached to precision in that register. There are clear parallels between the distribution of *own* and that of the semi-determiners (4.4.6) and the reflexive pronouns (4.12.1–2).

## 4.4.3 Demonstrative determiners

The **demonstrative determiners** *this/these* and *that/those* are closely related in meaning to the definite article. However, in addition to marking an entity as known, they specify the number of the referent and whether the referent is near or distant in relation to the speaker (cf. *here* v. *there*). In addition, the demonstrative determiners are stressed, whereas the definite article is almost always unstressed. The singular demonstrative determiners combine with both countable and uncountable nouns:

|  | singular | plural |
|---|---|---|
| near | *this book* | *these books* |
|  | *this money* | *these manners* |
| distant | *that book* | *those books* |
|  | *that money* | *those scissors* |

The reference of noun phrases with demonstrative determiners may be established on the basis of either the situation or the preceding or following text (cf. the situational, anaphoric, and cataphoric uses of the definite article; 4.4.1.3). Where the reference is textually determined, the demonstrative determiners may only retain a tinge of their original meaning, with *this/these* referring to matters of more immediate concern.

A **Situational reference**

Situational reference is very common in conversation, with the choice of demonstrative determiner reflecting the speaker's perception of distance. Compare:

> **This** cake's lovely. (CONV) <referring to the cake that the speaker is eating>
>
> Finish **that** cake if you want it. (CONV) <referring to the cake that the addressee is eating>
>
> **This** Julian person we're referring to is, is a complete and utter cripple. (CONV)
>
> Look at **that** man sitting there. (CONV†)

The choice of determiner may also reflect emotional distance, with *this/these* expressing greater empathy than *that/those*:

> You know I actually quite like **this** chap. (CONV)
> v.   I don't want **that** bastard. (CONV)

B **Time reference**

The use of the demonstrative determiners is not just a matter of physical location in relation to the speaker. Frequently they also express whether something is near or distant in time (cf. *now* v. *then*):

> They're buying a house **this** year in France. (CONV)
>
> They started at nursery **that** summer. (CONV)

C **Anaphoric reference**

In writing, the demonstrative determiners typically refer back to the preceding text:

> The simplest form of chemical bond, in some ways, is the ionic bond. Bonds of **this** type are formed by electrostatic attractions between ions of opposite charge. **This** attraction is exactly of the same nature as the attraction that makes hair stand up when some synthetic fabrics are drawn over it. (ACAD)
>
> She asked for her name not to be used because she wanted to protect her relationships with regular callers. The fragility of **those** relationships underlines the essential work done by the charity. (NEWS)

As in the present examples, the demonstrative determiners tend to refer anaphorically to the immediate textual context; see also 4.1.4.

D **Cataphoric reference**

The reference may be established through something following the demonstrative determiner:

> The unit of heat was defined as **that** quantity which would raise the temperature of unit mass of water, at standard atmospheric pressure, through one degree on some temperature scale. (ACAD)
>
> We apologize to **those** readers who did not receive the Guardian on Saturday. (NEWS†)

Such cataphoric reference is chiefly found with *that/those*; cf. cataphoric *the*, 4.4.1.3.

**E  Introductory *this/these***

There is a special conversational use where the demonstrative determiners *this/these* introduce new information, especially in telling a story or introducing a new topic:

> There's **this** one bloke, there's **this** one bloke yeah, he walks around with a grenade tied to his neck yeah? And **this** bloke goes, why does he walk around with a grenade, and he goes, a grenade tied to his neck? And he goes, well if this life gets too shit he's gonna pull the pin and see what the next one's like. (CONV)

> There was **this** really good looking bloke and he was like – we, we'd given each other eyes over the bar in **this** pub and Lottie goes, well if you don't hurry up with him, I'm gonna have him. <...> (CONV†)

Here the role of the demonstrative determiners is similar to the use of the definite article or personal pronouns at the beginning of a fictional text (cf. 4.4.1.3, 4.10.1.3).

## 4.4.3.1  Demonstrative determiners: distribution

**CORPUS FINDINGS ²**

➤ Individual demonstrative determiners have quite different distributions across registers:
  ➤ In the written expository registers, the proximate forms (*this/these*) are more common than the distant forms (*that/those*).
  ➤ The distribution of proximate and distant forms is roughly equal in conversation and fiction.
  ➤ The singular forms are more common than the plural forms.
  ➤ *This/these* are by far most common in academic prose.
  ➤ *That* is more common in conversation and fiction than in the other registers.

**DISCUSSION OF FINDINGS**

The higher frequency of the singular demonstrative determiners (*this/that*) reflects the higher overall frequency of singular nouns (4.5.6). The proximate forms tend to be more common overall because they signal both proximity and an immediate reference to the preceding text.

The distribution of proximate and distant forms is more similar in conversation and fiction, probably because the reliance on the immediate situation in conversation and fictional dialogue makes a proximate v. distant choice more natural.

In academic prose, where *this/these* are abundant, reference is often anaphoric, signalling a reference to the immediately preceding text. The use of these forms is primarily responsible for the high percentage of noun phrases with demonstrative determiners in this register (4.1.3–4).

There is some further discussion of demonstrative determiners along with the treatment of demonstrative pronouns in 4.14.

Table 4.13 **Distribution of demonstrative determiners; occurrences per million words**

each ● represents 500

| | CONV | FICT | NEWS | ACAD |
|---|---|---|---|---|
| *this* | ● ● ● ● | ● ● ● ● | ● ● ● ● | ● ● ● ● ● ● ● ● ● |
| *these* | ● | ● | ● | ● ● ● ● |
| *that* | ● ● ● ● | ● ● ● | ● | ● ● |
| *those* | ● | ● | | ● |

## 4.4.4 Quantifiers

Some determiners specify nouns in terms of quantity and are therefore called **quantifiers** (2.4.1). They combine with both indefinite and definite noun phrases. In the latter case they are generally followed by *of*. Compare:

| | |
|---|---|
| *all money* | *all (of) the money* |
| *some money* | *some of the money* |
| *much money* | *much of the money* |
| *all girls* | *all (of) the girls* |
| *some girls* | *some of the girls* |
| *many girls* | *many of the girls* |

Co-occurrence patterns with respect to countable and uncountable nouns are illustrated in 4.4.

Quantifiers can be broadly divided into four main groups:

**A  Inclusive**

*All* refers to the whole of a group or a mass; it combines with both countable and uncountable nouns. *Both* is used with reference to two entities with plural countable nouns:

> *I'm just fascinated by **all** those things.* (CONV)

> *Don't go to that awful man and spend **all** that money.* (FICT)

> ***Both** amendments were defeated.* (NEWS†)

*Each* and *every* refer to the individual members of a group and only combine with singular countable nouns. *Each* stresses the separate individual, *every* the individual as a member of the group. *Each* can be used with reference to two entities, but not *every*.

> *Throughout the proceedings two plainclothes policemen sat **each** side of 27-year-old Newall.* (NEWS†)

> *The book is divided into three parts. **Each** part consists of chapters grouped together according to their relation to the major concepts of the Earth's dynamics.* (ACAD)

> ***Every** minute of **every** day, hundreds of millions of tonnes of coal are burned.* (ACAD)

**B  Large quantity**

*Many* and *much* specify a large quantity; *many* with plural countable nouns, and *much* with uncountable nouns. They are typically used in negative contexts:

*There weren't **many** people there.* (CONV†)

*The girl wasn't paying **much** attention.* (FICT†)

Other determiners specifying a large quantity are *a great/good many* (with plural countable nouns), *a great/good deal of* (with uncountable nouns), *plenty of*, *a lot of*, and *lots of*. The last three combine with both uncountable and plural countable nouns. They are characteristic of casual speech:

*There were **lots of** people going through the tills.* (CONV†)

*"He's had **a lot of** trouble."* (FICT†)

### C   Moderate or small quantity

*Some* usually specifies a moderate quantity and is used with both uncountable and plural countable nouns:

*Insurance shares produced **some** excitement.* (NEWS)

***Some** performance curves will now be presented.* (ACAD†)

As regards the distribution of *some* as against *any*, see 3.8.6. *Some* also has other uses that need to be distinguished from the above:

1   *That is **some** horse!* (FICT†)

2   ***Some** 18 per cent of managing directors secured pay increases of over 20 per cent.* (NEWS†)

In the type illustrated in example **1**, *some* may also occur with singular countable nouns, is strongly stressed, and expresses approval or admiration ('quite a horse'). In **2** *some* is used as an approximating adverb before numerals (2.7.7.3C).

Determiners specifying a small quantity are *a few*, *few*, and *several* with plural countable nouns; and *a little* and *little* with uncountable nouns. *A few* and *a little* are close in meaning to *some*; *few* and *little* suggest that the quantity is less than expected. Compare:

*With **a little** care he had no difficulty whatever in putting his glass back on the table.* (FICT)

*Why do you take so **little** care?* (FICT)

*There were **a few** people sitting at the tables in the back.* (FICT†)

*Though it was not late there were **few** people about.* (FICT†)

### D   Arbitrary/negative member or amount

*Any* refers to an arbitrary member of a group or amount of a mass. It combines with both countable and uncountable nouns. *Either* has a similar meaning, but it is used with groups of two and combines only with singular count nouns. Both *any* and *either* are typically used in negative or interrogative contexts:

*There aren't **any** women.* (CONV)

*Got **any** money?* (CONV)

*There were no applications for bail for **either** defendant.* (NEWS†)

***Either** or both chromosomes may divide.* (ACAD†)

*No* and *neither* have negative reference, the former generally, the latter with reference to two entities:

***No** method for the precise manipulation of the embryo in utero has been devised.* (ACAD†)

***Neither** method is entirely satisfactory.* (ACAD†)

On *no*-negation and *not*-negation, see 3.8.2–4. The negative forms sometimes replace *any/either* in conversation and fictional dialogue (3.8.7.1).

For the multiple functions of determiners in other word classes, see 2.4.2.1.

### 4.4.4.1  Quantifiers: distribution

As determiner and pronominal uses are closely related, they have both been included in this distributional survey of quantifiers.

**CORPUS FINDINGS [2]**

➤ There is little variability in the distribution of quantifiers across registers, despite the fact that nouns are many times more common in the written registers than in conversation. (see Table 4.14)

Table 4.14  **Distribution of the four major categories for quantifiers; occurrences per million words**

each ● represents 500

|  | CONV | FICT | NEWS | ACAD |
|---|---|---|---|---|
| inclusive | ●●●●●●● ●●● | ●●●●●●● ●●● | ●●●●●● | ●●●●●●● ● |
| large | ●●●●● | ●●●●● | ●●●●● | ●●●●●● |
| moderate/small | ●●●●● | ●●●●● | ●●●● | ●●●●●●● |
| arbitrary/negative | ●●●●● | ●●●●●●● | ●●●●● | ●●●●● |

➤ There are wide differences in the distribution of individual quantifiers:
  ➤ In the 'inclusive' group, *all* is by far the most common form, especially in conversation and fiction. *Each* is relatively common in academic prose.
  ➤ In the 'moderate/small' group, *some* is by far the most common form, especially in academic prose.
  ➤ In the 'arbitrary/negative' group, *any* and *no* are by far the most frequent forms in all the registers: *no* is especially common in fiction.
➤ The following determiners occur less than 100 times per million words in all registers: *a good many, a good deal of, a great many, a great deal of, lots of, plenty of, fewer, fewest, least, either, neither.*

**DISCUSSION OF FINDINGS**

Some of the differences in the use of quantifiers may reflect their relative novelty, in historical terms. Those ending in *of*, such as *a lot of, lots of, plenty of*, and *a couple of* are recent developments from quantifying nouns. It is thus no surprise that these are relatively rare, and when they do occur, they are most typically found in conversation, or carry a strong overtone of casual speech when used. Compare the pattern of use of the semi-modals in the verb phrase (6.6).

Other differences reflect communicative preferences for different quantification meanings in the registers. The higher frequency of *many* and *some* in academic prose agrees with the need for expressing guarded generalizations. The more frequent use of *both* and *each* reflects the concern with precision in academic discourse. Conversation and fiction, on the other hand, have a tendency to opt for more categorical expressions (especially *all*). The very high frequency of

Table 4.15    **Distribution of individual quantifiers; occurrences per million words**

each ■ represents 200     □ represents less than 100

| | CONV | FICT | NEWS | ACAD |
|---|---|---|---|---|
| **inclusive:** | | | | |
| all | ■■■■■■ ■■■■■■ ■■■■■■ ■■■■ | ■■■■■■ ■■■■■■ ■■■■■ ■■ | ■■■■■■ ■■■■ | ■■■■■■ ■■■■■ |
| both | ■ | ■ | ■■ | ■■ |
| each | □ | ■■ | ■■ | ■■■■■ |
| every | ■■ | ■■ | ■■ | ■■ |
| **large:** | | | | |
| many | ■■ | ■■ | ■■■ | ■■■■■ |
| much | ■■■ | ■■ | ■ | ■ |
| more | ■■■■ | ■■■■ | ■■■■■ | ■■■■ |
| most | ■ | ■ | ■ | ■■■ |
| a lot of | ■■ | ■ | ■ | □ |
| **moderate/small:** | | | | |
| some | ■■■■■■ ■■■ | ■■■■■■ ■■ | ■■■■■ | ■■■■■■ ■■■■ |
| a few | ■ | ■■ | ■ | ■ |
| few | □ | □ | ■ | □ |
| a little | □ | ■ | □ | □ |
| little | □ | ■ | ■ | ■ |
| less | □ | □ | ■ | ■ |
| several | □ | ■ | ■ | ■■ |
| a couple of | ■ | □ | □ | □ |
| a number of | □ | □ | ■ | ■ |
| **arbitrary/negative:** | | | | |
| any | ■■■■■■ | ■■■■■■ | ■■■■ | ■■■■■■ ■ |
| no | ■■■■■■ | ■■■■■■ ■■■■■■ | ■■■■■ ■■ | ■■■■■ |
| none | □ | ■ | □ | □ |

the determiner *no* in fiction is consistent with the common use of *no*-negation in that register (3.8.4.2).

(For further discussion of the distribution of quantifiers, see the discussion of cardinal numerals in 4.4.5.)

## 4.4.5   Numerals

There are two main types of numerals: **cardinal numerals** (2.4.13.1) and **ordinal numerals** (2.4.13.2). Cardinals are clearly related to quantifying determiners (dealt with in the previous section), but differ from these in providing a numerical rather than a more general specification. Ordinals, on the other hand, specify nouns in terms of order and are more like the semi-determiners taken up in 4.4.6.

## 4.4.5.1 Numerals across the registers

Associated with their different types of specification, we find striking differences in the distribution of cardinals v. ordinals. For convenience both nominal and determiner uses are counted together in this survey, and occurrences in conversation are treated as alphabetic, though in speech they are actually neutral as to alphabetic or digit representation:

**CORPUS FINDINGS [2]**

➤ The cardinals are most common in news and academic prose; least common in fiction.

➤ When related to the overall frequency of nouns, the distribution of the cardinals turns out to be different. The extremes are one cardinal per seven nouns in conversation, as against one per 26 nouns in fiction.

➤ Except in fiction, cardinal numerals are more frequent than quantifiers (cf. 4.4.4.1).

➤ Alphabetical forms of cardinals predominate in fiction, while digital forms predominate in news and academic prose.

➤ The ordinals are far less common than the cardinals in all the registers; they are least frequent in conversation.

➤ The ordinals are predominantly written alphabetically.

**Figure 4.4**
**Distribution of ordinal v. cardinal numerals across registers**

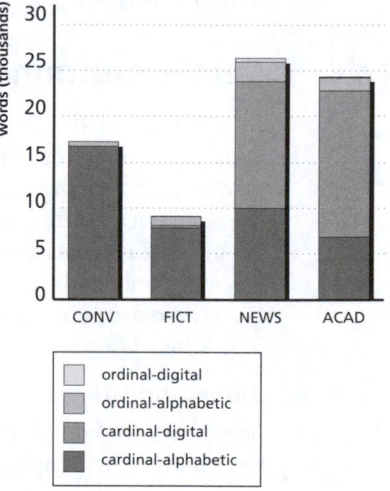

**DISCUSSION OF FINDINGS**

Fiction stands out by having the lowest frequency of cardinals, whether expressed in words per million or in relation to the overall frequency of nouns. It is the only register where the cardinals are less common overall than quantifying determiners; this is presumably because exact quantities are less important in the description of fictional worlds.

Given their informational purposes, it is not surprising that news and academic prose use cardinals more frequently than the other registers. However, when viewed in relation to the overall frequency of nouns, both the cardinals and the general quantifiers are even more common in conversation. In other words, conversation is more apt to specify nouns in terms of quantity (although it has fewer nouns overall). News and academic prose, on the other hand, make more frequent use of the definite article (4.4.1.6) and of anaphoric expressions containing a repeated noun or a synonym (4.1.3). These registers more typically mark nouns for identity, presumably because they are more topic bound.

Specification in terms of order, using ordinal numerals, is less common than specification in terms of quantity (using cardinals). In particular, the use of ordinals is restricted to those cases where there is explicit competition between different referents. Conversation has the lowest frequency of nouns, the least degree of competition between referents, and hence the lowest frequency of ordinals. At the other extreme, news has the highest frequency both of nouns and of ordinals.

The predominant alphabetical writing of the ordinals is evidence that they are perceived as ordinary words. Both positionally (4.4) and semantically, they are like semi-determiners (4.4.6). Moreover, they are almost always integrated in the text. By contrast, cardinals are often syntactically separated from the rest of the text, and either occur on their own (e.g. to mark items in lists) or in numerical expressions. Not surprisingly, the writing of the numerals as digits is most common in the expository registers: news and academic prose.

The writing of the numerals also varies with the particular forms involved, as shown in Chapter 2. Low numbers and round numbers are more likely to be written alphabetically (2.4.13.3).

## 4.4.6 Semi-determiners

In addition to the determiners proper, there are some determiner-like words which are often described as adjectives. They differ from central adjectives, however, in that they have no descriptive meaning and primarily serve to specify the reference of the noun. Moreover, they are characterized by special co-occurrence patterns with the determiners; in particular, most **semi-determiners** co-occur only with the definite article or with the indefinite article, but not both.

There are four major pairings of semi-determiners: *same* and *other*; *former* and *latter*; *last* and *next*; *certain* and *such*.

### A   *Same* and *other*

*Same* may be added after the definite article (less typically after demonstrative determiners) to emphasize that the reference is exactly to the person or thing mentioned before. Its role is comparable to that of *own* with possessive determiners (4.4.2):

> The **same** person was there with exactly the **same** message. (CONV)

> It is this **same** idea she develops here. (NEWS†)

*Other* is the opposite of *same* and specifies that the reference is to something or somebody different from the person or thing mentioned previously. It may be added after the definite article, the indefinite article (taking the form *another*), and possessive determiners, or it may occur as the only determiner in indefinite noun phrases.

> I saw how one fist beat into the palm of the **other** hand behind his back. (FICT)

> The company would still control large parts of the cellular market in **other** US cities. (NEWS)

> He's living with her and **another** girl, and **another** boy. (CONV)

### B   *Former* and *latter*

*Former* and *latter* may be added after the definite article (less typically after demonstrative determiners) to discriminate between the first and the second of two things or people already mentioned:

> *The separation between the owners of capital and the managers demonstrates the superfluousness of the **former** group, who now play no direct part in the productive process.* (ACAD)
>
> *Law as integrity is therefore more relentlessly interpretive than either conventionalism or pragmatism. These **latter** theories offer themselves as interpretations.* (ACAD)

*Former* and *latter* can also be used with reference to time:

> *The **former** jail infirmary was converted into offices.* (NEWS†)
>
> *They pinned the Derry side back in their own half for long periods during the **latter** stages.* (NEWS)

**C   *Last* and *next***

*Last* and *next* are like ordinal numerals (2.4.13.2, 4.4.5) in specifying items in terms of order, with respect to the speaking/writing situation (deictic reference) or in relation to some other point of reference. They regularly combine with the definite article or some other definite determiner (example 1), except when used in deictic time expressions, with present time as the situational point of reference (such as *last week, next Thursday*), as in **2**:

> 1  *I would like to think that this is not [his] **last** Olympics.* (NEWS)
>
> 2  ***Last** year, 767 works were sold to 410 people in four days.* (NEWS)

**D   *Certain* and *such***

*Certain* and *such* differ from the other semi-determiners in being used only in indefinite noun phrases. *Certain* singles out a specific person/thing or some specific people/things (cf. the role of the indefinite article, 4.4.1.1). *Such* refers to a person/thing or people/things of a particular kind (cf. the relationship to species nouns such as *kind*, 4.3.8).

> *I'm really referring to a **certain** Hindu scientist.* (FICT)
>
> *I would very much like to discuss **certain** ideas with you.* (FICT†)
>
> ***Such** a matrix is usually called a row matrix.* (ACAD†)
>
> ***Such** functions are not symmetrical.* (ACAD†)

**4.4.6.1   Other uses of the semi-determiners**

Apart from *certain*, the semi-determiners can also be used as pronouns, or they can combine like adjectives with *one(s)* to occupy a nominal position.

Semi-determiners used as pronouns:

> *Some sorts do and **others** don't.* (FICT)
>
> *Igneous rocks are divided on the basis of origin into intrusives and extrusives.* ***The former** are usually coarse grained; **the latter**, fine grained or glassy.* (ACAD)
>
> ***The next** he knew, he was dimly aware that his tongue was hurting.* (FICT†)
>
> *Morality is a collective property and must be studied as **such**.* (ACAD†)

Semi-determiner + *one(s)*:

> *So it might not be **the same one** at the top and bottom.* (CONV)
>
> *Do you want to hear **another one**?* (CONV)
>
> *If you screw the project up it doesn't matter too much cos you've got loads of **other ones**.* (CONV)

In addition to occurring as determiners and pronouns, some of these forms have other uses: *last* and *next* as adverbs (e.g. *When did you last see him?*), *certain* as an adjective (e.g. *Are you certain?*). *Such* has a range of uses, including classifier, intensifier, part of complex preposition, and part of complex subordinator (4.4.6.2).

## 4.4.6.2 Semi-determiners: distribution

As determiner and pronoun uses of the same forms are closely related, no distinction is made in the quantitative survey below.

In the case of *such*, the total frequency includes all uses of the form. However, four major uses can be distinguished:

Classifying *such* ('of this kind') cf. 4.4.6D:

> We believe, however, that **such** a theory is possible. (ACAD)

Intensifying *such* ('in a high degree'):

> He's **such** a flipping bastard. (CONV)

Complex preposition *such as* ('like'):

> There are crystals, of substances **such as** tourmaline, which are sensitive to the polarisation of light. (ACAD)

Complex subordinator *such that* ('so that'):

> That a generalization covers a multitude of items, **such that** it is impossible to nab each one, in no way makes the generalization unclear. (ACAD)

### CORPUS FINDINGS [2]

➤ The semi-determiners *same*, *other*, and *such* are especially frequent in academic prose.
  ➤ *Certain* is generally rare but also more common in academic prose than in the other registers.
➤ *Last* and *next* are most common in news, and least common in academic prose.
➤ *Such* in academic prose is used primarily as a classifier and as part of a complex preposition.

### DISCUSSION OF FINDINGS

The high frequency of many semi-determiners in academic prose agrees with the high degree of precision required in this register. This distribution is also consistent with the high frequency of some other determiners, especially *own* (4.4.2.1) and *each* (4.4.4.1). Note also the more frequent use in academic prose of emphatic reflexive pronouns (4.12.2), and of anaphoric expressions with repeated nouns (4.1.3).

Other semi-determiners are not predominant in academic prose. The even distribution of *another* across registers corresponds to the fairly even distribution of the indefinite article (4.4.1.6). The high frequency of *last* and *next* in news is due to their deictic use, which fits in with the communicative purpose of this register in reporting on recent and forthcoming events relative to the moment of publication. For these forms, academic prose is at the other extreme, presumably because it is the register which makes least use of reference to the immediate situation of writing with deictic forms (cf. the frequency of first- and second-person pronouns dealt with in 4.10.5). *The former and the*

Table 4.16  **Distribution of semi-determiners; occurrences per million words**

each ■ represents 100    □ represents less than 50

| | CONV | FICT | NEWS | ACAD |
|---|---|---|---|---|
| *same* | ■■■■■ | ■■■■■ | ■■■■ | ■■■■■■<br>■■■■ |
| *other* | ■■■■■■<br>■■■■■ | ■■■■■■<br>■■■■■■ | ■■■■■■<br>■■■■ | ■■■■■■<br>■■■■■■<br>■■■■■■<br>■■■■ |
| *another* | ■■■■■■ | ■■■■■■<br>■ | ■■■■■■ | ■■■■■■ |
| *others* | ■ | ■■■ | ■■ | ■■■■ |
| *former* | □ | □ | ■■ | ■ |
| *latter* | □ | □ | □ | ■■ |
| *last* | ■■■■■■<br>■■ | ■■■■■ | ■■■■■■<br>■■■■■■<br>■■■■■■<br>■■■■■ | ■■ |
| *next* | ■■■■■■ | ■■■■ | ■■■■■■<br>■■ | ■■ |
| *certain* | □ | ■ | □ | ■■■■ |
| *such* | ■■ | ■■■■■■ | ■■■■■ | ■■■■■■<br>■■■■■■<br>■■■■■■<br>■■■■■ |

Table 4.17  **Distribution of *such* by use; occurrences per million words**

each ■ represents 100    □ represents less than 50

| | CONV | FICT | NEWS | ACAD |
|---|---|---|---|---|
| classifier | □ | ■■■■ | ■■■ | ■■■■■■<br>■■■■■■ |
| intensifier | ■■ | ■■ | ■ | ■ |
| preposition | □ | □ | ■ | ■■■■■■<br>■ |
| subordinator | □ | □ | □ | ■■ |

*latter* are generally rare and restricted to the expository written registers. Furthermore they are widely perceived by users of English as marked by this association.

The high overall frequency of *such* in academic prose has various correlates. The subordinator *such that* is an option which is attested only in academic prose, where the complex preposition *such as* is also commonly used. Above all, academic prose has a very high density of classifying *such*, which is consistent with the high frequency of species nouns in that register (4.3.7).

At the other extreme, the low frequency of *such* in conversation is connected with the fact that only the intensifying function is common in that register. This same use is least represented in academic prose. The difference is consistent with the free expression of emotion in conversation (14.1.2.5), while academic prose is more impersonal and detached.

### 4.4.7    *Wh*-determiners

*Wh*-determiners are used as interrogative clause markers and relativizers.

*wh*-determiners as interrogative clause markers:

>   **Whose** *turn is it tonight?* (CONV)
>
>   **Which** *way are we going?* (CONV)

*wh*-determiners as relativizers:

>   *I had a girl* **whose** *dog was the bridesmaid.* (NEWS)
>
>   *The cabby refused and grabbed him by the arm, at* **which** *point the robber pulled free and ran off.* (NEWS)

See interrogative clauses (3.13.2.1) and relative clauses (8.7).

### 4.4.8    Determiner v. pronoun

There are close correspondences between determiners and pronouns. Some forms, such as the demonstratives *this, that, these, those,* can be used unchanged as determiners or pronouns. In other cases, there is a clear morphological parallel between determiners and pronouns, for example with the possessive forms: *my— mine, your—yours,* etc. (4.4.2, 4.11). There is also a close parallel in discourse function between personal pronouns and noun phrases with the definite article. The principal correspondences are:

| determiner class | pronoun class |
| --- | --- |
| the definite article (4.4.1.3) | personal pronouns (4.10) |
| possessive determiners (4.4.2) | possessive pronouns (4.11) |
| demonstrative determiners (4.4.3) | demonstrative pronouns (4.14) |
| quantifying determiners (4.4.4) | indefinite pronouns (4.15) |

In choosing between a pronoun and a noun phrase with determiner, the speaker/ writer can take into account the degree of precision that is required or desired. Where the identification is made clear by the linguistic or situational context, or where it can be stated only in very general terms, the natural choice is a pronoun rather than a full noun phrase.

   This choice is intimately connected with the characteristics and communicative purposes of texts. Conversation is embedded in a situation shared by the speaker and addressee; it can therefore be less specific and rely on implicit rather than explicit links and references. As a result, conversation is characterized by a very dense use of pronouns. A writer, on the other hand, must make sure that sufficient specification is given within the text, which leads to a higher frequency of full noun phrases. (The choice of pronouns v. full noun phrases is dealt with in detail in 4.1.2–4.)

## 4.5    Number

Countable nouns have both **singular** and **plural** forms, referring to one or more than one entity, respectively. Both singular and plural forms can also refer to a whole class of entities (4.4.1.4). **Number** is marked not only by inflection, but also by concord between subject and verb (3.9) and co-occurrence patterns between determiner and noun (4.4).

In most cases, plural formation conforms to the regular pattern described in 4.5.1. There are exceptions, however, and these are described in 4.5.2–4.5.4. In addition, some plurals have no corresponding singular form (4.5.5). The singular forms are more common overall and more widely distributed than the plural forms (4.5.6).

## 4.5.1    Regular plurals

The plural is regularly formed by the addition of the ending -(e)s, which is pronounced:

/s/     after voiceless consonants except /s, ʃ, tʃ/: cat—cats, map—maps, stick—sticks;

/z/     after vowels and voiced consonants except /z, ʒ, dʒ/: boy—boys, dog—dogs, girl—girls;

/ɪz/    after /s, z, ʃ, ʒ, tʃ, dʒ/: case—cases, house—houses, bridge—bridges.

In writing, the normal plural ending is -s. If the word ends in s, z, x, sh, or ch, the ending takes the form -es:

box—boxes, bush—bushes, match—matches.

If the word ends in a consonant plus -y, the ending is -ies:

copy—copies, fly—flies.

Otherwise, final -y takes the ending -s:

boy—boys, essay—essays.

Note also the plural of names: the Brodskys, the two Germanys.

With words ending in -o, there are two possible plural endings: -s and -es. However, individual words tend to be spelled with one pattern or the other.

## 4.5.1.1    Plurals of words ending in -o

**CORPUS FINDINGS** [2]

➤ The following words ending in -o take the plural ending -es at least 80% of the time: buffaloes, cargoes, echoes, heroes, mangoes, mosquitoes, mottoes, negroes, potatoes, tomatoes, tornadoes, torpedoes, vetoes, volcanoes.

➤ Most words ending in -o take the plural ending -s, although the majority of these words are rare. The following words take the plural ending -s at least 80% of the time: avocados, casinos, commandos, concertos, discos, embryos, Eskimos, jumbos, kilos, memos, pesos, photos, pianos, portfolios, radios, scenarios, shampoos, solos, stereos, studios, taboos, tacos, tattoos, trios, twos, videos, weirdos, zeros, zoos.

**DISCUSSION OF FINDINGS**

Nouns ending in a vowel letter + o (e.g. shampoo, video) and those which are in origin abbreviations (e.g. disco, photo) have plurals ending in -s. In addition, this is the regular pattern to which new words conform.

### 4.5.2 Irregular plurals

A small number of native words have irregular plural forms. The plural is formed through three major devices:

**A  Vowel change**

| | | |
|---|---|---|
| *man—men* | *foot—feet* | *tooth—teeth* |
| *woman—women* | *goose—geese* | *louse—lice* |
| *mouse—mice* | | |

Compounds ending in -*man* and -*women* behave like the simple forms, as in: *chairman—chairmen, policewoman—policewomen.*

*Foot* may take a zero plural in some contexts (4.5.4B). Moreover, *mouse* referring to the computer peripheral device can take a regular plural ending:

> *What they use up the school are proper computers, the screens and printouts and* **mouses**. (CONV)

**B  Adding -(r)en (in *children* combined with a vowel change)**

> *child—children*     *ox—oxen*

**C  Consonant change**

| | |
|---|---|
| *calf—calves* | *scarf—scarves* |
| *half—halves* | *sheaf—sheaves* |
| *knife—knives* | *shelf—shelves* |
| *leaf—leaves* | *thief—thieves* |
| *life—lives* | *wife—wives* |
| *loaf—loaves* | *wolf—wolves* |

Some words ending in -*f* take -*ves* in the plural, as shown above. The majority, including all nouns ending in -*ff*, take regular plural endings:

> *beliefs, chefs, chiefs, cliffs, proofs, puffs, reefs, roofs, serfs*

There is variation with a few forms:

> *dwarf—dwarfs/dwarves, hoof—hoofs/hooves,*
> *wharf—wharfs/wharves*

**D  The plural of *penny***

The plural *pence* is used in BrE to specify the price or value of something. The plural *pennies* refers to individual coins both in BrE and in AmE (where it means 'cents'), and is also used occasionally as a slightly humorous word for money (**3**).

1  *Pies were ten* **pence** *off for staff.* (FICT)
2  *He wants to put some* **pennies** *in a machine and he hasn't got any.* (CONV)
3  *Too many* **pennies** *spent on shuttle.* (NEWS) <headline>

*Pence* is outnumbered by far in BrE conversation by *p* (4.5.4B).

### 4.5.3 Latin and Greek plurals

Some words borrowed from Latin and Greek keep their foreign plural, or there may be alternation with regular plural forms.

A **Latin nouns ending in -us**

> *alumnus—alumni*     *nucleus—nuclei*
> *calculus—calculi*     *terminus—termini*
> *locus—loci*     *thesaurus—thesauri*

In the LSWE Corpus, the following words consistently take regular plural endings with *-es*: *apparatus, crocus, foetus*. Both regular and foreign plurals are found for: *cactus* and *syllabus*.

*Corpus* and *genus* derive from a different inflectional paradigm in Latin and take different plural forms: *corpora, genera*. *Corpus* also has the regular plural form *corpuses*.

B **Latin nouns ending in -um**

> *aquarium—aquaria*     *millennium—millennia*
> *curriculum—curricula*     *minimum—minima*
> *maximum—maxima*     *spectrum—spectra*
> *memorandum—memoranda*     *stratum—strata*

*Forums* and *stadiums* are preferred over the irregular forms *fora* and *stadia*. S-plurals are also attested for: *aquariums, curriculums, maximums, memorandums, millenniums, spectrums*.

The foreign plurals *data* and *media* have become dissociated from the original singular forms *datum* and *medium* and are variably treated as plural and singular nouns (see also 3.9.1.1):

> *We analysed [these]* **data** *ourselves.* (ACAD†)
> *[This]* **data** *is plotted in Figure 6.1.* (ACAD)
> **The media** *[have] been asked to stay away.* (NEWS)
> *When Arsenal aren't doing well* **the media** *[seems] to revel in it.* (NEWS)

C **Latin nouns ending in -a**

> *alga—algae*     *larva—larvae*
> *antenna—antennae*     *formula—formulae*

Both regular and irregular plurals are found with *antenna* and *formula*, but the irregular forms are predominant in both cases (though only regular forms were instanced in the conversation texts of the LSWE Corpus).

D **Latin nouns ending in -ex/-ix**

> *appendix—appendices*     *index—indices*

There is variation with the plural of *index*, usually correlating with a difference in meaning: the bibliographical meaning takes *-es* **1**, while the mathematical meaning takes *-ces* **2**:

> **1** *Citation* **indexes** *are a widely used method of tracking down other, later papers relevant to a query.* (ACAD†)
> **2** *The algebraic* **indices** *would be relatively easy to apply.* (ACAD†)

E **Greek nouns ending in -is**

> *axis—axes*     *hypothesis—hypotheses*
> *crisis—crises*     *oasis—oases*
> *diagnosis—diagnoses*     *thesis—theses*

**F**   **Greek nouns ending in -on**

> automaton—automata           ganglion—ganglia
> criterion—criteria           phenomenon—phenomena

*Criteria* and *phenomena* are occasionally used as singular forms:

> *Why is it a problem accepting this as a **criteria**, Caroline?* (CONV)
>
> *The **criteria** is that the songs have to have character.* (NEWS)

However, *criterion* and *phenomenon* are the preferred singular forms (occurring over 90 per cent of the time).

## 4.5.4   Zero plurals

Some nouns have a **zero plural**, i.e. they have no overt plural ending, though they have plural meaning and concord.

**A**   **Words for some animals**

> *They think they can kill a continent, people, trees, **buffalo**, and then fly off to the moon and just forget about it.* (FICT)
>
> *The **duck** leave small piles of finely-crushed mussel shells at their favoured resting sites.* (ACAD†)
>
> *Even now **trout** are being taken from the upper layers of the water and on more than one evening **fish** have surprisingly been caught on dry flies.* (NEWS)

Nouns which consistently take zero plurals include:

> *cod, deer, grouse, salmon, sheep.*

Ordinary *s*-plurals as well as zero plurals are found for: *buffalo, duck, fish*. The plural *fishes* is relatively uncommon compared with the zero plural. In cases of variation, the *s*-plural typically draws attention to the individual specimens, the zero plural to the animals as a group.

**B**   **Some quantifying nouns**

In BrE, the zero plural is used with the words *quid* (= pound, pounds) and *p* (= penny, pence), which are common in casual speech:

> *I get twenty **quid** for doing it.* (CONV)
>
> *Dad, have you got ten **p** for those?* (CONV)

*Foot* and *pound* may also occur in the zero plural after numerals:

> *The room's thirteen **foot** wide.* (CONV†)
>
> *Their shanks usually weigh about two and a half **pound**.* (CONV)

In British conversation, the zero plural is the predominant choice for these nouns, though it is normally considered non-standard (14.4.5.3F). The other registers use *feet* and *pounds*.

This pattern needs to be distinguished from *foot* and *pound* occurring more normally in complex numerical expressions such as:

> *That's nine **pound** twenty.* (CONV)
>
> *She was only four **foot** ten.* (FICT)

Furthermore the singular form is common for measure nouns in general in complex expressions premodifying a noun (cf. 4.6.1.1):

> *two **foot** square strips, a three-**mile**-square area, a five-**pound** note.*

The zero plural is also regularly used for *dozen, hundred, thousand, million* preceded by numerals:

> two **dozen** people, two **hundred** kids, fifty **thousand** dollars, 40 **million** new shares

but:

> **dozens** of people, **millions** of shares

### C   Other zero plurals

Other zero plurals include: *aircraft*; *dice*; words for people of nationalities in *-ese* such as *Chinese, Portuguese*; some words with bases ending in *-s* such as *series, species, means*.

## 4.5.5   Plural-only nouns and nouns in -s

**Plural-only** nouns do not have a singular-plural contrast, e.g. we have *scissors* but not *\*scissor*, except premodifying another noun where a bare form is regular, e.g. *scissor kick* (8.2). Alternatively, there may be a corresponding singular form, but with a different meaning. For example, *custom* is a regular countable noun, with the regular plural *customs*, in the sense of 'customary behaviour'. But *customs* in the sense of 'duties paid on goods' has no corresponding singular form and is best treated as a plural-only noun.

Most plural-only nouns are uncountable and do not combine with numerals (see C below for exceptions). They take plural concord (but see E for exceptions).

### A   Words denoting things consisting of two matching parts

Words in this group refer to tools and articles of clothing, such as *scissors* and *pants*:

> Where did you steal those **pants**? (FICT)

Other examples are: *pyjamas, shorts, trousers*; *binoculars, pliers, tongs*. Countable reference can be achieved by the use of the word *pair* (4.3.5).

### B   *Steps* and *stairs*

These denote an entire installation incorporating a set of matching individual parts:

> I can hear him on the **stairs**. (FICT)

The singular forms *step* and *stair* refer to the individual parts making up the steps/ stairs.

Countable reference for the whole unit is achieved by the unit noun *flight*, as in: *a huge flight of stairs, steep flights of steps*.

### C   *Cattle, clergy, people, police, staff*

Though not visibly plural in form, these take plural concord:

> Beef and store **cattle** and fat cows maintained their recent prices. (NEWS)
> Local **clergy** are hoping to hold a special commemorative service to mark the shutdown. (NEWS)
> **People** don't belch in this house. (CONV)
> **Police** are appealing for help from anyone who witnessed the incident. (NEWS†)
> The **staff** carry messages from guest to guest. (FICT)

*Cattle* combines with numerals (e.g. *a group of 36 cattle*). Countable reference can also be achieved by the use of a collective noun (*a herd of cattle*), a unit noun (*every head of cattle*), or by using a corresponding singular noun (*a cow/bull/bullock*).

*People* combines with quantifiers with plural reference (*many people, ten people*), but for singular reference it is necessary to resort to related nouns: *a man/woman/person*. However, *people* can also be treated as a regular countable noun in the sense of 'nation, tribe, race':

> *I have known it happen among savage **peoples**.* (FICT†)

*Police* is like *people* and *cattle* in combining with quantifiers with plural reference (e.g. *50 police*), although *policemen* and *police officers* are the preferred choices in this case. For singular reference, it is necessary to use a related word: *a policeman/policewoman/police officer/cop*, etc. Occasionally *police* combines with a singular verb; in these cases, the reference is collective:

> *The Royal Canadian Mounted **Police** was searching the airliner.* (NEWS†)

*Staff* can also combine with quantifiers with plural reference (e.g. *most staff*), while singular reference requires an expression such as *a staff member*. *Staff* is sometimes treated as a singular form, and the reference is then collective:

> *It also generally means that more money is spent and the **staff** is disrupted.* (ACAD)

### D  Other plural-only nouns

There are other words that occur as plural-only nouns:

> *The **surroundings** were beautiful and the food delicious.* (FICT)
>
> *Anyone bringing in more will be asked to confirm that their **goods** are not for reselling.* (NEWS†)
>
> *Pressed by the men, they offered various compromises at the April 1910 negotiations of which the **minutes** have been kept.* (ACAD)
>
> *Members jostled for the **remains** of unappetising-looking lettuce leaves that any self-respecting rabbit would have rejected.* (FICT)

*Archives*, which has sometimes been described as a plural-only noun, regularly occurs in the singular:

> *It's er going into an **archive**.* (CONV†)

### E  Forms with singular concord

Some nouns end in *-s* and look like plurals but actually behave like uncountable singular nouns; these include some words for games and diseases (e.g. *dominoes, draughts; measles, mumps*), as well as the noun *news*.

> *There's no **darts** tomorrow.* (CONV) <referring to a darts match>
>
> *My dear Alice, the symptoms of love are as clear as those of **measles**.* (FICT)
>
> *This **news** is brilliant.* (CONV)

Countable reference can be achieved with expressions such as: *a game of darts, an attack of measles, a piece of news*.

Another special group consists of nouns ending in *-ics* (e.g. *physics, mathematics*), which are regularly treated as singular when they refer to academic disciplines, but may behave like plural nouns in other senses (3.9.1.2).

## 4.5.6   Singular v. plural nouns: distribution

**CORPUS FINDINGS**

➤ The registers differ greatly in the proportion of singular to plural common nouns[3] (see Figure 4.5):

  ➤ Singular forms (including uncountable nouns) are more common overall than plural forms in all registers.

  ➤ Surprisingly, singular nouns are relatively frequent in conversation, although they are much more frequent in absolute numbers in news and academic prose.

  ➤ The differences are more striking with plural nouns: there are three to four times more plural nouns in the written registers than in conversation.

➤ Many individual nouns show a strong preference for either singular or plural forms:[2]

➤ The following selected nouns occur in the singular at least 75% of the time: *car, god, government, grandmother, head, house, theory.*

➤ The following selected nouns occur in the plural at least 75% of the time: *grandchildren, parents, socks, circumstances, eyebrows, onlookers, employees, perks.*

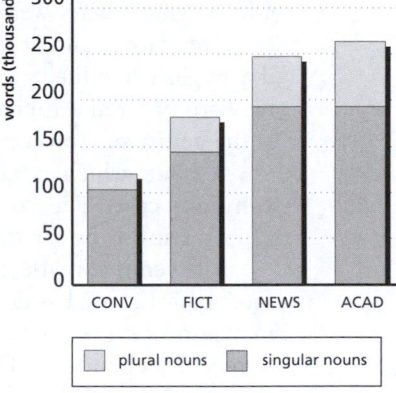

Figure 4.5

**Distribution of plural v. singular common nouns across registers**

---

**DISCUSSION OF FINDINGS**

The higher frequency of singular nouns agrees with their status as the unmarked form (which generally has the widest distribution). In addition, most uncountable nouns (4.3.2) usually have no number contrast and have singular forms only. (Most proper nouns are also restricted to singular forms, but these are not included in the Findings above.)

Moreover, with nouns that vary for number, the contrast is neutralized in some positions. Singular and plural forms do not usually contrast in premodifying position before another noun (8.2). In addition, there are many invariable collocations with singular nouns: *ask for trouble, hand in hand, from time to time, from top to toe,* etc.

The marked preferences for singular or plural forms associated with individual words reflect the communicative needs of the language user. With some entities it is more natural to refer to single instances, with others to two or more. The great majority of nouns, however, are more frequent in the singular than in the plural.

In general, the high frequency of singular nouns in conversation probably follows from the concern of speakers with individuals: a person, a thing, an event. Writers of academic prose, on the other hand, are more preoccupied with generalizations that are valid more widely (for people, things, events, etc.). This same tendency applies not only to nouns, but also to determiners and pronouns (4.4.3.1, 4.12.1, 4.14.1, 4.15.2.1).

# 4.6 Case

**Case** is a formal category of the noun which defines its relations to other units. In Old English there were four cases distinguished by inflections: nominative, genitive, dative, and accusative. Inflections have been much reduced in present-day English, and their role as syntactic signals has to a large extent been taken over by word order and function words. The only remaining case inflection for nouns is the **genitive**. However, some pronouns preserve more distinctions (4.10).

A noun which is not marked by a genitive inflection is said to be in the **common case**. The common case is used in a wide range of syntactic roles (2.7.1.1) and is by far the most frequent form of a noun (4.6.2).

The genitive marks the end of a genitive phrase (2.7.6). Genitive phrases are most typically used as **dependent** elements in noun phrases (4.6.3–4.6.6), but they may also occur without a following head noun (4.6.7, 4.6.8), and they are then termed **independent**. The fact that the genitive marks the end of a phrase is shown most clearly with so-called group genitives (4.6.9). Genitive phrases compete in meaning with postmodifying prepositional phrases, particularly *of*-phrases (4.6.12). A special type of construction combines both a genitive and an *of*-phrase (4.6.10).

## 4.6.1 The form of the genitive

The genitive of singular nouns is marked by the addition of a suffix which varies in pronunciation in the same way as the plural ending (4.5.1):

| | |
|---|---|
| /s/ | after voiceless consonants except /s, ʃ, tʃ/: *cat's, Jack's, Patrick's*; |
| /z/ | after vowels and voiced consonants except /z, ʒ, dʒ/: *boy's, girl's, men's*, etc.; |
| /ɪz/ | after /s, z, ʃ, ʒ, tʃ, dʒ/: *Charles's, George's, Ross's*, etc. |

The genitive suffix is marked off in writing by an apostrophe.

The genitive of regular plural nouns is shown in writing by the addition of an apostrophe:

*boys—boys', ladies—ladies'*

In speech there is no distinction between the genitive and the common case of regular plural nouns. Irregular plural nouns are marked in the same way as genitive singular forms and differ from the common case forms in both speech and writing:

*men—men's, women—women's*

In casual everyday writing, there is a good deal of variation in the use of the apostrophe. For example, the apostrophe is sometimes used to mark plural forms, especially of abbreviated or newly imported words, as in *video's* and *phone's*. This use is non-standard.

In careful writing, we find variation in how the apostrophe is used to mark the genitive particularly with proper nouns ending in -*s*:

***Charles's** grandfather always maintained that the aristocracy was becoming far too lax.* (FICT†)

*He is in many people's minds the next logical man to fill* **Charles'** *place.* (NEWS†)

*The prosperity of this part of the nation depends upon getting Senator* **Jones's** *bill enacted.* (FICT)

*The court heard the social services department received complaints of* **Mr Jones'** *ill-treatment.* (NEWS)

*Mrs Harvey had a different view of* **Nicholas's** *behaviour.* (NEWS)

*McAvennie nodded Grant's lob into* **Nicholas'** *path.* (NEWS†)

Most nouns of this type occur most often with *'s*.

## 4.6.1.1    Genitive v. common case

In certain contexts there is variation which is perhaps best regarded as involving a choice between genitive and common case (singular or plural), rather than between alternative spellings of the genitive.

One such situation arises with plural expressions of measure (4.6.6) with an uncountable head noun, where the choice could be seen as being between a genitive plural and a common case plural premodifying expression with no apostrophe:

*A man deserves* **a few weeks'** *holiday.* (FICT)

*All three men accused of raping a young woman at a local bar were released today on* **ten thousand dollars'** *bail.* (FICT)

v.   *This is the most serious of the offences in the Act, and is triable only on indictment and attracts a maximum penalty of* **ten years** *imprisonment.* (ACAD)

*He stood dumbstruck as they read the charges off to him and announced that he was being held on* **fifty thousand dollars** *bail.* (FICT)

There appears to be a great deal of variation with these forms, depending upon the particular collocation. For example, in the LSWE Corpus, the apostrophe is regularly used with expressions ending in *time* and most often omitted with *imprisonment*. Interestingly, the preferences differ depending upon the currency in *dollars' worth* v. *pounds worth* (perhaps a sign that the use of the apostrophe is more entrenched in some contexts in AmE).

Note that in singular expressions of measure the genitive, with an apostrophe, is regularly used: *an hour's discussion, a month's holiday* (cf. 4.6.6). With a countable head noun, the modifying noun is normally in the singular: *a two-week period, a five-year sentence, ten-dollar bills.*

For further examples of similar variation involving the genitive, see the account of classifying genitives (4.6.4.1) and independent genitives (4.6.8.1).

## 4.6.2    The frequency of genitive case forms

Most nouns rarely occur in the genitive. This is because the genitive is a marked form and has a very restricted syntactic role, while the common case is used in all other contexts.

The genitive frequency varies depending upon the type of noun (see also 4.6.12.2). Somewhat surprisingly, personal names do not have a consistently higher frequency as genitives than personal common nouns (such as *boy, women*).

The reason may be that personal names are used infrequently as parts of complex noun phrases. Instead they are more typically used on their own to realize a clause element. There is a slight tendency for the genitive plural to be less common than the genitive singular.

## 4.6.3 Specifying genitives

The most important function of the genitive phrase is to **specify** the reference of the noun phrase of which it is a part, in the same way as a determiner. The genitive phrase is, in fact, mutually exclusive with the central determiner groups (4.4). Compare:

> *a/the/that/the girl's* face

> but not: *\*the girl's that* face

The genitive phrase most typically is a definite noun phrase with specific reference, which also gives specific reference to the superordinate noun phrase. When the genitive phrase is paraphrased by a postmodifying prepositional phrase, the head of the noun phrase takes the definite article. Compare:

> *the girl's* face
>
> v.   *the* face *of the girl*

The genitive phrase may, however, have generic reference:

> *The client is always right. It is **the artist's** first axiom.* (FICT)

Less commonly, we find indefinite genitive phrases:

> 1  *He heard the clip-clop of **a horse's** hoofs behind him.* (FICT †)
>
> 2  *He had something of **a horse's** dreadful beauty.* (FICT †)

In **1** the reference is to a specific horse; in **2** the reference is generic, indicating something which is typical of a horse. The latter type gradually merges with the classifying genitive (4.6.4).

## 4.6.4 Classifying genitives

Some genitives have a **classifying** rather than a specifying function. Compare (with the whole noun phrase shown in *[]*) the following:

Specifying genitives:

> 1  *Several hours later **[the bird's** relieved owner]** arrived at the station, explaining the parrot had flown off as she took it to her grandchildren for a treat.* (NEWS)
>
> 2  *Even **[her two children's** clothes]** disappeared.* (NEWS)

Classifying genitives:

> 3  *His hair felt like **[a bird's** nest]**. He was a mess.* (FICT)
>
> 4  *Hoppity in Hartlepool is one of the few nearly new shops specialising just in **[children's** clothes]**.* (NEWS)

In **1** and **2** the reference is to the owner of a specific bird and the clothes of some specific children. In contrast, the genitives in **3** and **4** serve to classify the type of nest and clothes.

Classifying genitives differ in a number of respects from specifying constructions. First, they respond to the question 'What kind of ...?' rather than 'Whose ...?', which displays their similarity to adjectives and other such noun premodifiers, rather than to determiners. In fact they cannot be replaced by possessive determiners. Second, they can be preceded by determiners and modifiers of the whole noun phrase, rather than of the genitive noun alone: *a new bird's nest, new children's clothes*. This again is true also for adjective and noun premodifiers of nouns. Third, they form an inseparable combination with the following noun and do not usually allow an intervening adjective: *\*a bird's new nest, \*children's new clothes*. In this they resemble classifier adjectives (7.2.2) and noun premodifiers of nouns (8.2.2) which also are positioned closest to the head noun. Finally, they are frequently paraphrased by a *for*-phrase rather than an *of*-construction, as in *clothes for children*. Compare again constructions with noun premodifiers like *baby clothes*.

These characteristics reflect the close bond between a classifying genitive and the following head noun. The unity of classifying genitives and the head noun is also shown by the tendency for the combination to be single-stressed rather than pronounced as a phrase. Further, classifying genitives sometimes acquire idiomatic meanings (e.g. *a bull's eye, a hornet's nest*). Moreover, the spelling may be idiosyncratic: *bees wax* v. *hornet's nest*. In sum, many classifying genitive plus head noun combinations tend to behave more like compounds (4.8.2) rather than phrases (and they do in fact generally correspond to compounds in other Germanic languages).

### 4.6.4.1 Classifying genitives: use

Classifying genitives are commonly used with personal nouns, especially when they are in the plural form:

> *boys' camp, boys' clubs, a boys' school, a boys' home, girls' books, girls' coats, girls' names, girls' grammar school, a men's clothing store, men's suits, a men's team, the oldest women's club, women's clothing, women's magazines*

There is some uncertainty in the spelling of classifying genitives. For example, the following forms are all attested in the LSWE Corpus: *a bird's nest* (the most frequent form), *a birds' nest, a bird nest, birds' nests*.

## 4.6.5 Genitives of time

The **genitive of time** is used to specify location in time.

> *Have you read any of your letters about the poems in **last week's** Observer?* (CONV)

> *As far as we know, **yesterday's** job was only their second.* (FICT)

> *The Stock Exchange is investigating **Friday's** steep rise in the share price of Pearl Group.* (NEWS†)

> *Initial findings could be implemented by **this autumn's** statement on spending.* (NEWS)

This type occurs particularly in news, where location of events in time is obviously communicatively crucial (cf. 4.6.11).

Occasionally we find classifying genitives alternating with common case forms for some temporal nouns:

> *Her visitor had a strong pungent odor of a **winter's** day.* (FICT)

*All four children stood blinking in the daylight of a **winter** day.* (FICT†)

Temporal nouns are also common in measure expressions (4.6.6).

## 4.6.6 Genitives of measure

The **genitive of measure** is found in expressions of duration, distance/length, and value:

Duration
> *an hour's discussion, a minute's hesitation,*
> *a moment's consideration, a month's holiday,*
> *a second's delay, a year's sabbatical,*
> *two hours' sleep, ten minutes' duration.*

With plural forms (4.6.1) there is some variation in the use of the apostrophe.

Distance/length
> *I held the telephone at **arm's length** and stared at it.* (FICT)
> *They now kept **a stone's throw** to the left of the road.* (FICT†)

Value
> *She had to buy **fifty pounds'** worth.* (CONV)
> *Perhaps he took my thousand dollars and put me to sleep with **two dollars'** worth of ether.* (FICT)
> *In my book you're **a nickel's** worth of nothing.* (FICT)

Expressions with *worth* also often contain measure genitives which primarily express duration or amount:

> *There's only about **two weeks'** worth there!* (CONV)
> *There was **a quarter of hour's** worth of music.* (FICT)
> *Somebody on that other side had done **a whole wall's** worth of Uncle Ho himself.* (FICT†)

This occurs particularly in conversation and fiction.

Note that temporal expressions of duration may be used also to express distance, value, and amount in general:

> *Their huts were **12 hours'** journey from the nearest main road.* (NEWS†)
> *That's not **half an hour's** income to them.* (FICT)
> *I want **ten years'** supply of whisky.* (CONV†)

## 4.6.7 Elliptic genitives

Where the head noun is somehow recoverable, the genitive phrase may on its own fill a nominal position. Examples of such **independent genitives** include **elliptic genitives** where the complete noun phrase that one would reconstruct has not actually occurred elsewhere in the discourse, but can be inferred from the preceding context:

> *That isn't my [handwriting]. It's **Selina's**!* (FICT)
> *Albert, you are neglecting the [glasses]. **Mr Deane's** is almost empty, and so is **Monsieur Belmont's.*** (FICT)
> *If a [car]'s dirty, it's **a woman's.*** (NEWS)

These are generally specifying, but classifying constructions also occur:

> All the Turner girls preferred girls' *[toys]* to **boys'**. (FICT†)

The head noun of an elliptic genitive is occasionally recoverable from the following rather than preceding context:

> **Mahbub Ali's** was a *[name]* of power in Umballa. (FICT)
>
> **Bess's** was an old-fashioned country *[wedding]*. (FICT†)

This represents a rare, stylistically marked construction type (see also 4.11).

Elliptic genitives compete with *of*-phrases following a demonstrative pronoun (4.6.13).

## 4.6.8 Other independent genitives

In a special type of independent genitive, a full noun phrase, with a dependent genitive, is reduced when it recurs identically later in the text:

> A: *Yeah, I fancy going out anyway. I don't fancy sitting in* **Terry and Lindsey's flat** *all night.*
>
> B: *Oh no, I wasn't planning on staying at* **Terry and Lindsey's** *all night.* (CONV)
>
> **Parkinson's disease** *is a degenerative brain disorder that causes tremors and muscle rigidity among other symptoms.*
>
> <...> *Scientists at Synergen, based in Boulder, Colorado, have isolated and cloned a nerve growth factor that spurs cells specifically affected by* **Parkinson's** <...> (ACAD†)

Many independent genitives have become conventionalized, so that they need no supporting head noun in the context. They frequently refer to places, particularly to people's homes and to shops:

> *"We should be at* **Mom's** *in an hour", Roz surmised.* (FICT†) <house>
>
> *She's going to* **a friend's**. (CONV†) <house>
>
> *An open bottle of* **Jack Daniel's** *is on the candle table.* (FICT†) <whiskey>
>
> *The vast main concourse had the combined appearance of a football scrimmage and Christmas Eve at* **Macy's**. (FICT) <department store>

### 4.6.8.1 Independent genitives unsupported by the linguistic context

Independent genitives of this kind are found particularly in conversation, though this is the register with the lowest frequency of dependent genitives (4.6.11). This is in agreement with the general greater reliance of this register on non-linguistic situational reference and shared knowledge (cf. for example 4.4.1.5).

The connection with the genitive tends to become weakened with names of companies. For example, the following variants are all attested in the LSWE Corpus: *Marks and Spencer's, Marks and Spencers, Marks and Spencer, McDonald's, McDonalds, Woolworth's, Woolworths, Woolworth.*

## 4.6.9    Group genitives

The genitive suffix is attached to the last word of a genitive phrase. In the great majority of cases, the last word is the head of a noun phrase: *the **prince's** brother*, *the **clerk's** office*, etc. When the head of the genitive phrase is followed by a postmodifier, the suffix is attached at the end of the phrase, the so-called **group genitive**:

> She would be pleased to get back to her **mother-in-law's** house. (FICT)
>
> I have to accept **the clerk of the course's** decision. (NEWS) <reference is to a racecourse>
>
> **The father of five's** face was so badly busted he had to be fitted with a metal cage to keep the bones in place until they set. (NEWS)

The group genitive is chiefly used with more or less fixed collocations. When there is postmodification, the more common alternative is to resort to an *of*-phrase rather than an *s*-genitive (4.6.12.4).

> Other examples of group genitives are found with coordinate constructions:
>
> The new girls that were meant to be sleeping in there slept in **Zoey and Lucy's** room. (CONV)
>
> He had to take **a minute or two's** rest to recover his breath. (FICT)

The choice between a group genitive and two coordinated *s*-genitives may correlate with a difference in meaning. Compare:

> 1  *Sir David did not comment on **Britain and China's** war of words over Hong Kong's future.* (NEWS†)
>
> 2  *To set the tone for our discussion and to put planning and evaluation into proper perspective, we present **Berg and Muscat's** definition of planning.* (ACAD†)
>
> 3  *Not only do the World Cup organisers have to keep **England's and Holland's** supporters apart, they will also have to cope with Ireland's peaceful "green army", which could number 20,000.* (NEWS)
>
> 4  *The reason that **Schrodinger's and Heisenberg's** versions of quantum mechanics had seemed at first sight different from each other (see p. 14) was that they had chosen to use contrasting extreme possibilities.* (ACAD)

The group genitives in **1** and **2** clearly define the same phenomenon. By contrast, the reference of the coordinated *s*-genitives in **3** and **4** is to different supporter groups and different theories. Contrasts of this kind are, however, not consistently maintained. For example, **5** refers to different pairs of eyes:

> 5  ***Andrew and Horatia's** eyes met* (FICT)

while

> 6  ***Cedric's and Jane's** house* (FICT)

presumably refers to a single house.

Instead of a coordinated group genitive, it is also possible to use concatenated *of*-phrases, as in *the war of words of Britain and China over Hong Kong's future* (4.6.12.4).

## 4.6.10 The double genitive

The **double genitive** is a special construction which makes it possible for the same head noun to take a specifying genitive (or a possessive pronoun; 4.11) and another determiner. The head noun is most typically preceded by an indefinite article:

> *Aren't you having **a bun of mummy's** now?* (CONV)

> *This was **a good idea of Johnny's**.* (CONV)

> *The woman who owns Harte's is **a friend of ours**, well, **of my father's** and she's quite incredible.* (FICT)

> *Remember he's **a relative of Kupka's**, and close to his wife.* (FICT)

The definite article does not normally combine with the head noun of a double genitive. This is presumably because a noun phrase with the ordinary specifying genitive is anyway equivalent to a definite noun phrase (4.6.3), and would be used in preference to the double genitive: e.g. *Johnny's good idea* instead of \**the good idea of Johnny's*.

Apart from *a* and plural indefinite noun phrases, the double genitive is found commonly with demonstratives:

> *The child found herself permanently transported from her mother's two-room house to **this mansion of her father's**.* (FICT)

and on occasion with *wh*-determiners:

> ***What business of Winter's*** *was it that he'd had a mere half-bottle of champagne with his cold pheasant supper?* (FICT)

Partitive constructions and ordinary *of*-phrases are discourse alternatives to the double genitive (4.6.14).

## 4.6.11 Density of genitives

The following findings are based on the genitive forms of nouns, classified by the meaning of the genitivized noun, including both proper nouns and common nouns. Genitive forms of pronouns (e.g. *somebody's*, *another's*) are excluded. These are rare in all registers (apart from possessive determiners; cf. 4.4.2).

**CORPUS FINDINGS [9]**

➤ Dependent genitives are far more common in news than in the other registers (see Table 4.18).

Table 4.18 **Distribution of dependent genitives; occurrences per million words**

each ■ represents 500 □ represents less than 250

| genitive noun | CONV | FICT | NEWS | ACAD |
|---|---|---|---|---|
| personal | ■ ■ | ■ ■ ■ ■ ■ | ■ ■ ■ ■ ■ ■ | ■ ■ |
| collective | □ | □ | ■ ■ ■ ■ | □ |
| place | □ | □ | ■ ■ | ■ |
| time | □ | □ | ■ | □ |
| other | □ | ■ | ■ | ■ |

➤ Genitives based on nouns with human reference are more common than any other.
➤ Independent genitives are most common in conversation (occurring c. 500 times per million words) and extremely rare in academic prose.

**DISCUSSION OF FINDINGS**

The genitive frequency is far higher in news than in the other registers. This is true irrespective of the type of genitive noun, but the difference is particularly striking with non-personal nouns. The relatively high genitive density agrees with the high overall frequency of nouns in news (2.3.5). The genitive serves the purposes of journalism well, in allowing information to be presented in a concise manner:

> **Last week's** meeting of **the borough's** policy and finance committee was all but devoid of dissenting voices. (NEWS†)

> The England hooker, who has already said that he would have accepted only the usual expenses had he undertaken **this summer's** tour of the Republic marking **the South African Rugby Board's** centenary, has now been quoted as saying that "remuneration was mentioned." (NEWS)

The opposite extreme is conversation, where the genitive density is very low. Again this agrees with the overall frequency of nouns in the register (2.3.5). It is worth noting that the proportion of genitives with personal nouns is particularly high both in conversation and fiction, no doubt reflecting the fact that human beings are at the centre of interest in both registers.

The frequency of genitives in academic prose is surprisingly low in comparison with the overall density of nouns in that register (2.3.5). In part this reflects the subject matter of academic prose, where human beings and relationships play a less important role than in the other registers (cf. 4.6.12.2 for the use of *of*-phrases instead).

If we turn now to genitives without a following head noun, we find quite a different picture. Double and elliptic genitives are relatively rare in all registers. Other independent genitives are more frequent, but still rare compared with dependent genitives. Conversation makes the most frequent use of independent genitives, referring to shops, people's homes, etc.

The opposite tendencies observed in conversation and news fit in with the general characteristics of these registers (2.10); independent genitives reflect the greater simplicity of phrases in conversation, while the use of dependent genitives contributes to the phrasal complexity of news (see also Chapter 8).

## 4.6.12 Choice between *s*-genitives and *of*-phrases

There is frequently a choice between an *s*-genitive and a postmodifying structure. As with prenominal elements in general, the *s*-genitive is characteristically more compact and less explicit in meaning. The nature of the connection to the head noun is left unspecified with the *s*-genitive, whereas postmodifiers usually contain more signals of syntactic/semantic relationships. For example, compare the meanings expressed by the specifying genitive phrase and the postmodifier in the following two sentences:

> 1 *The Health Secretary posed for the lens of the famous photographer of beautiful women, Terry O'Neill.* **Terry's** *portrait [of our dishiest Cabinet*

> *Minister for years] will be used to spearhead European Drug Prevention Week in November.* (NEWS)
>
> 2 **Mrs. van Luyden's** *portrait [by Huntington] (in black velvet and Venetian point) faced that of her lovely ancestress.* (FICT)

The genitives in these two examples express different relationships: subjective in **1** and objective in **2**. These same relationships are marked by different prepositions in the postmodifiers: a subjective relationship is marked by *by* in **2**, while an objective relationship is marked by *of* in **1**.

S-genitives and postmodifying *of*-phrases often compete. In many cases, though, neither one is more explicit; both admit of a wide range of interpretations (4.6.12.3). For example, note how *s*-genitives and *of*-phrases are used in much the same manner in:

> *He is not aware of all that has happened, including the tragedy of **his mother's death**.* (NEWS†)
>
> *Freddie, who is still grieving **the death of his mother Hilda** three weeks ago, aged 82, is determined not to lose touch with his children this time.* (NEWS)
>
> **The car's owner**, *Salford University student Michael Afilaka, said <...>* (NEWS†)
>
> **The owner of the car** *was nowhere to be seen.* (FICT†)

In these examples we find the same head nouns, *death* and *owner*, combining with the same dependent nouns, *mother* and *car*, respectively.

However, the use of the *s*-genitive and postmodifying *of*-phrases is not indiscriminate. Rather, the choice between these two forms varies depending upon a number of factors, the most important of which are: register (4.6.12.1), the type of dependent noun (4.6.12.2), semantic relations between head and dependent phrase (4.6.12.3), the complexity of the dependent phrase (4.6.12.4), the information status of the dependent phrase (4.6.12.5), and specific collocations (4.6.12.6).

## 4.6.12.1    *S-genitives* and *of-phrases* overall

The registers vary greatly in the distribution of *s*-genitives and *of*-phrases. The following findings exclude *of*-phrases that could never be used as an alternative to an *s*-genitive. The excluded *of*-phrases include: phrases governed by preceding verbs or adjectives (*accused of, afraid of,* etc.); examples with fixed *of*-expressions (*in front of, because of,* etc.); and *of*-phrases preceded by numerals, quantifying determiners, unit nouns, collective nouns, quantifying nouns, or species nouns (*one of, some of, a piece of, a herd of, a box of, types of,* etc.). Although both *s*-genitives and *of*-phrases are not always possible choices in the remainder of cases, the differences among registers are nevertheless striking:

**CORPUS FINDINGS** [2]

➤ S-genitives are outnumbered by *of*-phrases in all registers.
➤ Conversation has by far the lowest frequency both of *s*-genitives and *of*-phrases.
➤ The distribution of the two construction types is strikingly different in news and academic prose:
  ➤ News has by far the highest frequency of the *s*-genitive;
  ➤ Academic prose has by far the highest frequency of *of*-phrases (and a surprisingly low frequency of *s*-genitives).

**DISCUSSION OF FINDINGS**

The register distribution of s-genitives and of-phrases is connected with the overall frequency of nouns (2.3.5, 4.1.2). As the frequency of nouns is low in conversation, we also get a low frequency of elements dependent upon nouns. Conversely, we get a much higher frequency of these elements in academic prose and news, and inter-mediate values for fiction.

The frequency of the s-genitive is particularly high in news, presumably because it represents a good way of compressing information. Note that this accords with the complexity of premodification in this register (8.2).

The fact that fiction makes more frequent use of s-genitives than academic prose probably reflects the types of nouns which are prevalent in these registers, with fiction using more nouns with human reference (4.6.12.2).

The far greater frequency of of-phrases in all registers may be due to a general preference for less compact structures. Postmodification produces a less dense and more transparent means of expression. For example, determiners and modifiers preceding an s-genitive noun may qualify either that dependent noun or the head of the noun phrase (related to the precise interpretation of the genitive as specifying, classifying etc.). Compare:

*[her two children's] clothes*    *the clothes of her two children*

*new [children's clothes]*        *new clothes for children*

The choice of the postmodifying structure makes it clearer which words go together; additional clarity may be provided by the choice of preposition. The postmodifying structure also opens up more possibilities of qualifying the dependent noun (4.6.12.4). This factor is important in accounting for the strikingly high frequency of of-phrases in academic prose.

The frequency of of-phrases represents the current state of a historical shift towards of that has been ongoing ever since Old English, where inflected genitives predominated.

**Figure 4.6**

**Distribution of *of*-phrases v. *s*-genitives across registers**

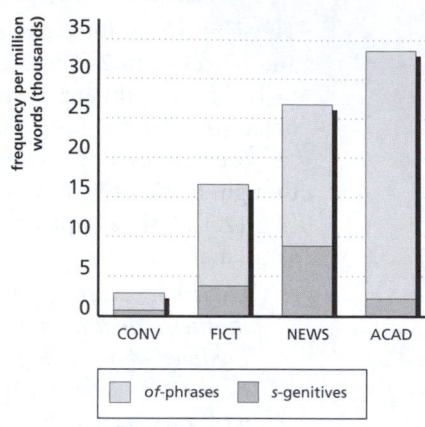

## 4.6.12.2    *S*-genitives and *of*-phrases and the dependent noun

The choice between s-genitives v. postmodifying of-phrases is influenced by the type of dependent noun.

**CORPUS FINDINGS** [1]

➤ Nouns with human/personal reference, especially proper nouns, tend to occur with the s-genitive rather than an of-phrase:

➤ selected nouns that occur in the s-genitive over 80% of the time: *Fred, Jane, Sarah, Tom;*

➤ selected nouns that occur in the *s*-genitive 61–80% of the time: *baby, girl, girls, student.*

➤ Nouns with inanimate concrete reference and abstract impersonal nouns tend to occur in an *of*-phrase rather than the *s*-genitive, as do some collective nouns for groups of people:

➤ selected nouns that occur in an *of*-phrase over 80% of the time: inanimate concrete nouns: *book(s), car(s), moon(s), tree(s), window(s), hotel(s), shop(s), house(s)*; abstract impersonal nouns: *freedom, idea(s), socialism*; collective nouns for groups of people: *club(s), college(s), committee(s).*

➤ Plural nouns are generally more likely to occur in *of*-phrases than singular nouns.

### DISCUSSION OF FINDINGS

The correlation of *s*-genitives v. *of*-phrases with the semantic domain of the noun is only partial. Given the right circumstances, we find personal nouns with postmodifying *of*-phrases and impersonal nouns with the *s*-genitive. The main conditioning factors are taken up in the sections below.

## 4.6.12.3 Meanings of *s*-genitives and *of*-phrases

Although both *s*-genitives and postmodifying *of*-phrases are used with a wide range of semantic interpretations, each expresses some preferred relations. In the case of the *s*-genitive, in specifying function (4.6.3), a division is usually made between the **possessive genitive 1**, the **genitive of attribute 2**, the **genitive of origin 3**, and the **subjective genitive 4**:

1 **The family's car** *was found abandoned at Andersonstown Crescent.* (NEWS)

2 *On occasions,* **Martha's courage** *failed her.* (FICT)

3 *A volume of* **Byron's poems** *lay before him on the table.* (FICT)

4 **Chiang's recognition** *of the priority of the spoken language explained why so few characters were pictographs and ideographs.* (ACAD)

Other relations commonly expressed by the *s*-genitive are time (4.6.5) and measure (4.6.6). In addition, *s*-genitives are commonly used with a classifying function (4.6.4).

Some preferred relations expressed by postmodifying *of*-phrases are **partitive 5**, **defining 6**, and **objective 7**:

5 **This section of the discussion** *concerns the use of sentence contexts in the recognition of words.* (ACAD†)

6 *I live in* **the city of Lahore.** (FICT†)

7 **The brutal murder of a child** *leaves a firm trace on the mind of a police officer like an indelible pen.* (NEWS)

In addition, *of*-phrases are commonly used after quantifying nouns (4.3.4-6) and species nouns (4.3.7).

The preferred uses of the two constructions are shown most clearly where they are both present in the same noun phrase:

8 **The Government's denial of the need for the draft directive** *is a clear breach of the welfare principle enshrined in the UN convention.* (NEWS)

9 *Both Dalgliesh and Massingham wondered how far* **Mrs. Bidwell's description of the quarrel** *given with the maximum dramatic effect, had been accurate.* (FICT)

10 *After* **yesterday's disclosure of the court action**, *the curator of the university's art collection spoke out in favour of its plans to sell one of the Torrie works.* (NEWS)

11 *At* **today's meeting of the 1922 Committee** *Mr Onslow will declare a leadership election open.* (NEWS)

In examples such as **8** and **9**, the *s*-genitive expresses a subjective relation, while the *of*-phrase expresses an objective relation. The *s*-genitive may also express a time relationship, while the *of*-phrase is objective **10** or subjective **11**.

Less commonly, the objective relationship is expressed by an *s*-genitive, and the subjective relation is expressed by a postmodifier:

12 *It was* **Cantona's exclusion by Leeds** *against Arsenal that led to his shock transfer last week.* (NEWS)

## 4.6.12.4 *S*-genitives and *of*-phrases and length

Six head nouns were analysed: *appointment, arrival, birth, murder, resignation, withdrawal.*

**CORPUS FINDINGS [2,10]**

➤ *S*-genitives are generally preferred for short dependent phrases, while *of*-phrases are preferred for longer dependent phrases.

Table 4.19 **Proportional use of *s*-genitives v. *of*-phrases for dependent phrases of different lengths, for selected head nouns**

each ■ represents 5%    ▫ represents less than 2.5%

| phrase | % use of *s*-genitive | % use of *of*-phrase |
|---|---|---|
| 1 word | ■■■■■■■■■■■■■ | ■■■■■■■ |
| 2 words | ■■■■■■■ | ■■■■■■■■■■■■■ |
| 3 words | ■ | ■■■■■■■■■■■■■■■■■■■ |
| 4+ words | ▫ | ■■■■■■■■■■■■■■■■■■■■■ |

**DISCUSSION OF FINDINGS**

Most typically, *s*-genitive constructions are used in one-word dependent phrases. In contrast, *of*-phrases are commonly used in much longer dependent phrases. Compare (with the whole noun phrase shown in *[]*):

*S*-genitive constructions

1 *[***The trustee's** *appointment] is effective from the date his appointment is certified by the chairman of the meeting.* (ACAD†)

2 *[***Mr Walsh's** *murder] came just 11 hours after the UFF shot dead four Catholics and injured a fifth man.* (NEWS†)

*Of*-phrases

> 3 *Commenting publicly after [the recent appointment **of a part-time woman and two men]** to a partnership comprising one woman and 30 men, the senior partner professed the firm "comfortable" with the "entirely natural progression of women".* (NEWS)

> 4 *A New Zealand man was recently sentenced to life imprisonment for [the murder **of an English tourist, Monica Cantwell]**.* (NEWS)

> 5 *Whitby Town Council is to meet representatives of Tees bus company over [the withdrawal **of the service to the port's St Andrew's Road area]**.* (NEWS)

> 6 *There was a further element to Mr McLean's rapidly boiling anger: [the sudden arrival **of Mr Uppal, who hitherto had taken no interest in the case]**.* (NEWS)

The *s*-genitives in these examples consist of just determiner/title plus noun. Where an *s*-genitive contains more than a single word, it is normally restricted to a simple structure (such as determiner + noun, or premodifier + noun).

*Of*-phrases, on the other hand, can be much more complex. The complexity of the dependent *of*-phrases in the above examples is due to coordination **3**, an appositional construction **4**, a postmodifying prepositional phrase **5**, and a relative clause **6**.

To sum up, complexity appears to be one of the main factors influencing the choice of *s*-genitives v. *of*-phrases. As on the clause level (11.1.3), there is a tendency for heavy and complex elements to be placed at the end.

## 4.6.12.5 *S*-genitives and *of*-phrases and information status

Choices within the noun phrase are dependent upon the wider context within which the noun phrase is embedded. This context determines whether elements may be regarded as given (rather than new) information, either because they have been introduced earlier in the text or because they are part of the general knowledge of the speaker/writer and the addressee (11.1.1).

Five head nouns are analysed: *appointment, arrival, murder, resignation, withdrawal*. Given information was identified here by mention in the immediately preceding text.

### CORPUS FINDINGS [2,10]

> ➤ *S*-genitives are generally preferred for presenting given information; *of*-phrases are preferred for presenting new information.

Table 4.20  **Proportional use of *s*-genitives v. *of*-phrases for presenting given v. new information, for selected head nouns**

each ● represents 5%

|  | % presenting given information | % presenting new information |
| --- | --- | --- |
| *s*-genitives | ● ● ● ● ● ● ● ● ● ● ● ● ● ● ● ● ● ● | ● ● ● ● ● |
| *of*-phrases | ● ● ● | ● ● ● ● ● ● ● ● ● ● ● ● ● ● ● ● ● ● |

**DISCUSSION OF FINDINGS**

*S*-genitives are typically used with reference to persons, things or phenomena which are given rather than new. In contrast, and even more markedly, postmodifying *of*-phrases more often introduce new entities into the discourse. The choice agrees with one of the main ordering principles on the clause level, viz. the information principle (11.1.1), stating that new information tends to be distributed later in the clause.

The relationship between the type of dependent noun phrase and the preceding context is shown very clearly in examples such as:

> *The renowned Aberdeen ballad-singer, Lizzie Higgins, died on Saturday in her native city at the age of 63. Lizzie was [the daughter **of a very famous mother, the late Jeannie Robertson, who after her "discovery" in 1953 was acclaimed internationally as the outstanding ballad-singer of modern times**]. [Lizzie's father] was the prize-winning piper Donald Higgins, whose influence on her musical development complemented that of her mother.*
> (NEWS)

The *of*-phrase in this example introduces a new referent (Lizzie's mother) and provides extensive new information about that referent. The *s*-genitive, on the other hand, contains only a reference to Lizzie, the person who is the theme of the text.

Where there is previous mention, *s*-genitives frequently express objective relationships (with, e.g. *appointment* or *murder*) as well as subjective relationships (with, e.g. *arrival* and *resignation*).

## 4.6.12.6  *S*-genitives and *of*-phrases in collocations

The distribution of *s*-genitives and postmodifying *of*-phrases is not just influenced by the general factors dealt with above. In addition, there are collocational patterns connected with individual nouns or specific groups of nouns. Collocations are common with classifying genitives (4.6.4.1) and genitives of measure (4.6.6). Other examples are: *death's door, life's work, nature's way, (out of) harm's way.*

The head noun *sake* is particularly productive in collocations with *s*-genitives: *for Christ's sake, for God's sake, for goodness' sake, for heaven's sake, for Pete's sake, for pity's sake, for safety's sake, for old times'/time's sake.*

## 4.6.12.7  Summary of choice between *s*-genitives and *of*-phrases

The choice of the *s*-genitive v. postmodifying *of*-phrases is a result of a complex interplay of factors. In addition to register (4.6.12.1), four factors have been identified which appear to influence strongly the choice of construction: the type of dependent noun (4.6.12.2), semantic relations between head and dependent phrase (4.6.12.3), the complexity of the dependent phrase (4.6.12.4), and the information status of the dependent phrase (4.6.12.5).

To generalize, we could say that the *s*-genitive is closely related to the subject of clauses, and *of*-phrases to objects. There is a similarity between position in the clause and in the noun phrase: early placement for subjects and *s*-genitives, late placement for objects and *of*-phrases. There is also a correspondence between the types of relations expressed, most clearly shown in the preference for the subjective relation of *s*-genitives and for the objective relation of *of*-phrases. There is an analogous difference in complexity and information status: subjects and *s*-genitives are characteristically less complex and more typically convey given information, while objects and *of*-phrases show the opposite tendency.

The type of dependent noun has traditionally been emphasized as the most important factor influencing this choice. The nouns which show the highest *s*-genitive frequency most typically refer to individual human beings. These are the entities which are most closely associated with agency, i.e. the semantic relation which is most characteristically associated with subjects. There is another subject-like characteristic of the nouns which tend to appear in the *s*-genitive: they refer to entities which are likely to be found as themes in texts. Similar associations are probably applicable to the higher *s*-genitive frequencies with singular (v. plural) nouns: individuals are more likely to attract the interest of speakers than groups. In other words, the role of the type of dependent noun appears to be connected with deeper underlying factors.

## 4.6.13 Choice between elliptic genitives and *of*-constructions

Constructions with *that/those* plus *of*-phrase are alternatives to elliptic genitives (4.6.7).

Elliptic genitives:

> *A more complete imagination than* **Philip's** *might have pictured a youth of splendid hope.* (FICT †)

> *Shareholders were told at the Bournemouth-based group's annual meeting yesterday that January reservations were 9.4 per cent up on* **last year's**. (NEWS †)

*that/those* plus *of*-phrase:

> *The coroner's report fixes her time of death, and* **that of Diana McKechnie**, *approximately two hours before the deaths of the five persons found fatally shot in the back room or office.* (FICT)

> *This year's first quarter sales are still below* **those of last year** *in the UK.* (NEWS †)

### 4.6.13.1 Elliptic genitives v. *of*-constructions: distribution

**CORPUS FINDINGS [2]**

➤ Elliptic *s*-genitives are characteristically used with nouns referring to humans. Constructions with *that/those* plus *of*-phrase occur with all kinds of nouns.

➤ The *of*-construction represents the majority choice in the written registers. In conversation, elliptic *s*-genitives are more common.

> ➤ *That/those* + *of*-phrase is extremely common in academic prose, but very rare in conversation.

**DISCUSSION OF FINDINGS**

The choice between the two construction types is partly governed by the same sorts of factors which apply to *s*-genitives v. *of*-phrases in general, e.g. in its

Table 4.21    **Distribution of elliptic *s*-genitives v. *that/those* plus *of*-phrase; occurrences per million words**

each ■ represents 20    □ represents less than 10

|  | CONV | FICT | NEWS | ACAD |
|---|---|---|---|---|
| elliptic *s*-genitive | ■■ | ■ | □ | □ |
| *that/those* + *of*-phrase | □ | ■■■■ | ■■■ | ■■■■■■■■■■■■■■ ■■■■■■■ |

relation to semantic domain of the noun (4.6.12.2). In the same way, the *of*-phrase is overall much more common than the *s*-genitive.

However, their distribution with respect to register differs from that of dependent *s*-genitives: elliptic *s*-genitives are most common in conversation, whereas news has by far the highest frequency of dependent *s*-genitives (4.6.12.1). This preference of conversation for elliptic *s*-genitives is in agreement with the generally common occurrence of ellipsis in this register (cf. 3.7 and 14.3.5).

In contrast, constructions with *that/those* plus *of*-phrase have a quite different distribution, more similar to that of *of*-phrases in general (4.6.12.1). However the extremes of frequency in conversation and academic prose are relatively far greater. Clearly *that/those* plus *of*-phrase is felt as overwhelmingly associated with careful expository writing and hence inappropriate to conversation.

## 4.6.14    Choice between the double genitive and related constructions

The double genitive, i.e. the type *a friend of Bob's* (4.6.10), competes with *of* + possessive pronoun constructions (*a friend of his*, 4.11.1), ordinary *of*-phrases (*a friend of Bob*), and with partitive constructions (*one of Bob's friends*).

### 4.6.14.1    The double genitive v. corresponding constructions with possessive pronouns

Constructions with *of* plus a possessive pronoun are often alternatives to double genitives:

    *a friend of hers* (FICT)
v.   *a friend of Deborah's*

**CORPUS FINDINGS 2**

➤ The double genitive is far less common than corresponding constructions with possessive pronouns.
➤ The construction with *of* plus a possessive pronoun is particularly common in fiction.

**DISCUSSION OF FINDINGS**

The very low frequency of the double genitive may in part be due to the fact that it competes with ordinary postmodifying *of*-phrases; in contrast, there is no such

Table 4.22    **Distribution of double genitives v. *of* + possessive pronouns; occurrences per million words**

each ■ represents 5      ⧠ represents less than 3

|  | CONV | FICT | NEWS | ACAD |
|---|---|---|---|---|
| double genitives | ■ | ■ | ⧠ | ⧠ |
| *of* + possessive pronoun | ■■■ | ■■■■■■■■■■■ | ■ | ⧠ |

alternative for the corresponding constructions with possessive pronouns. Thus compare:

> a friend of Deborah's    a friend of Deborah
> a friend of hers          *a friend of her

Moreover, because genitives tend to present given information (4.6.12.5), pronouns are a natural option.

The variant with *of* + possessive pronoun is particularly common in fiction. It also turns out that the majority of these constructions contain the demonstrative determiner *this* or *that*:

> "Did he ever strike you as being crazy **this brother of hers**?" (FICT)
>
> When I listen to you talk I feel you need a lot of good commonsense pumped into **that head of yours**. (FICT)

The demonstrative determiners in these examples are used with their main function of expressing nearness v. distance (4.4.3A). Such constructions are rare in news and academic prose, although they are occasionally used in conversation:

> **That bloody car of mine**, hear the trouble I had? (CONV)

In such examples the distance may be more psychological than physical: e.g. the speaker wishes to distance him/herself from the car problem.

Another characteristic of combinations with *this* and *that* is that they are much more varied than those opening with the indefinite article. Over half of the latter have the head noun *friend*, and many of the remaining nouns denote personal or social relationships (e.g. *acquaintance, associate, brother, colleague*):

> The woman who owns Harte's is **a friend of ours**. (FICT)
>
> This is **an old colleague of mine**. (FICT)

In contrast, constructions opening with *this* and *that* occur with a wide variety of head nouns, including: *bag, bed, boat, box, car, dog*, etc.

> And **this boat of yours** is she crewed? (FICT†)
>
> There's **that china dog of mine**. (FICT)

These two subtypes of the possessive pronoun construction thus seem to be used for different purposes. Constructions opening with *this/that* have an evaluating function which is typical of literary language. They are found with a wide variety of nouns and indicate a psychological attitude of closeness or distance on the part of the writer. Constructions opening with *a/an* are less common in fiction, but represent the predominant use in conversation. Collocational patterns are striking, with the great majority of instances containing *friend* or some other noun denoting a personal or social relationship.

## 4.6.14.2 The double genitive v. ordinary *of*-phrases

In double genitives, nouns denoting personal or social relationships (*colleague, friend, mate*) commonly occur as the head, and nearly all genitive nouns are either personal names or common nouns referring to people.

However, personal nouns are also found in ordinary postmodifying *of*-constructions. Compare:

> It was about **a cousin of my wife's**, Peter Ennals. (FICT)

> The Queen's grandfather, George V, was **a first cousin of Czar Nicholas II**. (NEWS)

> **A friend of my daughter's** went in the other week and bought a little table off her. (CONV†)

> He is twenty-three years old and **a friend of Charles Weymann**, the American pilot with the pince-nez. (FICT)

When the head noun does not denote a human relation, double genitives cannot normally be replaced by ordinary postmodifying *of*-constructions. Thus compare:

> a book of Alfred Beasley's      \*a book of Alfred Beasley
> a hat of Dickie's                \*a hat of Dickie

Three head nouns which allow both possibilities are analysed below: *cousin, friend, relative.*

### CORPUS FINDINGS ²

➤ Double genitives are generally preferred for short dependent phrases, while *of*-phrases are preferred for longer dependent phrases.

**Table 4.23   Proportional use of double genitives v. *of*-phrases for dependent phrases of different lengths, for selected head nouns**

each ■ represents 5%      □ represents less than 2.5%

| phrase | % use of double genitive of X | % use of *of*-phrase of X |
|---|---|---|
| 1 word | ■■■■■■■■■■■■■ | ■■■■■■■ |
| 2 words | ■■■■ | ■■■■■■■■■■■■■■■ |
| 3 words | ■■ | ■■■■■■■■■■■■■■■■■ |
| 4+ words | □ | ■■■■■■■■■■■■■■■■■■■ |

### DISCUSSION OF FINDINGS

The dependent phrase is normally very short in the case of double genitives, and frequently quite long with ordinary postmodifying *of*-phrases. Moreover, there is a characteristic difference in information status: the dependent noun phrase in double genitives is typically given, whereas ordinary postmodifying *of*-phrases tend to introduce new entities into the discourse. This is parallel to the general distribution of *s*-genitives v. postmodifying *of*-phrases (4.6.12.4-5). The conclusion is that the restrictions on the ordinary *s*-genitive and the double genitive are closely related.

### 4.6.14.3 The double genitive v. partitive constructions

Double genitives or corresponding constructions with possessive pronouns overlap with **partitive constructions** of the type illustrated in:

> "Kill **one of your sons** for me." (FICT)
>
> cf. ... **a son of yours**
>
> Diana, who was at the Cenotaph ceremony in London, has refused to go with her husband to a charity pop concert on Monday to watch **one of her favourite stars**, Phil Collins. (NEWS)
>
> cf. ... **a favourite star of hers**

Although the partitive constructions and the corresponding constructions with possessive pronouns convey much the same meaning, there are important differences. First of all, double genitives (and corresponding possessive constructions) sometimes do not allow a simple paraphrase by a partitive construction. This is, for example, true of:

> 1 "In fact, I'm **quite a fan of yours**." (FICT)
>
> 2 She was **a great friend of Kathleen's**. (FICT†)

A partitive paraphrase (quite one of your fans) is much less likely in **1**. In **2**, we could have a corresponding partitive construction (one of Kathleen's great friends), but it has a somewhat different meaning. The form in **2** does not imply that Kathleen has other great friends, but this is explicitly stated in the partitive construction.

Similarly, the opposite type of paraphrase is very often questionable:

> Could you spare me **just one of your beautiful pears**? (FICT)
>
> cf. *a beautiful pear of yours
>
> He was **one of her most promising pupils**. (FICT†)
>
> cf. ?a most promising pupil of hers
>
> She named him Patrick and **one of her 12 grandchildren** bears the same name in memory. (FICT)
>
> cf. *a 12 grandchild of hers

Another important difference is that partitive constructions show none of the collocational restrictions found with the double genitive and corresponding possessive constructions (4.6.14.1–2).

Partitive constructions explicitly pick out one or more entities from a well-defined group. This is not true of a great friend of mine or a good mate of Tony's, and it is definitely excluded with constructions such as that head of yours, that sweet little shop of Miss Adeane's. Thus each of the constructions has its own area of use and contextual fit.

## 4.7 Gender

**Gender** is a less important category in English than in many other languages. It is closely tied to the sex of the referent and is chiefly reflected in co-occurrence patterns with respect to singular personal pronouns (and corresponding possessive and reflexive forms). The main gender classes are:

| | example nouns | pronouns |
|---|---|---|
| personal/human: | | |
| masculine | *Tom, a boy, the man* | *he* |
| feminine | *Sue, a girl, the woman* | *she* |
| dual | *a journalist, the doctor* | *he, she* |
| non-personal/neuter: | *a house, the bird* | *it* |

The personal v. neuter distinction extends to other pronoun groups as well:

| | personal | neuter |
|---|---|---|
| indefinite | *-body/-one* | *-thing* (e.g. *nobody, no one, nothing*) |
| interrogative | *who* | *what* |
| relative | *who* | *which* |

Although there is nothing in the grammatical form of a noun which reveals its gender, there are lexical means of making gender explicit (4.7.1), and reference with a third person singular pronoun may make it apparent (4.7.2–3). However, gender is not a simple reflection of reality; rather it is to some extent a matter of convention and speaker choice and special strategies may be used to avoid gender-specific reference at all.

## 4.7.1 Lexical expression of gender

There are lexical pairs with male v. female denotation, chiefly among words for family relationships (*father—mother, uncle—aunt*, etc.), social roles (*king—queen, lord—lady*, etc.), and animals (*bull—cow, cock—hen*, etc.). The masculine-feminine distinction may also be made explicit by formal markers.

- gender-specific premodification:

  *I'm not in the market for a **male** nurse.* (FICT)

  *Whenever possible a **female** officer will attend.* (NEWS†)

- compounding with a gender-specific element:

  *It was ironic that during an Irish debate an **Englishman** had demonstrated such affection for a **Scotsman**.* (FICT)

  *Three teenage youths who attacked a lone **policewoman** were being hunted yesterday.* (NEWS)

- use of a gender-specific derivational ending:

  ***Actor** John Thaw was in a defiant mood yesterday.* (NEWS†)

  ***Actress** Vanessa Redgrave has arrived in Macedonia.* (NEWS†)

Note that while *-ess* is unambiguously a feminine marker, *-or/-er* is not always clearly a masculine-only marker, especially when there is no corresponding *-ess* form in common use (e.g. *sailor, teacher*). Many such words are widely perceived as having strong masculine overtones, however.

### 4.7.1.1 Words for masculine/feminine gender

**CORPUS FINDINGS [2]**

➤ English speakers and writers use far more words ending in *-man* than in *-woman*.

**Table 4.24** **Frequency of compound nouns ending in -*man* v. -*woman*; occurrences per million words**

each ● represents 20

.................................................................

nouns ending in -*man*    ● ● ● ● ● ● ● ● ● ● ● ● ● ● ● ● ● ● ● ●
                          ● ● ● ● ● ● ● ● ● ● ● ● ● ●

.................................................................

nouns ending in -*woman*    ● ●

➤ The LSWE Corpus contains only 38 different words ending in -*woman*.
  ➤ Most of these words have parallel terms ending in -*man*; the masculine forms are consistently many times more common.
  ➤ Only six words ending in -*woman* are at all common (see Table 4.25).

**Table 4.25** **Most common nouns ending in -*woman*, compared to parallel terms ending in -*man*; occurrences per million words**

each ■ represents 5    ▢ represents c. 1

|  | -*woman* | -*man* |
|---|---|---|
| *spokes-* | ■ ■ ■ ■ | ■ ■ ■ ■ ■ ■ ■ ■ ■ ■ ■ ■ ■ ■ ■ ■ ■ ■ ■ ■ ■ ■ ■ ■ ■ ■ ■ |
| *police-* | ■ | ■ ■ ■ ■ ■ ■ |
| *chair-* | ▢ | ■ ■ ■ ■ ■ ■ ■ ■ ■ ■ ■ ■ ■ ■ ■ ■ ■ ■ ■ ■ ■ ■ ■ ■ ■ |
| *business-* | ▢ | ■ ■ ■ ■ |
| *congress-* | ▢ | ■ |
| *horse-* | ▢ | ■ |

➤ Only seven words ending in -*woman* have no parallel term ending in -*man*: *beggarwoman, catwoman, charwoman, ghostwoman, needlewoman, slavewoman, sweeperwoman.*
➤ In contrast, there are dozens of words in the LSWE Corpus ending in -*man* with no parallel term ending in -*woman*: *airman, alderman, ambulanceman, anchorman, barman, boatman, cabman, cameraman, churchman, clergyman, coalman, conman, countryman, craftsman.*
➤ A similar distribution is found for words with gender-specific derivational endings, with most masculine forms being much more common than the parallel feminine terms.
➤ In the LSWE Corpus, there is only one -*ess* word without a corresponding masculine form: *seamstress.*

**DISCUSSION OF FINDINGS**

The great difference in the distribution of masculine and feminine terms reflects a continuing sex-bias in English language use and society more generally. There are two major factors that are associated with these patterns.

First, and most importantly, this skewed distribution reflects societal differences in the typical roles of men and women, where men still hold more positions of power and authority than women. Thus, for example, there are more spokesmen, chairmen, businessmen, congressmen, etc., than there are spokeswomen, chairwomen, businesswomen, congresswomen, etc. Because such social roles are of popular interest to speakers and (especially) writers, masculine terms are used more commonly than feminine terms.

Related to this difference, there is some evidence that speakers and writers simply make reference to men more often than women (see also the relative frequencies of *he* and *she*; 4.10.5). For example, there are considerably more references to *actors, hosts, stewards,* and *waiters* than there are to *actresses, hostesses, stewardesses,* and *waitresses,* even though women fill these roles in society at least as often as men.

Second, the differences in language use reflect a linguistic bias, because masculine terms can often be used as duals, to refer to both men and women, but not vice versa.

**Table 4.26**   **Most common nouns ending in *-ess* or *-er/-or*, compared to parallel terms; occurrences per million words**

each ● represents 5

Most common nouns ending in *-ess*:

| | feminine | masculine |
|---|---|---|
| *princess/prince* | ●●●●●●●●●●●●●● | ●●●●●●●●●●●●●●● |
| *actress/actor* | ●●●●● | ●●●●●●●●● |
| *mistress/master* | ●●● | ●●●●●●●●●●●●●● |
| *duchess/duke* | ●● | ●●●●● |
| *waitress/waiter* | ●● | ●●● |
| *countess/count* | ●● | ● |
| *goddess/god* | ● | ●●●●●●●●●●●● |
| *hostess/host* | ● | ●●●●●●●●● |
| *stewardess/steward* | ● | ●● |

**Table 4.27**   **Most common masculine nouns with feminine counterparts ending in *-ess* (excluding nouns listed in Table 4.26); occurrences per million words**

each ■ represents 5     □ represents less than 3

| | feminine | masculine |
|---|---|---|
| *clerkess/clerk* | □ | ■■■■■■■■■■■■■ |
| *doctress/doctor* | □ | ■■■■■■■■■■■■■■■■ ■■■■■■■■■ |
| *authoress/author* | □ | ■■■■■■■ |
| *priestess/priest* | □ | ■■■■■■■■ |
| *huntress/hunter* | □ | ■■■■■■ |
| *lioness/lion* | □ | ■■■■■■ |
| *songstress/singer* | □ | ■■■■■ |

In some cases, a masculine term is used when the specific referent is not identified:

*A Ford **spokesman** admitted the existence of an internal document.* (NEWS†)

In other cases, masculine terms are used to refer to women:

> *That's the view of Sheila Davidson, **chairman** of the Institute of Public Relations.* (NEWS)

> *Eyeline **spokesman** Rosie Johnson said: "We don't need a vast sum but without it, we'll be forced to close."* (NEWS)

> *Area **manager** Beth Robinson says: "Our business in Finaghy has steadily increased year by year."* (NEWS†)

> *Other guests at yesterday's opening, which was broadcast live by the radio station, included North-east Essex Euro-MP Anne McIntosh and **Mayor** of Colchester Mary Frank.* (NEWS)

It is worth noting that the uniquely feminine terms tend to refer to social roles of lesser status than most masculine terms. Thus, five of the seven feminine words with no masculine equivalent have meanings that are derogatory or denote menial social roles: *beggarwoman, charwoman, ghostwoman, slavewoman, sweeperwoman*. In addition, many of the terms in feminine/masculine word pairs are not in fact equivalent. Instead, the feminine term often denotes a lesser social role or something with a negative overtone compared with the masculine term. Compare:

| Feminine term | Masculine term |
|---|---|
| *spinster* | *bachelor* |
| *governess* | *governor* |
| *mayoress* <= the wife of a mayor> | *mayor* |
| *mistress* | *master* |
| *tigress* | *tiger* |
| *witch* | *wizard* |

## 4.7.1.2  Lexical means of expressing dual gender reference

Compounds ending in *-person(s)* and *-people* are sometimes used to express dual reference. Though mostly recent formations, these overcome issues of bias associated with the use of masculine forms in a dual gender function:

> *The rally will also be addressed by Amanda Hallaway, **chairperson** of the Youth Committee of the Northern Ireland Congress of Trade Unions.* (NEWS†)

> *Mrs Ruddock, who said she had been nominated as **spokesperson** for the wives, told reporters: <...>* (NEWS†)

> ***Salespersons** by the thousands have been laid off in the recession.* (FICT†)

In addition, the term *chair* is used as a neutral alternative to both *chairman* and *chairperson*:

> *"Law firms have not come to grips with the issues," says Geraldine Cotton, **chair** of the 5,500-strong English Association of Women Solicitors.* (NEWS)

**CORPUS FINDINGS** [2]

➤ The frequency of words ending in *-person/-persons/-people* is low compared with corresponding words with *-man* and *-men*.

> The only moderately common terms are: words occurring over 20 times per million words – *chairperson(s)*, *spokesperson(s)*; words occurring over ten times per million words – *salespeople*, *townspeople*.

**DISCUSSION OF FINDINGS**

The low frequency of these dual terms might be due to the fact that the LSWE Corpus does not contain text where legal requirements might have encouraged such forms, such as advertisements for jobs. Moreover it seems that equal opportunity legislation may not have much effect on the language generally.

## 4.7.2 Gender-specific v. dual gender pronoun reference

When referring to nouns of dual gender (*friend, individual, journalist, spokesperson*, etc.) and pronouns such as *anybody* there is a choice where the required pronouns have different masculine and feminine forms depending upon the sex of the referent (especially *he, his* v. *she, her*). Special problems arise, however, where the sex of the referent is unknown or irrelevant, as English has no dual third person singular pronoun. Traditionally, masculine pronouns have been used:

> Each [novelist] aims to make a single novel of the material **he** has been given. (ACAD†)

> Each [individual] is thus the recipient of the accumulated culture of the generations which have preceded **him**. (ACAD†)

Even though such masculine pronouns may be intended to have dual reference, readers often perceive the referent to be male. As a result, such use of masculine pronouns has come in for a great deal of criticism in recent years, and it has become increasingly common to use various strategies to avoid gender-specific reference.

Two major grammatical devices are used as alternatives to gender-specific reference:

### A Use of coordinated pronoun forms

> A [geologist] studying fossiliferous rocks in the field needs only an average knowledge of paleontology in order to make a fairly accurate estimate of the epoch in which the rocks **he or she** is studying belong. (ACAD)

> [Anyone] with English as **his or her** native language does not need other languages. (NEWS)

> Thus, the [user] acts on **his/her** own responsibility when executing **his/her** functions within **his/her** task domain. (ACAD)

### B Use of plural rather than singular forms

Plural co-referent pronouns and determiners are commonly used in both speech and writing:

> A: Not [everybody] uses **their** indicat– indicator.
> B: **They** don't use **their** indicators any more.
> A: No **they** don't. (CONV)

> [Everybody] remembers where **they** were when JFK was shot. (NEWS†)

*[Nobody] likes to admit that **they** entertain very little, or that **they** rarely enjoy it when **they** do.* (NEWS)

A way of avoiding a difference in number between co-referent forms is to opt consistently for the plural:

*Now they expect responsible [customers] to pay for **their** folly.* (NEWS)

### 4.7.2.1 Grammatical means for dual gender reference

**CORPUS FINDINGS** [2]

➤ Examples of coordinated *he/she* pronoun forms are relatively rare and restricted primarily to academic prose.

**Table 4.28** **Distribution of coordinated *he/she* pronoun forms; occurrences per million words**

each ■ represents 10 □ represents less than 5

|  | CONV | FICT | NEWS | ACAD |
|---|---|---|---|---|
| *he* or *she* | □ | □ | □ | ■■■ |
| *him* or *her* | □ | □ | □ | ■ |
| *his* or *her* | □ | □ | ■ | ■■■■ |
| *he/she* | □ | □ | □ | ■ |

**DISCUSSION OF FINDINGS**

The implication is that writers (and editors) of academic prose are particularly aware of a need to avoid gender bias. Indeed many academic journals explicitly mention this issue in their style sheets. Furthermore, the coordination solution has the exactness commonly associated with academic writing and coordination is generally common in this register anyway (cf. 2.4.7.3). However, coordination involves a length that might make it dispreferred in news and a clumsy feel that might make it less preferred in the other registers. By contrast any use of plural pronouns to refer to entities introduced with singular forms violates prescriptive rules of grammar, even where the singular forms refer to all members of a group, rather than a single entity, as do generic *a geologist* in 4.7.2A and *everybody* in the example in 4.7.2B. Consequently this solution is least likely to be adopted by academic writing, being a register much concerned with correctness.

## 4.7.3 Personal v. non-personal reference with pronouns

In a number of cases, the speaker can choose between personal (*he, she*) or non-personal reference (*it*). Personal reference expresses greater familiarity or involvement. Non-personal reference is more detached. There are four specific semantic domains where this choice is relevant.

In the following examples there is a three-way choice, and the non-personal option additionally overcomes any problems of ignorance or irrelevance of the sex of the living being that is referred to (cf. 4.7.2):

- *baby, child, infant*

    *One three-month-old [baby] managed to talk **its** parents into sending Santa a letter asking for some clothes.* (NEWS†)

    *We then need to reach in to that inner [child] and supply what **it** did not have, and heal **it**.* (NEWS)

    *Shortly before birth the developed [infant] reverses **its** position.* (ACAD†)

    v.  *The [baby] was lying on **his** back in **his** crib, perfectly content.* (FICT)

    *Poor [infant]! Why on earth did **her** people park such a kid as that at boarding school?* (FICT)

- *animals, especially pets*

    *You know that [cat] **it** scratched me.* (CONV)

    *The [dog] he bought in London from Ross and Mangles, the dealers in Fulham Road. **It** was the strongest and most savage in their possession.* (NEWS)

    v.  *The ship's [cat] was in every way appropriate to the Reach. **She** habitually moved in a kind of nautical crawl, with **her** stomach close to the deck.* (FICT†)

    *Only the [dog]'s determination to be reunited with **her** master kept **her** going.* (NEWS†)

In the following examples the choice is between feminine and non-personal only:

- *countries*

    *[Italy] announced **it** had recalled **its** ambassador to Romania for consultations.* (NEWS†)

    v.  *The only work a citizen can do for the good of the country is that of cooperating with the material revolution: therefore conspiracies, plots, assassinations, etc., are that series of deeds by which [Italy] proceeds towards **her** goal.* (NEWS)

- *ships*

    *The bow of the [ship] was punctured, and **its** forward speed was so great that a gash eighty-two feet long was made down the port side.* (FICT)

    v.  *A derelict [ship] turns over on **her** keel and lies gracefully at rest, but there is only one way up for a Thames [barge] if **she** is to maintain her dignity.* (FICT)

## 4.8 Noun formation

New nouns can be formed by **derivation** and **compounding**. Derived nouns are formed through the addition of derivational **affixes** (**prefixes** and **suffixes**), as in *disbelief* (*dis* + *belief*) or *treatment* (*treat* + *ment*). Compound nouns, on the other hand, are formed from two words combined to form a single noun (see noun derivational processes in 4.8.1 and noun compounds in 4.8.2).

## 4.8.1 Derived nouns

Noun derivational prefixes typically do not change the word class; that is, the prefix is attached to a noun base to form a new noun with a different meaning:

| base noun | derived noun with prefix |
|-----------|--------------------------|
| patient | outpatient |
| group | subgroup |

Noun derivational suffixes, on the other hand, often do change the word class; that is, the suffix is often attached to a verb or adjective base to form a noun with a different meaning. There are, however, also many nouns which are derived by suffixes from other nouns.

| | base form | derived noun with suffix |
|------------|-----------|--------------------------|
| adjectives: | abnormal | abnormality |
| | conventional | conventionalism |
| | effective | effectiveness |
| verbs: | agree | agreement |
| | break | breakage |
| | calculate | calculation |
| | deny | denial |
| | design | designer |
| nouns: | infant | infancy |
| | kitchen | kitchenette |
| | star | stardom |

Apart from derivation by affixes, there is also **zero derivation**, or **conversion**. Adjectives and verbs may be converted to nouns. Some typical meaning relationships are illustrated below, but note that the noun often acquires more specific meanings with conversion.

Affixes vary in frequency and productivity, i.e. the extent to which they are used to build new words. Noun derivational suffixes are generally more frequent and more productive than prefixes and will therefore be dealt with more fully below.

| conversion | base form | meaning | zero-derived noun |
|------------|-----------|---------|-------------------|
| adjectives (A): | hopeful | 'somebody who is A' | presidential **hopefuls** |
| | white | 'somebody who is A' | she knew the **whites** disliked her |
| | | 'something which is A' | you could see the **whites** of his eyes |
| verbs (V): | catch | 'act of V-ing' | he took a brilliant **catch** |
| | | 'something that is V-ed' | they had a fine **catch** of fish |
| | | 'something used for V-ing' | he loosened the **catch** and opened the window |
| | cheat | 'someone who V-s' | . . . accused him of being a **cheat** |
| | walk | 'act of V-ing' | we can go for a **walk** later |
| | | 'way of V-ing' | my walk was the **walk** of a gentleman |
| | | 'place for V-ing' | the **walk** stretches 154 miles |

## 4.8.1.1 Derivational prefixes used to form new nouns

The derivational prefixes listed below give the basic meaning of each prefix plus examples. Note that, being lexicalized units, prefixed nouns may acquire meanings which cannot be fully understood by combining the meanings of the prefix and the base. Prefixes also vary in their preference for hyphenation.

| prefix | examples |
| --- | --- |
| *anti-* ('against, opposite to') | *antiabortionist, anticlimax* |
| *arch-* ('supreme, most') | *arch-enemy, arch-priestess* |
| *auto-* ('self') | *autobiography, autograph* |
| *bi-* ('two') | *bicentenary, bilingualism* |
| *bio-* ('of living things') | *biochemistry, biomass* |
| *co-* ('joint') | *co-chairman, co-founder* |
| *counter-* ('against') | *counterargument, counterclaim* |
| *dis-* ('the converse of') | *disbelief, discomfort* |
| *ex-* ('former') | *ex-marxist, ex-student* |
| *fore-* ('ahead, before') | *forefront, foreknowledge* |
| *hyper-* ('extreme') | *hyperinflation, hypertension* |
| *in-* ('inside; the converse of') | *inpatient; inattention* |
| *inter-* ('between, among') | *interaction, intermarriage* |
| *kilo-* ('thousand') | *kilobyte, kilowatt* |
| *mal-* ('bad') | *malfunction, malnutrition* |
| *mega-* ('million; supreme') | *megabyte, megawatt; megastar* |
| *mini-* ('small') | *minibus, mini-publication* |
| *mis-* ('bad, wrong') | *misconduct, mismatch* |
| *mono-* ('one') | *monosyllable, monotheism* |
| *neo-* ('new') | *neomarxist, neo-colonialism* |
| *non-* ('not') | *nonpayment, non-specialist* |
| *out-* ('outside, separate') | *outpatient, outbuilding* |
| *poly-* ('many') | *polysyllable, polytheism* |
| *pseudo-* ('false') | *pseudo-democracy, pseudo-expert* |
| *re-* ('again') | *re-election, re-organisation* |
| *semi-* ('half') | *semicircle, semi-darkness* |
| *sub-* ('below') | *subgroup, subset* |
| *super-* ('more than, above') | *superhero, superset* |
| *sur-* ('over and above') | *surcharge, surtax* |
| *tele-* ('distant') | *telecommunications, teleshopping* |
| *tri-* ('three') | *tricycle, tripartism* |
| *ultra-* ('beyond') | *ultrafilter, ultrasound* |
| *under-* ('below; too little') | *underclass; underachievement* |
| *vice-* ('deputy') | *vice-chairman, vice-president* |

## 4.8.1.2 Some common derivational suffix patterns

Suffixes typically have less specific meanings than prefixes. The main contribution to meaning of many suffixes is that which follows from a change of grammatical class. In the list below, the word class of the base is identified by A (adjective), N (noun), and V (verb). Note that suffixed nouns often acquire meanings which cannot be fully understood by combining the meanings of the suffix and the base. Note also that there may be changes in spelling and pronunciation as a result of the derivational process, e.g. *infant* + *-cy infancy, deny* + *-al denial.*

| suffix | meaning(s) | examples |
|---|---|---|
| *-age* | 'collection of N' | *baggage, leafage, plumage* |
| | 'action/result of V' | *breakage, haulage, wastage* |
| | 'cost of N/V-ing' | *brokerage, haulage, postage* |
| | 'measure in N-s' | *acreage, mileage, tonnage* |
| | 'place for N' | *hermitage, orphanage, vicarage* |
| *-al* | 'action/instance of V-ing' | *arrival, burial, denial* |
| *-an, -ian* | 'person who lives in N' | *American, Estonian, Korean* |
| | 'language of N' | *Estonian, Korean* |
| | 'person associated with N' | *Darwinian, Victorian* |
| *-ance, -ence* | 'action or state of V-ing' | *adherence, assistance, resemblance* |
| | 'state of being A' | *abundance, dependence, ignorance* |
| *-ant, -ent* | 'person who V-s' | *assistant, consultant, student* |
| | 'something used for V-ing' | *coolant, defoliant, intoxicant* |
| *-cy* | 'state or quality of being A/N' | *accuracy, adequacy, infancy* |
| *-dom* | 'state of being A/N' | *boredom, freedom, stardom* |
| *-ee* | 'person who has been or is to be V-ed' | *employee, evacuee, trainee* |
| | 'person to whom something has been or is to be V-ed' | *assignee, licensee* |
| | 'person who V-s or has V-ed' | *escapee, retiree, standee* |
| | 'person who is A' | *absentee, devotee* |
| *-er, -or* | 'person who V-s' | *advertiser, driver, governor* (cf. 4.7.1) |
| | 'something used for V-ing' | *computer, filler, silencer* |
| | 'person concerned with N' | *astronomer, footballer, geographer* |
| | 'person living in N' | *cottager, Londoner, New Yorker* |
| *-ery, -ry* | 'action/instance of V-ing' | *bribery, robbery, thievery* |
| | 'place of V-ing' | *bakery, cannery, refinery* |
| | 'art/practice involving N' | *imagery, pottery* |
| | 'place for N' | *nunnery, piggery* |
| | 'collection of N' | *citizenry, jewellery, machinery* |
| | 'state or quality of being A/N' | *bravery, savagery, snobbery* |
| *-ese* | 'person living in N' | *Burmese, Japanese, Vietnamese* (cf. 4.5.4C) |
| | 'language of N' | *Burmese, Japanese, Vietnamese* |
| | 'language in the style of N' | *computerese, journalese, officialese* |
| *-ess* | 'female N' | *actress, baroness, lioness* |
| | 'wife of N' | *baroness, mayoress* (cf. 4.7.1.1) |
| *-ette* | 'small N' | *kitchenette, novelette* |
| *-ful* | 'amount that fills N' | *bucketful, handful, teaspoonful* (cf. 4.3.6.1F) |
| *-hood* | 'state of being A/N' | *childhood, falsehood, widowhood* |
| *-ician* | 'person concerned with N' | *mathematician, politician* |
| *-ie, -y* | 'diminutive or pet name for N' | *daddy, doggie, Johnny* |
| *-ing* | 'action/instance of V-ing' | *meeting, reading, singing* |
| | 'something that one V-s or has V-ed' | *building, painting, recording* |

| suffix | meaning(s) | examples |
|---|---|---|
| | 'place for V-ing'<br>'material for V-ing'<br>'material for making N' | crossing, dwelling, landing<br>binding, colouring, lining<br>coating, fencing, shirting |
| -ism | 'doctrine of N'<br>'movement characterized by A/N' | Buddhism, Marxism, Thatcherism<br>impressionism, realism, Romanticism |
| -ist | 'person believing in or following N/A-ism'<br>'person concerned with N' | Buddhist, impressionist, realist<br><br>biologist, physicist, violinist |
| -ite | 'person from N'<br>'person following N' | Moabite, Muscovite, Wisconsinite<br>Thatcherite, Trotskyite |
| -ity | 'state or quality of being A' | ability, purity, similarity |
| -let | 'small N' | bomblet, booklet, piglet |
| -ment | 'action/instance of V-ing' | development, encouragement, punishment |
| -ness | 'state or quality of being A' | blindness, darkness, preparedness |
| -ship | 'state of being N'<br>'skill as N' | citizenship, friendship<br>craftsmanship, statesmanship |
| -tion | 'action/instance of V-ing' | alteration, demonstration, resignation |
| -ure | 'action/instance of V-ing' | closure, departure, exposure |

## 4.8.1.3 Frequency of common noun derivational suffixes

The distribution of derived nouns, as of nouns in general, varies greatly across the registers.

**CORPUS FINDINGS [1, 17]**

➤ Conversation has by far the lowest number of derived nouns.
➤ With one exception (-ness in fiction), the relative frequency grows sharply as we move from conversation to fiction, news, and academic prose.
➤ The relative difference between registers is far sharper for derived nouns than for nouns overall (see Figure 4.1 in 4.1.2).

**Table 4.29** Frequency of the four most common derivational suffixes used to form abstract nouns; occurrences per million words

each ■ represents c. 500     □ represents fewer than 250

| | CONV | FICT | NEWS | ACAD |
|---|---|---|---|---|
| -tion | ■ | ■■■ | ■■■■■■■■■ | ■■■■■■■■■■■<br>■■■■■■■■■■ |
| -ity | □ | ■■ | ■■■■■ | ■■■■■■■■■■ |
| -ism | □ | □ | ■ | ■■ |
| -ness | □ | ■■ | ■ | ■ |

**DISCUSSION OF FINDINGS**

Noun phrases are less complex in conversation than in the written registers (2.10). The simplicity of noun phrases seems to be reflected not only in the high proportion of pronouns and other simple noun phrases (4.1.1.1, 4.1.2), but also in the preference for simple nouns. Furthermore, academic discourse is much more concerned with abstract concepts than the other registers, especially conversation. Consequently the distribution pattern of Table 4.29 is not entirely unexpected.

The special preference of fiction for derivatives in -*ness*, compared with the other registers, could be due to the fact that many such words derive from native adjectives denoting people's states of mind or character traits, which are the concern of much fictional narrative (e.g. *happiness*, *selfishness*). See also the end of 4.8.1.4.

## 4.8.1.4  Productivity of common noun derivations

Apart from differing in the frequency of occurrence of their tokens, derivational affixes also differ in their productivity, which can be assessed by considering the total number of noun lexemes (2.2.2) formed with the affix. In doing this, it is useful to distinguish between common and rare nouns, in that uncommon derived nouns are more likely to reflect either recent coinages gaining currency or an older coinage becoming obsolete. The following findings are based on analysis of academic prose only, which uses the most such words.

**Figure 4.7**  **Number of nouns formed with common derivational suffixes—academic prose**

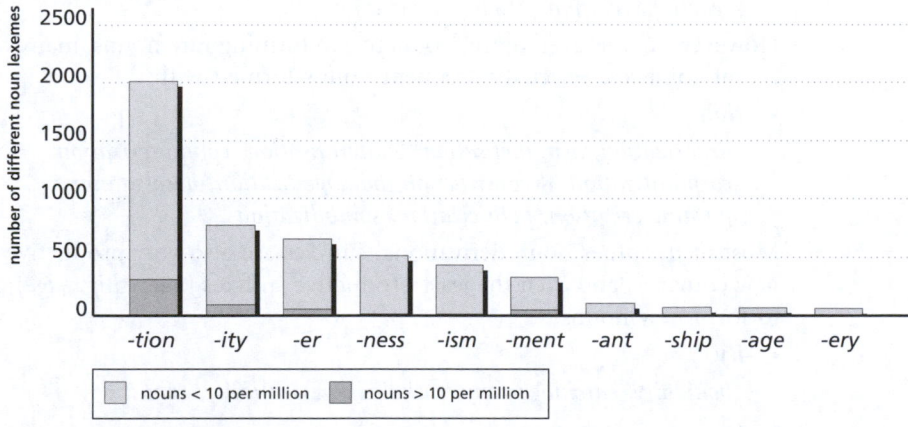

**CORPUS FINDINGS** [7]

➤ Noun derivational prefixes are considerably less productive than the derivational suffixes.
  ➤ Even the most productive noun derivational prefixes *sub-* and *co-* are used to form fewer than 50 different noun lexemes.
➤ There are extensive differences in the productivity of noun derivational suffixes:
  ➤ The suffix -*tion* is by far the most productive, both in terms of the total number of noun lexemes formed, and in terms of the number of relatively rare coinages (i.e. derived nouns occurring less than ten times per million words).
  ➤ Several other suffixes are relatively productive: -*ity*, -*er*, -*ness*, -*ism*, -*ment*.
➤ All noun suffixes are used mostly for forming relatively rare coinages.

## DISCUSSION OF FINDINGS

A reason why derivational prefixes are less productive than derivational suffixes is perhaps that many of them are of Greek origin, whereas almost all the suffixes listed in 4.8.1.2 are of Romance or native Germanic origin. Many Greek prefixes, such as *hyper-*, *mono-*, and *poly-*, arrived in English more recently and have been exploited for new lexical items mainly in specialized scientific areas. It is noticeable that the two most productive prefixes are in fact Latinate ones *co-* and *sub-*. Furthermore, apart from their more technical overtones, the prefixes often do not express anything that could not equally be conveyed, at little greater length, with a numeral or adjective premodifier of the noun. By contrast, the suffixes more often encapsulate a meaning that would be longer and clumsier to convey in another way, as attested by the complexity of their meanings glossed in 4.8.1.2 and their predominant class-changing nature (see further discussion below).

The top ranking of the suffix *-tion* for productivity is directly related to its top ranking for frequency (Table 4.29). Unlike the other noun affixes, it is used to form numerous high frequency nouns as well as rare coinages. For example, all the following noun lexemes formed with *-tion* occur more than 200 times per million words:

> *action, addition, application, association, communication, concentration, direction, distribution, education, equation, examination, formation, infection, information, instruction, operation, organization, population, production, reaction, relation, situation, variation*

However, *-tion* is even more productive in forming rare nouns, many of which are recent coinages. Selected infrequent nouns formed with:

- *-tion*

  > *arborization, arithmetisation, bilateralisation, computerization, corporatization, deconstruction, homogenization, necessitation, parameterization, politicization, solubilization*

Most of the other noun derivational suffixes are also very productive in forming new coinages, and even the least productive suffixes (e.g. *-ship*, *-age*) can be used to form new nouns:

- *-ity*

  > *benignity, carcinogenicity, catholicity, essentiality, robusticity*

- *-er*

  > *answerer, bioanalyser, cohabiter, condescender, demander, worrier*

- *-ness*

  > *aboutness, expertness, overcarefulness, repressiveness*

- *-ism*

  > *disabledism, kantianism, scapegoatism*

- *-ment*

  > *misassessment, piercement*

- *-ant*

  > *adulterant, arrestant, inheritant, odorant*

- *-ship*

  > *clientship, spokesmanship, studentship*

- *-age*

    *concubinage, personage, reassemblage.*

The derivational suffixes are most productive by far in academic prose than in the other registers, and they are far more common (4.8.1.3). Derived abstract nouns are essential in academic discussions, where frequent reference is made to abstract concepts and where actions and processes are often referred to in general terms rather in relation to a specific place and time. For such reference, it is convenient to use nominalizations, where the content of a clause (stripped of tense specification and other deictic elements) is compressed into a noun phrase. Following are some typical examples, with derived nouns shown in bold, and noun conversions shown in []:

    The **conventionalist** system lacks the **capacity** to reach anything like the **flexibility** of **pragmatism**, because any **relaxation** would inevitably involve the [defeat] of publicly encouraged **expectation**. (ACAD)

    The **interpretation** of laboratory data will always provide areas for some **disagreement**, since the prime **objective** is to detect [risk] of **deficiency** before clinical **evidence** of disease develops. Standards may also vary somewhat in **specificity** and **reproducibility** according to the methods used. (ACAD)

    A simple **categorization** of industrial [wastes] can be made on the basis of their hazardous nature including their **toxicity**, **flammability**, **explosivity**, **infectivity** and **corrosivity**. (ACAD)

It may seem puzzling that there should be a difference in productivity of nouns ending in *-ity* and in *-ness*, as both have the basic meaning 'state or quality of being A' (4.8.1.2). However, there are two differences which make *-ity* more productive (and more frequent, 4.8.1.3) in academic prose. First, for the most part, these suffixes occur in complementary distribution, with particular bases taking only one or the other:

    *callousness, calmness, carefulness*

but not

    *\*callosity, \*calmity, \*carefulity*

    *capability, captivity, celebrity*

but not

    *\*capableness, \*captiveness, \*celebriousness.*

This distribution is found because the Romance suffix *-ity* combines almost exclusively with bases derived from the Romance languages, which academic writing generally favours, while the native suffix *-ness* commonly combines both with originally native and non-native words. Second, while the words ending in *-ness* commonly denote qualities of persons and things, the *-ity* words predominantly denote qualities of abstract entities and abstract relations, which again are more the focus of communication in academic prose.

## 4.8.2 Formation of nouns through compounding

Another process used to form nouns is compounding: that is, two words (or sometimes more than two) are combined to form a single noun. In English, noun compounding is a highly productive process; some major patterns are illustrated by:

noun + noun: *bar code, database, eye-witness, fanlight, lamp post, logjam, shell-fish, spacecraft, suitcase*

noun + noun/verb-*er*: *dressmaker, eye-opener, fire-eater, screwdriver*

noun + verb-*ing*: *fire-fighting, housekeeping, window shopping, windsurfing*

adj + noun: *bigwig, blackbird, easy chair, greatcoat, quicksand, real estate*

verb + noun: *cookbook, dipstick, makeweight, swimsuit*

verb-*ing* + noun: *filing cabinet, filling station, mockingbird, printing-press, rocking chair*

verb + particle: *checkout, drop-out, go-between, handout, standby, writeoff*

particle + verb: *backlash, bypass, downpour, income, output, overspill*

*self* + noun: *self-control, self-esteem, self-indulgence, self-help, self-pity*

As is suggested by the above lists, practice varies as to whether to represent a compound as two orthographic words, one unbroken orthographic word, or a hyphenated word. Partly this is because there is no clear dividing line between compounds and free combinations. This is especially true of the most productive class, that of noun + noun compounds. The formation patterns for these are investigated in detail, as syntactic combinations, in 8.3.

## 4.8.2.1 Noun compounds in conversation and news in AmE

Table 4.30 presents the distribution of common noun compounds in AmE conversation and news, based on the frequency of compounds spelt as single words (i.e. with no intervening hyphen or space).

**CORPUS FINDINGS [7]**

➤ Compounds are much more frequent in news than in conversation: in fact just over twice as frequent (see Table 4.30).

Table 4.30 **Frequency of common noun compounds in AmE conversation and AmE news**

| frequency of forms | number of lexemes | |
|---|---|---|
| (times per million words) | CONV | NEWS |
| over 100 | 3 | 11 |
| 26–100 | 14 | 41 |
| 11–25 | 29 | 71 |
| 6–10 | 77 | 125 |
| total lexemes occurring over 5 times per million words | 123 | 248 |

➤ There are few really frequent compounds: about half of those that occur are in the least frequent category in news, and 63% in conversation.

➤ Noun + noun compounds are the most productive type structurally (see Table 4.31).

    ➤ However, news, more than conversation, exploits the different types: about two thirds of the lexemes are not noun + noun as against only half in conversation.

**Table 4.31**  **Classification of the most frequent noun compounds (occurring more than 10 times per million words) by structural type**

| | number of lexemes | | |
|---|---|---|---|
| | CONV | NEWS | examples |
| noun + noun | 24 | 47 | *bathroom, newspaper* |
| noun + verb/noun* | 0 | 12 | *gunfire, landslide* |
| noun + noun/verb-*er* | 1 | 6 | *dishwasher, firefighter* |
| noun + verb-*ing* | 1 | 1 | *thanksgiving, kidnapping* |
| verb/noun* + noun | 3 | 8 | *playboy, volleyball* |
| adjective + noun | 7 | 19 | *grandmother, highway* |
| verb + particle | 1 | 10 | *feedback, dropout* |
| particle + verb/noun | 7 | 13 | *outfit, downturn* |
| others | 2 | 7 | *broadcast, spokeswoman* |
| **total** | 46 | 123 | |

\* These are cases of compounding where one of the elements of the compound could be either a verb base or a noun, but where the underlying relationship is more appropriately expressed by a verb (e.g. *gunfire* implies 'Someone *fires* a *gun*').

**DISCUSSION OF FINDINGS**

It is not surprising that conversation uses fewer noun compounds than news, given the much lower overall frequency of nouns in conversation (2.3.5). The predominance of low-frequency compounds in both registers reflects a common finding of word frequency study generally: in a text often as many as half of the different words used (= types, 2.2.1) may occur only once. The greater variety of compound patterns in news fits in with the tendency of this register to use a more varied vocabulary, as evidenced by the high type-token ratio in this register (2.2.1).

Clearly noun + noun compounds are by far the most productive type. In fact, if one includes related or variant patterns (noun + verb/noun, noun + noun/verb-*er*, verb/noun + noun), then well over half the compounds in both registers are composed of two nominal elements. The next most common types of compound are those consisting of adjective + noun and those beginning or ending with a particle. The common compound type verb-*ing* + noun (e.g. *swimming pool*) does not appear in this table because it is very rare for such compounds to be spelt as a single word.

## 4.9    The role of pronouns in discourse

Most **pronouns** replace fully specified noun phrases and can be regarded as economy devices. Rather than giving a detailed specification, they serve as pointers to the surrounding (usually preceding) text or the speech situation. In addition, pronouns are used where the reference is unknown or very general (4.15), and for specific clause-binding functions (4.16).

## 4.10     Personal pronouns

**Personal pronouns** are function words which make it possible to refer succinctly to the speaker/writer, the addressee, and identifiable things or persons other than the speaker/writer and the addressee. There are corresponding series of personal pronouns, possessive determiners, possessive pronouns, and reflexive pronouns. Further, there is a distinction between **nominative** and **accusative case** for most personal pronouns (4.10.6). Table 4.32 summarizes these distinctions.

**Table 4.32**     **Personal pronouns and corresponding possessive and reflexive forms**

| person | personal pronoun | | possessive | | reflexive pronoun |
|---|---|---|---|---|---|
| | nominative | accusative | determiner | pronoun | |
| **1st** | | | | | |
| singular | *I* | *me* | *my* | *mine* | *myself* |
| plural | *we* | *us* | *our* | *ours* | *ourselves* |
| **2nd** | | | | | |
| singular | *you* | *you* | *your* | *yours* | *yourself* |
| plural | *you* | *you* | *your* | *yours* | *yourselves* |
| **3rd** | | | | | |
| singular | *he* | *him* | *his* | *his* | *himself* |
| | *she* | *her* | *her* | *hers* | *herself* |
| | *it* | *it* | *its* | – | *itself* |
| plural | *they* | *them* | *their* | *theirs* | *themselves* |

In spite of the name, personal pronouns may have both personal and non-personal reference. *I, me, you, he, she, him, her, we,* and *us* generally have personal reference, while *it* generally has non-personal reference (but see 4.7.3 for exceptions). The plural pronouns *they/them*, however, are commonly used with both personal and non-personal reference.

*They/them* with personal reference:

> **They** *should keep quiet for the time being.* (NEWS†)
>
> *"You don't like Poles very much, Uncle." – "I think on the whole I like* **them** *better than* **they** *liked me."* (FICT)

*They/them* with non-personal reference:

> *These impressions are not of a kind that occur in our daily life.* **They** *are extremely special* <...> (ACAD†)
>
> *Radio waves are useful as we can make* **them** *carry information by modulating* **them**. (NEWS)

## 4.10.1     Specific reference

Most typically, personal pronouns are used to refer to definite specific individuals identified in the speech situation (first and second person) or the preceding text (third person). However, the specific reference is often far from straightforward. In conversation, uncertainty can be cleared up in the course of the exchange:

> A: **We're** *coming to eat in a minute.*
> B: **We? You and who?** (CONV)

> A: **You** *wrote that.*
> B: **Who me?** (CONV)
> A: *I mean* **she's** *got a bit of a reputation. I suppose everyone has, but I hear about her a lot, in school and everything.*
> B: **Which one** *was that?*
> A: *Pardon?*
> B: **Which one** *was this?*
> A: **The skinny one**. (CONV)

However, whether in speech or writing, the interpretation of pronouns (as of definite noun phrases in general) requires a great deal of cooperation between the speaker/writer and the addressee (cf. also 4.4.1.3). The following sections address specific issues that arise in the interpretation of personal pronouns.

## 4.10.1.1 Problems in the use of first person plural pronouns

Whereas the first person singular pronoun (*I*) is usually unambiguous in referring to the speaker/writer, the meaning of the first person plural pronoun is often vague: *we* usually refers to the speaker/writer and the addressee (inclusive *we*), or to the speaker/writer and some other person or persons associated with him/her (exclusive *we*). The intended reference can even vary in the same context. For example, in a casual conversation, *we* can vacillate between meaning *I* + *you* v. *I* + somebody else (e.g. my family). In a political speech given by a member of the government, *we* may mean the government, or it can be used to refer to the government + the people.

By adding elements in apposition to the pronoun, speakers can make the meaning more explicit:

> "**We all** *believe in him,*" said the 18-year-old chairwoman. (NEWS†)
>
> **Us two, we** *don't use many, so I made, I made quiches.* (CONV)
>
> **We three guests** *stared into our glasses.* (FICT†)
>
> "**We Americans** *are spoilt,*" he said. (NEWS)

*We all* is particularly common, occurring about 45 times per million words in BrE conversation and 60 times per million words in AmE conversation.

Another method, which is found occasionally in conversation and fictional dialogue, uses prefaces or tags (3.4.3–4) to make the reference clear. They usually take the form *me and X* (cf. 4.10.6.4).

> **I and Vicki** *we don't really like caramels.* (CONV†)
>
> *We've got a bond in common,* **you and I.** (FICT)
>
> **Me and Sarah Jones** *we went up.* (CONV†)
>
> *Well, it was late, and* **me and my friend Bob**, *we'd been to a game.* (FICT†)

Usually, however, it is left to the addressee to infer the exact meaning of *we*.

The use of the first person plural is notable in academic prose, where *we* may refer to a single author, a group of authors, to the author and the reader, or to people in general:

> 1 **We** *spoke of Dirac's piece of chalk.* (ACAD†)

    2 *We are now able to understand why **our** information about the states of motion is so restricted in quantum mechanics.* (ACAD)

    3 *When **we** start talking **we** often cease to listen.* (ACAD)

In **1**, *we* refers to the author(s), while in **2** *we* refers primarily to readers (assuming that the author has understood this point all along). In **3**, the reference is to people in general.

    In some cases, academic authors seem to become confused themselves, switching indiscriminately among the different uses of *we*:

    4 *If **we** are tempted to choose conventionalism on the ground that it provides an acceptable strategy for reaching the most sufficient balance between certainty and flexibility, then **we** should choose pragmatism, which seems a far better strategy, instead. **We** can summarize. In the earlier part of this chapter **I** have argued <...>* (ACAD†)

The first two occurrences of *we* in this passage seem to refer to both reader and writer. However, the intended reference of the third occurrence is harder to pin down: in this case, *we* is contrasted with *I*, suggesting that the intended reference should continue to be reader and writer as opposed to the author. However, only the author is summarizing here, suggesting that both *we* and *I* refer to the writer excluding the reader.

    By choosing the plural pronoun *we* rather than *I*, a single author avoids drawing attention to himself/herself, and the writing becomes somewhat more impersonal. On the other hand, when *we* is used to include the reader, it has a rather different effect and the writing becomes more personal.

## 4.10.1.2    Problems in the use of second person pronouns

The second person pronoun *you* is similar to *we* in being used with different intended referents. In the first place, it is not always clear in present-day English whether the second person pronoun refers to one or more people. There are again means of making the reference more explicit (cf. 4.10.1.1):

    *And what did **you all** talk about?* (NEWS)

    ***You two** are being over optimistic.* (FICT)

    ***You imperialists** stick together, don't you?* (FICT)

    *Are **you guys** serious?* (FICT)

*You all* is particularly common, occurring around 50 times per million words in British conversation, and 150 times per million words in American conversation (including both *you all* and *y'all*; 14.4.5.2). *You two* is found about 40 times per million words in British conversation and 20 times per million words in American conversation. However, as with *we*, it is usually left to the addressee to infer who is included in the reference of *you*.

    The dialectal form *yous* is a second-person plural pronoun, filling the gap left by the absence of number contrast for *you* in modern standard English:

    *I am sick to death of **yous** – All **yous** do is fight and ruck and fight – do you ever see a house like it Albert?* (CONV)

A particular problem in the use of *you* is that it may refer to people in general, including the speaker/writer. This is found both in speech and writing:

    ***You**'ve got to be a bit careful when **you**'re renting out though.* (CONV)

> *I have got this little problem you see. Sometimes I forget. And the trouble with "sometimes" is that **you** never know when to expect it.* (NEWS)

### 4.10.1.3   Problems in the use of third person pronouns

The interpretation of third person pronouns frequently requires a good deal of work on the part of the addressee, particularly in conversation:

> *Nobody really likes, you know, snow snowmen and things like that. Okay? So we built this snowman round this rock and this car came back cos **he** came **he** just came in to hit **it** and **he** burst into and broke **his** bumper, this massive dent in **his** bumper and **he** drove round. Cos **they** did **it** to me before. I made another one in the park earlier. And **they** just drove in, knocked **it** over and ran out. So I put in a rock this time and **it** was so funny though.* (CONV)

Here we can infer that *he* is the driver of the car and *they* the people in the car. In two of the cases, *it* seems to refer to the snowman; in the other cases, the pronoun *it* refers more vaguely to what happened (*did it, it was so funny*).

In some cases, third person pronouns can be used without prior introduction (cf. a similar use of the definite article; 4.4.1.3):

> ***It** was the first dead body **he** had ever seen.* <opening of novel> (FICT)

> ***They** may please Barbara Cartland, but the true romantic scorns heart shaped chocolates, Chanel No. 5, sexy underwear and other fashionable cliches of romance.* (NEWS)

The use of initial pronouns in news texts serves to raise the reader's curiosity. In the novel, the inherent definiteness of personal pronouns means that people and entities are presented as if familiar, even though they have not been introduced, and the reader is forced to be instantly involved in the fictional world.

As with *we* and *you*, *they* can also be used with reference to people in general:

> *Ross duly appeared in a multi-million pound advertising campaign and the rest, as **they** say, is history.* (NEWS)

Other problems in using third-person pronouns were taken up in the discussion of gender (4.7.2–3).

## 4.10.2   Referring to people in general

When *we*, *you*, and *they* are used with reference to people in general (4.10.1.1–3), they tend to retain a tinge of their basic meaning. Another possible form for general reference is *one* which has no such personal overtones:

> ***One** cannot say it of a person. But if **one** could, **one** would say it of these young persons.* (FICT)

> ***One** can have too much of a good thing.* (NEWS)

> *So far as **one** can judge, the women's resistance movement was formed towards the end of June 1910.* (ACAD†)

*One* is virtually restricted to the written registers, and is perceived as a non-casual choice. See also 4.15.2B.

## 4.10.3   Special problems with collective nouns

Collective nouns can occur with both singular and plural personal pronouns and possessive determiners (cf. 4.3.4, 3.9.2.3):

1 *The Western Health Board has denied that **it** plans to close the accident and emergency unit at the Tyrone County Hospital.* (NEWS)

2 *The Hydro Board were playing tunes with **their** dams, and did a great deal to lessen the impact by holding back as much water as **they** could.* (NEWS)

3 *The planning committee decided on Monday evening to defer **its** decision.* (NEWS†)

4 *The committee has decided that **their** faithful followers should be the ones to vote on the club's fate.* (NEWS)

5 *The Government has made it clear that **it** may not use **its** power of veto.* (NEWS†)

6 *She said: "The message is that the UK government couldn't care less, **they** are just applying a Band-aid to a mortal wound."* (NEWS)

The singular pronoun *it/its* is the predominant choice with a collective noun. However, plural pronouns occur both in speech and writing. Note that we may find singular subject-verb concord and plural co-referent pronouns and determiners in the same context (as in **4**). (See also 3.9.2.3 on collective nouns.)

## 4.10.4 Special uses of *it*

There are three major non-referential uses of the pronoun *it* (as a **dummy pronoun**):

### A Empty subject/object

Empty *it* occurs where there are no participants to fill the subject slot (3.2.1.2), particularly in referring to weather conditions, time, and distance:

> *It's cold.* (CONV)

> *It is eight o'clock in the morning.* (NEWS)

> *It's a long way from here to there.* (FICT†)

*It* is occasionally also found as an empty object (3.2.4.2).

### B Anticipatory subject/object

*It* is inserted as subject where a clause has been extraposed (3.2.1.2 and Chapter 9):

> *Oh I was just thinking **it**'d be nice to go there.* (CONV)

> *It is not surprising that 90 per cent of the accidents are caused by excess speed.* (NEWS)

More rarely, *it* is used as an anticipatory object (3.2.4.2).

### C Subject in cleft constructions

*It* is found in cleft constructions placing focus on a particular element in the clause (11.6.1):

> *Oh Peter, **it**'s today you're going up to Melbourne, isn't it?* (FICT)

> *It was at this stage that the role of the DCSL became particularly important.* (ACAD)

*It* with ordinary specific reference and with vague contextual reference is illustrated in 4.10.1.3.

# 4.10.5  Personal pronouns: distribution

➤ Personal pronouns are many times more common than the other pronoun types (cf. 2.4.14).

➤ Personal pronouns are by far most common in conversation.

　➤ There are wide differences in the distribution of individual personal pronouns:

　➤ With the exception of *we/us*, forms which refer to the speaker and the addressee (*I/me, you*) are far more common in conversation (and to a lesser extent fiction) than in the other registers. *We* is more evenly distributed across registers.

　➤ Other forms with predominantly human reference (*he/him* and *she/her*) are most common in fiction and (to a lesser extent) conversation.

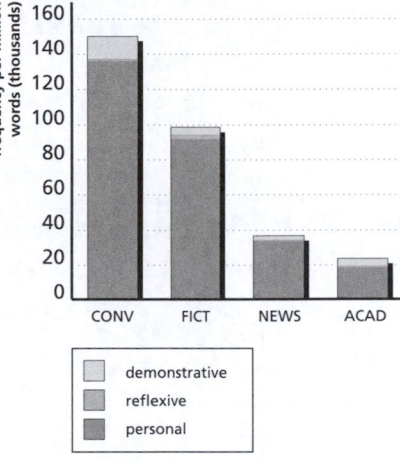

Figure 4.8
**Distribution of personal pronouns v. other pronoun types**

➤ The masculine pronouns (*he/him*) are more common than the corresponding feminine pronouns (*she/her*) in all registers.

➤ *It* (used for non-human reference) and *they/them* (both human and non-human reference) are also by far most common in conversation (and to a lesser extent fiction). *It* and *they/them* are also relatively common in news and academic prose.

➤ Except for *we/us* in academic prose, the plural in each person is consistently less common than the singular.

➤ The nominative forms of pronouns are more common than the corresponding accusative forms in all registers.

The high overall frequency of pronouns with human reference in conversation and fiction has to do with the general concern in those registers with individuals and their thoughts and actions. First and second person pronouns, referring to the speaker and the addressee, are naturally very common in conversation because both participants are in immediate contact, and the interaction typically focuses on matters of immediate concern. The same is true of the speech situations depicted in fictional dialogue. Frequencies are lower in fiction than in conversation, because narrative and descriptive passages are as important as dialogue.

In academic prose, on the other hand, human beings are a more marginal topic. News consistently has a higher frequency of pronouns with human reference than academic prose, because the actions and thoughts of people are frequently reported in news stories.

**Table 4.33**  **Distribution of individual personal pronouns; occurrences per million words**

each ■ represents 1,000     □ represents less than 500

| | CONV | FICT | NEWS | ACAD |
|---|---|---|---|---|
| *I* | ■■■■■■■■■■ ■■■■■■■■■■ ■■■■■■■■■ ■■■■■■■ | ■■■■■■■■■■ ■■■■■■ | ■■■■■ | ■■ |
| *me* | ■■■■ | ■■■■ | ■ | □ |
| *we* | ■■■■■■ | ■■■ | ■■■ | ■■■ |
| *us* | ■ | ■ | ■ | □ |
| *you* | ■■■■■■■■■■ ■■■■■■■■■■ ■■■■■■■■■ | ■■■■■■■■■■ ■ | ■■ | ■ |
| *he* | ■■■■■■■■■■ ■ | ■■■■■■■■■■ ■■■■■■■ | ■■■■■■■ | ■ |
| *him* | ■■ | ■■■■■ | ■ | □ |
| *she* | ■■■■■■■ | ■■■■■■■■■■ | ■■ | □ |
| *her* | ■ | ■■■ | ■ | □ |
| *it* | ■■■■■■■■■■ ■■■■■■■■■■ ■■■■■■■ | ■■■■■■■■■■ ■■■ | ■■■■■■■ | ■■■■■■■ |
| *they* | ■■■■■■■■■■ | ■■■■■ | ■■■■ | ■■■ |
| *them* | ■■■■ | ■■■ | ■ | ■ |

The unexpectedly high frequency of *we/us* in news and academic prose is connected with the multiple uses of this pronoun in written prose: to make generalizations, and to refer to the author or jointly to the author and reader (4.10.1.1).

The generally higher frequency of singular pronouns is related to the general frequency difference between singular and plural nouns (4.5.6).

The bias in the distribution of the masculine and feminine forms reflects traditional sex-role biases (4.7.1.1). The most extreme differences are found in news and academic prose, where masculine pronouns are over three times more common than feminine pronouns.

The large difference in frequency between nominative and accusative forms should be seen in relation to the general distribution of nouns v. pronouns with respect to syntactic role. Pronouns are associated particularly with subject position, i.e. the role carried by the nominative form (4.1.2).

An additional relevant factor, which applies particularly to conversation, is that nominative pronouns are repeated far more often than accusative forms. The pronoun *I* is repeated about 200 times per million words in conversation, while *he/she*, *we*, and *they* are all repeated more than 20 times per million words. In contrast, *me*, *him/her*, *us*, and *them* are almost never repeated.

The repetition of nominative forms can be quite extreme:

1  *I, I I, I got, I told you, I told you, Mick told me, I thought no you didn't.* (CONV)

2   *Oh yeah, **I, I I, I** really think that you can just go and buy driving licences over the counter just like that.* (CONV)

3   *We work, **we we** work shift work so **I I** mean – you know we get up at half past four in the morning.* (CONV)

4   *And **he he** got, he got my hand for five seconds and then **I I** got – I got his for ten something like that.* (CONV)

Interestingly, we sometimes find repeated personal pronouns (especially *I*) in fictional dialogue, and they reveal the same pattern as in conversation.

The grammatical subject is central in the planning of speech. Repetition of the subject (often together with the verb, as shown in **4**), as well as pauses and other disfluencies in the subject, is a sign of ongoing planning (see also 14.2.2.1).

## 4.10.6   Nominative v. accusative forms of personal pronouns

Most of the personal pronouns preserve a distinction between a **nominative** and an **accusative** case form: *I—me, he—him, she—her, we—us, they—them*. The distribution of the forms is generally straightforward: the nominative is used in subject position, while the accusative is used in object position and as the complement of prepositions. In some contexts, however, there is variation, and the general tendency is for the accusative forms to spread into contexts traditionally associated with the nominative case.

### 4.10.6.1   Pronoun choice after forms of *be*

After forms of *be* we find both nominative and accusative forms. This applies both to clauses where the pronoun is a simple subject predicative (as in **1-4**) and where it is the focus of a cleft construction (as in **5-8**):

1   *Hello gorgeous it's **me**!* (CONV)

2   *So maybe it's **I**, John Isidore said to himself.* (FICT)

3   *Oh it's **him** what's his name.* (CONV)

4   *Who spoke first? Was it at all sure it was **he**?* (FICT)

5   *Carlo immediately thought it was **me** who had died.* (FICT)

6   *The odds were that it was **I** who was wrong.* (FICT †)

7   *Some people say it was **him** that wrote it.* (CONV)

8   *It was **he** who had given Billy morphine.* (FICT)

**CORPUS FINDINGS** [2,11]

➤   Accusative forms are predominant after the copula *be*.
  ➤   However, cleft constructions in fiction and news generally have nominative forms followed by *who*.

**DISCUSSION OF FINDINGS**

Despite a traditional prescription based on the rules of Latin grammar, accusative forms are predominant in all registers where the relevant forms are found. In conversation, where indeed we might expect to find a change most advanced, they

Table 4.34    **Proportional use of nominative v. accusative pronouns (*I/he* v. *me/him*) in the construction *it* + BE + pronoun; as a percentage of the total post-copular pronouns in that register**

each ■ represents 5%    □ represents less than 2.5%

|  | % use of *I/he* | % use of *me/him* |
| --- | --- | --- |
| **CONV** | | |
| *it* BE pronoun *who* | □ | ■ |
| *it* BE pronoun *that*/zero | □ | ■ ■ ■ |
| *it* BE pronoun (final) | □ | ■ ■ ■ ■ ■ ■ ■ ■ ■ ■ ■ ■ ■ ■ ■ ■ |
| **FICT** | | |
| *it* BE pronoun *who* | ■ ■ ■ ■ ■ ■ ■ | ■ |
| *it* BE pronoun *that*/zero | □ | ■ |
| *it* BE pronoun (final) | ■ | ■ ■ ■ ■ ■ ■ ■ ■ |
| **NEWS** | | |
| *it* BE pronoun *who* | ■ ■ ■ ■ ■ ■ ■ ■ ■ ■ | |
| *it* BE pronoun *that*/zero | □ | ■ |
| *it* BE pronoun (final) | □ | ■ ■ ■ ■ ■ ■ ■ ■ |

are nearly universal. Even where cleft constructions occur in conversation, we usually find an accusative form, together with *that* or a zero connective.

In fiction and news, accusative forms are also the norm for subject predicatives following the copula *be*. However, cleft constructions generally have nominative forms followed by *who*. The nominative forms are presumably felt to be more correct, as they are typically coreferential with the subject of the following subordinate clause. It is also significant that in these registers *who* is often chosen to introduce the subordinate clause rather than *that* or zero connective, which are typical of casual speech.

## 4.10.6.2    Pronoun choice after *as* and *than*

We find more or less the same pattern after *as* and *than* (7.8) as after the copula *be*. Both nominative and accusative forms occur:

1  *She's as bad as **me** and you!* (CONV)
2  *You are closer to death than **I**.* (FICT)

Where there is a following verb, nominative forms are the regular option:

3  *She was half a head taller than **he** was.* (FICT)
4  *He knew a lot more than **I** did.* (FICT)

**CORPUS FINDINGS** [2,12]

➤  Accusative forms are predominant after *as/than*, especially in conversation.

**DISCUSSION OF FINDINGS**

The accusative forms are the only ones attested in conversation, where *as* and *than* seem to behave like prepositions rather than conjunctions introducing elliptic degree clauses. In fiction, nominative and accusative forms are fairly evenly divided. Both types are extremely rare in news and academic prose.

**Table 4.35** **Proportional use of nominative v. accusative pronouns (*I/he* v. *me/him*) in the construction *as/than* + pronoun**

each ■ represents 5%    □ represents less than 2.5%

| | % use of *as/than* + *I/he* | % use of *as/than* + *me/him* |
|---|---|---|
| CONV | □ | ■■■■■■■■■■■■■■■■■■■ |
| FICT | ■■■■■■■■■□ | ■■■■■■■■■■■ |

Instead, writers frequently opt for a full comparative clause (as in examples **3** and **4**), thereby avoiding a choice between a nominative and an accusative form.

Writers can also avoid a case choice by using a reflexive pronoun:

5 *When he learned that the young girl beside her was her daughter he judged her to be a year or so younger than* **himself**. (FICT)

6 *She was slightly smaller than* **himself**. (FICT†)

Such examples are found particularly in fiction.

### 4.10.6.3 Pronoun choice in coordinated noun phrases

Accusative forms are occasionally used in subject position, if the subject is realized by a coordinated noun phrase:

1 *But somehow I* **me and this other bloke** *managed to avoid each other.* (CONV†)

2 *"***Me and her mother** *split up about two years ago."* (NEWS)

3 *And* **you and me** *nearly – nearly didn't get on the train.* (CONV)

4 **Him and Ed** *stink, both of them.* (CONV)

Note how the speaker in **1** opts for an accusative form in the coordinate noun phrase, after starting out with a nominative form.

**Table 4.36** **Proportional use of nominative v. accusative pronouns (*I/he* v. *me/him*) in coordinated phrases**

each ■ represents 5%    each □ represents less than 2.5%

| | % of *I and X* | % of *X and I* | % of *me and X* | % of *X and me* |
|---|---|---|---|---|
| CONV | □ | ■■■■■■■■■■■ | ■■■■■■■■ | ■ |
| FICT | □ | ■■■■■■■■■■■■■■■ | □ | ■ |
| NEWS | ■■ | ■■■■■■■■■■■■■■ | ■ | □ |

| | % of *he and X* | % of *X and he* | % of *him and X* | % of *X and him* |
|---|---|---|---|---|
| CONV | ■■■■■■ | □ | ■■■■■■■ | ■■■■■ |
| FICT | ■■■■■■■■■■■■■■■■ | ■■ | □ | □ |
| NEWS | ■■■■■■■■■■■■■■■■■■ | □ | □ | □ |

**CORPUS FINDINGS** [2.13]

➤ Accusative forms in coordinated noun phrases are for the most part restricted to conversation.

➤ The accusative forms are predominantly found as the first element of a coordinated phrase.

➤ Nominative forms are the only ones attested in academic prose, and they are by far the most frequent choice in fiction and news.

➤ The nominative forms have different preferred orders in a coordinated phrase: *he* is almost always in first position, *I* is usually in second position.

**DISCUSSION OF FINDINGS**

The order preferences in coordinated noun phrases are connected partly with tact on the part of the speaker and partly with the weight and information status of the coordinated elements. Where pronouns are coordinated with full noun phrases, we would ordinarily expect the pronoun to be placed initially, as pronouns are unstressed and generally convey given information (cf. the ordering principles taken up in 11.1.1). This is the main pattern observed for *he*, but *I* is almost always placed second in the coordinate phrase. *I* represents a more considered choice, and it is felt to be more tactful to delay reference to the speaker; in addition, it is considered to be formally more correct, according to prescriptive grammar, to use a nominative form.

The almost-complete lack of accusative forms in the written registers, even though they are common in conversation, reflects the fact that writers are consciously aware of this choice, and that the accusative forms are stigmatized. Consider the following interaction:

> A: *But now, even on television, they say –* **you and me***!*
> B: **You and me***.*
> C: *Yeah, oh yeah!*
> A: *But I mean really the – the grammar – is* **you and I***!*
> C: *Yeah!*
> A: *And every time I hear it, I think well I didn't know I was taught to say* **you and me***.*
> D: *No no, Auntie Annie used to be a stickler on*
> A: **You and I***.*
> D: *how we talked!*
> C: *Yeah.* (CONV)

The influence of prescriptive grammar may also lead to an occasional hypercorrect use of nominative forms in contexts where the accusative form is the regular choice:

> *Well there's two left in there and that's not enough for* **you and I***.* (CONV)

> *So really it sounds the sort of thing that'll be nice for you and I to go really just to get away from the children.* (CONV)

> *Balthazar says that the natural traitors like* **you and I** *are really Caballi.* (FICT†)

As the coordinated noun phrases in these examples are the complement of a preposition, we expect accusative forms. Such examples of hypercorrect nominative forms are generally rare.

Reflexive pronouns are also found occasionally in coordinated noun phrases in subject position:

> **Paul and myself** *went up there didn't we?* (CONV†)

> *"***My three associates and myself** *are willing to put big money into the club to get the best players for the team."* (NEWS)

> *Only* **myself and my family** *are affected by it.* (NEWS)

Reflexive pronouns, which have no case contrast, provide a convenient way of avoiding a choice between a nominative and an accusative case form. Examples of this kind are generally rare and occur mainly in news.

## 4.10.6.4 Pronoun choice in peripheral and non-integrated noun phrases

Where a noun phrase is peripheral in a clause, accusative forms are commonly used. This applies to coordinated noun phrases occurring as specifications of the subject of the clause, either as prefaces (examples **1** and **2**; cf. 3.4.3) or as tags (examples **3** and **4**; cf. 3.4.4):

> 1 **You and me**, *we're three of a kind.* (CONV)

> 2 **Me and my friend Bob**, *we'd been to a game.* (FICT†)

> 3 *Here we are, then,* **me and Anna**, *starving romantically in the next best thing to a garret: a tiny room in a dreadful hotel near the Pantheon.* (FICT)

> 4 *We are blue with the cold, and I mean blue,* **Randy Stan and me and this Terry Lennox**. (FICT)

A reflexive pronoun is another possible option in these structures, as in **5** and **6**:

> 5 A: **Myself and Ronnie**, *this chap erm Peter's or Rupert's brother*
> B: *Yeah*
> A: *We went down by ourselves. Well, how we got down alive I'll never know.* (CONV)

> 6 *"By the way," he says, "we'll be over to see you soon,* **Estie and myself**.*"* (FICT)

Note how the accusative form *me* in **7** and **8** is used with much the same force as a reflexive pronoun:

> 7 **Me**, *I'm dozing even better than him.* (CONV)

> 8 *"You have started I suppose.* **Me**, *I was early."* (FICT)

Where the noun phrase is not integrated in a clause, accusative forms regularly occur, e.g. in answers to questions:

> 9 A: *Who told you?*
> B: **Me**.
> C: *And* **me**. (CONV)

> 10 A: *I mean he ain't a hundred percent fit.*
> B: *Who?*
> A: **Him**. (CONV)

11  A: *I think I would have dumped him overboard then!*
    B: *Oh! And* **me**. *And* **me**, *May.* (CONV)

### 4.10.6.5  Summary of factors affecting pronoun case choice

To summarize, accusative pronoun forms are used in a wider range of contexts than nominative forms. Accusative forms are generally used in conversation after *be*, after *as* and *than*, frequently in coordinated noun phrases in subject position, and normally in peripheral and non-integrated noun phrases. In addition, they are of course the regular choice in the typical accusative positions, i.e. as an object in a clause and as a complement in a prepositional phrase. In fact, the only position where nominative forms are regularly used in conversation is as a simple subject occurring next to the verb of the clause.

Fiction exhibits a more conservative use of the case forms, with a fairly high frequency of the nominative after *be* (chiefly in cleft constructions) and after *as* and *than*, while nominative forms are almost universal in coordinated noun phrases in subject position. Choices in news are fairly similar to those in fiction.

Academic prose, which has a very low overall frequency of pronouns, provides few examples of the relevant forms, with not a single example of the accusative being attested in the LSWE Corpus.

## 4.11  Possessive pronouns

Corresponding to the personal pronouns, there is a series of **possessive determiners** and **possessive pronouns** (see Table 4.32 in 4.10; note that *its* is only used as a determiner). Despite the term 'possessive', they are used for a much wider range of relationships than possession (just like the genitive of nouns—4.6.12.3). Possessive determiners were covered in 4.4.2: we deal here with possessive pronouns, which are typically used where the head noun is recoverable from the preceding context (in the same way as elliptic genitives; cf. 4.6.7):

> *Could be – the same [car] as – * **ours**. (CONV)
>
> *The [house] will be* **hers** *you see when they are properly divorced.* (CONV†)
>
> *Their [eyes] met,* **his** *coolly amused,* **hers** *dark with dislike.* (FICT)
>
> *Our [paths] cross* **theirs** *seldom, by chance or purpose.* (FICT)
>
> *We have different [problems].* **Yours** *is that you happen to be the chief law enforcement officer of this Commonwealth.* (FICT)
>
> *Writers have produced extraordinary work in [conditions] more oppressive than* **mine**. (NEWS)

The head noun may be recoverable from the following context:

> **His** *was not the kind of [face] to reveal weakness by showing surprise but his eyes widened fractionally.* (FICT)
>
> **Theirs** *was an unenviable [job].* (FICT†)
>
> *The manager was told when he was appointed that* **his** *was a pressure [job].* (NEWS†)

This is a rare, stylistically marked construction type, which is also found with the elliptic genitive (4.6.7).

Possessive determiners, not possessive pronouns, precede *own* (4.4.2), even when there is no head noun:

> A: *Well, she's got to pay so much for her bloody [clothes].*
> B: *She makes **her own**, a lot of them.* (CONV)

> *It's Bryony's [space suit], give her, otherwise she will be squeaking cos she wants **her own**. Here's yours James, you have **your own**, give that one to Bryony.* (CONV†)

> *It has a glorious [style] of **its own**, light yet biscuity.* (NEWS†)

Note that *its own* may occur without a following head noun, while *its* by itself has no corresponding use (cf. Table 4.32 in 4.10).

In special cases, possessive pronouns are used when no head noun can be recovered from the context (syntactically comparable with the independent genitives dealt with in 4.6.8):

> 1 *That's not **ours** to wash darling.* (CONV)
> 2 *Well, Tommy, he said, I wish **you and yours** every joy in life.* (FICT†)
> 3 *Why is **she and hers** always at the center of things?* (FICT)

The meaning here is roughly 'our task' **1**, 'you and your family/friends' **2**, 'she and her concerns' **3**.

Other special uses are *yours sincerely/truly*, as used in correspondence, and the construction type taken up in 4.11.1.

## 4.11.1 The type *a friend of mine*

In this construction, which is parallel to the double genitive (4.6.10), the possessive pronoun occurs in a postmodifying *of*-phrase.

> *Ha, look, look, there's **a friend of yours** across there.* (CONV)

> *I found **a pattern of hers**, jacket in white, in that bag.* (CONV†)

> ***Some friends of mine**'re going down to Central America for part of the summer.* (FICT)

The special advantage of this construction is that it makes it possible for a noun to be specified with both a determiner (e.g. an indefinite article or a quantifier) and a possessive marker, whereas this combination is not possible with possessive determiners (cf. \**a your friend* v. *a friend of yours*). It is also possible to form an indefinite plural like *friends of mine* (while *my friends* is definite).

Apart from combinations with the indefinite article and indefinite plurals, we find combinations with demonstrative determiners:

> ***This friend of ours** who lost his wife last year <...>* (CONV†)

> *Bride's in trouble with **that donkey of hers**, by appearances.* (FICT)

> *I'll blow **that house of theirs** up, she was thinking.* (FICT†)

See also the comparison of the double genitive and related constructions (4.6.14).

## 4.11.2 Possessive pronouns: distribution

There are important differences in the distribution of individual possessive pronouns across registers.

**Table 4.37  Distribution of possessive pronouns; occurrences per million words**

each ■ represents 20    □ represents less than 10

| | CONV | FICT | NEWS | ACAD |
|---|---|---|---|---|
| *mine* | ■■■■■■■■■■■■■■■ | ■■■■■ | ■ | □ |
| *ours* | ■■■■■ | ■ | ■ | □ |
| *yours* | ■■■■■■■■■■ | ■■■ | ■ | □ |
| *his* | ■■■ | ■■■■■ | □ | □ |
| *hers* | ■■ | ■■■ | □ | □ |
| *theirs* | ■ | ■ | ■ | □ |

**CORPUS FINDINGS [2]**

➤ Possessive pronouns are very rare compared with personal pronouns (see Figure 4.8 in 4.10.5) and possessive determiners (Table 4.12 in 4.4.2.1).

➤ First and second person possessive pronouns are by far the most common forms, especially in conversation.

➤ In the third person singular, masculine forms outnumber feminine ones.

**DISCUSSION OF FINDINGS**

Possessive pronouns are restricted in their grammatical distribution: they require a recoverable head noun, or they are limited to special construction types. This explains the low overall frequency of these forms in relation to personal pronouns. The distribution of individual possessive pronouns reflects differences in the speech situation and the topics of the texts. First and second person singular stand out in conversation just as do the corresponding personal pronouns (4.10.5) and possessive determiners (4.4.2.1). Third person singular forms are, as would be expected, most frequent in fiction, and we find the usual difference in frequency between male and female forms.

The higher frequency of possessive pronouns in conversation and fiction should be related to the frequency of genitives without a head noun (4.6.11) and to the overall prevalence of ellipsis in those registers (3.7).

## 4.12  Reflexive pronouns

The **reflexive pronouns** form a series corresponding to the personal pronouns and possessive forms (see Table 4.32 in 4.10). They have four main uses:

**A  Marking co-reference with the subject**

In their purely reflexive use, these pronouns mark identity with the referent of a preceding noun phrase within the same clause, usually in subject position. The reflexive pronoun carries a different syntactic role; it is typically an object or a complement in a prepositional phrase. Elements co-referent with the pronouns are marked in *[]*:

*[I]'m cooking for **myself** tonight.* (CONV)

*[We]'re all looking very sorry for **ourselves**.* (CONV)

*[She] made **herself** get up.* (FICT)

*[Universal envy] setting **itself** up as a power is only a camouflaged form of cupidity [which] re-establishes **itself** and satisfies **itself** in a different way.* (ACAD)

*As [traders] fall over **themselves** to dump the pound, the wise grow wary that a bear trap may await them further down the line.* (NEWS)

Reflexive pronouns may also be controlled by the (implied) subject of a non-finite clause. Compare:

1 *[He] wanted <implied: [him/he]> to prove to **himself** and to others this sort of crime could be successfully committed.* (NEWS)

2 *[He] wanted his big brother to treat **him** as an equal.* (FICT†)

In these examples we have embedded infinitive clauses after the matrix verb *want*. A reflexive pronoun is obligatorily chosen in **1**, as it is co-referent with the subject of *prove*. In **2**, the subject and the object of *treat* are not co-referent, and this explains the use of the personal pronoun.

Apart from the normal forms shown in Table 4.32 (4.10) there are other more specialized reflexive forms: *oneself*, which refers to people in general (cf. 4.10.2, 4.15.2B), and also occasionally *ourself* and *themself*:

3 *[One] does not wish to repeat **oneself** and the reader is referred to other parts of this book.* (ACAD†)

4 *[We] find **ourself** reexamining the ways we speak to, inform, and educate one another about health.* (ACAD†)

5 *You won't be the first or last man or woman [who] gets **themself** involved in a holiday romance.* (NEWS)

The use of *ourself* in example **4** may be due to the generic reference of *we*. *Themself* in **5** appears to fill the need for a dual gender singular reflexive pronoun (other examples co-occur with *someone* as subject).

B **Alternating with personal pronouns**

Reflexive pronouns are also found in contexts where there is no overt preceding co-referent subject in the same clause, so personal pronouns would be expected. Often there is a co-referent subject in a different finite clause:

*Bess and Mercy would go on in front, [she] supposed, then Rose and **herself**.* (FICT†)

*Everything [they] were saying was, Olivia thought, as boring as **themselves**.* (FICT†)

A: ***Myself** and Ronnie, this chap erm Peter's or Rupert's brother*
B: *Yeah.*
A: *[we] went down by ourselves.* (CONV)

Sometimes, however, there is co-reference only with an implied entity:

*Assume that the project will be directed by a competent researcher other than **yourself**.* (ACAD†) <*you* is the implied subject of imperative *assume*>

*He will go in the same as **myself**.* (CONV) <*I*, as the speaker, is situationally implied>

In examples of this type, reflexive pronouns are used as an alternative to personal pronouns. They occur particularly in contexts where there is case variation in personal pronouns (4.10.6).

**C Marking emphatic identity**

In this use, the reflexive pronoun is stressed and placed in apposition to an adjacent (or nearby) noun phrase. It has about the same effect as *own* when added to a possessive form (4.4.2, 4.11). That is, it underlines the identity of the referent and frequently has a selective function, picking out a particular referent from among several possible alternatives.

> 1 *[I]'ll do the preparation **myself**.* (CONV)
>
> 2 *Hm, **myself** [I] don't know, [I] might go.* (CONV†)
>
> 2 *Unfortunately [I] **myself** did not have this chance.* (FICT)
>
> 3 *[The airlines] **themselves** will next week step up their recruitment drive for pilots in North America and western Europe.* (NEWS)
>
> 4 *We are always forced back on seeking some control outside and greater than [the earth] **itself**.* (ACAD)

Emphatic reflexive pronouns are commonly placed immediately after the noun phrase they relate to. With subject noun phrases, they may also be placed later in the clause **1** or initially **2**. Late placement of *myself*, as in **1**, is the predominant choice in conversation. *I myself* is considerably more common than *myself I*; it is found chiefly in fiction.

The placement of emphatic reflexive pronouns is dealt with further in 4.12.2.

**D Empty reflexives**

Many verbs combine obligatorily or very frequently with a reflexive pronoun:

> *Jeffrey has not **availed himself** of the facility.* (NEWS†)
>
> *Henceforth Mr O'Reilly will conduct his business within the rules and regulations and **acquaint himself** with these regulations.* (NEWS†)

Here the reflexive pronoun is not independently referring, but follows from the choice of verb. See also 4.12.1.

# 4.12.1 Reflexive pronouns: distribution

**CORPUS FINDINGS [2]**

➤ The first and second person reflexive pronouns are generally more common in conversation and fiction than in the other registers.

➤ Third person forms with predominantly human reference (*himself, herself*) are much more common in fiction than in the other registers.

➤ Reflexive pronouns used for non-human reference (*itself* and often *themselves*) occur frequently in all written registers, but are generally rare in conversation.

> ➤ *Itself* and *oneself* are most common in academic prose (though numbers are small, the latter occurs twice as frequently as in any other register).

➤ Except for *ourselves* in academic prose (contrasted with *myself*), the plural in each person is consistently less common than the singular.

**DISCUSSION OF FINDINGS**

The reflexive pronouns are much less frequent than the corresponding personal pronouns (see Figure 4.8 in 4.10.5) because their uses are far more specialized. Fiction has by far the highest frequency of reflexive pronouns, and even matches or exceeds conversation in frequency of first and second person forms, where

**Table 4.38** **Distribution of reflexive pronouns; occurrences per million words**

each ■ represents 50      □ represents less than 25

| | CONV | FICT | NEWS | ACAD |
|---|---|---|---|---|
| *myself* | ■■■ | ■■■■■■■ | ■ | □ |
| *ourself* | □ | □ | □ | □ |
| *ourselves* | □ | ■ | ■ | ■ |
| *yourself* | ■■■ | ■■■ | ■ | ■ |
| *yourselves* | □ | □ | □ | □ |
| *himself* | ■ | ■■■■■■■■■■ ■■■■■■ | ■■■■■ | ■■ |
| *herself* | ■ | ■■■■■■■■ | ■ | ■ |
| *itself* | ■ | ■■■■ | ■■ | ■■■■■ |
| *oneself* | □ | □ | □ | □ |
| *themself* | □ | □ | □ | □ |
| *themselves* | ■ | ■■■■ | ■■■ | ■■■■■ |

conversation usually has higher frequencies. Otherwise the distribution of individual pronouns agrees broadly with the tendencies for the corresponding personal pronouns (4.10.5).

In all the registers the most common use is marking co-reference with the subject (4.12A). There are two possible reasons for the comparatively low frequency of reflexive pronouns in conversation. Emphatic reflexives (4.12C) are less common (see also 4.12.2). There are also differences with respect to the use of reflexive verbs (4.12D), i.e. verbs which obligatorily or very frequently combine with reflexive pronouns:

> *acquaint oneself with*, *address oneself to*, *apply oneself to*, *avail oneself of*, *commit oneself to*, *content oneself with*

Such verbs are more common in the written registers than in conversation, contributing to the low overall frequency of reflexive pronouns in that register.

## 4.12.2 Emphatic reflexive pronouns

**CORPUS FINDINGS** [2,14]

➤ Emphatic reflexive *himself* (4.12C) is by far most common in fiction, and relatively rare in conversation:

**Table 4.39** **Distribution of emphatic reflexive *himself*; occurrences per million words**

each ■ represents 50      □ represents less than 25

| | CONV | FICT | NEWS | ACAD |
|---|---|---|---|---|
| *himself* | □ | ■■■■ | ■ | ■ |

**DISCUSSION OF FINDINGS**

Emphatic reflexive *himself* is relatively rare in conversation, presumably because the speaker can resort to phonological means for emphasis. In addition, the emphatic pronoun rarely follows immediately after the co-referent noun phrase in conversation. A separation may be preferable because it agrees with the general tendency in English to place heavily stressed elements (in this case, the emphatic reflexive pronoun) late in the clause. A separation may also be easier because of the low density of nouns (2.3.5) and the low degree of phrasal complexity (2.10) in this register.

In contrast, emphatic reflexive pronouns in the written registers typically follow immediately after the noun phrase they relate to. This pattern is especially prevalent in academic prose, associated with the concern for precision in this register (note also the parallel in meaning and distribution of the reflexive pronouns and the emphasizer *own*; 4.4.2.1):

> Labour recruitment, remuneration, the conditions of work and [the worker] **himself** must all come under capitalist control. (ACAD)

> This explains why the representation of the totem is more sacred than [the totemic object] **itself**. (ACAD)

> [The subskills] **themselves** are not the purpose of the activity, but they must be developed to serve the needs of the higher-level complex activity. (ACAD)

# 4.13 Reciprocal pronouns

As with reflexive pronouns, the **reciprocal pronouns** *each other* and *one another* mark identity with the referent of a preceding noun phrase within the same clause, usually in subject position. They differ from reflexive pronouns in that the reference is to more than one entity and that there is a mutual relationship between the entities: *X and Y like each other* means that *X likes Y* and *Y likes X*.

> I don't think you like **each other** very much. (CONV)

> We always speak French to **each other**. (CONV)

> It is only by teaching respect for **one another** that different races can live peacefully together. (NEWS)

## 4.13.1 Reciprocal pronouns: distribution

**CORPUS FINDINGS** [2]

➤ The frequency of reciprocal pronouns is low relative to personal pronouns (see Figure 4.8 in 4.10.5).

➤ *Each other* is by far the more common form in all registers.

➤ *One another* is relatively common in fiction and academic prose.

**DISCUSSION OF FINDINGS**

The reciprocal pronouns are much less frequent than the personal pronouns, because they have a very specialized use. *One another* is characteristic of academic prose and fiction. As with generic *one* (4.10.2) and *oneself* (4.12.1) it is perceived

**Table 4.40** **Distribution of reciprocal pronouns; occurrences per million words**

each ■ represents 20   ☐ represents less than 10

|  | CONV | FICT | NEWS | ACAD |
|---|---|---|---|---|
| *each other* | ■■■ | ■■■■■■■■■■ | ■■■■ | ■■■■■ |
| *one another* | ■ | ■■■ | ■ | ■■ |

as a form suitable for careful writing rather than casual speech. *Each other* is the more neutral alternative. In addition, *each other* is strongly preferred when the reference is to two entities.

It is particularly surprising that reflexive and reciprocal pronouns are less common in conversation than in the written registers, while conversation far surpasses the other registers in the frequency of personal pronouns, possessive pronouns, and demonstrative pronouns. As regards reciprocal pronouns, this distribution must be connected with the lower plural frequency in conversation (4.5.6); if there are fewer plural referents, there will also be fewer reciprocal pronouns.

# 4.14   Demonstrative pronouns

The **demonstrative pronouns** relate to the personal pronouns in much the same way as the demonstrative determiners are related to the definite article:

| definite article | personal pronoun | demonstrative determiner | demonstrative pronouns |
|---|---|---|---|
| *the book* | *it* | *this/that book* | *this/that* |
| *the books* | *they* | *these/those books* | *these/those* |
| *the girl* | *she* | *this/that girl* | *(this/that)* |
| *the girls* | *they* | *these/those girls* | *(these/those)* |

In addition to marking something as known, the demonstrative forms specify whether the referent is near or distant in relation to the addressee. The basic distinction between the pronouns *this/that* and *these/those* is the same as that between the corresponding determiners (4.4.2).

The demonstrative pronouns have a number of special uses:

**A   Reference to humans**

Unlike the personal pronouns, the demonstrative pronouns are not used with reference to humans, except as an introductory subject in examples such as:

> Sally introduced them. "Danny, **this** is my friend Sarah." (FICT)

> **These** are the survivors. (NEWS)

Reference to humans normally requires a determiner plus a noun:

> Someone must know him, someone must have noticed a man, friend, lodger, neighbour, behaving oddly. She begged **that person, those people**, to come forward. (FICT)

**B   Reference of the singular forms**

The singular forms, similar to the personal pronoun *it* (4.10.1.3), may refer to a preceding clause or sentence, or more vaguely to the preceding text:

> *We are identifying children who have needs but we're not providing the resources to solve the problem. We are waiting until they crash land and **that** is no good.* (NEWS)

> *Will there not be a continuity of evolution implied, in contradiction to our postulated discontinuous collapse? Presumably the answer will be "yes" if we accept the premise of the question. **This** has led supporters of this particular point of view to deny the premise.* (ACAD)

*This* may also refer cataphorically to something later in the text:

> *Her story was **this**: she had a husband and child.* (FICT)

> ***This** is vintage Havel: creating a work that is both specific and universal, tragic and comic.* (NEWS)

The reference of *that* may be made clear by a postmodifying phrase or clause (cf. 8.1.2):

> *In the next ten years we shall be fortunate if we witness as productive a period for text research as **that** which has just ended.* (ACAD)

> *The unit of energy is the same as **that** for work.* (ACAD)

*That* here does not have its usual demonstrative force, but is equivalent to *the one* (see also 4.14.3).

## C Reference of the plural forms

The reference of the plural forms is generally clear:

> *A: What's wrong with communal changing rooms?*
> *B: **Those** are awful.* (CONV)

> *"For the first time, in Objective 1 areas, measures are being talked about in relation to health and education," he said. "We don't know in detail what **these** would involve. **These** are aspects we will be exploring precisely over the next few weeks and months."* (NEWS)

The reference of *those* (as of *that*; see B above) can be made even more precise by a postmodifying phrase or clause:

> *The insurance men were willing to admit that the safe driver is subsidising **those** who have accidents.* (NEWS)

> *The occupational categories are the same as **those** defined there.* (ACAD)

As with *that*, the form *those* in these examples does not have its usual demonstrative force, but is equivalent to *the ones* or *the people* (see also 4.14.3).

## D Sequences containing substitute *one/ones*

Reference to countable entities can be clarified by the addition of *one/ones* (syntactically, the demonstrative forms are determiners here, cf. 4.4.3):

> *A: That picture of a frog, where is it?*
> *B: I like **this one**.* (CONV)

> *A: I'm having er er lemon.*
> *B: Yes, I I was looking at **that one** just now. What's the other one down the bottom there?* (CONV)

This use is particularly common in conversation (4.15.2.1).

## 4.14.1    Demonstrative pronouns: distribution

**CORPUS FINDINGS** [2]

➤ Demonstrative pronouns are rare compared with personal pronouns (see Figure 4.8 in 4.10.5).

➤ As with personal pronouns, demonstrative pronouns are far more common in conversation than in the written registers.

   ➤ *That* in conversation (and to a lesser extent fiction) is by far the single most common demonstrative pronoun.

➤ The singular forms are more common than the plural forms in all registers.

➤ *This*, *these*, and *those* are slightly more common in academic prose than in the other registers.

**Table 4.41**    **Distribution of demonstrative pronouns; occurrences per million words**

each ■ represents 500    ☐ represents less than 250

|       | CONV | FICT | NEWS | ACAD |
|-------|------|------|------|------|
| *this* | ■ ■ ■ | ■ ■ ■ | ■ ■ | ■ ■ ■ ■ ■ |
| *these* | ■ | ■ | ☐ | ■ |
| *that* | ■ ■ ■ ■ ■ ■ ■ ■ ■ ■ ■ ■ ■ ■ ■ ■ ■ ■ ■ ■ ■ | ■ ■ ■ ■ ■ ■ | ■ ■ | ■ ■ |
| *those* | ■ | ☐ | ■ | ■ |

**DISCUSSION OF FINDINGS**

The demonstrative pronouns mark reference in terms of proximity, while the personal pronouns simply identify an entity as known. This more specialized use accounts for the much lower frequency of demonstrative pronouns in all registers.

The higher frequency of the singular forms is related to the higher overall frequency of singular nouns (4.5.6). The lack of a consistent pattern of proximate v. distant forms indicates that proximity is insufficient to account for the distribution of the demonstrative pronouns. The following sections take up special uses of *this/these* (4.14.2), *those* (4.14.3), and *that* (4.14.4).

## 4.14.2    *This/these* in academic prose

The high frequency of *this/these* both as determiners and as pronouns in academic prose is due to their use in marking immediate textual reference. Following is a typical example:

> We must accept that the positive part of conventionalism—that judges must respect the explicit extension of legal conventions—cannot offer any useful advice to judges in hard cases. **These** will inevitably be cases in which the explicit extension of the various legal conventions contains nothing decisive either way, and the judge therefore must exercise his discretion by employing extralegal standards.
>
> But it may now be said that, so far from being a depressing conclusion, **this** states precisely the practical importance of conventionalism for adjudication. On **this** account the positive part of that conception is the huge

> *mass of the iceberg that lies beneath the surface of legal practice.* **This** *explains why cases do not come to court when the conditions of my comically weak description of the explicit extension of our legal conventions are met, which is most of the time.* (ACAD)

See also the discussion of anaphoric expressions in 4.1.3.

### 4.14.3 *Those* with postmodifying phrases or clauses

The relatively high frequency of the pronoun *those* in academic prose is due to its cataphoric use with a postmodifying clause or phrase (4.14C): over 90 per cent of the tokens of *those* in news and academic prose occur with a post-modifier (cf. 8.1.2).

The pattern is somewhat different in fiction, where there are more demonstrative pronouns without postmodification. The distribution in conversation is the opposite, with *those* rarely taking a post-modifier.

See also the account of constructions with *that*/*those* plus *of*-phrases in 4.6.13.

### 4.14.4 The demonstrative pronoun *that* in conversation

The exceptionally high frequency of *that* in conversation may have a number of causes. The reference of *that* in conversation is usually fairly vague and fits in with the use of other vague expressions in conversation (14.1.2.3). Where there is a need, the speaker may clarify the reference by adding *one* (4.14D). Uncertainties can also be cleared up in the course of the exchange, as with other anaphoric expressions in conversation (4.4.1.3, 4.10.1.3).

In addition, *that* can be regarded as the stressed counterpart of *it*. Unlike the other personal pronouns, *it* can only be stressed in very special cases (e.g. the phrase *that's it*). Instead, *that* is used when there is a need to express contrast or emphasis.

Some more specialized structures, which are characteristic of conversation, contain the pronoun *that*. These include reversed *wh*-clefts (see also 11.6.3):

> **That's how** *they were doing it.* (CONV)

> **That's what** *I thought!* (CONV)

Other typically conversational structures which may contain the demonstrative pronoun *that* are tags (3.4.4):

> *It's just Rosie* **that** *is.* (CONV)

> *That's that's true* **that**. *That's what they do.* (CONV†)

The repetition illustrated in the last example is also important.

### 4.14.5 *That* in general

*That* is one of the most common and most flexible word forms in English. Here its demonstrative uses are compared with 'other' functions of this form, which include *that* as a complementizer, relative pronoun, and degree adverb (e.g. *It was that hot*).

**CORPUS FINDINGS** [15]

➤ In conversation *that* is primarily used as a demonstrative form, with a small minority of instances of other types, including the use as a degree adverb.

➤ The distribution between demonstrative and other uses is more even in fiction.

➤ The complementizer and relative pronoun uses are the dominant ones in news and academic prose.

**Table 4.42** **Proportional uses of *that*; percentage total occurrences**

each ● represents 5%

| | % demonstrative determiner | % demonstrative pronoun | % other |
|---|---|---|---|
| CONV | ● ● ● | ● ● ● ● ● ● ● ● ● <br> ● ● ● ● | ● ● ● |
| FICT | ● ● ● | ● ● ● ● ● ● | ● ● ● ● ● ● ● ● ● ● ● <br> ● |
| NEWS | ● ● | ● ● | ● ● ● ● ● ● ● ● ● ● ● <br> ● ● ● ● ● ● |
| ACAD | ● | ● ● | ● ● ● ● ● ● ● ● ● ● ● <br> ● ● ● ● ● ● ● |

**DISCUSSION OF FINDINGS**

*That* as complementizer or relative pronoun is relatively infrequent in conversation because the zero alternative is so often selected for these functions in that register, but not so much in the written ones (see 8.7.1 for relativizers and 9.2.8 for complementizers). Reasons for the frequent use in conversation of the demonstrative pronoun *that* have been given in 4.14.4 and there is discussion of the distribution of demonstrative determiner *that* in 4.4.3.1.

# 4.15 Indefinite pronouns

The **indefinite pronouns** refer to entities which the speaker/writer cannot or does not want to specify more exactly. Most of these pronouns were originally noun phrases consisting of a quantifier and a noun with a general meaning.

There are four main groups of indefinite pronouns, each derived from a quantifier:

the *every* group: *everybody, everyone, everything*
the *some* group: *somebody, someone, something*
the *any* group: *anybody, anyone, anything*
the *no* group: *nobody, no one, none, nothing*

The meaning of these pronouns is parallel to that of noun phrases with the corresponding determiners (4.4.4), except that the reference is to an indefinite person or thing. Compare:

*Father Christmas couldn't go to **every single child***. (CONV†)
*I've got to go around and talk to **everybody***. (CONV†)
*"He brought me **some natural food**."* (FICT)
*"I have brought **something** for you from Doctor Fischer."* (FICT)

*No observer* was present during the home observations. (ACAD†)
*No one* has a moral right to compensation except for physical injury. (ACAD)

Many of the forms used as quantifying determiners can also occur as pronouns (2.4.2.1 and 4.4.4.1).

**Table 4.43** **Distribution of indefinite pronouns (frequencies of the quantifiers *every*, *some*, *no*, and *any* are included for comparison); occurrences per million words**

each ■ represents 200     □ represents less than 100

| | CONV | FICT | NEWS | ACAD |
|---|---|---|---|---|
| *everybody* | ■ | ■ | □ | □ |
| *everyone* | ■ | ■ | ■ | □ |
| *everything* | ■■ | ■■ | ■ | □ |
| *every* (quantifier) | ■■ | ■■ | ■■ | ■■ |
| *somebody* | ■■ | ■ | □ | □ |
| *someone* | ■ | ■■ | ■ | ■ |
| *something* | ■■■■■■ | ■■■■■ | ■■■■■ | ■ |
| *some* (quantifier) | ■■■■■■■■ ■■ | ■■■■■■■ ■ | ■■■■■ | ■■■■■■ ■■■ |
| *anybody* | ■ | □ | □ | □ |
| *anyone* | ■ | ■ | ■ | □ |
| *anything* | ■■■ | ■■■ | ■ | □ |
| *any* (quantifier) | ■■■■■ | ■■■■■ | ■■■■ | ■■■■■■ |
| *nobody* | ■ | ■ | □ | □ |
| *no one* | □ | ■ | □ | □ |
| *none* | □ | ■ | □ | □ |
| *nothing* | ■■■ | ■■■■ | ■ | ■ |
| *no* (quantifier) | ■■■■■ | ■■■■■■■ ■■■■ | ■■■■■■ | ■■■■■ |

**Table 4.44** **Proportional use of pronoun-*body* v. pronoun-*one* in AmE and BrE fiction[4]**

each ● represents 5%

| | % use of pronoun-*body* | % use of pronoun-*one* |
|---|---|---|
| **AmE** | | |
| *any-* | ●●●●●●●●● | ●●●●●●●●●●● |
| *every-* | ●●●●●●●● | ●●●●●●●●●●● |
| *no-* | ●●●●●●●●●● | ●●●●●●●●● |
| *some-* | ●●●●●●●● | ●●●●●●●●●●● |
| **BrE** | | |
| *any-* | ●●●● | ●●●●●●●●●●●●●●●●● |
| *every-* | ●●●●●● | ●●●●●●●●●●●●●●●● |
| *no-* | ●●●●●●● | ●●●●●●●●●●●●●●● |
| *some-* | ●●●●● | ●●●●●●●●●●●●●●●● |

## 4.15.1 Indefinite pronouns: distribution

➤ All groups of indefinite pronouns are most common in conversation and fiction, and least common in academic prose.

➤ Pronouns ending in -*body* are most common in conversation; in contrast, pronouns ending in -*one* are preferred in the written registers.

➤ Pronouns ending in -*body* are more common in AmE than in BrE (see Table 4.44).

**DISCUSSION OF FINDINGS**

The indefinite pronouns and the corresponding determiners have different distributions (cf. 4.4.4.1). The high frequency of indefinite pronouns in conversation and fiction agrees with the common overall use of pronouns in these registers (2.4.14, 4.1.2). News and academic prose far more frequently opt for a more precise expression, consisting of a determiner plus noun.

The relatively high frequency in fiction of the *no*-group, both determiner and pronouns, is clearly connected with the frequent use of *no*-negation in this register (3.8.4.2).

The -*body* forms have more casual overtones and are slightly preferred in conversation, while -*one* forms (consistently with generic *one*, *oneself*, and *one another*) are somewhat more typical of the written registers. British fiction employs the less casual choice (-*one*) more widely than does AmE.

## 4.15.2 The pronoun *one*

Apart from being used as a numeral (2.4.13.1, 4.4.5), *one* has two main pronominal uses.

### A Substitute *one*

*One* may replace a countable noun that has been mentioned or is inferred from the context. A singular noun is replaced by *one*, a plural noun by *ones*.

1 *An artist cannot fail; it is success to be **one**.* (ACAD)

2 *Bookmakers William Hill are offering 8/11 on a rainy Christmas and 11/10 on a dry **one**.* (NEWS)

3 *What about, are we going to put that **one** in the sale this year, the **one** that's out in the shed?* (CONV)

4 *The **one** she actually cancelled was the **one** to her family because I had already cancelled the group **one**.* (CONV)

5 *It's like everything else in this world, he said. You get some bad **ones** and you get some good **ones**.* (FICT)

In **1** *one* replaces *an artist*, in **2** *Christmas*; in the other examples the exact reference is not made clear within the context provided. Substitute *one(s)* is often found after adjectives (**2**, **5**) and determiners (**3**, **4**, **5**), but also co-occurs with premodifying nouns (as in *the group one* in **4**). Note that *one* by itself substitutes for both indefinite determiner and noun in **1**.

### B Generic *one*

*One* is also used as a generic pronoun referring to people in general:

1 **One** *doesn't raise taxes with enthusiasm, but the alternative is public sector borrowing going through the roof.* (NEWS)

2 *Success and acclaim were seen as a means of validating **one's** existence.* (NEWS†)

3 **One** *could set **oneself** to endure forty-eight hours of almost anything, she told herself.* (FICT)

4 **One** *does not wish to repeat **oneself** unduly and the reader is referred to other parts of this book.* (ACAD†)

Note the possessive form *one's* in **2** and the reflexive form *oneself* in **3** and **4**. In **4**, *one* conveys a veiled reference to the author; this is characteristic of the impersonal style often adopted in academic prose. (It is also significant that the reader is addressed in the third person.)

## 4.15.2.1 The pronoun *one*: distribution

**CORPUS FINDINGS** [2]

➤ Substitute *one* is far more common in conversation than in the written registers.
➤ The singular forms are consistently more frequent than the plural forms.
➤ Generic *one* is far less common overall than substitute *one*.
   ➤ Generic *one* is restricted primarily to the written registers, especially fiction and academic prose.

**Table 4.45   Distribution of substitute and generic *one*; occurrences per million words**

each ■ represents 50      □ represents less than 25

|  | CONV | FICT | NEWS | ACAD |
|---|---|---|---|---|
| **substitute *one*:** | | | | |
| *this one* | ■■■■■■ | ■ | □ | □ |
| *these ones* | □ | □ | □ | □ |
| *that one* | ■■■■■■■■■■■■ | ■ | □ | □ |
| *those ones* | □ | □ | □ | □ |
| *the (other) one* | ■■■■■■■■ | ■■ | ■ | ■ |
| *the (other) ones* | ■■ | □ | □ | □ |
| *which one* | ■■ | □ | □ | □ |
| *which ones* | □ | □ | □ | □ |
| **generic *one*** | □ | ■■■■■■ | ■■ | ■■■■■■■■ |

**DISCUSSION OF FINDINGS**

The register distribution of substitute *one* is in broad agreement with the overall distribution of pronouns (2.4.14), although conversation and the written registers are even more sharply differentiated with substitute *one*. The special significance of substitute *one* is that it provides a general means of countable reference. The probable reason for the sharp differentiation is that conversation relies far more than the written registers on implicit links and references (4.1.3). The higher frequency of singular *one* is related to the higher overall frequency of singular nouns (4.5.6).

The register distribution for generic *one* deviates sharply from the overall distribution of pronouns. The probable reason why generic *one* is most common in fiction and academic prose is that it is perceived as an impersonal option (4.10.2), lacking the personal overtones attaching to the personal pronouns when used for referring to people in general (4.10.1.1–3), a use more characteristic of conversation and news.

The relatively high frequency of generic *one* in academic prose should be compared with the unexpectedly high frequency of *we* (4.10.5), and with the very high passive frequency in this register (6.4.1, 11.3.2). These are all connected with the preoccupation in academic work with making generalizations and with the wish to adopt an impersonal, objective style.

## 4.16 Other pronouns

*Wh*-pronouns (2.4.9) are used as interrogative clause markers and relativizers and are dealt with in connection with interrogative clauses (3.13.2.1) and relative clauses (8.7).

Quantifiers *many, all, a lot, few*, etc. occurring as pronouns are covered along with the determiner function of these forms (4.4.4.1).

Pronoun uses of *others, the latter, the last, such*, etc. are covered along with the semi-determiner function of these forms (4.4.6.2).

# 5

# Verbs

*See page xiii for contents in detail*

## 5.1  Major verb functions and classes

Verbs can have one of two major roles in a verb phrase: **main verb** or **auxiliary verb**. Main verbs, such as the verb *went* in the following example, can stand alone as the entire verb phrase:

> I **went** into the empty house. (FICT)

In contrast, auxiliary verbs, such as the verbs *can* and *be* in the following example, occur together with some main verb (in this case *cited*):

> Instances **can be** [*cited*] where this appears not to be the case. (ACAD)

Exceptions, where auxiliary verbs seem to function alone as verb phrases, include instances of ellipsis (3.7), where a repeated main verb is ellipted, and question and declarative tags (3.4.4).

There are three major classes of verbs: **lexical verbs** (also called **full verbs,** e.g. *run, eat*), **primary verbs** (*be, have,* and *do*), and **modal verbs** (e.g. *can, will, might*). These classes are distinguished by their roles as main verbs and auxiliary verbs. Lexical verbs comprise an open class of words that function only as main verbs; the three primary verbs can function as either main verbs or auxiliary verbs; and modal verbs can function only as auxiliary verbs.

- Lexical verbs, main verb function
  > Children and dogs **ran** from side to side almost underfoot. (FICT)
  > He barely **ate** or **slept** that night. (FICT)
- Primary verbs *be, have,* and *do*, main verb function
  > He **does** my washing. (CONV)
  > She **was** one of the few women to comment on Ashdown the hunk. (NEWS)
  > Every atom **has** a dense nucleus. (ACAD†)
- Primary verbs *be, have,* and *do*, auxiliary verb function
  > He **doesn't** look at the numbers. (CONV)
  > He **was** wearing a dark ski mask. (NEWS†)
  > The work it **has** stimulated **has** enriched the subject. (ACAD†)
- Modal verbs, auxiliary verb function
  > People thought he **might** have been joking. (NEWS)
  > He **would** probably like it softer. (NEWS)

In addition, verbs can be classified on the basis of their semantic domains (5.2.1) and valency patterns (copular, intransitive, and transitive; 3.5, 5.2.4). Finally, we make a fundamental distinction between simple lexical verbs (5.2) and the various kinds of multi-word verbs (phrasal verbs, prepositional verbs, and phrasal-prepositional verbs; 5.3).

## 5.1.1  Frequency of lexical, modal, and primary auxiliary verbs

**CORPUS FINDINGS** [1]

➤ Overall, lexical verbs are the most common class of verb in the LSWE Corpus, occurring over 100,000 times per million words (more than one word in ten).
➤ Primary auxiliary verbs and modal auxiliary verbs are also very common.

➤ Primary auxiliary verbs are about twice as common as modal auxiliary verbs.
➤ The primary verb *be* in its role as a main verb is the single most common individual verb, about as common as all the modal auxiliaries together.

**Figure 5.1**

**Overall distribution of verb types in the LSWE Corpus**

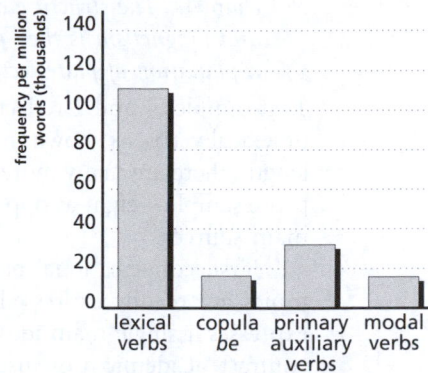

### DISCUSSION OF FINDINGS

The much higher frequency of lexical verbs reflects the fact that main verbs often occur without any auxiliary in simple tense forms (6.2), and in non-finite clauses (3.12).

Primary auxiliary verbs are more frequent than modal verbs because they express basic grammatical meanings of aspect and voice (6.3–4). In addition, the primary auxiliary verb *do* is obligatory in many questions and negative clauses. In contrast, modals express meanings related to stance (e.g. probability, permission, obligation), and similar meanings can alternatively be expressed by other lexical items (cf. 10.3, 12.3).

## 5.1.2 Distribution of lexical verbs and copula *be* across registers

### CORPUS FINDINGS [2]

➤ The verb types are not distributed evenly across registers:
  ➤ Lexical verbs are extremely common in fiction and conversation. They are less common in news, and considerably less common in academic prose.
  ➤ The copula *be* occurs most commonly in academic prose and least commonly in conversation.

**Figure 5.2**

**Frequency of lexical verbs and copula *be* across registers**

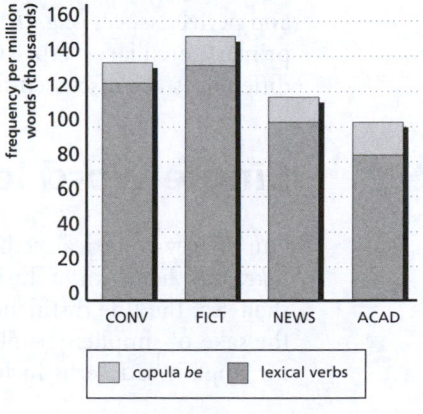

### DISCUSSION OF FINDINGS

Text samples 1 and 2 below illustrate the differing uses of verbs in conversation and academic prose, as the two varieties which show the greatest contrast. Lexical verbs are bold, and the copula *be* is given in *[]*.

Text sample 1: CONVERSATION

> A: *Those hyacinths in the corner are* **taking** *a long time to* **come out***, aren't they? I'd have* **thought** *the tulip in the coal scuttle, the tulips in the cauldron, I* **thought** *they'd* **had** *it, they were* **lying** *down completely.*
> B: *I* **know***, but they've* **straightened out***.* (CONV)

Text sample 2: ACADEMIC PROSE

> *Internal heat, volcanism, and the kinds of igneous and metamorphic rocks that are* **produced** *by thermal processes [are] the subjects of the first group of chapters. The structure of the interior as* **deduced** *from seismology, gravity, and magnetism is then* **explored**, *in preparation for a detailed systematic explanation of plate tectonics.* (ACAD)

Text samples 1 and 2 reflect the significant register differences in the frequencies of lexical verbs, as shown in Figure 5.2. Although the samples are nearly the same length, there are many more lexical verbs in the conversation than in the academic prose sample—eight as opposed to three. This difference seems to come from two main sources.

First, conversational partners talk a lot about actions and events, and these topics are readily expressed through frequent, short clauses. Often, each clause expresses a single main idea; and most of these clauses contain a lexical verb. In contrast, academic prose uses relatively few clauses and therefore few lexical verbs; the clauses in academic prose tend to be long, containing many noun phrases and prepositional phrases. Academic prose focuses more on the relations among entities than actions and events and thus contains elaborate noun phrases referring to those entities. This difference in purpose also accounts for the higher frequency of copula *be* in academic prose; a copula simply links a noun phrase to another noun phrase, adjectival phrase, or adverbial, rather than specifying a particular action (5.5).

Second, conversation commonly uses lexical verbs to frame the personal stance of the speaker (e.g. *I know, I think, I mean*). These verbs often occur with a following dependent complement clause (9.2.2); lexical verbs are rarely used in this way in academic prose.

As for primary auxiliary verbs, these two text samples illustrate an important difference not shown by the overall similarities in frequency. Conversation tends to use primary auxiliary verbs to mark progressive aspect (e.g. *they are taking*) and perfect aspect (e.g. *they've straightened*), whereas academic prose tends to use primary auxiliary verbs to mark passive voice (e.g. *they are produced*). These differences are discussed further in 6.3–5.

## 5.2    Single-word lexical verbs

Our survey of lexical verbs deals first with single-word verbs, such as *come* and *take*, and then with multi-word verbs (5.3) such as *come across* and *take up*. As we shall see, the fine distinction between the two types is sometimes fuzzy, and, for the sake of simplicity (unless otherwise indicated), all the frequency information for single-word verbs includes their use as components of multi-word verbs.

## 5.2.1    Classification of verbs into semantic domains

Although many verbs have more than one meaning, we have found it useful to classify verbs into seven major semantic domains: **activity verbs**, **communication verbs**, **mental verbs**, **causative verbs**, **verbs of simple occurrence**, **verbs of existence or relationship**, and **aspectual verbs**.

For the most part, the following classification of verbs is based on their core meanings (i.e. the meaning that speakers tend to think of first). However, it is important to note that many verbs have multiple meanings from different semantic domains, and in some cases a verb is most common with a non-core meaning. In those cases, the verb is listed in the category corresponding to its most typical use. For example, most speakers tend initially to think of the verbs *start*, *stop*, and *keep* as referring to physical activities, as in the following examples:

> We **stopped** at the market on the way back. (CONV)

> I'll **keep** the coins. (CONV)

> It must have been fifteen minutes before he got it **started**. (FICT)

However, these verbs more commonly have an aspectual meaning, concerned with the progress of some other action:

> And it was two o'clock when they **stopped** talking. (CONV)

> I **keep** doing garlic burps. (CONV)

> Her car **started** to overheat. (NEWS†)

As a result, these three verbs are listed under the aspectual category.

There are two kinds of problem case we should mention. First, for some verbs there is no single correct classification, since their core meanings can be considered as belonging to more than one category. For example, the verbs *hesitate*, *pretend*, *find*, and *resist* can be regarded as both activity verbs and mental verbs. The verbs *read*, *deny*, *confirm*, and *blame* can denote both communication acts and mental acts or states.

Also, some verbs can be used with different meanings belonging to more than one semantic domain. This is especially true of activity verbs, which often have secondary meanings in some other domain. For example, the verbs *contact* and *raise* can refer to physical activities or communicative acts, while the verbs *admit* and *consult* can refer to physical, communicative, or mental activities. The verbs *follow*, *gather*, *face*, and *overcome* can be physical or mental; *change*, *rise*, and *open* can refer to either a physical activity or a simple occurrence; *look* can refer to either a physical or mental activity or a state of existence (e.g. *you look happy*); and the verbs *make* and *get* can refer to physical activities, but they are also commonly causative in meaning.

Most verbs, however, have core meanings belonging to only one semantic domain. Sections 5.2.1.1–3 show how the most common verbs are distributed across these semantic domains (based on their core meanings and most common uses if they differ from the core meaning), while the extended meanings for selected verbs are discussed in 5.2.2.2.

## 5.2.1.1 Major semantic domains of single-word verbs

### A Activity verbs

Activity verbs primarily denote actions and events that could be associated with choice, and so take a subject with the semantic role of agent (3.2.1.1). Examples are *bring*, *buy*, *carry*, *come*, *give*, *go*, *leave*, *move*, *open*, *run*, *take*, *work*:

> Then you should **move** any obstacles before. (CONV)

> He **bought** biscuits and condensed milk. (FICT)

> The airline had **opened** the route on the basis that it would be the first of many. (NEWS)

> For two years he had **carried** a chalice around with him. (FICT)

> In many of these jobs, women are **working** with women only. (ACAD)

Activity verbs can be transitive, taking a direct object, or intransitive, occurring without any object (3.5, 5.2.4):

- Transitive activity verbs

  > Well **give** it to the dogs, they'll eat it (CONV)

  > Even the smallest boys **brought** little pieces of wood and threw them in. (FICT †)

- Intransitive activity verbs

  > They **ran**, on rubbery legs, through an open gate. (FICT †)

  > From Haworth they **went** to Holyhead and on to Dublin. (NEWS)

Many activity verbs can be used to express non-volitional actions, events, or static relations, in addition to volitional activities (5.2.3). For example, compare the non-volitional meanings in the sentences below with the volitional meanings of the same verbs illustrated above:

> New laws resulting from the Children Act **carry** a wide range of implications for voluntary groups. (NEWS †)

> During that time continents, oceans, and mountain chains have **moved** horizontally and vertically. (ACAD †)

> This will **give** the electron the chance to get over the hump. (ACAD †)

> Compulsory elementary education was **working** with a vengeance. (ACAD)

## B  Communication verbs

Communication verbs can be considered a special subcategory of activity verbs that involve communication activities (speaking and writing). Common communication verbs include *ask, announce, call, discuss, explain, say, shout, speak, state, suggest, talk, tell, write*:

> You **said** you didn't have it. (CONV)

> I **told** him he was a pain. (CONV)

> "Stop that", he **shouted**. (FICT)

> The old man, however, never **spoke** directly to him. (FICT)

> The organiser **asked** me if I wanted to see how the money was spent. (NEWS)

> He might find it impossible to **write** in the tone or theme he first took up. (ACAD †)

## C  Mental verbs

Mental verbs denote a wide range of activities and states experienced by humans; they do not involve physical action and do not necessarily entail volition. Their subject often has the semantic role of recipient (3.2.1.1). They include both cognitive meanings (e.g. *think* or *know*) and emotional meanings expressing various attitudes or desires (e.g. *love, want*), together with perception (e.g. *see, taste*) and receipt of communication (e.g. *read, hear*):

> I **think** it was Freddie Kruger. (CONV)

> I would **love** to kick it. (CONV)

> He did not **know** what he expected. (FICT)

> I **wanted** very much to give him my orange but held back. (FICT)

Many mental verbs describe cognitive activities that are relatively dynamic in meaning, such as *calculate, consider, decide, discover, examine, learn, read, solve,* and *study*:

> Mr Tench **examined** his companion again with surprise. (FICT)
>
> Curry has **decided** to by-pass the Italian Open to lend his support to the Senate Open. (NEWS†)
>
> We might even **discover** that he uses a lower number of abstract nouns than other writers of his time. (ACAD)
>
> Tillyard (1918b) has **studied** the hairs occurring on the wings of the most primitive groups of Holometabola. (ACAD)

Other mental verbs are more stative in meaning. These include verbs describing cognitive states, such as *believe, doubt, know, remember, understand,* as well as many verbs describing emotional or attitudinal states, such as *enjoy, fear, feel, hate, like, love, prefer, suspect, want*:

- Cognitive states

> Oh yeah, right we all **believe** that. (CONV)
>
> Somehow I **doubt** it. (FICT)
>
> I **remember** the way you used to bash that ball. (FICT)

- Emotional/attitudinal states

> I **feel** sorry for her. (CONV)
>
> He **hated** this weekly ritual of bathing. (FICT†)
>
> I **preferred** life as it was. (NEWS)

### D  Verbs of facilitation or causation

Verbs of facilitation or causation, such as *allow, cause, enable, force, help, let, require,* and *permit* indicate that some person or inanimate entity brings about a new state of affairs. These verbs often occur together with a nominalized direct object or complement clause following the verb phrase, which reports the action that was facilitated (9.4.2). For simplicity, we will simply refer to these verbs as **causative** verbs:

- Causative verbs with nominalized direct objects

> Still other rules **cause** the deletion of elements from the structure. (ACAD)
>
> This information **enables** the formulation of precise questions. (ACAD†)
>
> The I.U.P.A.C. system **permits** the naming of any alkane on sight. (ACAD†)
>
> Suction methods for obtaining solution **require** careful interpretation. (ACAD†)

- Causative verbs with following complement clauses

> What **caused** you to be ill? (FICT)
>
> This would **help** protect Jaguar from fluctuations in the dollar. (NEWS†)
>
> Police and council leaders agreed to **let** a court decide the fate of the trees. (NEWS†)
>
> This law **enables** the volume of a gas to be calculated. (ACAD†)
>
> The second dimension of interpretation then **requires** him to judge which of these readings makes the work in progress best. (ACAD)

### E   Verbs of simple occurrence

Verbs of simple occurrence primarily report events (typically physical events) that occur apart from any volitional activity. Often their subject has the semantic affected role (3.2.1.1). For simplicity, we will refer to these verbs as **occurrence** verbs. They include *become, change, happen, develop, grow, increase,* and *occur*:

> *The lights* **changed***.* (CONV)
>
> *The word of adults had once again* **become** *law.* (FICT†)
>
> *Resistant organisms may* **develop** *in the alimentary tract.* (ACAD†)
>
> *The term "feature" has* **occurred** *many times in this chapter.* (ACAD)

### F   Verbs of existence or relationship

Verbs of existence or relationship report a state that exists between entities. Some of the most common verbs of existence or relationship are copular verbs (5.5), such as *be, seem,* and *appear*. Such copular verbs are typically followed by a subject predicative and perform a linking function, so that the subject predicative directly characterizes the subject:

> *The problem* **is** *most acute in rural areas.* (NEWS)
>
> *All these uses* **seem** *natural and serviceable.* (ACAD)

The primary verb *be* is discussed in 5.4.1; copular verbs are discussed separately in 5.5.

Other verbs of existence or relationship are not copular verbs, but report a particular state of existence (e.g. *exist, live, stay*) or a particular relationship between entities (e.g. *contain, include, involve, represent*). We will refer to verbs of existence or relationship simply as **existence** verbs:

- State of existence

  > *I go and* **stay** *with them.* (CONV)
  >
  > *She had gone to* **live** *there during the summer holidays.* (FICT)
  >
  > *These varying conditions may* **exist** *in close proximity.* (ACAD†)

- Relationship

  > *Well she* **has** *a day off school.* (CONV)
  >
  > *The exercise will* **include** *random stop checks by police, and* **involve** *special constables and traffic wardens.* (NEWS)
  >
  > *Comparison with equation (3.3) shows that the area* **represents** *the work done per unit mass.* (ACAD)
  >
  > *They* **contained** *large quantities of nitrogen.* (ACAD†)

### G   Aspectual verbs

Finally, aspectual verbs, such as *begin, continue, finish, keep, start,* and *stop* characterize the stage of progress of some other event or activity, typically reported in a complement clause following the verb phrase (compare the meanings of progressive and perfective aspect; 6.3):

> *She* **kept** *running out of the room.* (CONV)
>
> *He couldn't* **stop** *talking about me.* (CONV†)
>
> *Tears* **started** *to trickle down his cheeks.* (FICT)
>
> *After another day, he* **began** *to recover.* (FICT)
>
> *The conventional turboprop will certainly* **continue** *to dominate the market for smaller aircraft.* (ACAD†)

**5.2.1.2** **Distribution of semantic domains**

We consider here the range of common verbs used in each semantic domain.

**CORPUS FINDINGS ¹**

➤ The most common verbs (i.e. verbs that occur at least 50 times per million words) are far from evenly distributed across the seven semantic domains.
  ➤ c. 50% of all common verbs are activity verbs (139 out of 281 common verbs).
  ➤ There are also many common verbs from the domains of mental verbs and communication verbs, but the other semantic domains have a relatively small membership.

Table 5.1    **Total number of common lexical verbs from each semantic domain (verbs that occur at least 50 times per million words)**

| semantic domain | number of lexical verbs | % of all common verbs |
|---|---|---|
| activity | 138 | 49 |
| mental | 53 | 19 |
| communication | 36 | 13 |
| existence | 22 | 8 |
| occurrence | 14 | 5 |
| causative | 10 | 4 |
| aspectual | 8 | 3 |

**DISCUSSION OF FINDINGS**

The range of verbs found across semantic domains reflects the kinds of topics that speakers and writers most commonly discuss. Although there are important differences across registers (5.2.1.3), English generally makes more distinctions (as represented by different verbs) among activity verbs than in any other domain. Speakers not only distinguish among a wider range of physical activities but commonly talk about those activities, repeatedly using verbs like *bring, buy, carry, come, follow, get, give, go, leave, look, make, meet, move, put, show, take, try, use, work.*

Communication, although a specialized type of activity, is an important semantic domain in its own right. Speakers of English distinguish among many types of communicative activities, and commonly report what someone has said or written using verbs such as *ask, call, say, speak, talk, tell, write.*

In addition to activities, speakers of English frequently report on their own opinions, wants, and feelings, and on those of other people, using such common mental verbs as *believe, consider, expect, feel, find, know, like, mean, need, see, think, want.*

**5.2.1.3** **Semantic domains of verbs**

**CORPUS FINDINGS ²**

➤ Overall, activity verbs occur much more commonly than verbs from any other semantic domain.

**Figure 5.3**
**Distribution of common verbs across semantic domains— conversation**

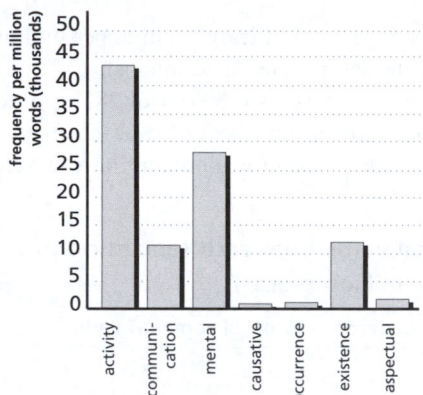

**Figure 5.4**
**Distribution of common verbs across semantic domains—fiction**

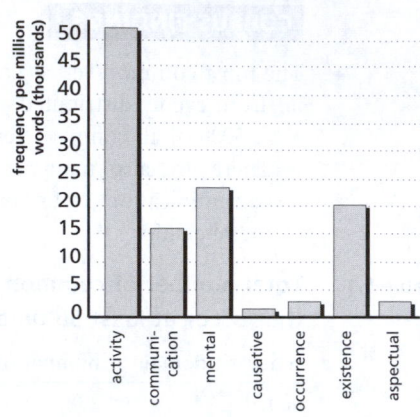

**Figure 5.5**
**Distribution of common verbs across semantic domains—news**

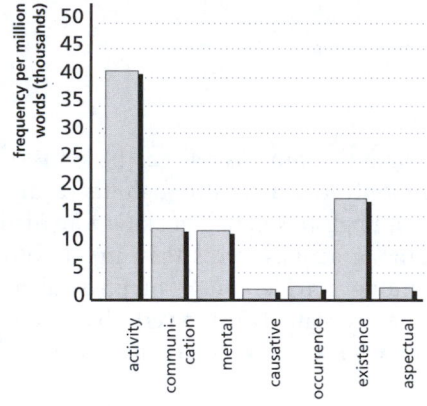

**Figure 5.6**
**Distribution of common verbs across semantic domains—academic prose**

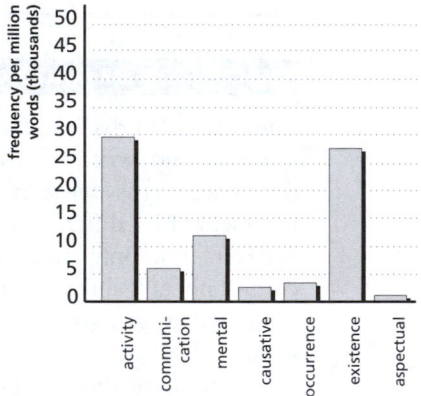

➤ Mental verbs and existence verbs are also notably common.

➤ Causative verbs, occurrence verbs, and aspectual verbs are relatively rare.

➤ The four registers use verbs from the seven semantic domains in quite different ways (see Figures 5.3–6):

   ➤ Activity verbs are most common in conversation, fiction, and news.

   ➤ Mental verbs are also particularly common in conversation and fiction.

   ➤ In contrast, existence verbs are notably common in fiction, news, and academic prose.

   ➤ In academic prose, existence verbs are almost as common as activity verbs.

   ➤ Academic prose also uses causative verbs and occurrence verbs somewhat more often than the other registers.

➤ The lexical diversity within each semantic domain differs across registers (see Table 5.2)[2,7].

**Table 5.2** **The most common lexical verbs in each semantic domain, including all verbs that occur more than 300 times per million words in at least one register; occurrences per million words**

over 2,000    over 1,000    over 500    over 300    over 200

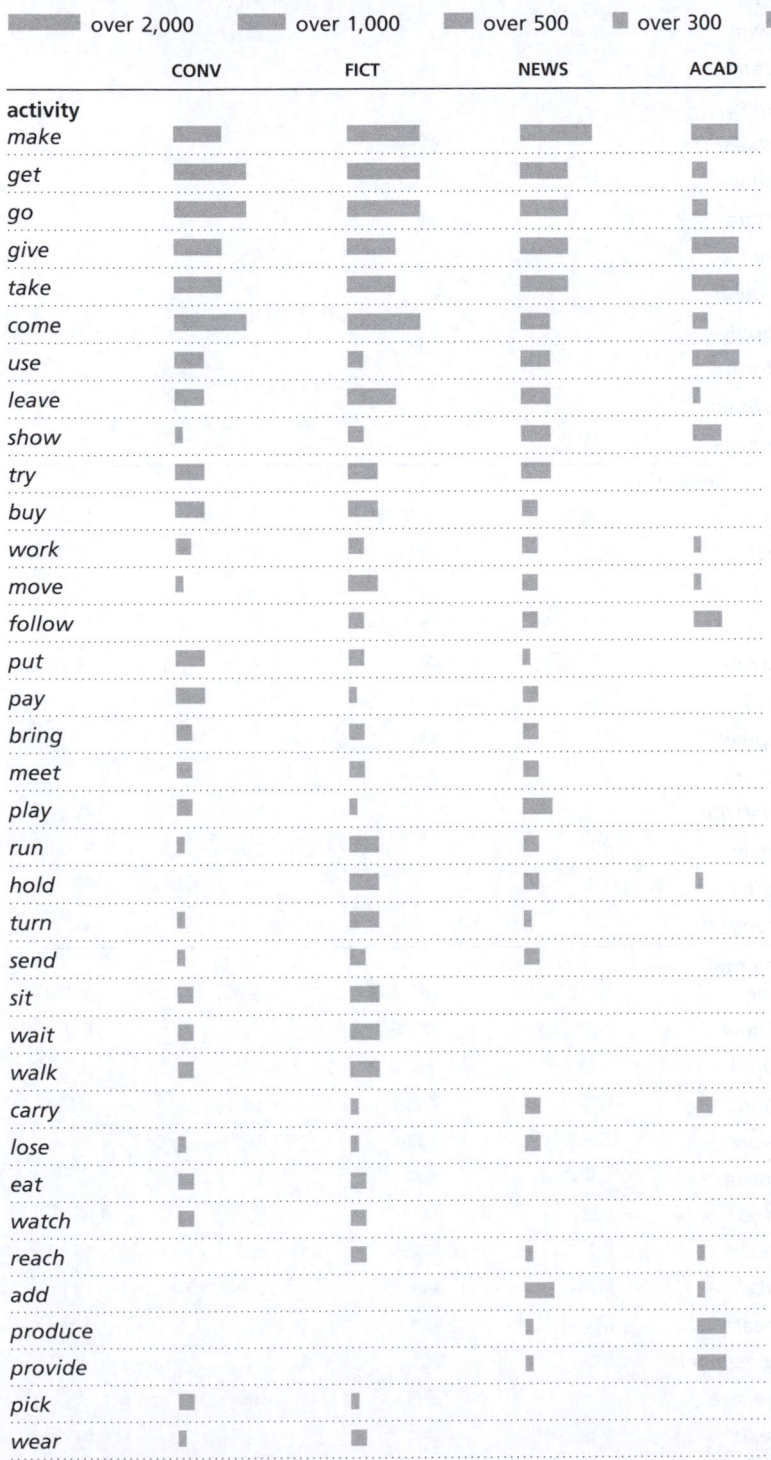

|  | CONV | FICT | NEWS | ACAD |
|---|---|---|---|---|
| **activity** | | | | |
| make | | | | |
| get | | | | |
| go | | | | |
| give | | | | |
| take | | | | |
| come | | | | |
| use | | | | |
| leave | | | | |
| show | | | | |
| try | | | | |
| buy | | | | |
| work | | | | |
| move | | | | |
| follow | | | | |
| put | | | | |
| pay | | | | |
| bring | | | | |
| meet | | | | |
| play | | | | |
| run | | | | |
| hold | | | | |
| turn | | | | |
| send | | | | |
| sit | | | | |
| wait | | | | |
| walk | | | | |
| carry | | | | |
| lose | | | | |
| eat | | | | |
| watch | | | | |
| reach | | | | |
| add | | | | |
| produce | | | | |
| provide | | | | |
| pick | | | | |
| wear | | | | |

Table 5.2    continued

| | CONV | FICT | NEWS | ACAD |
|---|---|---|---|---|
| open | | ■ | ▪ | |
| win | | | ■ | |
| catch | | ■ | | |
| pass | | ■ | | |
| shake | | ■ | | |
| smile | | ■ | | |
| stare | | ■ | | |
| sell | | | ■ | |
| spend | | | ■ | |
| apply | | | | ■ |
| form | | | | ■ |
| obtain | | | | ■ |
| reduce | | | | ■ |

**communication**

| | CONV | FICT | NEWS | ACAD |
|---|---|---|---|---|
| say | ▬▬ | ▬▬ | ▬▬ | ■ |
| tell | ▬ | ▬ | ■ | |
| call | ■ | | | ■ |
| ask | ■ | ▬ | ■ | |
| write | ▪ | ■ | ■ | ■ |
| talk | ▬ | ▪ | | |
| speak | ▪ | ▬ | | |
| thank | ■ | ▪ | | |
| describe | | | | ▬ |
| claim | | | ■ | |
| offer | | | ■ | |
| suggest | | | | ■ |

**mental**

| | CONV | FICT | NEWS | ACAD |
|---|---|---|---|---|
| see | ▬ | ▬ | ▬ | ▬ |
| know | ▬ | ▬ | ■ | ■ |
| think | ▬ | ▬ | ■ | ■ |
| find | ■ | ▬ | ■ | ■ |
| want | ▬ | ▬ | ■ | ▪ |
| mean | ▬ | ▬ | ▪ | ▪ |
| need | ■ | ▪ | ■ | ■ |
| feel | ■ | ▬ | ▪ | |
| like | ▬ | ■ | ▪ | |
| hear | ■ | ■ | ■ | |
| remember | ▬ | ■ | | |
| believe | | ■ | ▬ | |
| read | ▪ | ■ | | ▪ |

**Table 5.2    continued**

| | CONV | FICT | NEWS | ACAD |
|---|---|---|---|---|
| *consider* | | | ■ | ■ |
| *suppose* | ■ | ■ | | |
| *listen* | ■ | ■ | | |
| *love* | ■ | ■ | | |
| *wonder* | ■ | ■ | | |
| *understand* | | ■ | | ■ |
| *expect* | | ■ | ■ | ■ |
| *hope* | | ■ | ■ | |
| *assume* | | | | ■ |
| *determine* | | | | ■ |
| **causative** | | | | |
| *help* | ■ | ■ | ■ | ■ |
| *let* | ■ | ■ | | |
| *allow* | | | ■ | ■ |
| *require* | | | | ■ |
| **occurrence** | | | | |
| *become* | | ■ | ■ | ■ |
| *happen* | ■ | ■ | ■ | |
| *change* | ■ | ■ | ■ | ■ |
| *die* | | ■ | ■ | |
| *grow* | | ■ | | ■ |
| *develop* | | | | ■ |
| *occur* | | | | ■ |
| **existence** | | | | |
| *seem* | ■ | ■ | ■ | ■ |
| *look* | ■ | ■ | ■ | |
| *stand* | ■ | ■ | ■ | |
| *stay* | ■ | ■ | ■ | |
| *live* | ■ | ■ | ■ | |
| *appear* | | ■ | ■ | ■ |
| *include* | | ■ | | ■ |
| *involve* | | | ■ | ■ |
| *contain* | | | | ■ |
| *exist* | | | | ■ |
| *indicate* | | | | ■ |
| *represent* | | | | ■ |
| **aspectual** | | | | |
| *start* | ■ | ■ | ■ | ■ |
| *keep* | ■ | ■ | ■ | |
| *stop* | ■ | ■ | ■ | |
| *begin* | | ■ | ■ | ■ |
| *continue* | | | ■ | |

## Other common verbs

When * follows a verb in the lists below it indicates that it is more than twice as frequent in the passive as in the active form (6.4).

- **Activity verbs**

  Over 50 occurrences per million words—over 100 verbs, including:

  *arrange, beat, check, cover, divide, earn, extend, fix, hang, join, lie, obtain, pull, receive, repeat, save, share, smile, throw, visit*

  Over 20 occurrences per million words—over 120 verbs, including:

  *accompany, acquire, advance, be arrested\*, behave, borrow, burn, clean, climb, combine, control, defend, deliver, dig, be elected\*, encounter, engage, exercise, expand, explore*

- **Communication verbs**

  Over 50 occurrences per million words:

  *admit, announce, answer, argue, deny, discuss, encourage, explain, express, insist, mention, note, offer, propose, publish, quote, reply, report, shout, sign, sing, state, teach, warn*

  Over 20 occurrences per million words:

  *accuse, acknowledge, address, advise, appeal, assure, challenge, complain, consult, convince, declare, demand, emphasise, excuse, inform, invite, be named\*, persuade, phone, pray, promise, question, recommend, remark, respond, specify, swear, threaten, urge, welcome, whisper*

- **Mental verbs**

  Over 50 occurrences per million words:

  *agree, bear, care, choose, compare, decide, discover, doubt, enjoy, examine, face, forget, hate, identify, imagine, intend, learn, mind, miss, notice, plan, prefer, prove, realise, recall, recognise, regard, suffer, wish, worry*

  Over 20 occurrences per million words:

  *accept, afford, appreciate, approve, assess, blame, bother, calculate, conclude, celebrate, confirm, count, dare, deserve, detect, dismiss, distinguish, be estimated\*, experience, fear, forgive, guess, ignore, impress, interpret, judge, justify, observe, perceive, predict, pretend, reckon, remind, satisfy, solve, study, suspect, trust*

- **Causative verbs**

  Over 50 occurrences per million words:

  *affect, cause, enable, ensure, force, prevent*

  Over 20 occurrences per million words:

  *assist, guarantee, influence, permit*

- **Occurrence verbs**

  Over 50 occurrences per million words:

  *arise, be born\*, emerge, fall, increase, last, rise*

  Over 20 occurrences per million words:

  *disappear, flow, shine, sink, slip*

- **Existence verbs**

  Over 50 occurrences per million words:

  *deserve, fit, be located\*, matter, reflect, relate, remain, reveal, sound, tend*

Over 20 occurrences per million words:

*concern, constitute, define, be derived\*, illustrate, imply, lack, owe, own, possess, suit, vary*

- **Aspectual verbs**

  Over 50 occurrences per million words:

  *complete, end, finish*

  Over 20 occurrences per million words:

  *cease.*

**DISCUSSION OF FINDINGS**

## A Conversation

The common semantic domains of verbs in conversation reflect the typical communicative purposes of that register: talking about what people have done (activity verbs), what they think or feel (mental verbs), or what they said (communication verbs). In conversation speakers operate online, so they tend to rely on relatively few verbs from these domains, repeating the same common verbs frequently. The following conversational sample illustrates many of these characteristics:

> A: *Well I, I, I **asked** him what he **wanted** for Christmas.*
>
> B: *Yeah?*
>
> A: *and he **said get** me a padded shirt, he **said**, Joycie's **getting** me one he said and I **want** two.*
>
> B: *Oh.*
>
> A: *So that's what I **bought** him. – And I was **looking** in the <unclear> yesterday – and they **sell** them in You-Can't-Go-Wrong for five ninety-nine <unclear> for Robert.*
>
> B: *Mm. – Ten ninety-nine he **paid** for his. It's a nice, nice thick one though.*
>
> <...>
>
> A: *Anyway, erm – we **went** to the Ca= Polly hadn't **seen** them in the shops anywhere and **went** to Caerphilly market on Saturday morning <unclear> and as we were **coming** from it he **said look** there's a shirt you **want** for Robert there. – So I **thought** well in case I can't **get** them anywhere else <unclear> the market and he **said well we'll have one from here, twelve ninety-nine.** (CONV)

Apart from the primary existence verbs *be* and *have*, all main verbs in this conversation are from three semantic domains: activity verbs: *get, buy, sell, pay, go, come*; communication verbs: *ask, say*; mental verbs: *want, see, look, think, forget.* These verbs tend to be dynamic in meaning, and occur with animate subjects (typically personal pronouns such as *I, you, she/he*). Note that the most common verbs in this conversation are used repeatedly: *get, go, say, want.*

## B Fiction

Fiction has communicative purposes similar to those of conversation, reporting the physical activities of fictional characters, together with their thoughts/feelings and speech. In contrast to conversation, though, fiction shows extensive lexical diversity (and less repetition) in the choice of verbs. Authors of fiction have greater opportunity for careful production, and fictional texts are often valued for aesthetic purposes, resulting in a more varied selection of verbs. Consider the following text extract:

> Pod **made** a strange face, his eyes **swivelled** round towards Arrietty. Homily **stared** at him, her mouth open, and then she **turned**. 'Come along, Arrietty,' she **said** briskly, 'you **pop** off to bed, now, like a good girl, and I'll **bring** you some supper.'
>
> 'Oh,' **said** Arrietty, 'can't I **see** the rest of the borrowings?'
>
> 'Your father's **got** nothing now. Only food. Off you **pop** to bed. You've **seen** the cup and saucer.'
>
> Arrietty **went** into the sitting-room to **put** away her diary, and **took** some time **fixing** her candle on the upturned drawing-pin which **served** as a holder.
>
> 'Whatever are you **doing**?' **grumbled** Homily.
>
> '**Give** it here. There, that's the way. Now off to bed and **fold** your clothes, **mind**.'
>
> 'Good night, papa,' **said** Arrietty, **kissing** his flat white cheek. (FICT)

Although this sample from fiction is shorter than the conversation extract, it uses a much wider selection of activity verbs: *make, swivel, stare, turn, come, pop (off), bring, go, put, take, fix, serve, do, give, fold, kiss*. Apart from *pop*, none of these verbs are repeated in the sample. In addition, this text shows the use of communication verbs (*say, grumble*) and mental verbs (*see, mind*).

### C Academic prose

Academic prose is quite different from these other two registers. It usually reports relations among entities—both concrete and abstract—using simple statements of existence/relationship or occurrence. Academic prose reports relatively few physical, mental, or communication activities—and when such activities are reported, they are often attributed to some inanimate entity as subject of the verb (5.2.3). Consider the following text extract from an academic article:

> It has long been **recognized** that the wide fluctuations periodically **occurring** in acridid populations throughout the world are closely **linked** to weather conditions (Parker 1935; Dempster 1963); the major weather factors **involved are** apparently temperature and precipitation. <...>
>
> In an analysis of 10-years' survey data for Melanoplus sanguinipes (Fabricius) in five large areas in Saskatchewan, each **including** almost 8000 square miles, high correlation coefficients between population indices of adults and such weather factors as temperature, sunshine and rainfall **suggested** causal relationships (MacCarthy 1956). <...>
>
> Since the mechanisms responsible for such correlations **were** not obvious, a more detailed empirical approach was **used** to **investigate** the effects of various weather factors on grasshoppers. <...> While it was **found** that the early hatchling stage **was** extremely vulnerable to adverse weather conditions, the major influence of such conditions on the population as a whole **appeared** to be **exerted** upon egg production <...> (ACAD)

Existence verbs are the most common in this academic prose text: in addition to a repeated use of the copula *be*, this extract contains the existence verbs *linked, involved, including*, and *appeared*, all expressing abstract relations of various kinds. The text also shows an occurrence verb: *occurring*. Although there are some activity verbs, mental verbs, and communication verbs used in this text, the particular verbs chosen from these domains differ from those typically found in conversation and fiction: activity verbs: *used, found, exerted*; communication verbs: *suggested*; mental verbs: *recognized, investigate*.

## 5.2.2  Most common lexical verbs

### 5.2.2.1  Overall use of the most common lexical verbs

Figure 5.7  **Frequency of the most common lexical verbs in the LSWE Corpus (over 1,000 per million words)**

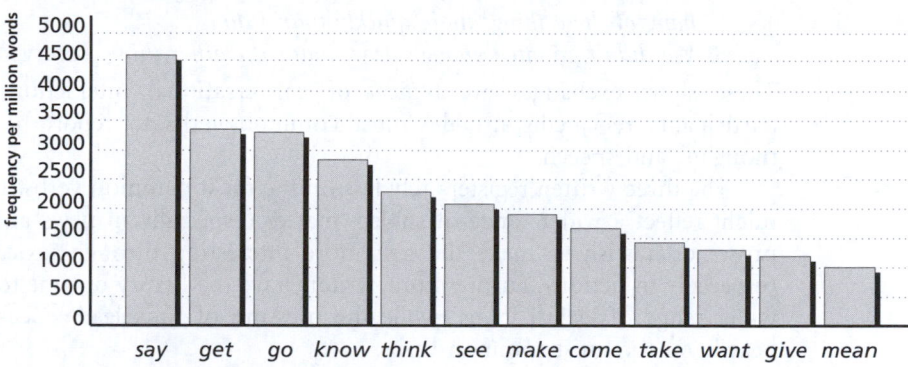

CORPUS FINDINGS [1,2]

➤ The 12 most common lexical verbs all occur over 1,000 times per million words (see Figure 5.7).

➤ These very common verbs are unevenly distributed across the semantic domains:
  ➤ six are activity verbs: *get, go, make, come, take, give*;
  ➤ five are mental verbs: *know, think, see, want, mean*;
  ➤ one is a communication verb: *say*, which is the single most common lexical verb overall.

➤ Taken as a group, the 12 most common lexical verbs occur much more frequently in conversation than in the other three registers (see Figure 5.8). They account for nearly 45% of all lexical verbs in conversation.

Figure 5.8
**Distribution of the most common lexical verbs v. other verbs**

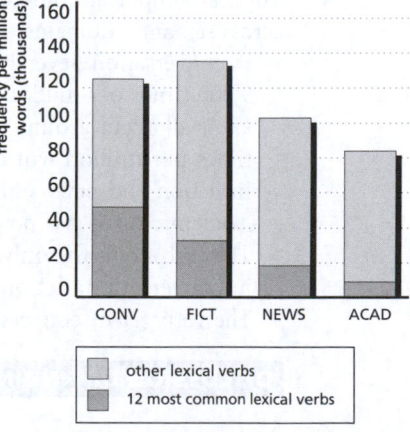

other lexical verbs

12 most common lexical verbs

➤ Conversely, this group of very common verbs occurs least commonly in academic prose, where they account for only 11% of lexical verbs.
(The primary verbs *be* and *have* are also extremely common expressing existence or relationship; 5.4.)

DISCUSSION OF FINDINGS

The following two excerpts illustrate speakers' heavy reliance on the 12 most common lexical verbs in conversation:

  A: *She and Cathy might like to* **come** *because she did* **say** *to me, how is Cathy and I* **said** *she was* <unclear>
  B: *She* **knows** *about Cathy's problem?*

> A: *Yes, she **said** so do you **think** Cathy would mind if I rang her? – and I **said** no I'm sure she wouldn't.* (CONV)
>
> A: *I used to **get** really nervous when I **came** to Chinese restaurants. I never **knew** what to choose.*
>
> B: *Really?*
>
> A: *But gradually over the years you **get** the hang of it. Some people **get** the hang of these things more quickly than I do.*
>
> B: *We didn't **go** often enough dear, that's the other thing.* (CONV)

These short exchanges are typical of conversational interaction, in which participants repeatedly use the most common verbs to report basic actions, thoughts, and speech.

The three written registers rely less on the most common verbs. In part, this might reflect a wider range of subject matter (especially in news and academic prose) or a wish to make the text more interesting through lexical variation (especially in fiction). Furthermore, writers have the luxury of time to draw on a wider range of lexical items, while the pressure of time leads speakers to rely heavily on the most common verbs.

## 5.2.2.2 Most common verbs in each register

**CORPUS FINDINGS** [2]

> ➤ There are important differences in the register distribution of the most common verbs across semantic domains (see Figures 5.9–12).
>> ➤ In conversation, several verbs occur with extremely high frequency: *get* occurs over 9,000 times per million words (almost once per minute on average); *say, go,* and *know* all occur around 7,000 times per million words; *think* occurs around 5,000 times per million words; *see, come, want,* and *mean* are also very common.
>> ➤ In fiction and news, only the verb *say* is extremely common.
>> ➤ Academic prose has no extremely high frequency verbs.
>> ➤ The verb *say* is the only verb to be extremely frequent in more than one register: in conversation, fiction, and news.
>> ➤ The verb *get* in conversation is the single most common verb in any register.

**DISCUSSION OF FINDINGS**

**A Say**

The verb *say* is the most common verb overall in the LSWE Corpus and the only verb to be extremely common in more than one register. No other communication verbs are included among the 12 most common verbs in the corpus. Thus, to report the speech of themselves and others, speakers and writers rely heavily on the single verb *say*. In all registers, this verb is most common in the past tense, in referring to a past utterance:

> *You **said** you didn't have it.* (CONV)
>
> *No use sitting about, he **said**.* (FICT)
>
> *He **said** this campaign raised "doubts about the authenticity of the eventual allegedly free choice".* (NEWS)

However, conversation differs from the written registers in that it also commonly uses *say* in the present tense (c. 35 percent of the time). Many of these occurrences

**Figure 5.9**
**Frequencies of the most common lexical verbs—conversation**

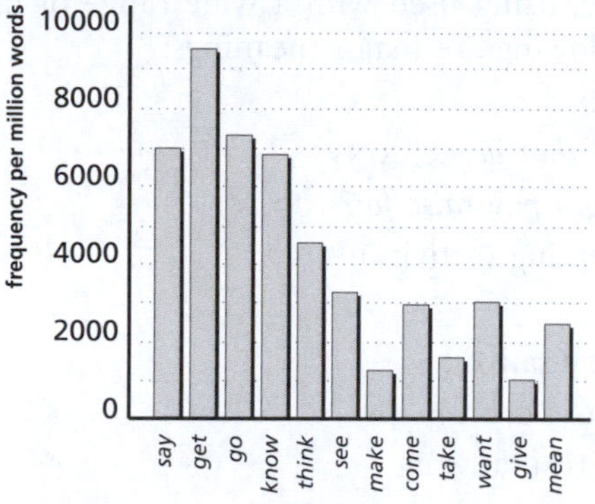

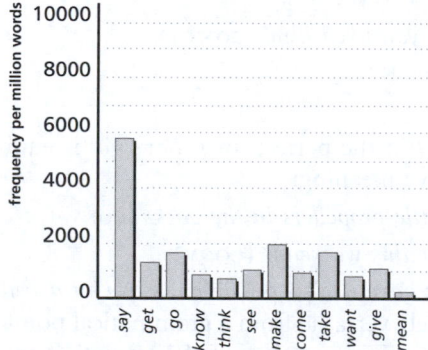

**Figure 5.10**
**Frequencies of the most common lexical verbs—fiction**

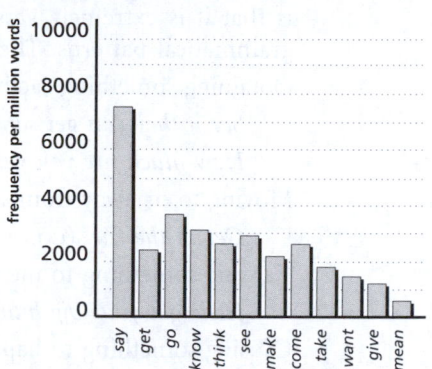

**Figure 5.11**
**Frequencies of the most common lexical verbs—news**

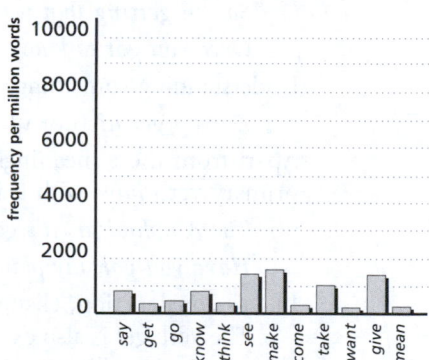

**Figure 5.12**
**Frequencies of the most common lexical verbs—academic prose**

are used to mark past speech reported as if in the present, with an effect of immediacy and personal involvement:

> So he **says**, *Oh my God!* (CONV)

> *Lisa **says** she don't want to come.* (CONV)

Present tense *say* is also commonly used to mark habitual behavior:

> *But she just **says** a lot of things like that.* (CONV)

> *Look mum, he **says** horrible things to me.* (CONV)

Interestingly, jokes in conversation commonly use present tense *say* for both of these functions:

> *And the daughter comes home from school one day and **says** mum I want to be like you.* (CONV)

> *And she **says** yes every time she got her bubble gum in, she **says** no when she ain't got the bubble gum in her mouth.* (CONV)

(For a discussion of *say* with complement clauses, see 9.2.2, and for its use in reporting clauses, see 11.2.3.6–7.)

**B  *Get***

The verb *get* goes largely unnoticed, and yet in conversation it is the single most common lexical verb in any one register. The main reason that *get* is so common is that it is extremely versatile, being used with a wide range of meanings and grammatical patterns. The following are major meanings:

Obtaining something (activity):

> *See if they can **get** some of that beer.* (CONV)
>
> *How much are you **getting** a pay raise for?* (CONV)

Moving to or away from something (activity):

> ***Get** in the car.* (CONV)

Causing something to move (causative):

> *Jessie **get** your big bum here.* (CONV)

Causing something to happen (causative):

> *Uh, I got to **get** Max to sign one, too.* (CONV)
>
> *It **gets** people talking again, right.* (CONV)

Changing from one state to another (occurrence; 5.5):

> *She's **getting** ever so grubby looking now.* (CONV)
>
> *So I'm **getting** that way now.* (CONV)
>
> *Once you **got** to know him you liked him.* (CONV †)

Understanding something (mental):

> *Do you **get** it?* (CONV)

Apart from these meanings, *get* in the perfect form *have got* is equivalent to the primary verb *have* with a stative meaning:

> *The Amphibicar. It**'s got** little propellers in the back.* (CONV)
>
> ***Have** you **got** any plans for this weekend?* (CONV)

In this construction, elision of *have* is also possible, as in *Got a pen?*

The verb *get* is also extremely versatile from a grammatical point of view. The above sentences illustrate its use in a number of the transitive and intransitive patterns discussed in 5.2.4.7. In addition, *get* serves a number of more specialized functions. *Have got* has the status of a semi-modal verb in the expression (*have*) *got to*, which is commonly contracted to *gotta* (6.6):

> *You **got to** take it.* (CONV)
>
> *I **gotta** go down there and work on school work all day.* (CONV)
>
> *Well, I've **gotta** do a few work jobs I guess.* (CONV)

*Get* further functions as a passive voice auxiliary verb when used in combination with a following past participle (6.4):

> *Did it really **get** [blown off]?* (CONV)

Finally, *get* occurs in idiomatic multi-word phrases (5.3.2.3, 5.3.4.2):

> *He was no good she says, she **got rid of** him.* (CONV)
>
> *But if you are white, you can **get away with** anything.* (CONV)

Given its versatility, it might seem surprising that *get* is not extremely common in all registers. It is relatively rare in most written registers because many of its uses have strong casual overtones which are avoided by more careful writers of informational prose.

**C   Give**

The verb *give* is one of the few lexical verbs that is relatively common in all registers. While this verb is used with activity meanings in most registers, it typically expresses relational or existence meanings in academic prose:

> *He's not gonna **give** it to you twice though.* (CONV)
>
> *She was too shy to **give** him more than a covert glance.* (FICT)
>
> *The vehicles will be **given** to the National Association of Boys' Clubs.* (NEWS)
>
> *A good method of analysis is one that **gives** a large correlation coefficient.* (ACAD)
>
> *K values are **given** in Fig. 2.5.* (ACAD)

**D   Other verbs**

Most of the other common activity verbs have skewed distributions across registers: *go* being most common in conversation but also common in fiction; *come* being most common in conversation and fiction; *make* and *take* being most common in news.

The activity verb *go* is extremely common in conversation and also very common in fiction. The verb *come*, which is related in meaning, is also most common in these two registers:

> *You're **going** so slow.* (CONV)
>
> *We might as well **go** and see Janet.* (CONV)
>
> *Here we **go**.* (CONV)
>
> *Then they **went** and sat in rocking chairs in the front room.* (FICT)
>
> *He took no heed of how fast the money **went**.* (FICT)
>
> *He **came** with Alan.* (CONV)
>
> *What **comes** next?* (CONV)
>
> *'Ma, the permit isn't going to **come**', he said.* (FICT)
>
> *Alan's turn **came**.* (FICT)
>
> (The verb *go* is also used in the semi-modal *be going to*; 6.6.)

In news and fiction, two other activity verbs are relatively common—***make*** and ***take***:

> *I thought I might **make** coffee for them all before I go.* (FICT)
>
> *They will also need to **take** the same long-term view.* (NEWS)

Like *get*, both of these verbs commonly occur as part of larger idiomatic expressions (5.3):

> *At 53, Jeffrey Archer's elevation to the Lords is his third and perhaps final chance to **make his mark** in politics.* (NEWS)
>
> *It was failing to **take advantage of** other changes.* (NEWS†)

It is noteworthy that two of the most common activity verbs often occur marking causation rather than physical activities—*get* and *make*:

> *We could **get** them organized up there.* (FICT)
>
> *Mr. Bland said members of his association **make** the collection of debts more efficient.* (NEWS)

The primary verb *have* can also occur with this function:

> *The problem continues to be that a religious-fascist state wishes to hire professional terrorists to **have** me killed.* (NEWS)

Mental verbs, especially *know*, *think*, *see*, *want*, and *mean*, are particularly common in conversation. These verbs report various states of awareness, certainty, perception, and desire. They typically occur with *I* or *you* as subject, and not infrequently occur together in the same utterance:

> *I **know** you didn't do it.* (CONV)
>
> *I **think** so.* (CONV)
>
> *I **think** it was a worm that it had in its mouth.* (CONV)
>
> *I **want** to **see** that flash intro again.* (CONV)
>
> *I **see** what you **mean**.* (CONV)
>
> *You **know** what I **mean**.* (CONV)
>
> *I **know** where you **mean**.* (CONV)
>
> *I really **wanted** her to wear it, you **know**?* (CONV)

Fiction, too, has relatively high frequencies of the verbs *know*, *think*, and *see*, which are often used in the narrative past tense to report the cognitions and perceptions of fictional characters:

> *She **knew** what had happened to them.* (FICT)
>
> *I **thought** I would go and see the Pope.* (FICT)
>
> *She **saw** the light again.* (FICT)

The mental (perceptual) verb *see* is also relatively common in academic prose, where it is used to report scientific observations, or to refer readers to related work in the same or in other publications:

> *The Type I disease is usually **seen** in calves grazed intensively.* (ACAD†)
>
> *There now exists an extensive literature on the construction of social indicators (**see**, for example, Knox 1978c).* (ACAD†)

For the use of these verbs across registers with complement clauses see Chapter 9, and for the use of *I think* etc. as comment clauses with a stance meaning see 10.3.2.1.

## 5.2.3 Verbs with animate and inanimate subjects

**CORPUS FINDINGS** [2,8]

➤ In conversation and fiction, the large majority of verbs, irrespective of semantic domains, occur with animate subjects.

➤ News and academic prose, however, show a higher proportion of verbs occurring with inanimate subjects.

➤ Notably, in academic prose:
  ➤ over 60% of all causative, occurrence, and existence verbs occur with inanimate subjects;
  ➤ over 30% of all activity verbs occur with inanimate subjects;
  ➤ even communication verbs (about 20%) and mental verbs (about 10%) are used with inanimate subjects.

➤ Some verbs from the activity, communication, and mental domains are particularly common with inanimate subjects (see Table 5.3).

➤ Other verbs occurring with an inanimate subject at least 20 times per million words:
  ➤ activity verbs—*bring*, *form*, *get*, *go*, *hold*, *move*, *reach*, *receive*, *reduce*, *turn*, *use*, *work*;

**Table 5.3** **Verbs occurring most commonly with an inanimate subject in academic prose**

| | approximate % of pronominal subjects | approximate % of full noun subjects |
|---|---|---|
| **activity** | | |
| apply | 50 | 99 |
| come | 45 | 60 |
| give | 45 | 85 |
| lead | 90 | 99 |
| make | 40 | 60 |
| produce | 55 | 99 |
| provide | 70 | 99 |
| show | 50 | 90 |
| take | 40 | 85 |
| **communication** | | |
| suggest | 70 | 99 |
| **mental** | | |
| mean | 60 | 80 |
| prove | 65 | 70 |

➤ communication verb—*explain*;
➤ mental verbs—*find, need*;
➤ existence—*stand*.

**DISCUSSION OF FINDINGS**

When we examine the kinds of noun phrases that occur as subjects of verbs, academic writing is exceptional in its tendency to use abstract rather than concrete and animate subjects. The core meanings of activity, communication, and mental verbs usually entail human subjects (agents or recipients; 3.2.1.1). Conversation and fiction, for the most part, rely heavily on these core meanings, so that these verbs typically occur with animate subjects in those registers (see examples in 5.2.3).

In academic prose, however, verbs from these same semantic domains commonly occur with inanimate subjects. The inanimate entity functioning as subject is often an abstraction that is somehow instrumental to the meaning of the verb. Further, instead of describing an activity or process, the verbs in these uses tend to describe static situations or relationships. In effect, they have become existence verbs, as in the following examples (with subject heads in *[]*).

Activity verbs:

Similarly the [findings] of the report **apply** equally to pupils in England and Wales (ACAD)

Social [science], [religion], and the [arts], **make** contributions. (ACAD)

Unfortunately, public [affairs] do not **provide** this degree of predetermination and control. (ACAD)

[Testing] usually **takes** the following three steps <...> (ACAD†)

Communication verbs:

> The [tenacity] of public opposition **suggests** a resistance profound enough to demand explanation. (ACAD)
>
> Yet [investigations] of the writing process **suggest** that there is more than one way to salvation. (ACAD)
>
> It was found that no structural [formula] could satisfactorily **explain** all the properties of certain compounds. (ACAD)

Mental verbs:

> The associated [dispersion] **means** that the free spectral range becomes a function of frequency. (ACAD)
>
> An odd [multiple], on the other hand, **means** that the pump is off-resonance. (ACAD†)
>
> [Experiments] in the Philippines (Palis and Calma 1948) **proved** that transplanted paddy develops faster. (ACAD†)

In addition, several of these activity verbs commonly have a causative or facilitative sense when used with inanimate subjects in academic prose:

> No field treatment can **make** a large difference to the out-turn of total rice. (ACAD†)
>
> It is doubtful that the mere pleasure their harmony **gives** to a selected happy few is worth such large public expenditure. (ACAD)
>
> Note that high sulfur residual oil **leads** to much greater emissions. (ACAD†)
>
> Y is little changed when the hydrogen bond **produces** the complex ZNY. (ACAD)

From the above examples it can be seen that verbs in academic prose are often associated with a following abstract complement, in addition to taking an abstract subject. The following element can be a direct object noun phrase with an abstract head:

> It was found that no structural formula could satisfactorily **explain** all the [properties] of certain compounds. (ACAD)

or a complement clause expressing a proposition:

> The insistence in this quotation on typicality **shows** [that the difference is not an absolute one]. (ACAD†)
>
> No test sequence can **prove** [that one product does completely conform to a standard]. (ACAD)

## 5.2.4   Valency patterns for single-word lexical verbs

Every verb can occur with specific patterns of clause elements, called **valency** patterns. All such patterns contain a subject and can contain additional adverbials. They are therefore differentiated by the core clause elements that follow the verb in a basic clause. (See 3.2 for the definitions of clause elements and their abbreviations [S], [P$_s$] etc.) There are five major patterns (cf. 3.5); [] demarcate the clause elements.

### A   Intransitive

**Intransitive** verbs occur in the SV pattern with no object or predicative complement:

> [More people <S>] [**came** <V>]. (FICT)

**B   Monotransitive**

**Monotransitive** verbs occur with a single direct object in the pattern SVO$_d$:

> [She <S>] [carried <V>] [a long whippy willow twig <O$_d$>]. (FICT†)

**C   Ditransitive**

**Ditransitive** verbs occur with two object noun phrases—an indirect object and a direct object—in the pattern SVO$_i$O$_d$:

> [Fred Unsworth <S>] [gave <V>] [her <O$_i$>] [a huge vote of confidence <O$_d$>]. (NEWS†)

**D   Complex transitive**

**Complex transitive**  verbs occur with a direct object noun phrase followed by either an object predicative (noun phrase or adjective) in the pattern SVO$_d$P$_o$, or by an obligatory adverbial in the pattern SVO$_d$A:

> It was natural to [call <V>] [them <O$_d$>] [photons <P$_o$>]. (ACAD)
>
> He reached out to [put <V>] [his hand <O$_d$>] [on the child's shoulder <A>]. (FICT)

In these examples the valency pattern illustrated is that of an infinitival dependent clause, so the subject is not explicit.

**E   Copular**

**Copular** verbs are followed by a subject predicative (a noun, adjective, or prepositional phrase) in the pattern SVP$_s$, or by an obligatory circumstance adverbial in the pattern SVA (5.5):

> [Carrie <S>] [felt <V>] [a little less bold <P$_s$>]. (FICT†)
>
> I wasn't planning on [staying <V>] [at Terry and Lindsey's <A>]. (CONV†)

Taken together, Patterns B, C, and D are the transitive patterns, which all require some type of object.

Verbs in all patterns can occur with optional adverbials:

- **Intransitive with optional adverbial** SV(+A)

  > He <S> went <V> to the corner shop <A>. (FICT)
  >
  > Then <A> they <S> fell <V> in the sea <A>. (FICT)

- **Transitive with optional adverbial** SV+O(+A)

  > He <S> ate <V> nearly all those chips <O> tonight <A>. (CONV)
  >
  > He <S> left <V> it <O> in the bushes <A>. (FICT†)

Many verbs can take more than one valency pattern. For example, *speak* and *help* can occur with either intransitive or transitive patterns:

- Intransitive

  > Simon **spoke** first. (FICT)
  >
  > Money **helped**, too. (NEWS)

- Transitive

  > The stewards all **spoke** French. (NEWS)
  >
  > As Australia's forward coach, Evans did great work when he **helped** Alan Jones. (NEWS)
  >
  > Study of the appropriate literature **helped** us to extend our background. (ACAD)

**5.2.4.1    Valencies of common verbs across semantic domains**

This section considers all verbs occurring at least 300 times per million words in at least one register (cf. Table 5.2). It excludes prepositional and phrasal verbs (5.3).

**CORPUS FINDINGS** [2,9]

➤  The large majority of notably common verbs in the LSWE Corpus occur with transitive patterns.
  ➤ c. 47% of these verbs occur with both transitive and intransitive patterns.
  ➤ c. 36% of these verbs occur with only transitive patterns.
➤  The number of common verbs taking transitive, intransitive, and copular patterns is not distributed evenly across semantic domains (see Table 5.4).

Table 5.4    **Transitive, intransitive, and copular patterns of common verbs, by semantic domain**

| domain | intrans-itive only | transitive only | copular only | transitive and intrans-itive | copular and intran-sitive | copular and transitive | all three |
|---|---|---|---|---|---|---|---|
| activity | 5 | 19 | 0 | 22 | 2 | 0 | 2 |
| communication | 0 | 6 | 0 | 6 | 0 | 0 | 0 |
| mental | 0 | 8 | 0 | 14 | 0 | 1 | 0 |
| causative | 0 | 3 | 0 | 1 | 0 | 0 | 0 |
| occurrence | 3 | 0 | 1 | 2 | 0 | 0 | 1 |
| existence | 2 | 5 | 2 | 1 | 3 | 0 | 0 |
| aspectual | 0 | 0 | 0 | 4 | 0 | 0 | 1 |
| **total** | 10 | 41 | 3 | 50 | 5 | 1 | 4 |

➤  Activity verbs
  ➤ Intransitive only: *fall, sit, smile, stare, wait*
  ➤ Transitive only: *add, bring, buy, carry, catch, give, hold, make, obtain, pick, produce, provide, put, reduce, send, spend, take, use, wear*
  ➤ Both intransitive and transitive: *apply, eat, follow, form, leave, lose, meet, move, open, pass, pay, play, reach, run, sell, shake, show, try, walk, watch, win, work*
  ➤ Both intransitive and copular: *come, go*
  ➤ Transitive, intransitive and copular: *turn, get*
➤  Communication verbs
  ➤ Transitive only: *describe, claim, offer, suggest, say, thank*
  ➤ Both intransitive and transitive: *ask, call, speak, talk, tell, write*
➤  Mental verbs
  ➤ Transitive only: *assume, determine, expect, find, like, mean, need, want*
  ➤ Both intransitive and transitive: *believe, consider, hear, hope, know, listen, love, understand, read, remember, see, suppose, think, understand, wonder*
  ➤ Both transitive and copular: *feel*
➤  Causative verbs
  ➤ Transitive only: *allow, let, require*
  ➤ Both intransitive and transitive: *help*

➤ Occurrence verbs
  ➤ Intransitive only: *die, happen, occur*
  ➤ Both intransitive and transitive: *change, develop*
  ➤ Copular only: *become*
  ➤ Transitive, intransitive and copular: *grow*
➤ Existence verbs
  ➤ Intransitive only: *exist, live*
  ➤ Transitive only: *contain, include, indicate, involve, represent*
  ➤ Both intransitive and transitive: *stand*
  ➤ Copular only: *(be), seem*
  ➤ Both intransitive and copular: *appear, look, stay*
➤ Aspectual verbs
  ➤ Both intransitive and transitive: *begin, continue, start, stop*
  ➤ Transitive, intransitive and copular: *keep.*

### DISCUSSION OF FINDINGS

Verbs occurring with transitive patterns are common across all semantic domains. In contrast, there are few exclusively intransitive verbs. Only three semantic domains have common verbs that are exclusively intransitive: activity verbs, occurrence verbs, and existence verbs.

Three common activity verbs report simple actions that do not take objects— *come, go,* and *wait:*

> I never used one before until I **came** here. (CONV)

> And then he **went** into the bathroom. (CONV)

> A figure in the shadows **waited**. (FICT)

Intransitive activity verbs can occur with adverbials, as in the first two of those examples. In some of these cases, it is difficult to decide whether the adverbial is optional or obligatory.

Occurrence verbs, which simply document that an event happened, constitute the only semantic domain to include more intransitive than transitive verbs:

> She **died** about two months later. (CONV)

> For a time yet he might **last**. (FICT)

> But this is not likely to **occur**. (NEWS)

> Confusion **arose** because Roding described a whelk under the name of Nucella lap ii/us. (ACAD†)

> Details of the circumstances at Neill's **emerged** only slowly and selectively. (ACAD)

A subset of existence verbs, describing simple states of existence, also occur as exclusively intransitive verbs:

> Oh it doesn't **matter** about that. (CONV)

> Most of the club members don't even **live** in the area. (NEWS)

> The effect can doubtless not **exist** without its cause. (ACAD)

## 5.2.4.2  Variation in verb valency patterns

It is common for grammarians to use terms like "intransitive verbs" and "transitive verbs", as if one verb normally takes just one pattern. However, the reality is different from this. Most common verbs allow more than one pattern, and some allow a wide range. More surprisingly, verbs that have the same potential range of valency patterns are often used in very different ways. That is, there are important differences in the extent to which a verb actually occurs with one or another pattern. In this section we illustrate these differences for several typical verbs with different valency pattern combinations, taken from different semantic domains.

The following are the main valency patterns distinguished in Tables 5.5–5.9:

| | |
|---|---|
| SV | intransitive pattern |
| SVA | copular pattern with obligatory adverbial |
| SV+A | intransitive pattern with optional adverbial |
| $SVO_d$ | monotransitive pattern with noun phrase as object |
| $SVP_s$ | copular pattern, with adjective phrase or noun phrase as the subject predicative element |
| $SVO_iO_d$ | ditransitive pattern, with both indirect and direct objects |
| $SVO_dP_o$ | complex transitive pattern, with adjective phrase or noun phrase as the object predicative |
| SV + complement clause | pattern with a complement clause following the verb |
| SVO + complement clause | transitive pattern with an object and a complement clause following the verb. |

The complement clause patterns are displayed separately, as it is often problematic whether they should be classed as monotransitive, complex transitive, or ditransitive. For example, a clause which fills the role of object semantically may not behave like an object syntactically. Similarly, it is often uncertain whether a noun phrase occurring between a verb and a following infinitive should be regarded as a direct object of the preceding verb, or part of the complement clause with the following infinitive. (See also 9.4.2.)

## 5.2.4.3  Intransitive and monotransitive patterns

**CORPUS FINDINGS** [3]

➤ Many verbs can take both intransitive and monotransitive patterns, but individual verbs differ considerably in their preference for one pattern over another.

**DISCUSSION OF FINDINGS**

### Stand

Intransitive SV+A, with a non-obligatory adverbial, is the most common pattern:

> I just **stood** there. (CONV)

SV occurring with no adverbials is the second most common pattern:

> As it **stands**, this operation requires three addresses. (ACAD†)

$SVO_d$ is found primarily in conversation and news:

> We must keep the score low to **stand** a chance. (NEWS†)

**Table 5.5**  **Percentage of verb tokens occurring with intransitive and monotransitive patterns, as well as with complement clauses**

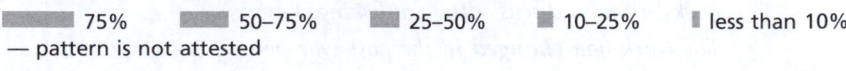

■ 75%   ■ 50–75%   ■ 25–50%   ■ 10–25%   ▐ less than 10%
— pattern is not attested

| | SV | SV+A (optional) | SVOd noun phrase | SV + complement clause |
|---|---|---|---|---|
| ***stand*** | | | | |
| CONV | 25–50% | 50–75% | 10–25% | — |
| FICT | 25–50% | 50–75% | <10% | <10% |
| NEWS | 25–50% | 25–50% | 10–25% | <10% |
| ACAD | 25–50% | 25–50% | <10% | <10% |
| ***change*** | | | | |
| CONV | 25–50% | <10% | 25–50% | — |
| FICT | 25–50% | <10% | 25–50% | — |
| NEWS | 25–50% | <10% | 25–50% | <10% |
| ACAD | 25–50% | <10% | 25–50% | — |
| ***meet*** | | | | |
| CONV | <10% | <10% | 50–75% | — |
| FICT | <10% | <10% | 50–75% | — |
| NEWS | <10% | 10–25% | 50–75% | — |
| ACAD | <10% | 10–25% | 50–75% | <10% |
| ***begin*** | | | | |
| CONV | 10–25% | <10% | <10% | 50–75% |
| FICT | 10–25% | <10% | <10% | 50–75% |
| NEWS | 25–50% | 25–50% | 10–25% | 25–50% |
| ACAD | 10–25% | 25–50% | 10–25% | 25–50% |
| ***try*** | | | | |
| CONV | 10–25% | — | 10–25% | 25–50% |
| FICT | 10–25% | — | 10–25% | 50–75% |
| NEWS | <10% | — | 10–25% | 50–75% |
| ACAD | <10% | — | <10% | 50–75% |

SV + complement clause is found primarily in fiction:

> Could you **stand** being alone with me for five or six days? (FICT)

## *Change* and *meet*

Transitive SVOd is the most common pattern:

> I want to **change** my clothes. (CONV)
> That is why you will never **change** the world. (FICT)
> The girl **met** Ellis while she was living in the home. (NEWS†)

SV is the second most-common pattern, especially for *change*:

> Because of this the neighbours of a junction will **change** and not be the same. (ACAD)

Intransitive SV with an optional adverbial is also found:

> *Representatives of Spain, France and Italy are to* **meet** *in Madrid in two weeks' time to discuss drug trafficking.* (NEWS)
>
> *The work had* **changed** *in the post-war period.* (ACAD†)

### *Begin* and *try*

Transitive SV + complement clause is the most common pattern:

> *He* **tried** *to attack the pit bull.* (CONV)
>
> *He* **began** *to scratch slowly in the armpit of his alpaca jacket.* (FICT†)

Transitive SVO$_d$ is less common:

> *Don't* **try** *it.* (CONV)
>
> *Mr Hawke's government has* **begun** *its controversial plan to compensate the three main domestic airlines.* (NEWS†)

Intransitive SV and SV+A (with an optional adverbial) are common for the verb *begin* in news and academic prose:

> *Martin Wood's course* **begins** *on 1 November.* (NEWS)

## 5.2.4.4 Intransitive, monotransitive, and complex transitive patterns

**CORPUS FINDINGS** [3]

➤ The simple monotransitive pattern is the most common for many of the verbs in this class.

➤ The same valency preferences tend to be found across registers.

**DISCUSSION OF FINDINGS**

### *See*

Monotransitive SVO$_d$(NP) is the most common pattern:

> *I can't* **see** *you.* (CONV)
>
> *A good mineralogical museum is a far better place to* **see** *good crystals.* (ACAD)

SV + complement clause is found primarily in academic prose:

> *We shall shortly* **see** *that pragmatism is less radical than this description makes it seem.* (ACAD)

Intransitive SV is found primarily in conversation and fiction:

> *I* **see**. (CONV)
>
> *He couldn't* **see** *very clearly.* (FICT)

Finally, a pattern found primarily in news is one where an object is followed by a complement clause (either an *ing*-participial clause or a bare infinitive; see also 9.4.2.1, 9.5.2.1):

> *The group does not* **see** *the position being reversed this year.* (NEWS)
>
> *I was disappointed to* **see** *him go.* (NEWS)

### *Call*

Complex transitive SVO$_d$P$_o$(NP) is the most common pattern:

Table 5.6 **Percentage of verb tokens occurring with intransitive, monotransitive, and complex transitive patterns, as well as patterns with complement clauses**

■ 75%　　■ 50–75%　　■ 25–50%　　■ 10–25%　　▮ less than 10%
— pattern is not attested

| | SV | SVO$_d$ noun phrase | SV + complement clause | SVO$_d$P$_o$ adjective | SVO$_d$P$_o$ noun phrase | SVO$_d$ + complement clause |
|---|---|---|---|---|---|---|
| ***see*** | | | | | | |
| CONV | ▮ | ■■ | ▮ | — | — | — |
| FICT | ▮ | ■■ | ▮ | — | — | ▮ |
| NEWS | ▮ | ■■ | ▮ | — | — | ■ |
| ACAD | ▮ | ■■ | ■ | — | — | ▮ |
| ***call*** | | | | | | |
| CONV | ▮ | ▮ | — | ▮ | ■■ | — |
| FICT | ■ | ▮ | — | ▮ | ■■ | — |
| NEWS | ▮ | ■ | — | ▮ | ■■ | — |
| ACAD | ▮ | ▮ | — | ▮ | ■■ | — |
| ***consider*** | | | | | | |
| CONV | ▮ | ■■ | ■ | ▮ | ▮ | ▮ |
| FICT | ▮ | ■■ | ■ | ■ | ▮ | ▮ |
| NEWS | — | ■■ | ■ | ▮ | ▮ | ▮ |
| ACAD | ▮ | ■■ | ▮ | ▮ | ▮ | ▮ |

> He **called** her a stupid idiot. (CONV)
> We **called** this property the 'internal energy'. (ACAD†)

Complex transitive SVO$_d$P$_o$(Adj) is also found:

> I'm soaking wet and you **call** it nice. (CONV)

Simple monotransitive and intransitive patterns are also found:

> Her father had **called** her one evening. (FICT†)
> Mating owls **called** through the darkness of valleys. (FICT†)

## Consider

All six patterns are found:

> The captain **considered** for a minute. (FICT) <SV>
> Now **consider** three contrasting experiments. (ACAD†) <SVO$_d$(NP)>
> They should urgently **consider** employing a good public relations firm. (NEWS†) <SV + complement clause>
> You **consider** her trustworthy? (FICT) <SVO$_d$P$_o$(Adj)>
> You **consider** it the safest and most prudent course for your men. (FICT†) <SVO$_d$P$_o$(NP)>
> She had **considered** this particular manifestation to be fabrication (FICT†) <SVO$_d$ + complement clause>

**5.2.4.5** ## Intransitive, monotransitive, and ditransitive patterns

For this class of verbs, we need to consider two additional patterns.

### SVO$_d$O$_i$ (PrepP)

This is the pattern where the indirect object follows the direct object and is realized by a prepositional phrase with *to* or *for*. These clauses can be analyzed in two alternative ways: (a) as a prepositional verb with direct object and prepositional object (as in 3.5.7; cf. 5.3.3), and (b) as a monotransitive verb with a direct object and a recipient adverbial (as in 10.2.1.7).

### SVO$_i$

This pattern superficially resembles the monotransitive pattern, but it has a noun phrase with the role of indirect object instead of direct object following the verb.

**CORPUS FINDINGS [3]**

➤ Individual verbs of this type can differ dramatically in their preferred valency patterns.
➤ Variation between verbs is far greater than any differences across registers.

Table 5.7 **Percentage of verb tokens occurring with intransitive, monotransitive, ditransitive, and complement clause patterns**

▰ 75%   ▰ 50–75%   ▰ 25–50%   ▪ 10–25%   ▮ less than 10%
— pattern is not attested

| | SV | SVO$_d$ (NP) | SV + complement clause | SVO$_i$O$_d$ (NP) | SVO$_d$O$_i$ (PrepP) | SVO$_i$ + complement clause | SVO$_i$ |
|---|---|---|---|---|---|---|---|
| ***tell*** | | | | | | | |
| CONV | <10% | <10% | <10% | 25–50% | — | 25–50% | 25–50% |
| FICT | <10% | 10–25% | — | 25–50% | — | 25–50% | 10–25% |
| NEWS | <10% | <10% | — | <10% | — | 50–75% | <10% |
| ACAD | <10% | 25–50% | — | 10–25% | <10% | 25–50% | <10% |
| ***promise*** | | | | | | | |
| CONV | 10–25% | <10% | 25–50% | 10–25% | — | 25–50% | — |
| FICT | 10–25% | 10–25% | 25–50% | <10% | <10% | 10–25% | <10% |
| NEWS | <10% | 25–50% | 50–75% | <10% | <10% | — | <10% |
| ACAD | — | 10–25% | 50–75% | <10% | — | <10% | — |

**DISCUSSION OF FINDINGS**

The SV + complement clause pattern is the most common one with *promise*:

> I'll **promise** *I will give you that.* (CONV)
> They **promised** *to write.* (FICT)

For *tell*, this pattern is possible but rare relative to the other patterns:

> You can **tell** *she's from London* (CONV)

In contrast, SVO$_i$ + complement clause is the most common pattern for *tell*; it is also relatively common for *promise*:

*You can't **tell** her to get off.* (CONV)

*He **told** the President that he was obliged to blow the whistle on them anyway.* (NEWS)

*I **promised** Dad that I would have a serious word with you.* (FICT)

Simple ditransitive SVO$_i$O$_d$(NP) is relatively common with both verbs, but more so with *tell*:

*Well I can't **promise** you that.* (CONV)

*They certainly couldn't **tell** her the truth.* (FICT†)

However, it is relatively rare with either verb to find the opposite order SVO$_d$O$_i$, where the indirect object is introduced by a preposition, typically *to* or *for* (11.2.4.1):

*It is against the will of God, who has **promised** everlasting life to all who believe in His holy name.* (FICT)

Both verbs can also occur with only an indirect object (SVO$_i$):

*Let me **tell** her.* (CONV)

*I've already **promised** Carey.* (FICT)

This pattern must be carefully distinguished from occurrences with simple monotransitive patterns (SVO$_d$):

*When her father's drunk enough he can't **tell** the difference.* (ACAD)

*Last week Mr. Badran **promised** further amnesties for political prisoners.* (NEWS†)

Finally, both verbs occur with intransitive patterns (SV):

*Yes, I **promise**!* (FICT)

*She said that only time would **tell**.* (NEWS)

## 5.2.4.6 Monotransitive and ditransitive but not intransitive patterns

**CORPUS FINDINGS** [3]

➤ Monotransitive use generally outweighs ditransitive with this class of verbs.

**DISCUSSION OF FINDINGS**

Simple monotransitive SVO$_d$ is the most common pattern in all registers for both verbs:

*Then we'll **bring** our friends.* (CONV)

*He **sent** his fondest love.* (ACAD)

Ditransitive SVO$_i$O$_d$(NP) is moderately common in conversation and fiction:

*I might not actually **send** you a real birthday card.* (CONV)

*Later, after dark, a boy **brought** him a plate of food.* (FICT)

The alternative ditransitive pattern SVO$_d$O$_i$(PrepP) is also moderately common, especially in the written registers:

*Rumours of closures has <sic> **brought** distress to residents.* (NEWS†)

*You cannot use it to **send** codes or characters to the printer.* (ACAD†)

The SVO + complement clause also occurs but is generally rare:

Table 5.8 **Percentage of verb tokens occurring with monotransitive, ditransitive, and complement clause patterns**

■■■■ 75%　　■■■ 50–75%　　■■ 25–50%　　■ 10–25%　　▮ less than 10%
— pattern is not attested

| | SVO_d (NP) | SVO_iO_d (NP) | SVO_dO_i (PrepP) | SVO + complement clause |
|---|---|---|---|---|
| ***bring*** | | | | |
| CONV | ■■■■ | ■ | ▮ | ▮ |
| FICT | ■■ | ■ | ■ | ▮ |
| NEWS | ■■ | ▮ | ■ | ▮ |
| ACAD | ■■■ | ▮ | ▮ | — |
| ***send*** | | | | |
| CONV | ■■ | ■ | ■ | ▮ |
| FICT | ■■ | ▮ | ▮ | ▮ |
| NEWS | ■■ | ▮ | ■ | ■ |
| ACAD | ■■ | ■ | ■ | — |

> He can never **bring** himself to lie down in the dingy bedroom. (FICT)
> Nearby machinegun fire **sent** us running indoors. (NEWS)

### 5.2.4.7　Verbs taking almost all patterns

**CORPUS FINDINGS [3]**

➤ A few verbs are exceptionally versatile in the patterns they allow.
➤ Monotransitive use typically constitutes the greatest proportion of occurrences.

Table 5.9 **Percentage of verb tokens occurring with each valency pattern, for selected verbs**

■■■■ 75%　　■■■ 50–75%　　■■ 25–50%　　■ 10–25%　　▮ less than 10%
— pattern is not attested

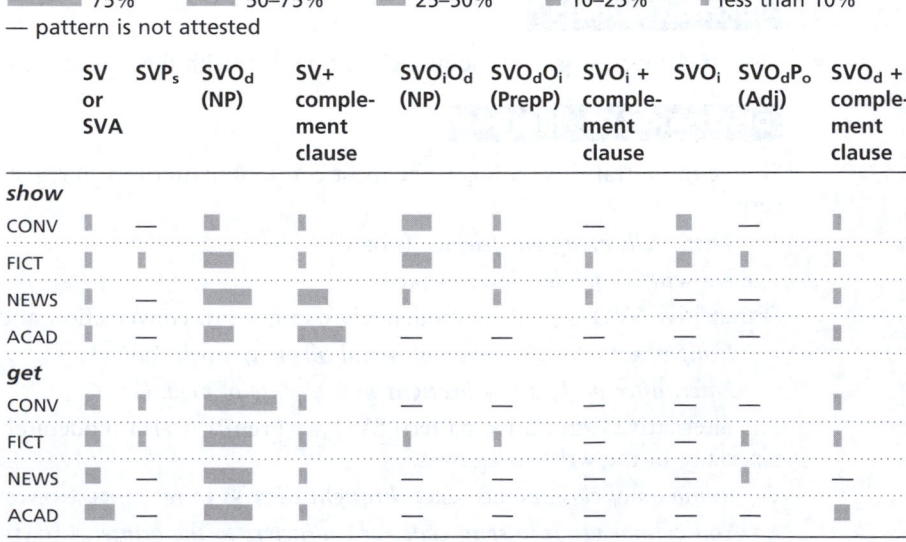

| | SV or SVA | SVP_s | SVO_d (NP) | SV+ complement clause | SVO_iO_d (NP) | SVO_dO_i (PrepP) | SVO_i + complement clause | SVO_i | SVO_dP_o (Adj) | SVO_d + complement clause |
|---|---|---|---|---|---|---|---|---|---|---|
| ***show*** | | | | | | | | | | |
| CONV | ▮ | — | ■ | ▮ | ■■ | ▮ | — | ▮ | — | ▮ |
| FICT | ▮ | ▮ | ■■ | ▮ | ■■ | ▮ | ▮ | ▮ | ▮ | ▮ |
| NEWS | ▮ | — | ■■ | ▮ | ▮ | ▮ | ▮ | — | — | ▮ |
| ACAD | ▮ | — | ■■ | ■■ | — | — | — | — | — | ▮ |
| ***get*** | | | | | | | | | | |
| CONV | ■ | ▮ | ■■■ | ▮ | — | — | — | — | — | ▮ |
| FICT | ■ | ▮ | ■■■ | ▮ | ▮ | ▮ | — | — | ▮ | ▮ |
| NEWS | ■ | — | ■■■ | ▮ | — | — | — | — | ▮ | — |
| ACAD | ■■ | — | ■■■ | ▮ | — | — | — | — | — | ■ |

**DISCUSSION OF FINDINGS**

The occurrence of patterns with *show* is more register-dependent than that of most verbs we have illustrated. In the case of *get*, the range of valency patterns matches the exceptional range of meanings the verb can have (5.2.2.2).

The following illustrates the patterns with each verb.

Intransitive SV:

> I could hear the letter crackling in my pocket and wondered if it **showed**. (FICT)
>
> Don't ask, you don't **get**. (CONV)
>
> Bruce! Go **get**! (CONV)

Copular SVA (with obligatory adverbial; *get* only):

> Either it **gets** through completely or it totally fails to do so. (ACAD)

Copular SVP$_s$ (with an adjective as predicative):

> In one particular quarter it **showed** black against a silvery climbing phosphorescence. (FICT†)
>
> The mug of coffee had not **got** any hotter. (FICT)

Monotransitive SVO$_d$ (with noun phrase as direct object):

> We should **show** understanding for the fear of our neighbours. (NEWS)
>
> Your dog's **got** brown teeth. (CONV)

Monotransitive SV + complement clause:

> Gamow **showed** that the quantitative formalism accounted for the experimental results. (ACAD†)
>
> So they used computer simulations instead, where they **get** to punch in all the assumptions. (NEWS†)

Ditransitive SVO$_i$O$_d$(NP):

> I want to **show** him the cover. (CONV)
>
> Why don't you go and **get** us both a pie. (FICT)

Ditransitive SVO$_d$O$_i$ (with indirect object in a prepositional phrase):

> Can I **show** this to Ian? (CONV)
>
> Noel brought out Michaels' papers again and **showed** them to me. (FICT)

Ditransitive SVO$_i$ + complement clause:

> Another glance **showed** me that it was carried on a stick by a man. (FICT†)

Ditransitive with only an indirect object SVO$_i$:

> Yeah I **showed** my mom. (CONV)
>
> I'll **show** you. (FICT)

Complex transitive SVO$_d$P$_o$ (with an adjective as object predicative):

> Even the ladies of our party, sitting in front, **showed** themselves mildly interested as Ted came by. (FICT)
>
> Her mother warned her not to **get** her clothes too dirty. (FICT)

Complex transitive SVO$_d$ + complement clause:

> But they still **show** boardroom salaries growing faster than middle management's. (NEWS)

*So I am trying to **get** the new librarian to push all those books into one section.* (ACAD)

### 5.2.4.8 General patterns

Several general patterns can be noted from the above accounts. First, the absence of register differences for the valency preferences of most verbs is striking. This is in direct contrast to the large register differences found for most grammatical features, including the relative frequencies of many lexical verbs themselves. This finding suggests that the need for different valency patterns is much more uniform than the need to express the meanings carried by the verb itself. (But see also Chapter 9 for details of register differences between these verbs with different types of complement clause pattern.)

It is also noteworthy that the shortest, simplest valency pattern—SV—is the exception rather than the norm. Instead, there is a strong preference for valency patterns that involve the verb plus two other elements. The overwhelmingly popular pattern is monotransitive SVO$_d$.

However, when the intransitive pattern does occur, it is often filled out with a second element: an optional adverbial SV+A. Furthermore, some verbs (such as *tell*) have as their default valency pattern one of the more complex types, in this instance SVO$_i$O$_d$.

Finally it is worth emphasizing that there are important differences in the occurrence of these patterns, in addition to the different valency potentials. Many reference sources list the possible patterns for each verb. However, it turns out that some of these patterns are commonly used, while others are relatively insignificant (although possible). For example, while *tell* and *promise* have essentially the same range of potential valencies, their exploitation of these patterns is strikingly different (see Table 5.7).

Such differences are connected to the extended meaning of each verb. For example, with *tell* it is important to specify both the content of the telling and who you told it to; with *promise* the content of the promise is most important and the addressee can be left out.

## 5.2.5 Regular lexical verb inflections

We turn now to the morphology of regular verbs in English (2.2.5.1, 2.3.2). Regular lexical verbs have only four morphological variants, involving three **suffixes** added to a **base**:

- The base form, without any affix, is used for infinitives, and present tense excluding 3rd person singular.
- The suffix -*(e)s* is used for 3rd person singular present tense.
- The suffix -*ing* is used for progressive aspect, all persons, and present participles.
- The suffix -*ed* is used for simple past tense and for past participles (i.e. in perfect and passive constructions), all persons.

For example:

| **base** | *look* | *move* | *try* | *push* | *reduce* |
|---|---|---|---|---|---|
| **-(e)s** | *looks* | *moves* | *tries* | *pushes* | *reduces* |
| **-ing** | *looking* | *moving* | *trying* | *pushing* | *reducing* |
| **-ed** | *looked* | *moved* | *tried* | *pushed* | *reduced* |

The suffixes are pronounced as follows:

- *-ing* is pronounced /ɪŋ/.
- *-(e)s* is pronounced /s/ after voiceless consonants except /s, ʃ, tʃ/: *hits, sleeps, looks, makes*; /z/ after vowels and voiced consonants except /z, ʒ, dʒ/: *tries, moves, falls, needs*; /ɪz/ after /s, z, ʃ, ʒ, tʃ, dʒ/: *passes, reduces, recognizes, pushes, massages, watches, manages.*
- *-ed* is pronounced /t/ after voiceless consonants except /t/: *watched, stopped, looked, reduced, pushed*; /d/ after vowels and voiced consonants except /d/: *tried, moved, called, caused*; /ɪd/ after /t,d/: *waited, wanted, included.*

In writing, the following spelling rules usually apply:

- If the base of the verb ends in the letters *s, z, x, sh,* or *ch,* the *-(e)s* ending takes the form *-es* rather than the default *-s*; for example: *pass—passes, push—pushes, watch—watches.*
- If the base of the verb ends in consonant + *e,* the final *e* is dropped before *-ing* or *-ed: reduce—reducing—reduced.* Compare a base ending in vowel + *e* : *agree—agreeing—agreed.*
- If the verb ends in a consonant + *y,* the endings *-(e)s* and *-ed* take the form *-ies* and *-ied* respectively: *copy—copies—copied, try—tries—tried.*
- Otherwise, final *-y* takes the usual endings *-s* or *-ed: play—plays—played.*

For details of consonant doubling when verbal inflections are added, see 5.2.5.1.

## 5.2.5.1   Consonant doubling of regularly inflected verbs

In addition to the spelling changes described in 5.2.5 for regular verb inflections, a single consonant letter at the end of the base is doubled before adding *-ing* or *-ed.* This normally occurs when the preceding vowel is stressed and spelled with a single letter:

| | | |
|---|---|---|
| *drop* | *dropping* | *dropped* |
| *admit* | *admitting* | *admitted* |
| *occur* | *occurring* | *occurred* |

When the preceding vowel is unstressed or spelled with two letters, there is no doubling of the final consonant in most cases:

| | | |
|---|---|---|
| *order* | *ordering* | *ordered* |
| *develop* | *developing* | *developed* |
| *fail* | *failing* | *failed* |
| *avoid* | *avoiding* | *avoided* |

One exception is that base-final *-s* can be doubled sometimes when preceded by an unstressed vowel; for example *focused* and *focussed* are both attested, although the spelling with single *s* is strongly preferred in the LSWE Corpus. By contrast, final *-m* preceded by an unstressed vowel is usually doubled: *program—programmed—programming.*

    More substantial variation arises with base-final *-l.* It is often doubled even when preceded by an unstressed vowel, and a number of English verbs have this pattern:

| | | |
|---|---|---|
| *cancel* | *cancelled* | *cancelling* |
| *model* | *modelled* | *modelling* |

## 5.2.5.2 Doubling of base-final *l* followed by *-ed* across dialects

**CORPUS FINDINGS** [4]

➤ Doubling of final *l* represents a sharp dialect difference between AmE and BrE: when verbs permit both single *l* and double *ll*, AmE is much more likely to use the alternative with a single *l* than BrE.

➤ This difference is remarkably uniform across registers, and differs little for individual verbs.

**Table 5.10** **Spelling variants in *l* and *ll* for verbs in AmE and BrE fiction and news**

**s** less than 50% with double *ll*   **dd** 50–75% with double *ll*   **DD** more than 75% with double *ll*

| | AmE fiction | BrE fiction | | AmE news | BrE news |
|---|---|---|---|---|---|
| dialled ~ dialed | dd | DD | cancelled ~ canceled | s | DD |
| labelled ~ labeled | dd | DD | dialled ~ dialed | s | DD |
| marvelled ~ marveled | s | DD | labelled ~ labeled | s | DD |
| signalled ~ signaled | s | DD | levelled ~ leveled | s | DD |
| swivelled ~ swiveled | s | DD | marvelled ~ marveled | s | DD |
| travelled ~ traveled | s | DD | modelled ~ modeled | s | DD |
| | | | signalled ~ signaled | s | DD |
| | | | travelled ~ traveled | s | DD |

**DISCUSSION OF FINDINGS**

This marked differentiation along dialect lines is a testament to the enduring power of the reform promoted by Noah Webster in the early 19th century in AmE, favoring single *l* in such cases. Indeed this choice makes the basic rule simpler, while BrE heavily favors a practice that makes verbs ending in *l* an exception to the general rule. Similar to the *-ize* v. *-ise* difference (5.2.7), this difference is widely perceived by speakers at a conscious level as an AmE v. BrE dialect marker.

## 5.2.6 Irregular lexical verb inflections

About 200 English verbs, including many common verbs, depart from the patterns described in 5.2.5 in having irregular morphological variants. Regular and irregular lexical verbs are identical in their morphology for *-(e)s* forms and *-ing* forms. Irregular verbs differ from regular verbs, though, in the formation of past tense and past participle forms.

### 5.2.6.1 Classes of irregular verbs

Seven main patterns are used to mark past tense and past participles in irregular verbs:

• Class 1 verbs take a voiceless *-t* = /t/ suffix to mark both past tense and past participles: this can replace a final *d* of the base; for example, *build—built*, *send—sent, spend—spent*. Or it may be added to the base; for example, *spoil—spoilt, learn—learnt*.

- Class 2 verbs take a *-t* or *-d* suffix to mark both past tense and past participle, with a change in the base vowel:

| base form | past tense | past participle |
|---|---|---|
| *feel* /fiːl/ | *felt* /fɛlt/ | *felt* |
| *keep* /kiːp/ | *kept* /kɛpt/ | *kept* |
| *leave* /liːv/ | *left* /lɛft/ | *left* |
| *mean* /miːn/ | *meant* /mɛnt/ | *meant* |
| *bring* /brɪŋ/ | *brought* /brɔːt/ | *brought* |
| *think* /θɪŋk/ | *thought* /θɔːt/ | *thought* |
| *sell* /sɛl/ | *sold* /səʊld/ | *sold* |
| *tell* /tɛl/ | *told* /təʊld/ | *told* |

- Class 3 verbs take the regular *-ed* suffix for past tense but the *-(e)n* suffix for past participles:

| base form | past tense | past participle |
|---|---|---|
| *show* | *showed* | *shown* (or *showed*) |

- Class 4 verbs have no suffix for past tense forms but take the suffix *-(e)n* for past participles, with a change in the base vowel for one or both:

| base form | past tense | past participle |
|---|---|---|
| *break* /eɪ/ | *broke* /əʊ/ | *broken* /əʊ/ |
| *choose* /uː/ | *chose* /əʊ/ | *chosen* /əʊ/ |
| *eat* /iː/ | *ate* /ɛ/ or /eɪ/ | *eaten* /iː/ |
| *fall* /ɔː/ | *fell* /ɛ/ | *fallen* /ɔː/ |
| *forget* /ɛ/ | *forgot* BrE /ɒ/ AmE /ɑː/ | *forgotten* BrE /ɒ/ AmE /ɑː/ |
| *give* /ɪ/ | *gave* /eɪ/ | *given* /ɪ/ |
| *grow* /əʊ/ | *grew* /uː/ | *grown* /əʊ/ |
| *know* /əʊ/ | *knew* /uː/ | *known* /əʊ/ |
| *see* /iː/ | *saw* /ɔː/ | *seen* /iː/ |
| *speak* /iː/ | *spoke* /əʊ/ | *spoken* /əʊ/ |
| *take* /eɪ/ | *took* /ʊ/ | *taken* /eɪ/ |
| *wear* /ɛː/ | *wore* /ɔː/ | *worn* /ɔː/ |

- Class 5 verbs have past tense and past participle forms marked only by a change in the base vowel:

| base form | past tense | past participle |
|---|---|---|
| *come* /ʌ/ | *came* /eɪ/ | *come* /ʌ/ |
| *begin* /ɪ/ | *began* /æ/ | *begun* /ʌ/ |
| *find* /aɪ/ | *found* /əʊ/ | *found* /əʊ/ |
| *get* /ɛ/ | *got* BrE/ɒ/ AmE/ɑː/ | *got* (AmE Class 4 *gotten*) BrE /ɒ/ AmE/ɑː/ |
| *hold* /əʊ/ | *held* /ɛ/ | *held* /ɛ/ |
| *hang* /æ/ | *hung* /ʌ/ | *hung* /ʌ/ |
| *meet* /iː/ | *met* /ɛ/ | *met* /ɛ/ |
| *sit* /ɪ/ | *sat* /æ/ | *sat* /æ/ |
| *stand* /æ/ | *stood* /ʊ/ | *stood* /ʊ/ |
| *win* /ɪ/ | *won* /ʌ/ | *won* /ʌ/ |

- Class 6 verbs have past tense forms and past participle forms identical to the base form:

  **base form   past tense   past participle**
  *cut*        *cut*        *cut*
  *hit*        *hit*        *hit*
  *let*        *let*        *let*
  *shut*       *shut*       *shut*

- Class 7 verbs have one or more completely unmatched forms:

  **base form   past tense       past participle**
  *go* /gəʊ/    *went* /wɛnt/   *gone* BrE /gɒn/ AmE /gɒn/

(See *CGEL* pp. 103–120 for a complete discussion and exhaustive listing of irregular verb forms in each pattern.)

## 5.2.6.2   Regular and irregular forms

Many irregular verbs have regular variants. In these cases, there are usually marked preferences for one alternative or another, influenced by several major factors.

**CORPUS FINDINGS [2,4]**

➤ For many verbs, regular and irregular variants can be used both as past tense verbs and as past participles.

➤ The relative preference for regular v. irregular variants differs for each verb and is influenced by register as well as grammatical use (see Table 5.11):
  ➤ The irregular variant is almost always preferred for the verbs *hang* and *light*, except that in BrE *hanged* is used for the 'death by hanging' sense.
  ➤ The irregular variant is also preferred for the verbs *leap*, *quit*, *spell*, *speed*, and *wed*, although both variants are rare in some registers.
  ➤ For five other verbs—*sneak*, *dive*, *knit*, *lean*, and *dream*—the regular form is generally preferred (although both variants are rare in some registers).

➤ Surprisingly, the transcriptions of conversation show the strongest overall preference for irregular variants.

➤ In expository registers (news and academic writing), the preferred variant for some verbs is influenced by grammatical function (past tense v. past participle):
  ➤ For *spoil*, the regular form is preferred for past tense, while the irregular form is preferred for past participles.
  ➤ For *burn*, however, the irregular form is preferred for past tense, while the regular form is preferred for past participles.

➤ AmE has a stronger preference for the regular variant of these verbs than BrE (see Table 5.12).

**DISCUSSION OF FINDINGS**

As we see from the findings, many factors can affect the choice between regular and irregular inflectional variants: register, dialect, grammatical function (past tense v. past participle), and the individual verb itself.

The expected historical trend is towards a greater use of the regular *-ed* pattern, and thus it is not surprising to find AmE more advanced in this respect than BrE. It is unexpected, however, to find conversation more conservative than the written registers in using the irregular forms.

Table 5.11 **Percentage use of irregular v. regular forms where both variants can be used as either past tense or participle**

R regular form used over 85% of the time
r regular (v. irregular) form used over 50% of the time
ir irregular (v. regular) form used over 50% of the time
IR irregular (v. regular) form used over 75% of the time
— Combined total of both regular and irregular forms is less than three per million

| | conversation | | fiction | | BrE news | | academic | |
|---|---|---|---|---|---|---|---|---|
| | past tense | past participle | past tense | past participle | past tense | past participle | past tense | past participle |
| snuck (v. sneaked) | – | – | R | – | R | – | – | – |
| dove (v. dived) | – | – | R | – | R | – | – | – |
| knit (v. knitted) | – | – | R | – | – | – | – | – |
| leant (v. leaned) | – | – | r | R | – | – | – | – |
| dreamt (v. dreamed) | – | – | r | r | r | – | – | – |
| spoilt (v. spoiled) | – | IR | – | ir | R | ir | – | – |
| learnt (v. learned) | ir | IR | r | r | r | r | r | r |
| burnt (v. burned) | IR | IR | r | r | r | r | ir | r |
| smelt (v. smelled) | IR | – | ir | ir | ir | – | – | – |
| spelt (v. spelled) | IR | IR | ir | – | ir | – | – | – |
| leapt (v. leaped) | – | – | ir | ir | IR | IR | – | – |
| hung (v. hanged) | IR | IR | IR | IR | ir | r | IR | – |
| quit (v. quitted) | – | – | – | – | IR | IR | – | – |
| sped (v. speeded) | – | – | IR | – | IR | – | – | – |
| wed (v. wedded) | – | – | – | – | IR | – | IR | – |
| lit (v. lighted) | IR | – | IR | IR | IR | – | – | – |

Table 5.12 **Percentage use in BrE v. AmE news of irregular v. regular forms where both variants can be used as either past tense or participle**

| | BrE news | | AmE news | |
|---|---|---|---|---|
| | past tense | past participle | past tense | past participle |
| leant (v. leaned) | – | – | R | – |
| dreamt (v. dreamed) | r | – | R | R |
| burnt (v. burned) | r | r | R | R |
| learnt (v. learned) | r | r | R | R |
| spoilt (v. spoiled) | R | ir | R | R |
| smelt (v. smelled) | ir | – | R | – |
| leapt (v. leaped) | IR | IR | r | R |
| spelt (v. spelled) | ir | – | R | R |
| lit (v. lighted) | IR | – | r | r |
| sped (v. speeded) | IR | – | IR | – |
| hung (v. hanged) | ir | r | IR | ir |
| quit (v. quitted) | IR | IR | IR | IR |

Overall frequency of the target verb is not a decisive factor influencing this choice. For example, *lean* and *learn* are high-frequency verbs that favor the regular variant, while *hang* is a high frequency verb that favors the irregular variant. At the other extreme, *sneak* is a relatively rare verb that favors the regular variant, while *spell* is a relatively rare verb that favors the irregular variant.

Some verbs allow a choice between regular and irregular variants only for past participles, the regular form being used consistently for past tense: *shorn* (v. *sheared*), *sewn* (v. *sewed*), *sown* (v. *sowed*), *swollen* (v. *swelled*), *shown* (v. *showed*). These verbs show a strong preference for the irregular form for the past participle, except for *shorn*, which has tended to lose its participial connection with *shear* and to develop a metaphorical usage:

> *In some fearful way this girl had* **shorn** *me of all my force morale.* (FICT†)

*Dive* is unusual in exhibiting variation only in the past tense (between *dived* and *dove*). The regular variant *dived* is used over 90 percent of the time in fiction and news (the only registers with sufficient occurrences to judge).

Some verbs have an alternation between two irregular forms marked by a vowel shift, with no regular *-ed* variant. For these verbs, although both variants are attested for all uses, the variant with the *a* vowel is uniformly preferred for past tense, while the variant with the *u* vowel is uniformly preferred for past participles: *rang/rung*; *shrank/shrunk*; *sprang/sprung*; *swam/swum*. Compare:

> *The Consul* **sprang** *to his feet instantly sober as a judge.* (FICT) <past tense>
>
> *A: He seems tall for his age.*
> *B: He really has* **sprung** *up.* (CONV†) <past participle>
>
> *He splashed into the water and* **swam** *until rocks and boulders rose before him.* (FICT) <past tense>
>
> *Local radio estimated that about 100 had* **swum** *to safety.* (NEWS) <past participle>

However, there is some tendency to confuse the functions of the two forms, for example with the verb *swim*:

> *When his dinghy blew out to sea, he* **swum** *after it, not realising the strength of the waves.* (FICT) <past tense>
>
> *They had* **swum** *from the harbour wall and emerged over the low side of the buoyed sampan.* (FICT) <past participle>

## 5.2.6.3 *Got* and *gotten*

The verb *get* has two irregular past participle variants that occur following *have*: *got* and *gotten*.

**CORPUS FINDINGS** [6]

➤ The combination *have + gotten* rarely occurs in BrE.
➤ In AmE conversation:
  ➤ *have + gotten* occurs c. 140 times per million words;
  ➤ *have + got* occurs c. 1000 times per million words (excluding instances of the semi-modal *have got to*);
  ➤ *got* not preceded by a form of *have* occurs c. 1800 times per million words.
➤ *Gotten* is somewhat less common in the written registers than in conversation in AmE.

**DISCUSSION OF FINDINGS**

The *got/gotten* alternation represents an important dialect difference between BrE and AmE, since it occurs only in the latter. If we limit the comparison just to verb phrases with a true perfect aspect meaning, the preference for *have gotten* in AmE is even stronger. This is because many occurrences of *have got* in AmE have a meaning roughly equivalent to *have* as a lexical verb, rather than *get* in the perfect aspect:

> *Look at that face. He **has**n't **got** any teeth.* (AmE CONV)

This example means 'He doesn't have any teeth/doesn't possess any teeth' rather than the true perfective use of *get* with the meaning 'He hasn't obtained any teeth'.

In contrast, *have gotten* almost always has a perfective meaning:

> *I can't believe Ginger's bike **has**n't **gotten** stolen yet.* (AmE CONV)

AmE conversation is unexpectedly conservative in retaining the irregular form *have gotten*.

Both the simple and the perfective meanings are typically realized by *have got* in BrE:

> ***Have** you **got** an exam on Monday?* (BrE CONV)
> *cf. Do you **have** an exam on Monday?*

> *We **have got** ourselves into a rut.* (BrE NEWS†)

Similarly, it should be noted that there are many cases in AmE where *have got* is used instead of *have gotten* to express the perfect:

> *It could **have got** put in storage or something.* (AmE CONV)

On lexical *have* v. *have got* see also 6.3.2.2, 3.8.2.1, 3.13.2.8A, and on semi-modal *have to* v. *have got to* see 6.6.2, 3.8.2.2, 3.13.2.8B.

## 5.2.7  Verb derivation

Derivational affixes can be added to existing words (the **base**) to form new verbs in English. **Prefixes** are attached to the front of the base, while **suffixes** are attached to the end of the base.

Verb derivational **prefixes** usually do not change the word class; that is, a verb prefix is attached to a verb root to form a new verb with a changed meaning:

| base verb | derived verb with prefix | base verb | derived verb with prefix |
|---|---|---|---|
| *like* | *dislike* | *cook* | *overcook* |
| *lead* | *mislead* | *seal* | *reseal* |
| *do* | *outdo* | *zip* | *unzip* |

Verb derivational **suffixes,** on the other hand, usually do change the word class; that is, a verb suffix is attached to a noun or adjective base to form a verb with a different meaning:

| adjective base | derived verb with suffix | noun base | derived verb with suffix |
|---|---|---|---|
| *active* | *activate* | *assassin* | *assassinate* |
| *simple* | *simplify* | *class* | *classify* |
| *actual* | *actualize* | *alphabet* | *alphabetize* |
| *black* | *blacken* | | |

### 5.2.7.1 Most frequent verb derivational affixes

There are many different derivational prefixes used to form new verbs in English. The most common derivational prefixes, in order of frequency of occurrence, are:

| prefix | examples |
|---|---|
| re- | *reabsorb, rearm, rebuild, redefine, refinance* |
| dis- | *disallow, disarm, disconnect, discontinue, dislike* |
| over- | *overbook, overcome, overeat, overhear, overreach* |
| un- | *unbend, uncouple, unfold, unload, unpack* |
| mis- | *misbehave, mishandle, misinform, mispronounce* |
| out- | *outbid, outdo, outgrow, outperform, outweigh* |

Other derivational prefixes include:

| | |
|---|---|
| be- | *befriend, behead, belittle, bewitch* |
| co- | *coexist, co-occur, co-star* |
| de- | *decode, defrost, delouse, deselect, devalue* |
| fore- | *foreclose, foresee, foreshadow, foretell* |
| inter- | *interact, interface, intermarry, intermix* |
| pre- | *precompile, predesign, prejudge, prepackage, pretest* |
| sub- | *subcontract, subdivide, subtitle* |
| trans- | *transact, transform, transplant* |
| under- | *undercut, underfund, undergo, undersell, undervalue* |

There are fewer derivational suffixes used for verb formation, although some of these are quite productive. The suffixes are listed below in order of frequency of occurrence:

| suffix | examples |
|---|---|
| -ize/-ise | *cannibalize, characterize, computerize, energize, formalize, itemize* |
| -en | *awaken, broaden, flatten, lengthen, moisten* |
| -ate | *alienate, captivate, differentiate, liquidate, pollinate* |
| -(i)fy | *beautify, codify, exemplify, notify, solidify* |

### 5.2.7.2 Productivity of verb derivational affixes

The productivity of an affix can be assessed by considering the total number of verb lexemes formed with the affix. In addition it is useful to distinguish between common and rare verb formations. Uncommon verbs formed with an affix are likely to be either recent coinages gaining currency, or older coinages becoming obsolete. Recent coinages show that an affix is productive, even if the verbs in question are not particularly frequent.

**CORPUS FINDINGS [5]**

➤ The verb derivational affixes are productive to different degrees:
  ➤ The prefix *re-* and the suffix *-ize* (or *-ise*) are by far the most productive, both in terms of the total number of verb lexemes formed and in terms of the number of relatively rare coinages.
  ➤ A considerable number of verbs are formed with the suffix *-en,* but relatively few of these verbs are rare.
  ➤ In contrast, a high proportion of the verbs formed with the affixes *mis-*, *over-*, and *un-* are rare verbs, even though there is not a large number of total verb lexemes formed with these affixes.

Figure 5.13 **Number of verbs with common derivational affixes—conversation**

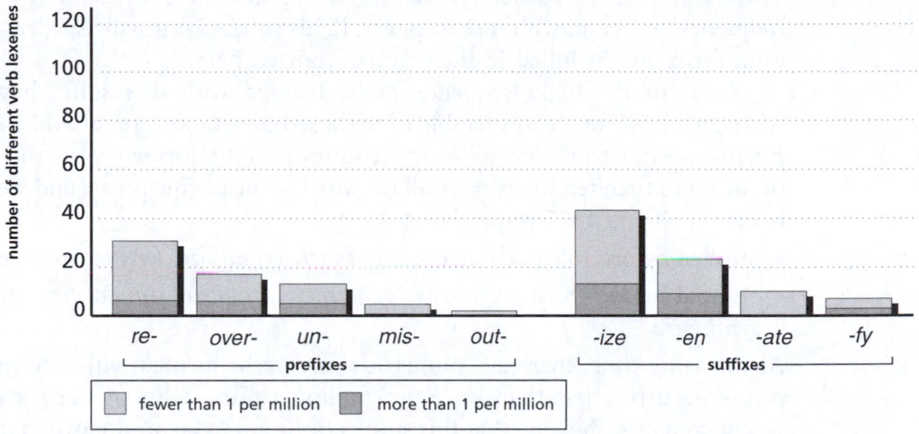

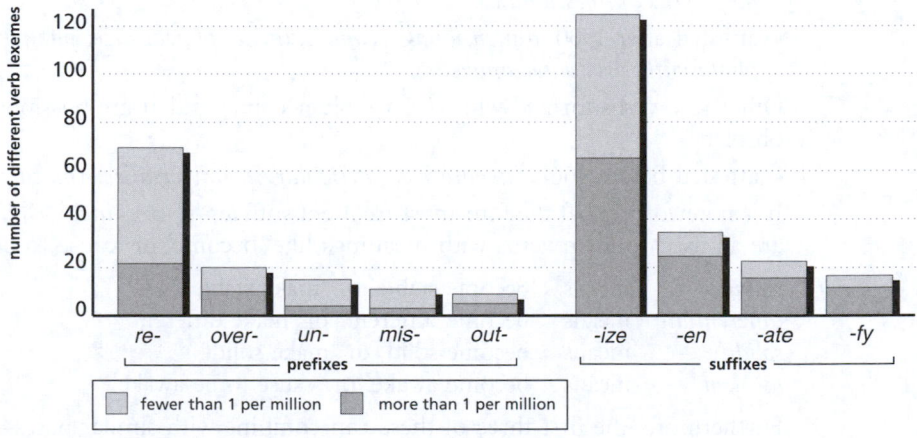

Figure 5.14 **Number of verbs with common derivational affixes—academic prose**

➤ There are important differences in the productivity of verb affixes across registers (see Figures 5.13–14):

   ➤ The suffix *-ize/-ise* in academic prose is by far the single most productive affix in any register.

   ➤ All three written registers are similar in using a large number of verbs formed with derivational affixes.

   ➤ In contrast, conversation uses few verbs formed with derivational affixes.

## DISCUSSION OF FINDINGS

There is a striking similarity between conversation and academic prose in the order of frequency of derivational affixes. This is in spite of the fact that these registers are at opposite extremes in terms of the productivity of verb derivation generally. (See 4.8.1 for noun derivational affixes.)

## A   The common suffixes

The suffix -*ize* is particularly common in academic prose, both with high frequency verbs and with rare coinages. (This suffix is normally spelled -*ise* in BrE; both forms are included in the counts reported here.)

Most of the high frequency verbs formed with this suffix have been in widespread use for a considerable time (based on citations reported in *The Oxford English Dictionary*). The following common verbs formed with the suffix -*ize* occur more than ten times per million words in academic prose, and were attested before 1650 and 1875 respectively:

- attested before 1650: *characterize, criticize, crystallize, fertilize, realize, specialize*
- attested before 1875: *emphasize, generalize, stabilize, standardize, summarize, synthesize.*

At the same time, there are numerous rare verbs formed with -*ize* in academic prose, occurring less than once per million words. Most of these are relatively recent coinages, showing that this suffix continues to be productive in its ability to create new forms:

- attested after 1845: *anthropomorphize, diagonalize, internalize, parasitize, polymerize, professionalize*
- attested after 1900: *dimensionalize, masculinize, phagocytize, phonemicize, photosynthesize, vasectomize.*

Other rare verbs formed with -*ize* are older coinages that are possibly becoming obsolete:

- attested before 1660: *inventorize, particularize, universalize, volatilize.*

It is noteworthy that the four most frequent suffixes— -*ize*, -*ate*, -*(i)fy*, and -*en*— are all used to form verbs with meanings like 'become' or 'cause to be':

| | | |
|---|---|---|
| *stabilize* | means | 'become stable' or 'make stable' |
| *differentiate* | means | 'become different' or 'make different' |
| *solidify* | means | 'become solid' or 'make solid' |
| *awaken* | means | 'become awake' or 'cause to be awake' |

Furthermore, the first three of these can combine with similar bases—especially ones of Latinate origin. In fact these suffixes can be used to form verbs from the same specific base, with different specialized meanings: e.g. *liquidize, liquidate,* and *liquefy.* Only the suffix -*en* differs in being rather restricted to bases of Germanic origin.

The productivity of these four derivational suffixes with similar meanings in academic prose is a testament to the central concern of this register with describing processes and cause-effect relations. These are not only processes and causations of a natural or physical kind (e.g. *crystallize, pollinate, solidify, flatten*) but also connected with academic discussion (e.g. *characterize, differentiate, exemplify, broaden*). However, the ongoing need to name new processes is being met primarily through verbs formed with -*ize*.

## B   The common prefixes

The prefix *re-* is extremely productive in both academic prose and news. Many verbs formed with *re-* have been in widespread use for a considerable time; for example, the verbs *reappear, reassure, rebuild, regain, renew, repay,* and *reproduce* are all attested before 1650, and they all occur over 100 times in the LSWE Corpus. These verbs reflect the importance of this prefix, but they do not in themselves prove that the prefix is still productive. However, as with *-ize*, there is also a high proportion of rare verbs formed with *re-*, and many of these are recent coinages serving the communicative needs of technical discourse:

> *recross, redeploy, redraft, redimension, reerect, reexcrete, rehouse, retitle, retransmit*

Unlike the common suffixes, the common prefixes each have a distinct meaning and are not in competition with each other. This can be one reason why the prefixes *over-, mis-,* and *un-* are used to form many different verbs that are not common, and so are very productive in constantly forming new verbs. It turns out that these rare verbs represent recent coinages as well as very old forms. For example, the following words are formed with the prefix *over-* (with dates determined from *The Oxford English Dictionary*):

- first attested after 1920: *overextend, overgraze, overprotect, overprovide*
- first attested before 1650: *overeat, overfeed, overpay, overshoot, overstay, overstrain, overtax, overweigh.*

## 5.3   Multi-word lexical verbs

There are four major kinds of multi-word combinations that comprise relatively idiomatic units and function like single verbs:

- verb + adverbial particle: **phrasal verbs**, e.g. *pick up*
- verb + preposition: **prepositional verbs**, e.g. *look at*
- verb + particle + preposition: **phrasal-prepositional verbs**, e.g. *get away with*
- other **multi-word verb** constructions, notably: verb + noun phrase (+ preposition) e.g. *take a look (at)*; verb + prepositional phrase, e.g. *take into account;* verb + verb, e.g. *make do.*

Phrasal verbs are multi-word units consisting of a verb followed by an adverbial particle (e.g. *carry out, find out,* or *pick up*). These adverbial particles all have core spatial or locative meanings (e.g. *out, in, up, down, on, off*); however, they are commonly used with extended meanings. In contrast, prepositional verbs consist of a verb followed by a preposition, such as *look at, talk about, listen to.* Phrasal-prepositional verbs contain both an adverbial particle and a preposition, as in *get away with.*

Phrasal verbs and prepositional verbs usually represent single semantic units that cannot be derived from the individual meanings of the two parts. As such, they are often simple lexical verbs that have similar meanings to multi-word verb units:

> *carry out → perform* or *undertake*      *look at → observe*
> *find out → discover*                              *talk about → discuss*

All the above structural combinations can also occur as **free combinations,** where each element has separate grammatical and semantic status. Free combinations consist of a verb followed by either an adverb that carries its own distinct meaning (e.g. *come down, go back*), or by a prepositional phrase functioning as an adverbial (e.g. *live in, sit on*). In practise, it is hard to make an absolute distinction between free combinations and fixed multi-word verbs; one should rather think of a cline on which some verbs, or uses of verbs, are relatively free and others relatively fixed.

The following section introduces the distinguishing characteristics of phrasal verbs and prepositional verbs. Then, we provide a detailed description of each type in 5.3.2–3. Phrasal-prepositional verbs are discussed in 5.3.4, while free combinations are discussed further in 13.4. Other multi-word verb constructions (like *take a look*) are introduced in 5.3.5 and then discussed more fully in 13.3.

## 5.3.1 Features distinguishing multi-word verb combinations

There are a number of semantic and structural criteria used to distinguish the various types of multi-word verb combinations. These criteria are fully described in *CGEL* (16.2–16), relating to adverb insertion, stress patterns, passive formation, relative clause formation, prepositional fronting, *wh*-question formation, and particle movement. The last two of these—*wh*-question formation and particle movement—are sufficient to distinguish among most instances.

Semantic criteria are useful for distinguishing between free combinations and multi-word constructions. With free combinations, each word has an independent meaning, while the meanings of multi-word verbs often cannot be predicted from the individual parts. This is especially important in distinguishing between intransitive phrasal verbs and free combinations with an adverb, since there are few reliable structural indicators. For example, the intransitive phrasal verbs *come on*, *shut up*, *get up*, *get out*, *break down*, *grow up*, and *set in* all have meanings beyond the separate meanings of the two parts. In contrast, both the verb and the adverb have their own meaning in intransitive free combinations like *come back*, *come down*, *go back*, *go in*, *look back*:

> If this was new, I wouldn't let people **go in**. (CONV)
>
> They'll send a letter to make an appointment for her to **go back**. (CONV†)
>
> **Come back**, or I'll fire. (FICT)
>
> And he was afraid to **look back**. (FICT)

Structural criteria are more important for combinations with a following noun phrase, to determine whether the combination is functioning as a phrasal verb, prepositional verb, or free combination. One important factor is the possibility of particle movement, the optional placement of the particle either before or after the object noun phrase. Nearly all transitive phrasal verbs allow particle movement, while such movement is not possible with prepositional verbs or free combinations:

> I've got to **get** this one **back** for her mom. (CONV)
>
> I went to Eddie's girl's house to **get back** my wool plaid shirt. (FICT†)
>
> K came back and **picked up** the note. (FICT)
>
> He **picked** the phone **up**. (FICT)

Compare the impossibility of particle movement with the following prepositional verbs:

> I'm **waiting for** somebody to come and get me. (CONV)
>
> I had never **thought about** them. (FICT)
>
> It was hard to **look at** him. (NEWS)
>
> Availability **depends on** their being close to the root (ACAD†)

Phrasal verbs with pronominal objects nearly always place the adverbial particle following the object:

> *Yeah I'll **pick** them **up**.* (CONV)
>
> *So I **got** it **back**.* (CONV)

Other factors influencing particle movement are discussed in 11.2.4.4.

*Wh*-question formation is an important test for distinguishing between prepositional verbs followed by an object, and free combinations followed by an adverbial prepositional phrase. With prepositional verbs, *wh*-questions are typically formed with *what* or *who*, indicating that the noun phrase following the preposition functions as the object of the prepositional verb:

> *What are you **talking about**?* (CONV)
>
> *What are you **listening to**?* (CONV)
>
> *Who are you **working with**?* (CONV)
>
> *Who was he **talking to**?* (CONV)
>
> *What are you **laughing at**?* (FICT)
>
> *What are you **waiting for**?* (FICT)

In contrast, *wh*-questions for free combinations are typically formed using the adverbial *wh*-words *where* and *when*, reflecting the adverbial function of the prepositional phrase following the verb:

- **Place**

  > **go to**: *Where were they going?* (FICT)
  >
  > **meet at**: *Where will we meet?* (FICT)
  >
  > **walk to**: *Where are you walking?* (CONV)

- **Time**

  > **go on/at**: *When are you going to Christie's?* (CONV)
  >
  > **play at**: *When are you playing?* (CONV)
  >
  > **leave on/at**: *When are you leaving?* (FICT)

These criteria do not always result in clear-cut distinctions among the categories: several verb combinations can function as more than one type, depending on the context; and some particular combinations can be interpreted as belonging to more than one category. Section 5.3.1.1 illustrates several of these problematic cases.

## 5.3.1.1 Multi-word combinations functioning as different structural categories

Many multi-word combinations can function as different structural categories in different contexts. The present section discusses four of these cases.

### A Intransitive phrasal verb v. free combination

Some combinations function as an intransitive phrasal verb when there is no following noun phrase, but as a free combination of verb + prepositional phrase functioning as an adverbial when there is a following noun phrase. The following sentences illustrate both uses for the combinations *stay on, fall in, fit in,* and *come in.*

Intransitive phrasal verbs:

> I *fell in*. (CONV)
>
> He just doesn't *fit in*. (CONV)
>
> I would like to *stay on* and honor my contract. (NEWS)
>
> Details of the crimes in Chelmsford were still *coming in* yesterday. (NEWS†)

Free combinations of verb + prepositional phrase:

> More than an inch of rain *fell in* a few hours. (NEWS)
>
> The mushroom was too big to *fit in* a special dryer at Purdue University's plant and fungi collection. (NEWS†)
>
> Many dealers were content to *stay on* the sidelines. (NEWS)
>
> For *coming in* the opposite direction was an endless flood of motor cyclists. (NEWS†)

## B Prepositional verb v. free combination

A second class of combinations with multiple functions involves verbs followed by prepositional phrases that can be interpreted as either prepositional verbs or as free combinations. In some cases this distinction is difficult to make, since it involves an interpretation of whether the noun phrase following the preposition is functioning as an object (referring to a person or thing) or as part of an adverbial (e.g. referring to a place or time). This duality of function is especially problematic with prepositions that can mark spatial relations, such as *in*, *on*, and *from*. When the noun phrase following these prepositions identifies a location or time, they function as free combinations (with *wh*-questions typically formed with *where* or *when*):

> A person resembling a poor clergyman or a poor actor *appeared in* the doorway. (FICT)
>
> The service of the Irish church *used in* Mount Jerome is simpler. (FICT†)
>
> Bert had *appeared on* the stairs. (FICT)
>
> Members are *coming from* Switzerland, Germany, Holland, ... (NEWS†)

However, when the noun phrase following these prepositions primarily identifies a person or thing, these same multi-word sequences can be considered prepositional verbs (with *wh*-questions formed with *who* or *what*):

> Susannah York and Anna Massey *appear in* the thriller The Man from the Pru. (NEWS)
>
> They are, however, widely *used in* the preparation of special cakes. (ACAD†)
>
> Would-be Barry Normans in Edinburgh are being given the chance to *appear on* a new movie review TV program. (NEWS)
>
> The first goal *came from* Tim Cliss. (NEWS)

## C Transitive phrasal verb v. prepositional verb v. free combination

A few combinations can actually serve three different functions: as transitive phrasal verb, prepositional verb, and free combination. Thus, consider the following examples with *put on* and *put in*.

Transitive phrasal verb function—the particle *on* or *in* can be placed either before or after the object noun phrase:

> I *put* my shoes *on*. (FICT)
>
> He had *put on* his spectacles. (FICT)

*Have you **put** any alarms **in** yet?* (CONV)

*You want someone young, hungry, and willing to **put in** a lot of hours.* (NEWS)

Prepositional verb function—the noun phrase following *on* or *in* marks *who* or *what*:

*They **put** handcuffs **on** me.* (FICT)

*That's because you didn't **put** vinegar **on** it.* (NEWS)

*I'm gonna **put** tomato puree **in** it.* (CONV)

*That's right. **Put** them **in** cold water.* (CONV)

Free combination—the prepositional phrase beginning with *on* or *in* marks *where* or *when*:

*Don't **put** it **on** the floor.* (CONV)

*She **put** it carefully **on** the table.* (FICT)

*I **put** them all **in** the deep freeze.* (CONV)

***Put** it **in** the microwave for two minutes.* (CONV)

### D  Intermediate uses

Other uses are intermediate and might be interpreted as belonging to multiple categories. For example, *come back* meaning to 'recover' or 'resume (an activity)' might be interpreted as either a free combination (since both *come* and *back* contribute independently to the meaning) or as a phrasal verb (since the combined meaning is somewhat different from the sum of the parts):

*Everton **came back** from a goal down to beat Blackburn 2–1.* (NEWS)

*It was not expected that Hanley, who returned from a summer in Australia with a bad pelvic strain, would **come back** before the New Year.* (NEWS)

Of these two examples, the second is probably judged more like a free combination than the first: it can, for instance, be paraphrased by 'go back'. However, neither of these examples is a free combination comparable to the following purely literal example of *come back*:

*When Jim went to the police station, officers told him to **come back** another day.* (NEWS)

## 5.3.2  Phrasal verbs

There are two major subcategories of phrasal verbs: intransitive and transitive. Examples of intransitive phrasal verbs include *break down, come along, come on, hold on, shut up*; examples of transitive phrasal verbs include *bring up, carry out, find out, pick up, point out, take out, turn on*.

Intransitive phrasal verbs:

***Come on**, tell me about Nick.* (CONV)

*Oh **shut up**! You're so cruel.* (CONV)

*But then this damn college kid asked if he could **come along**.* (FICT)

***Hold on**! What are you doing there?* (FICT)

*I just **broke down** in tears when I saw the letter.* (NEWS)

Transitive phrasal verbs:

*Did you **point out** the faults on it then?* (CONV)

> *Margotte rarely **turned on** the television set.* (FICT)
>
> *I ventured to **bring up** the subject of the future.* (FICT)

With transitive phrasal verbs the direct object can appear between the particle and the verb. This is the normal word order when the object is a pronoun (11.2.4.4):

> *Terri **turned** it **on**.* (CONV)
>
> *I just thought I would **point** it **out** to you.* (CONV)
>
> *The warden said that she would **turn** the heating **on**.* (ACAD†)

In addition, a few phrasal verbs are copular, such as *turn out, end up,* and *wind up*; 5.5.

## 5.3.2.1 Semantic domains of phrasal verbs

Phrasal verbs can be classified by semantic domain, based on their core meanings, using the same categories as simple lexical verbs (5.2.1). Like single-word lexical verbs, many phrasal verbs have multiple meanings. This is especially true of activity verbs, which often have secondary meanings in some other domain. For example, the phrasal verbs *make up, make out, sort out,* and *take in* can all refer to either physical or mental activities.

Physical activities:

> *So he **took** it **in** to be looked at.* (CONV)
>
> *I find myself obliged to **make up** ground.* (FICT)
>
> *I know you were **making out** with that German maid.* (FICT)
>
> *I pick them into a lard pail then **sort out** the dead twigs and leaves.* (FICT†)

Mental activities:

> *I used to **make up** stories for him.* (CONV)
>
> *She held up her wrist; on it he **made out** a small dark bruise.* (FICT)
>
> *"I would be delighted, Prime Minister," Andrew stammered, trying to **take in** the news.* (FICT)
>
> *It has given me time to **sort out** my priorities.* (NEWS†)

Similarly, *put down* and *take up* can refer to either physical or communication activities; *turn round* and *wake up* can have a causative meaning in addition to the simply physical activity sense; *keep up* and *set out* can have both activity and aspectual meanings. However, most phrasal verbs have core meanings in only one domain, and the following lists (5.3.2.3) are organized in those terms.

In addition, it is important to note that many combinations that function as phrasal verbs can also function as a prepositional verb or free combination (5.3.1.1). The information included in these sections is based on counts of their occurrences as phrasal verbs only.

## 5.3.2.2 Register distribution of phrasal verbs

**CORPUS FINDINGS 2**

➤ Overall, phrasal verbs are used most commonly in fiction and conversation; they are relatively rare in academic prose.

➤ In fiction and conversation, phrasal verbs occur almost 2,000 times per million words.

**Table 5.13**   **Overall frequency of phrasal verbs; per million words**

each ● represents 100

| | |
|---|---|
| CONV | ●●●●●●●●●●●●●●●●●●● |
| FICT | ●●●●●●●●●●●●●●●●●●●● |
| NEWS | ●●●●●●●●●●●●●● |
| ACAD | ●●●●●●●● |

**DISCUSSION OF FINDINGS**

The distribution pattern of phrasal verbs closely matches that for lexical verbs generally (cf. Figure 5.4), except that academic prose has fewer than would be expected. Thus, rather than being a marked feature of conversation, phrasal verbs are notably rare in academic prose. In their place, academic prose shows a much greater reliance on derived verbs and more specialized verbs generally (5.2.7).

## 5.3.2.3   The most common phrasal verbs

**CORPUS FINDINGS** [2]

➤  The large majority of common phrasal verbs are activity verbs (c. 75%); see Table 5.14.

➤  Other common verbs occurring more than ten times per million words:

  ➤  activity intransitive—*get on, look out, move in, step up, walk in;*

  ➤  activity transitive—*bring in, build up, fill in, keep up, pull up, pull down, put in, put up, set out, sort out, take away, take in, take out, turn on, wake up, work out;*

  ➤  mental transitive—*make out;*

  ➤  communication transitive—*bring up, call in;*

  ➤  occurrence intransitive—*break down, grow up, set in;*

  ➤  aspectual intransitive—*carry on, go ahead, hang on;*

  ➤  aspectual transitive—*keep on, start off.*

➤  There are relatively few common phrasal verbs from the domains of mental, communication, occurrence, and aspectual verbs.

➤  Intransitive phrasal verbs are particularly common in conversation and fiction, but extremely rare in news and academic prose.

➤  The intransitive verb *come on* in conversation is the single most common phrasal verb.

**DISCUSSION OF FINDINGS**

Overall, conversation and fiction show much greater use of the most common phrasal verbs than news and academic prose. This difference is especially noteworthy for intransitive phrasal verbs, which are extremely common in conversation and fiction, but extremely rare in news and academic prose. One reason for this difference is that most phrasal verbs are colloquial in tone. In fact, the most common intransitive phrasal verbs are activity verbs commonly used as directives, often occurring as imperatives. Since imperative clauses are far more common in conversation than the expository registers (3.13.4.2), it is not surprising that phrasal verbs used in this way are also rare in the expository registers:

Table 5.14    **Phrasal verbs by semantic domain across registers (including all phrasal verbs that occur over 40 times per million words in at least one register); occurrences per million words**

Legend: ▬ over 300 | ▬ over 200 | ▬ over 100 | ▪ over 40 | ▪ over 20

| | CONV | FICT | NEWS | ACAD |
|---|---|---|---|---|
| **activity intransitive** | | | | |
| *come on* | over 300 | over 200 | over 20 | |
| *get up* | over 200 | over 200 | | |
| *sit down* | over 100 | over 200 | | |
| *get out* | over 100 | over 100 | | |
| *come over* | over 100 | over 100 | | |
| *stand up* | over 20 | over 200 | | |
| *go off* | over 100 | over 20 | | |
| *shut up* | over 100 | over 20 | | |
| *come along* | over 20 | over 100 | | |
| *sit up* | over 100 | | | |
| *go ahead* | | | over 100 | |
| **activity transitive** | | | | |
| *get in* | over 200 | over 100 | over 100 | |
| *pick up* | over 100 | over 200 | over 100 | |
| *put on* | over 100 | over 100 | over 100 | over 20 |
| *make up* | over 20 | over 20 | over 100 | over 100 |
| *carry out* | | | over 200 | over 200 |
| *take up* | | over 20 | over 100 | over 20 |
| *take on* | | over 20 | over 100 | over 20 |
| *get back* | over 100 | over 20 | | |
| *get off* | over 100 | over 20 | | |
| *look up* | | over 200 | | |
| *set up* | | over 100 | over 20 | |
| *take off* | | over 100 | | |
| *take over* | | | over 100 | |
| **mental transitive** | | | | |
| *find out* | over 200 | over 100 | over 100 | over 20 |
| *give up* | over 20 | over 100 | over 100 | |
| **communication transitive** | | | | |
| *point out* | | over 20 | over 20 | over 200 |
| **occurrence intransitive** | | | | |
| *come off* | over 100 | over 20 | over 20 | |
| *run out* | over 100 | over 20 | | |
| **copular** | | | | |
| *turn out* | | over 100 | over 20 | over 20 |
| **aspectual intransitive** | | | | |
| *go on* | over 300 | over 200 | over 200 | over 100 |

> *You go and **sit down**!* (CONV)
>
> ***Shut up**! Just forget it.* (CONV)
>
> ***Go off** to bed now.* (CONV)
>
> *No, don't **get up**.* (FICT)
>
> ***Stand up** straight! People are looking!* (FICT)

Further, in declarative clauses these intransitive phrasal verbs tend to have human subjects:

> *No, he **came over** to the study.* (CONV)
>
> *He would **get up** at daybreak.* (FICT)
>
> *Crowe **sat up** and stared at Frederica.* (FICT)
>
> *I **sat down** behind my desk.* (FICT)

By far the most common phrasal verb in any register is intransitive *come on* as used in conversation. This verb has three major functions:

As an exclamatory exhortation to act:

> ***Come on**, let Andy do it.* (CONV)
>
> *I mean, **come on**, it's a bit obvious.* (CONV)

As a pre-departure summons to move:

> ***Come on**, we better go.* (CONV)
>
> ***Come on**, let's go.* (CONV)

Meaning 'to start' or 'become activated':

> *The heating didn't **come on** this morning.* (CONV)
>
> *Has that just **come on**?* (CONV)

The combination *go on* is the most common phrasal verb overall in the LSWE Corpus. This phrasal verb is common in all four registers, serving a number of different functions:

As an exclamatory exhortation to act (like *come on* above):

> ***Go on**. Stamp on it.* (CONV)
>
> *It's alright, rub it in. **Go on**!* (CONV)

To mark continued progression of a physical activity:

> *I just ignored her and **went on**. I didn't have time to talk.* (CONV)

To mark continuation of some general action (intransitive):

> *If it failed once, there's no point in **going on**.* (FICT)
>
> *As time **went on**, Liebig developed his thesis.* (ACAD†)

To mark continuation of some general action (transitive, taking a complement *ing-* or *to*-infinitive clause as direct object):

> *Labour would **go on** getting the public's support by constructing strong unity of purpose.* (NEWS†)
>
> *Bjornsson **went on** to study the newspapers of 11 countries.* (ACAD)

To mark unspecified activity, with a meaning similar to 'happen':

> *Think what's **going on**. It's dreadful.* (FICT)
>
> *There's such and such **going on**.* (CONV)

Transitive phrasal verbs are more evenly distributed across registers. For example, verbs such as *put on, make up,* and *find out* are relatively common in both conversation and the written expository registers:

> *Some people they read the top bit and read the bottom bit, and sort of **make up** the bit in the middle.* (CONV)

> *Because you might **find out** it works.* (CONV)

> *Haven't you **found** that **out** yet?* (FICT)

> *He **put on** his business suit and coat.* (FICT)

> *I haven't even been able to **put** my socks **on**.* (NEWS†)

> *For the modern mathematician these numbers would **make up** the ordered pair (V1, V2).* (ACAD)

Against the general trend, a few transitive phrasal verbs are even more common in written exposition than in conversation. These include *carry out, take up, take on, set up,* and *point out*:

> *It is common practice to **carry out** a series of design point calculations.* (ACAD†)

> *The rule also affected Henry Cotton, who **took up** the post at Royal Waterloo, Belgium, in 1933.* (NEWS†)

> *When the Spanish arm of the operation needed assistance he was asked to **take on** a supervisory role.* (NEWS)

> *The EIT was **set up** last year to help fund university research.* (NEWS†)

> *Gushchin (1934) **pointed out** many of the weaknesses of these attempts.* (ACAD†)

Finally, the combination *turn out* (discussed further in 5.5) is unusual in that it is a phrasal verb that can function as a copular verb:

> *Didn't my little pecan tartlets **turn out** very Julia Charles.* (CONV)

> *Auntie Madge and Jo would have several fits if any of us **turned out** sneaks.* (FICT)

### 5.3.2.4 Productivity of particular verbs and adverbial particles

**CORPUS FINDINGS** [2]

➤ A few lexical verbs are particularly productive in combining with adverbial particles to form phrasal verbs that occur frequently (see Table 5.15).

➤ Most of these verbs are additionally productive in forming a large number of different phrasal verbs.

➤ In addition, a few adverbial particles are particularly productive in combining with lexical verbs to form common phrasal verbs (see Table 5.16).

**DISCUSSION OF FINDINGS**

The verbs that are most productive in combining with adverbial particles to form phrasal verbs are among the most common lexical verbs in their own right. These extremely common verbs—*take, get, come, put, go*—are also unusually polysemous, so that they can combine with a range of adverbial particles:

| lexical verb | | selected adverbial particles |
|---|---|---|
| *take* | + | *apart, back, down, in, off, on, out, over, up* |
| *get* | + | *along, around, away, back, down, in, off, on, out, through, up* |
| *come* | + | *about, across, along, around, back, down, in, off, on, out, over, up* |
| *put* | + | *across, away, back, down, forward, in, off, on, out, over, through, up* |
| *go* | + | *about, along, down, in, off, on, out, over, through, up* |

This list also shows how a few adverbial particles are particularly productive in combining with lexical verbs to form phrasal verbs. All of the most productive verbs of Table 5.15 combine with the most productive particles listed in Table 5.16.

**Table 5.15**  **Number of phrasal verb types formed with eight common verbs**

| lexical verb | common phrasal verbs (over 10 per million) | total phrasal verbs listed in *LDOCE* |
|---|---|---|
| *take* | 7 | 9 |
| *get* | 6 | 18 |
| *put* | 5 | 15 |
| *come* | 4 | 18 |
| *go* | 3 | 15 |
| *set* | 3 | 10 |
| *turn* | 2 | 10 |
| *bring* | 2 | 12 |

**Table 5.16**  **Number of phrasal verb types formed with six common adverbial particles**

| adverbial particle | common phrasal verbs |
|---|---|
| *up* | 17 |
| *out* | 14 |
| *on* | 9 |
| *in* | 9 |
| *off* | 5 |
| *down* | 3 |

## 5.3.3   Prepositional verbs

All prepositional verbs take a prepositional object, i.e. the noun phrase occurring after the preposition (shown in brackets in the examples below). There are two major structural patterns for prepositional verbs:

**Pattern 1: NP + verb + preposition + NP**

It just **looks like** [the barrel]. (CONV)

I've never even **thought about** [it]. (CONV)

Britannia said he had **asked for** [permission to see the flight deck]. (NEWS)

A new telephone hotline will be established by York City Council to **deal with** [parking problems in the Barbican area]. (NEWS)

**Pattern 2: NP + verb + NP + preposition + NP**

> *No, they like to **accuse** women **of** [being mechanically inept].* (CONV†)
>
> *He **said** farewell **to** [us] on this very spot.* (FICT)
>
> *But McGaughey **bases** his prediction **on** [first-hand experience].* (NEWS†)
>
> *For example, the 'library manager' **reminded** members **of** [the procedures for ordering library stock].* (ACAD†)

Pattern 2 is also common with passive verbs, where the noun phrase corresponding to the direct object has been placed in subject position (6.4, 11.3):

> *I think the media is falsely **accused of** [a lot of things].* (CONV†)
>
> *cf. People falsely **accuse** the media **of** [a lot of things].*
>
> *The initiative is **based on** [a Scottish scheme].* (NEWS†)
>
> *cf. Someone **based** the initiative **on** [a Scottish scheme].*

Prepositional verbs have two competing structural analyses. On the one hand, they can be treated as simple lexical verbs followed by a prepositional phrase functioning as an adverbial (as in Chapter 10). This analysis is supported by the fact that it is usually possible to insert another adverbial between the verb and the prepositional phrase in Pattern 1:

> *She **looked** exactly **like** [Kathleen Cleaver].* (FICT)
>
> *I never **thought** much **about** [it].* (FICT)

However, the verb plus preposition can also be considered as a single unit—a 'prepositional verb'. From this perspective, the noun phrase following the preposition is analyzed as the object of the prepositional verb. One piece of evidence supporting this interpretation is the fact that, for many Pattern 1 prepositional verbs, the verb + preposition functions as a single semantic unit, with a meaning that cannot be derived completely from the individual meanings of the two parts. These two-word verbal units can often be replaced by a simple transitive verb with a similar meaning (5.3.1):

> ***looks like** [the barrel]* → ***resembles** the barrel*
>
> ***thought about** [it]* → ***considered** it*
>
> ***asked for** [permission]* → ***requested** permission*
>
> ***deal with** [parking problems]* → ***handle** parking problems*
>
> *I won't **stand for** [it]* → *I won't **tolerate** it*

Other structural arguments supporting this interpretation, including *wh*-question formation, are given in 5.3.1 and 3.5.5.

### 5.3.3.1 Semantic domains of prepositional verbs

Like other verb categories, prepositional verbs can be classified by semantic domain based on their core meanings, with many common prepositional verbs being polysemous. This is especially the case with activity verbs often used to refer to mental activities; for example, *deal with, get into, go through, look at, return to, arrive at, engage in, get at, get through, look into, derive NP from, reduce NP to, take NP as, take NP for.*

Further, it is important to keep in mind that many of the combinations used as prepositional verbs can also function as phrasal verbs or free combinations (5.3.1.1). For example *come from*, apart from its use as a prepositional verb, is also common as a free combination in conversation and fiction.

Furthermore, some prepositional verbs occur with both Patterns 1 and 2; for example, *apply (NP) to, connect (NP) with, provide (NP) for, ask (NP) for, hear (NP) about, know (NP) about*:

Pattern 1

> The regulations also **apply to** new buildings. (NEWS†)

Pattern 2

> They were cosmologists wrestling to **apply** quantum mechanics **to** Einstein's general theory of relativity. (ACAD)

Pattern 1

> But I've **asked for** much too much already. (FICT)

Pattern 2

> He **asked** Stan **for** a job. (CONV)

The counts in the following sections are based on occurrences of these combinations as prepositional verbs. The passive alternative of Pattern 2 is cited where this is more common than the active, although both alternatives are included in the counts.

## 5.3.3.2    Register distribution of prepositional verbs

**CORPUS FINDINGS** [2]

➤ Prepositional verbs are relatively common in all four registers, occurring almost 5,000 times per million words.
> ➤ They are particularly common in fiction.
➤ Prepositional verbs are three to four times more common than phrasal verbs (cf. Table 5.13).

**Table 5.17**   **Overall frequency of prepositional verbs across registers; per million words**

each ● represents 200

| | |
|---|---|
| CONV | ●●●●●●●●●●●●●●●●●●●●●●●● |
| FICT | ●●●●●●●●●●●●●●●●●●●●●●●●●●●●●● |
| NEWS | ●●●●●●●●●●●●●●●●●●●●● |
| ACAD | ●●●●●●●●●●●●●●●●●●●●● |

**DISCUSSION OF FINDINGS**

Compared with the distributional profile of verbs in general (Figure 5.4), fiction stands out as having an especially high frequency of prepositional verbs (see also 5.3.3.3). The fact that prepositional verbs are relatively common in academic prose shows that they do not have the same informal overtones as phrasal verbs.

Prepositional verbs have a higher frequency than phrasal verbs. Phrasal verbs have a limited set of adverbial particles available for their formation (5.3.2.4), all denoting location or direction. Prepositional verbs, on the other hand, draw on the full set of prepositions, including important forms denoting non-spatial relations, such as *as, with, for,* and *of*.

### 5.3.3.3  The most common prepositional verbs

➤ There are marked differences in the common prepositional verbs across registers (see Table 5.18).

➤ The verb *look at*, with its extreme frequency in conversation and fiction, is the single most common prepositional verb overall.

➤ *Say to* NP + quote is also extremely common in conversation (and to a lesser extent in fiction).

➤ Several other prepositional verbs are particularly common:
  - ➤ in fiction—*think of*;
  - ➤ in academic prose—*be used in, depend on, be based on, be associated with.*

➤ There are numerous common prepositional verbs in all domains except aspectual.

**Table 5.18**  **Prepositional verbs by semantic domain across registers (including all prepositional verbs that occur over 40 times per million words in at least one register); occurrences per million words**

Legend: ▇ over 400  ▆ over 300  ▅ over 200  ▄ over 100  ▪ over 40  ▫ over 20

| semantic domain | CONV | FICT | NEWS | ACAD |
|---|---|---|---|---|
| **activity**  Pattern 1: verb + preposition + NP | | | | |
| *look at* | over 400 | over 400 | over 40 | over 40 |
| *look for* | over 40 | over 100 | over 40 | over 20 |
| *go for* | over 100 | over 40 | over 40 | |
| *go through* | over 100 | over 40 | over 40 | |
| *wait for* | over 40 | over 100 | over 40 | |
| *deal with* | | over 40 | over 40 | over 200 |
| *pay for* | over 100 | over 20 | over 40 | |
| *get into* | over 40 | over 40 | over 20 | |
| *turn to* | | over 100 | over 20 | |
| *play with* | over 40 | over 20 | | |
| *stare at* | | over 100 | | |
| *glance at* | | over 40 | | |
| *smile at* | | over 40 | | |
| *play for* | | | over 40 | |
| *serve as* | | | over 40 | |
| **activity**  Pattern 2: verb + NP + preposition + NP | | | | |
| *be applied to* | | | over 40 | over 100 |
| *be used in* | | | over 20 | over 200 |
| *do* NP *for* | over 40 | over 20 | | |
| *be made of* | | over 40 | | over 20 |
| *be aimed at* | | | over 40 | over 20 |
| *send* NP *to* | | | over 40 | over 20 |
| *give* NP *to* | | | over 20 | over 40 |
| *be derived from* | | | | over 100 |
| *fill* NP *with* | | over 40 | | |

Table 5.18 **continued**

| semantic domain | CONV | FICT | NEWS | ACAD |
|---|---|---|---|---|
| be accused of | | | ■ | |
| be charged with | | | ■ | |
| be jailed for | | | ■ | |
| be divided into | | | | ■ |
| obtain NP from | | | | ■ |
| use NP as | | | | ■ |
| **communication**   Pattern 1: verb + preposition + NP | | | | |
| talk to | ■ | ■ | ■ | |
| talk about | ■ | ■ | ▪ | |
| speak to | ■ | ■ | ▪ | |
| ask for | ▪ | ■ | ■ | |
| refer to | | ▪ | ▪ | ■ |
| write to | ▪ | ▪ | ■ | |
| speak of | | ■ | | |
| call for | | | ■ | |
| **communication**   Pattern 2: verb + NP + preposition + NP | | | | |
| say to NP + Quote /say NP to | ■ | ■ | ■ | |
| be expressed in | | | | ■ |
| **mental**   Pattern 1: verb + preposition + NP | | | | |
| think of | ■ | ■ | ■ | ■ |
| think about | ■ | ■ | ▪ | |
| listen to | ■ | ■ | ▪ | |
| worry about | ■ | ■ | ▪ | |
| know about | ■ | ■ | | |
| hear of | ▪ | ■ | | |
| add to | | | ▪ | ■ |
| believe in | | ■ | | |
| occur to | | ■ | | |
| **mental**   Pattern 2: verb + NP + preposition + NP | | | | |
| be known as | | | ■ | ■ |
| be seen in | | ▪ | | ■ |
| be regarded as | | | ▪ | ■ |
| be seen as | | | ▪ | ■ |
| be considered as | | | | ■ |
| be defined as | | | | ■ |
| **causative**   Pattern 1: verb + preposition + NP | | | | |
| lead to | | ▪ | ■ | ■ |
| come from | | ▪ | ■ | ■ |
| result in | | | | ■ |
| contribute to | | | | ▪ |
| allow for | | | | ■ |

**Table 5.18**  **continued**

| semantic domain | CONV | FICT | NEWS | ACAD |
|---|---|---|---|---|
| **causative**  Pattern 2: verb + NP + preposition + NP | | | | |
| *be required for* | | | | ■ |
| **occurrence**  Pattern 1: verb + preposition + NP | | | | |
| *look like* | ■ | ■ | ■ | |
| *happen to* | ▪ | ■ | | |
| *occur in* | | | | ■ |
| **existence or relationship**  Pattern 1: verb + preposition + NP | | | | |
| *depend on* | ▪ | ▪ | ■ | ■ |
| *belong to* | | ■ | ▪ | ■ |
| *account for* | | | ▪ | ■ |
| *consist of* | | | | ■ |
| *differ from* | | | | ■ |
| **existence or relationship**  Pattern 2: verb + NP + preposition + NP | | | | |
| *be based on* | | | ■ | ■ |
| *be involved in* | | | ■ | ■ |
| *be associated with* | | | | ■ |
| *be related to* | | | ▪ | ■ |
| *be included in* | | | ▪ | ■ |
| *be composed of* | | | | ■ |

## Other common verbs (over ten occurrences per million words)

- Activity verbs—Pattern 1
  *apply for, arrive at, break into, connect with, engage in, get at, get over, get through, go on, laugh at, look after, look into, meet with, point to, stay with, succeed in, suffer from, work at, work for, work on, work with*
- Activity verbs—Pattern 2
  *attach* NP *to, do* NP *about, keep* NP *in, make* NP *for, make* NP *from, place* NP *in, provide* NP *for, put* NP *into, put* NP *on, reduce* NP *to, spend* NP *on, take* NP *from, use* NP *for*
- Communication verbs—Pattern 1
  *bet on, respond to*
- Communication verbs—Pattern 2
  *explain* NP *to, say* NP *about*
- Mental verbs—Pattern 1
  *agree with, conceive of, concentrate on, cope with, feel like, hear about, know of, sound like*
- Mental verbs—Pattern 2
  *add* NP *to, be faced with, hear* NP *from*
- Causative verbs—Pattern 1
  *call for*

- Occurrence verbs—Pattern 1
  *fall into, run into*
- Occurrence verbs—Pattern 2
  *be covered with*
- Existence or relationship verbs—Pattern 1
  *refer to* (over 40 occurrences per million words)
  *live with, rely on, stand for*
- Existence or relationship verbs—Pattern 2
  *be compared with, be involved with*
- Aspectual verbs—Pattern 1
  *begin with, enter into, start with*

➤ In conversation and fiction, most common prepositional verbs are activity, communication, or mental verbs (see Table 5.19).

➤ In contrast, nearly half of all common prepositional verbs in academic prose belong to the causative and existence verb domains.

➤ Academic prose also has many common activity and mental prepositional verbs.

Table 5.19 **Distribution of prepositional verbs across semantic domains, as a percentage of all common prepositional verbs in each register (based on the register distributions of Table 5.18; number of verbs given in parentheses)**

| semantic domain | CONV | | FICT | | NEWS | | ACAD | |
|---|---|---|---|---|---|---|---|---|
| activity | 38% | (9) | 41% | (16) | 41% | (18) | 33% | (14) |
| communication | 25% | (6) | 21% | (8) | 16% | (8) | 5% | (2) |
| mental | 25% | (6) | 23% | (9) | 18% | (8) | 19% | (8) |
| causative | 0% | (0) | 5% | (2) | 5% | (2) | 14% | (6) |
| occurrence | 8% | (2) | 5% | (2) | 2% | (1) | 3% | (1) |
| existence | 4% | (1) | 5% | (2) | 16% | (7) | 26% | (11) |
| **total** | 100% | (24) | 100% | (39) | 100% | (44) | 100% | (42) |

➤ Activity verbs and mental verbs are well represented in all registers, but there is a marked difference in their use of the two structural patterns (see Table 5.20):

➤ Conversation and fiction have a very strong preference for Pattern 1, with a single object (verb + preposition + NP).

➤ Academic prose has the opposite preference for Pattern 2, with double objects (verb + NP + preposition + NP); this pattern frequently occurs in the passive version: passive verb + preposition + NP.

### DISCUSSION OF FINDINGS

Because of the topics and purposes typical of conversation and fiction, these registers have many common prepositional verbs that are activity, communication, or mental verbs (similar to the distribution of single word verbs; 5.2.1.3). The most common of all, *look at*, is used in two main ways.

To direct the attention of others:

**Look at** *that great big tree stuck under the bridge!* (CONV)

**Look at** *me.* (FICT)

**Table 5.20**   **Distribution of prepositional verbs across structural patterns, as a percentage of all common prepositional verbs in each register (based on the register distributions of Table 5.18; number of verbs given in parentheses)**

| valency pattern | CONV | | FICT | | NEWS | | ACAD | |
|---|---|---|---|---|---|---|---|---|
| Pattern 1:<br>verb + preposition + NP | 92% | (22) | 87% | (34) | 64% | (28) | 43% | (18) |
| Pattern 2:<br>verb + NP + preposition + NP | 8% | (2) | 13% | (5) | 36% | (16) | 57% | (24) |
| **total** | 100% | (24) | 100% | (39) | 100% | (44) | 100% | (42) |

To describe actions involving sight:

> I want to **look at** the animals. (CONV)
>
> He ain't **looking at** her, is he? (CONV)
>
> I **looked at** that and thought it would be nice. (CONV)
>
> The boys **looked at** each other tearfully unbelieving. (FICT)

The communication verb *say NP to NP* is also very common, especially in conversation but also in fiction. This prepositional verb is used to report the content of speech (the direct object), while also identifying the addressee (the prepositional object). In many examples with *say to*, a clause is used to report what was said; this clause is often postponed to final position following the principle of end weight (11.1.3):

> I **said to** Russell [I will never ever take speed]. (CONV)
>
> I keep **saying to** Michael [it's so expensive]. (CONV)
>
> Anyway, I **says to** Di [I'm not doing any in this]. (CONV)

In some examples, the quoted speech is actually given as a separate main clause (cf. 3.11.5, 11.2.3.6–7):

> [Wow], Isidore **said to** himself. [It really sounds as if it's dying]. (FICT)

In conversation, this construction is often spread across two complete clauses with *say*: the first identifies the addressee and the second reports the speech quote:

> Did you hear what that man **said to** his little girl? He **said**, [oh look, there's two boys and a girl]. (CONV)
>
> I **said to** Nick, I **said** [I bet something happens at the ball]. (CONV)

Beyond these two especially frequent verbs, conversation and fiction use a number of other common prepositional verbs to mark physical activities, communication acts, and mental processes.

Activity:

> Couldn't he just **put** it **in** his bean bag? (CONV)
>
> Pity we couldn't **go for** a romp around a canal, isn't it? (CONV)
>
> Patrice held her breath, **waiting for** Lettie's reply. (FICT)
>
> He **stared at** me blankly, unbelievingly. (FICT)
>
> "I am **looking for** a man," the lieutenant said. (FICT)

Communication:

> Just **talk to** her. (CONV)
>
> I was **talking about** the old sort of diesel multiple unit. (CONV)
>
> He **spoke to** Paul in a bitter, controlled tone. (FICT†)

Mental:

> *What did they **think of** the brochure then?* (CONV)
>
> *And then of course I always **thought of** Laurel.* (FICT†)
>
> *I was **thinking about** the playgroup downstairs.* (CONV)
>
> *Since when does nobody **listen to** you?* (CONV)

Academic prose also uses several common prepositional verbs marking physical activities and mental states. However, these are mostly verbs that take the double object Pattern 2, and they are typically used in the passive voice. The most common of these is the prepositional verb *use* NP *in*:

> *We will continue to **use** Table 5.2 **in** our economic analysis.* (ACAD†)

Following the typical pattern, this verb is much more common in the passive voice: *(be) used in*. As is usual in the passive, the agent of the verb—the person doing the 'using'—is not specified. Rather, the thing being used is given prominence in relation to some particular use:

> *It can also sometimes be used to signify a disinfecting agent **used in** a weaker concentration.* (ACAD†)
>
> *The models of community **used in** this argument are ideal in several ways.* (ACAD)

Because academic writing focuses on the relations among inanimate entities, rather than the animate agent performing actions, there is a strong preference for using Pattern 2 prepositional verbs in the passive voice, often with a preceding modal verb. The following are other examples:

Activity verbs:

> *For example, the Message Type can **be derived from** its internal structure.* (ACAD)
>
> *Similarly other parts of the body may **be used as** bases to start from.* (ACAD†)
>
> *The method outlined could now **be applied to** a selected number of points along the blade length.* (ACAD)

Mental verbs:

> *This induced mustiness **is known as** Sierra rice.* (ACAD)
>
> *The electron may **be regarded as** a tiny mass carrying a negative charge.* (ACAD†)
>
> *All members of the specified Role Class **are considered as** possible senders of the received message.* (ACAD†)

For similar reasons, academic prose uses a number of common prepositional verbs of causation and existence, in addition to the verb *occur in*; these verbs typically show relations among entities rather than describing actions.

Causative verbs:

> *Further experimentation might **lead to** the identification of other difficulty factors.* (ACAD†)
>
> *Replacing the nonsense stems by English stems would have **resulted in** a grammatically correct sequence.* (ACAD†)
>
> *Patrons and brokers **contributed to** the widespread belief that a wastah (an intermediary) was the necessary means to contact.* (ACAD)

Existence verbs:

> It will **depend on** the purpose of, and audience for, the writing. (ACAD)
> Mental models **related to** the physical domain are therefore in general
> necessary. (ACAD†)

Occurrence verbs:

> It **occurs in** many manganese ore bodies and is usually associated with
> metasomatic activity. (ACAD)

## 5.3.3.4 Productivity of particular verbs and prepositions

**CORPUS FINDINGS** [2]

➤ A few lexical verbs combine with multiple prepositions to form common prepositional verbs, but (unlike the case of phrasal verbs) none of these verbs is particularly productive (see Table 5.21).

➤ In contrast, some prepositions are very productive in combining with lexical verbs to form prepositional verbs (see Table 5.22).

**Table 5.21** **Number of prepositional verb types formed with seven common verbs; based on all prepositional verbs occurring more than 10 times per million words**

| lexical verb | prepositional verbs |
|---|---|
| get | 5 |
| look | 5 |
| work | 4 |
| go | 3 |
| know | 3 |
| hear | 3 |
| use | 3 |

**DISCUSSION OF FINDINGS**

The most productive word forms used for prepositional verbs tend to be different from those used for phrasal verbs. Only the verbs *get* and *go* overlap on the two lists, while only *in* and *on* are productive as both adverbial particle and preposition. In general, there are a large number of verbs used to form prepositional verbs, and these are distributed widely across semantic domains. However, few individual verbs are very frequent or productive. In contrast, the verbs used to form phrasal verbs primarily refer to physical activities, and a few of these verbs are particularly frequent and productive. There is a similar contrast in the particles/prepositions used in these combinations. While all adverbial particles used with phrasal verbs have spatial/locative core meanings, a much wider range of prepositions is used to form prepositional verbs.

Table 5.22    **Number of prepositional verb types formed with 10 common prepositions; based on all prepositional verbs occurring more than 10 times per million words**

| preposition | prepositional verbs |
|---|---|
| *to* | 21 |
| *with* | 14 |
| *for* | 16 |
| *in* | 13 |
| *on* | 12 |
| *into* | 7 |
| *about* | 6 |
| *of* | 6 |
| *at* | 6 |
| *as* | 5 |

## 5.3.4    Phrasal-prepositional verbs

The third major type of multi-word verb has characteristics of both phrasal and prepositional verbs: phrasal-prepositional verbs consist of a lexical verb combined with an adverbial particle plus a preposition. As with prepositional verbs (5.3.1, 5.3.3), the complement of the preposition in these constructions functions as the direct object of the phrasal-prepositional verb (shown in *[]* below). There are two major structural patterns for phrasal-prepositional verbs.

**Pattern 1: NP + verb + particle + preposition + NP:**

> *Oh I shall* **look forward to** *[this] now.* (CONV)
>
> *But since there was no other mill, people had to* **put up with** *[such treatment].* (FICT)
>
> *Perhaps I can* **get out of** *[it] without having to tell her anything.* (FICT)
>
> *No one has been able to* **come up with** *[a product as lucrative and easy to market as opium].* (NEWS†)

**Pattern 2: NP + verb + NP + particle + preposition + NP:**

> *I could* **hand** *him* **over to** *[Sadiq].* (FICT)

Only a few phrasal-prepositional verbs can take two objects. Another is *put NP up to NP.*

Phrasal-prepositional verbs function as a semantic unit and can sometimes be replaced by a single transitive lexical verb with similar meaning:

> *put up with [such treatment]* → *tolerate [such treatment]*
>
> *get out of [it]* → *avoid [it]*
>
> *look forward to [this]* → *anticipate [this].*

## 5.3.4.1    Register distribution of phrasal-prepositional verbs

**CORPUS FINDINGS [2]**

The overall frequency of phrasal-prepositional verbs is here organized by semantic domain. As before, the passive variant is cited if that is more common than the active.

➤ Phrasal-prepositional verbs are somewhat more common in conversation and fiction, but they are particularly rare in academic prose (only about 50 per million words; see Table 5.23).

➤ In comparison with phrasal verbs and prepositional verbs, phrasal-prepositional verbs are generally rare (see Table 5.24).

**Table 5.23    Overall frequency of phrasal-prepositional verbs across registers; occurrences per million words**

each ● represents 50

| | |
|---|---|
| CONV | ● ● ● ● ● ● ● |
| FICT | ● ● ● ● ● ● ● ● |
| NEWS | ● ● ● ● |
| ACAD | ● |

**Table 5.24    Overall corpus frequency of multi-word verb types; occurrences per million words**

each ● represents 100

| | |
|---|---|
| phrasal verbs | ● ● ● ● ● ● ● ● ● ● ● ● ● ● ● ● |
| prepositional verbs | ● ● ● ● ● ● ● ● ● ● ● ● ● ● ● ● ● ● ● ● ● ● ● ● ● ● <br> ● ● ● ● ● ● ● ● ● ● ● ● ● ● ● ● ● ● ● ● ● ● ● ● ● ● |
| phrasal-prepositional verbs | ● ● ● |

**DISCUSSION OF FINDINGS**

Although phrasal-prepositional verbs are similar to prepositional verbs in their valency patterns, their register distribution is more similar to phrasal verbs (cf. Tables 5.13, 5.17, and 5.23). In particular, both phrasal verbs and phrasal-prepositional verbs are notably rare in academic prose. As the following sections show, phrasal-prepositional verbs are also similar to phrasal verbs in being used primarily for physical activities, in contrast to the wide range of meanings associated with prepositional verbs. The relative absence of phrasal-prepositional verbs in the occurrence, existence, and causative domains helps to account for their rarity in academic prose.

## 5.3.4.2    The most common phrasal-prepositional verbs

➤ Most common phrasal-prepositional verbs are activity verbs (see Table 5.25).
  ➤ The most frequent verb overall is *get out of*.
  ➤ *Come out of* and *get back to* are also relatively frequent.
➤ In the mental domain, *look forward to* is the most common verb.
➤ Very few phrasal-prepositional verbs are used commonly with two objects (Pattern 2); however, two passive verbs occur with moderate frequency in academic prose: *be set up in* and *be set out in*.

**DISCUSSION OF FINDINGS**

Most common phrasal-prepositional verbs are activity verbs, especially in conversation and fiction. The combination *get out of* is the most frequent, with two major uses.

Imperative:

> Just **get out of** my way. (CONV)
>
> **Get out of** there. (CONV)

Declarative:

> We have to **get out of** here. (FICT)

Several other activity phrasal-prepositional verbs are relatively common in these two registers:

> I've never heard a word **come out of** her mouth. (CONV)
>
> You can **go up to** full beam, can't you? (CONV)
>
> Stop yakking and **get on with** it! (CONV)
>
> Omi **came out of** his reverie. (FICT†)
>
> He said he would **get back to** me P.M. (FICT)
>
> Burns **went up to** the soldiers and started talking. (FICT)

Apart from these activity verbs, only the mental verb *look forward to* is relatively common across registers, occurring especially in fiction and news:

> She had been **looking forward to** this moment. (FICT)

In the case of news reportage, this verb typically occurs in direct or reported speech:

> We are **looking forward to** the game. (NEWS)
>
> He said he was **looking forward to** the results of the inquiry. (NEWS†)

Two other phrasal-prepositional verbs are relatively common in news reportage—*get back to* and *come up with*:

> It's going to take time for you to **get back to** full strength. (NEWS)
>
> The panel will be asked to **come up with** the best all-time team on earth. (NEWS)

Finally, although phrasal-prepositional verbs are generally rare in academic prose, the single verb *be set out in* (*set NP out in*) is commonly used to identify the source of information:

> These project objectives were **set out in** the first project report. (ACAD)
>
> There are three forms of statutory demand **set out in** Schedule 4. (ACAD†)

Table 5.25    **Phrasal-prepositional verbs by semantic domain across registers, including all prepositional verbs that occur over 10 times per million words in at least one register; occurrences per million words**

▓▓▓ over 40     ▓▓ over 20     ▓ over 10

| semantic domain | CONV | FICT | NEWS | ACAD |
|---|---|---|---|---|
| **activity** | | | | |
| *get out of* | ▓▓▓ | ▓▓▓ | ▓ | |
| *come out of* | ▓▓ | ▓▓▓ | ▓ | |
| *get back to* | ▓ | ▓▓ | ▓▓▓ | |
| *go up to* | ▓▓ | ▓▓ | | |
| *get on with* | ▓▓ | ▓ | ▓ | |
| *get away with* | ▓ | ▓ | ▓ | |
| *get off at* | ▓ | | | |
| *get off with* | ▓ | | | |
| *go out for* | ▓ | | | |
| *catch up with* | | ▓ | | |
| *get away from* | | ▓ | | |
| *go over to* | | ▓ | | |
| *hold on to* | | ▓ | | |
| *turn away from* | | ▓ | | |
| *turn back to* | | ▓ | | |
| *be set up in* | | | | ▓ |

other attested verbs:
*come in for, get back into, go along with, hand NP over to, keep up with, look out for*

| **communication** | | | | |
|---|---|---|---|---|
| *come out with* | ▓ | | | |

other attested verbs:
*bring NP up in*

| **mental** | | | | |
|---|---|---|---|---|
| *look forward to* | ▓ | ▓▓ | ▓▓ | |
| *come up with* | ▓ | ▓ | ▓▓ | |
| *put up with* | ▓ | ▓ | | |

other attested verbs:
*give in to*

| **occurrence** | | | | |
|---|---|---|---|---|
| *come down to* | ▓ | ▓ | | |

| **existence** | | | | |
|---|---|---|---|---|
| *be set out in* | | | | ▓▓ |

other attested verbs:
*be made up of, be cut off from*

**Table 5.25** **continued**

| semantic domain | CONV | FICT | NEWS | ACAD |
|---|---|---|---|---|
| causative<br>attested verbs:<br>*end up with* | | | | |
| aspectual<br>attested verbs:<br>*go on to, move on to* | | | | |

## 5.3.5 Other multi-word verb constructions

In addition to phrasal and prepositional verbs, there are three major types of idiomatic multi-word verb constructions:

- verb + prepositional phrase combinations
- verb + verb combinations
- verb + noun phrase combinations.

These combinations are introduced here but illustrated more fully in 13.3–4.

### A Verb + prepositional phrase combinations

First, several verb + prepositional phrase combinations have idiomatic status. These include combinations like *bear in mind, come as a surprise, fall in love, take into account,* and *take into consideration.* Such combinations function semantically as a coherent unit that can often be replaced by a single lexical verb (cf. 5.3.1B):

> *bear in mind* → *remember*
>
> *come as a surprise* → *surprise*
>
> *take into account / take into consideration* → *consider.*

For example:

> *I also have to **bear in mind** the interests of my wife and family.* (NEWS†)
>
> *The triumph **came as a surprise** to many.* (NEWS)
>
> *You have to **take into account** where the younger shoots are dominant.* (FICT)
>
> *The organization had to **take into consideration** human feelings and attitudes.* (ACAD†)

### B Verb + verb combinations

A second idiomatic category involves verb + verb combinations, such as *make do (with)* and *let NP go/be:*

> *You have to **make do**, don't you?* (CONV)
>
> *Patients had to **make do with** quiche or ham salad.* (NEWS†)
>
> *He was "very reluctant" to **let him go**.* (NEWS†)
>
> *I think it is time to **let it be**.* (NEWS)

**C  Verb + noun phrase combinations**

Third, there are a few semantically light verbs—such as *take*, *make*, *have*, and *do*—that combine with noun phrases to form set verbal expressions. In many cases, the combination also includes a following preposition:

> Yes, I'll **take care of** it. (FICT)
>
> It will **take time** to cut costs in the acquisitions. (NEWS)
>
> But you know how you **make fun of** me sometimes. (CONV)
>
> We don't **have a chance**. (NEWS)
>
> Do you want me to **do your hair**? (CONV)

The verbs in such examples can be followed by a deverbal noun, so that the verb + noun combination can sometimes be paraphrased by a simple verb corresponding to the noun:

> How can she **make a bet on** an unpublished author? (ACAD †)
>
> cf. How can she **bet on** an unpublished author?

However, in more idiomatic examples of this type, the alternative version does not mean the same:

> He went to the darkness of the bathroom to **take a leak**. (FICT †)
>
> cf. He went to the darkness of the bathroom to **leak**.

## 5.4  Main and auxiliary functions of primary verbs

The three primary verbs—*be*, *have*, and *do*—can serve as both main verbs and auxiliary verbs. They differ, however, in their particular main and auxiliary functions.

### 5.4.1  *Be*

As a main verb, *be* is the most important copular verb in English, serving to link the subject noun phrase with a subject predicative or obligatory adverbial (see also 3.5.2–3, 5.1.2, 5.5):

SVP$_s$(NP)

> You drank coffee like it **was** [water]. (CONV)

SVP$_s$(AdjP)

> The odds **are** [favourable enough]. (NEWS †)

SVA$_c$

> Well that's how we got acquainted so well because she **was** [in Olie's room] a lot. (CONV)

As an auxiliary verb, *be* has two distinct functions: marking progressive aspect and passive voice:

Progressive aspect:

> You**'re** going so slow. (CONV)
>
> The last light **was** fading by the time he entered the town. (FICT)

Passive voice:

> Shareholders will **be** advised of the outcome as soon as possible. (NEWS)
>
> Each **is** called a path or a history. (ACAD)

These two auxiliary uses of *be* can occur together in the same clause:

> A mutual investment fund for Eastern Europe **is being** launched today with the backing of Continental Grain. (NEWS†)

Progressive aspect and passive voice verbs are discussed further in 6.3 and 6.4. (*Be* is also a component of the semi-modal verb *be going to*; 6.6.)

## 5.4.2   *Have*

As a transitive main verb, *have* is as common as the most frequent lexical verbs in English (5.2.2). Across the four registers, *have* is most common in conversation and least common in academic prose. Within academic prose, though, *have* is more common than any of the lexical verbs.

In the same way as *get*, the main verb *have* can be used with various meanings marking many different kinds of logical relations.

Physical possession:

> One in three of these families **has** two cars. (NEWS)
>
> They **had** three tons of sugar. (FICT†)

Family connection:

> Her story was this: she **had** a husband and child. (FICT)
>
> Jim is aged 40 and **has** two children. (NEWS†)

Food consumption:

> The kids **had** "superhero sundaes" which turned out to be merely ice cream. (NEWS†)

Existential (cf. 11.4.9):

> But it really would be nice to **have** a young person about the house again. (FICT)
>
> cf. It would be nice if there was a young person about the house.

Linking a person to some abstract quality:

> You're gonna **have** problems with your feet. (CONV)
>
> Will you **have** enough to do? (CONV)
>
> I hope she **has** fun. (CONV)
>
> I **had** moments of indecision when I wanted to distribute the orange. (FICT)
>
> Her visitor **had** a strong pungent odor of a winter's day. (FICT)

Linking an inanimate subject to some abstract quality:

> In practical terms, the gates and fences probably **have** little advantage over the waist-high barrier. (NEWS†)
>
> Stylistics can **have** other goals than this. (ACAD†)
>
> In these extensions soil science will always **have** a major role. (ACAD†)

Marking causation:

> The problem continues to be that a religious-fascist state wishes to hire professional terrorists to **have** me killed. (NEWS)

Also the verb *have* has marginal semi-modal status in the expression **have to** (6.6.2):

> I'll **have to** blank it out. (CONV)

Further, *have* occurs in a number of idiomatic multi-word phrases (5.3.5 and 13.3.2):

> *I'll **have a look**.* (CONV)

*Have* serves only one auxiliary function: as the marker of perfect aspect:

> *Twenty years before, Charlie **had** passed a whole day from rising to retiring without a drink.* (FICT)

> *No one **has** ever seen anything like that before.* (NEWS)

Perfect aspect verbs are discussed further in 6.3.

## 5.4.3 *Do*

The verb *do* serves a number of functions: simple main verb, pro-verb, emphatic verb, and auxiliary verb in negative and interrogative constructions.

### 5.4.3.1 Main verb *do* in idiomatic expressions

As a main verb in transitive constructions, *do* has an activity meaning and appears in the $SVO_d$ and $SVO_iO_d$ patterns:

> ***Do** me a favour.* (FICT)

However, *do* more commonly combines with a following noun phrase to form relatively fixed, idiomatic expressions:

> *do* + **a bit, the job, the car, the dishes, time, some work, the wash, your hair.**

For example:

> *It **does the job**. It's not a bad little thing.* (CONV)

> *I went and **did the car**.* (CONV)

> *I'm used to it. I **do the dishes** every day.* (CONV)

Here *do* conveys minimal lexical content, merely referring to the performance of an activity that is relevant to the object noun phrase.

### 5.4.3.2 *Do* as pro-verb

#### A Transitive

*Do* also commonly functions as a **pro-verb**, substituting for some lexical verb. In one common pattern, *do* combines with a following pronoun *it* or *this/that* to form a transitive pro-verb construction:

> *I didn't **do it**.* (CONV)

> *Well that's why he **did it**.* (CONV)

> *That really hurts my ears when you **do that**.* (CONV)

> *We can't let you **do that**.* (FICT)

In some cases, pro-verb *do* can be identified as a substitute for a specific lexical verb, such as *cook* in the following:

> *But maybe she doesn't know how to cook, he thought suddenly. Okay, I can **do it**; I'll fix dinner for both of us. And I'll show her how so she can **do it** in the future if she wants.* (FICT)

In many other cases, though, pro-verb *do* + *it/this/that* substitutes for a series of actions or events, rather than referring to a specific preceding verb. This is especially the case in conversation:

> A: *Even Miss <teacher's name> hates him. – Now, well you see, she o~, we was having this discussion about education and she goes Are you cynical about education Terry? He goes no. She goes oh! She goes why? And he goes I don't know what cynical means.*
> B: *<laughs>*
> A: *I was saying ah no. And everyone in the class just cracked up. – Sometimes you woth– er whe– you wonder whether he **does it** on purpose. – He must **do it** on purpose, no one could be that thick.* (CONV)

In this conversation, the pro-verb expressions *does it* and *do it* refer to Terry's actions and speech, rather than substituting for a specific preceding verb.

## B Intransitive

*Do* in intransitive use, with no following object, substitutes for a verb or predicate (2.4.2.2):

> A: *He doesn't even know you.*
> B: *He **does**!* (CONV)

> A: *The top one doesn't look so evil.*
> B: *The bottom one **does**.* (CONV)

In many of these instances, *do* can be regarded as an auxiliary verb, because *not* (or *n't*) follows *do* in the corresponding negative form (cf. 5.4.3.6):

> A: *Does he know Bassam?*
> B: *No he **doesn't**.* (CONV)

> *I think his mom wants him to come back but his dad **doesn't**.* (CONV)

Hence although *doesn't* substitutes for a whole negative predicate here (*... but his dad doesn't want him to come back*), its grammatical role is simply that of an auxiliary verb.

Question tags (3.13.2.4) might be considered a special case of intransitive *do*:

> *But Fanny looked after you, **didn't** she?* (FICT)

> *This delay solves nothing, **does** it?* (FICT)

In BrE conversation, intransitive pro-verb *do* can also be used as a main verb:

> A: *You must have touched her up the wrong way*
> B: *Yeah, I **must've done**, mustn't I?* (CONV)

> A: *No, no signs of him resigning.*
> B: *Well they kicked him out.*
> A: *They **should have done**, but they won't.* (CONV)

In such instances it is more common for the substitution to be made by ellipsis rather than *do* (as in *They should have, but they won't*).

## 5.4.3.3 Register distribution of main verb and pro-verb *do*

**CORPUS FINDINGS** [2]

➤ Transitive *do* is particularly common in conversation.

**Table 5.26** **Transitive *do* across registers; occurrences per million words**

each ■ marks 100   □ marks less than 50

| | all forms of *do* + *it* | all forms of *do* + demonstrative pronoun | all forms of *do* + other noun phrase |
|---|---|---|---|
| CONV | ■■■■■■■■■ | ■■■ | ■■■■■■■■■■■ |
| FICT | ■■ | ■ | ■■■■ |
| NEWS | ■ | □ | ■■ |
| ACAD | □ | □ | ■■ |

➤ Intransitive pro-verb *do* is most common in conversation.
  ➤ It is also relatively common in fiction.
  ➤ It is rarely found in news or academic prose.

**Table 5.27** **Frequency of clause-final pro-verb *do* (marked by following punctuation or change of speaker turn) across registers; occurrences per million words**

each ■ marks 100   □ marks less than 50

| | *do* | *does* | *did* |
|---|---|---|---|
| CONV | ■■■■■ | ■ | ■■ |
| FICT | ■■■ | □ | ■ |
| NEWS | ■ | □ | □ |
| ACAD | □ | □ | □ |

**DISCUSSION OF FINDINGS**

Face-to-face communication, coupled with online production needs, result in the common use of pro-verb *do* in conversation. This device leaves implicit the exact referent of the verb, as well as following noun phrases, other complements, or adverbials in many cases. In conversation, speakers can rely on the shared situation together with the possibility for immediate clarification to identify the implied meaning (see 14.1.2.2–4). The following excerpt illustrates the extreme reliance on implicit meaning common in conversation:

> A: *Well I haven't got one of those.*
> B: *Yes.*
> C: *Go.*
> B: *Come on. You **do it** too.*
> A: *No, you **do it**.*
> B: *No, you **do it**.*
> C: *I've got a wicked joke.* (CONV)

### 5.4.3.4    Auxiliary *do* in emphatic function

As an auxiliary verb, **emphatic** *do* commonly serves a specialized function of emphasizing the meaning of the whole following predicate, whether in declarative or imperative clauses. Emphatic *do* cannot be combined with another auxiliary; in speech it is usually stressed:

> Well it **does** help if you say it twice. (CONV)
>
> Oh **do** shut up! (CONV)
>
> You **did** cut me. Look! (CONV)
>
> I **do** beg you to consider seriously the points I've put to you. (FICT)
>
> But in the final hour he **did** deliver the goods. (NEWS)
>
> They **do** share important attitudes about legal education. (ACAD)

### 5.4.3.5    Lexical associations of emphatic *do*

**CORPUS FINDINGS** [2]

➤ While emphatic *do* is most common in conversation and fiction, it is found in all four registers.

**Table 5.28**    **Frequency of emphatic *do* across registers; occurrences per million words**

each ● marks 50

|        | *do/does*   | *did*   |
|--------|-------------|---------|
| CONV   | ● ● ● ● ●   | ● ● ●   |
| FICT   | ● ● ●       | ● ● ●   |
| NEWS   | ● ●         | ●       |
| ACAD   | ● ●         | ●       |

➤ There are a few verbs that typically occur with emphatic *do*, and none of these is particularly common.

**DISCUSSION OF FINDINGS**

Emphatic *do* combines most commonly with the verb *have*, in all registers:

> I **did have** a protractor, but it broke. (CONV)
>
> So you are saying he **did have** a conscience? (FICT)
>
> They **did have** the consolation of team medal, however. (NEWS)
>
> But they **did have** a distinct legal life. (ACAD)

Many of the most common lexical verbs commonly occur with emphatic *do* (cf. Figure 5.7).

Emphatic *do* usually marks a state of affairs in contrast to some other expected state of affairs, which is by implication denied (cf. 11.1.2). This contrast can be explicitly marked by the use of connectives such as *but*, *however*, *nevertheless*, and *although*:

> But they **did say** four to five weeks on the coat, didn't they? (CONV)
>
> But he **did know** what he liked. (FICT†)

**Table 5.29** **Most frequent verbs that occur with emphatic *do*; occurrences per million words**

■ over 10    ▪ over 5

| | CONV | FICT | NEWS | ACAD |
|---|---|---|---|---|
| have | ■ | ■ | ■ | ■ |
| get | ■ | ■ | ▪ | |
| know | ■ | ■ | | |
| go | ■ | ▪ | | |
| look | ■ | ▪ | | |
| say | ■ | ▪ | | |
| want | ■ | ▪ | | |
| come | ▪ | ■ | | |
| feel | ▪ | ▪ | | |
| see | ▪ | ▪ | | |
| think | ▪ | ▪ | | |
| make | ▪ | ▪ | | |
| like | ▪ | | | |
| need | ▪ | | | |
| take | ▪ | | | |
| tell | ▪ | | | |
| work | ▪ | | | |
| believe | | ▪ | | |
| happen | | ▪ | | |
| hope | | ▪ | | |
| seem | | | ▪ | ▪ |
| occur | | | | ▪ |

> *I like a good sing-song when I'm having a bath, but I **do get** a bit loud and the neighbors can't hear the telly.* (NEWS)
>
> *Nevertheless, great changes **do occur** and have been well documented.* (ACAD)
>
> *Although individuals vary, there **does seem** to be a general developmental pattern revealed by miscue analysis.* (ACAD)

In other cases, the contrast is made across clauses without an overt connector:

> *I can't remember – I **do know** his name.* (CONV)
>
> *"Will he die?" "Some dogs **do get** over it, Wes."* (FICT)
>
> *Well, thought Alice, they are probably still sulky about last night. I **did go** too far I suppose. Well let them.* (FICT)
>
> *A: Or like yesterday when you <said> you stupid machine. He looked at you as if to say Jeez! She can swear!*
> *B: I wasn't swearing. Just said –*
> *A: I know.*
> *B: – stupid machine.*
> *A: I know. He **did**, he **did look** at you though.* (CONV)

A special use of emphatic *do* is in persuasive commands (which can be polite or impolite). Although this use is conversational, it occurs mainly in fictional dialogue rather than actual conversation:

> ***Do come*** *and see me some time.* (FICT)
>
> ***Do get*** *on with your work, Beth.* (FICT)

### 5.4.3.6 Auxiliary *do*-support in negatives and interrogatives

Finally, *do* functions as an auxiliary verb in negative and yes-no interrogative constructions with a lexical main verb. This use of *do* is known as *do*-support, because the *do* merely serves to mark the construction as negative or interrogative, without contributing any independent semantic content. Present or past tense is marked on the verb *do* in these constructions rather than the main lexical verb. Compare the following:

Negative **clauses:**

> *He **doesn't** like them.* (CONV)
>
> v.   *He likes them.*
>
> *I **didn't** realize it was from smoking.* (CONV)
>
> v.   *I realized it was from smoking.*

Interrogative **clauses:**

> ***Does*** *she honestly think that?* (FICT)
>
> v.   *She honestly thinks that.*
>
> ***Did*** *you see Andy today?* (CONV)
>
> v.   *You saw Andy today.*

See 3.8.2 on the negative and 3.13.2.8 on the interrogative.

## 5.5   Copular verbs

Copular verbs (or copulas) are used to associate some attribute, expressed by the **subject predicative** following the verb, with the subject of the clause (SVP$_s$ pattern, 3.5.3). For example, in the clause:

> *You're very stupid* (CONV)

*you* is the subject, and the adjectival phrase *very stupid* is the subject predicative, specifying an attribute of the person referred to by *you*. The copula *be* (contracted as *'re* in this case) links this attribute to the subject.

Many copular verbs can also be used to locate the subject of the clause in relation to time or place, expressed by an obligatory circumstance adverbial of position, duration, or direction (SVA pattern; 3.5.2).

Several verbs—like *go*, *grow*, and *come*—can function as either copular verbs or as intransitive or transitive verbs, depending on the context.

Transitive SVO:

> *So you said she started to **grow** sesame herbs.* (CONV)

Intransitive SV, with optional adverbial:

> *It was when Wharton Horricker and I **went** to Mexico.* (FICT)
>
> *He **came** from the far north.* (FICT†)

Copular SVP<sub>s</sub>:

> *It makes your teeth and your bones* **grow strong and healthy**. (CONV)
>
> *It's beginning to* **go bad** *for you.* (FICT)
>
> *Buckingham Palace still refused to* **come clean** *last night on the Di smear letter.* (NEWS)

In their copular function, these verbs link an attribute to the subject.

## 5.5.1 Verbs functioning as copulas

There are a number of verbs that can function as copulas. These fall into two main categories:

- current copular verbs—*be, seem, appear, keep, remain, stay*
- resulting copular verbs—*become, get, go, grow, prove, come, turn, turn out, end up, wind up.*

**Current copular** verbs identify attributes that are in a continuing state of existence:

> *I've just got to drink loads of coffee to* **keep** *awake.* (CONV)
>
> *We* **are** *all human.* (FICT)
>
> *I may have* **appeared** *a little short with my daughter that morning.* (FICT)
>
> *David Elsworth* **seemed** *quite satisfied with the performance of Barnbrook.* (NEWS)

Current copular verbs are mostly in the existence domain, except for a special sub-class that can be labelled **sensory copular verbs** because they report sensory perceptions: *look, feel, sound, smell, taste.*

> *I really do* **look** *awful.* (CONV)
>
> *Ooh that* **feels** *good.* (CONV)
>
> *They just* **sound** *really bad when they're recorded on.* (CONV)

In contrast, **resulting copular** verbs identify an attribute that happens as a result of some process of change:

> *She'll* **end up** *pregnant.* (CONV)
>
> *His breathing* **became** *less frantic.* (FICT)
>
> *My heart* **grew** *sick and I couldn't eat.* (FICT)

## 5.5.2 Complements of copular verbs

The complement of a copular verb can be either a subject predicative or an obligatory adverbial. Subject predicatives in the SVP<sub>s</sub> pattern can be realized by a noun phrase, adjective phrase, or prepositional phrase. In contrast, the obligatory adverbial in the SVA pattern is usually a prepositional phrase. The copular verbs *be, seem,* and *appear* take the widest range of patterns, occurring with complement clauses as well as adjectival and nominal complements; these patterns are discussed in 5.5.4 below.

Adjectival complements have been illustrated in 5.5.1. Although all copulas can take an adjective phrase as subject predicative, each copular verb is associated with a different set of adjectival complements, reflecting subtle differences in meaning. Section 5.5.3 describes the adjectives most commonly occurring with each copular verb (cf. 7.5).

Noun phrases as subject predicative also characterize or identify the subject (3.5.3):

> Prestatyn **seemed** [a dismal town]. (NEWS)
>
> She **became** [a pilot] and now flies jumbo jets. (NEWS†)
>
> Some companies could **end up** [losers] from the move. (NEWS†)
>
> We suggested that these roots **are** [special respiratory organs for supplying oxygen]. (ACAD†)

Prepositional phrases as subject predicative describe an attribute of the subject:

> But his wife Shelley **seemed** [in great shape] yesterday. (NEWS)
>
> I don't **feel** [in a mood for fireworks] (FICT)

Alternatively, prepositional phrases can have an adverbial meaning and indicate when or where something existed:

> It **was** [by the hospital]. It **was** [in the road of the hospital]. (CONV)

## 5.5.3    Register distribution of copular verbs and common predicative adjectives

**CORPUS FINDINGS** [2]

➤ The copula *be* is overwhelmingly the most common verb taking an adjectival complement, occurring over 20 times more often than any other copular verb.

➤ Copula *be* + adjective occurs over 5,000 times per million words for all registers (more than twice per page on average).

➤ This pattern is especially common in academic prose and fiction.

**Table 5.30**    **Frequency of copula *be* + adjective across registers; occurrences per million words**

each ● represents 500

| | |
|---|---|
| CONV | ●●●●●●●●●●● |
| FICT | ●●●●●●●●●●●●●●● |
| NEWS | ●●●●●●●●●● |
| ACAD | ●●●●●●●●●●●●●●●●●●●●●● |

➤ Apart from copula *be*, the verbs *become*, *get*, *look*, and *feel* are the four most common copular verbs taking an adjectival complement. These four have completely different register distributions (see Figures 5.15–18 and Table 5.31).

**Table 5.31**    **Frequency across registers of four common copular verbs**

| | CONV | FICT | ACAD |
|---|---|---|---|
| *become* + adjective | rare | relatively common | very common |
| *get* + adjective | very common | relatively common | rare |
| *look* + adjective | relatively common | very common | rare |
| *feel* + adjective | relatively common | very common | rare |

(In news, all four of these copular verb + adjective combinations are moderately common.)

Figure 5.15  **Frequencies of 12 copular verbs + predicative adjective—conversation**

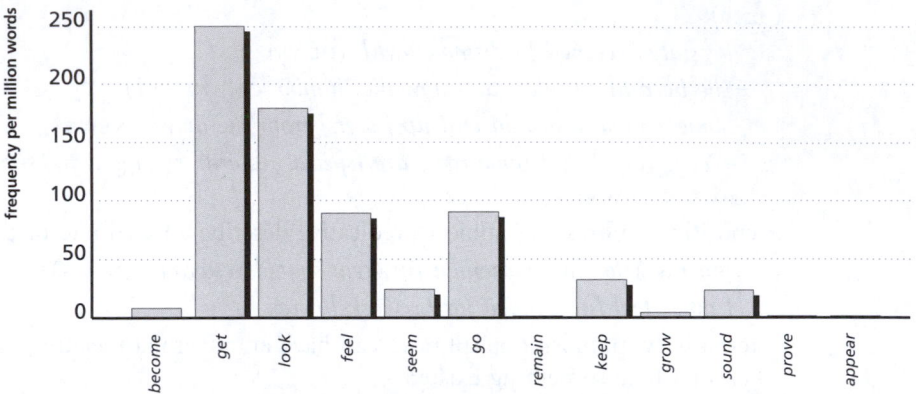

Figure 5.16  **Frequencies of 12 copular verbs + predicative adjective—fiction**

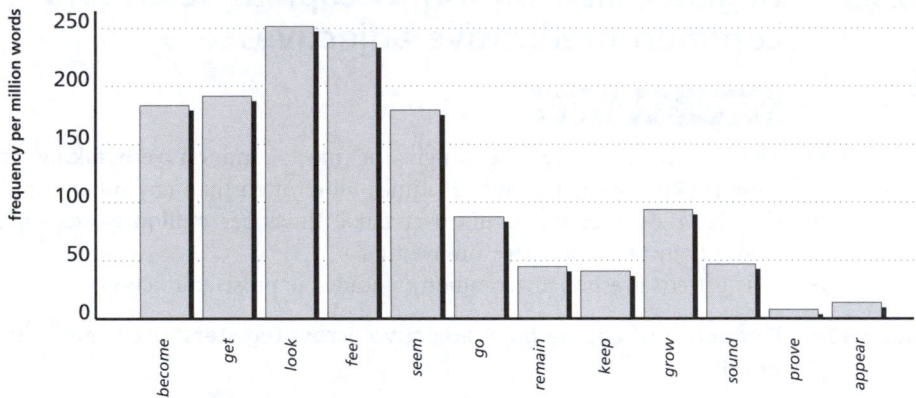

➤ The other copular verbs co-occur with fewer adjectives as subject predicatives, but each verb takes a different set, reflecting the different kinds of linking relations that they represent.

➤ There are a number of adjectives that are especially common as subject predicatives with the copula *be* (see Table 5.32).

  ➤ Many of these common adjectives are evaluative: *right*, *good*, *sure*, and *true*.

  ➤ There is noticeable complementarity between the common adjectives in conversation and those that are most common in academic prose.

### DISCUSSION OF FINDINGS

Sensory copular verbs are favored in fiction because of its topical concern with the feelings and appearances of characters in the narrative. The complementary distribution of copular verbs in conversation and academic prose, on the other hand, fits the general preference for short words of Germanic origin in conversation (note *get*, *look*, *feel*, *go*), in contrast to the preference for polysyllabic words of Latin-Romance origin in academic prose (note *remain*, *appear*, *become*). Overall, the high frequency of copular verbs in academic prose fits with its greater use of existence and occurrence verbs (5.2.1.3).

Figure 5.17  **Frequencies of 12 copular verbs + predicative adjective—news**

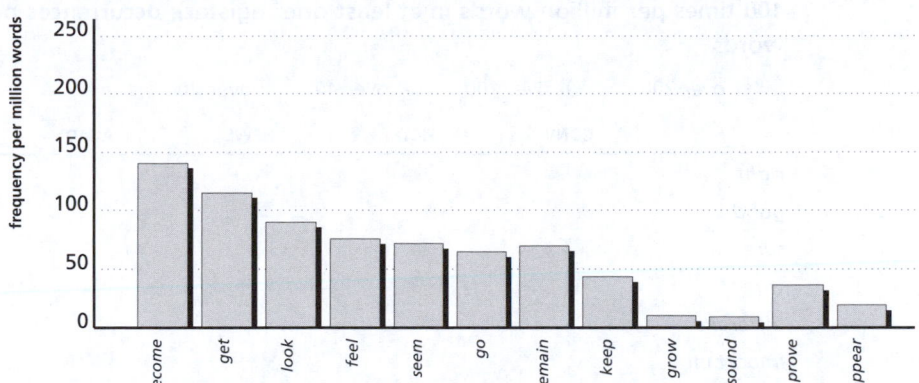

Figure 5.18  **Frequencies of 12 copular verbs + predicative adjective—academic prose**

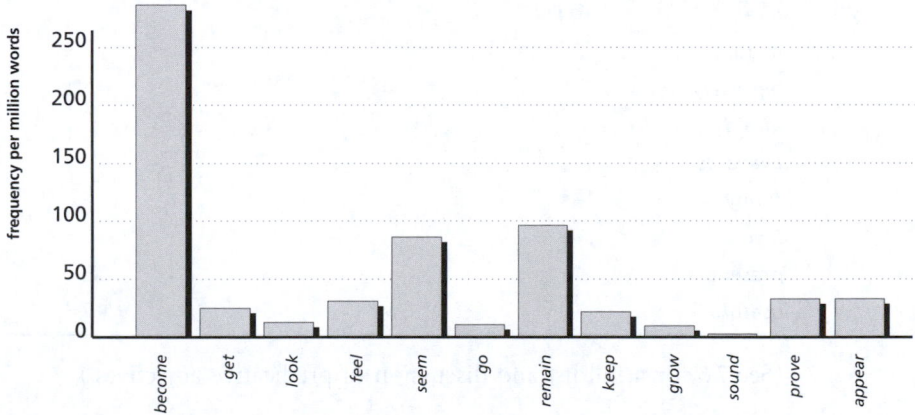

Several adjectives are common as subject predicatives with *be* in academic prose but rare in conversation. Many of these adjectives occur with a following complement clause, representing one of the major devices for expressing stance in academic prose (e.g. *sure, important, difficult, likely, necessary, possible*; 9.2.5.2, 9.4.5, 12.2, 12.4, 13.2.4.5).

The following sections focus on the copular verbs other than *be*, identifying the most common predicative adjectives co-occurring with each verb.

### 5.5.3.1  Current (non-sensory) copular verbs

Apart from *be*, the current copular verbs are associated with three primary semantic domains:

- likelihood—marked by *seem* and *appear*
- continuation of some current state—marked by *remain, keep, stay*
- personal attitudes—marked by *seem*

### A  *Seem* and *appear*

*Seem* is the most common of these current copular verbs. *Seem* is particularly common in fiction, combining with adjectival complements to mark personal

Table 5.32　**Most common adjectives as subject predicative of copula *be* (occurring over 100 times per million words in at least one register); occurrences per million words**

■ over 200　　■ over 100　　■ over 40　　▮ over 20

| | CONV | FICT | NEWS | ACAD |
|---|---|---|---|---|
| *right* | over 200 | over 200 | over 40 | over 20 |
| *good* | over 200 | over 100 | over 40 | over 20 |
| *sure* | over 100 | over 200 | over 40 | over 20 |
| *true* | over 40 | over 100 | over 20 | over 100 |
| *different* | over 40 | over 40 | over 20 | over 100 |
| *important* | | over 40 | over 100 | over 200 |
| *difficult* | | over 40 | over 40 | over 100 |
| *possible* | | over 40 | over 20 | over 200 |
| *likely* | | over 20 | over 100 | over 100 |
| *nice* | over 100 | over 40 | | |
| *dead* | over 40 | over 100 | over 20 | |
| *necessary* | | over 20 | over 20 | over 100 |
| *afraid* | over 20 | over 100 | over 20 | |
| *available* | | | over 100 | over 100 |
| *funny* | over 100 | over 20 | | |
| *lovely* | over 100 | | | |
| *present* | | | | over 100 |
| *useful* | | | | over 100 |

(See 7.5 for a full list and discussion of predicative adjectives.)

attitudes, often indicating some degree of surprise. The most common adjectives associated with this use are *absurd, full of* NP, *natural, odd, pleased, strange, surprised*:

> But today these dreams **seemed** [absurd and presumptuous]. (FICT)
> He **seemed** [full of chuckles] for a while. (FICT)
> It **seems** [odd] to me, that's all. (FICT)
> It **seemed** [strange] that it should still be there. (FICT†)
> He **seemed** [surprised] by that. (FICT)

*Seem* is also used commonly in fiction with the adjectives *possible* and *impossible* to mark degree of likelihood:

> It scarcely **seemed** [possible] that all this could ever be eaten. (FICT)
> Sometimes it **seemed** [impossible] that he should fail. (FICT)

In academic prose, *seem* is relatively common marking likelihood, especially with the adjectives *likely, unlikely, clear, obvious, possible, reasonable*. These are usually extraposed structures with a complement *that*-clause (3.6.4, 9.2.3):

> It **seems** [likely] that practical work in subjects such as CDT has helped to develop these skills for some students. (ACAD)
> It **seems** [clear] that more meals will be cooked over charcoal in the future. (ACAD†)

> It **seems** *[reasonable] to assume that it is approaching some stable,*
> *maintained course.* (ACAD†)

Assessment of epistemic stance is a major concern of academic prose, although it is usually not directly tied to the author (12.3–4). It is notable that stance is doubly marked in these constructions: by the copular verb *seem* and by adjectives such as *possible*, *likely*, and *reasonable*.

The copular verb *appear* is much less common than *seem*, but it has similar uses, being used in academic prose and news reportage to mark likelihood (or sometimes ability):

> *News Corp's last-minute $1.35bn offer for MGM-UA in September* **appeared**
> *[likely] to trigger an auction for the Los Angeles based group.* (NEWS)
>
> *The courts have* **appeared** *[willing] to go beyond the rules of natural justice.*
> (ACAD†)

### B  *Remain, keep,* and *stay*

The copular verbs *remain*, *keep*, and *stay* are all used to mark the continuation of some pre-existing state.

Of these three copular verbs, *remain* is the most common, especially in academic prose and news reportage. This verb is associated with static adjectives, simply reporting the absence of change, i.e. the continued existence of a static condition. In most cases this state of affairs does not involve humans. Adjectives typically used with *remain* are *unchanged, constant, intact, motionless, immobile, low, high, open, closed, controversial, uncertain, unknown, obscure*:

> *The cellular business* **remains** *[complex and uncertain].* (NEWS)
>
> *Next Friday's date for the final* **remains** *[unchanged].* (NEWS)
>
> *The angular momentum of the flow* **remains** *[constant].* (ACAD†)
>
> *The opening of the oviduct* **remains** *[intact].* (ACAD†)
>
> *The valve is allowed to* **remain** *[open].* (ACAD†)

*Keep* is used in all four registers, being least common in academic prose. Use of this copular verb implies a sense of agency, with the meaning that someone is actively maintaining something in its current state. Typical adjectives used as subject predicative with *keep* are *alive, awake, quiet, silent, secret, busy, fit, close, warm*:

> *It's funny how he manages to* **keep** *[awake].* (CONV)
>
> *He was just trying to* **keep** *[warm].* (FICT)
>
> *I* **kept** *[busy] and tried not to think about him.* (FICT)
>
> *They should* **keep** *[quiet] for the time being.* (NEWS)

*Stay* is by far the least common of the three copular verbs marking continuation. Like *remain*, the verb *stay* reports the continued existence of a static condition; but *stay* is similar to *keep* in that it usually reports situations that involve humans. Adjectives occurring with *stay* include *awake, dry, sober, alive, clear, loyal, healthy*:

> *I mean, if you* **stay** *[sober].* (CONV)
>
> *But she* **stayed** *[awake] long into the night.* (FICT)
>
> *Meanwhile Millie's mistress* **stayed** *[loyal] to her husband's ambitions.*
> (NEWS†)

## 5.5.3.2 Sensory copular verbs

The sensory copular verbs—*look, feel, sound, smell, taste*—report positive or negative evaluations associated with sense perceptions. The copular verb itself identifies the sense (e.g. sight, hearing, etc.), while the adjective occurring as subject predicative reports the evaluation. These copulas are less distinguished by their associated sets of predicative adjectives than the other current copular verbs. In fact, the general evaluating adjectives *nice, good,* and *bad* commonly occur as subject predicative to all five sensory copular verbs.

### A Look

The copular verb *look* is very common in fiction and relatively common in conversation, reporting the evaluation of physical appearance. In conversation, the adjective *nice* is notably common as subject predicative to *look*, occurring about once every 200 minutes (40–50 occurrences per million words). The combination *look good* is also relatively common in both conversation and fiction (over ten occurrences per million words):

> *Do I* **look** *[nice]?* (CONV)
> *It* **looks** *[nice], doesn't it?* (CONV)
> *That* **looks** *[good].* (CONV)

Other adjectives that repeatedly occur as subject predicative to *look* are: *awful, different, happy, lovely, pale, puzzled, sad, small, surprised, terrible, tired, well, young*:

> *Oh he does* **look** *[sad], doesn't he?* (CONV)
> *Quite frankly she* **looked** *[terrible].* (FICT)

This combination is commonly used to evaluate the physical appearance of the addressee:

> *You* **look** *[lovely].* (FICT)
> *You* **look** *[awful].* (FICT)
> *You* **look** *[happy].* (FICT)

### B Feel

The copular verb *feel* is very common in fiction and moderately common in conversation and news. This copular verb reports an assessment of physical or mental state of being, combining especially with the adjectives *ashamed, bad, better, cold, good, guilty, sick, sure, tired, uncomfortable, uneasy*.

Physical state of being:

> *It'll make you* **feel** *[better].* (NEWS)
> *And also I* **feel** *[sick] from the radiation.* (FICT)
> *My hands* **feel** *[cold].* (FICT)
> *It was then she began to* **feel** *[tired, drowsy].* (FICT)

Mental state of being:

> *I always* **feel** *[guilty] passing Mike's house.* (CONV)
> *I know it's daft but I do* **feel** *[bad] about it.* (CONV)
> *He* **felt** *[uneasy, apprehensive].* (FICT)
> *She no longer* **felt** *[ashamed] of her shabby cotton dress.* (FICT)

**C** *Sound*

The copular verb *sound* is moderately common in fiction and conversation. In its literal use, *sound* reports what the speaker has heard. However, because of the association of hearing with speech, *sound* has come to be used to report reactions to some previous idea or suggestion. This use is especially common in conversation, despite the objections of some prescriptivists. The adjectives *awful*, *angry*, *sad*, and *strange* recur with *sound* to report actual hearing perceptions, while *good*, *nice*, *silly*, *stupid*, and *interesting* are used in reaction to previous utterances.

Hearing perceptions:

> *She doesn't **sound** [angry] anymore.* (FICT)
>
> *He looked and **sounded** [awful].* (FICT)

Reaction to ideas:

> *A: I'm Cancer. What does it say about me?*
> *B: <reading> Market forces do not make the world go round. <... long quote ...> Indeed, the more selfless you can be this weekend, the better things will work out.*
> *A: Oh how nice. That **sounds** [good] to me.* (CONV)
>
> *A: I wanted to go, you know. I know it **sounds** [stupid], but I wanted to go.* (CONV)

**D** *Smell*

The copular verb *smell* is generally rare in all registers, but it is used occasionally in conversation and fiction. Not surprisingly, this verb reports the smells perceived by the speaker, using adjectives such as *awful*, *bad*, *funny*, *musty*, *odd*, *rotten*, *terrible*, *delicious*, *fresh*, *good*, *lovely*, *nice*:

> *The food **smelled** [good] to her.* (FICT)
>
> *It **smells** [funny] in there.* (CONV)

**E** *Taste*

The copular verb *taste* is quite rare. Its use is restricted to occasions in conversation and fiction that report taste perceptions, using adjectives like *awful*, *horrible*, *nice*, *wonderful*:

> *That boiled fruit **tastes** [nice].* (CONV)
>
> *The taste of them is just dreadful. They just **taste** [awful].* (CONV)

## 5.5.3.3 Resulting copular verbs

Although at first glance the verbs in this set seem very similar in meaning, they are in fact sharply differentiated by their specific meanings, collocational preferences, and register distributions.

**A** *Become*

The resulting copular verb *become* is extremely common in academic prose and relatively common in fiction; in contrast, *become* is quite rare in conversation. *Become* is used to focus on the process involved in reaching some resulting state. In academic prose, that resulting state most often relates to human understanding and ideas, viewed impersonally. The associated adjectives *clear* and *apparent* are most common (more than ten per million words), but there are a number of other adjectives that recur: *aware, difficult, evident, familiar, important, possible*:

> In the joint-stock company, the social character of production has **become** *[apparent].* (ACAD)
>
> It soon **becomes** *[clear]* that there is much more to comprehension than vocabulary. (ACAD†)
>
> This approach **becomes** *[difficult]* to use and understand when a large number of entities are displayed. (ACAD†)
>
> Performance and functionality only **become** *[important]* with release 3. (ACAD†)

Other adjectives recur as subject predicative with *become* marking situational changes relating to concrete substances. The adjective *available* in academic prose is most common with this function (more than ten per million words):

> Convenient sources of radiations and chemical mutagens **became** *[available]* about 1950. (ACAD†)

In fiction, *become* is usually tied to a specific person, describing some change in that person's state of awareness (especially with the adjectives *aware* and *clear*) or state of being (e.g. *become silent*):

> Raymond soon **became** *[aware]* that his strategy and hard work was paying dividends. (FICT)
>
> It all **became** *[clear]* to me when I reached street level. (FICT)
>
> I **became** *[silent]*, overwhelmed suddenly by the great gulf between us. (FICT†)

## B  Get

The resulting copular verb *get* is usually used to describe a human experience changing to a new state. Because it is so common, especially in conversation and fiction, *get* has a number of uses, describing both physical and mental changes. The adjectives *ready* and *worse* are the most common subject predicatives with *get*, but a number of other adjectives recur: *angry, bigger, better, bored, cold, dressed (up), drunk, lost, mad, mixed (up), old, older, pissed (off), sick, tired, upset, wet.* Most of these mark some affective or attitudinal stance:

> They helped Scott **get** *[ready].* (CONV)
>
> Well he's only gonna **get** *[worse].* (CONV)
>
> And if she doesn't win, she either **gets** *[upset]* and cries or **gets** *[angry].* (CONV)
>
> And people **get** *[pissed off]*, don't they? (CONV)
>
> In the end he had **got** *[mixed up]* in some shady affair. (FICT)
>
> The drizzle increased and Eddie **got** *[cold].* (FICT†)

## C  Go

The copular verb *go* with an adjectival subject predicative is typically used to describe a change towards some undesirable state. *Go* describes both changes experienced by humans and natural processes that happen to other things. This combination is relatively common in conversation and fiction. Three adjectival complements are relatively common with *go*—*crazy, mad, wrong* (occurring more than ten times per million words), while several other adjectives recur with this copular verb—*bad, cold, deaf, funny, limp, quiet, red, wild*:

*You don't want those back ones to **go** [bad].* (CONV)

*You can't **go** [wrong] with that, can you?* (CONV)

*Yeah I know. I would **go** [mad].* (CONV)

*Mama will **go** [crazy].* (FICT)

*Andrew felt his whole body **go** [limp].* (FICT)

## D Grow

The copular verb *grow* is used to describe gradual evolution, affecting both humans and other things; it focuses on the process of change as well as the result. The resulting attribute often makes an implicit comparison to some earlier state, through comparative adjectives ending in -*er*. Only fiction shows a moderately common use of *grow* + adjective. Recurrent adjectives following *grow* include *angry, big, bright, cold, dark, hot, large, old, pale, tall, tired, warm, weak*, as well as the comparative adjectives *bigger, darker, larger, louder, older, shorter, smaller, stronger, warmer, weaker, worse*:

*We should **grow** [old] here together.* (FICT)

*The wind dropped and it suddenly **grew** [cold].* (FICT)

*The girl's deep black eyes **grew** [darker].* (FICT)

*She continued to lose weight and **grow** [weaker].* (FICT†)

## E Prove

*Prove* with an adjectival complement is moderately common in academic prose and news, and is used to report an assessment that has been demonstrated. Recurring adjectives in this pattern are: *costly, decisive, difficult, fatal, necessary, popular, possible, successful, suitable, useful, wrong*. These combinations are often used with non-personal subjects:

*Looking for tourist highlights in Montepulciano can **prove** [difficult].* (NEWS)

*He was confident the units would **prove** [popular] with travellers.* (NEWS)

*Yet it has **proved** [necessary] to attempt this task.* (ACAD†)

*Such experiments may well **prove** [useful] in testing the universality of the "universal" routes to chaos.* (ACAD)

## F Come

The copular verb *come* with an adjectival complement is used to describe processes away from some static condition. This pattern is generally rare, occurring mainly in fiction and news. Recurring adjectives are: *alive, awake, clean, loose, short, true, unstuck*. *Come* often marks a change to a more favorable condition, complementing the use for copular *go*.

## G Turn

The copular verb *turn* + adjective is used to describe a change in appearance, especially a change in color: *black, brown, (bright) red, white, pale*. This combination is occasionally used in fiction but is otherwise rare:

*The canals in the suburbs appear to **turn** [black].* (FICT)

*She had **turned** [pale] and her voice shook.* (FICT)

## H Turn out, end up, wind up

Finally, there are three phrasal verbs used as resulting copular verbs: *turn out, end up*, and *wind up*. All three are generally rare.

*Turn out* is used to emphasize the end-point of a process, with a simple positive or negative evaluation: *turn out + good, nasty, nice, (all) right, wrong*:

> *A lot of times they **turned out** [wrong].* (FICT)

> *The marriage will **turn out** [all right].* (FICT)

*End up* and *wind up* are used to describe an unintended negative event or state resulting from someone doing something undesirable:

> *And this argument went on. Danny **ended up** in tears and I **ended up** really [angry].* (CONV)

> *And the young bucks who tore the place apart, challenging the far north with their frail planes, invariably **wound up** [dead].* (FICT)

> *He says Marilyn **ended up** [pregnant] after her affair with President Kennedy.* (NEWS)

> *But if you did manage to get her back with her husband again, I'm sure she would **end up** forever [suspicious, bitter and soured].* (NEWS)

## 5.5.4 Valency patterns of the copulas *be*, *seem*, and *appear*

The copular verbs *be*, *seem*, and *appear* are special in that they can take a wider range of valency patterns than the other copular verbs. In particular, the complement of these copular verbs can be an adjective phrase, noun phrase, prepositional phrase, or complement clause (*to*-infinitive or *that*-clause). With *be*, prepositional phrases can function as either a subject predicative or an obligatory adverbial, but with *seem* and *appear* only the former is possible (cf. 5.5.2). Despite the structural similarities, these three verbs have important differences in their preferred patterns.

### 5.5.4.1 Complement types with *be*, *seem*, and *appear*

**CORPUS FINDINGS** [2]

➤ Over 50% of the complements of the copular verb *be* are noun phrases. This structure is extremely common, occurring about 10,000 times per million words (or several times on every page of prose).
  - ➤ *Be* + adjective (phrase) is also very common.
  - ➤ *Be* + complement clause is relatively rare.
➤ The verbs *seem* and *appear* show the opposite pattern, usually occurring with a complement clause as subject predicative.
  - ➤ *Seem* and *appear* are less common with a noun phrase or adjective phrase as subject predicative.
➤ Overall, prepositional phrases are the least common complement type.

**Figure 5.19**
**Proportional use of structures as subject complement with *be*, *seem*, and *appear***

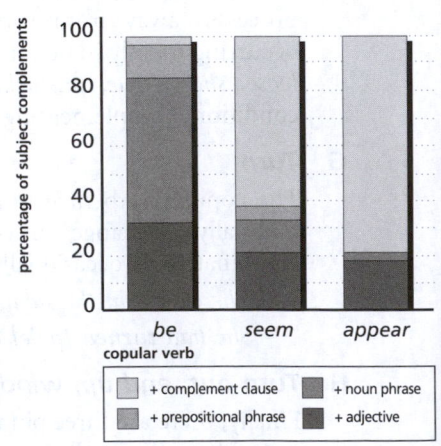

| | + complement clause | + noun phrase |
| + prepositional phrase | + adjective |

➤ Prepositional phrases account for just over 10% of all complements of *be*. Because the copula *be* is so common overall, this pattern occurs frequently (about 2,000 times per million words).

➤ Prepositional phrases account for less than 5% of all subject predicatives with *seem*.

➤ Prepositional phrases are not attested in the LSWE Corpus as subject predicatives with *appear*.

### DISCUSSION OF FINDINGS

## A  Noun phrase complement

Although the pattern of copular verb + adjective is productive for a wide range of copular verbs, the single most common copular pattern is the copula *be* followed by a noun phrase as subject predicative. In these structures, the noun phrase following *be* provides either a descriptive characterization of the subject noun phrase, or some identifying information (3.5.3).

Characterizing:

> This **is** [*a good example of how internal deviation can give prominence*]. (ACAD)

> The only consolation **was** [*a crowd at the Harvey Hadden Stadium*]. (NEWS†)

Identifying:

> The kernel **is** [*the part of the plant of greatest value*]. (ACAD†)

> AMP **is** [*the largest manager of private retirement funds in that country*]. (NEWS†)

> Maria suddenly broke out, "I'**m** [*his wife*]." (FICT)

*Seem* and *appear* can also occur with a noun phrase as subject predicative, although *appear* is rare in this pattern. While *be* is used for simple assertions, *seem* and *appear* are used to characterize the subject predicative as a perception that is not necessarily accurate:

> This **seems** [*a good idea*]. (FICT)

> Fujisankei, itself privately owned and independent, **seems** [*the ideal partner*]. (NEWS)

> This argument <...> might therefore **seem** [*a strong rival to my suggestion*]. (ACAD†)

> On one level it **appears** [*a simple matter*]. (ACAD†)

## B  Prepositional phrase complement

Prepositional phrases are much less common than noun phrases as copular complements, but this pattern does occur with *be*, and rarely with *seem*. With both copular verbs, a prepositional phrase as complement can be used to express an attribute or characterization (SVP$_s$ pattern). In addition, prepositional phrases with *be* can be used to express positional or directional meaning (SVA pattern).

Prepositional phrase expressing an attribute of the subject:

> She'**s** [*like the manager of a hotel*]. (CONV)

> Now he **seemed** [*in control*]. (FICT)

> Umuofia **was** [*in a festival mood*]. (FICT)

> Most of the time he **seems** [*like such a normal guy*]. (FICT)

> The film **is** [*about a getaway driver*]. (NEWS†)

*He **seems** [in great form].* (NEWS†)

*The resistive voltage drop **is** [in phase with the current].* (ACAD)

Prepositional phrase expressing positional or directional information:

*I wish you **were** [at the shack] with me last night.* (CONV)

*She got that top off the teapot while she **was** [on the toilet].* (CONV)

*Well, it's [in the cupboard].* (FICT)

*The houses **are** [in a conservation area].* (NEWS)

The verb *appear* with a prepositional phrase functions as an intransitive verb with an optional place adverbial:

*Then he **appeared** [in Zamosht, in the town itself].* (FICT)

*The two accused men are due to **appear** [before Chelmsford magistrates] today.* (NEWS)

**C  Complement clause complement**

In contrast to the typical patterns of complementation with *be*, the copular verbs *seem* and *appear* occur most commonly with a complement clause:

*This **seemed** [to work].* (FICT)

*In two short years the government has **seemed** [to lose its grip].* (NEWS)

*The inheritance of leaf angle **appears** [to be polygenic].* (ACAD)

This pattern also occurs frequently with the copula *be*, although it accounts for a small proportion of the total occurrences of *be*:

*The capital **is** [to be provided by the French government].* (NEWS†)

*But the danger **was** [that the pound would fall further than planned].* (NEWS)

These structures are described more fully in 9.2.4 and 9.4.4.

**5.5.4.2  Subject and complement types with *be***

The typical subjects and complements occurring with *be* differ in important ways across registers. See 5.5.3 above for discussion of adjectives as subject predicatives with *be*, and 9.2.4, 9.4.4 for discussion of complement clauses as subject predicatives. Here we take up the other two complement types of *be*—noun phrases and prepositional phrases—focusing only on their use in conversation and academic prose.

**CORPUS FINDINGS** [2]

➤ The types of subjects occurring with *be* differ in important ways across registers.
  ➤ Conversation has more pronouns.
  ➤ Academic prose has more full noun phrases.
➤ Conversation and academic prose are also very different in the typical noun phrases and prepositional phrases that occur as complements with *be*.
➤ Common noun phrases as subject predicative with *be*, occurring over 20 times per million words:
  ➤ Conversation: pronouns—*anything, it, me, mine, nothing, one, something, they;* full noun phrases—*crap, his/her name, home, no way, people, the matter, the thing, the time, the trouble, the way, time.*
  ➤ Academic prose: pronouns—*it, nothing, one, something;* full noun phrases—*an example, evidence, part, subject, the case, the number, the result.*

**Table 5.33** **Types of subject with *be* + adjective/NP/prepositional phrase in two registers; in percentages**

| conversation | *be* + adj | *be* + NP | *be* + PrepP |
|---|---|---|---|
| full noun phrase | 17 | 33 | 19 |
| personal pronoun | 38 | 19 | 45 |
| *it* | 28 | 21 | 26 |
| demonstrative pronoun | 15 | 14 | 7 |
| relative pronoun | 2 | 2 | 3 |
| *there* | – | 11 | – |
| **total** | **100%** | **100%** | **100%** |

| academic prose | *be* + adj | *be* + NP | *be* + PrepP |
|---|---|---|---|
| full noun phrase | 69 | 62 | 72 |
| personal pronoun | 5 | 4 | 7 |
| *it* | 17 | 7 | 11 |
| demonstrative pronoun | 3 | 6 | 5 |
| relative pronoun | 6 | 3 | 5 |
| *there* | – | 18 | – |
| **total** | **100%** | **100%** | **100%** |

➤ Common prepositional phrases as subject predicative with *be*, occurring over 20 times per million words:
  ➤ Conversation: *about it, at home, at school, at work, in bed, like that, like this, on holiday, on it, with you.*
  ➤ Academic prose: *in a position, of importance, of interest, of use, of value.*

**DISCUSSION OF FINDINGS**

In conversation, the majority of clauses with a copular verb have a pronoun as a subject. The following illustrate personal pronouns as subject, where the clause is used to give an opinion of a human being:

> *[He]'s very alert.* (CONV)
> *[I] must **be** a weakling.* (CONV)
> *[They]'re all great friends.* (CONV)

Similarly, there is a high frequency of *it* as subject, where the clause is used to assess a personal situation:

> *No, [it]'s nothing to do with you.* (CONV)
> *[It] **was** funny though.* (CONV)
> *Have you ever seen him do that flying spin kick? [It]'s brilliant, isn't it?* (CONV)

Demonstrative pronouns can have a similar function, reinforcing situational reference with a deictic emphasis:

> *[That] **wasn't** very nice.* (CONV)
> *[That] **is** the best one we've had.* (CONV)
> *It lasted twelve hours and [that] **was** the worst twelve hours I've had in my life.* (CONV)

The common noun and prepositional phrases occurring as subject predicatives in conversation reflect this register's reliance on circumstances for interpretation.

Many of the noun phrases in this class are referentially vague (e.g. *anything, nothing, something, the way, the thing*):

> *You see, that's [the thing] isn't it?* (CONV)
>
> *That's [the way] it has to be.* (CONV)
>
> *Well, there's [nothing] there to see.* (CONV)

The prepositional phrases commonly following the verb *be* in conversation provide spatial, comparative, or descriptive references similarly dependent on the immediate context:

Spatial complements (adverbial):

> *You should be [in bed].* (CONV)
>
> *He's [at work].* (CONV)

Comparative or descriptive complements (subject predicative):

> *Some people are [like that].* (CONV)
>
> *And his nose—it's still [like that].* (CONV)
>
> *I didn't know April showers were [like this].* (CONV)

In contrast, the copula *be* in academic prose usually specifies a logical relationship between referents, although the typical referent here is an abstract concept or process, rather than a concrete entity. The majority of subjects of the copula *be* in academic prose are full noun phrases having a specific referent:

> *[The seed] is unlikely to survive.* (ACAD†)
>
> *[Past politics] is decisive of present rights.* (ACAD†)
>
> *[Calcium] is essential for the growth of meristems.* (ACAD)
>
> *[The process of change in rock material, called weathering,] is a continuous and complex combination of destruction and synthesis.* (ACAD)

Similarly, subject predicatives in academic prose are also usually full noun phrases. The most common of these often identify the logical class or type to which the subject noun phrase belongs:

> *The latter is [an example of the case where not all nuclei in the spin system are coupled].* (ACAD)
>
> *This is particularly [the case] when a child has already developed guilt feelings.* (ACAD†)
>
> *Each point on this curve is [the result of a previous optimization.]* (ACAD†)

Two special types of subject with the copula *be* are non-referential: existential *there* and non-referential *it* (with existential clauses, clefts, and extraposition). These are discussed fully in 3.2.1.2, 3.6.3–4, 9.2.7, 9.4.7, 11.4, 11.6.

Finally, both conversation and academic prose have common subject predicatives that are attitudinal, marking the stance of the speaker/writer. In conversation, noun phrases like *crap* and *the matter* serve this function:

> *Yeah, it's [crap], isn't it?* (CONV)
>
> *What is [the matter] with you people?* (CONV†)

In academic prose, prepositional phrases (especially *of*-phrases) following *be* are often equivalent in meaning to adjectives, giving some evaluation that provides an impersonal indication of stance:

> *The right way of using the feet is [of importance] in all stepping.* (ACAD†)
>
> *But it was [of little value] to the girls.* (ACAD†)
>
> *It is [of interest] to consider the significance of the limiting values of A.* (ACAD)

# 6

# Variation in the verb phrase: tense, aspect, voice, and modality

## 6.1 Structure and meaning distinctions in the verb phrase

The most fundamental distinction among English verb phrases is between **finite verb phrases** (those which begin with a finite verb; 2.7.2) and **non-finite verb phrases** (those which contain only non-finite verbs).

This chapter concentrates on finite verb phrases, which in English vary with respect to the following six major structural distinctions (cf. 2.7.2, 5.1):

**tense**: *present or past (e.g. see(s) v. saw)*

**aspect**: *unmarked/simple, perfect, progressive (e.g. sees v. has seen v. is seeing), or perfect progressive (e.g. has been seeing)*

**voice**: *active or passive (e.g. sees v. is seen)*

**modality**: *unmarked (tensed) v. modal (e.g. sees v. will/can/might see)*

**negation**: *positive v. negative (3.8) (e.g. sees v. doesn't see)*

**clause structure type**: *declarative v. interrogative (3.13) (e.g. you saw v. did you see?).*

In this chapter we concentrate on the first four of these: tense, aspect, voice, and modality. These structural distinctions correspond to a number of semantic distinctions, as described in the following sections. However, there is no one-to-one correspondence between form and meaning in the verb phrase. Rather, a single structural variant can represent quite different meanings; and similar meanings can be expressed by different structural variants. This complex mapping between form and meaning is especially apparent in the marking of time distinctions.

For example, verbs structurally marked for the present tense can refer to events at the present time or at some time in the past:

Present (habitual) time with present tense:

*He **goes** there a lot.* (CONV)

Past time with present tense (the so-called **historic present**):

*Well I, I wanted just a small box like what you made. He wasn't satisfied with it—He **goes** and **makes** a big one as well.* (CONV)

Conversely, the same domain of meaning can be expressed by different structural options: for example, future time can be expressed with the present tense or with the modal *will*:

Future time with present tense:

*Goalkeeper Stephen Pears **goes** into hospital tomorrow for an operation on a cheekbone injury.* (NEWS†)

Future time with modal *will*:

*This part of the project **will go** ahead extremely rapidly.* (NEWS)

Similar mappings of structure and meaning can be found with the other distinctions marked in the verb phrase.

This chapter is organized around the primary structural distinctions marked in the verb phrase: tense (6.2), aspect (6.3), voice (6.4), combinations of aspect and voice (6.5), and modality (6.6). Each of these structural choices is discussed relative to the range of associated meanings.

## 6.2 Tense

In this section, for illustrative purposes we focus on the **simple** or **unmarked** present and past tenses (i.e. those which do not have marking for aspect or voice). However, the frequency data we present account for all cases of the present and past tenses, including those marked for aspect and voice.

## 6.2.1 Basic tense and time distinctions

From a structural point of view, English verbs are inflected for only two tenses: **present** and **past**. However, many verb phrases are not marked for tense. First, tense is not marked for imperative clauses (3.13.4) and non-finite clauses (e.g. *to*-clauses and *ing*-clauses as complement clauses; see 9.4–5). Beyond that, finite clauses can be marked for either modality or tense, but not both. Thus the presence of a modal verb precludes tense marking (although modal verbs sometimes express time distinctions; 6.6). Verb phrases which are marked for tense, but not for modality, will be referred to as **tensed**.

Present tense is unmarked morphologically, except for the suffix *(e)s* on the third person singular; past tense for regular verbs is marked with the suffix *-ed* (see 2.3.2 for an overview, and 5.2.6 for further discussion of irregular verbs). The two tenses typically refer to present and past time respectively:

Simple present tense referring to the present time:

> I **want** a packet of crisps. (CONV)
>
> Some recent field experimental evidence **suggests** that biotic interactions also can be important to grasshoppers. (ACAD)

Simple past tense referring to past time:

> Well I **rang** them up yesterday. (CONV)
>
> A few vultures **looked** down from the roof with shabby indifference. (FICT)
>
> We **examined** this question by excluding birds for 3 years from experimental plots in a semiarid grassland in Arizona. (ACAD)

Simple present tense referring to the present time has two major meanings: to describe a state existing at the present time, and to describe present habitual behavior.

Simple present tense referring to a state existing at the present time:

> I **want** a packet of crisps. (CONV)
>
> I **think** you might be wrong. (CONV)
>
> Plea by leaders as civil war **grips** Bosnia. (NEWS) <headline>
>
> Economists **fear** interest rate rise. (NEWS) <headline>
>
> Table 4.1 **shows** the composition of mucigel produced by Zea mays (maize). (ACAD)

Such a state may be temporary, as in the first two examples, or persist for a longer time, as in the last three examples.

Simple present tense referring to present habitual behavior:

> She's vegetarian but she **eats** chicken. (CONV)
>
> This is on one of those hikes that we **go** on. (CONV)

> There's this one bloke, he **walks** around with a grenade tied to his neck. (CONV)

> He **dances** and **moves** about a lot. (NEWS)

In addition, the simple present can report on an action ongoing at the time:

> Here **comes** your mother. (CONV)

> Oh, my goodness. There he **goes**. Look at him walk. (CONV) <talking about a toddler>

Past tense most commonly refers to past time via some past point of reference, especially in fictional narrative and description, where the use of the past tense to describe imaginary past happenings is a well-established convention. All past tense verbs are in bold in the following excerpt:

> The clock on the tower of St Michael-in-the-Moor **chimed** nine as he **came** onto the road. The milkman's van **was** on the green; Mrs Southworth from the Hall **was** at the pillar box, posting a letter. He **walked** on away from the green and the houses up the bit of the Jackley road from which Tace Way **turned** off. (FICT)

Additionally, there are functions of the past tense which relate more to present time, but with an added indication of stance. With verbs like *think*, *wonder*, and *want*, past tense can indicate a present time state of mind with a tentativeness that shows the speaker is being especially polite:

> **Did** you **want** a cup of tea? (CONV)

> Hi Peggy this is Ellen at Sports Spectrum, um, I **wanted** to let you know we got your swimsuit in. (CONV†) <telephone message>

Furthermore, in certain types of dependent clause, the simple past marks the hypothetical:

> And if you **were** in the mood we could at least go. (CONV†)

## 6.2.1.1 Simple present tense marking past or future time

Simple present tense is also used in special cases to refer to either past events or future events. The historic present tense, referring to past time, occasionally occurs in fiction (especially in colloquial narratives) to produce a more vivid description, as if the events were being enacted at the time of speech. This use is especially common in jokes, which are often told entirely in the historic present:

> A: I could tell you a really boring joke that goes on for ages.
> B: Go on then. Go on then.
> A: All right. There**'s** a fortune teller and the man **goes** to the fortune teller and the fortune teller **goes** <...> he **goes** I can't tell you. This is, this is, this is awful. All right, it's, it's worse than dying. He **goes** look, I'll write it down on an envelope, <...> So the man **goes** all right. The man **walks** home and the man**'s** depressed. He **walks** like this. <pause> He **has** to buy a new pair of trainers on the way home because he**'s dragging** his feet on the floor so much. So he **gets** in the house <...> (CONV)

<note this excerpt also contains straightforward examples of present tense referring to present time, e.g. in the reported direct speech>

The above excerpt also illustrates how this function of the historic present in conversational narratives is especially common with speech-act verbs (*say, go*). Other examples are:

> *No. He **says**, are you going home tonight. He thought I was going home to my parents.* (CONV)

> *And the guy driving the truck **says**, no we can't; we've got an important meeting.* (CONV)

> *And the daughter comes home from school one day and **says**, mum I want to be like you. And then the mum **goes**, okay dear, I'll go out and get some stuff.* (CONV)

While the use of present tense to refer to past time is strongly associated with conversational narratives, the use of present tense to refer to future time is related to grammatical rather than register factors. Nearly all occurrences of present tense referring to future time occur in one of two related grammatical contexts—either with an accompanying time adverbial that explicitly refers to the future, or in a conditional or temporal adverbial clause that has future time reference:

1 *It's open day on Wednesday.* (CONV)

2 *If I **refuse** to do what she **says** this time, who knows where my defiance will end?* (FICT)

3 *A new era **begins** for the bomb-damaged Ulster landmark when the curtain **goes up** on Jack and the Beanstalk in December.* (NEWS†)

4 *Although production will continue for many years yet, I feel it is time to record what historical production data is available before records **are** lost and memories **fade**.* (ACAD)

The simple present accompanied by an adverbial of time, as in 1, is used particularly where a future event is felt to be fixed and certain at the time of speech. Example 2 also illustrates a characteristic pattern, where the modal verb in the main clause (*will*) signals future time, thus providing a future context for the simple present in the dependent clause.

## 6.2.1.2 Past tense in reported speech

Past tense also has a common special use, when it is **backshifted** from the present in reported speech or thought. That is, reports of earlier speech or thought can be given in the past tense, when the original quote (in the case of speech) was presumably in the present tense. In these cases, the tense of the verb in the indirect quote is adapted to agree with the past tense of the reporting verb. When reporting the speech of others, there can be accompanying shifts in the person of pronouns; see 1 and 2 below:

1 *A girl at work said she **worked** at Woolworths.* (CONV)
  cf. direct speech '*I work at Woolworths*'.

2 *Then the next day he said he no longer **loved** me.* (CONV)
  cf. direct speech '*I no longer love you*'.

3 *And I thought I **was** going to go home early.* (CONV†)
  cf. original thought '*I am going to go home early*'.

4 *Abbey said there **was** a meeting planned to discuss the contract this week.* (NEWS)
  cf. direct speech '*There is a meeting ... next/this week*'.

  5 He thought they **wanted** to talk to him so he stopped and got out.
  (NEWS)
  cf. original thought '*They want to talk to me*'.

Note that the circumstances of the report may well be continuing (as in **1** and **2** above). That is, the girl may still work at Woolworths, and the speaker may no longer be loved, even at the time of the later conversation.

### 6.2.1.3 The marking of future time

As noted above, there is no formal future tense in English. Instead, future time is typically marked in the verb phrase by modal or semi-modal verbs such as *will, shall, be going to*:

  Even more precise coordination **will** be necessary. (FICT)

  We **shall** give an account of the Einstein-Podolsky-Rosen paradox. (ACAD†)

  And he**'s going to** see it. (CONV)

The semi-modal *be going to* can also be marked for tense. When combined with the past tense form of *be*, this verb marks reference to a projected future time dating from some point in the past; thus, the actual time reference can be before the present time, and the reference can be to a situation that never actually took place:

  I **was going to** be called Kate if I was a girl. (CONV)

  It was in the summer holidays and Matthew **was going to** start school.
  (CONV)

## 6.2.2 Register distribution of tense and modality

From a grammatical point of view, tense and modality comprise a single system, since all finite verb phrases (excluding imperatives) are marked for either tense or modality (but not both).

**CORPUS FINDINGS [1,2]**

➤ Overall, tensed verb phrases are much more common than verb phrases with modals.
  ➤ About 85% of all finite verb phrases in the LSWE Corpus are tensed.
➤ Overall, present tense verbs are somewhat more common than past tense verbs.
➤ The distribution of present and past tense verbs differs considerably across registers:
  ➤ Conversation and academic prose are alike in showing a strong preference for present tense forms.
  ➤ Fiction shows the opposite pattern, with a strong preference for past tense verbs.
  ➤ News uses both tenses to about the same extent (with slightly more present tense than past tense).
➤ Verb phrases with modals comprise 10–15% of all finite verb phrases in all registers.

**Figure 6.1**

**Frequency of present/past tense v. modal verbs across registers**

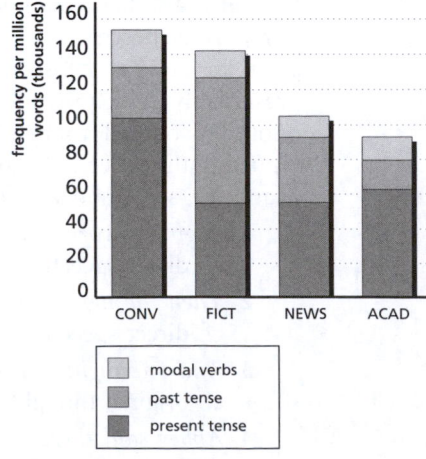

- modal verbs
- past tense
- present tense

**DISCUSSION OF FINDINGS**

The large majority of all finite verb phrases are tensed, while verb phrases with modal verbs are comparatively rare. Modals are used to express a speaker's or writer's stance, expressing either the degree of (un)certainty of the proposition, or meanings such as permission, obligation, or necessity (6.6). Without a modal verb, most verb phrases include only a marking of time orientation and not an overt expression of stance. However, in a sense the absence of a modal verb (or other stance marker) can itself be interpreted as a choice of stance, with the addressor attributing unquestioned validity to the proposition.

In some ways, present tense can be considered the unmarked form, occurring more frequently than past tense, and expressing a wide range of meanings. Present tense can be used to refer to events in the past, to present states, to present habitual behavior, or to future events. It is the verb form of 'all-inclusive time reference'. In contrast, past tense is used primarily to refer to states or events existing at some past time, excluding present and future.

The preference for present tense verbs is particularly strong in conversation and academic prose, but for quite different reasons. In conversation, the reliance on present tense reflects speakers' general focus on the immediate context, as illustrated by the following excerpts, where all present tense verbs are in bold:

A: Yeah, Laura**'s** in Robin's class.
B: Oh.
A: So er, anyway, I er – I**'ve** done this thing today, I**'ve** to come up with, I'll do this afternoon. I**'m** quite proud of it.
B: – What **do** you **do** at Dudley Allen then?
A: What the school?
B: Yeah. **Do** you –
A: No I**'m**, I**'m** only on the PTA.
B: You**'re** just on the PTA?
A: That**'s** it.
B: You **don't** actually work?
A: I **work** at the erm –
B: I **know** you **work** at Crown Hills, **don't** you?
A: Yeah. (CONV)

A: Excuse me, who**'s** that making that noise?
B: Oh look at monkeypooh, he**'s** got his tongue hanging out.
A: I **know**, and he always **sleeps** like that.
C: **Does** he?
A: Mm mmm.
B: Michael this **is** lovely.
C: You**'re** not planning on having <unclear>.
B: But that**'s** awful that you**'ve** done everything.
C: But, well – it **is** awful, I **agree**, but –
D: Well just stay there then.
A: **Do** you two **do** the cooking rather than go out?
C: Well it **depends**. (CONV)

As these excerpts illustrate, both of the two major functions of the simple present tense are common in conversation: to refer to current states (e.g. *Laura's in ...*, *I'm quite proud, I know, this is lovely*) and to refer to current habitual behavior (e.g. *What do you do, I work at ...*, *he always sleeps ...*, *do you two do the cooking*). These functions are associated respectively with two broad semantic categories of verbs: **stative verbs** (which typically denote stable states of affairs) and **dynamic verbs** (which denote events, acts, or processes with an inherent implication of completion).

In addition, the use of the present progressive above (*You're not planning ...*) refers to present intention, and the use of the present perfect (*I've done ...*, *You've done ...*, etc.) relates past events or states to the present situation. Because conversational concerns tend to be with the immediate here and now, speakers use present tense most of the time. In addition, as discussed in 6.2.1.1, speakers can use the present tense even when narrating past events.

Academic prose, on the other hand, uses the present tense not so much to focus on the immediate context, as to imply a lack of time restriction, with the present subsuming past and future time:

> A fault tree analysis **reveals** the logical connections existing between an undesired event in a technical system and component and operating failures which **lead** to it. In the case of safety analyses for process plants the undesired event usually **is** a fire, a release of toxic substances or an explosion. In other cases it **is** simply an outage of the system. The method of analysis **is** deductive and **is** normally used for calculating the probability of occurrence of the undesired event. A qualitative investigation of the system **is** a prerequisite for it. This **requires** knowledge about the dynamic behaviour of the system.
> (ACAD)

Here and elsewhere in academic writing, the present tense is used to convey the idea that these propositions are true, regardless of time (e.g. the method of analysis in the passage above will in some sense always be deductive). Further, the distinction between description of a state and habitual behavior is blurred in this register. In the above passage, both stative verbs (such as the copula *be* and the lexical verb *require*) and dynamic verbs (such as *lead* and *reveal*) are used to present propositional information that is generally valid whenever the states or events actually occur (cf. 5.2.1).

In contrast, as already noted, fiction writers use past tense verbs much more frequently than present tense verbs. In fact, many fictional narratives are written entirely in the past tense (shown in bold below), with present tense verbs being used only in the direct speech attributed to fictional characters (in *[]*):

> Roz **was** irritable as she **sat** across the table from Marge in the holiday filled coffee shop off the turnpike. The sounds of loud voices and ringing jingle of the cash register **resounded** sharply against her ears, causing her to become more impatient to leave. Hurriedly draining her cup, she **frowned** at Marge, who **had** hardly touched the coffee that she just **had** to have before traveling any farther.
> "Look, hon, we [have] to hurry. Mom['s] real together about serving Thanksgiving dinner on time."
> "All right—" Marge **replied**. (FICT)

## 6.2.3    Lexical associations of present and past tense

Many verbs have a strong association with either present or past tense.

➤ Many verbs occur most of the time in the present tense.

    The following lists include all relatively common verbs (verbs occurring over ten times per million words) in the LSWE Corpus that typically occur in the present tense:

> ➤ Verbs occurring over 80% of the time in the present tense: *bet, doubt, know, matter, mean, mind, reckon, suppose, thank.*

> ➤ Verbs occurring over 70% of the time in the present tense: *care, differ, fancy, imply, tend, want.*

➤ There are also many verbs that occur most of the time in the past tense. The following lists include all relatively common verbs (verbs occurring over ten times per million words) in the LSWE Corpus that usually occur in the past tense:

> ➤ Verbs occurring over 80% of the time in the past tense: *exclaim, eye, glance, grin, nod, pause, remark, reply, shrug, sigh, smile, whisper.*

> ➤ Verbs occurring over 70% of the time in the past tense: *bend, bow, lean, light, park, seat, set off, shake, stare, turn away, wave, wrap.*

**DISCUSSION OF FINDINGS**

The above lists show a basic difference in the most common verbs used in the two tenses. The present tense is strongly associated with verbs denoting mental and logical states (cf. mental verbs and existence verbs; 5.2.1–2) while the past tense is strongly associated with verbs denoting events or activities, especially bodily movements and speech acts (cf. activity verbs and communication verbs; 5.2.1–2).

    Many of the mental verbs strongly associated with the present tense express emotions or attitudes, especially in conversation (5.2.2.2). Common verbs of this type are *bet, care, doubt, fancy, know, mean, mind, reckon, suppose, thank, want*:

> I don't **want** one. (CONV)

> I **bet** he's starving for real grub. (FICT)

> But I **reckon** they have got it just right with the Mondeo. (NEWS)

In addition, many of the verbs associated with present tense refer to logical states; common verbs of this type are *differ, imply, tend, matter*:

> I don't suppose that **matters** really. (CONV)

> Customs **differ**, but the meaning's the same. (NEWS)

> The sequence **implies** a history of Muav sedimentation and burial. (ACAD†)

> Transplanting **tends** to reduce lodging. (ACAD)

In contrast, many of the verbs strongly associated with past tense describe human activities, e.g. *bend, bow, eye, glance, grin, lean, nod, park, pause, sit, set off, shake, shrug, sigh, smile, stare, turn away, wave*. A special subset of these are communication verbs used for reporting speech acts: *exclaim, remark, reply, whisper*. Fiction makes extensive use of both sets of verbs. Other less-common verbs that occur in the past tense over 80 percent of the time include *beckon, blush, chuckle, cough, duck, fold, frown, gasp, gesture, giggle, groan, growl, grunt, heave, limp, mumble, murmur, mutter, scramble, stagger, whistle, wink.* These all refer to typically human actions (e.g. bodily movements or creating noises). Human activities:

> She just **shrugged** her shoulders. (CONV)
>
> Rachael **glanced** at her uncle. (FICT)
>
> She **waved** to well-wishers at Sadler's Wells in London. (NEWS†)

Speech act verbs:

> Well he **whispered** to me last night, you know. (CONV)
>
> "A fine thing," Dr. Saito **remarked** to me. (FICT)

## 6.3 Aspect

From a semantic point of view, both tense and aspect relate primarily to time distinctions in the verb phrase. However, whereas **tense** refers primarily to past and present time orientation, **aspect** relates to considerations such as the completion or lack of completion of events or states described by a verb (cf. the aspectual main verbs in 5.2.2). The **perfect aspect** designates events or states taking place during a period leading up to the specified time. The **progressive aspect** designates an event or state of affairs which is in progress, or continuing, at the time indicated by the rest of the verb phrase.

Structurally, the two aspects in English are distinguished as follows: perfect aspect is marked by the auxiliary verb *have* + *ed*-participle; and progressive aspect is marked by the auxiliary verb *be* + *ing*-participle. Both aspects can be combined with either present or past tense.

**Perfect aspect present tense:**

> We **have written** to Mr. Steven, but he **has ignored** our letters. (NEWS)

**Perfect aspect past tense:**

> He **had seen** him picking purses. (FICT)

**Progressive aspect present tense:**

> No, she**'s going** by train. (CONV)

**Progressive aspect past tense:**

> That's why I **was thinking** I might hang onto the Volvo. (CONV)

In general terms, the present perfect is used to refer to a situation that began sometime in the past and continues up to the present. For example, the sentence

> But now she**'s gone** on holiday for a whole month. (CONV)

describes a past action (leaving for a holiday) that creates a situation (or result) that extends to the present. (The phrase *for a whole month* also implies a continuation into the future.)

Compared with present perfect aspect, past perfect aspect has a straightforward function—to refer to a time that is earlier than some specified past time:

> Two brothers told a court yesterday how they watched their terminally-ill mother "fade away" after she was given an injection.
>
> Widow Lilian Boyes, 70, **had** earlier **pleaded** with doctors to "finish her off," Winchester Crown Court heard. (NEWS)

Because there are important differences in meaning and function between the present perfect and the past perfect, they are each discussed in separate sections below: present perfect in 6.3.2.1–3 and past perfect in 6.3.2.4–5.

The progressive aspect is typically used to report situations or activities that are in progress at some point in time. The meaning and use of the progressive aspect is discussed in 6.3.3 below.

## 6.3.1 Perfect and progressive aspect across registers and dialects

In this section, we first look at the distribution of aspectually marked forms across registers in BrE, and then compare the patterns of use for AmE and BrE.

## 6.3.1.1 Register distribution of perfect and progressive aspect

Figures 6.2–4 show the distribution of simple, perfect, and progressive aspects across the four registers. Note that the perfect progressive aspect is omitted because of its rarity (less than 0.5 percent of all verb phrases).

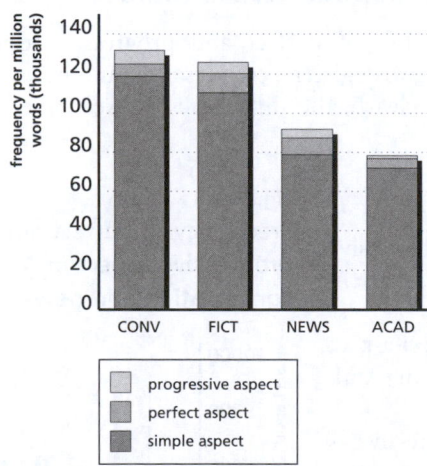

**Figure 6.2**
**Frequency of simple, perfect, and progressive aspect across registers**

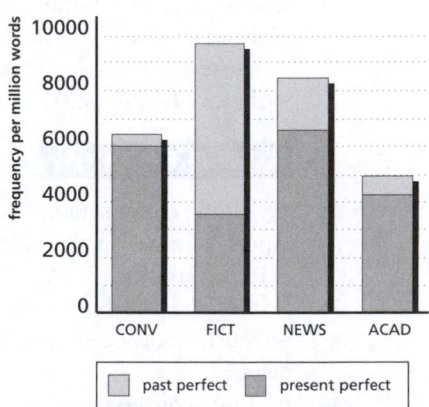

**Figure 6.3**
**Frequency of past perfect and present perfect aspect across registers**

**CORPUS FINDINGS** [2,7]

➤ Verbs phrases unmarked for aspect are overwhelmingly the most common in all four registers (about 90% of all verbs).
➤ While perfect aspect verb phrases are much less common than simple aspect verb phrases, they do occur relatively frequently in all registers (between 5% and 10%).
➤ Progressive aspect verb phrases are slightly less common than perfect aspect verb phrases.
➤ The usual tense of verb phrases marked for aspect differs across registers:
  ➤ The large majority of perfect and progressive aspect verb phrases in conversation, news reportage, and academic prose are in the present tense.

➤ Fiction shows the opposite preference—most perfect and progressive aspect verb phrases are in the past tense.

➤ Perfect progressive verb phrases (marked for both aspects, e.g. *has been waiting*) are rare in all registers, comprising less than 0.5% of all verb phrases (see also 6.5).

### DISCUSSION OF FINDINGS

The perfect and progressive aspects convey specialized kinds of meaning, and hence are less commonly used than simple present tense and past tense. The register preferences for present or past aspectual forms parallel the distribution of simple tense forms across registers (6.2.2). The perfect aspect is used to report events or states existing at an earlier time; they are most common in fiction and news.

**Figure 6.4**

**Frequency of past progressive and present progressive across registers**

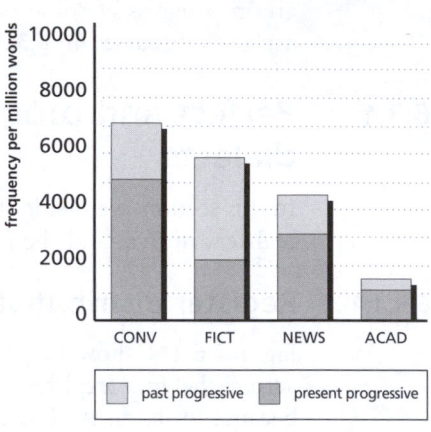

## 6.3.1.2 Perfect and progressive aspect across dialects

Figure 6.5 shows the distribution of perfect and progressive aspects in two registers in AmE and BrE. The two registers, conversation and news, were chosen as those most likely to reflect clearly the differences between the two regional varieties (1.3.2, 1.4.2).

### CORPUS FINDINGS [2]

➤ In AmE conversation, the progressive aspect is much more common than in BrE conversation.

➤ Conversely, in BrE news the perfect aspect is much more common than in AmE news.

➤ In AmE conversation, the progressive is about twice as common as the perfect.

➤ In marked contrast, in BrE news the perfect is about twice as common as the progressive.

### DISCUSSION OF FINDINGS

If we add the frequencies in the two registers together, there is a clear trend: AmE strongly favors the progressive in comparison with BrE (approximately in

**Figure 6.5**

**Frequency of perfect and progressive aspect in AmE v. BrE conversation and news**

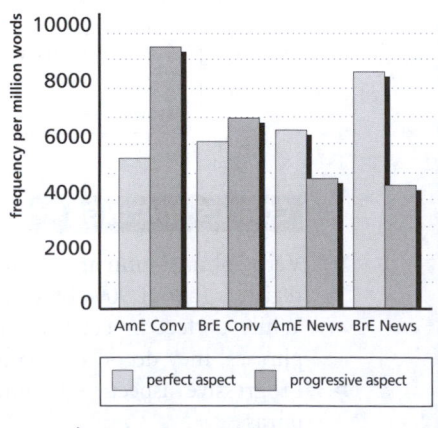

the ratio of 4:3), whereas BrE strongly favors the perfect in comparison with AmE (approximately in the same ratio of 4:3). However, when we break this down by register, a puzzling yet remarkable picture emerges. For each aspect, virtually the whole difference is accounted for by one register: conversation in the case of the progressive, and news in the case of the perfect. However, if we look more carefully at the other registers, they confirm the same trend, but to a much smaller degree. There is a slightly higher frequency of the progressive in AmE news than in BrE news, and a slightly higher frequency of the perfect in BrE conversation than in AmE.

The interpretation of these findings can only be highly speculative. The progressive has been in use for 500 years. AmE conversation often appears the most 'advanced' variety in our Corpus, so it would not be surprising if it was setting the trend in the increasing use of the progressive aspect as well. However, its vast difference in frequency between AmE conversation and BrE conversation is still surprising.

As for the perfect aspect, it has frequently been noted that AmE uses the past tense in contexts where BrE favors the present perfect, for example with *yet* or *already*:

> A: Hey, **did** you **read** through this yet?
> B: No not yet I **didn't**. I **didn't get** a chance. (AmE CONV)

> *We already **gave** him a down payment.* (AmE CONV†)

Nevertheless, this difference of usage does not seriously affect the frequencies in conversation. It remains a mystery why the marked difference of frequency shows up mainly in news. It might be relevant that American newspapers are renowned for a space-saving drive towards stylistic economy, and that the simple past usually requires one less word than the perfect.

## 6.3.2 Perfect aspect

Because the meaning and use of present perfect aspect differs in important ways from the past perfect, we discuss them separately in the following sections.

### 6.3.2.1 Lexical associations of present perfect aspect

The present perfect aspect is common in news, academic prose, and conversation (6.3.1.1). However, as shown by the verbs that commonly occur with the present perfect, these three registers use this tense-aspect combination in somewhat different ways (see Table 6.1).

**CORPUS FINDINGS** [2,4]

➤ The verb *been* is the most common present perfect form in all registers except conversation.
➤ The verb *has/have got* in BrE conversation is the single most common present perfect verb in any one register, occurring well over 2,000 times per million words; it rarely occurs in academic writing.
➤ In news and academic prose, several other verbs occur with the present perfect relatively frequently. The following lists include all relatively common verbs in these registers that occur with the present perfect more than 25% of the time.
  ➤ News reportage: *agree, appoint, campaign, circulate, criticise, draft, experience, pledge, prompt, vow, witness.*
  ➤ Academic prose: *criticise, document, implicate, master, report.*

Table 6.1    **Verbs that occur with the present perfect aspect over 40 times per million words in at least one register; occurrences per million words**

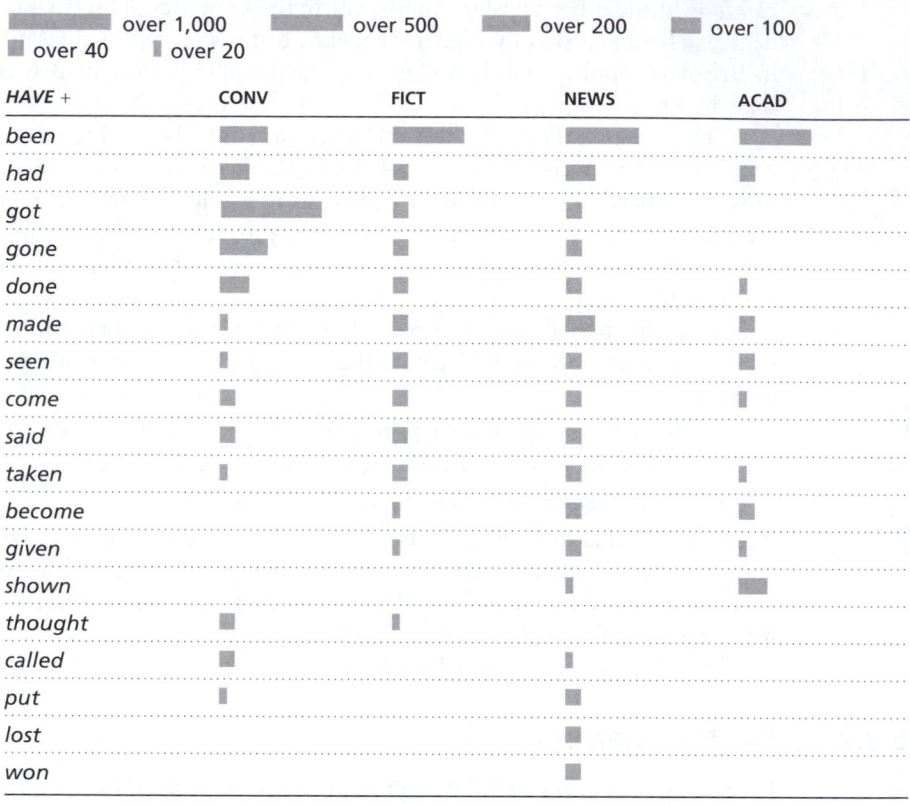

| HAVE + | CONV | FICT | NEWS | ACAD |
|--------|------|------|------|------|
| been | ■■■ | ■■■■ | ■■■ | ■■■■ |
| had | ■ | ▪ | ■ | ▪ |
| got | ■■■■■ | ▪ | ■ | |
| gone | ■■■ | ▪ | ▪ | |
| done | ■ | ▪ | ▪ | ▪ |
| made | ▪ | ■ | ■■ | ■ |
| seen | ▪ | ■ | ■ | ■ |
| come | ■ | ■ | ■ | ▪ |
| said | ■ | ■ | ■ | |
| taken | ▪ | ■ | ■ | ▪ |
| become | | ▪ | ■ | ■ |
| given | | ▪ | ■ | ▪ |
| shown | | | ▪ | ■■ |
| thought | ■ | ▪ | | |
| called | ■ | | ▪ | |
| put | ▪ | | ■ | |
| lost | | | ■ | |
| won | | | ■ | |

Legend: ■■■ over 1,000    ■■ over 500    ■■ over 200    ■ over 100    ▪ over 40    ▪ over 20

➤ At the other extreme, there are many verbs that hardly ever occur with the perfect. The following list includes all relatively common verbs in the LSWE Corpus that occur with the perfect less than 2% of the time: *accommodate, afford, aim, await, base, believe, bet, boil, compete, comprise, connect, consist, constitute, contain, correspond, cost, denote, depend, differ, distinguish, doubt, ensure, entitle, excuse, glance, illustrate, induce, inhibit, kiss, lean, let, matter, mind, need, nod, protect, quit, reckon, reflect, regulate, relate, remember, represent, require, resemble, scream, smell, smile, stare, suppose, thank, want, wave.*

### DISCUSSION OF FINDINGS

The perfect aspect combination *have/has been* is frequent and serves a variety of functions. Apart from its copular use, it can occur with a meaning similar to the perfect of *go*, as in:

> **Where the hell have you been?** (CONV)

> **We've been to a lot of seminars too.** (CONV)

Here *been* implies movement to a destination followed by return. Additionally *have/has been* functions as the auxiliary part of a passive verb phrase or (less commonly) of a progressive verb phrase:

> However once its position **has been determined** it is in a totally different state. (ACAD)

> Hunter Howerton, an American secret service agent, **has been reminiscing**
> about the days when counterfeiting was a specialist art form. (NEWS)

The present perfect of *get* and *have* are used in different ways in AmE and BrE; see
the detailed discussion of those differences in 6.3.2.2.

Otherwise, the most common main verbs with the present perfect aspect are
also some of the most common verbs overall: compare the list of Table 6.1 with
the list of most common lexical verbs in 5.2.2.2. Most of the verbs that are
common with perfect aspect denote physical or communicative activities with
consequences that can exist over an extended period of time; these verbs therefore
imply a resultant state in the present:

> He's **gone** home. (CONV)
>
> They've **done** so much. (CONV)
>
> Every time I've **said** something nasty about her, I'm sorry. (CONV)
>
> One of Czechoslovakia's most prominent dissidents **has gone** underground
> rather than face an appeal hearing. (NEWS†)
>
> The Indian High Commission **have made** a similar comment. (NEWS)
>
> Doctors in the region **have called** for a review of the prescription charge
> system. (NEWS†)

In academic prose, the present perfect is typically used with different verbs, to
imply the continuing validity of earlier findings or practices:

> Experiments **have shown**, however, that plants can obtain their nutrients at
> sufficient rates to maintain rapid growth. (ACAD†)
>
> This, as we **have seen**, is a stable arrangement. (ACAD†)
>
> It **has become** the usual practice to use only maintenance applications.
> (ACAD†)

By contrast, the verbs that rarely occur with the present perfect are mainly from
the mental and existence domains (5.2.2). These verbs refer to states that typically
exist at some past or present time but do not suggest any ensuing situation.

Mental states:

> He **needs** it for something. (CONV)
>
> He **wants** another piece. (CONV)
>
> But he **doubted** it. (FICT)
>
> She **believed** she would be safer as a public figure. (FICT)

Logical states:

> Each formation **comprises** a distinctive set of rock layers. (ACAD†)
>
> Again, this **represents** a transposition of tendencies. (ACAD†)
>
> Durkheim seeks to delimit what **constitutes** crime. (ACAD†)

Note, in this last example, the tendency to use the simple present tense even when
reporting the views and writings of scholars and scientists in the past (Durkheim
died in 1917).

Some activity verbs denoting bodily actions such as *glance, kiss, nod, scream,
smile* also rarely occur in the present perfect:

> She **glanced** at him shyly. (FICT)
>
> Judge Crawford **kissed** the woman on both cheeks. (NEWS)

These typically involve short-term events without long-term results.

## 6.3.2.2   Present perfect forms of *get* and *have* across dialects

This section considers further two of the most common present perfect verbs: *has/have got* and *has/have had*. Both verbs mark possession in a general sense. The frequency counts reported in this section exclude occurrences of *have got to*, which is considered as a semi-modal (6.6); however, they include all other occurrences of *got(ten)* (as copula, or transitive main verb, and passive auxiliary).

**CORPUS FINDINGS** [2]

➤ In BrE conversation, the combination *has/have got* is more common than either *got* or *have* occurring alone.

   ➤ An alternative form—*has/have gotten*—is restricted primarily to AmE conversation and rare compared to the other forms.

➤ Overall, perfect aspect *got* is much more common in BrE than AmE (even when including *gotten* with *got* in AmE); in contrast, simple present tense *has/have* (as transitive main verb) is much more common in AmE.

**Table 6.2**   ***Have, have got(ten)*, and *got* in AmE and BrE conversation; occurrences per million words**

each ● represents 100

| | has/have (main verb) | has/have got | has/have gotten | got (past tense or ed-participle) |
|---|---|---|---|---|
| AmE | ●●●●●●●●●●●● ●●●●●●●●●●● ●●●●●●●●●●● ●●●●●●●●●●● ●●●●●●●●● | ●●●●●●●●●●● | ● | ●●●●●●●●●●●● ●●●●●●●● |
| BrE | ●●●●●●●●●●● ●●●●●●●●●●● ●●●●●● | ●●●●●●●●●●● ●●●●●●●●●●● ●●●●●● | – | ●●●●●●●●●●● ●●●●●●●● |

➤ In addition, the present perfect of *have* is especially common in news as well as conversation (see Table 6.1).

**DISCUSSION OF FINDINGS**

The two most common present perfect aspect verbs (apart from *been*) both mark possession in a general sense: *has/have got* and *has/have had*. *Has/have got*, which is extremely common in BrE conversation, has a range of meanings roughly equivalent to the simple present tense of *have*:

   *Jones **has got** the letter.* (CONV)

   *I **have got** a problem actually.* (CONV)

   *She's **got** blond hair.* (CONV)

   *He's **got** a bad temper.* (CONV)

   *Angie I think we've **got** a leak.* (CONV)

It is also common to elide the perfect aspect marker (*has/have*) while retaining the *ed* form of the verb (*got*). In many cases, this expression has a meaning associated with perfect aspect *have + got*—indicating the current possession of something—rather than the past tense meaning that something was acquired:

   *You **got** more than thirty pence.* (CONV)

*Oh I **got** loads left.* (CONV)

*And then something else I **got** here is peanut butter pie.* (CONV)

In AmE conversation, the present tense form of *have* is much more commonly used to express this meaning than *has/have got*:

*This friend of mine **has** a vault in his house.* (AmE CONV)

*Santa Barbara **has** Republican tendencies.* (AmE CONV)

In addition, AmE makes a meaning distinction between *has/have got*, to refer to current possession, and *has/have gotten*, meaning that something has been acquired or that a change of state has occurred:

*And we still **haven't gotten** a damn pumpkin.* (AmE CONV)

*You know my daughter **has gotten** in trouble with this in school.* (AmE CONV)

In BrE, this perfect meaning is expressed by *have got*:

*She **has got** hold of some papers which seem to support her claim.* (BrE FICT)

In contrast, *have had* emphasizes the current relevance of some state that came into being in the past. This expression is especially common in conversation and news:

*Well, she**'s had** a miserable life.* (CONV†)

*I've **had** enough of this conversation.* (CONV)

*I **have had** a few years in which to practise cooking.* (NEWS)

*The Chancellor, who **has had** his troubles with the press, took his chance to hit back with obvious glee yesterday.* (NEWS)

### 6.3.2.3 Present perfect aspect v. simple past tense

Both the present perfect and the simple past tense are used to refer to an event or state in the past. In addition, both can be used to refer to a state of affairs that existed for a period of time. The primary difference in meaning between the two is that the present perfect describes a situation that continues to exist up to the present time, while the past tense describes a situation that no longer exists or an event that took place at a particular time in the past.

This meaning difference is often made explicit by time adverbials accompanying the main verb (see 10.2.1.2 on adverbials of time). With the past tense, these adverbials simply describe when the event or state occurred:

*I **saw** him [yesterday].* (CONV)

*[At that moment], Toby **knocked**.* (FICT)

*[One day, a few weeks ago], I **talked** with Dave about exactly that.* (FICT)

The most common time adverbial occurring with the simple past tense is *then*, which typically marks a simple progression of past events:

*And [then] they **said** have you heard of the paper? And I **said** yes but not as er as a window. [Then] they **said** well and [then] I **realized** that it was Fennite.* (CONV)

*He **picked** up Sammler's dark glasses and **returned** them to his nose. He [then] **unfolded** and **mounted** his own, circular, of gentian violet gently banded with the lovely Dior gold. [Then] he **departed**.* (FICT)

Other time adverbials with the simple past are often used to delimit a period or duration of past time, thus marking a clear ending point before the present time. Prepositional phrases headed by *in*, *during*, *throughout*, and *for* are commonly used for this function (e.g. *in 1976, in August, during the fall of 1988, throughout this period, for 30 minutes*):

> *[Throughout the rest of the week] we* **racked** *our brains.* (FICT)
>
> *I* **met** *Giovanni [during my second year in Paris].* (FICT)
>
> *[In 1988] the Long-term Credit Bank of Japan* **set up** *a joint investment advisory company.* (NEWS†)
>
> *Raper* **was jailed** *[for two years] and Allen [for six months].* (NEWS)

In contrast, adverbials indicating duration or a time period are used with present perfect to mark the beginning point or the duration of the period of time, but rarely indicate the ending time (which is assumed to be the present):

> *We've had it [since last January].* (CONV)
>
> *The bigger nations, for their part,* **have** *[already]* **developed** *systems of takeover supervision.* (NEWS)
>
> *Energy costs* **have risen** *in real money terms [since the early 1970s].* (ACAD†)

An exception is *now*, which is used to mark a contrast between the present situation and one obtaining in the past:

> *Turbojets* **have** *[now]* **been superseded** *by turbofans.* (ACAD†)

## 6.3.2.4  Lexical associations of past perfect aspect

**CORPUS FINDINGS** [2,3,4]

> ➤ Only *had been* is very common in all registers; other verbs are common in the past perfect only in fiction (see Table 6.3).
>
> ➤ In addition, several verbs in fiction occur in the past perfect a relatively high proportion of the time. The following are all the relatively common verbs in fiction that occur in the past perfect more than 25% of the time: *anticipate, deceive, encounter, inherit, taste, transform*.

**DISCUSSION OF FINDINGS**

Like past tense verb phrases, past perfect verb phrases are most common by far in fiction. The major semantic difference between them is that the past perfect refers to a time before the past time referred to by the simple past tense.

The most common verbs with the past perfect are some of the most common verbs overall, similar to the most common verbs with the present perfect (compare Table 6.3 with Table 6.1 and the lists of most common lexical verbs in 5.2.2.2). These are mostly verbs describing physical movements and other activities (e.g. *go, come, leave, make, take, do, bring, give, get*), speech acts (*say, tell*), and mental perceptions or thoughts (*see, hear, know*):

> *Nancy* **had gone** *with them.* (FICT)
>
> *He* **had taken** *it himself.* (FICT)
>
> *I kept remembering what Addy* **had said**. (FICT)
>
> *Rick* **had seen** *that before in androids.* (FICT)

**Table 6.3** **Distribution of the most common verbs with the past perfect aspect**

Verbs that occur with the past perfect aspect over 40 times per million words in at least one register; occurrences per million words

▰ over 100   ▪ over 40   ▮ over 20

| HAD + | CONV | FICT | NEWS | ACAD |
|---|---|---|---|---|
| been | over 40 | over 100 | over 100 | over 100 |
| gone | over 20 | over 100 | over 20 | |
| come | | over 100 | over 20 | |
| made | | over 100 | over 20 | |
| taken | | over 100 | over 20 | |
| done | over 40 | | over 20 | |
| left | over 40 | | over 20 | |
| had | over 40 | | | over 20 |

**verbs common in the past perfect only in fiction:**

| | | FICT | | |
|---|---|---|---|---|
| say | | over 100 | | |
| see | | over 100 | | |
| become | | over 40 | | |
| begin | | over 40 | | |
| bring | | over 40 | | |
| find | | over 40 | | |
| give | | over 40 | | |
| get | | over 40 | | |
| happen | | over 40 | | |
| hear | | over 40 | | |
| know | | over 40 | | |
| tell | | over 40 | | |
| turn | | over 40 | | |

## 6.3.2.5  Past perfect aspect v. simple past tense

**CORPUS FINDINGS** [2,3]

➤ The past perfect aspect has accompanying time adverbials a greater percentage of the time than does the simple past tense.
➤ Past perfect verb phrases often occur in dependent clauses.
➤ Taken together, these two factors (time adverbials and dependent clauses) account for c. 70% of all occurrences of past perfect verb phrases.

**DISCUSSION OF FINDINGS**

Because past perfect verb phrases are context dependent—referring to a time before a past time signaled elsewhere—it is sometimes difficult to identify their intended time reference. As a result, the time reference of the past perfect is often anchored by (a) time adverbials and (b) dependent clauses.

Time adverbials do this by overtly identifying a time frame (shown in *[ ]*) to be used in interpreting the reference of the past perfect:

> But too late; he **had** *[already]* **told** her. (FICT†)
>
> *[When he returned]* the priest **had** *[already]* **used** the special needle-sharp quill and ink. (FICT†)
>
> So he sat down and breathed deeply as the Zen teachers **had taught** him *[years ago].* (FICT)
>
> She **had seen** them *[once]* through the dining-room door. (FICT†)

When past perfect verb phrases occur in dependent clauses, the main clause provides the anchor for interpreting the time reference. In fiction, the past perfect is most common in adverbial clauses and complement clauses, while in academic prose the past perfect is most common in relative clauses.

**Figure 6.6**

**Percentage use of past perfect and simple past tense verbs in four grammatical contexts**

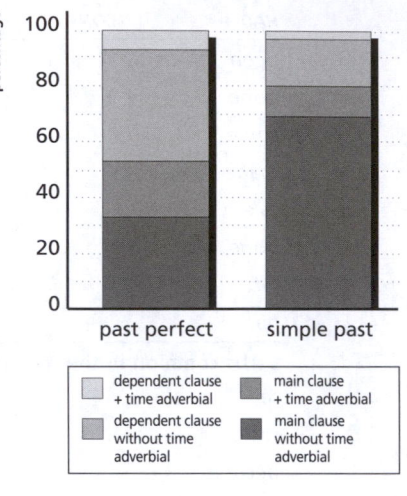

Past perfect in adverbial clause:

> When I **had sorted** that out, I shrugged. (FICT)
>
> When everyone **had drunk** two or three horns, Nwakibie sent for his wives. (FICT)

Past perfect in complement clause:

> It came almost as a shock to realize that her night **had been** peaceful. (FICT)
>
> Some people even said that they **had heard** the spirits flying and flapping their wings against the roof of the cave. (FICT)

Past perfect in relative clause:

> This finding was confirmed using lifetable analysis, with a 35 percent reduction in the proportion of ulcer relapses in patients who **had received** cisapride. (ACAD†)
>
> The 245-year-old was a remnant of the old-growth lodgepole pine that **had** originally **covered** the area of all three stands. (ACAD)

## 6.3.3 Progressive aspect

The progressive aspect is used to describe activities or events that are in progress at a particular time, usually for a limited duration. The present progressive aspect describes events that are currently in progress or are about to take place in the near future; the past progressive aspect describes events that were in progress or about to take place at some earlier time.

Present progressive aspect:

> **I'm looking** for an employee of yours. (FICT)
>
> What's she **doing**? (CONV)

Past progressive aspect:

>I **was** just **coming** back from Witham. (CONV)

>Well he **was saying** that he's finding it a bit difficult. (CONV)

Present progressive with future time reference:

>But she's **coming** back tomorrow. (CONV)

>I'm **going** with him next week. (FICT)

It is sometimes supposed that the progressive aspect occurs only with dynamic verbs describing activities or events. However, the progressive can also be used with verbs that describe a static situation. In this case, the progressive expresses the meaning of a temporary state that exists for a period of time:

>Chris **is living** there now. (CONV)

>I **was sitting** in my office smoking one of James's cigarettes. (FICT)

Some of the most common verbs occurring with progressive aspect are of this type.

## 6.3.3.1 Lexical associations of progressive aspect

Progressive aspect is most common in conversation and fiction (6.3.1.1). In conversation, most progressive verb phrases are in the present tense (c. 70 percent), while in fiction, most progressive verb phrases are in the past tense (c. 70 percent).

**CORPUS FINDINGS** [2,3,4]

➤ Common verbs in the progressive aspect come from several different semantic domains. These include dynamic verbs marking physical or communication activities, and stative verbs describing physical situations and mental, attitudinal, and perceptual states (cf. the activity verbs, communication verbs, and mental verbs discussed in 5.2.2.2).

➤ There are also several verbs that have a strong lexical association with the progressive aspect, occurring over 50% of the time as progressives. Most of these verbs refer to physical or communication activities.

➤ At the other extreme, many verbs from these same semantic domains hardly ever occur in the progressive aspect.

**Verbs referring to activities and physical events** (cf. activity verbs, 5.2.2.2):

• occurring over 80% of the time with the progressive, in conversation: *bleed, chase, shop, starve*

• occurring over 50% of the time with the progressive, in conversation and/or fiction: *dance, drip, head (for), march, pound, rain, stream, sweat*

• 40 other verbs that frequently occur with the progressive aspect (more than ten times per million words): e.g. *bring, buy, carry, come, cry, do, drive, eat, give, go, laugh, leave, make, move, pay, play, run, take, walk, work*

• rarely occurring with the progressive aspect (less than 2% of the time): *arrest, attain, award, dissolve, find, frighten, invent, rule, shut, shrug, smash, suck, suspend, swallow, throw, trap*

**Verbs referring to communication acts** (cf. communication verbs, 5.2.2.2):

• occurring over 80% of the time with the progressive, in conversation: *chat, joke, kid, moan*

- occurring over 50% of the time with the progressive, in conversation and/or fiction: *scream, talk*
- other verbs frequently occurring with the progressive aspect (more than ten times per million words): *ask, say, speak, tell*
- rarely occurring with the progressive aspect (less than 2% of the time): *accuse, communicate, disclose, exclaim, label, reply, thank*

**Verbs referring to mental/attitudinal states or activities** (cf. mental verbs, 5.2.2.2):

- occurring over 50% of the time with the progressive, in conversation and/or fiction:[4] *look forward, study*
- frequently occurring with the progressive aspect (more than ten times per million words): *hope, think, wonder*
- rarely occurring with the progressive aspect (less than 2% of the time): *agree, appreciate, associate, attribute, base, believe, conceive, concern, conclude, correlate, delight, desire, know, like, reckon, suspect, want*

**Verbs referring to perceptual states or activities** (cf. mental verbs, 5.2.2.2):

- frequently occurring with the progressive aspect (more than ten times per million words): *look, watch, feel, stare, listen*
- rarely occurring with the progressive aspect (less than 2% of the time): *detect, hear, perceive, see*

**Verbs referring to static physical situations** (cf. existence verbs, 5.2.2.2):

- occurring over 50% of the time with the progressive aspect, in conversation and/or fiction: *lurk*
- frequently occurring with the progressive aspect (more than ten times per million words): *wait, sit, stand, wear, hold, live, stay*

**Verbs of facilitation/causation or obligation** (cf. causative verbs, 5.2.2.2):

- rarely occurring with the progressive aspect (less than 2% of the time): *convince, entitle, guarantee, incline, induce, inhibit, initiate, inspire, interest, mediate, oblige, promise, prompt, provoke, render*

➤ Two verbs in conversation are notable because they occur as past progressives more commonly than present progressives: *was saying* and *was thinking*.
  ➤ *Was saying* is the only past progressive verb sequence to occur more than once every 100 minutes in conversation (over 100 times per million words).

### DISCUSSION OF FINDINGS

The verbs that are most frequent in the progressive aspect are also some of the most common verbs overall: thus compare Table 6.4 with the lists of most common lexical verbs in 5.2.2.2. *Be going* also functions as part of the semi-modal *be going to* (6.6); the counts reported here include only its use as a regular progressive aspect verb.

Many previous accounts of the progressive aspect describe it as occurring freely with dynamic verbs, while verbs with stative senses have been described as not occurring in the progressive. However, it turns out that both dynamic and stative verbs are included among the most common verbs in the progressive—and that both dynamic and stative verbs are included among the verbs that very rarely take the progressive.

Two characteristics distinguish the group of verbs commonly taking progressive aspect from the group that rarely occurs with the progressive:

First, the common progressive aspect verbs typically take a human subject as agent (3.2.1.1), actively controlling the action (or state) expressed by the verb. In contrast, some of the verbs that rarely occur in the progressive take a human subject as experiencer, undergoing but not controlling the action or state expressed by the verb. Other verbs in this group do not usually take a human subject at all.

Second, the action, state, or situation described by common progressive verbs can be prolonged. In contrast, the verbs that rarely occur in the progressive fall into two main groups: (a) those that refer to an action that is immediate, and (b) those that refer to a state that is not normally a continuing process.

The first distinguishing characteristic is most apparent with stative verbs. For example, the visual and auditory perception verbs *look*, *watch*, *stare*, and *listen*, which are all common with the progressive aspect, normally occur with a human agent controlling the visual or auditory perception:

> *He's **staring** at me now.* (CONV)
>
> *I **was looking** at that one just now.* (CONV)
>
> *And the police **are** always **watching**.* (FICT†)
>
> *I felt he **wasn't listening**.* (FICT)

In contrast, the verbs *see* and *hear*, which rarely occur in the progressive, describe perceptual states experienced, but not actively controlled, by the human identified in subject position:

> *I **saw** him the other day.* (CONV)
>
> *Yeah, I **heard** about that.* (CONV)

This difference is reflected in the fact that it is possible to 'stop looking/watching/staring/listening', but it is not reasonable to ask someone to 'stop seeing/hearing':

> *If only he would **stop staring** at her.* (FICT)
>
> *I **stopped listening** to Mavis.* (FICT)

However, the verb *see* does occasionally occur in the progressive in the expression *stop seeing* when it has the special meaning of 'having an ongoing relationship', which is presumably under the control of the subject:

> *'And I'll like it even more,' Rabbit says, 'when you **stop seeing** this greasy creep.'* (FICT†)

Similar factors are influential in distinguishing between progressive and non-progressive mental verbs. That is, verbs like *think* and *wonder*, which commonly occur with the progressive, can be interpreted as involving an active agent controlling the thought process. In contrast, verbs like *appreciate*, *desire*, *know*, *like*, and *want* are more typically interpreted as expressing a state experienced by someone:

> *You should **be wondering** why.* (CONV)
>
> *Oh, I **was** just **thinking**, it'd be nice to go there.* (CONV)
>
> *He **had been thinking** along the same lines.* (FICT)
>
> *I **was wondering** how often she did this.* (FICT†)
>
> v. *He didn't **know** why.* (FICT)
>
> *Naturally I **want** to help.* (FICT)

Other non-progressive verbs rarely occur with human subjects at all, because they describe a relationship between inanimate (often abstract) entities and often occur in the passive voice.

Relational verbs:

> This **concerned** the way in which electrons were ejected from metals. (ACAD†)

> This again **correlates** well with the light aerodynamic loading of this stage. (ACAD†)

Verbs typically occurring in the passive:

> Observable quantities can **be associated** with certain operators. (ACAD†)

> A financial estimate **was based** on these data. (ACAD)

Whether the verb can be regarded as reporting a process or not is also influential in distinguishing between progressive and non-progressive mental verbs. That is, verbs like *hope*, *think*, and *wonder* can be regarded as referring to processes having limited duration, and thus they occur commonly in the progressive. In contrast, verbs such as *believe*, *know*, *like*, and *want* are regarded as denoting mental states rather than processes, and thus they rarely occur with the progressive (see examples above).

Similarly, the static situations reported by verbs such as *stay*, *wait*, *sit*, *stand*, and *live* are often of short duration, so these verbs frequently occur with the progressive:

> Sandy's **staying** with her for a few days. (CONV)

> We **were waiting** for the train. (CONV)

> I **was standing** there the other night. (CONV)

> When I first came to this city as a young man, I **was living** in Furukawa. (FICT†)

This 'process' element of meaning is even more important, however, in accounting for the large number of dynamic activity verbs that rarely occur with the progressive. Stereotypical activity verbs (e.g. *bring*, *drive*, *move*, *play*, *walk*) refer to an action that can be prolonged over a period of time and thus commonly occur with the progressive:

> He **was driving** his van, delivering copies of First Rebel. (FICT)

> I dream I**'m running** along the street outside the school ... A lot of people **are chasing** after me. They**'re shouting**. (FICT)

In contrast, many dynamic verbs refer to an action that takes place instantaneously; for example, *shut*, *smash*, *swallow*, *throw*. Because these actions have virtually no duration, such verbs rarely occur in the progressive:

> The man **threw** me off the bus. (CONV)

> They **shut** the sliding doors behind them. (CONV)

> I **smashed** the electric light bulb. (FICT)

> He **swallowed** it down in one big gulp. (FICT)

It might be noted that several verbs of this type report the end-point of some process; for example, *attain*, *dissolve*, *find*, *invent*, *rule*. In these cases, the reference is still typically immediate, referring to a specific time when some result is achieved, rather than referring to the process leading up to that point:

*A disciplinary hearing in June **ruled** that Mr. Reid should be dismissed.* (NEWS†)

*Collett (1972), for example, **found** several directionally sensitive movement detectors in the brain.* (ACAD†)

The particular frequency of the verbs *saying* and *thinking* with the past progressive is puzzling. It seems that the use of the past progressive with these verbs (as in *She was saying ..., I was thinking ...*) conveys a more vivid imagery and a greater sense of involvement than the simple past tense (see also 14.4.4.5).

## 6.4 Active and passive voice

Transitive verbs are usually active, but can also occur in the passive voice (cf. 3.6.2). Since the active is the unmarked voice, and is copiously illustrated elsewhere in this chapter, we focus on passive verb phrases here.

Most passive constructions are formed with the auxiliary *be* followed by an *ed*-participle:

*Similarly, a polariser can **be shown** to act linearly.* (ACAD)

However, passive verb phrases can also be formed with the verb *get* in the role of auxiliary:

*It's about these people who **got left** behind in Vietnam.* (CONV)

Passive constructions are possible with most transitive verbs. The noun phrase in the role of subject in a passive construction usually corresponds to the noun phrase which is the direct object in the associated active construction:

1 *[The proposal] **was approved** by the Project Coordinating Team.* (ACAD)
   cf. *The Project Coordinating Team **approved** [the proposal].*

2 *To do so, [the cooling curves] **are plotted** for the two pure components.* (ACAD†)
   cf. *Someone **plotted** [the cooling curves].*

Example **1** also shows how the subject in the active version can be included in a *by*-phrase in the corresponding passive construction. The noun phrase in the *by*-phrase is commonly referred to as the **agent**, although it could also serve other semantic roles (3.2.1.1). The passive construction with a *by*-phrase is called the **long passive**. In contrast, the **short passive** (or **agentless passive**) does not have a *by*-phrase, as in **2** (see also 11.3.1).

Passive constructions are also commonly found with two-object (Pattern 2) prepositional verbs (5.3.3):

*[Dormancy] **is associated with** short duration.* (ACAD†)
cf. *Researchers **associate** [dormancy] **with** short duration.*

*[Elements] **are** usually **classified as** metals or non-metals.* (ACAD)
cf. *Researchers usually **classify** [elements] **as** metals or non-metals.*

In addition, the subject of a passive verb can correspond to the indirect object of a ditransitive verb (3.2.5), or the prepositional object of a two-place (Pattern 1) prepositional verb (3.2.6, 5.3.3).

Passive constructions form a fuzzy category, grading into *be* + predicative adjectives with stative meaning (3.5.3.1 and 5.5.2). For example, participial forms such as *delighted* and *excited* are clearly adjectival (7.2) rather than passive verbs:

> We *are delighted* with the result. (NEWS)

> I ought to *be excited*. (FICT†)

In contrast, forms such as *frozen* and *broken* are borderline cases; they are usually interpreted as stative in meaning, but it is also possible to infer an agent in many instances:

> The unity of the whole might *be broken*. (FICT†)

> The spell *was broken*. (FICT†)

> It is not known whether A. lapillus can withstand *being frozen* into sea ice. (ACAD)

The counts presented in the following sections are based on a relatively broad definition of passive, excluding only forms that are clearly adjectival in function (see also 11.3 on the **stative passive** v. **dynamic passive**).

## 6.4.1    Register distribution of active and passive voice

There are a number of factors influencing the use of the passive. Chapter 11 (11.3) deals with discourse factors influencing the choice between active and passive verbs (e.g. relating to the presentation of given and new information, and short v. long passives). The present section discusses the general register distribution of active and passive verb phrases; lexico-grammatical factors are covered in 6.4.2.

**CORPUS FINDINGS** [2,4]

> ➤ Passives are most common by far in academic prose, occurring about 18,500 times per million words.
>   > ➤ Passives are also common in news, occurring about 12,000 times per million words.
>   > ➤ Passives are most common in the registers that have the fewest total number of finite verbs.
> ➤ Proportionally, passives account for c. 25% of all finite verbs in academic prose.
>   > ➤ Passives account for c. 15% of all finite verbs in news.
> ➤ At the other extreme, passives account for only c. 2% of all finite verbs in conversation.
> ➤ The *get* passive is extremely rare (see 6.4.2.2).
>   > ➤ *Get* occurs only in conversation, except for an occasional example in colloquial fiction.
>   > ➤ Even in conversation, the *get* passive accounts for only about 0.1% of all verbs, and so is even less common than *be* passives.

**Figure 6.7**

**Frequency of finite passive v. non-passive verbs across registers**

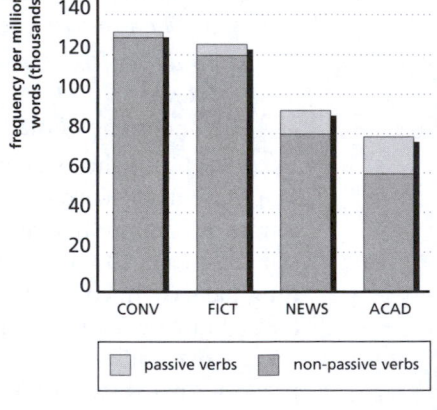

**DISCUSSION OF FINDINGS**

In many kinds of written expository prose, especially academic journal articles, passive constructions can be extremely frequent, with whole passages being written in the passive voice:

> *Three communities on a brackish marsh of the Rhode River, a sub-estuary of the Chesapeake Bay, **were exposed** to elevated carbon dioxide concentrations for two growing seasons beginning in April 1987. The study site and experimental design **are described** in Curtis et al. (1989a). One community **was dominated** by the perennial carbon 4 grass spartina patens ...* (ACAD)

One of the major functions of the passive is that it demotes the agent of the verb (often the person doing the action of the verb, cf. 3.2.1.1), while giving topic status to the affected patient (the entity being acted on, cf. 3.2.4.1). For example, the first two passive sentences in the above passage use short passives to omit the agent altogether, as can be seen from the corresponding active sentences:

> *[We, the researchers,] **exposed** three communities to elevated carbon dioxide concentrations.*

> *[We, the researchers,] **describe** the study site and experimental design in Curtis et al. (1989a).*

The short passive is in fact far more common than the long passive, and is widely used in academic writing to omit mention of the specific researcher(s). In part, this extensive use of passive constructions conveys an objective detachment from what is being described, as required by the Western scientific tradition. However, it might also be regarded simply as the expected style typical of much academic writing.

News has somewhat different reasons for the use of the passive, especially the short passive. Often the focus of a story is an event involving an affected person or institution, and the agent of this event may be easy to infer, uninteresting, or already mentioned. Hence, with a journalistic desire to save space and maximize what is novel, it is natural to omit these agents. For example, reference to 'the police' is omitted in an example like:

> *Doherty **was arrested** in New York in June.* (NEWS†)

In other instances the precise agent(s) may not be known, or they are not mentioned for legal reasons:

> *The officer **was beaten** and repeatedly **kicked** in the head.* (NEWS†)

By contrast, conversation, having a human-centered concern with people's actions, thoughts, and stances, usually does not demote the subject, who is often the speaker (11.3.1).

The *get* passive is clearly a recent innovation in English, and so not surprisingly is found almost exclusively in conversation (and consequently in dialog in fiction).

## 6.4.2 Lexical associations of the passive

In addition to register, lexical factors are strongly related to the choice between active and passive forms.

### 6.4.2.1 Verbs that commonly occur in the passive

**CORPUS FINDINGS ²**

➤ The passive forms of most verbs are most common in academic prose (Table 6.5); some exceptions are *be done, be born, be told, be said, be expected, be held.*

Table 6.5  **Frequency of particular lexical verbs with the passive (including all verbs that occur with the passive voice with overall corpus frequencies of more than 20 occurrences per million words); occurrences per million words**

Legend: ▬ over 300   ▬ over 200   ▬ over 100   ▪ over 40   ▪ over 20

| BE + | CONV | FICT | NEWS | ACAD |
|---|---|---|---|---|
| made | over 40 | over 40 | over 100 | over 300 |
| given | over 20 | over 40 | over 100 | over 200 |
| done | over 100 | over 40 | over 20 | over 40 |
| taken | over 20 | over 40 | over 100 | over 200 |
| used | over 20 | over 20 | over 100 | over 300 |
| found | | over 40 | over 100 | over 300 |
| seen | | over 40 | over 100 | over 200 |
| called | over 40 | over 40 | over 20 | over 100 |
| concerned | over 20 | over 20 | over 40 | over 100 |
| said | | over 40 | over 100 | over 40 |
| expected | | over 20 | over 200 | over 100 |
| put | over 40 | over 20 | over 20 | over 20 |
| told | over 20 | over 100 | over 100 | over 20 |
| known | | over 40 | over 40 | over 100 |
| set | | over 20 | over 100 | over 100 |
| left | | over 100 | over 40 | over 20 |
| held | | over 20 | over 100 | over 40 |
| born | over 20 | over 40 | over 40 | |
| asked | | over 20 | over 40 | over 20 |
| brought | | over 20 | over 40 | over 20 |
| prepared | | over 20 | over 40 | over 20 |
| based | | | over 40 | over 100 |
| described | | | over 40 | over 100 |
| determined | | | over 40 | over 100 |
| involved | | | over 40 | over 100 |
| needed | | | over 40 | over 100 |
| considered | | | over 20 | over 200 |
| shown | | | over 20 | over 200 |
| paid | over 20 | | over 40 | over 20 |
| forced | | over 20 | over 40 | over 20 |
| sent | | over 20 | over 40 | over 20 |
| drawn | | over 20 | over 20 | over 40 |
| kept | | over 20 | over 20 | over 40 |
| lost | | over 20 | over 20 | over 40 |
| reported | | | over 40 | over 20 |
| thought | | | over 40 | over 20 |

**Table 6.5**  **continued**

|  | CONV | FICT | NEWS | ACAD |
|---|---|---|---|---|
| *treated* |  |  | ■ | ■ |
| *understood* |  |  | ■ | ■ |
| *carried* |  |  | ▪ | ▨ |
| *required* |  |  | ▪ | ▨ |

➤ In addition, some verbs are common in the passive in a single register:

**academic prose**:

- occurring over 100 times per million words: *be + achieved, associated, defined, expressed, measured, obtained, performed, related*
- over 50 verbs occurring over 40 times per million words, including: *be + applied, calculated, chosen, compared, derived, designed, developed, discussed, examined, explained, formed, identified, illustrated, introduced, limited, noted, observed, presented, recognized, regarded, replaced, represented, studied, suggested*

**news**:

- occurring over 40 times per million words: *be + accused, announced, arrested, beaten, believed, charged, delighted, hit, injured, jailed, killed, named, released, revealed, shot, sold*

**conversation**:

- occurring over 40 times per million words: *be bothered*
- other less common passive verbs (over 20 occurrences per million words): *be + allowed, finished, involved, left, married, meant, stuck*

➤ In academic prose, there are many verbs that occur most of the time in the passive voice:

- occurring over 90% of the time: *be + aligned (with), based (on), born, coupled (with), deemed, effected, entitled (to), flattened, inclined, obliged, positioned, situated, stained, subjected (to)*
- over 40 verbs occurring over 70% of the time, including: *be + approved, associated (with), attributed (to), classified (as), composed (of), confined (to), designed, diagnosed (as), distributed, documented, estimated, extracted, grouped (with), intended, labelled, linked (to/with), located (at/in), plotted, recruited, stored, transferred, viewed.*

**DISCUSSION OF FINDINGS**

Lexical factors strongly influence the choice between active and passive: whereas some verbs normally take the passive voice, other verbs very rarely do so. A few verbs, like *be born* (referring to birth) and *be reputed*, occur idiosyncratically only in the passive:

> Brandon Lee **was born** in Oakland, California. (NEWS†)

> The deal **is reputed** to be worth £1m. (NEWS†)

Other verbs, like *be based on*, *be deemed*, *be positioned*, and *be subjected to*, are grammatical in both the active and passive voice, but they are used well over 90 percent of the time with the passive voice:

> The material **was deemed** faulty. (NEWS)

> *And anyone found guilty of drinking alcohol may* **be subjected to** *80 lashes of a cane.* (NEWS)

> *They* **were based** *on his book* **The Principles of Quantum Mechanics.** (ACAD†)

> *This part can then* **be positioned** *within another space.* (ACAD†)

In academic writing, many of the verbs that most commonly occur in the passive refer to aspects of scientific methodology and analysis:

> *The same mechanism* **was analysed** *on each.* (ACAD†)

> *The rate of profit can only* **be calculated** *with reference to both variable and constant capital.* (ACAD)

> *The air leaving the diffuser passages might* **be collected** *in a volute.* (ACAD†)

> *Their occurrence* **is measured** *in a few parts per million.* (ACAD†)

> *The test object clause will allow any object to* **be tested.** (ACAD)

Other passive verbs are used to report findings or to express logical relations:

> *These effects* **are believed** *to* **be associated with** *a disturbance of auxin metabolism.* (ACAD)

> *The rate constant can* **be interpreted** *in terms of entropy.* (ACAD)

> *Their presence must* **be regarded as** *especially undesirable.* (ACAD)

In news, a different set of verbs commonly occurs in the passive. Many of these report negative events that happened to someone, omitting mention of the person who performed the activity (cf. 6.4.1):

> *He* **was accused** *of using threatening or insulting behaviour.* (NEWS)

> *He* **was jailed** *for three months.* (NEWS)

> *In the shooting that followed Special Constable Goodman* **was killed** *and PC Kelly* **wounded.** (NEWS)

> *Everybody remembers where they were when JFK* **was shot.** (NEWS†)

> *Neither man* **was injured** *during the incident.* (NEWS)

In conversation, passives are generally rare. However, a few passive verbs are more frequent in conversation than in the written expository registers. The most common of these is the fixed phrase *can't be bothered*:

> *I* **can't be bothered** *really.* (CONV)

> *I* **can't be bothered** *to play the piano.* (CONV)

Otherwise, the passive verbs that are commonly used in conversation tend to be stative in meaning and often come close to adjectival functions; some of those could be alternatively analyzed as the copula *be* followed by a predicative adjective (3.5.3.1, 5.5.2–3, 7.2, 7.5):

> *It's gotta* **be done.** (CONV)

> *It* **was done** *so quietly that they hadn't time to object.* (CONV)

> *I* **was meant** *to go and play there.* (CONV)

> *I still shouldn't* **be allowed** *to train him.* (CONV)

> *Most of our garden will* **be finished** *one day.* (CONV)

**6.4.2.2**    **Verbs common with the *get* passive**

➤ The *get* passive is generally rare and restricted primarily to conversation (6.4.1).
➤ Only a few verbs are common with the *get* passive, even in conversation.
    ➤ Over 20 occurrences per million words: *get married*
    ➤ Over five occurrences per million words: *get* + *hit, involved, left, stuck.*

**DISCUSSION OF FINDINGS**

It is interesting to note that most of the verbs that are moderately common with *get* passives have negative connotations, conveying that the action of the verb is difficult or to the disadvantage of the subject. These verbs include *hit, left, stuck,* and sometimes *involved.*

Most of the verbs commonly occurring in the *get* passive in conversation, like many in the *be* passive, are used as stative passives. Thus, most of these constructions cannot take an agent specified in a *by*-phrase. However, use of the *get*-passive conveys a more dynamic sense than the *be*-passive. That is, the *be*-passive often simply describes a state, while the *get*-passive describes the process of getting into the state, with a resultant meaning similar to *become*. As we saw in 5.5, the copula *get* in this use is also typical of conversation, while the written registers, especially academic prose, would use *become* instead.

*Be* passive:

    *I was **married** for a couple of years in the seventies.* (CONV)
    *They **weren't involved** for that long.* (CONV)
    *You're gonna **be left** alone to get on with your job.* (CONV)
    *You wouldn't **be stuck** at home.* (CONV)

*Get* passive:

    *She **got married** when she was eighteen.* (CONV)
    *And then we start to **get involved** in local society.* (CONV)
    *It's about these people who **got left** behind in Vietnam.* (CONV)
    *My head **got stuck** up there.* (CONV)

**6.4.2.3**    **Verbs uncommon in the passive**

➤ There are many transitive verbs and single-object prepositional verbs (Pattern 1; 5.3.3) that very rarely occur in the passive voice. The following verbs occur in the passive voice less than 2% of the time:
  • single word transitive verbs: *agree, climb, dare, exclaim, guess, hate, have, hesitate, joke, lack, let, like, love, mind, pretend, quit, reply, resemble, survive, swear, thank, try, undergo, want, watch, wish, wonder, yell*
  • single-object prepositional verbs: *agree to/with, apologise to/for, belong to, bet on, come across/for, compete with, cope with, correspond to, glance at, laugh about/at, listen to, live like/with, look at/like, participate in, smile at, stay with, talk about/to, wait for/with.*

A number of transitive verbs usually occur in the active voice:

> He **has** money. (CONV)
>
> Sinead **wants** a biscuit. (CONV)
>
> I **lacked** the courage to be alone. (FICT)

Most of these verbs are grammatical in the passive voice:

> Justin Martin-Clarke **is wanted** in connection with the drugs-related shooting of a businessman in April. (NEWS)

However, in practice this use is extremely rare.

Many of these verbs typically take a post-verbal complement clause rather than a direct object noun phrase, effectively blocking the passive option:

> I **wished** I had a job like that. (CONV)
>
> He's also **agreed** to deal with a few other things. (FICT)
>
> I **pretended** to be another friend. (FICT)

In addition, single-object prepositional verbs (5.3.3) generally occur with the active voice, many of them very rarely taking the passive:

> They're all **waiting for** me. (CONV†)
>
> We can **smile at** them. (FICT)
>
> The eigenvectors must obviously **correspond to** special states. (ACAD)

However, there are a few single-object prepositional verbs that occur occasionally in the passive voice, with the subject corresponding to the prepositional object of the active version:

> Your sister, as a rule, can **be relied on** to remember when your birthday is. (FICT)
>
> Here in the hospital the manicurist **was sent for**. (FICT)

In contrast, two-object prepositional verbs generally take the passive voice, and many of these verbs even occur most of the time with the passive (such as associate X with Y, base X on Y, link X to/with Y; see 6.4.2.1). With these verbs, the passive subject corresponds to the direct object of the active version, suggesting that passive subjects are more readily formed from direct objects than prepositional objects.

# 6.5    Complex combinations of aspect and voice

English verb phrases can be marked for combinations of aspect and voice. That is, perfect aspect, progressive aspect, and passive voice can occur together in various combinations, presenting more specialized verbal meanings.

- ➤ The perfect passive is the only complex combination that is moderately common.
  - ➤ The present perfect passive occurs over 1,000 times per million words in academic prose and news.
  - ➤ The past perfect passive occurs about 500 times per million words in fiction.
- ➤ All other combinations of aspect and voice are generally rare.

**DISCUSSION OF FINDINGS**

Given the high frequencies for both perfect aspect and passive voice in academic prose and news, it is not surprising that the two are often used together. Typically, this combination retains the time orientation ('past with present relevance') of the perfect aspect while demoting the agent through use of the passive voice:

> He **has been jailed** for explosives offenses in Ulster and **has** previously **been denied** a visa. (NEWS)

> Since 1916 much government money **has been spent** on these developments. (ACAD†)

In fiction, perfect passives are also moderately common in the past tense:

> He **had been thrown** from a moving train. (FICT)

> Most of the lights **had been turned off** ... (FICT)

The two remaining combinations, both involving the progressive aspect, are attested but considerably less common. Perfect progressives are used occasionally in fiction, especially in the past tense:

> He **had been keeping** it in a safety deposit box at the Bank of America. (FICT)

> For months she **had been waiting** for that particular corner location. (FICT)

> God knows how long I**'ve been doing** it. **Have** I **been talking** out loud? (FICT)

The meaning of the perfect progressive here is to refer to a situation or activity in progress up to a particular time.

Progressive passives are used occasionally in news reportage and academic prose:

> A police spokesman said nobody else **was being sought** in connection with the incident. (NEWS†)

> These figures include only the budget as it was set up, since expenses therein **are** still **being incurred** while a budget for the future **is being prepared**. (ACAD)

Here the 'in progress' meaning of the progressive is combined with the change of focus associated with the passive.

## 6.6 Modals and semi-modals

As already noted (6.2.1), English verb phrases can be marked for either tense or modality, but not both. Nine **central modal** auxiliary verbs (2.4.4) are used to express modality: *can, could, may, might, shall, should, will, would, must*. These are invariant forms taking the role of auxiliary; they precede the negative particle *not* in negation (3.8.2) and precede the subject in *yes-no* questions (3.13.2.2). They are followed in the verb phrase by a bare infinitive verb (e.g. *can see, would go*). In general, modals cannot co-occur with each other in the verb phrase; however, some regional dialects allow modals in series (such as *might could* or *might should*).

Although the central modals form a homogeneous group, the boundary between modals and lexical verbs taking infinitive complementation is in some cases unclear.

First, there is a handful of **marginal auxiliary** verbs (e.g. *need (to), ought to, dare (to), used to*). These verbs can behave like modals in taking auxiliary negation and *yes-no* question inversion (*needn't, ought we to ...*, *She dare not*, etc.). However, such constructions are extremely rare and largely confined to BrE (3.8.2.3, 3.13.2.8C).

In addition, there are a number of fixed idiomatic phrases with functions similar to those of modals: *(had) better, have to, (have) got to, be supposed to, be going to*. Note that in orthographic representations of the spoken language, *better, gotta*, and *gonna* often occur as reduced forms of *had better, have got to*, and *be going to* (see also 14.1.2.9). A contraction of the preceding auxiliary can also appear (*'d better, 've gotta, 'm gonna*), but this is frequently omitted with *better* and *gotta*.

These expressions are called **semi-modals.** (Other terms used for these expressions are 'quasi-modals' and 'periphrastic modals'.) In the counts and discussions that follow we have included the three marginal auxiliaries other than *dare* as semi-modals.

Unlike the central modal verbs, many of the semi-modals can be marked for tense and person, and can occur as non-finite forms. In the infinitive, they can sometimes co-occur with a central modal verb or another semi-modal (cf. 6.8):

> He **had to** call the police. (CONV)
>
> I think the teachers **are gonna have to** be there. (CONV)
>
> I know you **have to** protect your eyesight. (FICT)
>
> The county council **will have to** ask colleges to bid for money on its behalf. (NEWS†)
>
> Maybe she **needs to** grow up a bit more. (CONV)
>
> You **might need to** get back quick. (FICT)
>
> He **needed to** be sure that current arrangements were working as well as possible. (NEWS†)

Beyond this there are a large number of other relatively fixed expressions with meanings similar to the modal auxiliaries; for example, *want to, be able to, be obliged to, be likely to, be willing to*. These differ from other semi-modals, however, in that the component parts contribute independently to the overall meaning of the phrase. Such expressions in relation to complement clauses following adjectival predicates are discussed further in 9.4.5.

The central modal verbs can be used to make time distinctions, even though they are not formally marked for tense. For example, the modals *will* and *shall*, and the semi-modal *be going to*, can be used to refer to future time (6.2.1.3):

> There **will** be no outcry from the corporate sector about the disarray in the accountancy profession. (NEWS)
>
> We **shall** deal with these questions in 4.4. (ACAD)
>
> It**'s going to** be hot. (CONV)

In addition, it is possible to group the central modals (except for *must*) into pairs with related meanings. These can in limited circumstances be used to distinguish between past time and non-past time:

| modals referring to non-past time | corresponding modals that can refer to past time |
|---|---|
| *can* | *could* |
| *may* | *might* |
| *shall* | *should* |
| *will* | *would* |

Compare, for example, the following pairs:

> *I think we **can** beat Glenavon.* (NEWS)

v. *In 1971 he thought he **could** help his brother in his illness by writing about their childhood.* (NEWS)

> *You know he'**ll** come.* (CONV)

v. *I knew I **would** put on weight.* (CONV)

The second example in each pair involves a backshifted time reference (cf. 6.2.1.2).

However, there are a number of other meaning distinctions made by these pairs of modals, with the main functions relating to speaker stance rather than the marking of time distinctions. For example, modals associated with past time are also associated with hypothetical situations, conveying overtones of tentativeness and politeness:

> *Could I sit here a minute, Joyce?* (CONV)

> *Could you sign one of these too? Would you mind?* (CONV)

For this reason, we regard modal verbs as unmarked for tense.

Modals and semi-modals can be grouped into three major categories according to their main meanings (excluding *used to*, which relates to past time).

- **permission/possibility/ability**: *can, could, may, might*
- **obligation/necessity**: *must, should, (had) better, have (got) to, need to, ought to, be supposed to*
- **volition/prediction**: *will, would, shall, be going to.*

Each modal can have two different types of meaning, which can be labeled **intrinsic** and **extrinsic** (also referred to as 'deontic' and 'epistemic' meanings). Intrinsic modality refers to actions and events that humans (or other agents) directly control: meanings relating to permission, obligation, or volition (or intention). Extrinsic modality refers to the logical status of events or states, usually relating to assessments of likelihood: possibility, necessity, or prediction.

There are two typical structural correlates of modal verbs with intrinsic meanings: (a) the subject of the verb phrase usually refers to a human being (as agent of the main verb), and (b) the main verb is usually a dynamic verb, describing an activity or event that can be controlled. In contrast, modal verbs with extrinsic meanings usually occur with non-human subjects and/or with main verbs having stative meanings.

Intrinsic meanings:

> *You **can**'t mark without a scheme. You **must** make a scheme.* (CONV)
> <obligation>

> *We **shall** not attempt a detailed account of linguistic categories in this book, but **will** use as far as possible those which are well enough known …* (ACAD†)
> <intention>

Extrinsic meanings:

> *You **must** have thought that you **must** have so much time.* (CONV)
> <necessity>

> *But in other cases his decisions **will** seem more radical.* (ACAD) <prediction>

It should be noted, however, that these correlates are not absolute. For example, the modal *might* often occurs in an extrinsic sense (marking possibility rather than permission) with both an animate subject and dynamic main verb:

> *Otherwise you **might** jeopardize the situation.* (CONV)

> *Or he **might** accept it but reach different conclusions.* (ACAD†)

Each of the modals is discussed in more detail below, describing its use preferences with intrinsic or extrinsic meanings in different registers.

## 6.6.1 Distribution of modals and semi-modals

**CORPUS FINDINGS** [1,2]

➤ The nine central modals differ greatly in frequency (see Figure 6.8):

Figure 6.8    **Frequency of modal verbs in the LSWE Corpus**

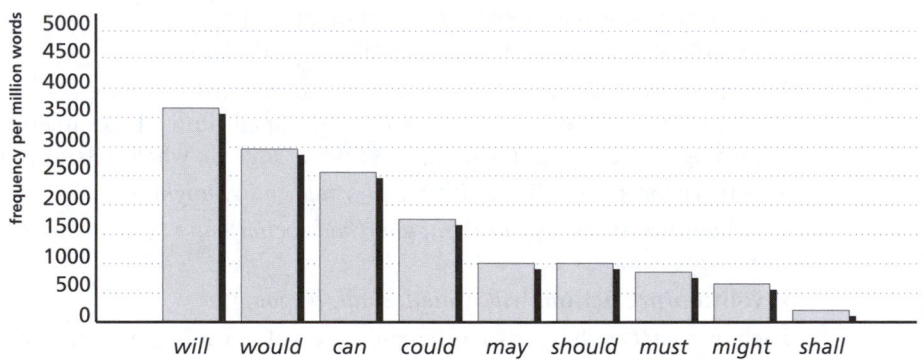

➤ The modals *can*, *will*, and *would* are extremely common.

➤ At the other extreme, the modal *shall* is relatively rare.

➤ Considering the pairs of central modals, the tentative/past time member is less frequent than its partner in all cases except *shall/should*.

➤ Modal and semi-modal verbs are most common in conversation, and least common in news and academic prose (see Figure 6.9).

   ➤ The register differences in the use of semi-modals are particularly striking: semi-modals are five times more common in conversation than they are in the written expository registers.

Figure 6.9
**Frequency of semi-modals and modals across registers**

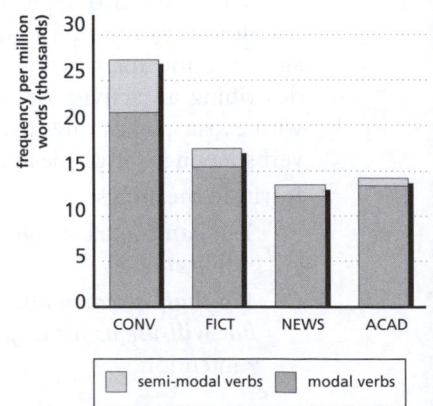

semi-modal verbs    modal verbs

➤ Semi-modal verbs are considerably less common than modal verbs.

**DISCUSSION OF FINDINGS**

To interpret the overall distribution of the modals and semi-modals properly, we must consider their use with intrinsic and extrinsic meanings. We discuss modal verbs marking permission/possibility/ability in 6.6.4.1, marking obligation/ necessity in 6.6.4.2, and marking volition/prediction in 6.6.4.3.

Overall, the greater frequency of both modals and semi-modals in conversation is understandable given that these forms mostly convey stance-type meanings (see Chapter 12). The predominance of semi-modal verbs in conversation has a historical explanation. The modals all pre-date the tenth century, while the semi-modals developed much more recently. The following historical data comes from the *The Oxford English Dictionary*:

• semi-modals attested before 1400: *need to, ought to, used to*
• semi-modals first attested between 1400 and 1650: *had better, have to, be going to*
• semi-modals first attested between 1650 and 1800: *be supposed to*
• semi-modals first attested after 1800: *better, (have) got to.*

As usual, it is not surprising to find linguistic novelty establishing itself in conversation first, and then spreading to the written registers. Academic prose, being the most conservative register in the LSWE Corpus, uses semi-modals least of all.

## 6.6.2 Individual modals/semi-modals across registers and dialects

(The semi-modal *ought to* is excluded from Figures 6.10–11, and from much subsequent discussion, because it is generally rare in comparison with the central modals; see Table 6.6. Examples of *ought to* can be found in 3.8.2.4 and 3.13.2.8D.)

**CORPUS FINDINGS** [1,2,8]

➤ In fiction and conversation, many modal verbs are more common in BrE than AmE (see Figures 6.10–11).
  ➤ This is especially the case for modals marking obligation/necessity—*must* and *should*—and modals marking volition/prediction—*will, would,* and *shall.*
➤ In contrast, semi-modals tend to be more common in AmE, especially *have to* and *be going to.*
  ➤ *(Had) better* and *(have) got to* as semi-modals are restricted primarily to conversation and are considerably more common in BrE than AmE.
  ➤ Modals marking permission/possibility and volition/prediction are considerably more common than those marking obligation/necessity.
➤ Most modals have strikingly different distributions across registers (see Table 6.6).
  ➤ *Can* and *could* are relatively common in all registers: *can* is extremely common in conversation and academic prose; *could* is particularly common in fiction.
  ➤ *May* is extremely common in academic prose; rare in conversation.
  ➤ *Must* and *should* are relatively common in academic prose.

Figure 6.10 **Frequency of necessity and prediction modal verbs in BrE and AmE conversation**

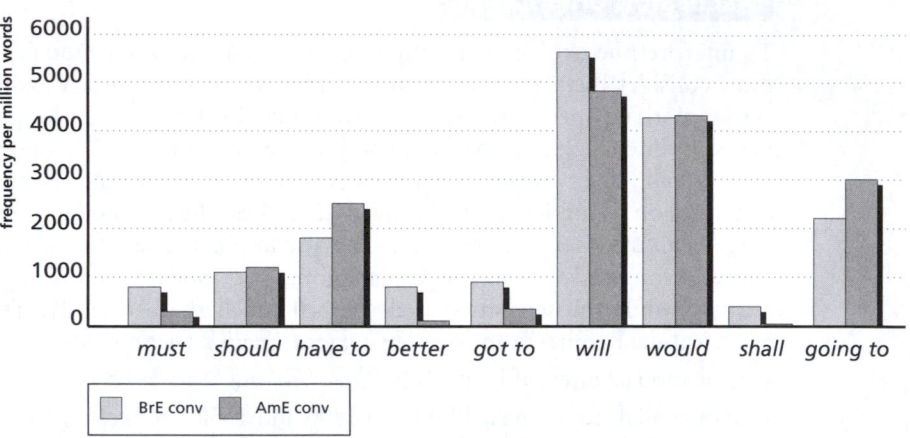

Figure 6.11 **Frequency of necessity and prediction modal verbs in BrE and AmE fiction**

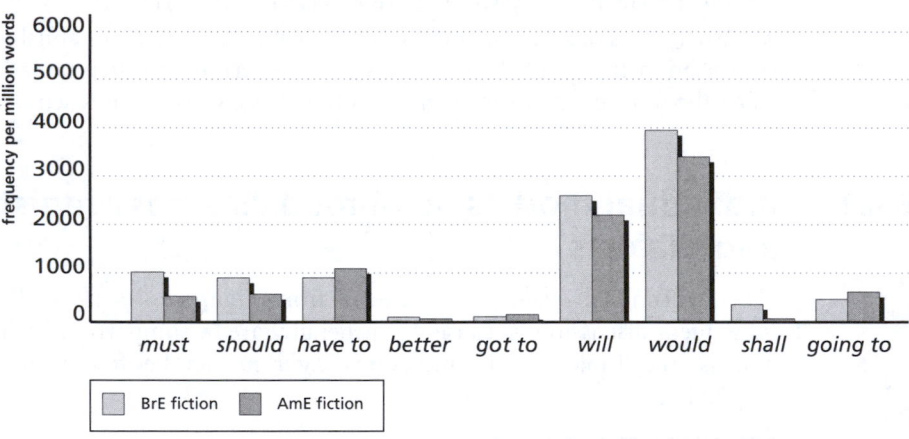

➤ *Will* and *would* are relatively common in all registers: *will* is extremely common in conversation and news reportage; *would* is extremely common in conversation and fiction.

➤ *Be going to* (including *gonna*) in conversation is the most common semi-modal; *have to* in conversation is also very common.

  ➤ The semi-modals *(had) better*, *(have) got to* (including *gotta*), and *used to* are also relatively common in conversation.

➤ *Have to* is the only semi-modal that is relatively common in the written expository registers as well as conversation and fiction.

### DISCUSSION OF FINDINGS

It is not surprising that the most recently developed semi-modals—*(had) better* and *(have) got to*—are common in conversation but virtually non-existent in written exposition. Interestingly BrE has been more innovative recently in the use of semi-modals than AmE. While the older semi-modal forms, such as *have to* and *be going to*, are considerably more common in AmE, the more recent semi-

**Table 6.6**     **Distribution of modal verbs across registers; occurrences per million words**

each ■ marks c. 200     □ marks less than 100

| | CONV | FICT | NEWS | ACAD |
|---|---|---|---|---|
| **permission/possibility/ability:** | | | | |
| *can* | ■■■■■■■ ■■■■■■■ ■■■■■■ ■ | ■■■■■■■ ■ | ■■■■■■ | ■■■■■■■ ■■■■■■ ■ |
| *could* | ■■■■■■■ ■■■ | ■■■■■■■ ■■■■■■■ | ■■■■■■■ | ■■■■ |
| *may* | ■ | ■■ | ■■■ | ■■■■■■■ ■■■■■■■ |
| *might* | ■■■ | ■■■■ | ■■ | ■■■ |
| **obligation/necessity:** | | | | |
| *must* | ■■■■ | ■■■■■ | ■■ | ■■■■■■ |
| *should* | ■■■■ | ■■■■ | ■■■■■ | ■■■■■ |
| *have to* | ■■■■■■■ ■■ | ■■■■■ | ■■■■ | ■■ |
| *(had) better* | ■■■ | ■ | □ | □ |
| *(have) got to* | ■■■ | □ | □ | □ |
| *need to* | ■ | □ | ■ | ■ |
| *(be) supposed to* | ■ | □ | □ | □ |
| *ought to* | □ | ■ | □ | □ |
| **volition/prediction:** | | | | |
| *will* | ■■■■■■■ ■■■■■■■ ■■■■■■ ■■■■■■ | ■■■■■■■ ■■■■■■ | ■■■■■■■ ■■■■■■ ■■■■■■ | ■■■■■■■ ■■■■ |
| *would* | ■■■■■■■ ■■■■■■■ ■■■■■■■ | ■■■■■■■ ■■■■■■■ ■■■■■ | ■■■■■■■ ■■■■■ | ■■■■■■■ |
| *shall* | ■■ | ■■ | □ | ■ |
| *be going to* | ■■■■■■■ ■■■■ | ■■ | ■ | □ |
| **past time:** | | | | |
| *used to* | ■■■ | ■ | □ | □ |

modals *(had) better* and *(have) got to* (also transcribed *gotta*) are more common by far in BrE conversation:

> You **better** go. (CONV)

> We**'ve got to** leave that till later on. (CONV)

> I **gotta** read this. (CONV)

The lower frequency of modals with obligation/necessity meanings probably has two sources. First, this relative rarity reflects a general tendency to avoid the face threatening force of expressions with an obligation meaning (cf. 6.6.4.2). In addition, semi-modals have become better established in this semantic domain, apparently replacing the modal verbs to a greater extent. Six different semi-modal verbs are used to express obligation/necessity (including all semi-modals first attested after 1650). *Have to* is the most common of these and is notable in that it is the only semi-modal to be used commonly in all four registers:

> Then he **has to** come and show me. (CONV)
>
> We **have to** catch him first. (FICT)
>
> He **had to** deal forcefully with Britain's Martin Brundle. (NEWS†)
>
> Some reflex actions **have to** be learnt. (ACAD†)

The semi-modals *be going to* and *used to* are different in that they are used primarily to mark time distinctions rather than personal stance. The semi-modal *be going to* is a common way of marking future time in conversation (and fictional dialog), but is rarely used in written exposition:

> We're **going to** wait. (CONV)
>
> I think I'm **going to** die. (FICT)

Finally, *used to* marks past habitual behavior or a past state; this semi-modal is particularly common in conversation:

> This was before I **used to** speak to her. (CONV)
>
> He **used to** sleep-walk. (CONV)

The sequence *used to* actually has multiple functions which must be carefully distinguished: as a semi-modal (described and counted in this section); as an adjective + preposition combination meaning 'accustomed to'; and as a passive lexical verb followed by a *to*-complement clause (where it would be pronounced differently from the other two in speech). While the semi-modal is particularly common in conversation, the complement clause use is notably common in academic prose:

> Water control may **be used to** reduce liability to lodging. (ACAD†)

In contrast, the adjectival use is more common in conversation:

> I'm **used to** it. I do the dishes every day. (CONV)

## 6.6.3 Lexical associations of modality

**CORPUS FINDINGS [2]**

Although tensed verb phrases are many times more common than verb phrases with a modal (see Figure 6.1), there are a number of individual verbs that occur predominantly with modals:

- over 60% of the time: *abide, admit, afford, appeal, assure, cope (with), discern, fathom, guarantee, handle, imagine, interact, resist, settle for, suffice, survive, tolerate*

- over 40% of the time: *account for, advise, aid, believe, benefit, claim, compete, continue, contribute, count on, debate, deduce, endanger, end up, expect, exit, focus, forgive, get over, grumble, harm, insure, jeopardise, muster, outweigh, overwhelm, pause, predispose, reach, rely, respect, settle for, solve, tempt, withstand.*

The verbs that show the strongest association with modal verbs (rather than tense) are mostly mental verbs. These mental verbs usually express various emotions, attitudes, or cognitive states that are intrinsically personal, and thus they commonly co-occur with modals expressing a personal stance. The modal verbs *can* and *could*, often combined with negation, are particularly common:

> You **can imagine** what it's like. (CONV)
>
> I mean as an acquaintance I **could tolerate** her. (CONV†)
>
> I **can't cope** with this. (CONV)
>
> I **can't abide** the dratted things. (FICT)
>
> I **could just discern** a faint nodding of the head. (FICT)
>
> The council **cannot afford** to maintain them. (NEWS†)

## 6.6.4  Extrinsic v. intrinsic uses of individual modals

In the following sections, each modal and semi-modal verb is discussed in more detail, describing its use preferences with intrinsic and extrinsic meanings in different registers. We concentrate on the registers of conversation and academic prose here, since these show the clearest contrasts.

### 6.6.4.1  The permission/possibility/ability modals

Figure 6.12  **Frequency of permission/possibility modals with intrinsic, extrinsic, and ability meanings**

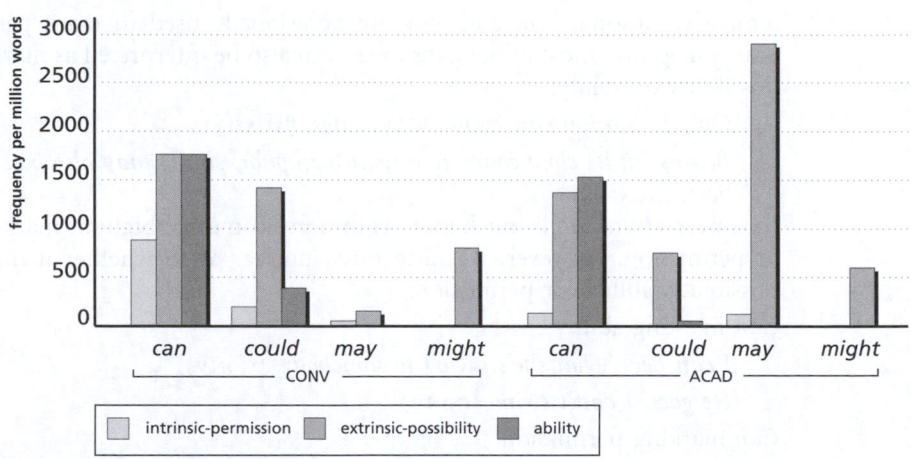

➤ In academic prose, three of the permission/possibility modals (*could*, *may*, and *might*) are used almost exclusively to mark logical possibility.
  ➤ *May* is extremely common in this function.
➤ *Can* in academic prose commonly marks both ability and logical possibility.
➤ Permission is rarely expressed in academic writing.
➤ Logical possibility is also the predominant use of these modals in conversation.

➤ *Could* and *might* are much more common expressing logical possibility than permission or ability.

➤ *May* is rarely used in conversation. When it does occur, it typically marks logical possibility rather than permission.

➤ *Can* differs from these other modals in that it commonly occurs with permission and ability meanings in conversation (in addition to its frequent use with possibility meanings).

### DISCUSSION OF FINDINGS

The meanings and use of the four permission/possibility modals are multi-functional to differing extents. At one extreme, *might* is used only to mark logical possibility; at the other extreme, *can* commonly marks permission, ability, and logical possibility.

In academic prose, *could*, *may*, and *might* usually express logical possibility:

*The two processes **could** well be independent.* (ACAD)

*The only problem **may** be that the compound is difficult to remove after use.* (ACAD†)

*Of course, it **might** be the case that it had been settled long before that.* (ACAD)

*Can* is especially ambiguous in academic prose, since it can often be interpreted as marking either ability or logical possibility:

*Dualism assumes that one **can** paraphrase the Sense of a text.* (ACAD†)

*These observations **can** be explained biochemically.* (ACAD†)

*However, using harvest index as a physiological indicator **can** be misleading.* (ACAD†)

Similarly, although *can* and *may* are occasionally used to mark permission in academic prose, most of these instances can also be interpreted as marking logical possibility or ability:

*Only legislation **can** establish tax rates.* (ACAD†)

*Because of its close connection with metaphor, simile **may** also be considered here.* (ACAD)

In conversation, *can* is much more common as an unambiguous marker of ability or permission. However, it is also often unclear as to whether it marks logical possibility, ability, or permission:

*Can* marking ability:

*I **can** hear what she's saying to somebody.* (CONV)

*He goes, I **can't** swim.* (CONV)

*Can* marking permission:

***Can** I have some?* (CONV)

***Can** I have a piece of paper please?* (CONV)

*You **can** read my book.* (CONV)

*Can* ambiguously marking logical possibility or ability (or permission):

*Listen here, I **can** pick you up from over here.* (CONV)

*I **can't** believe it.* (CONV)

*Well you **can** get cigarettes from there **can't** you?* (CONV)

*We **can't** sit on the stage cos there's crap raggers on the stage.* (CONV)

In contrast to the typical functions of *can*, the modal *could* usually marks logical possibility in conversation, expressing a greater degree of uncertainty or tentativeness:

> That **could** be her. (CONV)

> It **could** be anything you choose. (CONV)

In addition, *could* in conversation is also sometimes used to mark ability or permission:

*Could* marking ability:

> They asked me and I just **couldn't** refuse. (CONV)

> I **couldn't** feel my hand. (CONV)

*Could* marking permission:

> And we didn't know we **could** see her. (CONV)

> She had the nerve to ask me if she **could** sit at the end of our table. (CONV)

*Could* ambiguously marking logical possibility or ability:

> So you **couldn't** do it anyway. (CONV)

> Or you **could** do a legalized dope poster campaign. (CONV)

Interestingly, *may* is rarely used in conversation, where in most cases it expresses logical possibility:

> He **may** not see it as a joke. (CONV)

> That **may** be wrong, though. (CONV)

Despite a well-known prescription favoring *may* rather than *can* for expressing permission, *may* is especially rare in the sense of permission. Interestingly, many of the instances of *may* marking permission in the LSWE Corpus are produced by caregivers in conversations with children:

> Student: Please **may** I go to the toilet?
> Teacher: And I will speak to you individually. Now—individually. One at a time. Now—this is what you can do if you want to. You **may**—shh. Kevin. Kevin.
> Students: <many voices talking>
> Teacher: Yes Carl. You **may** do some maths if you want to.
> Student: No.
> Teacher: You **may** do your language work if you want to.
> Student: I thought you said anything.
> Teacher: If you don't want to do—either of those things—and you are—keen on writing a story, you **may** write.
> <...>
> Teacher: No you **may** not draw a picture. (CONV)

## 6.6.4.2 The obligation/necessity modals and semi-modals

**CORPUS FINDINGS** [2,9]

➤ Obligation/necessity modals and semi-modals are less common overall than the other modal categories.

**Figure 6.13**   **Frequency of obligation/necessity modals with intrinsic and extrinsic meanings**

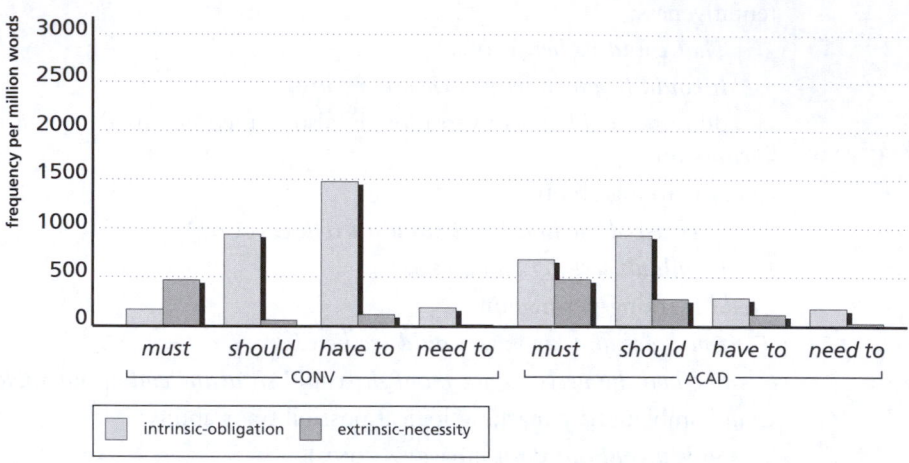

➤ Except for the modal *must*, all of these forms are used most of the time to mark personal obligation (rather than logical necessity).

  ➤ *Have to* in conversation is the most common form used to mark personal obligation.

  ➤ *Should* in both conversation and academic prose is relatively common marking personal obligation.

➤ *Must* is the only modal used commonly for both logical necessity and personal obligation.

  ➤ Surprisingly, *must* in conversation is used most of the time to mark logical necessity.

  ➤ *Must* in academic prose is somewhat more common marking personal obligation than logical necessity.

### DISCUSSION OF FINDINGS

Most of the time, obligation/necessity modals are used to mark personal obligation. This is especially the case with *should* and *have to* in conversation, with the semi-modal *have to* being used more commonly than any other form in this class:

> Well I **have to** get up at ten thirty in the morning to take this thing back. (CONV)

> What do we **have to** do? (CONV)

> You **should** relax. (CONV)

Personal obligation is also by far the most common meaning of these modals in academic prose. This is a surprising finding, in view of the otherwise impersonal tendency of this register:

> However one **should** not despise too hastily such hand-waving discussions. (ACAD)

> If the crop is to be harvested by machinery, varieties **should** be cultivated which do not readily shatter. (ACAD)

> Likewise, in the case of Lloyd George's great enemy, Neville Chamberlain, we **have to** await the completion of David Dilks's biography. (ACAD)

The modal *must* is particularly intriguing here because its distribution runs counter to the expectation of personal involvement: the extrinsic meaning of logical necessity is most common in conversation, while the intrinsic meaning of personal obligation is most common in academic prose.

*Must* marking logical necessity in conversation:

> *Your mum **must** not care.* (CONV)
>
> *It **must** have fallen out trying to fly.* (CONV)
>
> *Your feet **must** feel wet now.* (CONV)

*Must* marking personal obligation in academic prose:

> *I **must** now confess something which I kept back from you in Chapter 3.* (ACAD)
>
> *The permanence of dams already constructed **must** be ensured, states Gorrie (1954a) by carrying out whatever can be done to stop erosion.* (ACAD)
>
> *This is the sort of case in which judges **must** exercise the discretionary power described a moment ago.* (ACAD†)

The relative rarity of *must* marking personal obligation in conversation is probably due to the strong directive force this modal has when used in face-to-face interaction. The modal *should* provides a hedged expression of obligation that is typically regarded as more polite. In academic prose, since there is no individual addressee, the use of *must* meaning personal obligation is not interpreted as confrontational. Finally, both *must* and *should* are relatively common expressing logical necessity in academic prose:

> *It **must** surely be the case that the cat is competent to act as observer of its own survival or demise.* (ACAD)
>
> *All explanations of chemists **must** remain without fruit.* (ACAD†)
>
> *If the preceding work has been done with care there **should** be few, if any, off-types.* (ACAD)

## 6.6.4.3 The volition/prediction modals and semi-modals

**CORPUS FINDINGS** [2,9,10]

➤ In academic prose, volition/prediction modals are used most of the time to mark prediction.
  ➤ *Will* is particularly common and *would* is also relatively common expressing prediction.
  ➤ *Shall* is noteworthy in that it marks volition more often than prediction (although it is generally rare in both functions).
➤ In conversation, these modals are commonly used to mark both volition and prediction.
  ➤ *Would* is used particularly to mark both volition and prediction; *will* is also common with both meanings (and is often ambiguous).
  ➤ *Be going to* is particularly common marking volition but less commonly used to mark prediction.
➤ One striking observation is the heavily biased distribution of *be going to*, which is many times more frequent in conversation than in academic prose.

**Figure 6.14** **Frequency of volition/prediction modals with intrinsic and extrinsic meanings**

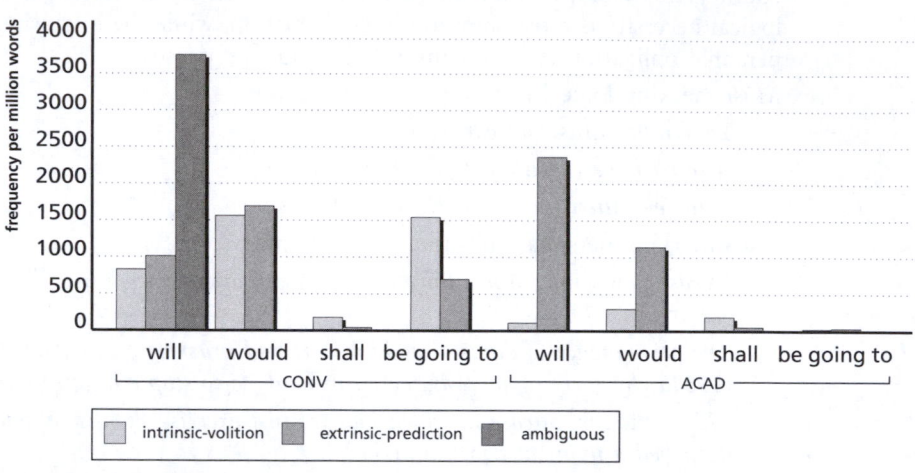

## DISCUSSION OF FINDINGS

The distinction between volition and prediction is often blurred. In conversation, *will* and *would* are commonly used to mark logical (extrinsic) prediction as well as personal volition (and prediction of one's own future actions). In the case of *would*, the meaning is past or hypothetical.

*Will* and *would* marking personal volition:

> *I'll come and show you it in registration Tuesday morning <...>*
> *I won't be here early enough to show you before school.* (CONV)
> *I would just read the book as well.* (CONV)
> *I would give it back.* (CONV)

*Will* and *would* marking prediction:

> *It won't be that difficult to do.* (CONV)
> *Will my coat be dry?* (CONV)
> *She would just feel better if she went out.* (CONV)

The semi-modal *be going to* in conversation is noteworthy because it is quite common but used mainly for marking personal volition:

> *I'm going to put my feet up and rest.* (CONV)
> *I said I was going to collect John's suitcase from Susan.* (CONV)

In contrast (but not unexpectedly) these verbs in academic prose rarely mark personal volition; instead they are used for predictions of events or states not involving personal agency. *Will* is extremely common in this function, and *would* is also relatively common:

> *Such deviations will often be the clue to special interpretations.* (ACAD†)
> *If the marble is not moving fast enough it will run out of kinetic energy before it reaches the top.* (ACAD†)
> *Cheap money would have the same effect by increasing private investment.* (ACAD†)

Finally the modal *shall* is worth noting because its use in academic prose (as well as in conversation) runs counter to prior expectations; although *shall* is generally rare, it is used most of the time to mark personal volition rather than prediction:

*I **shall** try to show that our political practices accept integrity as a distinct virtue.* (ACAD)

*We **shall** here be concerned with only s and p orbitals.* (ACAD)

In conversation, *shall* is typically used as a volitional modal in questions acting as offers or suggestions:

***Shall** we wait for them?* (CONV)

***Shall** I tell you who Sally fancies?* (CONV)

As these examples show, *shall* is generally used with a first-person subject.

## 6.7 Combinations of modal verbs with marked aspect or voice

Although modals cannot combine with tense, they can combine with marked aspect and voice.

Modal with passive voice:

*To produce the best results the plant **should be supplied** with water which carries no contamination.* (ACAD)

*A virus air filter has been developed which **can be fitted** by the exhaust outlet.* (ACAD†)

Modal with perfect aspect:

*Well it **would have been** easier.* (CONV)

*The demand for subject access **may have come** as a shock to the library profession.* (ACAD†)

Modal with progressive aspect:

*All these people I know **will be trying out** for the new series.* (CONV)

*This **has got to be moving** around this way.* (CONV†)

**Figure 6.15 Percentage of verb phrases with modals that have marked voice or aspect—conversation**

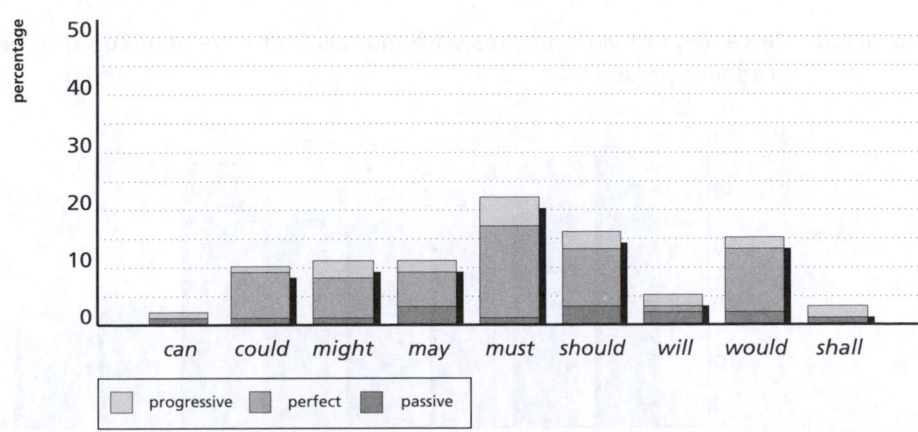

Figure 6.16   **Percentage of verb phrases with modals that have marked voice or aspect—fiction**

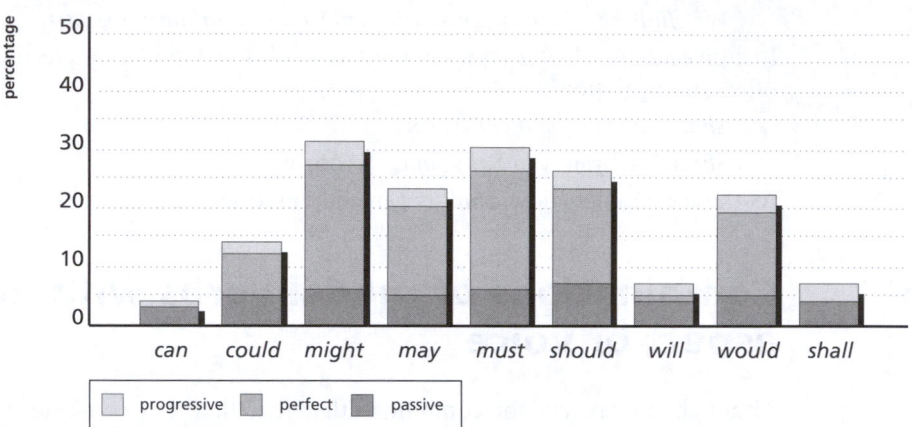

Figure 6.17   **Percentage of verb phrases with modals that have marked voice or aspect—news**

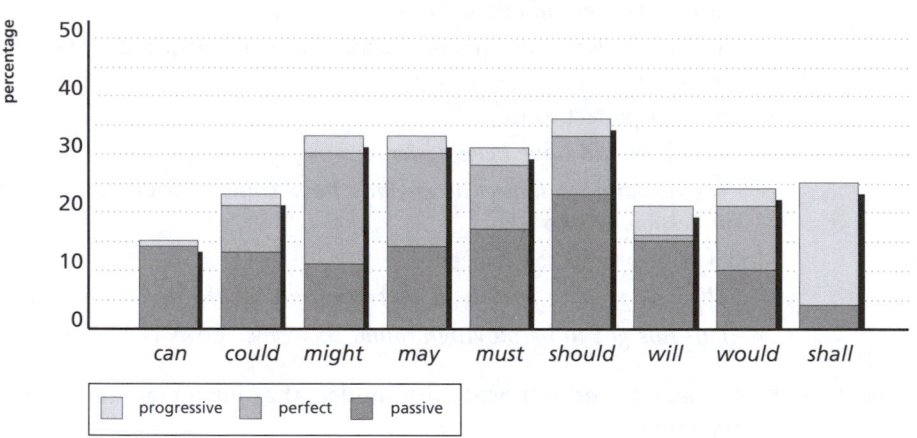

Figure 6.18   **Percentage of verb phrases with modals that have marked voice or aspect—academic prose**

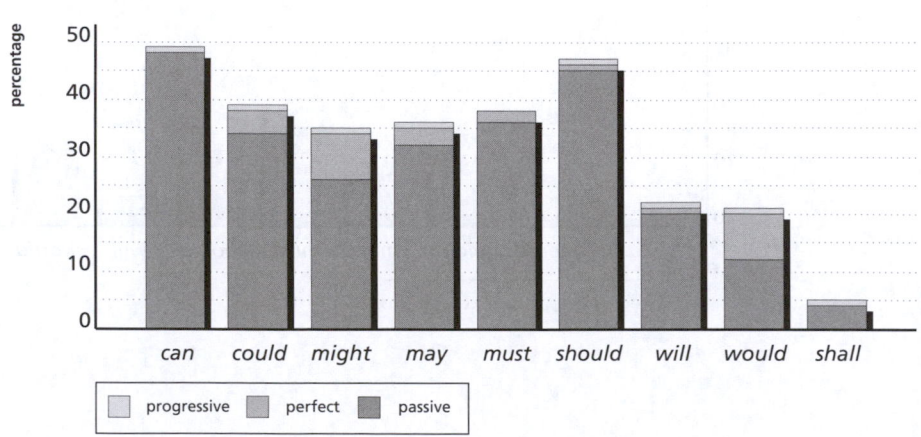

**CORPUS FINDINGS** [2]

➤ While the majority of modals do not co-occur with marked aspect or voice, particular modals show differing preferences for these combinations (see Figures 6.15–18).

➤ Passive voice with modals is rare in conversation and fiction, but relatively common for some modal verbs in academic prose.

  ➤ With the passive, *can* and *should* are particularly common; *could* and *must* are also fairly common.

  ➤ The volition/prediction modals (especially *shall*) are notably rare with passive voice, even in academic prose.

➤ Perfect aspect with modals is most common in fiction (and news).

  ➤ The permission/possibility modals *might* and *may* and the obligation/necessity modals *must* and *should* are the most common modal verbs with the perfect.

  ➤ In all registers, three modals with present/future time connotations—*can*, *will*, and *shall* very rarely occur with the perfect aspect; the two comparable modals with past time connotations—*could* and *would*—do occur with perfect aspect.

➤ Progressive aspect with modals is generally rare, with a few exceptions:

  ➤ the obligation/necessity modals in conversation, especially the semi-modal *be supposed to* (occurring with the progressive over 10% of the time); and

  ➤ the volition/prediction modals in news (note that the modal *shall* is rare in frequency but occurs a high percentage of the time with progressive aspect).

**DISCUSSION OF FINDINGS**

In many cases, the marked voice or aspect associations of a modal verb can be tied to its typical meanings. For example, *will*, *would*, and *shall* are rare with passive voice because they often mark volition/prediction and often overtly express the agent of the main verb. This is especially the case with *shall*, which is used most of the time to mark personal volition, with the human agent expressed as the subject of the verb (usually *I* or *we*):

> We **shall** hereafter refer to the results of this ordering as the Components of the Activity. (ACAD)

> We **shall** deal with chromatography in general in 6.3 of this chapter. (ACAD)

In contrast, the modals *can* and *could* commonly occur with passive voice, expressing a kind of logical possibility. These constructions are of two types: short agentless passives, or passives with a nominalized process given in the *by*-phrase. In both cases, the use of *can* and *could* with the passive avoids overt identification of the human agent of the main verb—the person who is able to carry out the reported action. As a result, the understood meaning is that the reported action or situation is logically possible.

Agentless passives:

> Each interpretation **can be seen** generally to flow through the abbreviated text as a whole. (ACAD)

> For example the effects of biological, physical and management factors on crop nutrition **can now be investigated**. (ACAD)

> The methods **could be refined** and made more accurate. (ACAD†)

Passives with a nominalized process given in the *by*-phrase:

> Its answer **can be illustrated** [by considering again the action of a polariser]. (ACAD)

> *Marked improvements in yield **can be obtained** in one or two seasons [by selection based upon a single character].* (ACAD)

> *The process **could be started** again after the chloroform was removed [by adding a little turbid extract of dry soil].* (ACAD†)

*Must* and *should* are also commonly used with passive voice in academic prose. This pattern corresponds to the surprisingly frequent use of these modals to mark obligation (rather than logical necessity) in academic prose. That is, these modals are used to express a kind of collective (personal) obligation, but the passive voice is used to avoid explicit identification of the person who is obliged to act:

> *Care **must be taken** to ensure that the diffusion in the stator is kept to a reasonable level.* (ACAD)

> *The angle of the diffuser vanes at the leading edge **must be designed** to suit the direction of the absolute velocity of the air at the radius.* (ACAD†)

> *It **should be noted** that the following scenario is nothing more than one of many potential scenarios.* (ACAD)

In fiction and news, the obligation/necessity modals *must* and *should* are relatively common with perfect aspect, where in the absence of tense the aspect marker serves to provide a past time reference. In contrast to the typical use of these modals in academic prose, in fiction and news this association of modal + perfect aspect usually marks logical necessity (rather than personal obligation). That is, the logically necessary events and situations are often those that occurred at some point in the past:

> *So the wind **must have blown** it here.* (FICT)

> *If the new tape is genuine, then the phone call made by Prince Charles **must have been** deliberately bugged.* (NEWS†)

> *It's more aerodynamic, the interior has been improved (although not nearly as much as it **should have been**) ...* (NEWS†)

In conversation, the use of the perfect with modals accounts for the surprisingly frequent use of *must* marking logical necessity:

> *There **must have been** about four hundred at the most.* (CONV)

> *If they say she's made a payment, she **must have made** a payment.* (CONV)

The possibility modals *might* and *may* are also common with the perfect expressing a certain degree of doubt about past events or situations:

> *Also he **may have had** quite a job finding it.* (FICT)

> *You can imagine what it **might have been** like.* (FICT)

> *Yet the markets **may have over-reacted** even more than usual.* (NEWS)

> *Yesterday he confessed he **might have forgotten** one.* (NEWS†)

Finally, relatively few modal forms occur at all with the progressive aspect. In conversation, the obligation/necessity modals (especially the semi-modal *be supposed to*) are relatively common with the progressive, marking a personal obligation or likely occurrence that is actually in progress or predicted to occur in the future:

> *She's **supposed to be coming** in.* (CONV)

> *Are you **supposed to be going** with him on holiday?* (CONV)

> *He **must be running** low.* (CONV)

In news, the volition/prediction modals are common with progressive aspect, marking future events or situations that will take place over (or after) a period of time:

> Next season, only one team **will be going** down from the First Division. (NEWS†)

The simple aspect *will go* in this context would suggest a strong volitional meaning. This pattern is particularly noteworthy with the modal *shall*, which is generally rare but occurs a high proportion of the time with the progressive aspect following first-person subjects:

> We **shall be campaigning** for the survival of local government in Cleveland. (NEWS)

> We **shall be meeting** with all parties in the near future. (NEWS†)

## 6.8    Sequences of modals and semi-modals

The semi-modals *have to*, *need to*, and *be going to* can occur in series following another modal or semi-modal:

> The researchers warn that they **will have to treat** many more patients before they can report a cure. (NEWS)

> I'm **gonna have to stay**. (CONV)

> These two **will need to rest** for a good long time. (FICT)

> I thought, perhaps, you **might be going to be married**. (FICT)

### CORPUS FINDINGS ²

➤ Modal + semi-modal sequences are by far most common with *have to*, in all four registers (see Table 6.7).
  ➤ Sequences of modal + *need to* are also relatively common.
  ➤ Sequences of modal + *be going to* are rare and restricted primarily to conversation and fiction.

### DISCUSSION OF FINDINGS

Sequences of modal + *have to* are relatively common in all four registers, especially in combination with volition/prediction modals:

> If I wanted to come, you see, I **would have to pay** again. (CONV)

> Because you**'re going to have to say** something. (CONV)

> He **would have to wait** a whole year again to taste it. (FICT)

> To succeed again they **will have to improve** their fitness and concentration. (NEWS†)

> If this programme is to make any sense we **shall have to find** a way to associate numbers with our operators. (ACAD)

Sequences of modal + *need to* are used less commonly; they are restricted primarily to academic prose and news:

> A complete theory **would need to accommodate** every element of physical reality. (ACAD†)

**Table 6.7** **Modal + semi-modal sequences occurring over 10 times per million words in at least one register; occurrences per million words**

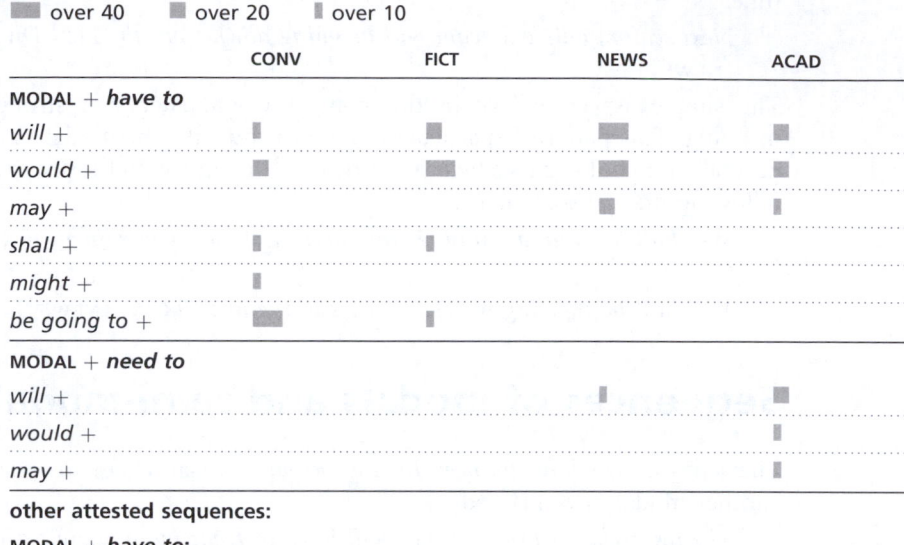

■ over 40　　■ over 20　　▌over 10

| | CONV | FICT | NEWS | ACAD |
|---|---|---|---|---|
| **MODAL + *have to*** | | | | |
| *will +* | ▌ | ■ | ■■ | ■ |
| *would +* | ■ | ■■ | ■■ | ■ |
| *may +* | | | ■ | ▌ |
| *shall +* | ▌ | ▌ | | |
| *might +* | ▌ | | | |
| *be going to +* | ■■ | ▌ | | |
| **MODAL + *need to*** | | | | |
| *will +* | | | ▌ | ■ |
| *would +* | | | | ▌ |
| *may +* | | | | ▌ |

**other attested sequences:**

**MODAL + *have to*:**

could have to, must have to, need to have to, should have to, used to have to

**MODAL + *need to*:**

be going to need to, can need to, might need to, must need to, shall need to, should need to

**MODAL + *be going to*** (rare; attested in fiction only):

may be going to, might be going to

> A utilitarian pragmatist **may need to worry** about the best way to understand the idea of community welfare. (ACAD)

> He **will need to jump** about 120 feet to clear the 20ft high wall. (NEWS†)

Finally, sequences of modal + *be going to* are rare, being attested only in fiction:

> Blackberry clearly thought that he **might be going to attack** them. (FICT)

> He thought I **might be going to slug** him. (FICT†)

> It **may be going to rain** before much longer. (FICT†)

It is noticeable that these complex verb phrases are on the whole less common in conversation than in the written registers, even though their semi-modal elements are generally more common in conversation. This could be due to the preference of conversation for shorter, less-complex structures. The only complex modal combination that occurs commonly in conversation is the one that combines the two most common semi-modals: *be going to have to*.

# 7

# Adjectives and adverbs

*See page xiii for contents in detail*

## 7.1 Overview

This chapter concerns the two lexical word classes of **adjectives** and **adverbs**, focusing on their basic forms, meanings, and syntactic roles. Further major aspects of adjectives are covered in 5.5 (their occurrence as predicatives with copular verbs), 8.2 (their occurrence as premodifiers in complex noun phrases), and Chapter 9 (their complementation by clauses). Adverbs are considered further in Chapter 10 with respect to their role as adverbials.

### 7.1.1 Use of adjectives and adverbs

Adjectives and adverbs are extremely common in all registers, but considerably less common overall than nouns and verbs, the other two lexical word classes. Further, these two word classes are distributed very differently across registers (see Figures 2.3 and 2.4 in 2.3.5): adjectives are most frequent in the written registers, especially academic prose, while adverbs are most frequent in conversation and fiction.

Interestingly, this distribution mirrors the distribution of nouns and verbs. Nouns, like adjectives, are most frequent in news and academic prose; while verbs, like adverbs, are most frequent in conversation and fiction. In large measure, these shared distributions reflect the most common uses of adjectives and adverbs: adjectives are frequently used to modify nouns, thus adding to the informational density of expository registers such as news and academic prose. In contrast, adverbs occur most commonly as clause elements (**adverbials**) and thus co-occur with lexical verbs in adding information to the relatively short (and therefore frequent) clauses of conversation and fiction. Text sample 1 illustrates the co-occurrence of adjectives and nouns in academic prose. Text sample 2 illustrates the co-occurrence of adverbs with verbs in conversation.

Text sample 1
Adjectives are **in bold**; nouns are marked with *[]*.

> Thus *[HIV] [infection] is **likely** to remain with us for the **foreseeable** [future]. The **full** [impact] of [HIV] [infection] will be felt over [decades]. The [virus] does not need to spread rapidly in a [population] to have a very **marked** and gradually **expanding cumulative** [effect]. The two **major** [factors] influencing the [risk] of **individual** [infection] are the [prevalence] of [HIV] [infection] and **individual** [behaviour].* (ACAD)

Text sample 2 (describing a "brain-dead hen")
Adverbs are **in bold**; lexical verbs are marked with *[]*.

> A: *And she [got] her feet stuck through netting – **so** she was [flapping] and the net was **just** [going] up and down!*
> B: *It's **quite** er*
> A: *No – that, that'll [give] way, that will be alright. Now as she, I [flapped] it, I [got] hold of it and I [flapped] it **so** it, I **sort of** [bounced] about, she **sort of** [bumped] along*
> B: *Yeah, you have to.*
> A: *Until she [got] onto that crossbar – and **then** she **just** [flew] **straight** back and did **exactly** the same thing **all over again** and I **just** [thought] – [sod] it! I [left] her on **there**!*

B: *Yeah.*

A: *And that she'll **just** have to [take] a chance **tonight**. Because she [saw] me [putting] the corn in and she [decided] she would [try] and [get] it – by [diving] through the black net – instead of [going] through the gate, like with a normal hen, you [know], this one's **obviously** brain-dead or*

B: *They are stupid that lot!* (CONV)

Text sample 1 not only illustrates the dense use of adjectives and nouns typical of academic prose, but also shows how a majority of the adjectives in academic writing occur as noun modifiers:

> ***foreseeable** [future]*
>
> ***full** [impact]*
>
> *a very **marked** and gradually **expanding cumulative** [effect]*

In contrast, as Text sample 2 illustrates, conversation tends to have relatively few nouns and adjectives, but many more verbs, corresponding to shorter but more frequent clauses. Adverbs commonly occur as adverbials in those clauses, resulting in a similar distribution for verbs and adverbs. This sample also illustrates the occurrence of adverbial particles in phrasal verbs, such as *bumped along*. These are not italicized, as they are regarded as separate from adverbs and dealt with elsewhere (2.4.6, 5.3.2).

Beyond these overall distributional patterns, there is considerable variation in the form and syntactic roles of both adjectives and adverbs. These are taken up in the two main sections following.

# 7.2 Defining characteristics of adjectives

**Central** adjectives are defined by their morphological, syntactic, and semantic characteristics (cf. 2.3.3, 2.7.3.1, 7.2.2):

### A Morphological

Many central adjectives can be inflected to show **degree of comparison**, as in *big, bigger, biggest* (7.7).

### B Syntactic

Central adjectives can serve both **attributive** and **predicative** syntactic roles. Adjectives in an attributive role modify nominal expressions, occurring as constituents of the noun phrase and typically preceding the head noun:

> *He hands me a pad: "Motion for production of all **scientific** [examinations]: all **underlying** [reports], spectographs, charts, **chemical** [analyses], et cetera."* (FICT)

Adjectives in a predicative role, on the other hand, characterize a noun phrase that is a separate clause element. They occur principally as subject predicatives following a copular verb (3.2.3, 5.5.3):

> *[That]'ll be quite **impressive**.* (CONV)

However they also occur as object predicatives (3.2.7):

> *Even Oscar Wilde called [it] **charming**.* (NEWS)

### C  Semantic

Central adjectives are descriptive, typically characterizing the referent of a nominal expression (e.g. **blue** and **white** *flag*, **unhappy** *childhood*). Further, they are **gradable** in meaning, that is, they can denote **degrees** of a given quality. This means they can be modified by an adverb of degree: *very* strange, *deeply* unhappy. They also take comparative and superlative forms (see A above).

Many of the most common adjectives are **central** adjectives that have all of these characteristics; they include adjectives of color (e.g. *black, red, dark*), adjectives of size and dimension (e.g. *big, small, long, thin*), and adjectives of time (e.g. *new, old, young*). Other adjectives are more **peripheral** in that they do not have all of the central defining characteristics above. Further, other word classes can be used in similar ways to adjectives (especially nouns, adverbs, and semi-determiners), so that the boundaries of the adjective category are not easy to draw in terms of these defining characteristics (2.2.6, 2.2.7, 2.3.6).

## 7.2.1  Attributive and predicative adjectives across registers

**CORPUS FINDINGS [2]**

➤ Across registers, attributive adjectives differ in frequency to a much greater extent than predicative adjectives.

➤ In conversation, attributive and predicative adjectives are both relatively rare.

➤ Attributive adjectives are much more frequent than predicative adjectives in the expository written registers.

➤ Predicative adjectives are somewhat more common in fiction than in the other registers.

**Figure 7.1**

**Distribution of attributive and predicative adjectives across registers**

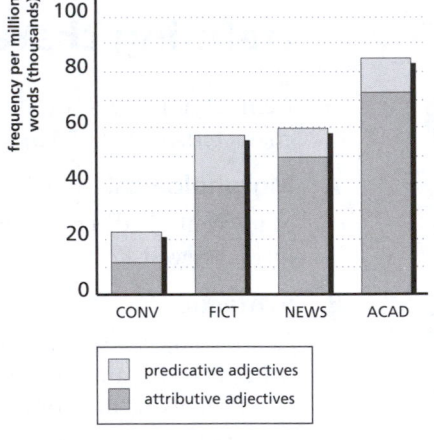

**DISCUSSION OF FINDINGS**

The greater frequency of adjectives in the written registers, especially in an attributive role, reflects the heavy reliance on noun phrases to present information. Attributive adjectives are one of the primary mechanisms used to pack additional information into noun phrases:

> He said the **former Yugoslav** republic could become a "**European** Lebanon" and fighting would spread beyond its frontiers if Bosnia crumbled into **separate ethnic** mini-states. (NEWS)

> With **economic** specialization and the development of **external economic** linkages, division of labour intensifies, a merchant class is added to the **political** elite, and **selective** migration streams add to the **social** and **ethnic** complexity of cities. (ACAD)

The roughly equal frequency of predicative and attributive adjectives in conversation is in keeping with the general reliance on a clausal rather than nominal presentation of information. For example, note the relatively dense use of predicative adjectives in the following conversational interaction:

> A: <...> getting a B is **good** enough for him.
> B: That's **great**.
> A: Especially for people in med school – I think a lot of them are so **used** to being –
> B: Super-achievers
> A: Super-achievers that they can't slow down, but, uh, Trey's not that way. He's real **laid back**. (CONV)

## 7.2.2 Central and peripheral adjectives

As already explained, central adjectives—such as *black, big, new*—all have the core defining characteristics of adjectives: they are descriptive in meaning, gradable, inflected morphologically, and can be used in both attributive and predicative roles. In contrast, Table 7.1 illustrates the ways in which other adjectives can be peripheral by not having one or more of the defining characteristics.

**Table 7.1    Variability in the defining characteristics of adjectives**

| morphological inflection | attributive role | predicative role | descriptive meaning | gradable | example |
|---|---|---|---|---|---|
| + | + | + | + | + | big |
| – | + | + | + | + | beautiful |
| – | + | + | ? | – | absolute |
| – | – | + | + | + | afraid |
| – | – | + | + | ? | alive |
| – | + | + | – | + | different |
| – | + | ? | + | ? | lone |
| ? | + | – | – | – | mere |

(Note that *mere* has a superlative form used only in a rhetorical sense: e.g. *hanging by the merest thread*.)

Many peripheral adjectives occur in only attributive or predicative syntactic roles (but not both). For example, *unable* is used only predicatively, while *mere* is used only attributively. Thus:

> Heisenberg was totally **unable** to answer them. (ACAD)
> cf. *An **unable** Heisenberg could not answer them.

> He had lost his reputation as a strong man, having been defeated twice by a **mere** boy. (NEWS)
> cf. *He had lost his reputation as a strong man, having been defeated twice by a boy who was **mere**.

However, these patterns are usually not absolute: rather, most peripheral adjectives show a strong preference for either an attributive or a predicative role, but do occasionally occur in the other role as well. For example, adjectives such as *able, aloof,* and *aware* usually occur in predicative position:

> *Clients will be **able** to trade electronically.* (NEWS†)
>
> *In some ways, you're **aloof** too.* (FICT)
>
> *Charlton is **aware** of the problem.* (NEWS†)

But attributive uses of these adjectives also occur:

> *a very **able** writer* (FICT)
>
> *a cool and **aloof** mood* (NEWS†)
>
> *an ever more **aware** consumer market* (NEWS†)

## 7.2.3 Adjectives strongly associated with attributive or predicative position

**CORPUS FINDINGS** [2,3]

➤ Adjectives beginning with the prefix *a-* show a strong preference for predicative position. All the following forms occur over 98% of the time as predicative adjectives: *abed, ablaze, abreast, afraid, aghast, aglow, alike, alive, alone, askew, asleep, aware.*

➤ Some other adjectives are also strongly associated with predicative position:
  ➤ Selected adjectives that occur predicatively over 95% of the time: *easier, glad, ill, impossible, ready, sure.*
  ➤ Selected adjectives that occur predicatively over 80% of the time: *anxious, evident, grateful, helpful, lucky, responsible, tired, unlikely, worse.*

➤ At the other extreme, the adjective *mere* is attested only in attributive position.

➤ Adjectives ending in *-al* (e.g. *political, chemical, industrial*; 7.9.2) also show a very strong preference for attributive position.
  ➤ For example, several of the most common adjectives ending in *-al* occur in attributive position over 98% of the time: *general, industrial, local, national, social.*

## 7.3 Semantic grouping of adjectives

It is useful to distinguish two broad semantic groups of adjectives: **descriptors** and **classifiers**. Descriptors are prototypical adjectives denoting such features as color, size and weight, chronology and age, emotion, and a wide range of other characteristics. They are typically gradable (see 2.3.3; also 7.2C above). In contrast, the primary function of classifiers is to delimit or restrict a noun's referent, by placing it in a category in relation to other referents. They are typically non-gradable. Classifiers can be grouped into subclasses, including relational, affiliative, and a miscellaneous topical class. Classifiers can be more or less descriptive in meaning: relational classifiers (such as *additional, final, similar*) have little descriptive content, while many topical classifiers (such as *chemical, medical, political*) provide descriptive content while also limiting the reference of the head noun.

Selected examples of adjectives belonging to these semantic domains are:

**A Descriptors**

**Color**—denoting color, brightness: *black, white, dark, bright, blue, brown, green, grey, red*

**Size/quantity/extent**—denoting size, weight, extent: *big, deep, heavy, huge, long, large, little, short, small, thin, wide*

**Time**—denoting chronology, age, frequency: *annual, daily, early, late, new, old, recent, young*

**Evaluative/emotive**—denoting judgements, affect, emphasis: *bad, beautiful, best, fine, good, great, lovely, nice, poor*

**Miscellaneous descriptive**—*appropriate, cold, complex, dead, empty, free, hard, hot, open, positive, practical, private, serious, strange, strong, sudden.*

## B Classifiers

**Relational/classificational/restrictive**—delimiting the referent of a noun, particularly in relation to other referents: *additional, average, chief, complete, different, direct, entire, external, final, following, general, initial, internal, left, main, maximum, necessary, original, particular, previous, primary, public, similar, single, standard, top, various, same* (note: *same* can alternatively be analyzed as a semi-determiner; 4.4.6)

**Affiliative**—designating the national or religious group to which a referent belongs: *American, Chinese, Christian, English, French, German, Irish, United*

**Topical/other** (e.g. giving the subject area or showing a relationship with a noun): *chemical, commercial, environmental, human, industrial, legal, medical, mental, official, oral, phonetic, political, sexual, social, ventral, visual.*

Some adjectives can serve as either classifier or descriptor. Below, the expressions in the left-hand column contain a classifying or restricting adjective, while those in the right-hand column a descriptor. Note that the descriptors are gradable and can be modified to show degree or extent (e.g. by *very*).

| Classifier | Descriptor |
|---|---|
| *modern* algebra | some *modern* authorities |
| *criminal* law | *criminal* activity |
| a *secondary* school | a useful *secondary* function |

In the discussions of attributive adjectives to follow, semantic groupings of adjectives are employed as a heuristic to help characterize the patterns across registers. However, very common adjectives typically designate a range of meanings. For example, in some expressions *old* is descriptive, denoting age (*an old radio, old newspapers*); in others it denotes affect (*poor old Rusty, good old genetics*). Similarly *poor* has two principal uses: emotive (*the poor devil, You poor bunny!*) and descriptive (*a poor country, in poor health*). Even the descriptive uses of *poor* carry different denotations, such as 'lacking adequate financial resources' and 'not good'.

Grammatical role can be associated with a particular meaning. Thus, the predicative use of *poor* typically refers to financial circumstances (*someone who's poor*), while the attributive use has a wider range of meanings, including the emotive meaning (*poor little bastards*). In addition, the characteristic uses of a given adjective often differ across registers. For example, in academic prose *poor* is generally descriptive, whereas in fiction it is commonly emotive.

## 7.4 Attributive adjectives

Attributive adjectives modify nominal expressions, preceding the head noun or pronoun. In most cases, they modify common nouns, as in the following examples (with **attributive adjectives** in bold and head nouns in *[]*):

> Yes, it's a **bad** *[attitude]*. (CONV)
>
> It's **rustic, knotty** *[pine]* with a **huge** *[fireplace]*. (FICT)
>
> One of the most **important** *[ways]* of achieving this is by the **regular** and **thorough** *[implementation]* of **planned** disinfection *[programmes]* in all livestock units. (ACAD)

Attributive adjectives can also modify proper place nouns, as in **old-fashioned Episcopalian** *[New York]*, **ancient** *[Mesopotamia]* and **pharaonic** *[Egypt]*. Less commonly, adjectives modify the name of a person, as in **little** *[Laura Davies]*, *the* **wretched** *[Paul]* or *the* **late** *[John C. Drennan]* (see also 8.1.2).

Particularly in exclamations, attributive adjectives can also modify a personal pronoun. Attributive adjectives with pronouns are not common in any register but occur occasionally in conversation and fiction. Although no adjective is frequent in this role, the adjectives *poor*, *lucky*, and *silly* are somewhat more common modifying personal pronouns than other adjectives:

> Ah! **Poor** you Helen! (CONV)
>
> Not like **poor** me. (FICT)
>
> **Lucky** you! (CONV)
>
> Oh of course—**silly** me. (CONV)
>
> "**Silly old** him," Lally laughed (FICT †)

As the following sentence from fiction suggests, such usage is stylistically marked:

> People called her **Little** Me because she had this ridiculous habit of saying things like "there'll just be the four of us, including **Little** Me". (FICT †)

See also 8.1.2.

## 7.4.1 Semantic domains of attributive adjectives

In this section and 7.4.2 we group adjectives into semantic domains based on their characteristic significance, even though meanings associated with other semantic categories can also occur. While this semantic grouping is useful for the interpretation of distributional patterns, it does not in any way influence the quantitative findings themselves.

**CORPUS FINDINGS** [2]

➤ The four registers use attributive adjectives from the major semantic domains in quite different ways (see Table 7.2):

➤ Descriptors are found in all four registers to varying extents.

> ➤ Fiction uses a greater number of descriptors than the other registers:

➤ Classifiers, on the other hand, are used primarily in the informational written registers:

> ➤ Academic prose shows a very heavy reliance on relational classifiers.
>
> ➤ Academic prose also uses more topical classifiers than any other register.
>
> ➤ News uses affiliative classifiers to a greater extent than the other registers.

Table 7.2  **Number of common attributive adjectives by semantic domain and register; occurrences per million words**

each ● represents 3 adjectives, each occurring at least 100 times

|  | CONV | FICT | NEWS | ACAD |
|---|---|---|---|---|
| **descriptors** | | | | |
| evaluative | ● ● | ● ● ● ● | ● ● ● | ● ● ● ● |
| size | ● | ● ● ● ● | ● ● ● | ● ● ● |
| time | ● | ● | ● ● ● | |
| color | ● | ● ● ● | ● | |
| miscellaneous | | ● ● ● | ● | ● ● |
| **classifiers** | | | | |
| relational | ● | ● ● | ● ● ● ● ● ● | ● ● ● ● ● ● ● ● ● ● ● ●<br>● ● ● ● ● ● ● ● |
| topical/miscellaneous | | | ● ● ● ● ● | ● ● ● ● ● ● ● ● ● ● ● |
| affiliative | | | ● ● ● | ● |

**DISCUSSION OF FINDINGS**

Although attributive adjectives functioning as descriptors are used in all four registers, fiction employs a greater number of these than the other registers. The semantic domains of size (e.g. *big*, *little*), color, and evaluation (e.g. *good*, *nice*) are most important in this register. Conversation also employs adjectives from all four major categories of descriptors, although it uses fewer of these forms (reflecting the general rarity in conversation of attributive adjectives). Time and affiliative adjectives are important in news, in addition to size and evaluative adjectives, perhaps not surprisingly given the typical subject matter of this register.

In academic prose, the descriptor categories of size and evaluation are relatively important (see also discussion in 7.4.2). However, the most striking pattern in academic prose, and to a lesser extent in news, is the extreme reliance on classifiers—especially relational adjectives (such as *different*, *general*, *major*), but also topical adjectives (such as *social*, *economic*).

All of these patterns can be better understood after considering the specific attributive adjectives that are most common in each register, taken up in the following section.

## 7.4.2  Most common attributive adjectives

**CORPUS FINDINGS [2]**

➤ The distribution of particular attributive adjectives differs considerably across registers (Table 7.3).
➤ In addition, many attributive adjectives are frequent in one register:

| | |
|---|---|
| in conversation | *bad* occurs over 100 times per million words |
| in fiction | *bad*, *short*, *young*, *bright*, *hot*, *cold*, and *empty* all occur over 100 times per million words. |

Table 7.3    **The most common attributive adjectives across registers (all attributive adjectives that occur more than 200 times per million words in at least one register); occurrences per million words**

██ over 500    ■ over 200    ▪ over 80

| semantic domain | CONV | FICT | NEWS | ACAD |
|---|---|---|---|---|
| **descriptors: size/amount** | | | | |
| *big* | ■ | ■ | ■ | |
| *little* | ■ | ■ | ▪ | |
| *long* | ▪ | ■ | ■ | ▪ |
| *small* | | ■ | ■ | ■ |
| *great* | | ■ | ■ | ■ |
| *high* | | ▪ | ■ | ■ |
| *low* | | ▪ | ▪ | ■ |
| *large* | | ▪ | ▪ | ■ |
| **descriptors: time** | | | | |
| *new* | ■ | ■ | ██ | ██ |
| *old* | ■ | ■ | ██ | ▪ |
| *young* | | ■ | ■ | ▪ |
| **descriptors: color** | | | | |
| *black* | ▪ | ■ | ▪ | |
| *white* | ▪ | ■ | ▪ | |
| *red* | | ■ | ▪ | |
| *dark* | | ■ | | |
| **descriptors: evaluative** | | | | |
| *good* | ■ | ■ | ■ | ■ |
| *best* | ▪ | ▪ | ■ | ▪ |
| *right* | ▪ | ▪ | ▪ | ■ |
| *nice* | ■ | ▪ | | |
| *important* | | | ▪ | ■ |
| *special* | | | ▪ | ■ |
| **classifiers relational** | | | | |
| *same* | ■ | ■ | ■ | ██ |
| *whole* | ▪ | ■ | ▪ | ■ |
| *different* | ▪ | ▪ | ▪ | ██ |
| *full* | | ▪ | ■ | ▪ |
| *general* | | | ■ | ■ |
| *major* | | | ██ | ■ |
| *final* | | | ■ | ▪ |
| *main* | | | ▪ | ■ |
| *single* | | | ▪ | ■ |
| **classifiers: topical** | | | | |
| *political* | | | ■ | ■ |
| *public* | | | ■ | ■ |

**Table 7.3**   **continued**

| semantic domain | CONV | FICT | NEWS | ACAD |
|---|---|---|---|---|
| *social* | | | ■ | ■ |
| *human* | | ■ | | ■ |
| *international* | | | ■ | ■ |
| *national* | | | ■ | ■ |
| *economic* | | | ■ | ■ |

in news
**affiliative**: *American, British, European, Scottish*
**topical**: *royal*

in academic prose
**evaluative**: *simple*
**relational**: *basic, common, following, higher, individual, lower, particular, similar, specific, total, various*
**topical**: *local, natural, normal, oral, physical, public, sexual*

### DISCUSSION OF FINDINGS

With few exceptions, the most frequent attributive adjectives in conversation are descriptors rather than classifiers. They are mostly monosyllabic and simple, consistent with the generally less-complex structures in this register. Semantically, most of these words characterize size, time, or personal evaluation. Of these, evaluative adjectives are the most common:

*That's a **good** film.* (CONV)

*He had this really **nice** cap.* (CONV)

*Especially if you can get the **right** price.* (CONV)

In fact, two of the adjectives grouped in other semantic categories typically have evaluative functions in conversation—*old* and *whole*:

*The **old** pig!* (CONV)

*Yeah. Same **old** stuff.* (CONV)

*I mean the **whole** thing would have to be redesigned.* (CONV)

See also the discussion of stance in 12.1.2.

As noted in 7.4.1, fiction uses a wider range of descriptor adjectives than any other register, taken from the full range of semantic domains. These forms add the descriptive detail characteristic of fictional narrative, illustrated in the following passage (with descriptor adjectives in bold):

*It was a **broad, low, heavy, ruddy, thick-featured, wool-haired, staring, bakefaced** man.* <...>

*But this was our Walter.*

*In a **black** raincoat, in a cap, **gray** hair bunched before the ears; his **reddish-swarthy** teapot cheeks; his **big mulberry-tinted** lips.* <...>

*He found **old** manuscripts and adapted or arranged them for groups performing **ancient** and baroque music.*

*His own **little** racket, he said.* (FICT†)

All adjectives in this passage are descriptors, with the possible exception of *baroque*.

Interestingly, several of the most common attributive adjectives in both conversation and fiction comprise contrasting pairs:

| | |
|---|---|
| size/amount | *big/little, large/small, long/short, high/low* |
| time | *new/old, young/old* |
| color | *black/white, bright/dark* |
| evaluative | *good/bad* |
| other descriptor | *hot/cold* |
| relational (classifier) | *same/different, full/empty* |

News employs a wider range of common adjectives than any other register, including numerous classifiers as well as descriptors. These adjectives serve the twin purposes of clearly identifying the referents of noun phrases and providing descriptive details about those referents. In the following excerpt, descriptor attributive adjectives are in bold, with classifiers marked by *[]*:

> It has never lost an artist from its record label, supposedly because it consists of many **small** and **friendly** *[individual]* companies. <...>
>
> Fujisankei, itself privately owned and independent, seems the **ideal** partner.
>
> But the question must remain as to whether a *[Japanese]* giant with five times the turnover of the Virgin group will be content to stay a minority player in the **long** term. (NEWS†)

Many of the most common attributive adjectives in news are words derived from, or closely related to, nouns, especially those ending in *-al*, such as *political* and *national* (cf. 7.9.2). Other denominal adjectives that occur frequently in news include *financial, industrial, legal, medical,* and *personal*. Such adjectives tend to be topical classifiers which delimit the domain of the head noun (*good* **financial** *planning*, a **medical** *doctor*).

Consistent with its communicative needs, academic prose shows an even greater use of classifiers, especially relational and topical adjectives:

Relational adjectives in academic prose:

> the **same** physical units, **basic** processes, **general** method, **whole** number

Topical adjectives in academic prose:

> **social** status, **human** nature, **sexual** development, **natural** law, **public** policy, **political** economy, **experimental** physics

Among other frequent attributive adjectives in this register are many that derive either from nouns (*environmental, experimental, functional, natural, sexual*) or from verbs (*considerable, continuous, various*).

Somewhat surprisingly, several evaluative attributive adjectives are also relatively common in academic prose. These adjectives are particularly productive in occurring with different head nouns:

| Evaluative adjective | Selected head nouns |
|---|---|
| *good* | *judges, readers, separation, communication, relations, fortune, yields, indication* |
| *important* | *changes, advances, step, part, consequences, respect, role, point, factor* |
| *special* | *cases, process, regulations, class, types, method* |
| *right* | *principles, level, relation, direction, answer, criteria* |

As in the other registers, several of the most common attributive adjectives in academic prose comprise contrasting pairs, including:

| | | |
|---|---|---|
| *large/small* | *long/short* | *young/old* |
| *low/high* | *final/initial* | *previous/following* |
| *general/particular* | *same/different* | *simple/complex* |
| *primary/secondary* | *necessary/possible* | *positive/negative* |

## 7.5 Predicative adjectives

Predicative adjectives have two syntactic roles: **subject predicatives** and **object predicatives** (2.7.3.1).

**Subject predicatives** complement a copular verb, characterizing the nominal expression in subject position. For example, the predicative adjective *nice* is an evaluation characterizing the subject pronoun *she* in the following sentence:

*She seems quite **nice** really.* (CONV)

Other examples of subject predicatives are given below:

*[That]'s **right**.* (CONV)

*[It] would be **easier, quicker,** and **cheaper**.* (FICT)

*[I]'m **afraid** [that]'s **impossible**.* (FICT)

*[The fans] became **restless** and [the soccer grapevine] was **alive** with names of likely successors to Mr Stringer.* (NEWS)

*[The tendencies] are not **significant** and get **weaker** when data are corrected for guessing.* (ACAD)

In contrast, **object predicatives** follow a direct object, making a predication about that noun phrase. In the examples below, the object predicative is italicized and the direct object preceding it is marked by *[]*:

*I said you've got all your [priorities] **wrong*** (CONV)

*I had [it] **right** the first time, didn't I?* (CONV)

*He did not find [her] **amusing**, and she found [him] **quite disastrously dull**.* (FICT)

*She had considered [it] **infinitely vulgar and debased**.* (FICT)

*She has since declared [herself] **bankrupt**.* (NEWS†)

*Pragmatism makes [it] **somewhat harder** [to predict what courts will do].* (ACAD†) <note the extraposition of the object in this example; see 3.6.4>

Many of the most frequent predicative adjectives typically occur with a phrasal complement or clausal complement of their own, such as a prepositional phrase, *to*-infinitive clause, or *that* clause (cf. 9.2.5, 9.4.5, 9.5.3). In the examples below, predicative adjectives are in bold and their complements marked by *[]*.

Predicative adjectives with phrasal complements:

*Well you're **good** [at remembering numbers].* (CONV)

*That's **nice** [of you].* (FICT)

*Is so much protection **necessary** [for life itself]?* (FICT)

*Powerful earphones are also **available** [to him].* (NEWS)

*To be **susceptible** [to systematic analysis], a system concept is **subject** [to several constraints]* (ACAD†)

Predicative adjectives with clausal complements:

*"You look **good enough** [to eat]," he said* (FICT†)

*I am **sure** [the warm affinities between Scots and Jews arise out of appreciation of herrings].* (NEWS)

*In horses, its prevalence is **difficult** [to establish].* (ACAD†)

In contrast, English grammar normally does not allow adjectives accompanied by prepositional or clausal complements to occur attributively.

## 7.5.1   Most common predicative adjectives

(See also Table 5.33 on predicative adjectives with *be*, and the detailed account in 5.5.3 of adjectives as predicatives with specific copular verbs.)

### CORPUS FINDINGS [2]

➤ The distribution of particular predicative adjectives differs considerably across registers (Table 7.4).

➤ Adjectives from the descriptor semantic domains predominate, while the affiliative and topical classifier domains are not represented.

➤ In general, there is little overlap with the list of common attributive adjectives (Table 7.3).

> ➤ However, the following adjecitves are common in both attributive and predicative positions: *nice, right, good, large, low, different,* and *full*.

➤ In addition, many predicative adjectives are common in a single register:

| | |
|---|---|
| in conversation | *alright, lovely* |
| in fiction | *alone, tired* |
| in news | *due* |
| in academic prose | *common, dependent, equal, equivalent, essential, greater, large, low, present, similar, useful* |

### DISCUSSION OF FINDINGS

Semantically, the most frequent predicative adjectives of conversation tend to be evaluative and emotive, e.g. *good, lovely,* and *bad. Right, alright,* and *sure* usually express agreement or confidence, as in *I'm sure.* The expression of disagreement (e.g. *you're wrong*) is less common.

The wide range of meanings that attaches to some very frequent adjectives cannot be overlooked here. For example, given its core meaning of 'humorous' or 'amusing', it may seem surprising to find *funny* among the most frequent predicative adjectives in conversation. However, *funny* carries a wide range of other meanings, including 'odd', 'spoiled', 'strange', 'noteworthy', 'peculiar', or 'out of sorts', as in these examples:

*She sounds **funny** on the phone. Most odd.* (CONV)

*Told you about her having that ... dish ... and it went **funny**.* (CONV)

***Funny** though how people are like that.* (CONV)

*I said I don't think she's **funny** I think she's idle!* (CONV)

*So she got a bit **funny** over it!* (CONV)

Table 7.4 **The most common predicative adjectives across registers (all predicative adjectives that occur more than 50 times per million words in at least one register) occurrences per million words**

Key: ■■■ over 100  ■■ over 50  ■ over 20

| | CONV | FICT | NEWS | ACAD |
|---|---|---|---|---|
| able | ■■■ | ■■■ | ■■ | ■■ |
| sure | ■■■ | ■■■ | ■ | ■ |
| right | ■■■ | ■■ | ■ | ■ |
| good | ■■■ | ■■ | ■■ | |
| nice | ■■■ | ■ | ■ | |
| true | ■■ | ■■ | ■ | ■■■ |
| wrong | ■■ | ■■ | ■ | ■ |
| bad | ■■ | ■ | ■ | |
| fine | ■■ | ■ | | |
| funny | ■■ | ■ | | |
| difficult | ■ | ■■ | ■■ | ■■■ |
| different | ■ | ■■ | ■ | ■■ |
| hard | ■ | ■■ | ■■ | ■ |
| afraid | ■ | ■■■ | ■ | |
| dead | ■ | ■■■ | ■ | |
| happy | ■ | ■■ | ■■ | |
| full | ■ | ■■ | ■ | |
| glad | ■ | ■■ | ■ | |
| possible | | ■■ | ■ | ■■■ |
| impossible | | ■■ | ■ | ■■ |
| ready | | ■■ | ■■ | ■ |
| aware | | ■■ | ■ | ■ |
| likely | | ■ | ■■■ | ■■■ |
| unable | | ■ | ■■ | ■ |
| important | | ■ | ■ | ■■■ |
| necessary | | ■ | ■ | ■■■ |
| clear | | ■ | ■ | ■■ |
| small | | ■ | | ■■ |
| available | | | ■■ | ■■■ |
| unlikely | | | ■■ | ■ |
| better | | ■ | ■ | ■■ |

Unlike many predicative adjectives in other registers, those in conversation typically lack complements. Even predicative adjectives such as *sure*, *true*, and *wrong*, which normally take clausal complements in the written registers, commonly occur without a complement in conversation:

Are you **sure**? (CONV)

*We'll find out what's **wrong**.* (CONV)

*Well yeah that's **true**.* (CONV)

Fiction has the highest frequency of predicative adjectives, in part because fictional descriptions sometimes include sequences of subject predicative adjectives, such as:

*The conscripts, apart from being **idle**, **homesick**, **afraid**, **uninterested**, **hot**, **sweating**, **bored**, **oversexed** and **undersatisfied**, were in better condition.* (FICT)

*What she intended to be was **gay**, **pleasure-giving**, **exuberant**, **free**, **beautiful**, **healthy**.* (FICT)

Semantically, the predicative adjectives in fiction tend to be descriptive of a state of mind or emotion (e.g. *afraid, aware, glad, happy, ready, sure, tired*). As with their use in conversation, *right* and *sure* tend to express (or solicit) agreement or confidence, while expression of disagreement, as represented principally by *wrong*, is far less frequent.

In news, most frequent predicative adjectives (such as *able* and *likely*) usually take clausal or phrasal complements. Thus, they provide a frame for making judgments and supplying information—both important functions of opinion pieces and news reports:

*Clients will be **able** [to trade electronically].* (NEWS†)

*Increasing controls are **likely** [to be imposed in this area].* (NEWS†)

In addition, since news writers often incorporate spoken quotations into their reports, many predicative adjectives of news occur in quoted speech:

*"So either way I go, it's **likely** to be **unpopular** with the other section."* (NEWS)

A notable feature of academic prose is the frequency with which intellectual claims are made, and predicative adjectives commonly provide a frame for such claims:

*It will be **clear** [that the presence of two slits is **essential** [to give an interference pattern]].* (ACAD)

Such predicative adjectives mark a kind of epistemic stance e.g. *true, clear, likely*, or an author's evaluative stance, e.g. *important, essential, difficult* (9.2.5, 9.4.5, 12.3).

In contrast to the sequences of predicative adjectives that often occur in a single clause in fiction, sentences that contain multiple predicative adjectives in academic prose typically have them in separate clauses:

*The feeling of comfort is **basic** [to a sense of well-being], but it is **difficult** [to define] and is often most **notable** [in its absence].* (ACAD)

*In horses, its prevalence is **difficult** [to establish] since infections rarely become **patent** although it is frequently incriminated as a cause of chronic coughing.* (ACAD)

# 7.6    Adjectives in other syntactic roles

Apart from their primary uses in attributive and predicative roles, adjectives can occur in a range of other syntactic roles, including **postposed nominal modifiers**

(7.6.1), **noun phrase heads** (7.6.2), **adjectives with a clause linking function** (7.6.3), **exclamations** (7.6.4), and **detached predicatives** (7.6.5). Adjectives also play a pivotal role in comparative clauses, as discussed in 7.8.

## 7.6.1 Postposed adjectives

An adjective that is a constituent of a noun phrase and follows rather than precedes the head is said to be **postposed** (i.e. it is a postmodifier).

Postposed adjectives are especially prevalent with indefinite pronoun heads (4.15, 8.1.2), such as *no one, anything,* and *somebody*:

> *It's a shame if you haven't got [anyone]* **musical** *here.* (CONV)

> *[Something]* **cold and refreshing** *actually.* (CONV)

> *We were both hungry for jury work, and therefore we agreed to try a dead-bang loser of a rape case on reassignment from [somebody]* **smarter**. (FICT)

> *Four-course meals that last four hours are marathons for [everyone]* **concerned**. (NEWS)

> *Try as they might, [no one]* **close** *to Frankie Howerd could ever improve his image.* (NEWS)

> *"I think they are doing [everything]* **possible** *to protect the workers."* (NEWS)

Certain adjectives, such as *involved, available,* and *concerned,* tend to be postposed after a noun head:

> *She was unacquainted with any of the [people]* **involved**. (FICT)

> *He said the only [details]* **available**, *apart from a death certificate, had come from Mr Garrod's family.* (NEWS)

> *The proposal seemed to be appropriate for the [school]* **concerned**. (ACAD†)

In addition, a number of fixed expressions contain postposed adjectives, e.g. *attorney general, heir apparent, notary public, Asia Minor.*

Finally, when the modifying adjective phrase is heavy (usually containing an adjectival complement), the adjective phrase will often follow its head noun:

> *It's a, a [lounge]* **not much bigger than the one we've got now**. (CONV)

> *He drew from the high soprano instrument [sounds]* **totally different from what we think of as saxophone tone**. (NEWS†)

In some of these cases, the head noun is both premodified and postmodified:

> *"McDeere is a* **great** *[student],* **dedicated, hardworking and ambitious**," *says Cruise of his character.* (NEWS)

> *The* **physiological** *[factors]* **involved in transplanting** *are somewhat obscure.* (ACAD†)

## 7.6.2 Adjectives as noun phrase heads

Some adjectives can serve as the head of a noun phrase. As the examples below illustrate, this quasi-conversion from adjective to noun is not complete, in that the adjective head does not ordinarily take a plural *-s* inflection, even when it has plural reference. In addition, as with adjectives (but not nouns) these forms can be modified by adverbs, as in **3** below. However, example **6** illustrates how they can also take premodifiers typical of nouns. Definite determiners are the norm for adjectives as noun phrase heads, although **5** illustrates an exception, where the determiner is a quantifier.

> 1 *Everyone picks on the **Welsh**, don't they?* (CONV)
>
> 2 *Why he was at Panglin with the **lazy** and the **lame**, the **fat**, the **indifferent**, the **leaning** and the **halt**.* (FICT)
>
> 3 *I think the contrast between the [very] **rich** and the [very] **poor** in this country is disgusting.* (FICT)
>
> 4 *But in politics the **unlikely** can happen.* (NEWS†)
>
> 5 *A policy which would require many **unemployed** either to find a job or to accept full-time training or higher education.* (NEWS†)
>
> 6 *These people may be the [real working] **poor**, the **elderly**, the [very] **young**, the **unemployed**, or the **transient**.* (ACAD)

In most cases, as these examples show, the adjective-headed noun phrase generically refers to people with the characteristic named by the adjective (4.4.1.4): thus *the elderly* refers to 'elderly people in general'.

## 7.6.3 Adjectives with a clause linking function

Adjectives—with or without accompanying modifiers—sometimes serve to link clauses or sentences to one another, as illustrated below:

> ***Worse** he had nothing to say.* (FICT)
>
> ***Even more important**, the prospect of a single currency would eliminate an enormous source of uncertainty for businesses.* (NEWS)
>
> ***Still more important**, children who grew up in elite homes enjoyed advantages that helped them maintain elite status.* (ACAD)

## 7.6.4 Adjectives as exclamations

Adjectives often serve as exclamations (3.13.3), especially in conversation and fictional dialogue:

> ***Great**! I need some of those.* (CONV)
>
> ***Good**! I like that.* (CONV)

Other examples in conversation:

> *Excellent! Bloody brilliant! Rough! Uncanny! Sorry! Alright! Oh horrible! Hilarious! Oh right! Oh dear! Amazing! Right! Lucky! Wonderful! Super! Super-duper!*

(A number of these could alternatively be regarded as inserts; 2.5).

Examples in fiction:

> *Ridiculous! Irrelevant! Stupendous! Good gracious! Miraculous! Glorious! Marvelous!*

Adjectives as exclamations also occur in headlines and captions in news writing, e.g. *Blinding! Hair-raising! Alive!*

## 7.6.5 Adjectives as detached predicatives

Adjectives can also occur as detached predicatives: syntactically free modifiers of a noun phrase (cf. 3.4.1). These structures are especially characteristic of fiction, and typically occur in sentence-initial position. Below, the detached predicative adjective phrases (with any complements) are in bold and the noun phrases they modify are enclosed in *[]*:

> **Slender and demure**, *[she] wore a simple ao dai.* (FICT†)
>
> **Green, bronze and golden** *[it] flowed through weeds and rushes.* (FICT)
>
> **Too tired to move**, *[she] stayed there.* (FICT†)
>
> **Delicate and light bodied**, *[it] is often confused with American blended whiskey and thus called rye.* (ACAD)

Detached predicatives can also occur in sentence-final position:

> *[Victor] chuckled,* **highly amused**. (FICT)

## 7.7 Comparative and superlative degree

Adjectives capable of representing degrees of a characteristic are said to be **gradable** and can be modified by degree adverbs. Most common adjectives, particularly from the descriptor semantic domains, are gradable:

> *They are* **so difficult** *to diagnose.* (FICT)
>
> *The two couples were* **very close**. (NEWS)
>
> *It is a* **very decorative** *plant.* (ACAD)

Gradable adjectives can also be specially marked to denote **comparative** and **superlative** degree. Whereas the base form of an adjective is formally unmarked for degree (e.g. *strong, famous*), these levels of degree can be marked either **inflectionally** or **phrasally** (7.7.2):

| | degree | |
|---|---|---|
| **type of marking** | **comparative** | **superlative** |
| inflectional | *stronger* | *softest* |
| phrasal | *more difficult* | *most famous* |

Non-gradable adjectives cannot be marked for comparative or superlative degree or modified by degree adverbs, such as *\*more previous, \*very motionless,* and *\*most continuous.* They can, on the other hand, often be modified by emphatic adverbs, as in:

> **quite** *motionless* (FICT)
>
> **really** *tremendous* (NEWS)
>
> **absolutely** *continuous* (ACAD)

Some non-gradable adjectives, however, cannot be modified even by emphatic adverbs, as in the ungrammatical *\*absolutely utter* or *\*quite previous.*

Classifier adjectives are generally non-gradable. For example, the adjective *dental*, as in *dental decay*, admits no comparison (*\*more dental, \*dentalest*) and no degree modification (*\*very dental*). Other non-gradable adjectives include: *countless, fateful, jobless, rightful, simultaneous, stainless, total, virtual.*

## 7.7.1 Gradable adjectives with *-er* and *-est*

Most common gradable adjectives are monosyllabic and marked for comparative degree by *-er* (e.g. *bigger*) and superlative degree by *-est* (e.g. *longest*).

Note that the addition of *-er* or *-est* can involve regular spelling changes to the adjective stem. Silent *-e* is omitted before adding the suffix (e.g. *safe, safer, safest*); a single final consonant is doubled after a single vowel letter (e.g. *dim, dimmer, dimmest*); and a final *-y* is changed to *-i-* if a consonant letter precedes it (e.g. *tidy, tidier, tidiest*). *Good* and *bad* have completely irregular comparative and superlative forms:

> **good** → **better** → **best**
>
> **bad** → **worse** → **worst**

In addition, *long, strong,* and *young* have an irregular pronunciation: before *-er, -est,* the consonant /g/ is pronounced.

## 7.7.2 Inflectional v. phrasal comparison

Gradable adjectives of one syllable usually take the inflectional suffix, except for a few forms such as *right, wrong,* and *real*. Longer adjectives usually take phrasal comparison, using the degree adverbs *more* and *most*, e.g. *more difficult, most important*.

In some cases, monosyllabic adjectives can alternatively take phrasal marking as well as inflectional. Examples of monosyllabic adjectives with phrasal marking are:

1 *"Wouldn't that be **more fair**?" she asked.* (FICT)
2 *"But Pavarotti is a little fuller in the face." And probably a little **more full** by now.* (NEWS) <note the use of monosyllabic *full* with both comparative forms>
3 *Our women were **more fierce** than our men.* (NEWS)
4 *"I think this is the one she is **most proud** of."* (NEWS)
5 *We recently had a PM even **more rude** than Paul Keating.* (NEWS)

A possible reason for the choice of the phrasal alternative here is that it makes the comparison more prominent; in speech, the comparison can additionally be stressed for emphasis.

Disyllabic adjectives vary considerably in occurrence with inflectional and phrasal comparison, depending on phonological or morphological characteristics. Disyllabic adjectives ending in the unstressed vowel *-y* are usually inflected for degree (as with *easy, easier, easiest*). Common examples usually taking *-er, -est* include:

> *angry, bloody, busy, crazy, dirty, easy, empty, funny, gloomy, happy, healthy, heavy, hungry, lengthy, lucky, nasty, pretty, ready, sexy, silly, tidy, tiny, wealthy*

Even trisyllabic adjectives in *-y* sometimes take inflectional comparison; forms such as *almightiest* and *unhappiest* are attested.

Adjectives ending with the suffix *-ly*, on the other hand, are more variable. For example, *earlier* is much more common than *more early* (in fact, *more early* is not attested in the LSWE Corpus), whereas *more likely* is much more common than *likelier*. Adjectives in *-ly* taking both types of comparison, with varying degrees of frequency, include:

> *costly, deadly, friendly, lively, lonely, lovely, lowly, ugly*

The following examples show the same *-ly* adjectives used with different forms of comparison:

> *She thought Blackpool would be probably somewhat **livelier** and possibly safer and cheaper than other resorts.* (NEWS)

v. *The photographer wanted something **more lively**, though, a picture of an actual capture.* (FICT)

> *When our reporter thanked him for the interview, Britain's **friendliest** bus driver said: "You are most welcome."* (NEWS)

v. *Thankfully I went to the South stand and found myself in the middle of the **most friendly** people I have ever met in my whole life.* (NEWS†)

Disyllabic adjectives such as *mellow, narrow, shallow,* and *yellow*, which end in an unstressed vowel, can also be inflected. Other disyllabic adjectives sometimes inflected are those ending in syllabic /r/ (AmE) or /ə/ (BrE) (e.g. *bitter, clever, slender, tender*), syllabic /l/ (e.g. *able, cruel, feeble, gentle, humble, little, noble, simple, subtle*), *-ere* (e.g. *severe, sincere*), and *-ure* (e.g. *secure* and *obscure*).

Several other classes of adjectives usually take phrasal comparison. These include gradable adjectives of two syllables with no internal morphology (e.g. *common*), adjectives longer than two syllables, adjectives ending in *-ful, -less, -al, -ive, -ous* (e.g. *useful, mindless, musical, effective, zealous*), and adjectives formed with *-ed* and *-ing* (so-called **participial adjectives**; e.g. *bored* and *tiring*).

### CORPUS FINDINGS [1,2]

➤ Individual polysyllabic adjectives with inflected degree marking are generally rare.
>  ➤ However, these forms occur considerably more often in fiction than in the other registers.
➤ Outside the categories of disyllabic adjectives normally allowing *-er* and *-est* the following forms have some general currency: *commoner, commonest, minutest, pleasantest, politest, handsomest*.
➤ The following forms are attested but must be regarded as exceptional: *artfullest, alivest, boringest, cursedest, darlingest, extremest, exactest, handsomer, honestest, intensest, profounder, profoundest, raggediest, solemnest, stupidest, vulgarest, wickedest*.
➤ The disyllabic adjective *quiet* is exceptional in that it is almost always inflected.

### DISCUSSION OF FINDINGS

Inflected superlative forms of polysyllabic adjectives are most common in fiction, where they often occur in the speech of rustic or uneducated characters and also often serve as noun phrase heads.

## 7.7.3 Inflectional comparison across registers

### CORPUS FINDINGS [2]

➤ Inflected comparative degree adjectives are about twice as frequent as inflected superlative degree adjectives.

➤ Superlatives in academic writing are surprisingly rare, given the overall frequency of adjectives in that register (see Figure 7.1).

**Table 7.5** **Distribution of inflected comparative and superlative forms across registers; occurrences per million words**

each ● represents 100

| | *-er* adjectives | *-est* adjectives |
|---|---|---|
| CONV | ●●●●●●●●●●● | ●●●●● |
| FICT | ●●●●●●●●●●●●●●●●●● | ●●●●●●●● |
| NEWS | ●●●●●●●●●●●●●●●●●● ●●●●●●● | ●●●●●●●●●●●●●●●● |
| ACAD | ●●●●●●●●●●●●●●●●●● ●●●●●●●●●●●●●●●●●● | ●●●●●●●●● |

➤ In addition, relatively few gradable adjectives occur commonly in an inflected form.
  ➤ Inflected comparative degree adjectives occurring at least 50 times per million words:
    in conversation—*best, bigger, cheaper, easier, older;*
    in fiction—*best, lower, older, younger;*
    in news—*best, better, biggest, greater, higher, highest, largest, latest, lower;*
    in academic prose—*best, better, earlier, easier, greater, greatest, higher, highest, larger, largest, lower, older, smaller, wider.*

**DISCUSSION OF FINDINGS**

The comparatively low frequency of superlatives in academic writing probably reflects a general reluctance to make extreme claims. In contrast, news reportage has the greatest frequency of superlatives, probably reflecting a focus on the extreme in the interests of attracting readers.

It is noticeable that the most commonly inflected adjectives all either have an evaluative meaning, or a descriptor meaning that can be used with evaluative overtones (e.g. *cheaper, older*).

## 7.7.4 Phrasal comparison with *more* and *most*

We turn now to adjectives taking phrasal comparison, with the adverb *more* or *most* preceding the base form:

> the **most intensive and sophisticated** *intelligence* (ACAD)

> a **more recent** *constitutive equation* (ACAD)

Other than those discussed in 7.7.2 above, disyllabic adjectives (such as *proper, limpid, rapid*) generally take phrasal markers of degree.

**CORPUS FINDINGS [2]**

➤ Only a few adjectives occur commonly with phrasal comparison.
➤ Academic writing has the most instances and conversation very few.
➤ In addition, some adjectives occur relatively frequently in one register with phrasal degree marking.

Table 7.6 **Number of common attributive adjectives by semantic domain and register; occurrences per million words**

over 100 ▪ over 50 ▪ over 20 ▪ over 10

| | CONV | FICT | NEWS | ACAD |
|---|---|---|---|---|
| *more important* | ▪ | | ▪ | ▪ |
| *most important* | ▪ | | ▪ | ▪ |
| *more likely* | | | ▪ | ▪ |
| *most likely* | | | ▪ | ▪ |
| *more difficult* | | | ▪ | ▪ |

➤ Phrasal degree adjectives occurring over ten times per million words in only one register:

in fiction—*most beautiful*;

in news—*most popular, most famous, more serious, most successful*;

in academic prose—*most common, more complex, more complicated, more convenient, more detailed, most effective, more efficient, more frequent, more general, more powerful, more recent, most significant, more sophisticated, most suitable, more useful, most useful*.

**DISCUSSION OF FINDINGS**

The relative infrequency of phrasal comparison reflects the generally lower frequency of polysyllabic adjectives, especially in conversation (7.4.2, 7.5.1). The greater use of phrasally marked adjectives in news and academic prose reflects the need to be more specific in the choice of descriptive and delimiting vocabulary, and therefore to use polysyllabic adjectives more frequently.

The relatively high frequency of *most important* in academic prose is surprising given the relative rarity of superlative adjectives in that register (7.7.3).

## 7.7.5 Doubly marked comparatives and superlatives

In conversation, adjectives are occasionally **doubly marked** for degree, carrying both inflectional and phrasal markers:

*This way, it's **more easier** to see.* (CONV†)

*Are Manchester United not the **most cockiest** fans going, aren't they?* (CONV)

*It's much **more warmer** in there.* (CONV)

*She's a bit **more nicer** than Mrs. Jones.* (CONV)

In a few cases, irregular comparative and superlative adjectives are also given the regular *-er* or *-est* inflection, with a resulting double comparison, as with *bestest* and *worser*:

*This is the **bestest** one you can read.* (CONV)

Such forms are stigmatized and generally considered unacceptable—unless they are used jokingly—in Standard English.

## 7.7.6    Adjectives with superlative or absolute meanings

With adjectives that have inherently superlative meanings—such as *dead*, *true*, *unique*, and *perfect*—degree marking can be considered redundant and even inappropriate. Thus, prescriptive opinion criticizes comparative or superlative marking with these adjectives, or their modification by *very*, *rather*, *so*, etc., claiming that they are non-gradable. However, degree marking with inherently superlative adjectives is not at all unusual in conversation; for example:

> I'll just – trim the **very** *[dead]* *ends off the side there.* (CONV)

> *That's* **very** *[true].* (CONV)

In fact, several instances of gradable *unique* and *perfect* are attested in the written registers:

> <...> *an eligible selfcontained gentleman's residence,* "**very unique.**" (FICT†)

> <...> *the* **most unique** *transportation and distribution system for time sensitive inventories.* (NEWS†)

> *It is quite likely that the population will be* **so unique** *that the project is not feasible.* (ACAD†)

> *He had truly never expected to find his ship* **so perfect***, so clean and cared for, and ready.* (FICT)

> *That it was* **more perfect** *to exist than not to exist, and that to exist as a matter of necessity was the* **most perfect** *of all.* (NEWS†)

> *The slates have* **more perfect** *planar partings.* (ACAD†)

## 7.8    Comparative clauses and other degree complements

Gradable words—particularly adjectives and adverbs—can have clauses and phrases of degree as their complements. **Comparative clauses** and **comparative phrases** are the most common of these constructions. In this section, we concentrate on **degree complements** following adjectives, postponing until 7.13.6 consideration of these constructions with adverbs.

When adjectives are used for comparison (7.7.1–6), the basis of comparison is often left implicit, so that the addressee must infer the basis from the wider context. For example, in the following sentence, readers must infer that the *momentum equation* analysis is being compared with (i.e. it is *more detailed* than) the analysis *using nj*:

> *This method of using nj to determine the critical pressure ratio yields results consistent with a* **more detailed** *analysis involving the momentum equation given in Ref. 5.* (ACAD)

To make the basis of comparison explicit, it is possible to use a comparative phrase or clause following the comparative adjective (cf. 3.11.4):

> *The treatment will be [a little more detailed]* **than the last chapter***, and sometimes [a little more detailed]* **than everyone will need.** (ACAD)

Such comparative expressions can be prepositional phrases (e.g. *than the last chapter*) or comparative clauses (e.g. *than everyone will need*).

There are six major structural types of degree complement. The first two (beginning with *than* and *as*) can be realized by either a phrase or a clause, while the other four are realized exclusively by clauses. Only the first type can involve an inflected comparative adjective; all other types rely on the use of a separate word, viz. a degree adverb: *more ... than, as ... as, so ... that, so ... as to, too ... to, ... enough ... to*.

A **Adjective-*er* + *than* + phrase/clause OR *more/less* + adjective + *than* + phrase/clause**

Phrase:

> *Truna's only [a tiny bit taller] **than me**.* (CONV)
>
> *Carrie was sure he must guess something was up but he seemed [less suspicious] **than usual**, perhaps because he was happier.* (FICT)
>
> *The magic potion was nothing [more sinister] **than Hawaiian Tropic sun tan oil**.* (NEWS)

(On the choice between *me* and *I* following *than*, see 4.10.6.2.)

Clause:

> *I did not want to go there if they were [poorer] **than we were**.* (FICT)
>
> *Although Eurotunnel's attitude to Trans Manche Link, the contractors' consortium, was [more conciliatory] yesterday **than has been the case**, there are still important differences to be settled.* (NEWS)
>
> *The result will be [less effective] **than would be achieved by a teacher in harmony with the unit**.* (ACAD†)

B **as + adjective + as + phrase/clause**

Phrase:

> *The last tinkle of the last shard died away and silence closed in [as deep] **as ever before**.* (FICT)

Clause:

> *It's a good place—I mean, [as good] **as you can get**.* (CONV)

C **so + adjective + that-clause**

> *The murder investigation was [so contrived] **that it created false testimony**.* (NEWS†)

D **so + adjective + as to-clause**

> *And if anybody was [so foolhardy as] **to pass by the shrine after dusk** he was sure to see the old woman hopping about.* (FICT)

E **too + adjective + to-clause**

> *For larger systems the bundles of energy were [too numerous] **to be countable**.* (ACAD)

F **adjective + enough + to-clause**

> *The stairs wouldn't be [strong enough] **to hold the weight**.* (CONV)

The degree complement construction can generally be omitted, leaving its content to be inferred. For example, *so* + adjective without a complement can be used with almost exclamatory force:

> *What was his mother like before she was **so shapeless** and his father was **so fat**?* (FICT†)

Similarly, in a suitable context, the examples of E and F above could be reduced to the following:

> *For larger systems the bundles of energy were **too numerous**.*
>
> *The stairs wouldn't be **strong enough**.*

## 7.8.1 Comparative constructions across registers

**CORPUS FINDINGS** [2]

➤ Comparative constructions of the type adjective-*er than* are by far the most common type of comparative expression in all registers (see Table 7.7).

**Table 7.7** **Distribution of comparative clauses/phrases across registers; occurrences per million words**

each ● represents 10

| | AmE CONV | BrE CONV | FICT |
|---|---|---|---|
| adjective-*er than* + | ●●●●●●●●●●● ●● | ●●●●●●●●●●● ●●● | ●●●●●●●●●●● ●●●●●●●●●● |
| *as* adjective *as* + | ●●●●●● | ●●●●●● | ●●●●●●●●●● |
| *so* adjective *that* + | ●●● | ● | ●●●●●●●●● |
| *so* adjective *as to* + | | | ● |
| *too* adjective *to* + | ●●● | ●● | ●●●●●●●●●● |
| adjective *enough to* + | ●●● | ●● | ●●●●●●●●● |

| | AmE NEWS | BrE NEWS | ACAD |
|---|---|---|---|
| adjective-*er than* + | ●●●●●●●●●●● ●●●●● | ●●●●●●●●●●● ●●●●●● | ●●●●●●●●●●● ●●●●●●●●●●● ●●●●●●●● |
| *as* adjective *as* + | ●●●●●● | ●●●● | ●● |
| *so* adjective *that* + | ●●●● | ●●● | ●● |
| *so* adjective *as to* + | | | ● |
| *too* adjective *to* + | ●●●● | ●●●●●● | ●●● |
| adjective *enough to* + | ●●●● | ●●●● | ●●●● |

(Note: the count for adjective-*er than* + does not include the pattern *more/less* adjective *than* +.)

➤ These constructions are considerably more common in academic prose than in the other registers.

➤ Overall, fiction uses more comparative constructions, as well as a wider range of construction types, than the other registers.

➤ There are only small differences between AmE and BrE in their preferences for particular comparative clause types.

**DISCUSSION OF FINDINGS**

Comparative constructions of the type adjective-*er than* are common in all registers. However, while most registers rely on a range of comparative constructions, academic prose is marked by its extremely frequent use of this single type of construction. Both phrases and clauses are found, although *than*-phrases are more common in academic prose than *than*-clauses:

Adjective-*er than* + phrase:

> But a small sample for comparison is [better] **than nothing at all**. (ACAD)
>
> Internodes are longer and sheaths relatively and progressively [shorter] **than the internodal length**. (ACAD†)
>
> The cost of installing the device would have been [higher] **than the discounted cost of the accident**. (ACAD†)

Adjective-*er than* + clause:

> Chemical manures are always [better and cheaper] **than dung is**. (ACAD)
>
> Distances were in fact reported as being [shorter] **than they were in reality**. (ACAD†)

The frequency of comparative phrases and clauses in academic writing reflects the importance of comparison as a means of understanding and explicating reality. It is difficult to explain the nature of something without describing how it resembles or contrasts with other, comparable things (cf. 7.7).

In general, degree complements are most common in fiction, with the greatest range of different devices. For example, the following forms represent just a small sample from a typical novel:

> The heroine of this song was threatened with something [worse] **than death**. (FICT†)
>
> I turned [redder] **than I was already**. (FICT)
>
> She looked formidable then, almost [as formidable as] **her mother**. (FICT)
>
> It was a shrub, almost a tree, and [as tall as] **I was**. (FICT)
>
> His personality was [so subdued] **that it seemed to fit in with anything he did**. (FICT)
>
> I mounted the black scaffold, which was almost [too hot] **to touch**. (FICT)
>
> I was [old enough] **to do it for myself**. (FICT)

The wide range of comparative constructions frequently used in fiction reminds us that comparison is not only an explanatory device, but a device of the imaginative construction of reality. One notable use of comparative constructions, especially in fiction and in conversation, is to present an extreme or exaggerated comparison which appeals to the imagination rather than to the reason:

> Extraordinary! ... Can't see anybody being [daft enough] **to believe it's gonna last when they marry someone for the tenth time**. (CONV)
>
> The sea came in with black waves [as high] **as church towers and mountains**. (FICT†)

## 7.9 Formation of adjectives

New adjectives can be formed with **derivational affixes** (7.9.2) and **compounding** (7.9.3). In addition, participial forms can be used as adjectives (2.7.2.1, 7.9.1).

### 7.9.1 Participial adjectives

Both *ing-* and *ed*-participle forms can be used as **participial adjectives**. Most of these—such as *promising, surprised,* and *determined*—can serve as main verbs as well as predicative and attributive adjectives. In most cases, then, participial adjectives can be analyzed as being derived from verbs (e.g. *following, working, alleged, frightened*). In some cases, though, nouns rather than verbs provide a more convincing base form, as with *interested* and *crowded*. In other instances, as with *uninteresting* or *unemployed*, a negative prefix attaches to the derived participial adjective (*interesting, employed*) rather than directly to the verb. In still others, the correspondence with a verb or adjective is more indirect, as with *outstanding, ashamed,* or *disabled* (cf. 7.9.3 for the occurrence of participial forms in compounds).

Participial adjectives vary greatly in how far they possess all the defining characteristics of adjectives (7.2). Examples such as *surprised* or *interesting* are gradable and can occur predicatively with a range of copular verbs (*become, seem* etc.). Others, such as *following* or *alleged*, are much more restricted; although they occur freely attributively, they are non-gradable and occur predicatively mainly with *be*, where they are often hard to distinguish from main verbs (cf. 2.3.6).

#### 7.9.1.1 Common participial adjectives

**CORPUS FINDINGS [1]**

➤ Many *ing*-participle forms, such as *boring* and *thrilling*, can serve as attributive and predicative adjectives.

➤ Similarly, *ed*-participle forms such as *confused* and *excited* can serve as attributive and predicative adjectives.

➤ In general, attributive uses outnumber predicative uses for both *ing-* and *ed*-participles.

➤ Selected common adjectives ending in *-ing* (occurring at least ten times per million words): *amazing, boring, corresponding, encouraging, exciting, existing, following, increasing, interesting, leading, missing, outstanding, promising, remaining, threatening, underlying, willing, working.*

➤ Selected common adjectives ending in *-ed* (occurring at least ten times per million words): *advanced, alleged, armed, ashamed, bored, complicated, confused, depressed, determined, disabled, disappointed, educated, excited, exhausted, frightened, interested, pleased, surprised, tired, unemployed, unexpected, worried.*

### 7.9.2 Derived adjectives

Many adjectives are derived by affixing an adjectival suffix (e.g. *-less, -ous*) to a base form. Denominal and deverbal adjectives are derived respectively from nouns (e.g. *cordless*) and verbs (e.g. *continuous*). The derivational suffix *-ive* marks adjectives related to nouns or verbs, although in many cases the derivations are no longer transparent:

| Noun | → | Derived adjective |
|---|---|---|
| *mass* | → | *massive* |
| *effect* | → | *effective* |

| Verb | → | Derived adjective |
|---|---|---|
| *elude* | → | *elusive* |
| *interpret* | → | *interpretive* |

In addition adjectives can be derived from other adjectives, especially by the negative prefixes *un-*, *in-*, and *non-* (e.g. *unhappy, insensitive, nonstandard*).

## 7.9.2.1 Common adjectives with derivational suffixes

➤ Derived adjectives are by far most common in academic prose.

  ➤ They are moderately common in news, and relatively rare in fiction and conversation.

➤ Derived adjectives formed with *-al* are overwhelmingly more common than adjectives formed with any other derivational suffix.

➤ Derived adjectives with *-ent*, *-ive*, and *-ous* are moderately common.

➤ Adjectives formed with *-ate*, *-ful*, *-less*, *-like*, and *-type* are relatively rare in all registers.

➤ Many individual derived adjectives are notably common.

**Figure 7.2**

**Frequency of derivational suffixes for adjectives across registers**

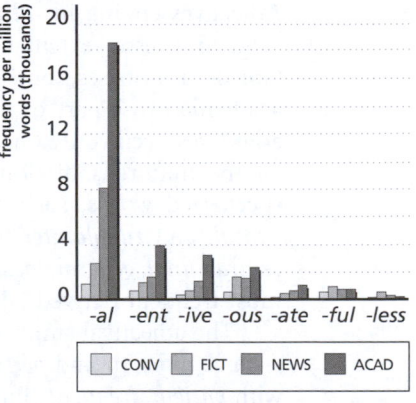

  ➤ Common adjectives with *-al*: occurring over 100 times per million words—*central, final, general, international, local, national, normal, political, real, royal, social, special*; occurring over 50 times per million words—*annual, equal, financial, individual, industrial, legal, medical, mental, natural, official, original, personal, physical, professional, sexual, total, usual*; occurring over 25 times per million words—*actual, additional, chemical, commercial, critical, crucial, environmental, essential, experimental, formal, functional, fundamental, historical, ideal, initial, internal, liberal, moral, oral, potential, practical, regional, substantial, technical, traditional, typical, unusual, visual, vital.*

  ➤ Common adjectives with *-ent*: occurring over 100 times per million words—*different, present*; occurring over 25 times per million words—*ancient, apparent, confident, current, decent, dependent, excellent, independent, permanent, recent, silent, sufficient, violent*; selected examples occurring over ten times per million words: *absent, adjacent, consistent, convenient, efficient, frequent, innocent, intelligent, magnificent, persistent, prominent, subsequent.*

  ➤ Common adjectives with *-ive*: occurring over 25 times per million words—*active, attractive, conservative, effective, expensive, massive, negative, positive, relative*; selected examples occurring over ten times per million words—*administrative,* *aggressive, alternative, cognitive, comprehensive, creative, distinctive, excessive, exclusive, extensive, impressive.*

➤ Common adjectives with *-ous*: occurring over 100 times per million words—*serious, various*; occurring over 25 times per million words—*anxious, conscious, continuous, curious, dangerous, enormous, famous, nervous, obvious, previous, religious.*

➤ Adjectives with *-ate*: occurring over 50 times per million words—*appropriate, private, separate*; selected adjectives occurring over ten times per million words—*accurate, adequate, immediate, intimate, moderate, unfortunate.*

➤ Adjectives with *-ful*: occurring over 50 times per million words—*beautiful, useful, successful, careful, awful, wonderful*; selected examples occurring over ten times per million words—*cheerful, doubtful, grateful, helpful, painful, peaceful, powerful.*

➤ Adjectives with *-less*: occurring over ten times per million words—*endless, helpless, homeless, useless.*

## DISCUSSION OF FINDINGS

Adjectives ending in *-al* are extremely common, particularly in academic prose (and to a lesser extent in news writing). Most adjectives in *-al* are formed on Greco-Latin bases, but many are familiar in everyday conversation. In the academic prose part of the LSWE Corpus, an exceptionally high number of *-al* adjectives occur only once, reflecting the high productivity of this suffix. Almost all the hundreds of nonce *-al* adjectives in the LSWE Corpus are extremely specialized words, such as *adrenocortical, carpopedal, epicontinental, icositetra-hedral*, and *tubulointerstitial*. In contrast, more familiar *-al* adjectives, such as *central, final, general, local, national, real, social, special*, and *total*, rank among the most frequent derived adjectives in all four registers.

The adjectival suffix *-ent* is also notably frequent. While some *-ent* adjectives such as *different* and *persistent* have transparent stem elements, others do not, as with *patient, frequent*, and *recent*. Adjectives in *-ive* similarly have several sources: some correspond to nouns in *-tion* (*active, relative, attractive, impressive*); some come from other nouns (*instinctive*); some are derived from verbs (*adaptive*); while others are more opaque, at least from a synchronic standpoint (*acquisitive, aggressive*).

By and large, *-ous* adjectives represent learned words, especially in expository writing. Hundreds of *-ous* adjectives occur only once in the LSWE Corpus, most of them highly specialized or technical (e.g. *floriferous, parenchymous, umbrageous*). In contrast, conversation uses *-ous* forms with descriptor meanings, such as *gorgeous, marvelous, fabulous, horrendous, obnoxious*, and *atrocious*.

Adjectives ending in *-ate* are again mostly of Latin origin and, with few exceptions, uncommon in everyday talk. In sharp contrast to the large number of *-al* adjectives occurring rarely in the LSWE Corpus, single-occurrence *-ate* adjectives number only two (*obdurate* and *roseate*); this suggests how much less-specialized the *-ate* adjectives are when compared with many *-al* adjectives.

Although generally rare, adjectives ending in *-ful* are distributed more evenly across registers. Just a score of *-ful* adjectives occur only once or twice in the LSWE Corpus, and like the more frequent forms, these rare adjectives have a relatively familiar and non-specialist ring (e.g. *prayerful, unmindful, neglectful*).

The limitation of such nonce occurrences almost exclusively to fiction suggests their principally imaginative use.

Adjectives ending in -*less* are uncommon as compared with the other derived adjective types considered above. Despite their relative scarcity as a group, -*less* adjectives are transparently interpretable, even those appearing only once in the LSWE Corpus. Their interpretability is a consequence of their resulting from a productive process, applied mostly to common nouns.

Although the suffixes -*like* and -*type* are even less common, they have interesting uses. They retain the meanings of *like* and *type* as separate words, and are therefore near the boundary between affixation and compounding. The suffix -*like* is particularly versatile in its ability to derive new adjectives from nouns. Its virtual absence from conversation and its relative frequency in academic prose and fiction suggest that -*like* is not entirely integrated into the system of English suffixation, and with few exceptions its application seems ad hoc rather than lexicalized. Examples in fiction include: *business-like, cat-like, child-like, dream-like, rocklike, sharklike, unladylike, workmanlike*; and in academic prose: *block-like, bristle-like, cone-like, cup-like, finger-like, granule-like, needle-like, plate-like, rib-like, rubber-like*.

Adjectives with -*type* are almost invariably hyphenated: *terrorist-type offenses, backward-type country*. A versatile suffix, -*type* can be added to common and proper nouns, as well as to adjectives and prepositions/adverbs: *A-type, backward-type, birthday-type, churchy-type, content-type, data-type, examination-type, Hollywood-type, immediate-type, Israeli-type, leasing-type, Mr-Smith-type, off-type, pyroxene-type, serpentine-type, storage-type, supermarket-type, textbook-type*.

## 7.9.3 Adjectival compounds

Compounds used as adjectives lend themselves to a compact and integrated expression of information. Formally, adjectival compounds take many shapes. Adjectives can be added to other adjectives as in *greyish-blue*. Compounds can also be composed of an adjective plus noun, as with *full-time* (adjective + noun) or *butterfly-blue* (noun + adjective), or an adjective plus adverb, as in *overly-protective*. As we see from these examples, the component elements can themselves be derived (e.g. *greyish, protective*).

Furthermore, many adjective compounds involve participial forms. For example, the compound *open-minded* is derived from a noun phrase (*open mind*) to which -*ed* has been suffixed. *Glass-topped* exemplifies a noun-noun compound (*glass top*) to which -*ed* has been suffixed. However, the element in an adjectival compound that is suffixed with -*ed* or -*ing* is most often a verb, as in: *sexually-transmitted, psychologically-disturbed, classroom-based*, and *world-renowned*.

The following lists exemplify the most common adjectival compound patterns, mostly from news. Note that we use hyphenation as our criterion for compound status, as a clear objective indicator, even though some non-hyphenated forms can also be considered compounds. In conversation, of course, the hyphen is at the discretion of the transcriber. Without hyphenation, some of these sequences could be treated as complex premodification (see 8.4). (We label as adverbs in these patterns words which are adjectival in form, though adverbial in function: **new**-*born*, **free**-*spending*.)

**Adverb + adjective:**

*already-tight, blisteringly-fast, critically-ill, environmentally-progressive, fiercely-competitive, grimly-familiar, highly-sensitive, hissingly-hot, politically-independent, highly-respectable, nearly-equal*

**Adverb + *ed*-participle:**

*carefully-honed, extensively-researched, fiercely-contested, ill-suited, internationally-acclaimed, lavishly-produced, new-born, newly-restored, psychologically-disturbed, recently-installed, sexually-transmitted, specially-adapted, strictly-controlled, strongly-worded, urgently-needed, well-timed, widely-held, carefully-planned, comparably-sized, ethnically-based, federally-insured, finely-wrought, highly-educated, neatly-shaved, newly-married, so-called, well-fed, well-organized, wondrously-carved*

**Adverb + *ing*-participle:**

*brightly-shining, constantly-changing, equally-damaging, free-spending, harder-hitting, rapidly-growing, slowly-sinking, slyly-charming, badly-fitting, constantly-grinning, early-maturing, slow-moving, straight-speaking, tightly-fitting*

**Reduplicative:**

*lovey-dovey, okey-dokey, curly-whirly, easy-peasy, wishy-washy, roly-poly, super-duper, even-stevens, oldy-worldy, goody-goody*

**Adjective + color adjective:**

*silvery-green, royal-blue, dark-blue, light-blue, gray-white*

**Adjective + other adjective:**

*sectoral-zonal, abdomino-perineal, infinite-dimensional*

**Adjective + *ed*-participle:**

*clean-shaven, ready-made, soft-textured, strait-laced, white-washed*

**Adjective + *ing*-participle:**

*biggest-selling, double-crossing, free-standing, funny-looking, good-looking, longest-serving, lovely-sounding, respectable-looking, sickly-smelling*

**Noun + adjective:**

*age-old, battle-weary, grease-free, iron-rich, life-long, sea-blue, sex-specific, subsidy-free, smoke-free, waist-high*

**Noun + *ed*-participle:**

*church-owned, classroom-based, dome-shaped, family-oriented, fuel-injected, germ-ridden, health-related, home-baked, horse-drawn, king-sized, moth-eaten, poverty-stricken, state-run, stroke-induced, US-oriented, wheelchair-bound, world-renowned*

**Noun + *ing*-participle:**

*confidence-boosting, eye-catching, God-fearin', hair-raising, law-abiding, life-prolonging, nerve-wracking, peace-keeping*

**Adjective + noun:**

*big-name, cutting-edge, double-digit, fast-food, free-market, front-row, full-time, general-purpose, hard-core, hi-tech, inner-city, large-scale,*

> *late-night, left-hand, long-distance, long-term, low-class, present-day,*
> *right-wing, short-term, single-storey, top-level, white-collar, working-class*

**Participle + adverbial particle:**

> *blown-out, boarded-up, left-over, paid-up, sawn-off.*

## 7.9.3.1 Distribution of adjectival compounds

**CORPUS FINDINGS** [2]

➤ Adjectival compounds are common in the written registers, especially news, but are relatively rare in conversation.

➤ They are far more common in attributive than predicative use.

➤ Adverb-adjective sequences comprise by far the most productive type of adjectival compound, especially in news.

➤ Reduplicative compounds are more productive in conversation than in the other registers.

**DISCUSSION OF FINDINGS**

Adjectival compounds represent compact, integrated forms of expression, which apparently are not easy to produce 'online' (except for lexicalized compounds such as *sugar-free, tongue-tied, old-fashioned, cross-eyed,* and *wishy-washy*). Reduplicative compounds are more numerous in conversation than in the other registers, possibly because they are lexicalized and supported by their euphony, as well as serving an emotive purpose.

Fiction has many more compounds used as adjectives than conversation. There is a general balance between uncommon formations (such as *gauzy-bearded, dashingly-clad, incompetently-suppressed*), and compounds that contain relatively frequent everyday elements (such as *slow-moving* and *easy-going*). Fiction also uses series of adjectival compounds more than other registers:

> *One day, after supper, he sat in the rocker by the stove, **bone-tired**,*
> ***river-whipped**, and fell asleep.* (FICT)

Adjectival compounds are abundant and frequent in news, which shows a particular partiality for adverb-adjective compounds. In addition, news writers use very frequent compounds consisting of numerals and nouns, such as *six-man, 24-hour,* and *second-round*. Many of the more frequent compounds in news are familiar enough to be viewed as lexicalized expressions, e.g. *high-speed* and *double-decker*.

Compounds formed with an *ed*-participle as the second element are especially common in news (e.g. *racially-motivated*). These forms provide an efficient way of compressing information into a two-word construction, as an alternative to a fuller clausal expression (often involving a relative clause), such as *an attack that was motivated by racism*. Below, the compound in bold in **1** avoids the relative clause marked in *[]* in **2**. In its original news text, **1** is immediately followed by **2**, suggesting that **1** captures for the writer a more integrated statement of the quoted words of **2**:

> **1** *In a speech before the ballot, Mr Kovac—whose career includes a stint as an economic adviser to Cuban leader Fidel Castro in the 1960s—said he was in favour of "**socially-oriented**" market policies.* (NEWS)

2  *"I agree with the principles of a market economy [which are socially oriented]," he told parliament.* (NEWS)

Examples **3** and **4** constitute a brief excerpt of a news report about a speech given by a French politician.

3  *Instead he proposed a new coalition spanning Socialists, ecologists, **reform-minded** Communists and **socially-conscious** centrists.* (NEWS)

4  *"What we want is a big, open, extrovert movement, [which is rich in diversity], [which even encourages it], a movement gathering all those [who share the values of solidarity and a goal of transformation]," he said.* (NEWS)

Taken together, **3** and **4** provide a tidy contrast between the use of adjectival compounds in writing (**3**) and of relative clauses in quoted speech (**4**). These examples indicate a likely motivation for the very frequent compounds of news: these constructions can be used to compress information into a two-word expression, which is typically integrated attributively within a noun phrase. Online, relative clauses seem to be somewhat easier to produce for certain kinds of information. On the other hand, the more compact expression of an attributive compound is aided by the planning and editing available to writers.

Compound attributive adjectivals are used in academic prose for essentially the same purpose that they serve in news, namely to permit complex modification within the noun phrase, thus avoiding the lengthier relative clauses that could convey the same information.

# 7.10  Adjectives in combination

Adjectives are sometimes used in sequences, especially in fiction. In addition, there are two special types of structure involving adjectives in combination: (a) repeated comparative adjectives (7.10.1) and (b) constructions beginning with the intensifiers *good and* and *nice and* (7.10.2).

## 7.10.1  Repeated comparative adjectives

Especially in fiction, two identical comparative adjectives are sometimes conjoined by *and*, forming a structure that denotes an ever-increasing degree of the adjective. For example, *funnier and funnier* is an expressive way of saying 'increasingly funny'. Typically, the repeated adjectives function predicatively after the copular verb *get*, *grow*, or *become*:

*His own need for food [grew] **slighter and slighter**.* (FICT†)

*Her visits to the country to see her son [became] **rarer and rarer**.* (FICT)

*Consequently, as the stakes [become] **bigger and bigger** in the playing of the game, the scruples will [become] **smaller and smaller**.* (NEWS†)

*'People who go to acid house parties are [getting] **younger and younger**.'* (NEWS)

*In the process false personality has to be [made] gradually **weaker and weaker**.* (ACAD)

More than one repetition is also possible:

*See the branches get **smaller and smaller and smaller**.* (CONV)

A related and more frequent structure for phrasal comparatives repeats *more*, conjoining it to itself with *and*:

> *So things are getting **more and more** – [fraught]* (CONV †)
>
> *Eventually it'll get **more and more** [computer wise].* (CONV †)
>
> *It got **more and more** [popular] strangely enough.* (CONV)

**CORPUS FINDINGS 2**

➤ Conjoined identical comparative adjectives are rare in all registers, but most common in fiction.

➤ There is a slight tendency for inflected sequences in conversation as against phrasally compared variants in academic prose.

**Table 7.8**  **Distribution of repeated adjectives across registers; occurrences per million words. (Based on analysis of 14 common adjectives in repeated sequences: *funnier, bigger, smaller, slighter, rarer, younger, weaker, better, brighter, darker, hotter, lighter, stronger*, and *worse*.)**

each ● represents c. 2

|  | CONV | FICT | NEWS | ACAD |
|---|---|---|---|---|
| adjective + *er and* adjective + *er* | ● ● | ● ● ● ● | ● ● | ● |
| *more and more* adjective | ● | ● ● ● ● ● | ● ● | ● ● ● |

**DISCUSSION OF FINDINGS**

The overall greater frequency of these structures in fiction suggests that they are more a device of descriptive narrative than spontaneous speech.

## 7.10.2  The intensifiers *good and* and *nice and*

Conjoined sequences beginning with *good and* or *nice and* often serve to intensify the degree of the second adjective. This so-called 'pseudo-coordination' is characteristic of predicative rather than attributive uses, as in *Everything looks nice and burnt*! Sequences of this type are especially common in fictional dialogue and natural conversation.

The following examples, all from fictional dialogue, illustrate the intensifying effect of these sequences when in predicative position:

> *'You're going to be **good and sorry** you grabbed Nurse Duckett by the bosom.'* (FICT)
>
> *'Furthermore, we'll end this conversation when I'm **good and ready**.'* (FICT)
>
> *'I'm **good and sick** of it,' Tom said.* (FICT)
>
> *I'll be **nice and pissed**.* (CONV)
>
> *Good for your teeth. Makes your teeth **nice and strong**!* (CONV)
>
> *'The police want a local lab **nice and handy**, and who's to blame them?'* (FICT)

In contrast, similar sequences in attributive position do not carry this same intensifying force:

*There are many **good and prosperous** people here.* (FICT†)

*Her former lover is a **good and supportive** friend.* (NEWS†)

*But, to quote one of Maggie's very own **good and faithful** servants <...>* (NEWS†)

Note that the attributive (non-intensifying) uses tend to combine *good* with another adjective carrying favorable connotations (e.g. *faithful, prosperous*), whereas predicative uses favor adjectives carrying negative connotations (e.g. *sorry, sick*). With *nice*, the intensifying use holds for favorable and unfavorable adjectives alike. In both BrE and AmE conversation, *nice and* is far more frequent than *good and*. There are over 30 occurrences per million words for *nice and* + adjective v. only about two occurrences per million words for *good and* + adjective.

## 7.11  Overview of adverbs

In a clause, adverbs can either be integrated into an element of the clause or function themselves as an element of the clause. In the first case, the adverbs serve as **modifiers**; in the second, they are **adverbials**.

Most commonly, adverbs that are integrated into another element of the clause modify an adjective or another adverb, as in the following examples (the modified word is marked with *[]*):

1  *I am **almost** [positive] she borrowed that off Barbie!* (CONV)

2  *First, health service managers must be able to price their services **reasonably** [accurately] for trading purposes.* (NEWS)

In **1** the adverb *almost* modifies the adjective *positive*, while in **2** the adverb *reasonably* modifies the adverb *accurately*.

In contrast, examples **3** and **4** illustrate adverbs that are themselves elements of the clause:

3  *I think she'll be married **shortly**.* (CONV)

4  ***Possibly** the Wesleyan Church tolerated outside unions unofficially, in a way that the Anglican Church did not.* (ACAD)

In **3** the adverb *shortly* provides further information about the time for the entire clause *she'll be married*. In **4** *possibly* conveys the level of certainty for the entire following clause. Thus, these adverbs are not integrated into another element within the clause; rather, they are adverbials. It is important to note that the same adverbs that function as modifiers can also function as adverbials. For example, the adverbs in **5** and **7** are modifiers, while the same adverbs in **6** and **8** are adverbials:

5  *To put on a grey shirt once more was **strangely** [pleasing].* (FICT)

6  ***Strangely**, it is in this area that the greatest fears concerning CAD exist.* (ACAD)

7  *This apparently complicated expression for pull-out torque gives the **surprisingly** [simple] characteristic shown in Fig 5.8.* (ACAD)

8  ***Surprisingly**, the choked voice resumes.* (FICT)

The overall distribution of adverbs and adjectives across registers is discussed in 2.3.5 (see Figures 2.3 and 2.4) and in 7.1. The following sections discuss adverbs in terms of their forms (7.3.2), their syntactic roles (7.3.3), and their semantic categories (7.3.4). Adverbials are dealt with in detail in Chapter 10, which includes an account of the use of adverbs as adverbials. Thus, although this section introduces information about adverbs as adverbials, we concentrate here on structural information about adverbs and on findings related to the use of adverbs as modifiers.

# 7.12 The form of adverbs

## 7.12.1 Formation of adverbs

Adverbs are sometimes characterized as ending in *-ly*. While this is true of some adverbs, the class is far more diverse in form. There are four major formal categories of adverbs, and each category also contains substantial variation within it.

### A Simple adverbs

Simple adverbs are single words that are not formed from compounds or derivational affixes. Examples include *well, too, rather, quite, soon*, and *here*. Other simple adverbs are clearly related to other word classes: *fast* and *long* can be adjectives; *down* and *round* can be used as prepositions (but contrast these forms with adverbial particles; 2.4.6); *today* and *tomorrow* can be used as nouns. In addition, some simple adverbs originated as compounds, but the independent meaning of the two parts is no longer transparent (e.g. *already, indeed*).

### B Compound adverbs

Compound adverbs are formed by combining two or more elements into a single word. Examples include adverbs such as *anyway (any + way), nowhere (no + where)*, and *heretofore (here + to + fore)*.

### C Adverbs derived by suffixation

Many adverbs are formed by suffixing *-ly* to the base form of an adjective, such as *clearly* formed from the adjective *clear*. Note, however, that not all adverbs ending in *-ly* are formed by the addition of *-ly* to an adjectival form. Some adverbs are derived from adjectives that already end in *-ly*: e.g. *weekly, fatherly*. In these cases the adverb is normally formed by zero derivation, i.e. by adding nothing to the adjective form: *weekly*, not *\*weeklily, fatherly* not *\*fatherlily*.

The productivity of the *-ly* suffix can be seen from some unusual *-ly* adverbs used in both spoken and written texts. Even the expository registers, rarely thought of as showing creativity, include rare adverbs derived from adjectives with an *-ly* suffix. Examples include:

> *Oh yes, it went very **jollily**.* (CONV)

> *You're doing **spiffily**.* (CONV)

> *Every 20 minutes or so, the play **guffawingly** alludes to the non-arrival of some long-ordered calculators.* (NEWS)

> *Channel 4 has in any case taken on the mantle of the senator for adult-intelligent viewing: in other words, the place where you can watch **randily** beneath a thinnish veneer of knowledge and a deeper understanding of self.* (NEWS)

> *All phenols can act **bactericidally** or **fungicidally**.* (ACAD†)
>
> *Twenty-six patients with Barret's columnar lined lower oesophagus were diagnosed by endoscopic documentation of the squamocolumnar junction being **circumferentially** more than 3 cm above.* (ACAD†)

In addition to *-ly*, other suffixes are used to form adverbs. Two relatively common ones are *-wise* and *-wards*. The suffix *-wise* is added to some nouns (e.g. *piecewise*), and the suffix *-ward(s)* to some nouns (e.g. *homewards*, *seawards*) and prepositions (e.g. *onward*, *afterwards*).

## D Fixed phrases

There are also some fixed phrases which are used as adverbs. These phrases are invariant in form, and the component words rarely retain their independent meaning. Examples include *of course*, *kind of*, and *at last*.

## 7.12.1.1 Adverb forms

Considering all adverb forms that occur over 50 times per million words, Figure 7.3 breaks down the proportion in each register that falls into each class.

### CORPUS FINDINGS [1,2]

➤ Common adverbs are distributed differently over the four form categories, and, more significantly, over the four registers.

➤ Simple forms and *-ly* suffixes account for the greatest percentage of frequently occurring adverbs in all four registers.

  ➤ Conversation and academic prose represent opposite extremes of use: in conversation, over 60% of the common adverbs are simple forms, and only about 20% *-ly* forms; in academic prose, about 55% of the common adverbs are *-ly* forms, and slightly over 30% simple forms.

➤ Other suffixes, fixed phrases, and compound forms occur much less commonly in all four registers.

**Figure 7.3**

**Morphological forms of common adverbs—proportional use by register**

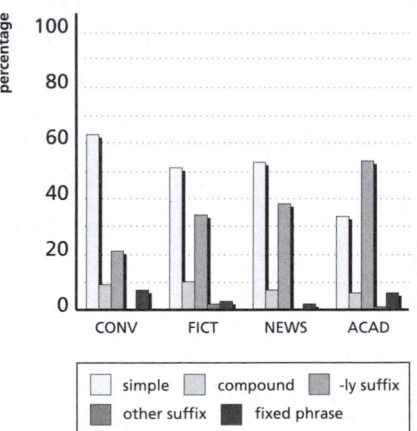

### DISCUSSION OF FINDINGS

Simple adverbs and *-ly* adverbs have different complexity and typical uses, resulting in their differing distributions across registers. In conversation, many simple adverbs are adverbials used to establish time or place relationships; they include items such as *again*, *always*, *already*, *far*, *here*, *never*, *now*, *soon*, *still*, *then*, and *yet*. Certain modifying adverbs are also common, such as *very*, *rather*, *quite*, and *pretty*. Examples include:

> *And a lot of women that are on fertility drugs **now**?* (CONV)
>
> *But we couldn't, didn't walk too **far** today.* (CONV)
>
> *It's **quite** nice yeah yeah.* (CONV)
>
> *That's **pretty** good.* (CONV)

In contrast, adverbs formed with the *-ly* suffix are mostly derived from adjectives. In academic prose, these adverbs are used for a variety of purposes. Many have to do with stance, that is, with the author's attitude towards the proposition in the clause (cf. 10.3). Often these forms comment on the likelihood of a proposition, its generalizability or its expectedness, with adverbs such as *generally, possibly, probably, certainly,* and *obviously*:

> **Obviously** *this is an overstatement.* (ACAD†)

> *Expressive movement would be out of place, unprofitable and* **possibly** *dangerous.* (ACAD) <implying 'possibly expressive movement would be dangerous'>

> *The second group contains both brown and grey soils with shallow (***generally*** less than 10 cm) surface horizons.* (ACAD†)

In addition, *-ly* adverbs in academic prose are used in descriptions of processes or conditions, or in instructions:

> *The solubility decreases* **rapidly** *as the temperature falls.* (ACAD†)

> *The passage is almost* **entirely** *in third-person narration.* (ACAD)

> *Examine footnotes* **carefully**. (ACAD)

Academic prose also commonly uses *-ly* adverbs as modifiers:

> *Acclimatization is* **relatively** *unimportant.* (ACAD†)

> *The paper by Donchin et al. is a* **particularly** *good methodological critique of research in this area.* (ACAD)

Generally these modifiers differ from those typical of conversation, many of which are simple and perceived as appropriate to casual speech (e.g. *pretty* and *rather*).

Also in academic prose, modifiers with *-ly* suffixes are used to express precision or estimation with measurements:

> *After* **exactly** *five years the tree that had grown up weighed 169 pounds and about three ounces.* (ACAD)

> **Approximately** *60 percent of the community are of Polish and Russian ancestry.* (ACAD†)

Differences in the choice of modifiers between conversation and academic prose are discussed further in 7.13.1.1.

It is interesting to note that, overall, fiction also uses many different descriptive *-ly* adverbs, although few of these are notably common (occurring over 50 times per million words). Rather, fiction shows great diversity in its use of *-ly* adverbs. In describing fictional events and the actions of fictional characters, writers often use adverbs with specific descriptive meanings:

> *All three adults giggled* **easily** *and at everything,* **absentmindedly** *fingering small silver spoons.* (FICT†)

> *He was smiling* **benignly***, almost* **fatherly***, at her.* (FICT†)

The slightly higher proportion of compound adverbs in conversation and fiction partly reflects a difference in formality and precision between these two registers and the expository written registers. The compound adverbs in conversation and fiction tend to express vague meanings or be informal terms: e.g. *sometimes, anywhere, everywhere, anyway,* and *maybe*. Fiction also uses compound adverbs to indicate location, such as *inside* and *upstairs*:

*I'll – put them **somewhere**. (CONV)*

*If it's **anywhere** it'll be here. (CONV)*

*Mama herself would more often than not stand to eat, **sometimes** out of the pot. (FICT†)*

*I went **upstairs** uneasily and knocked on his door. (FICT)*

A final point of interest concerns the slightly greater proportional use of fixed phrases in conversation and academic prose over fiction and news. The specific phrases used in conversation and academic prose are very different, however. Conversation uses the hedges *sort of* and *kind of*, as well as forms such as *o'clock*, *at least*, and *as well*. Academic prose, on the other hand, is notable for its foreign phrases (particularly the Latin abbreviations *i.e.*, *e.g.* and *etc.*) and linking adverbials (e.g. *in general, in particular*; see 10.4 for more discussion of these).

## 7.12.2    Adverbs and adjectives with the same form

In some cases, an adverb has the identical form as a related adjective. For example, *fast* is an adjective in **1** below, while in **2** it is an adverb.

>    1   ***Fast** guys tire, a basketball coach once said of his own high-rise team, but big guys don't shrink. (NEWS)*
>
>    2   *One looter, a woman who did not run **fast** enough, was shot dead. (FICT)*

In addition, particularly in informal situations, forms that are usually used as adjectives can sometimes be used as adverbs. In many of these cases, the *-ly* suffix of the more accepted adverb form is omitted. For example, the following adverbs in conversation could instead have the forms *slowly, quickly,* and *smoothly*:

*The big one went so **slow**. (CONV)*

*Well it was hot but it didn't come out **quick**. (CONV)*

*They want to make sure it runs **smooth** first. (CONV†)*

From a prescriptive point of view, this use of the adjective form is often stigmatized as non-standard. However, in some instances this usage is widespread, particularly in colloquial AmE (see Tables 7.9 and 7.10).

In addition, *good* is sometimes used as an adverb in place of the prescriptively correct adverb *well*:

*They go **good** with baggy jeans. (CONV)*

*"It's running **good** now." (FICT)*

When used as an adverb, *good* is typically an adverbial, as in the above examples. However, other adverbs that have the same form as adjectives occur as modifiers. One example is the modifier *real* used in place of the more prescriptively correct *really*:

*It came out **real** [good]. (CONV)*

### 7.12.2.1    *Good* and *real* as adverbs

**CORPUS FINDINGS** [2,3]

➤   *Good* is commonly used as an adverb (as an alternative to *well*) in AmE conversation.
>    ➤   This usage is rare in BrE conversation and in the written registers.

**Table 7.9**   **Distribution of *good* functioning as an adverb across registers and dialects; occurrences per million words**

each ■ represents c. 10     □ represents less than 10     – unattested in that register

| BrE CONV | AmE CONV | FICT | NEWS | ACAD |
|----------|----------|------|------|------|
| □ | ■ ■ ■ ■ ■ | □ | □ | – |

➤   In BrE conversation, it is very rare for *real* to be used as a modifier of an adjective; the
adverb *really* is very common.

➤   In AmE conversation, the adverb *really* is extremely common.

➤   *Real* is also very common as an adverb in AmE conversation,
almost as frequent as *really* in BrE conversation.

**Table 7.10**   **Distribution of *real* and *really* functioning as adverbs in conversation, across dialects; occurrences per million words**

each ● represents c. 20

| | BrE CONV | AmE CONV |
|---|---|---|
| *real* | ● | ●●●●●●●●●●●●●● |
| *really* | ●●●●●●●●●●●●●●●●●● | ●●●●●●●●●●●●●●●●●●●●●●●●●●● ●●●●● |

**DISCUSSION OF FINDINGS**

Only AmE conversation has a notable use of *good* as an adverb. This use is rare
but attested in BrE conversation, as well as in fiction and news (in direct speech or
quotations from interviews). Clearly, this is a casual speech form, favored by
Americans. Typical examples include:

> *It just worked out **good**, didn't it?* (AmE CONV)
>
> *Bruce Jackson, In Excess' trainer said, "He ran **good**, but he runs **good** all the
> time. It was easy."* (AmE NEWS)

Both BrE and AmE conversation use *really* to modify a variety of adjectives. The
four most common collocates with *really* are *good*, *nice*, *bad*, and *funny* (all
occurring over 20 times per million words):

> *This looks **really** [good] this little—thing.* (BrE CONV)
>
> *But he's always, he's always making **really** [funny] comments.* (BrE CONV)
>
> *You couldn't tell from looking at him but he was driving a **really** [nice] car.*
> (AmE CONV)
>
> *The alternative is to live with my parents which I know is a bad idea, a
> **really** [bad] idea.* (AmE CONV)

On the other hand, only AmE conversation uses *real* with a variety of adjectives.
The most common collocates, occurring over five times per million words, are:
*good*, *nice*, *hard*, *bad*, *big*, and *easy*:

> *It would have been **real** [bad] news.* (AmE CONV)
>
> *That's one of the **real** [hard] things ...* (AmE CONV†)
>
> *She's a **real** [nice] girl.* (AmE CONV)

Interestingly, the same speaker may alternate between *really* and *real* in close proximity:

> *I have a **really** [good] video with a **real** [good] soundtrack.* (AmE CONV)

## 7.12.3 Comparative and superlative forms

Adverbs can be marked inflectionally for **comparative** or **superlative** degree (e.g. *fast, faster, fastest; hard, harder, hardest*). Comparative and superlative forms are used more commonly for adjectives than adverbs (7.7.3). Superlative forms are very rarely used as adverbs, while comparative forms are occasionally used. Examples include:

1 *I just kept working **harder** and **harder*** (NEWS†)
2 *The creature sank **farther**, retreating, turning.* (FICT)
3 *He went to the altar every first Friday, sometimes with her, **oftener** by himself.* (FICT†)

In some cases, an adverb can be made comparative either with the use of *more* or with the *-er* inflection. For example, **3** above illustrates the use of *oftener* where *more often* could also be used. This choice appears to be related to register and authorial style. *Oftener* occurs only in fiction, and then is used by only a small number of writers (only seven of the almost 150 fiction authors in the LSWE Corpus). It occurs in both narrative and dialog:

> *We didn't always go to the same bar, but **oftener** to Victor's than anywhere else.* (FICT)

> *"Thanks. I wish it might happen **oftener**," said the visitor in his easy arrogant way.* (FICT)

In contrast, the other registers use only *more often*:

> *I love live theatre, of course, I really ought to go **more often**.* (CONV)

> *Other officials said the sweeps come about once a week, maybe **more often**.* (NEWS†)

All of the registers tend to use *more often* when the adverb is followed by *than*:

> ***More often** [than] usual her head looked up as she swam from bank to bank.* (FICT†)

> *In fact, **more often** [than] not, it will be found that the work of mass selection must be repeated annually.* (ACAD)

# 7.13 Syntactic roles of adverbs

## 7.13.1 Adverbs modifying adjectives

One of the primary functions of adverbs is to modify adjectives, as in these examples:

> *I'm **rather** [partial] to parsnips.* (CONV)

> *I was **utterly, hopelessly, horribly** [glad].* (FICT)

> *He is a **deeply** [sick] man.* (NEWS†)

> *This is **slightly** [larger] than the calculated value.* (ACAD†)

Usually, adverbs precede the adjectives that they modify, but postmodification also occurs. The adverbs *enough* and *ago* must be placed after the adjectives they modify, but other adverbs can also be postposed:

> Down came the dry flakes, *[fat]* **enough** and *[heavy]* **enough** to crash like nickels on stone. (FICT)
>
> That seems so *[long]* **ago**. (FICT†)
>
> It is *[rich]* **nutritionally** with high calcium content. (ACAD)
>
> Several preparations are *[available]* **commercially**. (ACAD†)

In cases such as the last it becomes difficult to differentiate between occurrence as postmodifier and as adverbial, since this adverb can be separated from the adjective (cf. *Several preparations are [available] to us* **commercially**.)

## 7.13.1.1 Adverbs modifying adjectives in conversation and academic prose

Registers vary greatly with respect to the adverb + adjective pairs that commonly occur (cf. 7.12.1.1). We focus here on the two contrasting registers of conversation and academic prose.

**CORPUS FINDINGS [2]**

➤ Conversation (in both dialects) has higher frequencies of adjective with modifying adverb combinations than academic prose does.

➤ Academic prose, in contrast, has more diversity in the adjectives and adverbs that collocate.

➤ The following are the most common collocations:

> ➤ Occurring over 100 times per million words—AmE Conv: *pretty good, really good*; BrE Conv: *very good, very nice*.
>
> ➤ Occurring over 50 times per million words—AmE Conv: *too bad, very good*; BrE Conv: *quite good, really good*.
>
> ➤ Occurring over 20 times per million words—AmE Conv: *real good, real quick, really bad, really nice, too big, very nice*; BrE Conv: *pretty good, quite nice, really nice, too bad, fair enough*; Acad: *more general, quite different, significantly different, significantly higher, statistically significant, very difficult, very important, very large, very low*.

**DISCUSSION OF FINDINGS**

The higher frequency of adverb + adjective combinations in conversation (in both dialects) and their greater diversity in academic prose is typical of the general contrast between conversation and the expository registers. Conversation usually has less diversity in word choice: see, for example, 10.2.4.3 on the diversity in circumstance adverbials; cf. also 2.2.1 in general.

For the most part, adverb + adjective pairs in conversation have a single type of modifier, i.e. a degree adverb (7.14.2.4). The degree adverbs *quite, real, really, too, pretty,* and *very* are especially common. This group of adverbs and the adjectives that they typically modify—e.g. *bad, good, nice*—are vague or informal words. The adverb modifiers in academic prose also include degree adverbs, especially *more, quite,* and *very*. However, the adjectives modified by these forms have more to do with specific characteristics than general value judgments (e.g. *different, higher, difficult).* In addition, several of the pairs in academic prose refer to statistical measurements, such as *significantly different/higher* and *statistically significant.*

These general trends are illustrated in the following examples:

Conversational:

> *That sounds **very** [good].* (AmE CONV)
>
> *That looks **pretty** [good].* (AmE CONV)
>
> *Really, I, I fancy Emma cos she's a **very** [nice] girl.* (BrE CONV)

Academic:

> *He found it **very** [difficult] to regain his usual level of activity because his arthritis seemed worse after the operation.* (ACAD†)
>
> *The hospital mortality at 21 days for those who received streptokinase was not **significantly** [different] from the control group.* (ACAD†)
>
> *The **statistically** [significant] interaction between condition of retention and visual field of presentation was held to confirm the hemispheric locus of visual and verbal codes.* (ACAD)

Degree adverbs as modifiers are discussed further in 7.14.2.4

## 7.13.2 Adverbs modifying other adverbs

Adverbs also serve as modifiers of other adverbs:

> *They'll figure it out **really** [fast].* (CONV)
>
> *The do-it-yourself builder **almost** [always] uses a water-repellent plywood, oil-tempered hardboard or fibre-cement sheet.* (ACAD†)

### 7.13.2.1 Adverbs modifying adverbs in conversation and academic prose

Here we exemplify the range of use of adverb + adverb combinations by considering only the most common combinations in conversation (AmE and BrE) and academic prose:

> **CORPUS FINDINGS** [2]

➤ Adverbs are less common as modifiers of other adverbs than as modifiers of adjectives.

➤ The following are the most most common collocations.

  ➤ Occurring over 100 times per million words—AmE Conv: *right now.*

  ➤ Occurring over 50 times per million words—AmE Conv: *pretty much, right here, right there, so much, very much*; BrE Conv: *very much*; Acad: *much more.*

  ➤ Occurring over 20 times per million words—AmE Conv: *much better, much more, pretty soon, pretty well, really well, too much, very well*; BrE Conv: *too much*; Acad: *much less.*

  ➤ Occurring over ten times per million words—AmE Conv: *so fast, so well*; BrE Conv: *just now, just there, much better, quite well, really well, right now, very often*; Acad: *almost certainly, almost entirely, very much, very often.*

**DISCUSSION OF FINDINGS**

In both conversation and academic prose, modifying adverbs in the most-common collocate pairs often show a concern for qualifying amounts of something or for qualifying a comparison. Thus, conversation includes common pairs such as *very much*, *much better*, and *much more*, while academic prose includes *very much*, *much more*, and *much less*. Examples of these items include:

1 *Oh, you're going to do **much better**.* (AmE CONV)

2 *Thank you **very much** for listening.* (BrE CONV)

3 *I admitted, however, that internal skepticism offers a **much more** powerful challenge to our project.* (ACAD)

4 *It is **much less** easy when one has to explain the simultaneous extinction of several unrelated groups.* (ACAD)

As examples **3** and **4** illustrate, in academic prose the adverbs *more* and *less* in the pairs *much more* and *much less* are usually themselves modifiers of a following adjective.

With the use of *pretty much* in AmE conversation, it is sometimes difficult to differentiate between the meaning of a decrease in intensity and a hedge (7.14.2.6):

5 *What they did in India was study Sanskrit, which is **pretty much** a waste of time.* (AmE CONV)

6 *Like I'm **pretty much** in awe of it when I see it.* (AmE CONV)

In **5**, *pretty much* could signal either that the study of Sanskrit was mostly—but not entirely—a waste of time, or that 'waste of time' is not a precisely accurate choice of words. In **6**, *pretty much* could be interpreted as meaning 'I'm in slight but not great awe', or that the phrase *in awe* is somehow imprecise. (In fact the entire proposition in **6** is marked as imprecise with the hedge *like* at the beginning of the clause.)

Conversation also shows a concern for time and place, particularly in the use of *right* in AmE as a modifier to suggest exactness, and occasionally in the similar use of *just* in BrE:

*I really couldn't keep him in my apartment **right** [now].* (AmE CONV)

*She already got a twenty percent tip **right** [here].* (AmE CONV)

*And the whatchacallems are **right** [there], see?* (AmE CONV †)

*Can you see a little spark of green **just** [there]?* (BrE CONV)

*I think we'll put it off **just** [now], Grant.* (BrE CONV)

Conversation also commonly uses adverb modifiers that occur with *well* to describe either quality or thoroughness:

*Well that's how we got acquainted **so** [well] because she was in Olie's room a lot.* (AmE CONV)

*You could remember that number **pretty** [well].* (AmE CONV)

*England did **really** [well], didn't they?* (BrE CONV)

In contrast to conversation, academic prose has two common pairs with *almost* as modifier, both serving to soften a claim:

*This decline is **almost** [certainly] partly due to the increased disease incidence.* (ACAD)

*The passage is **almost** [entirely] in third-person narration.* (ACAD)

As in these examples, the modifier *almost* allows academic authors to make strong but not absolute claims.

## 7.13.3 Adverbs modifying other elements

Although adverbs that are used as modifiers most commonly modify adjectives or other adverbs, they can also serve as modifiers of noun phrases (or parts of noun phrases), prepositional phrases, particles, and numerals or measurements:

> *"It came as **quite** [a surprise]," said one.* (NEWS) <premodifier of noun phrase>
>
> ***Almost** [nobody], it seemed, could eat what they were given.* (FICT†) <modifier of pronoun>
>
> *I've done **about** [half] a side.* (CONV) <modifier of predeterminer>
>
> *But there's a hell of a lot—**well** [into their seventies].* (CONV) <modifier of prepositional phrase>
>
> *It's really filled the room **right** [up].* (CONV) <modifier of particle of phrasal verb>
>
> *It is still not clear whether the **approximately** [250] people still listed as missing include those whom ex-detainees say were still alive in May.* (NEWS) <modifier of numeral>
>
> *Tosi (1984:27–34, Figure 3) estimates that **roughly** [one-quarter to one-third] of the total surface area of four sites in "prehistoric Turan" was devoted to different craft activities.* (ACAD) <modifier of numerical expression>

As with adjective and adverb modifiers, most of these adverbs occur as premodifiers. However, postmodification also occurs, especially with locative information about a noun phrase:

> *Thus, in [the ammonia example] **above**, if ammonia, NH$_3$, is allowed to escape from the reaction system, the reaction cannot achieve equilibrium.* (ACAD) <postmodifier of noun phrase>

For some of these functions, only a small set of adverbs is used. For instance, few adverbs apart from *right*, *well*, and *directly* are commonly used to modify prepositions.

## 7.13.4 Adverbs as complements of prepositions

Another function of adverbs is to serve as the complement of a preposition. Consider the following examples, with the preposition in *[]* and the adverb in bold:

> 1 *You can't go [through] **here** can you?* (CONV)
> 2 *There's another sweatshirt lurking [under] **there** that I didn't see.* (CONV)
> 3 *But I'm seeing all this [from] **above**.* (FICT†)
> 4 *[Until] **now**, I did not realize how much of a ski lesson is spent not skiing.* (NEWS†)
> 5 *[Before] **long**, he met a pretty singing cowgirl from Texas who went by the name of Dale Evans.* (NEWS)
> 6 *Its importance has often been recognized [since] **then**.* (ACAD†)

As these examples demonstrate, the adverbs serving as complements of prepositions usually denote place (as in **1–3**) or time (**4–6**). For problems of overlap with constructions with adverbial particles see 2.4.6.2.

## 7.13.5   Adverbs as clause elements: adverbials

There are three major types of adverbials: circumstance adverbials, stance adverbials, and linking adverbials (see 3.2.8 for the basic distinction; and also Chapter 10).

**A** **Circumstance adverbials** add information about the action or state that is described in the clause, giving details about factors such as time, manner, and place:

> They're gonna be **there** Mom. (CONV)
>
> He took it in **slowly** but **uncomprehendingly**. (FICT †)

**B** **Stance adverbials** convey the speaker/writer's assessment of the proposition in the clause. They include comments about:

- the **epistemic** conditions on the clause, e.g. the level of doubt/certainty with *maybe, probably*:

  > His book **undoubtedly** fills a need. (NEWS)

- the speaker/writer's **attitude** towards the proposition, e.g. *unfortunately* or *surprisingly*:

  > Then, **amazingly**, he would turn over the microphone to his daughter Maureen and give her equal time to speak on behalf of the amendment. (ACAD)

- the **style** in which the proposition is being conveyed, e.g. *honestly* or *frankly*:

  > And he sounded a bit low, **quite frankly**, to me yesterday on the phone. (CONV)

**C** **Linking adverbials** serve to connect stretches of text—phrases, sentences, paragraphs or longer:

> The weight of bureaucracy still hangs a trifle heavy. **Nevertheless**, the review represents substantial progress. (NEWS)
>
> Most of our rural people do not have radio or television and a large proportion are illiterate. **Therefore** we had to use approaches that do not depend on the mass media or on literacy. (ACAD)

As the above examples illustrate, all three kinds of adverbials can be realized by adverbs or adverb phrases. Chapter 10 gives a detailed account of adverbials.

## 7.13.6   Adverbs with degree complements

The clauses and phrases which occur as **degree complements** with adjectives (7.2.7) also occur with adverbs (marked with *[]* below). Of the six major structural types of degree complement listed in 7.8, the first two can be phrasal or clausal structures, while the others are clausal only. The whole adverb phrase functions as an adverbial in all of the examples below.

**A** **Adverb-*er* +** *than*-**phrase/clause OR** *more/less* **+ adverb +** *than*-**phrase/clause**

Phrase:

> *He rode it [oftener]* **than ever**. (FICT)
>
> *Generally speaking, those higher in occupational status suffered [less acutely]* **than those lower down**. (ACAD)

Clause:

> *We expected this to happen [much quicker]* **than it did**. (NEWS)
>
> *It could happen [more quickly]* **than anyone expects**. (NEWS†)
>
> *Ford and Beach's study of nearly two hundred societies concluded that in virtually all of them sex is regarded as something the woman does for the man. He needs it [more urgently]* **than she does**. (ACAD)

As the examples show, this structure can include inflectional or phrasal marking of comparative degree on the adverb (i.e. *quicker* v. *more quickly*).

**B** *as* **+ adverb +** *as*-**phrase/clause**

Phrase:

> *The normal scan must be resumed [as quickly]* **as possible**. (ACAD)

Clause:

> *I didn't do [as well]* **as I wish that I had**. (CONV)
>
> *"I don't know where you got the idea I was ill," I said [as heartily]* **as I could**. (FICT)

**C** *so* **+ adverb +** *that*-**clause**

> *It happened [so fast]* **that I didn't even realise I had fallen off**. (CONV)
>
> *He wanted it [so urgently]* **that he fidgeted in his chair**. (FICT)

**D** *so* **+ adverb +** *as to*-**clause**

This structure occurs most commonly with the adverb *far*:

> *He went [so far]* **as to write home some vague intimation of his feelings about business and its prospects**. (FICT)
>
> *My new found anti-regulatory spirit goes [so far]* **as to object to the movement in Congress to set the rates that Cable TV companies can charge**. (NEWS)

**E** *too* **+ adverb +** *to*-**clause**

> *Through the open window the voice of the beauty of the world came murmuring, [too softly]* **to hear exactly what it said**. (FICT†)
>
> *The situation has deteriorated [too far]* **to repair**. (NEWS†)

**F** **Adverb** *enough* **+** *to*-**clause**

> *It couldn't turn [quickly enough]* **to follow them**. (FICT)
>
> *At least four people were bitten [seriously enough]* **to be hospitalized**. (NEWS)
>
> *How it is done is less important than learning something [well enough]* **to share it in collective life**. (ACAD†)

As with adjectives as head, the degree adverb in all of these constructions can also occur without the following degree complement construction, for example:

> You shouldn't go to bed **too early**! (CONV)

## 7.13.7 Adverbs standing alone

In conversation (and direct reports of dialogue in other registers), adverbs can stand alone as structurally unconnected elements (see 3.15 and 14.3.4), and even as complete utterances. In some cases, the adverbs are related to elliptted forms of previous sentences, as in:

> The kitten's gone crazy. No, totally I mean it. **Totally** and **utterly**. (CONV)
> <i.e. The kitten has gone totally and utterly crazy.>
> A: Getting there.
> B: Yeah.
> A: **Slowly** but **surely**. (CONV) <i.e. I am getting there slowly but surely.>

Adverbs as utterances can also serve to express—or emphasize—agreement or concurrence:

> A: What you could afford you had.
> B: **Exactly**. **Exactly**. (CONV)
>
> A: In other words the skills of a counselor?
> B: Yes. Yes.
> C: **Definitely**. **Definitely**. (CONV)

Adverbs can also be used as questions. Often, these adverbs are stance adverbials of actuality or style of speaking:

> A: You can still vote if you lost it.
> B: **Really**?
> A: They should have your name on the roster. (CONV)
>
> A: You're supposed to put the lid on, otherwise it won't switch off.
> B: **Seriously**?
> A: Yeah. (CONV)
>
> A: Have you got any on that?
> B: No.
> A: **Honestly**?
> B: Honestly! (CONV)

Some of the above examples illustrate that adverbs can serve not only to pose questions, but also to answer them. Other examples include:

> A: It's warm isn't it. By the radiator.
> B: **Probably**. (CONV)
>
> A: Are they that good?
> B: **Definitely**. Only band I want to see playing—in the world. (CONV)

Again, most adverbs answering questions are stance adverbs.

# 7.14 Semantic categories of adverbs

## 7.14.1 Importance of context in the semantics of adverbs

As with adjectives (7.3) and verbs (5.2.1), many adverbs have meanings that vary with context of use. First, some adverbs have both literal and more metaphorical meanings. For example, *perfectly* can be used in its literal meaning of 'in a perfect manner': e.g. *perfectly arranged*; *perfectly fits the bill*. However, more commonly it is used in a more metaphorical sense to mean 'completely': e.g. *perfectly normal*; *perfectly safe*.

Other adverbs can be used with distinctly different meanings. For example, the adverb *just* has a wide range of meanings:

- denoting closeness in time: e.g. *the horse had just had its foal*
- increasing the intensity of a following element: e.g. *just dreadful, just what I wanted*
- decreasing intensity of a following element: e.g. *just 4.5 points down*
- signalling manner: e.g. *it'll just stop* (i.e., 'by itself').

The adverb *far* has a literal meaning with distance (*too far up the road*), a metaphorical meaning with time (*so far, with Christmas not that far off*), and a third meaning of intensification (*a far better atmosphere, far more numerous*). Thus, the meaning of an adverb is often context-dependent.

## 7.14.2 Description of semantic categories

Adverbs cover a wide range of semantic categories. The following discussion identifies seven main categories, as well as discussing other less common meanings.

### 7.14.2.1 Place

**Adverbs of place** can show position, direction, or distance:

> *He loves it **there**.* (CONV) <position>
>
> *It hopped **backward** among its companions.* (FICT†) <direction>
>
> *"Don't worry, he can't have gone **far**."* (FICT) <distance>

As in the above examples, adverbs of place are typically adverbials (10.2.1.1). They can also occur occasionally as the first word in compound adjectives (7.9.3):

> *Only four of the **forward**-[looking] components were positive.* (NEWS)
>
> *The changes made in Map 3.0 are **far**-[reaching].* (ACAD)

However, in these cases it would not be appropriate to consider the adverb to be an independent modifier, since the following participle could not occur alone as an -*ing* adjective: *the looking components* and *The changes ... are reaching* do not make sense.

### 7.14.2.2 Time

Adverbs convey information about **time** in four ways: position, frequency, duration, and relationship:

> 1 *She doesn't say go away very much **now**.* (CONV) <time position>

2 *They looked intently at him,* **then** *at each other,* **then** *executed a smart about-face.* (FICT) <time position>

3 **Recently** *deserted by her husband she's found it hard enough to make ends meet in the past.* (NEWS) <time position/relationship>

4 *She* **always** *eats the onion.* (CONV) <time frequency>

5 *Worse still, the product itself is* **often** *dull and unchanging.* (NEWS) <time frequency>

6 *She will remain a happy memory with us* **always**. (NEWS) <time duration>

7 *When they took the old one out it was* **already** *in seven separate pieces!* (CONV) <time relationship>

These examples illustrate two characteristics common in the semantics of adverbs of time. First, a single adverb can incorporate more than one temporal meaning. In example **3**, *recently* conveys both a sense of a point in the near past and a time relationship (i.e. more recent than other events). Secondly, the same adverb can have different temporal meanings, depending on its context of use. In **4**, *always* refers to frequency (i.e. each time there's an onion, she eats it). In **6**, *always* refers more to duration: she will endure as a happy memory with us from now and continuing for ever. Clearly the semantic domain of the verb in the clause is important for interpreting the adverb: *eat* refers to an activity which can be performed repeatedly, *remain* is a stative verb of existence (5.2.1.1).

## 7.14.2.3  Manner

Many adverbs express information about how an action is performed. Many—though not all—**manner adverbs** have *-ly* suffixes, taking their meanings from the adjectives from which they are derived. Examples include:

*He really believed that because we were hitch-hiking, we were whores and that we would* **happily** *go to his house.* (CONV†)

**Automatically** *she backed away.* (FICT)

*But sentiment recovered* **quickly**. (NEWS†)

*There could be no doubt that EPR, as we shall* **acronymically** *refer to them, had drawn attention.* (ACAD†)

However, other adverbs of manner are not *-ly* adverbs:

*You can run* **fast** *but not here.* (CONV)

*They were riding* **abreast** *down the railway lines.* (FICT†)

*To perform* **well** *it has to be tightly targeted to cope with quite a narrow band of frequencies.* (NEWS)

*Recorded interviews and reports of observations were transcribed* **verbatim** *and checked for accuracy before analysis.* (ACAD)

The above examples illustrate manner adverbs used as adverbials. Many manner adverbs are also used as modifiers of participial premodifiers of a noun, providing descriptive information that is integrated into a noun phrase:

*By the dark waters of Buda, her tears dropping hotly among the* **quietly** *[flowing] dead leaves.* (FICT†)

*In a* **fast** *[moving] first half the teams appeared to cancel each other out in mid-field.* (NEWS)

> *The Russian leader threw the **carefully** [arranged] welcome into chaos.*
> (NEWS†)

These combinations can also be analyzed as compound adjectives, an analysis which the presence of a hyphen between the adverbs and participle would render more persuasive (7.9.3).

Occasionally manner adverbs also occur as modifiers within compound predicative adjectives:

> *They are **fast**-[moving], colourful, noisy, and as good if not better than anything you can buy for home computers.* (NEWS)
> *But it is clean, **well**-[lighted] and you can be certain it will be well tended.* (NEWS)

Certain *-ly* adverbs that can act as manner adverbials often take on the role of degree adverbs when they are used as modifiers. Consider, for example, the difference between **1** and **2** below:

> **1** *The day which ended **terribly** at the presidential palace started badly at the same venue.* (NEWS)
> **2** *He's a **terribly** [imaginative] businessman.* (FICT)

In **1**, the adverbial *terribly* is used to describe a bad situation. However, in **2** there is nothing terrible about the imaginativeness of the businessman; rather, the modifier *terribly* emphasizes the extent of his imaginativeness. This type of semantic change is particularly apparent with adverbs that have negative meanings as adverbials, but lose their negative value as modifiers (e.g. *awfully*, *terribly*).

### 7.14.2.4 Degree

**Adverbs of degree** describe the extent to which a characteristic holds. They can be used to mark that the extent or degree is either greater or less than usual or than that of something else in the neighboring discourse. They occur as both adverbials and modifiers. Examples of degree adverbs functioning as adverbials include:

> *It's insulated **slightly** with polystyrene behind.* (CONV)
> *Those letters from you, it got so I **almost** believed they were really written to me.* (FICT)
> *They **thoroughly** deserved a draw last night.* (NEWS†)
> *Fluids were withheld **completely** for 4 hours prior to surgery.* (ACAD†)

Adverbials of extent/degree are discussed further in 10.2.1.5.

### A Amplifiers/intensifiers

Traditionally, degree adverbs that increase intensity are called **amplifiers** (or **intensifiers**). Some of these modify gradable adjectives and indicate degrees on a scale. They include *more, very, so, too, extremely,* and *good and* (7.10.2); *[]* below marks the head word:

> *Our dentist was **very** [good].* (CONV)
> *We both thought you were marvellous. And **so** [kind] to let us come to the party afterwards.* (FICT)
> *Most will be **extremely** [cautious] until new case law defines the extent of the new Act.* (NEWS)

Other amplifiers indicate an endpoint on a scale. These include *totally*, *absolutely*, and *quite* (in the sense of 'completely'):

> But snow and ice accumulate in a **totally** *[different]* way from sediment. (ACAD)

> **Completely** *[cold]* and *[unemotional]*. (FICT†)

These amplifiers are used with some gradables (those denoting a scale that can be thought of as having a fixed end, such as *different*, *sure* and *possible*) and also some non-gradables (7.2).

*How* is also used as a degree adverb in exclamative clauses (3.13.3):

> A: *Well it ain't the child's fault.*
> B: *No.*
> A: **How** *[cruel]!* (CONV)

> **How** *[ironic]* that Hays is launching one of the biggest non-privatisation share offers to the public at a time when the party is in trouble. (NEWS)

This use of *how* as an amplifier typically introduces ironic comments in conversation:

> A: *This guy came reeling down the hallway completely plastered, uh, and the manager told me, oh, don't worry about him. He lives here, but he's completely harmless, and he sits out front, on the grass, right in front of the door to my apartment and drinks.*
> B: **How** *[lovely]*. (CONV)

As noted above, adverbs that can also be used as manner adverbials sometimes lose their literal semantic value when they are used as amplifiers. Thus consider:

> 1 *New York's an **awfully** [safe] place.* (FICT)

> 2 *And Carl was **perfectly** [awful].* (FICT)

In **1**, *awfully* does not mean 'in an awful way'; it simply increases the intensity of *safe*. In **2**, *perfectly* takes on its more metaphorical sense of 'absolutely' (7.14.1). *Dead* is another adverb used in colloquial situations to modify adjectives. Clearly, *dead* has lost its literal meaning in such cases:

> It's **dead** *[easy]*. (CONV)

> It's **dead** *[nice]*. (CONV)

> He is **dead** *[serious]* all the time. (CONV)

## B Diminishers/downtoners

Degree adverbs which scale down the effect of the modified item are sometimes called **diminishers** (or **downtoners**). As with intensifiers, many indicate degrees on a scale and apply to gradable adjectives. They include *less*, *slightly*, *somewhat*, *rather*, and *quite* (in the sense 'to some extent'):

> 3 *A **slightly** [cold] start gave way to wonderful contrasts of feeling.* (NEWS)

> 4 *Consequently, Marx often uses the term Klasse in a **somewhat** [cavalier] fashion.* (ACAD†)

Some of these adverbs are related to hedges (discussed below as stance adverbs). That is, they convey some sense that the use of the modified item is not precisely accurate. For example, in **3** and **4** above, *cold* and *cavalier* appear not to be absolutely exact in describing *the start* and *a fashion*. However, we make a distinction between the items that primarily modify intensity (degree adverbs) and items that primarily mark imprecision or estimation (hedges such as *kind of*).

As can be seen in the above discussion, *quite* can occur with both gradables and non-gradables, but often with a different meaning. With gradables whose meaning does not imply any absolute end-point of the scale it usually means 'to some extent':

> **quite** *nice* (CONV)

With non-gradables it has the meaning mentioned earlier, 'completely':

> **quite** *motionless* (FICT)

However, there are many adjectives with which *quite* can be used in both its senses for example:

> *I was* **quite** *[confident] that it would stay in.* (CONV†)

*Confident* can be interpreted as gradable or as an absolute state. Thus, *quite confident* could indicate either moderate or complete confidence. Intonation would likely make the interpretation easier in the actual spoken version. However, in practice it has often been impossible to decide which of the senses of *quite* is being used, and they have been conflated in the counts below.

Similar to diminishers, other degree adverbs may indicate lesser degree in terms of falling short of the endpoint on a scale, e.g. *almost*, *nearly*, *pretty*, and *far from*. These also occur with some non-gradables (7.2).

> *Mr Deane's glass is* **almost** *[empty].* (FICT)

For discussion of the use of amplifiers and diminishers with supposedly non-gradable adjectives, see 7.7.6.

## 7.14.2.5 Additive/restrictive

**Additive** adverbs show that one item is being added to another—either at a clausal level, as in **1** and **2**; or at a phrasal level, as in **3**:

> 1 *Oh, my dad was a great guy,* **too**. (CONV)
>
> 2 *The formula* **also** *shows the number of moles of atoms of each element in one mole of molecules.* (ACAD)
>
> 3 *I can hear the hatred, but* **also** *the need.* (FICT)

Even when they occur as adverbials at clause level, additive adverbs typically single out one particular part of the clause's meaning as being 'additional' to something else (often implied). For example, out of context, **1** is ambiguous between two senses: '*My dad* (in addition to someone else) was a great guy' and 'My dad was *a great guy* (in addition to being some other kind of person)'. That is, the focus in this case can be either on the subject or on the subject predicative (cf. the scope of negators, 3.8.5).

**Restrictive** adverbs such as *only* are similar to additive adverbs in that they focus attention on a certain element of the clause. They serve to emphasize the importance of one part of the proposition, by restricting the truth value of the proposition either primarily or exclusively to that part:

> *The idea of anybody, Marge* **especially**, *liking that wall-eyed ox in preference to Dickie made Tom smile.* (FICT)
>
> **Only** *those who can afford the monthly payment of $1,210.05, plus $91.66 a month during probation, can be ordered to pay.* (NEWS)

Sections 10.2.1.6 discusses further considerations with additive and restrictive adverbials, the majority of which are adverbs. The close connection between the restrictive and degree categories is also discussed in 10.2.1.6.

### 7.14.2.6 Stance

Adverbs can be used to realize all three types of stance: epistemic, attitude, and style. These are exemplified below; detailed discussion is in 10.3.

### A Epistemic stance adverbs

- Adverbs can show levels of **certainty** or **doubt**:

  *No it's alright I'll **probably** manage with it.* (CONV)

  *My ideas about food are **definitely** passé.* (NEWS)

- Adverbs can comment on the **reality** or **actuality** of a proposition:

  ***Actually** I'm not very fussy at all.* (CONV)

  *If I like the music enough, I **really** could care less who the people are.*
  (AmE CONV) <*could care less* occurs commonly in AmE speech for the more literally true *couldn't care less*>

- Adverbs can be used to show that a proposition is based on some **evidence**, without specifying the exact source:

  *She was a rosycheeked, very unassuming, and simple woman, who smiled easily and talked with difficulty, and for the rest lived **apparently** a servile life of satisfaction and content.* (FICT)

  *The supernumerary instar is **reportedly** dependent on the density of the parental population.* (ACAD)

- Adverbs can be used to show the **limitations** on a proposition:

  *Our losses were **mainly** due to promotional activity from our rivals.*
  (NEWS†)

  ***Typically**, the front top six teeth will decay because of the way the child has sucked on its bottle.* (NEWS)

- Adverbs can be used to convey imprecision. These adverbs are also called **hedges**:

  *It was **kind of** strange.* (CONV)

  *I ain't seen this series I just **sort of** remember from the last series.* (CONV)

  *The ratio of clerks to total employees in the same manufacturing industries **roughly** averages 9%.* (ACAD†)

Many hedges occur as adverbials; however, hedges are also very common as modifiers of phrases and words. In conversation they can show the imprecision of word choice, as in the following example where *a little flaming fire thing* is clearly imprecise:

*They'd bring **like** [a little flaming fire thing].* (CONV†)

Hedges are also very common with numbers, measurements, and quantities. These forms are also called **approximators**, and typically function as modifiers of numerical or other quantifying expressions (cf. 2.7.7.4):

*They were suing Kurt for **like** [seventy thousand] dollars.* (CONV)

*So now I needed a job that I could do for **approximately** [four months].*
(FICT)

*About [15] families attended the first meeting.* (NEWS†)

*Prices were lower across the board, with **nearly** [all] blue-chip stocks losing ground.* (NEWS)

The category of hedges also overlaps with stance adverbs that convey uncertainty. For example, the use of *maybe* in the following sentences shows the imprecision of the following measurements:

*See it's come to me **maybe** – [eleven o'clock, half-past eleven] in the morning.* (CONV)

*We see 50, **maybe** [100] new Wine Racks in a year's time.* (NEWS)

### B  Attitude stance adverbs

These adverbs tell a speaker's or writer's attitude towards a proposition:

*I lost the manual that goes with it, **unfortunately**.* (CONV)

***Surprisingly**, the dividend rates of some pretty solid companies equal and sometimes exceed rates available from bonds and certificates of deposit.* (NEWS)

***Curiously**, an (at first sight) almost diametrically opposed argument may be advanced without contradicting the above.* (ACAD)

All of these attitude stance adverbs function as adverbials; see 10.3 for further discussion.

### C  Style stance adverbs

Style stance adverbs comment on the manner of speaking which the speaker is adopting: for example, is the speaker (or writer) using the language sincerely, frankly, or simply?

*Crackers she is, that woman! **Honestly**! She's crackers!* (CONV)

***Frankly**, Dee Dee suspects that in this instance she may also be a victim of lookism, i.e., discrimination against persons who do not measure up to an arbitrary, unrealistic and sexist standard of beauty.* (NEWS†)

***Quite simply**, life cannot be the same.* (NEWS†)

Like adverbs that show attitude, these style stance adverbs function as adverbials and are covered in more detail in 10.3.

## 7.14.2.7  Linking

Linking adverbs serve to make semantic connections between spans of discourse of varying length, thus contributing to the cohesion of discourse. They function as adverbials and are covered in more detail in 10.4. For their distinction from coordinators see 2.4.7.2. We briefly exemplify the different semantic categories here.

### A  Enumeration and addition

*For Braverman, Taylor's 'scientific management' rested on three principles. **First**, management must systematically investigate and acquire knowledge and information <...>. **Secondly**, the knowledge acquired by management is used for <...>. **Thirdly**, <...>* (ACAD†)

***Additionally**, the serum potassium level may be useful as a differential point.* (ACAD†)

**B   Summation**

> ***Altogether***, *Rose Milton was as unlike as possible to the stage or novelist's conception of a lady's maid.* (FICT)
>
> ***Overall***, *there are several major issues confronting us on the media front right now.* (NEWS)

**C   Apposition**

> *It must be remembered that evaluation usually takes place while another, more primary, activity is going on—**namely**, that of the service program.* (ACAD)
>
> *A third decision criterion is becoming increasingly popular: the payback period, **i.e.** the length of time it will take for the present value of accumulated net benefits to equal the total capital conversion costs.* (ACAD†)

**D   Result/inference**

> *But facing me in the nets for two winters, he got to know my bowling inside out and by the end of our stay in Cape Town he was hammering me all around the practice area. **Therefore**, I suppose I should claim some credit for Graham currently being one of the best batsmen against spin in the world.* (NEWS)
>
> *They need to propel themselves upwards and it is that moment of suspension coming between their force upwards and the force of gravity downwards that is so important. **Thus** it is possible to fly onto and off apparatus as separate tasks.* (ACAD†)

**E   Contrast/concession**

> *A: They're just ground beef.*
> *B: It's really gross **though**.* (CONV)
>
> *The police would like another chance to talk to Michaels about those responsible, namely his friends from the mountains. **Alternatively** they want us to put certain questions to him.* (FICT)
>
> *And the month before he left, he had made several long distance phone calls to Arizona and Ohio. Police, **however**, would not say where they were concentrating their search.* (NEWS)

**F   Transition**

> *Someone had the idea that if he walked along prodding the ground with his shovel, he could make the clams squirt ahead of him. Everyone else was doing the same thing, everyone but the old timers. One old timer told me later that the constant prodding kept the clams lying low until the tide came back in. **Incidentally**, out of some 40 or 50 people on the beach that day, the only ones with clams carried small hand shovels.* (NEWS)
>
> *In other words, the width of the band of wavelengths thus required will be inversely proportional to x; as the latter narrows, the former must widen. **Now**, de Broglie, when he hypothesized matter waves, related their wavelength to the particle momentum through the equation $p = h/\lambda$.* (ACAD)

## 7.14.2.8    Other meanings

In addition to the categories specified above, adverbs occasionally realize other meanings. For example, consider the following:

> 1  *The technical achievement of opening a vessel measured* **angiographically** *was similarly successful for both groups of patients.* (ACAD)
>
> 2  *When there is a funeral, the body is washed* **symbolically** *as part of the service.* (NEWS)

In **1**, *angiographically* could be considered a manner adverb, but more specifically it shows **means**; that is, it specifies the method by which the vessel was measured. (See 10.2.1.3 for more on adverbials of means.) In **2**, the adverb makes clear that the purpose of the body washing is symbolic, and it could therefore be considered a **purpose** adverb. The semantic categories of means and purpose, as well as certain other categories identified for adverbials in Chapter 10, are more commonly realized by structures other than adverbs; however, adverbs are occasionally used for these semantic categories.

One adverb which does not fit into any of the above categories is the courtesy adverb, *kindly*. It functions similarly to the insert *please* to mark politeness overtly in requests. It is used most commonly in fiction, and in requests lends itself to an ironic (i.e. impolite) interpretation:

> *In any case,* **kindly** *ask the authorities to call off their search.* (FICT)
>
> *"In the meantime, will you two* **kindly** *stop yapping, and try to give me some ideas of what we should do to keep the kids quiet this afternoon," commanded Beth.* (FICT)
>
> **Kindly** *attend to what I say and not to what Mr Shelly says, sir.* (FICT)

## 7.14.3    Semantic domains of adverbs in conversation and academic prose

**CORPUS FINDINGS** [2,3]

➤  In conversation, the majority of common adverbs fall into three semantic domains: time, degree, and stance.

➤  In contrast, a greater number of the common adverbs in academic prose are from the semantic domains of degree and linking (see Table 7.11).

**DISCUSSION OF FINDINGS**

The distribution of semantic categories of adverbs is in many cases closely related to patterns of use for semantic categories of adverbials (10.2.2, 10.3.1.5, 10.4.1.8).

First, in conversation (both AmE and BrE) many common adverbs fall in the time (and to a lesser extent place) categories. *Here, there, then,* and *now* are especially common. This is to be expected in that their meanings are all deictic— i.e. they can only be defined relative to the time and place of a particular utterance (e.g. *now* = 'at the time of speaking'). These and other adverbs are typically used as adverbials; their use and the contrast between conversation and academic prose are further discussed in 10.2.5.

Table 7.11  **Most common adverbs groups by semantic domain in BrE and AmE conversation and in academic prose; occurrences per million words**

(Listing all adverbs that occur at least 200 times per million words, including both modifier and adverbial functions.)

■ over 1,000     ▪ at least 200

| semantic domain | BrE CONV | AmE CONV | ACAD |
|---|---|---|---|
| **place adverbs** | | | |
| *here* | ■ | ■ | ▪ |
| *there* | ■ | ■ | |
| *away* | ▪ | ▪ | |
| **time adverbs** | | | |
| *now* | ■ | ■ | ▪ |
| *then* | ■ | ■ | ▪ |
| *again* | ▪ | ▪ | ▪ |
| *always* | ▪ | ▪ | ▪ |
| *still* | ▪ | ▪ | ▪ |
| *today* | ▪ | ▪ | |
| *never* | ▪ | ▪ | |
| *ago* | ▪ | ▪ | |
| *ever* | ▪ | ▪ | |
| *just* | ▪ | ▪ | |
| *yesterday* | ▪ | ▪ | |
| *already* | | ▪ | ▪ |
| *sometimes* | | ▪ | ▪ |
| *yet* | ▪ | | |
| *later* | | ▪ | |
| *often* | | | ▪ |
| *usually* | | | ▪ |
| **manner adverbs** | | | |
| *together* | | ▪ | |
| *significantly* | | | ▪ |
| *well* | | | ▪ |
| **degree adverbs** | | | |
| *very* | ▪ | ▪ | ▪ |
| *really* | ▪ | ▪ | |
| *too* | ▪ | ▪ | |
| *quite* | ▪ | | ▪ |
| *exactly* | | ▪ | |
| *right* | | ▪ | |
| *pretty* | | ▪ | |
| *real* | | ▪ | |
| *more* | | | ▪ |
| *relatively* | | | ▪ |

**Table 7.11** **continued**

| semantic domain | BrE CONV | AmE CONV | ACAD |
|---|---|---|---|
| **additive/restrictive adverbs** | | | |
| *just* | ■ | ■ | ■ |
| *only* | ■ | ■ | ■ |
| *even* | ■ | ■ | ■ |
| *too* | ■ | ■ | ■ |
| *else* | ■ | ■ | |
| *also* | | ■ | ■ |
| *especially* | | | ■ |
| *particularly* | | | ■ |
| **stance adverbs** | | | |
| *of course* | ■ | ■ | ■ |
| *probably* | ■ | ■ | ■ |
| *really* | ■ | ■ | |
| *like* | ■ | ■ | |
| *actually* | ■ | ■ | |
| *maybe* | ■ | ■ | |
| *sort of* | ■ | ■ | |
| *perhaps* | ■ | | ■ |
| *kind of* | | ■ | |
| *generally* | | | ■ |
| *indeed* | | | ■ |
| **linking adverbs** | | | |
| *then* | ■ | ■ | ■ |
| *so* | ■ | ■ | ■ |
| *anyway* | ■ | ■ | |
| *though* | ■ | ■ | |
| *however* | | | ■ |
| *e.g.* | | | ■ |
| *i.e.* | | | ■ |
| *therefore* | | | ■ |
| *thus* | | | ■ |

Secondly, there are a higher number of common adverbs serving a linking function in academic prose than in conversation. Their frequency reflects the importance in academic prose of marking the connections between ideas and explicitly showing the development of logical arguments. These forms function as adverbials and are discussed further in 10.4.

The difference in the use of stance adverbs between conversation and academic prose is also covered in the discussion of stance adverbials in 10.3. However, it is important to note here that some of the common stance adverbs of conversation are also used to modify adjectives and noun phrases:

*Angie's one is really **like** [hot] and will dry things.* (CONV)

*And at that stage my plaster that I'd had on after the er op had only been off **perhaps** [a fortnight].* (CONV)

*You can still find that in Mexico in **sort of** [hacienda-like] places and ranchos.* (CONV)

*<...> when I go away away, visiting, I mean, **like** [a week].* (CONV†)

In the additive/restrictive category, most of the very common items are adverbials (see discussion in 10.2.5). However, one item classed as additive (although it might arguably be placed in the 'other meanings' category) is not an adverbial. The characteristically conversational adverb *else* is used as a postmodifier of indefinite and *wh*-pronouns (4.15.1, 4.16):

*If we run out of toilet rolls right, [someone] **else** can buy them cause I bought the last two lots.* (CONV)

*[Everybody] **else** doing okay right now?* (CONV)

*I thought I had [something] **else** to show you up there.* (CONV)

*[What] **else** happened at school today?* (CONV)

This type of vague language is more typical of conversation than the written registers (see 14.1.2.3).

The semantic category of manner is notable for having very few common adverbs, even though adverbs of manner are common overall (10.2.2). The great diversity of manner adverbs results in few commonly recurring items. The three adverbs that are relatively common—*together*, *significantly*, and *well*—tend to have general meanings or more than one meaning; that is, they can be applied to very diverse contexts. For example, in the following samples, *together* is used to describe: **1** people living in the same house; **2** exercises being brought into sequence with each other; and **3** individuals standing side by side:

**1** *We're going to have to live **together**.* (CONV)

**2** *Teach each one individually, then put those two **together**.* (CONV)

**3** *Stand **together**.* (CONV)

*Significantly* is used in academic prose both in a general sense to show importance (or lack of importance) and in the more specific statistical sense:

*Without **significantly** lengthening the book we have added new material to most chapters.* (ACAD)

*Overall decreases of breeding differ **significantly**.* (ACAD)

The common degree adverbs are dealt with in more detail in 7.15. However, one item deserves discussion here: *right*, which occurs frequently in AmE conversation as a modifier of adverbials of place and time. It typically modifies prepositional phrases of position and the adverbs *there* and *now*:

*He said maybe **right** [in the city].* (AmE CONV)

*He takes that little hammer thing **right** [there] and whacks me.* (AmE CONV)

*But he, uh, they're in this really hairy lawsuit **right** [now].* (AmE CONV)

Both *well* and *right* are also very common as discourse markers in conversation (3.4.5). These usages as inserts (2.5) are distinguished from the use of *well* and *right* as adverbs (see also 14.3.3.3).

# 7.15    Discourse choices for degree adverbs as modifiers

Speakers and writers have a variety of degree adverbs to choose from in modifying adjectives. In some cases, the degree adverbs have slightly different meanings. Consider the following examples:

> *The highly priced Basmati varieties of rice, produced in Pakistan and India, are* **strongly** *[aromatic].* (ACAD)

> *Obligations of fraternity need not be* **fully** *[voluntary].* (ACAD†)

In the above examples, *strongly* and *fully* clearly are not interchangeable.

However, in many cases, there is little semantic difference between the degree adverbs. Thus, the adverbs could be exchanged in the following pair of sentences with little or no change in meaning:

> *That's that's—***completely** *[different].* (CONV)

> *It's* **totally** *[different].* (CONV)

Even for similar degree adverbs, there are differing preferences across registers and associations with different adjectives. The following subsections describe the use of amplifiers (7.15.1) and other modifying adverbs of degree (7.15.2) in BrE conversation, AmE conversation, and academic prose.

## 7.15.1    Amplifiers in conversation and academic prose

**CORPUS FINDINGS [2,3]**

➤ Conversation uses a wider range of common amplifiers than academic prose.
➤ AmE and BrE conversation have a similar profile of frequency except that:
  ➤ *so, totally, really,* and *real* are more common in AmE
  ➤ *bloody* and *absolutely* are more common in BrE.

**DISCUSSION OF FINDINGS**

Conversation uses a range of informal amplifiers which are generally not used in academic prose. They include: *bloody* (in BrE conversation), *damn, incredibly, terribly, real* (especially in AmE conversation), and *really*:

> *You're stupid, you're* **bloody** *[stupid]!* (BrE CONV)

> *He'll look* **really** *[sweet].* (BrE CONV)

> *It's* **terribly** *[slow] today.* (BrE CONV)

> *I got that speeding ticket and now I'm making* **damn** *[sure] I don't speed.* (AmE CONV)

> *It's probably* **real** *[easy] to use.* (AmE CONV)

> *It's* **incredibly** *[annoying].* (AmE CONV)

See 7.12.2.1 for the use of *real* and *really* across dialects.

As illustrated in the above examples, various adjectives are modified by these amplifiers. The most common have to do with positive value judgments (*good, cool, nice*), though negative judgments (*awful, bad, stupid*) are also relatively common.

Table 7.12 **Distribution of most common amplifiers (immediately preceding adjectives) in BrE and AmE conversation and in academic prose; occurrences per million words**

each ● represents 50

| | BrE CONV | AmE CONV | ACAD |
|---|---|---|---|
| *very* | ●●●●●●●●●● ●●●●●● | ●●●●●●●●●● ●● | ●●●●●●●●●● ●● |
| *so* | ●●●●●●●●●● ●● | ●●●●●●●●●● ●●●●●●●● | ●●●●● |
| *really* | ●●●●●●● | ●●●●●●●●●● ●● | |
| *too* | ●●●●●● | ●●●●●● | ●● |
| *real* | | ●●●●●● | |
| *completely* | ● | ● | ● |
| *absolutely* | ●● | ● | |
| *totally* | ● | ●● | |
| *damn* | ● | ● | |
| *bloody* | ●● | | |
| *extremely* | | | ●● |
| *highly* | | | ●● |
| *entirely* | | | ● |
| *fully* | | | ● |

Other amplifiers occurring c. 10 times per million words: *incredibly, perfectly, strongly, terribly.*

In contrast to conversation, academic prose makes more frequent use of the amplifiers *entirely, extremely, fully, highly,* and *strongly*:

> But the publication of Darwin's theory of biological evolution gave an **entirely** [new] stimulus to the elaboration of organicist theories. (ACAD)

> Indeed it is **extremely** [difficult] to establish any truly satisfactory system of defining the limits of these functions. (ACAD)

> The office slave boasts a waist and slender figure, while the navvy rolls along, a **fully** [developed] man of bone and muscle. (ACAD†)

> The **highly** [complex] process of adjustment to infection is determined by many variables. (ACAD)

> When both calmodulin and GTP are present, a **strongly** [biphasic] curve is produced with a peak activity at $1.1 \times 10^{-4}m$. (ACAD)

Most of these amplifiers are used to express the degree of intensity of a specific characteristic—newness, difficulty, development, complexity, and biphasicity in the above examples. In academic prose, there are fewer collocations with the more general positive or negative value judgments found in conversation.

Three of the most common amplifiers frequently occur in both conversation and academic prose: *very, so,* and *too*. These degree adverbs are used with a large variety of adjectives, though in conversation the most common collocates with *very* are again general positive words (*good, nice*):

> That sounds **very** *[good]*. (CONV)

> He's a **very** *[nice]* person and I like him. (CONV)

AmE and BrE conversation are similar in their common collocates with *too*: *bad, big,* and *late*. However, BrE conversation shows more of a tendency for *too bad* to be used in negative constructions (identifying something as 'not too bad'), while AmE conversation shows a tendency to use *too bad* in positive constructions:

> They are damp but they don't feel **too** *[bad]*. (BrE CONV)

> That's really **too** *[bad]*. (AmE CONV)

Several collocates of *too* occur commonly in both conversation and academic prose: *early, easy, hard, late, little, long, low, small.* In all registers, *too* + head functions as a kind of comparative construction (7.8, 7.13.6), describing the degree of a characteristic as excessive relative to the requirements of a particular set of circumstances:

> The doctor said it was **too** *[late]*. The damage had been done. (CONV)

> Her blood count was **too** *[low]* so we couldn't have it. (CONV)

> The general surrender of personality and autonomy it contemplates would leave people **too** *[little]* room for leading their own lives rather than being led along them. (ACAD)

*So* is more common in AmE conversation than in BrE conversation:

> A: Are you looking for a job?
> B: Yeah.
> A: It's **so hard** isn't it?
> B: I know, it's a nightmare. (AmE CONV)

The compound amplifier *ever so*, however, is found in conversation only in BrE, where it is quite frequent as a means of emotive intensification:

> I mean he was a super chap, really lovely chap, **ever so nice**. (BrE CONV)

## 7.15.2 Degree modifiers other than amplifiers in conversation and academic prose

Apart from amplifiers, modifying degree adverbs have a varied semantic effect (7.14.2.4).

**CORPUS FINDINGS 2,3**

➤ Academic prose uses a wider range of common adverbs of these types than conversation.

➤ The use of these adverbs in BrE and AmE conversation is similar, with the exception of *quite* and *pretty*:

> ➤ BrE conversation has a much higher frequency of *quite*, and AmE conversation has a much higher frequency of *pretty*.

**Table 7.13** **Distribution of most common amplifiers (immediately preceding adjectives) in BrE and AmE conversation and in academic prose; occurrences per million words**

Each ● represents 50

| | BrE CONV | AmE CONV | ACAD |
|---|---|---|---|
| quite | ● ● ● ● ● ● ● | ● | ● ● ● |
| pretty | ● ● | ● ● ● ● ● ● ● ● ● | |
| nearly | ● ● | ● ● | |
| rather | ● | | ● ● |
| relatively | | | ● ● ● ● |
| fairly | | | ● ● |
| slightly | | | ● ● |
| almost | | | ● |
| somewhat | | | ● |

Other non-amplifier degree adverbs occurring c. 10 times per million words: *moderately*.

**DISCUSSION OF FINDINGS**

Considering the dialect difference with respect to *quite* and *pretty*, many of the same collocates that occur with *quite* in BrE conversation occur with *pretty* in AmE conversation: *bad, big, cheap, easy, expensive, funny, high, interesting*:

> She's **quite** *[big]*. (BrE CONV)
>
> I guess they're **pretty** *[big]*. (AmE CONV)
>
> It's **quite** *[easy]* actually. (BrE CONV)
>
> Is it a system that would be **pretty** *[easy]* to learn? (AmE CONV)
>
> It was **quite** *[funny]*. (BrE CONV)
>
> So that was **pretty** *[funny]*. (AmE CONV)

The adjectives *good* and *sure* occur commonly in both dialects with *quite* and *pretty*. A difference between the dialects, however, is that AmE conversation tends to use *quite sure* exclusively in negative contexts, where *pretty sure* is impossible (that is, one cannot say *I am not pretty sure*). BrE conversation, on the other hand, uses *quite sure* in both positive and negative contexts. Examples of *quite good*, *pretty good*, and *pretty sure* in both dialects:

> I bet it's actually **quite** *[good]*. (BrE CONV)
>
> It's supposed to be **quite** *[good]*. (AmE CONV)
>
> We are really doing a **pretty** *[good]* job. (BrE CONV)
>
> But it seems like you have a **pretty** *[good]* relationship with Nicole. (AmE CONV)
>
> I'm **pretty** *[sure]* we must have paid it. (BrE CONV)
>
> I'm **pretty** *[sure]* I brought it upstairs. (AmE CONV)

Examples of *quite sure* in both dialects:

> She was probably **quite** *[sure]*. (BrE CONV)
>
> I think so, I'm not **quite** *[sure]*. (BrE CONV)
>
> I wasn't **quite** *[sure]* what her purpose in life was. (AmE CONV)

*You're never **quite** [sure] which goal they're trying to achieve.* (AmE CONV)

The reason for this difference appears to be that BrE favors the more intensifying use of *quite*, which can be used with adjectives which indicate the end-point of a scale, such as *right*, *true*, and *sure*. Thus in *quite right*, *quite sure*, and *quite true*, *quite* has a force similar to 'entirely' or 'absolutely' and is not close in meaning to *pretty sure*. This use is relatively rare in AmE, except when a negative precedes *quite*; in both dialects, in fact, negator + *quite*, meaning 'not entirely', is not uncommon.

Academic prose has more variety in the use of non-amplifier adverbs of degree, although no individual form is as frequent as *pretty* or *quite* in conversation. Such adverbs in academic prose modify a range of adjectives:

> *In fact more accurate calculations lead to **almost** [identical] maximum efficiencies.* (ACAD†)
>
> *In general, then, recent evidence points to conceptual or linguistic difficulties of a **fairly** [high] level.* (ACAD)
>
> *The ventral interradial plates are **slightly** [smaller] than the dorsal plates.* (ACAD)
>
> *These temperatures tend to be **somewhat** [lower] than those in common practice.* (ACAD)

As the above examples illustrate, several of the collocations in academic prose have to do with marking the extent of comparison between two items (e.g. *slightly smaller, somewhat lower*). Likewise, specifying the amount of difference appears to be an important function for degree adverbs in academic prose; the adjective *different* is a common collocate with several modifying adverbs:

> *The laws of thermodynamics, like Newton's laws of motion, are **quite** [different] in kind.* (ACAD†)
>
> *The most striking feature of these results is that they are **rather** [different] from those reported in the great majority of studies.* (ACAD†)
>
> *The European study asked a **slightly** [different] question.* (ACAD†)
>
> *Carburettor icing is **somewhat** [different] as it can occur in very hot weather conditions.* (ACAD)

Compared with conversation, academic prose is also notable for its use of *relatively*. The use of this adverb also indicates the importance of comparisons in this register:

> 1 *However, the morphology is still **relatively** [simple].* (ACAD†)
>
> 2 *In any **relatively** [stable] society, there exists an equilibrium between the mode of production, the social relations, and the "superstructure".* (ACAD†)
>
> 3 *Amphiboles occur characteristically in the plutonic rocks and in general are **relatively** [unimportant] minerals of the volcanic rocks.* (ACAD)

The use of *relatively* in these examples implies that measuring certain characteristics—simplicity in **1**, stability in **2**, and importance in **3**—depends on comparison with other members of a group.

*Quite* is also used notably in academic prose (though not as commonly as in BrE conversation). Besides modifying a variety of adjectives describing characteristics (e.g. *common, distinct, large, small*), the collocates of *quite* in academic prose also include adjectives marking stance (*clear*, *likely*, *possible*), for example:

> It is **quite** *[likely] that the population will be so unique that the project is not feasible.* (ACAD†)

# More complex structures

# 8

# Complex noun phrases

## 8.1 Overview

**Noun phrase** can be used as a cover term for two major types of construction: noun-headed phrases and pronoun-headed phrases. It also sometimes has a wider sense for which we use the term **nominal** (4.1).

The basic canonical structure of the noun-headed phrase includes four major components (4.2), of which two are optional: determiner + (premodification) + head noun + (postmodification and complementation). See Table 8.1.

**Table 8.1** **Major components of the noun-head phrase**

| determiner | premodifiers | head noun | postmodifiers |
|---|---|---|---|
| the | *industrially advanced* | *countries* | |
| a | *small wooden* | *box* | *that he owned* |
| a | *market* | *system* | *that has no imperfections* |
| the | *new training* | *college* | *for teachers* |
| the | | *patterns* | *of industrial development in the United States* |
| | | | **complement** |
| the | | *fact* | *that I haven't succeeded* |

The basic canonical structure of the pronoun-headed phrase is similar, except that it usually cannot include a determiner: (determiner) + (premodifiers) + head pronoun + (postmodifiers). See Table 8.2.

**Table 8.2** **Major components of the pronoun-head phrase**

| determiner | premodifiers | head noun | postmodifiers |
|---|---|---|---|
| | | *I, you, she* | |
| *a/the* | *big* | *one* | *in town* |
| | | *anyone* | *who is willing to listen* |
| | | *those* | *who take the trouble to register* |

Chapter 4 describes the obligatory elements in these basic structures, focusing on the different types of nouns and pronouns, as well as the types of determiners and the marking of number, case, and gender in the noun phrase. Chapter 4 and this chapter overlap slightly in at least three areas. First, there is a fuzzy borderline between some types of compound nouns (4.8.2) and structures with premodification of noun heads (8.3). Second, some genitives are more like premodifiers than determiners (4.6.4). Third, the consideration of genitives (4.6.10–14), of possessive pronouns (4.11.1), and of quantifying nouns (4.3.4–7) involved substantial coverage of *of*-phrases following noun heads as types of postmodification (8.9). However, noun phrases can be expanded in far more ways and often involve multiple premodifiers and postmodifiers.

There are several different types of premodifiers and postmodifiers. **Premodifiers** include primarily adjectives, participial modifiers, and other nouns:

Adjective as premodifier (7.4, 8.2)

   *a **special** project* (CONV)

   *an **internal** memo* (NEWS)

Participial premodifiers (8.2)

    **written** *reasons* (NEWS)

    **hidden** *variables* (ACAD)

    **detecting** *devices* (ACAD)

Noun as premodifier (8.2–3)

    *the* **bus** *strike* (CONV)

    *the* **police** *report* (NEWS)

Participial premodifiers, such as those illustrated above, are typically adjectival (7.9.1); but in some cases they have the character of noun rather than adjective modifiers, and in yet other cases their word-class membership is unclear (2.3.6). In this chapter we do not attempt to sub-classify these *-ing* and *-ed* forms as adjectival or nominal, but treat them as a separate category of premodifiers.

    **Postmodifiers** include primarily relative clauses, *ing*-clauses, *ed*-clauses, *to*-infinitive clauses, prepositional phrases, and noun phrases in apposition.

Relative clause as postmodifier (8.7)

    *that job* **I was doing last night** (CONV)

    *the penny-pinching circumstances* **that surrounded this international event** (NEWS)

*Ing*-clause as postmodifier (8.8.1)

    *the imperious man* **standing under the lamppost** (FICT)

*Ed*-clause as postmodifier (8.8.1)

    *a stationary element* **held in position by the outer casing** (ACAD)

*To*-infinitive clause as postmodifier (8.8.2)

    *enough money* **to buy proper food**. (FICT)

Prepositional phrase as postmodifier (8.9)

    *doctors* **at the Johns Hopkins Medical School** (NEWS)

    *compensation* **for emotional damage** (ACAD)

Noun phrase in apposition as postmodifier (8.10)

    *the Indian captain,* **Mohammed Azharuddin** (NEWS)

**Complement clauses** are distinct from postmodifiers in structure and meaning, though they also occur following noun heads (see also 8.14). They involve primarily special kinds of *that*- and *to*-clauses:

    *the idea* **that he was completely cold and unemotional** (FICT)

    *a chance* **to do the right thing** (FICT)

Occasionally adverbs can also be premodifiers or postmodifiers in noun phrases (7.13.3):

    *the* **nearby** *guards* (FICT†)

    *a block* **behind** (FICT†)

Also adjectives occasionally postmodify (7.6.1).

    As noted above, multiple premodifiers and postmodifiers can be added to a noun phrase, providing the potential for complex structures. For example, in the outer-bracketed noun phrase in the following sentence, the head noun *study* is followed by two postmodifiers: *of intraspecific variability* and *focused on developmental physiology*:

*Since most taxonomists agree about its monospecific status, [a **study** of intraspecific variability focused on developmental physiology] may be undertaken on a large scale.* (ACAD†)

The internal structure of this noun phrase is ambiguous, since potentially *focused on developmental physiology* could postmodify either *study* or *variability*. However, semantically it is much more likely that the study, not variability, is focused on physiology. With this meaning, both postmodifiers directly modify the head noun *study*, as in Figure 8.1.

Figure 8.1  **Complex noun phrase with ambiguous structure: analysis I**
**NP = noun phrase   PP = prepositional phrase**

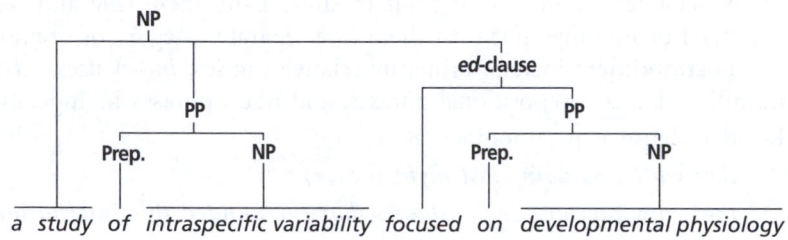

With the second meaning, the participle clause (*focused on developmental physiology*) is embedded and modifies the head noun *variability* rather than *study*, as in Figure 8.2.

Figure 8.2  **Complex noun phrase with ambiguous structure: analysis II**
**NP = noun phrase   PP = prepositional phrase**

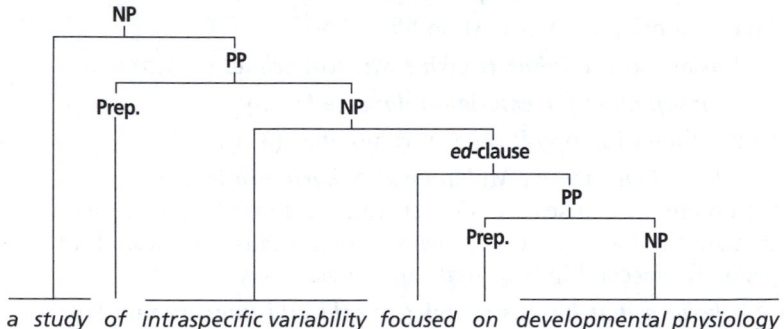

In principle, there is no limit to the complexity of noun phrases. The following two examples illustrate noun phrases even more complex than those above. The noun *trend* is the head noun of the complex phrase in **1**, while *prerequisites* is the head noun in **2**. To highlight the complexity of these examples, all premodifiers are given in SMALL CAPS while postmodifiers are marked by *[]*. The outer boundaries of the complex noun phrase are marked by {}. Subscripts $_a$, $_b$, etc. indicate levels of embedding; in **2**, subscripts $_{b1}$, $_{b2}$, etc. indicate embedding at the same level. Example **1** is also represented by a tree diagram in Figure 8.3:

   **1** *There has been* {a **trend** [$_a$towards CHRONIC, INSIDIOUS and COMPLEX
      *groups* [$_b$of diseases [$_c$caused by organisms [$_d$which are often NORMAL
      inhabitants [$_e$ of the ANIMAL body$_e$]$_d$]$_c$]$_b$]$_a$]}. (ACAD)

**Figure 8.3**    **Structure of a noun phrase with complex postmodification**
**NP = noun phrase   PP = prepositional phrase**

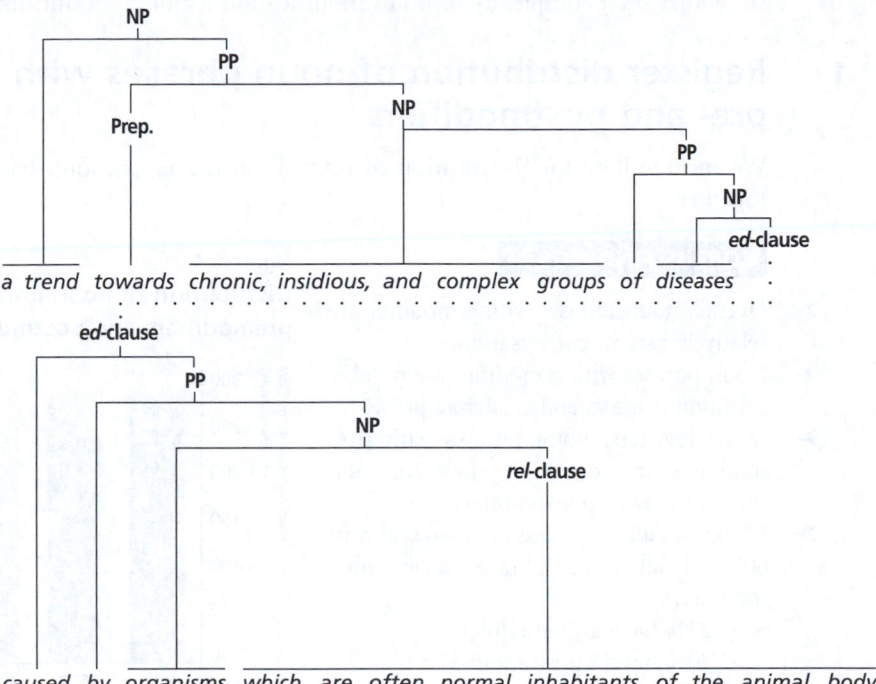

2  *Ideally environmental pollution is avoidable provided {certain* WELL
   RECOGNIZED ***prerequisites*** [ₐ *for* EFFICIENT CAPTIVE RECYCLING [ᵦ₁*of*
   NONRENEWABLE *materials* [𝒸₁ *of production𝒸₁*]ᵦ₁] *and* STRICT *control*
   [ᵦ₂ *of* POLLUTANT *emissions* [ᵦ₃ *into the environment* ᵦ₃]ᵦ₂]ₐ]} *are*
   *fulfilled.* (ACAD)

In their clause structures, neither of these sentences are particularly complex. The
first example consists only of a simple main clause with copula *be* as the main
verb; the second includes only a matrix clause (. . . *pollution is avoidable* . . .) and
one adverbial clause (*provided prerequisites are fulfilled*). The complexity in both
cases is contained in the noun phrase occurring after the main verb. These noun
phrases include multiple premodifiers and postmodifiers, which present a wealth
of additional propositional information beyond that presented by the matrix
clause itself. In many cases, postmodifiers are embedded, modifying a noun in
another postmodifier instead of the top-level head noun. For example, the
following statements are implied in one way or another by the complex noun
phrase in **2** (with *prerequisite* as head):

- certain prerequisites are well recognized
- the prerequisites in question relate to captive recycling of materials
- the captive recycling must be efficient
- the recycled materials are nonrenewable
- the prerequisites in question also relate to the control of emissions
- these emissions must be strictly controlled
- these emissions are pollutant

- the release of the emissions into the environment must be controlled.

Although these examples are particularly complex, the following sections will show that such complexity of noun modification is not at all unusual in English.

## 8.1.1 Register distribution of noun phrases with pre- and postmodifiers

We include here the distribution of noun-headed and pronoun-headed phrases together.

➤ Overall, noun phrases with a modifier are relatively rare in conversation.

➤ Noun phrases with a modifier are notably common in news and academic prose.

➤ In all registers, noun phrases with pre-modifiers are somewhat more common than those with postmodifiers.

➤ Proportionally in academic prose, almost 60% of all noun phrases have some modifier:
   ➤ c. 25% have a premodifier;
   ➤ c. 20% have a postmodifier;
   ➤ an additional 12% have both.

➤ Conversation represents the opposite extreme, with only c. 15% of all noun phrases having any modifier.

**Figure 8.4**

**Distribution of noun phrases with premodifiers and postmodifiers**

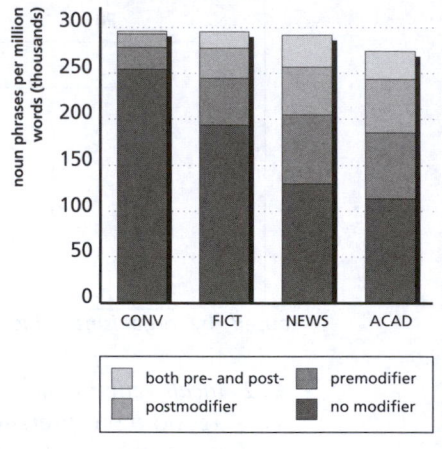

**DISCUSSION OF FINDINGS**

Overall, the complexity of noun phrases increases across the registers in a familiar order, with conversation at one extreme and academic prose at the other. The following two text samples, from a conversation and an academic text, illustrate these differences; all noun phrases are in *[]*:

Text sample 1: CONVERSATION

> A: *[Trouble] is [granny] does [it] and [she]'s got [loads of time]. [She] sits there and does [them] twice as fast as [me]. [I] – what [I] like doing, [I] like [the pictures].*
> B: *Yes.*
> A: *So [I] don't mind doing [the pictures]. If [she]'d do [the sleeves] and [the back] for [me], [I]'d be very grateful.*
> B: *Yeah.*
> A: *Whereas [she] can't stand doing [the pictures], cos [it] takes [her] [too much time].*
> B: *[It]'s like doing [tapestry].*

Text sample 2: ACADEMIC PROSE

> *In studying [his continuous transformation groups ([groups whose elements depend upon a system of continuously varying parameters satisfying certain*

*differentiability conditions])]* [Lie] *was led naturally to study [some non-commutative, non-associative algebras subsequently named after him: [Lie Algebras]].*

Even the visual impression created by these two excerpts is dramatically different: almost every word in the academic excerpt belongs to some noun phrase, while less than half of the words in the conversational excerpt are contained in noun phrases. At the same time, the conversational excerpt has more noun phrases than the academic text (despite the small proportion of text given to noun phrases). Most of these noun phrases have concrete referents—specific people, places, or things. Pronominal forms are also extremely common in conversation.

The use of these forms reflects the heavy reliance on a shared situation and shared personal knowledge for understanding. As a result, speakers in conversation typically use referring expressions with minimal modification, knowing that the listener will have no trouble identifying the intended referent (see also 4.1).

In contrast, the academic excerpt has only three non-embedded noun phrases, but two of these are complex with extensive modification (including modification in embedded noun phrases). These noun phrases are listed below, with premodifiers given in SMALL CAPS and postmodifiers given in *[]*:

1  *his* CONTINUOUS TRANSFORMATION **groups** [(**groups** [$_a$*whose elements depend upon a system* [$_b$*of* CONTINUOUSLY VARYING *parameters* [$_c$*satisfying* CERTAIN DIFFERENTIABILITY *conditions*$_a$]$_b$]$_c$])]

2  *some* NON-COMMUTATIVE, NON-ASSOCIATIVE **algebras** [*subsequently named after him*]: *Lie* [*Algebras*]

Such structures are typical of academic prose, where a majority of all noun phrases have some modifier. Much of the new information presented in academic texts is packaged as modifiers in noun phrases, resulting in a very high density of information.

The pattern in news is similar to that in academic prose, but with a slightly greater preference for premodification. This could be due to the space limitations of news reportage, since premodifiers are generally shorter than postmodifiers (cf. the use of *s*-genitives v. *of*-phrases; 4.6.12).

It is somewhat surprising to note that premodifiers and postmodifiers have a similar distribution across registers. It might be expected that some registers would show a much greater bias towards reliance on either premodifiers or postmodifiers. Instead, we find both types of noun modification to be extremely common in written expository registers, while both types are relatively rare in conversation.

## 8.1.2    Co-occurrence of modifiers with head noun types

Pronouns are slightly more frequent than nouns in conversation (see Figure 4.1); in contrast, nouns are by far more frequent than pronouns in written non-fiction registers. The amount of pre- and postmodification also depends on the type of noun phrase head. In Figures 8.5 and 8.6, we compare seven types of head: the pronoun *one*, common nouns, indefinite pronouns, the demonstrative pronoun *those*, other demonstrative pronouns, proper nouns, and personal pronouns.

**Figure 8.5**  **Percentage use of modifiers occurring with head noun types in conversation**

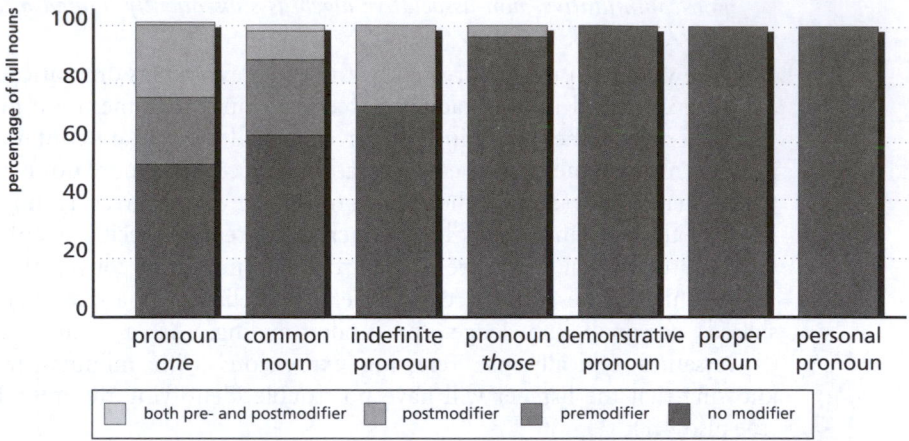

**Figure 8.6**  **Percentage use of modifiers occurring with head noun types in academic prose**

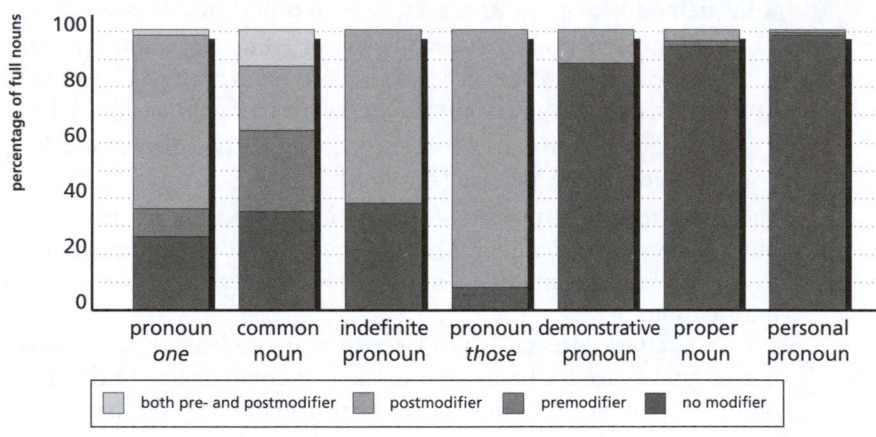

**CORPUS FINDINGS [1,2]**

➤ Proportionally, there is a general cline among the head types in the extent to which they co-occur with modifiers.

➤ Four types commonly take a modifier (ordered according to their preference for modification): pronoun *one*, demonstrative pronoun *those* (in written registers only), common nouns, and indefinite pronouns.

➤ Three other head types very rarely occur with a modifier: proper nouns, demonstrative pronouns (apart from *those*), and personal pronouns.

➤ The head types also differ in their co-occurrence with premodifiers v. postmodifiers (see Table 8.3).

➤ Postmodifiers are much more versatile in combining with different head types than premodifiers.

➤ Common nouns are the only head type taking premodifiers more commonly than postmodifiers.

➤ Proper nouns rarely take a modifier, except in news, where c. 20% of all proper nouns take some kind of modifier: 5% with premodifier; 5% with postmodifier; 10% with appositive.

Table 8.3    **Co-occurrence of premodifiers v. postmodifiers with different head noun types**

| head type | use with premodifiers | use with postmodifiers |
|---|---|---|
| common noun | common | common |
| pronoun *one* | moderate | very common (in writing) |
| indefinite pronoun | rare | common |
| proper noun | rare | rare (except news) |
| personal pronoun | rare | rare |
| demonstrative pronoun | rare | rare |
| *those* | unattested | very common (in writing only) |
| other demonstrative pronoun | unattested | relatively rare |

**DISCUSSION OF FINDINGS**

**A    Common nouns and personal pronouns**

Common nouns are the most frequent type of noun phrase head, and they are also the most productive head type freely occurring with both premodifiers and postmodifiers. (The major kinds of common noun are described fully in 4.3.)

Personal pronouns are also extremely common, especially in conversation. However, they represent the opposite end of the continuum from nouns in the extent to which they take modifiers: examples of a personal pronoun with either a premodifier or a postmodifier are quite rare:

> *But it's getting too late for [little]* **me**. (FICT)

> **She** *[who sat here before me] had not wasted her time, as I was doing.* (FICT)

It is interesting to note that common nouns and personal pronouns also occupy opposite poles in terms of their informational characteristics. Nouns are often used to refer to a new referent that is previously unknown to the listener/reader. Thus pre- and postmodifiers are used to help identify the reference of the noun and provide descriptive details.

In contrast, personal pronouns are used to refer to a specific entity (often a person) known to the listener/reader, either from the previous text or from the wider situational context. Consequently, there is usually no need for a modifier to anchor the reference or provide elaborating details.

However, there are three exceptions to this general practice. First, speakers in conversation sometimes use premodifiers with personal pronouns non-restrictively to register an emotive attitude, as in *poor you* or *little me*, often in exclamations (7.6.4). Second, when fiction writers want to emphasize an attribute of a known character, the character can be referred to with a personal pronoun, and the attribute can be given in either a premodifier or a postmodifying clause:

> *It was funny to see her helpless and despairing,* **she** *[who always took things so lightly].* (FICT†)

> **He** *[who had been healthy, firm-fleshed, virile], lay now on his hospital bed a skeleton with eyes.* (FICT)

Finally, personal pronouns can take a postmodifier when the pronoun has generic rather than specific reference, that is, referring to people in general, usually in relation to a general truth:

> **He** [who wants to jump out] should jump out now. (NEWS)
>
> **He** [who can], does. **He** [who cannot], teaches, wrote George Bernard Shaw. (NEWS)

The pronoun *he* has often been used for this function in the past, while many speakers and writers now use the pronouns *she/he* or *they* for generic reference (4.7.2).

## B The pronoun *one*

There are two distinct uses of the pronoun *one*: substitute *one*, which has specific reference, and generic *one* (4.15.2). These behave quite differently with respect to modification.

Substitute *one* stands in for a noun or noun-headed expression, is on its own indefinite in reference, and is similar to common noun heads in that it freely takes both pre- and postmodifiers. In conversation, *one* is usually of this type. When the specific reference is clear from the context, *one* often occurs with no modifier at all:

> I only bought **one** today. (CONV) <indefinite>
>
> **This one** takes a bit longer. (CONV) <marked definite by determiner *this*>

Elsewhere in conversation, a pre- or postmodifier is used to identify 'which one' is intended:

> You know **the one** [she ran off with]. (CONV)
>
> He's got **a** [horrible] **one** [that he hardly ever wears]. (CONV)
>
> **The last one** [I had] was at least four years ago. (CONV†)

In contrast, in academic prose the pronoun *one* is used with both specific and generic reference. When it has generic reference, *one* usually occurs with no modifier, being used in general statements that refer to some unspecified person:

> **One** cannot simulate the process by which facility closings and sitings take place. (ACAD)

When the pronoun *one* has specific reference in academic prose, it is usually directly anaphoric, substituting for a previously used noun phrase, with the modifier providing new descriptive details about that referent:

> The idea is **a** [strange] **one**. (ACAD†)

Postmodifiers are used more commonly than premodifiers for this purpose, since they can be longer and thus provide more descriptive information:

> A black body is **one** [that perfectly absorbs, and then re-emits, all radiation falling upon it]. (ACAD)
>
> The transition from agrarian, handicraft production to an industrial economy founded upon the factory and the machine was **one** [which began in Britain towards the end of the eighteenth century]. (ACAD)

## C Other indefinite pronouns

As with common nouns and the substitute pronoun *one*, other indefinite pronouns (4.15) commonly take a modifier and allow both pre- and postmodifiers. However, postmodifiers are overwhelmingly more common with this head type.

Premodifiers occur mostly with the indefinite pronoun *something*. The expression *a/that certain something* recurs in the LSWE Corpus, marking an unspecified special quality, while other combinations are more innovative:

> There was always **a certain something** in Ignatius Gallaher that impressed you in spite of yourself. (FICT)

> But they don't have **that certain something**. (NEWS†)

> His side clearly lacked **that [extra] something**. (NEWS†)

> There you go man. **No [big] something**. (CONV)

(Note that *certain* can alternatively be treated as semi-determiner; 4.4.6.)

Premodifiers with the other indefinite pronouns are even less common and more innovative in nature:

> Because each has nothing to say, the mirrored buildings simply reflect **a [bigger] nothing**. (NEWS)

> If you were shining it into **[pure] nothing**, you wouldn't see anything. (CONV)

> A: And er they're er they're going to have cold breakfast.
> B: They'll have **[cold] everything** there. (CONV)

In contrast, the full range of indefinite pronouns commonly take a postmodifier. This pattern is especially common in the written registers, but it is also relatively common in conversation. Here the postmodifier serves to constrain the pronoun's range of reference:

> She said she couldn't remember **anything [about it]**. (CONV)

> I was just saying **something [like that]**, **something [cheap]**. (CONV)

> Crusaders had **nothing [of note]** to show in the first half. (NEWS†)

> We have tried to impart **something [about the motivations of contemporary geologists]**. (ACAD†)

> But today, over thirty years after Basset's book appeared, is there **anything [new to say about 1931]**? (ACAD)

> Nonlinear systems theory is of great importance to **anyone [interested in feedback systems]**. (ACAD)

In addition, a special class of *wh*-pronouns formed with *-ever* occurs in fused relative clauses with similar meaning. In these constructions, the head and relativizer are combined into a single pronoun form, followed by the remainder of a postmodifying relative clause (see nominal relative clauses, 3.11.1, 9.3.1):

> **Whoever [killed her]** will be sent to prison. (NEWS)

> **Whoever [accused my husband]** is a liar. (FICT)

> The most effective way to teach Laura is to take her away from **whatever [she is doing wrong]**. (NEWS†)

> I'll do **whatever [you say]**. (FICT)

## D Proper nouns and other naming expressions

Proper nouns (4.3.3) and other naming expressions usually do not occur with a modifier, since the name itself clearly refers to a specific person, place, or institution. However, names can take both pre- and postmodifiers (both marked by *[]*):

> *[old]* **Dr. Stoddard** (FICT)
>
> **Irene Rushton** *[of Denton Square]* (FICT)
>
> **Aunt Mabel**, *[who was very proud of the house]* (FICT)
>
> *the [world-famous]* **Universal Studios** *[in Florida]* (NEWS)
>
> *the Soviet team* **Stroitel Kiev**, *[who were to play in this year's World International Club Championships]* (NEWS)

When a modifier is used, it serves one of two purposes: to help to identify a known referent, for readers who might not be familiar with that person or thing; or to add new descriptive information about the referent. These two functions are associated respectively with restrictive and non-restrictive modification (cf. 8.5), although in many cases this distinction is not clear.

In news, proper nouns are relatively common with modifiers serving both of the above functions. In addition, news makes extensive use of appositives to clarify the reference of a proper noun (8.10):

> **Princess Alice**, *[Duchess of Gloucester]* (NEWS)
>
> **Heiko**, *[a 19-year-old factory worker]* (NEWS)
>
> **Voronezh**, *[a dour city of 850,000 people in the great Russian heartlands]* (NEWS)

In many constructions, it is difficult to determine whether such elements should be analyzed as premodifiers, appositives, or titles:

> *Secretary of State Warren Christopher* (NEWS)
>
> *former Industry Minister Peter Vigger* (NEWS)
>
> *the French financial group Paribas* (NEWS)
>
> *Dedham councillor George Williams* (NEWS)
>
> *Sizewell B project manager Jim McFarlane* (NEWS)

## E   Demonstrative pronouns

Demonstrative pronouns differ from other head types in that they take only postmodifiers. In fact, apart from the demonstrative pronoun *those*, these forms rarely take any modifier at all. The four demonstrative pronouns differ considerably in their ability to take a postmodifier: the pronouns *this* and *these* are extremely rare with any modifier; the pronoun *that* occasionally takes a postmodifier; while the pronoun *those* is extremely common with a postmodifier, especially in writing. When postmodified, *that* and *those* function more like substitute forms than demonstratives (4.14.3–4).

The demonstrative pronoun *that* occasionally precedes a relative clause, but much more commonly it takes an *of*-phrase as postmodifier:

> *The simplest covalent structure is* **that** *[of diamond].* (ACAD)

The rarity of relative clauses with the demonstrative pronoun *that* can be attributed in part to the fact that the form *that* also serves as a relative pronoun, and English tends to avoid sequences of identical forms. Hence any relative clause postmodifying *that* usually begins with the relative pronoun *which*:

> *He might throw some light on* **that** *[which is so dark to us].* (FICT)

The sequence *that which* introducing a relative clause is usually close in meaning to *what* introducing a nominal relative clause.

When it takes a postmodifier, demonstrative pronoun *that* usually occurs as a prepositional object or as subject predicative to a copular verb.

Demonstrative pronoun *that* as prepositional object:

> *In practice we may find it difficult to separate the hardware of the data manipulation unit from* **that** *[of the control unit].* (ACAD)

> *They describe a different event from* **that** *[which the author chose to describe].* (ACAD†)

Demonstrative pronoun *that* as subject predicative to a copular verb:

> *The other problem is* **that** *[of sealing between the two streams].* (ACAD) <where *that* refers to 'the problem'>

> *The simplest form of tribal society is* **that** *[which follows a migratory existence].* (ACAD†) <where *that* refers to 'the form of tribal society'>

In contrast, the demonstrative pronoun *those*—referring to people or things—freely takes a postmodifying *of*-phrase or relative clause identifying the reference of the pronoun. In conversation, the pronoun *those* typically has deictic meaning, referring to something in the situational context, and therefore rarely takes a modifier. In written prose, however, it usually has either a substitute function (meaning 'the ones'), or else an unspecific personal meaning ('the people in general'). Thus, it usually occurs with a postmodifier (normally a restrictive relative clause—8.7) to identify the intended reference:

*Those* with restrictive relative clause as postmodifier:

> *He soon discovered that every movement by the man, even* **those** *[which were obviously stupid], functioned along lines of scientific exactitude.* (FICT†)

> *A state may have good grounds in some special circumstances for coercing* **those** *[who have no duty to obey].* (ACAD)

*Those* with *of*-phrase as postmodifier:

> *They sat erect, conscious of their uniforms, styled like* **those** *[of the post-1843 Prussian army].* (FICT)

> *This may be smugly satisfying to* **those** *[of us] [who sit on the sidelines].* (NEWS)

## 8.1.3 Discourse distribution of noun phrase types in academic prose

The occurrence of premodification or postmodification not only relates to register and the head of the noun phrase. It also crucially depends on the role the noun phrase is playing in the ongoing discourse. In 4.1 we reviewed the discourse roles of simple noun phrases, focusing on the choice among pronouns, definite noun phrases, proper nouns, and indefinite noun phrases to refer to entities on first v. later mention. The following analysis looks in more detail at the roles of noun phrases with pre- and postmodification with first and later mentions in academic prose.

**CORPUS FINDINGS [5]**

➤ Noun phrase types are distributed in a systematic way within texts:
  ➤ Noun phrases with postmodifiers are used most commonly for first mentions of a referent in a text.

➤ Noun phrases with premodifiers and simple nouns are used for both first and subsequent mentions.

➤ Pronouns are used primarily for subsequent mentions.

**Table 8.4**   **Noun phrase type in relation to 1st, 2nd, or 3rd mention in academic prose**

| form | 1st mention | 2nd mention | 3rd mention |
|---|---|---|---|
| N + postmodifier | 19 | 9 | 9 |
| premodifier + N | 26 | 23 | 32 |
| premodifier + noun + postmodifier | 13 | 3 | 3 |
| simple noun | 28 | 37 | 29 |
| proper noun | 6 | 3 | 4 |
| nominalization | 2 | 3 | 3 |
| pronoun | 6 | 22 | 20 |
| total | 100 | 100 | 100 |

**DISCUSSION OF FINDINGS**

Although it is by no means an absolute rule, repeated references to an entity tend to follow the same progression of noun phrase types across texts:

N + postmodifier > premodifier + N > simple noun > pronoun

For example, consider the repeated references to *systems* and *behaviours* in Text sample 1. (Noun phrases with *systems* or *behaviours* as head are shown in bold):

Text sample 1: DETERMINISTIC SYSTEMS

> **Deterministic dynamical systems of three or more dimensions** *can exhibit* **behaviours of the type generated by the rotating taffy machine**. *Despite their determinism,* **the behaviours generated** *look extremely random. This is what it means to say that* **such systems** *are effective mixing devices. The discovery of chaos suggests that the question of whether* **a given random appearing behaviour** *is at base probabilistic or deterministic may be undecidable.*
>
> *Nevertheless it is useful and justified to look at* **living systems** *from the functional point of view. This is due to the enormous asymmetry between existence and nonexistence.* **Some biological systems** *are so organised that* **they** *remain in the game of life.* **Others** *go out of existence.* (ACAD)

References to *behaviours* in this excerpt progress from noun phrases with postmodifiers to a premodified noun phrase:

> behaviours of the type generated by the rotating taffy machine → the
> behaviours generated → a given random appearing behaviour

References to *systems* follow a similar progression, beginning with a noun phrase having both pre- and postmodifiers, followed by a simple noun reference, premodified noun phrases, and finally pronominal references:

> deterministic dynamical systems of three or more dimensions → such systems
> → living systems → some biological systems → they → others

This progression represents a gradual decrease in fullness of expression over the course of a text. First mentions tend naturally to be more elaborated, so as to establish the intended reference and provide the salient descriptive details about that referent. Postmodification provides more elaborated ways of attaching information for this purpose than premodification. Subsequent mentions become progressively more economical and reduced, to the extent that the intended reference is clearly established. Departures from the expected progression are influenced by factors such as the distance between referring expressions, the informational prominence of an expression, and the need to provide additional identifying or descriptive details. However, in most cases, the above progression of noun phrase types generally holds. For example, consider the references to *societies* in Text sample 2 and to *accumulations* in Text sample 3.

Text sample 2:

> *If aggression and violence are part and parcel of what it means to be human, then why is it that there exist **societies where aggressive or violent behaviour is conspicuous by its absence**? It was with such questions in mind that, in 1985, we invited a group of social anthropologists who had fieldwork experience in **societies which, for whatever reason, they described as "peaceful"** to attend an informal seminar to discuss the issues involved in interpreting **such societies**.* (ACAD)

Text sample 3:

> *At many fossil sites there are **great accumulations of small mammals**. **These** can tell us a great deal about past environments and climate during the time of their accumulation, but there are many ways by which **small mammal accumulations** occur in the natural world.* (ACAD)

In other cases, a simple noun or simple premodified noun phrase is repeated throughout a text because it is the accepted term for the entity being discussed. For example:

> ***Education** is recognized, in law, to be essential to life. No one will die from lack of **education** as he will from lack of food or basic health care. It seems that **education** is not even essential to happiness.* (ACAD†)

> *A prevalent, though completely erroneous, idea often held by students and laymen is that **theory** is synonymous with speculation. The mistaken view is that **theory** refers to ideas which have never been tested. This unfortunate way of thinking that **theory** is purely speculative leads to a division.* (ACAD)

The following illustrates referential chains with repeated premodified noun phrases (***elderly people*** and ***social workers***):

> *The aim of this book is to foster good social work practice with **elderly people** and their families. The first chapter sets out to clarify our understanding of **vulnerable elderly people** in relation to their families <...This book> is addressed primarily to **social workers** and social work aids. It is recognized that **old people** and their families are disadvantaged in the amount of care and attention paid to them by **social workers**. However, some of the disinterest of **social workers** reflects the inherent ageism in our society.* (ACAD)

Here there are two interwoven referential chains involving humans, so neither could be reduced to pronominal reference (they), following the expected pattern, without causing confusion.

## 8.2   **Structural types of premodification**

There are four major structural types of premodification in English:

- general adjective: **big** pillow, **new** trousers, **official** negotiations, **political** isolation
- *ed*-participial modifier: **restricted** area, **improved** growth, **fixed** volume, **established** tradition
- *ing*-participial modifier: **flashing** lights, **growing** problem, **exhausting** task
- noun: **staff** room, **pencil** case, **market** forces, **maturation** period.

In addition, determiners, genitives (or possessive nouns), and numerals serve to specify the reference of noun phrases; these features are described more fully in 4.4, 4.6, and 2.4.13.

A premodifier can usually be re-phrased as a postmodifier. For most adjectival and participial forms, this re-phrasing is straightforward, involving the use of a copular relative clause with a predicative adjective or a related verb phrase:

| | |
|---|---|
| *a big pillow* | a pillow which is big |
| *a restricted area* | an area which is restricted |
| *established tradition* | a tradition which has been established |
| *flashing lights* | lights which are flashing |

However, the re-phrasing of noun premodifiers is not at all straightforward, because noun + noun sequences can represent many different meaning relations, with no overt indication of which meaning is intended in any given case. For example, consider the range of meaning relations expressed by the following noun + noun sequences:

| | |
|---|---|
| *plastic trays* | trays made from plastic |
| *wash basins* | basins used for washing |
| *law report* | report about the law |
| *company management* | the management of a company |
| *commission sources* | sources in the commission |
| *elephant boy* | boy who resembles an elephant |

In fact such structures often represent more than one possible meaning relation. For example, *elephant boy* could also refer to a 'boy who rides on an elephant' or a 'boy who takes care of elephants'. In 8.3 we examine these and other meaning relations, having first discussed the dividing line between noun + noun sequences and noun compounds.

In summary, premodifiers differ from postmodifiers in two major ways: first, premodifiers are consistently more condensed than postmodifiers, using many fewer words (often a single word) to convey similar information; but second, premodifiers are much less explicit in identifying the meaning relationship that exists between the modifier and head noun. This reliance on implicit meaning relationships is most evident in the case of noun + noun sequences.

## 8.2.1 Structural types of premodification across registers

➤ Overall, noun phrases with premodifiers are three to four times more common in expository written registers than in conversation.
  ➤ Premodifiers are most common in news and academic prose.
➤ Common adjectives (i.e. non-participial adjectives) are the most common category of premodifier in all registers.
  ➤ Premodifying adjectives are extremely common in academic prose.
➤ Nouns are also very common as premodifiers, especially in news and academic prose.
  ➤ Nouns account for almost 40% of all premodifiers in news, and c. 30% of all premodifiers in academic prose.
➤ The other premodifier categories are relatively uncommon in comparison with adjectives and nouns.
  ➤ *ed*-participial modifiers are somewhat more common in academic prose than in the other registers.

**Figure 8.7**
**Frequency of premodifier types across registers**

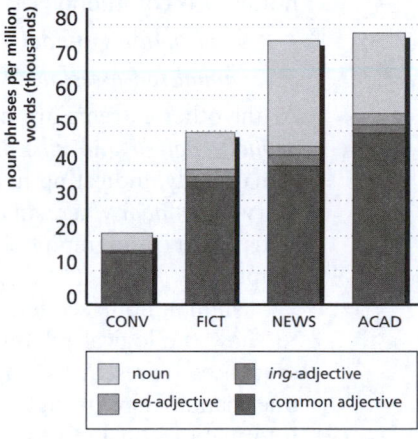

**DISCUSSION OF FINDINGS**

Adjectives are by far the most common type of noun premodifier. This undoubtedly relates to the fact that they come from many different semantic classes, including color, size/extent, time/age/frequency, and affective evaluation. (See Chapter 7 on the semantic categories and structural types of adjectives.)

Nouns are the second most common type of noun premodifier in all registers, occurring with particularly high frequencies in news and (to a lesser extent) academic prose. These constructions express a wide range of meaning-relationships in a succinct form, although the exact relationship is often not explicit. Apparently the great need for brevity in news favors this kind of premodification, even at the cost of less explicitness. In the following section, we survey the meaning relationships, expressed by noun + noun sequences.

## 8.3 Meaning relations expressed by noun + noun sequences

It is arguable that certain noun + noun sequences (e.g. *law report*) are more appropriately treated as noun compounds (4.8.2). However, the division between a noun compound and a sequence of noun modifier + noun head is in actuality a cline. Stress placement is one criterion for separation: initial stress, as in '*heart attack* (with the major stress on *heart*) is a characteristic of noun compounds. Stress on the second element, as in *glass 'bottle* (with the major stress on *bottle*), occurs with noun + noun sequences.

Orthography is also a strong indicator: at one extreme are compounds written as a single word, such as *seaweed* and *waterbed*, while hyphenated words such as *milk-yield* and *steam-hammer* have intermediate status. Hyphenated nouns also commonly serve as a premodifier of some other noun:

> *plum-pudding* **model**

> *annual soil-assessment* **competition**

At the other extreme are noun + noun sequences written as two words, such as *asphalt rooftop* and *silk necktie*, where the first noun functions as a modifier semantically, indicating in this case the substance from which something is made (cf. *wooden door* where an adjective performs this function). We have adopted the criterion of orthographic separation in identifying noun + noun sequences in this chapter.

Noun + noun sequences contain only content words, with no function words to show the logical relations between the two parts. As a result, noun + noun sequences represent two opposite extremes of communicative priorities. On the one hand, they bring about an extremely dense packaging of referential information; on the other hand, they result in an extreme reliance on implicit meaning, requiring addressees to infer the intended logical relationship between the modifying noun and head noun. In fact, noun + noun sequences are used to express a bewildering array of logical relations, including the following (where the head noun is labeled $N_2$ and the premodifying noun $N_1$):

- **Composition**: $N_2$ is made from $N_1$; $N_2$ consists of $N_1$, e.g. *glass windows* → windows made from glass: *word classes, protein granules, fact sheets, egg masses, metal seat, plastic beaker, zinc supplement, tomato sauce, satin dress, water supplies*

- **Purpose**: $N_2$ is for the purpose of $N_1$; $N_2$ is used for $N_1$, e.g. *pencil case* → case used for pencils: *safety device, search procedure, reference values, worship services, war fund, nursery program, extortion plan, chess board, radio station, brandy bottle, patrol car, Easter eggs, picnic ham, leg room*

- **Identity**: $N_2$ has the same referent as $N_1$ but classifies it in terms of different attributes, e.g. *women algebraists* → algebraists who are women: *conventionalist judge, men workers, consultant cardiologist, member country, exam papers, compression process, grant aid*

- **Content**: $N_2$ is about $N_1$; $N_2$ deals with $N_1$, e.g. *algebra text* → a text about algebra; *probability profile* → profile showing probability; *currency crisis* → crisis relating to currency: *sex magazines, market report, set theory, sports diary, prescription chart, success rates, credit agreement, intelligence bureau, explosives charges, interest group, speech impediment, color adjectives*

- **Source**: $N_2$ is from $N_1$, e.g. *irrigation water* → water that comes from irrigation: *crop yield, farmyard manure, plant residues, fault blocks, computer printout, Pentagon proposals, whale meat, press release, court messengers*

- **Objective Type 1**: $N_1$ is the object of the process described in $N_2$, or of the action performed by the agent described in $N_2$, e.g. *egg production* → X produces eggs: *waste disposal, paddy cultivation, root development, case study, water loss, taxi driver, child cruelty, curio sellers, corn farmer, computer users*

- **Objective Type 2**: $N_2$ is the object of the process described in $N_1$, e.g. *discharge water* → water that has been discharged: *substitute forms, pilot projects*
- **Subjective Type 1**: $N_1$ is the subject of the process described in $N_2$; $N_2$ is nominalized from an intransitive verb, e.g. *child development* → children develop: *leaf appearance, eye movement, management buy-out*
- **Subjective Type 2**: $N_2$ is the subject of the process described in $N_1$, e.g. *labor force* → a force that labors/is engaged in labor
- **Time**: $N_2$ is found at the time given by $N_1$: *summer conditions, Sunday school, Christmas raffle*
- **Location Type 1**: $N_2$ is found or takes place at the location given by $N_1$: *corner cupboard, roof slates, Paris conference, home areas, world literature, church square, surface traction, tunnel trains, thigh injury, heart attack, industry sources, administration officials*
- **Location Type 2**: $N_1$ is found at the location given by $N_2$, e.g. *notice board* → a board where notices are found: *job centre, sushi bar, staff room, theme park*
- **Institution**: $N_2$ identifies an institution for $N_1$, e.g. *insurance companies* → companies for (selling) insurance: *ski club, egg industry*
- **Partitive**: $N_2$ identifies parts of $N_1$: *cat legs, rifle butt, family member*
- **Specialization**: $N_1$ identifies an area of specialization for the person or occupation given in $N_2$; $N_2$ is animate, e.g. *finance director* → director who specializes in finance: *Education Secretary, gossip columnists, football fans, estate agent, management consultant.*

Some sequences can be analyzed as belonging to more than one category. For example, *heart attack* and *thigh injury* could be considered as Objective Type 1, in addition to Location Type 1.

In addition, there are numerous noun + noun sequences that do not fit neatly into any of the above categories. For example, the expression *riot police* might be understood as expressing a 'purpose' relationship, but there is an additional component of meaning: these are police used to control riots, not simply police for (creating) riots! Other noun + noun sequences express a range of meaning relations in addition to the above major categories:

| noun + noun | meaning |
|---|---|
| *computation times* | times required for computation |
| *voice communication* | communication using voice |
| *retail outlets* | outlets which sell retail  merchandise |
| *union assets* | assets belonging to a union |
| *media events* | events reported by the media |
| *confidence trick* | trick based on gaining one's confidence |
| *jet streams* | streams resembling jets |
| *bank holiday* | holiday observed by banks |
| *pressure hose* | hose able to withstand pressure |
| *pressure ratios* | ratios measuring pressure |

## 8.3.1 Noun + noun sequences across registers

A few premodifying nouns are extremely productive in their ability to combine with multiple head nouns. For example, the noun *family* as a premodifier is used with a wide range of head nouns representing many different kinds of semantic relations, including: *family affair, family argument, family background, family barbecue, family car, family company, family doctor, family entertainment, family friend*. There are large differences among the registers in their use of these extremely productive premodifying nouns. Figure 8.8 plots the number of premodifying nouns that are productive in combining with many head nouns, in each register. Two levels of productivity are distinguished: nouns that are used in more than 50 different noun + noun sequences, and nouns used in more than 100 different noun + noun sequences.

**CORPUS FINDINGS ²**

➤ News has by far the greatest number of premodifying nouns that are productive in combining with many head nouns.
  ➤ Academic prose also has many productive premodifying nouns.
➤ The productivity of a premodifying noun does not necessarily correspond to frequency.
➤ In news:
  ➤ Only four premodifying nouns are both extremely productive (combining with more than 100 different head nouns) and extremely frequent (occurring as a noun modifier over 100 times per million words): *government, police, home, world.*
  ➤ The premodifiers *government* and *police* actually combine with more than 200 different head nouns.
➤ 12 premodifying nouns are extremely productive (more than 100 combinations) and relatively frequent (over 50 occurrences as a noun modifier per million words): *business, car, city, council, family, health, labor, market, party, record, security, TV.*
  ➤ The premodifier *family* combines with more than 200 different head nouns.
➤ An additional 11 premodifying nouns are extremely productive (combining with more than 100 different head nouns) but relatively rare (occurring as a noun modifier less than 50 times per million words): *cash, club, community, computer, drug, food, future, safety, school, state, tax, water.*
➤ c. 150 additional premodifying nouns are relatively productive (more than 50 combinations); most of these occur as a noun modifier less than 50 times per million words and can be grouped into one of a few major semantic domains. For example:

> **business**: *bank, company, consumer, insurance, management, price, trade*
> **the media**: *film, media, newspaper, press, telephone, television*
> **other institutions**: *church, county, court, hospital, office, prison*
> **sports**: *football, soccer, sports, star, team*

**Figure 8.8**

**Productivity of premodifying nouns**

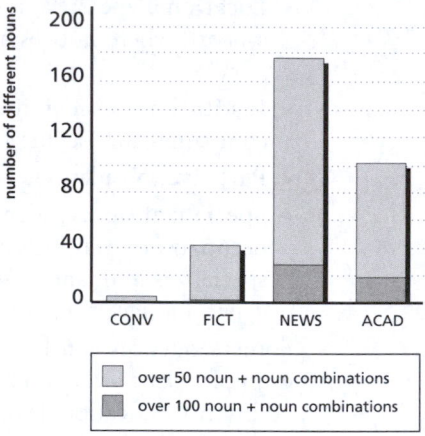

number of different nouns

| | over 50 noun + noun combinations |
| | over 100 noun + noun combinations |

> **conflict:** *army, defence, terrorist, war*
> **time:** *day, holiday, morning, night, summer, weekend*
> **people:** *baby, child, fellow*
> **health concerns:** *cancer, death, emergency.*

➤ Academic prose also has numerous productive premodifying nouns:
  ➤ 18 premodifying nouns are extremely productive (more than 100 combinations); most of these are relatively frequent (over 50 occurrences as a noun modifier per million words): *cell, class, community, computer, family, government, group, information, language, library, research, school, state, surface, system, test, time, work.*
  ➤ About 85 additional premodifying nouns are relatively productive (more than 50 combinations); for example: *acid, case, blood, classroom, farm, health, labor, population, root, student, term, unit, user, welfare.*
➤ Conversation represents the opposite extreme to news, with only four premodifying nouns that are relatively productive (more than 50 combinations): *car, Christmas, school, water.*

### DISCUSSION OF FINDINGS

Some nouns are particularly productive as nominal premodifiers. Several relate to major institutions, especially government, business, and the media, which are central concerns of news. For example:

> **government** + *action, agencies, approval, bonds, control, decision*
> **business** + *administration, cards, community, dealings, empire, ideas*
> **TV** + *ads, appearance, cameras, channel, crew, documentary, licence*

In conversation, only four nouns are notably productive as noun premodifiers. Typical combinations with these nouns reflect the everyday topics of conversation:

> **car** + *accident, door, insurance, keys, park, seat, wash*
> **Christmas** + *cake, card, day, decorations, list, presents, tree*
> **school** + *book, children, clothes, fees, holidays, trips*
> **water** + *balloon, bottle, fight, leak, line, pressure, pump, rates*

The premodifiers *school* and *water* are also extremely productive in news, although the most common combinations are different from those found in conversation, having characteristically a more institutional focus:

> **school** + *activities, boards, budget, care, leavers, pupils, work*
> **water** + *authorities, bill, companies, industry, levels, privatisation*

Overall, the extremely productive use of nouns as premodifiers in news results in a very dense, integrated packaging of information. The frequent use of these forms might be motivated in part by space-saving considerations, since a single noun + noun sequence typically conveys a complex meaning in condensed form. However, as already noted, the dense use of these forms places a heavy burden on readers, who must infer the intended logical relationship between the modifying noun and head noun (as described in the last section). It is probably for this reason that news relies primarily on premodifying nouns from those semantic domains most commonly associated with current events (such as government, business, education, the media, and sports). These are areas where news writers can reasonably expect readers to have well-developed pragmatic knowledge, and so be able to decode noun + noun relationships without too much difficulty.

## 8.3.2 Plural nouns as premodifiers

Plural nouns can occur as premodifiers, such as **carpets** *retailer*, **cities** *correspondent*, **drugs** *business*, **trades** *union*, **residents** *association*.

> **CORPUS FINDINGS** [1,2]

➤ Plural nouns have a much more restricted distribution than singular nouns as premodifiers.

➤ Plural premodifying nouns are much more common in news than the other registers.
  - ➤ In conversation and fiction, only one premodifying plural noun combines with more than 20 different head nouns: *police*.
  - ➤ In academic prose, only two premodifying plural nouns combine with more than 20 different head nouns: *police*, *women*.
  - ➤ In contrast, news has numerous productive premodifying plural nouns.

➤ Plural premodifying nouns are more productive in BrE than AmE. This difference is most evident in news.
  - ➤ Many of the most productive plural nouns (combining with more than 20 different head nouns) are common in both BrE and AmE: *appeals, arms, arts, cattle, communications, customs, personnel, police, sales, savings, securities, sports, rights, systems, telecommunications, women*. For example:

    **arms** + *race, scandal, supplier, treaty*

    **arts** + *center, editor, festival, society*

    **sales** + *force, gain, increases, tax*

    **savings** + *account, banks, deposits, institutions*

    **women** + *candidates, drivers, ministers, voters*

  - ➤ Four other plural nouns are notably productive in BrE but rarely occur in AmE news: *drugs, games, jobs, schools*. For example:

    **drugs** + *administration, ban, business, companies, problem, trade*

    **games** + *room, show*

    **jobs** + *crisis, losses, market*

    **schools** + *athletics, football, programmes*

  - ➤ Numerous other pre-modifying plural nouns are moderately productive in BrE news (combining with at least five different head nouns). Some of these are also moderately productive in AmE news: *antiques, awards, chemicals, drinks, firearms, girls, boys, kids, ladies, mergers, payments, points, singles, stores*. For example: *antiques dealer, chemicals division, drinks menu, points scheme, singles title*

  - ➤ However, many of these moderately productive pre-modifying nouns are rarely, if ever, used in AmE: *animals, borders, careers, clothes, complaints, courts, highways, parents, pensions, profits, roads, students, talks, wages*. For example: *animals shelter, borders police, careers office, courts correspondent, highways department, pensions schemes, profits growth, roads budget, students president, talks proposals, wages council*.

➤ There are also certain head nouns that commonly occur with plural premodifying nouns. Most often these head nouns denote a person's job or occupation, or a unit or organization connected with a particular type of activity.

➤ Head nouns that commonly take a plural pre-modifying noun, referring to a person's job or occupation: *adviser, agent, analyst, assistant, clerk, commissioner, director, engineer, manager, officer, official, operator, specialist*. For example: *corporate affairs director, operations director, public relations director, technical services director.*

➤ Head nouns that commonly take a plural premodifying noun, referring to a unit or organization: *court, tribunal; board, commission, committee, panel; business, market; department, division, group, section, sector; affiliate, company, firm, giant, manufacturer, supplier*. For example: *boilers and radiators division, building properties division, construction materials division, inns and taverns division.*

### DISCUSSION OF FINDINGS

In news reportage, nouns abound and there is often complex premodification. Noun phrases are suited to the main purpose of news reportage: to convey a maximum of information as concisely as possible. The high frequency of plural first-elements in noun + noun constructions fits into this general pattern.

Complex premodification can accommodate a great deal of information, but with the risk that the compression might create problems of interpretation. The plural ending can serve as a signal to guide the reader in unraveling the structure of a complex noun phrase. It is no coincidence that these structures are especially associated with complex first-elements (see B below).

Apart from this general consideration, there are five specific factors which seem to influence the retention of the plural form of premodifying nouns:

**A The noun modifier only has a plural form or has a distinctive meaning associated with its plural (see 4.5.5)**

Examples of this type are:

> *arms accord, arts administrator, customs officer, explosives factory*

However, some nouns which ordinarily have only a plural form do sometimes lose the plural ending in noun + noun constructions:

> *billiard ball, scissor kick, trouser leg*

**B The noun modifier is itself complex**

Where there is a complex first element as noun pre-modifier (rather than a simple first noun), the tendency towards keeping the plural ending increases:

> *At Tesco's you've got fifty feet of **baked beans** shelves.* (CONV†)
>
> *Growth-hungry **pubs and hotels** group Greenalls has wrestled a tiny profits improvement out of a difficult year.* (NEWS)
>
> *Airline boss Richard Branson is on the verge of victory after claiming a "**dirty tricks**" campaign had been waged against Virgin Atlantic.* (NEWS)
>
> *A bit more will be said of particular features of the metalinguistic and **possible-worlds** proposals.* (ACAD†)

The motivation for the use of the plural form in these sequences is that it provides a clear signal of the structure of a complex noun phrase.

In addition, some plural nouns, such as *affairs, relations, resources, rights, services, skills, standards,* and *systems,* are almost always premodified themselves, and thus they retain the plural form when used in pre-modification:

> *the State Department's* **consular affairs** *bureau* (NEWS)
>
> *Labour's chief* **foreign affairs** *spokesman* (NEWS)
>
> *the* **customer relations** *department* (CONV)
>
> *the Senate* **Foreign Relations** *Committee* (NEWS)

**C   The noun modifier or the whole noun phrase is a proper name**

Constructions with plural first-elements frequently appear in names:

> *He had his house painted by the FBI* **Exhibits** *Section.* (NEWS†)
>
> *Post Office chief executive Bill Cockburn said 15,000 jobs will be lost in the Royal Mail and another 1,200 from its* **Counters** *division.* (NEWS)

In some cases, it is not clear whether the second-noun is part of the name or not; thus note that *division* is not capitalized in the second example. If the name is limited to the first-element and does not include the second-noun, we naturally expect a plural form, as names do not generally change with syntactic context.

**D   The noun modifier is quoted speech**

A plural first-element can be used as a quotation which is not to be changed. Sometimes we find quotation marks explicitly inserted in the text:

> *Toyota's* **"terms"** *scheme sums up what the manufacturers say they are offering.* (NEWS†)
>
> *The "input" group would probably come from the junior staff working on existing clerical procedures, the* **"operations"** *group would comprise the present machine operators.* (ACAD†)

In other cases, quotation is indicated by an initial capital; the reference in the following example is to a section headed 'Remarks' in a book on biology:

> *O. bacata is distinguished from O. pachaphylax under the* **Remarks** *section of that species.* (ACAD)

**E   The noun phrase is part of a news headline**

Plural first-elements are common in newspaper headlines:

> *Armagh* **car-parts** *theft* <discussing a robbery of car parts>
>
> **Homes** *plan* <discussing a plan to build houses>
>
> **Shares** *probe* <discussing a rise in the price of stockmarket shares>
>
> **Rules** *change on pets likely* <discussing a change in rules>

The use of plural first-elements clearly has to do with the main purpose of headlines: to compress information as succinctly as possible. Headlines are concise, context-bound expressions, whose exact interpretation is dependent upon the following text. They go further than other types of texts in allowing plural first-elements. Thus many noun + noun constructions with plural first-elements are recorded only in headlines.

## 8.4   Noun phrases with multiple premodifiers

Many noun phrases have two-word premodification, and noun phrases with longer sequences of premodifiers also occur:

two-word premodification:

> ***funny whistling*** *noises*
> ***quite pale*** *skin*
> ***settled legal*** *practice*
> *the two* ***mutually perpendicular*** *directions*

three-word premodification:

> ***genuine, nonstrategic legal*** *rights*
> *the* ***greatest British theoretical*** *physicist*
> ***high sulphur soil*** *areas*

four-word premodification:

> ***very finely grained alluvial*** *material*
> *the* ***formerly self-sufficient rural feudal*** *economy*
> ***naked, shameless, direct, brutal*** *exploitation*
> *a* ***totally covered, uninsulated pig*** *house*
> *an* ***unusually thick naturally-colored*** *cardigan*

## 8.4.1    Length of sequences of premodifiers

**CORPUS FINDINGS** [2,3]

➤ Premodifiers generally are most common in written expository registers; they are relatively rare in conversation.

➤ However, all four registers are very similar in their proportional use of premodification by length:

> ➤ 70–80% of premodified noun phrases have only a single premodifier.
> ➤ About 20% of premodified noun phrases have two-word premodification.
> ➤ Only about 2% of premodified noun phrases have three- or four-word premodification.

➤ In news, longer premodifier sequences are slightly more common.

**Figure 8.9**
**Distribution of premodification by length**

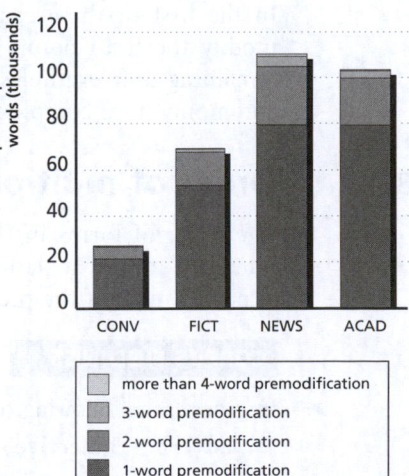

**DISCUSSION OF FINDINGS**

The use of multiple premodifiers is certainly very efficient, packing dense informational content into as few words as possible (when compared with the use of postmodifiers or separate clauses). However, the use of multiple premodifiers places a heavy burden on readers and listeners, since the logical relations among constituents must be inferred.

    In fact, it is rare for all the multiple words in a premodification sequence to modify the head noun directly; rather, premodifier sequences usually have embedded relations, with some words modifying other premodifiers instead of the head noun. In a few cases, the meaning relations among constituents are truly ambiguous. For example, out of context, the noun phrase *two more practical principles* has two distinct interpretations:

>*[two more] [practical] principles*
>
>'two additional principles that are practical'
>
>*two [[more] practical] principles*
>
>'two principles that are more practical'

Most noun phrases are not ambiguous. However, many different structural/ logical relations are possible, and in each case the reader must infer the intended meaning. For example, consider the contrasting relations among constituents in the following noun phrases with three-word premodification:

>*the [[one-time prosperous] [[market] town]]*
>
>*the [[controversial] [offshore investment] portfolios]*

The number of possible logical relationships increases dramatically with each additional premodifier. Thus, noun phrases with four-word premodification can manifest any of a large number of logical relations among constitutents. Each of the five noun phrases with four-word premodification given below represents a different set of logical relations:

>$[_a[_{b1}naked_{b1}]$, $[_{b2}shameless_{b2}]$, $[_{b3}direct_{b3}]$, $[_{b4}brutal_{b4}]$ $exploitation_a]$
>
>$[_a[_{b1}$ very $[_c finely\ grained_c]_{b1}]$ $[_{b2}alluvial_{b2}]$ $material_a]$
>
>the $[_a[_{b1}formerly\ self\text{-}sufficient_{b1}]$ $[_{b2}rural_{b2}]$ $[_{b3}feudal_{b3}]$ $economy_a]$
>
>a $[_a[_{b1}totally\ covered_{b1}]$, $[_2uninsulated_{b2}]$ $[[_c pig_c]$ $house]_a]$
>
>an $[_a[_{b1}unusually\ thick_{b1}]$ $[_{b2}naturally\text{-}colored_{b2}]$ $cardigan_a]$

In the first of these examples, all four words in the premodification directly modify the head noun. This type of structuring is very rare, however. As the remaining four examples illustrate, multiple words in the premodification more commonly have complex logical/structural relations among themselves.

## 8.4.2 Order of multiple premodifiers

The order of forms in the premodification is dictated in the first place by the intended meaning. However, the order is also strongly influenced by the structural type of the premodifiers.

**CORPUS FINDINGS [2,3]**

➤ In general, the following order of premodifiers is preferred:

>**adverb + adjective + color adjective + participle + noun + head noun**

Table 8.5 shows the percentage of occurrences for pairs of premodifiers in the predicted order. (For example, when a noun phrase has both an adverb and an adjective, the order adverb + adjective + head noun occurs in over 95% of all instances, while the order adjective + adverb + head noun occurs less than 5% of the time.)

➤ The pair-wise ordering tendencies are not equally strong.
>➤ The pattern is most closely followed by adverbs.
>➤ The pattern is least consistently adhered to by participles in sequence with adjectives or noun premodifiers.

**Table 8.5**      **Percentage of occurrences for pairs of premodifiers**

| Adv + Adj + color Adj + participle + N + head N | | | | | | percentage use of order |
|---|---|---|---|---|---|---|
| Adv + Adj | | | | | + head N | > 95 |
| Adv | | | + participle | | + head N | > 95 |
| | Adj + color Adj | | | | + head N | > 85 |
| | Adj | | participle | | + head N | > 65 |
| | Adj | | | + N | + head N | > 85 |
| | | color Adj + participle | | | + head N | > 60 |
| | | color Adj | | + N | + head N | > 80 |
| | | | participle | + N | + head N | > 55 |

DISCUSSION OF FINDINGS

Although there are no absolute rules governing the order of premodifiers, there are many strong tendencies. First, there is an overall tendency for the most noun-like modifiers to occur closest to the head noun. Thus, nouns tend to occur closer to the head than participial modifiers or adjectives. This structural tendency has a semantic correlate: positions closest to the head noun will be filled by modifiers describing attributes that are more integral to the identification, classification, or description of the head noun referent. The following noun phrases illustrate both of these tendencies.

Adjective + noun + head:

> *mature rice grain, spontaneous mutation rate,*
> *thick winter overcoat, true life stories*
> *bright canvas bags*

Color adjective + noun + head:

> *black plastic sheet, black leather jacket,*
> *red address book*

Participial modifier + noun + head:

> *increased disease incidence, an experienced woman worker, broken bicycle*
> *wheels, a limiting diffusion factor, an increasing mortgage burden*

In general, participial modifiers tend to occur closer to the head noun than adjectives:

Adjective + participial modifier + head:

> *considerable fertilizing value, traditional feeding programs, rare shopping trips,*
> *ancient stuffed armchair*

However, the order participial modifier + adjective + head noun is also relatively common:

> *increased nutritional support, the estimated average magnitude, concerned*
> *local authorities, breathtaking natural beauty*

In part this variation is due to the fact that *ing*-participles can range from being more adjective-like to more noun-like (2.3.6), both in meaning and grammatical characteristics. The latter will be more prone to occur nearer the head, in the same way as ordinary premodifying nouns (see *shopping* and *feeding* in the examples above).

In other cases, the observed ordering preferences reflect embedded modification, with forms modifying other premodifiers rather than directly modifying the head noun. For example, adverbs regularly modify a following adjective or participial modifier, resulting in their strong ordering preference:

Adverb + adjective + head noun

> a *[really hot]* day, a *[quite big]* man, a *[rather blunt]* penknife, a *[thoroughly satisfactory]* reply

Adverb + participial modifier + head noun

> these *[fully grown]* men, *[generally accepted]* principles, an *[extremely varied]* and *[immensely pleasing]* exhibition

Some sequences like these, especially adverb + participle, are hyphenated and so qualify as compound adjectives (7.9.3).

The order noun + participial modifier + head noun is a special case of embedded modification. As shown above, premodifying nouns generally have a stronger structural and semantic association with the head noun than participial modifiers, and thus they tend to occur closest to the head. However, when a premodifying noun modifies a participial modifier (rather than the head noun), it tends to precede that participial modifier, which then occurs closest to the head noun. In the first two examples below, the noun + participle combination expresses a semantic object + verb relation:

Noun + participial modifier + head noun:

> *[information processing]* activities, *[hypothesis testing]* process, *[barrier bred]* animals

In most cases, this kind of sequence of premodifiers is hyphenated, reflecting the separate constituency of the noun + participle combination, which as a whole premodifies the head noun. In fact, such sequences can be considered as adjectival compounds (7.9.3):

> *English-speaking world, stomach-turning trepidation,*
> *self-fulfilling prophecy, class-based categorizations, tree-lined avenues,*
> *egg-shaped ball*

Finally, the ordering of color adjectives following other adjectives deserves special mention. Although this ordering does not follow from any of the above general factors, it does represent a strong ordering tendency (occurring over 85 percent of the time):

Adjective + color adjective + head noun:

> *dry white grass, clear blue eyes, shabby black clothes.*

## 8.4.3 Coordinated premodifiers

The preceding sections have described how sequences of words in the premodification can represent a large number of different structural/logical relations, with forms often modifying other premodifiers instead of the head noun. As a result, there is much structural indeterminacy, leading to the possibility of incorrect interpretations. One way to reduce this indeterminacy, while retaining the dense packaging of information found with premodifiers, is to use coordinated premodifiers. This construction makes the logical relations among premodifiers explicit, with each one directly modifying the head noun:

> *black and white cat*
>
> *hot and hardening mud*
>
> *arrogant and unattractive man*
>
> *physical and sexual abuse*

## CORPUS FINDINGS [2]

➤ *And*-coordinated adjectives—adjective *and* adjective—are very common only in academic prose.
  ➤ *And*-coordinated adjectives are extremely rare in conversation.
  ➤ Surprisingly, *and*-coordinated adjectives are also relatively rare in news, making news very different from academic prose in this regard.
➤ *Or*-coordinated adjectives—adjective *or* adjective—are much less common than *and*-coordinated adjectives.
  ➤ They are moderately common in academic prose, but rare in the other registers.

### Figure 8.10
**Frequency of coordinated premodifiers across registers**

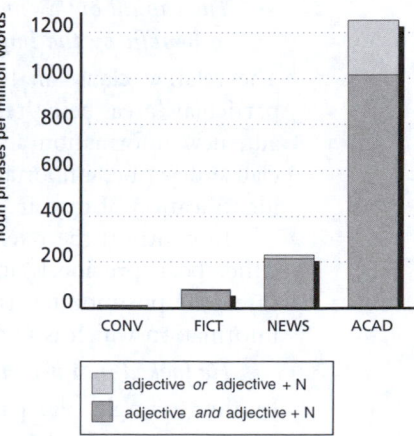

## DISCUSSION OF FINDINGS

In the majority of cases, premodifiers coordinated with *and* in academic prose are used to identify two distinct attributes that are qualities of a single referent:

> *unskilled and disposable workforce*
>
> *strict and systematic discipline*
>
> *complex and technical legislation*
>
> *precise and effective solutions*
>
> *pleasing and efficient surroundings*

However, with plural and uncountable heads, *and*-coordinated premodifiers are also commonly used to identify two different (mutually exclusive) referents, such as:

> *spoken and written styles*
>
> *male and female workers*
>
> *British and American spelling*

*Or*-coordinated premodifiers can also have two interpretations. In some cases, either one, or both, of the two attributes can be applied to a given referent:

> *racial or religious cohesion*
>
> *familiar or preplanned activities*

In other cases, though, the coordinator connects two attributes that are mutually exclusive, so that only one can characterize a given referent:

> *dead or dying larvae*
>
> *petroleum or coal-based hydrocarbon matrices*

On the limitations of what can be coordinated in this way, see 2.3.6B.

## 8.5    Restrictive v. non-restrictive postmodifiers

Postmodifiers are used with one of two main functions: **restrictive** or **non-restrictive** modification. Restrictive postmodifiers serve to identify the intended reference of the head noun:

> *The capital outlay may not be justified by the area* **which may be expected to benefit by the improvement**. (ACAD)

The relative clause in this sentence has a restrictive function, identifying the particular 'area' being referred to. In many cases, restrictive relative clauses also add new information about the head noun; thus, in this example, the relative clause describes important characteristics of the area, in addition to providing identification of that area.

In contrast, the reference of head nouns with non-restrictive modifiers has either been previously identified or is assumed to be already known. In these cases, the postmodifier is an independent unit that adds elaborating, descriptive information which is not required to identify the head:

> *He looked into her mailbox,* **which she never locked**. (FICT)

In this example, the particular mailbox intended is clearly identified by the possessive pronoun *her*, and the non-restrictive relative clause is used to provide additional, descriptive information (about the mailbox never being locked).

In writing, non-restrictive postmodifiers are usually separated from the head noun by a comma, while no punctuation is used with a restrictive postmodifier. However, with indefinite noun heads, there is little if any difference in meaning dependent on the use of a comma. Compare:

> *I caught a bus in the square* **which just happened to have Collioure on the front**. (FICT)
>
> v.   *I caught a bus in the square,* **which just happened to have Collioure on the front**.

In spoken language, where there are no punctuation marks, intonation and pauses serve many of the same functions. However, without the aid of a prosodic transcription, it is very difficult to determine whether a restrictive or non-restrictive sense was intended. (In fact, this distinction is notoriously difficult to make even with the aid of prosody.) For example, either of the two *wh*-relative clauses in the following utterance could easily be interpreted with restrictive or non-restrictive meaning:

> *And there's another one on the market* **which I can't remember the name of which costs a lot more**. (CONV)

Due to the difficulties in classifying indeterminate cases, there is no way to study the distribution of restrictive and non-restrictive postmodifiers directly. However, postmodifiers separated from the head noun with a comma (or other punctuation such as dashes or parentheses) can easily be distinguished from those with no punctuation. Therefore, the following sections use punctuation-separation as a working definition of non-restrictive postmodifiers. Because our spoken corpus is not annotated for prosodic features, we do not attempt to distinguish between restrictive and non-restrictive postmodifiers in conversation. Further, we compare only restrictive v. non-restrictive relative clauses (although other structural types are discussed in 8.6; for the same distinction in premodification see 8.1.2D).

## 8.5.1 Distribution of restrictive v. non-restrictive relative clauses

**CORPUS FINDINGS [2]**

➤ Overall, restrictive relative clauses are much more common than non-restrictive clauses (marked by a comma) in all written registers.
➤ However, the relative proportion of the two types varies somewhat by register:
  ➤ Non-restrictive relative clauses make up only about 15% of all relative clauses in fiction and academic prose;
  ➤ Non-restrictive relative clauses make up about 30% of all relative clauses in news.

**DISCUSSION OF FINDINGS**

Post-nominal modifiers are usually used to help identify the reference of the head noun (restrictive), rather than for elaborating functions (non-restrictive). The information added by non-restrictive clauses is often tangential to the main point of the text (in addition to being non-essential for the identification of the head noun). This is especially the case in news, where non-restrictive clauses are used to add information of potential interest but not directly related to the news story. For example, consider the following concluding sentences from a financial news article about negotiations for the sale of the firm Whyte & Mackay by the company Brent Walker:

> *Brent Walker said it expected the buyout negotiations "would be successfully completed shortly."*
> *Brent Walker bought Whyte & Mackay from Lonrho earlier this year for £180m in a deal that included four French vineyards, **which are also for sale for as much as £60m**.* (NEWS)

In this excerpt, the fact that the four French vineyards are for sale does not help the reader identify the reference of the vineyards, and it is not really relevant at all for the story being reported here. Instead, this is a tacked-on piece of information that might be of interest to some readers.

Similar uses of non-restrictive relative clauses are also common in news when the head is a proper noun:

Figure 8.11

**Frequency of restrictive v. non-restrictive relative clauses across registers**

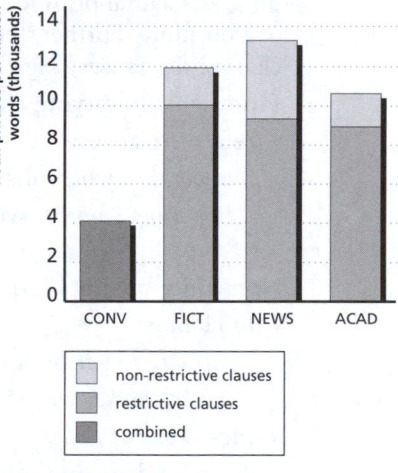

*Richards,* **who did not attend yesterday's badly disrupted squad session at the Stoop,** *is to have dye injected into his injured shoulder to show up the extent of the damage.* (NEWS)

In constructions of this type, the identity of the head noun is well-known to readers, and the non-restrictive relative clause is used to add newsworthy but often incidental information about that referent. This pattern is moderately common in news, resulting in a proportionally greater use of non-restrictive modifiers in that register.

## 8.6 Major structural types of postmodification

There are several different types of postmodifier, including both clauses and phrases. Clausal postmodifiers can be either finite, referred to as **relative clauses**, or non-finite. Further, there are three different types of non-finite postmodifying clauses: *to*-**clauses**, *ing*-**clauses**, and *ed*-**clauses** (3.12.1–3):

**Finite postmodifying clauses**

- **relative clauses:**

    *a footpath* **which disappeared in a landscape of fields and trees** (FICT)

    *beginning students* **who have had no previous college science courses** (ACAD)

**Non-finite postmodifying clauses**

- *to*-**clauses:**

    *the way* **to get to our house** (CONV)

    *one of the key contenders* **to mount a rescue bid for Ferranti** (NEWS)

- *ing*-**clauses:**

    *rebels* **advancing rapidly southwards** (NEWS)

    *a structure* **consisting of independent tetrahedra** (ACAD)

- *ed*-**clauses:**

    *fury* **fanned by insensitive press coverage** (NEWS)

    *products* **required to support a huge and growing population** (ACAD)

**Noun complement clauses**, which differ both structurally and semantically from other postmodifying clauses, are dealt with in 8.12–14.

**Prepositional phrases** are the main type of non-clausal postmodifier.

**Prepositional phrase as postmodifier:**

   *a phone* **with a couple of buttons on it** (CONV)

   *evidence* **for a second victory by Jenny Pitman in the Grand National** (NEWS) \<headline\>

In addition, three less-common types of phrase are used as postmodifiers: adverb (phrase), adjective (phrase), and emphatic reflexive pronoun in apposition. (For more on adjective and adverb phrases as postmodifiers, see 7.6.1, 7.13.3; for emphatic reflexives, see 4.12.2.)

**Adverb (phrase):**

   *He was just trapped in there with apparently no way* **out**. (NEWS)

   *Grace and Cordelia and Carol are up ahead, I am a block* **behind**. (FICT)

**Adjective (phrase):**

> President Bush will reiterate he wants a smooth transition and will cooperate in any way **possible**. (NEWS)

> The extremely short duration varieties **common in India** were not used in West Africa. (ACAD†)

**Reflexive pronoun:**

> He **himself** paid two fruitless visits to the site of a camp near Torzhok. (NEWS)

> The airlines **themselves** will next week step up their recruitment drive. (NEWS†)

Although the majority of postmodifying structures are restrictive (see Figure 8.11 in 8.5.1), most of these structural types of postmodifier can occur with non-restrictive as well as restrictive functions.

**Non-restrictive relative clauses:**

> The goat, **which had slid about during the transfer**, regarded him with bright-eyed perspicacity. (FICT)

> Davis, **who won the world title for the sixth time in May**, decided not to compete. (NEWS†)

**Non-restrictive *ed*-clauses:**

> A converted farm building, **donated by Mr. and Mrs. Tabor**, has been turned into a study room filled with photographs and displays. (NEWS)

> The distinction between public and private law, **espoused in many pluralist accounts**, is largely bogus. (ACAD)

**Non-restrictive *ing*-clauses:**

> Both writing and reading are enormously complex skills, **involving the coordination of sensory and cognitive processes**. (ACAD)

> Style variation is intrinsic to the novel's satiric-epic picture of Victorian urban society, **concentrating on the capitalist house of Dombey**. (ACAD)

**Non-restrictive prepositional phrases:**

> The great tall library, **with the Book of Kells and of Robert Emmet**, charmed him. (FICT)

> The sale, **for a sum not thought to be material**, marks the final dismemberment of Metro-Cammell Weymann. (NEWS)

> Certain of the soils on the east derived from limestones and schists, **with mixed sandstones and shales**, are alkaline in reaction and poor in nitrogen. (ACAD)

Finally, there is one other type of postmodifier that is almost always non-restrictive in function: the **appositive noun phrase** (see 8.10):

> The rebels, **the Tigrayan People's Liberation Front** (TPLF) (NEWS)

> a Soviet Deputy Defence Minister, **General Varrenikov** (NEWS)

> both types of eggs (**diapause and non-diapause**) (ACAD)

## 8.6.1 Postmodifier types across registers

➤ Prepositional phrases are by far the most common type of postmodification in all registers (see Figure 8.12).

   ➤ The frequency of prepositional phrases as postmodifiers forms a scale: relatively rare in conversation to extremely common in academic prose.

   ➤ At the same time, the proportion of prepositional phrases is fairly constant: prepositional phrases make up 65–80% of all postmodifiers in all registers.

➤ There is more variability among the other postmodification types (see Figure 8.13):

   ➤ Most postmodifiers are generally rare in conversation.

   ➤ Relative clauses are relatively frequent in all three written registers.

   ➤ Proportionally, they are most common in fiction (c. 70% of all non-prepositional postmodifiers).

   ➤ *Ing*-clauses are moderately common in all three written registers (10–15% of all non-prepositional postmodifiers): *ing*-clauses are most frequent in academic prose.

   ➤ *Ed*-clauses and appositive noun phrases are considerably more common in written non-fiction than in the other registers: *ed*-clauses are more common in academic prose than in any other register (both in terms of frequency and proportionally).

➤ Appositive noun phrases are frequent in both academic prose and news.

➤ *To*-clauses are relatively rare in all registers.

**Figure 8.12**

**Prepositional v. other postmodification across registers**

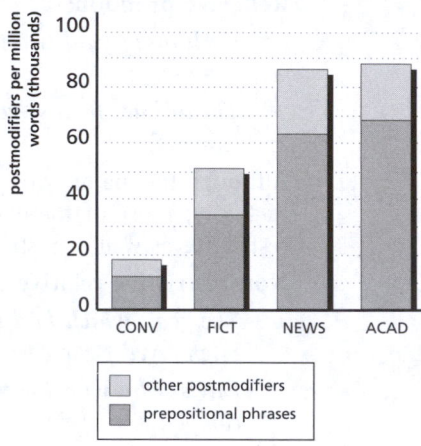

**Figure 8.13**

**Non-prepositional postmodifier types across registers**

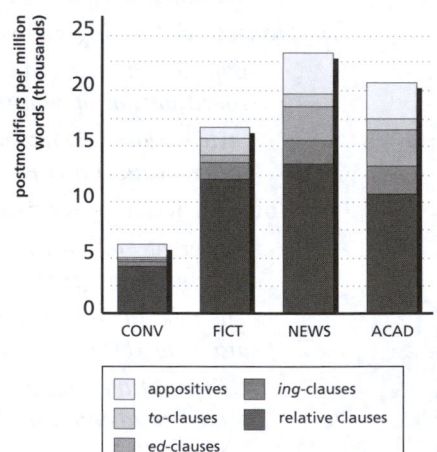

Postmodifiers are generally rare in conversation. Further, when they are used in this register, they often have a special grammatical function not seen in the written registers: they can occur outside the regular clause structure, modifying a dislocated noun phrase (see 3.4.3–4) and clarifying the reference of some nearby pronoun. For example (with the relevant noun phrases and co-referential pronouns in *[]*):

Cos [Brenda, **whose horse I ride up at Bridley**]—I was telling [her] <...>
(CONV)

[That old boy **that I spoke to**], when his—[he] was with his daughter.
(CONV)

Like [this girl Tracy **that he got on with really well**], I mean I, I really
disliked [her], [this girl **that Claire knows**]. (CONV)

*To*-clauses as postmodifiers are exceptional in that they are proportionally more
common in conversation than in writing. They are frequently used with general
head nouns and have a future planning orientation:

Father's got a lot of things **to tell you**. (CONV)

I'll remember which way **to go**. (CONV)

There's just a lot **to think about**. (CONV)

At the opposite extreme from conversation, postmodifiers are extremely common
in academic prose. Prepositional phrases are the most common of these, often
occurring in extremely dense, embedded sequences. In the following text extract,
prepositions at the start of postmodifiers are underscored, while other
postmodifiers are marked by *[]*; the boundaries of unembedded noun phrases
are marked by *{}*.

{Mortality **among** stocks **of** eggs [stored outdoors in the ground]} averaged
70%; {eggs [collected the following spring from a large number **of** natural
habitats **in** the central part **of** the province]} suffered {a 46% reduction **in**
viability [which could only be attributed to this exposure **to** cold]}. {Further
evidence **of** the association **of** winter egg mortality **with** sub-zero temperatures
and snow cover} was reported by {Riegert (1967a)}. (ACAD)

In academic prose, prepositional phrases as postmodifiers allow a very dense
packaging of referential information in a text, typically characterizing non-human
entities in relation to other non-human entities. They are more compact than
clausal postmodifiers and commonly occur in sequences. The hierarchical
embedding relations found with such sequences are often complex. However, they
are less compact, and more explicit about the relationships involved, than
equivalent sequences of noun premodifiers (8.4).

Relative clauses differ from prepositional phrases as postmodifiers in both
their communicative characteristics and their register distribution. In fiction and
news, relative clauses are commonly used to identify or describe a person.

Relative clauses characterizing humans:

someone **whom I had never seen before** (FICT)

a man on the platform **whose looks I didn't like** (FICT)

a 20-year-old woman **who has been missing for a week** (NEWS)

When they are used to characterize inanimate objects, relative clauses commonly
do so by linking those objects to a person. Further, relative clauses in fiction and
news typically use dynamic verbs describing actions, in contrast to the static
presentation of information associated with prepositional phrases.

Relative clauses characterizing an inanimate head:

one of those mixed-up salads **which men will eat with complete docility in
restaurants** (FICT)

the boiling pot of gravy **which fell upon his foot** (FICT)

the 1988 event **which left her on the verge of a nervous breakdown** (NEWS)

The structural variations of relative clauses are dealt with in the subsections of 8.7. Other types of clausal postmodifier are generally less common, although postmodifying *ed*-clauses are relatively frequent in academic prose, corresponding to the common use of the passive voice in this register (8.8.1). Finally, appositive noun phrases are relatively common in both news and academic prose; the communicative characteristics of these constructions are described in 8.10.

## 8.7 Postmodification by finite relative clause

When discussing relative clauses, we will refer to three major components: the **head noun**, the **relativizer** (a relative pronoun or relative adverb), and the **gap**. The relativizer anaphorically refers to the same person or thing as the head noun, which is often also called the **antecedent** (3.11.3). One of the less-obvious defining characteristics of relative clauses is that they are always missing a constituent, which corresponds in meaning to the head noun. The structural location of this missing constituent is referred to as the 'gap'. Thus, in the relative clause construction

*the diamond earrings **that Mama wore***. (FICT)

The head noun phrase is *the diamond earrings*; the relative pronoun *that* refers to the earrings, and the gap occurs in the direct object position, after the verb *wore*. That is, the underlying meaning of the relative clause is that 'Mama wore the diamond earrings'.

There are numerous structural variants possible with relative clauses, and these are described in detail in the following sections. The most obvious of these involves the choice of relativizer (8.7.1), either a relative pronoun—*which, who, whom, whose,* and *that*—or a relative adverb—*where, when,* and *why*. The relative pronoun can sometimes be omitted altogether (the **zero relativizer**). Further, the gap can correspond to almost any clause element in the relative clause (8.7.2) while the head can function as any clause element in the matrix clause (8.7.3). Finally, relative clauses with adverbial gaps occur with a particularly wide range of variants; these are thus dealt with in a separate section (8.7.4).

## 8.7.1 The discourse choice among relativizers

In Standard English, relative clauses can be formed using eight different relativizers: *which, who, whom, whose, that, where, when,* and *why*:

*The lowest pressure ratio **which will give an acceptable performance** is always chosen.* (ACAD†)

*There are plenty of existing owners **who are already keen to make the move**.* (NEWS)

*There was a slight, furtive boy **whom no one knew**.* (FICT)

*It was good for the fans, **whose support so far this season has been fantastic**.* (NEWS)

*Well, that's the only way **that this can be** <...> **assessed**.* (CONV†)

*I could lead you to the shop **where I bought it**.* (FICT)

*He was born in another age, the age **when we played not for a million dollars in prize money**.* (NEWS)

> *There are many reasons **why we may wish to automate parts of the decision process**.* (ACAD)

In addition, the relativizer can be omitted with many relative clauses (referred to as the zero relativizer):

> *The next thing **she knows**, she's talking to Danny.* (CONV)

> *Gwen gave the little frowning smile **she used when she was putting something to someone**.* (FICT†)

To some extent the choice of relativizer is determined grammatically by the role of the gap in the relative clause. Thus, the pronoun *whom* and the zero relativizer (with rare exceptions) are used only with non-subject gaps; the pronoun *whose* is used only with possessive/genitive gaps; and the relative adverbs *where*, *when*, and *why* are used only with adverbial gaps. However, the choice among relativizers is influenced by a number of additional factors discussed in 8.7.1.2–9. These other factors include: register, restrictive v. non-restrictive function, and animate (human) v. non-animate head noun. In addition, non-standard dialects include other relativizers, which are briefly covered in the following section.

## 8.7.1.1 Variant relativizers in non-standard dialects

There is considerable dialect variation in the range of relativizers used in conversation. For example, the form *as* is sometimes used as a relativizer:

> *Well I know one person **as**'ll eat it.* (CONV)

The *wh*-word *what* is somewhat more common as a relativizer in BrE conversational texts, although it is much rarer than the standard forms *who*, *which*, and *that*:

> *And you see that truck **what just went by**.* (CONV)

> *Gotta make sure she's got the book **what I had last week**.* (CONV)

> *I'll get off to shop and get her the stuff **what she wants**.* (CONV)

> *You know that thing **what you fill up with liquid**.* (CONV)

> *We've got a bottle of apricot wine **what we've had for about twelve years**.* (CONV)

For the rest of this account we consider only the standard set of relativizers.

## 8.7.1.2 Distribution of relativizers across registers

There is a complex set of interrelated factors influencing the choice among relativizers, resulting in striking differences in their distributions. Later sections provide a detailed discussion of these factors, while the overall patterns are introduced here.

**CORPUS FINDINGS [2]**

➤ Three relativizers stand out as being particularly common: *who*, *which*, and *that*.
➤ The zero relativizer is moderately common.
➤ The remaining five—*whom*, *whose*, *where*, *when*, and *why*—are considerably less common.
  ➤ The relativizer *why* is particularly rare in all registers.
➤ The relativizers *which* and *that* are the most common overall, but they have notably different distributions across registers (see Figures 8.14–17):

Figure 8.14  **Frequency of relativizers in conversation**

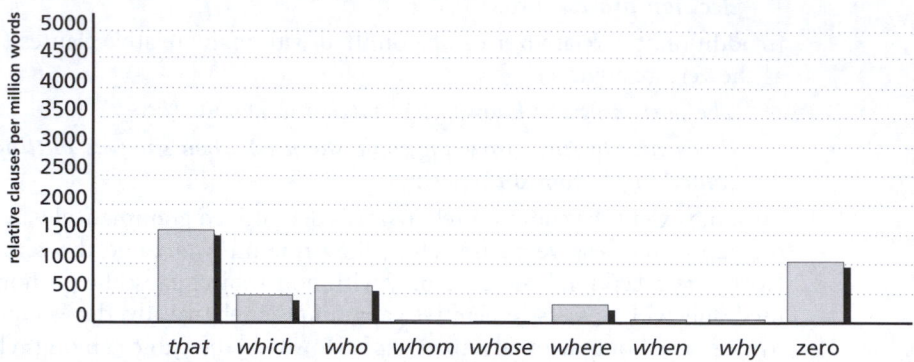

Figure 8.15  **Frequency of relativizers in fiction**

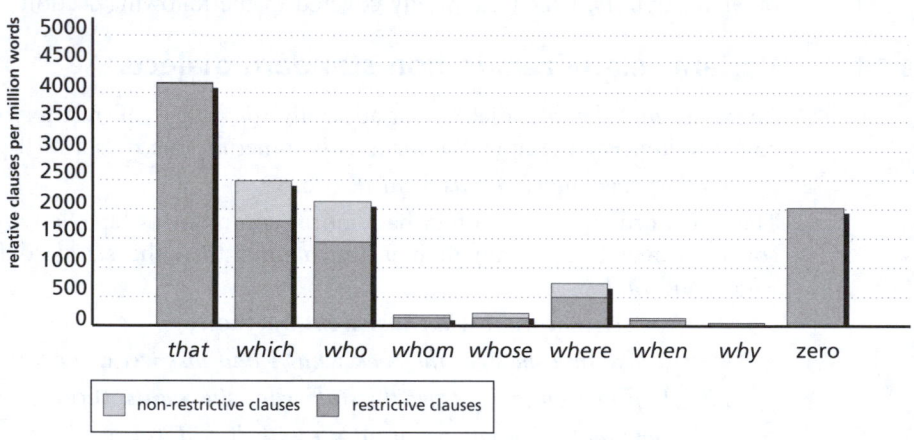

Figure 8.16  **Frequency of relativizers in news**

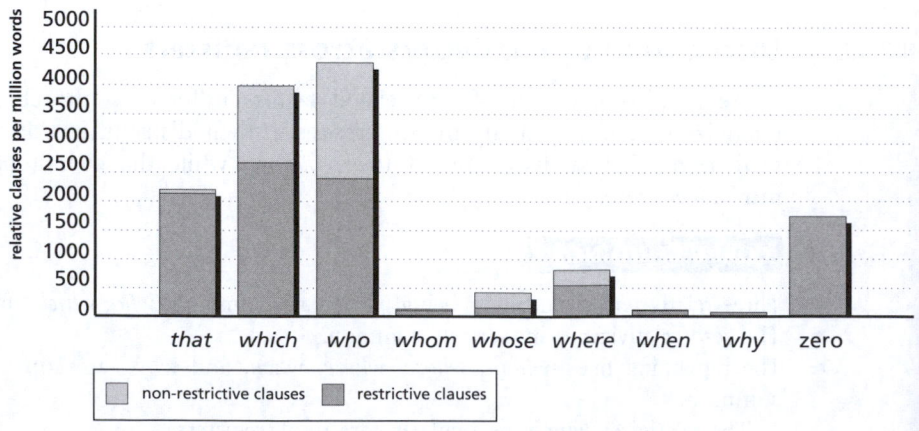

**Figure 8.17   Frequency of relativizers in academic prose**

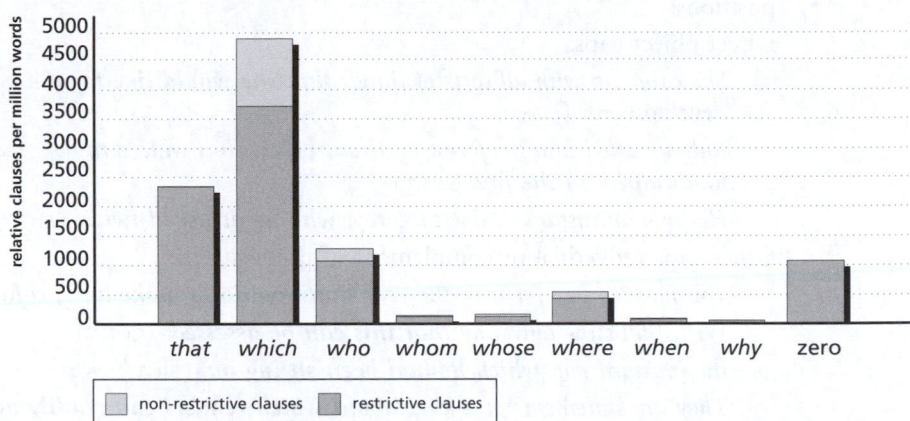

➤ *Which* in academic prose is the most frequent relativizer in any register. *That* is also common in this register, but considerably less so than *which*.

➤ In news and fiction, *that* and *which* both occur as relativizers with moderately high frequencies. *Which* is more common than *that* in news; *that* is somewhat more common than *which* in fiction.

➤ In conversation, *which* is relatively rare, while *that* is moderately common.

➤ *Who* is actually more common than either *which* or *that* in news.

➤ *Who* is also relatively common in fiction.

➤ Relativizer omission is most frequent in fiction, but proportionally most common in conversation.

➤ *Where* is by far the most common of the five remaining relativizers, having relatively high frequencies in fiction, news, and academic prose.

➤ The relativizers also differ in the extent to which they are used with restrictive v. non-restrictive clauses:

➤ *Which* and *where* are commonly used with non-restrictive clauses in all written registers.

➤ At the other extreme, *that* is very rarely used with non-restrictive clauses.

➤ *Who* and *whose* in news occur a high proportion of the time with non-restrictive clauses. *Whose* in news is the only relative pronoun to be used more commonly with non-restrictive than with restrictive clauses.

**DISCUSSION OF FINDINGS**

The relativizers *that* and *which*, and to a lesser extent *who*, are the most flexible in their use, in terms of the gap positions in which they can occur and the meanings that they can express. As a result, they are by far the most frequent forms. The most common use of all three pronouns is with subject gaps.

Subject gaps:

> *Do you want a cup of tea **that's been brewing for three days?*** (CONV)

> *The lowest pressure ratio **which will give an acceptable performance** is always chosen.* (ACAD†)

> *There are merchant bankers **who find it convenient to stir up apprehension.*** (NEWS†)

However, all three of these relative pronouns can also be used with other gap positions:

Direct object gaps:

> She came up with all sorts of things **that she would like for the new development**. (CONV)
>
> Ralph trotted into the forest and returned with a wide spray of green **which he dumped on the fire**. (FICT)
>
> He took an instant dislike to Leroy, **who he attacked twice**. (FICT†)

Other gaps (adverbial or complement of preposition):

> You have to pay for it in the year **that you don't make any profit**. (CONV)
>
> Well, that's the only way **that this can be assessed**. (CONV)
>
> the mustard pot, **which he had been sitting on**. (FICT†)
>
> They are statements of a kind **about which readers can readily agree**. (ACAD)
>
> <...> the guy **who I buy the Mega stuff off**. (CONV†)

In contrast, the other relativizers are restricted to a specific gap position and are thus rarer overall: *whom* and zero to non-subject gaps; *whose* to possessive/genitive gaps; and *where*, *when*, and *why* to adverbial gaps.

*Who* is also restricted in meaning in that it occurs only with animate (usually personal/human) head nouns. In contrast, the pronouns *that* and *which* usually occur with inanimate head nouns, but in certain circumstances they can also occur with animate heads (see 8.7.1.3). This difference means that *that* and *which* are more common than *who* in most registers, since inanimate head nouns taking a relative clause are generally more common than animate heads with a relative clause. In conversation and fiction, animate references are most commonly made with either a personal pronoun or proper name, which rarely allow modification with a relative clause (8.1.2). In academic prose, there are relatively few animate references at all. However, the communicative focus of news, with its emphasis on humans, results in a more frequent use of relative clauses with the pronoun *who*:

> a 20-year-old woman **who has been missing for a week** (NEWS)

Finally, the register distribution of *which* v. *that* v. the zero relativizer also reflects the stylistic associations of these forms. The relative pronouns beginning with the letters *wh* are often considered to be more literate and appropriate to careful language; the pronoun *that* and the zero relativizer have a more colloquial flavor and are preferred in conversation.

## 8.7.1.3   *Who* v. *which*, *that*, and zero

The relative pronoun *who* is distinctive in that it is used almost exclusively with an animate (human) head.

**CORPUS FINDINGS** [4]

➤ In the written non-fiction registers, relative clauses with human head nouns usually take the relativizer *who* (see Table 8.6).

Table 8.6 **Choice of *who, which, that*, and zero following selected human head nouns in news and academic prose**

| head noun | % use with *who* | % use with *which* | % use with *that* | % use with *zero* |
|---|---|---|---|---|
| *people, boys, children teenager(s), student(s)* | c. 90 | less than 1 | less than 5 | less than 10 |
| *person, man, men, woman, women, boy, girls, girls* | c. 70–80 | less than 1 | less than 5 | less than 25 |

➤ In conversation, a different pattern is observed: *that* is much more common with human head nouns, almost as common as *who* (Table 8.7).

Table 8.7 **Choice of *who, which, that*, and zero following selected human head nouns in conversation**

| head noun | % use with *who* | % use with *which* | % use with *that* | % use with *zero* |
|---|---|---|---|---|
| *people, woman, women, man, men, girl, girls, boy, boys* | less than 50 | less than 1 | 30–40 | 10–20 |
| *person* | c. 40 | less than 1 | c. 30 | c. 30 |

**DISCUSSION OF FINDINGS**

The relative pronoun *who* occurs almost exclusively with human heads and, in the written registers, there is a very strong tendency for a relative clause with human head noun to use *who* rather than *which* or *that*:

> They all seemed to have relatives **who had been involved in scandals in London hotels**. (FICT)

> Team Millar rider McWilliams, **who is still looking for a 500 Grand Prix finish**, had a constructive finish. (NEWS)

At the other extreme, the relative pronoun *which* rarely occurs with an animate head. Although *which* is attested in conversation as a relative pronoun with animate heads, this occurs so rarely that it might be considered a speech error:

> She's just the type of person **which everybody would avoid to speak to**. (CONV)

By contrast, relative clauses with *that* freely occur with animate heads, especially in conversation. In fact, for many head nouns referring to humans, *that* is almost as common as *who* in conversation:

> I had more friends **that were boys**. (CONV)

> <…> all those poor people **that died** (CONV†)

> <…> those two women **that had the operations** (CONV†)

> <…> that man **that I went to that time** (CONV†)

> <…> that girl **that lives down the road** (CONV†)

> <…> all these children **that like to go to the library** (CONV†)

These same head nouns also commonly take a zero relativizer in conversation:

> Who's the ugliest person **you've ever seen**? (CONV)

> I thought of a girl **I used to know called Louise**. (CONV)

The head noun *child* in fiction is somewhat exceptional in that it occurs occasionally with the relativizer *that* instead of *who* in fiction. A closer examination of these cases shows that *child* can be used non-personally, as if children are treated more like objects than persons (4.7.3A):

> *He is like a child **that doesn't know what it wants**.* (FICT) <note the anaphoric pronoun *it*>
>
> *There's a child **that quickens in you**.* (FICT)
>
> *... a child **that was given to Mrs. Gredge**.* (FICT†)

### 8.7.1.4  *Who* v. *whom, that,* and zero

Both *who* and *whom* are usually used with human head nouns; the choice between these relative pronouns relates primarily to the gap position rather than a meaning difference.

**CORPUS FINDINGS** [4]

In general, with human head nouns:

➤ *who* occurs usually with subject gaps (over 95% of the time); very rarely with non-subject gaps (less than 2% of the time).

➤ *whom* and zero occur only with non-subject gaps (which are much less common than subject gaps).

➤ *that* can occur with either subject or non-subject gaps.

➤ With non-subject gaps referring to humans, the most common choice by far is zero. This pattern holds for both written and spoken registers.

Table 8.8   **Choice of relativizer with selected human head nouns and non-subject gaps in the LSWE Corpus**

| head noun | % use with *whom* | % use with *that* | % use with zero relativizer |
|---|---|---|---|
| *person, people, woman, women, man, men, girl, girls, boy, boys* | 5–10 | 5–10 | 80–90 |

**DISCUSSION OF FINDINGS**

The relativizers *who* and *whom* are both used with animate head nouns, but the choice between them is clear-cut: *who* is usually used with subject gap positions, while *whom* is used with non-subject gaps.

*Who* with subject gap:

> *Harry Ford, **who now lives in Santa Fe, New Mexico**, met those **who helped him**.* (NEWS†)
>
> *This gentleman is the doctor **who examined the body**.* (FICT)

*Whom* with non-subject gap:

> *They lived in America and had one child, a girl **whom they idolized**.* (FICT)
>
> *Ms Sayeed should not be condemned for the crimes of her father, **whom she denounced as a traitor**.* (NEWS†)

While *who* can also occur with object gaps, this option is rare (and stigmatized in written texts):

*There's a girl **who I work with** who's pregnant.* (CONV)

*That* is more commonly used than *who* as a viable alternative to *whom*. This choice is especially preferred in colloquial discourse, apparently to avoid the formal overtones of *whom*, and possibly to avoid making a choice between *who* and *whom*:

*There might be people **that we don't know of**.* (CONV)
<note the stranded preposition: 2.7.5.3>

*She took up with the first boy **that she came near to liking**.* (FICT)

*Then the woman **that they actually caught and pinned down** would not have been Margot.* (FICT)

However, with non-subject gaps it is much more common to completely avoid the choice among relative pronouns by omitting the relativizer altogether. Interestingly, this alternative is the preferred choice in both spoken and written registers:

*You're one person **I can talk to**.* (CONV)

*She was the most indefatigable young woman **he had ever met**.* (FICT)

*He's one of the most unpretentious people **I've met**.* (NEWS†)

For the most part, *that* and the zero relativizer are alternatives to *whom* only with restrictive relative clauses; non-restrictive clauses with animate head nouns and non-subject gaps almost always take *whom*:

*This man, **whom Elethia never saw**, opened a locally famous restaurant.* (FICT†)

*Ivan said Sue, **whom he met two years ago**, had spent almost every hour with him during and since the operation.* (NEWS)

## 8.7.1.5 *Which* v. *that*

The relativizers *which* and *that* are similar in their grammatical potential. They are both grammatical with a wide range of gap positions and with animate or inanimate heads.

However, the preceding sections have identified a number of important differences in their actual patterns of use, which we summarize here.

With animate heads, *which* is rare, while *that* is more common, especially in conversation. A more important difference is that *which* commonly occurs with non-restrictive relative clauses—25 percent to 35 percent of the time, depending on the register. In contrast, *that* rarely occurs with non-restrictive clauses. When *that* does mark a non-restrictive clause, it often occurs in a series of postmodifiers and is used for special stylistic effect (especially in fiction):

*Here one might say to those sliding lights, those fumbling airs, **that breathe and bend over the bed itself**, here you can neither touch nor destroy.* (FICT)

*He gazed at the yellow, stained wall with all the spots which dead bugs, **that had once crawled**, had left.* (FICT†)

*I am talking about an organization that probably few of you have heard of, **that can and will provide to some, perhaps to some of you, a year of travel, cultural refreshment and excitement you'll remember a long time**.* (FICT)

Stylistic association is another important factor, leading to marked register differences. *Which* has more conservative, academic associations and is thus preferred in academic prose: 70 percent of the academic texts in the LSWE Corpus use *which* for restrictive clauses more commonly than *that*. In contrast, *that* has more informal, colloquial associations and is thus preferred in conversation and most contemporary fiction: 75 percent of the fiction texts in the LSWE Corpus use *that* for restrictive clauses more commonly than *which*.

In addition, dialect differences and the grammatical type of the head noun are important factors.

**CORPUS FINDINGS ²**

➤ In contrast to BrE, AmE news shows a marked preference for *that* over *which* in restrictive clauses (see Table 8.9).

Table 8.9    **The relativizers *that* and *which* in American and British news; occurrences per million words**

each ● represents 200

| | AmE NEWS | BrE NEWS |
|---|---|---|
| restrictive *that* | ●●●●●●●●●●●●●●●●●●●● | ●●●●●●●●●●●● |
| restrictive *which* | ●●●● | ●●●●●●●●●●●●● |
| non-restrictive *which* | ●●●●●●● | ●●●●●●● |

➤ Relative clauses with *that* are about twice as frequent in AmE conversation as in BrE conversation. Relative clauses with *which* are about equally common in both AmE and BrE conversation.

➤ Relative clauses with demonstrative pronouns as head usually take the relativizer *which* (Table 8.10).

➤ Relative clauses with indefinite pronouns as head usually take the relativizer *that* or zero.

Table 8.10    **Pronoun heads followed by *which*, *that*, or zero**

| head noun type with relativizer | % use with *which* | % use with *that* | % use with zero |
|---|---|---|---|
| demonstrative pronoun | 85 | 5 | 10 |
| indefinite pronoun | 10 | 45 | 45 |

**DISCUSSION OF FINDINGS**

The AmE preference for *that* over *which* reflects a willingness to use a form with colloquial associations more widely in written contexts than BrE.

The form *that* is used for a wide range of grammatical functions in English, including relativizer, demonstrative pronoun, demonstrative determiner, and complementizer. As a result, when the head of a relative clause is a demonstrative pronoun, the relativizer *that* is strongly dispreferred, as it would create a sequence of two identical or like elements (cf. 8.1.2E). This pattern holds for all four demonstrative pronouns (*this, that, these, those*).

Dispreferred pattern, with *that*:

> *What's [this]* **that I'm looking at?** (FICT)

Preferred pattern, with *which*:

> *I recognized a silence like [that]* **which pervades a church after a service.** (FICT)

In contrast, relative clauses with indefinite pronouns as head have a strong preference for *that*, instead of *which* as the relativizer. The motivation for this preference might relate to the colloquial associations of indefinite pronouns (4.15.1).

Dispreferred pattern, with *which*:

> *There is [something]* **which everybody can do to alleviate the problem.** (NEWS)

> *The local authority committee member tends to go in dread of [anything]* **which may scandalise the electorate.** (ACAD)

Preferred pattern, with *that*:

> *It's just [something]* **that we can't do** *I'm afraid.* (CONV)

> *So it wouldn't want to do [anything]* **that would stuff it out.** (NEWS)

However, it is equally common for relative clauses with indefinite pronouns as head to omit the relativizer altogether:

> *I'll give you [anything]* **you want** *my darling.* (CONV)

> *He has [something]* **he wants to say to you.** (FICT)

> *There could be a call from [someone]* **you haven't heard from in some time.** (NEWS)

### 8.7.1.6 Discourse choice between *whose* and *of which*

The relativizer *whose* has a syntactic role comparable to the possessive determiners (*my, your,* etc.; 4.4.2) and is typically used to mark a possessive relationship between a human head noun and some other noun phrase, with the two together comprising the gap in the relative clause:

> *And we also know that there's at least one and maybe two other white males* **whose names we do not know.** (FICT)

Thus, the underlying meaning of the relative clause in this case, with the gap included, is: 'We do not know the males' names'.

By extension, *whose* can be used to mark possessive relations with collective entities, such as corporations, government agencies, clubs, societies, and committees (see the comparable use of the genitive with collective nouns—4.6.12.2):

> *A shipping group,* **whose profits dived last year by nearly a third,** *has told shareholders to expect an even lower result for 1993.* (NEWS)

In fact, *whose* can be further used to mark other genitive relationships with completely inanimate, sometimes abstract, head nouns:

> *There is a way of proceeding in conceptual matters* **whose method is to define away any inconvenient difficulty.** (ACAD)

> *He might argue that this consensus provides an abstract convention* **whose implicit extension includes the proposition** <...> (ACAD†)

An alternative to *whose* with inanimate head nouns is the phrase *of which*:

> Some of the particles cluster into aggregates, clods or crumbs, **the size distribution of which determines the soil structure.** (ACAD)
> cf. ... **whose size distribution determines the soil structure**

An alternative way of introducing a relative clause with *of which* is to front only the prepositional phrase *of which*, leaving the rest of the noun phrase to follow it in its normal position in the relative clause:

> He joined a dining-club **of which the motto was, The Whole, The Good, and The Beautiful.** (FICT)
>
> Reynolds also appears as the central Figure in Zoffany's group portrait of all 36 founder members of the Royal Academy, **of which he was first President.** (NEWS)

Finally, a genitive relation can also be marked by using a postmodifying prepositional phrase with the preposition *with* (8.9).

## 8.7.1.7 *Whose* v. *of which* across registers

➤ Both the relativizer *whose* and the alternative *of which* are extremely rare in conversation.

➤ The relativizer *whose* is moderately common in all written registers.

➤ Overall, the alternative *of which* is considerably less common than *whose*.
  ➤ In contrast to this general pattern, *of which* occurs almost as often as *whose* in academic prose.

➤ In news, *whose* usually marks a possessive relationship with a human head noun (70% of the time).
  ➤ 25% of the time *whose* is used with head nouns referring to collective entities (corporations, sports teams, etc.).

➤ The pattern of use in academic prose is strikingly different: 75% of the occurrences of *whose* modify an inanimate head noun.

**Figure 8.18**
**Distribution of *of which* and *whose* in relative clauses**

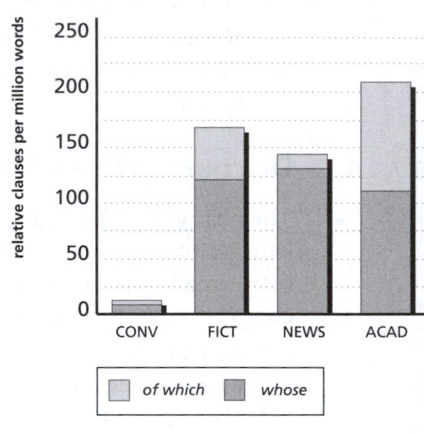

In news, the relativizer *whose* is used commonly to mark possessive relations with a human head noun:

> "Well, there is a choice," says Graham Poole, **whose grandfather started the shop in 1895.** (NEWS)
>
> He was only eight when Bruce Lee, **whose 1973 film Enter the Dragon made him an international film star,** died mysteriously. (NEWS)

In addition, news reports often contain information about collective entities with human associations, such as corporations, government agencies, sports teams, and societies, and these commonly occur as head with the relativizer *whose*:

> The bid is being resisted by Pearl Group, **whose Chairman, Einion Holland, has described the offer as "derisory"**. (NEWS†)

> We assumed that the US Army was blocking off La Boca from the Panama Defence Force, **whose local headquarters is only about 300 yards from our house**. (NEWS†)

Since there are comparatively few inanimate references in news, there are correspondingly few occurrences of *whose* or *of which* with an inanimate head noun.

In contrast, academic prose deals primarily with inanimate entities and so has relatively high frequencies of both *of which* and *whose* used with an inanimate head noun:

> These grey and brown soils of heavy texture often occur as a Gilgai complex, **the puff component of which may be referred to as calcareous, crumbly soils**. (ACAD)

> This wheel drives a similar but smaller wooden-toothed wheel, **the other end of which carries a large open-spoked wheel**. (ACAD†)

> They knew that only another planet, **whose orbit lay beyond those already recognized**, could explain the behavior of the nearer planets. (ACAD)

> A crystal is a piece of matter **whose boundaries are naturally formed plane surfaces**. (ACAD)

It is notable that academic prose makes such wide use of *whose* in this way, despite the folk belief that *whose* should be restricted to personal antecedents.

### 8.7.1.8 Discourse choice of the zero relativizer

Speakers and writers can opt to omit the relativizer altogether in restrictive relative clauses, thereby avoiding the choice among relativizers. This alternative is possible in Standard English whenever the gap is not in subject position. For example,

> the only shiny instrument **he possessed** (FICT)

> the way **the man used to watch him** (FICT)

Also, in some conversational varieties, there is a marginally non-standard usage in which the relativizer is omitted with the gap in subject position. This variant occurs most commonly when the main clause has an existential *there* construction:

> There's people **think he was murdered**. (CONV)

> All these kids are growing up, yeah, thinking there's this bunny **dropped eggs, Easter eggs all over the place**. (CONV)

> Cos I think there's more women **drive now than ever they used to**. (CONV)

> There's a nice little stream **runs through the valley**. (CONV)

> There's a lot of people **won't let you do it**. (CONV)

> There aren't many people **say that nowadays**. (CONV)

**CORPUS FINDINGS [2,3]**

➤ The zero relativizer occurs about twice as frequently in fiction as in conversation and academic prose.

   ➤ Surprisingly, the frequency of relativizer omission is about the same in conversation and in academic prose.

➤ Proportionally, relativizer omission is by far most common in conversation:

   ➤ About 25% of all relative clauses in conversation omit the relativizer.

   ➤ Only c. 10% of the restrictive relative clauses in academic prose omit the relativizer.

➤ A grammatical factor—the subject of the relative clause—has a strong influence on relativizer omission:

   ➤ When the subject of the relative clause is a pronoun, 60–70% of relative clauses have the relativizer omitted.

   ➤ When the subject of the relative clause is a full noun phrase, 80-95% of relative clauses retain the relative pronoun.

   ➤ Surprisingly, these grammatical constraints hold equally for all four registers.

**Figure 8.19**
**Restrictive relative clauses with relative pronoun retained v. omitted, across registers**

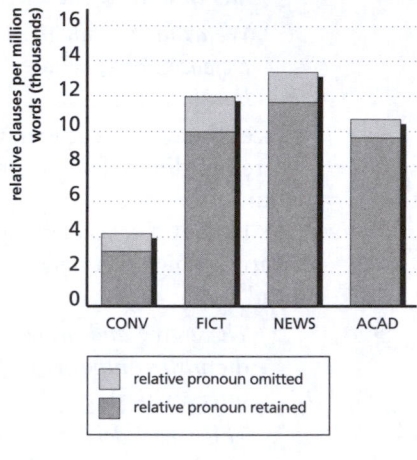

relative clauses per million words (thousands)

relative pronoun omitted
relative pronoun retained

**DISCUSSION OF FINDINGS**

Although the zero relativizer is found in all four registers, it has colloquial associations and thus is more common in conversation and fiction than in the expository registers. However, since relative clauses are many times more frequent in fiction than conversation, zero is by far most common in fiction. Although many examples occur in the quoted speech of fictional characters, the zero relativizer is also very common in fictional narrative.

Fictional speech:

> *Here I can make any sound **I like**.* (FICT)
>
> *I do beg you to consider seriously the points **I've put to you**.* (FICT)
>
> *I confess I have got plans **you may find a little startling**.* (FICT)

Fictional narrative:

> *her curiosity about the herds of cattle **she saw grazing*** (FICT)
>
> *a lot of the people **she knew*** (FICT)
>
> *the names **his mother had remembered from the past*** (FICT)
>
> *a rather ugly tie **his father had lent him*** (FICT)

In contrast to fiction, conversation uses few relative clauses overall, and has a lower frequency of the zero relativizer. Proportionally, though, the zero relativizer is very common in conversation, occurring in one of every four relative clauses. Approximately half of all these relative clauses have gaps in subject position (8.7.2), making a relativizer virtually obligatory. Thus the relativizer is actually omitted in about half of the relative clauses that permit this option in conversation:

> *that person **she was with*** (CONV)
>
> *all the music **we like*** (CONV)
>
> *the way **the people are dressed*** (CONV)
>
> *the slippers **you lost*** (CONV)

The frequent use of the zero relativizer in news and academic prose is somewhat surprising. Although the relativizer is omitted only 10-15 percent of the time in these registers, the frequency of this option is relatively high, due to the overall frequent use of relative clauses. As in the other registers, the choice to omit the relativizer results in a less formal style, often bringing a more colloquial tone to dense informational prose:

> *the only way **the inquiry could be properly conducted*** (NEWS)
>
> *a post **the writer earned through work as an editor*** (NEWS)
>
> *a country **they had sought to leave*** (NEWS)
>
> *the convictions **these arguments try to explain*** (ACAD)
>
> *a claim **a wise cynic can easily refute*** (ACAD)
>
> *the way **we acquire knowledge*** (ACAD)

In all registers, the zero relativizer is strongly favored by the presence of a personal pronoun as subject in the relative clause. This is because most pronouns distinguish between subject (nominative) and object forms (e.g. *I*, *she*, *he* v. *me*, *her*, *him*), and so the presence of a subject pronoun unambiguously marks the beginning of a new clause. Thus, these pronouns provide a grammatical clue for the beginning of the relative clause, even without the relativizer:

> *the only choice **we've got*** (CONV)
>
> *things **they want to emphasize*** (CONV)
>
> *the way **I like it for myself*** (FICT)
>
> *the kind of organisation **she likes*** (NEWS)
>
> *the apparatus **he used*** (ACAD)

In contrast, a full noun phrase can fill many grammatical slots and thus provides no indication of a clause onset. As a result, the zero relativizer is strongly disfavored when a full noun phrase occurs as subject of the relative clause. See 9.2.8 for a discussion of similar factors influencing the omission of complementizer *that*.

## 8.7.2 Grammatical role of the relative clause gap

### CORPUS FINDINGS[2]

➤ Subject gaps in the relative clause occur more commonly than non-subject gaps:
  - ➤ In conversation and fiction, c. 55% of all relative clauses have subject gaps.
  - ➤ In news and academic prose, c. 75% of all relative clauses have subject gaps.

### DISCUSSION OF FINDINGS

Because the relativizer occurs initially in a relative clause, subject gaps preserve the standard subject + verb + object/predicative/adverbial order in the relative clause, while non-subject gaps result in a clause element being displaced from its normal position. Subject gaps are therefore considered easier to process and are more common. It is thus surprising that conversation and fiction use relative clauses with non-subject gaps more commonly than written non-fiction.

In general, subject noun phrases tend to refer to given entities, while object noun phrases tend to provide new information (11.2.1). Thus, the subject of a relative clause will typically be known, and often a human participant. When a non-subject element is gapped, the primary function of the relative clause is to associate the head noun with that known entity given in the subject position. Constructions of this type are considerably more common in conversation and fiction than in written exposition:

> the store **that Robin made** (CONV)
>
> people **that they owe money to** (CONV)
>
> a friend **to whom I am deeply attached** (FICT)
>
> the conditions **from which she had fled** (FICT)

In contrast, when the gap is in subject position, it is likely that non-subject noun phrase elements in the relative clause will provide new information, in addition to identifying the reference of the head noun. This pattern fits the informational purposes of written exposition, and thus these constructions are most common in news and academic prose:

> clocks **which kept accurate time at sea** (NEWS)
>
> hundreds of Falkirk fans **who are demanding that the Deans sell their shares in the club** (NEWS)
>
> ways **that could be construed as aggressive** (ACAD)
>
> fine particles **which are swept up into the upper convecting layer across the interface** (ACAD)

(Note how passive constructions are used to create subject gaps in the last two examples.)

### 8.7.2.1 Relative clause gaps in conversation

There are other variants relating to the gap position in relative clauses that occur primarily in conversation. These characteristics are associated with the difficulties of online production, sometimes resulting in constructions that might be considered non-standard or even a disfluency (14.2).

First of all, relative clauses in conversation sometimes do not have a gap at all; instead, a **resumptive pronoun**, which is co-referential with the head noun, fills the gap position (marked *[]*):

> There was a case of one girl **who back in 1968 [she] killed two boys when she was eleven.** (CONV)
>
> Usually they give you a, a thing to return it, you know, a thing **that you don't want [it].** (CONV)
>
> A: But look at that Denise, Pam's friend –
> B: yeah.
> A: the – about the little boy **that they think [he]'s dead.** (CONV)
> A: Are these leeks?
> B: Things **that I don't know what [they]** – yes, I think. (CONV)

In addition, relative clause constructions in conversation are often complex, with deeply embedded gap positions. Most commonly, the gap in such constructions occurs in a complement clause embedded in the relative clause. In the examples below, the gap position is marked with <–> and the complement clause with *[]*:

> There's so many things **that I know** *[I want to learn* <–>*]*. (CONV)

> And we bought her a video of The Little Mermaid **which we know** *[she wants* <–>*]*. (CONV)

> I mean something **which I think** *[as a committee we should be in agreement with* <–>*]*. (CONV)

> Things **that I think** *[*<–>*] shouldn't be done on the health service]* are breast implants. (CONV)

> That's the bit **that we don't tend** *[to know so much about* <–>*]*. (CONV)

The existence of such constructions in conversation is surprising, since structural complexity is stereotypically associated with written exposition rather than speech. However, among the types of structural complexity that are characteristic of conversation is the heavy use of complement clauses (9.2.6, 9.4.6). Relative clauses with embedded gaps are a related type of complexity. In formal writing, they would be regarded as awkward at best, whereas in conversation, they are perfectly acceptable and not at all unusual.

## 8.7.3 Subject v. non-subject head nouns

The head noun to which a relative clause is attached also has a grammatical role in a higher clause (subject, direct object, indirect object, etc.).

### CORPUS FINDINGS [3]

➤ Head nouns of relative clauses rarely occur in subject position in the matrix clause (only 10–15% of the time across registers).

### DISCUSSION OF FINDINGS

Although the head noun of a relative clause can occur in any position, the most important distinction is between subject and non-subject heads.

Subject head nouns:

> *[Systems]* **which give detailed prompts** *appear to be very helpful to the inexperienced user*. (ACAD)

> The *[volunteer]*, **whom we shall call Mary**, *said the biggest asset of the Samaritans is their ear*. (NEWS)

Non-subject head nouns:

> Well that's the only *[way]* **that this can be assessed**. (CONV)

> Now they were on the long *[incline]* **that led to the bridge**. (FICT)

As the above examples illustrate, relative clauses with subject heads disrupt the matrix clause—hearers/readers must process the relative clause before reaching the main verb of the matrix clause. As a result, subject noun phrases rarely contain a relative clause as postmodifier. On the other hand, relative clauses with non-subject heads occur after the matrix clause verb; this position is strongly preferred because it does not interrupt the flow of the matrix clause and is in keeping with the principle of end weight (11.2.1).

## 8.7.4 Relative clauses with adverbial gaps

There are four major structural variants for relative clauses with adverbial gaps. The choice that conforms most to prescriptive tradition is to use the relativizer *which* preceded by the preposition that marks the adverbial element in the relative clause:

    1 *the apartments **in which no one lives*** (FICT)

    2 *the endless landscape **from which the sand is taken*** (FICT)

In these constructions, the preposition + relativizer stands for the entire prepositional phrase in the relative clause. Thus, the relative clause in **1** has the meaning 'no one lives in the apartments', and the relative clause in **2** has the meaning 'the sand is taken from the endless landscape'.

A second option for adverbial gaps is to leave the preposition stranded (2.7.5.3) in the relative clause, marking the site of the gap. The relativizer is often omitted with this option:

    *the one **that old James used to live [in]*** (FICT)

    *some of the houses **I go [to]*** (CONV)

The third option is simply to omit the preposition altogether, providing no surface marker of the adverbial gap. The relativizer is also often omitted in these structures:

    1 *the time **that I began*** (FICT)

    2 *the day **that he left*** (CONV)

    3 *the way **I look at it*** (CONV)

    4 *a place **I would like to go*** (CONV)

Finally, there are three relative adverbs that specifically mark adverbial gaps: *where* for place adverbials, *when* for time adverbials, and *why* for reason adverbials (cf. 10.2.1). These forms do not need to occur with a preposition, since they substitute for an entire adverbial (while the other relativizers substitute only for a noun phrase):

    *the area **where the chapels have closed*** (CONV)

    *one day **when she was at school*** (FICT)

    *the other reason **why the ambulance workers have lost out*** (NEWS)

For other types of adverbial gap, there is no available relative adverb. For example, there is no relative adverb for manner adverbials: *\*the way how I look at it.*

## 8.7.4.1 Relative adverbs across registers

**CORPUS FINDINGS 2**

➤ In most registers, *where* is by far the most common relativizer used for relative clauses with adverbial gaps.

➤ In academic prose, the preposition + relativizer sequence *in which* is equally common.

    ➤ The preposition + relativizer sequence *to which* is also comparatively common in academic prose.

**Table 8.11**   **The most common relativizers for relative clauses with adverbial gaps; occurrences per million words**

each ● represents 50

| | CONV | FICT | NEWS | ACAD |
|---|---|---|---|---|
| *where* | ●●●● | ●●●●●●●●●●● ●● | ●●●●●●●●●●● | ●●●●●●●●●●● |
| *when* | ● | ●● | ● | ● |
| *why* | ● | ● | ● | ● |
| *in which* | | ●● | ● | ●●●●●●●●●●● |
| *to which* | ● | | | ●●● |
| *from which* | ● | | | ● |
| *at which* | | | | ● |
| *on which* | ● | | | ● |

➤  Other structural options for relative clauses with adverbial gaps are generally much less common (8.7.4.2).

### DISCUSSION OF FINDINGS

The relative adverb *where* occurs commonly in all four registers with adverbial gaps. However, the registers use different head nouns with relative clauses of this type. Similar lexico-grammatical patterns are found for the relative adverbs *when* and *why*. These are all described fully in 8.7.4.2.

Relativizers in the form preposition + *which* are common only in academic prose. Unlike the relative adverbs, these relativizers occur with many different head nouns (also described in 8.7.4.2).

A less common relativizer option is to strand the preposition at the gap position (see 2.7.5.3). This variant is occasionally used in conversation, often with the relativizer omitted:

> That would be the very last place **that Marion and I would want to go** *[to]*. (CONV)

> What about that place **we were going to stay** *[at]*. (CONV)

Usage handbooks have traditionally warned against the use of such stranded prepositions. However, it is in fact much more common to omit the preposition altogether in these constructions, a practice generally overlooked by the handbooks.

Examples of preposition omission with *that* or zero as relativizer are easily found in the written registers as well as in conversation:

> That's a place **that we don't want to take you.** (CONV)

> One place **you can get a percent discount** (CONV)

> the time **I saw her in the police station** (CONV)

> When's the last time **you got a letter from Jamie?** (CONV)

> the reason **that I got up to ten stone** is because of Christmas. (CONV)

> the place **that Jacobus took him** (FICT)

> It was the first day **that Mr. Andrew didn't come.** (FICT)

> the day **that the wall was opened** (NEWS)

*the last time **that automatic budget cuts, mandated by the Gramm-Rudman-Hollings deficit-cutting law, took effect*** (NEWS)

*the reason **that he was not better known*** (FICT)

### 8.7.4.2 Head nouns taking relative clauses with adverbial gaps

**DISTRIBUTIONAL FINDINGS** [2]

➤ A few head nouns corresponding to major adverbial categories—especially *place*, *time*, *day*, *reason*, and *way*—are particularly common for relative clauses with adverbial gaps.

➤ Relative clauses with the head nouns *time* and *way* are exceptional in that they commonly occur with the preposition omitted.

➤ The heads *place*, *time*, and *reason* are very commonly followed by their corresponding relative adverbs.

**DISCUSSION OF FINDINGS**

#### A Place head nouns with *where*

Although the relative adverb *where* occurs commonly in all four registers with adverbial gaps, the registers use different head nouns with relative clauses of this type. In conversation, fiction, and news, these head nouns typically refer to physical locations:

*that place **where they had the used goods sale*** (CONV)

*the hospital **where she spent 63 hours*** (NEWS)

This association is strongest in fiction:

*the place **where the savages had vanished*** (FICT)

*my back room, **where I used to smoke and write my letters*** (FICT)

In academic prose, in contrast, relative clauses with *where* are typically used to mark logical rather than physical locations:

*the kind of situation **where this type of work is helpful*** (ACAD)

*another case **where the initial and final values of p and T are the same*** (ACAD)

*the points **where further inquiry needs to be made*** (ACAD)

This pattern holds even with the head noun *area*, which has a literal meaning referring to a physical location but is often used to refer to a knowledge domain:

*Specialist nurses have particular expertise in one field of nursing, usually in an area **where the patient and family need teaching and support***. (ACAD†)

*Farmers were slow to see management as an area **where training could help***. (ACAD)

#### B Time head nouns

The relative adverb *when* is much less common than *where* overall, although it does frequently occur with the head noun *time* in all four registers:

*I can't think of a time **when I would be going by myself***. (CONV)

Table 8.12 **Head nouns most commonly occurring with relative clauses that have adverbial gaps; occurrences per million words**

■ over 100  ■ over 40  ■ over 20  ■ over 10  ▌ over 5

| | CONV | FICT | NEWS | ACAD |
|---|---|---|---|---|
| **place head nouns:** | | | | |
| *place + where* | over 10 | over 40 | over 10 | over 5 |
| *place + preposition + which* | | over 5 | | |
| *place + zero* | over 5 | over 10 | | |
| *area(s) + where* | | | over 10 | over 20 |
| *area(s) + preposition + which* | | | over 5 | over 10 |
| *room(s) + where* | over 5 | over 20 | | |
| *room(s) + preposition + which* | | over 5 | | |
| *situation + where* | | | over 5 | over 20 |
| *situation + preposition + which* | | | | over 10 |
| *house + where* | | over 10 | over 5 | |
| *point + where* | | over 5 | | over 10 |
| *case(s) + where* | | | | over 20 |
| *spot + where* | | over 5 | over 5 | |
| *country + where* | | | over 5 | over 5 |
| *bit + where* | over 5 | | | |
| *hospital + where* | | | over 5 | |
| *condition(s) + where* | | | | over 5 |
| *example(s) + where* | | | | over 5 |
| **time head nouns:** | | | | |
| *time(s) + when* | over 20 | over 20 | over 20 | over 20 |
| *time(s) + preposition + which* | | | | over 10 |
| *time(s) + zero* | over 100 | over 40 | over 20 | over 5 |
| *day(s) + when* | over 10 | over 10 | over 20 | over 5 |
| *day(s) + preposition + which* | | over 5 | | |
| *day(s) + zero* | over 10 | over 10 | over 5 | |
| *occasion(s) + when* | | over 5 | over 5 | over 5 |
| *moment(s) + when* | | over 5 | over 5 | |
| *bit + when* | over 5 | | | |
| *season + when* | | | over 5 | |
| *case(s) + when* | | | | over 5 |
| *period(s) + when* | | | | over 5 |
| **reason head nouns:** | | | | |
| *reason + why* | over 10 | over 20 | over 20 | over 20 |
| *reason + zero* | over 10 | over 5 | over 5 | |

**Table 8.12    continued**

| ▬ over 100 | ▬ over 40 | ▪ over 20 | ▪ over 10 | ▪ over 5 | |
|---|---|---|---|---|---|
| | | **CONV** | **FICT** | **NEWS** | **ACAD** |
| **manner head nouns:** | | | | | |
| *way* + *that/which* | | ▪ | ▪ | ▪ | ▬ |
| *way* + *in which* | | | | | ▬ |
| *way* + zero | | ▬ | ▬ | ▪ | ▬ |

> *That summer marked the time* **when their carefree childhood really ended.** (FICT†)
>
> *The launch comes at a time* **when Rover's share of the record UK car market is slipping.** (NEWS)
>
> *It occurred at a time* **when abolitionist leaders hoped for improved treatment of slaves.** (ACAD)

Relative clauses with the head noun *time* are even more common with the zero relativizer and no preposition. This pattern holds for fiction and news, as well as for conversation:

> *You say that every time* **you come in this door.** (CONV)
>
> *I have the authority to leave any time* **I want.** (FICT)
>
> *It's time* **they paid the money back.** (NEWS)

Equivalent forms with prepositions would be difficult to form in many of these cases (e.g. *every time at which you come in this door*). Examples also occur in academic prose:

> *The activity checklist is completed each time* **the activity changes.** (ACAD†)

But generally this register retains the conservative preference for *wh*-forms seen in earlier sections.

**C    Head nouns common with both *when* and *where***

A few head nouns are moderately common with both *where* and *when* as relative adverb. In conversation, the head noun *bit*, referring to a part of a movie or story, commonly occurs with both relativizers:

> *You know the bit* **where the man jumps inside Whoopie Goldberg.** (CONV)
>
> *But the bit* **when he's finished that.** (CONV)

Similarly, in academic prose the head noun *case(s)* can occur with either *where* or *when*:

> *The contrastive nature of linguistic categories is clear in cases* **where the category label contains two words.** (ACAD)
>
> *One of the main applications of the scan score is in difficult cases* **when accurate estimation of disease activity will have important therapeutic implications.** (ACAD)

**D    *Reason***

The relativizer *why* commonly occurs with only one head noun—*reason*:

> *You are the reason* **why I left school.** (CONV)

> *The ramshackle Whitley Council negotiating machinery is the other reason* **why the ambulance workers have lost out**. (NEWS)
>
> *The major reason* **why these researchers have reached different conclusions is that they have used competing criteria**. (ACAD†)

This combination is common in all four registers, especially in the relatively fixed expression *There is no reason why*:

> *There's no reason* **why you shouldn't go out for a drink with him**. (CONV)
>
> *There is no reason* **why differing model forms cannot be used to provide differing pictorial displays**. (ACAD)

In conversation, as might be expected, the head noun *reason* is relatively common with the zero relativizer:

> *That's the reason* **he can't go**, *you see*. (CONV)

**E** *Way*

The head noun *way* is exceptional in several respects. It is used when the gap in the relative clause represents a manner adverbial and is many times more common as a head noun—in all registers—than any other form discussed in this section (cf. the use of *way* as a head noun with a *to*-clause as postmodifier; 8.8.2.1). However, there is no relative adverb marking manner, corresponding to the use of *where*, *when*, and *why* with other adverbials. In academic prose, with its general preference for preposition + *which*, a manner adverbial gap is commonly marked by the relativizer sequence *in which*:

> *The way* **in which this happens** *gives important information on the inner organization*. (ACAD)
>
> *It is not the only way* **in which a person can be brought before a court**. (ACAD)

In conversation and the non-academic written registers, though, it is much more common simply to omit the preposition. In some cases, the relativizer *that* is used:

> *They're not used to the way* **that we're used to living**. (CONV)
>
> *Children were no longer treated in the formal and distant way* **that they had treated their daughter**. (FICT)

However, because *way* as a head noun is so strongly associated with a manner adverbial gap, these relative clauses usually occur with both the relativizer and the preposition omitted:

> *That's not the way* **you do that**. (CONV)
>
> *I like the way* **it comes out**. (CONV)
>
> *I can't stand the way* **you androids give up**. (FICT)
>
> *He was sorry about the way* **it had ended**. (NEWS)

Surprisingly, this pattern is found in academic prose as well as in the more colloquial registers:

> *the way* **the book is used** (ACAD)
>
> *the way* **the tetrahedra are linked** (ACAD)
>
> *the way* **we all accept that it is wrong to torture babies** (ACAD)

**F    Head nouns with preposition + *which***

Unlike relative adverbs, *in which* and *to which* occur with a wide range of different head nouns, particularly in academic prose:

> *a state **in which they both take definite values*** (ACAD)
>
> *an apparatus **in which pairs of protons are produced*** (ACAD)
>
> *the growth period **in which it occurs*** (ACAD)
>
> *the natural and social world **in which he lives*** (ACAD)
>
> *the extent **to which the Burma crop is rainfed*** (ACAD)

In many of these cases, preposition + *which* could be replaced with a relative adverb *where* or *when*. However, there is no common prepositional sequence that corresponds in meaning to the relative adverb *why*.

# 8.8    Postmodification by non-finite clause

There are three major types of non-finite postmodifying clauses: *ing*-clauses, *ed*-clauses, and *to*-clauses (3.12). The first two types are also termed **participle clauses**, and the third is also termed an **infinitive clause** or a **to-infinitive relative**. All three types have non-finite verbs, which are not inflected for tense. Participle clause postmodifiers always have subject gap positions, and often have close paraphrases with relative clauses (cf. 8.8.1.1):

> *selections **retained from the second year*** (ACAD)
> cf. *selections **which are retained from the second year***
>
> *young families **attending the local clinic*** (NEWS)
> cf. *families **who/which are attending the local clinic***

In contrast, *to*-clause postmodifiers can have either subject or non-subject gaps. Subject gap:

> *I haven't got friends **to beat him up** though.* (CONV)
> cf. *'Friends will beat him up.'*

Non-subject gap:

> *I had a little bit **to eat**.* (CONV) <direct object: *'I ate a little bit'*>
>
> *I'll remember which way **to go**.* (CONV) <direction adverbial: *'I can go that way'*>
>
> *Get angry! We've both got a lot **to be angry about**.* (FICT) <complement of preposition: *'We are angry about a lot'*>

Note that the subject is generally not expressed in these clauses, regardless of the gap position (8.8.2).

## 8.8.1    Participle clauses as postmodifiers

Both *ing*-clauses and *ed*-clauses can function as postmodifying participle clauses. *Ing*-clauses:

> 1  *A military jeep **travelling down Beach Road at high speed** struck a youth **crossing the street**.* (FICT†)
> 2  *Interest is now developing in a theoretical approach **involving reflection of Alfvén waves**.* (ACAD)

*Ed*-clauses:

> **3** *The US yesterday welcomed a proposal* **made by the presidents of Colombia, Peru and Bolivia.** (NEWS)
>
> **4** *It can be derived using the assumptions* **given above.** (ACAD)

The verbs in *ed*-clauses correspond directly to the passive in finite clauses. Thus, in **3** and **4** the meaning can be paraphrased as *A proposal was made* and *Assumptions were given*. In contrast, although the verbs in *ing*-clauses might appear to correspond to finite progressive aspect verbs, in fact they do not always do so. In **1** a paraphrase *A jeep was travelling* <...> is quite possible. However, in **2** it would be highly unusual to find a finite clause progressive form *the theoretical approach is/was involving* <...> Instead, the nearest equivalent clause would be *The theoretical approach involves* <...>.

## 8.8.1.1 Passive and *-ing* forms of verbs in postmodifying participle clauses v. relative clauses

As discussed in 8.6.1, both types of postmodifying participle clauses are most common in academic prose, with *ed*-clauses being considerably more common than *ing*-clauses.

### CORPUS FINDINGS [2]

➤ Most postmodifying clauses with a verb in *-ing* or passive voice are participle clauses.
> ➤ Less than 5% of the postmodifying clauses with verbs in *-ing* are full relative clauses.
> ➤ Similarly, in most registers, less than 5% of the postmodifying clauses with a passive voice verb are full relative clauses.
> ➤ In academic prose, c. 10% of the postmodifying clauses with a passive voice verb are full relative clauses.

➤ Although postmodifying participle clauses are most frequent in academic prose, only a few verbs are particularly common in these constructions.
> ➤ Common verbs in *ing*-clauses—over 100 occurrences per million words: *being, containing, using*; over 50 occurrences per million words: *concerning, having, involving*.
> ➤ Common verbs in *ed*-clauses—over 100 occurrences per million words: *based, given, used*; over 50 occurrences per million words: *caused, concerned, made, obtained, produced, taken*.

➤ In academic prose, many of the verbs that commonly occur in *ing*-clauses (more than 20 times per million words) rarely occur as main clause progressive verbs: *arising, concerning, consisting, containing, corresponding, involving, relating, requiring, resulting*.

### DISCUSSION OF FINDINGS

In the majority of cases, a participle clause (instead of a full relative clause) will be used whenever an *-ing* verb form or a passive verb occurs in a postmodifying clause. However, there are different reasons for this tendency. With *-ing* verb forms, the primary factor seems to be structural: many of the most common *-ing* verbs occurring in postmodifying clauses are stative in meaning (verbs of existence/relationship; 5.2.2). As a result, these verbs rarely, if ever, occur as full progressive verbs, and thus a full relative clause containing a finite progressive form is not truly an option. For example, none of the following postmodifiers could normally be re-phrased with a full relative clause containing a progressive verb:

> *a matter* **concerning the public interest** (ACAD)
>
> *an affidavit* **containing all the basic factual material** (ACAD)
>
> *initiatives* **involving national and local government authorities** (ACAD)
>
> *a society* **consisting of educated people** (ACAD)
>
> *water stress* **resulting in stomatal closure** (ACAD)
>
> *the data* **relating to married male clerks** (ACAD)

In contrast, postmodifying *ed*-clauses are often used when a full relative clause with a passive verb is a viable alternative. In these cases, the preference for participle clauses seems to be economy, since they convey essentially the same meaning as a full relative clause but use fewer words.

This preference raises the question of why full relative clauses with a passive verb are used at all. Three discourse factors seem to be influential here. First, a full relative clause is used whenever tense, perfect aspect, or modality are important (since these distinctions cannot be marked in a postmodifying participle clause):

> *The mistaken view is that theory refers to ideas* **which have never been tested**. (ACAD†)
>
> *Now 48 sites* **which could be maintained by local authorities** *have been identified.* (NEWS)

Second, a full relative clause is preferred whenever the postmodifier is separated from the head noun. In the following examples, the subject noun phrase is discontinuous, with the relative clause being placed after the predicate of the main clause (head noun in *[]*):

> *Valuable [contributions] towards botanical classification have been made in India,* **which are discussed later.** (ACAD†)
>
> *Between 1770 and 1800 [work] was done on the effect of vegetation on air* **that was destined to revolutionize the ideas of the functions of plants**. (ACAD†)

Finally, full relative clauses are required with non-subject gaps:

> *A strain* **the purity of which is determined by morphological characters** *need not necessarily be so for other characters.* (ACAD†) <possessive/genitive gap>
>
> *The latter carries two parallel endless ropes, joined by spacing bars,* **to which are attached a series of water containers**. (ACAD) <prepositional object gap>

## 8.8.2 *To*-clauses as postmodifiers

Like participle clauses, *to*-clauses are a type of non-finite postmodifying clause. In two major respects, however, *to*-clauses are more flexible than participle clauses. First, they can occur with both subject and non-subject gaps; and second, in the case of non-subject gaps, they can occur with an overt subject noun phrase.

*To*-clauses with subject gap:

> *Its absence was a factor* **to be taken into account.** (NEWS†)

*To*-clauses with object gaps:

> *Papa dressed in his Sunday suit and hat was a sight **to see**.* (FICT)
> *There is one further matter **to confess**.* (ACAD)

*To*-clauses with adverbial gaps:

> *They'd take a long time **to dry**.* (CONV)
> *We shall have to find a way **to associate numbers with our operators**.* (ACAD†)

*To*-clauses with prepositional object gap:

> *She's had a lot **to put up with**.* (CONV)
> <Note the stranded preposition; 2.7.5.3.>

*To*-clauses with an overt subject (introduced by *for*):

> *That'll be the worst thing **for us to do**.* (CONV) <object gap>
> *Really now is the time **for you to try and go**.* (CONV) <time adverbial gap>
> *There was no possible way **for the pilot to avoid it**.* (ACAD) <manner adverbial gap>

With adverbial and prepositional object gaps, a further option is a *to*-clause introduced by a preposition and a relative pronoun:

> *Engineers have a good helping of functional grey matter **with which to devise theories**. They also need the conditions **in which to test them**.* (NEWS)

## 8.8.2.1 Structural types of postmodifying *to*-clause

**CORPUS FINDINGS** [2,3]

➤ The overwhelming majority of *to*-clauses (over 90%) do not have a subject given in a *for*-phrase.
➤ All three major gap positions—subject, object, and adverbial—are relatively common (each occurring between 25% and 40% depending on the register)
  ➤ Many of the *to*-clauses with subject gaps have passive verbs.
➤ A few head nouns with general meanings are particularly common with *to*-clauses.
  ➤ This is especially the case in conversation—occurring over 50 times per million words: *time*; occurring over 20 times per million words: *thing, way*; occurring over ten times per million words: *place(s), stuff, a lot*.
  ➤ In academic prose, only two head nouns are notably common taking a *to*-clause (over 20 per million words): *way* and *time*.

**DISCUSSION OF FINDINGS**

The most common head nouns taking a *to*-clause are associated with object and adverbial gap positions. The nouns associated with object gaps are generalized in meaning and especially common in conversation:

> *Well I mean this is a horrible thing **to say**, but <...>* (CONV†)
> *I've got stuff **to sort out** anyway.* (CONV)
> *Friday evening I didn't have a lot **to drink**.* (CONV)

Common head nouns associated with adverbial gaps cover the three major domains of *time*, *place*, and manner (*way*)—(similar to the common heads occurring with relative clause adverbial gaps; 8.7.4.2):

> *There's not enough time **to get it out and defrost it**.* (CONV)
>
> *But it's certainly a nice place **to live**.* (CONV)
>
> *That's no way **to talk to Sean**!* (CONV)

In most cases, *to*-clauses do not contain an overt subject marked with *for*. Instead, as the above examples show, *to*-clauses are generally preferred when the subject of the postmodifying clause is easily predicted from the context.

Post-nominal *to*-clauses with *time* and *way* as head noun and adverbial gaps are also relatively common in written exposition:

> *They themselves had insufficient time **to offer this kind of support**.* (ACAD)
>
> *Feynman offers us a simple way **to see that this happens**.* (ACAD)

(Compare the treatment of *to*-clauses acting as adverbials in 10.1.2)

A wider range of head nouns takes *to*-clauses with subject gaps, although no individual noun is particularly common:

> *She's not gonna be the kind of person **to say no**.* (CONV)
>
> *I think she should be earning enough money **to pay a taxi**.* (CONV)
>
> *Therefore any measures **to discourage the refugees** would be wrong.* (NEWS)
>
> *There is evidence **to suggest that they had indeed been introduced before this**.* (ACAD†)

## 8.9 Postmodification by prepositional phrase

Prepositional phrases are by far the most common type of postmodifier in all registers (8.6.1). In many cases, prepositional phrases can be re-phrased as full relative clauses with nearly equivalent meaning. Prepositional phrases beginning with *with* often correspond to full relative clauses with the main verb *have*:

> *continuous-time feedback systems **with chaotic behaviour*** (ACAD)
>
> *cf. systems **which have chaotic behaviour***
>
> *varieties **which have a long maturation period*** (ACAD)
>
> *cf. varieties **with a long maturation period***

Some other prepositional phrases can be re-phrased as a full relative clause with the copula *be* and a prepositional phrase complement:

> *the main substantive problem **which is at the root of Durkheim's concern*** (ACAD)
>
> *cf. the main problem **at the root of Durkheim's concern***
>
> *documents **which were in his possession*** (NEWS)
>
> *cf. documents **in his possession***
>
> *the car keys **that were on the table*** (ACAD)
>
> *cf. the car keys **on the table***

However, these equivalencies hold only for selected functions of the prepositions, so that many occurrences of prepositional postmodifiers cannot be re-phrased as relative clauses; for example:

> *the problems **at its ISC Technologies subsidiary*** (NEWS)
>
> *this list **of requirements*** (ACAD)
>
> *turbulence **in lasers and other optical systems*** (ACAD)
>
> *the same effect **on the final state*** (ACAD)

## 8.9.1    Common prepositions in postmodifying prepositional phrases

As we have seen in 8.6.1, prepositional phrases are by far the most common type of postmodifier in all registers, although they are much more frequent in the written non-fiction registers than in conversation and fiction. We look first at the choice of preposition; it turns out that only a few prepositions are common in these constructions.

**CORPUS FINDINGS [2,3]**

➤ Although prepositional postmodifiers are most common by far in the written expository registers, the proportional use of individual prepositions is very similar across registers.

**Table 8.13    Prepositional phrases as postmodifiers**

| preposition | percentage of prepositional postmodifiers |
|---|---|
| of | 60–65 |
| in | 8–10 |
| for | 3–5 |
| on | 3–5 |
| to | 3–5 |
| with | 3–5 |

➤ Six prepositions account for c. 90% of all prepositional phrases as postmodifiers.
➤ An additional six prepositions each account for c. 1% of all prepositional phrases as postmodifiers: *about, at, between, by, from, like.*
➤ All other prepositions are relatively rare in prepositional postmodifiers (e.g. *above, after, among*).

**DISCUSSION OF FINDINGS**

The majority of postmodifying prepositional phrases begin with the preposition *of*. This is due to the extremely wide range of functions served by this preposition:

• After quantifying collectives (4.3.4): *a set of books*
• After unit nouns (4.3.5): *a piece of cake*
• After container nouns (4.3.6.1A): *our bottle of champagne*
• After nouns denoting shape (4.3.6.1B): *a pile of money*
• After nouns of measure (4.3.6.1C): *a yard of cloth*
• After quantity nouns (4.3.6.1D): *loads of work*
• After *pair* and *couple* (4.3.6.2): *a couple of hours*
• After nouns in *-ful* (4.3.6.1F): *a mouthful of food*
• After species nouns (4.3.7): *these kinds of question*
• After quantifying determiners (4.4.4): *a lot of trouble*
• In double genitives (4.6.10): *a cousin of my wife's*

- In constructions comparable to genitives (4.6.12): *the owner of the car, the city of Lahore, the brutal murder of a child*
- In partitive constructions (4.6.14.3): *one of your sons.*

(With quantifying determiners, the real head of the structure may be regarded as the noun following *of* rather than preceding it, so these are not true instances of postmodification; see 4.3.8).

In addition, *of*-phrases have a range of uses in expressing a close semantic relationship between the head noun and the following noun phrase, where there are parallels with noun and adjective premodification (8.2), rather than with the genitive:

> *facades* **of Portland stone** (FICT) cf. *stone facades*
>
> *ten words* **of English** (FICT) cf. *English words*
>
> *the color* **of chocolate** (FICT) cf. *chocolate color*
>
> *secretaries* **of companies** (FICT)
>
> *the Ministry* **of Defence** (NEWS)
>
> *wonderful contrasts* **of feeling** (NEWS)
>
> *a woman* **of very strong high moral values** (NEWS)
>
> *the population* **of embryos** (ACAD)
>
> *the National Union* **of Clerks** (ACAD)
>
> *your style* **of interpretation** (ACAD)
>
> *26 Bishops* **of the Church of England** (ACAD)

Further, many of the most common recurrent lexical bundles in academic writing include *of*-phrases (13.2.4.1; 13.2.4.3).

Prepositional phrases beginning with *in* also represent a number of meanings, ranging from physical location to various logical relations:

> *the mess* **in his bedroom** (CONV)
>
> *the third largest trucking firm* **in the midwest** (FICT)
>
> *the longest touchdown* **in the history of the school** (FICT)
>
> *the co-chairman's faith* **in the project** (NEWS)
>
> *the rapidly deteriorating trend* **in cashflow** (NEWS)
>
> *maintenance of health* **in the long term** (ACAD)
>
> *a resulting decrease* **in breeding performance** (ACAD)

The two fiction examples above illustrate the use of *in* following a superlative adjective (*largest* and *longest*) to restrict the scope of the superlative (such examples could alternatively be analyzed as postponed adjective complements; 2.7.3.2).

Prepositional phrases beginning with *for, on, to,* or *with* are less common than *of* or *in*, but they are similarly versatile in representing a range of meanings:

> *a school* **for disabled children** (CONV)
>
> *the arrangements* **for tomorrow** (FICT)
>
> *a cure* **for AIDS** (NEWS)
>
> *the search* **for new solutions** (ACAD)
>
> *a mole* **on his head** (CONV)
>
> *a lot* **on the Sunset Strip** (FICT)
>
> *his most wounding attack* **on the tabloids** (NEWS)

> *limitations **on unit size*** (ACAD)
> *their first trip **to Scotland*** (NEWS)
> *a legal right **to compensation*** (ACAD)
> *one apparently attractive answer **to that question*** (ACAD)
> *some cheese **with garlic*** (CONV)
> *the man **with the megaphone*** (FICT)
> *a sensible relationship **with the West German mark*** (NEWS)
> *solids **with low melting points*** (ACAD)

## 8.9.2   Choice of prepositional phrase v. relative clause

**CORPUS FINDINGS** [2,3]

➤ Full relative clauses are rare in comparison to prepositional postmodifiers.
  ➤ Full relative clauses with main verb *have*, or with the copula *be* + preposition, occur less than 100 times per million words in all registers. (By comparison, prepositional phrases as postmodifiers occur around 68,000 times per million words in academic prose.)

**DISCUSSION OF FINDINGS**

Many postmodifiers with *of* cannot be paraphrased as a full relative clause (e.g. **these kinds which are of questions*). Furthermore, even the less common prepositions are still much more frequent in prepositional phrase postmodifiers than clausal alternatives.

Although full relative clauses are much less common than prepositional postmodifiers, there are certain discourse factors that favor those alternatives. The most important of these is the need to convey non-restrictive meaning.

Non-restrictive relative clause with copula + preposition:

> *Then he set off for Simon's house, **which was at the other end of the lane**.* (FICT)

> *He said the resident, **who is in her late 70s**, had been very confused.* (NEWS†)

Non-restrictive relative clause with *have*:

> *Quinn, **who had a disappointing game despite those two efforts on goal**, was taken off after 70 minutes.* (NEWS)

> *With animals like moles, **which have tough and durable skins**, the periods involved are longer.* (ACAD†)

In a number of cases, relative clauses of this type are not separated from the head noun with a comma, although they are still clearly non-restrictive in meaning:

With copula + preposition:

> *She went one day to the tiny public library **which was in a room with stained glass windows at the back of the Town Hall**.* (FICT†)

> *The soldier denies the murder of 18-year-old Karen Reilly **who was in the car with her friend Martin Peake**.* (NEWS†)

With *have*:

> *There is a vast amount of interference between the contributions of neighbouring paths* **which have a tendency to cancel each other out**. (ACAD)

> *Aroma Rices* **which have a marked aroma** *are prized in India and Pakistan.* (ACAD†)

A second factor favoring the use of a full relative clause is a past tense form crucial to the intended meaning:

> *DMB and B Result,* **which had a link with a big international agency,** *went bust recently.* (NEWS†)

> *When two veins coalesce the cell* **that was between them** *becomes obliterated.* (ACAD)

> *The lower-income groups also consumed amounts of iron* **that were below the standard**. (ACAD†)

Finally, full relative clauses are preferred whenever the postmodifier is separated from the head noun (identified in *[]* below); in these cases, parsing ambiguity could result from the use of a prepositional phrase:

> *Please forget the [words] I said,* **which have no application whatever to you.** (FICT)

> *First half [profits] from Prudential* **which were in line with the City's forecasts** *lifted the shares.* (NEWS†)

> *We are planning to appoint a mix of hands-on [people] with vision and commitment* **who have knowledge and expertise.** (NEWS†)

# 8.10 Postmodification by appositive noun phrase

**Appositive noun phrases** (or noun phrases in apposition) differ from other kinds of postmodifiers in that they have equivalent status with the preceding (head) noun phrase. Thus, the order of head noun phrase and appositive noun phrase could normally be reversed to produce an equally grammatical construction with essentially the same meaning. Compare:

> *the dissident playwright,* **Vaclav Havel** (NEWS)

> *Vaclav Havel,* **the dissident playwright**

As these examples illustrate, appositive noun phrases are typically non-restrictive in meaning; they provide descriptive information about the head noun but are not needed to identify the reference of the head noun. However, appositive noun phrases can also be used in a restrictive sense. For the most part, this use is confined to cases where the second noun has a metalinguistic function, referring to a word, phrase, or expression:

> *[The term]* **'pre-embryo'** *is used to describe this stage.* (NEWS)

> *[The word]* **gossip** *itself actually means 'God's kin'.* (NEWS)

In these examples, the order of noun phrases cannot be reversed.

# 8.10.1 Appositive noun phrases in news and academic prose

➤ Appositive noun phrases are common in news and academic prose, both in terms of their absolute frequency, and proportionally (accounting for over 15% of all postmodifiers in those registers; see Figure 8.13 in 8.6.1).
➤ In news, over 90% of all appositive constructions involve a proper noun.
  ➤ The majority of these constructions have human reference.
➤ In academic prose, appositive noun phrases are used for a wider range of functions.
  ➤ Approximately 65% of the time, appositive noun phrases in academic prose are used to modify a proper noun or a technical name. However, these constructions rarely have human reference.

**DISCUSSION OF FINDINGS**

Appositive noun phrases are a maximally abbreviated form of postmodifier. In contrast to clausal postmodifiers (relative or non-finite clauses), appositive noun phrases include no verbs at all. Thus, these postmodifiers are favored in the registers with highest informational density.

In news, with its focus on the actions of human participants, appositive noun phrases are used primarily to provide background information about people. Most of these constructions include both a proper noun and a descriptive noun phrase, but these two elements can occur in either order.

Proper noun + descriptive phrase:

> *Dr. Jan Stjernsward, chief of the World Health Organisation Cancer Unit* (NEWS)
>
> *Vladimir Ashkenazy, one of the world's greatest pianists* (NEWS)
>
> *Mr. Pyotr Luchinsky, the new first secretary* (NEWS)

Descriptive phrase + proper noun:

> *The Environment Secretary, Mr. Chris Patten* (NEWS)
>
> *the Labour Party's housing spokesman, Mr. Clive Soley* (NEWS)

In academic prose, appositive noun phrases have a wider range of uses, although they rarely characterize humans. Moreover, unlike in news, appositives in academic prose are commonly given in parentheses () following the head noun (cf. 3.4.2):

> *Schedule 4 to the rules contains both an application and an affidavit (Forms 6.4 and 6.5).* (ACAD†)

Appositive noun phrases have a number of specific uses in academic prose. First, they are commonly used to provide an explanatory gloss to a technical reference or name of some entity:

> *another technique (the 'Wheeler linkage')* (ACAD)
>
> *the mill (a term introduced by Babbage)* (ACAD)
>
> *the optical propagation direction (z-direction)* (ACAD)

Second, they are commonly used to introduce acronyms:

> *Kinetics Technology International (KTI)* (ACAD)

> *the arithmetic and logical unit (ALU)* (ACAD)
>
> *IAS (Institute of Advanced Studies)* (ACAD)
>
> *PMSG (pregnant mare's serum gonadotropin)* (ACAD)

Short convenience labels for variables or parts of diagrams are also commonly introduced with an appositive noun phrase:

> *the valves on the pressure side (V1 and V2)* (ACAD)

In many cases, these constructions appear as restrictive modifiers (with no comma or parentheses):

> *a circle C* (ACAD)
>
> *a point P* (ACAD)
>
> *reflectivity R* (ACAD)

Similarly, chemical or mathematical formulas are commonly given as appositive noun phrases:

> *fayalite, Fe$_2$SiO$_4$* (ACAD)
>
> *hydrogen chloride, HCl* (ACAD)
>
> *the current contents of the program counter (n+1)* (ACAD)
>
> *bicarbonate-buffered culture medium (MI$_6$ + BSA)* (ACAD)

Finally, appositive noun phrases are often used for a list of items included in some class:

> *essential nutrients (manganese, copper and zinc)* (ACAD)
>
> *the various life-history events (i.e. oviposition, hatching and maturation)* (ACAD)

## 8.11   Noun phrases with multiple postmodifiers

Postmodification often includes multiple structures, which can represent either a series of forms modifying a single head noun or embeddings (or combinations of both). In academic writing, the postmodification can become especially long and complex. For example, in the following sentence, the postmodifier complex following the head noun *source* includes multiple prepositional phrases, relative clauses, and *ing-* and *ed-*participle clauses, together with a high-level split in apposition (marked by the ':'):

> *Theoretically it can serve as [a source] **of ideas and insights which are of particular relevance for the formulation of principles: ideas emerging from disciplines devoted to the study of language and learning which might bear upon the definition of language as subject.*** (ACAD)

Figure 8.20 gives a schematic representation of the structural relations among these modifiers.

In most cases, a postmodifier will modify the immediately preceding noun, which can be embedded inside higher level postmodifiers. In other cases, though, two postmodifiers can occur in series modifying the same head noun, so that the second postmodifier is removed from the head noun. Thus, in the above sentence, the final relative clause (*which might bear upon ...*) modifies the head noun *ideas*, even though there is an extended sequence of intervening postmodifiers (a participle clause—*emerging from disciplines*—with embedded postmodifiers).

Figure 8.20  **Structural relations among modifiers in a complex noun phrase**

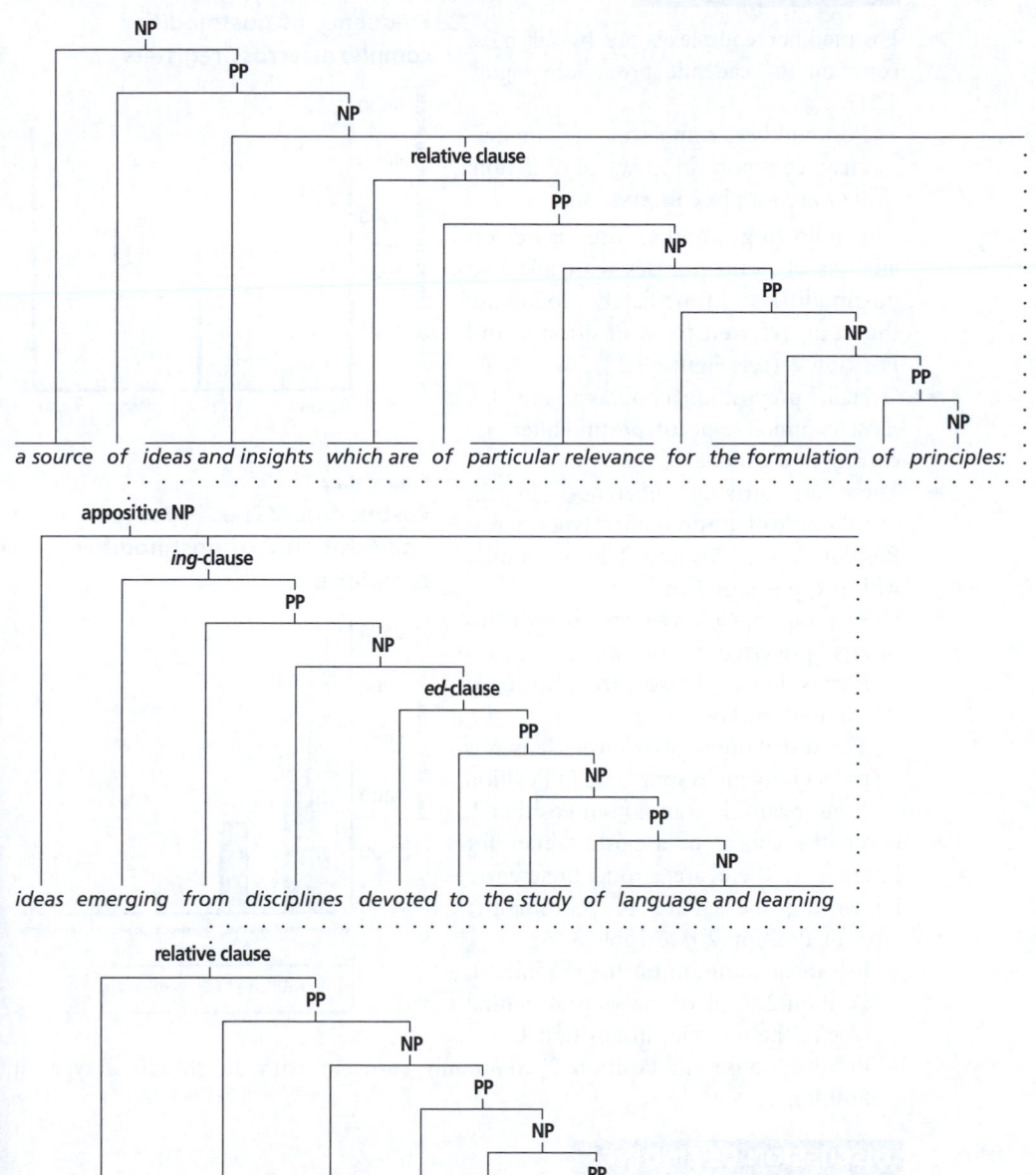

## 8.11.1   Order of constituents in postmodifier complexes

For the purposes of this section, we define a **postmodifier complex** as a combination of postmodifiers, whether they represent one postmodifier embedded in another or a series of postmodifiers modifying a single head noun.

➤ Postmodifier complexes are by far most common in academic prose (see Figure 8.21).

➤ Postmodifier complexes are moderately common in news and fiction; they are rare in conversation.

The following findings are based on analysis of noun phrases with just two postmodifiers immediately following the head, referred to as Position 1 and Position 2 (see Figure 8.22).

➤ Overall, prepositional phrases are the most common type of postmodifier occurring in a complex.

➤ There are striking differences in the distribution of postmodifier types across Position 1 and Position 2 in a complex with two postmodifiers:

➤ Prepositional phrases are overwhelmingly preferred in Position 1.

➤ Prepositional phrases are also most common in Position 2.

➤ The distribution of relative clauses is particularly interesting: rare in Position 1, but relatively common in Position 2.

➤ Given the choice of a postmodifier for Position 1, there are strong preferences influencing the choice of postmodifier type for Position 2 (see Table 8.14).

➤ It is most common for the modifier in Position 2 to be of the same structural type as the modifier in Position 1.

➤ Relative clauses in Position 2 commonly co-occur with all structural types in Position 1.

**Figure 8.21**

**Frequency of postmodifier complexes across registers**

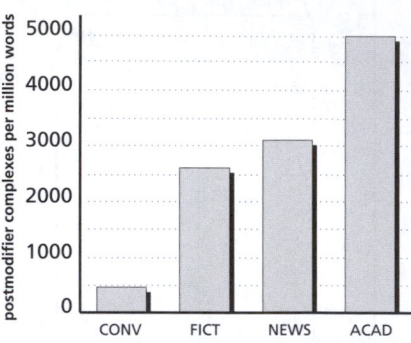

**Figure 8.22**

**Postmodifier types in Position 1 and Position 2 of postmodifier complexes**

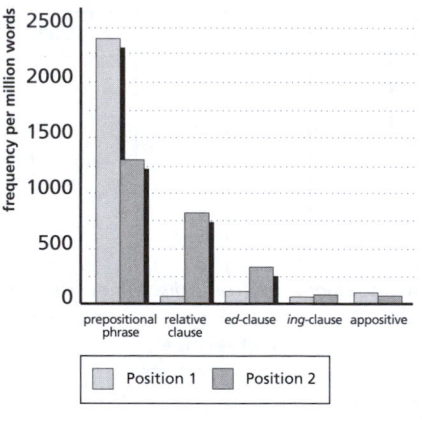

**DISCUSSION OF FINDINGS**

Noun phrases with complex postmodifier complexes are relatively common in academic prose. The example in 8.11, as well as examples **1–4** below, illustrate some of the combinations of postmodifiers typical of academic writing. Noun phrases with multiple postmodifiers are in bold in the following examples, with the head noun phrase in []. All the examples illustrate the use of prepositional phrases and relative clauses in postmodifier complexes. In addition, they illustrate *ed*-participle clauses (**2**) and an elaborate appositive structure (**3**).

1 *Terms such as Geist or representation collective have no satisfactory English equivalents, and themselves express [some of the differences]* **in social development between Britain, Germany and France which are touched upon in the book**. (ACAD)

**Table 8.14** **Proportional use of common postmodifier types in Position 2, for each structural type in Position 1**

■ more than 50 percent ▮ more than 25 percent

(For example, the first row should be read as follows: when the first modifier in a sequence of two postmodifiers is a prepositional phrase, over 50 percent of the second modifiers will also be a prepositional phrase, and over 25 percent of the second modifiers will be a relative clause.)

| | position 2 | | | |
|---|---|---|---|---|
| position 1 | prepositional phrase | relative clause | ed-clause | appositive noun phrase |
| prepositional phrase | ■ | ▮ | | |
| relative clause | | ■ | | |
| ed-clause | | ▮ | ▮ | |
| appositive noun phrase | | ▮ | | ■ |

2 *To some extent this is true, due as he pointed out to [the double-thinking]* **of those of us who retain inhibitions and hang-ups born of earlier years** *and [the mixture]* **of fascination and revulsion connected with sex which lies so deep in many of us.** (ACAD)

3 *The chapters in this section of the reader consider [various aspects]* **of teaching and learning that have come under increased official scrutiny by central state agencies in recent years, particularly the curriculum of schools, the assessment of pupil performance in school and the quality of teaching itself.** (ACAD)

4 *What were [the dynamics]* **within the religious-intellectual traditions which committed some adherents to public action for reform and provided theological rationales which sustained antislavery over many years?** (ACAD)

As these examples show, prepositional phrases are particularly common in postmodifier complexes. In some cases, writers construct extremely dense sequences of prepositional phrases, such as:

*We similarly use the notations to denote the substitution* **of (lists of) expressions for (equal length lists of) variables in (lists of) expressions.** (ACAD)

More commonly, writers employ relatively simple structures with two prepositional phrases:

*The main difficulties which are posed concern the rendition* **of culturally specific German or French terms into English.** (ACAD)

*These figures serve to underline the increasing orientation* **of western society to information and information processing activities.** (ACAD)

*A sociological description might discuss the utilisation* **of such devices for social purposes.** (ACAD)

These examples also illustrate a general pattern that holds across all postmodifier types: the tendency for the second postmodifier in a complex to be of the same structural type as the first postmodifier.

*Ed*-clause + *ed*-clause:

> *Large clear diagrams* **drawn on sugar paper and covered with transparent film** *are particularly useful teaching aids.* (ACAD)

> *It was spacious with a high ceiling* **painted with cherubs and decorated with flowers.** (FICT)

Appositive noun phrase + appositive noun phrase:

> *At the last election the Labour MP,* **Mildred Gordon, a left-winger** *beat the Liberal Alliance candidate.* (NEWS†)

> *Judy Gaselee,* **wife of Nick, chairman of the village Conservative Association,** *invited Newbury candidate* <...> (NEWS†)

An equally important tendency is for the second postmodifier in a complex to be a relative clause, regardless of the structural type of the first postmodifier. Examples **1–4** above all illustrate this tendency. Other examples include:

> **5** *Firemen needed police support as they tackled a car* **in the driveway which had been set on fire.** (NEWS)

> **6** *Most countries have a written document* **known as "the constitution" which lays down the main rules** <...> (ACAD†)

> **7** *The ambivalence* **of feeling and thought which is bound to exist at any time of change** *has been seized upon.* (ACAD†)

Relative clauses are particularly common in this function because they provide the most overt surface marking of their postmodifier status (by means of the relativizer); therefore, even when they are distant from the head, they are easily recognized as postmodifiers. In contrast, postmodifying prepositional phrases usually modify the immediately preceding noun.

Thus, the two most common structural types occurring in postmodifier sequences serve very different functions. Prepositional phrases are typically embedded structures, modifying the immediately adjacent noun contained in the preceding postmodifier. In contrast, relative clauses provide an additional modifier for some earlier head noun, usually on the same hierarchical level as other intervening postmodifiers. In some cases, there can be numerous postmodifiers intervening between a head noun and the final relative clause, as with the second relative clause, in **1** and **2** above.

# 8.12   Noun complement clauses v. nominal postmodifiers

On the surface, relative clauses and **that-complement clauses** of nouns can appear to be identical. Similarly postmodifying *to*-clauses look superficially like **to-complement clauses**. However, they represent very different structural relations. Thus compare the following two sentences, both with the noun *report* as head.

Postmodifying relative clause:

> *Peter reached out for the well-thumbed [report]* **that lay behind him on the cupboard top.** (FICT)

Noun complement clause:

> Other semiconductor stocks eased following an industry trade group's [report] **that its leading indicator fell in September**. (NEWS†)

Postmodifying clauses serve to identify the reference of the head noun, or to add some descriptive information about that noun. Structurally, postmodifying clauses are not complete (i.e. they have a gap), and they could not stand on their own as independent sentences. Thus, the relative clause in the above example has a gap in subject position: the underlying meaning of the relative clause is that 'the report lay behind him', but *the report* is not mentioned in the clause itself. In contrast, noun complement clauses actually present the complete content of the head noun, in this case what was in the report: 'the trade group's leading indicator fell'. This principle applies generally: complement clauses differ from post-modifying clauses in that they do not have a gap corresponding in meaning to the head noun.

## 8.13 Structural types of noun complement clause

There are two major types of noun complement clause: *that*-clauses and *to*-infinitive clauses (cf. 9.1.1–2). In the following examples, the head is placed in *[]* and the complement clause is italicized.

*That*-clauses:

> There were also [rumors] **that Ford had now taken its stake up to the maximum 15 per cent allowed**. (NEWS†)

> These figures lead to an [expectation] **that the main application area would be in the office environments**. (ACAD)

*To*-clauses:

> You've been given [permission] **to wear them**. (CONV)

> Legal peers renewed their attack on the Government's [plans] **to shake up the legal profession** yesterday (NEWS)

The complementizer *that* cannot be omitted in *that* complement clauses controlled by nouns, making these clauses different from most other types of *that*-clauses (including *that*-complement clauses controlled by verbs and adjectives, as well relative clauses with relativizer *that*).

That-clauses are finite (with marked tense) while *to*-clauses are non-finite. Note that the *to*-clauses have missing subjects that can be reconstructed from the context (similar to postmodifying *to*-clauses, 8.8.2). However, they do not have gaps corresponding to the heads (*permission* or *plans*).

In addition, there are several other less common types of noun complement clause. For example, *of* + **ing-clauses** are often used with similar meaning:

> He had no [intention] **of singing at anyone's twenty-first birthday**. (FICT)

> The exchanged protons have about the same [chance] **of having the same or opposite spin orientations**. (ACAD†)

**Dependent *wh*-interrogative clauses** (cf. 9.3) can also function as noun complement clauses:

> There was no [question] **who was the star**. (FICT)

> *We always come back to the same [question]* **why the devil won't he show himself.** (FICT)

In addition to the simple pattern noun + *wh*-clause shown above, there are two structural variants for *wh*-interrogative clauses. The first uses the preposition *of* followed by the *wh*-clause:

> *I also want the Government to look at the wider [issue]* **of what happens to British aid and credit going into Ghana.** (NEWS)

> *But the [question]* **of who will pay the multi-million dollar bill** *is unanswered.* (NEWS†)

> *We will then lack any appropriate [explanation]* **of why a vote for a checkerboard solution is wrong.** (ACAD†)

> *Table 4.22 gives [examples]* **of how valencies can be used to find the formulae of simple compounds.** (ACAD)

> *We have only the most general [notion]* **of how the first continents formed.** (ACAD)

The second option uses the preposition *as to* followed by the *wh*-clause. This option is used primarily with the *wh*-interrogative word *whether*:

> *Recent studies have posed the [question]* **as to whether there is a link between film violence and real violence.** (NEWS)

> *Masters and men were deeply divided over the substantive [issue]* **as to whether women should be employed at all.** (ACAD†)

Finally, it should be noted that complement clauses can be used in non-restrictive functions:

> *It was a pleasing thought,* **that I might soon be moving in more exalted circles.** (FICT)

> *This revolving of him in her mind led invariably to the same end, the same fear,* **that he would go away from Hilderbridge without her seeing him.** (FICT)

> *Clinton's second allegation,* **that there has been collusion between the security forces and Protestant para-military groups,** *is based on a very few isolated cases.* (NEWS)

> *This thought,* **of why Jasper consented to let her sleep here,** *made her mind swirl.* (FICT†)

Although non-restrictive complement clauses are rare, they are somewhat more common in academic prose than in the other registers:

> *The recognition that a text may set up its own secondary norms leads to a further conclusion,* **that features of language within that text may depart from the norms of the text itself.** (ACAD)

> *Hence they avoid giving an actual analysis of their principal claim,* **that a mental event is identical with a neural event.** (ACAD†)

> *The contrary assumption,* **that common sense will take wholly indistinguishable mental events to be different thoughts,** *strikes me as remarkable.* (ACAD)

## 8.13.1 Noun complement clause types across registers

**CORPUS FINDINGS** [2,3]

➤ Compared with the frequencies of post-modifiers, noun complement clauses are only moderately common.
  ➤ Complement clauses controlled by verbs or adjectives are also much more common than noun complement clauses (cf. Chapter 9).
➤ The major types of noun complement clause have the same general distribution across registers:
  ➤ rare in conversation;
  ➤ most common in expository writing.
➤ *To*-clauses are particularly common in news.
➤ *That*-clauses are most common in academic prose.
➤ *Of* + *ing*-clause constructions are slightly less common than the other two types in all registers.
➤ *Wh*-interrogative clauses (all variants) are comparatively rare in all registers.

**Figure 8.23**

**Distribution of noun complement clause types across registers**

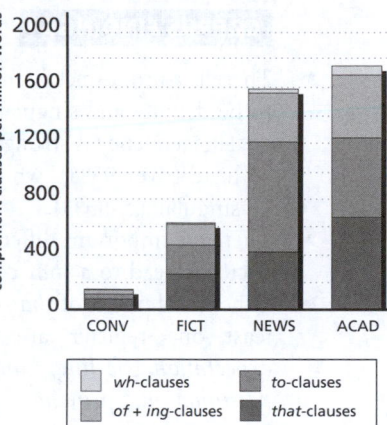

**DISCUSSION OF FINDINGS**

Noun complement clauses are controlled by a closed set of head nouns, in contrast to postmodifying clauses, which can occur with almost any head noun. This lexical restriction of complements helps account for the much greater frequency of postmodifiers.

Most of the head nouns with noun complement clauses mark some abstract (nominalized) stance towards the proposition in the complement clause, including assessment of the certainty of the proposition, the source of the information, or other speaker/writer attitudes towards the proposition. Similar functions are more commonly served by complement clauses controlled by verbs or adjectives (see Chapter 9). This difference is most striking in conversation: whereas complement clauses controlled by verbs and adjectives are more common in conversation than in any other register, noun complement clauses are the least common in conversation. In contrast, noun complement clauses are most important in the non-fiction written registers. The following section shows that many of the same roots can be used to control both noun and verb complement clauses.

There are also systematic differences in the register distribution of particular types of noun complement clauses, with *to*-clauses being especially common in news, and *that*-clauses being especially common in academic prose. These preferences relate to the sets of nouns that can control each type of complement clause (8.14).

## 8.14    Head nouns taking noun complement clauses

### 8.14.1    Head nouns taking *that*-clauses

**CORPUS FINDINGS** [2]

➤ There is a pronounced tendency for the noun phrases taking noun complement clauses to be definite and singular.
  ➤ This tendency is strongest with *that*-clauses: almost all *that*-clauses have a singular head (over 95%), while most *that*-clauses have heads that are both definite and singular (c. 85%).
➤ There are important differences across registers in the particular nouns that commonly occur as head to a *that* complement clause (see Table 8.15).
➤ Other head nouns of *that*-complement clauses, occurring over twice per million in at least one register are: *assertion, comment, contention, conviction, discovery, expectation, feeling, implication, impression, indication, opinion, perception, presumption, principle, probability, proposition, realisation/realization, reason, remark, requirement, result, rumor/rumour, statement, suspicion, thesis.*

**DISCUSSION OF FINDINGS**

*That*-clauses functioning as noun complements are one of the primary devices used to mark stance in academic prose. In these constructions, the *that*-clause reports a proposition, while the head noun reports the author's stance towards that proposition. Two primary kinds of stance information are given by the most common head nouns:

• an assessment of the certainty of the proposition in the *that*-clause, as with *fact, possibility, claim, notion, assumption, hypothesis, rumor*:

> But there remained the very troublesome *[fact]* **that leguminous crops required no nitrogenous manure.** (ACAD†)

> There is a *[possibility]* **that this morphology represents an ancestral great ape character.** (ACAD†)

• an indication of the source of the knowledge expressed in the *that*-clause. Three primary sources can be distinguished: linguistic communication, as with *claim, report, suggestion, proposal, remark*; cognitive reasoning, as with *assumption, hypothesis, idea, observation*; personal belief, as with *belief, doubt, hope, opinion.* For example:

> This conforms conveniently with Maslow's (1970) *[suggestion]* **that human motivation is related to a hierarchy of human needs.** (ACAD)

> The survey was aimed at testing a *[hypothesis]* **that happily-married couples tend to vote more conservatively.** (ACAD†)

> Their frustrations were the product of their *[belief]* **that the leadership was not responding adequately to the party's "crisis".** (ACAD†)

Many of these head nouns are nominalized equivalents of verbs or adjectives that can control *that*-complement clauses (cf. 9.2). In fact, 14 of the 23 most common

**Table 8.15** **Abstract nouns taking *that*-complement clauses; occurrences per million words**

(All head nouns that occur more than ten times per million words in at least one register)

Legend: ▰ over 50　▪ over 20　▪ over 10　▪ over 5

| | CONV | FICT | NEWS | ACAD |
|---|---|---|---|---|
| *fact* | over 5 | over 20 | over 20 | over 50 |
| *idea* | over 5 | over 10 | over 5 | over 10 |
| *hope* | | over 10 | over 20 | over 5 |
| *possibility* | over 5 | | over 10 | over 20 |
| *doubt* | | over 20 | | over 20 |
| *impression* | | over 10 | over 10 | over 5 |
| *suggestion* | | | over 20 | over 10 |
| *belief* | | | over 10 | over 10 |
| *sign* | over 5 | | over 10 | over 5 |
| *conclusion* | over 5 | | over 5 | over 10 |
| *claim* | | | over 10 | over 10 |
| *ground(s)* | | | over 10 | over 10 |
| *view* | | | over 10 | over 10 |
| *fear* | | over 10 | over 5 | |
| *knowledge* | | over 10 | over 5 | |
| *news* | over 5 | | over 10 | |
| *sense* | over 5 | | | over 10 |
| *report* | | | over 10 | over 5 |
| *notion* | | | over 5 | over 10 |
| *assumption* | | | | over 20 |
| *thought* | over 10 | | | |
| *hypothesis* | | | | over 10 |
| *observation* | | | | over 10 |

head nouns listed above are of this type. Most of these nouns have corresponding verbs (rather than adjectives)—*hope, doubt, suggestion, belief, conclusion, claim, fear, knowledge, sense, report, assumption, thought, hypothesis, observation*:

> Lagrange seemed to cherish [hopes] **that his work would show the way to the solution of the general quintic.** (ACAD)
> cf. I just [hope] **that I've plugged it in properly.** (CONV)

> There seems to be an automatic [assumption] **that a single division on a scale represents a single unit of some kind.** (ACAD)
> cf. She had always idly [assumed] **that there was some system.** (FICT)

The only common head noun derived from an adjective is *possibility*:

> But there remains a [possibility] **that gregarious Desert Locusts might become less viable.** (ACAD†)
> cf. It is [possible] **that she has just decided to leave the area.** (NEWS)

As illustrated by the above examples, the expression of stance is backgrounded in noun complement clauses. With verb complement clauses, the subject of the controlling verb is often a human agent or experiencer, so that the stance reported by the verb can be attributed directly to that person. In contrast, the stance conveyed by a controlling head noun is not normally attributed to anyone, so that readers must infer that the noun reports the stance of the writer.

The opposite distributions of verb complement clauses (preferred in conversation) and noun complement clauses (preferred in academic writing) can thus be attributed to two factors. First, conversation has an overall preference for verbal rather than nominal structures, while academic prose shows the opposite pattern, preferring to integrate information in noun phrases. Second, the differing primary purposes of conversation and academic prose are at least as important here: conversational participants are interested in each others' personal feelings and attitudes, and thus stance is expressed prominently and directly attributed to participants. In contrast, academic writers are generally much more interested in the information being conveyed than personal attitudes; thus, when stance is expressed, it tends to be backgrounded and not directly attributed to the author.

The strong preference for definite head noun phrases with complement clauses is a further way of backgrounding the reported stance, since it carries the implication that the noun phrase is known information. In most cases, readers will not in fact know the information being presented. However, the use of the definite article suggests that the proposition is generally known, backgrounding the stance rather than presenting it as new information that is open to challenge.

## 8.14.1.1 Head nouns that take both *that*-complement clauses and relative clauses

**CORPUS FINDINGS** [2]

➤ Many nouns can potentially take either a relative clause or a complement clause. In actual use, though, the nouns that are common with a *that*-complement clause rarely take a *that*-relative clause.

   ➤ For the following nouns, a post-nominal *that*-clause functions as a complement clause over 99% of the time—in academic prose: *possibility, doubt, belief, assumption*; in news: *hope, doubt, suggestion.*

➤ The head noun *fact* is complicated in that it occurs with extraposed constructions and relative clause constructions, in addition to its frequent use with noun complement clauses.

➤ Nouns that are less common with a complement clause tend to be more flexible, taking both complement clauses and relative clauses.

   ➤ In academic prose: *idea/hypothesis/suggestion/sign* + *that*-clause represents a noun complement clause c. 70–80% of the time; *reason/conclusion* + *that*-clause represents a noun complement clause c. 60% of the time; *result* + *that*-clause represents a noun complement clause only c. 20% of the time.

➤ Other registers show different preferences.

**DISCUSSION OF FINDINGS**

The combination 'noun + *that*' is ambiguous, introducing either a complement clause or a relative clause. For the less common head nouns taking a *that* complement clause, both possibilities regularly occur.

Complement clause:

> A second [reason] **that probability samples are so important** is from the point of view of internal validity. (ACAD)

Relative clause:

> But that would be a case of our having a competing or countervailing [reason] **that conflicted with our main positive reason for not killing or stealing**. (ACAD)

However, the head nouns that occur most commonly with a complement clause (such as *possibility*, *doubt*, *impression*, *belief*) almost never occur with relative clauses. For other head nouns, there are often strong register-specific preferences. For example, the head noun *knowledge* occurs 80 percent of the time with a *that* complement clause in fiction, but it occurs 80 percent of the time with a *that* relative clause in academic prose.

Complement clause in fiction:

> His plans were suddenly brought to a head by his [knowledge] **that Sir Charles was about to leave the hall on the advice of Dr. Mortimer**. (FICT)

Relative clause in academic prose:

> We use stereotypical 'labels' to make sense of other people, based on cues or [knowledge] **that we have about them**. (ACAD)

The head noun *fact* is exceptional in this regard. On the one hand, the noun *fact* in academic prose is by far the most common head noun that takes a noun complement clause. However, the combination of *fact* followed by a *that*-clause also commonly represents an extraposed construction rather than a noun complement clause (9.2.7):

> It is an accepted fact that people associate showrooms with pressure. (NEWS)

> It is an experimental fact that any property can be expressed as a function of two other independent properties. (ACAD†)

Further, the head noun *fact* also occasionally takes a relative clause:

> The overall figure would be even higher, a [fact] **that is to be explained, in part at least, by Zhou Youguang's use of a larger syllabary**. (ACAD†)

> A [fact] **that becomes clear**, however, was that the addition of heparin undoubtedly raised the incidence of bleeding. (ACAD)

(On *the fact that* in subject position, see 9.2.7.)

In short, although some nouns have become specialized as complement clause heads, there is a good deal of variation for most head nouns.

## 8.14.2 Head nouns taking *to*-clauses

**CORPUS FINDINGS** [2]

➤ There are important differences across registers in the distribution of nouns that commonly occur as head to a *to*-complement clause, shown in Table 8.16.

**Table 8.16** **Abstract nouns with *to*-clauses as complement; occurrences per million words**

(All head nouns that occur more than ten times per million words in at least one register)

▨ over 50    ▨ over 20    ▪ over 10    ▪ over 5

| | CONV | FICT | NEWS | ACAD |
|---|---|---|---|---|
| *chance* | over 20 | over 50 | over 50 | over 5 |
| *attempt* | | over 20 | over 50 | over 50 |
| *effort* | | over 20 | over 10 | over 20 |
| *ability* | | over 10 | over 20 | over 50 |
| *opportunity* | | over 10 | over 10 | over 20 |
| *desire* | | over 20 | over 5 | over 5 |
| *decision* | over 5 | | over 20 | over 5 |
| *plan* | over 5 | | over 20 | over 5 |
| *power* | over 5 | | over 10 | over 20 |
| *right* | | | over 20 | over 20 |
| *tendency* | | over 5 | over 5 | over 20 |
| *failure* | | | over 10 | over 20 |
| *capacity* | | | over 5 | over 50 |
| *inability* | over 5 | | over 5 | over 10 |
| *bid* | | | over 20 | |
| *permission* | | over 5 | over 10 | |
| *commitment* | | | over 10 | over 5 |
| *determination* | | | over 10 | over 5 |
| *intention* | | | over 10 | over 5 |
| *refusal* | | | over 10 | over 5 |
| *willingness* | | | over 5 | over 10 |
| *battle* | | | over 10 | |
| *proposal* | | | over 10 | |
| *scheme* | | | over 10 | |

➤ Less common head nouns, occurring over twice per million in at least one register, are: *agreement, authority, confidence, deal, duty, freedom, incentive, inclination, invitation, obligation, plot, potential, promise, readiness, reluctance, responsibility, temptation, threat, wish.*

Unlike *that*-clauses, the head nouns with *to*-clauses do not typically present a stance towards the complement clause. Instead, the common head nouns taking *to*-clauses represent human goals, opportunities, or actions; for example, *chance, attempt, effort, ability, opportunity, decision, plan, bid*. These meanings fit the purposes of news, with a focus on human goals and actions rather than on the attitudes of the writer:

> We need to give decent people a [chance] **to elect a sensible council**. (NEWS)
>
> The leader's gunshot wounds are taking their toll, complicating [efforts] **to persuade him to surrender**. (NEWS)
>
> Last year the society's committee made a [decision] **to relaunch** in a [bid] **to attract more members**. (NEWS)

At the same time, the head nouns taking *to*-clauses are similar to those taking *that*-clauses in that many of them are nominalized equivalents of verbs or adjectives controlling *to*-complement clauses. Of the 24 most common head nouns listed above, 15 are of this type. Ten of these have corresponding verbs that control *to*-clauses:

> *attempt, decision, desire, ailure, intention, permission, plan, proposal, refusal, tendency;*

while an additional five are derived from adjectives:

> *ability/inability, commitment, determination, willingness.*

Thus compare:

> He chastises Renault for their [failure] **to respond to BMW's challenge**. (NEWS†)
>
> v.  He [failed] **to notice that it made Wilson chuckle**. (FICT)
>
> The sense of betrayal has been deepened by London's [refusal] **to acknowledge any moral responsibility**. (NEWS†)
>
> v.  And he [refused] **to stay in Manhattan watching television**. (FICT)
>
> Such an order should be made only where there is evidence of the defendant's [ability] **to pay**. (NEWS)
>
> v.  I've never been [able] **to determine that for sure**. (FICT)

## 8.14.3  Head nouns taking *of* + *ing*-clauses

➤ There are important differences across registers in the distribution of nouns that commonly occur as head to *of* + *ing*-clause as complement; shown in Table 8.17.

➤ Less common head nouns, occurring over five times per million in at least one register, are: *act, aim, business, consequence, difficulty, dream, evidence, example, experience, fear, job, matter, necessity, opportunity, option, policy, principle, probability, question, sign, verge*.

Table 8.17   **Abstract nouns with *of* + *ing*-clauses: occurrences per million words**

(All head nouns that occur more than ten times per million words in at least one register)

▬▬ over 100    ▬▬ over 50    ▬ Over 20    ▪ over 10    ▌ over 5

| | CONV | FICT | NEWS | ACAD |
|---|---|---|---|---|
| *way* | over 20 | over 50 | over 50 | over 100 |
| *chance* | over 10 | over 10 | over 20 | over 10 |
| *idea* | over 5 | over 20 | over 10 | over 10 |
| *cost* | | | over 20 | over 20 |
| *intention* | | over 10 | over 10 | over 5 |
| *hope* | | over 5 | over 20 | over 5 |
| *means* | | over 5 | over 5 | over 20 |
| *method* | | | over 5 | over 50 |
| *task* | | over 5 | over 10 | over 10 |
| *danger* | | over 5 | over 10 | over 5 |
| *possibility* | | | over 5 | over 20 |
| *effect* | | | over 5 | over 20 |
| *problem* | | | over 5 | over 20 |
| *process* | | | over 5 | over 20 |
| *risk* | | | over 5 | over 20 |
| *point* | over 5 | over 10 | | |
| *habit* | | over 10 | over 5 | |
| *prospect* | | over 5 | over 10 | |
| *experience* | | | over 5 | over 10 |
| *purpose* | | | over 5 | over 10 |
| *result* | | | over 5 | over 10 |
| *thought* | | over 10 | over 5 | |
| *charge* | | | over 10 | |
| *advantage* | | | | over 10 |
| *form* | | | | over 10 |
| *importance* | | | | over 10 |
| *practice* | | | | over 10 |
| *system* | | | | over 10 |

## DISCUSSION OF FINDINGS

Several of the head nouns that take *of* + *ing*-clauses can also take another type of complement clause. (In contrast, there is almost no overlap between the head nouns taking *that*-clauses and the head nouns taking *to*-clauses.) For example, the following head nouns are common with both *of* + *ing*-clauses and with *that*-clauses:

   *idea, hope, possibility, sign, thought.*

Compare:

> *Feynman discusses the [idea]* **of putting a lamp between the two slits to illuminate the electrons.** (ACAD)

v. *Then a door is opened for the more threatening [idea]* **that some principles are part of the law because of their moral appeal.** (ACAD)

> *So we have no [hope]* **of finding here a common reason for rejecting checkerboard solutions.** (ACAD)

v. *There is every [hope]* **that this will continue.** (ACAD†)

Fewer head nouns can take both an *of* + *ing*-clause and a *to*-clause, but they include two of the most common nouns with both constructions: *chance* and *intention*.

Compare:

> *Also one increases the [chance]* **of revealing similarities between superficially distinct objects.** (ACAD)

v. *BOAC never had a [chance]* **to establish commercial operations on any scale.** (ACAD†)

> *This writer has served on review teams and has had every [intention]* **of giving each proposal a thorough reading.** (ACAD)

v. *Mr. Rawlins announced his [intention]* **to leave Sturge at some time in the future.** (NEWS)

Finally, there are some head nouns that can control only *of* + *ing*-clauses, such as *cost*, *task*, and *problem*:

> *They presented the move as a contribution by the Government to the huge [cost]* **of improving water quality.** (NEWS)

> *It therefore seems logical to begin the [task]* **of disentangling the relationship between movement and urban structure.** (ACAD)

The head noun *way*, which is by far the most-common head noun in this category, also occurs only with an *of* + *ing*-clause construction. This combination, however, is structurally ambiguous, in that it can be interpreted as either a complement clause or as a postmodifying construction with an adverbial gap. In fact, most of these constructions could be paraphrased with a postmodifying *to*-clause (8.8.2):

> *I have other [ways]* **of keeping fit.** (CONV)
> *cf. other ways to keep fit.*

> *He had no [way]* **of preventing the wheels from spinning off.** (FICT)
> *cf. no way to prevent the wheels ...*

> *However, this is not the only [way]* **of introducing the concept of an integral.** (ACAD)
> *cf. the only way to introduce the concept ...*

Similar ambiguities arise in the structural interpretation of constructions with the head nouns *method* and *means*:

> *The development of statistical [methods]* **of assessing error in biological experiments** *was also a major advance.* (ACAD)

> *All these provide indirect [means]* **of converting solar energy to forms of energy which are useful to us.** (ACAD)

## 8.14.4 Head nouns taking *wh*-interrogative clauses

*Wh*-interrogative clauses are much less common than the preceding types and restricted mostly to occurrence with the head noun *question*.

The *of* + *wh*-clause variant is actually more common than simple *wh*-clauses as noun complements, especially in news and academic prose. Further, it occurs with a wider range of head nouns. These include nouns referring to:

**speech communication**—*question, story, explanation, description, account, discussion*

**exemplification**—*example, indication, illustration*

**problems**—*problem, issue*

**cognitive states or processes**—*knowledge, understanding, sense, analysis, idea, notion.*

For example:

*The [question]* **of how to resolve the fear which so many people have in Hong Kong** *was omitted.* (NEWS)

*She has offered her plight as an [example]* **of what is happening to many small producers.** (NEWS)

*This presents the [problem]* **of how to handle the case where a message is presented to another user 'for inspection' only.** (ACAD)

*We have no [knowledge]* **of where it came from.** (NEWS)

# 9

# The form and function of complement clauses

# 9.1 Overview

## 9.1.1 Complementation by clauses

**Complement clauses** are a type of dependent clause used to complete the meaning relationship of an associated verb or adjective in a higher clause. For example, the *that*-clause in

> I thought **that it looked good**. (CONV†)

is a complement clause to the verb *thought*, specifying the content of the speaker's thinking. The verb *thought*, which we refer to as the **main clause verb**, is said to **control** the *that* complement clause.

Complement clauses are also sometimes called **nominal clauses** (3.11.1) because they typically occupy a noun phrase slot as subject, object, or predicative (3.2). For example, the *that*-clause in the following sentence functions as the direct object of the verb *said*:

> I said **that I wasn't perfect**. (CONV†)

Complement clauses can also be controlled by an adjectival predicate rather than a lexical verb in the main clause. The *that*-clause in the following sentence is complement to the adjectival predicate *careful*:

> I've gotta be careful **that I don't sound too pompous**. (CONV†)

In this chapter, we use the term **predicate** as a cover term for the two major elements that can control a complement clause: either a lexical verb or a copula + adjective. (Nouns can also control a complement clause; 8.12–14.)

## 9.1.2 Structural types of complement clause

There are four major structural types of complement clause: ***that*-clauses** (9.2), ***wh*-clauses** (9.3), ***to*-infinitive clauses** (9.4), and ***ing*-clauses** (9.5). They are distinguished on the basis of their internal structure and **complementizer** (e.g. *that* or *to*). All can complement both verbs and adjectival predicates.

*That*-clauses and *wh*-clauses are finite clauses (3.10–11). Thus, they include tense or modality distinctions and must have a subject.

*that*-clause:

> They warned him **that it's dangerous**. (CONV†)

*wh*-interrogative clause:

> I couldn't think **what it was**. (CONV)

*That*-clauses can occur with or without a *that* complementizer:

> I thought **it was a good film**. (CONV)
> cf. I thought **that it was a good film**.

*To*-clauses and *ing*-clauses are non-finite and thus do not include tense distinctions or modals (3.12).

*to*-clause:

> We wanted **to talk in front of my aunt**. (FICT)

*ing*-clause:

> He began **crunching it gently but firmly**. (FICT†)

Non-finite clauses often omit the subject, especially when the subject of the nominal clause refers to the same entity as the subject of the main clause (as in the examples above).

In addition, there are non-finite complement clauses which occur with an infinitive verb form (as in *to*-clauses) but no complementizer:

> Surrey police say the film would help **identify participants at the weekend party**. (NEWS)

These **bare infinitive clauses** are treated below as a special subclass of infinitive clauses.

Infinitive clauses can also occur in combination with *wh*-clauses:

> She never knows **how to just say no**. (CONV)

Finally, *ed*-clauses can also function as verb complements:

> I got **the door unlocked**. (FICT†)

> Western Union must have got **the names reversed**. (FICT†)

> They had **carnival rides trucked in and installed on the great green lawns**. (FICT†)

Only a few main clause verbs can control *ed*-clauses: they include *got*, *had*, *want*, *need*, *see* and *hear* (11.3.1).

## 9.1.3 Grammatical positions of complement clauses

Where the controlling predicate is a verb, complement clauses of all structural types can occur in both **pre-predicate** (subject) position and **post-predicate** (e.g. direct object) position (except bare infinitive clauses and *ed*-clauses, which occur only in post-predicate position).

Subject, preceding the verb predicate (9.2.7, 9.4.7):

> **That they are already struggling** troubles Graham Taylor. (NEWS)

> **What is good among one people** is an abomination with others. (FICT)

> However, **to say all other courses are impossible** is not to say this course is possible. (NEWS)

> **Walking the back nine** confirms what all the fuss is about. (NEWS†)

Direct object, following the verb predicate (9.2.2, 9.3.2, 9.4.2, 9.5.2):

> They conclude **that the change was cynical and opportunistic**. (NEWS†)

> You know **what I call my mom**. (CONV)

> They are trying **to hold it together**. (CONV†)

> I'm not going to start **going on cross-country runs at my age**. (FICT)

In addition, complement clauses can serve as subject predicative to a copular verb. In these cases, the complement clause further identifies or describes the subject of the main clause:

> One of the reasons could be **that some of the people are socially and economically deprived**. (NEWS†)

> The industry's premise is **that we can recognize information presented below our threshold of awareness**. (NEWS)

> That's **what the case is all about**. (NEWS)

> The immediate reason for his return is **to give two charity concerts**. (NEWS†)

> Publicity is **communicating**. (General prose)

Similarly, clauses complementing adjectival predicates can occur in both pre-predicate position and post-predicate position.

Pre-predicate position:

**That it would be unpopular with colleges or students** *was obvious.* (NEWS)

**What a single mother represents** *may seem touchingly attractive.* (NEWS)

**To attempt to forecast the effects of changing regulations on a national scale** *is very difficult.* (ACAD)

**Her coming** *was quite useless.* (FICT)

Post-predicate position (9.2.5, 9.4.5, 9.5.3):

*If they vote against the governor, I feel very confident* **that Republican state organizations would finance an opponent.** (NEWS)

*I'm not sure* **when it's open.** (CONV†)

*Everybody's glad* **to have him around.** (CONV)

*The Prime Minister appeared confident* **of winning an overall majority.** (NEWS†)

However, in actual use complement clauses rarely occur in the pre-predicate position. Instead, *that*-clauses and *to*-clauses have a structural alternative to pre-predicate clauses—called **extraposition** (3.6.4, 9.2.3, 9.2.5.2, 9.2.7, 9.4.3, 9.4.5.3, 9.4.7)—which is more common:

*It just never crossed their minds* **that it might happen.** (CONV†)
*cf.* **That it might happen** *just never crossed their minds.*

*It's good* **to see them in the bath.** (CONV†)
*cf.* **To see them in the bath** *is good.*

*It had taken him 26 years* **to return.** (NEWS†)
*cf.* **To return** *had taken him 26 years.*

*It seems odd* **that I should be expected to pay for the privilege of assisting in this way.** (NEWS)
*cf.* **That I should be expected** ... *(seems odd)*

Extraposed constructions are also possible with *wh*-clauses:

*It was not immediately clear* **how the Soviet leadership could enforce such a ruling.** (NEWS†)

In an extraposed structure, the dummy pronoun *it* fills the slot preceding the main clause verb, and the complement clause occurs after the main clause verb or adjectival predicate. In these constructions, the *it* is not referential (3.2.1.2), and the complement clause functions as logical subject of the main clause.

# 9.2    *That*-clauses

## 9.2.1    Discourse functions of *that*-clauses

*That* complement clauses occurring in post-predicate position are commonly used to report the speech, thoughts, attitudes, or emotions of humans. In these constructions, the subject of the main clause refers to the human participant, the lexical verb or adjectival predicate presents the type of reporting (e.g. speech or thought), and the *that*-clause presents the reported speech, thought, or attitude:

> *He said **that nine indictments have been returned publicly in such*** ***investigations.*** (NEWS)
>
> *I think **Stuart's gone a bit mad*** (CONV)
>
> *I was quite confident **that it would stay in very well*** (CONV)

Extraposed *that*-clauses and *that*-clauses in subject position involve a main clause that often reports an attitude or stance which is not overtly attributed to any person. This is usually the attitude of the speaker or writer of the text, even though the author does not assume explicit responsibility for the attitude:

> *It is certain **that the challenges ahead are at least as daunting as anything*** ***the cold war produced.*** (NEWS)
>
> *It was obvious **that no subjects could perceive the movement at a normal*** ***distance.*** (ACAD†)
>
> *It is vitally important **that both groups are used to support one another**.* (ACAD†)

In non-fiction writing, it is not unusual to find a complex series of *that*-clauses, representing various kinds of coordination and embedding, with post-predicate as well as extraposed constructions:

> *I think [that President Reagan believed [[that not only was the government* *the problem], but [that it was rare indeed [that government could be a* *positive force in solving the problem]]]].* (NEWS)

For the most part, the verbs and adjectival predicates taking *that*-clauses in post-predicate position represent different semantic domains from those taking *that*-clauses in other positions. In both cases, though, there is a relatively restricted set of controlling verbs and adjectives, which belong to relatively few semantic classes.

## 9.2.2 Post-predicate *that*-clauses controlled by verbs

The verbs that take a *that*-complement clause in post-predicate position fall into just three major semantic domains: **mental verbs**, mainly of cognition (e.g. *think, know*), but including a few with emotive/affective content (e.g. *hope* and *wish*); **speech act verbs** (e.g. *say, tell*); and **other communication verbs** that do not necessarily involve speech (e.g. *show, prove, suggest*) (cf. the verb classes in 5.2.1–2). We will look first at the structural patterns with *that*-clauses, and then in more detail at these lexical associations.

### 9.2.2.1 Structural patterns

There are three possible structural patterns for verbs taking a *that*-clause in post-predicate position (cf. 3.5.4–7, 5.2.4).

**Pattern 1: verb + *that*-clause**
(e.g. *agree, ask*)

> 1 *I didn't agree **that he should be compelled to do singing**.* (CONV)

**Pattern 2: verb + NP + *that*-clause**
(e.g. *tell, persuade*)

> 2 *I persuaded myself **that something awful might happen**.* (FICT)

**Pattern 3: verb + *to* NP + *that*-clause**
(e.g. *suggest*)

   **3** *I suggested to Miss Kerrison* **that she sit down on the chair and wait.**
      (FICT)

*That*-clauses do not occur following prepositions. However, some of the simple verbs that take *that*-clauses correspond to the prepositional verbs taking noun-headed phrases:

   *Pattern 1:* **agree + *that*-clause**          **agree to** + NP

   *Pattern 2:* **advise** + NP + ***that*-clause**     **advise** + NP + **of/about** NP

Similarly, the complements of Pattern 3 verbs occur in a different order with a noun-headed phrase:

   *Pattern 3:* **suggest** + **to** NP + *that*-clause   **suggest** + NP + **to** NP

Most of the verbs taking Pattern 2 can also occur in the passive voice with a *that*-clause:

   **4** *He was told* **that she had checked out of the hospital.** (FICT†)

All verbs taking Pattern 3 can also occur with Pattern 1. For example, compare **3** with **5**:

   **5** *I suggested* **that she sit down on the chair and wait.**

(For discussion of the subjunctive in **5**, see the end of 9.2.2.2.)

   In addition, many verbs can occur with both Pattern 1 and Pattern 2:

   *I promise* **that we will take great care of him.** (FICT†)
   *cf. I promise you* **that we will take great care of him.**

A few verbs can occur with all three patterns (e.g. *write, cable, wire*):

   *I wrote* **that I would be satisfied with any old freighter.** (FICT†)
   *cf. I wrote him* **that I would be satisfied with any old freighter.**
   *cf. I wrote to him* **that I would be satisfied with any old freighter.**

The second of these options with *write* is largely restricted to AmE.

   Finally, a few verbs of affect are used in the pattern verb + *it* + *that*-clause:

   *He doesn't like* **it that she poses as a Catholic.** (FICT)

In this pattern, the pronoun *it* and the *that*-clause are co-referential. This pattern is rare in the LSWE Corpus and thus not considered further below.

## 9.2.2.2    Controlling verbs, by semantic domain

**CORPUS FINDINGS 1**

➤ Nine verbs are notably common taking *that*-clauses in post-predicate position (Figure 9.1).

   ➤ Two verbs are extremely common in this function: *think* and *say*. The verb *know* is also very common.

   ➤ Six of the seven most frequent verbs taking *that*-clauses are cognition verbs: *think, know, see, find, believe, feel.*

   ➤ *Guess* is also extremely common with *that*-clauses in AmE conversation (see Figure 9.2).

   ➤ In addition, three communication verbs are notably common: *say, show,* and *suggest.*

➤ 27 other verbs are relatively common controlling a *that*-clause (see Table 9.1).

**Figure 9.1**   **Overall frequencies of the most common verbs controlling *that*-clauses**

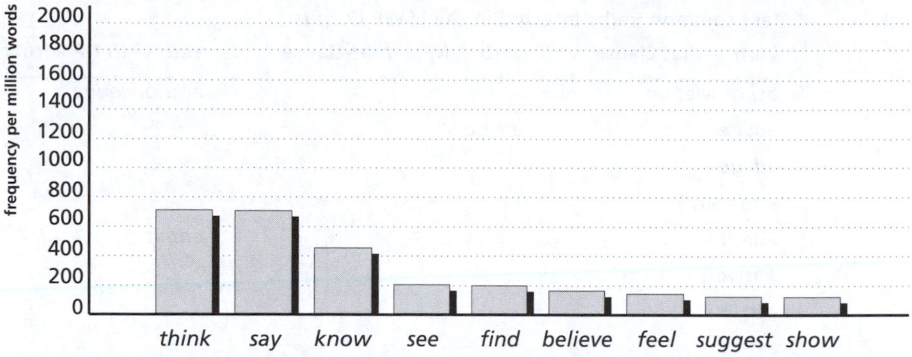

**Table 9.1**   **Common verbs controlling a complement *that*-clause, by frequency and structural pattern**

**Mental verbs, mainly of cognition**

All having the structure: **verb + *that*-clause**

**notably common verbs** (more than 100 per million words):

*believe, feel, find, guess* (AmE), *know, see, think*

**relatively common verbs** (more than 20 per million words):

*assume, conclude, decide, doubt, expect, hear, hope, imagine, mean, notice, read, realize, recognize, remember, suppose, understand, wish*

**other verbs attested in the LSWE Corpus:**

*accept, anticipate, ascertain, calculate, conceive, consider, detect, determine, deduce, deem, discover, dream, estimate, fancy, fear, figure, foresee, forget, gather* (= 'understand'), *hold* (= 'believe'), *hypothesize, intend, judge, learn, maintain, mind, observe, perceive, plan, predict, pretend, presume, presuppose, prefer, reckon, recollect, reflect, resolve, recall, sense, speculate, suspect, trust, worry*

**Speech act verbs**

**notably common verbs** (more than 100 per million words):

| verb + *that*-clause | verb + NP + *that*-clause | verb + to NP + *that*-clause |
|---|---|---|
| *say* | | *say* |

**relatively common verbs** (more than 20 per million words):

| verb + *that*-clause | verb + NP + *that*-clause | verb + to NP + *that*-clause |
|---|---|---|
| *admit* | | *admit* |
| *agree* | | |
| *announce* | | *announce* |
| *argue* | | |
| *bet* | *bet* | |
| *insist* | | *insist* |
| | *tell* | |

**Table 9.1** **continued**

less common verbs attested in the LSWE Corpus:

| verb + *that*-clause | verb + NP + *that*-clause | verb + *to* NP + *that*-clause |
|---|---|---|
| acknowledge | | acknowledge |
| advise | advise | |
| allege | | |
| add ('say') | | |
| admit | | admit |
| answer | | |
| ask | | |
| assert | | |
| boast | | boast |
| charge | | |
| complain | | complain |
| contend | | |
| claim | | |
| concede | | concede |
| confess | | confess |
| confide | | confide |
| cry | | cry |
| declare | | declare |
| demand | | |
| deny | | |
| emphasize | | emphasize |
| explain | | explain |
| express | | express |
| forewarn | forewarn | |
| grant | | grant |
| hint | | hint |
| imply | | imply |
| | inform | |
| mention | | mention |
| mutter | | mutter |
| | notify | |
| order | | |
| | persuade | |
| point out | | point out |
| proclaim | | proclaim |
| promise | promise | |
| propose | | propose |
| protest | | |
| remark | | remark |
| | remind | |
| reply | | reply |

**Table 9.1** **continued**

**less common verbs attested in the LSWE Corpus—continued**

| verb + *that*-clause | verb + NP + *that*-clause | verb + *to* NP + *that*-clause |
|---|---|---|
| report | | report |
| respond | | respond |
| shout | | shout |
| state | | state |
| stress | | stress |
| swear | | swear |
| testify | | testify |
| urge | | |
| vow | | vow |
| warn | warn | |
| whisper | | whisper |

## Other communication verbs

**notably common verbs** (more than 100 per million words):

| verb + *that*-clause | verb + NP + *that*-clause | verb + *to* NP + *that*-clause |
|---|---|---|
| show | show | |
| suggest | | suggest |

**relatively common verbs** (more than 20 per million words):

| verb + *that*-clause | verb + NP + *that*-clause | verb + *to* NP + *that*-clause |
|---|---|---|
| ensure | | |
| indicate | | indicate |
| prove | | prove |

**less common verbs attested in the LSWE Corpus:**

| verb + *that*-clause | verb + NP + *that*-clause | verb + *to* NP + *that*-clause |
|---|---|---|
| affirm | | |
| arrange | | |
| | assure | |
| bear | | |
| cable | cable | cable |
| certify | | |
| check | | |
| confirm | | |
| convey | | convey |
| | convince | |
| demonstrate | | demonstrate |
| guarantee | | |
| note | | |
| petition | petition | |
| (tele)phone | (tele)phone | |
| postulate | | |

Table 9.1    **continued**

less common verbs attested in the LSWE Corpus—continued

| verb + *that*-clause | verb + NP + *that*-clause | verb + *to* NP + *that*-clause |
|---|---|---|
| pray | | pray |
| | reassure | |
| recommend | | recommend |
| record | | |
| require | | |
| reveal | | reveal |
| signify | | signify |
| submit | | submit |
| teach | teach | |
| wager | wager | |
| wire | wire | wire |
| write | write | write |

**DISCUSSION OF FINDINGS**

## A    Mental verbs, mainly of cognition

The most common use of *that* complement clauses is clearly to report people's mental states and processes:

> We felt **that between us we'd got over twenty years experience of working with children**. (CONV†)

> My mother thought **that firmness should come into it**. (FICT†)

> He knew **that nothing Garth said would surprise him**. (FICT)

> I believe **that God exists**. (NEWS)

> I imagine **that many honest people would sympathize with Weatherhead**. (NEWS†)

> Political leaders in all parties recognise **that Germany is moving towards reunification**. (NEWS†)

> We also saw **that densities of liquids are much higher than those of gases**. (ACAD)

> W. L. Bragg found **that a pattern of diffraction corresponded to one that would be formed by reflection of the X-ray beam**. (ACAD)

The most frequent mental verbs with *that*-clauses include some of the most frequent verbs in English (e.g. *think* and *know*; 5.2.2.2). The majority of these verbs denote states or processes of thought (e.g. *know, think, conclude, suppose*). A smaller number express emotions (e.g. *feel, hope*) or receptive processing of communication (*read, hear*).

Mental verbs with *that*-clauses are an important device used to express stance. For example, verbs such as *think, feel*, and *assume* convey a sense of possibility combined with uncertainty, while verbs such as *know, find*, and *see* convey a definite sense of certainty. Compare:

> **I think it's gotta be through there**. (CONV)

> I know **I told you**. (CONV)

**B   Speech act and other communication verbs**

The other common use of *that*-clauses is to report what somebody said:

> She said **that it's lovely to wear.** (CONV)
>
> Fatty had told him **that he looked the type.** (FICT†)
>
> Tonight Mr. Terence had promised **that several hot-shots from American recording companies would be in the audience.** (FICT)
>
> Besides, aid workers argue **that cutting any aid will only result in more poppies.** (NEWS)
>
> The police say **that they haven't the time or resources to worry about hashish.** (NEWS†)

Clauses giving the content of speech (without *that*) can be preposed to a topic position before the subject of the main clause (3.11.5, 11.2.3.6). This construction is most commonly found in news:

> **The downing of two U.S. helicopters by a pair of American warplanes over Iraq occurred despite a host of systems designed precisely to avert that kind of mistake,** Pentagon officials said Thursday. (NEWS)
>
> **Throughout the selection process, Kearse's name has been one of the few that Clinton consistently has had under serious consideration,** Administration officials say. (NEWS)

Other communication verbs, reporting information in ways that do not necessarily involve speech, often indicate the degree of certainty associated with the reported information. For example, verbs such as *show*, *prove*, and *demonstrate* mark a high degree of certainty, while a lesser degree of certainty is expressed by verbs such as *suggest*, *indicate*, and *postulate*:

> They suggest **that he could become the country's national president.** (NEWS†)
>
> Empirical data show **that similar processes can be guided quite differently by users with different views on the purposes of communication.** (ACAD)
>
> First we prove **that Banach spaces contain uncomplemented subspaces.** (ACAD)
>
> Information from the planetary probes indicates **that all the terrestrial planets have undergone differentiation.** (ACAD)

In addition, some communication verbs can be used with a *that*-clause to propose a potential course of action (rather than report information):

> 1   The medicine-man then ordered **that there [should be] no mourning for the dead child.** (FICT)
>
> 2   We ask **that this food [be] blessed.** (CONV†)

*That*-clauses with this use occur with either the modal *should* (as in **1**), or an uninflected subjunctive verb form (as in **2**; cf. 3.9). Other verbs that can occur in this pattern are *advise* and *insist*.

## 9.2.2.3   Common controlling verbs across registers

**CORPUS FINDINGS 2**

➤  The single most common verb controlling *that*-clauses is *think* in conversation.

**Figure 9.2**
**Frequencies of the most common verbs controlling *that*-clauses—conversation**

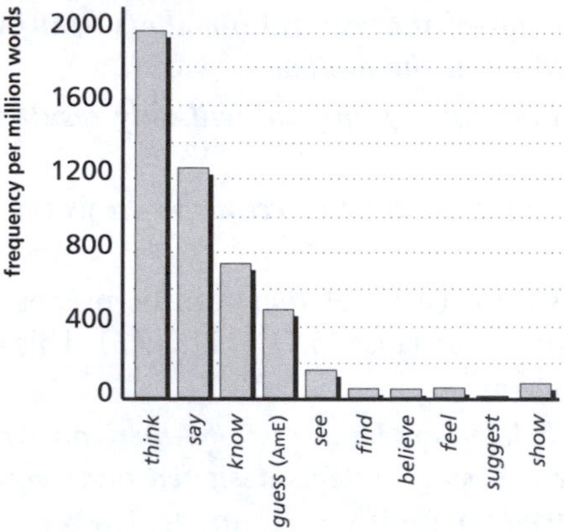

**Figure 9.3**
**Frequencies of the most common verbs controlling *that*-clauses—fiction**

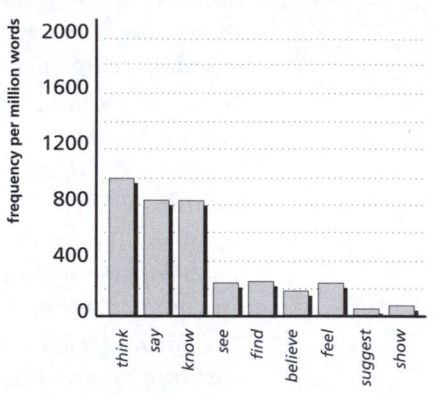

**Figure 9.4**
**Frequencies of the most common verbs controlling *that*-clauses—news**

**Figure 9.5**
**Frequencies of the most common verbs controlling *that*-clauses—academic prose**

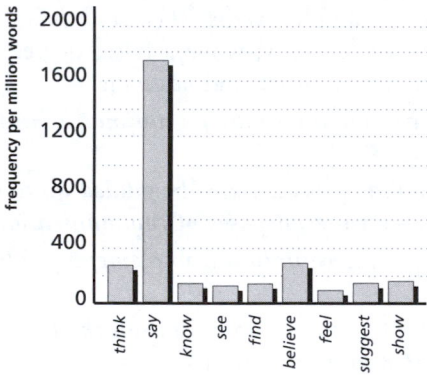

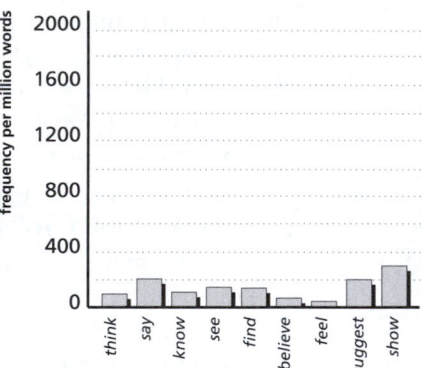

➤ *Say* in news and conversation is the second most common verb controlling *that*-clauses.

➤ *Know* is also notably common in conversation and fiction.

➤ *Guess* is more restricted in distribution, being particularly frequent only in AmE conversation.

➤ Academic prose has the least frequent use of these forms.

   ➤ However, the verbs *suggest* and *show* are moderately common in academic prose.

➤ Eight other verbs are notably common (more than 100 occurrences per million words) in at least one register: *mean, suppose, realize, hear, hope, assume, ensure, indicate* (see Table 9.2).

➤ In general, mental verbs controlling *that*-clauses are especially frequent in fiction (and to a lesser extent conversation).

➤ In contrast, communication verbs controlling *that*-clauses (apart from *say*) are most frequent in academic prose (and to a lesser extent news).

**Table 9.2** **The most common verbs controlling a complement *that*-clause by semantic domain and register; occurrences per million words**

Legend: ▰ over 600  ▰ over 200  ▪ over 100  ▎ over 20

| semantic domain | CONV | FICT | NEWS | ACAD |
|---|---|---|---|---|
| **mental/cognition** | | | | |
| *know* | over 600 | over 600 | over 100 | over 20 |
| *think* | over 600 | over 600 | over 200 | over 20 |
| *guess* (AmE) | over 200 | over 100 | | |
| *see* | over 100 | over 200 | over 100 | over 100 |
| *find* | over 20 | over 200 | over 100 | over 100 |
| *believe* | over 20 | over 100 | over 200 | over 20 |
| *mean* | over 100 | over 100 | over 20 | over 20 |
| *suppose* | over 100 | over 100 | | over 20 |
| *feel* | over 20 | over 200 | over 20 | over 20 |
| *realize* | over 20 | over 100 | over 20 | over 20 |
| *hear* | over 20 | over 100 | over 20 | |
| *hope* | over 20 | over 100 | over 20 | |
| *assume* | | over 20 | over 20 | over 100 |
| **speech act** | | | | |
| *say* | over 200 | over 200 | over 200 | over 100 |
| **other communication** | | | | |
| *show* | over 20 | over 20 | over 100 | over 200 |
| *suggest* | | over 20 | over 100 | over 200 |
| *ensure* | | | over 20 | over 100 |
| *indicate* | | | over 20 | over 100 |

**DISCUSSION OF FINDINGS**

## A Cognition verbs

The extremely high frequency of the verb *think* with *that*-clauses in conversation is largely due to the use of the clause *I think* to report one's own personal thoughts:

*I think* **we picked it** (CONV†)

*I think* **that's why you can't clean them** (CONV)

*I don't think* **he does too much in the furniture business** (CONV†)

In contrast, fiction commonly uses a wide range of mental verbs to describe the thoughts and other cognitive states of fictional characters:

*She thought* **that I gloated over their downfall.** (FICT)

*He knew* **that if he touched it, it would be as soft as silk.** (FICT†)

*She saw* **that it was a moose with a body as big as a truck.** (FICT)

*He looked at the wound and found* **that it had stopped bleeding.** (FICT†)

*He felt* **that something else was going to happen tonight.** (FICT†)

As already noted, *guess* is very common with a *that*-clause in AmE conversation and fiction:

> I **guess** I should probably call Michele. (CONV)

> I **guess** they didn't hear anything. (FICT)

The verb *believe* also reports a cognitive state, but is more common in news than the other registers:

> The Secretary of State, Mr. Jim Baker, and probably Mr. Bush, believe **that there are trustworthy deals to be done**. (NEWS)

> Federal Interior Minister Aitzaz Ahsan, whose portfolio includes narcotics control, believes **that an armed intervention is not a panacea to end the traffic**. (NEWS)

Academic writers consider it less relevant or appropriate to report personal thoughts, so mental verbs are least common in academic prose.

**B   Speech act and other communication verbs**

The speech-act verb *say* shows a different register distribution with *that*-clauses: it is extremely common in news and conversation, and very common in fiction. Its frequent use in news reflects the fact that the pronouncements of public figures are considered newsworthy:

> Mr. Kenneth Clarke, the Health Secretary, yesterday said **that the latest pay offer made last Friday was worth 9 per cent**. (NEWS†)

Academic prose shows a moderately frequent use of communication verbs such as *show*, *ensure*, and *indicate*. These verbs are often used with a non-personal subject to report a stance that is not overtly associated with the thoughts or feelings of human observers:

> Other models show **that this state of affairs may have been reached only a few hundred million years after Earth's formation**. (ACAD†)

> Measured values at present indicate **that the chain modulus of polyethylene is certainly higher than 280 Gpa**. (ACAD)

## 9.2.3   Verbs taking extraposed *that*-clauses

There are fewer verbs controlling extraposed *that*-clauses, and correspondingly the overall frequency of extraposed constructions is much lower than that of *that*-clauses in post-predicate position. The copula *be*, functioning as a predicate in combination with various noun phrases, is the most common verb taking extraposed *that*-clauses:

> It's a wonder **he's got any business at all**! (CONV)

Similarly, the copular verbs *seem* and *appear* are relatively common:

> It seemed however **that in-pig sows showed more stress than empty ones**. (ACAD)

> It now appears **that I will be expected to part with a further portion of my income as a graduate tax**. (NEWS†)

Other verbs taking extraposed *that*-clauses are *follow* used intransitively, and passive voice verbs such as *be found*, *be known*, *be assumed*, *be said*, and *be shown*:

> It follows **that frequentist probability is conceptually inadequate for the design or licensing of hazardous facilities**. (ACAD)

It has been shown **that sites near the mushroom bodies control the production of normal song-rhythms.** (ACAD†)

## 9.2.4 Subject noun phrases with subject predicative *that*-clauses

When a *that*-clause serves as subject predicative to a copular verb, it also identifies or describes the subject of the main clause. These constructions often describe the nature of some problem:

[The problem] is **that the second question cannot be answered until Washington comes up with a consensus on the first.** (NEWS)

[The problem about heroin] is **that the money is so good that even good people do it.** (NEWS)

[The only problem] may be **that the compound is difficult to remove after use.** (ACAD)

A second common use of subject predicative *that*-clauses is to present reasons, results, or conclusions:

Another reason to use Ohio as a surrogate for the country as a whole is **that the data base for hazardous waste generation and flow for the state are fairly good.** (ACAD)

The net result is **that foreign money has frequently ended up fertilising or irrigating opium fields.** (NEWS†)

Our first conclusion at this point was **that it is necessary to support the specification and application of regulations and patterns in groups.** (ACAD)

A third use is to present accepted facts or truths:

The truth is **that the country is now specialising more in processing and marketing.** (NEWS)

The set of nouns that occurs as subjects in such clauses is similar to the set that takes noun complement clauses (8.14).

## 9.2.5 *That*-clauses controlled by adjectival predicates

The adjectives that control a *that* complement clause all convey stance, falling into three major semantic domains: degrees of certainty (e.g. *certain, confident, evident*); affective psychological states (e.g. *annoyed, glad, sad*); and evaluation of situations, events, etc. (e.g. *appropriate, odd, good, important, advisable*).

For the most part, the adjectives that control post-predicate *that*-clauses are different from those that control extraposed *that*-clauses.

Post-predicate *that*-clause:

1 *I'm glad* **that I found you again.** (FICT)

Extraposed *that*-clause:

2 *It's nice* **that people say it to you unprompted.** (CONV)

However, a few adjectives (e.g. *certain, sad*) can control both post-predicate and extraposed *that*-clauses. In the following sections, we describe the sets of adjectives that take these two major types of *that*-clause.

### 9.2.5.1 Adjectival predicates taking post-predicate *that*-clauses

**CORPUS FINDINGS** [1]

➤ *That*-clauses controlled by adjectival predicates are much less common than *that*-clauses controlled by verbs.

➤ Only one adjectival predicate—*be sure*—is relatively common, occurring more than ten times per million words in the LSWE Corpus.

➤ Numerous other adjectives occur less commonly with a post-predicate *that*-clause:

   ➤ **Certainty adjectives**—*certain, confident, convinced, positive, right, sure*

   ➤ **Affective adjectives**—*adamant, afraid, alarmed, amazed, amused, angry, annoyed, astonished, (un)aware, careful, concerned, depressed, disappointed, distressed, disturbed, encouraged, frightened, glad, grateful, (un)happy, hopeful, hurt, irritated, mad, pleased, proud, reassured, relieved, sad, (dis)satisfied, sensible, shocked, sorry, surprised, thankful, uncomfortable, upset, worried.*

**DISCUSSION OF FINDINGS**

Certainty adjectives indicate the degree of certitude of the proposition presented in the *that*-clause. These constructions typically have a human subject in the main clause, and they attribute the feeling of certainty to that person:

> *I'm sure* **that they'd got two little rooms on the ground floor** (CONV†)

> *The minister is confident* **that Pakistan could deflect western pressure.** (NEWS)

In other cases, the certainty adjective can reflect the writer's assessment of a position held by some third person:

> *They are undoubtedly right* **that it has now become clear that the government will not pay for the expansion it desires.** (NEWS†)

Affective adjectives similarly co-occur with human subjects, presenting a personal attitude or feeling towards the proposition in the *that*-clause:

> *I'm afraid* **it brings the caterpillars in.** (CONV)

> *I'm sorry* **I hit you just now.** (FICT)

> *Ellen was pleased* **that Tobie had remembered.** (FICT†)

> *The president himself can hardly have been surprised* **that his own head was now being demanded on a platter.** (NEWS†)

Although a few of these adjectives have close counterparts among the emotive mental verbs that take *that*-clauses (e.g. *afraid/fear, worried/worry*; see 9.2.2.2), the two sets are mostly complementary in their coverage of this semantic domain.

### 9.2.5.2 Adjectival predicates taking extraposed *that*-clauses

**CORPUS FINDINGS** [1]

➤ Four adjectival predicates are relatively common controlling extraposed *that*-clauses: *clear, (un)likely, (im)possible, true*. These forms occur more than ten times per million words in the LSWE Corpus.

➤ Many other adjectives occur less commonly with an extraposed *that*-clause.

➤ **Certainty adjectives:** *accepted, apparent, certain, clear, correct, doubtful, evident, false, inevitable, (un)likely, obvious, plain, (im)possible, probable, right, true, well-known.*

➤ **Affective or evaluative adjectives:** *(un)acceptable, amazing, anomalous, annoying, appropriate, astonishing, awful, (in)conceivable, curious, disappointing, dreadful, embarrassing, extraordinary, (un)fortunate, frightening, funny, good, great, horrible, incidental, incredible, indisputable, interesting, ironic, irritating, (un)lucky, natural, neat, nice, notable, noteworthy, noticeable, odd, okay, paradoxical, peculiar, preferable, ridiculous, sad, sensible, shocking, silly, strange, stupid, sufficient, surprising, tragic, (un)typical, unfair, understandable, unthinkable, unusual, upsetting, wonderful.*

➤ **Importance adjectives:** *advisable, critical, crucial, desirable, essential, fitting, imperative, important, necessary, obligatory, vital.*

### DISCUSSION OF FINDINGS

Adjectival predicates with extraposed *that*-clauses mark a stance or attitude towards the proposition in the *that*-clause. In most cases, this predicate represents the attitude of the speaker/writer, although it is not overtly attributed to that person.

Certainty adjectives are the most common adjectival predicates controlling extraposed *that*-clauses, indicating the extent to which the speaker/writer regards the embedded proposition as *certain, obvious, likely, possible,* etc.:

> *It has been clear for some time **that the demands of the arms control process would increasingly dominate military planning**.* (NEWS)

> *But already it is certain **that the challenges ahead are at least as daunting as anything the Cold War produced**.* (NEWS)

> *It is obvious **that direct chilling of the udder depends as much on the thermal properties of the floor as on the air temperature**.* (ACAD†)

> *It is unlikely **that any insect exceeds about twice this velocity**.* (ACAD)

The affective/evaluative adjectives mark other assessments or attitudes towards the proposition in the *that*-clause. Some adjectives, such as *appropriate, fortunate, good, great, lucky, nice, wonderful,* have positive connotations; others, such as *awful, bad, disappointing, dreadful, horrible, unfortunate, unlucky, sad, tragic,* have negative connotations. Other such adjectives are not strongly positive or negative, but indicate an emotional response such as surprise, interest, or amusement (e.g. *amazing, astonishing, funny, incredible, interesting, natural, odd, peculiar, strange, surprising, unusual*):

> *It is good **that our clan holds the Ozo title in high esteem**.* (FICT†)

> *It's horrible **that he put up with Claire's nagging**.* (CONV†)

> *It is tragic **that so many of his generation died as they did**.* (FICT†)

> *It is unfair **that one sector of the water industry should be treated more favourably than another**.* (NEWS†)

> *It is conceivable **that this critical stage would not be reached before temperatures began to rise again in the spring**.* (ACAD)

Several evaluative adjectives can occur with an extraposed *that*-clause having a hypothetical sense, proposing a course of action that should be followed rather than simply evaluating a proposition reported as a fact. These constructions are marked by *should* or subjunctive verb forms:

> It is preferable **that the marked cells [should be] identical in their behaviour to the unmarked cells.** (ACAD†)

> It is sensible **that the breeding animals [receive] the highest protection.** (ACAD†)

Necessity or importance adjectives also control extraposed *that*-clauses usually with *should* or an uninflected subjunctive verb form, reflecting the writer's belief that a proposed course of action is essential or important. These forms are most common in academic prose:

> It is essential **that the two instruments should run parallel to the microscope stage.** (ACAD†)

> It is vital **that leaking water is avoided.** (ACAD†)

> It is important **that it be well sealed from air leakage.** (ACAD†)

> It is desirable **that it be both lined and insulated.** (ACAD†)

## 9.2.6    Register distribution of *that*-clause types

**CORPUS FINDINGS** [2,3]

➤ Over 80% of all *that*-clauses occur in post-predicate position controlled by a verb.

➤ Post-predicate *that*-clauses after verbs are most common in conversation and very common in fiction and news (but less common in academic prose).

➤ Post-predicate *that*-clauses controlled by adjectival predicates are also most common in conversation.

➤ Extraposed *that*-clauses are moderately common in news and academic prose (but rare in fiction and conversation).

➤ *That*-clauses in subject position are rare in all registers.

➤ Subject predicative *that*-clauses are moderately common in news and academic prose (but rare in fiction and conversation).

**Figure 9.6**

**Frequencies of *that*-clause types in the LSWE Corpus**

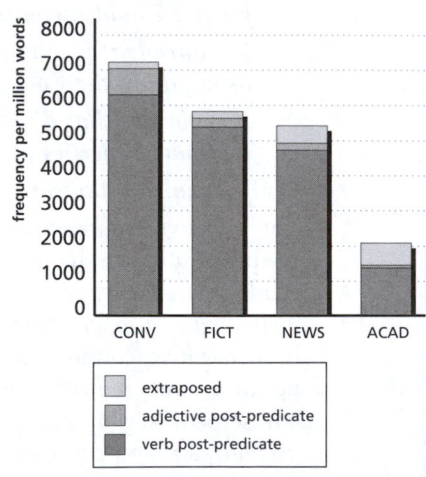

## DISCUSSION OF FINDINGS

These distributional patterns reflect the communicative needs of each register in relation to the major discourse functions of *that*-clauses.

Post-predicate *that*-clauses controlled by verbs are used most commonly to report indirect speech or mental states. These clauses typically have two major characteristics: a personal, human noun phrase as subject of the main clause, and an active voice verb as the predicate. These features make post-predicate *that*-clauses particularly suited to conversation.

The following excerpt from a conversation illustrates the repeated use of *that*-clauses to serve the purposes of interpersonal communication. Note especially the frequent use of *that*-clauses with verbs such as *think*, *know*, and *reckon*, to present various thoughts and attitudes, plus the use of *that*-clauses with verbs such as *tell* and *say* (marked by *[ ]*) to report speech acts:

Text sample 1: DISCUSSING SCHOOL EXPERIENCES

> B: *So this is where you two get all this supposedly <sic> cleverness.*
>
> A: *Supposedly, when I, when I [told] Nicola the other day **that you [reckon] that I don't do enough work**, she says cor blimey – she was shocked she was, shocked –*
>
> B: *I don't think er, I don't [think] **you do do work, enough work**, either of you really – if they ever brought it back, it'll be a lot different than what it was then – it'd be easy wouldn't it? –*
>
> A: *It wouldn't have been easier*
>
> B: *Well it would, it would have, it'd be easier, I [think] **it would***
>
> A: *Not to everybody it wouldn't*
>
> B: *Well I think, I think, I [think] **to be honest they've all got easier** –*
>
> A: *I'd [say] **they'd got harder**, you should see some of the things we do in maths mum, it's not easy*
>
> B: *No I know **that it's not easier now**, you know, but I [think] **that would be easier** wouldn't it?*

At the other extreme, extraposed *that*-clauses controlled by adjectival predicates, as well as *that*-clauses in subject predicative position, have the opposite structural and functional characteristics: an impersonal, non-human noun phrase as subject of the main clause; a main clause predicate representing a static relation or attribute; a heavy, complex *that*-clause that includes other embedded phrases and clauses.

Constructions with these characteristics are relatively rare. When they are used, they are most likely to occur in the expository prose registers (news and academic prose), which often report static information in an impersonal manner. The following examples from a single academic prose text (a biology textbook) illustrate the use of extraposed *that*-clauses to mark likelihood and other stances in an impersonal manner:

> *It now seems unlikely **that this depends on an oriented layer of wax molecules subject to disruption at a critical transition temperature**.* (ACAD)
>
> *It is possible **that variations in the colour and intensity of light reflected from these structures help to confuse predators as to the size and distance of the insect**.* (ACAD)
>
> *It is now generally accepted **that wings arose, perhaps in the early Devonian, as lateral expressions of thoracic terga**.* (ACAD)
>
> *It is perhaps more likely **that they were associated with locomotion from the beginning**.* (ACAD)
>
> *It is interesting **that in Stenobothrus rubicundus the same nervous mechanism can induce two different activities**: <...>* (ACAD†)

## 9.2.7 Pre-predicate v. extraposed *that*-clauses

Two of the major structural types of *that*-clause can be considered alternative variants of one another: pre-predicate subject *that*-clauses and extraposed *that*-clauses.

Pre-predicate *that*-clause:

> 1 *That Saints managed to cause an upset with nothing more than direct running and honest endeavour* bodes well for Great Britain. (NEWS)

Extraposed *that*-clause:

> 2 *Maybe it annoys them **that you don't fit their image of a fairy princess**.* (FICT)
>
> cf. *That you don't fit their image of a fairy princess* annoys them.

In both of these structures, the *that*-clause functions as the logical subject.

A third related construction has a subject noun phrase that begins with *the fact that*:

> 3a *The fact that the medical technicians were available* does not make the government's conduct any less offensive. (NEWS)

Structurally, the *that*-clause in these constructions acts as complement to the noun *fact* (8.12–14). However, the meaning in such cases is usually equivalent to the analogous sentence with a pre-predicate *that*-clause. Compare **3a** with **3b**:

> 3b *That the medical technicians were available* does not make the government's conduct any less offensive.

Both pre-predicate *that*-clauses and subject noun phrases beginning with *the fact that* present the proposition in the *that*-clause as factual or generally accepted information.

Overall, extraposed *that*-clauses are much more common than pre-predicate *that*-clauses, and they should thus be regarded as the unmarked choice.

However, there are four grammatical and discourse factors that can favor the choice of a pre-predicate *that*-clause over an extraposed clause: register, information structure, grammatical complexity, and topic and personal style. These are discussed in 9.2.7.1–4.

## 9.2.7.1 Register factors

**CORPUS FINDINGS** [2,3]

➤ Pre-predicate *that*-clauses are rare in all registers. They occur 10–20 times per million words in academic prose and news, while they are virtually non-existent in conversation.

> ➤ Subject noun phrases beginning with *the fact that* are also rare, occurring with about the same overall frequency as pre-predicate *that*-clauses.

> ➤ In contrast, extraposed *that*-clauses are considerably more frequent: they occur overall more than 200 times per million words, rising to more than 500 times per million words in academic prose (Figure 9.6).

**DISCUSSION OF FINDINGS**

The preference for extraposed over pre-predicate *that*-clauses reflects the general preference for 'light' subjects in English. There is a strong tendency to use short, non-complex constituents in subject position, and to shift 'heavy', complex constituents towards the end of a sentence (see 11.1.3 on the principle of end-weight).

From a processing perspective, pre-predicate *that*-clauses are disruptive, because the embedded complement clause must be produced and understood before reaching the main clause predicate. In extraposed constructions, this order is reversed, so that the main clause predicate precedes the embedded *that*-clause. Because they are not operating under production constraints, writers can choose to disregard the preference for placing heavy constituents after the main clause predicate, instead using pre-predicate *that*-clauses when they serve other discourse functions. However, because speakers are constrained by online production and comprehension needs, pre-predicate *that*-clauses are extremely rare in spoken unplanned discourse.

## 9.2.7.2 Information structure

**CORPUS FINDINGS** [3]

➤ In nearly every case when a pre-predicate *that*-clause is used, it presents information as if it is factual or generally accepted, and provides an anaphoric link to the preceding discourse.

**DISCUSSION OF FINDINGS**

One of the main uses of pre-predicate *that*-constructions is to present information about a referent as factual. Hence in pre-predicate *that*-clauses, the subject is a given referent, providing a direct anaphoric link to the preceding discourse; further, the predicate of the *that*-clause provides some fact or generally accepted information about that referent. For example:

> There are many players who might win the Masters, many who could. But the feeling about Faldo is that if he is at the top of his game, he should win it.
>     **That he is ranked only No 4 in the world at the moment** is due to the eccentricity of the system. His first Masters win has now slipped from his ranking points. (NEWS)

In this example, the subject of the pre-predicate *that*-clause is the pronoun *he*, an anaphoric reference to *Faldo*. The *that*-clause then presents the fact that Faldo is ranked No 4 in the world, which would quite likely be familiar information to readers of the golfing columns in newspapers.

Pre-predicate *that*-clauses are used in a similar way in academic prose:

> One of the triumphs of radioactive dating emerged only gradually as more and more workers dated meteorites. It became surprisingly apparent that all meteorites are of the same age, somewhere in the vicinity of 4.5 billion years old <...> **That there are no meteorites of any other age, regardless of when they fell to Earth,** suggests strongly that all meteorites originated in

> *other bodies of the solar system that formed at the same time that the Earth did.* (ACAD)

Here the *that*-clause summarizes information that could be deduced from the text itself, as the basis for the following assertion about the origin of meteorites.

In most occurrences of a pre-predicate *that*-clause, it would be possible to add *The fact that* at the beginning of the clause with little change in meaning or discourse function. Thus, the following examples beginning with *The fact that* can be compared to the pre-predicate *that*-clauses illustrated above:

> *On day two of MP-TV Nicholas Ridley was scheduled to make a live appearance before the cameras—or, as it turned out from his speech, a dead appearance <...>. Apart from an extra lick of oil on his hair, he had made no concessions to the cameras.*
> **The fact that Mr Ridley looked awful on television** *is not entirely his fault. After the novelty of the first day, the omissions and the limitations of the rules governing the coverage are beginning to look more glaring.* (NEWS†)

> *The GT4 test was taken by almost every pupil who participated in the project trials <...>. The items were selected so as to give a quick overview of performance in relation to a range of topics <...>.*
> **The fact that 14 of the 29 questions were answered correctly by 30 per cent or more of the lowest band** *suggests that there is a range of questions within the conceptual grasp of all or practically all the lowest band of attainers.* (ACAD†)

## 9.2.7.3 Grammatical factors

**CORPUS FINDINGS 2,3**

➤ In a majority of cases when pre-predicate *that*-clauses are used, the main clause predicate is followed by a complex construction comprising multiple phrases or clauses.

**DISCUSSION OF FINDINGS**

An additional factor favoring the use of pre-predicate *that*-clauses is the concomitant use of complex phrases and/or clauses following the main clause predicate.

There are two major kinds of complex structures that favor the use of a *that*-clause in pre-predicate position. First, a main clause with a complement clause in object position strongly favors the use of pre-predicate over extraposed *that*-clauses: see several of the examples in 9.2.7.2 and the following (with the post-predicate complement clause in *[]*):

> **That a stimulus can be processed either verbally or non-verbally** *helps [to make sense of those otherwise anomalous findings in which verbal stimuli give rise to a Lvf superiority].* (ACAD)
> **That the windscreen wipers started to work** *can properly be said [to have been caused by a set of things including the state of the wipers' mountings and the smooth surface of the windscreen as well as the switch's being flipped].* (ACAD)

Second, a main clause with its verb followed by a series of complex noun phrases or prepositional phrases favors the use of pre-predicate over extraposed *that*-clauses. The complex phrases are highlighted by *[]*:

> **That the restrictions are at last to be lifted** in part reflects *[universal acknowledgement that terror of the communications revolution has been a prime contributor to the technological backwardness of the country]*. (NEWS)

> **That this egg mortality was not due to parental ageing** was indicated *[by the similar trends taking place in pods laid by old or young adults]*. (ACAD)

In addition, some examples combine post-predicate phrasal elements with a complex complement clause:

> **That a Lvf superiority in reaction time emerged at 100 msec.**, however, was taken *[by Moscovitch et al.]* *[to mean that the right hemisphere had some advantage with respect to a more stable representation of the stimulus]*. (ACAD)

Pre-predicate *that*-clauses are favored in these cases because they are easier to process. If the *that*-clause were extraposed it would follow the other complex post-predicate constituents. This would place a great burden on the short-term memory of the receiver, who would need to process all intervening constituents before finally reaching the logical subject of the main clause (i.e. the extraposed clause).

## 9.2.7.4 Topic and style

Topical domain and personal style also influence the choice of pre-predicate *that*-clauses over extraposed constructions.

**CORPUS FINDINGS** [3]

➤ Sports writers have a stylistic preference for pre-predicate *that*-clauses:
  ➤ about 60% of the pre-predicate *that*-clauses found in news are from sports articles (seven out of 12 examples in a million-word sample), even though sports reportage comprises only c. 15% of the news writing in the sample.
➤ Some authors have a strong stylistic preference for pre-predicate *that*-clauses and clauses beginning with *the fact that*.
  ➤ 60% of all pre-predicate *that*-clauses found in academic prose are from four texts (nine out of 15 examples in a million-word sample), even though these texts comprise only c. 7% of all academic prose in the sample.
  ➤ 62% of all clauses beginning with *the fact that* found in academic prose are from four texts (13 out of 21 examples in a million-word sample), even though these texts comprise only c. 7% of all academic prose in the sample.
➤ Authors who have a strong stylistic preference for pre-predicate *that*-clauses also tend to favor clauses with *the fact that*:
  ➤ Six texts use both constructions. Although these texts comprise only c. 11% of all academic prose in the sample, they contain 73% of all pre-predicate *that*-clauses (11 out of 15 examples) plus 62% of all clauses beginning with *The fact that* (13 out of 21 examples).

**DISCUSSION OF FINDINGS**

The stylistic preference for pre-predicate *that*-clauses in sports reportage has been illustrated in the preceding sections (e.g. example **1** in 9.2.7). Other examples include:

> *That the 49ers' injury-ravaged defensive secondary was exploited by the Vikings (2–1)* was no shocker. (NEWS†)

> *That he won a points decision against the Californian Mark Wills at Wembley* will give them some reassurance that the British heavyweight champion could give a reasonable account of himself. (NEWS†)

Individual stylistic preferences probably play a role with many of the features covered in the grammar. However, the influence of individual preference is especially noticeable with rare features (like pre-predicate *that*-clauses).

## 9.2.8 Retention v. omission of the *that* complementizer

Another major discourse choice associated with *that*-clauses is whether to keep or to omit the *that* complementizer. From a semantic perspective, these alternatives are freely available choices, having no effect on meaning:

> I hope **you realised they said a few words on there.** (CONV)
> cf. I hope *[that]* you realised *[that]* they said a few words on there.

However, there are a number of discourse factors that influence the retention v. omission of *that*.

### 9.2.8.1 Register factors

**CORPUS FINDINGS [3]**

➤ In conversation, the omission of *that* is the norm, while the retention of *that* is exceptional.

➤ At the opposite extreme, retention of *that* is the norm in academic prose.

**DISCUSSION OF FINDINGS**

These distributional patterns correspond to the differing production circumstances and communicative purposes found in the four registers. Conversations are spoken and produced online; they typically have involved, interpersonal purposes; and they generally favor the reduction or omission of constituents that can be easily reconstructed. These characteristics are associated with omission rather than retention of *that* as the norm. Academic prose has the opposite characteristics: written, careful production circumstances; an expository, informational purpose; and a general preference for

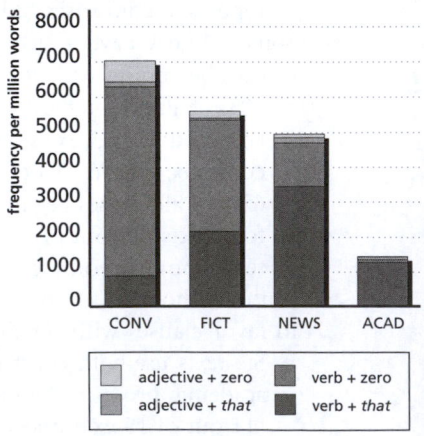

Figure 9.7
**Frequency of *that* retention v. omission, by register**

*that* retention is the norm in academic prose.

## 9.2.8.2 Discourse factors favoring *that* omission

**Figure 9.8** **Percentage of *that* omission—influence of discourse factors**

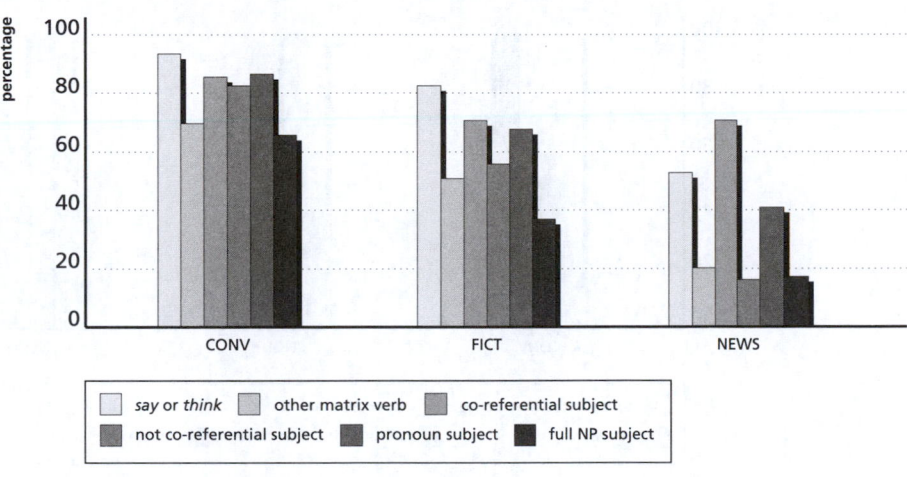

### CORPUS FINDINGS [2,3]

➤ The omission of *that* is favored by three grammatical characteristics that conform to the most common discourse uses of *that*-clauses:
  ➤ The use of *think* or *say* as the main clause verb (v. other less common verbs);
  ➤ The occurrence of co-referential subjects in the main clause and *that*-clause (v. non-coreferential subjects);
  ➤ The occurrence of a personal pronoun subject (v. a noun-headed phrase) in the *that*-clause.
➤ The influence of these factors is strongest in news. (Academic prose is not considered here, since clauses with *that* omission are so rare in that register.)

### DISCUSSION OF FINDINGS

The following sentences illustrate all three of the characteristics conducive to *that*-omission: (a) *think* or *say* as the main clause verb; (b) co-referential subjects; and (c) a personal pronoun subject in the *that*-clause:

> *I think* **I'll make a shopping list today** (CONV)
> *I thought* **I might look.** (FICT†)
> *You said* **you didn't** (CONV)
> *I said* **I bought them yesterday** (CONV)
> *He said* **he probably would not have come back before President Gorbachev launched his Perestroika policy**. (NEWS)

To the extent that a construction conforms to these typical characteristics, hearers/readers can anticipate a *that*-clause without the explicit marking by *that*. These factors are least influential in conversation, where *that* omission is already the overall norm. Conversely, they are most influential in news, which shows an overall preference for *that* retention.

### 9.2.8.3 Discourse factors favoring *that* retention

**Figure 9.9** Percentage of *that* retention—influence of discourse factors

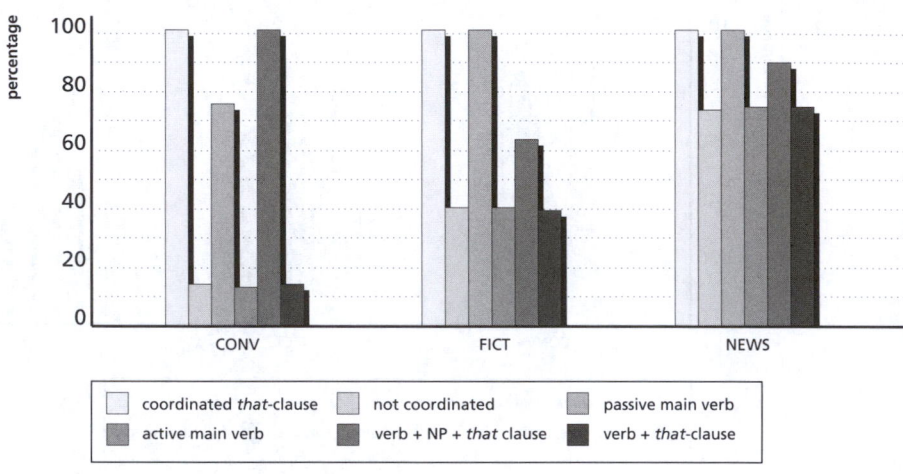

| | coordinated *that*-clause | not coordinated | passive main verb |
| active main verb | verb + NP + *that* clause | verb + *that*-clause |

**CORPUS FINDINGS** [2,3]

➤ The retention of *that* is favored by grammatical characteristics that are not typical of *that*-clauses, such as:
  ➤ The use of coordinated *that*-clauses;
  ➤ The use of the passive voice in the main clause;
  ➤ The presence of an intervening noun phrase between the main clause verb and the *that*-clause (Pattern 2 in 9.2.2.1).
➤ The influence of these factors is strongest in conversation.

**DISCUSSION OF FINDINGS**

The construction types just mentioned are packaged in such a way that it would be difficult to recognize the presence of a *that*-clause if it were not overtly marked by *that*. Each factor is illustrated below.
The use of coordinated *that*-clauses:

> *Mr. Gorbachev agreed* **that the NATO and the Warsaw Pact would be maintained [and] that the transatlantic members of the Western Alliance—the U.S. and Canada—would play a vital role in the common European home.** (NEWS)

> *The major conclusion of both studies was* **that the nation and particularly the state of Florida must quickly reduce their large reliance on foreign oil [and] that conservation measures and increased reliance on the abundant national supply of coal were the major alternatives.** (ACAD)

A passive in the main clause:

> *Western leaders [were convinced]* **that NATO's steadfastness had been crucial in bringing the communist bloc in from the cold.** (NEWS†)

> *I [was told]* **that both the new right and those who support the government's view had been excluded.** (NEWS†)

An intervening noun phrase between the main clause verb and the *that*-clause:

> *The second U.S. reaction was to reassure [the West Germans]* **that Washington was happy to leave the details in Bonn's hands.** (NEWS†)
>
> *They warn [him]* **that it's dangerous** (CONV)

The influence of these factors is least strong in news, since *that* retention is the norm in that register. Conversely, they are most influential in conversation, where *that* omission is the expected norm apart from other considerations.

# 9.3     *Wh*-clauses

## 9.3.1     Structural types of *wh*-clauses

*Wh*-complement clauses can be either dependent **interrogative clauses** or **nominal relative clauses**. The same set of *wh*-words is used with both, except that *whether* is unambiguously interrogative (9.3.2.4–5).

The clearest type of **wh-interrogative clause** is used with verbs such as *ask* and *wonder* to present an indirect question:

> *Jill was asking* **what happened.** (CONV†)
>
> *I wonder* **what that could be about.** (CONV)

In contrast, **nominal relative clauses** can be paraphrased by a general head noun modified by the *wh*-clause functioning as a relative clause:

> *Yes. Burbidge Road. Which is* **where Carlos used to live.** (CONV)
> cf. *Which is the* **place where** *Carlos used to live.*
>
> **"Whoever sorts Eagle out** *will make a lot of money," Mr Fitton said.* (NEWS)
> cf. *"The* **person who** *sorts Eagle out ..."*
>
> **What baffles me** *is how few of them can spell.* (NEWS)
> cf. *The* **thing that** *baffles me ...*
>
> *It says that judges should follow* **whichever method of deciding cases will produce** *[what they believe to be the best community for the future].* (ACAD†)
> cf. *... the* **method** *of deciding cases* **which** *will produce the* **thing that** *they believe to be ....*

This last example contains two nominal relative clauses as direct objects: one (marked by *[]*) is embedded in the other.

A third, less common type of *wh*-clause has an **exclamative** function, and is introduced by either the intensifier *how* followed by an adjective, or by the predeterminer *what*:

> *He still remembered* **how wonderful it had been.** (FICT)
>
> *I was thinking* **how nice you are, what a good actor,** *and* **what a nice man.** (FICT†)

*Wh*-complement clauses can occur in subject as well as object position with verbs:

> *What could be at work there* is an actual enmity towards the very structure of society. (FICT)
>
> *How to read the record* is the subject of much of this book. (ACAD)
>
> *What we come to* is this. (ACAD)
>
> *Why the NTSB was not invited to participate in the investigation by the Mexican authorities* is not known. (ACAD†)

In addition, *wh*-clauses occur in subject predicative position. This function is particularly common in conversation and fictional dialogue, with the demonstrative pronoun *that* filling the subject slot (and the copula *is* typically contracted to *'s*):

> *That's* **what I'm saying**. (CONV)
>
> *That's* **what we could call her**. (CONV)
>
> *That's* **what the other ones were**. (CONV)
>
> *That's* **why I bought the refill**. (CONV†)
>
> *That's* **why I asked her**. (FICT)
>
> *That's* **how it was on my old show**. (FICT)

*Wh*-clauses can be controlled by adjectival predicates as well as verbs, and they can occasionally be extraposed.

Adjectival predicate + *wh*-clause:

> *I'm not sure* **when it's open for anybody**. (CONV)
>
> *You'd be amazed* **what they do**. (CONV)
>
> *She wanted to be careful* **what she said**. (FICT†)

*Wh*-clause + adjectival predicate:

> **How the return of a Labour government would affect the political calculations in Northern Ireland** *is difficult to foresee*. (NEWS)

Adjectival predicate + extraposed *wh*-clause:

> *It was incredible* **what had happened to them**. (FICT)
>
> *It seemed incredible* **how much had happened**. (FICT)
>
> *It was not immediately clear* **how, if at all, the Soviet leadership could enforce such a ruling**. (NEWS†)

Finally, unlike *that*-clauses, *wh*-clauses can be complements of prepositions and objects of prepositional verbs:

> *She was amazed at* **how exhausted she was**. (FICT)

## 9.3.2    Post-predicate *wh*-clauses controlled by verbs

The verbs that most commonly control *wh*-clauses in post-predicate position can be grouped into six major semantic domains: speech act verbs (e.g. *tell* NP, *say*, *explain*), other communication verbs (e.g. *show*, *write*), cognition verbs (e.g. *know*, *think about*, *remember*), perception verbs (e.g. *see*, *look at*), verbs of attitude and emotion (e.g. *agree with*, *condemn*, *like*, *hate*), and aspectual verbs (e.g. *start*, *stop*, *finish*). (Compare the semantic domains of verbs in 5.2.1–2.)

We will first review the structural patterns found with *wh*-clauses, and then look at the lexical associations in more detail.

### 9.3.2.1 Grammatical patterns

The following are the two most important grammatical patterns available for *wh*-complement clauses in post-predicate position. (cf. 3.5, 5.2.4)

**Pattern 1: verb + *wh*-clause**

(e.g. *know, remember, see*)

> *I don't know **what they are**.* (CONV)
>
> *I can remember **how I used to be**.* (FICT†)

**Pattern 2: verb + NP + *wh*-clause**

(e.g. *ask, show, tell*)

> *I didn't tell you **what Emma thought**.* (CONV)
>
> *I want you to show me **where the car went off**.* (FICT†)

A variant of Pattern 1 has prepositional verbs:

> *It depends whether you actually think about **what you're seeing and what you're reading**.* (CONV)

However, some prepositional verbs omit the preposition with some types of *wh*-clause:

> *Sabina stood wondering **what their relationship was**.* (FICT)
>
> *cf. Sabina stood wondering **about** it.*

A variant of Pattern 2 similarly has three place prepositional verbs, e.g. *remind + NP + of wh*-clause.

> Some verbs in both patterns can additionally take **wh-infinitive clauses**:
>
> *I would tell them **where to go**.* (CONV)
>
> *She never knows **how to just say no**.* (CONV)
>
> *One of these days I'll really show you **how to play**.* (FICT)
>
> *You must also understand **how to check their accuracy at recognised stages**.* (ACAD†)

### 9.3.2.2 Controlling verbs, by semantic domain

**CORPUS FINDINGS** [1]

➤ *Know* is overwhelmingly the most common verb controlling a *wh*-clause.

➤ Five other verbs are notably common with *wh*-clauses: *see, tell* (NP), *wonder, ask, understand*.

➤ The primary verb *do* as a lexical verb is common with *what*-clauses in conversation (occurring c. 20 times per million words), but much less frequent in the other registers.

➤ Four of the six relevant semantic domains contain verbs that occur frequently controlling *wh*-clauses (see Table 9.3).

**Figure 9.10** **Frequencies of the most common verbs controlling *wh*-clauses**

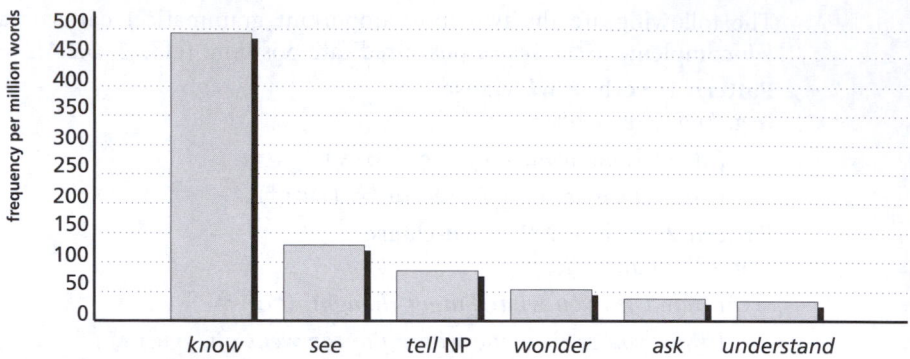

**Table 9.3** **Frequency of verbs controlling a complement *wh*-clause, by semantic domain; occurrences per million words**

▢ over 50    ▢ over 20

**Speech act verbs**

*ask* ▢    *tell* (NP) ▢

**other verbs attested in the LSWE Corpus:**

*argue, ask (NP), confess, contradict, criticize, debate, disclose, discuss, enquire, emphasize, explain, express, inquire (about/into), offer (NP), point out, query, question, relate, repeat, report, say, sing, state*

**Other communication verbs**

*show* (NP) ▢

**other verbs attested in the LSWE Corpus:**

*define, demonstrate, describe, dictate, indicate, prove, record, reveal, signify, teach (NP), write*

**Cognition verbs**

*know* ▢    *remember* ▢    *think (of / about)* ▢    *understand* ▢    *wonder* ▢

**other verbs attested in the LSWE Corpus:**

*anticipate, ascertain, assess, believe, calculate, consider, concentrate on, confirm, compare, decide, detect, determine, discover, establish, estimate, fathom, figure (out), find out, foresee, forget, gather, guess, imagine, learn, ponder, plan, plot, predict, realize, recognize, reconsider, reflect (on), be reminded of / remind NP of, study*

**Perception verbs**

*see* ▢

**other verbs attested in the LSWE Corpus:**

*hear, listen to, look (at), note, notice, observe, perceive, read, watch*

**Verbs of attitude and emotion**

*accept, agree with, approve, beware of, brood over, care, condemn, condone, cope with, doubt, dread, endorse, feel, give a damn, hate, laugh at, like, loathe, love, respect*

**Aspectual verbs**

*complete, end, finish, start, stop*

**DISCUSSION OF FINDINGS**

Almost any transitive verb can control a post-predicate *wh*-clause functioning as a nominal relative clause, including numerous verbs with concrete activity meanings:

> You give him **what he wants**. (FICT)
>
> The birds gathered round to eat **what was left**. (FICT)
>
> She pointed to **where the blue-roofed cave had been**. (FICT†)
>
> She also won **what they call oratory**. (FICT†)
>
> Most of Emecheta's life has been a fight to get **what she feels is her due**. (NEWS)

The lexical verb *do* is also relatively common followed by a *what*-clause, especially in conversation and fictional dialogue:

> Do you think I should've stuck to that or just done **what I did**? (CONV)
>
> If then they've made a mistake, you have done **what you are told**. (CONV)
>
> You can start doing **what you want then**. (CONV)
>
> That'll enable me to get on doing **what I've got to do**. (CONV†)
>
> He has done **what he could**. (FICT)

Although nominal relative *wh*-clauses can be controlled by almost any transitive verb, the most common verbs with *wh*-clauses are from some of the same semantic domains as those with *that*-clauses—especially communication and mental verbs. However, many specific verbs are common with only one type of clause.

In the domain of speech-act communication, only *tell* is common with both *that*- and *wh*-clauses. Most speech act verbs are grammatical with *wh*-clauses, including *say* (which is very common with *that*-clauses).

Speech act verbs with a *wh*-clause:

> Did dad tell you **what happened this morning**? (CONV)
>
> I told him **where to turn off the boulevard**. (FICT†)
>
> He had to ask her **why she had lied for him**. (FICT†)
>
> I just said **what I thought**. (FICT†)
>
> This conference should be discussing **why this bankrupt policy isn't working**. (NEWS)
>
> We will briefly explain **how these may be established**. (ACAD)

In the domain of mental verbs (including cognition and perception), several verbs are common controlling both *wh*- and *that*-clauses: *know*, *think* (*of / about*), *see*, *understand*, and *remember*.

Cognition verbs with a *wh*-clause:

> I know **what she said**. (CONV)
>
> No one knew **where she was again**. (FICT)
>
> I could never remember **how to do them**. (CONV)
>
> Suddenly she understood **why Gabby had been so uptight that morning**. (FICT)

Perception verbs with a *wh*-clause:

> Well you can't see **where he was sick anywhere**. (CONV)

> *Oh, look **what I've done**.* (CONV)

> *Sammler noticed now **how his widow tended to impersonate him**.* (FICT)

Finally, it is worth noting that several verbs from the cognition and other communication domains deal with 'discovery and description', especially in academic prose:

Cognition:

> *We need to discover **what they believe about AIDS**.* (ACAD)

> *Thus the programmer can establish **when a transput operation is complete**.* (ACAD†)

Other verbs of this type are *ascertain, compare, confirm, detect, determine, figure out, gather*.

Other communication:

> *I'll just show you **what was on there before**.* (CONV)

> *He describes **how the National Committee is organized**.* (ACAD†)

Other verbs of this type are *define, demonstrate, indicate, prove, record, reveal, signify*.

### 9.3.2.3    Common controlling verbs across registers

**CORPUS FINDINGS ²**

➤ By far the most common verb controlling *wh*-clauses is the verb *know* in conversation. *Know* is also very common with *wh*-clauses in fiction.

➤ *Wh*-clauses are more common in conversation than in the other registers:
  ➤ Three verbs besides *know* are moderately common with *wh*-clauses: *see, tell* NP, *wonder*.
  ➤ Another six verbs are relatively common with *wh*-clauses: *ask, understand, show, remember, think, look*.

➤ *Wh*-clauses are also relatively common in fiction.

➤ *Wh*-clauses are relatively rare in news and academic prose.

**DISCUSSION OF FINDINGS**

By far the most common use of *wh*-clauses is with the verb *know* in conversation, where it is usually used to report that the speaker (*I*) does *not* know something:

> *I don't know **what's happening**.* (CONV)

> *I don't know **where they are**.* (CONV)

> *I don't know **how you get any enjoyment out of doing that**.* (CONV)

(Compare the frequent use of *I think* + *that*-clause (9.2.2.3) in conversation to indicate lack of certainty.) The verb *know* is also common in quoted speech in fictional dialogue and in news:

> *I don't know **what to say**.* (FICT)

> *I don't know **how to thank you**.* (FICT)

> *I don't know **how people are going to get through the winter**.* (NEWS)

The verb *see* is also notably common with *wh*-clauses in conversation. This combination sometimes reports literal perceptions of seeing:

**Table 9.4** **The most common verbs controlling a complement *wh*-clause by semantic domain and register; occurrences per million words**

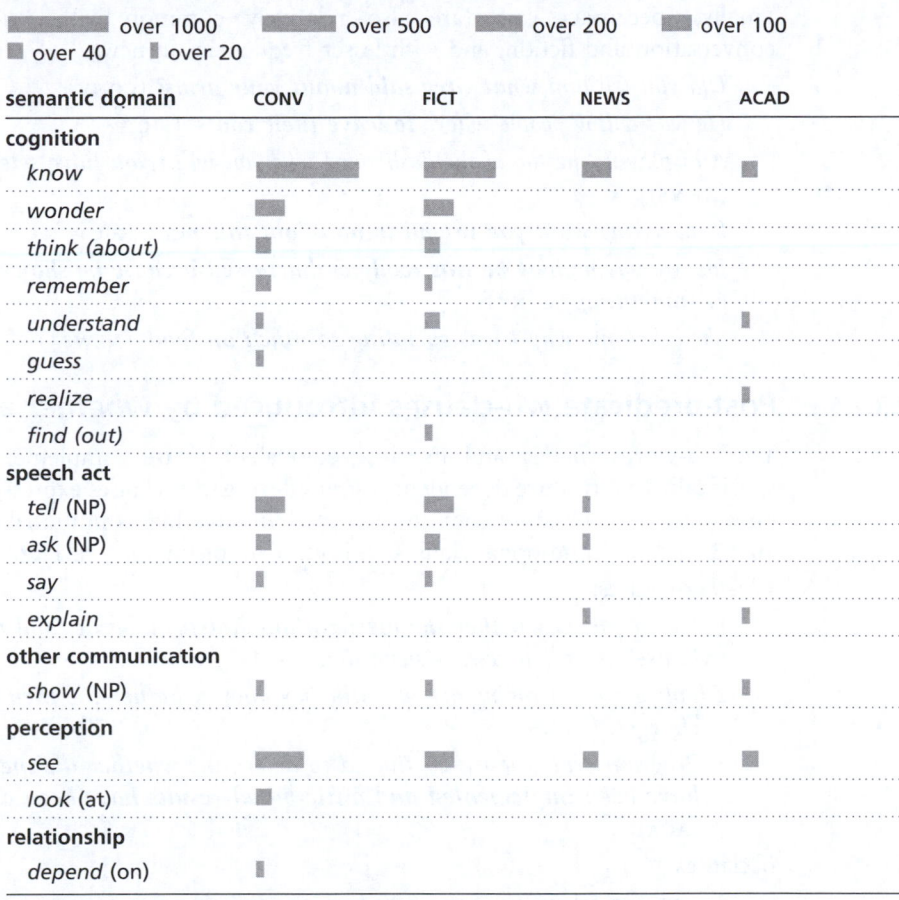

| semantic domain | CONV | FICT | NEWS | ACAD |
|---|---|---|---|---|
| **cognition** | | | | |
| *know* | ▇▇▇ | ▇▇ | ▆ | ▪ |
| *wonder* | ▇ | ▇ | | |
| *think (about)* | ▪ | ▪ | | |
| *remember* | ▪ | ▪ | | |
| *understand* | ▪ | ▪ | | ▪ |
| *guess* | ▪ | | | |
| *realize* | | | | ▪ |
| *find (out)* | | ▪ | | |
| **speech act** | | | | |
| *tell* (NP) | ▇ | ▇ | ▪ | |
| *ask* (NP) | ▪ | ▪ | ▪ | |
| *say* | ▪ | ▪ | | |
| *explain* | | | ▪ | ▪ |
| **other communication** | | | | |
| *show* (NP) | ▪ | ▪ | | ▪ |
| **perception** | | | | |
| *see* | ▇ | ▇ | ▪ | ▪ |
| *look* (at) | ▪ | | | |
| **relationship** | | | | |
| *depend* (on) | ▪ | | | |

Legend: over 1000, over 500, over 200, over 100, over 40, over 20

> *I couldn't see **what they were doing**.* (CONV)
>
> *I didn't even look to see **what it was**.* (CONV)

More commonly, though, it is used metaphorically in a cognitive sense to mean 'find out':

> *I'll see **what cash I've got left**.* (CONV)
>
> *So we'll see **what transpires this time**.* (CONV)

The expression *see what I/you mean* is particularly common in conversation:

> *I can see **what you mean**.* (CONV)
>
> *Do you see **what I mean**?* (CONV)

Other verbs of cognition, such as *wonder*, *think* (*about/of*), *remember*, and *understand*, are relatively common with *wh*-clauses in both conversation and fiction:

> *She's sitting there wondering **what's going on**.* (CONV)
>
> *I couldn't think **what it was**.* (CONV)
>
> *I could never remember **how to do them**.* (CONV)

> *You should wonder **why she wants me around**.* (FICT)
>
> *Sethe smiled just thinking about **what the word could mean**.* (FICT)

Finally, speech-act verbs are also relatively common with *wh*-clauses in conversation and fiction, and with lesser frequencies in news:

> *Did you tell him **what Greg said about your arms**?* (CONV)
>
> *He was telling people **where to leave their coats**.* (FICT)
>
> *A display at the top of the dashboard tells you **what you have selected**.* (NEWS)
>
> *I am asking **what you intend to do about this man**.* (FICT†)
>
> *Joe was saying **how he was really embarrassed because he showed y– mom or something**.* (CONV)
>
> *She asked me **why I was spending so much on food**.* (NEWS†)

### 9.3.2.4 Post-predicate *wh*-clauses introduced by *whether* and *if*

The *wh*-word *whether* and its close equivalent *if* are complementizers used specifically to introduce dependent *yes/no* interrogative clauses expressing indirect questions. (For the more common use of *if*, in adverbial conditional clauses, see 10.2.8, and for conditional clauses without a subordinator, see 11.2.3.5.)

*Whether*-clauses:

> 1 *He wondered **whether the mestizo had stolen his mule**, and reproached himself for the necessary suspicion.* (FICT)
>
> 2 *Police are not taking action until they know **whether the men face charges**.* (NEWS)
>
> 3 *Program evaluation is conducted to determine **whether the methods have been implemented and anticipated results have been achieved**.* (ACAD)

*If*-clauses:

> 4 *Ask him when they were here last. See **if he's got a tongue**. See **if he's such an idiot as he looks**.* (FICT)
>
> 5 *Sir: Mr Stephen Campbell (letters, 5 October) asks **if he is alone in thinking that personal injury awards should be increased in relation to libel awards**.* (NEWS†)
>
> 6 *One of the most common problems encountered is simply deciding **if two components in a machine clash**.* (ACAD)

In all the above examples, it would be possible to substitute *if* for *whether* or vice versa without changing the meaning of the sentence.

With the verb *ask* (see **5** above), the *whether/if* clause functions as an indirect speech report of a *yes/no* question (3.13.2.2). There is also a variant of the *whether/if* clause which corresponds to an alternative direct question (3.13.2.3):

> 7 *When they reached Duck Bank, Mynors asked her **whether** they should go through the marketplace **or** along King Street, by the bottom of St Luke's Square.* (FICT)

Alternative question constructions are also found with an elliptical negative clause *or not*:

> *I don't care **whether you want to play an instrument or not**.* (CONV)

In alternative question constructions with an elliptical negative clause, the *or not* can also directly follow the complementizer *whether*:

> We do not ask **whether or not** an axiom is 'true', just as we don't ask if the rules of chess are 'true'. (ACAD)

In this case, *if* could not be substituted for *whether*. In general, alternative interrogative clauses are strongly associated with *whether*, although alternative clauses with *if* do occasionally occur:

> I don't know **if** she was upset **or** her eyes were watering because of the smoke. (NEWS)

> It really doesn't matter **if** I'm a nice guy **or** not. (NEWS)

As many of the above examples illustrate, *whether/if* clauses are frequently used with a negative in the main clause—almost invariably so in the case of negative-oriented controlling verbs such as *care*, *matter*, and *mind*:

> I don't **care** if you're serious or not. (CONV)

> Doesn't **matter** whether – whether it's a boy or a girl. (CONV)

> I don't **mind** if the goals are spread around. (NEWS)

One of the most common verbs taking *whether/if* clauses is *know*, which also occurs predominantly in the negative:

> We do not **know** whether all those infected will ultimately develop AIDS. (ACAD†)

## 9.3.2.5  Common verbs controlling *whether*- and *if*-clauses

**CORPUS FINDINGS** [2]

➤ *If*-clauses as interrogative clauses are more frequent than *whether*-clauses.
➤ However, it is notable that fewer verbs (of any frequency) are found with *if*-clauses than with *whether*-clauses.
  ➤ The predominance of *if*-clauses is overwhelmingly due to the high frequency of three verbs: *know*, *wonder*, and, above all, *see*, especially in conversation.
➤ *Know* is also very common with *whether*-clauses in conversation.
➤ While *whether*-clauses are fairly evenly spread across the four registers, *if*-clauses are especially frequent in conversation but rare in academic prose.

**DISCUSSION OF FINDINGS**

There is a clear stylistic difference between interrogative *if*-clauses, which are strongly favored in the more colloquial style of conversation and fiction, and interrogative *whether*-clauses, which are more neutral in their stylistic range.

The three verbs that are very frequent with *if*-clauses—*see*, *wonder*, and *know*—are used most commonly in conversation and fiction. (*See* here has the meaning of 'finding out' an answer):

> Dad, try this on and **see if** it fits. (CONV)

> They had approached Barlow to **see if** he would be prepared to contribute. (FICT†)

> Oh I **wonder if** they will I **wonder if** they will close our school down cos there's exams next week. (CONV)

Table 9.5  **Frequency of common verbs controlling a complement *whether*-clause, by register; occurrences per million words**

each ● represents 5

| | CONV | FICT | NEWS | ACAD |
|---|---|---|---|---|
| *know* | ● ● ● ● ●<br>● ● ● ● ●<br>● ● ● ● ●<br>● ● | ● ● ● | ● ● | ● ● |
| *decide* | ● | ● | ● ● ● | ● ● |
| *see* | ● | ● | ● | ● ● |
| *wonder* | ● ● | ● ● ● ● ● | | |
| *mind* | ● ● | ● | | |
| *care* | ● | ● | | |
| *say* | ● | | ● | ● |
| *remember* | ● | | | |
| *ask* | | ● | ● | ● |
| *tell* | | ● | | |
| *doubt* | | ● | | |
| *determine* | | | ● | ● ● ● ● |
| *consider* | | | ● | ● |
| *establish* | | | | ● |
| *indicate* | | | | ● |
| *investigate* | | | | ● |
| *judge* | | | | ● |
| *determine* | | | | ● |
| *find out* | | | | ● |

> *Hm, impact sprinklers for two ninety-three each.* **Wonder if** *they're worth taking home* <...> (CONV)
>
> *I really don't* **know if** *that's such a good idea.* (CONV)

*See* tends to be associated with the addressee's state of mind, especially in the use of the imperative as in the first example. *Wonder* and *know*, on the other hand, tend to be associated with the speaker's state of mind, typically occurring with the subject *I*.

The surprisingly high frequency of *know whether* is probably due to its use with alternative interrogatives, especially in conversation:

> *And you know, sometimes we don't find out from others, people don't let us* **know whether** *we've succeeded* **or not***.* (CONV)
>
> *Sometimes, as he walked, he did not* **know whether** *he was awake* **or** *asleep.* (FICT)

Table 9.6 **Frequency of common verbs controlling a complement *if*-clause, by register; occurrences per million words**

each ● represents 5

| | CONV | FICT | NEWS | ACAD |
|---|---|---|---|---|
| *see* | ●●●●●●●● ●●●●●●● ●●●●●●● ●●●●●● | ●●●●●●● ●●● | ●●●● | ●● |
| *wonder* | ●●●●●●● ●●●● | ●●●●●●● ●●●●●● | ●● | |
| *know* | ●●●●●●● ●●●●●●● ●●●● | ●●●●●●● | ●●● | |
| *ask* | ●● | ●●● | ●●● | |
| *matter* | ●● | ● | | ● |
| *doubt* | ● | ● | | ● |
| *mind* | ●● | ● | | |
| *care* | ● | ● | | |
| *remember* | ● | | | |
| *determine* | | | | ● |
| *find out* | | | | ● |

# 9.4 Infinitive clauses

## 9.4.1 Overview

Infinitival complement clauses serve a wide range of functions: in addition to reporting speech and cognitive states, they are commonly used to report intentions, desires, efforts, perceptual states, and various other general actions. Similar to *that*-clauses, infinitive clauses can occur in either post-predicate or subject position, and in a variety of other structures as illustrated in 9.1.3, although they are by far most common in the post-predicate position.

## 9.4.2 Post-predicate infinitive clauses controlled by verbs

The verbs taking *to*-clauses in post-predicate position can be usefully grouped into ten major semantic classes (subsets of the domains in 5.2.1–2): speech act verbs (e.g. *ask, tell, warn*); other communication verbs (e.g. *show, prove*); cognition verbs (e.g. *assume, consider, expect, find*); perception verbs (e.g. *feel, see, hear*); verbs of desire (e.g. *hope, wish, like*); verbs of intention or decision (e.g. *decide, choose, plan*); verbs of effort (e.g. *try, manage, fail*); verbs of modality or causation (e.g. *help, let, persuade, get*); aspectual verbs (e.g. *start, continue, cease*); verbs of existence/occurrence, some with a probability meaning (e.g. *seem, appear, happen, turn out*). We first examine the structural patterns of infinitive clauses, and then consider the lexical and register associations in more detail.

### 9.4.2.1   Grammatical patterns

Five major grammatical patterns are possible with the verbs that control an infinitive clause in post-predicate position.

**Pattern 1: verb + *to*-clause**
(e.g. *try, hope*):

> *I'm just trying **to get away early.*** (CONV†)
>
> *The new promoters hope **to make prototypes at $299,000 each*** (NEWS)

**Pattern 2: verb + NP + *to*-clause**
(e.g. *tell, believe, enable, expect*):

> *It enables the farmer **to maintain uniform and near constant conditions in the house.*** (ACAD†)

**Pattern 3: verb + *for* NP + *to*-clause**
(e.g. *ask, love, arrange, wait*)

> *Hire a Daily Mirror van and wait for Mrs Jones **to arrive.*** (CONV†)

**Pattern 4: verb + bare infinitive clause**
(e.g. *dare, help, let*)

> *Thirteen thousand Ovambos on strike, that time, and the police didn't dare **touch them** because of United Nations.* (FICT)
>
> *It could have helped **clarify a number of issues.*** (NEWS†)

(On the construction with *dare*, see 3.8.2.3 and 9.4.10.)

**Pattern 5: verb + NP + bare infinitive clause**
(e.g. *have, feel, help*):

> *I'll have Judy **do it.*** (CONV)
>
> *He actually felt the sweat **break out now on his forehead.*** (FICT)

Many of the verbs in Pattern 2 (verb + NP + *to*-clause) also have corresponding passive forms, referred to as Pattern 2P:

**Pattern 2P: *be* verb-*ed* + *to*-clause**

> *PCBs are generally considered **to be carcinogenic.*** (ACAD)
>
> cf. *Researchers generally consider PCBs **to be carcinogenic.***

Verbs that are prepositional with a noun-headed phrase usually occur without those prepositions when they control a *to*-clause (as with *that*-clauses; 9.2.2.1).

> *Pattern 1: **hope for** + NP*        ***hope** + **to**-clause*
>
> *Pattern 2: **warn** + NP$_1$ + **of** NP$_2$*    ***warn** + NP$_1$ + **to**-clause*

However, there is a complication with Pattern 3 verbs. For some, the *for*-phrase should be considered part of the *to*-clause (e.g. *mean, love, hate*); these verbs do not occur elsewhere as two-place prepositional verbs with *for* (3.5.5). However, many others should be considered as prepositional verbs, including *ask for, call for, pray for, long for, plan for, arrange for,* and *wait for.*

There are many further complications with the grammar and semantics of post-verbal infinitive clauses. A more detailed discussion of these verb patterns is taken up in 9.4.2.2–5.

### 9.4.2.2   Pattern 1: verb + *to*-clause

Three major sub-types can be distinguished for Pattern 1 verbs:

**Type 1**

Although infinitive clauses in the pattern verb + *to*-clause have no overt subject, the implied subject of the *to*-clause is usually the same as the subject of the main clause. This relationship can be seen from a comparison of *to*-clauses with analogous sentences having a *that*-clause:

> *I didn't claim **to be an authority**.* (CONV)
> *cf. I didn't claim **that I was an authority**.*

> *Widmer said he hoped **to sell Brabham**.* (NEWS†)
> *cf. Widmer said he hoped **that he could sell Brabham**.*

**Type 2**

The verb *say* is exceptional when it occurs in the pattern verb + *to*-clause, in that the implied subject of the *to*-clause refers to the speaker (rather than the main clause subject):

> Mr. Bryant said **to put it through to you**. (FICT)
> *cf. Mr. Bryant said **that I should put it through to you**.*

> *Jerry said **to tell you how sorry he is**.* (FICT)
> *cf. Jerry said **that I should tell you how sorry he is**.*

> He said **to give you rum punches**. (FICT)
> *cf. He said **that I should give you rum punches**.*

In both Types 1 and 2, the *to*-clause is effectively analogous to the direct object of the main clause verb.

**Type 3**

Verbs of probability or simple fact (9.4.2.7) control a special type of grammatical construction involving **subject-to-subject raising**. In these constructions, the noun phrase that occupies the subject slot in the main clause is interpreted logically as the subject of the *to*-clause, but not as the logical subject of the main clause. Rather the entire *to*-clause is the logical subject of the main clause. Thus, the sentence:

> 1 *The prize pupil, however, turned out **to have another side to his character**.* (NEWS)

has a meaning equivalent to an extraposed construction with a *that*-clause:

> 2 *It turned out **that the prize pupil had another side to his character**.*

See 9.4.9 for a fuller discussion of raising constructions.

### 9.4.2.3    Pattern 2: verb + NP + *to*-clause

The two noun phrases in clauses having the structure NP$_1$ + verb + NP$_2$ + *to*-clause can represent three different semantic/structural relations:

**Type 1**

In Type 1, NP$_2$ functions as both the direct object (or indirect object) of the main clause verb and the subject of the *to*-clause:

> *I told grandma **to make me and Tim some more**.* (CONV†)

In this case, the noun phrase *grandma* functions as both the indirect object of the main clause verb *told*, as well as the subject of the *to*-clause (i.e. *grandma should make some more*). Compare the equivalent:

> *I told grandma **that [she] should make me and Tim some more**.*

Many of the verbs taking this structure occur as distransitive or three-place prepositional verbs with simple noun-headed phrases (as direct, indirect, or prepositional objects 3.5.4–7). They include some speech-act verbs such as *ask*, *tell*, and *warn*, as well as many verbs of modality or causation, such as *allow*, *dare*, *encourage*, *force*, *help*, *order*, *permit*, *persuade*, *require*, and *tempt*:

> *I think you can ask the council **to take it away or something*** (CONV†)
>
> *"I sprinkle a little around and tell the demons **to leave**."* (NEWS)
>
> *But please encourage other people **to have some**.* (CONV)
>
> *He had persuaded a woman **to come into the laundry room of the house**.* (FICT†)
>
> *Too many options within a single program tempt the teacher **to try and use all of them in too short a period**.* (ACAD)

### Type 2

In Type 2, the NP$_2$ functions grammatically as direct object (pronouns take the accusative case) while the *to*-clause functions as object predicative. However, in terms of meaning, NP$_2$ functions logically only as the subject of the *to*-clause:

> *Rechem believes the results **to be unscientific**.* (NEWS†)
> cf. *Rechem believes them **to be unscientific**.*

In this example, the noun phrase *the results* functions in meaning only as the subject of the *to*-clause (i.e. *the results are unscientific*). *The results* is not semantically the object of the main clause verb *believes*; in fact, such an interpretation would result in the incorrect inference that *Rechem believes the results*.

Verbs taking this structure occur as complex transitive verbs with simple noun-headed phrases (i.e. with a direct object and object predicative; 3.5.8). These include cognition verbs, such as *assume*, *believe*, *consider*, *understand*; many verbs of intention, desire, or decision, such as *choose*, *expect*, *like*, *need*, *prefer*, *want*, *wish*; as well as verbs of discovery (*find*):

> *In a sense, he considered the trip **to be a medical necessity**.* (FICT)
>
> *We want the student **to share some of the excitement and exhilaration triggered by recent discoveries**.* (ACAD†)
>
> *He was enjoying this little exchange, and he expected Sam **to enjoy it also**.* (FICT†)
>
> *In nylon he found the Voigt average **to be closest to experimental data**.* (ACAD)
>
> *She said that she would like her mother **to stay with her**.* (ACAD†)

### Type 3

In Type 3, NP$_2$ functions as the indirect object of the main clause verb, but NP$_1$ is the implied subject of the *to*-clause (in addition to being the subject of the main clause). The verb *promise* is the only major verb following this pattern:

> *Ollie has promised Billy **to take him fishing next Sunday**.* (FICT)

### Combinations of Types 1 and 2

For some controlling verbs, NP$_2$ can be interpreted as belonging to either a Type 1 or a Type 2 structure. The following examples contrast two sentences for the verbs *allow* and *enable*. With these verbs, a Type 1 interpretation is more plausible with an animate NP$_2$ (in which case the animate noun phrase functions as both object of the main clause and subject of the *to*-clause). On the other hand, a Type 2 interpretation is more plausible with an inanimate NP$_2$ (in which case the inanimate noun phrase functions only as subject of the *to*-clause).

Animate post-verbal NP:

> *She allowed Michael **to settle her in the barrow**.* (FICT†)
>
> *Silk Slippers may not enable Sangster **to challenge the Arab supremacy**.* (NEWS)

Inanimate post-verbal NP:

> *He must not allow this unusual barrier **to stop him from fighting through to his river**.* (FICT†)
>
> *Barley malt enables starch **to be converted to sugar**.* (ACAD†)

### 9.4.2.4 Pattern 2P: NP$_2$ + passive verb + *to*-clause

Many verbs taking the structure NP$_1$ + verb + NP$_2$ + *to*-clause allow corresponding passive constructions in which the NP$_2$ becomes the subject of the main clause:

Active:

> **1a** *His wife Lavinia had [asked] estate manager Mr Brian Ealey **to raise the alarm at 9.20pm when he did not return**.* (NEWS)
>
> **2a** *Cecilia eventually [forced] the social workers **to come up with an alternative**.* (NEWS†)
>
> **3a** *We [assume] the variable x **to be subjective**.* (ACAD†)
>
> **4a** *He did not [believe] this last remark **to be true**.* (FICT)

Passive:

> **1b** *Every man of Umuofia was [asked] **to gather at the market-place tomorrow morning**.* (FICT)
>
> **2b** *A 1987 Naval Academy graduate who says he was [forced] **to quit the Navy because of his homosexuality** is refusing demands that he pay for his education.* (NEWS)
>
> **3b** *An unemployed teenager sharing a house with the family was [assumed] **to have a separate, and often lower, income**.* (NEWS†)
>
> **4b** *Tens of thousands of phantom azalea bushes and geraniums are [believed] **to be alive and growing in the gardens of Northern Ireland**.* (NEWS)

Interestingly, the passive alternative is possible with both Pattern 2 Type 1 verbs (e.g. *tell*) and Type 2 verbs (e.g. *believe*).

There are some verbs, such as *want*, *get*, *cause*, and *prefer*, which take only the active form with an object NP (no passive counterpart is possible):

> *Do you [want] daddy **to talk to you**?* (CONV)
>
> *If we [got] Terry **to do that** we'd be well away.* (CONV)
>
> *She said that she would [prefer] the nurse **to obtain any necessary information from her mother**.* (ACAD†)
>
> *A further electric shock [causes] the frequency **to rise again several minutes or more**.* (ACAD†)

Finally, with verbs such as *be claimed*, *be said*, and *be thought* only the passive form commonly takes a *to*-clause:

*The costs are claimed **to be about £2.5bn**.* (NEWS†)

*Of the various materials used, wooden slats, asphalt, rubber mats or damp straw can be said **to be neutral types of floor**.* (ACAD†)

*In Ceausescu's Romania, even the ashtrays are thought **to have ears**.* (NEWS†)

<h3>9.4.2.5    Pattern 3: verb + for NP + to-clause</h3>

Several verbs occur in the pattern verb + *for* NP + *to*-clause:

*She waited **for** the little antelope **to protest**.* (FICT†)

*He stared at the misty window, longing **for** the night **to pass**.* (FICT)

*The society called **for** consumers **to take conservation measures to save water**.* (NEWS†)

Most of these verbs are prepositional, in which the preposition is an integral part of the verbal predicate. In addition, some verbs of desire optionally take *for* + NP before a *to*-clause:

*I would like Sir Alec **to carry on**.* (FICT)

v.   *But I would like **for** you **to do one thing** if you would.* (FICT)

*Certainly, but I should hate you **to forget that he has scored more runs in Test cricket than any other Englishman**.* (BrE NEWS)

v.   *I'd hate **for** all that stuff **to go bad**.* (AmE CONV)

<h3>9.4.2.6    Register distribution of verb patterns</h3>

Figure 9.11 shows occurrences with both active and passive main clause verbs, for all verbs except *be*.

**CORPUS FINDINGS** [2,3]

➤ Pattern 1: verb + *to*-clause is by far the most-common pattern for infinitive clauses in all four registers.
   ➤ This pattern is particularly common in fiction (and to a lesser extent in news).
➤ Pattern 2: verb + NP + *to*-clause is the second most-common pattern for infinitive clauses in all four registers.
   ➤ Proportionally, this pattern accounts for c. 20–25% of the post-predicate infinitive clauses in news and academic prose.
➤ Pattern 2P: *to*-clause with passive main clause verb is rare in conversation and fiction, but occurs with moderate frequencies (over 200 times per million words) in news and academic prose.
➤ Pattern 5: verb + NP + bare infinitive clause has the opposite distribution—rare in news and academic prose, but occurring with moderate frequencies (over 200 per million words) in conversation and fiction.

**Figure 9.11**
**Frequency of verb patterns for *to*-clauses across registers**

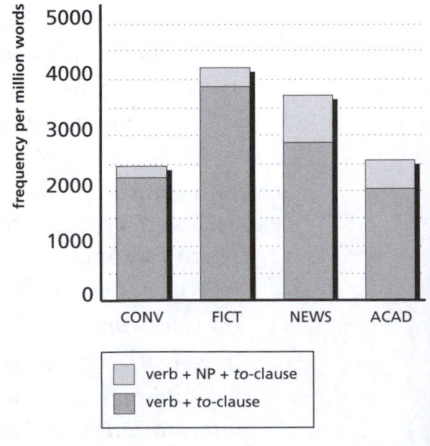

➤ Pattern 3: verb + *for* + NP + *to*-clause is rare in all four registers in BrE.
   ➤ It is somewhat more common in AmE conversation.
➤ Pattern 4: verb + bare infinitive clause is rare in all four registers.

**DISCUSSION OF FINDINGS**

In general, infinitive clauses are considerably more common in the written registers than conversation. This is in marked contrast to the register distribution of *that*-clauses and *wh*-clauses, which are both most common in conversation (9.2.5 and 9.3.2.3). This difference can be explained in part by the much greater range of verbs that can control *to*-clauses (9.4.2.7).

Bare infinitive clauses occur with only a few controlling verbs, and as a result they are much less common than *to*-clauses. With *to*-clauses, the simple Pattern 1 (verb + *to*-clause) is by far the most common. At the other extreme, Pattern 3 is rare, especially in BrE. However, it is slightly more common in AmE conversation, as in:

    *I would just like for you* **to live without my income.** (AmE CONV)

## 9.4.2.7   Controlling verbs, by semantic domain

The lists of verbs in Table 9.7 are organized by three criteria: semantic domain, structural pattern, and frequency of occurrence.

**Figure 9.12**   **Overall frequencies of the most common verbs controlling *to*-clauses**

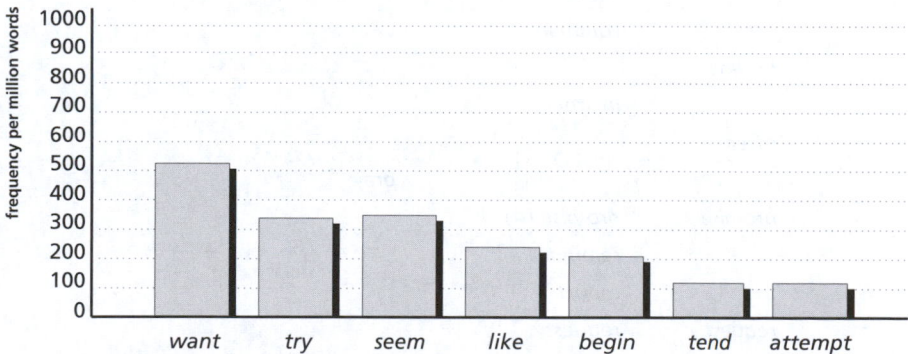

**CORPUS FINDINGS ¹**

Several general patterns are apparent from Table 9.7:
➤ Verbs taking bare infinitive clauses in post-predicate position come from just two of these semantic classes—perception verbs, and verbs of modality or causation.
➤ Pattern 3, with *for* NP, occurs with only selected verbs.
➤ Patterns 1 and 2 are the most widespread across verbs and domains; many verbs can take both patterns.

Table 9.7    **Verbs controlling infinitive clauses in post-predicate position; occurrences per million words**

■ over 100    ■ over 50    ▌over 20

((A) marks Pattern 2 verbs that occur primarily or exclusively in the active; (P) marks Pattern 2P verbs that occur primarily or exclusively in the passive)

### Speech act verbs:

| Pattern 1 verb + to-clause | Patterns 2 and 2P verb + NP + to-clause (or be verb-ed + to-clause) | Pattern 3 verb + for NP + to-clause | Pattern 4 verb + bare infinitive clause | Pattern 5 verb + NP + bare infinitive clause |
|---|---|---|---|---|
| **common verbs:** | | | | |
| ask | ask ▌/ be asked ▌ | ask | | |
| **other verbs attested in the LSWE Corpus:** | | | | |
| | advise | | | |
| beg | beg | | | |
| | beseech | | | |
| | call | call | | |
| claim | be claimed (P) | | | |
| | challenge | | | |
| | command | | | |
| decline | | | | |
| | invite | | | |
| offer | | | | |
| | | pray | | |
| promise | promise (A) | | | |
| | remind | | | |
| | report | | | |
| request | request | | | |
| say | be said (P) | | | |
| | tell / be told | | | |
| | urge | | | |
| | warn | | | |

### Other communication verbs:

| Pattern 1 verb + to-clause | Patterns 2 and 2P verb + NP + to-clause (or be verb-ed + to-clause) | Pattern 3 verb + for NP + to-clause | Pattern 4 verb + bare infinitive clause | Pattern 5 verb + NP + bare infinitive clause |
|---|---|---|---|---|
| **common verbs:** | | | | |
| prove | prove ▌/ be proven / be proved | | | |

**Table 9.7** **continued**

other verbs attested in the LSWE Corpus:

| | |
|---|---|
| | *show* |
| | *teach* |
| | *convince* |

**Cognition verbs:**

| Pattern 1<br>verb +<br>*to*-clause | Patterns 2 and 2P<br>verb + NP +<br>*to*-clause (or<br>*be* verb-*ed* +<br>*to*-clause) | Pattern 3<br>verb + *for* NP<br>+ *to*-clause | Pattern 4<br>verb + bare<br>infinitive<br>clause | Pattern 5<br>verb + NP +<br>bare infinitive<br>clause |
|---|---|---|---|---|

common verbs:

| | | | | |
|---|---|---|---|---|
| *expect* | *expect* ■<br>/ *be expected* ▌ | | | |
| | *find* ■ / *be found* | | | |
| *learn* ▌ | | | | |

other verbs attested in the LSWE Corpus:

| | | | | |
|---|---|---|---|---|
| | *assume* | | | |
| | *believe* | | | |
| | *consider* | | | |
| | *estimate* | | | |
| *forget* | | | | |
| | *imagine* | | | |
| | *judge* | | | |
| | *know* | | | |
| | *presume* | | | |
| *pretend* | | | | |
| *remember* | | | | |
| | *suppose* | | | |
| | *take* | | | |
| | *be thought* (P) | | | |
| | *trust* | | | |
| | *understand* | | | |

**Perception verbs:**

| Pattern 1<br>verb +<br>*to*-clause | Patterns 2 and 2P<br>verb + NP +<br>*to*-clause (or<br>*be* verb-*ed* +<br>*to*-clause) | Pattern 3<br>verb + *for* NP<br>+ *to*-clause | Pattern 4<br>verb + bare<br>infinitive<br>clause | Pattern 5<br>verb + NP +<br>bare infinitive<br>clause |
|---|---|---|---|---|

verbs attested in the LSWE Corpus:

| | | | | |
|---|---|---|---|---|
| | *be felt* (P) | | | *feel* |
| | *be heard* (P) | | *hear tell* | *hear* |
| | *see* | | | *see* |
| | | | | *watch* |

**Table 9.7    continued**

### Verbs of desire:

| Pattern 1 verb + to-clause | Patterns 2 and 2P verb + NP + to-clause (or be verb-ed + to-clause) | Pattern 3 verb + *for* NP + to-clause | Pattern 4 verb + bare infinitive clause | Pattern 5 verb + NP + bare infinitive clause |
|---|---|---|---|---|
| **common verbs:** | | | | |
| *like* ■ | *like* (A) | *like* | | |
| *want* ■ | *want* ■ (A) | | | |
| *need* ■ | *need* | | | |
| *wish* ■ | *wish* (A) | | | |
| *hope* ■ | | | | |
| **other verbs attested in the LSWE Corpus:** | | | | |
| *(cannot) bear* | | *(cannot) bear* | | |
| *care* | | *care* | | |
| *dare* | *dare* (A) | | *dare* | |
| *desire* | | | | |
| *dread* | *dread* (A) | *dread* | | |
| *hate* | *hate* (A) | *hate* | | |
| *love* | *love* (A) | *love* | | |
| *long* | | *long* | | |
| *prefer* | *prefer* (A) | *prefer* | | |
| *regret* | | | | |
| *(cannot) stand* | | *(cannot) stand* | | |

### Verbs of intention or decision:

| Pattern 1 verb + to-clause | Patterns 2 and 2P verb + NP + to-clause (or be verb-ed + to-clause) | Pattern 3 verb + *for* NP + to-clause | Pattern 4 verb + bare infinitive clause | Pattern 5 verb + NP + bare infinitive clause |
|---|---|---|---|---|
| **common verbs:** | | | | |
| *decide* ■ | | | | |
| *agree* ■ | | *agree* | | |
| *intend* ■ | *intend* | *intend* | | |
| *mean* ■ | *mean* | *mean* | | |
| *prepare* ■ | *prepare* / be prepared ■ | | | |

**Table 9.7**     **continued**

**other verbs attested in the LSWE Corpus:**

| | | |
|---|---|---|
| aim | | |
| consent | | consent |
| choose | choose | |
| | design | |
| hesitate | | |
| look | | look |
| plan | | plan |
| refuse | | |
| resolve | | |
| | schedule | |
| threaten | | |
| volunteer | | |
| wait | | wait |

**Verbs of effort:**

| Pattern 1 | Patterns 2 and 2P | Pattern 3 | Pattern 4 | Pattern 5 |
|---|---|---|---|---|
| verb + to-clause | verb + NP + to-clause (or be verb-ed + to-clause) | verb + for NP + to-clause | verb + bare infinitive clause | verb + NP + bare infinitive clause |

**common verbs:**

| | | | | |
|---|---|---|---|---|
| attempt | | | | |
| try | | | | |
| fail | | | | |
| manage | | | | |

**other verbs attested in the LSWE Corpus:**

| | | | | |
|---|---|---|---|---|
| bother | | | | |
| endeavor | | | | |
| seek | | | | |
| strive | | | | |
| struggle | | | | |
| venture | | | | |

**Verbs of modality or causation:**

| Pattern 1 | Patterns 2 and 2P | Pattern 3 | Pattern 4 | Pattern 5 |
|---|---|---|---|---|
| verb + to-clause | verb + NP + to-clause (or be verb-ed + to-clause) | verb + for NP + to-clause | verb + bare infinitive clause | verb + NP + bare infinitive clause |

**common verbs:**

| | | | | |
|---|---|---|---|---|
| | allow /be allowed | allow | | |
| | enable /be enabled | | | |
| get | get (A) | | | |
| | require /be required | | | |

Table 9.7 **continued**

other verbs attested in the LSWE Corpus:

| | | | | |
|---|---|---|---|---|
| *afford* | | | | |
| | *appoint* | | | |
| *arrange* | | *arrange* | | |
| | *assist* | | | |
| | *authorize* | | | |
| | *cause* | | | |
| | *compel* | | | |
| | *counsel* | | | |
| | *defy* (A) | | | |
| *deserve* | | | | |
| | *drive* | | | |
| | *elect* | | | |
| | *encourage* | | | |
| | *entitle* | | | |
| | *forbid* | | | |
| | *force* | | | |
| | | | | *have* |
| *help* | *help* (A) | | *help* | *help* |
| | *inspire* | | | |
| | *instruct* | | | |
| | *lead* | | | |
| | *leave* | | | |
| | | | *let* | *let* |
| | *be made* (P) | | *make do (with)* | *make* |
| | *oblige* | | | |
| | *order* | | | |
| | *permit* | | | |
| | *persuade* | | | |
| | *prompt* | | | |
| | *raise* | | | |
| | *summon* | | | |
| | *tempt* | | | |
| *vote* | | | | |

**Aspectual verbs:**

| Pattern 1 | Patterns 2 and 2P | Pattern 3 | Pattern 4 | Pattern 5 |
|---|---|---|---|---|
| verb + *to*-clause | verb + NP + *to*-clause (or *be* verb-*ed* + *to*-clause) | verb + *for* NP + *to*-clause | verb + bare infinitive clause | verb + NP + bare infinitive clause |

common verbs:

| | | | | |
|---|---|---|---|---|
| *begin* ▨ | | | | |
| *continue* ▪ | | | | |
| *start* ▪ | | | | |

**Table 9.7** **continued**

**other verbs attested in the LSWE Corpus:**

*cease*

*commence*

*proceed*

**Verbs of probability and of simple fact (with subject raising):**

| Pattern 1<br>verb +<br>to-clause | Patterns 2 and 2P<br>verb + NP +<br>to-clause (or<br>be verb-ed +<br>to-clause) | Pattern 3<br>verb + for NP<br>+ to-clause | Pattern 4<br>verb + bare<br>infinitive<br>clause | Pattern 5<br>verb + NP +<br>bare infinitive<br>clause |
|---|---|---|---|---|
| **common verbs:** | | | | |
| *seem* ▬▬ | | | | |
| *tend* ▬▬ | | | | |
| *appear* ■ | | | | |

**other verbs attested in the LSWE Corpus:**

*come*

*happen*

*turn out*

➤ Seven verbs are notably common in the pattern active verb + *to*-clause: *want, try, seem, like, begin, tend, attempt* (see Figure 9.12).
  ➤ The verb *want* is especially common in this pattern.
  ➤ These verbs come from four semantic domains—verbs of desire (*want* and *like*), verbs of effort (*try* and *attempt*), verbs of probability (*seem* and *tend*), and an aspectual verb (*begin*).

**DISCUSSION OF FINDINGS**

The frequencies of specific verbs with infinitive clauses can be explained by a combination of factors, including the communicative importance of the semantic domain, whether the verb can only be complemented by an infinitive clause, and, where it can also control a *that*-clause, the differences in meaning that can be conveyed with the two kinds of complementation. It is notable, for instance, that six of the seven most frequent verbs do not control *that*-clauses at all.

The following paragraphs discuss the discourse functions of verbs controlling *to*-clauses in each of the ten major semantic domains.

(1) Speech act verbs controlling a post-predicate infinitive clause are used to give indirect reports of directives (e.g. commands, requests):

*I [asked] the telephone operators* **to connect me with his friend.** (FICT†)

*I [warned] Nwankwo* **to keep a sharp eye and a sharp ear.** (FICT)

*I should have [told] Walter* **to let him go.** (NEWS)

*Rep. Tom DeLay, R-Texas, [challenged] colleagues* **to be truthful about whether a commission would help resolve the complex matter.** (NEWS)

With *to*-clauses, these verbs express indirect commands (imperatives). As such, they complement the use of speech-act verbs introducing indirect questions and exclamatives with *wh*-clauses (9.3.2.2), and their use to convey indirect statements with *that*-clauses (9.2.2.2).

(2) 'Other communication' verbs serve to report findings, indicating that the proposition presented in the *to*-clause should be accepted as known information:

*Peter Briggs, who [proved]* **to be an astute campaign manager,** *has resigned his membership.* (NEWS)

*Trace concentrations have been [shown]* **to interfere seriously with the breeding performance of male mice.** (ACAD†)

(3) Cognition verbs represent mental states or attitudes, often indicating the epistemological status of the information presented in the *to*-clause:

*The laws were [believed]* **to include Lithuania's announcement last week of separate Lithuanian citizenship.** (NEWS†)

*International football was [considered]* **to be of paramount importance to the status of Rugby League.** (NEWS†)

*Voigt (1910) in considering polycrystalline assembles [assumed] strain* **to be uniform throughout the mixture.** (ACAD)

*We [expect]* **to find adequate specification methods and techniques.** (ACAD)

*Differences in hardness were [found]* **to make it easy to distinguish between minerals that look similar.** (ACAD)

(4) Perception verbs are a special subset of mental verbs that represent sense perceptions rather than other mental states or attitudes. This category includes only four verbs, *feel, hear, see,* and *watch,* which typically occur with bare infinitive clauses (Pattern 5):

*I didn't [feel] the wind* **do it** *either.* (CONV)

*I went in just in time to [hear] Christopher* **say well I'm having all grandpa's money when he's dead not you.** (CONV)

*I mean often times you [see] teams* **equalize immediately.** (CONV)

In addition, the verbs *feel, hear,* and *see* can occur as passives controlling a *to*-clause:

*Non-tournament expenditure is also [felt]* **to be excessive in some areas.** (NEWS)

*Trevor Brooking, that most mild-mannered of radio reporters, was [heard]* **to utter the word "awful" on the air.** (NEWS)

*In some rocks the minerals can be [seen]* **to have crystal faces.** (ACAD†)

The verb *see* can also control a *to*-clause with a direct object noun phrase. This construction often has a metaphorical meaning:

*That is, one explanation [sees] the right ear advantage* **to be the result of stimulating a particular ear.** (ACAD)

(5) Several common verbs mark various kinds of desire. These verbs can also be regarded as a subset of mental verbs, representing an attitudinal stance towards the envisioned action contained in the *to*-clause. Most verbs of this type represent a positive stance (e.g. *wish, hope, like, love*), but a few of these verbs convey negative stance (e.g. *dread, hate*):

> *She [wants]* **to see drugs tested on convicted murderers.** (CONV†)
>
> *We [need] a support teacher* **to go there.** (CONV)
>
> *We'd [love]* **to come.** (FICT†)
>
> *This is not a government which [likes]* **to ask fundamental questions.**
> (NEWS)
>
> *They [hope]* **to heighten their appreciation of nature.** (ACAD†)
>
> *When we [wish]* **to distinguish among several levels of storage in a**
> **computer,** *we will refer to this basic level as main or primary store.* (ACAD†)
>
> *She [hated]* **to say the words,** *for fear of bringing him pain.* (FICT)

The verb *want* is noteworthy here for its extremely frequent use with a *to*-clause. In fact, *want* + *to*-clause is acquiring semi-modal status in English, as reflected by its common reduction to *wanna* + verb in conversation (6.6).

(6) Verbs of intention or decision might also be regarded as a subset of mental verbs, involving a resolve, plan, or decision to carry out some action:

> *They didn't [plan]* **to have two wives,** *it just happened.* (CONV)
>
> *There is not much to do here, but do you [intend]* **to continue upcountry?**
> (FICT)
>
> *France has [decided]* **to cut off aid to the Comoros Islands.** (NEWS†)
>
> *Rail fares are [scheduled]* **to soar in the next few years.** (NEWS)
>
> *Iverson (1962) [designed] the APL language* **to describe hardware at this**
> **level.** (ACAD†)

(7) There are relatively few verbs of effort, but four of these are notably common: *try, attempt, manage,* and *fail.* This set of verbs is constrained grammatically, occurring only in Pattern 1, Type 1:

> *I'm just [trying]* **to get my bearings.** (CONV)
>
> *Kemp [tried]* **to hide his sigh of relief.** (FICT†)
>
> *Somehow he [managed]* **to stand at an angle.** (FICT†)
>
> *Governments and airlines had [failed]* **to learn lessons from the incident.**
> (NEWS)
>
> *Since we [attempt]* **to support work in an office environment,** *we have been*
> *studying methods proposed in organization research.* (ACAD†)

(8) Verbs of modality or causation form the largest class of verbs controlling infinitive clauses in post-predicate position. In addition, these verbs come from all five grammatical patterns, but especially Pattern 2, Type 1. The meaning of these verbs normally involves two participants (in addition to the *to*-clause), with one participant permitting, facilitating, requiring, or causing the other to undertake the action expressed in the *to*-clause:

> *How could I [get] him* **to agree to go?** (CONV†)
>
> *I [persuaded] Hawkbit* **to join us.** (FICT†)
>
> *He had [convinced] Gene Lopwitz* **to put up $600 million of Pierce and**
> **Pierce's money to buy the Giscard.** (FICT)
>
> *I would [allow] the Press Council* **to play its proper role.** (NEWS†)
>
> *It [enables] geologists* **to distinguish the relative ages of formations that are**
> **only a few meters thick.** (ACAD†)

Four of the verbs taking bare infinitive clauses (Pattern 5) mark some kind of facilitation or causation: *have*, *help*, *let*, and *make*:

> I *[helped]* a young girl **get an old lady onto the train**. (CONV)
>
> If you *[let]* Kitty **cross the line once**, all hell breaks loose. (FICT†)
>
> The thought *[made]* Kramer **twist his lips in a smile**. (FICT†)
>
> I'll *[have]* Alicia **bring something up**. (FICT)
>
> The political machine won votes by *[having]* precinct captains **talk to each voter in a neighborhood**. (NEWS†)

(The verbs *have* and *help* in the pattern verb + NP + bare infinitive clause are sometimes considered to be more common in AmE than BrE; see 9.4.10.1. However, they are attested relatively rarely in both dialects in the LSWE Corpus.)

The verb *help* is particularly noteworthy in that it can occur with four of the five possible structural patterns.

*Help* + *to*-clause:

> Congress helped **to keep the peace**. (CONV†)

*Help* + NP + *to*-clause:

> A person can help another person **to get well**, can't they? (CONV)

*Help* + bare infinitive clause:

> Key testimony has been broadcast live on television and radio to help **keep the city fully abreast of the proceedings**. (NEWS)

*Help* + NP + bare infinitive clause:

> Lammers helped me **persuade Van Heeren to let you in tonight**. (FICT†)

(9) Aspectual verbs characterize the state of completion of the event or activity described in the *to*-clause, for example, whether the action is beginning, ending, or in progress. Aspectual verbs occur only in Pattern 1:

> His pen *[began]* **to fly over the paper** as he sketched rapidly. (FICT†)
>
> Nearly half a billion Indian voters yesterday *[started]* **to choose their next government**. (NEWS)
>
> Moscow *[continues]* **to value the Warsaw Pact as a military buffer**. (NEWS)
>
> On his view the fact that it *[ceased]* **to be a probability**, and did occur, is something that might not have happened. (ACAD)

(10) Finally, verbs of probability and of simple fact indicate that the proposition presented in the *to*-clause has a certain degree of likelihood (*appear*, *seem*, *tend*), or that the proposition is simply an accepted fact/occurrence (*come*, *happen*, *turn out*):

> Miss Adeane *[appeared]* **to have become rather deaf**. (FICT)
>
> This Lebanese atrocity *[seems]* **to be a great boost to Gen. Aoun**. (NEWS†)
>
> Recent theories *[tend]* **to be Neo-Laplacian**. (ACAD†)
>
> The world No. 3 from Australia also *[happens]* **to be the president of the International Squash Players Association**. (NEWS)
>
> Most of the early ages *[turned out]* **to be too high**. (ACAD†)

The verb *come* occurs in this construction only with a specialized sense related to *come about* or *happen*:

> The Brandenburg Gate has [come] **to symbolize the division between East and West**. (NEWS†)

Some of these verbs are also moderately frequent in the alternative extraposed pattern with *that*-clauses (9.2.3, 9.4.9).

## 9.4.2.8 Interaction between the semantic and grammatical characteristics of controlling verbs

The grammar and semantics of verbs controlling post-predicate infinitive clauses are complex: these verbs occur in six grammatical patterns and represent ten major semantic classes.

Many semantic classes allow only a restricted set of structural patterns. Perception verbs primarily take bare infinitive clauses. Verbs of effort and aspectual verbs occur only in the verb + *to*-clause pattern. Verbs of probability occur only in verb + *to*-clause constructions which are instances of subject-to-subject raising.

Conversely, some grammatical patterns occur only with a restricted set of semantic categories. Bare infinitives occur only with perception verbs or some verbs of modality or causation; subject-to-subject raising only with verbs of probability or simple fact.

At the other extreme, some semantic classes are extremely productive. For example, verbs of modality or causation comprise 37 verbs, including verbs with all six grammatical patterns.

In addition, individual verbs can follow different patterns. We noted in 9.4.2.7 that the verb *help* takes four of the five possible grammatical patterns. The verbs *ask* and *mean* can occur in any of the four structural patterns with a *to*-clause:

Verb + *to*-clause:

> We can always ask **to put them away for a week**. (CONV)

Verb + NP + *to*-clause:

> He should ask the Prime Minister **to open negotiations to enter the Exchange Rate Mechanism**. (NEWS†)

*Be* + verb-*ed* + *to*-clause:

> European transport ministers meeting in Paris will today be asked **to approve radical plans for tax and financial incentives**. (NEWS†)

Verb + *for* NP + *to*-clause:

> To continue the parallel, Mr Crosby will probably ask for Liverpool **to take their appointed place at Wembley next month**. (NEWS)

It is much more common, though, for a verb to control only one or two patterns. Thus, verbs such as *choose, desire, expect, need, prefer, promise, want,* and *wish* occur in two patterns.

Verb + *to*-clause / verb + NP + *to*-clause:

> I don't want **to have a broken nose!** (CONV)
>
> I don't want that dog **to come in**. (CONV†)

Similarly, verbs such as *arrange, long, plan, agree,* and *consent* occur in two patterns.

Verb + *to*-clause / verb + *for* NP + *to*-clause:

> *Are you planning* **to eat that tray?** (CONV)

> *They must be able to plan for sufficient waste management capacity* **to serve their industrial base.** (ACAD†)

The verb *dare* (see 9.4.10) can control either a *to*-clause or a bare infinitive:

> *I don't think she would dare* **say anything to me about it.** (CONV)

> *He no longer dared* **to irrigate the entire acre,** *or the greenness of new grass would betray him.* (FICT)

Finally, many verbs take only one of the grammatical patterns. For example, verbs such as *aim, decline, hope, refuse, regret, attempt, fail,* and *try* occur only in the pattern verb + *to*-clause. Verbs such as *tell, urge, warn, imagine, trust, allow, authorize, enable, permit,* and *persuade* occur only in the pattern verb + NP + *to*-clause (or the corresponding passive).

## 9.4.2.9 Common controlling verbs across registers

**CORPUS FINDINGS** [2]

➤ Verbs that commonly control post-predicate *to*-clauses are distributed differently across semantic domains and across registers (see Table 9.8).
  ➤ The written registers commonly use verbs from many different semantic domains in combination with a *to*-clause.
  ➤ Conversation is much more restricted, commonly using only verbs of desire (*want, like*), plus the verbs *try* and *seem*.
➤ Frequencies for the most common verbs with Pattern 1 are displayed in Figures 9.13–16:
  ➤ In conversation, the combination *want* + *to*-clause occurs more frequently than any other verb controlling an infinitive clause in any register. Three other verbs are relatively common in this pattern: *try, seem,* and *like*.
  ➤ In fiction, the combination *want* + *to*-clause is also extremely common. Three other verbs are notably common: *try, seem,* and *begin*.
  ➤ In news, no single verb is extremely common controlling a *to*-clause, but five verbs are relatively frequent: *want, try, seem, fail,* and *appear*.
  ➤ Individual verb + *to*-clause combinations are much less common in academic prose, but five verbs are relatively frequent: *seem, appear, tend, try, want*.
➤ Frequencies for the most common verbs in Patterns 2 and 2P are displayed in Table 9.9:
  ➤ The active verb pattern: verb + NP + *to*-clause, and the passive verb pattern: *be* + verb-*ed* + *to*-clause, are much less common overall than the pattern: verb + *to*-clause. However, there are a few verbs that take these patterns with relatively high frequencies.
  ➤ *Expect* is the only verb that is common in the pattern verb + NP + *to*-clause in all four registers.
  ➤ *Expect* + NP + *to*-clause is particularly common in news.
  ➤ The verb *allow* is common with this pattern in fiction, news, and academic prose.
  ➤ In academic prose, *enable* and *require* are also relatively common.
  ➤ In conversation, both Patterns 2 and 2P are generally rare.
➤ Passive verbs are less common controlling post-predicate *to*-clauses than active verbs.

Figure 9.13

**Frequencies of the most common verbs controlling *to*-clauses— conversation**

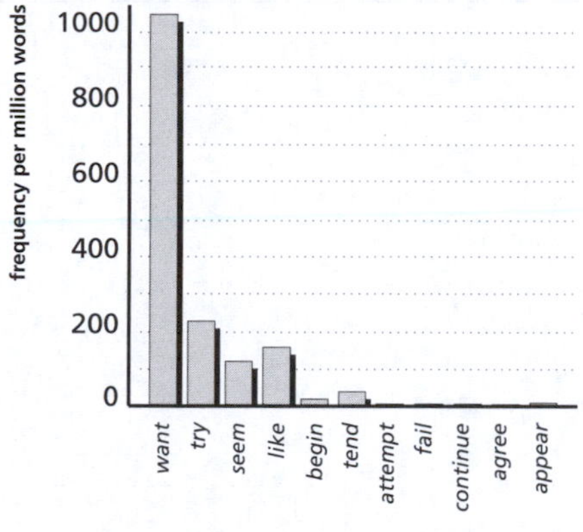

Figure 9.14

**Frequencies of the most common verbs controlling *to*-clauses—fiction**

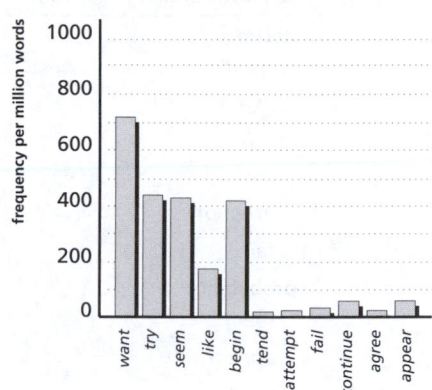

Figure 9.15

**Frequencies of the most common verbs controlling *to*-clauses—news**

Figure 9.16

**Frequencies of the most common verbs controlling *to*-clauses— academic prose**

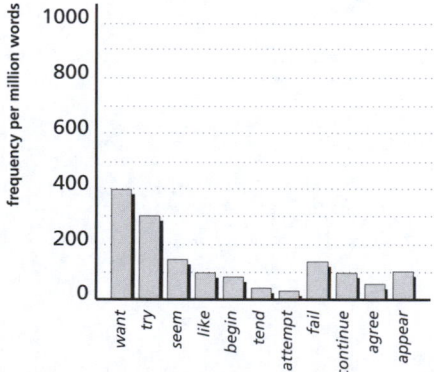

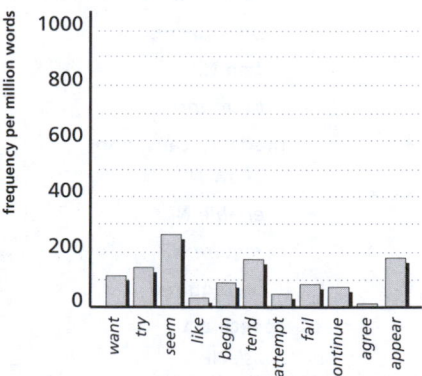

➤ In academic prose, two passive verbs are common with a *to*-clause: *be found* and *be required*.

➤ Three common verbs occur more frequently in the passive with a *to*-clause than in the active: *be expected* in news, and the verbs *be found* and *be considered* in academic prose.

**DISCUSSION OF FINDINGS**

*To*-clauses in post-predicate position typically perform specific functions in different registers, and these functions are reflected in the controlling verbs that are common in each register. In conversation, the verb *want* functions as a general expression of personal desire. In most conversations, it is topically relevant for participants to express their own personal desires (*I want* X) or less commonly the personal desires of others (*she/he/they want(s)* X):

Table 9.8    **The most common verbs controlling a complement *to*-infinitive clause, by semantic domain and register; occurrences per million words**

■ over 400    ■ over 200    ■ over 100    ▮ over 50

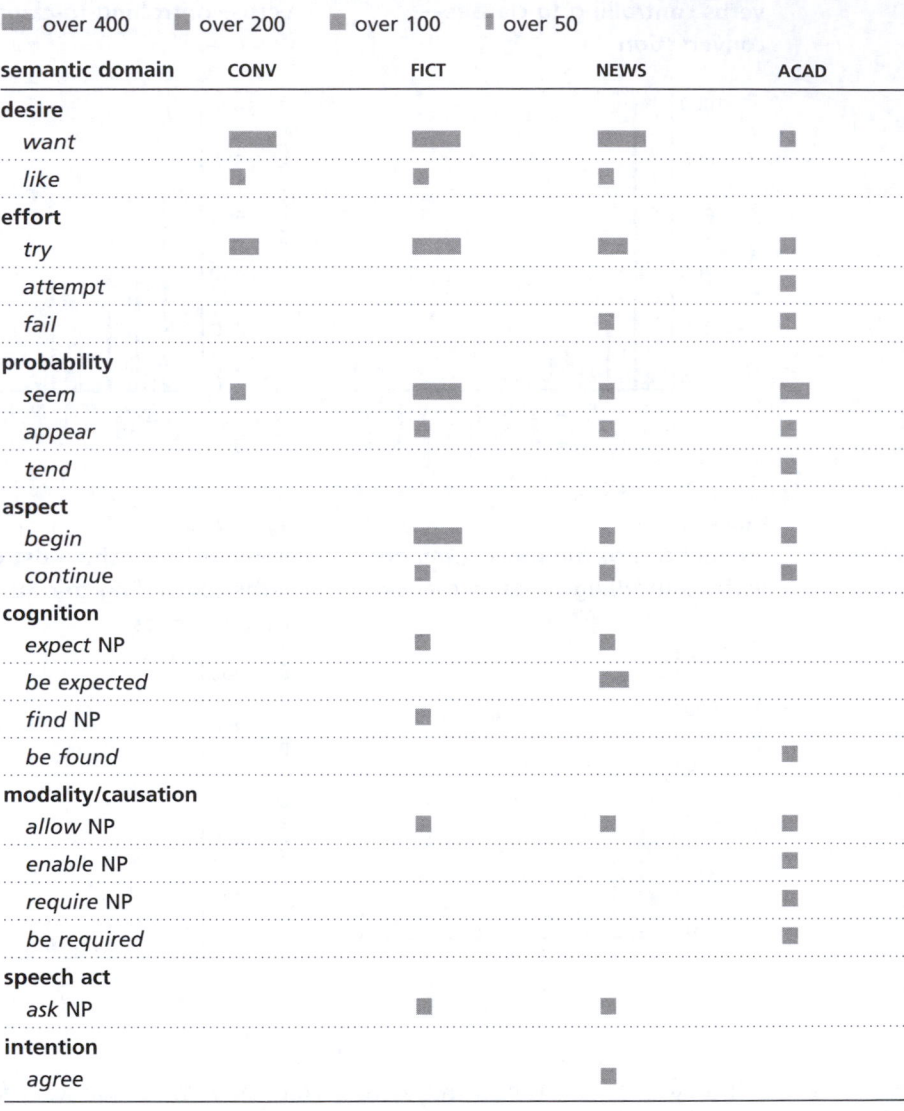

| semantic domain | CONV | FICT | NEWS | ACAD |
|---|---|---|---|---|
| **desire** | | | | |
| *want* | over 400 | over 400 | over 400 | over 50 |
| *like* | over 50 | over 50 | over 50 | |
| **effort** | | | | |
| *try* | over 200 | over 200 | over 100 | over 50 |
| *attempt* | | | | over 50 |
| *fail* | | | over 50 | over 50 |
| **probability** | | | | |
| *seem* | over 50 | over 200 | over 50 | over 100 |
| *appear* | | over 50 | over 50 | over 50 |
| *tend* | | | | over 50 |
| **aspect** | | | | |
| *begin* | | over 100 | over 50 | over 50 |
| *continue* | over 50 | | over 50 | over 50 |
| **cognition** | | | | |
| *expect* NP | | over 50 | over 50 | |
| *be expected* | | | over 100 | |
| *find* NP | | over 50 | | |
| *be found* | | | | over 50 |
| **modality/causation** | | | | |
| *allow* NP | | over 50 | over 50 | over 50 |
| *enable* NP | | | | over 50 |
| *require* NP | | | | over 50 |
| *be required* | | | | over 50 |
| **speech act** | | | | |
| *ask* NP | | over 50 | over 50 | |
| **intention** | | | | |
| *agree* | | | over 50 | |

> *I want **to get one of my shoes on the way out.*** (CONV†)
> *I wanted **to go and get something.*** (CONV)
> *I didn't want **to go to assembly really.*** (CONV)
> *I don't want **to have a broken nose.*** (CONV)
> *She wanted **to see dad.*** (CONV)
> *He probably wants **to speak to you.*** (CONV)

In addition, speakers commonly question the desires of their interlocutors:

> *Do you want **to go in the water?*** (CONV)
> *Do you want **to stay there?*** (CONV†)

These same functions are common in fictional dialogue:

Table 9.9 **Verbs commonly occurring in the pattern verb + NP + *to*-clause, by voice and register; occurrences per million words**

▭ over 100   ▪ over 50   ▌ over 20

| | CONV active | CONV passive | FICT active | FICT passive | NEWS active | NEWS passive | ACAD active | ACAD passive |
|---|---|---|---|---|---|---|---|---|
| *expect* | ▌ | | ▪ | | ▭ | ▭ | ▌ | ▌ |
| *allow* | | | ▪ | | ▌ | | ▭ | |
| *find* | | | ▪ | | ▌ | | ▌ | ▪ |
| *require* | | | | | ▌ | ▌ | ▪ | ▪ |
| *enable* | | | | | ▌ | | ▪ | |
| *ask* | ▌ | | | | ▌ | | | |
| *prove* | | | | | ▌ | | ▌ | |
| *consider* | | | | | | | | ▌ |

> *I want **to jump into a tub of hot water first**.* (FICT)
>
> *I don't want **to come**.* (FICT)
>
> *Do you want **to come along**?* (FICT)

In addition, fictional narrative often reports the desires of characters with constructions of this type:

> *Jane wanted **to jump up and down and scream with excitement**.* (FICT†)
>
> *He wanted **to know more about it**.* (FICT)

Verbs of effort are most common in fiction and news, where they typically report people's attempts (or failures):

> *He had tried **to get through for hours**.* (FICT)
>
> *She attempted **to smile**.* (FICT†)
>
> *She had failed **to appear in court**.* (FICT†)
>
> *Military officers have tried **to seize power six times**.* (NEWS†)
>
> *He attempted **to withdraw from international judo by offering his resignation**.* (NEWS†)
>
> *The police have failed even **to recognize the nature of the problem**.* (NEWS)

Similarly, aspectual verbs are most common in fiction and news, where they typically report the state of progression for some process or activity:

> *Harry was beginning **to think that Bill was obsessed with Sandy**.* (FICT†)
>
> *He continued **to stare at her**.* (FICT)
>
> *Even ambulance staff not suspended are beginning **to feel the pinch**.* (NEWS†)
>
> *He maintained that ambulance crews were continuing **to answer 999 calls**, even though they were suspended.* (NEWS†)

In contrast, the verbs *tend* and *appear* are typical of subject-raising verbs of probability in that they occur most frequently in academic prose:

> *The cloud tended **to flatten into a disk**.* (ACAD)
>
> *Neither the sex nor the strain of donor rats appears **to be important**.* (ACAD)

The verb *expect*, in the patterns verb + NP + *to*-clause and *be* + verb-*ed* + *to*-clause, is most common in news, where it reports on future predicted events:

> *A senior opposition source said that he expected Forum ministers* **to be in office by the weekend.** (NEWS†)

> *Greece's overall debt is expected* **to exceed the nation's gross domestic product for 1989.** (NEWS†)

> *Heavy fighting with government troops was expected* **to break out soon.** (NEWS)

Verbs of modality/causation, such as *allow*, *enable*, and *require*, are especially common controlling *to*-clauses in academic prose:

> *An autumn-like pattern, or even a constant day length, will allow the body* **to develop properly before the bird starts laying.** (ACAD)

> *The WHO System will enable a worldwide user network* **to have access to an AIDS data bank.** (ACAD)

> *The mass of the swivelling grip requires considerable stress* **to rotate or move it into the axial position.** (ACAD†)

## 9.4.3 Verbs taking extraposed *to*-clauses

There are few verbs that control extraposed *to*-clauses, the most common being the copular verb *be* when it combines with a predicative noun phrase or prepositional phrase to make up a complex main clause predicate:

> *It's up to you* **to make an appointment.** (CONV)

> *It is for others* **to offer moral guidance to the newly prosperous Pharisees.** (NEWS)

> *It is still an adventure* **to travel down the river of the Colorado river in a small boat.** (ACAD)

The verb *help* also occurs with moderate frequency controlling extraposed *to*-clauses:

> *It may also help* **to set out some educational objectives against which the ideas will be tested.** (ACAD†)

The verb *take*, in the sense of *require*, can combine with object noun phrases to control extraposed *to*-clauses:

> *It takes a little time* **to get a visa to Mexico.** (FICT)

> *It had taken him twenty-six years* **to return.** (NEWS†)

> *It takes resources* **to counteract pollution.** (ACAD†)

In these constructions, the object noun phrase specifies the requirement (*twenty-six years, resources, a little time*), and the *to*-clause indicates the action that depends on that requirement.

## 9.4.4 Subject noun phrases and subject predicative *to*-clauses

*To*-clauses serving as subject predicative to a copular verb are relatively common (around 400 per million words in the written registers). Similar to *that*-clauses in this role, subject predicative *to*-clauses further identify or describe the subject of the main clause. In these constructions, the subject noun phrase can refer to a range of abstract referents:

> *[Their hope]* is **to succeed as the consolidator of post-Thatcherism**. (NEWS)
>
> *[The only safe course]* is **to protect human life from the beginning**. (NEWS)
>
> *[The Soviet leader's main concern]* is **to avoid an "artificial" acceleration of the process**. (NEWS)
>
> *[The answer]* is probably **to run him on a left hand track**. (NEWS)
>
> *[The last thing I want]* is **to be a laughing stock among local farmers**. (NEWS)
>
> *[Their function]* is **to detect the cries of predatory bats**. (ACAD)
>
> *[The mouse's natural response]* is **to move away from the handler**. (ACAD)

There are, however, three major uses of subject predicative *to*-clauses that occur more systematically. First, these constructions are used to frame a series of points in a discussion:

> *[A fourth challenge]* is **to develop management arrangements within hospitals**. (NEWS)
>
> *[The first step in any such calculation]* is **to write the equation for the reaction**. (ACAD)

Second, subject predicative *to*-clauses are often used to introduce an *aim*, *objective*, *plan*, *goal*, *purpose*, *strategy*, *task*, or *idea*:

> *[The inevitable short-term aim]* is **to affect the decisions of would-be migrants**. (NEWS)
>
> *[Our major aim]* is **to reach beginning students in geology**. (ACAD†)
>
> *[The plan]* is **to turn Ross into a mini-conglomerate**. (NEWS†)
>
> *[The SHV objective]* is **to end up with a significant stake in Burmah**. (NEWS)
>
> *[Our objective]* is **to give an introduction to this broad field of knowledge**. (ACAD)
>
> *[The purpose of this chapter]* is **to describe some of the available techniques**. (ACAD†)

Third, subject predicative *to*-clauses are commonly used to introduce a method or way of doing something. This use is especially common in academic prose:

> *[The most convenient and safest way of storing and retrieving them]* is **to stack the dishes on narrow Perspex trays**. (ACAD†)
>
> *[The best method for recovering eggs]* is **to use the flushing method described in Section 2.2**. (ACAD)
>
> *[An alternative method for isolating advanced Icms]* is **to allow blastocysts to hatch**. (ACAD†)
>
> *[An alternative technique for this stage of oocyte maturation]* is **to collect freshly ovulated oocytes from the fallopian tubes**. (ACAD)

Finally, subject predicative *to*-clauses are occasionally used where the subject itself is also a *to*-clause, making for a balanced sentence structure pivoted round the copular verb (9.4.7):

> *[To be European in France]* is **to think globally about a French-led political Europe which will challenge the power of Japan and America**. (NEWS)

## 9.4.5 *To*-clauses controlled by adjectives

*To*-clauses occur with adjective predicates in post-predicate, pre-predicate, and extraposed positions. Adjectival predicates controlling *to*-clauses come from seven major semantic domains.

Adjectives controlling post-predicate *to*-clauses:

- degree of certainty (e.g. *certain, due, unlikely, sure*)
- ability or willingness (e.g. *able, determined, keen, reluctant*)
- personal affective stance (e.g. *afraid, glad, surprised, sorry*)
- ease or difficulty (e.g. *easy, hard*)
- evaluation (e.g. *good, convenient, foolhardy, useless*)
- habitual behavior (e.g. *unaccustomed, used*)

Adjectives controlling extraposed *to*-clauses:

- necessity or importance (e.g. *important, essential*)
- ease or difficulty (e.g. *easy, hard*)
- evaluation (e.g. *good, convenient, foolhardy, useless*)

Bare infinitives do not occur with adjectives, but in some cases *for*-phrases are possible, to make explicit the subject of the *to*-clause:

> Whatever the ideological preoccupations of the prime minister, it is impossible *[for the government]* **to take no view.** (NEWS†)

### 9.4.5.1 Grammatical patterns

Similar to verbs controlling *to*-clauses, a combination of adjective + *to*-clause can represent four different grammatical patterns:

**Pattern 1**

The simplest situation is where the absent subject of the *to*-clause is understood to be the same as the subject of the main clause:

> *Millar was obstinately determined* **to change the content of education.** (NEWS)

**Pattern 2**

Degree of certainty adjectival predicates occur with subject-to-subject raising (like verbs of probability in 9.4.2.2). The pre-predicate noun phrase in these structures should be interpreted as the subject of the *to*-clause and not as the main clause subject, which is logically the entire subject + *to*-clause. Thus, compare the following example to analogous sentences:

> *The government is unlikely* **to meet the full cost.** (NEWS†)
> v. **For the government to meet the full cost** *is unlikely* <pre-predicate *to*-clause>
> **That the government will meet the full cost** *is unlikely.* <pre-predicate *that*-clause>
> *It is unlikely* **that the government will meet the full cost.** <extraposed *that*-clause>

In contrast, this sentence does not imply that *The government is unlikely.* (See also 9.4.9.)

**Pattern 3**

Adjectives of ease or difficulty occur in constructions referred to as **object-to-subject raising**. With this pattern, the implied object of the *to*-clause is placed in the subject position of the main clause. Once again the logical subject of the main clause is the entire object + *to*-clause:

> *Without those powers, computer hacking would be almost impossible* **to prove**. (NEWS†)

Here it is **not** implied that *computer hacking would be almost impossible*; rather, the whole proposition of the *to*-dependent clause is the implied subject:

> **To prove computer hacking** *would be almost impossible.*

The logical subject of the *to*-clause in such instances usually has generic reference: *... impossible for one/people/anyone to prove*. The following example further illustrates these characteristics (cf. 9.4.8):

> *He would be very difficult* **to reach**. (FICT†)
> *cf.* **For people/someone/us to reach him** *would be very difficult.*

Prepositional objects in *to*-clauses may also be raised in the same way with these adjectives:

> *You're easy* **to cook for**. (CONV)
> *cf. It is easy* **to cook for you**.
> **To cook for you** *is easy.*

**Pattern 4**

Finally, some adjectives of evaluation occur in structures that resemble Patterns 2 or 3, except that they do not require a *to*-clause in order to be grammatically complete:

> 1 *You're lucky* **to be alive**. (FICT)
>
> 2 *That would be very bad* **to do**. (FICT)

In **1** the implied subject of the *to*-clause corresponds to the grammatical subject of the main clause, while in **2** the implied object of the *to*-clause corresponds to the grammatical subject of the main clause. In both cases, the *to*-clause can function as the logical subject of the main clause:

> **For you to be alive** *is lucky* / **That you are alive** *is lucky.*

> **For us/someone to do that** *would be very bad.*

However, these structures differ from Patterns 2 and 3 respectively in that the uncomplemented forms *You are lucky* and *That would be very bad* are also possible as implications of **1** and **2**.

A third variant is similar to **2** in that the grammatical subject of the main clause functions as the implied object of the *to*-clause:

> 3 *They were good* **to eat**. (FICT†)

This structure also allows the uncomplemented implication *They were good*. However, in this case the alternative paraphrases result in a different meaning:

> (**For us**) *to eat* **them** *was good.*
> *It was good* (**for us**) *to eat* **them**.

## 9.4.5.2    Adjectives taking post-predicate *to*-clauses

**CORPUS FINDINGS [1]**

➤ Only one adjectival predicate is notably common controlling *to*-clauses in post-predicate position: *(un)likely*. This form occurs more than 50 times per million words in the LSWE Corpus.

➤ Other adjectival predicates occurring more than ten times per million words in the LSWE Corpus are: *(un)able, determined, difficult, due, easy, free, glad, hard, ready, used, (un)willing*.

➤ Other adjectival predicates attested in the LSWE Corpus:

> **Degree of certainty:** *apt, certain, due, guaranteed, liable, (un)likely, prone, sure*.

> **Ability or willingness:** *(un)able, anxious, bound, careful, competent, determined, disposed, doomed, eager, eligible, fit, greedy, hesitant, inclined, keen, loath, obliged, prepared, quick, ready, reluctant, (all) set, slow, (in)sufficient, welcome, (un)willing*.

> **Personal affective stance:** *afraid, amazed, angry, annoyed, ashamed, astonished, careful, concerned, content, curious, delighted, disappointed, disgusted, embarrassed, free, furious, glad, grateful, happy, impatient, indignant, nervous, perturbed, pleased, proud, puzzled, relieved, sorry, surprised, worried*.

> **Ease or difficulty:** *awkward, difficult, easy, hard, (un)pleasant, (im)possible, tough*.

> **Evaluation:** *bad, brave, careless, crazy, expensive, good, lucky, mad, nice, right, silly, smart, (un)wise, wrong*.

> **Habitual behavior:** *(un)accustomed, (un)used*.

**DISCUSSION OF FINDINGS**

### A    Degree of certainty

Degree of certainty adjectives indicate the degree of certitude or likelihood ascribed to the proposition in the *to*-clause; they generally exhibit structure Pattern 2 and occur with subject-to-subject raising. For example:

> *The Congress is virtually certain **to declare itself independent of the Soviet Party**.* (NEWS)
> cf. *It is virtually certain **that the Congress will declare itself independent of the Soviet Party**.*

> *I'm certain **to regret it**.* (FICT)
> cf. *It's certain **that I will regret it**.*

Other certainty adjectives are of the same type but do not readily occur with extraposed paraphrases:

> *They were due **to get one**.* (CONV)

> *He's liable **to be a bit amorous**.* (CONV)

> *He was sure **to see the old woman hopping about**.* (FICT†)

The adjectives *likely* and *unlikely* are especially common with subject-to-subject raising (9.4.9):

> *They are likely **to have been made by different processes**.* (ACAD†)

> *Most of the countries with viable alcohol programmes are likely **to belong to this group**.* (ACAD)

## B Ability or willingness

Adjectives of ability or willingness concern the ability, preparedness, or commitment of the subject to carry out the action described in the *to*-clause. These adjectives generally occur as structure Pattern 1, with the grammatical subject of the main clause functioning as logical subject of both the main clause and *to*-clause:

> *After a few weeks of this, I can guarantee you'll be unable **to wait to get out for your Sainsbury's session**.* (NEWS†)
>
> *He doesn't seem actually willing **to move out**.* (CONV)
>
> *I'm ready **to take over in Dave's place**.* (FICT†)
>
> *The embryos are less inclined **to skid about**.* (ACAD†)
>
> *Both Ford and GM were "clearly anxious **to improve their slumping image in this market**."* (NEWS)

Several adjectives in this domain are moderately frequent: (*un*)*able*, (*un*)*willing*, *determined*, and *ready*.

## C Personal affective stance

A relatively large number of adjectives are used with a *to*-clause to mark personal stance, although only *glad* and *free* have notable frequency. These adjectives present some affective stance towards the proposition in the *to*-clause and occur with structure Pattern 1, with the subject noun phrase referring to the person experiencing the affective state:

> *About the rest I am content **to be agnostic**.* (NEWS)
>
> *Not everybody's going to be glad **to have him around**.* (FICT†)
>
> *I'm sorry **to hear about you**.* (CONV)
>
> *I'm a little surprised **to be accused of poor taste**.* (FICT†)
>
> *We're quite happy **to rent for a while**.* (CONV)
>
> *Gabby was afraid **to say anything more**.* (FICT)

## E Ease or difficulty

Adjectives in this class provide the speaker's assessment of the ease or difficulty of the task described in the *to*-clause; they occur with object-to-subject raising (Pattern 3; cf. 9.4.8). *Easy*, *difficult*, and *hard* are all notably frequent:

> *They're easy **to steal**.* (CONV)
>
> *Jobs were hard **to come by**.* (FICT†)
>
> *PCBs are biologically difficult **to degrade**.* (ACAD†)

In extraposed paraphrases the logical object appears in the *to*-clause:

> *It is biologically difficult **to degrade PCBs**.*

## E Evaluation

Adjectives in this class present a range of evaluations or assessments of the action or situation described in the *to*-clause (structure Pattern 4). Although several of these are very frequent adjectives, none is notably common with *to*-clauses:

> *This one is nice **to smell**.* (CONV†)
>
> *You'd be silly **to decorate it**.* (CONV)
>
> *Katharine was smart **to have her wits about her**.* (FICT†)
>
> *This food wouldn't be bad **to wake up to**.* (FICT†)

Although there is some similarity in their meanings, *to*-clauses controlled by these evaluation adjectives differ semantically and structurally from *to*-clauses controlled by personal stance adjectives. Personal stance adjectives describe the feelings or emotions held by the person referred to in the subject noun phrase. In contrast, evaluation adjectives present an external evaluation of the entire proposition. The major structural difference between these constructions is that evaluation adjectives mostly allow analogous constructions with a subject *to*-clause (structure Pattern 4), while comparable constructions are not possible with personal stance adjectives (structure Pattern 1).

With most evaluation adjectives, the subject of the main clause is co-referential with the implied (but omitted) subject of the *to*-clause:

> *Perhaps he's wise **to cast things of the world aside**.* (FICT†)
>
> *cf. Perhaps it is wise [of / for him] **to cast things of the world aside**.*

However, for some other evaluation adjectives, the subject of the main clause is co-referential with the implied (but omitted) object of the *to*-clause (rather than the subject of the *to*-clause):

> *The test was expensive **to produce**.* (ACAD†)
>
> *cf. It was expensive for someone **to produce [the test]**.*

### F  Habitual behavior

A few adjectives are used to mark habitual behavior, occurring in structure Pattern 1 but with obligatory *to*-complements. *Used* is the most frequent:

> *She was not accustomed **to eating this time of day**.* (FICT†)
>
> *"I'm a lawyer. I'm used **to suppressing my feelings**."* (NEWS)

## 9.4.5.3  Adjectival predicates taking extraposed *to*-clauses

**CORPUS FINDINGS [1]**

➤ Three adjectival predicates are relatively common controlling extraposed *to*-clauses: *(im)possible*, *difficult* and *hard*. These forms occur more than ten times per million words in the LSWE Corpus.

➤ Adjectives from three major semantic domains are attested with extraposed *to*-clauses:
**Necessity or importance:** *essential, important, necessary, vital.*
**Ease or difficulty:** *difficult, easier, easy, hard, tough.*
**Evaluation:** (General) *bad, best, better, good, nice, wonderful, worse*; (Specific) *(in)appropriate, awkward, convenient, criminal, cumbersome, desirable, dreadful, foolhardy, fruitless, improper, interesting, logical, (un)reasonable, right, safe, unseemly, sick, smart, stupid, surprising, useful, useless, wise, wrong.*

**DISCUSSION OF FINDINGS**

There are considerably more adjectives than verbs that can control extraposed *to*-clauses; many adjectives can control both extraposed and post-predicate *to*-clauses. The adjectives in all three major semantic domains are used to mark an impersonal stance or attitude towards the proposition in the *to*-clause.

A   **Necessity and importance**

Necessity or importance adjectives regularly control extraposed rather than post-predicate *to*-clauses:

> *I'm sure it's not necessary* **to ask you not to pass any information on to the Communists.** (NEWS)

> *If the development of the unit spans a long period it will be essential* **to make use of the new developments of this kind.** (ACAD)

> *If you want peace it is important* **to stay cool.** (NEWS)

> *As always it was vital* **to preserve the atmosphere of the commonplace.** (FICT)

B   **Ease and difficulty**

Adjectives marking ease or difficulty can control extraposed *to*-clauses as well as *to*-clauses in post-predicate position (Pattern 3). *Difficult* and *hard* are common in both:

> *It's very very difficult* **to separate these topics out and teach that one as a topic.** (CONV)

> *Moreover, it is notoriously difficult* **to predict the costs of major infrastructural projects.** (NEWS†)

> *It's hard* **to know where she learns her lines.** (FICT)

> *It can be tough* **to attract people.** (NEWS†)

> *It is easy* **to see that the model ignores some fundamentally important variables.** (ACAD†)

> *It is possible* **to love, and to aid thy neighbor, without state intervention.** (NEWS)

C   **Evaluation**

Evaluation adjectives with extraposed *to*-clauses come from two major subclasses: adjectives marking general goodness or badness, and adjectives marking some more specific evaluation or assessment.

Adjectives marking goodness or badness indicate a generalized positive or negative stance towards the proposition in the extraposed *to*-clause. These adjectives include: *bad, best, better, good, nice, wonderful, worse*:

> *It's good* **to see them in the bath.** (CONV†)

> *It'd be better* **for him to put that fire on at night time.** (CONV)

> *It was bad* **to be prodigal.** (FICT†)

Other evaluation adjectives represent more specific assessment or evaluation of the proposition in the *to*-clause:

> *It was awkward* **to move elbows and clap in such a crowd of people.** (FICT)

> *For the purposes of this paper it is convenient* **to consider four major categories of uncertainty.** (ACAD†)

> *It is reasonable, in this light,* **to consider an area that is typical in many ways of the industrial United States.** (ACAD†)

> *It's not safe* **to run down there.** (FICT)

> *However, for our purposes it is useful* **to emphasize three roles.** (ACAD)

> *It is wrong* **to suppose that they can be kept in grossly fluctuating or humid conditions**. (ACAD†)

# 9.4.6 Grammatical distribution of *to*-clauses

**CORPUS FINDINGS** [2,3]

➤ Over 60% of all *to*-clauses occur in post-predicate position controlled by a verb. The major patterns across registers are summarized below:

|  | CONV | FICT | NEWS | ACAD |
|---|---|---|---|---|
| post-predicate *to*-clause complementing a verb | common | very common | very common | common |
| post-predicate *to*-clause complementing an adjective | rare | moderately common | common | moderately common |
| extraposed *to*-clause complementing a verb | rare | rare | relatively rare | rare |
| extraposed *to*-clause complementing an adjective | rare | moderately common | moderately common | common |
| subject *to*-clause | rare | rare | rare | rare |
| subject-predicative *to*-clause | rare | moderately common | moderately common | moderately common |

**DISCUSSION OF FINDINGS**

These distributional patterns reflect the differing discourse functions typically served by each type of *to*-clause. Post-predicate *to*-clauses controlled by verbs are typically used to report the activities, desires, and other thoughts or emotions of human participants:

> *I want* **to do it**. (CONV)

> *You started* **to eat that one**. (CONV†)

> *Dr. Gruner asked Uncle Sammler* **to read a few items from the Market Letter**. (FICT)

> *Okonkwo encouraged the boys* **to sit with him in his obi**. (FICT†)

> *Mrs. Carol Bentley, a 44-year-old Presbyterian Republican opposed to abortion, tried* **to ignore the fuss**. (NEWS)

> *Carpenter (16) found highly nonlinear cases* **to be chaotic**. (ACAD†)

> *Pelseneer (1926) considered the broadest specimens* **to be females**. (ACAD†)

Because fiction, news, and conversation focus on such concerns, post-predicate *to*-clauses controlled by verbs are most common in those registers.

*To*-clauses controlled by adjectives are more static, often describing a stance or attitude towards the proposition in the *to*-clause. For this reason, these structures are more common in written informational registers than in either conversation or fiction.

**Figure 9.17**
**Frequencies of *to*-clause types—conversation**

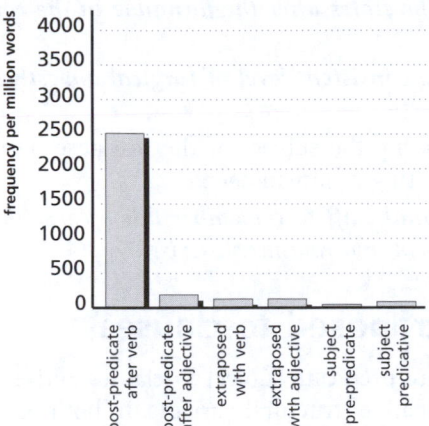

**Figure 9.18**
**Frequencies of *to*-clause types—fiction**

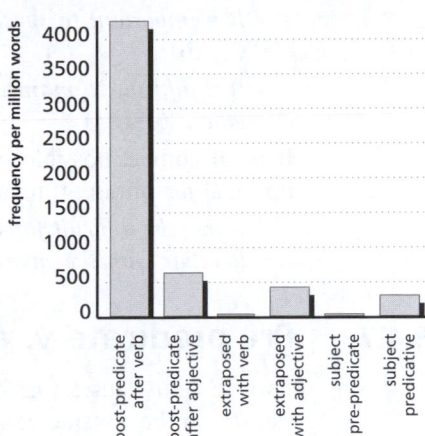

**Figure 9.19**
**Frequencies of *to*-clause types—news**

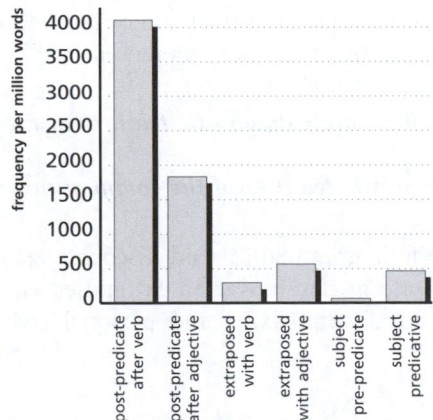

**Figure 9.20**
**Frequencies of *to*-clause types—academic prose**

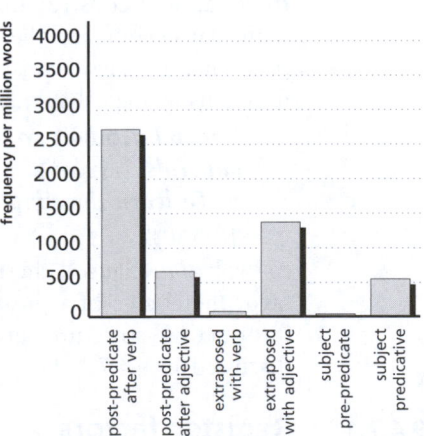

Post-predicate *to*-clauses controlled by adjectives often describe a stance held by some person regarding their own activities (reported in the *to*-clause). This use is relatively common in news:

> *Sir Anthony is willing* **to provide a focal point for discussion**. (NEWS†)

> *The researchers reported they have been able* **to pluck the five genes that produced the toxin out of the pertussis bacterium**. (NEWS)

> *Advertisers said they were delighted* **to see many of their proposals reflected in the Government's approach**. (NEWS)

> *Mr. Beregovoy has been quoted as saying that he is not ashamed* **to be called a social democrat**. (NEWS)

In contrast, extraposed *to*-clauses controlled by an adjective present a stance that is not directly attributed to anyone. This detachment suits academic prose:

*Above a certain temperature it is impossible* **to liquefy a gas.** (ACAD)

*In these circumstances it is essential* **to ensure that the foster mother has finished giving birth.** (ACAD†)

*It is important* **to specify the states after the formulae in the equation.** (ACAD)

*It is difficult* **to maintain a consistent level of surgical anaesthesia with ether.** (ACAD†)

It is, of course, possible to specify the subject of the *to*-clause by means of an optional *for*-phrase, thus indicating a human agent:

*It may be difficult* **for hospital staff to remember this** *because they are familiar with the environment and routines.* (ACAD)

## 9.4.7 Pre-predicate v. extraposed *to*-clauses

As with *that*-clauses (9.2.7), pre-predicate subject *to*-clauses and extraposed *to*-clauses can be considered alternative structural variants. In both of these, the *to*-clause functions semantically as the logical subject.

Pre-predicate clauses precede the main clause verb, occupying the normal position for subjects:

**To be without it** *was to be in some way dead.* (FICT)

In extraposed constructions, the dummy pronoun *it* fills the slot preceding the main clause verb, and the *to*-clause occurs after the main clause verb or adjectival predicate. In these constructions, the *it* is not referential, and the *to*-clause functions as logical subject of the main clause:

*It is still necessary* **to learn the simple diagnostic features of the common minerals.** (ACAD†)

*cf.* **To learn the simple diagnostic features of the common minerals** *is still necessary.*

As with *that*-clauses, there are four grammatical and discourse factors that can favor the choice of a pre-predicate *to*-clause over an extraposed clause: register, information structure, grammatical complexity, and personal style. These are discussed in 9.4.7.1–4.

### 9.4.7.1 Register factors

**CORPUS FINDINGS** [2,3]

➤ Pre-predicate/subject *to*-clauses are relatively rare in all registers. While extraposed *to*-clauses occur more than 500 times per million words in most written registers, pre-predicate *to*-clauses occur fewer than 50 times per million words. (See Figures 9.17–20.)

➤ However, pre-predicate *to*-clauses are somewhat more common in academic prose (occurring between 30 and 40 times per million words); they are especially rare in conversation.

**DISCUSSION OF FINDINGS**

Although pre-predicate *to*-clauses are more common than pre-predicate *that*-clauses, they are still rare relative to extraposed *to*-clauses. Extraposed constructions should be regarded as the unmarked choice whenever a *to*-clause functions as logical subject of a main clause.

As with pre-predicate *that*-clauses (9.2.7), the overall avoidance of pre-predicate *to*-clauses reflects the general avoidance of 'heavy' pre-predicate subjects in English (11.1.3).

From a processing perspective, pre-predicate *to*-clauses are disruptive, because the embedded complement clause must be processed before reaching the main clause predicate. Because they are not operating under severe production constraints, writers can choose to disregard the preference for placing heavy constituents after the main clause predicate, instead using pre-predicate *to*-clauses when they serve other discourse functions.

## 9.4.7.2 Information structure

**CORPUS FINDINGS [3]**

➤ In nearly every case when a pre-predicate *to*-clause is used, it marks the information in the *to*-clause as being topical and is anaphoric to the preceding discourse.

➤ In many cases, pre-predicate *to*-clauses are used in a series, to highlight a parallel development of topics across sentences.

**DISCUSSION OF FINDINGS**

One of the main uses of pre-predicate *to*-clauses is to overtly mark the information in the *to*-clause as being part of the current topic, providing a direct anaphoric link to the preceding discourse:

> There is one exception, however: the Hahn-Banach Theorem, in its two forms (analytic and geometric), is given in its largest setting; **to do so** does not require more work, and will be useful. (ACAD)

In this example, the *to*-clause refers to the entire proposition already given before the semicolon. Here the *to*-clause is directly anaphoric as well as the topic of the following main clause.

In addition, pre-predicate *to*-clauses are sometimes used in sequences to present a topical progression of connected ideas, foregrounded and presented in parallel structures for effect:

> 1 He advanced into the room and sat in the armchair. I felt incensed, yet helpless. **To order him to leave** would be overdramatic yet perhaps I should. **To pull the bell-rope and ask for help** would be even more so. (FICT)
>
> 2 <...> the law also allowed the seizure of all assets, not simply those related to a specific offence. 'The US law in this respect seems greatly excessive,' he said. '**To take away the profits of crime** is one thing; **to seize assets that have no connection with crime** is another. (NEWS)
>
> 3 Yet in all these random examples, which are each dimensions of the new Europe, it wouldn't occur to the participants for one second that they are

*being European <. . .>* **To expect Europe to become a single warm cultural bath** *is simply to mistake the nature of the European, and indeed any other, identity.*

*To be European in France* *is to think globally about a French-led political Europe which will challenge the power of Japan and America.* **But to be European in Lithuania or Scotland** *is to assert your nationality and the wish to get Moscow or London off your back.*

*To be European in Italy* *is a logical extension of what is already assumed to be one's natural multiple identity within a family, a city, a region and a nation.* **And to be European in southern England**, *is to make a political statement against Thatcherism, philistinism, and English insularity.* (NEWS)

These examples illustrate a dual use of pre-predicate *to*-clauses: (a) to provide a cohesive link to the preceding discourse, and (b) to emphasize topical parallelism across sentences. For example, the preceding context in **3** provides numerous illustrations of the diversity across European cultures. The first pre-predicate *to*-clause in this series contains familiar information and makes a direct cohesive link to those illustrations. The remaining subject *to*-clauses then form a chain predictably referring to a succession of European nationalities. These pre-predicate *to*-clauses are used to show topical parallelism across sentences, contrasting the meaning of 'being European' in different cultural settings.

## 9.4.7.3    Grammatical complexity

**CORPUS FINDINGS** [3]

➤ In a majority of cases when pre-predicate *to*-clauses are used, the main clause predicate is a complex construction comprising a verb followed by one or more phrases or clauses.

➤ The single most-common construction of this type is the subject predicative structure: *to*-clause + *be* + *to*-clause.

**DISCUSSION OF FINDINGS**

A third major factor favoring the use of pre-predicate *to*-clauses is the associated use of a complex construction, comprising one or more phrases or clauses, following the main clause predicate. Extraposition is avoided in this case because it would add yet another clause to the complex post-predicate structure.

The most common structure of this type takes the form *to*-clause + *be* + *to*-clause, where extraposition is effectively excluded because a direct succession of two *to*-clauses would result (see **3** in 9.4.7.2):

**To expect Europe to become a single warm cultural bath** *is simply [to mistake the nature of the European identity].* (NEWS†)

Constructions of this type account for over 30 percent of the pre-predicate *to*-clauses in fiction. There are two common variants. The first involves a simple identifying predicative relationship with a tensed copular verb (3.5.3):

*To*-clause + *is/was* + *to*-clause:

**To prevail** *is [to be recharged].* (FICT)

*To prosecute such cases* was *[to be part of the garbage-collection service].* (FICT†)

The second variant uses the verb phrase *would be*:

*To*-clause + *would be* + *to*-clause:

*To dwell on those empty shelves* would be *[to miss the point].* (FICT)

*To say otherwise* would be *[to deny reality].* (FICT)

These structures are relatively common in news, especially with the tensed copular verb (cf. the examples in **3** in 9.4.7.2 above):

*To enter Romania* is *[to sink into a bad dream].* (NEWS)

*To argue otherwise* is *[to betray millions of people].* (NEWS†)

There are also many other kinds of complex main-clause predicates that co-occur with pre-predicate *to*-clauses:

*To accept a US mediation plan* means that an Israeli-Palestinian meeting is now likely in the New Year. (NEWS)

*To include that issue in the forthcoming Student Loans Bill* would make the measure hybrid and deny it any prospect of a swift passage through Parliament. (NEWS)

*To produce large numbers of new plants vegetatively* would require large numbers of parent plants and correspondingly large tanks and floor space. (ACAD)

*To describe the positions and velocities of atoms in a polymer* requires choosing a set of global axes, defining a continuum, with reference to which we may describe the positions and velocities of the atoms. (ACAD)

*To go into details as to the retrofitability of these oil boilers* would require an extensive study which not only gives consideration to the detailed characteristics of these boilers but also the ambient air quality standards of the varying regions and the state and local emission standards. (ACAD)

## 9.4.7.4 Stylistic preference

**CORPUS FINDINGS** [3]

➤ Some authors, in both academic prose and fiction, have a strong stylistic preference for pre-predicate *to*-clauses.

  ➤ Most of the pre-predicate *to*-clauses found in a million word sample of academic prose (54 out of 61 examples) occur in 13 texts, even though those texts comprise only c. 23% of the sample.

  ➤ One academic prose text has 20 of the 61 attested examples. Seven other academic prose texts have three or more examples each.

➤ A similar stylistic preference is found with a few fiction authors.

**DISCUSSION OF FINDINGS**

These patterns reflect the fondness that some writers have for particular structures, over and above more general discourse factors. In this instance, parallel and balanced structures might be used primarily for rhetorical effect.

## 9.4.8 Object-to-subject raising v. extraposed *to*-clauses with adjectives

There are three main structural options with *to*-clauses complementing adjectival predicates of ease or difficulty (e.g. *easy, difficult, hard, impossible, tough*; 9.4.5). Pre-predicate *to*-clause:

> **To seek to eliminate it from the environment** *is impossible.* (NEWS)

Extraposed *to*-clause:

> *It may not be easy* **to check that the conditions are satisfied.** (ACAD†)

Post-predicate *to*-clause with object-to-subject raising:

> *It was difficult* **to find.** (CONV)

These three variants are roughly equivalent in meaning. Thus compare:

> *They're hard* **to get.** (CONV†)
> **To get them** *is hard.*
> *It is hard* **to get them.**

*To*-clauses in pre-predicate position are generally rare, and the discourse factors favoring pre-predicate v. extraposed *to*-clauses are discussed in 9.4.7. The present section discusses the factors influencing the choice between object-to-subject raising and extraposition. There are three major grammatical and discourse factors that can influence this choice: register, grammatical and information packaging factors, and personal style.

### 9.4.8.1 Register factors

**CORPUS FINDINGS [2,3]**

➤ Overall, object-to-subject raising is slightly more common than extraposition for *to*-clauses controlled by adjectival predicates of ease or difficulty

➤ *To*-clauses with these adjectives are most common in academic prose. This generalization holds for both extraposed *to*-clauses and object-to-subject raising constructions.

➤ Constructions with *difficult* and *easy* are considerably more common than constructions with other ease or difficulty adjectives.

➤ The proportion of extraposed *to*-clauses compared to object-to-subject raising constructions is about the same in both conversation and academic prose.

Table 9.10  **Frequency counts per million words of *to*-clause constructions with the four most common adjectives of ease or difficulty**

|  | CONV | | | ACAD | | |
|---|---|---|---|---|---|---|
|  | raised | extraposed | % raised | raised | extraposed | % raised |
| **controlling adjective** | | | | | | |
| *easy* | 10 | 6 | 63 | 36 | 26 | 58 |
| *hard* | 14 | 9 | 61 | 4 | 4 | 50 |
| *difficult* | 6 | 6 | 50 | 79 | 52 | 60 |
| *impossible* | 1 | 2 | — | 4 | 24 | 17 |

**DISCUSSION OF FINDINGS**

Since extraposed constructions and object-to-subject raising constructions occur in roughly the same proportions, neither should be considered the unmarked case. Rather, the two constructions serve different discourse functions and are used for complementary purposes. The fact that these constructions occur in the same proportions in both conversation and academic prose suggests that similar discourse factors are operative across registers.

## 9.4.8.2 Grammatical complexity and information packaging

Grammatical and information-packaging factors work together in influencing the choice between extraposition and object-to-subject raising.

**CORPUS FINDINGS** [3]

➤ In nearly all structures with object-to-subject raising, the implied object of the *to*-clause presents given information and provides an anaphoric link to the immediately preceding discourse.

  ➤ In these structures, the raised noun phrase is typically a pronoun or a simple noun phrase without modifiers.

➤ In contrast, extraposed structures are used when the implied object of the *to*-clause presents new information.

  ➤ In these structures, the object of the *to*-clause is typically a complex structure, comprising another complement clause or a noun phrase with complex modifiers.

**DISCUSSION OF FINDINGS**

The following short text passages illustrate the combined influence of grammatical and information packaging factors influencing the use of object-to-subject raising:

A: *Rob's is August.*

B: *Rob's is August, yeah. Sixth of August is Robin. It's only a week after yours. [It] should be easy* **to remember.** (CONV) <discussing birth dates>

A: *Yeah, [it]'s very difficult* **to cut.** (CONV) <discussing squashy bread>

A: *And then I fell out of the swing.*

B: *[That] wasn't easy* **to do.** (CONV)

*The ideal cellular marker should be cell-autonomous; it should not affect behavior of the marked cells in any way; it should be stably expressed; and [it] should be technically easy* **to demonstrate.** (ACAD†)

*Should the marked chromosome constitute the inactive X, however, [it] <i.e. the chromosome> is reasonably easy* **to observe as the darkest and longest chromosome in the cell.** (ACAD)

*The second approach <...> necessitates the building of special-purpose assembly and iterative routines <...> [This] is difficult* **to achieve on current commercial turnkey systems.** (ACAD†)

> *All the cylindrical surfaces are displayed only as two circles joined by a start line. As [this representation] is difficult for the draughtsman* **to interpret**, *mesh lines have been inserted.* (ACAD†)

In the majority of these cases, the raised noun phrase is a pronominal form (e.g. *it, this, that*). These forms refer directly either to an inanimate constituent identified in the preceding discourse (e.g. 'the squashy bread', 'Robin's birth date', *the ideal cellular marker, the marked chromosome*) or to some proposition given in the immediately preceding discourse (e.g. 'falling out of a swing', 'building a special-purpose assembly and routines'). In a few cases, a simple anaphoric noun phrase is used instead of a pronoun, as in the last example above.

In other cases, a noun phrase has been topicalized for a series of phrases or clauses, and is ellipted altogether from the raised construction. In the following examples <–> marks the slot where the raised noun phrase would occur:

> *[The ideal cell lineage marker] should be cell localized, cell autonomous, stable, ubiquitous, <–> easy* **to detect** *and developmentally neutral.* (ACAD)

> *Better approximations … have been developed … [They] involve higher derivatives and <–> are therefore somewhat less easy* **to apply**. (ACAD†)

In contrast, extraposed constructions have the opposite characteristics: heavy, complex noun phrases, which present new information, occurring as object of the *to*-clause. In these cases, the alternative construction with object-to-subject raising would have a 'heavy' subject noun phrase, resulting in a dispreferred packaging of information:

> *It is difficult* **to imagine a direct advantage conferred by shell banding for survival in waveswept conditions**. (ACAD†)

> *However, it is not difficult* **to demand a speed of calculation beyond the performance of currently available microcomputers**. (ACAD†)

> *Where such a situation does prevail it will not be easy* **to evaluate the effects of the graduated tests from those of the greater relevance of the new curriculum and the enthusiasm engendered by teachers with a belief in the efficacy of the change**. (ACAD)

In other cases, the object of the extraposed clause is itself a complex complement clause:

> *It is easy* **to see (Figure 4–11) that for a folded sequence of layers, the oldest beds would be found at depth in the core (or central axis) of the anticline and the youngest rocks on the surface over the axis of the syncline**. (ACAD)

> *However, in such cases it is difficult* **to decide whether the variation reflects real differences in the intensity of diapause or whether these pods are composed of eggs**. (ACAD†)

## 9.4.8.3   Stylistic preference

**CORPUS FINDINGS [3]**

➤ Some authors have a strong stylistic preference for *to*-clauses complementing adjectival predicates of ease or difficulty.

➤ For example, five academic prose texts, which comprise only 9% of all academic prose in a million-word sample, contain numerous examples of extraposition as well as object-to-subject raising.

**DISCUSSION OF FINDINGS**

This finding is consistent with findings elsewhere in this chapter (e.g. 9.2.7.4, 9.4.7.4) that choices related to complementation are especially subject to individual preference.

## 9.4.9    Subject-to-subject raising v. extraposed *that*-clauses

Two structural options are possible with complement clauses controlled by verbs of probability and simple fact (*seem, appear*), certainty adjectives (*likely, unlikely, certain, sure*), and passive voice mental verbs of Pattern 2, Type 2 (e.g. *be found, be assumed*): subject-to-subject raising v. extraposition with a *that*-clause (9.2.3, 9.4.2.2–4, 9.4.5.1, 9.4.6). For example:

    1   *The rate for the North American continent has been estimated **to be about 0.03 mm/year.*** (ACAD†)

v.    2   *It has been estimated **that the rate for the North American continent is about 0.03 mm/year.***

The following subsections consider the discourse factors influencing the choice between these structural alternatives.

### 9.4.9.1   Information packaging

In most constructions with subject-to-subject raising, the main clause subject is directly anaphoric:

    1   *Andy really surprises me <...> **Andy** seems **to know everything.*** (CONV)

    2   *The first thing he thought of when he woke up was Marge <...> **She** wasn't likely **to take a taxi to Naples.*** (FICT)

*Andy* in **1** and *She* in **2** are both identified in the immediately preceding discourse. Subject-to-subject raising serves to position this anaphoric element in sentence-initial position, making a direct cohesive link with the preceding discourse.

    Many of the analogous constructions with extraposed *that*-clauses also have directly anaphoric referents as the subject of the *that*-clause:

    3   *He stopped. I wanted to say that it seemed to me **that he had taken a most peculiar road out of his trouble.*** (FICT)

    4   *She held it with delight and relief at the sight of the still clinging butterfly <...> It seemed to her **that the butterfly was quite happy in its warm cage.*** (FICT)

    5   *Hermit crabs often utilise empty Nucella shells—but it is unlikely **that they obtained their "home" by killing and eating the original owner.*** (ACAD)

    6   *It is common practice to turn ewes and lambs out of doors as soon as possible to minimize the disease risk especially of enteric disease, even though it is likely **that the lambs will be below the lower critical temperature for lambs born in winter or early spring.*** (ACAD)

In many of these cases, the subject noun phrase in the *that*-clause is pronominalized (*he* in **3**, *they* in **5**), and in other cases the subject noun phrase is a repetition of an earlier noun phrase (*the butterfly* in **4**, *the lambs* in **6**). Thus, although subject-to-subject raising is used to place topical information in sentence-initial position, this is not the primary discourse factor motivating the choice between extraposed and raising structures.

Raising structures with passive verbs are different in structure and function: the subject of the main clause is often a heavy constituent that presents new information. Example **1** in 9.4.9 and **7** below illustrate these characteristics:

7 *The release of gases from the interior due to internal heat and chemical reaction* is generally thought *to be the primary source* (ACAD)

## 9.4.9.2 Register factors

**CORPUS FINDINGS** [2]

➤ In all registers, subject-to-subject raising is used for the overwhelming majority of complement clauses controlled by the verbs *seem/appear* or by the adjectival predicates *likely*, *unlikely*, *certain*, and *sure* (see Table 9.11).

**Table 9.11** **Frequency per million words of *to*-clause constructions with the most common verbs and adjectival predicates of probability**

| register | *appear* raised | extraposed | % raised | *seem* raised | extraposed | % raised |
|---|---|---|---|---|---|---|
| CONV | 5 | 0 | 100 | 126 | 0 | 100 |
| FICT | 70 | 0 | 100 | 413 | 22 | 95 |
| NEWS | 152 | 2 | 99 | 143 | 2 | 99 |
| ACAD | 150 | 2 | 99 | 119 | 4 | 97 |

| | *be likely* raised | extraposed | % raised | *be unlikely* raised | extraposed | % raised |
|---|---|---|---|---|---|---|
| CONV | 5 | 0 | — | 0 | 0 | — |
| FICT | 13 | 1 | 93 | 2 | 3 | — |
| NEWS | 176 | 3 | 98 | 35 | 4 | 90 |
| ACAD | 106 | 8 | 93 | 13 | 6 | 77 |

| | *be certain* raised | extraposed | % raised | *be sure* raised | extraposed | % raised |
|---|---|---|---|---|---|---|
| CONV | 0 | 0 | — | 1 | 0 | — |
| FICT | 1 | 2 | — | 6 | 0 | — |
| NEWS | 20 | 3 | 87 | 10 | 0 | 100 |
| ACAD | 2 | 1 | — | 1 | 0 | — |

➤ Only fiction shows a moderate frequency (22 per million words) of extraposed *that*-clauses with *seem*.

Subject-to-subject raising must be considered the unmarked option with probability verbs or certainty adjectival predicates. Since subject position is the preferred slot for given or topical information, it is typical to 'raise' the subject of the complement clause to sentence initial position, filling the subject slot of the main clause.

Fiction, having the highest overall use of *seem* with complement clauses, shows a moderate frequency of extraposed *that*-clauses with *seem*. Similarly, news and academic prose, having the highest overall use of *likely* and *unlikely* with complement clauses, show moderate frequencies of extraposed *that*-clauses controlled by *(un)likely*.

However, as the following sections show, the factors influencing the use of the extraposed option with *seem* are different from those influencing the use of the extraposed option with *(un)likely*.

## 9.4.9.3 Clauses with *seem* and *appear*

**CORPUS FINDINGS** [2,3]

➤ Over 98% of all extraposed *that*-clauses following *seem* have a prepositional phrase intervening between *seem* and the *that*-clause.

**DISCUSSION OF FINDINGS**

A single structural pattern accounts for almost all the extraposed *that*-clauses controlled by *seem*: the pattern *seem* + *to* NP + *that*-clause. The intervening *to*-phrase serves to attribute the perception of likelihood to some person:

> *It seemed [to him]* **that his home life was disintegrating all at once.** (FICT†)

> *At first, it seemed [to the village gossips]* **that both couples were happy enough.** (FICT)

> *Indeed it seemed [to us]* **that this "local theory" was the topic in which the most significant progress was made in recent years.** (ACAD)

In other instances, the intervening prepositional phrase has the form *from* NP and marks the source of the information rather than the person having the perception of likelihood. This alternative construction occurs most commonly with the verb *appear*:

> *It appears [from initial observations]* **that storage of viable sperm is limited to a period of two or three months.** (ACAD†)

> *It appears [from literature]* **that the seriousness of the societal consequences of an incident is judged to increase with the square of the number of people killed.** (ACAD†)

In most structures with subject-to-subject raising, the *to*-infinitive clause occurs immediately after the verb *seem*. If there was an intervening prepositional phrase in these structures, it would disrupt the logical association between the main clause subject and the *to*-clause. Also, the repetition of *to* after a *to*-phrase could be deemed awkward. Thus an intervening prepositional phrase following *seem* favors an extraposed *that*-clause over a *to*-clause with subject-to-subject raising.

## 9.4.9.4 Clauses with *likely* and *unlikely*

**CORPUS FINDINGS [2,3]**

➤ All extraposed *that*-clauses controlled by *(un)likely* have a modal verb or are marked for tense, adding a component of meaning that would not be possible with a *to*-clause.

➤ In academic prose, 42% (five out of 12 examples in a million-word sample) have a modal verb. The remaining instances are marked for present or past tense.

➤ In news, 100% (seven out of seven examples in a million-word sample) have a modal verb.

**DISCUSSION OF FINDINGS**

For constructions controlled by *(un)likely*, subject-to-subject raising is preferred unless there is a need to explicitly mark modality or tense in the complement clause. Since modality and tense cannot be marked in an infinitive clause, an extraposed *that*-clause must be used under these circumstances.

The majority of the constructions with extraposed *that*-clauses have a modal verb. The modal *will*, typically marking future time, is most common:

> *It is likely **that North Korea will channel investment to areas that can be contained**.* (NEWS)

> *It is likely **that wheelchairs will be excluded from future London marathons**.* (NEWS†)

> *It is unlikely **that such complications will colour Britain's political map in the foreseeable future**.* (NEWS†)

> *It is unlikely **that pollen will be transmitted from one plant to another**.* (ACAD)

Other modal verbs, such as *would* and *might*, are also used occasionally:

> *Coopers were told that a name for the new firm had not been decided, but that it was likely **that it would start with Coopers**.* (NEWS)

> *It is likely **that a moose to the right might be discerned easier than if it appears on the left side**.* (ACAD†)

Finally, some extraposed *that*-clauses are marked explicitly for past or present tense. In some cases, these constructions also have a more complex noun phrase serving as subject of the *that*-clause:

> *The report states that it is likely **that more than half of all conventional gas reserves that will be ultimately produced in the United States have already been produced**.* (ACAD)

> *It is likely **that this line of objection, that objects or contents are sometimes missing, has another wholly different root**.* (ACAD†)

## 9.4.10 *To*-clause v. bare infinitive clause with *dare* and *help*

Two main clause verbs can control either a *to*-clause or a bare infinitive: *dare* and *help*. (*Dare* can also be considered a marginal auxiliary; 6.6). In interrogative and negative structures, the choice between *to*-clause and bare infinitive clause is available only when *dare* is used as a lexical verb rather than as an auxiliary (3.8.2.3, 3.13.2.8C).

*dare*:

> Would he dare **to suck a sleeve**? (FICT)
>
> I don't think she would dare **say anything to me about it**. (CONV)

*help*:

> The legislation on unofficial strikes would help **to prevent disruption of essential services**. (NEWS†)
>
> It is hoped that this monograph will help **fill this void**. (ACAD†)

Since *help* is more common and occurs freely with both bare and *to*-infinitive complements, we focus on *help* primarily in this account.

### 9.4.10.1 Dialect factors

**CORPUS FINDINGS** [2]

➤ There are clear dialect differences in the preferred form of infinitive clauses following the verbs *dare* and *help*:

> ➤ AmE has an especially strong preference for the pattern verb + bare infinitive, although the bare infinitive is more common than the *to*-infinitive in both dialects.
>
> ➤ The bare infinitive is particularly dominant in the pattern verb + NP + infinitive clause.

Table 9.12   *Help* **followed by an infinitive clause in BrE and AmE (conversation and news) with or without an intervening noun phrase; occurrences per million words**

each ■ represents 5     each □ represents less than 3

| | |
|---|---|
| **BrE CONV:** | |
| *help* + to-clause | ■ |
| *help* + bare infinitive | ■ ■ ■ ■ |
| **AmE CONV:** | |
| *help* + to-clause | □ |
| *help* + bare infinitive | ■ ■ ■ ■ ■ ■ ■ ■ □ |
| **BrE NEWS:** | |
| *help* + to-clause | ■ ■ ■ ■ ■ ■ ■ ■ |
| *help* + bare infinitive | ■ ■ ■ ■ ■ ■ ■ ■ ■ ■ ■ ■ ■ ■ ■ ■ ■ ■ ■ ■ ■ ■ ■ ■ |
| **AmE NEWS:** | |
| *help* + to-clause | ■ ■ |
| *help* + bare infinitive | ■ ■ ■ ■ ■ ■ ■ ■ ■ ■ ■ ■ ■ ■ ■ ■ ■ ■ ■ ■ ■ ■ ■ ■ ■ ■ ■ ■ |

**DISCUSSION OF FINDINGS**

The following illustrates the tendency in AmE for bare infinitive in the pattern *help* + NP + infinitive clause:

> *His proposal includes tax vouchers and deductions to [help] millions of uninsured and underinsured Americans* **buy private medical coverage.** (AmE NEWS)
>
> *Brenner [helps] the individual* **understand his problems.** (AmE NEWS)
>
> *He [helped] her* **achieve success.** (AmE NEWS)

## 9.4.10.2  Register factors

**CORPUS FINDINGS** [2]

➤ *Help* + *to*-clause and *help* + bare infinitive clause are distributed differently across registers:
  ➤ In academic prose, c. 55% of all infinitive clauses controlled by *help* are bare infinitive clauses.
  ➤ In conversation, fiction, and news, bare infinitives predominate (occurring 75–80% of the time).

**DISCUSSION OF FINDINGS**

In both news and academic prose, infinitive clauses controlled by *help* are typically used to describe a process that is facilitated (or 'helped') by some other factors.

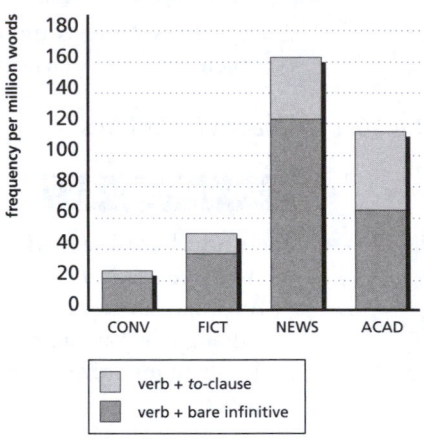

Figure 9.21

**Frequencies of *help* + *to*-clause v. bare infinitive clause, by register**

Legend: verb + to-clause; verb + bare infinitive

Bare infinitive clauses:

> *Lederle, based in Wayne, N.J. also is giving $1 million to the Children's Health Fund to help* **bring health care to homeless families and children.** (NEWS)
>
> *Key testimony has been broadcast live on television and radio to help* **keep the city fully abreast of the proceedings** *and to show the wheels of justice turning.* (NEWS)
>
> *The Conversion costing methods described in this study and in references could be applied to explore alternatives to help* **identify the most reasonable conversions.** (ACAD)

*To*-clauses:

> *We are way behind in taking the necessary measures that will help* **to prevent this kind of tragedy happening again.** (NEWS)
>
> *In the blowfly Phormia this system helps* **to regulate feeding.** (ACAD)
>
> *The noise may help* **to achieve a global optimum corresponding to correct recognition.** (ACAD†)

The unmarked choice with *help* is to use the bare infinitive. Academic prose goes against this trend, using *to*-clauses and the bare infinitive with roughly equal frequency. This pattern reflects the general preference for greater elaboration and explicitness of form in academic writing.

### 9.4.10.3 The pattern *to help* + infinitive

**CORPUS FINDINGS** [2]

➤ When the verb *help* is itself in a *to*-clause, a following bare infinitive clause is strongly preferred to a following *to*-clause.

➤ In news, 85% of all infinitival complement clauses in this context are bare infinitives.

➤ In academic prose and fiction, all infinitival complement clauses in this context are bare infinitives.

**DISCUSSION OF FINDINGS**

The verb *help* commonly occurs embedded in a *to*-clause while at the same time controlling a following infinitive clause. In these cases, a bare infinitive clause is strongly preferred over a *to*-clause, to avoid the sequence of *to* +

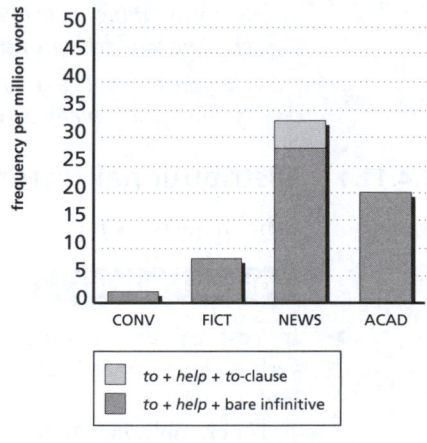

**Figure 9.22**

**Frequencies of *to* + *help* followed by *to*-clause v. bare infinitive clause, by register**

verb + *to* + verb. This preference holds regardless of whether the clause *to* + *help* functions as a complement clause or an adverbial *to*-clause of purpose. While such *to*-clause sequences do occasionally occur in news, in academic prose and fiction the second clause in a sequence is almost always a bare infinitive clause.

> US military police units might be forced to stay in Panama for at least a year to help **keep the peace**. (NEWS†)

> It can be used to help **ensure that all pupils are involved in the game**. (ACAD†)

> This was to help **promote the name of the small private college located on the outskirts of the city**. (FICT)

> v. There was a pressing need for more judges to help **to reduce the increasing delays**. (NEWS†)

The effect of this grammatical factor is strongest in academic prose, where bare infinitive clauses are generally less common. In this register, when bare infinitive clauses do occur, it is often when the controlling verb *help* is itself in a *to*-clause:

> Much of the substance of these studies can be utilized to help **provide approximate answers**. (ACAD†)

> They can be used to help **detect clash of a moving mechanism during operation**. (ACAD)

## 9.4.11 *Try* + *to* + verb v. *try* + *and* + verb

There is an additional alternation with infinitives which is found only with the controlling verb *try*: *try* + *and* + verb. This pattern alternates with the standard pattern of *try* + *to* + verb:

> He'll probably **try and wrestle it away from me.** (CONV)
> cf. He'll probably **try to wrestle it away from me.**

> One has to **try and find out what has happened.** (FICT)
> cf. One has to **try to find out what has happened.**

This discourse choice is not available when the verb *try* occurs with inflections such as *-ing* or *ed*:

> She was trying **to prove a point.** (FICT†)
> cf. *She was trying **and proving a point.**

> Do you remember when we tried **to make fluffy dogs?** (CONV)
> cf. *Do you remember when we tried **and made fluffy dogs?**

### 9.4.11.1 Distributional factors

(The frequencies reported here include all inflected forms of *try*.)

**CORPUS FINDINGS** [2,3]

➤ In most registers, the structure *try* + *to* + verb is much more common than *try* + *and* + verb.
  ➤ For example, in fiction, *try* + *to* + verb occurs over 400 times per million words; *try* + *and* + verb occurs less than 20 times per million words.
  ➤ In news and academic prose, *try* + *and* + verb is rare (less than ten times per million words).
  ➤ In conversation, the structure *try* + *and* + verb (80 times per million words) is closer to the frequency of *try* + *to* + verb (200 times per million words).

➤ *Try* + *and* + verb is often used when the verb *try* is itself in a *to*-clause (Figure 9.23).
  ➤ In news and academic prose, nearly all occurrences of *try* + *and* + verb are in this context.
  ➤ In conversation, 45% of occurrences of *try* + *and* + verb are in this context.

➤ In addition, *try* + *and* + verb is used more in BrE than in AmE.
  ➤ In fiction, *try* + *and* + verb occurs c. 20 times per million words in BrE but c. 2 per million words in AmE.

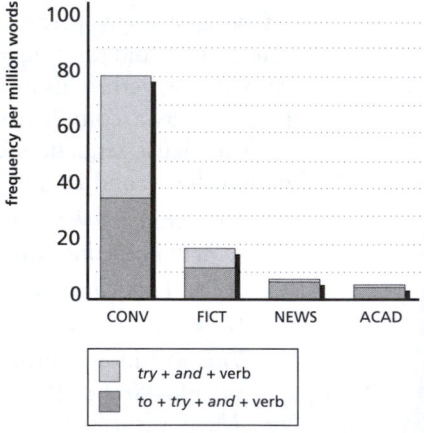

**Figure 9.23**
**Frequency of *try* + *and* + verb in two grammatical contexts, by register**

Legend:
- □ *try* + *and* + verb
- ■ *to* + *try* + *and* + verb

**DISCUSSION OF FINDINGS**

Overall, *try + to + verb* must be considered the usual, unmarked choice (cf. 9.4.2.9). *Try + and + verb* is a colloquial structure that is relatively common in conversation but generally avoided in formal written registers. When used in fiction, it typically appears in the dialogue of fictional characters:

Conversation:

> *Well we did **try and mend it several times**.* (CONV)
>
> *Can you **try and keep still**?* (CONV)
>
> *I'm going to **try and get the three o'clock train**.* (CONV)

Fiction:

> *I'll **try and come tomorrow**.* (FICT)
>
> *Just think of that, and **try and get that into your fat head**.* (FICT)

Nearly all occurrences of *try + and + verb* in news and academic prose are used to avoid a sequence of *to*-clauses:

> *He had practiced putting on his kitchen floor at home during the winter **to try and prepare himself for the greens**.* (NEWS)
>
> *It follows that any teacher persuaded to adopt the innovation must be willing and able to explore modifications to his repertoire in order **to try and achieve the hoped-for improvement in his pupils' understanding**.* (ACAD†)

# 9.5 *Ing*-clauses

## 9.5.1 Overview

Like *that*-complement clauses and infinitive complement clauses, *ing*-complement clauses serve a wide range of functions. They are used most commonly in conjunction with an aspectual verb in the main clause (e.g. *begin, start, stop*), but they are also used to report speech acts, cognitive states, perceptions, emotions, and various other actions.

Although they are most common by far in post-predicate position, *ing*-clauses can also occur in subject and subject predicative positions.

Subject:

> ***My having had what I describe as a mental image of Charlotte Street*** *was necessitated by one or another of certain neural events.* (ACAD†)
>
> ***Reflecting on this and related matters*** *took him past his stop and almost into Dinedor itself.* (FICT)

Subject predicative:

> *The movement's greatest hour was **fighting against an attack on the movement**.* (General prose)

In post-predicate position, *ing*-complement clauses can be controlled by either a verb or adjectival predicate in the main clause.

## 9.5.2     Post-predicate *ing*-clauses controlled by verbs

The verbs taking *ing*-clauses in post-predicate position can be grouped into the following major semantic classes: verbs of aspect or manner (e.g. *begin, keep, delay*); communication/speech-act verbs (e.g. *suggest, talk about*); cognition verbs (e.g. *consider, decide about*); perception verbs (e.g. *see* NP, *imagine*); verbs of affective stance (e.g. *like, detest, worry about*); verbs of description (e.g. *be used for, describe, find* NP); verbs of effort, facilitation, or hindrance (e.g. *try, prevent* NP, *assist in*); verbs of (dis)agreement or (dis)approval (e.g. *permit, allow, agree to*); verbs of avoidance and obligation (e.g. *avoid, resist, be stuck with*); verbs of offense, punishment, or apology (e.g. *accuse* NP *of, catch* NP, *apologize for, condemn*); verbs of required action (e.g. *need, want*). We will first review the relevant structures of post-predicate *ing*-clauses, then examine their associations with these verb classes.

### 9.5.2.1     Grammatical patterns

There are two major grammatical patterns available for *ing*- complement clauses in post-predicate position.

**Pattern 1: verb + *ing*-clause**
(e.g. *begin, remember*):

     1   *He began **paging through old newspapers**.* (FICT†)

     2   *I remember **reading this book**.* (CONV)

**Pattern 2: verb + NP + *ing*-clause**
(e.g. *see, find*):

     3   *When you see **a geek walking down the street**, give it a good throw.* (CONV)

     4   *Don't be surprised to find **me sitting on the tee in the lotus position**.* (NEWS)

With most verbs taking Pattern 1, the implied subject of the *ing*-clause is identical to the subject of the main clause; thus in **1** and **2**, *he* was 'paging through old newspapers', and *I* was 'reading a book'. The exception is verbs of required action, where the subject of the main clause corresponds to the implied direct object (or prepositional object) in the *ing*-clause:

     *That does need **fixing**.* (CONV)

The implied subject of the *ing*-clause in such cases is generic or reconstructed from the context.

     In Pattern 2 structures, the post-verbal NP functions logically as subject of the *ing*-clause, as well as direct object of the main clause. (Alternatively, the entire *ing*-clause can be considered as the direct object in these structures.)

     In a variant on this pattern possible with some verbs, the post-verbal NP is in the possessive or genitive form:

     *I won't report on **your wearing a non-reg shirt here**.* (FICT)

When the possessive form is used, the NP functions only as subject of the *ing*-clause, and the entire *ing*-clause functions as direct object of the main clause verb. As this example shows, the verb taking an *ing*-clause can also be a prepositional verb.

## 9.5.2.2 Controlling verbs, by semantic domain

It should be noted that some verbs are classified differently here from their classifications in earlier sections. This happens when they have different meanings with *ing*-clauses from those with other complements. For example, *want* with an *ing*-clause denotes required action, while *want* with a *to-* or *wh*-clause denotes desire.

**CORPUS FINDINGS** [1]

➤ Six verbs are notably common taking *ing*-clauses in post-predicate position.
  ➤ Five of these verbs are most common in Pattern 1 (verb + *ing*-clause): the aspect or manner verbs *begin*, *keep (on)*, *go (around/on)*, *start*, and *stop*.
  ➤ One of these verbs is most common in Pattern 2 (verb + NP + *ing*-clause): the perception verb *see*.
➤ An additional six verbs are relatively common controlling an *ing*-clause (over 20 occurrences per million words; see Table 9.12): five verbs in Pattern 1 (*come*, *remember*, *sit*, *spend (time)*, *be used for*) and one verb in Pattern 2 (*hear*).

**Figure 9.24**

**Frequencies of the most common verbs controlling *ing*-clauses**

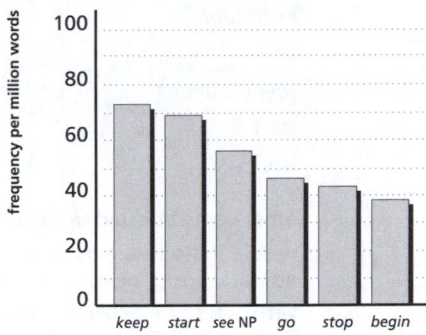

**DISCUSSION OF FINDINGS**

### A Aspect and manner

Verbs of aspect or manner are the most common verbs controlling post-predicate *ing*-clauses. With these verbs, the *ing*-clause conveys something of the meaning of the progressive aspect (i.e. the idea of an activity in progress for a limited time; 6.1, 6.3.3).

Aspectual verbs (5.2.1–2) provide a discourse frame for the event or activity described in the *ing*-clause, indicating its start, completion, or persistence:

> *East German border workers last night began* **demolishing the top of the Berlin Wall at the Brandenburg Gate**. (NEWS†)
>
> *In those days, people started* **predicting what computers, so called 'electronic brains', could be useful for in the future**. (ACAD)
>
> *All the polls stopped* **interviewing early on Wednesday afternoon**. (NEWS)
>
> *Gizzmo keeps* **trying to persuade me to go with her**. (CONV)
>
> *We'll keep on* **following you around**. (CONV)
>
> *Sometimes he went on* **working by himself all through the afternoon**. (FICT†)

Aspectual verbs are common with *ing*-clauses because their meanings concern the delimitation of actions that go on over time—relating to the starting point (e.g. *start*, *postpone*), the end point (e.g. *stop*, *quit*), or their progress (e.g. *keep on*, *continue*, *resume*).

Table 9.13  **Verbs controlling a post-predicate *ing*-clause, by semantic domain and structural pattern; occurrences per million words**

▪ over 40   ▌ over 20

### Verbs of aspect or manner

| verb + *ing*-clause | verb + NP + *ing*-clause |
|---|---|
| **common verbs:** | |
| *begin* ▪ | |
| *come* ▌ | |
| *go (around/on)* ▪ | |
| *keep (on)* ▪ | |
| *sit* ▌ | |
| *spend (time)* ▌ | |
| *start* ▪ | *start* |
| *stop* ▪ | *stop* |

**other verbs attested in the LSWE Corpus:**

**verb + ing-clause** – *burst out, cease, commence, continue, delay, be done, finish, hesitate, postpone, quit, remain, resume, stand*
**verb + NP + ing-clause** – *delay, postpone*

### Communication/speech act verbs

**verbs attested in the LSWE Corpus:**

**verb + *ing*-clause** – *acknowledge, complain about/of, mention, propose, recommend, renounce, report, suggest, talk about, talk* NP *into, urge, be warned about/warn* NP *about*
**verb + NP + *ing*-clause** – *acknowledge, complain about/of, discuss, emphasize, insist on, mention, propose, recommend, report, suggest, talk about, be warned about/warn* NP *about*

### Cognition verbs

| **common verbs:** | |
|---|---|
| *remember* ▌ | *remember* |

**other verbs attested in the LSWE Corpus:**

*believe in, conceive of, concentrate on, consider, contemplate, decide about, forget about, mean, recall, study, think about/of*
**verb + NP + *ing*-clause** – *believe in, conceive of, concentrate on, consider, contemplate, decide about, forget about, recall, recognize, think about/of*

### Perception verbs

| **common verbs:** | |
|---|---|
| | *hear* ▌ |
| *(can't) see* | *see* ▪ |

**other verbs attested in the LSWE Corpus:**

**verb + *ing*-clause** – *dream of, envisage, envision, experience, imagine, picture*
**verb + NP + *ing*-clause** – *dream of, envisage, envision, experience, feel, imagine, notice, observe, overhear, overlook, perceive, picture, sense, smell, spot, visualise, watch*

Table 9.13    **continued**

### Verbs of affective stance

**verbs attested in the LSWE Corpus:**

**verb** + *ing*-clause – *(cannot) bear, (don't) care for, be concerned about, brood over, celebrate, count on, delight in, deplore, detest, dislike, dread, endure, enjoy, be engrossed in, (can't) face, favor, fancy, feel like, hate, be interested in/interest NP in, like, loathe, love, (don't) mind, miss, prefer, regret, relish, resent, can't stand, tire of, tolerate, welcome, worry about*

**verb** + **NP** + *ing*-clause – *admire, (cannot) bear, (don't) care for, be concerned about, brood over, celebrate, count on, delight in, depend on, deplore, detest, dislike, dread, endure, enjoy, (can't) face, favor, fancy, hate, be interested in/interest NP in, like, loathe, love, (don't) mind, miss, prefer, regret, relish, rely on, resent, can't stand, tire of, tolerate, want, welcome, worry about*

### Verbs of description

| verb + *ing*-clause | verb + NP + *ing*-clause |
|---|---|
| **common verbs:** | |
| *be used for* ▌ | *be used for* |

**other verbs attested in the LSWE Corpus:**

**verb** + *ing*-clause – *amount to, be associated with/associate NP with, be based on/base NP on, consist of, describe, be to do with, be engaged in/engage NP in, entail, be found by, include, involve, be involved in/involve NP in*

**verb** + **NP** + *ing*-clause – *account of, amount to, be associated with/associate NP with, be based on/base NP on, consist of, describe, depict, detect, be to do with, discover, entail, find, hide, highlight, identify, ignore, include, involve, be involved in/involve NP in, leave, photograph, record*

### Verbs of effort, facilitation, or hindrance

**verbs attested in the LSWE Corpus:**

**verb** + *ing*-clause – *be achieved by/achieve NP by, adapt to, (can't) afford, aim at, assist in/assist NP in, bother/bother NP over, cope with, deal with, discourage, eliminate, facilitate, get <e.g. + going/moving>, handle, have (trouble/difficulty), (can't) help, hinder, inhibit/inhibit NP from, keep NP from, be obtained by/obtain NP by, overcome, prevent (NP) (from), risk, save NP from, succeed in, try*

**verb** + **NP** + *ing*-clause – *be achieved by/achieve NP by, adapt to, (can't) afford, aim at, assist in/assist NP in, bother NP over, cope with, deal with, discourage, eliminate, facilitate, get, handle, (can't) help, hinder, limit, overcome, prevent (from), restrict, risk, save NP from, support*

### Verbs of (dis)agreement or (dis)approval

**verbs attested in the LSWE Corpus:**

**verb** + *ing*-clause – *accept, agree to, allow (for), approve of, begrudge, defer, deserve, disagree with, disapprove of, permit*

**verb** + **NP** + *ing*-clause – *accept, accommodate, agree to, allow (for), approve of, begrudge, disagree with, disapprove of, endorse, permit*

### Verbs of avoidance and obligation

**verbs attested in the LSWE Corpus:**

**verb** + *ing*-clause – *avoid, escape (from), evade, necessitate, neglect, refrain from, resist, shun, be stuck (with)/stick NP with, withstand*

**verb** + **NP** + *ing*-clause – *avoid, necessitate, need, require, resist, be stuck with/stick NP with, withstand*

Table 9.13    **continued**

**Verbs of offense, punishment, or apology**

**verbs attested in the LSWE Corpus:**

**verb + *ing*-clause** – *accuse NP of/be accused of, admit, admit to, apologize for, be arrested for/arrest NP for, be blacklisted for/blacklist NP for, be blamed for/blame NP for, be caught, be cited for/cite NP for, condemn, confess (to), defend, deny, forgive, justify, repent, be suspected of/suspect NP of*

**verb + NP + *ing*-clause** – *admit to, apologize for, be blamed for/blame NP for, catch, condemn, confess to, defend, forgive, justify*

**Verbs of required action**

**verb + *ing*-clause** – *need, require, want*

---

Manner verbs are an important subtype of this semantic class. With these verbs, the *ing*-clause describes action which progresses along with the action or state of the main clause verb:

> *She came **toddling in**.* (CONV)
> *He sat **shivering on the chair** till daylight.* (FICT †)
> *We went **sailing in the afternoon**.* (FICT)

### B    Communication/speech act

Speech-act verbs, which are less common with *ing*-clauses, give indirect reports of statements made by either the speaker or by others:

> *She complained of **feeling feverish** and went early to bed.* (FICT)
> *They talk about **building more**.* (CONV)
> *She had never mentioned **having a religion**.* (FICT)
> *Mr. Etzioni also suggests **forbidding anyone from gathering background information about the jurors**.* (NEWS)
> *Schafer (1967) reported **finding a significant asymmetry in the electrical activity of the brain**.* (ACAD †)

### C    Cognition

Cognition verbs identify the proposition in the *ing*-clause as representing some mental state or process:

> *I don't even remember **telling you that**.* (CONV)
> *I was thinking of **doing a teddy*** (CONV)
> *I can't conceive of **somebody getting killed and injuring another person because of being too damn stupid to drive carefully**.* (FICT †)
> *We therefore consider **building an architecture round character string manipulation**.* (ACAD †)

### D    Perception

Perception verbs present sense perceptions rather than other mental states or attitudes:

> *I hear **it going beep beep**.* (CONV)
> *I could almost see **the sap rising to nourish it**.* (FICT)
> *We can feel **the blood coursing through our veins again**.* (NEWS)

These verbs also take bare infinitive clauses (9.4.2.7), where the meaning would be subtly different. While the *ing*-clause suggests an action that goes on for some time, the infinitive clause can imply one that happens briefly or just once (e.g. *I hear it go beep beep*).

**E   Affective stance**

Verbs of affective stance comprise one of the largest classes of verbs controlling post-predicate *ing*-clauses, although none is especially frequent. Most of these verbs present either a positive stance (e.g. *enjoy, like, love, prefer, welcome*) or negative stance (e.g. *detest, endure, hate, loathe, regret, resent*) towards the proposition in the *ing*-clause.

> *They don't like **taking them out**.* (CONV)
>
> *I hate **doing that**.* (CONV)
>
> *One might resent **going up there**.* (CONV)
>
> *I love **going there**.* (FICT)
>
> *I think really he preferred **slipping off quietly** in the end.* (FICT)
>
> *He immediately regretted **thinking any such thought**.* (FICT)
>
> *I enjoyed **going beyond the last putt**.* (NEWS†)

**F   Description**

Verbs of description comprise a broad class of verbs used to report previous findings or simple descriptions:

> *Frequently she would find **herself gazing absently at the side of the girl's face**.* (FICT†)
>
> *In China, a great number of workers are engaged in **pulling out the male organs of rice plants using tweezers**.* (NEWS†)
>
> *The experiment consists of **applying stress by pushing down on one end of a sample of rock with a piston**.* (ACAD†)

**G   Other**

The remaining verb classes are more specialized in meaning and comprise verbs from opposite semantic domains, such as facilitation and hindrance, agreement and disagreement, avoidance and obligation.

Verbs of effort, facilitation, or hindrance characterize attempts to facilitate or hinder completion of the action described in the *ing*-clause:

> *Well he couldn't help **being a miserable sod**.* (CONV)
>
> *You ought to try **taking some of them**.* (CONV)
>
> *Even the Arab world, which had tried to prevent **the UN turning Libya into an international pariah**, grudgingly acceded to the UN Security Council.* (NEWS†)
>
> *It also assists in **helping to buffer the indoor environment against sudden fluctuations outside**.* (ACAD)

Verbs of (dis)agreement or (dis)approval express various positive or negative assessments of the proposition in the *ing*-clause:

> *When it approved of **enabling secondary action**, it meant 'strike anywhere'.* (NEWS†)
>
> *This is a very popular instruction, since it allows **counting without disturbing an accumulator**.* (ACAD)

Verbs of avoidance or obligation convey a sense of obligation/necessity, or its avoidance, in relation to the action reported in the *ing*-clause:

> We don't need **you getting in the way**. (CONV)
>
> President Islam Karimov is trying to use slightly more subtle forms of repression to avoid **deterring the growing army of businessmen and politicians from abroad**. (NEWS†)
>
> The government has signalled its determination to resist **raising the 14 per cent base rate**. (NEWS†)

Verbs of offense, punishment, or apology are a specialized semantic class including a relatively large number of verbs taking *ing*-clauses. These verbs describe various social and personal responses to some offense that is reported in the *ing*-clause:

> I was going to apologize for **being stupid on Sunday**. (CONV†)
>
> They haven't been caught **doing it**. (FICT†)
>
> She admitted **causing the dog unnecessary suffering**. (NEWS†)
>
> Mr. Ashdown said he could be blamed for **forcing a second election**. (NEWS†)

Finally, a small number of verbs express required action, marking the *ing*-clause as an action that needs to be done. These verbs control *ing*-clauses with a passive sense, so that the main clause subject corresponds to the implied object of the *ing*-clause:

> It's the only one that really wanted **repairing**. (CONV†)

### 9.5.2.3 Common controlling verbs across registers

**CORPUS FINDINGS** [2]

➤ The single most common verb controlling *ing*-clauses is *keep* in conversation (see Figures 9.25–28).

➤ Start + *ing*-clause in conversation is also very common.

➤ Fiction has the widest distribution of different verbs commonly controlling *ing*-clauses.

➤ Academic prose has the least frequent use of these forms. However, the verb *be used for* is most common in academic prose.

➤ Seven of the ten most frequent verbs with *ing*-clauses are from the semantic domain of aspect or manner verbs (*keep, start, go, stop, begin, spend* (*time*), *come*).

➤ Nine other verbs are moderately common in at least one register (see Table 9.14).

**DISCUSSION OF FINDINGS**

Verbs of aspect or manner, which are the most common verbs controlling *ing*-clauses, are particularly frequent in conversation and fiction. The verb *keep* functions as a kind of progressive marker, emphasizing that the action described in the *ing*-clause is continuous or recurrent. This combination is especially common in conversation:

> She keeps **smelling the washing powder**. (CONV)
>
> His brake lights keep **flashing on**. (CONV†)
>
> You'll just have to keep on **doing it**. (CONV)

A near synonym, which is also colloquial, is *go on*:

> The guard went on **sleeping**. (FICT†)

**Figure 9.25**
**Frequencies of the most common verbs controlling *ing*-clauses— conversation**

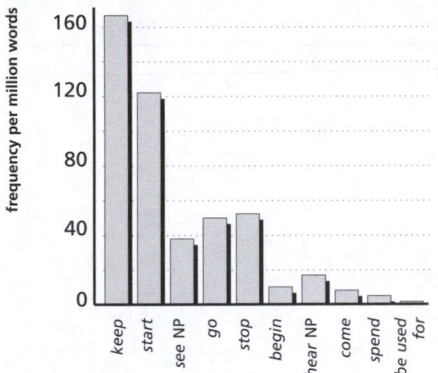

**Figure 9.26**
**Frequencies of the most common verbs controlling *ing*-clauses— fiction**

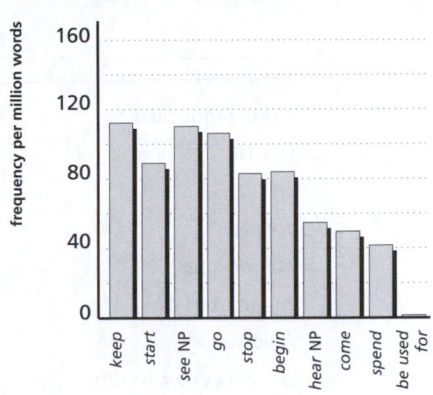

**Figure 9.27**
**Frequencies of the most common verbs controlling *ing*-clauses— news**

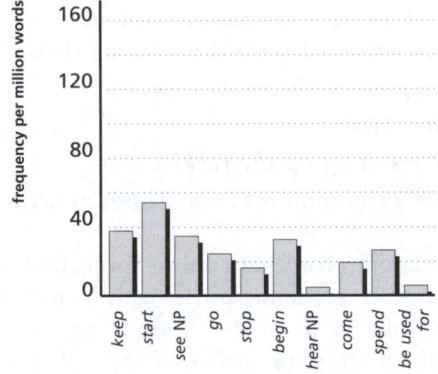

**Figure 9.28**
**Frequencies of the most common verbs controlling *ing*-clauses— academic prose**

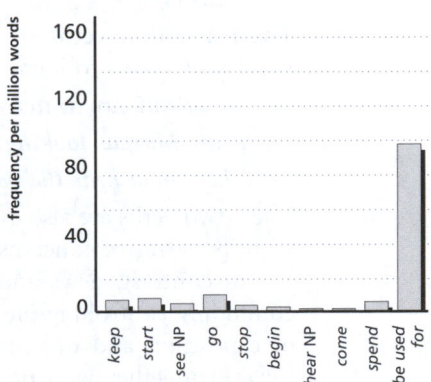

The verbs *start* and *stop*, denoting the beginning or end of an activity, are frequent in both conversation and fiction. However, *begin* is common only in fiction:

> *You can start **doing what you want** then.* (CONV)
>
> *A dog began **barking**.* (FICT)
>
> *Ralph had stopped **smiling**.* (FICT†)

News also has moderate frequencies of aspectual verbs controlling *ing*-clauses (especially *start*, *begin*, and *keep*).

The verbs *go*, *come*, *sit*, and *stand* are commonly used with *ing*-clauses, especially in fiction, to mark the manner in which an action was done. *Go* and *come* indicate the direction of movement (away from or towards some place), while *sit* and *stand* denote stationary but on-going states:

> *I went **looking for it**.* (CONV)
>
> *Peter went **shopping for a play pen**.* (FICT)

Table 9.14   **Moderately common verbs taking an *ing*-clause complement (more than 30 occurrences per million words), excluding the ten most common verbs (see Figures 9.25–28)**

■ over 30     ▪ over 20

|                     | CONV | FICT | NEWS | ACAD |
|---------------------|------|------|------|------|
| *remember*          | ■    | ■    |      |      |
| *think (about/of)*  | ■    | ■    |      |      |
| *get* NP            | ■    | ▪    |      |      |
| *sit*               | ▪    | ■    |      |      |
| *feel* NP           |      | ■    |      |      |
| *stand/stood*       |      | ■    |      |      |
| *be accused of*     |      |      | ■    |      |
| *involve*           |      |      |      | ■    |
| *be achieved by/with* |    |      |      | ■    |

> *One of the children came **running after him**.* (FICT)
>
> *All morning they sat **waiting in the sun**.* (FICT†)
>
> *The two police guards stood **peering in the direction of the commotion**.* (FICT†)

The perception verbs *see* and *hear* are commonly used to mark the sensory perceptions used to identify the activity described in the *ing*-clause:

> *I suddenly saw **water rushing down the wall**.* (CONV)
>
> *I saw **Marcus looking at me**.* (FICT)
>
> *They could hear **the waves breaking on the rocks**.* (FICT)

These two verbs are also especially common with *ing*-clauses in fiction, consistent with its narrative concerns.

In contrast, news and academic prose have more specialized sets of verbs commonly controlling *ing*-clauses. In academic prose, with its primary purposes of exposition and description, only verbs of description (e.g. *be used for* and *involve*) together with one verb of effort (*be achieved by/with*) are particularly common with *ing*-clauses:

> *Some method of refrigeration is used for **cooling the milk in all bulk tanks**.* (ACAD)
>
> *In a sense information theory involves **specifying a context**.* (ACAD†)
>
> *This is achieved by **saving information at the beginning of the subroutine**.* (ACAD†)

News is the only register to use verbs of offense or punishment frequently with an *ing*-clause, reflecting the common theme of 'crime and punishment' in news reporting:

> *He is accused of **conspiring with Mohammed Haque, a BCCI manager, to mislead the bank's auditor**.* (NEWS†)
>
> *George Helaine, a Belgian, is accused of **organising the shipment from Morocco**.* (NEWS†)
>
> *All are charged with **violating official secrets laws, an offense that carries a maximum three-year prison term and fines up to $27,000**.* (NEWS)

## 9.5.3    Adjectival predicates controlling *ing*-clauses

➤ The most common adjectival predicate with an *ing*-clause in post-predicate position is *capable of* (occurring over 20 times per million words).

➤ Several other adjectival predicates are relatively common in this construction.

    ➤ In most of these, the adjective is followed by a preposition (which could also have a noun phrase as its complement): *afraid of, available for, aware of, bad about/at, confident of, crucial for/in, different from, effective at/in, good at, great at, important for/in, incapable of, intent on, interested in, necessary for, responsible for, sorry about, successful at, suitable for, tired of, useful for/in*

**DISCUSSION OF FINDINGS**

Most of the adjectives that control an *ing*-clause convey either an affective stance or some other evaluation:

> *These people were not afraid of **signing papers**.* (FICT†)

> *I'm sorry about **being in a mood Saturday**.* (CONV)

> *I could see she was confident of **handling any awkward situation that might arise**.* (FICT†)

> *It is true that young rabbits are great migrants and capable of **journeying for miles**.* (FICT†)

> *There is no reason why women should not be good at **selling cars**.* (NEWS)

> *Colombian traffickers are responsible for **processing and smuggling 80 percent of the cocaine sold on U.S. streets**.* (NEWS†)

> *Mineralogy and texture are also useful in **subdividing the sedimentary rocks**.* (ACAD)

## 9.5.4    Post-predicate *ing*-clauses across registers

➤ Overall, *ing*-clauses in post-predicate position are most common in the written registers (especially fiction) and least common in conversation.

➤ *Ing*-clauses following adjectival predicates are most common in academic prose.

**DISCUSSION OF FINDINGS**

The non-finite complement clauses—*to*-clauses as well as *ing*-clauses—are predominantly a feature of written language. In contrast, the finite complement clauses (*that*-clauses and *wh*-clauses) are most common in conversation. Like *to*-clauses, *ing*-clauses

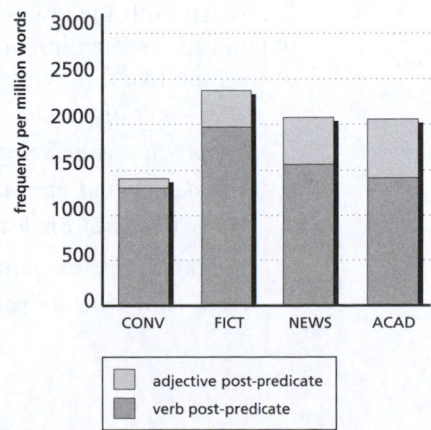

**Figure 9.29**
**Frequencies of *ing*-clause types across registers**

controlled by verbs are most common in fiction, while *ing*-clauses with adjectival predicates are commonly used in academic prose to express various kinds of impersonal stance.

## 9.5.5  Objective v. possessive NP with *ing*-clauses

In structures with Pattern 2, verb + NP + *ing*-clause, the post-verbal NP can occur in either an objective or possessive/genitive form:

> *Did you mind **me saying it**, Stephen?* (FICT)
>
> *And maybe you won't mind **my saying that you're getting a little old for studying**.* (FICT†)

However, it is not the case that all verbs of Pattern 2 allow the possessive alternative. Verbs such as *keep, have, get, leave, find, want, catch*, and many perception verbs cannot take a following possessive noun phrase:

> *I'm sorry to keep **you waiting**.* (FICT)
>
> *I won't have **you waiting on me hand and foot**.* (FICT)
>
> *I walked out and left **him sitting there**.* (FICT†)
>
> *She caught **him glancing at her**.* (FICT†)

### 9.5.5.1  Register distribution

**CORPUS FINDINGS** [2,3]

➤ The objective case is used for the overwhelming majority (over 90%) of noun phrases occurring in the pattern verb + NP + *ing*-clause.
  ➤ Only fiction shows a moderate frequency (less than ten per million words) of possessive forms in this pattern.

**DISCUSSION OF FINDINGS**

In spite of a prescriptive tradition favoring the possessive form, the objective case must be considered the unmarked choice for the post-verbal noun phrase in the pattern verb + NP + *ing*-clause. The preponderance of non-possessive forms is partly due to the fact that some Pattern 2 verbs (e.g. *keep, have, leave, find, catch*) cannot take a following possessive noun phrase.

When both the objective and possessive forms are permitted, the possessive option focuses attention on the action described in the *ing*-clause. In contrast, use of the objective form emphasizes the person doing the action:

> *They don't appreciate **my being called here**.* (FICT)
>
> *I appreciate **your being there**.* (FICT)
>
> *You don't mind **my calling you Toni**, do you?* (FICT)
>
> *We've discussed **his leaving his money to various charities**.* (FICT)

v.  *She could hear **me putting on my clothes in the dark**.* (FICT)

> *We couldn't picture **you walking so far**.* (FICT)

> *She might not want **me barging in on a special occasion like that**.* (FICT)
>
> *It is hard to imagine **him leading a crusade for Meadowell**.* (NEWS)

## 9.6 Ellipsis and pro-form substitution in post-predicate complement clauses

When the content of a complement clause is clear from the preceding discourse, various forms of ellipsis or substitution can be used for post-predicate clauses. With *to*-clauses and *wh*-clauses, the complement clause itself can be ellipted, while the complementizer (*to* or a *wh*-word) is usually retained:

> *A: Are we having that tonight too?*
> *B: If you **want to**.* (CONV)
> *i.e. If you want to have that tonight.*
>
> *He fell asleep up there—I don't **know how**.* (CONV)
> *i.e. I don't know how he fell asleep.*

In contrast, ellipsis is not possible with post-predicate *that*-clauses, but the pro-forms *so* or *not* can be used to substitute for the entire clause:

> *A: Oh, you tasted it before, didn't you?*
> *B: I don't **think so**.* (CONV)
> *i.e. I don't think I tasted it before.*
>
> *A: Is the dog going to jump?*
> *B: I **hope not**.* (CONV)
> *i.e. I hope that the dog is not going to jump.*

Almost any verb that can take a post-predicate *to*-clause or *wh*-clause can also take the ellipted form of those clauses. However, relatively few verbs permit substitution of *so* or *not* for a *that*-clause.

### 9.6.1 Verbs occurring commonly with ellipsis and pro-form substitution

**CORPUS FINDINGS** [2]

➤ Ellipsis and pro-form substitution in post-predicate complement clauses occurs primarily in conversation.
➤ Relatively few verbs occur commonly with either of these patterns.

**DISCUSSION OF FINDINGS**

Despite the greater potential for ellipsis with *to*-clauses and *wh*-clauses, there are in fact few verbs that commonly occur with an elliptic complement clause. With each type of ellipsis or substitution, there is a single verb that is especially common: *want* + *to*, *know* + *wh*-word, and *think* + *so*. These are the single most common verbs with each relevant complement type in general (Figures 9.1, 9.10, 9.12):

> *You can go if you **want to**.* (CONV)
> *I couldn't fall asleep till four last night—I don't **know why**.* (CONV)

Table 9.15 **Frequency of verbs co-occurring with complement clause ellipsis or substitution, by structural pattern and register; occurrences per million words**

each ● represents 10

**verbs frequently taking an elliptic to-infinitive clause:**

| | CONV | FICT | NEWS | ACAD |
|---|---|---|---|---|
| **verb + to** | | | | |
| want | ●●●●●●●●●● | ●●●● | | |
| try | ● | | | |
| like | ● | | | |

**verbs frequently taking an elliptic wh-infinitive clause:**

| | CONV | FICT | NEWS | ACAD |
|---|---|---|---|---|
| **verb + wh-word** | | | | |
| know | ●●●●●●● | ●●● | | ● |
| wonder | ● | ● | | |
| remember | ● | | | |
| tell NP | ● | | | |

**verbs frequently co-occurring with so and not as substitutes for post-predicate that-clauses:**

| | CONV | FICT | NEWS | ACAD |
|---|---|---|---|---|
| **verb + so** | | | | |
| think | ●●●●●●●●●● ●●●●●●●● | ●●●●● | | |
| say | ●● | ●●●● | ● | |
| hope | ●● | ●● | | |
| suppose (BrE) | ●● | ● | | |
| guess (AmE) | ●● | ● | | |
| **verb + not** | | | | |
| hope | ● | | | |
| guess (AmE) | ● | | | |

> A: *Have they found him?*
> B: *I don't know—I don't* **think so**. (CONV)

The verbs *try* and *like* are also moderately common with an ellipted *to*-clause, while *wonder*, *remember*, and *tell* NP are moderately common with an ellipted *wh*-clause:

> A: *Keep him in line.*
> B: *I'll* **try to**. (CONV)
> A: *I took a shower early this morning and I feel like I didn't shower.*
> B: *I* **wonder why**. (CONV)

*Like* + *to* usually follows the modal verb *would*:

> A: *Did you use my toothbrush again?*
> B: *Well, I would* **like to**. (CONV)

*Tell* + NP + *wh*-word most commonly occurs in the relatively fixed expression *I'll tell you what*. However, this combination is also found in expressions such as *just tell me when* and *I can't tell you why*.

The construction *think* + *so* usually occurs with a first person pronoun as subject and is used to indicate an epistemic stance, expressing a lack of certainty about some previous proposition (cf. 12.3.1):

> *I really think your dad is going to be her executor. I'm not sure, but I really* **think so**. (CONV)

> A: *Is she still living there?*
> B: *Yeah, I* **think so**. (CONV)

> *'Mister Johnny's not mad.' 'No. At least I don't* **think so**.*' (FICT)

The main clause verbs *hope, suppose*, and *guess* co-occurring with *so* similarly mark epistemic stance. *Suppose* is relatively common in this function in BrE conversation, while *guess* is relatively common in AmE:

> A: *You have to write your name down every time.*
> B: *Yeah, I* **suppose so**. (BrE CONV)

> A: *The medicine is slowing down the disease.*
> B: *Yeah, I* **guess so**. (AmE CONV)

The main clause verb *say* + *so* is used for indirect reported speech rather than marking stance. As a result, this combination is more common in fiction than any other register:

> *But he always found fault with their effort, and he* **said so** *with much threatening.* (FICT)

> *'He'll just weep for joy when I tell him,' she said. 'Well, if you* **say so**,*' Albert said doubtfully.* (FICT)

The pro-form *not* is considerably less common as a *that*-clause substitute than *so*. Only two verbs are moderately common co-occurring with *not*—*hope* and *guess* (the latter in AmE):

> A: *We're not having too early a lunch, are we?*
> B: *I* **hope not**. (CONV)

> A: *You don't think the Cardinals are doing very well at all, are they?*
> B: *Not that bad. I* **guess not**. (AmE CONV)

## 9.7 Choice of complement clause type

There are structural parallels among the four types of complement clause: each type can complement both verbs and adjectives, and each type occurs in subject, post-predicate, and subject predicative positions. At the same time, there are grammatical and discourse factors that distinguish among the four types. These can be considered under four headings: register distribution, structural factors, and semantic factors (discussed in 9.7.1), and lexical factors (discussed in 9.7.2).

## 9.7.1    Register distribution, structural factors, and semantic factors

**CORPUS FINDINGS** [2,3]

### A   Register distribution

➤ Overall, *that*-clauses and *to*-clauses are more than twice as common as *wh*-clauses and *ing*-clauses.

➤ Finite complement clauses, i.e. *that*-clauses and *wh*-clauses, are most common in conversation, followed by fiction. They are relatively rare in academic prose.

   ➤ In contrast, non-finite complement clauses, i.e. *to*-clauses and *ing*-clauses, are most common in fiction, followed by news and academic prose. They are relatively rare in conversation.

### B   Structural factors

➤ The large majority of *that*-clauses and *wh*-clauses occur in post-predicate position after verbs. In contrast, a much higher proportion of *to*-clauses and *ing*-clauses are controlled by adjectival predicates.

   ➤ This trend is most pronounced for *to*-clauses in academic prose, with over half of all occurrences being controlled by adjectives.

   ➤ Extraposed constructions and subject predicative constructions are more common with *to*-clauses than with *that*-clauses. For *to*-clauses, extraposition is more common with adjectives than with verbs.

   ➤ These trends are again most pronounced in academic prose, where extraposed and subject predicative *to*-clauses are particularly common. (In this register, extraposed *to*-clauses after adjectives are over twice as common as post-predicate *to*-clauses after adjectives, and over ten times as common as extraposed *to*-clauses after verbs.)

### C   Semantic factors

➤ The four complement clause types are not equally productive in the range of verbs that they occur with:

   ➤ At one extreme, *that*-clauses combine with relatively few verbs from only three major semantic domains. However, some of these verb + *that*-clause combinations are extremely common.

   ➤ *That*-clauses in combination with the verbs *think* (especially in conversation) and *say* (especially in news) are far more common than any other combination of verb + complement clause.

   ➤ At the other extreme, *to*-clauses and *ing*-clauses combine with a large number of different verbs from many semantic domains.

**DISCUSSION OF FINDINGS**

The following two text samples illustrate the different ways that *that*-clauses and *to*-clauses are used in conversation and academic prose:

Text sample 1: CONVERSATION

   *A: I said how's your revision going, cos I knew **she was doing revision**, she went cccckkk I try a maths paper and I can't do that, and I <unclear> a*

> *chemistry paper and I can't do that and I really <growl>. I said I think* **you need a break.** *<laugh> I think* **you need [to go and do something else for a little while]** *– I said cos if you keep looking over thinking* **you can't do it,** *have a break and go back to it afterwards. You just get really despondent*
>
> B: *Yeah.*
>
> A: *and fed up and think* **you can't do it** *and you go blank and then you can't touch anything you – and you know* **it's hard.** (CONV)

Text sample 2: ACADEMIC PROSE

> *The above means are not able* **to represent an office procedure or an activity in a way which would allow automation of the co-ordination required for execution.** *There are no methods for representing the interworking of the different description techniques and it should be noted* **that it may be necessary [to model the same activity more than once redundantly and in parallel by different means].** *In particular, it must be possible* **to model the interworking of roles (to be represented by organigrams or job profiles), flow charts and forms.** (ACAD)

The conversation sample illustrates a dense use of *that*-clauses in post-predicate position, most commonly controlled by the verb *think*. The subject of *think* is typically *I* or *you*, so that the construction directly represents the thoughts of the speaker or hearer.

In contrast, the academic prose sample illustrates the very different kinds of complement clause commonly found in informational written prose: a predominance of *to*-clauses rather than *that*-clauses; adjectives as well as verbs, from a wide range of semantic domains, as controlling elements; relatively frequent use of extraposition; non-animate noun phrases acting as subject of the main clause.

## 9.7.2    Lexico-grammatical factors

**CORPUS FINDINGS** [2,3]

➤ A few verbs can control all four types of complement clause: e.g. *remember, believe* (NP), *agree* (*to/with*), *warn* (NP *about*).

➤ Some verbs can control *that*-clauses and *to*-clauses but not *ing*-clauses: e.g. *hope, decide, wish, say, expect* (NP).

➤ Some verbs can control *that*-clauses and *ing*-clauses but not *to*-clauses: e.g. *imagine, mention, report, suggest, admit* (*to*), *understand* (*about*).

➤ A large number of verbs can control *to*-clauses and *ing*-clauses but not *that*-clauses: e.g. *begin, start, like, love, prefer, hate, try, attempt, need, want.*

➤ Finally, some verbs can control only one type of complement clause (excluding nominal relative clauses):

   ➤ Verbs such as *conclude, speculate, guess, argue,* and *assert* control only *that*-clauses.

   ➤ Verbs such as *consent, prepare, fail, refuse,* and *hesitate* control only *to*-clauses.

   ➤ Verbs such as *keep (on), finish, miss,* and *be used for* control only *ing*-clauses.

**DISCUSSION OF FINDINGS**

Nominal relative clauses are exceptional in that they occur with almost any verb. Otherwise, each complement clause type occurs with a particular set of verbs, although there is considerable overlap. The following sections consider additional factors influencing the choice among clause types when they are controlled by the same verb.

## 9.7.3 *That*-clauses v. non-finite clauses

**CORPUS FINDINGS** [2,3]

➤ For verbs that can control both *that*-clauses and non-finite clauses in the pattern verb + complement clause, *that*-clauses are used when: (1) the subject of the complement clause is not co-referential with the subject of the main clause; or (2) the complement clause includes a modal verb.

➤ Almost all occurrences of the verbs *agree*, *hope*, and *remember* with *that*-clauses have one or both of these characteristics (see Table 9.16).

Table 9.16 **Factors influencing the choice of *that*-clause after *agree*, *hope*, and *remember*; occurrences per million words**

each ■ represents 5     □ represents less than 3

| | *that*-clause subject not co-referential | modal verb in *that*-clause | both modal verb and not co-referential | neither |
|---|---|---|---|---|
| ***agree* + *that*-clause** | | | | |
| CONV | □ | □ | □ | □ |
| FICT | ■■■■■ | ■■■ | ■■■ | □ |
| NEWS | ■■■■■■■■ | ■■■ | ■■■ | □ |
| ACAD | ■■ | ■ | ■ | □ |
| ***hope* + *that*-clause** | | | | |
| CONV | ■ | ■ | ■ | □ |
| FICT | ■■■■■■ | ■■■■ | ■■■■ | □ |
| NEWS | ■■■ | ■■■ | ■■■ | □ |
| ACAD | ■ | ■ | ■ | □ |
| ***remember* + *that*-clause** | | | | |
| FICT | ■■■■■ | ■ | ■ | □ |
| NEWS | ■ | □ | □ | □ |
| ACAD | ■■■■■ | ■■ | ■■ | □ |

➤ For verbs that can control both *that*-clauses and non-finite clauses in the pattern verb + NP + complement clause, *that*-clauses are used when: (1) the subject of the complement clause is expressed by a complex noun phrase; or (2) the complement clause includes a modal verb.

*That*-clauses allow the expression of meanings not possible with *to*-clauses or *ing*-clauses: their verbs have tense or modality, and the subject of the *that*-clause does not have to be co-referential with the subject of the main clause. For verbs such as *agree*, *hope*, and *remember*, the implied subject of a post-predicate *to*-clause or *ing*-clause is always co-referential with the subject of the main clause. In contrast, the overwhelming majority of *that*-clauses controlled by these verbs have subjects that are not co-referential:

> *The others had finally gone along with him and agreed **that Demerest would personally write the report**.* (FICT)

v. *He agreed **to let her go out**.* (NEWS)

> *I hope **that you were happy while you were here**.* (FICT†)

v. *Anyway I hope **to see you**.* (CONV)

> *Remember **that fortune and misfortune should be left to heaven and natural law**.* (FICT)

v. *When you come down, remember **to do so with dignity**.* (FICT†)

> *I remember **growing those on the roof of the shelter**.* (CONV)

Complement clauses controlled by verbs such as *expect* and *believe* have expressed subjects with both *that*-clauses and with *to*-clauses occurring in the pattern verb + NP + *to*-clause. In these cases, *that*-clauses are commonly used (in addition to their use for tense and modality) when the subject of the complement clause is a complex noun phrase (enclosed in *[]*):

> *Only 12 per cent believed **that [roads through sites of natural beauty or historical interest] should be built as planned**.* (NEWS)

> *We believe **that [the computer's ability to generate quasi-random numbers] is educationally most important**.* (ACAD)

> *Ministers expect **that [at least one quarter of the entire flotation] will be bought by small British investors**.* (NEWS)

> *It is to be expected **that [any effects due to hemispheric asymmetry] will interact with social and personality factors**.* (ACAD)

v. *She genuinely believed **[it] to be worse than it really was**.* (NEWS)

> *City analysts expect **[it] to pass its final dividend**.* (NEWS†)

> *You expect **[most candidates] to make you offers and promises**.* (NEWS)

## 9.7.4 Infinitive v. *ing*-clause

➤ For verbs that can control both *to*-clauses and *ing*-clauses, but not *that*-clauses, semantic factors influence the choice.

> ➤ In general, a *to*-clause has a meaning that is more hypothetical or potential than the meaning of the corresponding *ing*-clause (with the same verb). However, the specific meaning difference between a *to*-clause and an *ing*-clause depends on the particular controlling verb.

➤ For example, c. 75% of the occurrences of *like* + *to*-clause in fiction and news are preceded by *would* (see Table 9.17). In contrast, *ing*-clauses rarely occur with a hypothetical meaning.

Table 9.17 **The co-occurrence of *would* with *like* + *to*-clause or *like* + *ing*-clause (in fiction and news); occurrences per million words**

each ■ represents 10    □ represents less than 5

| | *would like* + *to*-clause | *like* + *to*-clause | *would like* + *ing*-clause | *like* + *ing*-clause |
|---|---|---|---|---|
| FICT | ■■■■■■■■■■ | ■■■■ | □ | ■■ |
| NEWS | ■■■■■■■ | ■ | □ | ■ |

## DISCUSSION OF FINDINGS

The meaning differences between *to*-clauses and *ing*-clauses can be illustrated from consideration of four verbs from different semantic domains: *like*, *remember*, *try*, and *start*.

The greater focus on hypothetical or potential events associated with *to*-clauses is relatively easy to identify with verbs of desire (e.g. *like*, *love*, *hate*). In fact, a hypothetical meaning is often expressed structurally; these verbs with a *to*-clause typically co-occur with the modal *would*:

> *I would like **to cooperate**.* (FICT)
>
> *He thinks he would like **to play on Friday morning**.* (NEWS)

v.  *I used to like **being married very much**.* (FICT)

> *I like **creating things**.* (NEWS)

The verb *remember* can be used to illustrate verbs of cognition that control both *to*-clauses and *ing*-clauses. In most cases, the event described in a *to*-clause after *remember* has not actually occurred; rather, this combination is typically used to present a directive or to indicate potential compliance with some expected action. Directives:

> *Try and remember **to bring an electric drill up**.* (CONV)
>
> *You've got to remember **to pull them down**.* (CONV)

Potential compliance:

> *I must remember **to take that film out**.* (CONV)
>
> *He must remember **to tell her he was sorry**.* (FICT)

In contrast, an *ing*-clause controlled by *remember* usually describes an event that has actually occurred:

> *I remember **going late at night**.* (CONV)
>
> *I just remember **giving it to someone**.* (FICT)

There is another kind of meaning difference between *to*-clauses and *ing*-clauses following verbs of effort, such as *try*. With both types of clause, the action presented in the complement clause is usually potential in meaning. The major difference is that *try* + *ing*-clause usually proposes a general solution to a problem, while *try* + *to*-clause usually presents a specific action that a person attempts to do:

> *You ought to try **taking some of them**.* (CONV)
>
> *I would say you might try **going to bed early**.* (FICT†)

v.  *I didn't try **to hide it**.* (CONV)

> *I try* **to be a cheerful person**. (FICT)
>
> *Don't try* **to deny it**. (FICT)

Finally, the meaning difference between *to*-clauses and *ing*-clauses controlled by aspectual verbs (e.g. *start, begin*) is even more subtle, and in some cases the two seem to be virtually interchangeable. In many of these cases, though, there is again a difference in potentiality between the two complement clause types. For example, *start + to*-clause can indicate an intention to begin an action, although the following discourse shows that the action itself was not in fact carried out:

> *But now and again she would start* **to say something** *and then she would sort of find an easier way to say it.* (CONV)
>
> *He started* **to answer**, *then shrugged.* (FICT)
>
> *I started* **to ask him what he was doing home**, *but he pulled me into the room.* (FICT)

In contrast, *start + ing*-clause generally indicates that the event in question has truly begun to happen:

> *The complaints have started* **coming in already**. (FICT)
>
> *I started* **smoking** *when I was thirteen or fourteen in the barn with my buddies.* (FICT)
>
> *She was a patient of his before I started* **seeing him**. (FICT)

# 10 Adverbials

## Adverbials

*See page xiii for contents in detail*

# 10.1 Overview

Adverbials are elements of clauses with three major functions: to add circumstantial information about the proposition in the clause, to express speaker/writer stance towards the clause, or to link the clause (or some part of it) to some other unit of discourse.

Although the relationship between an adverbial and the rest of the clause can differ, as described in 10.1.4, it is important to distinguish adverbials from other features which have similar structures but are constituents of a phrase rather than elements of a clause. For example, **1–3** below are adverbials, but **4** and **5** are not:

1 *I keep walking **in this rubbish**.* (CONV)

2 *She grinned **widely**.* (FICT)

3 ***In all honesty**, $300 million is not going to make a fundamental change.* (NEWS)

4 *The £3,000 prize **in the women's event** went to Bev Nicholson.* (NEWS)

5 ***Widely** varying types of land are cultivated.* (ACAD)

The prepositional phrase *in this rubbish* in **1**, and the adverb *widely* in **2**, provide circumstantial information for their respective main verbs (*walking* and *grinned*). In **3** the prepositional phrase *in all honesty* provides the speaker's comment about the entire subsequent clause. All three of these examples are thus elements of their clauses and are adverbials. In contrast, the prepositional phrase *in the women's event* in **4** modifies the noun *prize*, while the adverb *widely* in **5** modifies the adjective *varying*. These examples are therefore only constituents of a noun phrase and adjective phrase, and are not adverbials.

Adverbials differ from other clause elements in a number of ways. Consider the following text samples (*[]* are used to distinguish adjacent sequences of adverbials).

6 ***As I say**, we were **eleven hundred feet above sea level** and we er **really** moved [**here**] [**because er I could not stand the er the bad weather**].* (CONV)

7 ***In spite of great efforts by their authors**, these books **usually** contain a number of fallacies and errors that are **in due course** passed on [**repeatedly**] [**by later writers of other books**] <...> **Unfortunately**, these authors lack <...>* (ACAD†)

These samples illustrate many of the important characteristics of adverbials:

- They perform a variety of functions. Some add information about the circumstances of an activity or state described in a clause (e.g. *here*, *usually*), while others give a speaker's comment on the proposition of a clause (e.g. *unfortunately*). Still other adverbials serve connective functions (e.g. *as I say* marking a restatement of an earlier utterance).

- They fulfill a variety of semantic roles. Even in the short excerpts above, for example, adverbials are used to express location (*eleven hundred feet above sea level*, *here*); reason (*because ...*); concession (*in spite of ...*); time (*usually*, *in due course*, *repeatedly*); agency (*by later writers*); and attitude (*unfortunately*).

- They are realized by a wide range of syntactic forms. The above samples include adverbials realized by adverbs (e.g. *here*, *usually*, *unfortunately*), prepositional phrases (e.g. *in spite of great efforts, in due course*), and clauses (*as I say, because …*). They may also be realized by noun phrases.

- They can be placed in a variety of positions. The above samples illustrate adverbials in the initial position of a clause (e.g. *as I say*), in one variant of the medial position—i.e. before the main verb but after the subject (e.g. *really, usually*), and in final position (e.g. *here, repeatedly, by later writers …*). Adverbials can also be placed between the main verb and obligatory final clausal elements.

- Multiple adverbials can occur in a clause. In **7**, for example, the first clause (the main clause) has two adverbials (*in spite of …* and *usually*) and the subordinate clause has three adverbials (*in due course, repeatedly, by …*).

- Finally, most adverbials are optional (the only exceptions are associated with certain verbs that require adverbial complementation; see 5.2.4, 3.5.2, 3.5.9). For example, the first sentence in the academic prose sample above would be well-formed without the adverbials:

  *These books contain a number of fallacies and errors that are passed on.*

Because a wide range of structures and functions is included in adverbial modification, not all adverbials exhibit all of these characteristics to the same extent. Thus, each of these characteristics, the relationships among them, and the association patterns with registers are discussed in depth in this chapter. We begin in the following sections with a general introduction to adverbials, giving overviews from three perspectives: the functional classes of adverbials (10.1.1), the syntactic forms of adverbials (10.1.2), and their positions in clauses (10.1.3). Variation in the relationship of adverbials to other clause elements is also further discussed in 10.1.4.

## 10.1.1 The three classes of adverbial

Adverbials can be divided into three major classes by their functions: **circumstance adverbials**, **stance adverbials**, and **linking adverbials**. Although each class is an element of a clause, the classes differ in the extent to which they are integrated into the clause structure and the amount of variability in the precise functions of the class.

**Circumstance adverbials** are the most varied class, as well as the most integrated into the clause structure. Circumstance adverbials add information about the action or state described in the clause, answering questions such as 'How, When, Where, How much, To what extent?' and 'Why?'. They include both obligatory adverbials, as in the first example below, and optional adverbials, as in the second:

> *And where were you this morning then? You weren't **in Geography**.* (CONV)

> *Writers on style have differed **[a great deal] [in their understanding of the subject]**.* (ACAD)

Furthermore, circumstance adverbials can have scope over differing amounts of the clause. They may modify an entire clause (in this case with a dependent clause within it):

> ***After intensive tests**, they believe the AIDS virus had been eradicated from the patient's body.* (NEWS)

Or they can have scope only over the predicate of the clause, as in the following example where the prepositional phrases add information only about the verb *sitting*:

> He was even now sitting *[beside her] [on the sofa]*. (FICT)

Special cases of circumstance adverbials with even more limited scope are discussed in 10.1.4, while circumstance adverbials are described in detail in 10.2.

The second class of adverbials is **stance adverbials**. Stance adverbials convey speakers' comments on what they are saying (the content of the message) or how they are saying it (the style). Stance adverbials fall into three categories: **epistemic**, **attitude**, and **style**.

Epistemic stance adverbials focus on the truth value of the proposition, commenting on factors such as certainty, reality, sources, limitations, and precision of the proposition:

> Well she **definitely** looks at her mobile. (CONV)
>
> It is very sad **really**, he added. (NEWS)
>
> **From my perspective**, it was a clear case of abuse. (NEWS)
>
> Travelling these days, especially on a low budget, is **supposedly** aided by the plethora of guidebooks, travel companions and survival kits. (NEWS)
>
> **On the whole**, sons-in-law were in better paid jobs than their fathers-in-law. (ACAD)
>
> Arphai pseudonietana and Psoloessa texana **apparently** were much more abundant in the wet summer of 1990 than in preceding years. (ACAD†)

Attitude stance adverbials express the speaker's attitude towards or evaluation of the content:

> The Yard's wonder boy, **appropriately**, descends from the clouds. (FICT)
>
> **To my surprise** the space devoted to the kinetic sculptures had a lively and progressive atmosphere. (NEWS†)
>
> **More importantly**, they do not provide information about the chemical composition of the substance. (ACAD)
>
> **Fortunately** this is far from the truth. (ACAD)

Finally, style stance adverbials convey a speaker's comment on the style or form of the utterance, often clarifying how the speaker is speaking or how the utterance should be understood:

> Well, yes, **technically speaking**, I guess it is burnt. (CONV)
>
> That proves at least that Cassetti or Ratchett, as I shall continue to call him, was certainly alive at twenty minutes to one. At twenty-three minutes to one, **to be precise**. (FICT)
>
> **Quite frankly**, we are having a bad year. (NEWS)
>
> I'm not sure if the princess held a gun to Charles's head, **figuratively speaking**. (NEWS†)

In most cases, as in all of the above examples, stance adverbials have scope over the entire clause; that is, the adverbial provides a comment on the content or style of the entire proposition (but see 10.1.4 for a discussion of special cases with more limited scope). In addition, unlike some circumstance adverbials, stance adverbials are always optional. Stance adverbials are covered in detail in 10.3.

The third class of adverbials is **linking adverbials**. Linking adverbials have a more peripheral relationship with the rest of the clause than circumstance adverbials typically do. Rather than adding additional information to a clause, they serve a connective function. They make explicit the relationship between two units of discourse, as in the following examples:

1 *They were kid boots at eight shillings a pair. He,* **however,** *thought them the most dainty boots in the world, and he cleaned them with as much reverence as if they had been flowers.* (FICT)

2 *Some hospitals use their own ethics committees to settle such cases, but a hospital's biases could creep into its committee's decisions, Ms. Yuen says.* **Furthermore,** *the committee's decision wouldn't be legally binding and wouldn't shield a physician from liability.* (NEWS)

3 *Now clearly, such semiotics are often manipulated <...>.* **Nonetheless,** *these Latin and North American "ethno-semantics" capture an important sense in which capitalistic labor is "unproductive" in a material sense.* (ACAD)

4 *My objectives in this work are twofold:* **first,** *to set out a precise yet comprehensive analysis <...>* (ACAD†)

As the above examples illustrate, linking adverbials can connect units of discourse of differing sizes. The linked units may be sentences, as in **1** and **2**. The units may also be larger than the sentence, as in **3** where *nonetheless* connects the subsequent sentence with several preceding sentences about *such semiotics*. Finally, **4** exemplifies a linking adverbial connecting a *to*-clause to the preceding main clause.

Linking adverbials can express a variety of relationships, including addition and enumeration, summation, apposition, result/inference, contrast/concession, and transition. These semantic roles as well as the structure and use of linking adverbials are described in detail in 10.4.

## 10.1.1.1 Frequency of the three classes of adverbial

**CORPUS FINDINGS** [1]

➤ Adverbials are very common in all four registers.
  ➤ They are most common in fiction and least common in news and academic prose.
  ➤ Conversation falls between the two extremes.
➤ In all four registers, circumstance adverbials are by far the most common class of adverbial.
➤ Stance adverbials are more common in conversation than the other registers, although they account for less than 10% of all adverbials in that register.
➤ Linking adverbials are most common in academic prose, but they account for less than 10% of all adverbials in that register.

**DISCUSSION OF FINDINGS**

Although in most cases they are optional, adverbials are a common feature of discourse relative to many other features. For example, adverbials are four to eight times more common than modal verbs (cf. 6.6.1); they are only slightly less common than lexical verbs in conversation, fiction, and news, and they are slightly more common than lexical verbs in academic prose (cf. 5.1.2).

In many cases, the information in adverbials, though grammatically optional, is crucial for fully understanding the proposition in a clause. In each of the following, for example, the adverbial is an important part of the speaker's or writer's message:

> *She threw a chair **at someone?*** (CONV)

> *It was getting dark **when Alice woke**.* (FICT)

> *Residents are hoping a children's play area will be established **on land at the Fron Heulog Estate, Bodffordd, Anglesey**.* (NEWS)

> *Researchers use their special expertise **to exploit and test the latest technology** and **to provide much needed reliable and accurate knowledge about system performance, use, and acceptance**.* (ACAD)

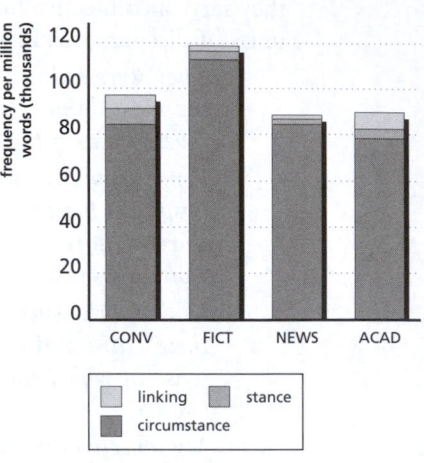

**Figure 10.1**

**Frequencies of adverbial classes in four registers**

It is thus not surprising that adverbials are a relatively common feature in English. The great variety of functions and meanings that can be expressed by adverbials (10.2.1, 10.3.1, 10.4.1), as well as their ability to co-occur in clauses (10.2.7) adds to their frequency.

Circumstance adverbials have the most varied functions of the classes of adverbials, since they can add all types of circumstantial information (e.g. place, time, process, extent). It is thus also not surprising that they are the most common class of adverbial. Fiction makes particularly frequent use of circumstance adverbials as it creates an imagined world. Adverbials are commonly used to describe the environment, the characters, and the action, and to make narrative relationships clear:

> *Color flamed [**vividly**] [**in a profusion of variegated reds and oranges**] intermingled **with magenta and purple**.* (FICT)

> *Ralph had no interest in business matters, which was evident [**at the cotton mill**] [**this morning**]. **Possessing a literary bent**, he stood out **like an abolitionist in the south**.* (FICT†)

> *The real difference between the president and myself may be that I ended **with too large an appreciation of the moon**, for I looked [**down the abyss**] [**on the first night I killed**].* (FICT)

> *Soon another clock began, **on a loud, decisive note**. **In a leisurely fashion** it gave an indisputable eight. **Then** I knew things were awry.* (FICT)

Although the other registers use circumstance adverbials for similar purposes, in general they have less emphasis on description, which is reflected in a lower frequency of circumstance adverbials.

In conversation, on the other hand, the slightly more frequent use of stance adverbials relates to the personal, interactive nature of this register. Speakers use stance adverbials to convey their judgments and attitudes, to claim the factual nature of what they are saying, and to mark exactly how they mean their utterances to be understood:

> I think you'd **probably** have a shot at your yellow. (CONV)

> There's **certainly** a fancy clubhouse. (CONV)

> I **actually** come from the Dales. (CONV)

> Put one in, put the pill in, put another one in. Yeah, **literally!** (CONV)

Finally, linking adverbials are used slightly more commonly in academic prose because this register tends to have an emphasis on conveying logical coherence and building arguments. Linking adverbials allow the writers to mark the development of their arguments, relating one proposition to another—for example, explicitly showing contrasts, restatements, and conclusions:

> All herbivore populations can grow to the points where resources become limiting, and competitive exclusion becomes likely. **However,** predators potentially can reduce herbivore numbers and eliminate competition among them. (ACAD)

> We chose the first viewpoint, **that is,** to look at activities and the regulations required by a group of people to cooperatively execute a particular activity. The model we want to develop should **therefore** allow specification of such regulations. (ACAD)

## 10.1.2 Syntactic realizations of adverbials

Adverbials are realized by a variety of syntactic forms. These are exemplified below:

- Single adverbs and adverb phrases

  > Oh she **never** does anything does she? (CONV)

  > We know each other **very well** and **frankly** we would have preferred to come out of the hat **first**. (NEWS)

- Noun phrases (including single nouns)

  > Well I went to that wedding **Saturday**. (CONV)

  > The man came to stay with them for a few weeks **each year**. (FICT)

- Prepositional phrases

  > The man came to stay **[with them] [for a few weeks]** each year. (FICT)

  > **In this chapter** three of the most important approaches are examined. (ACAD)

- Finite clauses

  > I had to turn it off earlier **because Rupert was shrieking**. (CONV)

  > **If you read these stories day by day,** you simply don't realize how many there are. (NEWS)

- Non-finite clauses. These include four major sub-classes:

*Ing*-clauses

  > He got up and refilled the teapot, then his cup, **adding a touch of skimmed milk**. (FICT†)

  > **Using an IBM 3090 supercomputer with 12 interconnected processing units and with a memory capacity of more than five billion characters of information,** the supercomputer center will explore new ways to connect even more advanced supercomputers. (NEWS)

*Ed*-clauses

> Now **added to that**—*by our wall*—*there was this ruddy great lorry again.* (CONV)
>
> *We measured a seasonal total of 56.99 cm precipitation in the two caged rain gauges,* **compared to 56.78 cm on the open plots**. (ACAD)

*To*-infinitive clauses

> *She called me* **to say a lawyer was starting divorce proceedings**. (FICT)
>
> **To reintroduce us to the joys of story telling round the log fire**, *Signals rounded up a slightly disconcerting group of five contemporary writers, all strange to me.* (NEWS)

Verbless clauses

> *One practice is to designate protons* **as if less than this**. (ACAD)
>
> *The author apologizes* **where appropriate**. (ACAD†)

## 10.1.2.1 Syntactic realizations of the three adverbial classes

### CORPUS FINDINGS [1,2]

➤ In terms of overall frequency, prepositional phrases are the most common syntactic realization of adverbials.

➤ Adverbs are also relatively common as adverbials.

➤ In comparison, finite clauses, non-finite clauses, noun phrases, and adverb phrases are relatively rare.

**Table 10.1** **Overall frequency distribution of syntactic forms of adverbials; occurrences per million words**

each ■ represents 5,000     ◻ represents less than 2,500

| | |
|---|---|
| adverbs | ■ ■ ■ ■ ■ ■ |
| adverb phrases | ◻ |
| noun phrases | ■ |
| prepositional phrases | ■ ■ ■ ■ ■ ■ ■ ■ ■ |
| finite clauses | ■ ■ |
| non-finite clauses | ■ |

➤ In terms of proportional use, only circumstance adverbials show a strong preference for prepositional phrases.

  ➤ Single adverbs account for about 20% of circumstance adverbials.

➤ In contrast, stance adverbials show a strong preference for single adverbs.

  ➤ About half of stance adverbials are realized by single adverbs.

  ➤ Prepositional phrases and finite clauses each account for about 15–20% of stance adverbials.

➤ Linking adverbials display the strongest association with a single syntactic form: almost 80% of the linking adverbials are realized by single adverbs.

### DISCUSSION OF FINDINGS

The high frequency of prepositional phrases as adverbials is due to their common use as circumstance adverbials (by far the most common class of adverbials; 10.1.1.1). Prepositional phrases are particularly suited to use as circumstance adverbials because they allow a wide range of meanings of this sort to be expressed.

The prepositions themselves can convey a wide variety of relationships and the complement of the preposition can be selected to express the specific content of the phrase. Even a small number of examples can illustrate the widely variable uses for prepositional phrases as circumstance adverbials.

Identification of location:

> *You're not **from this area** though are you?* (CONV)

Specification of the respect in which action of the verb is relevant:

> *I wish they'd stop going on **about Christmas**.* (CONV)

Identification of an agent:

> *French astronomers report that a vast, hitherto-unknown galaxy at the very edge of the universe has been purchased **by Japanese investors**.* (NEWS)

Expression of result:

> *Two patients died **as a consequence of the complications**.* (ACAD)

The meanings expressed by circumstance adverbials and the uses of other syntactic forms are discussed further in 10.2.1.

Unlike circumstance adverbials realized by a prepositional phrase, many stance and linking adverbials have a more fixed meaning. For example, the same single adverbs expressing comments of certainty/doubt and style are repeatedly used as stance adverbials in clauses with very different content:

> *That's **probably** why I've been getting low.* (CONV)
>
> *If he had shouted class or guilt after it, it would **probably** have answered.* (NEWS†)
>
> *These factors are **probably** important in the development and regeneration of the nervous system.* (ACAD)
>
> *Well that's true **of course**.* (CONV)
>
> *There must be a limit to how much cloth you can cram into any one house, but **of course** it's disposable.* (FICT)
>
> *I do not, **of course**, wish to argue that the writing of the authors discussed in this book represent the only significant streams of social thought.* (ACAD†)
>
> ***Frankly** I think that's very bad.* (CONV)
>
> ***Frankly** I don't know why I sit here drinking with you.* (FICT)
>
> ***Frankly**, few societies would have tackled even the choreography of this week's presentation.* (NEWS)

Interestingly, the finite clauses and prepositional phrases realizing stance adverbials also tend to be more fixed expressions than the prepositional phrases realizing circumstance adverbials:

**Figure 10.2**

**Syntactic realizations of adverbial classes**

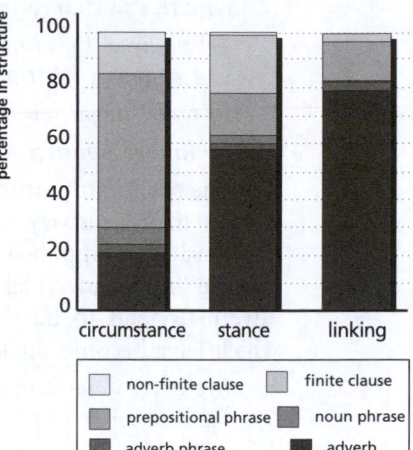

*If you want my opinion, the old boy's a terrifically distinguished citizen of Wales.* (FICT†)

*Egypt, it seems, is not preparing or more realistically, does not have the resources to change the environment.* (NEWS)

*Yet many of the crowd were kept interested by the possibility of victory, which is, I suppose, what derbies are about.* (NEWS)

*In fact I might not even need to vacuum the floor.* (CONV)

*By any reckoning, Alun has done some good things.* (FICT)

The particularly strong preference of linking adverbials for single adverbs also reflects their relatively fixed nature and more restricted repertoire. The same relationship (exemplified below with contrast or concession) is often marked with a single linking adverbial in texts with very different content. These fixed linking adverbials tend to be single adverbs (including some multi-word expressions which have become single words, such as *nevertheless*):

*I've never done it in the office, I've always gone, I've always probably gone in the canteen or in the of– in the, in the wagon thing <...> and yet I'm being nailed.* (CONV)

*It filled me with fear, and yet I longed to be nearer to it.* (FICT)

*She would not let me take her home no doubt because she was ashamed of her house in these slums. Nevertheless, she spoke wonderfully about her childhood.* (FICT)

*A further £13 a week goes on fuel. Nevertheless, families still manage to set aside £40.90 a week for leisure goods and services.* (NEWS)

*The 29 other defendants were found not guilty and acquitted. Only eight were released, however, because the other 21 face a second trial for "economic crimes".* (NEWS†)

*Biliary endoprosthesis insertion for choledocholithiasis is an important alternative means of establishing drainage in selective cases <...>. Caution must be exercised, however, in patients with an in situ gall bladder.* (ACAD)

Prepositional phrases used as linking adverbials, like those for stance adverbials, also tend to be more fixed phrases than those used as circumstance adverbials:

*"Gossip is mischievous, light and easy to raise, but grievous to bear and hard to get rid of." In other words, mud sticks.* (NEWS†)

*While further compounding the small numbers problem, there were interesting differences between the two course types. For example, specialist students of control were almost twice as likely to be in work than those pursuing control in conversion mode.* (ACAD)

*The promiscuous princess quickly becomes a pawn. As a result, the aging princess becomes bitter and cynical about men.* (ACAD)

Further details about the syntactic realizations of stance adverbials can be found in 10.3.2 and about linking adverbials in 10.4.2.

## 10.1.3 Positions of adverbials in the clause

As described in 10.1, an important characteristic of adverbials is that they can occur in a variety of positions in a clause. Four major positions can be distinguished, with some positions including more than one variant. It is also possible for more than one adverbial to occur at each of the positions.

## A Initial

The adverbial is in the first position in the clause, occurring before the subject or other obligatory elements of the clause:

> *In the nature of things, a good many somebodies are always in hospital.* (FICT)

> *[Generally], [however], the plants under consideration have been annuals, seedlings or cuttings of perennials grown under controlled conditions.* (ACAD)

## B Medial

This includes all positions between obligatory initial and final clausal elements. Several more specific positions can be distinguished. First, adverbials can be placed between the subject and the beginning of the verb phrase:

> *Jean **never** put anything away.* (CONV)

> *Mr. Chris Patten, the environment secretary, **yesterday** moved to mitigate the effects of the inland revenue revaluation.* (NEWS)

When an operator (3.2.9) is present, the adverbial can be placed after the operator before the main verb:

> *Carrie had **often** dreamed about coming back.* (FICT)

> *The utilisation of computers is not **of course** limited to business.* (ACAD)

Adverbials can also be placed after the main verb but preceding other obligatory elements of the clause, such as obligatory adverbials, subject predicatives, and direct objects. When this placement occurs with *be* as a main verb, it can be considered a special case of placement immediately after the operator:

> *It is **still** three weeks away.* (CONV)

> *For it is **no longer** a casino.* (FICT)

However, adverbials are also occasionally placed after other main verbs:

> *Kathy Acker's off-the-shoulder dress displayed **to advantage** her collection of off-the-shoulder tattoos.* (NEWS)

In this example the adverbial precedes the direct object of *displayed*.

## C Final

The adverbial is in the final position in the clause, after all obligatory elements (though it may not be the last element if there are other final adverbials in the same clause):

> *And he's trailing some **[in the back window] [as well]**.* (CONV)

> *There was an extensive literature on agriculture in Roman times which maintained a pre-eminent position **until comparatively recently**.* (ACAD)

## D Other speaker main clause

In conversation and occasionally in dialog in fiction, speakers will co-construct clauses or clarify each others' speech so that one speaker adds an adverbial to another speaker's utterance, for example:

> *A: I mean you don't have to pay for those.*
> *B: Oh **for the films*** (CONV)

In these cases, when the second utterance is clearly an adverbial relating to the first speaker's utterance, the position is identified as **other speaker main clause**.

In some cases, particularly due to the fragmented nature of conversation, adverbials occur without a main verb in a clause. In the following excerpt, for example, the meaning clearly is 'your potato fork is on the table', but it is impossible to assign a precise position to the adverbial:

> *Are you gonna have a potato fork? There you are.* **On the table***.* (CONV)

In cases such as this, the position of the adverbial has not been classified.

## 10.1.3.1 Frequencies of positions of adverbials

**CORPUS FINDINGS** [1,3]

➤ In overall frequency, final position is by far the most common position of adverbials.
➤ Initial and medial positions are relatively common, while adverbials connected to other speakers' main clauses are rare.

**Table 10.2** **Overall frequency distribution for positions of adverbials; occurrences per million words**

each ■ represents 2,000    ▫ represents less than 1,000

| | |
|---|---|
| initial | ■■■■■■■ |
| medial | ■■■■■■■■■■ |
| final | ■■■■■■■■■■■■■■■■ |
| | ■■■■■■■■■■■■■■■ |
| other speaker main clause | ▫ |

Figure 10.3 displays, for each class of adverbial, the percentage of the adverbials occurring in each position. Because other speaker main clauses are so rare, this position is omitted from the figure.

➤ Each class of adverbial has a strong preference for a different position:
  ➤ Circumstance adverbials in final position.
  ➤ Stance adverbials in medial positions.
  ➤ Linking adverbials in initial position.

**DISCUSSION OF FINDINGS**

The high frequency of final position overall is due largely to circumstance adverbials' preference for this position. This preference is associated with the fact that many circumstance adverbials complete the meaning of the verb (in the basic clause patterns with obligatory adverbials, SVA$_c$ and SVO$_d$A$_c$; 3.5.2, 3.5.9). As such, they must follow the verb. In the following examples, the adverbials must be placed in final position in their clauses:

**Figure 10.3**
**Positions of adverbial classes**

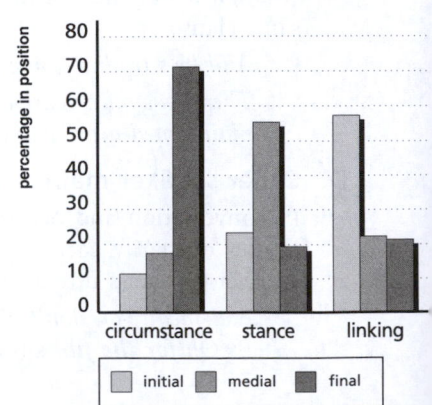

> Whoever put this plant **on the stairs** didn't realize we've got silly people like you in the house. (CONV)
>
> How can I thank you **for acceding to my request?** (FICT)

Other circumstance adverbials, however, can be placed in initial and medial positions:

> It's **only** three weeks, isn't it? (CONV)
>
> Deutsche Bank, the giant German banking group, will **today** make a move into the British fund management market. (NEWS)
>
> **Here** there was an intention to devise the necessary conditions for the most efficient and effective method of administration. (ACAD)

Factors associated with the positions of circumstance adverbials include semantic category, syntactic structure, and length. These are examined in 10.2.6 (for adverbials realized by structures other than clauses) and in 10.2.8.6 (for clausal adverbials).

Since stance adverbials typically have scope over the proposition of the entire clause, they can be placed more freely in all positions. The position which accounts for the highest percentage of stance adverbials—medial—has a number of variants. Medial stance adverbials are most commonly realized with the adverbial placed immediately after the operator:

> We'll **perhaps** change them when you get home. (CONV)
>
> They are **probably** there now. (CONV)
>
> I shall **definitely** be at the airport to meet you. (FICT)
>
> The defendant would, **in all probability**, have been forced to give consideration then to the making of a claim. (NEWS†)
>
> There is **actually** a very sound reason why Ray chose this amount. (NEWS)

Medial position is also commonly realized with the stance adverbial placed immediately after the subject. This position occurs in clauses both with and without an operator.

Clauses with an operator:

> They **certainly** have made a breakthrough in understanding the effect of light in humans. (NEWS)
>
> Caring workers **generally** are 'entrusted' with a burden of responsibility which many people would find impossible. (ACAD)

Clauses without an operator:

> The word gossip itself **actually** means 'God's kin'. (NEWS)
>
> That, **of course**, means plenty of the flaky white stuff. (NEWS)

In addition, initial and final positions are used with stance adverbials of all sorts, though stance adverbials commenting on the style of the clause are particularly common in initial position:

Stance adverbials in initial position:

> But **personally** I find it quite a relief. (CONV)
>
> Well **honestly** I I don't know. (CONV)
>
> **Of course**, I did not have any illusion that my heroism was equal to his. (FICT)

Stance adverbials in final position:

> *A: Did you take that out or did I?*
> *B: It was already out **actually**.* (CONV)

> *And then there had come this Belgian stranger all the way from England, **it seemed**.* (FICT)

> *Still, the new 911 is a better car than the old one, **as you'd expect**.* (NEWS)

Many forms used as stance adverbials can appear in all positions. Thus, in the examples below, *apparently* occurs in initial position in **1**, medial position immediately following the subject in **2**, medial position immediately following the operator in **3**, and final position **4**:

> **1** *Well **apparently** she said it stands her in good stead.* (CONV)
> **2** *Arphia pseudonietana and psoleoessa texana **apparently** were much more abundant in the wet summer of 1990.* (ACAD)
> **3** *The throne is **apparently** in no danger at all.* (NEWS)
> **4** *Words helped them, **apparently**.* (FICT)

Clearly, of the three classes, stance adverbials are the most mobile. However, there are also several important associations between the positions of stance adverbials and registers; these are covered in 10.3.4.

Linking adverbials are most often used in initial position, so that the connection between two clauses is clearly signalled as the reader or hearer moves from the first clause to the second. In the following text samples, for instance, the reader's or hearer's processing of the discourse is facilitated by the initial linking adverbials specifically marking the relationship between clauses—a relationship which is additive in **5**, contrastive in **6**, and listing in **7**:

> **5** *You go, you're going too slow. **Besides**, if you didn't understand how to do that <...>* (CONV)
> **6** *The bookmakers, showing unusual generosity, gave them a 44-point advantage on the handicap betting list. **Instead**, with only 10 minutes left, Dewsbury led 12–6 and a genuine upset was in the offing.* (NEWS)
> **7** *One is the role of the masses of third world indigenous peoples <...>. **Secondly**, it addressed the issue of the importance, in our models of economic development, of cultural factors.* (ACAD)

However, certain linking adverbials also commonly occur in final position:

> *What's the matter? It's confidential **anyway**.* (CONV)

> *They're digging in aren't they? Loosen it a bit **then**.* (CONV)

> *Feedback systems are common in both the natural world and the works of man. It is reasonable to model predator-prey systems as feedback systems, **for example**.* (ACAD)

It turns out that the use of final position, as well as the more rarely used medial positions, have important associations with register, semantic role, and the particular linking adverbial being used. These factors are considered in 10.4.4.

## 10.1.4   Adverbial variation in relation to other elements

As explained in 10.1, one of the distinguishing characteristics of adverbials is that they are elements of clauses, not constituents of phrases. However, the exact status of adverbials relative to other clausal elements varies. Some of this variation has been noted above (10.1.1). For example, some circumstance adverbials have scope over the entire proposition in a clause, while others primarily complete the meaning of the verb. Similarly, some linking adverbials serve to connect whole paragraphs, while others link main and non-finite clauses. However, certain adverbials deserve further attention because they have an even more subordinate relationship to clause elements.

All three classes of adverbials contain items that, through their meaning and position, can focus on a particular part of the clause, rather than being an equal element in the clause. For circumstance adverbials, these items most commonly serve to restrict or minimize the meaning of some other element of the clause:

  1 *It's **just** a hassle.* (CONV)

  2 *I was **only** joking.* (CONV)

  3 *The kids had "superhero sundaes" which turned out to be **merely** ice cream.* (NEWS†)

In these examples, the effect of the adverbial is focused on the immediately following element in the clause—in **1** on *a hassle*, in **2** on *joking*, and **3** on *ice cream*. Such items therefore have a more subordinate relationship to the clause than adverbials that have scope over the entire proposition. Often, this more subordinate relationship is associated with less mobility than other adverbials allow. For instance, it is not possible to say, *\*It's a hassle just.* Nevertheless, these items are not simply constituents of phrases; for example, it is possible to move *just* to follow the subject (*It just is a hassle*). Such items are therefore included as adverbials in this chapter.

Stance adverbials may also focus on a particular clause element:

  4 *It was all that running around that made it **sort of** hurt.* (CONV)

  5 *In short, I am **literally** disintegrating.* (FICT†)

In **4** *sort of* emphasizes the imprecision of the term *hurt* and in **5** *literally* seems to refer specifically to the disintegration. They are thus more local in scope than many stance adverbials. However, they are not integrated into the structure of a phrase; it is possible to move *sort of* to a position before the verb (*… that sort of made it hurt*) or to final position (*… that made it hurt sort of*), or to move *literally* to initial position (*Literally, I am disintegrating*) without substantially altering the meaning. Thus, these items too are considered adverbials.

In contrast, consider the hedging adverbs *approximately* and *about* in **6** and **7**:

  6 *Coverage is scheduled to begin at **approximately** 3 p.m. EDT.* (NEWS)

  7 ***About** 300 striking officers gathered on a downtown street.* (NEWS†)

In **6** *approximately* clearly modifies *3 p.m.* and in **7** *about* modifies *300*. Adverbs such as these are therefore not considered adverbials.

Finally, certain linking adverbials have more local functions in that they connect clauses to phrases or phrases to phrases:

  8 *The principles of care for many of the patients in the ward may be similar, **e.g.** the preparation carried out pre-operatively to ensure the safety of patients undergoing surgery.* (ACAD)

  9 *He recorded what was really there in the rocks, **that is to say** repeated and sudden changes in environments and extinctions of animals and plants.* (ACAD)

In **8**, *e.g.* links a noun phrase to the main clause; in **9**, *that is to say* links the following noun phrase to the direct object in the main clause (*what was really there in the rocks*). Although these structures are less clearly elements of a clause than many linking adverbials, they continue to function as linking adverbials do, showing how the writer is connecting two units of discourse. They are therefore included as adverbials in the analyses of this chapter.

## 10.2 Circumstance adverbials

We begin by looking overall at the semantic subcategories and syntactic realizations of circumstance adverbials (10.2.1–3). We then move on to consider aspects of circumstance adverbials realized as structures other than clauses (10.2.4–6), the ordering of adverbials when several occur in series (10.2.7), and circumstance adverbials realized as clauses (10.2.8).

### 10.2.1 Semantic categories of circumstance adverbials

Seven major semantic categories can be identified for circumstance adverbials, with several of the major categories having subcategories within them:
- Place: distance; direction; position
- Time: position in time; duration; frequency; temporal relationship
- Process: manner (subcategories: manner proper; comparison; accompaniment); means; instrument; agent
- Contingency: reason/cause; purpose; concession; condition; result
- Extent/degree: amplifier; diminisher
- Addition/restriction: addition; restriction
- Recipient
- Other

Each category, as well as the overlap among categories and certain ambiguous forms, is introduced below.

#### 10.2.1.1 Place

**Place** circumstance adverbials can convey **distance**, **direction**, or **position**.

Distance adverbials typically answer the question 'How far?', and include both general descriptions of distance and specific measurements:

> I had to go **a long way** to put the camp behind me. (FICT)

> He had travelled **some miles**, his horse and he. (FICT)

> A woman who fell **50 feet** down a cliff was rescued by a Royal Navy helicopter. (NEWS)

Direction adverbials describe the pathway of an action. Some give a general orientation of the direction (e.g. *southwards*), while others describe direction from a point of origin (e.g. *from here*) or towards a destination (e.g. *to the capitol*):

> And they went **from here** about – nine-ish, I suppose? (CONV)

> The Ethiopian army is failing to halt northern rebels advancing rapidly **[southwards] [to the capitol and its vital lifeline road]**. (NEWS)

> *You will admit that when you bring dung **into the field** it is to return to the soil something that has been taken away.* (ACAD)

Position adverbials occur most often with stative verbs. However, as the following examples illustrate, they also occur with communication and activity verbs (e.g. *discuss* and *build up*):

> *It would be, be cold **up there**.* (CONV)
>
> *A Panamanian passenger bus lay **in a ditch**.* (NEWS)
>
> *The implications of this comparison will be discussed further **in Section 2.4**.* (ACAD)
>
> *In the process an information model is built up **on a computer database*** (ACAD†)

## 10.2.1.2 Time

**Time** circumstance adverbials are used to convey four time-related meanings.

First, these adverbials can indicate **position in time**, telling when an event took place:

> *I'll see you all **tomorrow night**.* (CONV)
>
> *Perhaps we can put that right **in January**.* (NEWS)
>
> *It is not uncommon **nowadays** to have many hundreds of cattle in one building.* (ACAD)

Another meaning of time adverbials is **duration**, describing how long an event lasted:

> *I wouldn't like to go **for a week** in silence.* (CONV)
>
> *It lasted **years**.* (CONV)
>
> *Some observers are predicting the imminent collapse of the military regime which has ruled Ethiopia **for fifteen years**.* (NEWS)

Time adverbials can also convey **frequency**, describing how often an event occurs:

> *I know but you don't have to do it **every single day**, do you?* (CONV)
>
> *They wouldn't want to wash **very often**, would they.* (CONV)
>
> ***Occasionally** she would like to gaze out the window.* (FICT)
>
> *Soon he was working **once or twice a week** round the local pubs.* (NEWS†)
>
> *Furthermore, the term register is **sometimes** used to refer to <...>* (ACAD†)

Finally, time adverbials can convey the **temporal relationship** between two events/states:

> *I want to er clean the floor **before I take a load of stuff in**.* (CONV)
>
> ***After this** the conversation sank for a while into mere sociability.* (FICT)
>
> *Note that the store location accessed **still** contains a copy of the information.* (ACAD†)

## 10.2.1.3 Process

**Process** circumstance adverbials cover a wide range of semantic roles and are a less unified group than place or time adverbials.

The most common subcategory of process adverbials is **manner**, which describes the way in which something is done:

We were **frantically** doing that painting. (CONV)

I found myself writing **slowly**, and rewriting, **[piecemeal]**, **[endlessly]**. (FICT)

This is blue-sky country where they play their music **in that western way**. (NEWS†)

Adverbials of **comparison** can also be considered manner adverbials, comparing the manner of a state or action relative to another:

There are few better exponents of the art of looking **as though life is a complete grind**. (NEWS†)

Then I would go through the refrigerator **like a vacuum cleaner**, sucking in whatever there was. (FICT)

The lip curled **like a snail's foot**, the left nostril gaped. (FICT)

We also include under manner those adverbials that show **accompaniment**. As the following examples illustrate, these adverbials lie along a continuum from clearly conveying manner to encompassing more ambiguous meanings:

1  I had dinner **with Clay** the other night. (CONV†)

2  I would feel safer leaving **with somebody else** anyway. (CONV)

3  He's coming downstairs **with two sleeping bags over the top of his head**. (CONV)

Some occurrences, such as examples **1** and **2**, contain adverbials that show physical accompaniment. Though they are not always obvious answers to a 'How?' question, they can be replaced with the opposite manner adverbials such as *independently* or *by myself* and thus fit the manner category most clearly. However, other occurrences, as in **3**, are more ambiguous. In some sense, the adverbial in **3** conveys information about the manner of 'coming downstairs', but the precise semantic relationship between the adverbial and the rest of the clause is difficult to define. See 10.2.1.9 for further discussion of ambiguity in the meanings of circumstance adverbials.

Process circumstance adverbials also include the subcategory of **means**—that is, adverbials telling the means by which an activity or state was accomplished:

The US, as the country of origin for the uranium, had originally insisted that shipments be made **by air**. (NEWS)

We examined this question **by excluding birds for 3 years from experimental plots**. (ACAD)

Further, process adverbials include **instrument** adverbials, describing the item used to undertake a task:

Well you can listen to what you've taped **with headphones**. (CONV)

She tried a bottle; when it could not suck from the bottle she fed it **with a teaspoon**. (FICT†)

He wrenched up a piece of the road **with splintering finger-nails**. (FICT†)

Finally, agentive adverbials specify the **agent** of an action and are used with passive constructions (corresponding to the subject of an active voice construction; 3.2.1.1):

The naked crooks of his knees were plump, caught and scratched **by thorns**. (FICT)

Empirical data show that similar processes can be guided quite differently **by users with different views on the purpose of the communication**. (ACAD)

## 10.2.1.4 Contingency

Like the category of process, **contingency** is a more diverse category than time and place. This category covers circumstance adverbials that show how one event or state is contingent upon another, including: **cause**, **reason**, **purpose**, **concession**, **condition**, and **result**.

Despite the diversity in the category, several of the subcategories are closely related. In particular, cause and reason both answer the question 'Why?'. Traditionally, cause has been associated with a relatively objective statement, as in **1**, while reason has implied a more subjective assessment, as in **2**:

1 *He was buried under bricks, and died **of head injuries**.* (NEWS)

2 *He's quite frightened **cos he doesn't know you**.* (CONV†)

In the majority of cases, however, it is difficult to judge the level of objectivity and thus to discern between cause and reason, as with the following examples:

*Well I can imagine other people wearing big earrings **because they're super confident**.* (CONV)

***Because Allitt opted not to go into the witness box**, the defence case lasted just two and a half days.* (NEWS†)

For this reason, further analyses in this section conflate the cause/reason subcategories.

Purpose adverbials can be paraphrased as 'for the purpose of', as in the following examples:

*I've got to talk to you **to explain what we're doing**.* (CONV)

*They were pussy cats, and although some of them carried weapons, the knives were just **for show**.* (FICT)

*Other life insurers sought to increase their distribution networks, either increasing their branches or their personnel in a variety of ways **in order to market their products in increasingly competitive environments**.* (NEWS)

Purpose adverbials are also closely related to reason adverbials; it is possible, for instance, to paraphrase the first example above as 'The reason I've got to talk to you is to explain what we're doing.'

Concessive circumstance adverbials are used to express material that runs counter to the proposition of the rest of the clause or, in the case of adverbials realized as clauses, counter to the proposition in the main clause:

*1700 miners have been out for seven months and, **despite intimidation**, no one has gone back to work.* (NEWS)

***Although it has been used by others**, this book is written for beginning students who have had no previous college science courses.* (ACAD†)

*I suppose I wanted her timeless, **though there is no such thing on earth**.* (FICT)

Conditional adverbials express the conditions which hold on the proposition of the main clause, including both positive and negative conditions:

*And **if you were in the mood** we could at least go.* (CONV†)

***If she smiles** it will be at your hairline.* (CONV)

*These people cannot operate **unless they receive support**.* (NEWS†)

> *Should a variety prove unsuitable under a given set of climatic and soil conditions*, continuous cultivation is unlikely to render it more tolerant to these unfavorable conditions. (ACAD)

### 10.2.1.5 Extent/degree

**Extent/degree** circumstance adverbials tell the extent to which a proposition holds, answering questions such as 'How much/many?' and 'To what extent?'

Extent/degree adverbials can show amounts, either in exact terms or more generally:

> *She's getting on **a bit** now.* (CONV)
>
> *Our estimate puts government losses in the past four weeks **at 22,000 killed, captured, or deserted**.* (NEWS)
>
> *The government had predicted that rateable values would rise **by about seven times**.* (NEWS†)

They can either amplify the intensity of the clause proposition, sometimes called **amplifiers** or **intensifiers**, or lower the intensity, also called **diminishers**.

Amplifiers (see 7.14.2.4A):

> *In places the grass was gone **altogether**.* (FICT†)
>
> *She looked **very much** like her mother.* (FICT)
>
> *The idea is for them eventually to be restored **completely**.* (NEWS†)

Diminishers (see 7.14.2.4B):

> *You know, I think you can fix it by pulling the prongs out **a little bit**.* (CONV)
>
> *He **hardly** dared to look at what was framed in the hole in the sheet.* (FICT)
>
> *The land tenure system varies **slightly** from place to place.* (ACAD†)

### 10.2.1.6 Addition/restriction

**Additive** adverbials, show that a current proposition is being added to a previous one:

> 1 *Someday you'll be old, **too**, Carol.* (CONV†)
> 2 *Known in Bolivia as the 'Minister of Cocaine', Mr. Arce Gomez **also** has a grisly human rights reputation.* (NEWS†)
> 3 *The tycoon, who is **also** chairman of Dublin-based independent newspapers, now has a 1.3 shareholding.* (NEWS†)

It is important to note that these additive circumstance adverbials have a slightly different focus from linking adverbials of addition (10.4.1.1). Unlike linking adverbials, additive circumstance adverbials do not serve primarily to link units of discourse. Rather, their primary purpose is to show that one bit of propositional content is being added to a previously mentioned idea or entity. In **1**, for example, the speaker is saying that Carol, as well as some other previously mentioned person, or as well as having some other attribute, will some day be old. However, both additive circumstance adverbials and linking adverbials of addition contribute to the cohesion in a text, and at times the two may be difficult to distinguish.

**Restrictive** adverbials emphasize that the proposition is true in a way which expressly excludes some other possibilities:

> *A heart born **especially** for me, Jackie used to tease.* (FICT)

*The villagers say jokingly that **only** a sick man would choose such a remote place to build.* (FICT)

*That is, the time taken to access a store location in order to store or retrieve information is constant and **in particular** is independent of the particular location being accessed.* (ACAD†)

In some cases, adverbials combine qualities of both the restrictive and extent/ degree categories. Particularly the adverb *just*, common in conversation, often seems to have qualities of both restricting the action and lessening the intensity:

*I **just** want to show you the tape I bought.* (CONV)

*It's **just** that he wanted to see Jenny in front of everyone else* (CONV)

*Well they **just** fell behind you know.* (CONV)

The role of *just* is discussed further in 10.2.5.

A feature shared by additive and restrictive adverbials is that, unlike many other adverbials, they often cannot be moved without affecting their meaning in the clause. The position of the adverbial is important in determining what element of the clause is the focus of the addition or restriction. Thus, the following pairs of sentences are not equivalent:

*A heart born **especially** for me, Jackie used to tease.* (FICT)
***Especially** a heart born for me, Jackie used to tease.*

*Mr. Arce Gomez **also** has a grisly human rights reputation.* (NEWS†)
***Also** Mr. Arce Gomez has a grisly human rights reputation.*

### 10.2.1.7 Recipient

**Recipient** adverbials (including what are sometimes called **benefactive** adverbials, typically expressed by *for*-phrases) identify the target of an action. In the majority of cases, the recipient is a person or group of people:

1 *Did you hear what happened **to me**?* (CONV)
2 *Yeah well you used to do that **to me**.* (CONV)
3 *Okay and then I'll just write the check **for you**.* (CONV)
4 *OHA will present the referendum results **to the Democrat-controlled Legislature**.* (NEWS)

However, other animate and even inanimate objects can occur in recipient adverbials, as in **5** and **6**:

5 *Special cages have been developed **for wild mice**.* (ACAD)
6 *I think we're getting that **for our house**.* (CONV)

Recipient adverbials occur both in contexts that show volition (**3–6** above) and those that do not, as in **1**. Some instances analyzed in this chapter as recipient adverbials could be analyzed alternatively as instances of prepositional verbs with objects (see 5.3.3).

### 10.2.1.8 Other semantic relationships

Certain circumstance adverbials do not fit well within any of the above categories. These adverbials have less clearly defined semantic relationships with the rest of the clause. In many cases, they serve in some way to show in what **respect** the action or state described in the clause is relevant or true. Consider the following examples:

1 *It's lovely in here – sheltered* **from the wind.** (CONV)

2 *Each one fled at once the moment the house committed what was* **for him** *the one insult not to be borne or witnessed a second time.* (FICT)

3 *<...> but we would point out that if the council goes ahead* **with the plan,** *it will be ratepayers who are going to bear the cost.* (NEWS†)

In **1**, the adverbial specifies in what respect the participants are sheltered (i.e. *from the wind*); in **2**, the adverbial specifies the person with respect to whom the insult is said by the author to be unbearable (*for him*); and in **3**, the adverbial specifies in what respect the council is going ahead (*with the plan*). Describing the exact relationship between the adverbial and the rest of the clause in such cases is difficult, however. Some adverbials that could alternatively be analyzed as prepositional verb + prepositional object are difficult to classify:

*I might have been concerned* **about my hair.** (CONV†)

*She could not bring herself to speak* **about what was disturbing her.** (FICT)

*Other studies focus* **on new kinds of pavement that would help break the grip of ice.** (NEWS)

*People always protest* **against new forms of taxation.** (NEWS)

*The movements of the eye adjust* **to that function.** (ACAD)

*They argued that an interpretation in terms of the relative potency of crossed and uncrossed pathways could not account* **for this result.** (ACAD)

Some of these verb + adverbial combinations specify topics (e.g. *be concerned about ...*, *speak about ...*, *focus on ...*). However, they also add information about actions in other ways (e.g. *protest against ...*, *adjust to ...*, *account for ...*). In fact, the preposition may depend more on the choice of verb rather than being a free choice on its own. Structures of this type actually represent a cline, ranging from clear instances of prepositional verb + prepositional object at one extreme to clear instances of verb + adverbial prepositional phrase at the other extreme.

## 10.2.1.9 **Overlap and ambiguity**

Although many circumstance adverbials clearly fit only one of the seven major semantic categories, not all occurrences of circumstance adverbials are so clear cut.

First, there are many cases in which adverbials fit primarily into one category, but have secondary roles that fit another semantic category. Manner adverbials in particular often include aspects of another semantic category; for example, *slowly* and *quickly* in the examples below are not only descriptions of the manner of an action, but can also be interpreted as describing duration:

*I've started but it's going* **rather slowly.** (CONV)

*They evidently expected him to go* **quickly.** (FICT)

Other manner adverbials can include a meaning of extent/degree:

*They have no desire to investigate this matter* **properly.** (NEWS)

*The disease pattern has changed* **radically.** (ACAD)

In addition, certain adverbials have extremely ambiguous meanings. The ambiguity in the use of *just* as restrictive and extent/degree was noted above. *Ing-*clauses often present an even greater problem for interpretation. These clauses typically have an implicit and somewhat ill-defined relationship with the main clause. Consider the following:

1  *Watching him as the days went by*, the guilty collector had noticed signs of physical and moral decline. (FICT)

2  *Three weeks ago Swedish and Scottish police searched Talb's flat in Uppsala, **removing fifteen bags of clothing**. (NEWS)

3  *The result of the operation is placed in the accumulator, **destroying its previous contents**. (ACAD)

In **1**, the adverbial clause could be interpreted as showing a concurrent time relationship (i.e. while watching him, the collector noticed the decline) or as giving a reason (i.e. because he watched him, the collector noticed the decline). In **2** and **3**, the adverbial clause could be interpreted as describing a result, a concurrent time relationship, or an event that happened in a time sequence. The distribution and uses of this semantically ambiguous form, termed **supplementive clause**, is discussed further in 10.2.8.1 and 10.2.8.2.

Circumstance adverbials can also serve functions similar to linking adverbials. Much of the information in circumstance adverbials creates cohesion with information that has come before. For example, the time adverbials *then* and *meanwhile* show the connection between the events in the previous clause and the subsequent clause:

He plonked the bottle on the table, and shambled muttering round the corner. ***Then*** *he put his head back into sight.* (FICT)

*The 21 sambas originally submitted were whittled to one.* ***Meanwhile****, seamstresses and tailors all over Rio made costumes.* (NEWS)

With adverbials such as these, the connective function is made semantically, through the circumstantial information which indicates time relationships. Thus, they are still categorized as circumstance adverbials.

The circumstance categories of addition and contingency also occasionally exhibit similarities with linking adverbials (see 10.2.1.6 for discussion of the former, and 10.4.1 for linking adverbials in general).

## 10.2.2  Distribution of semantic categories

In Figure 10.4, the 'others' category includes recipient and extent/degree adverbials, as well as the items classified as 'other' above.

### CORPUS FINDINGS [1]

➤  Place, time, process, and contingency are the four most common categories of adverbials in all four registers; however, their order of frequency varies across registers:
  ➤ In conversation, time and place are almost equally the most common.
  ➤ In fiction, place, process, and time are all frequent, following that order.
  ➤ In news, time dominates, followed by place, then process.
  ➤ In academic prose, only process stands out.
➤  Within the category of process adverbials, manner is by far the most common subcategory in all four registers.
  ➤ Agentive adverbials are moderately common only in news and academic prose.
  ➤ The means and instrument subcategories are rare in all four registers.

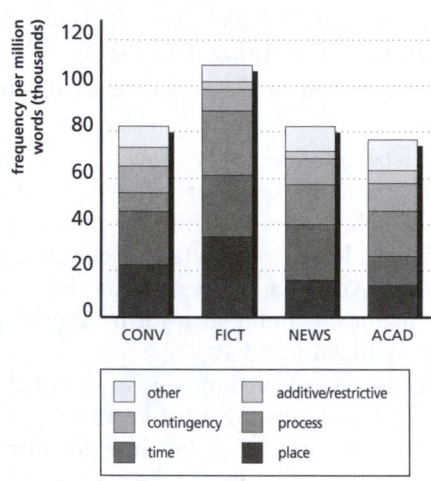

**Figure 10.4**
**Frequency of semantic categories for circumstance adverbials, by register**

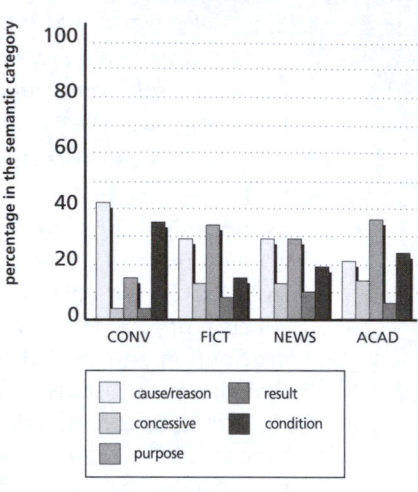

**Figure 10.5**
**Semantic categories of contingency circumstance adverbials**

➤ Within the category of contingency, cause/reason, purpose, and condition are the most common subcategories in all four registers; however, their proportional use varies across registers:
  ➤ In conversation, cause/reason and condition dominate.
  ➤ In fiction and news, cause/reason and purpose are most common.
  ➤ In academic prose, purpose is most common, followed equally by cause/reason and condition.

**Table 10.3**    **Proportional breakdown of subcategories within process adverbials within each register**

each ■ represents 5%     ▢ represents less than 2.5%

| | manner | agent | means and instrument |
|---|---|---|---|
| CONV | ■■■■■■■■■■■■■■■■■■■ | ▢ | ▢ |
| FICT | ■■■■■■■■■■■■■■■■■■■ | ■ | ▢ |
| NEWS | ■■■■■■■■■■■■■ | ■■■ | ■■ |
| ACAD | ■■■■■■■■■■■■ | ■■■ | ■■■ |

**DISCUSSION OF FINDINGS**

The distribution of semantic categories for circumstance adverbials reflects the major concerns of the four registers. Conversation is concerned to a large extent with the actions of interlocutors or other people. Place and time adverbials provide important information about the location and time of these actions:

> *I have to be [at her house] [at seven o'clock].* (CONV)

> *Well, they're <the police> just doing their job. Otherwise, people would park [anywhere] [all the time].* (CONV)

> *I still need to do a couple more drawings.* (CONV)

Fiction, on the whole, is more concerned with description than conversation is. As noted in 10.1.1.1, the circumstance adverbials in fiction are often used to create an imaginary setting and narrate characters' actions, as in this example:

> *[Now] [for the first time] he touched her skin, the skin of her forehead* **with his fingertips**. *<...> His instinct was to lift her up and carry her* **[down the hillside] [to the village]**. *He was strong enough to do that* **without effort**.
> (FICT)

In this passage, place adverbials identify locations and directions (*down the hillside, to the village*). The process adverbials (the instrument adverbial *with his fingertips* and the manner adverbial *without effort*) describe actions, while time adverbials clarify the sequence of events (*now, for the first time*). The multiple adverbials, even in this short passage, all work together in creating the fictional description.

News is particularly concerned with current events. Time adverbials are therefore commonly used to make clear when events happened or to give background leading up to the current event. Process adverbials provide information about how actions were undertaken (manner adverbials) and who was responsible (agentive adverbials). Place adverbials fill in details about the location of the story or actions that took place as part of the story. Thus, the adverbials help to provide the information typically considered important in news stories: when, how, who, where?

> *The first Pakamacs were made* **[by a Manchester company] [in 1949]**. **Within 15 years**, *60,000 were being sold* **a week**, *and they were exported* **to more than 60 countries**. *But production stopped* **[in the Eighties] [when they became unfashionable]**. *Now S Casket, the Manchester firm which bought the brand name* **in 1988**, *is unleashing a new version* **on the rained-upon British**. (NEWS)

Seven of the ten adverbials in this sample relate to time. Furthermore, use of the agentive adverbial allows mention of the agent, even though it is not particularly important to the story (and thus is not used as the subject of the clause). In addition, the example illustrates how information about location can be included in structures other than adverbials (e.g. *a Manchester company, the rained-upon British*), which contributes to the lower frequency of place adverbials relative to time adverbials in news.

In academic prose, the use of adverbials contributes to making information more precise. Process adverbials are commonly used to give details about how things are done, and to provide descriptions of the results of studies:

> *Approximately equal amounts of each are powdered and mixed together* **thoroughly**. (CONV)

> *This approach is then illustrated* **conceptually** *by discussion of a central issue in Marxist anthropology, the analysis of work.* (ACAD)

> *In the scirpus community, root growth was* **evenly** *distributed throughout the 15-cm profile.* (ACAD†)

> *<...> and 7 of these responded* **significantly** *and* **positively** *to the experiment by 1990 (table 1).* (ACAD†)

As in news, agentive process adverbials are also used in academic prose to identify agents when passive voice is used:

> One community was dominated **by the perennial carbon 4 grass Spartina patens**. (ACAD†)
>
> Amongst the most influential criticisms have been those made **by Child (1972)**. (ACAD†)
>
> The disparity in number of phonetics identified **by these scholars** reflects the differences of opinion. (ACAD†)

See 11.3 for further discussion of the passive voice.

Although contingency adverbials are relatively common in all four registers, particular subcategories are preferred in each one, further reflecting their different communicative concerns. Thus, conversation's greater use of reason and condition adverbials is also consistent with its concern for participants' actions. These adverbials often clarify the reasons for or conditions on interlocutors' actions.

Contingency adverbials giving reasons:

> I haven't been using the crutches **because I can't walk on them very well**. (CONV)
>
> I'm going to wash all the cafeteria itself as well **cos that's a bit grubby**. (CONV)
>
> It's not a good idea **because Richard's got a streaming cold and James hasn't**. (CONV)

Contingency adverbials giving conditions:

> **If I wash up all this stuff**, somebody else can dry it. (CONV)
>
> Put some carrots in **if you want**. (CONV)
>
> **If I would have known you were going** I would have got you to get me the nut ones. (CONV)

Rather than reporting conditions on actions, fiction and news more commonly use contingency adverbials to convey the purposes and cause/reasons associated with characters' feelings or with events. Such adverbials are used primarily in description and in reported speech:

> "They gave me a bag of oats **to start us out**." (FICT)
>
> She was teasing him as if he were one of the little ones but he didn't mind **because she was looking happy again**. (FICT)
>
> "Serious efforts must now be made by all concerned **in order to get the demobilization process quickly back on track**." (NEWS)
>
> Most of the providers refused to let him in **because they smelled something fishy**. (NEWS)

Finally, the greater use of purpose adverbials in academic prose corresponds to explicit identification of the purpose of certain procedures or passages of text:

> But now let us climb slowly down the stratigraphical column **to see what other widespread facies we can find**. (ACAD)
>
> However, **to begin to understand the application layer standards** it is necessary to be aware of some of the different entities within the layer. (ACAD)
>
> **In order to help such children**, it is necessary to introduce novel and artificial procedures to assist learning. (ACAD)

The use of contingency circumstance adverbials is further discussed in 10.2.8.1.

**10.2.3    Overview of syntactic realizations of semantic categories**

Adverbials can take a wide range of syntactic forms (10.1.2). However, the different semantic categories of circumstance adverbials are not associated equally with these different syntactic forms. The present section provides an overview of the preferred syntactic realizations for each semantic role, while more detailed issues about syntactic forms—including their frequencies and register patterns—are addressed in 10.2.4. Figure 10.6 displays, for the six most common semantic categories, the percentage of the occurrences realized by each syntactic form. Within process adverbials, only manner adverbials are included, since they dominate this category in all four registers. Nearly all recipient adverbials are realized as prepositional phrases, and thus they are not included in Figure 10.6.

**Figure 10.6    Syntactic realizations of semantic categories for circumstance adverbials**

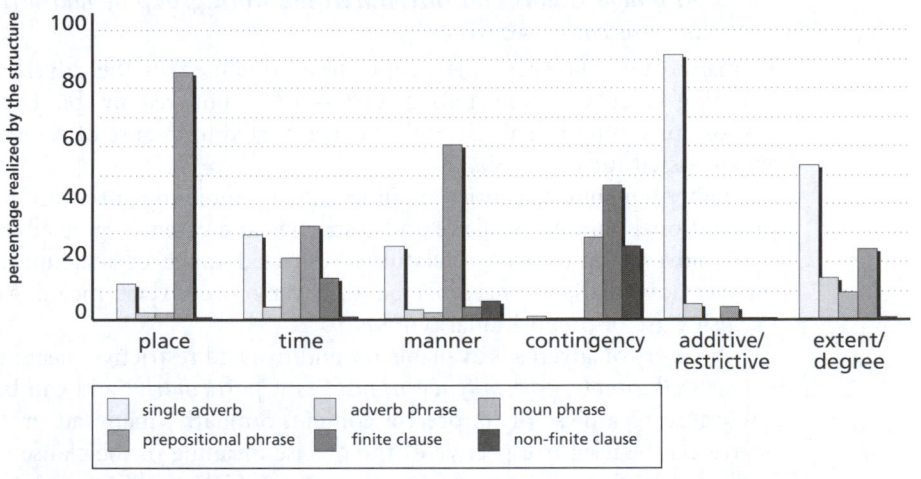

➤   Each semantic role for circumstance adverbials has different preferred structural realizations:

➤   Place is realized overwhelmingly by prepositional phrases.

➤   Time is realized mainly by single adverbs or prepositional phrases, but no single structure dominates.

➤   Process (manner) is realized by prepositional phrases, and to some extent single adverbs.

➤   Contingency is realized by finite clauses, and to some extent prepositional phrases and non-finite clauses.

➤   Additive/restrictive is realized almost completely by single adverbs.

➤   Extent/degree is realized by single adverbs, and to some extent by prepositional phrases.

➤   Recipient is realized by prepositional phrases.

### DISCUSSION OF FINDINGS

Most semantic roles favor non-clausal structural realizations. Contingency adverbials are exceptional in that they favor clauses over non-clausal structures. It is possible to convey contingency relationships with prepositional phrases, as in the following examples, where purpose is expressed with *for*, reason with *on account of* and *because of*, and concession with *in spite of*:

> Do it **for fun**. (CONV)

> My auntie wouldn't let me blow **on account of my asthma**. (FICT)

> **Because of the takeover moves** the meeting was cancelled. (NEWS)

> **In spite of these criticisms**, it is generally accepted that trade-off models do offer some valuable insights. (ACAD†)

However, it is far more common to use clauses for contingency adverbials:

> 1 **If his targets weren't killers**, he wouldn't sell guns. (NEWS)
> 2 **Although Galois had introduced the word group** he had used it inconsistently. (ACAD)

In many cases like these the proposition contained in the adverbial clause—requiring a subject and tensed verb—could not readily be encoded in a prepositional phrase. This and other issues related to the use of clausal adverbials are discussed further in 10.2.8.

Other semantic categories are differentially suited to realization by adverbs or prepositional phrases. Additive and restrictive and extent/degree adverbials favor single adverbs and cover a relatively restricted range of meanings. Place and manner adverbials, on the other hand, cover more diverse meanings and make extensive use of prepositional phrases.

A variety of adverbs is available for additive and restrictive meaning (e.g. *also*, *too*, *as well*, *simply*, *especially*, *even*, *just*, *only*, *particularly*) and can be used with any clause regardless of its precise content. Similarly, many adverbs of extent/degree can be used irrespective of the precise meaning of the clause (e.g. *almost*, *badly*, *hardly*, *increasingly*, *slightly*). These adverbials are illustrated in 10.2.1.5–6.

Prepositional phrases, on the other hand, allow the information in the adverbial to connect more specifically with the clause content (cf. 10.1.2). This is particularly useful for place and manner adverbials, so that even when similar spatial or manner relationships are expressed, they can be adapted to the context:

> We were now flying **to the moon**. (FICT)

> He had beaten the pickpocket **to the door**. (FICT)

> Before I could shout a warning he did indeed vomit, then slid down **to the deck**. (FICT)

> If the Colombian government someday decides to fight for the peace of our nation **in a sovereign and courageous way** <...> (NEWS†)

> It therefore makes sense to analyse urban morphology **in an historical context**. (ACAD†)

The semantic category of time is noteworthy in that it has a particularly wide range of syntactic realizations. Prepositional phrases are typically used to indicate specific times:

> **On Monday morning** Raymond put in a bid for the house. (FICT†)

> **On February 25**, Guppy flew to New York. (NEWS)

*This anxiety is aggravated by the common, but non-serious, symptoms which are so common **after the attack**.* (ACAD)

Single adverbs are used for times whose interpretation is tied to the context or situation (e.g. *then, later, today, now*), particular time frequencies (e.g. *weekly, monthly*), as well as more vague references to time (e.g. *sometimes, occasionally*):

*You're in for a treat **today** Barry.* (CONV)

*Matthew appeared **occasionally** in riding clothes.* (FICT)

*Maybe **then** the tide of violence will subside.* (NEWS†)

Noun phrases are also used to convey particular points in time (e.g. *this evening, last month, next year*) and duration or frequency (e.g. *every day, all year*):

*I'll go **this evening**.* (CONV)

*But everyone knew that Papa saved **all year** for that day.* (FICT†)

***Every day**, if possible, allot time at your desk to sorting and filing everything you have collected since the previous day.* (ACAD†)

Finite clauses are also used to show time relationships between one event and another:

***When they came to the car**, Penelope handed J.D. the keys.* (FICT)

*However, she was then arrested **after she called the family again**.* (NEWS)

*Have the language helper say the word correctly **after you have said it**.* (ACAD)

Even non-finite clauses are used (though very rarely) for time adverbials when the subject of the adverbial clause may be understood from context:

*They are more plausible **when taken as responses to a question about dependent conditionals**.* (ACAD)

*All these may be experienced in simple ways **before using more difficult pieces of apparatus**.* (ACAD)

In the first example the subject of *taken* is the subject of the main clause, *they*. In the second example the subject of *using* is the same unstated participant that is the agent of the passive verb phrase in the main clause.

## 10.2.4 Syntactic realizations of circumstance adverbials (excluding clauses)

This section discusses a number of important issues regarding the syntactic realizations of circumstance adverbials, focusing on structures other than clauses. See 10.2.8 for coverage of adverbials realized as clauses. See also the discussions of overall distribution in 10.1.2, and the overall distribution of syntactic realizations across semantic categories in 10.2.3.

### 10.2.4.1 Semantic categories within syntactic forms

The same general distribution of syntactic forms used as circumstance adverbials (10.1.2) is found in all four registers, with prepositional phrases by far the most common, adverbs second, noun phrases third, and adverb phrases rare. However, further breakdown of the syntactic forms by register and by semantic category provides additional insight into the patterns of use.

Figures 10.7 and 10.8 display the frequencies of the three most common non-clause structures in their six most common semantic roles in conversation and academic prose.

## CORPUS FINDINGS [1]

➤ Compared to academic prose, conversation has twice as many single adverbs and many more noun phrases used as circumstance adverbials, but a lower frequency of prepositional phrases.

➤ A particularly large proportion of the adverbs in conversation is used for the semantic categories of time and addition/restriction.

➤ Noun phrases are used predominantly for time adverbials in conversation. Noun phrases as circumstance adverbials are very rare in academic prose.

➤ The majority of prepositional phrases in conversation are used for place information. In academic prose, prepositional phrases are distributed more evenly over place and manner, though place is slightly more common.

## DISCUSSION OF FINDINGS

The broad semantic patterns described above are discussed in more detail in 10.2.3. However, there are additional patterns worth noting.

The higher frequencies of adverbs and noun phrases in conversation reflect certain characteristics typical of conversation. The first is a preference for shorter adverbials, as measured by the number of words. Single adverbs are only one word in length; noun phrase adverbials in conversation average two words in length. Furthermore, the single adverbs and short noun phrases are often expressions which are understood from context (e.g. *here*, *last time*) or vague expressions (e.g. *a little*, *a bit*), both characteristic of conversational discourse:

*What's this fancy building **here** David?* (CONV)

*He doesn't want cherries. **Last time** we had a—I remember having a row about this **before**.* (CONV)

**Figure 10.7**

**Frequency of semantic categories for each structural realization—conversation**

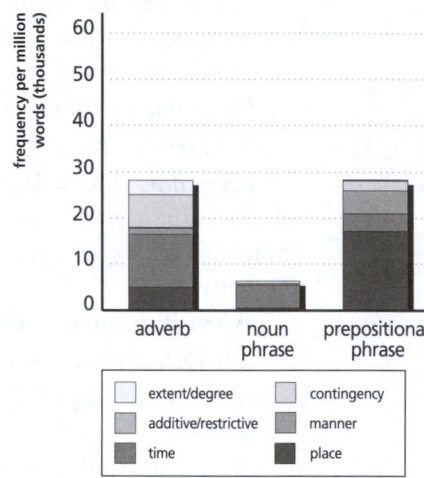

**Figure 10.8**

**Frequency of semantic categories for each structural realization—academic prose**

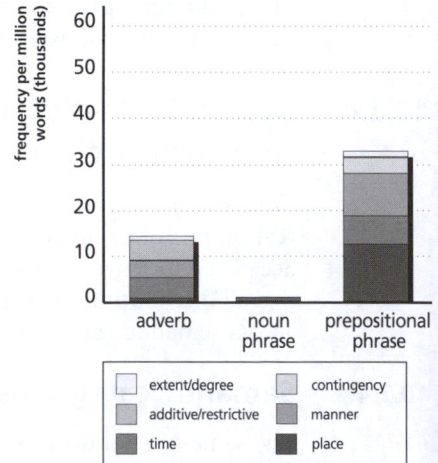

> *Well, she's **a bit** down. And **then** she's got the one from Charrid, you know,*
> *being rejected **again**.* (CONV)

The preference for shorter phrases in conversation is also discussed in 10.2.4.2 and
2.10.

In addition, it turns out that particular single-adverb forms are the most
common recurring adverbials in conversation. Many of these items are concerned
with time or with addition/restriction. The frequency of a few particular items
thus contributes greatly to the overall frequencies of adverbs and to the
associations with particular semantic categories. These items are discussed in
10.2.5.

Finally, the small but notable use of prepositional phrases of extent/degree in
academic prose reflects this register's concern with accurate, precise portrayals of
information. At times, exact measurements are given:

> *After age 35, the percentage increased **to 75%**.* (ACAD)

> *An increase in T from 15 to 40°C reduces the efficiency **by about 2–5 per***
> ***cent**.* (ACAD†)

In other cases in academic prose, prepositional phrases of extent/degree are used
to soften a claim:

> *The respect they can command depends **to a very considerable extent** on the*
> *degree to which they take account of the real world.* (ACAD)

> *The built environment is **to a large extent** a product of the social, economic*
> *and technological conditions prevailing at the time of its construction.* (ACAD)

These prepositional phrases can be similar in effect to epistemic stance adverbials
(10.3.1.1), though they more clearly give circumstantial information to answer the
question 'To what extent?'

## 10.2.4.2   Length of prepositional phrases

In 10.2.4.1 we noted that conversation has a preference for shorter syntactic
forms. This preference is particularly apparent in the distribution of prepositional
phrases across registers.

**CORPUS FINDINGS** [1]

➤ The great majority of prepositional
phrases in conversation are two or three
words in length.

➤ The proportion of short prepositional
phrases decreases from fiction to news to
academic prose.

➤ Prepositional phrases of six words or more
are very rare in conversation. In contrast,
they account for a substantial proportion
of all prepositional phrases in the written
registers, especially news and academic
prose.

Figure 10.9
**Length of prepositional phrase**
**circumstance adverbials by register**

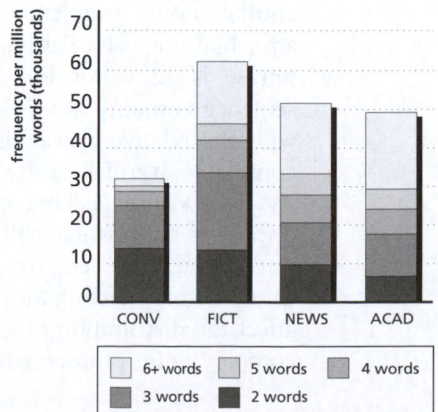

CONV    FICT    NEWS    ACAD

☐ 6+ words   ▨ 5 words   ▥ 4 words
▦ 3 words    ■ 2 words

**DISCUSSION OF FINDINGS**

In conversation, most adverbial prepositional phrases are simple constructions. That is, the noun or pronoun serving as the complement of the preposition typically has no modifier:

> *Did you want me to get it **for you**?* (CONV)
>
> *They're all going **to college**.* (CONV)
>
> *Well just keep quiet and we'll talk **[about it]** **[in a minute]**.* (CONV)
>
> *Charlie came up **to us** this morning.* (CONV)

As can be seen in the above examples, pronouns—which are common in conversation (4.1.2)—often function as the object of the preposition in conversation (e.g. *you*, *it*, *us*). Their use contributes to the short length of the phrases in this register.

Fiction, too, often has short prepositional phrases which contain no or few nominal modifiers:

> *No one called it **by that name** but that was how the boy thought **about it**.* (FICT)
>
> ***On the streets**, he was tense, quick, erratically light and reckless.* (FICT †)

However, the more descriptive nature of fiction also leads to the use of longer, more complex prepositional phrases as circumstance adverbials:

> *A yellow dressing gown, ungirdled, was sustained gently behind him **on the mild morning air**.* (FICT)
>
> *But she diverted his reasoning **with a question which startled him**.* (FICT)

The expository written registers most commonly have complex prepositional phrases as circumstance adverbials; these often include prenominal and postnominal modifiers within the phrase. For example, consider the following passage from academic prose:

> *This book is written **in the belief that there is a widespread feeling among sociologists that contemporary social theory stands in need of a radical revision**. Such a revision must begin **from a reconsideration of the works of those writers who established the principal frames of reference of modern sociology**.* (ACAD)

The first sentence in this extract includes an adverbial prepositional phrase that contains a noun complement clause (*that there is ...*) which itself includes another noun complement clause (*that contemporary social theory ...*) and an adverbial prepositional phrase (*in need of a ...*). In total, the complete adverbial phrase is 22 words long. The adverbial prepositional phrase in the second sentence contains two postnominal prepositional phrases and a relative clause, with the relative clause also including postnominal prepositional phrases. This complete adverbial phrase is 19 words long.

This dense packing of information into noun phrases and prepositional phrases is not possible with the real-time production constraints of conversation, nor would these lengthy prepositional phrases be easy for hearers to process. Thus, factors affecting the production and decoding of complex noun phrases also affect the distribution of adverbial prepositional phrases. For more on the use of complex noun phrases across registers see Chapter 8.

**10.2.4.3** **Diversity in adverb and prepositional phrase circumstance adverbials**

This section explores the diversity of lexical items which realize the two most common syntactic structures of circumstance adverbial: adverbs and prepositional phrases. Figures 10.10 and 10.11 compare the number of different expressions (the types) per 100 tokens of each semantic-structure type, for conversation and academic prose. Prepositional phrase type-token ratios are calculated by considering the preposition and the head noun that is the complement of the preposition, regardless of any modifiers. Semantic categories with too few tokens to be meaningful are omitted from the figures.

**Figure 10.10**
**Diversity in adverb and prepositional phrase circumstance adverbials—conversation**

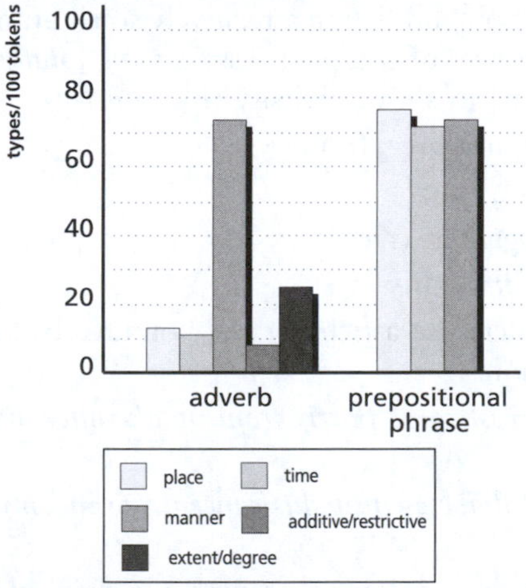

**Figure 10.11**
**Diversity in adverb and prepositional phrase circumstance adverbials—academic prose**

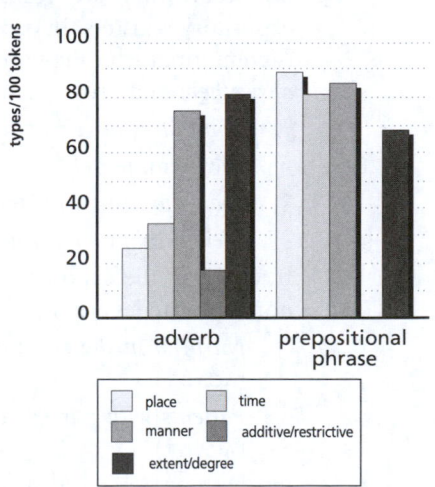

**CORPUS FINDINGS** [1]

➤ In general, circumstance adverbials realized as single adverbs exhibit much less diversity than those realized as prepositional phrases.
➤ Within single adverbs, manner adverbials are more diverse than the other categories.
➤ In academic prose, extent/degree adverbs also vary greatly.
➤ Among prepositional phrases in academic prose, the extent/degree category is slightly less diverse than the other semantic categories.

**DISCUSSION OF FINDINGS**

The most common adverbs used as circumstance adverbials (10.2.5) fall into the semantic categories of place, time, and additive/restrictive (including *here* and *there*; *now* and *then*; *also* and *only*). The repeated use of these items creates the low type-token ratios for these categories.

In contrast, adverbs that express manner include more variety in all registers. Many different kinds of manner can be expressed, and this class of adverbs is very productive, often derived from adjectives. Descriptions of manner in all registers are thus as diverse as the following:

> You two think **quietly** a minute. (CONV)
>
> Students do **well** in class if they have a lot of this. (CONV)
>
> He looked **proudly** where Macalister pointed. (FICT)
>
> The screams echoed **shrilly** along the corridor. (FICT)
>
> The big striker timed his run **perfectly** to glance a header past Oleg Karavaev. (NEWS)
>
> It's a menu that appears to blend **neatly** the fresh, straightforward cuisine of Vietnam with the French colonial influence. (NEWS)
>
> If the data are collected **systematically** and with care, they certainly offer more information. (ACAD†)
>
> Leguminous crops behave **abnormally**. (ACAD)

Extent/degree adverbs are not common as adverbials (10.2.5), but when they do occur, they are realized quite differently across the non-expository and expository registers. In conversation and fiction a relatively small number of items is common, including both measures of completeness (e.g. *all, totally, completely, altogether*) and more vague terms to show intensity (e.g. *much*):

> Computers have just **totally** took over. (CONV)
>
> I was **completely** taken aback. (FICT)
>
> Soon the rains will stop **altogether**. (FICT)
>
> Well I didn't care **much** for it. (CONV)

In contrast, the expository registers use a richer variety of adverbs to convey the non-absoluteness of a proposition:

> Nitrogen in the grain at harvest came **partly** from uptake after anthesis. (ACAD†)
>
> Patients with partial central diabetes insipidus concentrate **incompetely**. (ACAD†)

Furthermore, extent/degree adverbs are used to strengthen a claim of importance, both with precise terms and more general ones:

> It can be seen that thrust decreases **significantly** with increasing altitude. (ACAD)
>
> I believe that my analysis departs **considerably** from some of the established works in the field. (ACAD†)

Given the large number of prepositions and nouns in English, many different prepositional phrases are possible. Section 10.2.3 notes that one of the advantages of prepositional phrases is their adaptability to different specific content. Thus, the generally higher type-token ratios for prepositional phrases are not surprising. Time and extent/degree prepositional phrases make slightly greater use of repeated preposition + noun combinations, however, resulting in marginally lower type-token ratios than for manner and place ones.

Time prepositional phrases often contain the same nouns to show duration or points in time, frequently in combination with the prepositions *at, for,* and *in,* resulting in frames such as:

> at ___ time, at ___ point, for ___ moment, for ___ week(s), for ___ year(s), in ___ minute(s), in ___ week(s), in ___ year(s)

As the following examples show, these expressions of time are found in all registers:

> We were in Catterick **for two years**. (CONV)

> **For many years** it was recognized in Asia that rice varieties can be divided into two classes. (FICT)

> The Picasso painting has belonged **for more than 50 years** to a collector who kept its existence secret. (NEWS†)

> **For about twenty-five years**, people had to live with the dilemma. (ACAD)

> I'm not gonna shave **for three weeks**. (CONV)

> He walked about **for weeks** wired to a police tape recorder. (NEWS†)

> Ploughing finished, the land may be left **for three or four weeks**. (ACAD)

In conversation and news, prepositional phrases with *on* + a day of the week are also common:

> I spoke to him **on Wednesday**. (CONV)

> **On Sunday**, the city instead brought in some 5,000 schoolchildren who banged cymbals and beat drums as part of ceremonies to encourage civic enthusiasm. (NEWS†)

In academic prose, extent/degree prepositional phrases often use the preposition *to* in combination with *extent* or *degree(s)* (as a general term or measurement of temperature) and with other measurement terms (e.g. *meters, centimeters, centigrade*):

> But we know that people disagree **to some extent** about the right principles of behavior. (ACAD)

> These emphases were found **to different degrees** among the various categories of friendship identified by high school students in that study. (ACAD)

> It then rose **to 54.6 centimeters** in 1990. (ACAD)

Other preposition + noun combinations used to convey time and extent/degree are illustrated in 10.2.3 and 10.2.4.

## 10.2.5  Most common circumstance adverbials

**CORPUS FINDINGS** [4]

➤ All of the most common circumstance adverbials fall into three semantic categories: additive/restrictive, time, and place.

➤ Nearly all of the most common adverbials are single word adverbs.

➤ Relative to the other registers, conversation (both BrE and AmE) and to a lesser extent fiction have especially high frequencies of the adverbs *just* (in restrictive, not time, sense), *now*, *then*, *here*, and *there*.

➤ BrE news is particularly marked by a high frequency of the time adverb *yesterday*, while AmE news has a very high frequency of the days of the weeks used as time adverbials.

➤ Academic prose is marked by the relatively high frequencies of the additive adverb *also* and the restrictive adverb *only*; in general, though, academic prose has relatively low frequencies for most items.

➤ *Also* is more common in the expository registers, *too* in conversation and fiction.

Table 10.4 **Most common circumstance adverbials across registers and dialects; occurrences per million words**

each ■ represents 200      □ represents less than 100

| | CONV (AmE & BrE) | FICT | NEWS (AmE & BrE) | ACAD |
|---|---|---|---|---|
| **single adverbs** *additive/restrictive* | | | | |
| just | ■■■■■■■ ■■■■■■ ■■■■■■■ ■■ | ■■■■■■ | ■■■■ | ■ |
| only | ■■■■ | ■■■■■ | ■■■ | ■■■■■■■ |
| also | ■ | ■■ | ■■■■■■ | ■■■■■■■ ■■ |
| even | ■■■ | ■■■■ | ■■ | ■■■ |
| too | ■■■ | ■■ | ■ | □ |
| **time** | | | | |
| then | ■■■■■■■ ■■■■■■ | ■■■■■■■ ■■■■ | ■■■ | ■■■ |
| now | ■■■■■■■ ■■■ | ■■■■■■■ ■■■ | ■■■■■ | ■■ |
| never | ■■■■ | ■■■■■■ | ■■ | ■ |
| again | ■■■ | ■■■■■■ | ■■ | ■ |
| always | ■■■ | ■■■ | ■ | ■ |
| still | ■■■ | ■■■■ | ■■■ | ■ |
| today | ■■■ | □ | ■■ | □ |
| yesterday | ■ | □ | ■■■■ | □ |
| already | ■ | ■ | ■■ | ■ |
| ever | ■ | ■■ | ■ | □ |
| sometimes | ■ | ■ | ■ | ■ |
| often | □ | ■ | ■ | ■■■ |
| usually | ■ | □ | ■ | ■■ |
| **place** | | | | |
| there | ■■■■■■■ ■■■■■■■ ■■■■■ | ■■■■■■■ | ■ | □ |
| here | ■■■■■■■ ■■■■ | ■■■■■■ | ■ | ■■ |
| **noun phrase** *time* | | | | |
| this morning | ■ | □ | ■ | □ |
| words for days of the week (combined) | □ | □ | ■■■■■■■ | □ |

**Table 10.4** **continued**

| | AmE CONV | BrE CONV |
|---|---|---|
| **single adverbs** *additive/restrictive* | | |
| just | ■■■■■■■■■■■■■■ ■■■■■■■■■■■■■ | ■■■■■■■■■■■■■■ ■■ |
| only | ■■■ | ■■■■ |
| also | ■ | ■ |
| even | ■■■■ | ■■ |
| too | ■■■■■ | ■ |
| **time** | | |
| then | ■■■■■■■■■■■■■ | ■■■■■■■■■■■■■■■ |
| now | ■■■■■■■■ | ■■■■■■■■■■■ |
| never | ■■■■ | ■■■■ |
| again | ■■ | ■■■ |
| always | ■■■ | ■■■ |
| still | ■■■ | ■■■ |
| today | ■■■ | ■■ |
| yesterday | ■ | ■ |
| already | ■ | ■ |
| ever | ■■ | ■ |
| sometimes | ■ | ■ |
| often | ▢ | ▢ |
| usually | ■ | ■ |
| **place** | | |
| there | ■■■■■■■■■■■■■■ ■■■■■ | ■■■■■■■■■■■■■■ ■■■ |
| here | ■■■■■■■■■■■■■ | ■■■■■■■■■ |

| | AmE NEWS | BrE NEWS |
|---|---|---|
| **single adverbs** *additive/restrictive* | | |
| just | ■■■ | ■■■■ |
| only | ▢ | ■■■■■ |
| also | ■■■■■■■ | ■■■■■ |
| even | ■■■ | ■■ |
| too | ■ | ▢ |
| **time** | | |
| then | ■■■ | ■■■ |
| now | ■■■■ | ■■■■■ |
| never | ■■ | ■■ |
| again | ■ | ■■ |

Table 10.4   **continued**

|  | AmE NEWS | BrE NEWS |
|---|---|---|
| **single adverbs** *additive/restrictive* | | |
| *always* | ■ | ■ |
| *still* | ■■■ | ■■■ |
| *today* | ■■■ | ■■ |
| *yesterday* | ■ | ■■■■■■■ |
| *already* | ■ | ■□ |
| *ever* | ■ | ■ |
| *sometimes* | ■ | □ |
| *often* | ■ | ■ |
| *usually* | ■ | □ |
| **place** | | |
| *there* | ■■ | ■ |
| *here* | ■■ | ■ |
| **noun phrases** *time* | | |
| *this morning* | □ | ■ |
| *words for days of the week (combined)* | ■■■■■■■■■■■■■ | □ |

## DISCUSSION OF FINDINGS

The most common adverbials in conversation correspond to distinctive characteristics of conversational discourse. First, the very common word *just* not only fulfills the primary semantic purpose of restriction, but also has more subtle functions that are especially useful in face-to-face interactions. The primary semantic role as a restrictive adverb is clear in the following examples, where *just* is used to focus on the part of the clause for which the truth value of the proposition is most important:

   *You're **just** a number on a damn computer.* (CONV)

   *It's **just** crazy!* (CONV)

   *I **just** can't believe it.* (CONV)

When used with imperatives, *just* has a somewhat different function, conveying a strong sense of 'I'm not asking so much, only this one thing' or 'Don't argue; simply do as I say':

   ***Just** keep the water boiling.* (CONV)

   *Now, now **just** sit down!* (CONV)

   ***Just** stay there.* (CONV)

   ***Just** give me some of them.* (CONV)

However, in another context, *just* has the effect of softening what is being said. This occurs particularly when people are justifying their or others' actions, or making a claim on another's attention:

> Oh I **just** wondered – **just** wondered who it could be. (CONV)

> I'm **just** correcting her! (CONV)

> She's **just** that way. (CONV)

> Let me **just** show you this. (CONV)

As these examples show, the slightly different impacts that *just* can have make it a useful adverbial for a variety of contexts in conversation. In many cases, its function overlaps with that of stance adverbials (10.3).

Several of the other most common adverbial forms in conversation are used for deictic reference to the situation of utterance. The frequent use of *now* in conversation reflects its concern with current matters:

> I should get a cup of tea **now** shouldn't I? (CONV)

> It's sort of run down **now** and no use in trying to build it up again. (CONV)

> They're both making a lot of money **now** so they figured they'd invest. (CONV)

*Then* is used as a pro-form, referring to a time known to the conversants by the context (= 'at that time'), or, quite commonly, to mark the next event in a sequence (= 'after that'):

> If I would've known **then** what I know now, I wouldn't even let you operate. (CONV)

> And **then** you have to tense your toes and **then** you relax, **then** you tense <...> (CONV†)

> And **then** he goes into my bedroom and **then** he shuts the door and locks himself in. (CONV)

Finally, the adverbials *here* and *there* show the use of deictic place reference in conversation, and the use of *there* to substitute for a place already named in the conversation:

> What's she doing **here**? (CONV)

> Well, no one was **here** at the weekend. (CONV)

> Come **here**! (CONV)

> Your drink's **there**. (CONV)

> It's gonna stay **there** until it rots. (CONV)

> I think I've had a meal **there** years ago. (CONV)

In fiction, the use of *here*, *there*, *now*, and *then* is similar to conversation, though referring to the fictional world of the text rather than the real world. *Never* and *again*, which are more common than in conversation, are used especially in giving background about characters' activities. *Never* fills in information about a fictional character's past experience and *again* typically highlights repetition in the narration of their activities:

> He had **never** seen the woman before in his life. (FICT)

> There was **never** any unpleasantness and she was tireless in the work she had to do. (FICT†)

> **Again** she shuddered nervously, grimacing in awareness of saying something wrong. (FICT)

*By Monday morning at eight o'clock I was in the gym **again**, working out.* (FICT)

In both expository registers, the common additive adverbial *also* serves to mark information being added to previous information:

*Davies, who won the world title for the sixth time in May, decided not to compete in the first two ranking events in Hong Kong and Bangkok. He **also** did not compete in the European Open and will be absent from the Dubai Classic, which are **also** ranking events.* (NEWS)

*The local gin, akpeteshi, is normally distilled from palm wine, but may **also** be distilled from sugar-cane juice or pineapple juice.* (ACAD)

*In addition, we have **also** included descriptions of methods used to ensure the reproduction of aquatic plants under cultivation.* (ACAD)

In fiction, the meaning of addition is spread more evenly over two adverbs, *also* and *too*, with *also* carrying a more formal tone:

*But real was **also** brutal.* (FICT)

*There was **also** his prolonged vigour to marvel at.* (FICT)

*This **also** was a great gain.* (FICT)

*Too* is used more informally, often in dialog or reports of dialog:

*"They took it up the hill and burned it, **too**."* (FICT)

*"If anyone else gets hold of that letter it will be a bad look-out for her and me and perhaps for you, **too**."* (FICT)

*He said he was going to lunch at the Blue Lagoon and would she come **too**.* (FICT†)

Interestingly, this use of *too* is actually more common in fictional dialog than in conversation.

Among the time adverbs in news, the most common ones show the emphasis on current information: the days of the week, *yesterday* and *now*. Absolute items, such as *always* and *never*, are less common. BrE news often uses *yesterday* to identify when an event occurred:

***Yesterday** Barclays and Lloyds announced they wanted to join Switch, the debit card network <...>* (BrE NEWS†)

*A Tory Council **yesterday** failed in a High Court bid to halt a teacher's boycott of school tests.* (BrE NEWS)

*A 49-year-old man went on trial **yesterday** accused of attempting to kill an Essex traffic policeman.* (BrE NEWS)

In contrast, AmE news more commonly identifies the day of the week:

*A former Miss America revealed **Thursday** in Denver a dark family secret <...>* (AmE NEWS†)

*Midland, Texas, set a record high **Sunday** for the date with a reading of 103 degrees.* (AmE NEWS)

*The president said **Tuesday** he would continue his fight to get Congress to reduce the capital gains tax.* (AmE NEWS)

Although days of the week are also mentioned in the BrE news reports, they tend to be more often incorporated into prepositional phrases than noun phrases as adverbials (e.g. *on Sunday, for Tuesday's trip*).

In news generally, *now* marks a change from previous events, showing the latest newsworthy event or telling readers what they can expect next:

> Councilors have **now** called for a full investigation before any action is taken. (NEWS)

> And he said there was **now** further evidence to discredit a principal witness in the case as a liar and a cheat. (NEWS)

> There is **now** talk of an interest rate cut some time this week. (NEWS)

> The competition **now** goes into winter hibernation. (NEWS)

Three adverbs are more common in academic prose than the other registers (in addition to *also* discussed above): *only*, *often*, and *usually*. The use of these forms reflects the care taken in this register to convey information precisely. The restrictive adverb *only* typically limits the truth value of a statement to certain circumstances:

> Black phosphorous **only** occurs at high pressures. (ACAD)

> The Hahn-Banach Theorem given in 1 is valid **only** for linear functionals. (ACAD)

> Its proper specification has **only** been given for some simple cases. (ACAD)

The time adverbs *often* and *usually* are commonly used to describe typical events or conditions that hold most, but not all, of the time:

> **Often**, complete extinction does not occur. (ACAD)

> The condition behind the deviation is **often** rectifiable by counselling or psychotherapy. (ACAD)

> Doing theoretical physics is **usually** a two-step process. (ACAD)

> It is **usually** (although not in all circumstances) for the prosecution to prove that any act was carried out in bad faith. (ACAD†)

These adverbs contribute to academic authors' ability to make clear the generalizability of their statements, and their meaning is thus related to that of stance adverbials.

## 10.2.6 Position of circumstance adverbials

Overall, circumstance adverbials usually occur in final position (10.1.3). Conversation, fiction, news, and academic prose are all very similar in this overall distributional pattern. However, several factors influence the choice to use other positions. These factors include: the semantic category of the adverbial (10.2.6.1); the syntactic structure of the adverbial (10.2.6.2); and the length of the adverbial (10.2.6.2). Throughout these sections we concentrate on non-clausal circumstance adverbials, since their distribution is somewhat different from adverbials realized by clauses, which very rarely occur medially. The positions of clausal adverbials are covered in 10.2.8.6.

## 10.2.6.1 Associations between positions and semantic categories

**CORPUS FINDINGS 1**

➤ Many semantic categories have a strong preference for final position. These include place and all the process categories: manner, agent, instrument, and means.

➤ Initial position is used with time and contingency adverbials (15–20%), although the majority of occurrences of these semantic categories are placed finally.

➤ Medial position has marked use with the additive/restrictive, extent/degree, and (to a lesser extent) time and manner categories.

Table 10.5 **Associations between position and semantic category for non-clausal circumstance adverbials**

each ■ represents 5%      □ represents less than 2.5%

| semantic category | % in initial position | % in medial position | % in final position |
|---|---|---|---|
| instrument | □ | □ | ■■■■■■■■■■ ■■■■■■■■■■ |
| agent | □ | ■ | ■■■■■■■■■■ ■■■■■■■■■ |
| place | ■ | ■ | ■■■■■■■■■■ ■■■■■■■■ |
| means | ■■ | ■■ | ■■■■■■■■■■ ■■■■■■□ |
| contingency | ■■■ | ■■ | ■■■■■■■■■■ ■■■■■ |
| manner | ■ | ■■■ | ■■■■■■■■■■ ■■■■■ |
| time | ■■■■ | ■■■■■ | ■■■■■■■■■■ ■ |
| extent/degree | ■ | ■■■■■■■■■■ | ■■■■■■■■■■ |
| additive/restrictive | ■■ | ■■■■■■■■■■ ■■■■■ | ■■ |

---

### DISCUSSION OF FINDINGS

Adverbials from different semantic categories vary with respect to the relationship that they typically have with the other elements in their clause. Some categories, such as place, contain numerous adverbials that complete the valency pattern of certain common main verbs (e.g. *put*). Some categories, such as additive/restrictive, tend to have scope over only a part of the clause, rather than the complete clause. Other categories contain adverbials that are used to frame a stretch of discourse longer than a clause. These varying relationships have a strong influence on the placement of adverbials from the various semantic categories.

## A Preference for final position

The most important factor favoring final position has to do with the close tie between some adverbials and the main verb. Many of the adverbials of place, manner, agency, instrument, agent, and means have scope over the predicate rather than the whole clause and/or occur with verbs whose valency patterns require adverbials (5.2.4).

Place:

> I'm **at Willy's** right now. (CONV) <obligatory in clause pattern SVA$_c$>
>
> I can't get you **over there** in that car. (CONV) <obligatory in clause pattern SVO$_d$A$_c$>
>
> The state court of appeals met **in both locations**. (NEWS)

Manner:

> It was just flowing along **smoothly**. (CONV)
>
> The nun interrupted, her jaw set **at its firmest**. (FICT†)
>
> In dealing with the health in the modern livestock unit it is essential to ensure that the unit is planned **on the right lines** from the outset. (ACAD)

Instrument:

> <...> and our baggage would be brought later **with the wagonette**. (FICT†)
>
> It has often been noted that while barbarians fight **with hatchets**, civilised men fight **with gossip**. (NEWS)

Agent:

> Topaz had Amossy's fierce, unyielding spirit and hadn't been broken **by the indifference and contempt shewn to her**. (FICT†)
>
> It allows the young to study the beliefs and attitudes held **by the adherents of these religions** and also **by humanists**. (NEWS)
>
> There has been a trend towards chronic, insidious and complex groups of diseases caused **by organisms which are often normal inhabitants of the animal body but which circumstances allow to become pathogenic**. (ACAD†)

Means:

> I can't get you over there **in that car**. (CONV)
>
> <He> removed the dangerous Sanjay Manjrekar **with his third delivery**. (NEWS)
>
> They have been given a confidence and liveliness **through the influence of a common interpretation of quantum theory**. (ACAD)

Moving most of these adverbials to a position other than final—when it is possible—is a very marked choice (e.g. *In that car I can't get you over there*). Certain positions are not possible at all; for example, *I'm at Willy's* cannot be changed to *\*At Willy's I am*.

However, it should also be remembered that some adverbials in these semantic categories do occur in positions other than final. For example, initial place adverbials can have scope over the entire clause and be used to set the scene for the following description:

> **On the other side of the fence**, the upper part of the field was full of rabbit holes. (FICT)

In a different way, place adverbials may be fronted and accompanied by subject-verb inversion (11.2.3.1):

> **Alongside the platform at Aleppo** stood the train grandly designated in railway guides as the Taurus Express. (FICT)

The last example also illustrates how, in some contexts, place adverbials can be positioned before other obligatory elements of the predicate (i.e. medially). In the dependent *ed*-clause it is the *as*-phrase rather than the place adverbial that is the required complement of the main verb, *designate*.

Manner adverbials are also placed in initial and medial positions:

***Decisively**, he pushed open the door of the florist's shop and went inside.* (FICT)

*He was a fish that Welch had more than once **vainly** tried to land.* (FICT)

*I remember **vaguely** seeing it.* (CONV†)

Initial placement can have the effect of making the scope of the manner adverbial seem to be the entire clause, including the subject, rather than just the predicate: we interpret the first example as attributing decisiveness as much to the subject *he* as to the action of pushing open the door. However, in spite of these possibilities, final position is clearly the most typical case for these semantic categories.

Contingency adverbials also show a strong preference for final position. All the subcategories of this semantic category frequently occur in final position, as the following examples illustrate:

*I really don't think he would risk his friendship with Sal **because of a girl**.* (CONV) <reason>

*She, too, like her husband, seemed strangely resigned, **despite her superficial agitation**.* (FICT) <concession>

*The embattled Australian entrepreneur, Alan Bond yesterday struck a deal with a rival businessman, John Spalvins, **in an attempt to save his teetering business empire**.* (NEWS) <purpose>

*The difference is often not even mentioned in textbooks, **with the result that the learner may be ignorant about it and keeps sounding foreign**.* (ACAD) <result>

## B  Higher proportional use of initial position

The semantic categories in this group—time and contingency—both use initial position for a notably higher percentage of their occurrences than the other semantic categories do. The function of these initial adverbials varies slightly between the two categories, but they are similar in having scope over the entire clause.

Initial time adverbials typically are used to set up a new time setting for the subsequent discourse:

*****As far back as 700 BC**, Hesiod was saying of it: "Gossip is mischievous, light and easy to raise, but grievous to bear and hard to get rid of."* (NEWS)

*****From the time it reached its fully articulated form in the middle twenties of this century** it has been used daily by an army of honest toilers with consistently reliable results.* (ACAD)

The initial position also gives added salience to the time adverbial. This position is therefore also used with adverbials that identify particularly significant points in time or points in sequences of events through time:

*****Eight thirty tonight** we're either committing suicide or murder, one of the two.* (CONV)

*****In that moment** Franklin Field did a wonderful thing. He moved from the bridge, through the gap in the wall, and walked down the towpath. **In that moment** he decided not to go to work.* (FICT)

*She's come <...> in the smallest truck that U-Haul would rent her, from New Jersey.* **Before that** *she was in North Carolina.* **Before that,** *Calcutta, India.* (FICT)

The non-clausal contingency adverbials that appear in initial position tend to be from two sub-categories – concession and purpose:

**In spite of the circumstances which had brought me to Ashington Grange,** *I could not help but be thrilled.* (FICT)

**Despite modern-day technology,** *no better materials have been developed which will do the job as well.* (NEWS)

**Despite its accumulation by plants,** *chlorine is required in relatively low concentrations.* (ACAD)

**For detailed discussions of the definition of a system,** *the meaning of feedback, and other issues we have glossed over, consult the control theory literature.* (ACAD†)

**For notes on this act and these rules,** *reference should be made to the eighth edition of this book.* (ACAD)

Initial concessive adverbials note contrary conditions before presenting the reader with the rather surprising information of the main clause. Initial purpose adverbials often have ties to the previous discourse—in the examples above, the term *system* and *this act and these rules*. Thus, they help to create coherence before going on to the main clause. A high proportion of initial position is also characteristic of finite clauses of concession, though not of non-finite clauses of purpose (10.2.8.6).

Finally, adverbials of respect, which are used to limit or define the universe of discourse for the entire following proposition, also tend to be used in initial position:

1 **As for worship, or religious observance as the legislation calls it,** *I agree entirely with Marjorie B. Clark that "compulsory acts of worship can never be educationally justified."* (NEWS)

2 **With respect to those employees that remain technically dominant,** *Larson notes that even "they do not control key financial decisions."* (NEWS†)

These initial respect adverbials tend to occur in the written registers rather than in conversation. In addition, they can be interpreted as having functions similar to both linking adverbials and stance adverbials. For example, 1 can be seen as having a textual linking function, marking the introduction of a new topic, though this is not the primary purpose as clearly as for linking adverbials (10.4). In a sense, 2 provides information about the perspective from which the proposition of the rest of the clause is true, although it does not serve to limit the truth value of the clause as clearly as stance adverbials do (10.3).

## C  Marked use of medial positions

Two semantic categories show a marked preference for medial positions: additive/restrictive and extent/degree. These categories have two characteristics in common: they often apply to a particular part of the clause, and they are often one- or two-word adverbials. Because they focus on a particular part of the clause, medial positions can be important to show clearly the scope of the adverbial.

For example, in the following medial examples of restrictive adverbials, the placement of the adverbial highlights its relevance to the following word(s):

1  *I was **only** asking.* (CONV)

2  *If you read these stories day by day you **simply** don't realize how many there are.* (NEWS)

3  *Well I, I wanted **just** a small box like what you made. He wasn't satisfied with it – He goes and makes a big one as well.* (CONV)

Thus **1** downplays the speech act of asking, **2** focuses on the negative (that you do *not* realize), **3** draws attention to the requested limitation to *a small box* and no more.

Though prescriptive rules often state that additive/restrictive adverbials should immediately precede the element that is semantically in focus, this is frequently not the case:

4  *I **only** bought one today.* (CONV)

5  *He **only** told his name to an Italian painter named Carlino.* (FICT†)

In **4** the focus is likely on either *one* or *today*, but *only* precedes *bought*. In **5** the intended emphasis seems to be that he told his name *to an Italian painter* and nobody else, even though *only* precedes *told*. Even in academic prose the additive/restrictive adverbial may not immediately precede the focused item:

<...> *it is the main aim of this chapter to present and investigate current knowledge about sociological effects of computer systems. In doing so, we **also** hope to be able to show that computer technology does not always cause inevitable changes in the social environment.* (ACAD)
*cf. ... we hope to be able to show also that ...*

Medial placement is similarly important with many extent/degree adverbials. Consider for example:

6  *Last week, Jarman hadn't **quite** decided whether they were to talk to the audience or simply sleep through the exhibition's four-day run.* (NEWS)

7  *Traditionally, with apprenticeships and jobs **almost** assured at 16, there was <...>* (NEWS†)

In **6**, the placement of *quite* makes clear that the decision was not complete, and in **7** the placement of *almost* makes clear that it relates to *assured*, not, for example, *at 16*. In these cases, because the adverbial focuses on the following element of the clause, its position is very restricted.

In contrast, where extent/degree adverbials give measurements or descriptions of the entire predicate, final position is more common:

*I guess I won't be able to help you **very much**.* (CONV)

*I like it **best of all**.* (FICT)

*In some cases, the aim of nursing care may be to promote adaptation to the new situation, as previous function has not been restored **completely**.* (ACAD)

The association between length and medial positions is discussed in further detail in 10.2.6.2. We note here, however, that time adverbials occurring in medial positions also tend to be short structures, usually single adverbs. Items marking a point in time (such as *now, today, yesterday*) and time frequency (e.g. *always, never, often, rarely*) often occur before the main verb:

*I **always** thought that I reminded him too much of my mom.* (CONV)

*Jean **never** put anything away.* (CONV)

> Mason **now** faces a re-trial on the wounding and affray charges. (NEWS)
>
> An expert witness **yesterday** blamed a doctor's error of judgment for the death of an unborn child. (NEWS)
>
> Crops **rarely** experience constant environments. (ACAD)

Some of these adverbs are among the most commonly used circumstance adverbials (10.2.5).

## 10.2.6.2 Relationships between position, grammatical structure, and length

In addition to the influence of semantic category, the position of circumstance adverbials is influenced by the grammatical structure and the length (in number of words) of the adverbial. These two factors are in many cases closely connected and are handled together in this section.

**Table 10.6** **Association between position and grammatical structure for circumstance adverbials realized as single words or phrases**

each ■ represents 5%    □ represents less than 2.5%

| | % in initial position | % in medial position | % in final position |
|---|---|---|---|
| **grammatical structure** | | | |
| *conversation:* | | | |
| adverb | ■■■ | ■■■■■■■■ | ■■■■■■■■■ |
| noun phrase | ■■ | ■ | ■■■■■■■■■ ■■■■■■■ |
| prepositional phrase | ■ | □ | ■■■■■■■■■ ■■■■■■■■■ ■ |
| *academic prose:* | | | |
| adverb | ■■ | ■■■■■■■■■ ■■■■■■ | ■■■ |
| prepositional phrase | ■■■ | ■ | ■■■■■■■■■ ■■■■■■ |

(Noun phrases are omitted from academic prose because there are too few occurrences for meaningful analysis. The findings for fiction and news are very similar to academic prose.)

---

**CORPUS FINDINGS [1]**

### Associations between positions and structures

➤ In all four registers, adverbs as circumstance adverbials are more likely to be used in medial positions than the other grammatical forms. This trend is particularly notable for the written expository registers.

➤ Noun phrases occur most commonly in final position; however, fiction and news have a higher percentage of noun phrases in initial position (about 20%) than conversation does.

➤ The vast majority of prepositional phrases occur in final position in both the written registers and conversation.

➤ For all grammatical forms, conversation has a slightly higher proportion of adverbials used in final position.

## Associations between positions and lengths

➤ In initial position, the preference for one-word adverbials decreases sharply from conversation (over 75%) to fiction (30%) to news (c. 20%) to academic prose (c. 15%).

➤ In initial position in academic prose, long adverbials (three words or more) are actually more common than one-word adverbials.

➤ In medial positions there is a strong preference for one-word adverbials in all registers.

➤ In final position:

➤ Most adverbials in conversation (over 85%) are one to three words long;

➤ In contrast, over 60% of the adverbials in academic prose are more than four words long.

**Figure 10.12**

**Associations between position and length in non-clausal circumstance adverbials—conversation**

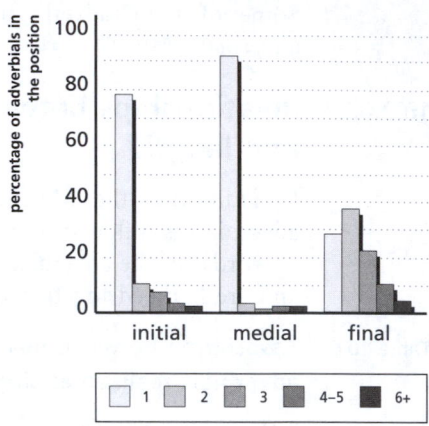

**Figure 10.13**

**Associations between position and length in non-clausal circumstance adverbials—academic prose**

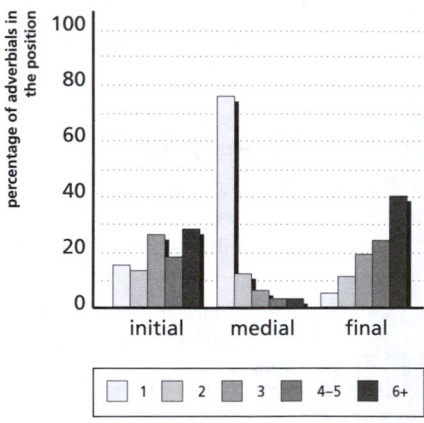

## DISCUSSION OF FINDINGS

In medial positions, adverbials interrupt the flow of obligatory components of the clause. For example, they may separate the subject from the verb, the auxiliary verb from the main verb, or the verb from its complement. It is thus not surprising that these positions have a strong preference for one-word adverbials. Furthermore, because single adverbs are the most common one-word adverbials, it is not surprising that medial adverbials are usually realized as adverbs.

To illustrate the impact of long medial adverbials, consider the following example:

> *The NCSC says the agreement may contravene the takeover code* **by effectively changing control of Bell without shareholder approval**. (NEWS)

Two medial positions are possible, either between the auxiliary and main verb or between the verb and object:

> *The NCSC says the agreement may* **by effectively changing control of Bell without shareholder approval** *contravene the takeover code.*

> *The NCSC says the agreement may contravene* **by effectively changing control of Bell without shareholder approval** *the takeover code.*

However, even if commas were used to show this interruption, the change to medial position results in a clause that is more difficult for the reader to process.

The semantic categories of additive/restrictive and extent/degree commonly occur in medial position (10.2.6.1). Furthermore, these semantic categories are commonly realized as single adverbs (10.2.3). Thus, one strong association between position, length, grammatical structure, and semantic category can be seen in the use of one-word adverbs of addition/restriction or extent/degree occurring in medial position:

> It **only** wants milk and stirring. (CONV)

> The cost of introducing new products at Inex Visions **also** impacted on margins. (NEWS†)

Furthermore, the additive/restrictive and extent/degree adverbials are some of the most common circumstance adverbials (10.2.5); thus, the high frequency of medial position is due largely to the use of a few recurring items. A few common time adverbs are also often used in medial positions. Notable among these is the most common adverb in BrE news, *yesterday*:

> Salomon Brothers **yesterday** placed <...> (BrE NEWS†)

> The Takeover Panel **yesterday** rapped <...> (BrE NEWS†)

> Farmers Group of insurance companies, the California subsidiary of Bat Industries, **yesterday** said <...> (BrE NEWS†)

> It was reported **yesterday** that <...> (BrE NEWS†)

> Democrats declared **yesterday** that <...> (BrE NEWS†)

In addition, even other semantic categories which have a strong preference for final position tend to be realized by single-word adverbs when they do occur in medial positions, as illustrated by these manner adverbials:

> He **abruptly** pointed at Rick. (FICT†)

> <...> but she **flatly** refused a fee <...> (FICT†)

> The ex-England bowler **badly** burned his arm <...> (NEWS†)

> This group evolved a distinctive culture, accumulated wealth and other resources, and **quickly** established itself as a new elite. (ACAD)

> He was directed, **silently**, to look downward. (FICT)

Noun phrases are most commonly used to express the semantic role of time (10.2.3). When they occur in initial position, these noun phrases often introduce the time setting for the subsequent discourse:

> **One day** I left the Yale on the latch accidentally, and when I came back I found a brand-new shelf, with a brass rod below it, high up in the shallow recess beside the fire. (FICT)

> **Two years ago**, Joseph Smith was stepping out of a Brooklyn crack house in a druggy haze when he spotted his three-year-old daughter <...>. **Today** Mr. Smith <...> (NEWS†)

Finally, it is somewhat surprising that initial prepositional phrases are more common in the written registers than in conversation. In many cases, these have a cohesive function, with the prepositional phrase using some information given in the previous discourse as the starting point for the next sentence. This phenomenon occurs with initial prepositional phrases as purpose adverbials (10.2.6.1) and is also used with place adverbials.

> 1 *It's glassy and be-tiled, green as an iceberg.* **Across the street from it** *is known territory.* (FICT) <note the subject verb inversion; 11.2.3>
>
> 2 *This approach was used in 40 such patients. <...>* **In seven patients with severe cholangitis** *no attempt was made to extract the stones.* (ACAD)

Initial position can also be used to highlight surprising or noteworthy information contained in the prepositional phrase and establish it as the basis for the proposition in the main clause:

> **By substituting tar (like a thick black oil) for paint**, *he intends to prompt thoughts about tar as both preservative and something more sinister.* (NEWS†)

> **In the extensive research undertaken for the book** *it became clear that a number of particular issues posed the greatest challenges to potential returners and to prospective employers.* (ACAD)

Such long initial phrases are rare in conversation, where the constraints of real time make it difficult both to compose such long introductory phrases and to process them. In fact, phrases of such length do not account for a large proportion of the adverbials in any of the positions for conversation. In contrast, the precise information given in the expository registers, often including quite long postnominal modification within adverbial prepositional phrases, leads to longer prepositional phrases (cf. 10.2.4.2).

## 10.2.7 Circumstance adverbials in series

As noted in 10.1, multiple circumstance adverbials can occur in the same clause. This section considers the frequency and ordering of circumstance adverbials occurring in series, such as:

> 1 *It's going **[slowly] [now]**.* (CONV)
>
> 2 *A few vultures looked down **[from the roof] [with shabby indifference]**.* (FICT)
>
> 3 *It intends to fly **[from Chicago's O'Hare airport] [to Stansted]**, **[via JFK airport, New York]**.* (NEWS)

Examples **1** and **2** illustrate **heterosemantic series**: **1** with a manner adverbial followed by a time adverbial, and **2** with a place adverbial followed by a manner adverbial. Example **3** illustrates a **homosemantic series** with three place adverbials in sequence.

The only series with notable frequencies (at least 400 occurrences per million words) consists of combinations of the most common semantic categories: time, place, and manner. These categories are therefore the focus of discussion below. The analyses include only contiguous adverbials (i.e. without other clause elements intervening). In addition, the analyses focus on sequences in final position, the position in which the vast majority of the series occur. Certain patterns typically occurring in other positions are noted, however.

## 10.2.7.1    Heterosemantic place, time, and manner series

**Figure 10.14**
**Order of place and time adverbials in series**

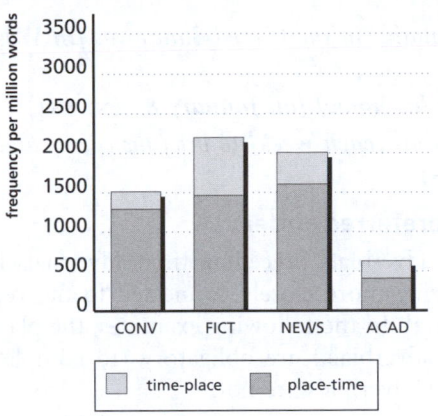

**Figure 10.15**
**Order of manner and time adverbials in series**

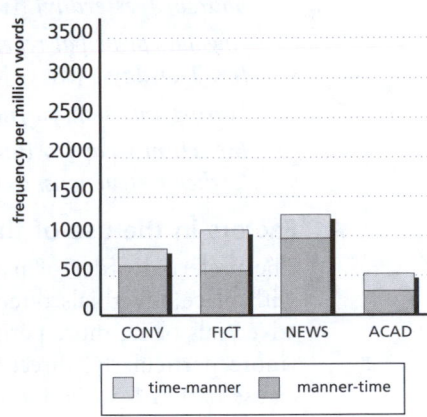

### CORPUS FINDINGS [1]

➤ Sequences of time and place adverbials are relatively common in fiction, news, and, to a lesser extent, conversation.
  ➤ In all four registers, the order of place adverbial + time adverbial is strongly preferred.
➤ Series of manner and time adverbials are less common than time and place series.
  ➤ In conversation and news, there is a marked preference for manner adverbials to occur before time adverbials.
  ➤ In fiction there is no strong preference for either order.
➤ Manner and place adverbials are the most common series in fiction.
  ➤ They are less common in the other registers and are, in fact, very rare in conversation.
  ➤ Fiction has a clear preference for manner adverbials to precede place adverbials.

**Figure 10.16**
**Order of manner and place adverbials in series**

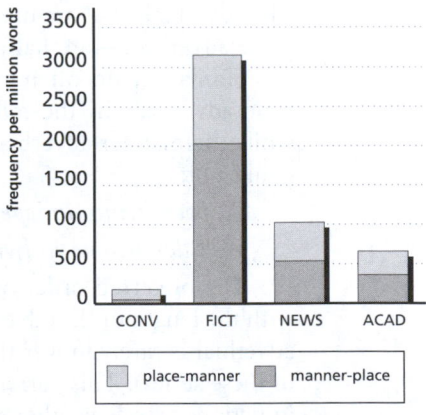

### DISCUSSION OF FINDINGS

In general, the frequency of these adverbial series is consistent with the most common semantic categories in each register (10.2.2). Conversation continues to show a particular concern with place and time, while fiction pays attention to manner as well as place and time.

However, news shows a slightly different pattern. Considered individually, manner adverbials are the most common category in news; but in series, place and time adverbials are most common. This distribution is not particularly surprising, since a report of the place and time of an event is often important in establishing the background of a news story. Often, the place and time are reported in the same clause:

> *Trading in the French financial group Paribas was suspended [on the Paris bourse] [yesterday].* (NEWS†)
>
> *Angola's principal representative in the United States was [in Washington] [on Tuesday].* (NEWS†)
>
> *Feering was stopped [near his home] [on January 8].* (NEWS†)
>
> *Mr. Hunt went [to Rampton] [each week] to brief his clients and receive further instructions.* (NEWS)

## A Factors in the use of the preferred orders

The preferred order of place adverbials preceding time adverbials is consistent with place adverbials often being more closely connected to the verb and time adverbials being more peripheral. In the following examples, the place adverbials (more particularly, direction adverbials) are obligatory (to complete the $SVA_c$ clause pattern), while the time adverbials are not:

> *This is like confession. You know save you going [to church] [on a Sunday].* (CONV)
>
> *Peggy wraps the robe [around herself] [again].* (FICT)
>
> *A van carrying migrant farm workers ran off a foggy rural road and plunged [into a murky canal] [today].* (NEWS†)

The adverbials that are more closely integrated with the meaning of the verb—the place adverbials—are naturally placed adjacent to the verb.

Similar factors often influence the ordering of manner + time adverbials. The time adverbials in the following examples could be moved to initial position, while the manner adverbials—which are more closely associated with the verb—could not:

> *I'd been living [independently] [for about two years].* (CONV)
>
> *Well don't come in [with the coat] [tomorrow].* (CONV)

The preferred order of manner before place in fiction is strongly associated with the length of the adverbials and the principle of end weight (11.1.3). The first adverbial is rarely longer than the second adverbial in fiction (less than 5 percent of these series). This corresponds to the frequent use of single adverbs of manner in fiction, as well as other shorter manner adverbials and long place adverbials. In fiction and the other registers, a single manner adverb typically occurs before a long place adverbial:

> *There is pride of ownership in that grin lifted [shyly] [to the farmer's gaze].* (FICT)
>
> *It was 4 a.m. and Holly had just sunk [wearily] [into the custom-made king-sized waterbed].* (FICT)
>
> *No raincoated figure skulks [furtively] [in the shadowy corners of the Groucho Club], hissing "Martin Amis is in. Pass it on."* (NEWS)
>
> *<...> this 150-page document due next month should be read [avidly] [across the province].* (NEWS†)
>
> *But now let us climb [slowly] [down the stratigraphical column].* (ACAD)

### B    Factors in the use of the dispreferred orders

The use of the dispreferred orders (i.e. time before place, time before manner, and place before manner) is associated with several factors, most notably: the length of the adverbials; a focus on particular information; presenting a sequence of events; and the adverbials' semantic closeness to the verb.

Commonly, the use of the dispreferred orders conforms to the principle of end-weight (11.1.3). It is rare for the first item in the sequence to be longer than the second. For example, for time + place sequences, the second adverbial is longer than the first in over 80 percent of all occurrences (c. 90 percent in news, and almost 100 percent in academic prose). Thus, the order of time + place is often used when a short time adverbial would be lost or its meaning misconstrued if it were placed after a long place adverbial:

> <...> *he advanced* **[once again]** **[towards the long table that stood in front of the speaker's chair between the two front benches which faced each other a mere sword's length apart]**. (FICT†)

> *I believe that this story, which came at the very start of my writing career, reflected feelings about San Fernando which were to be expressed* **[later]** **[in the novel, The Year in San Fernando]** <...> (FICT†)

In many cases, the time adverbials that precede place adverbials are single word adverbs, such as *still*, *again*, and the very common *yesterday* in BrE news.

> *I don't even know if you're* **[still]** **[in Rome]**. (FICT)

> *Of course I do hope I see you* **[again]**, **[in the States or anywhere else]**. (FICT)

> <...> *the seventh film, Asterix and the Big Fight, opened* **[yesterday]** **[in the West End]**. (NEWS†)

In the other dispreferred orders—time preceding manner, and place preceding manner—the second adverbial is also typically longer than the first:

> *Are you going up* **[tonight]** **[with your da]** *like?* (CONV)

> *I have escaped* **[to this island]** **[with a few books and the child, Melissa's child]**. (FICT)

In some cases, the dispreferred order also corresponds with the first item in the series being more important to the overall message of the clause or adjacent clauses. Thus, consider these examples in which time adverbials precede place adverbials:

> 1  *Maya is drinking her first bourbon tonight because Vern left* **[today]** **[for San Francisco State]**. (FICT)

> 2  *Grappling* **[every day]** **[with the sea]** *has dulled for Frank the adventure of peering into its close green depths.* (FICT)

> 3  *He selected a huge armful of mimosa, brilliant yellow and sweetly fragrant, flown in* **[that morning]** **[from Nice]**, *he was informed.* (FICT)

> 4  <...> *provincial leaders would reconvene* **[this morning]** **[in Ottawa]**. (NEWS†)

In each of these sentences, the most important information concerns the time of the events. In **1**, the reason for Maya drinking *tonight* is that Vern left *today*, not that he went to San Francisco State. In **2**, it is the frequency of Frank's grappling with the sea that accounts for his dulled sense of adventure. In **3**, the freshness of the flowers is emphasized by their having been flown in *that morning*. In **4**, interestingly, the fact that the meetings are taking place in Ottawa has already been established in the news article, and thus the only new information provided by the adverbials is the time when the leaders will reconvene (*this morning*). Example **4** thus provides a contrast with the typical ordering of information in clauses (i.e. with new information following given information; 11.1.1).

Time adverbials also precede place and manner adverbials when they are marking a sequence of events. This pattern is particularly noticeable with the time adverb *then* used before manner adverbials:

5 *Bryant said, "I think I'll talk to the Rosen organization myself, while you're away." He eyed Rick, [then], [silently].* (FICT)

6 *He looked at her [then], [closely].* (FICT)

7 *<...> and [then] [slowly] he got his chin over it.* (FICT†)

8 *The software [then] [automatically] returns the selected document to the fax machine.* (NEWS)

As it conveys a sequence of events, *then* not only expresses a meaning of time, but also serves a cohesive function. In addition, when placed in final position, these series give special emphasis to the manner adverbial, typically setting it off from the rest of the clause with a comma, as in **5** and **6**.

Finally, in sequences where place adverbials precede manner adverbials, the place adverbials may also be more integrated into the clause structure. Particularly in fiction, place adverbials are often obligatory, while manner adverbials add extra description:

*<...> a bird, a vision of red and yellow, flashed [upwards] [with a witch-like cry].* (FICT†)

*<...> the gigantic red evening, whose reflection bled away in the deserted swimming pools scattered [everywhere] [like so many mirages] <...>* (FICT†)

These place adverbials are typically adverbials of direction.

## 10.2.7.2  Homosemantic place, time, and manner series

**CORPUS FINDINGS** [1]

➤ In general, homosemantic series of adverbials (place-place, time-time, and manner-manner) are less common than heterosemantic sequences (cf. Figures 10.14–16).
➤ The exception is place-place series in fiction, which are notably common and more frequent than place-time combinations in that register.

**Table 10.7**  **Relative length of first and second adverbials in homosemantic series (all registers combined)**

each ● represents 5%

| order | 1st adverbial is longer | 2nd adverbial is longer |
|---|---|---|
| place-place | ● ● ● ● | ● ● ● ● ● ● ● ● ● ● ● ● ● ● ● ● ● ● |
| time-time | ● ● ● | ● ● ● ● ● ● ● ● ● ● ● ● ● ● ● ● ● ● |
| manner-manner | ● | ● ● ● ● ● ● ● ● ● ● ● ● ● ● ● ● ● ● ● ● |

➤ In all three kinds of homosemantic series, the most typical order has the shorter adverbial preceding the longer.

### DISCUSSION OF FINDINGS

In most homosemantic series, the second adverbial is longer than the first:

> It's *[still] [three weeks away].*
> (CONV) <time + time>

> *Miss Tish had taken Miss Monti [upstairs] [to the little parlor opening to the balcony off from her bedroom].* (FICT) <place + place>

> *Her arm was raised [high] [in a clenched fist].* (FICT) <manner + manner>

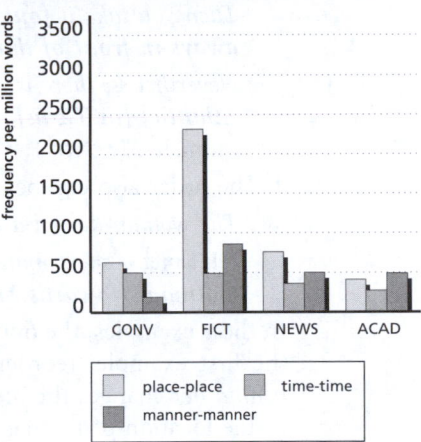

Figure 10.17

**Frequencies of homosemantic circumstance adverbials in series**

However, a variety of other factors influences the order of place + place and time + time series.

## A  Place-place sequences

For place-place series there are four particularly important factors:

1  The most common sequence of place-place adverbials shows movement from a source to a goal, or in a direction to a goal:

> *The packed assembly switched its gaze [from the speaker] [to the far end of the chamber].* (FICT†)

> *They had detached themselves from the torrent of peoples that in prehistory had poured [out of China] [onto the countless islands of the Pacific].* (FICT†)

> *The BAE 1000 will be able to fly up to 15 passengers direct [from London] [to the West Coast of the United States, Rio de Janeiro or Singapore] with one stop off.* (NEWS)

> *The dramatic development of transplant surgery brought this issue [out of the restrained polemics of academia] [into the hurly-burly of public discussion].* (ACAD)

In the last example the source and goal are metaphorical rather than physical ones.

2  The order of adverbials can also reflect the physical sequence of movement:

> *He moved [from the bridge], [through the gap in the wall], and walked down the towpath.* (FICT)

> *One of the doors led to the dining room, one to the side verandah, and the other [down broken marble steps] [into a tangled and overgrown garden].* (FICT)

In the second example the movement is potential, for anyone using the door being described.

3  Place-place sequences also often move from an adverbial with more general
    reference to a more specified location:

> I've found another tin opener *[here]* *[in the erm in the shed]*. (CONV)

> Then you take it *[outside]* *[under that first streetlight back up the street*
> *aways in front of that green house]*. (FICT)

> Nevertheless, there is even worse to come, for *[on the other side of the*
> *Atlantic]* *[in Texas]*, we find the Austin Chalk of the same age and
> character. (ACAD†)

4  The order also can be determined by a need for communicative clarity.

> The woman darted a wild-eyed glance *[behind her]* *[into the bar]*. (FICT)

> Paul met a short man with a long red beard stumping along *[behind the*
> *footman]* *[towards Margot's study]*. (FICT†)

In these examples, the opposite order changes the meaning of the clause. Thus, in
the first example, reordering the adverbials as *a wild-eyed glance into the bar*
*behind her* changes the meaning such that *behind her* is then understood to refer
to the location of the bar, rather than where the woman darted the glance.

## B  Time-time sequences

Five factors are particularly noteworthy in the order of time-time series.

1  Many of the first items in these series express frequency or duration, while
    the second gives a position in time:

> She's not been asleep *[a minute]* *[all night]*. (CONV)

> So he's got that job *[all the time]* *[now]*. (CONV)

Relationship in time is also expressed by *still* before a time-position adverbial:

> We'd be in the water *[still]* *[at six]*. (CONV)

> The move's *[still]* *[in six days]*, neh? (FICT)

2  In some cases, both time adverbials specify position in time, with the first
    referring to time in the day and the second to a longer period, especially the
    day itself:

> I thought Tracy and Sharon used to get drunk *[at lunchtime]* *[on a Friday]*
> and have a punch up. (CONV)

> Well they know I'm coming *[sometime]* *[today]*. (CONV)

> I went off to work *[at nine o'clock]* *[each morning]*. (FICT)

> Doctor Fischer will see Mr Jones *[at five o'clock]* *[on Thursday]*. (FICT)

> A lone masked gunman called to the house *[around 9:40 pm]* *[on Monday]*.
> (NEWS†)

3  *Now* and *then* are often placed before other time adverbials. They are often
    used to establish a point in time and are followed by a prepositional phrase
    describing duration:

> I felt right faint *[then]* *[for a minute]*. (CONV)

> She's been out *[now]* *[for twenty minutes]*. (CONV)

> This has been his custom *[now]* *[for years]*. (FICT†)

> Paul D had not trembled since 1856 and *[then]* *[for eighty-three days in a*
> *row]*. (FICT)

> The longer you leave it the more likely you are to profit from the upward
> trend in equities established *[now]* *[for nearly a century]*. (ACAD)

4 There are also certain time-time sequences, primarily in academic prose, in which the second adverbial functions like an appositive of the first (cf. 8.10). That is, the second adverbial restates the time introduced by the first. These series tend to occur initially:

> But *[today]*, *[over thirty years after Bassett's book appeared]*, is there anything new to say about 1931? (ACAD)

> *[In 1928]*, *[a year after it was published]*, a reviewer from Northwestern University said that it should be required reading for every graduate student. (ACAD†)

> *[In 1934]*, *[one year after Adolf Hitler came to power in Germany at the head of mass movement]*, the American sociologist Herbert Blumer published an "outline of collective behavior". (ACAD†)

5 Finally, one particular adverb—*again*—is placed before many different kinds of time adverbials. These series fit the criterion of the shorter adverbial preceding the longer; however, the use of this particular adverb is especially notable in both conversation and news:

> And then I'm up *[again]* *[at five]*. (CONV)

> So she said she would come *[again]* *[tomorrow]*. (CONV)

> Stocks edged higher *[again]* *[yesterday]*. (NEWS†)

> The liner QE2 will cruise *[again]* *[on October 4]* after repairs. (NEWS†)

## 10.2.7.3  Series of three and more adverbials

Grammatically, there is no limit to the number of adverbials that can be used in a series, though of course there is a limit to the number that the reader or addressee can follow. Series of three or more adverbials in conversation tend to be fairly short and concrete, often referring to place and time, as are many series in fiction, especially in dialog:

1 *I have to be [at her house] [at seven o'clock] [Thursday]*. (CONV)

2 *He'll be [in court] [tomorrow morning] [at Enfield]*. (FICT)

Fiction also uses series longer than two that incorporate manner adverbials with time and place:

3 *I was [here], [with Uncle Nick], [thirty years ago]*. (FICT)

4 *Hari strode [endlessly] [back and forth] [behind the bars]*.(FICT)

The expository registers have more widely varied series, including both longer adverbials and differing semantic categories:

5 *A coaching session for senior women footballers is to be held [at the racecourse ground in Wrexham] [between 6.30pm and 8pm tomorrow] [as part of a community sports programme]*. (NEWS) <place (position) + time (duration) + manner>

6 *Lord Justice Ralph Gibson said that neither the plaintiff nor the defendant applied [to the court] [at any time before judgment] [for an order under order 5, rule 52]*. (NEWS†) <place (direction) + time (position) + purpose>

7 *It then rose [to 54.6 centimeters] [in 1990], [due to an unusually wet summer]*. (ACAD) <degree + time (position) + cause>

**8** *The Roman literature was collected and condensed [into one volume]*
*[about the year 1240] [by a senator from Bologna, Petrus Crescentius,*
*whose book was one of the most popular treatises on agriculture of*
*any time, being frequently copied* <...> *].* (ACAD†) <place (direction)
+ time (position) + agent>

Regardless of the number of adverbials in the series or their semantic
categories, the general factors outlined above still influence the order of the
adverbials. For example, in **1**, **2**, **3**, **7**, and **8** the adverbial that is more integrated
with the verb, either as an obligatory complement or in collocational specificity, is
placed adjacent to the verb, before the other adverbials. As a result, the general
preferred order for pairwise sequences is common in the longer series as well;
thus, place adverbials occur before time adverbials in many of the examples above.
In addition, samples **6**, **7**, and **8** illustrate the longest adverbials appearing last in
the series.

Placement in series can of course also be used for emphasis, or physically to
show the sequence of events. The following homosemantic place series from
fiction describes a sequence of events, and, typical of such series, it also includes a
coordinating conjunction before the last adverbial:

*J.T. and the rest of the crowd followed me [out of the house], [up the street*
*to the streetlight] and [in front of the green house].* (FICT)

## 10.2.8 Clauses as circumstance adverbials

Semantic category, grammatical form, and positional distribution are all
important in understanding clausal circumstance adverbials as well as those
realized as single words and phrases. However, analyses of clauses include slightly
different foci: clauses include additional semantic categories; they have several
different syntactic realizations; and they rarely occur in medial position. In
addition, many clauses include the use of a subordinator.

This section focuses on issues related specifically to clausal forms. First the
semantic categories of clauses are broken down in detail (10.2.8.1–2). Then the
distribution and roles of the different forms of clauses are examined (10.2.8.3–4),
and issues specific to non-finite clauses are covered (10.8.5). Positions of clauses
are then discussed (10.2.8.6). Finally, variation in the use of subordinators is
covered (10.2.8.7–12).

### 10.2.8.1 Semantic categories of circumstance adverbial clauses

As with non-clausal adverbials, adverbial clauses, both finite and non-finite, are
used to realize time, place, manner, and contingency semantic categories. Section
10.2.1 illustrates these uses of adverbial clauses. The following are additional
examples.

Time adverbial:

**When the units are sold**, *the city expects to recover all but its $825,000*
*initial investment.* (NEWS)

Place adverbial:

*And* **wherever you go** *there's such a ordeal.* (CONV)

Manner adverbial:

> He smoothed the short sprays of leathery green leaves between his finger and thumb **as if their texture might tell him something**. (FICT)

Contingency adverbial of reason:

> She should have jumped on it **because it would be a way for her to make friends and meet people**. (CONV)

Contingency adverbial of condition:

> Well, I'm going to feel lucky **if my car isn't towed**, I think. (CONV)

Clauses are also used for the less common semantic role of showing in what respect the remainder of the proposition is relevant:

> **As dinosaurs go**, they were the biggest of the big. (NEWS)

> **As far as farmers are concerned** tree planting has not been integrated into their work patterns or land management. (NEWS)

In discussing the semantic categories of adverbial clauses, it should also be noted that clauses of condition can be further divided into three subcategories. First, they can present an **open condition** (also often called 'real'); that is, the clause does not specify whether the condition is fulfilled or not:

> Read the paper **if you don't believe me**! (FICT)

> **If the consequences of a wrong decision are potentially very great (as in medical diagnosis or Air Traffic Control)** the decision-maker is likely to look for cautious (and probably inefficient) strategies. (ACAD)

Second, conditional clauses can present a **hypothetical condition** (also often called 'unreal'), specifying that the condition is not fulfilled:

> I would **if I was you**. (CONV)

> In fact, I've got relatives in Romania and **if I were still there**, I'd be a vampire because of my red hair and blue eyes, or brown eyes. (CONV) <note the use of subjunctive 'were' here>

> **If I could correct this** I certainly would. (NEWS)

Less commonly, adverbial clauses present a **rhetorical condition**. These clauses take the form of a conditional, but combined with the main clause, they make a strong assertion:

> You may think that I want to destroy the milk boards, but **if you believe that you will believe anything**. (NEWS)

In this example, the rhetorical conditional and its associated main clause function as a statement meaning 'You should not believe that'.

In addition to the above semantic categories, adverbial clauses fit other semantic categories that are not found with non-clausal structures. Clauses can be used to show **preference**, typically with the subordinator *rather than*:

> It's crazy, it's crazy, if only people again'd sit back and look at it and see exactly what's happening, **rather than saying it serves them right**. (CONV)

> Planners working on Santa Cruz's 15-year general plan are recommending the city build more condominiums and apartments in urban areas **rather than sacrifice rural open spaces**. (NEWS)

> In the meantime it might be worthwhile to spend more time thinking how we might build humans into systems **rather than designing them out in the pursuit of technical advances**. (ACAD)

Clauses can also be used to convey **proportion**. These adverbial clauses are mostly introduced by *the* + comparative, and require a correlative *the* + comparative form in the main clause (2.4.8.2), marked here in *[]*:

> *The more Katheryn probed, [the more] Sally squirmed as she gave her version of what had gone on that night.* (FICT)

> *You're out to shock and **the more you astound and astonish people** [the happier] you'll be.* (NEWS)

Furthermore, there is a type of non-finite adverbial clause which cannot be clearly classified into any one semantic category. These **supplementive clauses**, typically *ing*-clauses, have been designated as a separate category (cf. 10.2.1.9):

1 *He shook his head, **still gazing at the patterns of sunshine on the grass outside the hut.*** (FICT)

2 ***Having stuffed the onionskin carbons in his briefcase**, Rick left his superior's office and ascended once more to the roof and his parked hovercar.* (FICT)

3 *She was very much as she had expected to be, **having found in her marriage nothing to surprise her nor to cause her the least distress.*** (FICT)

In these structures, the relationship between the supplementive adverbial clause and main clause is left indeterminate. For example, we might interpret all three of the above examples as denoting time relationships: concurrent time in **1**; and a series of events in **2** and **3**. However, the adverbial clause in **1** could also be considered a manner adverbial, and the adverbial clauses in **2** and **3** could be interpreted as reason clauses. Thus, rather than try to specify a single meaning for such clauses, we simply acknowledge them as showing a circumstance that supplements the action or state in the main clause.

## 10.2.8.2 Distribution of clausal semantic categories

The use of adverbial clauses tends to be concentrated in certain semantic categories, which differ across registers, as shown in Figures 10.18 and 10.19. Note that Figure 10.19 provides a detailed breakdown of clause types in the 'other' category shown in Figure 10.18.

### CORPUS FINDINGS [1]

➤ The overall distribution of adverbial clauses across registers is similar to the relative distribution of circumstance adverbials generally, with fiction well ahead of the other registers (Figure 10.1).

➤ There are considerable differences in the preferred semantic categories of clauses across the registers:

➤ Condition clauses are most common in conversation, and moderately common in academic prose.

➤ Purpose clauses are most common in academic prose and news.

➤ Reason/cause clauses are common only in conversation.

➤ Time clauses are very common in fiction and news.

➤ Supplementive clauses are very common in fiction, relatively rare in news and academic prose, and almost non-existent in conversation.

➤ Although not particularly frequent overall, two other categories have marked distributions across registers: manner clauses are considerably more common in fiction than in the other registers; concessive clauses are notably more common in the written registers (especially news and academic prose) than conversation.

**DISCUSSION OF FINDINGS**

Each of the most common semantic categories in each register plays an important role in fulfilling the communicative needs of the register.

A **Conversation**

With respect to conversation, condition, reason/cause, and time are particularly common categories. With clauses of condition, speakers explicitly mark the conditions on the truth of what they are saying, including both real and unreal conditions:

> *If we move some of these off the table* we'll have more room to do our pictures. (CONV)
>
> Now *if you were using this* this is what we would do. (CONV)
>
> I mean *if I knew for the fact that I was gonna get this job at the hospital* I would pay for it. (CONV)
>
> *If we could afford it* we'd get one. (CONV)

Conditional clauses are also used when giving commands or making suggestions to others:

> You can hold her *if you want*. (CONV)
>
> You can leave it right there *if you want*. (CONV)
>
> Well you can stop being a fusspot *if you don't mind*. (CONV)

Figure 10.18

**Frequencies of semantic categories of circumstance adverbial clauses**

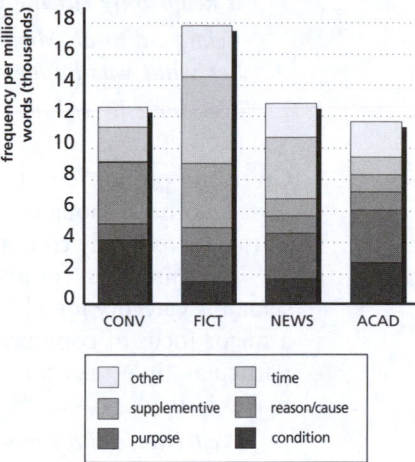

Figure 10.19

**Breakdown of frequencies for 'other' categories of circumstance adverbial clauses**

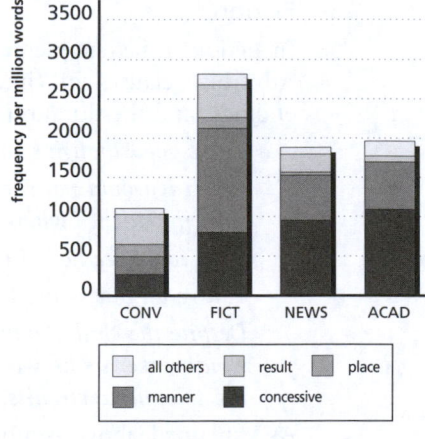

The conditional clause mitigates the force of the suggestion or command, making it the hearer's choice. In some cases, however, the apparent choice is clearly not to be taken literally. The last example above, for instance, was said to a child as a definite request to stop fussing.

The reason/cause clauses in conversation are used as speakers explain their thoughts, feelings, and activities. *Cos* in these examples represents a reduced spoken form of *because*:

*We were laughing about it.* **Cos I was telling them that we were sick of seeing the rain and that.** (CONV)

*I'll probably go down and see Dennis, get er – a nut – so I can get it level* **cos it keeps only cutting on half of the side.** (CONV)

*Velma called on Monday, erm,* **[because I rang her up on Sunday to tell her what was happening]**, **[cos** *I mean* **she didn't know it]**. (CONV)

*Well honestly I, I don't know* **because I haven't been in the discussions.** (CONV)

Given the proportion of conversational discourse that is spent explaining one's own or others' thoughts, feelings, and actions, it is not surprising that reason/cause is a relatively common semantic role for adverbial clauses in conversation.

The third most common category for conversation, time, is also an important semantic category for all circumstance adverbials generally. As discussed in 10.2.2, a major focus of conversation is who will do what when. Rather than naming a particular time (e.g. *this morning, yesterday, in two hours*) clauses are used to make particular times clear in relation to other times and activities:

*Well I was thinking we could – you know, leave it on* **while we're on the job.** (CONV)

*Could you bring in a couple ashtrays* **when you come in** *love?* (CONV)

*I want to er clean the floor* **before I take a load of stuff in.** (CONV)

**After I'd choked for half an hour** – *she went to sleep.* (CONV)

**Before you came home** – *the white cat came back!* (CONV)

## B Fiction

In fiction, time, supplementive, and manner clauses are all relatively common. Adverbial clauses of time are particularly useful for describing beginnings, endings, and the duration of activities, or for describing concurrent events:

*These good thoughts carry me* **until I'm right downtown.** (FICT)

*When it would not suck from the bottle she fed it with a teaspoon, fretting with impatience* **when it coughed and spluttered and cried.** (FICT)

*Tom could see her in tears* **as she wrote it.** (FICT)

*You've all but stopped working* **since she's around.** (FICT)

*Despite the chill, damp air, Philip was sweating heavily beneath his light windbreaker* **as he waited impatiently for his call to work its way through the telephone circuits.** (FICT)

As explained above, supplementive clauses leave the relationship between the adverbial clause and main clause inexplicit. This lack of explicitness makes the clauses very useful in fiction, which requires descriptive details to create an imaginary world, but does not have the need for the explicitness of the more expository registers. The supplementive clauses often describe happenings subsidiary to, or accompanying, the main narrative. Besides implying time and reason/cause relationships, as was illustrated above, they can also be used to give the narrator's interpretation of events:

*He began to puff at his pipe, no doubt* **arranging his opinion in his mind.** (FICT)

*Oh we can't take credit where it isn't due, protested the man from the mafia,* **enjoying himself.** (FICT)

Supplementive clauses are also used to give additional description of an action:

> *Dangling the keys in front of everybody's nose, I unlocked the caddy.* (FICT)
>
> *She would carry her nightlight into his bedroom and crouch by the cot for an hour or more, [her eyes fixed on his sleeping face], [her restlessness soothed by his peace].* (FICT†)
>
> *The conductor came along the aisle, waving his arms.* (FICT)

The manner clauses used in fiction also increase the amount of description. They are often comparative in nature and sometimes depend on descriptive similes:

> *He nodded to himself, pulled his torn and slashed tunic around him as though warding off the cold shadows.* (FICT)
>
> *I turned to face her, very quickly, as though strong hands on my shoulders had turned me around.* (FICT)
>
> *Sarah's head was aching as if it had taken a direct hit from a sledgehammer.* (FICT)

Other manner clauses give more literal details about the action:

> *There followed an orgy of shopping as Lovat had predicted.* (FICT)
>
> *He shook his head, as if reproving her, but his smile was fond.* (FICT)
>
> *He took to pacing the streets of London, very often in the poorer areas, in all weathers, alone, seldom speaking to anyone but staring, staring as if he had never seen a poor person in his life before.* (FICT)

## C  News

In news, time and purpose clauses are frequently used. Section 10.2.2 discusses the important role of time adverbials in the register of news. As it turns out, clauses that mark time are particularly useful in two ways. First they can describe certain events in relation to others:

> *The Chelsea player damaged cruciate ligaments in the game and faces more surgery before he can return to action.* (NEWS)
>
> *Gold was slightly easier yesterday, ending in London at $362.00/$362.50 an ounce after the dollar surged.* (NEWS†)
>
> *Staff and students are turning the world of learning upside down during Alternative Learning Week as they try out inventive ways of teaching and learning.* (NEWS)

Secondly, clauses with the subordinator *when* allow a more complete description of a time than is possible with adverbs, noun phrases and prepositional phrases:

> *When he is not on the golf course, he is making large sums as a company director.* (NEWS)
>
> *Interpol joined the hunt for Katie when fears grew that the youngster had already fled abroad.* (NEWS)
>
> *And when a relief worker asked Nicholson to take her to England, he agreed.* (NEWS)
>
> *Some newspapers are already running at a loss in the hope that they will move back into profit when the economic situation improves.* (NEWS)

Purpose clauses reflect the need for news stories to explain motivations behind events:

*Tendring Council's dog owners pack has been put together **to tackle a range of pooch problems including strays, fouling and dangerous dogs.*** (NEWS)

*DBCM is an offshoot of Deutsche Bank Capital Management International, founded in 1983 **to offer fund management primarily to international companies with operations in West Germany.*** (NEWS)

*Further tests are underway at Baltimore, in California and at Seattle's Cancer Research Center, **to see if the treatment can be repeated on other patients.*** (NEWS)

Like purpose clauses, some of the less common semantic categories, such as reason/cause, supplementive, and condition, are also important in providing explanatory information or background material for a news story.

Reason/cause clause:

*British Rail said the train was halted **because there was no relief guard.*** (NEWS)

Supplementive clause:

*Shares in Tokai, the eighth largest bank in the world, are due to begin trading today, **following the route pioneered by Fuji Bank in 1987.*** (NEWS)

Concessive clause:

*The elections were peaceful, **though hampered by delays in the delivery of ballots and the opening of poll booths.*** (NEWS)

Condition clause:

*It would make more money from a casino-hotel **if Louisiana approved landbased gambling.*** (NEWS)

## D  Academic prose

In academic prose, purpose and condition clauses are notably common, and concessive clauses are somewhat more common than in the other registers. The purpose clauses tend to appear in texts or sections of texts that present procedures or make recommendations for improving conditions:

*Changing the planting date and use of shelter belts have also been suggested **to protect the crop.*** (ACAD)

***In order to help such children**, it is necessary to introduce novel and artificial procedures to assist learning.* (ACAD)

*This is the sort of case in which judges must exercise the discretionary power described a moment ago, **to use extralegal standards to make what conventionalism declares to be new law.*** (ACAD)

*More air must be bled from the compressor **to cool the hotter power turbine.*** (ACAD)

Both conditional and concessive clauses are important in the presentation of arguments in academic prose. Conditions are often used to introduce or develop arguments:

***If aggression and violence are part and parcel of what it means to be human**, then why is it that there exist societies where aggressive or violent behavior is conspicuous by its absence?* (ACAD) <note the use of correlative *then* in the main clause>

> *Often the analyst is left with an uncomfortable feeling that more could have been achieved **if the situation had been approached more methodically**.* (ACAD)

> *Unless they can get people in the organization to do what must be done, they will not succeed.* (ACAD)

Concessive clauses are often used to show the limitations of certain facts, events, or claims:

> *It is possible to separate one from the others, **though in certain situations one aspect may be more involved**.* (ACAD)

> ***Although we could not separate scirpus roots from the roots of spartina and distichilis**, a comparison of the rooting profiles <...> indicated an increase in root growth by scirpus.* (ACAD†)

> *A number of field experiments have demonstrated the importance of such "keystone predators", **although the great majority of studies have centered on marine and freshwater ecosystems**.* (ACAD)

Taken together, clauses of condition and concession are important contributors to the development of arguments, which is a significant goal of academic writing.

Conditional clauses serve an additional role in academic prose, however. Besides functioning in the presentation of arguments, they play an important part in specifying the conditions under which facts hold:

> ***If light is moving in the direction labelled z in the figure**, it has two distinct possibilities of polarisation.* (ACAD†)

> *No significant distress has been recorded when pigs inhale air containing 20 000 ppm (2 per cent) carbon dioxide **if normal quantities of oxygen are present**.* (ACAD)

> ***If the phase excitation is changed** it is this other pair of rotor teeth which align with the newly-excited stator teeth.* (ACAD)

Finally, although they are not common, it is interesting to note that supplementive clauses are used in academic prose—a register often noted for the precision of its communication of information. These clauses often occur in descriptions of procedures; the relationship between the supplementive clause and the proposition of the main clause remain semantically inexplicit:

> *The important thing to remember is to have implicit faith in the instrument indications, **ignoring any contrary physical sensations**.* (ACAD)

> *The reheat fuel/air ratio would have to be calculated accurately **remembering that the fuel is burnt not in air but in the combustion gases from the main combustion chamber**.* (ACAD)

> *Hence, the enclosing box excursion domains can be extracted and investigated **yielding the spatial relationships between member parts**.* (ACAD)

## 10.2.8.3  Syntactic forms of circumstance adverbial clauses

Five major types of adverbial clause can be distinguished: finite clauses, *ed*-clauses, *ing*-clauses, *to*-clauses, and verbless clauses (10.1.2). These types differ in their overall frequencies and in their distribution across registers.

## 10.2.8.4 Distribution of clausal syntactic forms

➤ In all four registers, finite clauses are by far the most common type of circumstance adverbial clause.

> ➤ In conversation, finite clauses account for almost 90% of all circumstance clauses.

➤ *To*-clauses are the next most common circumstance clause type overall. They are most common in academic prose, and their frequency decreases across news, fiction, and conversation.

➤ *Ing*-clauses are the third most common type overall; they are particularly common in fiction, but extremely rare in conversation.

➤ *Ed*- and verbless clauses are rare in all four registers.

**Figure 10.20**
**Frequencies of syntactic forms for circumstance adverbial clauses**

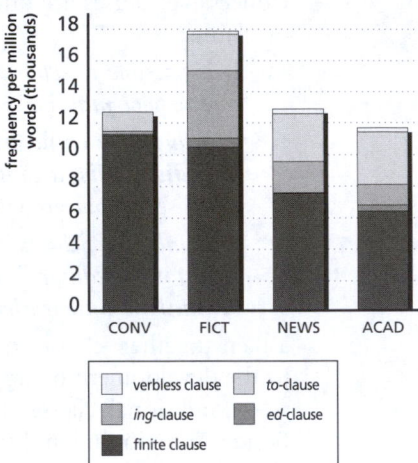

Finite clauses have several advantages over the other types of adverbial clause, allowing them to be adapted to a wide range of uses.

### A Semantic roles

First, finite adverbial clauses generally require a subordinator and can be used to express clearly a great variety of semantic relationships, including time, manner, reason/cause, result, concession, and condition. The adverbial clause is in *[]* in the following examples and the subordinator is in bold.

Time:

> Well [*after* you've taken tax and insurance back] you see, you've lost about three hundred, three fifty. (CONV)

Manner:

> He undid his sash and ripped off his sopping kimono and, [*as though* it were defiled], hurled it in a ditch. (FICT)

Reason/cause:

> If so, it will be a gamble, [*because* he flopped on his only previous international appearance in Saudi Arabia]. (NEWS)

Result:

> It was windy, [*so that* the leaves now and then brushed open a star, and the stars themselves seemed to be shaking and darting light and trying to flash out between the edges of the leaves]. (FICT)

Concession:

> [*Although* apprentices wasted a lot of time in their early years], most of them had picked up enough of the trade to be useful typesetters long before the seven years were up. (ACAD)

Condition:

> [*If you had really short hair*] *you'd dress exactly the same as her wouldn't you?* (CONV)

In some cases it is possible to use subordinators with non-finite, including verbless, clauses:

> [*Although a creature of the wilds*] *the primrose had a leaning towards civilization, and preened and smiled in a jam-jar in some cottage window without resentment, living quite a week* [*if given water*]. (FICT)

> *It's about showing compassion for the planet we live on and trying to hand on as much beauty and good-will as we possibly can to future generations;* [*while improving our own quality of life*]. (NEWS)

However, only a small percentage of non-finite clauses actually include subordinators (10.2.8.8), so non-finite adverbial clauses often lack the clarity of relationship with the main clause that finite clauses incorporate.

In contrast to finite clauses' semantic adaptability, many non-finite clauses are semantically limited. This limitation is most notable for *to*-clauses. In all four registers, nearly all adverbial *to*-clauses express purpose, with the purposive meaning being sometimes overtly marked by the subordinator *in order* + *to* (the form *to* in this case is the infinitive marker and not strictly part of the subordinator).

## B Overt subject

A second advantage of finite clauses is that they contain an overtly stated subject. Therefore, the subject of the adverbial can be different from the subject of the main clause, expressing its own circumstantial information. In the following examples, the adverbial clause is marked in [], while the subjects of both the adverbial clause and the main clause are given in bold:

> [*When* **the call** *first came in from Fraxilly*], **I** *didn't accept it.* (FICT)

> *But* [*when* **all the arts journalists in London** *start fluffing up their tail feathers in unison*], **the effect** *is not so much of natural compulsion as of chummy conspiracy.* (NEWS)

> **Yamagata's (1958) investigations** *established the fact that the number of tillers and ears increase with the intensity and quantity of light,* [*while* **Stansel** *found (1967) that favourable yield response to high levels of nitrogen occurs only when the crop receives high light levels*]. (ACAD)

In contrast, non-finite clauses usually do not contain subjects:

> *I borrowed a portable phone* [*to ring Waterloo*] [*to complain*]. (NEWS)

> *More than a century ago J.S. Mill argued for universal education on moral grounds,* [*holding that it would manifestly increase the general balance of pleasure over pain, happiness over* **unhappiness**]. (NEWS)

With these non-finite adverbial clauses, the subject of the adverbial clause must normally be the same as that of the main clause (i.e. 'I ring Waterloo and I complain'; 'J.S. Mill was holding that ...'), but see 10.2.8.5.

## C Tense/modality marking

Finally, finite clauses also allow the verb phrase in the adverbial clause to be marked for a different tense or modality from the main clause, options which are not possible with non-finite clauses. Such differences in verb characteristics are commonly needed with a variety of semantic relationships, including time, purpose, concession, and reason. In the following examples, the adverbial clause is marked in *[]*, while the verb phrases of both the adverbial clause and the main clause are given in bold:

> *Last Saturday we* **were** *frantically* **doing** *that painting [before it* **got** *dark].* (CONV) <time>

> *[Since Bassett's book* **was published**], *biographies of most of the main protagonists* **have appeared**. (ACAD) <time>

> *The personal allowances* **are being increased** *[so that this* **will take** *a lot of lower paid people out of tax <…> ]* (CONV†) <purpose>

> *The president's pet legislative project* **is** *in trouble again on Capitol Hill [even though congressional support* **seemed** *to be building at the end of last year].* (NEWS†) <concession>

> *It* **might be argued** *that children experience difficulties in the area of language development [precisely because the normal developmental processes* **have broken down**]. (ACAD) <cause>

The difference in tense and modality is essential in hypothetical conditional clauses; hypothetical meaning is expressed in the subordinate clause by the past tense, whereas in the main clause it is expressed by *would* or some other modal auxiliary:

> *Well you* **might get** *some facts right [if you* **did**]! (CONV)

> *[If London* **had been given** *time to study these], it* **would have seen** *that Smurfit is looking well placed in a world market notoriously prone to cyclical demand.* (NEWS)

> *[If that* **were** *true], it* **would** *perhaps* **support** *the conclusion that a different conception of a condition-set for an effect enters into our beliefs and proceedings.* (ACAD†) <note the use of subjunctive 'were' here>

In sum, then, finite clause's use of subordinators, explicit subjects, and finite verb phrases allow them to be used much more widely than non-finite clauses.

**D** *To*-clauses

As noted above, *to*-clauses—the second most common adverbial clause structure—are almost always used to convey purpose:

> **To smooth the way**, *the school has taken special steps.* (NEWS)

> *It would be inappropriate to divert scarce funds* **in order to support the kind of specialised provision which the college would offer**. (NEWS†)

> *Reforming is the process whereby straight-run gasoline is cracked* **in order to raise the octane number**. (ACAD)

The higher proportion of *to*-clauses in academic prose and news is thus tied to their higher use of purpose adverbials generally (Figure 10.18).

The only other notable use of *to*-clauses is to show results. This use is most common in news, particularly in sports reportage:

> *Dick Johnson and John Bowe of Australia, in a Ford Sierra, led from the start yesterday* **to win the Bathurst 1,000-km touring car race**. (NEWS†)

> *Internazionale shrugged off defeat by Malmo* **to beat the leaders, Roma, also by 3–0**. (NEWS)

**E** *Ed-* **and** *ing-***clauses**

The only other clause type with notable frequency is the *ing*-clause. Almost 90 percent of all adverbial *ing*-clauses are supplementive clauses (10.2.8.1). Hence the register patterns of *ing*-clauses and supplementive clauses are very similar.

Finally, although rare, *ed*-clauses are most commonly associated with supplementive clauses in academic prose and fiction. Some of these supplementive clauses, especially in academic prose, add information by making a comparison:

> Now about half of women who work in social welfare are parttime, **compared to 38% in the private sector.** (ACAD†)

> In this case the static position error is 2/3 degree, **compared to the 8 degree error when the load is directly coupled.** (ACAD†)

In fiction, these supplementive clauses are often added descriptors of a participant in the narrative, and occur both with subjects and without:

> He looked like a man born with the Tory party in mind, **[his patrician head set on an aristocratic frame, [a mane of hair combed meticulously]].** (FICT)

> I went on waiting, **tinged with doubt.** (FICT)

## 10.2.8.5  Dangling participles

A well-known prescriptive rule forbids the use of the so-called **dangling** or **unattached participle**, i.e. a non-finite circumstantial *ing*-clause with an understood subject that differs from that of the main clause. Consider the following examples:

> **Leaving the road,** they went into the deep resin-scented darkness of the trees. (FICT)
> cf. with dangling participle: **Leaving the road,** the deep resin-scented darkness of the trees surrounded them.

> **After trying to sneak their plans through,** Renfrewshire Enterprise are now trying to defuse the situation. (NEWS)
> cf. with dangling participle: **After trying to sneak their plans through,** an attempt is being made by Renfrewshire Enterprise to defuse the situation.

As the second, hypothetical, example of each pair shows, dangling participles can lead to impossible or absurd interpretations if taken literally, though readers can most often guess the implied meaning. In the first example, the dangling participle version has *the deep resin-scented darkness* as subject of the main clause, and so implies that it is the darkness rather than the people that left the road. In the second example the direct implication is that *an attempt* tried to sneak their plans through.

As we see from these examples, dangling participles can arise both when a subordinator is included and when one is not. Furthermore, non-equivalence of subjects in the two clauses can also arise with all types of non-finite adverbial clauses, not just *ing*-clauses.

In certain situations the rule that a non-finite adverbial clause must have the same subject as the main clause is relaxed. The following are examples.

- Adverbial clauses (especially conditional clauses) for which the understood subject is an entire clause implied by the main clause:

> *If necessary, you can take over.* (FICT)

The verbless adverbial clause here is equivalent to *If it is necessary for you to take over*, where *for you to take over* is the notional subject of *is*.

- Adverbial clauses which describe main clauses that have non-referential *it* as subject:

> *When writing the formulae of both covalent molecules and ionic compounds, it is often useful to use the valency of an atom, ion or group of atoms.* (ACAD)

Here we assume the subject of the adverbial clause to be the same unstated, generic people who 'use the valency of an atom …'.

- Adverbial clauses in formal scientific writing where the short passive is used:

> *To study drivers' visual scanning behavior in relation to game detection, a series of field experiments was performed.* (ACAD)

Here the subject of *study* in the adverbial clause corresponds to the omitted agent of *performed* in the main clause, and is understood as 'us' or 'the researchers'.

- Adverbial clauses in instructions with main clauses that contain imperatives:

> *Write out the dialog changing vocabulary items.* (ACAD)

Here the subject of the imperative *write* is in fact the same as that of *changing* in the dependent clause, i.e. 'you'.

## 10.2.8.6  Positions of adverbial clauses

Adverbial clauses can be placed in two main positions relative to the main clause with which they are associated – initial and final (i.e. before or after the main clause).

Initial position:

> **1** *When the elevator creakily arrived he rode it not to his own floor but to the lower level on which the new tenant, Pris Stratton, now lived.* (FICT)
>
> **2** *To succeed again they will have to improve their fitness and concentration.* (NEWS)

Final position:

> **3** *She had begun to experience dizziness and tightness of the chest when she bent down.* (FICT†)
>
> **4** *I borrowed a portable phone to ring Waterloo.* (NEWS)

A small number of adverbial clauses occur in medial positions:

> **5** *A man who, if necessary, can make certain Evan Kendrick is given the truth.* (FICT)

Most of these medial circumstance clauses are short and verbless, and often occur in marked constructions such as parenthetical comments or non-clausal material (3.15) like the noun phrase in **5** above. Although medial positions are hypothetically possible with many clauses, the resulting constructions are very difficult to process even with short clauses. For example, compare the following hypothetical sentences with **4** above:

> *I, to ring Waterloo, borrowed a portable phone.*
>
> *I borrowed, to ring Waterloo, a portable phone.*

Occurrences of medial adverbial clauses are too rare for meaningful quantitative analysis; in this section we therefore focus on the choice between initial and final positions for adverbial clauses.

In conversation, final adverbial clauses are sometimes not contiguous with their main clauses because of another speaker's comment; however, we have analyzed these cases consistent with utterances that do not have interruptions. For example, in the following extract, the reason clause is analyzed in final position, despite the intervening *yeah*:

A: *Well, I guess it wasn't too much, but it was, it was a lot for me*
B: *Yeah.*
A: ***Because I didn't expect it***, *you know.* (CONV)

In addition, some adverbial clauses are added by an interlocutor to another speaker's main clause. When occurrences are frequent enough for meaningful analysis, these are identified as 'other speaker main clause' below.

## A   Positions of non-finite and verbless clauses

### CORPUS FINDINGS [1]

➤ In all registers, the large majority of non-finite clauses are in final position.
➤ The written registers have a slightly higher proportion of non-finite clauses placed initially than conversation does.

**Table 10.8**   **Positions of non-finite and verbless circumstance adverbial clauses across registers**

each ● represents 5%

|       | initial position | final position |
|-------|------------------|----------------|
| CONV  | ●                | ●●●●●●●●●●●●●●●●●●●● |
| FICT  | ●●●●             | ●●●●●●●●●●●●●●●● |
| NEWS  | ●●               | ●●●●●●●●●●●●●●●●●● |
| ACAD  | ●●●              | ●●●●●●●●●●●●●●●● |

### DISCUSSION OF FINDINGS

Clearly, final position is the unmarked choice for non-finite adverbial clauses in all registers. All the syntactic forms of non-finite clauses and all semantic categories typically occur in final position:

*He lifted his head and saw the coffee and drank some slowly, **not looking at me**.* (FICT)

*That figure is remarkable **when compared to just 87,000 during the first six months of last year**.* (NEWS)

*In the northern areas of Japan seedlings are raised in hotbeds **in order to produce satisfactory growth despite the low temperature**.* (ACAD)

Given the strong preference for final position, it is interesting to ask under what conditions adverbial clauses are ever placed in initial position, and particularly why fiction and academic prose have slightly higher proportions in initial position.

In fiction, the most common non-finite clauses are *ing*-clauses; these are usually supplementive clauses with an unspecified semantic role (10.2.8.4). This clause type occurs in initial position with slightly more than average frequency for all non-finite clauses in fiction.

In initial position, *ing*-clauses have two important ways of contributing to a narrative. Sometimes the adverbial clause introduces an activity or state of some duration, while the main clause describes a one-time event within the time frame of that activity or state:

> Now, **hiding beneath a bit of desert rock**, *he nodded to himself*. (FICT)
>
> **Getting slowly to his feet** *Inspector Garland faced Phil Resch and said,* *"Have you wanted to test me, too?"* (FICT†)
>
> **Whistling**, *he began to cut new wood for the window frame*. (FICT)
>
> In the bedroom, **getting her keys off the bureau**, *Toni glanced into the mirror*. (FICT)

These adverbial clauses set up a larger frame of activity within which the action of the main clause takes place. A similar meaning can be expressed using a finite adverbial clause with the subordinator *while* or *as* together with progressive aspect (e.g. *while he was hiding beneath a bit of desert rock, he nodded to himself*). However, as discussed previously, without overt subordinators, the precise semantic role of these adverbials is left less explicit.

The initial supplementive clauses can also be used to show a sequence of events. In these cases, the action in the adverbial clause happens prior to the action of the main clause:

> **Rising and going into the bedroom**, *Pris reappeared carrying a pen and a scrap of paper*. (FICT†)
>
> **Opening the inner door** *he nodded to his superior, who was busy on the phone*. (FICT)
>
> **Seating himself in a nearby chair** *he unzipped his briefcase*. (FICT)

In this use, the adverbial clauses provide a descriptive link which makes a character's new action coherent; in the first example above, for instance, it would not make sense for Pris to reappear with pen and paper without first disappearing by rising and going into the bedroom.

In contrast to the initial position clauses, supplementive clauses in final position often give more specific details or additional information about the action in the main clause:

> *She blinks,* **closing her eyes against the snow**. (FICT)
>
> *He echoed her phrase,* **applying it to himself**: *What am I to do?* (FICT)
>
> *The three of us used to sleep in one big bed and keep each other awake most of the night,* **giggling and speculating on the mysteries and wonders of Christmas morning**. (FICT)
>
> *He launched into a tirade of abuse against the Government,* **complaining that they were looking more like Tories every day**. (FICT)
>
> *"Oh all right, then," she said,* **concealing her disappointment**. (FICT)

However, when used with speaker tags in fiction, the supplementive clauses in final position often have a similar function to clauses in initial position, showing an activity of longer duration during which something is said:

> *"I know everything,"* Richards said, **grinning**. (FICT)
> *"Okay,"* he said, **nodding**. (FICT)
> *"I guess we're near the kitchen,"* he said, **eyeing Francesca**. (FICT)

In academic prose, many of the initial non-finite clauses are *to*-clauses of purpose, the most common form of non-finite clause in that register (10.2.8.4). One common function of these initial *to*-clauses in academic prose is to give a lead into the next stage of discussion, by stating its purpose:

> **To assess the impact on education**, *we turn to some specific cases.* (ACAD)
> **In order to estimate the possibilities of a driver to detect animals**, *it is necessary to discuss the importance of different sources of information for the driving task.* (ACAD)
> **In order to evaluate enthalpies of compounds**, *it is necessary to know the absolute enthalpies of the elements present in these compounds.* (ACAD)

In addition, initial purpose clauses can provide a cohesive link with the previous discourse:

> **In order to achieve these growth rates** *factors other than solar radiation must be non-limiting.* (ACAD)
> **In order to satisfy criterion (iii)** *the physiological and/or biochemical functions should be known.* (ACAD)
> **To remember these latter two definitions** *the author uses the mnemonics rest and rota.* (ACAD)

Thus, in these examples, the noun phrases in the initial adverbial clauses (*these growth rates, criterion (iii)*, and *these latter two definitions*), are items mentioned in the immediately preceding discourse.

## B   Positions of finite clauses

**CORPUS FINDINGS [1]**

➤ Whereas all types of non-finite clause are uniformly preferred in final position, the different types of finite clause are distributed in different ways.

➤ Concessive clauses show a slight preference for final position; this preference is shared across all registers.

➤ Conditional and time clauses have different positional distributions in conversation v. the three written registers:
> ➤ Conditional clauses in conversation have no strong preference for either position. In the written registers, there is a slight preference for initial position.
> ➤ Time clauses in all registers have a preference for final position, but the preference is stronger in the written registers.

➤ Reason/cause clauses exhibit a markedly different distributional pattern from all the other categories:
> ➤ Conversation and fiction have a very strong preference for final position.
> ➤ In news and academic prose only about 60% of these clauses occur in final position.

➤ The most common type of finite adverbial clause added by one speaker to another's utterance is that expressing condition, followed by clauses of reason/cause.

**DISCUSSION OF FINDINGS**

One of the most striking, though quantitatively small, differences in adverbial clause use across registers concerns adverbial clauses added to other-speaker main clauses in conversation. The face-to-face nature of conversation makes it possible

Table 10.9    **Positions of finite circumstance adverbial clauses**

each ■ represents 5%     □ represents less than 2.5%

**finite clauses of concession—all registers combined**

| | initial position | final position |
|---|---|---|
| | ■■■■■■■■ | ■■■■■■■■■■■■ |

**finite clauses of condition—conversation v. written registers**

| | initial position | final position | other speaker |
|---|---|---|---|
| CONV | ■■■■■■■■■ | ■■■■■■■■■ | ■■ |
| written | ■■■■■■■■■■■ | ■■■■■■■■ | |

**finite clauses of time—conversation v. written registers**

| | initial position | final position | other speaker |
|---|---|---|---|
| CONV | ■■■■■■■■■ | ■■■■■■■■■■■■ | □ |
| written | ■■■■■ | ■■■■■■■■■■■■<br>■■■ | |

**finite clauses of reason/cause—CONV/FICT v. NEWS/ACAD**

| | initial position | final position | other speaker |
|---|---|---|---|
| CONV/FICT | ■ | ■■■■■■■■■■■■<br>■■■■■■ | ■ |
| NEWS/ACAD | ■■■■■■■■ | ■■■■■■■■■■■■ | |

for one participant to add circumstances on to another participant's utterance. Often this occurs with conditional clauses, where a second speaker adds a condition qualifying the truth value of the first speaker's assertion:

> A: *And then they can appeal*
> B: ***If they wish.***
> A: *Yeah.* (CONV)

Interestingly, the first speaker often repeats the conditional clause, showing acceptance of the condition:

> A: *The only way it could matter is that somebody breathes the information to*
> *– if they could get hold of a card, and get into an office, they could*
> *actually use the information to make a payment.*
> B: ***If they knew how.***
> A: *If they knew how.* (CONV)

> A: *There are certain programmes which you can er put in eight eight eight*
> *and you get captions.*
> B: *Ah ye – yes, **if that's available.***
> A: *If it's available.* (CONV)

> A: *You'll study like mad – revise like mad and come out with a C.*
> B: ***If I'm lucky.***
> A: *If you're lucky.* (CONV)

Concessive clauses are also at times added to other-speakers' main clauses, as are reason clauses:

> A: *They wouldn't shore that up because there are only about eight houses up there, so it doesn't pay them to* <unclear>
> B: **Although they own that bit**
> A: *Al-although they own that bit*
> B: **or are responsible for it**
> A: *or are responsible* (CONV) <concessive>
>
> A: *The races that we call primitive are the ones that are conserving the world.*
> B: **Cos they adapt to it.** (CONV) <reason>

Although not common, these clauses illustrate the negotiation of meaning and the co-construction of discourse typical of conversation. Adverbial clauses can even be a speaker's complete turn as the discourse is built. (See further discussion of the organization of conversation in 14.3.)

Unlike non-finite clauses, finite clauses appear relatively often in both initial and final positions. A number of interacting factors affect the choice between these two positions. Similar influences occur across registers and across semantic categories, although their combined effect results in the different distributions described above. Three influences are discussed below, although in many cases these factors are related. Factors with particular importance for different registers or semantic classes are noted.

## A Cohesion and information structuring

Many finite adverbial clauses in initial position contain given information, referred to in the preceding discourse, while the main clause presents new information:

> A: *I say that'll give them something to talk about.*
> B: *Well yeah—**While they're talking about me** they're leaving someone else alone.* (CONV)

> *It's not the rummy that aggravates my blood pressure. **If there were no cards**, there would still be the stock market, and **if there weren't the stock market**, there would be the condominium in Florida.* (FICT†)

> *The houses were perched precariously up the hillsides* <...> ***Because it was so hilly** the area seemed constantly to be in a dark blue haze.* (FICT†)

In contrast, when the main clause contains given information, the adverbial clauses, with new information, tend to be in final position:

> *But you see Penny's got no compassion, **although she's my sister**.* (CONV) <during a discussion of personality characteristics of Penny>

> *Neither will need to become a forced seller **if the property market gets really nasty**.* (NEWS†) <after an explanation of two companies' good business footing>

> *The rest is easy **if one can find someone who knows the prices of such things as secretaries, pocket calculators or whatever is needed**.* (ACAD) <explaining the steps in a process>

When adverbial clauses with given information are in initial position, they can also serve important cohesive functions. For example, in the expository registers, many initial reason clauses use previously given (or inferrable) information as a reason for the new information in the main clause. The reason clause thus serves as a bridge between the previous discourse and the new information in the main clause:

> *Because there are children and therefore the woman has obviously been part of a couple at some point,* there is an assumption that in her single state she is critical, cynical and undermining of couples around her. (NEWS) <after introducing the idea of a single mother>

> *Because one did not know how accurately the clock had been ticking during the processes of weighing,* one could not know precisely the times at which movements of the shutter occurred between which the radiation was released. (ACAD) <after establishing that there were uncertainties in the rate of the clock>

Initial concessive clauses, too, often contain material which has been discussed previously:

> *Even though he is a long way out of the handicap* he has the ability to spring a shock. (NEWS)

> Thus, *although we are wary of claiming too much for statistical analysis,* we would regard it as an essential and important tool in stylistic description. (ACAD)

Initial clauses can also provide contrast with the preceding discourse. In the following example, the reason clause puts strong emphasis on people's misbehavior as opposed to the supposedly well-controlled intentions of the drug:

> You're supposedly meant to feel good for so long and then it's meant to wear off and there's meant to be no hangover effects or nothing and that's why it's a designer drug and that's why it—you know, it's supposed to be so good <...> But *because people mess about so much* it kills. (CONV)

## B Framing subsequent discourse

A second influence on the position of adverbial clauses is the role the adverbial plays in framing subsequent discourse. Those clauses that set up a frame for several subsequent sentences tend to be in initial position. This is a particularly important function for initial time clauses, which introduce the following discourse by giving its setting:

1 *When I took Katie to school this morning* <...> I had to drag her into school! She was screaming! She wants <...> teacher to take her off, teacher to take her off me. She was crying, I said I want to go home! I want to go home! (CONV†)

2 *When anyone's like that with me or with one of my friends* she just sits there looking at you because, cos she's big, she's kind of threatening sometimes, you know what I mean? She's sitting there with a fag hanging out her mouth. She just sits there staring at him saying you make any funny moves you'll see what you get. (CONV)

3 *When the president sent Congress his 419-page epistle on the economy Tuesday,* all the hits from yesteryear were playing once again: Tax cuts to stimulate growth. Balanced budgets down the road just a bit, accomplished without the need for higher taxes. Promises of economic growth as far as the eye can see. Just as they did with Reagan's economic outlooks, the critics griped. (NEWS)

As the above examples demonstrate, the setting can be a specific time (as in **1** and **3**) or a more generalized time whenever certain conditions are met (as in **2**, and thus the clause is also related to the semantic category of condition).

Since many stories are told in the course of conversation, the use of initial time clauses is particularly noteworthy in that register. However, setting up frames is also a particularly important function of the initial condition clauses in the written registers. Many of these clauses set up hypothetical conditions, the potential consequences of which are then discussed in the main clause:

> And **if Miss Luft hadn't gotten to a phone** he probably would have killed her and then eventually he would have come sniffing around after me. (FICT)

> **If Senna had not either won the race or finished second**, he would have been out of the championship. (NEWS)

> **If, contrary to my argument, conventionalism did fit our legal practices**, would it provide a sound or even decent justification of them? (ACAD)

The initial condition clauses are also important for presenting options and their meaning, especially as procedures are explained in academic prose:

> The melting point is determined. **If it is not sharp and is lower than that of the two separate samples**, then the samples are not identical. **If, on the other hand, the melting point is sharp and is not lowered** then the two samples are identical. (ACAD)

The difference between the framing function of initial clauses and the typical functions of final clauses can be seen in the following examples, where the adverbial clauses add certain circumstantial information to the main clauses but do not set up a frame for the subsequent discourse:

> Kerry, come back **when you've got some trousers that actually fit**, okay? (CONV)

> I'm tense; excuse me **if I talk too much**. (FICT)

> The site is particularly important **because it is one of the few such castles to have developed out of an earlier Norman stone-built ring-work fort**. (NEWS)

## C Structural considerations

Structural considerations also influence the positions of finite clauses. The length of the adverbial clause and whether or not it is located within another dependent clause can affect the position. For example, the following reason clause could not be placed in initial position without making the resulting sentence extremely difficult to process:

> The life jackets failed to inflate **because Milo had removed the twin carbon dioxide cylinders from the inflating chambers to make the strawberry and crushed-pineapple ice-cream sodas he served in the officers' mess hall and had replaced them with mimeographed notes that read: 'what's good for M & M Enterprises is good for the country.'** (FICT)

Similarly, placing adverbial clauses into initial position when they are within other embedded clauses can create problems for processing. Consider:

> Officials claim there is an accident risk at the site **because the pumps swing out over the pavement and delivery tankers stick out into the road**. (NEWS)

> *Concern continued yesterday that the Chancellor might not be able to guarantee that 15 per cent base rates were the peak **if sterling came under pressure again**.* (NEWS)

Placing either of these adverbials into initial position in their clauses (i.e. *Officials claim because the ...* and *Concern continued yesterday that if sterling came ...*) delays the subject of the embedded clause and makes the sentences more difficult to understand.

## 10.2.8.7 Subordinators and adverbial clauses

Subordinators are used to introduce adverbial clauses, as in the following examples (with the subordinator in *[]*):

> *It's not a bundle of laughs [**because**], you know, **that really must be difficult**.* (CONV)
>
> *[**When**] he had landed on the roof of his building he sat for a time, weaving together in his mind a story thick with verisimilitude.* (FICT)

In the case of most finite adverbial clauses, such as the examples above, a subordinator must be used. Many semantic categories have multiple subordinators; reason clauses can be introduced with *because*, *since*, or *as*, for example.

Clauses in a few semantic categories have alternative forms for finite clauses. A conditional can be made, for example, using subject-operator inversion rather than the subordinator *if* (11.2.3.5):

> *But **were he to come**, he would most likely be invited before the summit starts.* (NEWS) <Note the use of subjunctive 'were' here.>

Non-finite clauses usually occur without a subordinator:

> *They had gone there **to liquidate his father-in-law's estate**.* (FICT)
>
> ***Given a probability sample**, well known statistical procedures can be readily applied.* (ACAD)

However, they also occur with subordinators:

> *[**When**] asked by journalists recently about the refugee problem, he said, "What refugee problem?"* (NEWS)
>
> *His big disappointment in the Ryder Cup was losing to Ronan Rafferty on the final day [**after**] twice putting the ball into water.* (NEWS)

With adverbial clauses, then, speakers and writers have choices in whether to use a subordinator and in which particular subordinator to use. In this section we address specific issues related to their use. We consider the frequency of subordinators with non-finite clauses (10.2.8.8), the most common subordinators with clauses (10.2.8.9), and several discourse choices related to subordinator use (10.2.8.10–12).

## 10.2.8.8 Subordinators with non-finite adverbial clauses

**CORPUS FINDINGS [1]**

➤ In all four registers, most non-finite adverbial clauses do not have subordinators.
➤ Academic prose has the largest proportion of non-finite clauses occurring with subordinators.

Table 10.10 **Use of non-finite circumstantial adverbial clauses with and without subordinators**

each ● represents 5%

|  | with subordinator | without subordinator |
|---|---|---|
| CONV | ● ● | ●●●●●●●●●●●●●●●●●●●● |
| FICT | ● ● | ●●●●●●●●●●●●●●●●●●●● |
| NEWS | ● ● ● | ●●●●●●●●●●●●●●●●●● ● |
| ACAD | ● ● ● ● ● | ●●●●●●●●●●●●●●● ● |

### DISCUSSION OF FINDINGS

The expository written registers place a higher premium on precision and explicitness in the communication of information. Since the subordinators make the relationships between the adverbial clause and the main clause very explicit, these registers tend to use proportionally more subordinators with non-finite clauses.

Subordinators of purpose (*in order + to, so as + to*), time (*before, after, while,* etc.), and similarity/comparison (*as though, as if*) are particularly common types of subordinators with the non-finite clauses. In academic prose, purpose clauses are relatively common, and are frequently introduced with *in order + to* in both initial and final position:

> Hence **in order to explain the existence of religion** we must discover the basics of the general energy which is the fount of all that is sacred. (ACAD)

> **In order to make use of a real number x** we must know how to combine it with other real numbers y, z. (ACAD)

> There are hundreds of questions to be asked **in order to find a satisfactory answer to the general question.** (ACAD)

> We need to stretch our thinking **in order to develop new possibilities.** (ACAD)

The subordinator *so as + to* usually occurs with clauses in final position, in both news and academic prose:

> The ground crew even crawled into the unpressurized luggage compartments and wheel wells **so as not to be left behind.** (NEWS)

> The items were selected **so as to give a quick overview of performance in relation to a range of topics including number concepts, measures, spatial concepts, algebra, graphs and number patterns.** (ACAD)

In fiction and conversation, on the other hand, it is more typical for a purpose clause to begin with only the infinitive marker:

> That's what he's gonna do, give it all up he said, **to have my kid normal.** (CONV)

> I know you finally told me about him **to get rid of me.** (FICT)

> I should say, **to explain this,** that beer-can aluminum is soft and sticky, as metals go. (FICT)

This is entirely consistent with the pattern of omission of complementizer *that* (9.2.8.1) and relativizer omission (8.7.1.9).

Without the explicit subordinator, the adverbial *to*-clause is structurally no different from many *to*-clauses used as complements of a verb or, in some cases, an adjective (9.4), or a noun (8.14.2):

> *I forgot **to take one down to the place with me**.* (CONV)

> *It may be tough **to attract people**.* (NEWS†)

> *We need to give decent people a chance **to elect a sensible council**.* (NEWS)

The subordinators *in order + to* and *so as + to* often make the meaning of the adverbial clause instantly recognizable and prevent any potential misinterpretation.

Academic prose and news also tend to be more overt about time relationships in non-finite clauses. Section 10.2.8.1 discusses the frequent use of supplementive clauses in fiction, which—without subordinators—leave their relationship to the main clause unspecified. For example, in the following sentence, the adverbial clause seems to imply both 'after' and 'because':

> *Mr. Duffy, however, had a distaste for underhand ways and, **finding that they were compelled to meet stealthily**, he forced her to ask him to her house.* (FICT)

In academic prose, in contrast, time meanings with non-finite clauses are often made explicit:

> *The trustee can ignore any creditors who have not lodged proofs of debts, **after receiving notice of the trustee's intention to declare a final dividend on a specified account**.* (ACAD)

> *It is customary to ignore the latter effect **when discussing 'resonance'**.* (ACAD)

> ***Before showing the use of matrices** we must first set up an algebra defining the various operations of addition, subtraction, multiplication, and so on.* (ACAD)

> *In religion men participate vicariously in an unreal, fantasy world of harmony, beauty and contentment, **while living in a practical everyday world of pain and misery**.* (ACAD†)

It is easy to understand, too, why news reports must be explicit about time relationships, since the sequence of events can be important to understanding the story:

> *He first entered Sweden the following year **after obtaining a visa through its Damascus embassy**.* (NEWS)

> ***Before leaving Capitol Hill for her meeting with the president**, she stepped onto the floor of the Senate, which suspended business and applauded her.* (NEWS)

> *He was accused of molesting a 14-year-old boy whom he had been counselling **while working as a school chaplain**.* (NEWS)

Finally, for all three of the written registers, it is important to note the use of the subordinators *as if* and *as though* with non-finite clauses. These subordinators indicate that the adverbial clause is showing similarity but is not to be taken factually. They are used with *ing*-clauses in the role of manner adverbials, especially in fiction:

> *He used to when he was just a kitten stand and stare up at us **as if asking a question**.* (FICT)

> He suspected the criminal was aware that a tall old white man (passing as
> blind?) had observed, had seen the minutest details of his crimes. Staring
> down. **As if watching his own heart surgery.** (FICT)

In addition, these subordinators are used with purpose *to*-clauses. Particularly in
academic prose and news, they have the important role of showing that the stated
purpose is not verified fact:

> **As if to prove that the National Hunt supermen that brought off this
> latest feat are in fact human**, Pipe admitted that he got it badly wrong over
> his assessment of In-keeping. (NEWS)

> Perhaps they satisfied their own curiosity by reciting creation myths to their
> young, **as if to put behind them the primeval chaos of an unknown
> creation.** (ACAD†)

> The brevity of the sentence "and then I was left alone with my ship, anchored
> at the head of the Gulf of Siam" contrasts with the complexities of the
> preceding scenesetting sentences, **as if to emphasize the insignificance of the
> lonely narrator against his background, the sea.** (ACAD†)

## 10.2.8.9  Most common subordinators across registers

**CORPUS FINDINGS** [4]

➤ Only 15 subordinators occur at least 200 times per million words in at least one of the
registers.

➤ The semantic categories of reason and condition have the least diversity in commonly
used subordinators.

  ➤ A single subordinator dominates in each category: *because* with reason clauses, and
  *if* with condition clauses.

➤ The semantic category of time shows the most diversity in commonly occurring
subordinators.

➤ Although frequencies vary slightly, the AmE registers follow the same patterns as the
BrE registers.

  ➤ The greatest difference is that AmE news has a slightly higher frequency of *as* used
  for manner and for time than BrE news.

➤ Conversation shows a marked tendency to use just one subordinator very frequently for
each semantic category.

➤ Fiction and news make most use of the range of common time subordinators, but with
a slightly different profile of frequencies.

**DISCUSSION OF FINDINGS**

The patterns of use for the most common subordinators are influenced by four
primary factors: the diversity of relationships within a semantic category, the
number of subordinators, discourse choices made by writers and speakers, and
particular semantic domains emphasized by certain registers.

Time subordinators express several different semantic relationships, including 'time before', 'time after', and 'same time'. The two registers that have the
most time adverbial clauses, fiction and news (10.2.8.2), also have the highest
frequencies of these subordinators. *When* is common in all four registers:

> And **when we had that, uh, birthday party there**, they did up her hair and
> put a ribbon in it and did her nails. (CONV)

**Table 10.11  Most common circumstance adverbial subordinators across registers and dialects; occurrences per million words**

each ■ represents 200     □ represents less than 100

| | CONV (AmE & BrE) | FICT | NEWS (AmE & BrE) | ACAD |
|---|---|---|---|---|
| *time* | | | | |
| when | ■■■■■■■ ■■ | ■■■■■■■ ■ | ■■■■■■■ ■■ | ■■■■ |
| as | ■ | ■■■■■ | ■■ | □ |
| after | ■ | ■■ | ■■■■ | ■ |
| before | ■ | ■■■ | ■■ | ■ |
| while | ■ | ■■■ | ■■ | □ |
| until | ■ | ■ | ■ | ■ |
| since | ■ | ■ | ■ | □ |
| *manner* | | | | |
| as (including *as if* and *as though*) | ■ | ■■■ | ■■ | ■ |
| *reason* | | | | |
| because/cos | ■■■■■■■ ■■■■■ | ■■■■■ | ■■■■ | ■■■■■ |
| since | □ | ■ | □ | ■■ |
| *concessive* | | | | |
| though (including *even though*) | ■ | ■■■ | ■ | ■ |
| although | □ | ■ | ■ | ■■■ |
| while | □ | □ | ■■ | ■■ |
| *condition* | | | | |
| if | ■■■■■■■ ■■■■■■■ ■■■ | ■■■■■■■ ■■■■■■ | ■■■■■■■ | ■■■■■■■■ ■■■■ |
| unless | ■ | □ | □ | ■ |

| | AmE CONV | BrE CONV |
|---|---|---|
| *time* | | |
| when | ■■■■■■ | ■■■■■■■■■■ |
| as | ■ | ■ |
| after | ■ | ■ |
| before | ■ | ■ |
| while | ■ | ■ |
| until | ■ | ■ |
| since | ■ | □ |

Table 10.11 **continued**

|  | AmE CONV | BrE CONV |
|---|---|---|
| *manner* | | |
| as (including *as if* and *as though*) | ■ | ■ |
| *reason* | | |
| because/cos | ■■■■■■■■■■ | ■■■■■■■■■■<br>■■■■■ |
| since | □ | □ |
| *concessive* | | |
| though | □ | ■ |
| although | □ | □ |
| while | □ | □ |
| *condition* | | |
| if | ■■■■■■■■■■<br>■■■■■ | ■■■■■■■■■■<br>■■■■■■■■■ |
| unless | ■ | ■ |

|  | AmE NEWS | BrE NEWS |
|---|---|---|
| *time* | | |
| when | ■■■■■■■ | ■■■■■■■■■ |
| as | ■■■ | ■ |
| after | ■■■ | ■■■■■ |
| before | ■■ | ■■ |
| while | ■ | ■■ |
| until | ■ | ■ |
| since | ■ | ■ |
| *manner* | | |
| as (including *as if* and *as though*) | ■■■ | ■ |
| *reason* | | |
| because/cos | ■■■ | ■■■■ |
| since | □ | □ |
| *concessive* | | |
| though | ■ | ■ |
| although | ■ | ■ |
| while | ■■ | ■ |
| *condition* | | |
| if | ■■■■■■ | ■■■■■■■ |
| unless | □ | □ |

**Table 10.11** **continued**

| other attested subordinators: | |
| --- | --- |
| time | once, till, whenever, whilst, now that, immediately (BrE), directly (BrE) |
| place | where, wherever |
| manner (including similarity and comparison) | like |
| purpose | so (that), in order that |
| reason | as, for, with, in that |
| result | so (that), such that |
| concession | whereas, whilst |
| exception | except that, save that, but that |
| condition and contingency | as long as, in case, in the event that, lest, on condition that, once, provided (that), whenever, wherever, whether |
| preference | rather than |

> *He was astonished* **when Pauli responded to their music with rough and rude Berlin slang.** (FICT)

> **When the sting was first announced last summer,** *the U.S. Attorney said it could eventually result in indictments against more than 100 people.* (NEWS)

> *Success rates are no higher* **when the test item is placed in context.** (ACAD)

The other subordinators describing concurrent events, *as* and *while*, are more common in fiction than the other registers:

> **As you stand holding your glass** *you see into the bedroom.* (FICT†)

> *The river swilled him along,* **while he whistled in happiness.** (FICT)

Compared to other registers, news is particularly marked in its use of *after*, where it often provides background information about prior events, following presentation of the main story line:

> 1 *In a related case, four Trinity College Dublin student leaders were cleared of contempt* **after the society sought to have them jailed for alleged breaches of an earlier injunction restricting distribution of literature on abortion services.** (NEWS)

> 2 *A Coroner's comments have goaded health bosses into issuing new guidelines* **[after a mentally handicapped woman died [after fracturing her skull]].** (NEWS)

> 3 *Teenager Matthew Bown is being hailed as a hero for saving a toddler from drowning* **after the child plunged into a fast-flowing stream.** (NEWS)

In 2 we see how news reportage can relate a whole series of events in reverse order with successive *after*-clauses in final position. Furthermore, *after* in news can also have strong overtones of cause as in 2 or the following:

> *He abandoned the attack* **after the woman screamed and bit him several times.** (NEWS)

*While* can also show time relations important to a news story:

> **While Nikki is at college,** *her children will be attending a local school.* (NEWS)

For the semantic category of condition, there is less choice in subordinators. Habitual condition can be introduced with *wherever* and *whenever*:

> **Whenever any job was vacant** *a friend was always ready to give him the hard word.* (FICT)

Conditional subordination can also be shown with inverted word order under certain circumstances (10.2.8.12). However, in many cases *if* is the only subordinator that can be used, as in the following example:

> *You can drink your orange* **if you like**. (CONV)

> **If you needed a ton of dynamite at point X**, *you didn't want to bring it down 800 kilometers away.* (FICT)

> **If that is the mathematical straw which breaks the camel's back for you**, *don't worry.* (ACAD)

Condition is a relatively common semantic category for circumstance clauses in all registers, and it is thus not surprising that the subordinator *if* is common in all four registers.

The semantic categories of reason and concession present users with more choices in subordinator use. Reason can be expressed with *because, since,* or *as*:

> *The leaflet angered parents, staff and governors* **because they said it was full of misleading statements and the individuals who produced it had not identified themselves.** (NEWS)

> *In fact, she wished the dinner to be particularly nice,* **since William Bankes had at last consented to dine with them.** (FICT)

> **As temperature is clearly associated with heat**, *it might be one of the properties.* (ACAD)

However, *because* is by far the most common reason subordinator in all four registers. It is also the only one of the three subordinators that unambiguously refers to reason, and is therefore the most clear choice. *As* and *since* can both refer to time, and *as* can also refer to manner. See 10.2.8.10 for further discussion of *since* and *as*.

For concessive relationships, users also have a choice between *though* and *although* (and *while*, which is described further in 10.2.8.10). When used as subordinators, *though* and *although* are synonymous. Either could have been used in the following:

> **Though his eyes took note of many elements of the crowd through which he passed** *they did so morosely.* (FICT)

> *Carden Park is proof that 49 year-old Broome is not a man of compromises,* **though it is not his greatest project.** (NEWS)

> **Although I felt a little lonely**, *my exaltation of the morning had not worn off.* (FICT †)

> *They claim the pamphlet is true,* **although they contest Lord Aldington's interpretation of it.** (NEWS)

Both of these subordinators occur in all four registers, although the registers show different preferences of use. Conversation and fiction show a slightly greater use of *though* (concessive clauses are, however, uncommon in conversation generally). News shows no particular preference. In academic prose, *although* is about three times as frequent as *though*. *Although* seems to have a slightly more formal tone to it, fitting the style of academic prose:

> *Although this is a practical proposal*, the way in which we have described it is not free from idealised elements. (ACAD)
>
> *Although some of them may seem trivial by any rational accounting*, they are not negligible in the social relations of industry. (ACAD)
>
> Under state mediation various occupations are increasingly incorporated into the organizational framework of government agencies, *although these take different forms which are a result of the prior historical development of the occupation*. (ACAD)

The greater use of *although* by writers of academic prose may also result from an attempt to distinguish this subordinator from the common use of *though* as a linking adverbial in conversation (10.2.8.11).

Finally, in fiction, the subordinator *as* is notable for introducing clauses of manner. The descriptive details provided by manner adverbials have been noted as an important element in fiction (10.2.2 and 10.2.8.2). The higher frequency of *as* in fiction over the other three registers again reflects this importance.

> She glanced downwards, *just exactly as she had on the day I'd come for the room*. (FICT)
>
> She knew the pictures were needed as evidence, but still, it always seemed so heartless and cruel, making them turn this way and that, *as though they were posing for some grim version of a wedding album*. (FICT)
>
> Within him an actual hatred once more manifested itself toward his electric sheep, which he had to tend, had to care about, *as if it lived*. (FICT)

## 10.2.8.10 Common subordinators with multiple semantic roles

Three of the most common subordinators are items that can express more than one semantic relationship: *as* can be used for manner, time, or reason; *since* can express time or reason; *while* can express time or concession. However, the preferred semantic roles for each of these subordinators varies across registers.

### A *As* used for manner, reason, and time

**CORPUS FINDINGS** [4]

➤ Conversation and academic prose most commonly use *as* to show manner relationships, while fiction and news more commonly use *as* to express time.

➤ In all four registers, *as* is used least as a reason subordinator. However, the proportion for reason is consistently higher in BrE than AmE.

**DISCUSSION OF FINDINGS**

The use of *as* for time clauses in fiction is illustrated in 10.2.8.9 above. In news, *as* is less frequent overall, but its use for time clauses is also proportionally high. *As*-clauses are often used to give context for a news story, explaining when the action took place, or to show sequences of events:

> An armed robber was mugged of his loot *as he made his getaway*. (NEWS)
>
> A pensioner was raped early yesterday *as she returned home from a church service*. (NEWS)
>
> <...> *as he turned the corner* he was shot in the back. (NEWS†)

**Table 10.12** **Proportional breakdown of semantic categories for the subordinator *as* across dialects and registers**

each ■ represents 5%     □ represents less than 2.5%

| | manner | reason | time |
|---|---|---|---|
| AmE CONV | ■■■■■■■■■■■ | □ | ■■■■■■■■■ |
| BrE CONV | ■■■■■■■■■■■■ | ■■ | ■■■■■■ |
| FICT | ■■■■■■■ | ■ | ■■■■■■■■■■■■ |
| AmE NEWS | ■■■■■■■■ | □ | ■■■■■■■■■■■ |
| BrE NEWS | ■■■■ | ■ | ■■■■■■■■■■■■ ■■ |
| ACAD | ■■■■■■■■■■■■■ | ■■ | ■■■■■ |

> *As they entered the salon*, *the two gunmen ran past a group of children on their way home from school*. (NEWS)

In some cases, the clauses introduced with *as* blend semantic roles. One event happening at the same time as another can also imply that the one event is the reason for the other:

1 *She kept her head down **as she spotted the newsmen**.* (BrE NEWS)

2 ***As details of the respective bids were unveiled in London and Delhi,** Today's revelations that the TCCB has been outmanoeuvred by the sub-continent were confirmed.* (BrE NEWS)

In these examples, the adverbial clauses seem to give the reason for the state in the main clause, in addition to describing concurrent events. Thus, in **1** it is implied that she kept her head down because she spotted the newsmen, and in **2** the revelations were confirmed because the bids were unveiled.

Neither conversation nor academic prose have particularly high frequencies of manner adverbial clauses, but when they are used in these registers, the clauses often take the subordinator *as*:

> *All of a sudden **as they like to do in Birmingham station**, all the trains are coming in on different platforms from usual.* (CONV†)

> *It is essential to add that plate tectonics has crept into this matter **as it has into every other aspect of the earth sciences**.* (ACAD)

Finally, it is interesting that both BrE conversation and academic prose use *as* for reason proportionally more than the other registers:

> *You can't ignore it – it's the first thing a buyer will, a buyer's survey will pick up, especially **as it was mentioned in our survey**.* (BrE CONV)

> *Did you tell him, **as he's threatened to come home**?* (BrE CONV)

> ***As a declaration will not quash a decision**, it cannot be used to challenge a decision.* (ACAD†)

> *<...> but **as they were not an extension of the central government**, their hold was weakened with the introduction of national policies and the strengthening of the formal organisation of the district administration.* (ACAD†)

## B *Since* used for reason and time

**CORPUS FINDINGS** [4]

➤ Conversation and news more commonly use *since* for time.
➤ Academic prose and, less markedly, fiction more commonly use *since* for reason.
➤ AmE conversation has a slightly higher use of *since* for reason than BrE conversation.

**Table 10.13** **Proportional breakdown of semantic categories for the subordinator *since* across dialects and registers**

each ● represents 5%

| | reason | time |
|---|---|---|
| AmE CONV | ● ● ● ● ● | ● ● ● ● ● ● ● ● ● ● ● ● ● ● ● ● ● ● ● |
| BrE CONV | ● ● ● | ● ● ● ● ● ● ● ● ● ● ● ● ● ● ● ● ● ● ● ● |
| FICT | ● ● ● ● ● ● ● ● ● ● ● ● ● | ● ● ● ● ● ● ● ● ● |
| AmE NEWS | ● ● ● ● ● | ● ● ● ● ● ● ● ● ● ● ● ● ● ● ● ● ● |
| BrE NEWS | ● ● ● ● ● ● | ● ● ● ● ● ● ● ● ● ● ● ● ● ● |
| ACAD | ● ● ● ● ● ● ● ● ● ● ● ● ● ● ● ● ● ● ● ● | ● |

**DISCUSSION OF FINDINGS**

In conversation, the subordinator *since* is usually used to mark time:

> **Since Billy's come around** *that's all we've been talking about.* (CONV)

> *Is it six weeks* **since we saw the last one then**? (CONV)

> *It's like, it's like fourteen years* **since the favourite won the National**. (CONV)

The relative absence of *since* marking reason in conversation is surprising because reason is a generally common category for adverbial clauses in conversation (10.2.8.2). However, conversation has a strong preference for *because* to be used with reason clauses (10.2.8.9). It is interesting to note that the use of *since* marking reason is somewhat more prevalent in AmE conversation than BrE conversation:

> *You do it* **since you're the best at this game**. (AmE CONV)

> *I was intent on not dealing with any crap about eating lunch with them* **since normally we're not invited**. (AmE CONV)

In contrast, *since* overwhelmingly marks reason in academic prose:

> **Since field capacity corresponds to a suction of about 5 to 10 kpa depending upon the soil type**, *much of the available water is in pores that are inaccessible to roots or root hairs.* (ACAD)

> *The application of isotopes in biochemistry has also been particularly fruitful,* **since they offer a means of identifying intermediates and the 'brickwork' of the final products**. (ACAD)

> *The converse is obvious,* **since the norm-topology is stronger than (e,e)**. (ACAD †)

In general, academic prose does not have as many time adverbials as the other registers. Furthermore, there tend to be few passages in academic prose specifically describing time duration up to the present. It is not particularly surprising, therefore, that *since* would rarely refer to time in this register.

Fiction and news show more variability in the use of *since*. The proportional uses in news again reflect the importance of time in reporting news events. However, fiction has a considerably higher proportion of reason clauses with *since*:

> *I could not tell her **since I did not myself know**.* (FICT)
>
> *And **since we had nothing really to do**, our reluctance went away bit by bit.* (FICT†)
>
> *I'll press-gang some helpers for you, but I do want you there, Wheeler, **since you're the only one who knows what's what**.* (FICT)
>
> *They've never had a curate; couldn't get one, **since they're few and far between these days**.* (FICT†)

Uncharacteristically for its use of adverbials, fiction here behaves more like academic prose than conversation.

## C   *While* used for concession/contrast and time

### CORPUS FINDINGS [4]

➤ Almost all occurrences of *while* as a subordinator in conversation express time. In contrast, over 80% of the occurrences in academic prose marks concession/contrast.

➤ Fiction and news are much more similar to conversation than academic prose in their use of *while*.

➤ There are no noteworthy differences between AmE and BrE in their preferences for *while* marking time or concession/contrast.

**Table 10.14** **Proportional breakdown of semantic categories for the subordinator *while* across registers**

each ■ represents 5%     ☐ represents less than 2.5%

| | concession/contrast | time |
|---|---|---|
| CONV | ☐ | ■■■■■■■■■■■■■■■■■■ |
| FICT | ■■ | ■■■■■■■■■■■■■■■■ |
| NEWS | ■■■■■■■ | ■■■■■■■■■■■■■■ |
| ACAD | ■■■■■■■■■■■■■■■■ | ■■ |

### DISCUSSION OF FINDINGS

In academic prose, *while* is occasionally used to show a time relationship, particularly in descriptions of procedures or case reports:

> *She said that the pain was a little better after the pethidine she had been given and she was able to rest quietly **while she waited to be taken to theatre**.* (ACAD)
>
> *In a second study left handers were observed in the speaking condition and **while humming**.* (ACAD)

However, *while* used in an adverbial clause of concession is far more common, contrasting information in the main clause and the adverbial clause:

> *While high turbine temperatures are thermodynamically desirable* they mean the use of expensive alloys and cooled turbine blades leading to an increase in complexity and cost. (ACAD)

> *Nearly all the 17-detosteroids in females are synthesized by the adrenal glands, **while in the male one-third is produced by the testes and two-thirds by the adrenals**.* (ACAD)

In conversation and fiction, *while* is relatively rare as a concessive, even though in fiction the general frequency of concessive clauses is quite substantial. Fiction clearly relies more on *though* to express concession and uses *while* as a time adverbial subordinator; for the possible factors involved in conversation, see 10.2.8.11. Additional examples of *while* as a time subordinator include:

> *Just mind your head a minute **while I open the cupboard**.* (CONV)

> *Enjoy yourself **while you're having a baby**?* (CONV)

> *It was good stuff **while it lasted**.* (FICT)

## 10.2.8.11 *Though* as subordinator v. linking adverbial

Although the form *though* is among the most common subordinators, it can also be used as a linking adverbial. As a subordinator, *though* introduces a concessive circumstance clause as we have seen above:

> 1 *The elections were peaceful, **though** hampered by delays.* (NEWS†)

As a linking adverbial, *though* marks a contrastive relationship between two units of discourse (similar to the linking adverbial *however* or the coordinator *but*):

> 2 *<...> few <of these studies> have considered the different economic and organizational context of state management. There are exceptions, **though**.* (ACAD†)

> 3 *A: You just have to try and accept it, I guess.*
> *B: It's kind of hard sometimes **though**, isn't it?* (CONV)

In the following, counts of *though* as a subordinator include occurrences of *even though*.

### CORPUS FINDINGS [4]

➤ *Though* is much more common overall in conversation and fiction than in news and academic prose.

➤ In the use of *though*, conversation is very different from all three written registers.
  ➤ Most occurrences of *though* in conversation are as a linking adverbial.
  ➤ In the written registers, the vast majority of the occurrences are as a subordinator.

### DISCUSSION OF FINDINGS

*Though* as a linking adverbial is found primarily in conversation, where its

**Figure 10.21**

**Use of *though* as linking adverbial and subordinator**

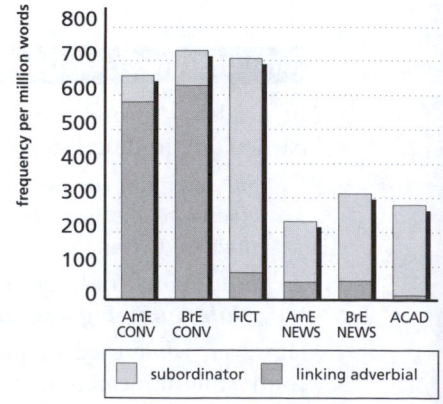

frequency far exceeds that of *though* as subordinator:

1 *Jeez. Oh, maybe I won't go. I should **though**, I feel that I should.* (CONV)

2 *It was one year she could've done without the invitation **though** isn't it?* (CONV)

3 A: <...> *the grammar schools, in the grammar school like your dad went to I mean it was, it was a really, you know it was a grammar school, it wasn't anything like it is now.*

B: *Well, there were two grammar schools in Lincoln **though** weren't there?* (CONV)

A possible factor at work is that considerable forward planning is required to construct a sentence with a concessive adverbial clause. The speaker has to have two propositions in mind, together with a realization that one runs counter to the other, before starting to speak. This is not easy to manage in the online production of speech.

We may also relate to this the frequency of *but* in conversation, which is also greater than in the expository registers (2.4.7.3) and in fact ten times that of *though. But* also allows for a somewhat delayed indication of incompatibility, though not as delayed as that afforded by linking *though* in final position. Compare with **1**: *Maybe I won't go, but I feel I should.*

*Though* as a linking adverbial is also sometimes used in writing that is informal or intended to resemble speech. For example, in fiction linking *though* occurs in informal descriptions or dialog, and in news passages it occurs with other informal language (e.g. note the use of colloquial *romp*, in the final example below):

*I may be exaggerating about the machine gun **though**: I don't think they had one between them.* (FICT)

*Morning came, and I got up. That doesn't sound particularly interesting or difficult, now does it? I bet you do it all the time. Listen, **though**, I had a problem here.* (FICT)

*When, **though**, you marry into the Royal Family, one romp too many means headlines you and they could very well do without.* (NEWS)

Surprisingly, *though* is also sometimes used as a linking adverbial in more formal written prose, for example:

*All old Mali had actually ever done **though**, was appropriate his fair share of what he had hoed and sweated to grow.* (FICT)

*Right now, **though**, he faces the most critical time in his managerial career.* (NEWS)

The linking adverbial *however* is far more common than *though* in academic prose and carries the same contrastive meaning (10.4.1.5). The use of *though* appears to be a marked stylistic choice by certain authors.

### 10.2.8.12 Conditional clauses with *if* v. subject-operator inversion

In conditional clauses with *had*, *were*, and *should*, it is possible to mark the adverbial clause with subject-operator inversion, rather than use the subordinator *if* (11.2.3.5):

***Had it not been for human kindness*** *he would have ended up in a pork pie.* (NEWS)

> *Were he to deflect the challenge by dissolving parliament*, it would confirm he had not properly learnt the lessons of April's disturbances. (NEWS)

> *Should the patient be the person who had attended to the business and financial side of family life*, then there will have to be a reversal of roles. (ACAD)

Each of these conditional clauses could be introduced with the subordinator *if* used with regular subject-operator order. All three of these verbs regularly occur in clauses introduced with *if*:

> *If I had touched her* it might have been a different thing! (CONV)

> *If you should ask him why he's drinking*, he'll tell you it's because he's ashamed of his daughter. (FICT)

> *If I were to die here*, I would be dried out by the wind in a day. (FICT)

**CORPUS FINDINGS** [5]

> ➤ In all registers, conditionals with *had* and *were* are very rarely marked by subject-operator inversion. (The findings for these two verbs are combined because they are very similar.)

> ➤ In news and academic prose, conditionals with the verb *should* are marked by subject-operator inversion in slightly over half of all occurrences.

>> ➤ Overall, however, conditionals with *should* are relatively rare (c. 5–15 occurrences per million words).

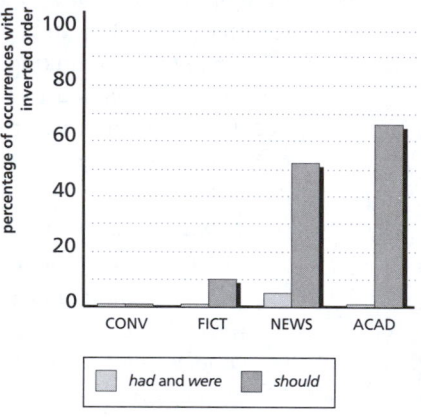

**Figure 10.22**

**Percentage of conditional clauses marked with subject-operator inversion**

**DISCUSSION OF FINDINGS**

The use of subject-operator inversion rather than the subordinator *if* is restricted for the most part to clauses with the modal verb *should* in the more formal, expository registers:

> *Should things go well*, it would be nice to see the likes of Darren Patterson and Keith Rowland getting a run. (NEWS)

> Even jobs which have been successfully relocated in areas such as East Kilbride, increasing employment opportunities, could end up being moved away again *should they be privatised*. (NEWS)

> *Should the marked chromosome constitute the inactive X*, however, it is reasonably easy to observe as the darkest and longest chromosome in the cell. (ACAD)

> *Should the change in relationships bring about an unexpected clash with yet another component domain*, then it may be sufficient to display only the excursion boxes. (ACAD)

Inversion of subject and operator occasionally occurs in conversation:

> 1 Erm – *should the house go up in smoke*, Theresa across the road – run to her. (CONV)

> 2 *Had I sat down and thought about it* I *could have said well er what I thought, you know.* (CONV†)

However, such inversion is generally rare and used by only a few speakers in conversation. In general, *should* is not widely used for conditionals in conversation but the further rarity of inversion in conversation is likely related to the lack of time for planning. The use of subject-operator inversion requires specific verb choice, and in many instances speakers are still deciding on verbs (and subjects) even as they are producing a conditional clause:

> *so she, she, if it weren't, if she has him to build her own suite – Is, if they we – if he's left* <...> (CONV†)

> *Whereas if he had, if he sold them as separate houses* <...> (CONV†)

> *If you haven't, if you worked – if you haven't worked at the – sorry?* (CONV)

In contrast, example **1** above comes from a more prepared passage than is typical of many conversations—running through a list of information for a babysitter. Other occurrences of subject-operator inversion in conversation occur with fixed phrases, as in the following example quoted from a television show:

> *Should you wish to accept this mission* <...> (CONV†)

# 10.3    Stance adverbials

Stance adverbials have the primary function of commenting on the content or style of a clause or a particular part of a clause (cf. 10.1.1). Stance adverbials are much less common than circumstance adverbials (10.1.1.1). In fact, most sentences in English do not contain stance adverbials. Rather, they are statements made without overt stance markers:

> *They went to some park in Ann Arbor and got an ice cream and sat around, walked around Ann Arbor and then went back to the car and got their stuff.* (CONV)

> *The Queen of England will race a horse in the United States for the first time in 35 years at Arlington International Racecourse.* (NEWS)

Of course, even circumstance adverbials can imply some comment on the form or style of a proposition. For example, the following circumstance adverbials can be interpreted as showing the speaker/writer's assessment of the situation:

> 1 *The disease pattern has changed **radically**.* (ACAD)

> 2 *I was **only** asking.* (CONV)

In **1**, the use of *radically* shows the writer's assessment of the change—that whatever amount it is exactly, it is radical. In **2**, *only* conveys the speaker's attitude that asking should not be taken as a very serious or intrusive action.

However, with stance adverbials, the author/speaker's attitude or comment on the content is much more overt:

> 3 *Ruth was **definitely** at Goosehill School.* (CONV)

> 4 *It was funny, though, how Christmas **undeniably** brought out the gentler, kinder aspects of human nature.* (FICT)

> 5 ***Regrettably**, last night's audience was a meagre one, but what they got was impressive.* (NEWS)

In these examples, statements of certainty (*definitely*, *undeniably*) and the attitude of regret (*regrettably*) are overtly stated. Furthermore, stance adverbials are frequently distinguishable by their greater potential mobility and prosodic separation from the rest of a clause (10.1.3.1, 3.2.8.2).

It should also be noted that stance can be conveyed with constructions other than adverbials. These other stance devices include nouns (e.g. *the fact that* ...), modal auxiliaries and main verbs (it *may* be, it *seems* that ...), and adjectives (e.g. it is *likely* that ...). In conversation paralinguistic features such as prosody and loudness can also function as markers of stance. See Chapter 12 for further discussion of the marking of stance.

## 10.3.1 Semantic categories of stance adverbials

Stance adverbials fall into three major semantic categories: **epistemic**, **attitude**, and **style**. Epistemic stance adverbials and attitude stance adverbials both comment on the content of a proposition. Epistemic markers express the speaker's judgment about the certainty, reliability, and limitations of the proposition; they can also comment on the source of the information. Attitude stance adverbials convey the speaker's attitude or value judgment about the proposition's content. Style adverbials, in contrast, describe the manner of speaking.

### 10.3.1.1 Epistemic stance adverbials

Epistemic adverbials are the most diverse category of stance adverbials. Typically they convey one of the following six major areas of meaning:

### A Doubt and certainty

Doubt and certainty adverbials show the speaker's certainty or doubt about the proposition in the clause. They include both absolute judgments of certainty and indication of belief in various levels of probability.

Expressing certainty:

> **No doubt** his bifocals added to this impression, as did his nonchalant gait and slouchy posture. (FICT)
>
> That sort of gossip **certainly** should be condemned. (NEWS†)
>
> During the action the person will **undoubtedly** have certain feelings towards it and gain satisfaction from achievement. (ACAD)

Expressing some level of doubt:

> In spite of that it was **probably** more comfortable than the home they'd left anyway. (CONV)
>
> And **perhaps** the soul thrived on its sufferings. (FICT)
>
> **Maybe** it is true, **maybe** it isn't. (NEWS)

Others epistemic stance adverbials of certainty or doubt include:

> *arguably, decidedly, definitely, incontestably, incontrovertibly, most likely, very likely, quite likely, of course, I guess, I think.*

### B Actuality and reality

Actuality and reality adverbials comment on the status of the proposition as real-life fact:

> **In fact** I'm taller than the doors. (CONV)

> *Everybody remembers where they were when JFK was shot and now a new round of "Who **Really** Killed the President" books are coming out.* (NEWS†)

> *Not all the evidence by any means concurs with the view that women were **actually** superior to men in some respects.* (ACAD)

*In actual fact*, *for a fact*, and *truly* are other typical stance adverbials of reality or actuality.

## C Source of knowledge

Adverbials of source of knowledge show the source of the information reported in the associated proposition. These adverbials include adverbs such as *evidently*, *apparently*, *reportedly*, and *reputedly* which allude to evidence supporting the proposition:

> **Evidently**, *the stock market believes that matters will not rest there and Pearl's share price raced up 87p to 639p.* (NEWS)

> *Today it was the dish towel she'd brought with her.* **Apparently**, *Rosie had interrupted her in the middle of some chore.* (FICT)

These adverbials may also identify a specific source:

> *Egypt's nuclear power industry is still in the design phase, but **according to Mr. Kandil**, nuclear power was the only clean energy alternative for Egypt.* (NEWS)

> **As Wardell (1986) notes**, *once managerial decisions are known they then become the basis on which groups lower down the hierarchy organize their resistance and responses.* (ACAD†)

Occasionally a finite clause, usually with the subordinator *because*, is used to state evidence for the main clause:

> *It doesn't work apparently.* **Cos Jim who was in there last year said it didn't work when he was there**. (CONV)

Here the adverbial clause does not provide the reason for the breakdown; rather, it gives evidence to support the claim that the machine has broken down. It can be interpreted, in fact, as providing the specific information supporting the more general adverbial *apparently*.

## D Limitation

Epistemic adverbials can mark the limitation of the proposition:

> **In most cases** *he would have been quite right.* (FICT)

> *Its footage is **mainly** licensed world-wide to film makers for inclusion in features and documentaries.* (NEWS)

> **Typically** *there is a pair of ganglia in each segment of the body.* (ACAD)

Other stance adverbials commonly used to mark limitation include: *generally*, *largely*, *in general* and *in most cases*.

In comparison with these stance adverbials, circumstance adverbials of respect limit the application of a proposition in somewhat different ways (10.2.1.8).

## E Viewpoint or perspective

Epistemic adverbials can mark the viewpoint or perspective from which the proposition is true:

> **In our view** *it would be a backward step.* (NEWS)

> **From our perspective**, *movement success is paradoxical.* (ACAD)

Such stance adverbials often include a possessive pronoun, as in the above examples and the expression *in my opinion.*

### F Imprecision

A number of epistemic adverbials are used to show that the proposition being conveyed is somehow imprecise:

> Men were **like** literally throwing themselves at me. (CONV)
>
> It kept **sort of** pouring out of his pocket, my brother said. (FICT)
>
> Indeed, the only real drawback, **if you can call it that**, is that people are continually coming up and congratulating us on our victory over England. (NEWS)

As in the examples above, the adverbials showing imprecision can be focused on a particular element of the clause—e.g. marking the word *drawback* as questionable. Other expressions typically used as stance adverbials of imprecision include: *about, kind of, roughly,* and *so to speak.*

All of these markers of imprecision can be considered **hedges**—a classification that also includes non-adverbial items, and which is not always easily distinguishable from degree (7.14.2.4).

## 10.3.1.2 Attitude adverbials

Attitude adverbials tell of the writer's or speaker's attitude toward the proposition typically conveying an evaluation, value judgment, or assessment of expectations:

> **Unfortunately** I have too many of them but someday you'll be old too. (CONV†)
>
> **Fortunately**, during my first few months here, I kept a journal. (FICT†)
>
> Born to salty, honest East End folk – this was hinted at, the script **sensibly** avoiding the risk of fleshing them out – he had risen in the city. (NEWS†)
>
> Later cretaceous chalks (still contemporaneous with the European development) are found in Arkansas, Mississippi and Alabama. And **most surprising of all**, much farther away still in western Australia, we have the gingin chalk of late cretaceous age. (ACAD†)

Often these adverbials can be restated as *to*-clauses or *that*-clauses with adjectives describing attitude, e.g. *It is fortunate/unfortunate that ...,  I think it sensible that ...,  It is surprising that ...* (cf. 9.2.4.2). A wide variety of attitudes, judgments, and expectations can be conveyed; items are as semantically diverse as the following:

Accordance with expectation—*as might be expected, inevitably, as you might guess, to my surprise, astonishingly*

Evaluation—*conveniently, wisely, sensibly, unfortunately, quite rightly, even worse, disturbingly*

Judgment of importance—*even more importantly*

In addition, the adverb *hopefully* is sometimes used as an attitude stance adverbial:

> **Hopefully** it's self-explanatory. (CONV)
>
> **Hopefully** their detective will be equally lost as to where to find him. (FICT)
>
> Jose Ramon, a new chef who arrived at the Guernica two months ago, will **hopefully** maintain these high standards. (NEWS)

> **Hopefully** *this problem will be solved when the group is thoroughly revised.* (ACAD)

In these examples, the meaning might be glossed as *I am hopeful that ....* Although writing manuals often warn against this use of *hopefully*, it occurs in the more formal registers of news and academic prose, as well as in conversation and fiction.

### 10.3.1.3 Style adverbials

Stance adverbials focused on style, comment on the manner of conveying the message (e.g. *frankly, honestly, truthfully*):

> *Well* **honestly** *I, I don't know.* (CONV†)

> **Quite frankly**, *he looked terrible.* (FICT)

> **More simply put**, *a feedback system has its inputs affected by its outputs.* (ACAD)

Often these stance adverbials can be glossed as: 'I am being X when I say ...'; e.g. *I am being honest when I say I don't know.* In this way, style adverbials are more focused on the speaker than are epistemic and attitude adverbials, although all three convey a speaker's or writer's stance. Other typical style adverbials include: *confidentially, figuratively speaking, in a word, in short, putting it bluntly, strictly, technically speaking, truthfully.*

Finite clauses are also occasionally used as style adverbials, often with the subordinator *if*:

> *Is it a fact that you have refused to take any fee for the work you are doing,* **if you don't mind my asking**? (FICT)

> *I have to say that in terms of violent crime generally the amount of it in the United Kingdom is small compared with that in other countries and,* **if I may say so**, *here in Washington.* (NEWS)

Such clauses are not as easily glossed, but they clearly show that the speakers view themselves as speaking bluntly or in a potentially offensive way.

### 10.3.1.4 Ambiguity with other adverbial classes

Certain stance adverbials can have ambiguous or multiple functions.

#### A Stance adverbial v. circumstance adverbial or degree modifier

The most commonly occurring ambiguity concerns whether an item is a stance adverbial or a circumstance adverbial of extent/degree (or in some cases, not an adverbial at all, but an adverb integrated into the structure of a phrase as a modifier).

The adverb *really*, for example, is particularly difficult to analyze. Certain instances do seem clearly to have the epistemic stance meaning 'in reality' or 'in truth', particularly when the adverb appears in initial and final positions:

> **Really** *you've noticed the difference?* (CONV)

> **Really**, *we have more than enough of everything.* (FICT)

> *"I was a dirty little bitch,* **really**.*"* (FICT)

> *I had no choice* **really**. (NEWS)

> *But of course there wasn't any doubt about it* **really**. (FICT)

Where *really* occurs medially, it often also has an epistemic stance meaning with propositions that concern absolute characteristics, such as being *alive* in **1**, or obtaining *all carbon dioxide* in **2**:

> 1 *Was Molly ever **really** alive alive-oh?* (NEWS)
>
> 2 *<...> it must be admitted that we have no proof that plants **really** do obtain all their carbon dioxide in this way.* (ACAD†)

However, in medial positions with gradable propositions, determination of the meaning can become even more difficult. In the following examples, *really* could have the stance meaning of 'in reality' or it could be interpreted as intensifying a verb or adjective, with the approximate meaning 'very (much)':

> *It's **really** wonderful.* (CONV)
>
> *Susie's **really** excited about that backyard.* (NEWS)
>
> *The numbers **really** took off in the late 1890s.* (ACAD†)

Even the wider context may not clarify which meaning the speaker/writer intended in such cases.

Sometimes, items that appear to be stance adverbials limiting the truth of propositions could alternatively be interpreted either as adverbials of extent or of time frequency. In the following, *mainly* and *largely* could be interpreted to mean 'to a great extent' or even 'usually' in addition to being epistemic stance adverbials:

> *Any reciprocal learning will depend **mainly** on what Japanese companies choose to make available.* (NEWS)
>
> *The great scholars also are **largely** ignored for their craft skills.* (ACAD)

## B Stance adverbial v. linking adverbial

Stance adverbials can also have a connective function, like linking adverbials. The use of *in fact*, for example, often not only shows actuality, but also connects the proposition to a preceding sentence, which it strengthens or makes more specific.

> *I went up and heard the jazz at the Crown last night. <...> **In fact** I was quite a busy little bee last night.* (CONV)
>
> *Men's legs needn't be the same length <...> **In fact** very few people's legs are exactly the same length.* (CONV)
>
> *She's never seen him on the porch. **In fact**, there's no chair to sit on.* (FICT)
>
> *The Tory tactic of trying to scare those they claim to be dissenters from switching to another party is laughable. **In fact**, traditional Tory support is holding.* (NEWS)
>
> *Irrigation implies not only an adequate and controlled water supply, but also efficient drainage of excess water when desirable. The supply and control of water, **in fact**, is the most important aspect of irrigated paddy cultivation.* (ACAD)

## C Stance adverbial v. discourse marker

At times, the interpretation of an item as a stance adverbial or as a discourse marker is not clear-cut. Consider *like* in the following example:

> *She **like** said that they would.* (CONV)

Here it is difficult to tell whether to interpret *like* as having no particular lexical meaning (a discourse marker, 3.4.5) or as a stance adverbial, showing that the proposition is being conveyed imprecisely (a hedge). Since discourse markers most commonly occur in conversation, Chapter 14 discusses them and their relationship to stance adverbials more fully.

## 10.3.1.5   Distribution of semantic categories

➤ Conversation contains by far the highest frequency of stance adverbials.
  ➤ Surprisingly, stance adverbials are also relatively common in academic prose.
  ➤ News has the lowest frequency of stance adverbials.
➤ In all four registers, epistemic adverbials are much more common than attitude or style adverbials.
➤ Style adverbials are more common in conversation than the other registers.
➤ Attitude adverbials are slightly more common in news and academic prose than conversation and fiction.

Figure 10.23

**Frequency of stance adverbials across registers**

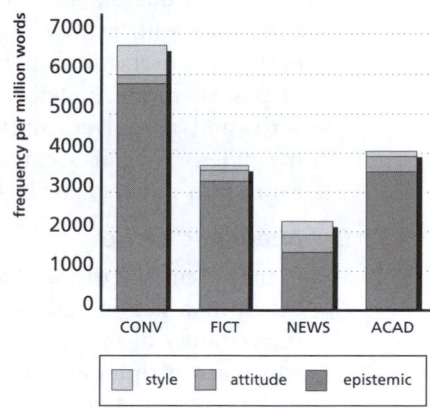

**DISCUSSION OF FINDINGS**

### A   Conversation

The higher overall frequency of stance adverbials and the higher frequency of style adverbials in conversation are consistent with the general communicative characteristics of conversation: the focus on interpersonal interactions and the conveying of subjective information. Speakers commonly use stance adverbials in the following ways.

To emphasize the actuality or reality of what they are saying:

*But I, I know **for a fact** there ain't.* (CONV)

*That door looks miles away but I mean **in actual fact** it's not very far.* (CONV)

*When you phone your order and they say twenty past they **really** mean twenty past don't they.* (CONV)

*Yeah **actually** I'm using a walker.* (CONV)

*Did you **actually** do a whole fifty?* (CONV)

To mark some level of doubt in what they are saying:

*Landlords have **probably** been quite pleased to get a decent tenant.* (CONV)

***Maybe** you're right.* (CONV)

***Perhaps** that's why she didn't go to sleep.* (CONV)

To mark certainty:

*You **definitely** don't want to go over tomorrow?* (CONV)

*And then **of course** money is floating round very quickly.* (CONV)

*It **certainly** changed my life.* (CONV)

To mark the imprecise nature of their communication:

*We always dragged it out, it's **like** gross and decrepit.* (CONV)

> *It's one of those things that **sort of** puts a little query in your mind.* (CONV†)

In addition, participants in conversation use style stance adverbials to tell others how they are speaking, as in the following examples:

> *Put one in, put the pill in, put another one in. Yeah, **literally**!* (CONV)

> *No **seriously** you have to move up one.* (CONV)

> ***Honestly**, I've got a headache.* (CONV)

One might wonder why conversation does not also have the most frequent use of attitude stance adverbials, since speakers in conversation are certainly concerned with expressing their attitudes and evaluations. The answer may lie partly in conversation's particularly high frequency, relative to the other registers, of post-predicate *that*-clauses following verbs and adjectives (9.2). Many of the verbs and adjectives controlling such clauses convey evaluative or emotional meanings. Thus it seems that conversation tends to use a clausal means of expression rather than the more condensed form afforded by stance adverbials.

**B   Academic prose**

It may seem surprising that academic prose uses stance adverbials to a greater extent than fiction and news. Academic prose, however, is often concerned with the certainty of information, and with giving some evidence of sources, both of which are at times achieved with stance adverbials:

> *There is **probably** no important cereal crop that is more influenced by environment than paddy.* (ACAD)

> *It was **definitely** established that bacteria bring about putrefaction, decomposition and other changes.* (ACAD†)

> *For example, interspecific competition for food may occur in some, but **apparently** not all, grasshopper assemblages.* (ACAD)

> *Nor, **evidently**, was Beccaria himself a towering figure of his time.* (ACAD†)

In contrast to conversation, many stance adverbials in academic prose also have to do with limitations on the propositions:

> *The mature males are **generally** less than 1.0 cm long.* (ACAD)

> *Inheritance was due **in most cases** to one or two genes.* (ACAD)

> ***In most instances** the contexts were thought to be appropriate to pupils in schools in different locations.* (ACAD)

Some of the stance adverbial in academic prose also make clear the perspective from which a proposition is true:

> ***To our knowledge** there have been no reports on the belowground responses to elevated carbon dioxide of mature perennials growing under field conditions.* (ACAD)

> ***From our perspective**, the criteria of social movement are cognitive.* (ACAD)

**C   News and academic prose**

Finally, it is interesting that news and academic prose both contain slightly more attitude adverbials than the other registers. In news, many of these adverbials occur in reviews, where the point of the text is largely to convey attitude.

From a music review:

> ***As you'd expect** strong traces of the surging Pixies sound remain.* (NEWS)

From a restaurant review:
> Again **unfortunately** the only thing lacking was people. (NEWS)

Quotations from sources also contain attitude adverbials:
> "It's too far from us. **Fortunately**, The New York Times *and other newspapers showed maps. So people know where the problem was,"* he said. (NEWS)

However, attitude adverbials occur in news reports as well:
> *Ironically, while the computer industry is struggling to regain its footing, some of the nation's largest software makers posted record earnings for the second quarter.* (NEWS)

> *Surprisingly, Northern Ireland has the third highest death rate from skin cancer in the world.* (NEWS)

Manuals, textbooks, and technical reports in academic prose include author's attitudes about material, and sometimes comments about what is surprising or expected:
> *The trouble is that for the most widely used magnetic material – iron – ix is not a constant. Not only that but its value depends on H, but,* **even worse**, *it depends on the previous history of the sample.* (ACAD) <note the secondary linking function of the stance adverbial, by virtue of it being a comparative form>

> **Unfortunately** *some recorded samples were lost.* (ACAD)

> **Predictably**, *the terse prose of Hemingway is found to lack the transformational complexities typical of Faulkner.* (ACAD)

> **As might be expected**, *very few came from middle-class suburbs.* (ACAD†)

## 10.3.2  Syntactic realizations of stance adverbials

Every type of adverbial structure reviewed in 10.1.2 is possible for the realization of stance adverbials.

Single word adverb:
> *They had* **evidently** *been too scared of their autocratic director to record such an unlikely phenomenon.* (ACAD†)

Adverb phrase:
> *But* **quite frankly** *I can't see myself ever getting—given the same sort of circumstances.* (CONV)

Prepositional phrase:
> *His bedside manner was,* **in a word**, *menacing.* (NEWS)

Noun phrase:
> *Some will* **no doubt** *accuse Jarman of shock tactics along Warhol lines.* (NEWS†)

Finite clause:
> *Well, then, I have come here to heal myself,* **if you like to put it that way**. (FICT)

Non-finite clause:
> **Based on studies of crop plants and native species grown under controlled conditions**, *root growth often responds at least as much, and perhaps more, to elevated carbon dioxide than does shoot growth.* (ACAD)

Multi-word stance adverbials are often more fixed and conventionalized than circumstance adverbials. Hence, fixed phrases such as *of course* and *sort of* can be considered single adverbs, since they function as a unit and never vary in form. In contrast, the expression *in fact* shows variability (e.g. *in actual fact*) and is therefore considered a prepositional phrase.

Stance adverbials can also be realized as adjectival phrases, although this structure is very rare (see also 7.6.3).

## 10.3.2.1 Distribution of syntactic forms

**Figure 10.24 Syntactic realizations of stance adverbials**

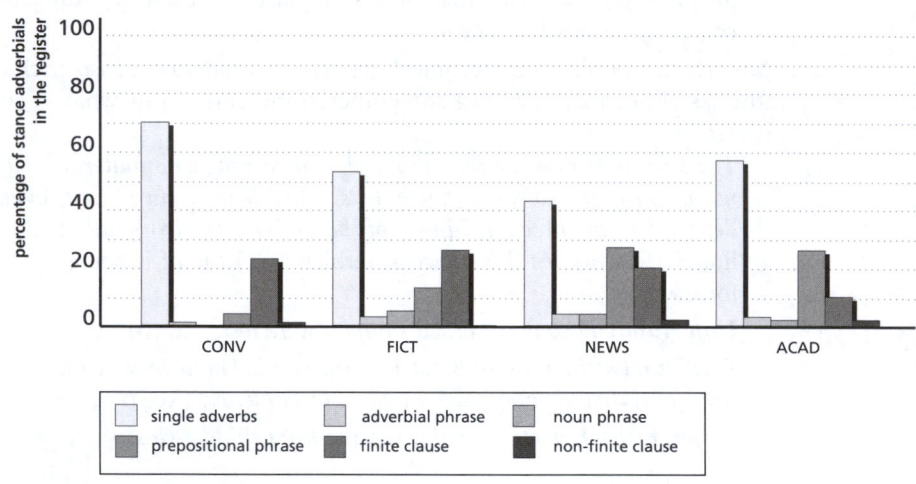

➤ In all four registers, single adverbs account for the highest percentage of stance adverbials.

➤ Finite clauses are the second most common structural form of stance adverbials in conversation and fiction.

➤ Prepositional phrases are the second most common form in news and academic prose.

**DISCUSSION OF FINDINGS**

### A Single-word adverbs

Single adverbs can be used to convey virtually every kind of stance meaning with respect to a proposition.

Certainty or doubt:

*I shall **definitely** be at the airport to meet you.* (FICT)

***Maybe** this damp weather has taken away my enterprise or my book has.* (FICT)

*The arts community has always gone in for manic attention-seeking, **of course** – the oxygen of publicity (to borrow a phrase) being crucial to its survival.* (NEWS)

Actuality or reality:

> A: *You can't see it there can you?*
> B: *What?*
> A: *The cream.*
> B: *No. Well I wasn't looking for it **actually**.* (CONV)
>
> *And he doesn't eat much **really** does he?* (CONV)

Evidence, particularly with *apparently* and *evidently*:

> *You know about this meteor crater in Flagstaff. That **apparently** is why you go to Flagstaff.* (CONV)
>
> *The terms of the settlement **evidently** also require both sides not to talk about the matter publicly.* (NEWS)

Limitation:

> ***Generally** a new broom sweeps clean.* (NEWS†)

Imprecision in the communication of a proposition:

> *Oh yeah, see how people **sort of** natter on.* (CONV)
>
> *They **like** didn't know anything about the city.* (CONV)
>
> *You **kind of** have to nail him to the wall.* (NEWS)

Single adverbs are also used as attitude adverbials, conveying an attitude towards the proposition or giving a judgment about it:

> *I have **inevitably** covered a great deal of familiar ground.* (ACAD)
>
> ***Unbelievably**, the court was told that they would not help the defence case – a demonstrable falsehood that could have landed the three in jail.* (NEWS)
>
> ***Amazingly** he was permitted to witness the illicit luftwaffe build-up of the mid-thirties, the preparations in East Prussia for the drive on the USSR, and much else.* (NEWS)

Finally, single adverbs can be used to communicate the style of speaking (most commonly in conversation, but in other registers as well):

> *Well, **frankly**, I would rather have a little mud than a hatchet thrown at my back.* (NEWS)
>
> *"**Confidentially**, Scheisskopf, I'm not too happy with Colonel Cargill."* (FICT)

Given these varied functions of single adverbs, it is not surprising that they are the most common realization of stance adverbials for all four registers. In addition, the most commonly used individual stance adverbials tend to be single adverbs (10.3.3).

## B Prepositional phrases

The functions of prepositional phrases as stance adverbials are more limited than single adverbs. In news and academic prose they tend to be used for functions which are less important in conversation and fiction, thus accounting for their greater use in the two expository registers.

In news, prepositional phrases are often used to convey the source of information, especially with the preposition *according to*:

> *Venezuela has paid more than $900m dollars in overdue interest on its public sector debt to commercial banks, **according to Chase Manhattan**.* (NEWS)
>
> ***According to later reports** Gerard Harte was suspected of triggering the Ballygawley bomb.* (NEWS)

> *The driver of the small truck and four family members in the car were killed when fire engulfed the two vehicles, **according to Sgt. Rick Fields**. (NEWS)*

Academic prose often uses prepositional phrases to qualify claims. This includes limiting the generality of the proposition:

> ***In general**, then, recent evidence points to conceptual or linguistic difficulties of a fairly high level. (ACAD)*

> ***On the whole**, however, philosophers have ignored this possibility. (ACAD)*

It may also involve explicitly stating that the author's viewpoint is being presented:

> *The remainder of the chapter selects three topics which are, **in the author's view**, the most important and/or mature in the field. (ACAD)*

> *In fact I must emphasize again that, **in my view**, the early Uniformitarians were the theoreticians and the Catastrophists were the careful field observers. (ACAD)*

News and academic prose also use prepositional phrases for style adverbials, although these are relatively rare (10.3.1.5):

> *But what of the car's performance capabilities? **In short**, they're very impressive. (NEWS)*

> *It is, **in a word**, more modernist. (ACAD)*

> *The answer, **in brief**, is the method of empirical inquiry, at its best the method of science. (ACAD)*

On the other hand, all four of the registers use prepositional phrases in marking the actuality of propositions, particularly with expressions that include the word *fact*:

> *At the moment I am therefore due **in actual fact** two weeks holiday. (CONV)*

> *But as Pod well knew, **in actual fact** it would be several hours before they dropped into bed. (FICT†)*

> ***In fact**, the hijack was a plot hatched between the two presenters to Fox listeners, some of whom phoned to find out what was going on. (NEWS)*

> ***As a matter of fact**, at this very moment a theory of those systems satisfying A2, A3, A4, M2 and one of the axioms in D is in the process of establishing itself as worthy of independent study. (ACAD)*

A less common use of prepositional phrases is to show doubt or attitude with the more informal expressions *for all I/we know/care*. These are most common in fiction, but they also occur in news and conversation:

> *She might chuck me in tonight **for all I know**. (CONV)*

> *"And, **for all we know**, he may be giving her a message to take to Reuben." (FICT)*

> *"To tell you the truth, Mr Willis, I am so glad to see him up there with the snowy clouds about him that he may dance a jig **for all I care**!" (FICT)*

> *And **for all I know** it might well have been composed rather than written. (NEWS†)*

## C   Finite clauses

With respect to the use of finite clauses, the higher percentage in conversation and fiction is due largely to the use of comment clauses (3.11.6). These finite clauses usually have a first person pronoun subject and no subordinator, and are used explicitly to mark a proposition as the speaker's opinion, or to convey some level of personal doubt or certainty.

When these expressions are integrated into the clause structure, they usually occur as a main clause taking a *that*-complement clause (e.g. *I think that . . .*; 9.2). When they are not integrated into the clause structure, they are finite clause stance adverbials:

> *I'm going to get a new one for the basement **I think**.* (CONV)
>
> *It'll come out in the wash **I guess**!* (CONV)
>
> *You'd wear that more than I would **I bet**.* (CONV)
>
> *This room's not been used in years, **I would say**.* (FICT)
>
> *Well, he has had to be careful so long, watching every tiny little thing he does, **I suppose**.* (FICT)
>
> *We have, **I believe**, paid more attention to sentimental Goldsmith and Richardson than lively old Fielding and Smollett!* (FICT)

In fiction, finite clauses are also occasionally inserted to show doubt or possibility, especially with the clause *who knows*:

> *Apart from anything else, you'll feel more relaxed if you do. And **who knows**, he might pick up on that, and relax himself.* (FICT)
>
> *They fantasise that if they had parents like yours, they'd sit on their backsides and eat chocolates, and hell, **who knows**, maybe they resent you because you don't.* (FICT)

In addition, conversation has finite stance clauses with *because* that give the evidence for the speaker's claim:

> *He's seriously deficient in what he should be learning **cos - he should know that at least**.* (CONV)

News and academic prose more commonly use comment clauses to show the source of information—sometimes vaguely and sometimes specifically:

> *Ratepayers in Ards may have to foot the bill if the district council goes ahead with a proposal not to charge for collecting rubbish from orange halls, **it has been disclosed**.* (NEWS)
>
> *The view that organizations are rational structures set up to achieve their goals in the most efficient way has been legitimated, **Albrow has claimed**, on the erroneous assumption that Weber associated rationality with efficiency.* (ACAD)

The comment clauses *it seems* and *it appears* also allude to some evidence supporting the proposition, although at the same time they introduce a certain level of doubt:

> *The new 1.8i engine is worth a second glance, **it seems**.* (NEWS)
>
> *For, by 1841, he had worked out not only his theory of the origin of species, natural selection, but also, **it seems**, his theory of generation (or reproduction, including heredity, variation so on), pangenesis.* (ACAD)
>
> *Wallace, **it appears**, created a model for scientific sociology which has an elitist appeal rather than the pluralistic one desired in the present project.* (ACAD)

Finally, finite clauses are often used to show recognition of the audience's knowledge or expectations:

*The net result was she had to do most of the work, the finished products were,* **as one might expect**, *completely professional.* (FICT)

*Still, the new 911 is a better car than the old one,* **as you'd expect**. (NEWS)

**As you might expect**, *there are several groups for the various different application areas.* (ACAD)

*This,* **as you might guess** *is called "systematically contributing to the field's knowledge base."* (ACAD)

In news and academic prose, the use of the subject *you* in these clauses creates a more involved text, overtly attributing an attitude to the reader.

## D Adverb phrases, noun phrases, and non-finite clauses

These other syntactic forms all have more limited functions as conveyers of stance. Adverb phrases, when they do occur, tend to be a combination of an adverb such as *quite*, *rather*, or *most* modifying an adverb of attitude or likelihood:

*They* **most likely** *wouldn't be able to give you the help as well.* (CONV)

**Quite likely** *he's not even a doctor.* (FICT)

*Beer is,* **quite rightly**, *Britain's favorite Friday night drink.* (NEWS)

*"These appointments are stressful and* **quite honestly** *something like this just makes it even more traumatic," she said.* (NEWS)

**Rather surprisingly**, *Friedman (1976) has found that in Gryllus assimilis the ultrastructure of the cells is* <...> (ACAD†)

*These often technical books may give a great amount of information on species which cannot even be cultivated under aquarium conditions or,* **even worse**, *about plants which turn into pesty weeds.* (ACAD†)

Noun phrases are uncommon as stance adverbials, with the exception of the phrase *no doubt*:

*These rows and rows of blue balloons – so* **no doubt** *it was a boy that was being christened.* (CONV)

*The thing* **no doubt** *would have happened differently to another man.* (FICT)

*But many people would* **no doubt** *argue that the current "anything goes as long as it sells papers" style goes too far the other way.* (NEWS)

*At the same time, readers will* **no doubt** *continue to be inventive in harnessing the insights of teachers and the tools of linguistic analysis.* (ACAD)

Finally, when non-finite clauses occur as stance adverbials, they tend to be style adverbials conveying how the speaker/writer is communicating:

*I don't know* **to tell you the truth**. (CONV)

*There's still a good deal of forest left,* **comparatively speaking**, *anyhow.* (FICT)

*We feel that if we did not pursue this second transplant it would be like,* **to put it bluntly**, *pulling the plug on her.* (NEWS)

**Generally speaking**, *you get what you pay for in a kitchen.* (NEWS)

**To put it less charitably**, *it has been a hotch-potch approach in which any variable deemed by the researcher to be even vaguely relevant has been thrown into the statistical melting pot.* (ACAD)

## 10.3.2.2   Sentence relatives as stance adverbials

Although not common, another syntactic structure deserves mention when discussing the syntactic realization of stance adverbials: **sentence relatives**, such as:

> *I've got Tuesday morning off now, **which is quite good**.* (CONV)

In this structure, a relative clause (e.g. *which is quite good*) refers back to the entire proposition (*I've got Tuesday morning off now*), rather than modifying a head noun like most relative clauses (see 8.7).

Sentence relatives are most commonly used to convey an attitude or value judgment about a proposition, as in the following examples:

> *We seem to be taking on more than hopefully the old, the old wages at the moment, **which is encouraging**.* (CONV)
>
> *A: But if we, what she has done is soured the relationship between Claire and Steve, and also between Claire, Steve*
> *B: and herself.*
> *A: Yes. **Which is a shame** because like, we all, we all get on really well with William.* (CONV)
>
> *Mom washed her hands of Kitty after the last incident, **which isn't as heartless as it sounds**.* (FICT)
>
> *'It's terribly common,' said Margot, 'but it rather impresses the young ladies, **which is a good thing**.'* (FICT)
>
> *The herring was to the Eastern European Jew what potatoes were to the Irish, **which is surprising, for the herring is a salt-water fish and in Russia and Poland one rarely got a glimpse of the sea**.* (NEWS)

Sentence relatives are also used to comment on the truth or likelihood of a proposition:

> *Okay, supposedly she claims that he hit her and winded her and she screamed after she was winded, yeah, **which is an impossibility** anyway but that's okay.* (CONV)
>
> *No risk for me; all I have to do is walk in and laser him. Assuming, of course, that he's in his apartment, **which isn't likely**.* (FICT)
>
> *If equations [7.11] and [7.12] were valid they would imply that v and s are zero under these condition, **which is obviously untrue**.* (ACAD)

## 10.3.3   Most common stance adverbials across registers

**CORPUS FINDINGS** [4]

➤ All of the most common stance adverbials mark epistemic stance.
➤ Three adverbials are especially common across all registers: *of course*, *perhaps*, and *probably*.
➤ In general, conversation has the highest frequencies of the most common adverbials.
   ➤ Conversation, compared with the other registers, has particularly high frequencies of adverbials marking actuality (*actually*, *really*) and imprecision (*sort of*, *like*, and *kind of*).
   ➤ AmE conversation differs from BrE conversation in having much higher frequencies of *maybe*, *kind of*, and *like*. In contrast, BrE conversation shows a preference for *sort of*.
   ➤ AmE news and BrE news show essentially the same patterns of use here.

➤ In general, fiction has the second highest frequencies of the most common adverbials. *Really* and *perhaps* are the most common items.

➤ At the other extreme, news has the lowest frequency for most of these items. *According to* + NP is the only adverbial used with a higher frequency than in the other registers (especially in AmE news).

➤ In academic prose, *perhaps*, *probably*, *of course*, and *generally* are the most common stance adverbials.

### DISCUSSION OF FINDINGS

## A Adverbials of doubt and certainty

The common use of *perhaps* and *probably* in all registers corresponds to one of the most important functions of stance adverbials: showing the doubt or certainty of the proposition (or part of the proposition). Both of these adverbs are general terms that occur commonly in conversation (with *probably* over twice as common as *perhaps*):

> You've **probably** wiped it off now. (CONV)
>
> We can **probably** leave packing until next week. (CONV)
>
> **Perhaps** I'll have two, cos I'm a pig. (CONV)

A difference between BrE and AmE conversation in this semantic area concerns the use of *maybe*. Though it is used in both dialects, it is far more common in AmE. Speakers use *maybe* to mark uncertainty in many situations where *probably* and *perhaps* could also be used, including giving possible explanations for events, interpreting the outcome of events, and considering future actions:

> **Maybe** she was in California or something. (AmE CONV)
>
> Well, but **maybe** it's good that he learns this right now instead of at, in his twenties. (AmE CONV)
>
> **Maybe** I'll put half of 'em out in the beginning and half of 'em out in the middle. (AmE CONV)

In fiction, *probably* and *perhaps* are often used in dialogue, imitating their use in conversation. They are also used in descriptions given through a character's eyes rather than by an omniscient narrator:

> "She **probably** thinks you're Rod Stewart," sneered Brian. (FICT)
>
> "You **probably** know that much better than I do." (FICT)
>
> He was **probably** just short of six feet tall, with a football player's physique. (FICT)
>
> Ellen thought that **perhaps** Jackie had been crazy to leave all of that and come to live with her in a cramped apartment on her salary. (FICT)

News and academic prose also use *probably* and *perhaps*, with predictions, suppositions, explanations, and interpretations that have not been clearly proven:

> He travelled widely in the early 1970s, **probably** more widely than any other world leader. (NEWS)
>
> The fact that relations between it and Fleet Street aren't as cosy as they once were **perhaps** makes it easier for the Government to introduce the tax at present. (NEWS†)

**Table 10.15** **Most common stance adverbials across registers and dialects; occurrences per million words**

each ■ represents 100   □ represents less than 50   ( ) marks semantically ambiguous occurrences which could also be interpreted as extent/degree adverbs

| | CONV (AmE & BrE) | FICT | NEWS (AmE & BrE) | ACAD |
|---|---|---|---|---|
| *epistemic—doubt/certainty* | | | | |
| probably | ■■■■■■■ | ■■■ | ■■ | ■■ |
| maybe | ■■■■■ | ■■ | ■ | □ |
| perhaps | ■■ | ■■■■■ | ■ | ■■■ |
| of course | ■■ | ■■■■ | ■ | ■■ |
| certainly | ■ | ■■ | ■ | ■ |
| definitely | ■ | □ | □ | □ |
| *epistemic—actuality* | | | | |
| really | ■■■■■■■■■ ■■(■■■■) | ■■■■■ | ■(■) | ■ |
| actually | ■■■■■■■ | ■ | ■ | ■ |
| in fact | ■ | ■ | ■ | ■ |
| *epistemic—imprecision* | | | | |
| like | ■■■■■■■■ | □ | □ | □ |
| sort of | ■■■■ | □ | □ | □ |
| kind of | ■■ | □ | □ | □ |
| *epistemic—source of information* | | | | |
| according to + NP | □ | □ | ■■ | ■ |
| *epistemic—limitation/perspective* | | | | |
| generally | □ | □ | □ | ■■ |

| | AmE CONV | BrE CONV |
|---|---|---|
| *epistemic—doubt/certainty* | | |
| probably | ■■■■■■■■■ | ■■■■■■ |
| maybe | ■■■■■■■■ | ■■ |
| perhaps | ■ | ■■ |
| of course | ■■ | ■■■ |
| certainly | ■ | ■ |
| definitely | ■ | ■ |
| *epistemic—actuality* | | |
| really | ■■■■■■■■■■ (■■■■■■) | ■■■■■■■■■■■ (■■■) |
| actually | ■■■■■■■ | ■■■■■■ |
| in fact | ■ | ■ |

**Table 10.15 continued**

| | AmE CONV | BrE CONV |
|---|---|---|
| *epistemic—imprecision* | | |
| *like* | ■■■■■■■■■■■ ■■■ | ■■ |
| *sort of* | ■■ | ■■■■■■ |
| *kind of* | ■■■■ | □ |
| | | |
| *epistemic—source of information* | | |
| *according to* + NP | □ | □ |
| | | |
| *epistemic—limitation/perspective* | | |
| *generally* | □ | □ |

> *This level is **probably** sufficient to cause clinical disease in susceptible adult animals or to upset the normal functioning of the gastric mucosa in cow.* (ACAD)

> ***Perhaps** their probosces are not long enough to reach the most succulent parts of the prey by any other means.* (ACAD)

*Of course* is used primarily for two effects. First, it indicates the certainty of a proposition. However, it also implies that the audience already knows—or will readily accept—the information:

> *The television is **of course** infernally clever.* (CONV)

> *I went to climb the ladders though **of course** they are staircases and broad at that to the afterdeck and quarterdeck.* (FICT)

> ***Of course**, things happen in politics for more than one reason.* (NEWS)

> *The above statistics refer, **of course**, to the opportunities for clerks in the first 3 decades of the present century.* (ACAD)

## B Adverbials of actuality

Adverbials marking actuality are also very common in conversation. Far more than in the other registers, conversants make a point of identifying propositions as factual or real, with *actually* and *really*:

> 1 *I've **actually** got very strong teeth.* (CONV)
> 2 *Are they **actually** supposed to make money off it or is it just supposed to be a break even thing or are they quite happy?* (CONV)
> 3 *Well, to tell you the truth I didn't **really** see him cos it was dark when he got in the car.* (CONV)
> 4 *That's all she could move. It **really** was.* (CONV)
> 5 *I **really** do feel sorry for that dog.* (CONV)

The only written register that uses *really* relatively commonly (though much less so than conversation) is fiction. In this register, *really* is often used in dialog or for characters' reflections on states or events; thus, as in conversation, *really* indicates the character's perception of actuality:

> *But now he realized that his anger had never **really** left him.* (FICT)

> *"I **really** have to go now."* (FICT)

> *Twenty-four years ago. Had it **really** been so long?* (FICT)

> *In Home Economics, which **really** means cooking and sewing, I've learned how to install a zipper and make a flat-fell seam.* (FICT)

## C Adverbials of imprecision

In conversation, stance adverbials also mark imprecision in the words used for describing a proposition. BrE conversation displays a preference for *sort of*:

> *It's **sort of** an L in shape of an O.* (BrE CONV)
>
> *We **sort of** were joking about it.* (BrE CONV)
>
> *A lot of people think those people are **sort of** back in the tenth century or something.* (BrE CONV)

AmE conversation more commonly uses *like* and *kind of*:

> *I always thought that I reminded him too much of my mom and **like** depressed him.* (AmE CONV)
>
> *There's **like** no place to put the stuff.* (AmE CONV)
>
> *She's **kind of** a rich, really rich woman with all this time on her hands.* (AmE CONV)
>
> *Now she's getting fractures in her back, her bones are **kind of** cracking.* (AmE CONV)

In both AmE and BrE conversation, *like* is also used in other functions; for example, it often serves as an approximator (e.g. *I looked for **like** three weeks*, cf. 7.14.2.6) and to introduce direct speech (e.g. *We're **like** I wonder what he meant by that?*). *Kind of* can also serve as a diminisher (e.g. *It's **kind of** hard to boss people around*, cf. 7.14.2.4).

## D Adverbials of source of knowledge

In addition to the most common adverbials described above, the use of *according to* + NP in news is noteworthy, since it reflects the singular emphasis in news on stance adverbials that show the source of knowledge. *According to* is used with sources that range from specifically named people and publications to sources identified only by their location:

> ***According to Mr K**, it all started with an argument with a customer over a faulty toy in an Easter egg last year.* (NEWS)
>
> ***According to the liquidator of the stockbroking firm which crashed as a result of the Farrington stead failure**, the summons for her arrest was issued that year.* (NEWS)
>
> *One person in 10 failed to spell any word correctly **according to the Gallup survey of 1,000 adults**.* (NEWS)
>
> *But drinkers will get off reasonably lightly, **according to reliable Westminster sources**.* (NEWS)

The adverbial *according to* + NP is much less common in other registers. In conversation, when *according to* + NP is used, it tends to distance the speaker from the proposition, as though the speaker does not want to be considered responsible for the information or does not agree with it:

> *Well it should dry out later **according to the weather forecast**.* (CONV)
>
> *I was leading Margaret astray **according to Eileen**.* (CONV)
>
> *I think it's a brown one. **According to Mary** it looked brown.* (CONV)

## 10.3.4 Positions of stance adverbials

**CORPUS FINDINGS [1]**

➤ All four registers display a preference for stance adverbials in medial positions.
➤ Relative to the other registers, conversation has a higher percentage of stance adverbials in final position and a lower percentage in initial position.
➤ Relative to the other registers, news has a particularly high percentage of stance adverbials in initial position.
➤ Relative to the other registers, academic prose has a very low percentage of stance adverbials in final position.

**Table 10.16 Positions of stance adverbials across registers**

each • represents 5%

| | % in initial position | % in medial position | % in final position |
|---|---|---|---|
| CONV | • • • | • • • • • • • • • • • | • • • • • • • |
| FICT | • • • • • | • • • • • • • • • • • | • • • • |
| NEWS | • • • • • • • | • • • • • • • • • • • | • • |
| ACAD | • • • • • • | • • • • • • • • • • • • | • |

**DISCUSSION OF FINDINGS**

Virtually every semantic category of stance adverbial can be placed in medial positions. Adverbials conveying certainty, likelihood, and actuality are often placed immediately before or after the operator. In this position, the adverbial emphasizes its relationship to the state or action described by the verb or, sometimes, the negator *not*:

> I **really** don't understand it darling. (CONV)

> The machine will **no doubt** tell you. (CONV)

> For some months Wallace had **actually** practiced law. (FICT)

> He repeated the act (the greenkeeper would **probably** say it was vandalism) at the 14th green. (NEWS)

> Someone who **most certainly** will not be having trouble keeping up with his mortgage repayments is Lord Hanson. (NEWS†)

> But this **definitely** does not involve the application of a deterministic philosophical materialism to the interpretation of the development of society. (ACAD)

Stance adverbials of imprecision also commonly occur before the main verb—either following an operator or when no operator is present—marking the predicate as imprecise:

> Do you **sort of** pay the whole lot first? (CONV)

> And he **like** rants and raves. (CONV)

> It has all **sort of** fermented inside him and makes him sound a bit mad at times. (FICT)

Markers of evidence are also often placed between the subject and verb:

> They just **apparently** built up huge quantities of dry bird droppings. (CONV)

> *He came late and,* **according to Lizzie***, had a bath and went straight to bed.*
> (FICT)
>
> *The answer,* **it seems***, is that next to nothing is known about it.* (NEWS)
>
> *A complete Pterygote ovipositor,* **according to the interpretation of Scudder (1971)** *consists of <...>* (ACAD†)

Adverbials limiting the generalizability of propositions or conveying perspective are also often placed in medial positions.

Limiting generalizability:

> *The primary lesion is* **generally** *treated with pituitary surgery.* (ACAD)
>
> *On the one hand, there is the emotional or subjective relation, which* **in most cases** *provides one of the important reasons for studying the particular object in the first place.* (ACAD)

Conveying perspective:

> *"Some such rumour,* **I believe***, reached me once long ago."* (FICT†)
>
> *This,* **in my view***, is totally wrong and contrary to my notions of natural justice.* (NEWS)
>
> *The chief contribution of recent sedimentary studies,* **in my opinion***, has been the demonstration of lateral rather than vertical sedimentation.* (ACAD)

These types of stance adverbials account for a large proportion of the occurrences of pre-verbal position in news and academic prose.

Attitude and style stance adverbials also occur in medial positions, often immediately following the subject:

> *At the time my mother* **fortunately** *never thought of selling his books.*
> (FICT†)
>
> *The second goal* **amazingly** *didn't come until the second half, courtesy of a goalkeeping lapse from Devine.* (NEWS)
>
> *Under normal circumstances, when the by-line Gerald R. Ford appears, I* **frankly** *don't bother to read it.* (NEWS)

In addition to the range of semantic roles that can occur medially, the examples above also illustrate that all syntactic structures—single adverbs, adverb phrases, prepositional phrases, noun phrases, finite clauses, and non-finite clauses—can occur in medial positions.

The higher percentage of final position in conversation, fiction, and news than in academic prose corresponds largely to the more frequent use of finite comment clauses in those registers (10.3.2.1). Many examples of this type are given in 10.3.2.1. Others include:

> *It's going to be about three* **I suppose***, isn't it?* (CONV)
>
> *"Most of the others didn't,* **I guess***."* (FICT)
>
> *Door-to-door salesmen are posing as Fire Brigade representatives to sell potentially lethal fire extinguishers,* **it has been disclosed***.* (NEWS)

The higher percentages of initial stance adverbials in fiction, news, and academic prose over conversation correspond to the use of prepositional phrases and certain style and attitude stance adverbials which are rare in conversation. For example, many of the uses of *according to* + NP occur initially, both in news and in the other written registers:

> *According to this book*, I'm supposed to be caught in a whirlwind of teenage emotions. (FICT)
>
> *According to the magazine*, 29 of the top 50 paper millionaires in 1988 have since lost money on paper. (NEWS)
>
> *According to experts of moose behavior*, it is not unusual for moose to stand still by the side of the road before they suddenly enter the carriageway. (ACAD)

Other stance expressions, such as *in fact, in short, in brief*, and even *in a word* commonly occur in the written registers in initial position:

> *In fact*, Carpetworld has a range of quality wool mixture twist carpets. (NEWS†)
>
> *In short*, the place looked dead. (FICT)
>
> *In brief*, all things about our wooden world have altered for the better. (FICT)
>
> *In a word*, they were won over. (ACAD)

The initial placement of these stance adverbials also highlights their secondary role as linking adverbials (which tend to occur in initial position; 10.1.3.1, 10.4.4). These adverbials serve to introduce a condensation or reinforcement of previous statements; the adverbial marks not just the nature of the clause, but also its connection to the previous discourse.

Finally, many of the attitude adverbials in news and academic prose are placed in initial position:

> *Wisely*, the Leinster Council decided to make the game all ticket. (NEWS)
>
> *Predictably*, the "night of fun" presented by the British Music Hall Company to open the Festival of Comedy generally appealed to the older age group. (NEWS)
>
> *Ironically*, however, the sociologists are correct on one important point. (ACAD)
>
> *Not surprisingly*, errors in complex systems tend to be more catastrophic when they occur but are usually very difficult to discover in advance. (ACAD)

## 10.3.5 Other discourse functions of stance adverbials

Stance adverbials can serve a variety of discourse functions in addition to conveying epistemic, attitudinal, and style meanings.

The cohesive function served by some stance adverbials has been discussed in previous sections. In addition, certain stance adverbials are important to the interactive nature of conversation. For example, a speaker can use *no doubt* or *of course* to mark shared familiarity with the interlocutor, as in this comment after a forecast for clear weather:

> But *no doubt* we'll have a few showers. (CONV)

Stance adverbials can also be used to soften disagreement. For instance, after one interlocutor lists Sophie as a *weird name*, the other responds:

> Sophie. Well that's not *really* a weird name. (CONV)

The insertion of *really* mitigates the force of the disagreement. Similarly, epistemic stance markers can soften a suggestion:

> Well I was thinking we could *perhaps* take her to Blagden Hall now that's open. (CONV)
>
> And then you could *perhaps* – tinkle the ivories. (CONV)

Epistemic stance markers can also be used for emphasis:

> *I need the person to go with because **definitely** you need a person to go with.* (CONV)

In this example the reason clause does not give a reason; it simply restates the idea of the main clause with a stance adverbial conveying certainty.

The above examples serve to illustrate the point that stance adverbials can be multi-functional in discourse. Though these functions can be important in all registers, they are often most obvious in conversation (see 14.1.2.4–5).

# 10.4 Linking adverbials

As described in 10.1.1, the primary function of linking adverbials is to state the speaker/writer's perception of the relationship between two units of discourse. Because they explicitly signal the connections between passages of text, linking adverbials are important devices for creating textual cohesion, alongside coordinators and subordinators (2.4.7–8).

## 10.4.1 Semantic categories of linking adverbials

A variety of different relationships can be marked by linking adverbials. We distinguish six general semantic categories, described below.

### 10.4.1.1 Enumeration and addition

Linking adverbials can be used for the **enumeration** of pieces of information in an order chosen by the speaker/writer and for the **addition** of items of discourse to one another. Linking adverbials used for enumeration include ordinal numbers such as *first* and *second*, and adverbs such as *finally* and *lastly*, as well as other structures such as prepositional phrases:

> *This new structure must accomplish two special purposes. **First**, as a part of overcoming the division of Europe there must be an opportunity to overcome through peace and freedom the division of Berlin and of Germany. **Second**, the architecture should reflect that American's security remains linked to Europe.* (NEWS)

> *We are already acquainted with six properties which may be used to describe the thermodynamic state of a system: pressure, volume, temperature, internal energy, enthalpy, and entropy <...> **Lastly**, entropy S was shown to be a property as a consequence of the First Law.* (ACAD)

> *He couldn't bring himself to say what he thought. **For one thing**, she seldom stopped to listen. **For another**, he doubted that he could make himself clear.* (FICT)

In some cases the order of enumeration follows real-life logical or time sequence orders but this need not be so. For example, in the last sample above, the pieces of information could have been enumerated in the opposite order.

Other enumerating adverbials include: *firstly, secondly, thirdly (etc.), in the first/second place, first of all, for one thing, for another thing, to begin with, next.*

In some cases, linking adverbials simply mark the next unit of discourse as being added to the previous one:

*These include peroxidase, catalase and some dehydrogenases, as well as the cytochromes which function prominently as electron carriers in photosynthesis and respiration.* **In addition**, *a cytochrome is one of three prosthetic groups* <...> (ACAD†)

*Mr. Justice Hirst said that the criteria in determining whether an overseas company had established a place of business in Great Britain were summarised in Palmer's Company Law, 24th edn (1987) page 1658.* **Further**, *a visible sign or physical indication was not essential.* (NEWS)

Note how in the first example the addition is directly that of the writer while in the second it is attributed to Mr. Justice Hirst. Furthermore, *further* in the second example links not to the entire preceding sentence, but just to the reported speech clause following *said*.

Additive linking adverbials may also show explicitly that the second item is similar to the first:

*Feedback tends to be used to stabilise systems, not to randomise them.* **Similarly**, *natural systems would probably evolve to avoid chaos.* (ACAD)

Other additive linking adverbials include *also, by the same token, further(more), likewise,* and *moreover*.

## 10.4.1.2 Summation

Adverbials marking **summation** show that a unit of discourse is intended to conclude or sum up the information in the preceding discourse:

**In sum**, *then, to account for a synchronic assimilation from [k] to [t] under this view, the processes of tier promotion and complex segment simplification must apply along with the spreading of the assimilation feature.* (ACAD)

**To conclude**, *we may place the three notions of saliency in an ordered relation as follows:* <...> (ACAD†)

Other summative adverbials include *all in all, in conclusion, overall, to conclude,* and *to summarize*.

## 10.4.1.3 Apposition

Adverbials of **apposition** show that the second unit of text is to be treated either as equivalent to or included in the preceding unit (cf. appositive noun phrases, 8.10).

An appositive linking adverbial can be used to show that the second unit is to be taken as a restatement of the first, reformulating the information it expresses in some way or stating it in more explicit terms:

*I looked into my Being, all that lovely light and rotting nerve, and proceeded to listen.* **Which is to say**, *I looked out deep into that shimmer of past death and new madness.* (FICT†)

*The current edition* <...> *shows that road users cover their track costs by a factor of 2.4 to 1.* **In other words** *users of all types pay almost two and a half times as much in taxes as is spent on all road costs.* (NEWS)

> *Our model allows the predefinition of who, **i.e.** which Communicator, may exchange when, **i.e.** at what point of time, what, **i.e.** which message, with whom, **i.e.** with which Communicator.* (ACAD)

> *All the items would have low omission rates among the bottom 20 per cent band of attainers nationally; **that is**, they would not deter this group of pupils, who would be willing to have a go at them.* (ACAD)

In many cases, the second unit of text is an example. It is therefore presented as information that is in some sense included in, rather than exactly equivalent to, the previous text (marked in *[]*):

> *She understood [the parameters of the picnics all too well]. **E.g.** they could not go to the beach because of the sand.* (FICT)

> *If a population becomes highly entrained, [its diversity is greatly reduced]. **For example**, the age structure could become very narrow.* (ACAD)

> *It's also an opportunity to say that [the US supermarket papers are streets ahead when it comes to headline writing]. **For instance**: "Man Explodes on Operating Table" (the Globe, California).* (NEWS)

*Namely* and *specifically* are other linking adverbials typically conveying apposition.

## 10.4.1.4  Result/inference

Linking adverbials in the **result/inference** category show that the second unit of discourse states the result or consequence—either logical or practical—of the preceding discourse:

> *This year's commitment we will not reach this year. **Therefore**, we'll be into deficit!* (CONV)

> *I once acquired a set of recordings of a Bach piano concerto. I was very fond of it, but my mother was forever criticizing and chastising my poor taste <...>. **Consequently**, I now hardly listen to Bach.* (FICT)

> *As the spatial file contains all the geometric relationships necessary to specify the body, this can be used to generate any pictorial view. It is **thus** not necessary to produce an engineering drawing specifically for the purpose of showing everyone what it looks like.* (ACAD)

Other typical resulive linking adverbials are *as a result, hence, in consequence,* and *thus.* In conversation this category is also commonly realized by *so.* In some cases, *so* clearly marks a resultive relationship:

> 1  *He's being a zombie, **so** he's coming downstairs with two sleeping bags over the top of his head and knocking everything over.* (CONV)

> 2  *Oh well you've seen it anyway, **so** I won't put it on.* (CONV)

In both of these examples, *so* introduces the result of the event which has already been stated in the first clause. *So* clearly has the same meaning as other resultive adverbials, and could, for example, be replaced with *therefore.*

However, *so* does not always have such a clear role. At times, it appears to be used to show the result of something understood from the context that is not available to analysts of a written transcription. In the following example, *so* could relate to some accompanying action that is not put into words (presenting a finished product, putting away tools, closing a book, etc.) which suggests work is finished:

> *Okay **so** that's that.* (CONV)

In such situations, however, it is impossible to be sure of the correct interpretation. Furthermore, in still other cases, *so* appears to have little semantic content of its own. Instead, it functions more as a discourse marker (3.4.5). For example, in the following excerpt, *so* simply marks the return to a story after an intervening description of a truck and the listener's acknowledgment of understanding the description:

> A: *Now added to that by our wall there was this ruddy great lorry again. It's a great big thing with an open back right? We – a long*
> B: *yeah*
> A: *open back.* **So** *they park that up on the pavement by our wall.* (CONV)

In the following Corpus analyses, we have included only clearly resultive occurrences of *so*. (See also 2.4.7.2 on the classification of *so*.)

The result/inference category also includes inferential linking adverbials, which mark one idea as an inferred result of another:

> *He works late. How am I supposed to get there* **then**? (CONV)

In this example, *then* marks the connection between the idea of the first clause (his working late) and the speaker's problem of getting to another location. However, this connection is not as overtly stated as with many resultive adverbials (e.g. *He works late;* therefore, *he cannot drive me there.*)

## 10.4.1.5  Contrast/concession

The category of **contrast/concession** is broader than many other categories of linking adverbials, containing items that in some way mark incompatibility between information in different discourse units, or that signal concessive relationships. Some adverbials clearly mark contrasts, alternatives, or differences:

> *Administration officials, notably the White House Chief of Staff and Deputy Treasury Secretary, were irked by his independence.* **On the other hand**, *Taylor reportedly is well-regarded by Treasury officials for his low-key, out-of-the-limelight style.* (NEWS)

> *Many statutory water companies are already saddled with high borrowings.* **In contrast**, *the water authorities are going into the private sector flush with cash.* (NEWS)

> *Potassium ions might be more readily translocated from zones of high concentration to zones of low concentration within the root system although there is no evidence for this.* **Alternatively**, *there might be a threshold concentration of all nutrients.* (ACAD†)

Other adverbials more clearly mark a concessive relationship, showing that the subsequent discourse expresses some reservation about the idea in the preceding clause:

> A: *Wish I could afford a new car, I would love a nice new car! We won't be able to afford one for a couple years yet.*
> B: *You could afford a Mini* **though**. (CONV)

> *Now that the lawyers have taken over, science will never be able to reach a verdict, and* **anyway** *it no longer matters.* (NEWS)

In some cases, elements of contrast and concession are combined in uses of linking adverbials:

> Until recently hypobiosis was not considered to be a feature of this genus. **However**, there is now ample evidence in temperate areas that hypobiosis plays an important part in the epidemiology, the seasonal occurrence being similar to that of Ostertagia spp. (ACAD)

> They were economically active; **yet**, as the workshops were closed down one after another, they had few places to go to be active. (ACAD)

Other examples of contrast/concession linking adverbials can be grouped according to their primary meaning (see also the discussion of *though* in 10.2.8.11):

> focus on contrast—*conversely, instead, on the contrary, in contrast, by comparison*

> focus on concession—*anyhow, besides, nevertheless, still, in any case, at any rate, in spite of that, after all.*

## 10.4.1.6 Transition

These linking adverbials mark the insertion of an item that does not follow directly from the previous discourse. The new information is not incompatible with what it is linked to (as in 10.4.1.5) but rather it is signalled as only loosely connected, or unconnected. That is, these adverbials mark the **transition** to another, usually tangential, topic. Certain occurrences of *now* and *meanwhile* are transition linking adverbials, as are the following:

> "It reminds one of some story in Punch. Did you know there was a place called Punch in Kashmir **by the by**?" (FICT)

> It seems clear that there is nothing for it but to go back and attack the first difficulties again. **Incidentally**, one way to motivate yourself if things do get sticky is to imagine that you have to explain the subject to the class the next day. (ACAD)

> I'm coming by yesterday, and he goes oh **by the way** I'm coming to the cinema on Saturday with you, I said, you what! (CONV)

## 10.4.1.7 Overlap of linking adverbials and other adverbial classes

We have described linking adverbials as having a primary function of marking the relationship between two units of discourse. It is important to note, however, that linking adverbials can have functions that overlap with those of circumstance and stance adverbials. For example, consider the following use of *thus*:

> When the democratically-elected Colombian senate rejected Mr. Roosevelt's proposal because the money offered was too low, he sponsored the invasion instead. **Thus** Panama gained its independence from Colombia and the Canal Zone was born. (NEWS)

In this passage, *thus* marks the second sentence as containing the result of the first. However, it can also be interpreted as a circumstance adverbial, equivalent to *in this way*.

Some occurrences of linking adverbials also blend functions of stance adverbials. Certain summative linking adverbials, in particular, not only mark summation, but also include the sense of a style stance adverbial, because the summative statement is a brief analysis of a situation. In the following passage, *in sum* seems closely related to the stance adverbial *in brief*:

*Inevitably it <the crucial question> must be answered in such a way as to produce either a kind of dualism or a true monism. In the former case, mental indispensability cannot be achieved by what is on hand. In the latter case, the upshot is Local Idealism <...>. Identity Theories, **in sum**, face a defeating dilemma.* (ACAD†)

Finally, a possible overlap of linking adverbials with discourse markers was discussed in connection with *so* in 10.4.1.4. See 10.2.1.9 and 10.3.1.4 for additional discussion of the overlap between adverbial classes.

## 10.4.1.8 Distribution of semantic categories

➤ Linking adverbials are considerably more common in conversation and academic prose than in fiction and news.
➤ Academic prose and conversation are also similar in having a large proportion of their linking adverbials in the semantic category of result/inference.
➤ Academic prose uses enumerative/additive/summative and appositional adverbials more commonly than the other registers.
➤ Conversation, fiction, and academic prose share a similar level of frequency of contrast/concession adverbials, which are less common in news.
➤ Transition adverbials are rare in all registers.

**Figure 10.25**

**Frequency of linking adverbials across registers**

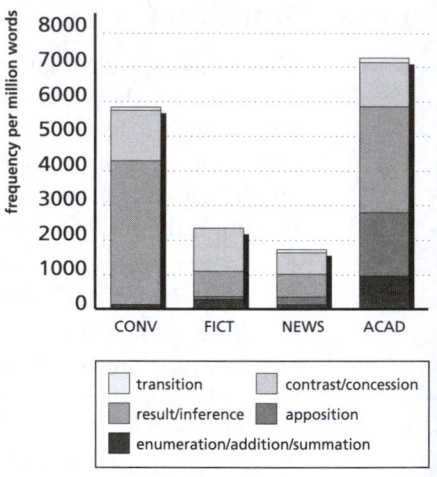

**DISCUSSION OF FINDINGS**

### A  Academic prose

A very important aspect of academic prose is presenting and supporting arguments. The higher frequency of linking adverbials in academic prose not only reflects this communicative need but also the characteristic choice of this register to mark the links between ideas overtly, as these arguments are developed. In some texts, especially as arguments are concluded, each of a series of sentences will begin with a linking adverbial, for example:

***To summarize**, there is no class of healthy ruminant for which the direct effects of low air temperature per se are likely to cause intolerable stress in the temperate and cool zones of the world. **Moreover**, the effects of air temperature on food conversion efficiency below the critical temperature are likely to affect only the smallest animals and at a time when their daily intake is very small relative to lifetime requirements. **Thus** there are no sound economic grounds for providing any more environmental control for the healthy animal than shelter from excessive air movement and precipitation.* (ACAD)

A single sentence may even contain more than one linking adverbial:

> There must, **in addition**, be some reason why water excretion by the kidney has failed, **however**, since ingestion of hypotonic fluid does not ordinarily lead to progressive dilution of body fluids. (ACAD)

All semantic categories of linking adverbials are useful in academic prose for developing arguments or signalling the connection between specific information and an author's point. The most common category, result/inference, marks the conclusions that the writer expects the reader to draw (as in the example above: *Thus, there are no sound economic grounds …*). Result/inference adverbials are also used to connect the writer's claim to supporting facts:

> The Census of Production includes only manufacturing industries, in which only one third of women are employed. We do not **therefore** have a comprehensive picture of women's, and especially their parttime, employment patterns. (ACAD)

> The sulphur compounds in the atmosphere comprise mainly sulphur dioxide derived from the combustion of sulphur containing fuels, and sulphate from sea spray. **As a result**, deficiency usually occurs in crops grown at great distances from these sources. (ACAD)

Appositional linking adverbials are by far most common in academic prose. They are used as connectors for examples that support more general claims, and with restatements that clarify previous statements:

> What empirical evidence there is tends to support this proposition. Brown and Holmes (1971), **for example**, have demonstrated that patterns of social contacts and vacancies visited in the research for a new home were much more compact and localized. (ACAD†)

> The embedding i is an isomorphism on its image, therefore a weak isomorphism (**that is**, (f,f) and (e,e) restricted to F coincide; see b) of the previous proposition, and <...> (ACAD†)

Contrastive/concessive linking adverbials highlight contrasting information, which often lead to main points that academic authors want to make:

> The elements of design and their interconnection into the process network are relatively easy to recognize and generalize, and so produce a common basis for all design activities. It is **however** the subtler aspects of weight, control and role which 'colour' the process. (ACAD†)

> These experiments do not support the notion that poor readers are unlikely to use context when reading, and go some way to suggesting that it is the poor readers who rely on context to aid their weak word-recognition skills. The good readers, **in contrast**, seem to recognise words so quickly that the beneficial (or harmful) effects of context do not have time to take effect. (ACAD)

Finally, enumerative/additive and summative adverbials help to structure the information in academic prose, giving readers clear signposts of where they are in the text:

> There are two related senses in which social facts are 'external' to the individual. **Firstly**, every man is born into an on-going society which already has a definite organisation or structure <...> **Secondly**, social facts are 'external' to the individual in the sense that <...> (ACAD†)

> *In conclusion, this 6-year study of the population dynamics of Locusta has not only determined the probable course of the beginning of an outbreak but has pointed the way to the forecasting of outbreaks.* (ACAD†)

## B News

The other expository written register, news, uses far fewer linking adverbials than academic prose. When it does use them, however, it tends to emphasize the same relationships as academic prose. Contrast/concession and results are the most commonly marked:

> *It was true that the chains' capacity for negotiating good deals made it hard for the family-run business to keep going, and they had many letters offering businesses for sale, and the price of shops was coming down all the time.* **On the other hand** *specialists could thrive.* (NEWS) <contrast>

> *Sir Alec Guinness is probably the world's best known actor,* **yet** *he claims to be the only one who can walk down a street unrecognised.* (NEWS) <concession>

> *British Rail management has said that it is time to start thinking about the passengers – "customer orientation" – but does not seem to have any other ideas for improvement. It is not surprising,* **therefore**, *that most people assume that under private ownership services would be fewer, and charges would be higher.* (NEWS) <result>

Appositional linking adverbials also give additional clarification of information in news:

> *Stopping distance –* **that is**, *the time it takes for the brain to register the need to stop and the time it takes for the brake to take effect – is at 70 miles an hour a frightening 315 feet.* (NEWS)

Much more commonly in news, however, the relationships between ideas are left implicit or encoded in other ways besides linking adverbials. Reports of events are more common and arguments rarer in news, and thus fewer linking signals are needed than in academic prose. Sequences of events are reported with respect to their relationship in time, not with linking adverbials. Resultive relationships are easily inferred based on common knowledge and experience. For example, consider the following passage:

> *Police hunting the killer of a champion Ayrshire cow believe it may have been slashed to death by a jealous farmer. The 11-year-old cow was found dead in its paddock at a remote farm near Gargrave, North Yorkshire, yesterday. A post-mortem revealed it had bled to death after being slashed on the udder with a sharp instrument, severing a main artery. The cow, worth thousands of pounds, had been champion of several shows and was due to appear at the National Dairy Event in Warwickshire next weekend.* (NEWS)

Here no argument is presented. Furthermore, there is no need to state overtly that the police investigation resulted from the cow being slashed to death, or that the other farmer's jealousy stemmed from the cow's championships; such connections are easily inferrable with the background knowledge of most readers.

## C Fiction

Fiction, too, tends to leave most textual relationships unmarked by linking adverbials. When used, contrastive/concessive adverbials are the most common:

> *I've gone to shrinkers for years, and have they cured me of anything? They have not. They have put labels on my troubles, **though**, which sound like knowledge. It's a great comfort and worth the money.* (FICT)

> *The morning had been bright and clear, but in the afternoon, the sky's glaze grew shrouded with warning signs. **Still**, despite the threatening clouds, she held to the hope that the somberness would eventually lift.* (FICT)

Fiction also uses resultive linking adverbials occasionally, especially *so*:

> *They didn't have an empty bed in your ward, **so** I pulled my rank and chased him back here into mine.* (FICT)

> *Billy's father-in-law laughed and laughed at that, and he begged the quartet to sing the other Polish song he liked so much. **So** they sang a song from the Pennsylvania coal mines.* (FICT †)

Most resultive relationships, however, are not signalled with linking adverbials. Rather, cause and result are inferred from a chronological sequence. In the following passage, for example, we are clearly meant to think that the man's action is the result of the child's beginning to cry:

> *The child had begun to cry. He went to her and bent over her, giving her a handkerchief. He put an arm around her shoulders and kept it there for a moment.* (FICT)

However, no linking adverbial (such as *as a result* or *in consequence*) signals this cause-result connection.

## D Conversation

It is surprising that linking adverbials are more common in conversation than fiction or news. In large part, this higher frequency is due to the relatively high frequency of *so* and *then* as result/inference linking adverbials:

> *I don't want there to be any misunderstanding, and he, he said explain. **So** I had to lie.* (CONV)

> A: *He said he didn't want to go out with, he didn't want to come with you in the holidays. He just didn't.*
> B: ***Then** why did he ask me out?* (CONV)

> *Well you've got your dungarees on **so** you're all ready.* (CONV)

> *It might not get dark until eleven o'clock at night and it gets light at about four o'clock in the morning. **So** you get extra daylight then.* (CONV)

The patterns of use for *so* and *then* in conversation are discussed further in 10.4.3.1 and 10.4.4.

The higher proportion of contrastive/concessive linking adverbials in conversation is similarly due to a high frequency of two items: *anyway* and *though* (10.4.3.1). However, other contrastive linking adverbials are used occasionally in conversation, including even some items generally considered more associated with expository writing, such as *nevertheless* and *however*:

> *But – **nevertheless** it's better the devil you know!* (CONV)

> *Oh, and er the cat was lurking around – **however**, it had gone somewhere else.* (CONV)

> *The only thing is in a place like that they're more likely to be Tory. **However**, Jim says he'll take them.* (CONV)

## 10.4.2 Syntactic realizations of linking adverbials

Linking adverbials can be realized by all of the syntactic structures listed in 10.1.2. Some examples of typical items include:

Single adverbs—*anyway, however, nevertheless, so, though, therefore*

Adverb phrases—*even so, first and foremost, more precisely*

Prepositional phrases—*by the way, for example, in addition, in conclusion, on the other hand*

Finite clauses—*that is, that is to say*

Non-finite clauses—*added to that, to conclude*

In this section we focus on the syntactic realizations of the two registers with the most frequent use of linking adverbials: academic prose and conversation.

## 10.4.2.1 Distribution of syntactic forms

**CORPUS FINDINGS [1]**

➤ In both conversation and academic prose, the majority of linking adverbials are realized by single adverbs.
  ➤ In conversation, almost all linking adverbials are single adverbs.
  ➤ In academic prose, prepositional phrases are also relatively common as linking adverbials.

**Figure 10.26**
**Syntactic realizations of linking adverbials in conversation and academic prose**

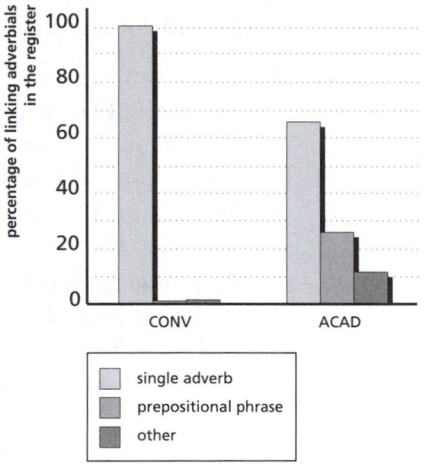

**DISCUSSION OF FINDINGS**

Single adverbs are the most numerous and semantically varied structure that realizes linking adverbials. Every semantic category can be realized by a number of adverbs. Furthermore, the most common linking adverbials are almost exclusively adverbs (10.4.3.1). It is thus not surprising that adverbs account for the vast majority of linking adverbials.

Academic prose, however, differs in its use of linking adverbials in certain ways which give it a more varied structural profile than conversation. First of all, academic prose emphasizes certain semantic categories which are expressed by numerous prepositional phrases as linking adverbials (as well as some clausal adverbials). In addition, as seen with circumstance and stance adverbials, academic prose includes more variety in its selection of linking adverbials.

Academic prose expresses appositional linking relationships more commonly than conversation does (see Figure 10.25 in 10.4.1.8), and many appositional linking adverbials are realized by prepositional phrases. Exemplification is often introduced with *for example* or *for instance*, and reformulation with *in other words*:

> *When glucose is metabolized, **for example** to produce energy, it is converted to lactate or pyruvate.* (ACAD)

> *In some of these are found certain ingenious speculations that have been justified by later work. Such, **for instance**, is Palissy's remarkable statement in 1563.* (ACAD†)

> ***In other words**, they swing from a Mediterranean to an Atlantic orientation.* (ACAD)

Restatements can also be introduced with clauses:

> *Such claims about our ordinary beliefs are commonly depended on in asserting free will, **which is to say** indeterminist accounts of decision and action.* (ACAD)

> *Originally, many computer-based systems were viewed as having the role predominantly of providing the 'design paperwork'. **That is to say** they operated in such a way to either confirm the proposed design or to generate the engineering information for production.* (ACAD)

Enumerative/additive and summative adverbials are also more common in academic prose than conversation, and many adverbials in these categories are prepositional phrases:

> ***In addition**, increased exploration of the rooting space or greater mycorrhizal activity could improve plant nutrient status.* (ACAD†)

> ***In conclusion**, I wish to emphasize that all the charge rearrangements discussed in this section occur very fast.* (ACAD†)

> ***In sum**, customary and outside unions between elite men and nonelite women opened the resources of the elite to the women and their children.* (ACAD)

Addition and summation are also occasionally realized by clauses:

> *Some general explanation is surely needed for such a wide distribution of such a unique facies during a comparatively short period of geological time. **What is more**, there has been no other deposit quite like it either before or since.* (ACAD)

> ***To sum up**, the purpose of the present project was initially to make an applied study of some aspects of driver behaviour which might be relevant in the evaluation of measures to prevent wildlife accidents.* (ACAD)

In both conversation and academic prose, a large proportion of the linking adverbials are used for result/inference and contrast/concession. Conversation, however, repeatedly uses a few single adverbs—especially *so* and *then* for result/inference, and *anyway* and *though* for contrast/concession (10.4.3.1). Academic prose also uses a few single adverbs commonly (e.g. *however, therefore, thus*), but other structures are also used, particularly prepositional phrases:

Result/inference:

> *Their primary audiences may differ, as may some of their aims and **in consequence**, their modes of analysis and communication.* (ACAD)

> *Both poor and lower middle class families are the victims of a partly inadvertent war by America's elites against the indispensable sanctions and sacrifices of life in families. **As a result**, more and more families are becoming bitter toward welfare.* (ACAD)

Contrast:

> *In many cases, the spin system embraces the complete molecule, e.g. is a six-spin system.* **On the other hand**, *a molecule may consist of two (or more) parts 'insulated' from each other.* (ACAD†)

> *For well-watered crops of pigeonpea dry matter production and the amount of radiation intercepted were linearly related <...>* **In contrast**, *dry matter production by monocropped and intercropped groundnuts was not linearly related to the amount of intercepted radiation.* (ACAD†)

The greater diversity in the use of linking adverbials in academic prose than conversation is further discussed in 10.4.3.

## 10.4.3 Most common linking adverbials

### 10.4.3.1 Most common linking adverbials in conversation and academic prose

**CORPUS FINDINGS [4]**

➤ Four linking adverbials are especially common in conversation. Two of these mark result/inference: *so* and *then*. The other two mark contrast/concession: *anyway* and *though*.

> ➤ AmE conversation differs from BrE in having a higher frequency of *so* and a lower frequency of *then*.

➤ Academic prose does not have any linking adverbials occurring as frequently as *so* and *then* in conversation, but several linking adverbials occur with notable frequencies: *however, thus, therefore,* and *for example*.

**DISCUSSION OF FINDINGS**

The above lists show the greater diversity for linking adverbials in academic prose than conversation. While conversation has four very common items (in the semantic categories of result/inference and contrast/concession), academic prose has several moderately common items—four in result/inference (*then, therefore, thus, hence*) and five in contrast/concession (*however, rather, yet, nevertheless, on the other hand*). In general, the heavy reliance of conversation on just a few high-frequency linking adverbials is similar to its heavy reliance on just a few subordinators for circumstance adverbial clauses (10.2.8.9).

The four common items in conversation play important roles in the development of conversational discourse. *So* is often used in narrative accounts in conversation. It moves the story along, making clear how one event follows from another. The recounting of some stories involves the repeated use of *so*, as with the following excerpts.

Describing a visit to the dentist:

> *He twisted it and a fragment of the tooth came off and hit me straight in the eye.* **So** *I've got I've got a little pinprick in my eye.* **So** *I'm just hoping I'm not gonna get an infection in it.* (CONV)

Describing a problem with small shoes:

> *She's got very wide feet <...>. She bought these new leather shoes quite a while ago, but even they and they were the widest she could buy, but they*

**Table 10.17** **Most common linking adverbials in conversation and academic prose; occurrences per million words**

each ■ represents 100      □ represents less than 50

| single adverbs | BrE CONV | ACAD |
|---|---|---|
| *so* | ■■■■■■■■■■■■■■■■ ■■■■■ | ■■ |
| *then* | ■■■■■■■■■■■■■■■■ | ■■■■ |
| *though* | ■■■■■ | □ |
| *anyway* | ■■■■■ | □ |
| *however* | □ | ■■■■■■■■■■■■■■ |
| *thus* | □ | ■■■■■■■ |
| *therefore* | □ | ■■■■■■ |
| *e.g./eg* | □ | ■■ |
| *i.e./ie* | □ | ■■ |
| *first* | □ | ■ |
| *finally* | □ | ■ |
| *furthermore* | □ | ■ |
| *hence* | □ | ■ |
| *nevertheless* | □ | ■ |
| *rather* | □ | ■ |
| *yet* | □ | ■ |
| **prepositional phrases** | | |
| *for example* | □ | ■■■■■ |
| *for instance* | □ | ■ |
| *in addition* | □ | ■ |
| *on the other hand* | □ | ■ |
| **finite clauses** | | |
| *that is* | □ | ■ |

| single adverbs | AmE CONV |
|---|---|
| *so* | ■■■■■■■■■■■■■■■■ ■■■■■■■■■■■■■■■■ |
| *then* | ■■■■■■■■ |
| *though* | ■■■■■ |
| *anyway* | ■■■■■ |

needed stretching, **so** Joanne got one of these shoe stretching things <...> even that wasn't filling it, **so** she stuck a spud down the end of it. (CONV†)

*Then* is often used when one participant sums up an inference based on another speaker's utterance:

> A: *Oh, Dad is sixty-one.*
> B: *Is he? Well **then** she must be sixty.* (CONV)

In some cases, particularly in BrE conversation, *then* is part of a question, asking for confirmation of the inference that has been made:

> A: *Well she's gonna have that knocked into an archway through to a dining room*
> B: *Oh right, lovely <...> So the third bedroom would go right across that extension **then**?* (CONV)
> A: *No all of his tail has gone, he's broken his tail*
> B: *Oh dear, did someone pull it out **then**?* (CONV)

*Then* also occurs with commands or suggestions to another participant in the conversation:

> A: *It's the spears don't work – they slide off the spears that's the problem.*
> B: *Well use your spoon **then**.* (CONV)
> A: *Have a cup of tea? – Put the kettle on **then**.* (CONV)

In almost all occurrences in conversation, *then* is used without a conditional clause, although the condition is implicit, or it has been included in the other participant's utterance. In the last two examples above, for instance, the complete ideas are:

> *If you have a problem using the spears on the fork, then use your spoon.*
> *If you want a cup of tea, then put the kettle on.*

*Though* is used in conversation as speakers mark contrasts between one clause and another:

> *So it should have everything, I still think that it's a bit expensive **though**.* (CONV)
> *They've got loads of dressy things for girls, not for boys **though**.* (CONV)

In addition, *though* can be used to make a link between speakers. The second speaker can mark his thoughts as differing from the previous speaker's, while at the same time not disagreeing with what has been previously said (cf. the discussion in 10.4.1.5):

> A: *That one's a nuisance.*
> B: *That one's alright **though**.* (CONV)
> A: *She's on morphine anyway <...>*
> B: *Poor old Wynn.*
> C: *Yeah, sounds er*
> A: *They told, Diane told me the other night **though**, she's had three years that she shouldn't have had.* (CONV)

*Anyway* also has important interactional functions in conversation. It is often used by speakers as they move to their main point, marking the preceding discourse as less important, especially when there has been some confusion expressed in the preceding discourse:

> A: *cos it wasn't in the er, in the first aid drawer.*
> B: *I don't think we've unpacked it from when we went -*
> A: *I can't remember unpacking it – it's not in the er – in the ski bag.*
> B: *<unclear> worry about*
> A: *Can always get another one **anyway**.* (CONV)

> A: *When we had the er – ITV, you know, over Christmas it said in there it was on Central but when I turned it on it wasn't at all.* **Anyway,** *we'll see.* (CONV)
>
> A: *Chris Jones over in Chester office, see if, that one would, oh mind you there isn't a chair there is there? Mind you is Jonathan away?*
>
> B: *There's this chair here. Jonathan's not here.*
>
> A: *Is Jonathan away?*
>
> C: *Yes, two day – a day and a half or something, two days?*
>
> A: *Right. So, you know, there's desks around* **anyway** *that you could use.* (CONV)

With *anyway* (as well as *so*), the functions of linking adverbials become closely connected with the functions of discourse markers; these have interactional functions but lose the lexical content of adverbials.

## 10.4.3.2 Stylistic preferences for linking adverbials

In academic prose, individual author preferences are also influential in the choices among linking adverbials. To mark contrast, *however* is uniformly preferred. However, choices among the result adverbials *therefore*, *thus*, and *hence* and the appositional adverbials *for example*, *for instance*, and *e.g.* exhibit more variability by author.

### CORPUS FINDINGS [4]

➤ *Hence, therefore,* and *thus* show marked distributions in their use across texts:
  ➤ Most occurrences of *hence* (over 70%) are in a few academic texts (c. one fifth of all academic prose texts).
  ➤ Most academic texts show a clear preference for either *thus* or *therefore*, usually using one choice at least twice as often as the other.

➤ *For example* is by far the most common appositional linking adverbial in academic prose, but the use of *for instance* and *e.g.* varies greatly by text:
  ➤ Most occurrences of *e.g.* (over 80%) are in a few academic texts (c. one fifth of all academic prose texts).
  ➤ Most occurrences of *for instance* (over 60%) are also in a few academic texts (c. one tenth of all academic prose texts).

### DISCUSSION OF FINDINGS

*Therefore, thus,* and *hence* are in most cases interchangeable. For example, in the following samples, any of the three linking adverbials could be used with no change in meaning:

> <...> *the Venezuelan government has encouraged the Piaroa to form larger communities in downriver positions closer to the administrative centre.* **Thus,** *although I use the present tense, the physical organization of communities and the economic organization that I discuss are more relevant to the pre-1970 period.* (ACAD)
>
> *Macro-functions are the governing principles of stylistic choice in both literary and non-literary language. And* **hence,** *to understand stylistic values in literature, we have to pay attention to the functional properties* <...> (ACAD†)

Individual authors' preferences often account for the choices between these adverbials. In particular, those authors using *hence* will repeatedly use this form when other linking adverbials could have been used, as in the following examples occurring within a few lines of each other in a single text:

> *The emission of electrons by a light sensitive surface, i.e., the conversion of light energy to electrical energy is virtually instantaneous.* **Hence,** *PM tubes have a very rapid response time.*
>
> *In continuous flow analyzers, all specimens flow through the same tubing.* **Hence,** *carry-over or cross-contamination can occur in continuous flow analyzers if suitable precautions are not taken.*
>
> *These positively charged ions are themselves highly hydrated.* **Hence** *when a current is applied, the positively charged ions move toward the cathode carrying water molecules with them.* (ACAD)

In many cases *for example, e.g.,* and *for instance* are also interchangeable, as in the following examples:

> *Tolerance of low water potential depends on many other factors (***e.g.*** osmotic adjustment and leaf morphology) not simply related to the photosynthetic pathway.* (ACAD)
>
> *<...> interesting pointers are emerging both in relation to reading and to writing (see,* **for instance,** *Byron et al., 1981 and Hoey, 1983).* (ACAD†)

*E.g.* is slightly more restricted in its use than the other two items, since it is rarely used in initial position, where *for example* and *for instance* regularly occur:

> *<...> assessments of root elongation in relation to penetrometer resistance give pressures very much greater than those suggested by Goss.* **For example,** *Fig 4.6 shows that penetration of cotton roots into 2.5 cm thick cores of four soils was <...>* (ACAD†)
>
> *<...> this means that there is very little standardization in either the stimuli or the recording of the responses.* **For instance,** *if the interviewer is carrying out an interview with an old inhabitant of the village <...>* (ACAD†)

While the use of *for instance* appears more a matter of author style, the use of *e.g.* is often associated with textbooks to add specific examples of technical terms:

> *A more complex medium containing serum (***e.g.*** Dmem + 10% Fcs) is required for this subsequent development.* (ACAD)
>
> *Each ward usually has clerical and domestic staff as well as nurses, and sometimes specialist nurses are called upon (***e.g.*** the stoma care nurse).* (ACAD)

Usually, examples given with *e.g.* illustrate background information rather than the main ideas; as a result, many occurrences are within parentheses.

## 10.4.4   Positions of linking adverbials

**CORPUS FINDINGS [1]**

> ➤ In both conversation and academic prose, the most common position for linking adverbials is initial.
> ➤ In conversation final position is the second most common position; medial positions are very rare.

➤ In academic prose, medial positions account for the second highest proportion of occurrences; final position is rare.

**Table 10.18 Positions of linking adverbials in conversation and academic prose**

each ■ represents 5%     ▫ represents less than 2.5%

| | % in initial position | % in medial position | % in final position |
|---|---|---|---|
| CONV | ■■■■■■■■■▫ | ▫ | ■■■■■■■ |
| ACAD | ■■■■■■■■■ | ■■■■■■■ | ■■ |

### DISCUSSION OF FINDINGS

As noted in 10.1.3.1, the use of initial position allows linking adverbials to mark explicitly the connection between units of discourse at the point when the connection is usually being made—i.e. between clauses or units larger than clauses. The adverbial identifies for the reader or hearer exactly how the subsequent discourse is to be understood in relation to the previous discourse:

> The bars may be used at about hip height, where the children can transfer their weight from the floor to the bars using various parts of the body in turn. **For example** they can start from the feet on the floor to the seat on the bar, then turn <...> (ACAD†)

> Water plants are a source of food for fish, water snails, and other aquatic animals which are, in turn, eaten by man <...>. **In addition**, aquatic vegetation provides shelter and breeding grounds for fish as well as oxygenating the water and absorbing compounds from the water. (ACAD)

Initial position can thus be considered the unmarked position for linking adverbials.

One of the most common linking adverbials in conversation—*so*—cannot occur in any position other than initial. For example, it would be impossible to change the placement of *so* in clauses like the following:

> I mean Strawberry's Hill's about—twenty five, twenty minutes, like the station, walk away. **So** it's easier to go to Witham. (CONV)

> People on the West Coast are a lot more relaxed <...>. **So**, it would be scarier to take a job on the East Coast, that's for sure. (CONV)

The adverb *so* accounts for a large proportion of the linking adverbials in initial position in conversation.

The high proportion of adverbials in final position in conversation is associated with three frequently occurring forms: *then*, *anyway*, and *though*. *Then* and *anyway* can also occur in initial and medial positions, and *though* can occur in medial positions (in initial position, *though* is a subordinator rather than a linking adverbial). However, all three of these adverbials in conversation are most commonly placed in final position:

> A: I bought some, Nick's bought two
> B: Oh she's gotta buy some **then**. I'll tell her. (CONV)

> A: And I think she's stealing stuff as well <...> stealing stuff. From the house.
> B: Does she still live at home **then**? (CONV)

A: *I missed it yesterday.*

B: *Why?*

A: *Cos I didn't watch it. I was doing something else.*

B: *No well you didn't miss much **anyway**.* (CONV)

A: *They said I would end up in Woolworths and <...> and I would have six kids with runny noses. <...>*

B: *Well you taught them didn't you?*

A: *Did I? I'm only down the road.*

B: *Haven't got any snotty kids **though**.* (CONV)

A: *She wasn't there.*

B: *No she was listening **though**.* (CONV)

None of these linking adverbials associated with final position in conversation occur frequently in academic prose. Instead, the common linking adverbs in academic prose—*therefore*, *thus*, and *however* tend to occur in medial positions (when not in initial position). In particular, these forms often occur immediately following the subject:

*Einstein, **therefore**, set to work to try to demolish the accepted version of quantum mechanics.* (ACAD)

*The support of Group Communication **thus** requires: the availability of already existing interchanged information <...>* (ACAD†)

*These characteristics, **however**, are dependent on other variables such as the conditions of pressure and temperature at entry to the compressor and the physical properties of the working fluid.* (ACAD)

These forms also occur in other medial positions, as follows.

Immediately following an operator:

*Scientific work to improve further agricultural production must **therefore** concentrate on the identification of constraints.* (ACAD)

*It is **thus** necessary to generate a model in which the final design is achieved by iteration and tested against the major constraints of shape, function and manufacturing.* (ACAD)

*Monopoly was **however** justified by reference to universalistic and objective criteria of recruitment and achievement.* (ACAD†)

Between a verb and complement clause:

*It would appear **therefore** that in this particular soil type a gravimetric moisture content of about 6.0% is required before water becomes generally available to the eggs.* (ACAD)

*It should be realized, **however**, that high-stage pressure ratios imply high Mach numbers and large gas deflections in the blading.* (ACAD†)

# Grammar in a wider perspective

# 11

# Word order and related syntactic choices

## 11.1 Overview

In this chapter we are concerned with the way clauses are adapted to fit the requirements of communication. The principal syntactic means are:

- word order (11.2)
- the passive (11.3)
- existential *there* (11.4)
- dislocation (11.5)
- clefting (11.6)

These devices are crucial for making clauses fit in with the context, thereby building a coherent text that conveys emphasis and related stylistic effects where required and eases the processing for the receiver. They may all be seen as means of re-arranging the information in a clause in different ways to achieve some such purpose (or frequently a combination of such purposes) which other structural options would not in that instance do successfully. Consequently we will, during the course of the chapter, utilize concepts such as the following, which are relevant to explaining the discourse functions of syntactic devices such as those above:

- information flow: given/topical v. new information
- focus and emphasis, including end focus and double focus
- contrast
- intensification
- weight, including end-weight and balance of weight.

Although these do not exhaust the relevant functions that need to be mentioned, they are the most important and are briefly introduced in 11.1.1–3. Others include irony, surprise, and similar stylistic effects.

Choices also vary depending upon register, reflecting differences in communicative needs and stylistic norms. In registers where a varied use of language is valued, e.g. in fiction and journalism, choices may sometimes simply be due to a desire to achieve stylistic variation.

## 11.1.1 Information flow

In any clause, some elements normally express, or refer back to, information that is familiar from the preceding discourse, i.e. **given**, while others present **new** information. There is a preferred distribution of this information in the clause, corresponding to a gradual rise in information load. This could be called the **information principle**:

> 1 *Inside the house Mr Summers found a family of cats shut in the bathroom.*
> (NEWS)

On the one hand, the clause is grounded in the situation and the preceding discourse, where *the house* and *Mr Summers* have already been mentioned; on the other, it carries the communication forward by telling us about what Mr Summers *found*. Thus, the clause characteristically opens with given or background information and ends with new information.

Normal reliance on this organization simplifies both the planning of the speaker and the decoding of the hearer. It may be seen as contributing to the

**cohesion** of text, since the given information is closest to that which it connects back to and the new information is very often taken up in the succeeding discourse. Devices such as those described in this chapter may be selected as appropriate in order to achieve this optimal information distribution. There has already been some discussion of such options in other chapters (e.g. 10.2.8.6 on initial placement of finite adverbial clauses and 9.4.7.2 on *to*-complement clauses).

However, it is clearly not true that the climax of information is necessarily at the end of the clause. For example, in many cases we find clauses opening with new information:

> 2 *A rectangular conference table and four chairs, of a type provided for senior public servants, stood between the tall windows.* (FICT)

In this example, the indefinite noun phrase in subject position expresses new information.

In the study of information flow it is necessary to view clauses in context. **Structural parallelism** between neighbouring clauses also plays a part (11.2.2.1, 11.2.3.2, 11.2.3.3).

Furthermore, placement of different types of information is not the only aspect at issue. Information may also be suppressed entirely (11.3.2), or fragmented (11.5), in order to serve the needs of discourse.

## 11.1.2 Focus, emphasis, contrast, and intensification

In any clause there is normally at least one point of **focus**, which is related in speech to the place where nuclear intonation/stress would fall, and whichever clause element includes this point thereby gains some prominence or emphasis. The general principle governing the placement of focus is that of **end focus**, i.e. that focus is normally placed on the last lexical item of the last element in the clause (i.e. *bathroom* in **1**). Thus if the information principle is being observed, it is new information in this last element that is highlighted in this way.

It is quite possible in speech to stress, and thereby place focus on, words in other positions in a clause, and indeed on more than one, where special emphases need to be conveyed. There is a variety of ways in which elements at the start of a clause may gain focus, and it is these that are most important in this chapter. For example, where a locative adverbial is placed before the subject, as in *Inside the house* in **1**, typically it (or more strictly its last lexical item *house*) will be focused. Thus the clause overall achieves **double focus**. Similarly in **2** a very long subject phrase, and a non-restrictive modifier, may each have their own focus, so this sentence could have three focal elements, those ending with *chairs*, *servants*, and *windows*. Dependent clauses often have their own focus. It is also possible to have clauses with a single focus in initial position.

In general, it seems accurate to identify two major potential points of prominence in the clause: the beginning and the end. Compare the natural prominence of the first and last elements in pronouncing a series: *one, two, three, four; English, German, Latin, and French*. Devices such as those dealt with in this chapter are commonly used to place elements in such a way that more than one is focused, in order to convey desired emphases and various stylistic effects.

The terms **intensification** and **contrast** apply to special cases of **emphasis** arising when elements are in focus. If what is focused in initial position is an adjective or adverb, the prominence it achieves is similar to that provided by adding an intensifying adverb premodifier (7.14.2.4):

> *Brilliant that was!* (CONV)

Here *brilliant* is intensified by being in initial focused position rather as if the speaker had said *That was totally brilliant!* On the other hand, a contrast is involved when the emphasized part is so treated as to highlight its difference from some parallel entity, which is usually explicitly mentioned in a neighbouring clause:

> *It's not the bikers – it's the other vehicle that's on the road.* (CONV†)

Here *the other vehicle* is not only in focus, but also contrasted with *the bikers* in a preceding clause with a parallel structure. The meaning involved is similar to that of coordinator *but* and concessive adverbial clauses (10.2.1.4).

## 11.1.3 Weight

In any clause, elements are frequently of different size and complexity, or **weight**. For instance, a noun phrase realizing the subject or object clause element may be a single pronoun or a complex structure with pre- and postmodifiers, the latter containing embedded clauses. There is a preferred distribution of elements in the clause in accordance with their weight called the **principle of end-weight**: the tendency for long and complex elements to be placed towards the end of a clause. This eases comprehension by the receiver, who does not then have the burden of retaining complex information from earlier in a clause in short-term memory while processing the remainder. Since heavy elements typically also carry a substantial new information load, the information principle and the principle of end-weight often reinforce one another.

Devices such as those dealt with in this chapter are commonly used to achieve end placement of weighty elements, and some options discussed in other chapters serve the same purpose (e.g. extraposition of complement clauses in 9.2.7 and 9.4.7).

The organization of the clause is not just a matter of end-weight, however. As in example **2** above we sometimes find very heavy elements at the beginning of the clause as well. By making appropriate use of both of the most prominent points in the clause, i.e. the beginning and the end, the speaker/writer can at the same time vary the focus and emphasis of the message and produce structures with a **balance** of weight at the ends.

## 11.2 Word order

The term **word order** is most often used to refer to the order of the elements in the clause, elements which are, of course, often each realized by phrases or clauses rather than just one word each: subject, verb, objects, predicatives, and adverbials.

English word order has often been described as **fixed**. It is certainly true that the placement of the core elements of the clause is strictly regulated. Yet there is variation, even in the core of the clause. Consider this passage from a fiction text:

> *It was beautiful grey stone mellowed by the years. There was an archway in the centre and **at the end of the west wing was a tower with battlements***

*and long narrow slits of windows which looked rather definitely out of place with the rest of the house which was clearly of a later period*. (FICT)

This is a description of a house, and the house is the topical starting-point in both sentences. The portion in bold illustrates an unusual or **marked** choice of word order: the clause opens with a circumstance adverbial, identifying a location in the house, followed by inversion of the subject (*a tower ...*) and the verb (*was*). This word order contributes to the maintenance of a consistent perspective. It is also significant that the author chose a *there*-construction to open the same sentence (11.4).

The word order of English clauses is determined by the interaction of a number of factors. First and most important, however, word order is used as a grammar signal.

## 11.2.1 Grammatical principles of word order

In order to study the discourse functions of word order and its variations, we need to understand the nature of the normal or unmarked order which may be altered to meet particular requirements of information flow or weight distribution, or to convey a special effect of emphasis. Fundamentally word order is used as a grammar signal in English in the following four ways:

A Clause elements appear in a preferred order in relation to each other: the subject before the verb, the verb before its complements, etc.—SV, SVA, $SVP_s$, $SVO_d$, $SVO_p$, $SVO_iO_d$, $SVO_dO_p$, $SVO_dP_o$, $SVO_dA$ (cf. 3.5).

B Independent interrogative clauses are signalled through subject-operator inversion (with the exception of clauses with a *wh*-word as subject, e.g. *Who did it?*; cf. 3.13.2.1. Subject-operator inversion is also obligatory after certain other elements when placed initially, such as *never* (11.2.3.2).

C All clause elements realized by *wh*-words are regularly placed in initial position. This applies to all *wh*-clauses, whether they are independent interrogative or exclamative clauses, or dependent nominal, or relative clauses. (However, if there is more than one such clause element in a clause, only one is placed in initial position, e.g. *Who did what?*)

D Phrases are normally continuous. This could be called the **principle of contact**. (There are, however, cases where the principle of contact is broken; see 2.7.1.2, 2.7.2.2, 2.7.3.2.)

These grammatical principles frequently operate in agreement with other ordering principles (11.1.1–3):

*She's had a miserable life.* (CONV †)

Here we have the regular SVO order, and the clause also conforms to the information principle and the principle of end-weight. Thus the unmarked order serves all the needs of communication. In the sections below, however, we are specially concerned with marked word order, where core clause elements are placed in an unusual position to achieve cohesion, emphasis, or some other stylistic effect. The main types are fronting of elements which are normally found in post-verbal position and inversion of subject and verb (11.2.2–3), while there is less variation in the placement of the core elements at the end of the clause (11.2.4). The much greater flexibility of adverbials is described in 10.1 and 10.1.3.

## 11.2.2 Fronting

Fronting refers to the initial placement of core elements which are normally found in post-verbal position. There are patterns which differ in stylistic effect and in register distribution. A full understanding is not possible without also considering variation in the order of the subject and the verb (11.2.3).

The main discourse functions of fronting are:

- organizing information flow to achieve cohesion
- expressing contrast
- enabling particular elements to gain emphasis

Apart from the grammatically conditioned initial placement of *wh*-words (cf. 11.2.1), fronting of core elements is virtually restricted to declarative main clauses, and is relatively rare in English.

### 11.2.2.1 Fronted objects and other nominals

When an object is placed in initial position, the subject is not moved (i.e. there is no subject-verb inversion).

The subject is generally a personal pronoun. The fronted object is often a demonstrative pronoun or a complement clause.

#### A Noun phrases as fronted objects

Demonstrative pronouns often occur as fronted objects:

1 *Sandy moves ahead. "**This** I do not understand," he said.* (FICT)

2 *I put in the day on the job, which I like, and I go home at night. **That** I also like.* (FICT)

The fronting in such examples can partly be accounted for by the information principle, since the clause opens with given information: the pronouns refer anaphorically to the preceding text. In examples with *such*, there is a similar reference to the preceding text:

***Such a blunder** I had now committed.* (FICT)

*Why didn't you tell me? **Such things** you must tell me.* (FICT)

However, givenness alone is insufficient as an explanation of fronting. Notice that an unstressed object pronoun (e.g. *it, him, them*) never occurs in initial position, and the fronted demonstrative pronouns in examples **1** and **2** would normally be stressed if spoken aloud. Fronting therefore also signals emphasis and allows focus to be placed on two elements in a clause in a way that would not be so easy with the unfronted equivalent. It would be difficult, for example, to show in writing, or indicate by stress in speech, that both *understand* and *this* were focal in the version with unmarked order *I do not understand this*—compare example **1** above.

In addition, contrast is often involved with elements in other clauses, as in the following examples, which contain other types of fronted objects:

*Bess was satisfied with her hair, but **her freckles** she regarded as a great and unmerited affliction.* (FICT)

***Some things** you miss because they're so tiny you overlook them. But **some things** you don't see because they are so huge.* (FICT)

***Some things** you forget. **Other things** you never do.* (FICT)

In the first two of these examples, the contrast is made explicit not only by the reference to both contrasted entities, but also through the conjunction *but*. In the last example there is close parallelism of the clause structures which also highlights the contrast.

### B Complement clauses as fronted objects

A second type of object fronting contains a complement clause:

> **That he has prepared his speech** I do not believe for there was not even one shorthandwriter in the hall. (FICT)

> **What it was that changed this conclusion,** I don't remember. (FICT)

> **Why he came this way** I will probably never know. (FICT)

> **How he would use that knowledge** he could not guess. (FICT†)

> Unfortunately, eating was her weakness. **Whether this was congenital, stemmed from growing up around a grocery store, or nerve induced,** she sometimes wondered. (FICT)

All these complement clauses contain pronouns referring back to the preceding text, signalling a connection with given information, although they also contain substantial new information. But the fronting goes completely against the principle of end-weight: note particularly the long *whether*-clause in the last example. Additionally, most of these examples contain a negative main clause, so that the fronting seems to bring about a kind of double focus: on the matter reported in the complement clause and on the negation in the main clause. That is, both clauses receive equal emphasis and are contrasted, which would not be the case if the dependent clause was in its usual position at the end.

There can be a similar element of contrast when the main clause is positive, and structured in a parallel way to the fronted clause:

> **What she had wanted,** she was to have. (FICT)

> **What they can do,** we can do. (FICT)

In the first example, the contrast is in the verb (*want* v. *have*); in the second example, the contrast is in the subject (*they* v. *we*). There is a similar double focus in example **2** in A above.

Note also the co-occurrence of a fronted complement clause and a co-referent demonstrative pronoun in the following example:

> **Whether she's involved in this hootenanny, that** I do not know. (FICT)

### C Fronted nominals in general

The same factors which govern the fronting of objects apply more generally to the fronting of nominals which have other syntactic roles:

> 1 Question's whether they can prove it. **That** I tend to doubt. (FICT)

> 2 "Pretty strange, huh?" **That** it is. I nod sadly. (FICT)

> 3 **Whether Nancy was there or not,** she could not be certain, looking from one to the other in her mind's eye. (FICT)

The fronted element in **1** is a direct object of an embedded infinitive clause, in **2** it is a subject predicative (see also 11.2.2.2C), and **3** illustrates a fronted nominal clause functioning as adjective complement.

Some passages have fronted nominals which are in parallel structures and contrasted, even though they serve different syntactic roles. For example, in **4** the parallel forms are a complement of the noun *idea* and a direct object of *know*; in 5, they are a noun phrase as prepositional object and a prepositional phrase.

> 4 **What he was doing here** *I have no idea.* **Why he came this way** *I will probably never know. But he* <...> (FICT†)

> 5 **Some things** *he could not vouch for (his friends had told him), but* **of others** *he had had personal experience.* (FICT)

### D  Single-focus structures

Although the prime purpose of nominal fronting generally seems to be to take advantage of both of the main focal points in the clause (the beginning and the end), we also find structures with focus exclusively on the fronted element:

> *Only one saucepan we had! – And it was stew every day if we didn't go out for dinner!* (CONV)

Here, when spoken aloud, there would typically be no stress on either word in the non-fronted part of the clause—*we had* (cf. similar structures with fronted predicatives in 11.2.2.2C). By contrast, in most of the examples of fronting above there would typically be focus on the non-fronted part of the clause, often the verb, as well.

## 11.2.2.2  Fronted predicatives

Fronting of predicatives may be accompanied by inversion of subject and verb (11.2.3.1), as in A and B below, or not, as in C.

Fronting of predicatives with inversion of subject and verb is more common than without. The subject is usually not light in weight (i.e. not a pronoun).

### A  Predicative fronting with subject-verb inversion

Subject predicatives in initial position generally contain an element of comparison with respect to the preceding context which forms a cohesive link. The predicative is given in bold and the inverted subject placed in *[]* in the examples below:

> *The hens in the next garden: their droppings are very good dressing.* **Best of all** *though are [the cattle], especially when they are fed on those oilcakes.* (FICT)

> **Far more serious** *were [the severe head injuries]; in particular a bruising of the brain.* (NEWS)

> *But time-wise the gap between them may well be much more important than the time-span between them.* <...> **Even more important**, *perhaps, is [the realisation that all through this long history, the environmental belts have hardly changed their positions or their nature].* (ACAD†)

In the last example, for instance, the comparative *even more important* implies *than this*, where *this* links anaphorically to the preceding context; furthermore, importance is an issue which has already been introduced in the preceding context and is therefore given information. A similar connecting link is found in examples with *also* and *such* (in the case of *such*, the initial element could arguably be analysed as subject):

> **Also** *popular for travelling are [quilted, overblown pseudo-ski jackets in pink or blue that look like duvets rampant].*
> (NEWS)

*Under stress, Sammler believed, the whole faltered, and parts (follicles, for instance) became conspicuous. **Such** at least was [his observation].* (FICT)

*It's rotten luck for a prolific writer of talent to be known for only one work, a masterpiece which overshadows any later writing. **Such** was [the fate of Stella Gibbons].* (NEWS)

The reference to the preceding context may also be made through a definite noun phrase expressing given information:

*A group of councillors, along with council officials from North Down, recently met with representatives from the Board to discuss the move. **Present at the meeting** were [outgoing Mayor Ellie McKay, deputy mayor Jane Copeland <...>]* (NEWS†)

*<...> are noted in a number of research reports. **Not least among these reports** are [those of Brake (1980), Rudduck and Hopkins (1984), <...>]* (ACAD†)

The organization of these examples is in agreement with the information principle, opening with a reference to what is already known (the *meeting* and the existence of *reports*) and ending with the introduction of new information (the identity of those present at the meeting or the specific reports).

## B  Special cases of predicative fronting

Two special types of predicative fronting are illustrated in the examples below. The first group contains proportion clause combinations (10.2.6.1) marked by pairs of phrases with *the*, where fronting of the correlative phrases almost always occurs:

1 *I think the better the players are treated in these respects, **the more enthusiastic** is [their response to the challenges before them].* (NEWS†)

2 *The more general the domain, **the more general, selective and tentative** are [the statements about its style].* (ACAD)

3 *The more firmly he tells them and the country that, as Prime Minister, he and not they will rule, **the more likely** [it] is that he will eventually reach Downing Street.* (NEWS)

4 *The larger the base **the easier** [it] will be to perform the action.* (ACAD†)

When the subject is long and heavy, there is subject-verb inversion (as in **1** and **2** above); clauses with a subject pronoun often have no inversion, as in the extraposed structures of **3** and **4** above (where, following the principle of end-weight, the complements of *likely* and *easier* are not fronted along with them).

The second special type of predicative fronting, with subject-operator inversion (11.2.3.2), frequently affects adjectives premodified by intensifier *so* introducing a *that*-comparative clause (7.8), which is not fronted:

***So preoccupied** was [she] at this moment, she was unaware that Diana was standing in the arched doorway to the sitting room.* (FICT)
*cf. She was so preoccupied at this moment that she was unaware ...*

***So ruthless** was [the IRA] in its all-out onslaught against the police and the Army, it didn't care who got in its way.* (NEWS)

***So different**, however, are [the theories of the schools] from the practice of ordinary business—every establishment, too having peculiarities of its own—*

*that much which he learned in the former will have to be unlearned in the latter.* (ACAD)

## C Fronting of predicatives with subject-verb order

Where the subject is an unstressed pronoun, we find the same pattern without inversion as with fronting of direct objects, and often with a single focus on the initial element:

***Right** you are!* (CONV)

*They're tiles. **Horrible** they are!* (CONV)

***Bloody amazing** it was!* (CONV)

***Pink as a fingernail** it was, and sprinkled with glittering chips.* (FICT)

The fronting has an intensifying effect, which is often strengthened by the choice of words (*horrible*, *bloody amazing*, etc.), or by emphatic stress when spoken (reflected by exclamation marks). Furthermore, the fronted material is new rather than old information.

Fronted predicatives with initial focus are related to structures with declarative tags (3.4.4C):

*You're a little devil you are!* (CONV)

*Oh God, it was magic it was!* (CONV)

*It's terrible it is!* (CONV)

If the subject pronoun and the copular verb are ellipted, as is frequently the case (3.7.5), we get a structure with a fronted predicative, e.g. *A little devil you are* or *Terrible it is*.

The following examples illustrate a special type of pattern with focus on the initial element:

*A: No, their surname isn't anything even similar to that.*

*B: No.*

*A: Because – **Jones** – their name is!* (CONV)

***Poplars** it was called was it?* (CONV)

*I don't know what her name is. **Dot** I think her name is.* (CONV)

***Peter Harronson**, he said he was called.* (FICT)

The initial predicative in these examples highlights the main purpose of the utterance—establishing the name of a person or place—and therefore contains the new information. The rest of the structure follows almost as an afterthought, contains given information, and is not in focus, even though it may contain extensive lexical material. Note that the predicative may belong to an embedded clause (as in the last two examples).

## D Fronted objects v. predicatives

The choice to front objects or predicatives differs in important ways. Object fronting is typically chosen when there is a communicative need to emphasize or contrast a clause element. Both the fronted element and the verb are strongly focused. In contrast, fronting of predicatives is basically cohesive. The clause opens with a reference to the preceding text, followed by a light-weight verb, which is in turn typically followed by a long and heavy subject introducing new information. Furthermore, in the unfronted, uninverted version of such a clause, both the same elements could be focused, or stressed in speech if required: there is no gain in capability to focus an additional element in the fronted version such as is obtained with fronted objects.

Furthermore, the structures differ with respect to weight distribution. With fronted objects, the end of the clause is light, because both the object and the subject precede the verb (OSV). With fronted predicatives there is a much more balanced distribution, as such fronting is usually accompanied by inversion of the subject and the verb (PVS). The subject, as in the examples in A, is often a substantial noun phrase rather than a single word, so the outcome is a clause with more or less equal weight at both ends. This accords better with the principles of weight distribution in English than does a clause with weight only at the front. For register differences see 11.2.2.7.

### 11.2.2.3 Fronted infinitive predicates

In a finite clause it is possible to place in front of the subject the main verb, with everything that follows it in normal clause order. The fronted element then constitutes a non-finite predicate (in the traditional sense of that term; 3.2). There are three main types of **fronted non-finite predicates**, corresponding to the three types of non-finite verb forms: predicates beginning with a bare infinitive (discussed in the present section), those beginning with an *ing*-participle, and those beginning with an *ed*-participle (discussed in 11.2.2.4).

Infinitive predicates are fronted with the remainder of the verb phrase without inversion of the subject (which is usually short). The operator, which renders the clause as a whole finite, with other auxiliary verbs, if any, remains in the normal position after the subject and takes the form of *do* in the absence of any other auxiliary verb.

One situation where infinitive predicates may be fronted is when they repeat or **echo** a previous verb (or predicate):

1 *I had said he would come down and* **come down** *he did.* (FICT)

2 *But, as he said, it had to be borne, and* **bear it** *he did.* (FICT†)

3 *Who better to help her than her father's old friend and distant relative, Eamonn Casey? And* **help her** *he did – into his bed.* (FICT)

Since an echoed element has, of course, already occurred previously, the echo is not providing new information so the fronting of it serves the information principle and is explicitly cohesive. However, the fronting also serves to emphasize the repeated element, since it would be more usual to ellipt such a repetition. For example, compare with **1**:

*I had said he would come down and he did.*

In fact the fronting brings about a double focus in the clause, such as we have seen with other types of fronting above, in this case placing emphasis on both the lexical verb and the final auxiliary verb. Thus both the meaning of the lexical verb (or the entire non-finite predicate) and the truth of the proposition can be focused separately in a way not possible in non-fronted versions. In **3** there is really a triple focus, because part of the predicate—*into his bed*—is not fronted along with the earlier part of the predicate—*help her*—but postponed for emphatic effect so that it occupies the end focus position in the clause.

Fronted infinitive predicates are also found outside echo contexts with similar double focus:

> *Hit **my bloody shoe** that will!* (CONV)
>
> ***Work*** *I must, and for money.* (FICT)

Note the similarity of effect of structures with fronted infinitive predicates and declarative tags (3.4.4C):

> *You'll get a smack you will!* (CONV)

With initial ellipsis of the type that often happens in speech, this would become identical to a structure with a fronted infinitive predicate *Get a smack you will.*

While fronting is a fairly marginal phenomenon with infinitive predicates, it is far more general with other non-finite forms (11.2.2.4).

## 11.2.2.4  Fronted *ed-* and *ing*-predicates

Fronting of *ed-* and *ing*-predicates is accompanied by inversion of the subject and the non-fronted portion of the verb phrase.

### A  Fronted *ed*-predicates

Examples of fronted *ed*-predicates, with subject in *[]*:

> 1  *Nothing on the walls, with one exception: **Tacked over the bed** was [a yellowed, deckel-edged photograph].* (FICT†)
>
> 2  ***Pasted to his pointed head, its overlapping cap of bone already springing apart under the elastic scalp**, was [a mat of thick black hair].* (FICT)
>
> 3  ***Enclosed** is [a card for our permanent signature file which we request you to sign and return to us].* (FICT)
>
> 4  *There were a couple of framed photographs on the walls, <...> **Also framed on the wall** was [a small inspirational legend in steely letters on a grey background].* (FICT†)
>
> 5  ***Also billed to appear as a special mystery guest** is [Vivacious Val].* (NEWS)

As might be expected, since participles as main verbs shade off into adjectives (7.9.1), these structures behave similarly to classic examples of predicative fronting (11.2.2.2A). Through fronting and subject-verb inversion, we get balance of weight between the fronted element and the subject. The order agrees with the information principle since there is generally a reference to the preceding context early in these structures: note the occurrence of definite noun phrases in the fronted *ed*-predicates of **1**, **2**, and **4**, and the use of *also* in examples **4** and **5**. The whole structure prepares for the introduction of new information in the final focus position, occupied by the subject.

A different effect is found with the more stylistically coloured fronting of *gone*, though the inversion ensures end-weight and end focus on the information in the subject, which often relates to an institution or customary event of a past time:

> 6  ***Gone** was [the vamp, the English schoolboy]. Instead, she appeared in clogs, a long granny dress of an old-fashioned print and sleazy texture, with a purple velvet cape.* (FICT)
>
> 7  ***Gone** were [the crises that had once produced banner headlines]. There were no mysterious murders to baffle the police <...>* (FICT†)
>
> 8  ***Gone** are [the days when the average man would be happy with soap on a rope in his Christmas stocking]. Now he is more likely to ask for a body spray or shower gel.* (NEWS)

**9** *Gone* is [*the sanctity of the family meal*]. *Irretrievably altered* is [*the role of Mom, the nurturer*]. (NEWS)

Here the initial element does not contain an explicit reference to the preceding text and the clauses end with a definite rather than an indefinite noun phrase, often with generic reference.

B **Fronted *ing*-predicates**

Fronted *ing*-predicates are used under much the same conditions as the regular type of fronted *ed*-predicate. Note the following example, which contains an instance of each:

**10** *The money was left on the parapet of a bridge carrying the track over an old dismantled railway line, the Dove Valley Trail.* ***Waiting below*** *was [Michael Sams, who had left a tray on the bridge parapet for the money].* ***Attached to it*** *was [a sash cord, linked to a rope hanging down to the track].* (NEWS)

As with fronted *ed*-predicates, fronted *ing*-predicates regularly open with elements conveying given information, so that the main clause ends with the introduction of new information:

**11** *Billy beamed lovingly at a bright lavender farmhouse that had been spattered with machine-gun bullets.* ***Standing in its cock-eyed doorway*** *was [a German colonel].* (FICT†)

**12** ***Waiting for him behind the Speaker's chair and out of sight of the other members*** *was [the leader of the opposition, Sir Alec Douglas-Home, who also shook him warmly by the hand].* (FICT)

**13** ***Coming to Belfast this month*** *are [The Breeders and Levellers], while next month sees Jethro Tull in Town.* (NEWS)

**14** ***Standing on the step*** *was [Father James Morrow, the Roman Catholic priest and pro-life activist who has threatened to bring a private prosecution for murder against the anguished couple if their son is allowed to die]. Father Morrow felt it his duty to try to appeal face to face to Tony's parents to allow their son to live.* (NEWS)

In **14** we clearly see the progression from a place known through the preceding text to the person who is introduced and serves as the starting-point in the following sentence.

If we examine the non-fronted paraphrases of clauses with initial *ing*-predicates, we sometimes find that they would actually be expected to contain a non-progressive verb form:

**15** ***Standing on the sand*** *is a beach hut built like a mini-mosque.* (FICT)

**16** *They suffered 25 per cent performance-related pay cuts, dropping to £996,000 and £740,700 respectively.* ***Also suffering*** *was Sir Derek Alun-Jones, chairman of Ferranti International Signal, the troubled electronics company.* (NEWS)

**17** *He is keen to catch up with family and friends, especially his 91-year-old mum Dolly Simmons who lives in Bebington.* ***Also living on the Wirral*** *are brother Stanley, 72, and sister Dorothy Jones, 68, and Audrey Duncan, 66.* (NEWS)

The hut in **15** was presumably not temporarily placed on the beach; hence a non-progressive form would be expected: *A beach hut … stood on the sand*. In **16** and

17, the preceding sentence contains non-progressive forms of the same verbs. In other words, we do not seem to be dealing here only with progressive aspect verbs that have been moved to initial position. We may note that the main verb in the non-progressive verb phrase could not readily be fronted in such instances as an infinitive predicate, because of the length of the subject and the quite different communicative effect that would be produced (cf. 11.2.2.3): e.g. *Stand on the sand a beach hut did.

In other cases, fronted *ing*-predicates behave much like adverbials, which may take the form of *ing*-clauses (10.2.1.9), and may occur fronted with subject-verb inversion (10.2.6, 11.2.3.1):

> **18** **Standing on the corner outside the petrol station on Park Lane** *stood a young girl smiling at him invitingly, her white leather mini skirt so short it might have been better described as a handkerchief.* (FICT)
>
> **19** *There on one side were three large bedrooms and a bathroom,* <...> *and on the far side this one bedroom.* **Adjoining it** *was the side verandah where* <...> (FICT†)
>
> **20** *There,* **standing at the bar of the Commons**, *was the victor of the first by-election since* <...> (FICT†)

Neither of the first two examples allows a straightforward paraphrase with a progressive verb phrase. *Standing* in **18** clashes with *stood*; it is in fact redundant and can be left out without loss of meaning, leaving a prepositional phrase as a place adverbial. *Adjoining* in **19** could easily be replaced by the complex preposition *next to*. Finally, note how the *ing*-predicate in **20** is used as a non-restrictive amplification of the preceding place adverbial *there*.

Initial *ing*-predicates—like *ing*-constructions in general—are chameleon-like structures. But whatever the correct structural analysis may be, it is quite clear what work these initially placed *ing*-constructions do: they connect with given information and provide the frame or setting for the situation described in the clause, especially the new information given in the grammatical subject.

## 11.2.2.5 Fronting in dependent clauses

Apart from syntactically conditioned fronting, which is completely regular in *wh*-clauses (cf. 11.2.1), fronting in dependent clauses is restricted to special structures with the subordinators *as* and *though*. It can, however, be related to types of fronting which occur more generally. Consider the following (with the dependent clause shown in *[]*):

> **1** *[Try as she might to make it otherwise], the sycamores beat out the children every time and she could not forgive her memory for that.* (FICT)
>
> **2** *Modern penitentials won't be of much use to future historians of the twentieth century, but eleventh-century penitentials might be, [rich as they are in the prejudices of our enlightened age—particularly the inferior status of women].* (NEWS)
>
> **3** *[Astounded though she was], Francesca was thrilled and excited.* (FICT)
>
> **4** <...> *the proponents of more traditional solutions to the problem of universals, [unsuccessful though they have been in their own proposals], have made trouble for the solution in terms of individual properties.* (ACAD†)

We may note that the fronting of the main verb in **1** and of the predicative adjectives in **2–4** occurs without subject-verb inversion, in a similar way to independent clause occurrences (11.2.2.3 and 11.2.2.2C). Furthermore, complements are often not fronted along with their controlling words (e.g. the *to*-infinitive complement of *try* in **1** and the *in*-prepositional complements in **2** and **4**), thus avoiding an unsatisfactorily front-weighted clause.

The main purpose of placing the fronted forms where they are in these structures, in a conspicuous position preceding the subordinators, is clearly to emphasize them. In **1**, **2**, and **4** the special effect is lost if the fronted element is placed in the unmarked position (using subordinator *though* in place of *as*, which only occurs with fronting) because it is then no longer focussed by being in initial or final position. End focus would naturally fall on a later word in the complement, such as *otherwise* in **1**: *Though she might try to make it otherwise, ....*

It is no coincidence also that these clauses are generally concessive, and the emphasis may involve contrast, as in **3**, between the adjective predicated of *Francesca* in the dependent clause and those predicated of her in the main clause.

## 11.2.2.6 Fronting in exclamations

Exclamative clauses introduced by *wh*-words have syntactically conditioned fronting (3.13.3) and thus do not belong in the survey here. However, there are declarative main clauses which have exclamatory force and mirror the structure of exclamative clauses, though there is no *wh*-word. Note the fronted predicatives and objects in the following examples, where *such* is used in much the same way as *what*:

> **Such a rich chapter** *it had been, when one came to look back on it all!*
> (FICT)

> **Such a gift** *he had for gesture. He looked like a king in exile.* (FICT)

> *And she thought:* **Such a sure hand** *my son has with people.* (FICT)

Note that this use of *such* is quite different from the cohesive uses illustrated earlier (11.2.2.1A, 11.2.2.2A). Compare also:

1 **Charming** *you are!* (FICT)
2 **How brave** *you are!* (FICT)
3 **Some diet** *that is!* (CONV)
4 *And* **what a great night** *that was!* (FICT)

Here the exclamation marks reflect the similarity in speech act function. Fronting in exclamations may express irony and sarcasm, as in **1** and **3** above. The exclamative force is particularly strong with the single-focus types of fronted objects (11.2.2.1D) and predicatives (11.2.2.2C).

## 11.2.2.7 Fronting: distribution

**CORPUS FINDINGS** [2]

➤ Fronting of core elements is relatively rare (excluding syntactically conditioned fronting in *wh*-clauses):
  ➤ c. 50–100 occurrences per million words in conversation and news;
  ➤ c. 200–300 occurrences per million words in academic prose and fiction.
➤ The overall frequency is less than half of that found for inversion.

➤ Fronted predicatives are most common, followed by fronted objects and other nominals.

  ➤ In academic prose, most examples represent predicative fronting with subject-verb inversion, used for cohesive purposes. The same is true of news.

  ➤ In fiction, all types of fronting are found, although object fronting is the most common type.

  ➤ Predicative fronting is less frequent than in academic prose.

  ➤ In conversation, fronting is generally rare, but most examples represent object fronting.

## DISCUSSION OF FINDINGS

Though the frequencies are generally low, there appears to be a tendency for fronting to be used for different purposes in the registers. These differences correspond to differences in the communicative goals of expository prose on the one hand, as against conversation and fictional prose on the other.

Academic prose style favours a dispassionate form of expression, so does not require devices that convey special emphases. However, it does put a premium on explicitness of cohesion, which may be enhanced by predicative fronting:

> In the Peruvian case study that follows, the degree to which marketwomen are independent petty commodity traders or are undergoing proletarianization is problematic. **Also problematic** is [the degree to which gender may be playing a part in the proletarianization process]. (ACAD)

> The close resemblance of the Newark Series along the eastern seaboard of the U.S.A. to the Triassic deposits of western has already received some comment. **Equally striking** is [the similarity of the structures in which these sediments are preserved]. (ACAD)

In both these examples the fronting serves to juxtapose items which through semantic repetition cohesively tie the sentences together (*problematic—problematic*, and *received some comment—striking*); see also the discussion and examples in 11.2.2.2A.

Conversation and fiction, by contrast, strive for greater impact and stylistic effect, so we find types of fronting which chiefly convey special emphasis and contrast—especially fronting of objects (11.2.2.1) but also some fronting of predicatives (11.2.2.2C):

> "No wet beds. **That** I won't stand." (FICT)

> **Whether it would fire after being in the river,** I can't say. (FICT)

> A: What act– what actually does the price include? – Does it does it?
> B: **That** I couldn't tell you. (CONV)

> A: Dad!
> B: Have stew!
> A: **Stew** we had last night. (CONV)

> **Whether they've got tables and stuff like that** I'm not sure. (CONV)

However, these structures do occur in the other registers as well:

> **Whether Moore was actually offered money or not** I have no idea. (NEWS)

> It concedes that some actual judicial decisions and practices are very different from those a conventionalist would make or approve: **these** it is prepared to count as mistakes. (ACAD)

In general, though fronting of core elements is relatively rare in present-day English, it is an important option, because of the special effects it may have—which may be all the more conspicuous because of the comparative rarity.

## 11.2.3   Inversion of subject and verb or operator

**Inversion** (3.6.1.1) is closely connected with fronting (11.2.2). Centuries ago, English was predominantly a verb-second language: the verb was placed in second position in the clause, whether it was preceded by the subject or by some other clause element. The latter case caused inversion of subject and verb. In present-day English, the subject generally stays before the verb—with the exception of interrogative clauses—whether there is some other pre-verbal element or not.

Nevertheless, given the right circumstances, inversion does occur in present-day English outside interrogative clauses. There are two main types:

- **Subject-verb inversion** or **full inversion** (11.2.3.1), where the subject is preceded by the entire verb phrase (or whichever portion of it remains if the main verb part of it is fronted, as in 11.2.2.4).
- **Subject-operator inversion** or **partial inversion** (11.2.3.2), where the subject is preceded by the operator rather than by the main verb or a full verb phrase. As in independent interrogative clauses, the auxiliary *do* is inserted, if there is no other verb that can serve as operator. The remainder of the verb phrase follows the subject, if included.

Both types are triggered by some element other than the subject being placed in clause-initial position. Yet the behaviour of the two types is quite different, as we shall see below. Furthermore, there is a great deal of variety in inversion patterns, some of which are obsolescent, reflecting differences both in form and communicative effect.

In general, inversion serves several discourse functions:

- cohesion and contextual fit (especially: subject-verb inversion)
- placement of focus (end focus and double focus)
- intensification (especially: subject-operator inversion).

Through skilful use of fronting combined with inversion, the speaker/writer can exploit the potential of the two most prominent positions in the clause: the opening and the end. The resulting structures adapt the clause to the context or produce some special stylistic effect (or both at the same time).

### 11.2.3.1   Subject-verb inversion

#### A   Use of subject-verb inversion

Subject-verb inversion is found most typically under the following circumstances:

- The clause opens with an adverbial, especially one of place, providing the background or setting for a situation. This adverbial often links the clause explicitly to the preceding text through a definite noun phrase. The opening element may also be a subject predicative linked to the preceding text.
- The verb is intransitive or copular and has less weight than the subject. It often expresses existence or emergence on the scene.

- The clause ends with a long and heavy subject introducing new information, often as an indefinite noun phrase, which may be further developed in the following text.

In other words, these structures conform to the requirements of the information principle and the end-weight principle (11.1.1 and 11.1.3).

The contextual fit of clauses with subject-verb inversion is such that a simple reordering of subject and verb is generally excluded for a clause in its context:

> *I do her worm for her, when her teacher isn't looking. Then I draw a diagram of the worm, cut open, beautifully labelled. After that* **comes the frog**. *The frog kicks and is more difficult than the worm, it looks a little too much like a person swimming.* (FICT)

Here it is hardly possible to reorder the subject and the verb (?*After that the frog comes*), in part because light-weight verbs are not generally used in final position. The only possible alternative order would be: *The frog comes after that*. This is less effective than the word order found in the text, which starts with a reference to the preceding text (*after that*) and moves on to the new referent (*the frog*), which is in its turn the starting-point of the following sentence. The order in the text also underlines the temporal sequencing of the events narrated.

## B   Opening place adverbial

Place descriptions with overt or implied anaphoric elements are common with subject-verb inversion (subject-verb inversion is in bold, while the initially placed triggering elements are given in *[]*):

> *[On one long wall]* **hung a row of Van Goghs**. (FICT†)
>
> *A massive mirror, framed in intricately-chased silver, hung above a carved pine chest, and [in its glassy depths]* **trembled reflections of the entire area**. *[Next to it]* **stood a silver urn bursting with branches of red berries**. (FICT)
>
> *[On the horizon]* **is a field of view overgrown with nettles**. (NEWS†)
>
> *They found an extension to the drawing room with thigh-high cannabis plants growing in polythene bags full of compost. [Nearby]* **was a 400-square-yard warehouse with more plants flourishing in conditions controlled by artificial lighting and automatic watering systems**. (NEWS)

In the following passage we find several instances of such **locative inversion**:

> *The seating blunder saw the Queen sitting with French president François Mitterand on her right. [Then]* **came the Princess of Wales** *on his right. The Duke of Edinburgh was opposite the Queen, sitting next to EEC chief Jacques Delors—and with his back to Charles. [Opposite him on one of the three tables set out for the lavish dinner]* **was Prime Minister John Major**. *[On the third table]* **sat Princess Anne** *in between the prime minister of Greece, Constantine Mitsotakis, and Irish prime minister, Albert Reynolds.* (NEWS)
>
> <note that *then* in the second sentence indicates place rather than time>

The distribution of information often reflects how a scene is observed (as in the above example). Note the following description of the streets moving by:

> *This was Amsterdam Avenue, with the cross streets moving slowly by. [There]* **goes Eighty-seventh**. *[Here]* **comes Eighty-eighth**. (FICT)

*Here* and *there* define a place as proximate v. distant from the point of view of the speaker and are often found in inversion structures:

*[Here]'s the bag.* (CONV)

*[Here] comes the first question.* (FICT)

*[There]'s the dog. Call the dog.* (CONV)

Locative *there* (as in the last example) should be distinguished from existential *there*, though a comparison between the two constructions is instructive (11.4.8).

A special type of place element triggering subject-verb inversion is an adverbial particle indicating direction:

*Worry, worry, Alice sat worrying. [In] came Jasper, smiling jaunty, stepping like a dancer.* (FICT†)

*Billy opened his eyes, and [out] came a deep, resonant tone.* (FICT)

*[Back] came the pompous reply:* <...> (NEWS†)

*When Sam tugged the rope, [down] came the money and he rode off with it in his scooter, leaving £2,500 in his haste to get away.* (NEWS)

*And this being a boiling Bank Holiday Monday the British are burning: [out] comes the sun, [off] come the clothes.* (NEWS)

This type of structure is unusual in that the opening element does not indicate a background or setting, but is strongly focused. It is used in dramatic narration, to emphasize a sudden change or event.

Descriptions with place adverbials are particularly common with subject-verb inversion in fiction and news texts, especially the type realized by a full prepositional phrase. The inversion type with *here* and *there* is also common in conversation. The type with a fronted adverbial particle is particularly frequent in fiction; see also 11.4.8.

## C Opening time adverbial

The opening adverbial may also be one of time, frequently *then* introducing a new event:

*For a moment nothing happened. [Then] came voices all shouting together.* (FICT)

*[Then] came the turning point of the match.* (NEWS)

*[Again] came the sounds of cheerfulness and better heart.* (FICT)

*[First] came the scouts, clever, graceful, quiet.* (FICT)

*[Next] came the Chaplain.* (FICT)

*[Now] comes the business of sorting out the returned forms.* (NEWS)

Most of these adverbials imply reference back to preceding, given, information.

## D Other types of opening adverbials

In academic prose, where there is less scope for place description and narration, we find examples such as the following:

*Formaldehyde may be generated in various ways. [Among these] is heating a solution of formaldehyde in a* <...> (ACAD†)

*[Among the more recent myological studies] are those by* <...> (ACAD†)

*[With incorporation, and the increased size of the normal establishment], came changes which revolutionized office administration.* (ACAD)

*[Within the general waste type shown in these figures] exists a wide variation.* (ACAD)

These abstract locative examples agree broadly with the other adverbial patterns described above: they also generally contain anaphoric links with the preceding text. However, these fronted locatives may be quite long, so the overall weight distribution of the clause is one of balance rather than end-weight.

**E  Fronted predicatives and fronted *ed-* and *ing-*predicates**

Clauses with subject-verb inversion may open with a fronted predicative (11.2.2.2) or with a fronted *ed-* or *ing-*predicate (11.2.2.4). The information flow in these construction types is much the same as in clauses with opening adverbials.

**F  Complex verb phrases**

The verb phrase preceding the subject may be complex, provided that it is lighter than the following subject; for example (with verb phrase in bold and subject in *[]*):

*Best of all* **would be** *[to get a job in Wellingham].* (FICT†)

*Among the sports* **will be** *[athletics, badminton, basketball, <...>].* (NEWS†)

*Also noted* **will have been** *[the 800 metres run by under-15 Claire Duncan at Derby and the under-17 100 metres hurdling of Jon Haslam (Liverpool) which also gained Northern silver].* (NEWS†)

*Here* **is provided** *[a patchwork of attractive breeding sites, which <...>].* (ACAD†)

Note that the verb phrase is not split with subject-verb inversion, as is the rule with subject-operator inversion (11.2.3.2).

**G  Variation in type of subject**

Unlike subject-operator inversion, which is syntactically obligatory with particular elements in initial position (11.2.3.2), subject-verb inversion varies with the complexity and information value of the subject and the verb. Compare:

1 *Then* **the night came up** *in dark blue vapour from the snow.* (FICT)
2 *Then* **the words came out** *in a rush.* (NEWS)

v. 3 *Then* **came the call from Sergio Leone**. (FICT)
4 *Then* **came the turning point of the match**. (NEWS)

The regular subject-verb order is the natural choice in **1** and **2**, where the subject is a simple definite noun phrase and the verb is accompanied by elements complementing the verbal meaning. In contrast, inversion is just as natural in **3** and **4**, where there is a simple intransitive verb followed by a longer and more informative subject.

Subject-verb inversion is excluded with a light-weight pronoun as subject, although ordinary subject-verb order is often possible:

*On one long wall* **hung a row of Van Goghs**. (FICT†)
cf. *On one long wall hung it/they.
But: ?*On one long wall it/they hung.*

*Then* **came the turning point of the match**. (NEWS)
cf. *Then came it.
But: *Then it came.*

Although inversion is most typically found with long and/or indefinite noun phrases in subject position, we also find examples such as:

*Watch out! [Here]* **comes Amanda***!* (CONV)

*And [then]* **came that clap of thunder***.* (FICT)

*[Here]* **comes the rub***.* (NEWS)

*Sitting together on a settee as they faced hostile questioning, Bill Clinton seemed at first to be struggling as he was tackled over the Flowers affair. Then [in]* **leapt Hillary***.* (NEWS)

Such inversions frequently seem to convey an element of suspense and surprise.

## 11.2.3.2  Subject-operator inversion

### A  Use of subject-operator inversion

Subject-operator inversion, or partial inversion, differs from subject-verb inversion (11.2.3.1) in a number of ways:

- Inversion may occur with both transitive and intransitive verbs. Especially with the former, there is often a weighty predicate occupying end position in the clause.
- The opening elements triggering subject-operator inversion are much more restricted.
- Inversion is obligatory where the triggering elements are found and occurs both with light-weight unstressed subject pronouns and with noun-headed subjects.

In addition, the effect of the two types of inversion is quite different, as illustrated below.

### B  Negative or restrictive opening elements

Subject-operator inversion is found after opening negative or restrictive coordinators or adverbials, such as: *neither, nor, never, nowhere, on no condition, not only, hardly, no sooner, rarely, scarcely, seldom, little, less, only.* In the following examples, inversion is marked in bold and triggering elements are marked by *[]*:

1  *A: I haven't got a copy of club rules.*
   *B: [Nor]* **have I***.* (CONV)
2  *And she said, you know, [on no account]* **must he** *strain.* (CONV)
3  *[Nor]* **was there** *the faintest scent of ink or the cherry gum and oak bark from which it was made. Nothing.* (FICT)
4  *[Not before in our history]* **have so many strong influences** *united to produce so large a disaster.* (NEWS)
5  *Judged simply in statistical terms these were stunning. [Rarely, if ever],* **do we** *find such a consensus across area and social class.* (NEWS)
6  *[Rarely]* **are all the constraints on shape, function and manufacturing** *clearly defined at the commencement of the activity. [Even less]* **are they** *understood and their effect, one on another, recognized by the designer.* (ACAD)

Due to the prominent placement, there is an intensification of the force of the negative/restrictive element. Note how the effect is underlined even further by other devices in most of these examples: the expression *the faintest* and the following sentence fragment *Nothing* in **3**; the use twice of intensifier *so* in **4**; the addition of *if ever* in **5**; and the parallel structures in the two sentences in **6**.

Subject-operator inversion after most initial negative/restrictive elements has a rhetorical effect and is virtually restricted to writing. However, subject-operator inversion after initial *nor* or *neither* is found in conversation as well as in the written registers. Note also the colloquial expression *no way*:

> Oh [*no way*] **do I** want to take that. (CONV)
>
> And if the case went to trial, there wasn't a damn thing Katheryn could do to stop them. And [*no way*] **could she** get Sarah to understand that. (FICT)

*No way* expresses strong negation and is obligatorily placed in initial position.

### C Order and negative scope

Inversion is found only if the negative scope affects the whole of the clause. Thus there is no inversion in:

1. **No doubt** *he will issue his instructions.* (FICT)
2. **Not surprisingly**, *most studies have concerned themselves with ill effect, notably that of emotional stress.* (ACAD)
3. **Not many years ago**, *it seemed that almost all readability research, and almost all research in linguistics confined itself to the analysis of units no larger than a sentence.* (ACAD)

In **1** and **2** the negation is part of the stance adverbial only, while in **3** it is part of the modification of the time adverbial. The main statements are thus expressed in positive terms (e.g. *he will issue* ...).

Occasionally, we find differences in ordering—and in some cases meaning—with the same or similar forms. Compare:

Forms with normal word order:

4. [*In no time at all*] **the hotels would** *be jammed to the doors.* (FICT)
5. *I could have gone there.* [*Only*] **I didn't**. *I didn't care.* (FICT)
6. *In the winter, sometimes,* [*rarely*], **you can** *hear the thunder of a siren but it is another country.* (FICT)

Forms triggering inversion:

7. [*At no time*] **did he** *indicate he couldn't cope.* (NEWS)
8. [*Only then*] **did he** *feel better.* (FICT)
9. [*Rarely*] **can two sets of forwards** *have covered so much ground.* (NEWS†)

*In no time* in **4** clearly does not affect the positive nature of the statement: we still conclude that the hotels would be jammed to the doors, while in **7** the implication is he did not ever indicate that he couldn't cope. Example **5** illustrates the use of initial *only* without inversion in the sense of 'but' or 'except', rather than in its customary restrictive adverb use (7.14.2.5) as in **8**. Finally, **6** illustrates the use of *rarely* meaning 'occasionally, sometimes' rather than 'not very often' (note the following comma, marking a looser connection with the clause). In most examples, however, initial *rarely* does trigger inversion.

### D Degree expressions with *so* and *such*

There is subject-operator inversion after opening elements consisting of the degree adverb *so* followed by an adjective or adverb (see also the examples of fronted *so*-elements in 11.2.2.2B):

> He refused to stir. [*So greatly*] **had he** suffered, and [*so far gone*] **was he**, that the blows did not hurt much. (FICT)
>
> [*So badly*] **was he** affected that he had to be taught to speak again. (NEWS)

The pattern has a degree expression in initial position, usually accompanied by a following comparative complement clause (7.8, 7.13.6). The effect of the pattern is a further intensification of the degree expression.

Compare similar examples with subject-verb inversion triggered by clause-initial *such*:

> [Such] **is the confusion** aboard this vessel I can find no one who has the authority to countermand this singularly foolish order. (FICT)

> [Such] **is the gravity of the situation** that it has already sparked an international incident. (NEWS)

## 11.2.3.3  Inversion after the linking forms *so*, *nor*, and *neither*

Inversion can occur after initial *so* when it is used as a pro-form pointing back to the predicate of a preceding clause (2.4.2.2):

> 1  A: *We used to watch that on T.V.*
>    B: *Yes, [so]* **did I**. (CONV)

> 2  A: *French oral's a doddle.*
>    B: *Is it?*
>    A: *Yeah, [so]* **is German reading**. (CONV)

> 3  *Gail's in, and [so]* **is Lisa**. (CONV)

> 4  *She despised him; [so]* **did Prue Ramsay**; *[so]* **did they all**. (FICT†)

> 5  *As infections increased in women, [so]* **did infections** *in their babies.*
>    (NEWS)

This inversion pattern usually includes no part of the verb phrase other than the inverted operator. The pattern expresses semantic parallelism and could be paraphrased with subject-verb order plus additive *too*, e.g. *I did too* in **1**.

This use of *so* is clearly different from initial *so* in degree expressions (11.2.3.2D). The initial *so* in these examples stands for given information, and so has a cohesive effect; it is also in initial position, and so emphasizes the parallelism between the clauses. The subject is the main new communicative point of the clause and is placed in the end focus position after the verb. The result is a structure with double focus.

Clauses with the initial pro-form *so* are closely related to structures with initial *nor* and *neither*, which express parallelism with respect to a preceding negative clause (cf. 11.2.3.2B):

> 6  *She hadn't known much about life, [nor]* **had he**. (FICT)

> 7  *The generalization's truth, if it is true, is not affected by how we count things in question, and [neither]* **is its falsehood** *if it is false.* (ACAD)

The meaning could be paraphrased with subject-verb order plus *either*, e.g. *… and he hadn't either* in **6**. Again the inversion pattern produces both a cohesive link and a double focus which emphasizes the parallelism.

Unlike *no* and *neither*, *so* is sometimes found with subject-verb order:

> 8  *Aye, he's a bastard, [so]* **he is**. (CONV)

> 9  *Have we a file? Yes [so]* **we have**. (FICT†)

> 10  *"I saw it distinctly, sir! You threw salt over your shoulder!" "[So]* **I did**,
>     *sir, I confess it."* (FICT)

In these instances the verb is in end focus rather than the subject. The effect is not of adding a proposition parallel to that which has gone before but of emphatically affirming the same proposition implied in the preceding clause; note the combination with *aye* and *yes* in **8** and **9**.

### 11.2.3.4  Special cases of inversion in independent clauses

Some uses of inversion are highly restricted and usually confined to more or less fixed collocations. Types A and B described below are remnants of earlier uses and carry archaic literary overtones.

#### A  Formulaic clauses with subjunctive verb forms

The combination of the inflectionless subjunctive and inversion gives the highlighted expressions below an archaic and solemn ring:

> ***Be it proclaimed*** *in all the schools Plato was right!* (FICT)

> *If you want to throw your life away,* ***so be it****, it is your life, not mine.* (FICT)

> *"I, Charles Seymour, do swear that I will be faithful, and bear true allegiance to Her Majesty Queen Elizabeth, her heirs and successors according to law,* ***so help me God****."* (FICT)

> ***Long Live King Edmund****!* (FICT)

> ***Suffice it to say*** *that the DTI was the supervising authority for such fringe banks.* (NEWS)

#### B  Clauses opening with the auxiliary *may*

The auxiliary *may* is used in a similar manner to express a strong wish. This represents a more productive pattern:

> ***May it be pointed out*** *that the teacher should always try to extend the girls helping them to achieve more and more.* (FICT†)

> ***May God forgive you your blasphemy****, Pilot. Yes.* ***May he forgive you*** *and open your eyes.* (FICT†)

> *The XJS may be an ageing leviathan but it is still a unique car.* ***Long may it be so****!* (NEWS)

> ***Long May She Reign****!* (NEWS)

#### C  Imperative clauses

Imperative clauses may contain an expressed subject following *don't* (3.13.4.1).

### 11.2.3.5  Inversion in dependent clauses

Although inversion is basically a main clause phenomenon, we do find it in dependent clauses (see also 11.2.3.6A). In most cases, this kind of inversion is closely related to the types discussed above.

With the exception of F below, which is a colloquial conversational choice, these patterns are restricted to formal writing.

#### A  Subject-verb inversion with opening adverbials

The formal conditions and the effect of the inversions illustrated below clearly parallel subject-verb inversion in main clauses following place adverbials and adverbial particles (11.2.3.1):

> *She pointed to an impressive but imitation oak desk [at which]* ***sat a prissy, tiny, bespectacled individual****.* (FICT†)

> *In the centre of the green was a pond, beside it was a wooden seat [on which]* **sat two men** *talking.* (FICT)
>
> *The bee <...> was working hopefully, curled in the very kernel of the bloom, when [in]* **came the kindly officer's little finger.** (FICT†)
>
> *He and the club's solicitor and director, Maurice Watkins, sat either side of Edwards while [on the flanks]* **were placed two more lawyers.** (NEWS†)

### B Subject-operator inversion with opening negatives/restrictives

Subject-operator inversion can penetrate into dependent clauses under the same circumstances and with the same effect as in main clauses (11.2.3.2):

> *Mr Teague said that [at no time]* **was Paul Jones** *ever hit with a cane or whip, [at no time]* **was he** *tied upside down and hit.* (FICT†)
>
> *Introspection suggests that [only rarely]* **do we** *consciously ponder the pronunciations of words.* (ACAD)

### C Clauses introduced by *as* and *than*

Inversion involving an operator on its own is found in formal writing in comparative clauses introduced by *as* and *than*, provided that the subject is heavier than the verb. In addition, inversion also occurs in other *as*-clauses:

Comparative clauses:

> 1 *Independent agencies are in a better position to offer personal service* **than are those tied to big chains**, *believes managing director Daphne Armstrong.* (NEWS)
>
> 2 *The liquid products are fractionally distilled, and refined in the same way* **as are the petroleum fractions**. (ACAD)

Other *as*-clauses:

> 3 *They chatted about Hollywood, and Charlotte was fascinated,* **as were the other guests**. (FICT)
>
> 4 *The contraceptive cap can also spark the syndrome,* **as can a wound infection**. (NEWS)
>
> 5 *It would be agreeable to pass it by,* **as have many inquiries into determinism pertaining to decisions and actions**. (ACAD)
>
> 6 *At least it is only two kisses and not three,* **as is the Russian custom**. (NEWS†)

Clauses of this latter kind (adverbials of manner, 10.2.8.1) are often reminiscent of inversion with the pro-form *so*, which may account for the inversion. We might closely paraphrase 3 with: *... (as) Charlotte was fascinated, so were the other guests* (cf. 11.2.3.3, example 5). In 6 the pattern is similar to a non-restrictive relative clause introduced by *which*: *..., which is the Russian custom*.

### D Hypothetical conditional clauses

In formal writing we find conditional clauses marked by inversion rather than by a subordinator. This is restricted to clauses introduced by *had*, *should*, and subjunctive *were*:

> *"I would be more hopeful," Sandy said, "***were it not for the problem of your testimony.***"* (FICT)
>
> **Were it running more slowly**, *all geologic activity would have proceeded at a slower pace.* (ACAD)

> *He would have accepted only the usual expenses **had he undertaken this summer's tour marking the South African Rugby Board's centenary**.* (NEWS†)
>
> ***Should either of these situations occur**, wrong control actions may be taken and a potential accident sequence initiated.* (ACAD)

In all of these cases, it is possible to use a paraphrase with *if*, which is the more common option. For example, we could re-word the first sentence above as follows (with a subjunctive or an indicative verb form): *... if it were/was not for the problem of your testimony*. See also 10.2.8.12.

### E Alternative and universal conditional clauses with subjunctive verbs

In the examples below, the dependent clauses can be paraphrased by *whether it/he/they be/is/are* introducing a clause providing two alternative possible conditions:

> *When the going gets tough, it's these people who react best – **be it at a natural disaster, accident or sudden emergency**.* (NEWS)
>
> *His passion is really for the others he writes about, **be they as famous as Brecht or as obscure as his landlady**.* (NEWS†)
>
> *They have brought out a range of confectionery for the man in your life, **be it father or partner**.* (NEWS)

Examples such as the following are paraphrasable with an uninverted *whatever* clause, expressing a universal condition:

> *La Bruyère strikes one as a naturally timid man who has somewhat desperately made up his mind to utter his whole self, **come what may**.* (ACAD)

These patterns of inversion are remnants of constructions which at one time were more widespread. They are highly restricted and carry a literary overtone.

### F Dependent interrogative clauses with inversion

Dependent interrogative clauses are normally introduced by a *wh*-word, and regularly have ordinary subject-verb order (3.11.1). A more informal alternative, without a connecting link, is found in colloquial English:

> *One lady thought we were turfing – and she said **could we turf the lawn for her**.* (CONV)
>
> *And she said **would we like these shirts**.* (CONV)
>
> *And then he said try it again and she rang and she asked, she said **had the cheques come**.* (CONV)
>
> *The young man who had seen Mac in Westmoreland Street asked **was it true that Mac had won a bet over a billiard match**.* (FICT)
>
> *She needed a backing guitarist and asked Kieran, who she had met once or twice on the road, **would he help out**.* (NEWS)

This pattern represents a compromise between direct and indirect speech. It preserves the subject-operator inversion of the independent interrogative clause, but pronouns have been adjusted and verb forms backshifted to the reporting situation. For example, compare in the last example the direct speech form: *Will you help out?* Note that the examples with *said* require a change of reporting verb if they are rephrased as ordinary indirect questions:

Direct speech:

>   *She said, "Can/Could you turf the lawn for me?"*

Semi-direct:

>   *She said could we turf the lawn for her.*

Indirect speech:

>   *She asked whether we could turf the lawn for her.*

The compromise form expresses a more direct report than ordinary dependent interrogative clauses.

## 11.2.3.6 Inversion in reporting clauses

### A Types of reporting clauses

Reporting clauses are appended to direct reports of a person's speech or thought and are on the borderline between independent and dependent clauses (3.11.5). Such clauses contain some kind of reporting verb, either a straightforward verb of speaking/thinking (e.g. *say, think*) or a verb identifying the manner of speaking (e.g. *mutter, shriek*), the type of speech act (e.g. *offer, promise*), the phase of speaking (an aspectual verb such as *begin, continue*), etc. Such clauses frequently have inversion:

>   *"That's the whole trouble,"* **said Gwen, laughing slightly.** (FICT)
>
>   *"It's the fuel,"* **said the chauffeur,** *"dirt in the pipe."* (FICT)
>
>   *"It's a good thing you are here at last <...>"* **began Mabel.** (FICT†)
>
>   *"I'd be delighted to pair with you,"* **continued Charles.** (FICT)
>
>   *Fifties and post-impressionist,* **thought Alexander, connecting.** (FICT)
>
>   *Sketching,* **says Uderzo,** *is a fast process.* (NEWS)
>
>   *Councils,* **argues Mr Cawley,** *are being hit by an unenviable double whammy.* (NEWS†)
>
>   *Escapes halved,* **declares Group 4.** (NEWS)
>
>   *A positive evil,* **fumed Derek Jarman.** (NEWS)

As shown by the examples, quotation marks identifying the reported text are often missing (especially in news).

In news, reporting clauses can also be used for attributions of written text:

>   *Where farming used to be the only viable source of income, hundreds of people have found regular work,* **reveals Plain Tales from Northern Ireland.** (NEWS†)
>
>   *The wave of strikes that has gripped France for a month showed some signs of abating yesterday as prison officers agreed to go back to work,* **writes Sarah Lambert.** (NEWS)

Inversion is found in medial or final reporting clauses containing a simple verb and a noun-headed subject. But subject-verb order occurs under the same conditions:

>   *"Are we to gather that Dreadnought is asking us all to do something dishonest?"* **Richard asked.** (FICT)
>
>   *"You can ask one or two of them to stay behind for a drink, if you like,"* **Laura said,** *"if there's anyone possible."* (FICT)

> *Increasing work loads, job insecurity and changes at work are taking their toll on nurses' health, **a report shows today**.* (NEWS)

Reporting clauses may be characterized not only in terms of their inversion (or not) and position relative to the reported clause (initial, medial, or final), but also in terms of their complexity (left expansion, right expansion, no expansion):

Final position; right expansion:

> *"Do you in point of fact want us to say that Dreadnought doesn't leak?" **asked Richard patiently**.* (FICT)

## B   Strong preference for uninverted order

For obvious reasons, reporting clauses are chiefly found in fiction and news, whether with or without inversion (11.2.3.7).

Subject-verb order is virtually the rule where one or more of the following three conditions apply:

The subject is an unstressed pronoun:

> *"The safety record at Stansted is first class," **he said**.* (NEWS)

The verb phrase is complex (containing auxiliary plus main verb):

> *"Konrad Schneider is the only one who matters," **Reinhold had answered**.* (FICT)

The verb is followed by a specification of the addressee:

> *There's so much to living that I did not know before, **Jackie had told her happily**.* (FICT)

To some extent, the conditions of inversion in reporting clauses are similar to those applying more generally to subject-verb inversion (11.2.3.1), reflecting the weight and communicative importance of the subject v. the verb: whichever is placed last becomes relatively more prominent.

However, inversion in reporting clauses is occasionally found with subject pronouns:

> *I said I think something's gone wrong with the auto bank machine, **says I**.* (CONV†)

> *"We may all be famous, then," **said he**.* (FICT)

Note the fixed combination *says I* which is used by some speakers in reporting a conversation. The sequence *say I* with the grammatically correct verb form is not attested in the LSWE Corpus.

Where clauses identifying the source of some quoted text precede the text reported, they have a more independent status and subject-verb order is typical, regardless of the relative weight of the subject and the verb:

> ***Standing, Rick said**, "Can I take Dave Holden's notes with me?"* (FICT)

> ***She said**: "Elderly people often have smaller groups of friends and family to support them."* (NEWS)

However, subject-verb inversion is sometimes found in initial position in news:

> ***Said a pollster**: "Frenchmen still like to believe that they are the world's greatest lovers."* (NEWS)

> ***Says Murray**: "I was in my room with a pal and after several drinks I started doing conjuring tricks."* (NEWS†)

## 11.2.3.7 Reporting clauses in fiction and news

➤ Reporting clauses are very common in fiction and news (including clauses with inversion (VS word order) and those with regular SV word order) (see Table 11.1).
  ➤ Reporting clauses occur over 5,000 times per million words in fiction.
  ➤ Reporting clauses occur over 2,000 times per million words in news.
➤ Final position for reporting clauses is preferred in both registers.
  ➤ News uses initial reporting clauses to a greater extent than fiction.
➤ The majority of reporting clauses have no expansion.
  ➤ When they are expanded, right expansion is strongly preferred over left expansion, especially with reporting clauses in final position.

**Table 11.1** **Position and complexity of reporting clauses in fiction and news; as a percentage of the total in that register**

each ■ represents 5%    □ represents less than 2.5%

| FICT complexity | initial | position medial | final |
|---|---|---|---|
| no expansion | ■ | ■■ | ■■■■■■■ |
| left expansion | ■ | □ | □ |
| right expansion | ■ | ■ | ■■■■■■ |
| left & right expansion | □ | □ | □ |

| NEWS complexity | initial | position medial | final |
|---|---|---|---|
| no expansion | ■■■■ | ■■ | ■■■■■■■ |
| left expansion | ■■ | □ | □ |
| right expansion | ■ | □ | ■■■ |
| left & right expansion | □ | □ | □ |

➤ In fiction, both SV and VS word orders are used for reporting clauses, with a slight preference for the regular SV order.
➤ In news, inversion (with VS word order) is strongly preferred over the regular SV order.
➤ With both word orders, most reporting clauses are not expanded, but fiction makes slightly greater use of a wider range of expansion types than does news.

### A Position and complexity of the reporting clause

Although the total number of reporting clauses is far higher in fiction than in news, the same positions are preferred in both registers: final > initial > medial. In other words, writers seem to prefer to leave the quoted element intact and place the reporting clause either at the end or the beginning. This accords with a clausal version of the principle of contact (11.2.1) and undoubtedly makes processing easier. Final and initial position also provide more possibilities for expansions (see below).

Table 11.2   **Order of subject and verb, with expansions, in final reporting clauses in fiction and news; as a percentage of the total in that register, excluding clauses with pronouns as subject**

each ■ represents 5%     □ represents less than 2.5%

| FICT expansion | word order SV | VS |
|---|---|---|
| none | ■■■■■■■ | ■■■■■ |
| adverbial | ■ | ■ |
| *ing*-clause | ■■ | ■■ |
| other | ■■ | □ |

| NEWS expansion | word order SV | VS |
|---|---|---|
| none | ■■ | ■■■■■■■■■■■■■■ |
| adverbial | ■■ | □ |
| *ing*-clause | □ | □ |
| other | □ | □ |

Final position is preferred in both registers, though more strongly so in fiction than in news. We may interpret this as follows: most typically the quoted text is the main communicative point, and the reporting clause is tagged on at the end. When read aloud, the reporting clause will normally receive less stress. This ordering seems to go against the information principle (11.1.1), but there are other cases where subsidiary elements are added at the end, e.g. vocatives (3.4.6, 3.13.4) and tags (3.4.4, 11.5.2). These are all elements having to do with discourse management.

Reporting clauses in initial and final position often contain expansions of different kinds. Final reporting clauses often have right expansions, including time adverbials (e.g. *said yesterday*), manner adverbials (e.g. *asked patiently*), a specification of the addressee (e.g. *told her*), and *ing*-clauses. The last type is particularly common in fiction:

> "*That's the whole trouble,*" **said Gwen, laughing slightly**. (FICT)

> "*Answer the private line for me, Alice,*" **Mattie said, throwing off her coat**. (FICT)

In contrast, initial reporting clauses often have left expansions, which can also include time adverbials, place adverbials, a specification of the addressee, and *ing*-clauses:

> **To the mother she said**: "*You should be happy, they bring luck to the household.*" (FICT)

> **After new talks succeeded, Ball said**: "*Sometimes agents' demands exceed what the players want.*" (NEWS)

> **At Marseilles airport, one customs officer said**: "*You can bring in anything you like – including drugs or weapons.*" (NEWS)

Reporting clauses rarely include both a left and a right expansion:

*Faking and dodging, he says before she can speak,* "Tell the darker of your boy-friends here I thought he promised to pull out when he got a stake." (FICT)

## B  The order of subject and verb in reporting clauses

Reporting clauses with pronoun subjects take subject-verb order. Similarly, the overwhelming majority of reporting clauses in initial position take subject-verb order. In contrast, there is more variability with final reporting clauses, with the overall distribution of subject-verb order and inversion being about equal. However, subject-verb order is slightly preferred in fiction, while inversion is strongly preferred in news. Although the number of examples is low, there seems to be a slight tendency for postmodification in the subject noun phrase to pull in the direction of inversion, presumably because it is easier to accommodate a heavier subject in end position in the clause.

Reporting clauses in fiction contain more expansions than those in news. Where there is a specification of the addressee, we only find subject-verb order. Time and manner adverbials also seem to pull in the direction of subject-verb order. On the other hand, *ing*-clauses seem not to have a marked effect on the choice of order.

## C  Register differences

Reporting clauses are used for different purposes in fiction and news. There is a much higher frequency of reporting clauses in fiction, because dialogue is central in that register, and there is a constant speaker shift. Furthermore, fiction commonly reports thoughts. Quotation in news reportage is less pervasive and normally represents fewer voices (in each news report).

It is notable that reporting clauses are more often placed in initial position in news than they are in fiction. This is no doubt connected with the need to introduce new speakers and writers in news reportage:

**Last night an executive director of Bond Corp, Peter Lucas, attacked the NAB Move:** "If that's the way business can expect bankers to behave, God help Australia." (NEWS)

**A sure-footed City scribbler Tim Congdon of Gerrard & National writes:** "The 1980s will be remembered as a decade of remarkable growth in all forms of credit." (NEWS)

**A Regional Health Authority spokesman said:** "It is superior in design to older models." (NEWS)

Expansions are in general more common in fiction than in news, particularly with reporting clauses in final position. This reflects the greater need in fiction to specify the manner and circumstances of speaking. In news, the focus is more on the content of the report.

The overall preference for subject-verb order v. inversion is quite different in the two registers: in fiction, a preference for subject-verb order, in news, a preference for inversion. To some extent, the greater reliance on subject-verb order in fiction may be connected with the more common occurrence of expansions. Where there are expansions after the verb, subject-verb order produces a more balanced structure, both from the point of view of weight and information flow.

There is also a striking difference between the registers as regards previous mention of the subject referent. In fiction, the subject referent has been mentioned before in the great majority of cases (c. 90 per cent). This is because a fictional text normally deals with a number of characters who appear regularly throughout the text. In news, on the other hand, new referents are regularly brought in with each story. It is possible that the need to introduce new referents has led to a convention favouring more use of inversion, with the subject placed after the verb in accordance with the information principle (11.1.1).

It has to be kept in mind, however, that there is also considerable variation within each register. This is an area where there is a great deal of freedom for individual choice.

## 11.2.3.8  Inversion in general: distribution

**CORPUS FINDINGS [2]**

➤ Inversion is relatively rare (excluding syntactically conditioned inversion in interrogative clauses):
  ➤ c. 300–400 occurrences per million words in conversation;
  ➤ c. 500–600 occurrences per million words in academic prose;
  ➤ over 1,000 occurrences per million words in fiction and news.
➤ Inversion is overwhelmingly a main-clause phenomenon: over 90% of all inversions in conversation, fiction, and, news occur in main clauses.
  ➤ c. 75% of all inversions in academic prose occur in main clauses.
  ➤ In fiction and news, inversion is most common in reporting clauses (over 50% of the total occurrences).

**DISCUSSION OF FINDINGS**

In spite of its relative rarity, inversion is an important option. Inversion is usually so strongly conditioned by context that it is impossible to normalize the order without affecting the contextual fit of the clause or without loss of stylistic effect.

Inversion is more frequent in the written registers than in conversation, with the highest frequency in fiction. In general, we may assume that writers of fiction make more use of the resources of the language, including options which were formerly in more frequent use.

Subject-verb inversion is the main inversion type found in fiction, particularly for description of settings, where inversion is a natural option (11.2.3.1). Subject-operator inversion is virtually restricted to the written registers, presumably because it is usually a deliberate rhetorical choice.

At the other extreme, inversion is least common in conversation, with dependent-clause inversion being especially rare. Conversation is spontaneously produced, and leaves less room for planning and varying the use of language resources. In addition, conversation is at the forefront of linguistic change and is thus less likely to make use of features which were previously more frequent in the language. Nevertheless, inversion is quite a normal option in conversation with certain more-or-less fixed patterns: *here's . . ., here are . . ., there's . . .* (with locative *there*), *and so is . . ., so am I.*

The strong association of inversion with main clauses can be interpreted as follows: independent clauses are the main means of carrying the communication forward. Their syntactic independence correlates with greater possibilities of internal variation and adaptation to context. Dependent clauses, on the other hand, must fit into the superordinate syntactic structure and are less free to adapt to contextual requirements. The regular presence of a link at the beginning of a dependent clause restricts the freedom of the other elements. It is also likely that the greater regularity of ordering in dependent clauses facilitates the recognition of complex structures. The slightly greater preference for dependent-clause inversions in academic prose reflects the greater opportunity for careful planning in that register (cf. the examples in 11.2.3.5).

Overall, inversion cannot be adequately studied as a purely syntactic phenomenon. We must consider the interplay between syntax, lexis, and register variation. Further, it is necessary to take into account non-syntactic factors which influence the ways in which clauses are adapted to context or varied for focus and emphasis.

## 11.2.4 Word-order options at the end of the clause

By and large, there is little variation in the order of the core elements at the end of the clause. The following survey focuses on the order of direct and indirect objects (11.2.4.1–2), direct objects and object predicatives (11.2.4.3), and objects of phrasal verbs (11.2.4.4).

The order of core elements at the end of the clause is governed by the same sorts of principles which determine word-order in general (11.1.1–3, 11.2.1). The word-order options at the end of the clause make it possible, within the limits set by syntax, to choose an order which brings about a desired distribution of information, weight, and focus.

### 11.2.4.1 The placement of direct and indirect objects

#### A Choice between the SVO$_i$O$_d$ and SVO$_d$O$_p$ patterns

Ditransitive verbs frequently allow two semantically equivalent patterns with a direct object (given in bold in the examples below) plus a second object noun phrase:

Indirect object + direct object (3.5.6):

1 *I'll fix [you]* **some tea** *later.* (FICT)
2 *Although it awarded [him]* **medals**, *the Academy never granted [him]* **the membership that was his life's ambition**. (NEWS†)

Direct object + preposition *to* or *for* + prepositional object (3.5.7):

3 *I'll fix* **it** *[for you].* (FICT)
4 *The Pentagon has yet to bite the bullet and recently awarded* **$419 million in contracts** *[to Westinghouse and ITT Avionics Division].* (NEWS†)

The bracketed phrases in **1** and **3** express a **benefactive** relation, in **2** and **4** a **recipient** relation. The choice between these two-word order patterns is partly determined by the valency potential of the individual lexical verb (5.2.4) and partly by other factors.

#### B The SVO$_i$O$_d$ and SVO$_d$O$_p$ patterns in relation to length

One relevant factor is the length of the direct and the indirect object. Three common lexical verbs which allow both a prepositional and a non-prepositional pattern were selected for a detailed study of this factor: *give, offer,* and *sell*.

➤ With the verbs *give*, *offer*, and *sell*, the pattern indirect object + direct object is about four times more common than the pattern direct object + preposition + prepositional object.

➤ With the non-prepositional pattern, there is a clear length effect, with the indirect object being very short in most instances.

➤ Length appears to be a less important factor with the prepositional pattern.

**Table 11.3** **Length of direct object and other object phrase in two word-order patterns, for the verbs *give, offer,* and *sell***

each ● represents 5%

**pattern: indirect object + direct object**

| | length of noun phrase | | |
|---|---|---|---|
| | **1 word** | **2 words** | **3+ words** |
| direct object | ● ● ● | ● ● ● ● ● ● ● | ● ● ● ● ● ● ● ● ● ● ● |
| indirect object | ● ● ● ● ● ● ● ● ● ● ● ● ● ● ● ● ● ● ● | ● ● | ● |

**pattern: direct object + recipient *to*-phrase**

| | length of noun phrase | | |
|---|---|---|---|
| | **1 word** | **2 words** | **3+ words** |
| direct object | ● ● ● ● ● ● ● ● ● ● ● ● ● ● | ● ● ● ● ● | ● ● ● ● |
| *to*-phrase | ● ● ● ● ● ● ● ● ● ● | ● ● ● ● ● ● | ● ● ● ● ● |

**DISCUSSION OF FINDINGS**

The length distribution of phrases in the non-prepositional pattern is in agreement with the principle of end-weight (11.1.3): the indirect object, which comes earlier in the clause, tends to be much shorter than the direct object. The indirect object also tends to be less informative: over 50 per cent of all indirect objects are realized by personal pronouns (v. less than 5 per cent of the direct objects). Thus, the early placement of the indirect object also agrees with the information principle (11.1.1).

Turning to the prepositional pattern, we note that the slight tendency for the direct object to be shorter than the noun phrase following *to* in the prepositional pattern is also in agreement with the principle of end-weight. Moreover, it is slightly more likely that the direct object will be realized by a personal pronoun. However, to account more fully for the choice of the *to*-phrase, we must turn to other sources of explanation.

In some cases, the *to*-phrase may be chosen because it is felt to be a clearer marker of syntactic relationships than word order. This factor becomes more important with longer noun phrases following *to*. Thus, the prepositional pattern is actually more common than the non-prepositional pattern when the noun phrase following *to* is two words or more in length.

The use of a *to*-phrase to clarify syntactic relationships is also shown by the seemingly unnecessary preposition in examples such as the following, where the long direct objects are placed in the position of end focus:

> *This irregularity in her features was not grotesque, but charming, and gave **to Anastasia's face** a humor she herself did not possess.* (FICT)

> *These include principally the discovery of America and the rounding of the Cape, which gave **to commerce, to navigation, to industry**, an impulse never before known.* (ACAD)

Examples of this kind are very rare and are characteristic of more formal writing.

The choice of a *to*-phrase to clarify syntactic relationships is also seen in pronoun sequences; see 11.2.4.2

## 11.2.4.2 Pronoun sequences as direct and indirect object

### A Discourse choice between patterns with pronouns

Where both the direct and the indirect object are realized by personal pronouns, there are three major patterns:

Indirect object + direct object:

> *Give **me it**, you little cow!* (CONV)

> *Well, they won't give **him it** straightaway.* (CONV†)

Direct object + *to*-phrase:

> *I'll give **it to him** tomorrow.* (CONV†)

> *"Give **it to me**, Pauli."* (FICT)

Direct object + indirect object:

> *Give it Nat – good girl, give **it me**.* (CONV†)

> *"Do let me give **it him**," she said.* (FICT)

### B Indirect object patterns with pronouns

**CORPUS FINDINGS [1]**

➤ Pronoun sequences as direct and indirect object occur almost exclusively in conversation and fiction.

➤ The prepositional construction (e.g. *give it to me*) is by far the most frequent (in contrast to the overall rarity of the prepositional pattern with full noun phrases, as reported in 11.2.4.1).

➤ The non-prepositional construction with the direct object in first position (e.g. *give it me*) is found both in conversation and fiction.

➤ The non-prepositional construction with the indirect object in first position (e.g. *give me it*) is virtually restricted to conversation.

**Table 11.4** **Distribution of pronoun sequences as direct and indirect object across registers; occurrences per million words**

each ■ represents 10     □ represents less than 5

| | CONV | FICT | NEWS | ACAD |
|---|---|---|---|---|
| indirect object + direct object | ■■■■ | □ | □ | □ |
| direct object + *to*-phrase | ■■■■■■■■■ | ■■■■■■■ | ■ | □ |
| direct object + indirect object | ■■ | ■ | □ | □ |

**DISCUSSION OF FINDINGS**

The overall distribution of these pronoun sequences across registers reflects the general differences in the frequency of pronouns, which are far more common in conversation and fiction than in the other registers (2.4.14).

As personal pronouns do not differ in givenness or length, the distribution across the three word-order patterns cannot be explained in terms of the information principle or the principle of end-weight. We may assume that the prepositional pattern is preferred because the syntactic relationship is more clearly marked (cf. 11.2.4.1), particularly in view of the two possible word orders when there is no such marker. Furthermore, it makes it easier to stress, and let the end focus fall on, the prepositional phrase than it does with a bare personal pronoun, where the recipient needs to be emphasized.

The fairly high frequency in conversation of the default order, with the indirect object preceding the direct object, reflects the tendency of conversation to conform to the most common overall pattern. The opposite order is least frequent, presumably because the syntactic relationships are not clearly marked. It is significant that this pattern is almost exclusively found with *it* as direct object; while *it* is naturally construed as a direct object, other personal pronouns (like *them*) could just as easily be interpreted as an indirect or a direct object.

## 11.2.4.3 Clauses with direct objects and object predicatives

### A Discourse choice between the $SVO_dP_o$ and $SVP_oO_d$ patterns

A direct object regularly precedes the object predicative (3.5.8), but may be postponed to end position under particular circumstances. In the following example, the object predicative is given in *[]*, and the postponed direct object is marked in bold:

> *Each region has a responsibility to create and make [available]* **a collection of contemporary work**. (NEWS†)
>
> cf. *... has a responsibility to create a collection of contemporary work and make it available.*

The object predicative is light in such cases in comparison with the direct object, which is long and complex. Where the direct object is a pronoun or a short noun-headed phrase, it must precede the object predicative.

### B Object predicative patterns

**CORPUS FINDINGS [1]**

➤ Regular placement of the direct object before the object predicative is by far the more common option. Postponement of the direct object is found most often in news and academic prose.

➤ There is a sharp differentiation by length: a postponed direct object is long; a regularly placed direct object is short.

**Table 11.5** **Distribution of regular order v. postponement for selected clauses: combinations of the verb *make* + direct object + object predicative containing *available*, *clear*, *plain*, or *possible*; occurrences per million words**

each ■ represents 10    □ represents less than 5

| | CONV | FICT | NEWS | ACAD |
|---|---|---|---|---|
| *make* NP ADJ | ■ | ■■■■■■■■■■ | ■■■■■■■■■■ ■■■■■■■ | ■■■■■■■■■■ |
| *make* ADJ NP | □ | ■ | ■■■■ | ■■■ |

**Table 11.6** **Length of the direct object with regular word order v. postponement for selected clauses: combinations of the verb *make* + direct object + object predicative containing *available*, *clear*, *plain*, or *possible* (in all registers combined); occurrences per million words**

each ■ represents 10    □ represents less than 5

| | length of the direct object, in number of words | | | | |
|---|---|---|---|---|---|
| | 1 word | 2 words | 3 words | 4 words | 5+ words |
| *make* NP ADJ | ■■■■■■■■ ■■■■■■■■ ■■■■■■■■ ■■■■■■■ | ■■■■■ | ■ | □ | □ |
| *make* ADJ NP | □ | □ | □ | □ | ■■■■■■■■ |

### DISCUSSION OF FINDINGS

The principle of end-weight (11.1.3) is important in favouring postponement of the direct object, which occurs almost exclusively when the direct object is long and complex. Postponement occurs particularly in the registers with the highest degree of phrasal complexity, i.e. news reportage and academic prose.

In contrast, the direct object is often a pronoun in conversation and fiction:

*I can make **you** [available] to people, yeah?* (CONV †)

*He made **it** [impossible].* (FICT)

Postponement is an important means of clarifying syntactic relationships, particularly where the direct object contains a clause:

*It is intended to make [clearer] **the targets which pupils need to aim for**.* (ACAD †)

*That this is a matter of decision, of a kind, does not make [indeterminate] **either the idea of a solid thing or the generalization that all the solid things on my table are inflammable**.* (ACAD)
*cf. ... does not make the idea indeterminate.*

The word order in these examples shows beyond doubt that the bracketed adjectives are not part of the following clause.

Where the whole of the direct object is a clause, two different patterns are used. In the first pattern, there is a dummy pronoun (*it*) in the ordinary object position, and the clause is obligatorily placed in extraposition:

*He made it impossible for her to do anything.* (FICT)

*My husband has made it clear he doesn't agree to me going.* (NEWS)

In the second pattern, *make clear* seems to be treated like a complex verb (cf. *make sure, make certain*):

*But he made clear it was not a sacking offence.* (NEWS†)

## 11.2.4.4 The placement of objects of phrasal verbs

### A Discourse choice between mid-position and post-particle placement

Direct objects of two-place phrasal verbs may be placed before or after the adverbial particle. In the following examples, the adverbial particle is given in brackets, and the direct object is marked in bold:

1 *Why do you like picking [up] **the telephone** so much?* (CONV)

2 *How fast can you pick **it** [up]?* (CONV)

Where the direct object is a pronoun (as in **2**), it is normally placed between the verb and the particle; this order will be called mid position. The ordering in **1** will be called post-particle position.

### B Full noun phrase object placement with phrasal verbs across registers in relation to length of object

**CORPUS FINDINGS** [1]

➤ For pronominal direct objects, mid-position placement is the norm (being chosen well over 90% of the time).

➤ For direct objects with full noun phrases, mid-position placement is by far most frequent in conversation.

  ➤ Proportionally, it is used over 60% of the time with phrasal verbs in that register.

  ➤ In contrast, mid-position placement is used less than 10% of the time with phrasal verbs in the written registers, where absolute frequencies are also smaller than in conversation.

➤ Mid-position placement is much more common with full noun phrase direct objects of two to four words in length, rather than longer objects, in all registers.

**Table 11.7** Distribution of mid-position placement of direct objects (excluding pronouns) of different lengths for selected phrasal verbs: *bring out, bring up, carry out, carry up, make out, make up, take out, take up*; occurrences per million words

each ■ represents 10    □ represents less than 5

| length of the direct object | CONV | FICT | NEWS | ACAD |
|---|---|---|---|---|
| 1 word | ■■ | ■ | ■ | □ |
| 2 words | ■■■■■■■■■ ■■■■■■■■ | ■■■■■■■ | ■■■■■ | ■ |
| 3–4 words | ■■■■■■ | ■■ | ■ | □ |
| 5+ words | ■■ | □ | □ | □ |

➤ There is considerable variability among individual phrasal verbs in their preference for mid-position placement.
  ➤ *Carry out* and *make out* have almost exclusively post-particle objects.
  ➤ At the other extreme, *bring up* and *take out* have more or less equal preference for the two positions.

**Table 11.8**  **Use of post-particle placement v. mid-position placement of the direct object (excluding pronouns) with particular phrasal verbs; occurrences per million words[7]**

each ■ represents 50     □ represents less than 25

| | post-particle placement | mid-position placement |
|---|---|---|
| *carry out* | ■■■■■■■■■■■ | □ |
| *make out* | ■■■ | □ |
| *take up* | ■■■■■■■■■ | ■ |
| *bring out* | ■■■ | ■ |
| *make up* | ■■■■■■■■■ | ■■ |
| *bring up* | ■■ | ■■ |
| *take out* | ■■■■■ | ■■■■ |

### DISCUSSION OF FINDINGS

Phrasal verbs with a primarily idiomatic sense, such as *carry out* and *make out* (where the particle *out* rarely has its literal meaning), prefer an order where the two elements of the phrasal verb are adjacent. In contrast, phrasal verbs where the particle has its literal spatial meaning (e.g. *take out*) more often take the direct object in mid position, leaving the particle at the end—i.e. in the typical position for a place adverbial. This tendency applies separately to the same verb when used in idiomatic v. literal spatial meanings. Compare:

  1 *Now carry [out]* **the instructions**. (FICT)
  2 *The Germans carried* **the corpse** *[out]*. (FICT)

Notice that in literal **2** we can say that the result of the action is that 'the corpse is out', while it is certainly not true that 'the instructions are out' as a result of the action in idiomatic **1**. This accounts for the greater naturalness of mid position with spatial uses, while the idiomatic type just as naturally prefers an order where the two parts of the phrasal verb are adjacent. The difference between spatial and idiomatic uses is, however, not absolute, as the order is dependent upon a number of interacting factors.

One consequence of the late placement of the particle with phrasal verbs used literally, is that it is still common for objects of several words in length to precede the one-word particle. However, the overall finding for word length of object accords to some extent with the principle of end-weight (11.1.3) in that very long objects are placed after the short adverbial particle.

Mid position seems to be strongly preferred where the particle is followed by an adverbial. In the examples below it is also favoured by the literal sense of the combination:

   3 *Paul took **his friend** [up] to the top floor.* (FICT)

   4 *She took **Liam** [out] to the park.* (FICT†)

   5 *Last week a husband took **his wife** [out] for a drive.* (NEWS†)

Examples **3** and **4** illustrate a common type where the adverbial particle is followed by an adverbial of direction. The two adverbials are semantically related and are naturally placed together. In **5**, the adverbial specifies the purpose of the action.

   What seems to happen in all these cases is that the direct object is placed in a less prominent position to allow focus to fall more clearly on the main communicative point given at the end of the clause, in agreement with the information principle (11.1.1).

   The distribution of mid position across registers follows the order of registers we have observed elsewhere, with the careful expository style of academic prose at the opposite extreme from conversation. Formal prose seems to resist the splitting up of the verb and the adverbial particle, and observe the principle of end-weight especially strongly (11.1.3); the frequency of mid position is low overall, but especially so with long direct objects. In contrast, conversation commonly uses mid position, even with long direct objects; for example (with following adverbials again):

   *Can't believe it, my mum brought **food for my brother** [up] today.* (CONV)

   *Take **that little bit of wire** [out] down there.* (CONV)

   *If you put the tab sign back on, it brings **all those vitamin Cs, fibres and fats** [up] as well.* (CONV†)

Where the direct object is realized by a clause, mid position is excluded:

   *Can't make [out] **where this school is**.* (CONV)

   cf. *\*Can't make where this school is out.*

Mid position is marginally possible where the direct object contains a relative clause; more commonly, the direct object is placed in end position, or the relative clause is postponed, thus resulting in a split noun phrase:

   *He had taken **two nails** [out] **that he couldn't see**.* (CONV†)

   cf. *He had taken out two nails that he couldn't see.*

   *?He had taken two nails that he couldn't see out.*

Conversation opts for a high frequency of mid position because clauses are generally short and because the connection between the verb and the adverbial particle can be marked by intonation: it is notable that the adverbial particle may often be in end focus, though focus is normally associated with lexical words. At the same time, the verb and the particle bind together the predication. It is also significant that pronouns are extremely common as direct objects in conversation (4.1.2, 4.10.5).

C  **Placement of pronoun objects with phrasal verbs**

Single pronouns are almost invariably placed in mid position. End position does occur exceptionally, however:

   *We'll have to wash [up] **these**.* (CONV)

The reason for end position here is probably that *these* is contrastive (i.e. 'these but not others in the discourse situation'), and would be end-focused with special stress.

   There is one pronoun category which is more commonly found in end position, i.e. indefinite pronouns. Compare:

Mid position with indefinite pronouns:

> *I would never pick **anybody** [up].* (CONV)
>
> *He should get **someone** [out] to paint it.* (FICT)

End position with indefinite pronouns:

> *He's going to – er – pick [up] **somebody** somewhere.* (CONV†)
>
> *He sent [out] **someone** to capture the bounty hunter.* (FICT†)

The word order preferences with these pronouns are the same as for noun-headed phrases, i.e. mid position is predominant in conversation and end position in fiction. Instances in news and academic prose are few.

Where the pronoun has postmodification, end position is the normal choice:

> *They didn't smash [up] **anything valuable**.* (CONV)
>
> *I think Mama was afraid I would blurt [out] **something that would betray her secret**.* (FICT)

In other cases, the pronoun is in mid position and a relative clause is postponed until after the particle:

> *"We think Brian might have seen something or found **something** [out] **that someone was afraid he would come home and tell us**," said Mr McDermott.* (NEWS)

## 11.3    The passive

The passive involves a restructuring of the clause (3.6.2), and thus it is not a simple order variation. It takes two forms: the **long passive** where the **agent** is expressed in a *by*-phrase **1**, and the **short passive** where the agent is left unexpressed **2**:

> **1** *As recently as last year, **Anderson was asked by the Ugandan government** to advise on the restructuring of the civil service there, following the turmoil of recent years.* (NEWS)
> *cf. ... the Ugandan government asked Anderson ...*
>
> **2** *In 1975 **Anderson was appointed** the first EEC delegate in Southern Africa.* (NEWS†)
> *cf. ... X appointed Anderson ...*

The passive agent is often the agent of the verbal action in the semantic sense, though it may fulfil other semantic roles such as experiencer (3.2.1.1). The availability of the passive option is subject to a number of constraints, chiefly connected with the nature of the verb. See 6.4 for general frequency information on the passive, and the association between verbs and the passive.

Primarily the passive serves the discourse functions of:

- cohesion and contextual fit through
    ordering of information
    omission of information (especially short passive)
- weight management (especially long passive).

## 11.3.1    Types of passive construction

Passives occur in both finite and non-finite constructions.

### A Finite constructions

- Short passive with stative verb
  Stative passives describe the state resulting from an action, rather than the action itself:

  Andy **may be adopted** or something like that. (CONV)

  It had made Sammler feel like a fool to go immediately to a phone booth on Riverside Drive. Of course the phone **was smashed**. (FICT)

  This structure forms a cline with the copular verb + participial adjective clause pattern (SVP$_s$).

- Short passive with dynamic verb
  Dynamic passives describe an action rather than the resulting state:

  It **was stolen** from my car. My car **was broken into**. (CONV†)

  Whichever system **is used** it is vital that leaking water **is avoided**. (ACAD)

- Get-passives

  No, you don't pass or fail. You **get given** marks. (CONV†)

  You**'re getting spoiled**, he says. (FICT)

- Long passives

  I'm **influenced by** all kinds of things. (CONV†)

  Her Royal Highness **was received by** the Austrian Ambassador. (NEWS†)

Finite constructions also include forms preceded by semi-modals and other auxiliary equivalents: has to be done, need to be taken, used to be written, etc.

### B Non-finite constructions

- Postmodifier of noun, short passive

  That would be the cause of death, I think, heavy blow from a piece of lead piping **wrapped** in a sock. (FICT†)

  The major weather factors **involved** are apparently temperature and precipitation. (ACAD†)

- Postmodifier of noun, long passive

  If, further, he feels that the free market policies and values **embraced by** Mrs Thatcher have done much to create a divided nation, **dominated by** Pharisees, he should feel free to offer his opinion. (NEWS)

  Let us look at an example **given by** Baillieul et al. (ACAD†)

For ed-clauses postmodifying nouns see 8.8.1.

- Infinitive or ed-clause complement of a verb, short passive

  1 My dad's having all the locks **changed**. (CONV†)

  2 We know with some confidence that if greenhouse gases continue **to be emitted** in their present quantities, we will experience unprecedented rates of sea-level rise. (NEWS)

- Infinitive or ed-clause complement of a verb, long passive

  3 That the windscreen wipers started to work can properly be said **to have been caused by** a set of things including <...> (ACAD†)

  4 More simply put, a feedback system has its inputs **affected by** its outputs. (ACAD)

The passive form in verb complements may lack a subject (**2**, **3**), or it may be immediately preceded by an overt subject (**1**, **4**).

- Other non-finite constructions, short passive

    **5** *But there is no debate, and any decisions are likely **to be taken**, piecemeal and by default.* (NEWS) <*to*-infinitive complement of an adjective>

    **6** *He looked like a man born with the Tory party in mind, his patrician head **set** on an aristocratic frame, a mane of fair hair **combed** meticulously into place.* (FICT) <supplementive adverbial *ed*-clause, 10.2.9.1>

- Other non-finite constructions, long passive

    **7** *Senhora Neto-Kiambata had the honour of **being received by** The Prince of Wales and The Prince Edward.* (NEWS) <*ing*-clause complement of a preposition>

    **8** *The club looked like a palace, a heavy Baroque building writhing with nymphs and naiads, its portals **supported by** a quartet of herculean pillars.* (FICT) <supplementive adverbial *ed*-clause, 10.2.8.4E>

Other non-finite constructions include forms in a variety of syntactic positions. As with verb complements, the passive form may lack a subject (**5**, **7**), or it may be immediately preceded by an overt subject (**6**, **8**).

## 11.3.2 Passives across syntactic positions and registers

The following distributional analysis excludes idioms such as *be bound to*, *be supposed to*, *get rid of*, *as opposed to*, which do not admit of any active-passive variation. Also excluded are forms containing clear cases of participial adjectives, chiefly denoting emotional states: *excited*, *pleased*, *scared*, *upset*, *worried*, etc. These allow modification by *very*, which is not possible with clear passives (7.9.1). However, it is difficult to draw a clear borderline with respect to stative passives in finite constructions (illustrated in A above).

> **CORPUS FINDINGS** [2]

➤ Short passives are predominant in all syntactic positions.

➤ Short dynamic *be*-passives are sharply differentiated by register, with conversation and academic prose at the opposite poles.

➤ Short stative *be*-passives are less frequent than dynamic *be*-passives and show far less variation by register.

➤ Long passives are most common in news and academic prose.

➤ Passives as postmodifiers of nouns are also most common in academic prose.
  ➤ The proportion of long passives compared to short passives in this position is higher than in finite clauses (especially in news and fiction).

➤ Passive verb complements are infrequent and usually short.
  ➤ These constructions are slightly more common in conversation than in the other registers.

➤ Passives are also infrequent in other non-finite positions.

Table 11.9   **Distribution of passive types across registers; occurrences per million words**

each ■ represents 500      □ represents less than 250

| finite constructions | CONV | FICT | NEWS | ACAD |
|---|---|---|---|---|
| **short passives** | | | | |
| with stative verb | ■■ | ■■ | ■■ | ■■■ |
| with dynamic verb | ■■ | ■■■■■ | ■■■■■■■ ■■■ | ■■■■■■■ ■■■■■■■ ■■■■■■ |
| *get*-passive | □ | □ | □ | □ |
| other copula | □ | □ | □ | □ |
| **long passives** | □ | ■ | ■■■ | ■■■ |

| non-finite constructions | CONV | FICT | NEWS | ACAD |
|---|---|---|---|---|
| **postmodifier in NP** | | | | |
| short passives | □ | ■■ | ■■■ | ■■■■■■■ |
| long passives | □ | ■ | ■■ | ■■ |
| **verb complement** | | | | |
| short passives | ■■ | ■ | ■ | ■ |
| long passives | □ | □ | □ | □ |
| **other constructions** | | | | |
| short passives | □ | ■ | ■■ | ■ |
| long passives | □ | □ | □ | □ |

## DISCUSSION OF FINDINGS

The most basic passive pattern is the short dynamic *be*-passive in finite clauses. The choice of a long passive is influenced by a number of discourse factors, described further in 11.3.3.

The main purpose of the short dynamic passive is to leave the initiator of an action (the agent) unexpressed. This may be because the agent is unknown, redundant, or irrelevant (i.e. of particularly low information value). The need to leave the agent unexpressed varies with register.

Academic prose shows the most frequent use of such short dynamic passives:

> In an experimental facility without breeding animals the health status **can be restored** if healthy animals **are issued** into a clean fumigated or disinfected room, and the infected room **is** gradually **emptied** as experiments **are terminated**. It is essential during the period that the clean and infected room are both in use that a strict barrier **is maintained** between them. Once the room **has been emptied** it **can be** thoroughly **cleaned** and **disinfected** or **fumigated**. (ACAD)

Academic discourse is concerned with generalizations, rather than the specific individuals who carry out an action. If expressed, the agent would be a generic pronoun or noun phrase in such examples: ... *can be restored by us/one/ researchers/laboratory workers*. Its omission also means that the verb phrase is more often in clause final position, characteristic of new information. This is often quite appropriate: for example in the above passage we can see, especially towards the end, that much of the new information is in fact conveyed by the verbs.

The generic nature of the omitted agent is shown clearly in the following passage where there is a switch from passive to active voice accompanied by the use of generic *we* as subject:

> *Stylistics, simply defined as the (linguistic) study of style,* **is** *rarely* **undertaken** *for its own sake, simply as an exercise in describing what use* **is made** *of language. [We] normally study style because we want to explain something* <...> (ACAD†)

The concern with generalizations in academic prose is reflected not only in the common use of the short passive, but also in the high frequency of plural nouns (4.5.6) and the subject pronouns *one* (4.15.2) and *we* (4.10.1.1).

News is also marked by a high frequency of short dynamic passives, although only about half as many as in academic prose. In news, the concern is usually with specific events rather than with generalizations. The reason for the suppression of the agent is not that it is generic; the agents are specific, but their identity is either not at issue or it does not need to be stated:

> *Jobless Frank Mason* **was cleared** *last night of attempting to kill a man in a street. Mason, of Bramston View, Witham,* **was acquitted** *of attempting to murder 27-year-old Adrian Hawes, but the jury failed to reach a verdict on alternative charges of wounding with intent and causing actual bodily harm. The charges arose from an incident in Cypress Road, Witham, on January 19 last year when three men got out of a car and set about Mr Hawes. He* **was punched**, *and* **kicked** *to the ground and* **stabbed** *three times in the back.* (NEWS)

> *The first serious prospect of a cure for Aids, rather than a treatment which delays its effects, has emerged when no trace of the Aids virus* **was found** *during the post mortem on a patient who* **had been treated** *with the standard AZT drug and a bone marrow transplant.* (NEWS)

With *was cleared* and *was acquitted* in the first example, and *was found* and *had been treated* in the second example, the agent follows from shared cultural frameworks of knowledge to do with lawcourts and hospitals. In the case of *was punched/kicked/stabbed*, the identity of the agent is recoverable from the preceding context.

In fiction, short dynamic passives are used when the agents are unknown, or their identity is regarded as irrelevant:

> *By a curious coincidence my father and mother* **were** *both* **killed** *on the same night that I lost my hand; they* **were buried** *under the rubble of a house in West Kensington while my hand* **was left** *behind somewhere in Leadenhall Street close to the Bank of England.* (FICT)

> *Late one morning in June, in the thirty-first year of his life, a message* **was brought** *to Michael K as he raked leaves in De Waal Park. The message, at third hand, was from his mother: she* **had been discharged** *from hospital and wanted him to come and fetch her.* (FICT)

It is remarkable that the passive frequency is lowest in conversation and fiction, although these are the registers with the highest frequency of lexical verbs (2.3.5). The strong predominance of active verbs in conversation and fiction should be seen in relation to the high frequency of personal pronouns, particularly of forms with exclusively human reference (4.10.5). Presenting actions in relation to agents is a natural consequence of the focus on human beings in these registers.

Interestingly, stative *be*-passives and passive verb complements deviate from the main trend in that they are relatively common in conversation and fiction. Notice that a stative *be*-passive does not describe an action. The focus is on the result, not on the agent and the action. Stative *be*-passives are like constructions with copular *be* plus adjective, and it is not surprising that they behave differently from dynamic *be*-passives.

The distribution of passive verb complements is remarkable, as they are actually most common in conversation. Most instances of this type are controlled by the causative verbs *have* and *get*:

> *Oh, has Kathy had **her hair done**?* (CONV)

> *I'd never get **my letters written** anyway.* (CONV†)

In such causative constructions the initiator of the action is given in the subject of the main clause, and they therefore do not deviate from the general tendency in conversation to express both the agent and the action.

## 11.3.3 The long passive

The long passive preserves the information of the corresponding active clause, but presents it in a different order. It is therefore reasonable to expect that the choice may be influenced by the same types of factors as affect pure word-order variations. Two such factors are especially important: length of subject v. agent phrase (11.3.3.1) and givenness of subject v. agent phrase (11.3.3.2). (The following description focuses on long passives in finite clauses.)

## 11.3.3.1 Length of subject v. agent phrase in long passives

**CORPUS FINDINGS [2,5]**

➤ There is a clear tendency for the subject to be shorter than the agent phrase in long passives.
➤ Subjects are more evenly distributed across the length categories than are agent phrases.
  ➤ Agent phrases rarely consist of a single word, while long subjects are by no means uncommon.

**Table 11.10 Length (in number of words) of subject v. agent phrase in long passives as a percentage of all long passives**

each ■ represents 5%    □ represents less than 2.5%

| length of subject (number of words) | length of agent phrase (number of words) | | |
| --- | --- | --- | --- |
| | 1 | 2–3 | 4+ |
| 1 | ■ | ■■■ | ■■■■ |
| 2–3 | □ | ■ | ■■■ |
| 4+ | ■ | ■ | ■■■■ |

**DISCUSSION OF FINDINGS**

The choice of the long passive can to a large extent be accounted for by the principle of end-weight (11.1.3), i.e. the tendency to place heavy elements towards the end of the clause. In the following examples, the subject is given in bold and the agent phrase marked by []:

> In two minutes **he** was surrounded [by a ring of men]. (FICT)

> After the judgment, **Mr Ashton** was approached [by a group of irate depositors] and questioned about the return of their money. (NEWS)

> **The Roman Literature** was collected and condensed into one volume about the year 1240 [by a senator of Bologna, Petrus Crescentius, whose book was one of the most popular treatises on agriculture of any time]. (ACAD†)

Nevertheless, the principle of end-weight is clearly insufficient in itself to account for the choice of the long passive. The subject and the agent phrase are often equally long, and sometimes the subject even exceeds the agent phrase in length. As the following section shows, information status is also an important factor for this discourse choice.

## 11.3.3.2  Givenness of subject v. agent phrase

Subject and agent phrases can be classified according to their information status, using a broad three-way division: given, given/new, and new. The intermediate category is required to handle multi-word phrases which include elements of both given and new information:

> 1 **The mourners** were led [by his widow, Stephanie, and his children, Roberta and Dean]. (NEWS)

> 2 **One such chain of events, leading to the 1968 plague/upsurge**, has been described to this meeting [by Dr. Symmons]. (ACAD†)

In **1**, the agent phrase brings in new information at the same time that *his* refers back to the man whose burial is reported in the text. The use of *such* in **2** relates to the preceding context, but the subject also introduces new information.

**CORPUS FINDINGS 2,5**

➤ Subjects and agent phrases are more sharply distinguished by information status than by length (cf. 11.3.3.1).
➤ In the majority of cases, the subject has a higher level of givenness than the agent phrase.
➤ Subjects vary more in information status than agent phrases.
➤ About 90% of the agent phrases bring in new information.

**Table 11.11  Subject v. agent phrases in long passives classified by givenness as a percentage of all long passives**

each ■ represents 5%     □ represents less than 2.5%

| subject | agent phrase given | given/new | new |
|---|---|---|---|
| given | ■ | ■ | ■■■■■■■■■ |
| given/new | □ | □ | ■■■■ |
| new | □ | □ | ■■■■ |

**DISCUSSION OF FINDINGS**

The use of the long passive agrees very well with the information principle (11.1.1): most commonly, the subject contains given information and the agent new information:

1 *Richard, like a good commander, sensed the uneasiness of the meeting, even through the solid teak partition. **He** would never, if he had taken to the high seas in past centuries, have been caught napping [by a mutiny].* (FICT)

2 *This memorial exhibition combines his explosively colourful paintings with sculptures by his father, Jacob Epstein, and <...> has been organised, following his mother's death, [by her friend, Beth Lipkin, to whom most of the pictures were left].* (NEWS†)

3 ***That similar relationships occur with these two species under field conditions in Saskatchewan*** *was suggested [by Pickford (1960, 1966a)].* (ACAD)

The second sentence in **1** naturally opens with a reference (in subject position) to the man mentioned in the preceding sentence; it then moves on to the new point being made. The choice of the passive in **2** provides a smooth continuation, preserving the subject of the preceding clause (which is actually omitted because it is identical) and ending with the long informative agent phrase. The very long subject in **3** is in blatant conflict with the principle of end-weight, but it agrees with the information principle. While the agent is new, *similar* and *these* provide explicit links between the subject and the preceding text.

It is less common for the subject and the agent phrase to have the same information value. In the following examples, both the subject and the agent phrase convey given information; the choice of the passive makes it possible to keep the same subject as in the preceding clause:

6 *He appealed for anyone who saw the three youths <...> The woman's ordeal started when she answered a knock on the back door of her house and <...> was confronted **by the three**.* (NEWS†)

7 *The social order involves both subjective human activity and objective social structure, men produce society and <...> are produced **by it**.* (ACAD†)

The need to consider the wider context is clear where both the subject and the agent phrase convey new information. Such examples are found in news, where stories appropriately begin with references to the people featured in the text:

8 ***The Chief Justice of Greece's Supreme Court, Yannis Grivas****, was appointed **by President Sartzetakis** yesterday to head a caretaker government which will conduct fresh elections, probably on 5 November. His government will be sworn in today. <...>* (NEWS)

9 ***Gary "Cat" Johnson, the coach of the season in 1987–88****, has been dismissed **by the Leicester Riders**. Leicester have won just one of their 11 Carlsberg League games this season but the club suggested that the reason for the dismissal was Johnson's unwillingness to involve himself in the club's junior programme. "I don't believe that," Johnson said yesterday. <...>* (NEWS)

## 11.3.4 Comparison of discourse functions of the long and short passive

The passive is traditionally described as a formal and impersonal choice. The formality is consistent with the distribution among registers, with high frequencies in academic prose and with conversation at the opposite extreme. Nevertheless, all passive patterns do not behave in the same way (11.3.2). In particular, the conditions of use are quite different for the short dynamic passive and the long passive.

The short dynamic passive makes it possible to eliminate the participant that would have been expressed in the subject of the corresponding active construction, i.e. normally the agent. As the agent is most typically human, it is no doubt correct to describe the short dynamic passive as impersonal. Significantly, its distribution across registers is a mirror image of the distributional patterns for the personal pronouns. It is also significant that the short passive frequently reflects a perspective maintained in long stretches of text (see the examples in 11.3.2).

The long passive preserves all the information that would be expressed in the corresponding active construction; therefore it cannot be described as impersonal. Unlike the short passive, it is hardly ever maintained in long stretches of text, explaining why long passives are far less common overall than short passives.

Because of these differences between short and long passives, long passives should be considered as competing with the corresponding active constructions rather than with short passives. The active construction is the more frequent choice in describing a situation involving an agent, an action, and an affected participant, presumably because it represents a natural way of viewing things (from originator to goal). The affected participant is chosen as subject if the context makes it a more natural starting-point than the agent, especially if it is given in the context and is less informative than the agent (11.3.3.2).

Although the conditions of use appear to be quite different, the long and the short passive are alike in their tendency to place given information in subject position. This is, however, true of subjects in general and is not limited to passive constructions (cf. 4.1.2).

## 11.4 Existential *there*

Existential *there* (3.6.3) is a formal device used, together with an intransitive verb, to predicate the existence or occurrence of something (including the non-existence or non-occurrence of something). Most typically, a clause with existential *there* has the following structure:

> *there* + *be* + indefinite NP (+ place or time position adverbial)

For example:

1 *A man goes in the pub.* **There***'s a bear sitting in the corner. He goes up to the, he goes up to the bartender. He says, why is* **there** *a bear sitting over there?* (CONV)

2 **There** *are around 6,000 accidents in the kitchens of Northern Ireland homes every year.* (NEWS)

The noun phrase following *be* is usually indefinite and referred to as the **notional subject**. Clauses with existential *there* may be called existential clauses. The main discourse function of existential clauses is to present new information (11.4.7).

## 11.4.1 The grammatical status of existential *there*

Existential *there* is a function word which has developed from the locative (position) adverb *there*. It differs from locative *there* in the following respects:

- phonologically, it is normally reduced to /ðə(r)/;

- the original locative meaning is lost;

- syntactically, it functions as a grammatical subject rather than as an adverbial.

The syntax and semantics of existential *there* are especially clear where it co-occurs with *here* or locative *there*:

    1 ***There**'s more gravy [here].* (CONV)

    2 ***There**'s still no water [there], is **there**?* (CONV)

As existential *there* can be used—without any apparent contradiction or tautology—in the same clause as *here*, as in **1**, or locative *there*, as in **2**, it clearly has the status of an empty grammatical element (cf. *it* of extraposition).

    Syntactically, existential *there* behaves like a grammatical subject: it is placed before the verb in declarative clauses and can be used in question tags, as in **2**. The subject status of existential *there* is also indicated by the strong tendency in conversation to use a singular verb regardless of the number of the notional subject (3.9.1.5). Existential *there* may further precede the verb in infinitive and *ing*-clauses:

    3 *N may be too large for **there** to be room for that number.* (ACAD†)

    4 *The paramedics arrived just in time, and there was some question of **there** being brain damage this time.* (FICT)

    5 *In sulphate soils there are very rapid fluctuations in pH values according to changes in the water regime, **there** being a very rapid drop on drying due to oxidation changes.* (ACAD)

Such non-finite existential clauses are rare, occurring primarily in academic prose (*ing*-clauses occur fewer than 10 times per million words; infinitive constructions are even less common). However, the use of these constructions further testifies to the subject status of existential *there*.

    It is also worth noting that existential *there* shows the same types of repetition patterns as subject pronouns (4.10.5, 14.2.2):

    6 ***There there** are two ways of tackling it.* (CONV†)

    7 ***There**'s **there**'s two girls' names there.* (CONV)

Such repetition with existential *there* occurs about 40 times per million words in conversation.

## 11.4.2 Variation in the verb phrase

The vast majority of existential clauses contain a form of the verb *be*, which may be preceded by auxiliaries or semi-modals: *has been, will be, is to be, is supposed to be, used to be*. *Be* may also appear in a *to*-infinitive complement of a lexical verb with the force of a hedge: *happen to be, tend to be, appear to be, is said to be*, etc.

(Strictly, in many of these instances, *there* has been raised from the lower clause like any other subject—9.4.2.2, 9.4.2.4):

> *[There]* **used to be** *a – a house on the end of the common up at Clarendon Road.* (CONV†)
>
> *If you want to know, [there]* **is supposed to be** *a plot between you and me to get hold of his wealth.* (FICT)
>
> *[There]* **seem to have been** *a lot of people who took up painting for a while and then dropped it.* (NEWS†)
>
> *[There]* **is said to be** *a mismatch between the mother tongue and the target language at these points.* (ACAD)

Existential clauses may contain verbs other than *be*, chiefly intransitive verbs denoting existence or occurrence:

> *Somewhere deep inside her [there]* **arose** *a desperate hope that he would embrace her.* (FICT†)
>
> *[There]* **came** *a roar of pure delight as it closed around him and carried him on.* (FICT)
>
> *[There]* **seems** *no likelihood of a settlement.* (NEWS†)
>
> *[There]* **seems** *little reason to interfere.* (NEWS†)
>
> *In all such relations [there]* **exists** *a set of mutual obligations in the instrumental and economic fields.* (ACAD)

## 11.4.2.1  Verb constructions other than simple *be*

**CORPUS FINDINGS** [1]

➤ Complex verb constructions in existential clauses are generally rare.
  ➤ Those with *seem* are relatively more common, especially in fiction.

**Table 11.12  Distribution of selected complex verb constructions with *be* in existential clauses; occurrences per million words**

each ■ represents 5    □ represents less than 3

|  | CONV | FICT | NEWS | ACAD |
|---|---|---|---|---|
| *seem to be* | ■ | ■■■ | ■ | ■■ |
| *appear to be* | □ | □ | □ | ■■ |
| *be supposed to be* | ■ | □ | □ | □ |
| *used to be* | ■■ | □ | □ | □ |

➤ Existential clauses without *be* are rare and make up a very small proportion of all existential clauses: less than 5% in fiction and academic prose, and less than 1% in news and conversation.
  ➤ The verb *exist* is the most frequent single alternative to *be*, but almost entirely in academic prose.
➤ In fiction, unlike the other registers, there is a fairly wide range of verbs used in existential clauses, including: *arise, ascend, break out, emerge, erupt, float, flow, flutter*, etc.

**Table 11.13** **Distribution of the most common simple verbs other than _be_ in existential clauses; occurrences per million words**

each ■ represents 5      ▢ represents less than 3

|        | CONV | FICT | NEWS | ACAD |
|--------|------|------|------|------|
| _seem_ | ▢ | ■■ | ■■ | ■ |
| _come_ | ▢ | ■■■■■ | ▢ | ▢ |
| _occur_ | ▢ | ▢ | ▢ | ■■ |
| _exist_ | ▢ | ▢ | ▢ | ■■■■■■■■■■ |

### DISCUSSION OF FINDINGS

The variation in fiction is characteristic of this register's tendency to use a greater variety of lexical items for stylistic effect (cf. 2.2.1.2). In contrast, there is less variation in news and academic prose, and only one (unusual) occurrence of an existential clause without _be_ in conversation:

> I don't think they're every twelve minutes. [There] **hasn't gone** an eighteen <i.e. bus> _up_ yet. (CONV)

Academic prose, with its predilection for Latinate words, shows a tendency to use _exist_ in addition to its less formal-sounding synonym _be_.

Exceptionally, we may find a transitive verb used together with existential _there_:

> Well then, on some corner of Time's beach, or on the muddy rim of one of her more significant rivulets, [there] **have been washed together** casually and indifferently a number of features that Nature had tossed away as of no use to any of her creations. (FICT)

> [There] **seized him** a fear that perhaps after all it was all true. (FICT†)

The language in these examples is stylistically marked, but the existential clause is typical in that it contains an indefinite notional subject following the verb.

Overall, although combinations occur with other verbs, existential clauses are overwhelmingly associated with the verb _be_.

## 11.4.3   The notional subject

The notional subject is typically an indefinite noun phrase, with a noun or an indefinite pronoun as head. The noun phrase is often complex:

> [There] is **something extra and a little heroic** about him. (FICT†)

> [There] must be **an enormous sense of isolation, of being aware of being let down.** (NEWS)

> [There] is in fact **a formalism** to hand **which perfectly expresses the idea of superposition.** (ACAD)

The head of the noun phrase may be followed by a non-finite clause:

> There's [a bear **sitting in the corner**]. (CONV)
> cf. A bear is sitting in the corner.

> There are [344 military plants **being converted to peaceful uses**]. (NEWS)
> cf. 344 military plants are being converted to peaceful uses.

> *There are [two scales of temperature **used in science**]. (ACAD)*
> *cf. Two scales of temperature are used in science.*

These constructions can be viewed as expansions of a simple finite clause with the verb *be* as progressive or passive auxiliary. They occur in all the registers and with a wide range of main verbs, transitive as well as intransitive. As regards complex notional subjects, see also 11.4.6. The notional subject is occasionally a definite noun phrase or a proper noun (see also 11.4.7). Examples are found in all registers:

> *I think there's gonna be six this time. [There]'s **Raymond and his wife and his wife Sherry's, I think, brother and his wife and** <...> (CONV†)*
>
> *I would say that Faye and Roberta represent an extreme. Then [there] were **Mary and Reggie**. (FICT†)*
>
> *First [there] was **the scandal of Fergie romping with John Bryan, pictured exclusively in the Mirror**. (NEWS)*
>
> *[There] is also **the group of non-benzenoid aromatic compounds**. (ACAD)*

Existential *there* constructions with a definite notional subject tend to occur when a series of elements is introduced, often marked explicitly by a conjunction or a linking adverbial (e.g. *first*) or additive adverbial (e.g. *too*).

Finally, there is a special use where the notional subject contains the demonstrative determiner *this* or *these* (4.4.3E), often found in joke-telling:

> *Dad, [there] was **this alien**. He had these enormous hands and silver eyes, and he was really ugly. (CONV)*
>
> *[There]'s **these three men** and they're walking through the desert. (CONV†)*

These constructions occur primarily in conversation (about 50 instances per million words) and occasionally in fiction.

## 11.4.4 Adverbial expansions

Existential clauses often contain a time or place adverbial, because things exist or happen in the context of time and place. However there are other adverbials which are essential to the existential clause:

> 1 *Because natural gas is an environmentally clean fuel, there is great interest **on the part of many scientists and policy makers** to assess its availability. (ACAD)*

The adverbial is usually at the end of the clause:

> *I said, well, there's a wheelbarrow **down there**. (CONV)*
>
> *"There's a cat **here under the casket**," she called to her brother. (FICT)*
>
> *There are no trains **on Sundays**. (NEWS†)*

However, clause-initial placement is also possible:

> ***Near the peak** there were no more trees, just rocks and grass. (FICT)*
>
> ***Inside the hall** there was piled a large assortment of packages and parcels and small articles of furniture. **On every item** there was a label tied. (FICT)*

The ordering is conditioned by the same factors that affect the placement of time and place adverbials in general (10.2.6). In the two fiction examples above, the adverbials are tied to the preceding text and the clause ends with the indefinite notional subject, which contains new information. The ordering is therefore in agreement with the information principle (11.1.1).

We may also find the adverbial in mid position, chiefly in fiction and with verbs other than *be*:

> There rose **to her lips** *always some exclamation of triumph over life when things came together in this peace, this rest, this eternity.* (FICT †)

> And in another second, had our contact lasted, I was certain that there would erupt **into speech, out of all that light and beauty,** *some brutal variation of Look, baby, I know you.* (FICT)

Mid position, like initial position, allows the main focus to fall on the indefinite notional subject, in agreement with the information principle.

Finally, it is possible for an adverbial in final position to have part of a complex notional subject postponed after it, so that it splits the notional subject and is no longer in final position. We term this **initial-end** position. See example **1** above, and the following:

> There's nothing **in there** *to reach.* (FICT †)
> *cf. There's nothing to reach in there.*

As regards the use and placement of adverbial expansions in existential clauses, see also 11.4.6–7.

## 11.4.5    Existential and locative *there*

**CORPUS FINDINGS** [1]

➤ While the registers differ sharply in the distribution of locative *there*, differences are far less marked for existential *there*.
➤ The distribution of locative *there* reveals a familiar pattern, with conversation and academic prose at the opposite poles.

**Table 11.14    Distribution of existential v. locative *there* across registers; occurrences per million words**

each ■ represents 500      □ represents less than 250

|  | CONV | FICT | NEWS | ACAD |
|---|---|---|---|---|
| existential *there* | ■■■■■■ | ■■■■■■ | ■■■■ | ■■■■■ |
| locative *there* | ■■■■■■ | ■■■ | ■ | □ |

**DISCUSSION OF FINDINGS**

The distribution across registers of locative *there* reflects the degree of dependence on situation. Conversation is embedded in a setting shared by the speaker and the addressee, where it is natural to make references in terms of *here* and *there*. The same is true of fictional dialogue.

In the other registers there is no such shared spatial context. The frequency of locative *there* is particularly low in academic prose, due to its abstract nature. Where locative *here* and *there* do occur in academic prose, they tend to refer to the text rather than the setting: *here we will only give a brief overview, references for further reading given there*, etc.

In contrast, existential *there* is commonly needed in all registers, although there are slight differences in distribution; see also 11.4.7.

## 11.4.6 Simple v. complex existential clauses

Variation in existential clauses relates to two major characteristics: adverbials which are essential for the meaning of the existential clause (chiefly time and place adverbials) and postmodifying elements in the notional subject.

**CORPUS FINDINGS** [6]

➤ Existential clauses generally contain either a complex notional subject or an adverbial expansion.
  ➤ Minimal existential clauses, i.e. clauses which lack both adverbial expansions and subjects with postmodification, are most common in conversation, with academic prose at the other extreme.
➤ Adverbial expansions are most common in conversation, while the written registers are characterized by notional subjects with postmodification.
  ➤ Place adverbials are the most common type of adverbial expansion.
  ➤ Postmodification often takes the form of prepositional phrases and relative clauses.

Table 11.15 **Use of structural expansions in existential clauses; as a percentage of all existential clauses in that register**

each ■ represents 5%    □ represents less than 2.5%

|  | CONV | FICT | NEWS | ACAD |
|---|---|---|---|---|
| no expansion | ■■■■■ | ■■■■ | ■■■ | ■■ |
| **postmodifier in the notional subject** | | | | |
| prepositional phrase | □ | ■■ | ■■■■ | ■■■ |
| relative clause | ■■ | ■ | ■ | ■■ |
| other | ■■ | ■■■■■ | ■■■■■ | ■■■■■ |
| **essential adverbial** | | | | |
| place adverbial | ■■■■■■ | ■■■ | ■■■■ | ■■ |
| other adverbial | ■■ | ■■ | ■■ | ■■ |
| **both postmodifier and adverbial** | ■■ | ■■ | ■ | ■■■ |

➤ Final position for adverbials is by far the most common choice in clauses that have a notional subject without postmodification.
➤ Where the notional subject has postmodification, preferences are less clear. Most often, however, the adverbial is placed towards the end of the clause, either in final position, or in initial-end position.

**DISCUSSION OF FINDINGS**

Two essential elements of existential clauses contain little information: the grammatical subject *there* and the verb *be* (in most cases). As a result, we naturally

**Table 11.16** **Placement of adverbial expansions in existential clauses; as a percentage of all existential clauses with adverbials**

each ■ represents 5%       □ represents less than 2.5%

| | position of the adverbial | | | |
|---|---|---|---|---|
| | initial | initial-end | final | other |
| clause with postmodifier | ■ | ■■ | ■■ | □ |
| clause with no postmodifier | ■ | □ | ■■■■■■■■■■■■■ | □ |

expect the rest of the clause to be more informative. This information is given in the notional subject and, optionally, in an adverbial expansion.

In the written registers, where phrases tend to be complex (2.10), notional subjects with postmodification are more common. In news and academic prose, the high frequency of prepositional phrases in existential clauses agrees with the generally high frequency of prepositions (2.4.14). Adverbial expansions are most common in conversation, which has the highest frequency of adverbs (2.3.5).

Minimal existential clauses occur most frequently in conversation, where there is a tendency to present information in smaller chunks and where information is more often left unexpressed, for the addressee to infer. These minimal structures commonly occur with negation:

> **There isn't any other way** dad? (CONV)

> **There's no bus.** (CONV)

> Yeah, **there really is no excuse**, is there? (CONV)

Existential clauses also often lack adverbial expansions in fiction and news. Where such expansions occur, they most commonly specify existence or occurrence in relation to a place. Place adverbials may be missing because the place is irrelevant or implicit:

> You don't have the personnel, and **there are priorities, political pressures.** (FICT)

> The judges said **there was no indication that the exemption was "other than a genuine response" to the terrorist situation.** (NEWS)

Adverbials are regularly placed at the end of an existential clause, which is the most common position for place adverbials in general (10.2.6). Where there is a notional subject with postmodification, the adverbial is often placed in other positions, either initially (see examples in 11.4.4) or in initial-end position, preceding a postmodifier of the notional subject:

> 1 *There's stuff **in here** we need.* (CONV)

> 2 *In most cases a syllable is represented by only one character, but there are many cases **among the 558** in which the same syllable is written in more ways than one.* (ACAD†)

In most of these cases, the postmodifier is a clause. The initial-end position makes it clear that the adverbial is not part of the following clause, and is also in agreement with the information principle (11.1.1) and the principle of end-weight (11.1.3), because the final postmodifying clause is frequently more complex and/or informative than the adverbial. For example, we understand from the ordering of **1**, assuming stress falls in the default position placing end-focus on *need*, that the key new point being made is that *we need* the stuff, rather than that the stuff is *in here*.

## 11.4.7 Discourse functions of existential clauses

It is generally said that existential *there* is used to present or introduce new elements into the discourse. This agrees with the typical occurrence with an indefinite notional subject. Nevertheless, definite notional subjects do occur (11.4.3). Moreover, existential *there* is by no means necessary to introduce new elements into the discourse. Consider this example, taken from a book on language learning:

> 1 *If you have a picture of a view, the following statements might be made:*
> **There** is a church. **There** is a river. **There** is a path. **There** are trees.
> **There** are flowerbeds. The church is reflected in the water. The trees are
> <...>. The flowers are under the trees. The trees are on both sides of the
> river. The church is in the distance.
>
> Paragraph: The picture is of a river with trees on both sides, and with
> flowerbeds under the trees. A path on the right leads to a church in the
> distance. The trees and the church are reflected in the water.* (ACAD†)

The object of the exercise is to teach students to write a coherent paragraph. When the individual statements are transformed into a prose passage, all examples of existential *there* disappear. Next consider again:

> 2 *A man goes in the pub. **There**'s a bear sitting in the corner. He goes up to
> the, he goes up to the bartender. He says, why is **there** a bear sitting over
> there?* (CONV)

Notice that existential *there* is not used in the first sentence, although a new person is introduced into the discourse: *a man*. But it is used twice in connection with *a bear*. Significantly, the bear is the main protagonist in the story which the speaker is beginning to tell. Furthermore, when spoken, stress would fall on *bear*, which would be in end-focus position in both its clauses.

Given examples of this type, we can conclude that existential *there* is used to focus on the existence or occurrence of something (including the non-existence or non-occurrence of something). As definite noun phrases refer to known entities or phenomena, whose existence is not at issue, existential *there* is most typically used with indefinite notional subjects. The use of existential *there* is in agreement with the information principle (11.1.1), as it serves to delay, and prepare the ground for, new information later in the clause.

One context where it is appropriate to focus on the existence of something is at the beginning of a story. The fairy-tale opening is well-known:

> 3 ***Once upon a time there were three bears***. *Mama bear, Papa bear, baby
> bear – [They] all went for a walk down the woods.* (CONV) <mother
> reading to child>

When used for an opening line in a conversational narrative, the notional subject in an existential clause commonly takes a demonstrative pronoun (see also 11.4.3):

> 4 ***There was this really good-looking bloke*** *and [he] was like – We, we'd
> given each other eyes over the bar in this pub and Lottie goes, well if you
> don't hurry up with [him] I'm gonna go and have [him], if you don't*

*hurry up, you know, and just like marched over. I said, Charlotte give me a break.* (CONV)

5 **There was this rattling sound**. *I placed [it] coming from the kitchen, right? I was thinkin' [it] was Jill coming to bug me to shoot her up again* <...> (FICT†)

6 **There was this wonderful little old lady called the tissue collector**. *[She] was grey haired, quite dumpy with a white coat on and [she] came to collect sperm if you wanted it stored.*

   *[She] came up in front of my parents and said: "Would you like to take this home, put a sample in it and we'll do a sperm count for you?" [She] hands over this little jar and [she] says: "It has to be brought back warm."* (NEWS)

Note also this example from a fictional text:

7 **In the Piazza San Michele on the waterfront at Livorno there is a statue of Ferdinand I**. *At each corner of the pedestal on which the archduke stands, a bronze figure of a naked African slave is chained. For this reason [the statue] is often referred to as I Quattro Mori.* **There is an inscription on the pedestal**, *[the last part of which] reads in Italian as follows:* <...> (FICT†)

What is signalled in all these cases is that something is to be the focus of interest, and it is then picked up by later references in the text.

Another way of using existential *there* as a springboard in developing the text is when it is used to introduce a series of elements:

8 **There are many types of aid to medical decision making available**. *[The earliest ones] used actuarial data and produced recommendations derived from statistical decision theory* <...> (ACAD†)

9 **There are three basic rules to consider in planning a farm enterprise**: <...> (ACAD†)

Frequently, existential *there* constructions occur in a series:

10 *But* **there was** *a stillness about Ralph as he sat that marked him out:* **there was** *his size, and the attractive appearance; and most, obscurely, yet most powerfully,* **there was** *the conch.* (FICT)

11 *It was like heaven.* **There was** *candlelight, and* **there were** *bunks with quilts and blankets heaped on top.* **There was** *a table with a bottle of wine and a loaf of bread and a sausage on it.* **There were** *four bowls of soup.* **There** *were pictures of castles and lakes and pretty girls on the walls.* (FICT)

12 *To reduce the number of wildlife accidents, three categories of possible countermeasures have been discussed. First* **there are** *measures to reduce the populations of game, for example by shooting more animals during the hunting season. Second,* **there are** *measures to prevent animals from entering the carriageway, for example by use of fences or repelling mirrors. In the third category* **there are** *measures intended to make road-users change their driving behaviour, for example signs warning for game-crossings.* (ACAD)

Existential *there* constructions introducing a series of elements seem to focus particularly on the fact that there is a sequence of items, rather than on each individual item.

It may seem strange that definite notional subjects should occur at all in existential *there* constructions. The effect of the existential *there* in some of these cases is to bring something already known back to mind, rather than asserting that it exists:

**13** A: *You won't get so much for twenty-five pound in Marks and Spencers.*
B: *Well, it's not that. What do they sell that you want?*
A: **There's the food place**, *isn't there?* (CONV)

**14** *"Do you know the town of Makara? Is there a medical station there?"*
*But he said that Makara patients had always been brought to him at*
*Kodowa. There wasn't even a trained nurse, only a couple of midwives.*
*Then he brightened.* **"There is the cotton factory,"** *he said.* (FICT)

**15** *The hours of liberty are long, full of wonder and narrow escapes,*
*precautions, hidden devices and daring.* **There was the bull in the river**
**field to be avoided, the idiot boy in the Gate Lodge to tease until his**
**frenzies frightened her and she had to run.** (FICT)

Given that nouns are generally least common in conversation (2.3.5), it is somewhat surprising that existential *there* (used as a special introductory device for nouns) is most common in that register. The reason for the high frequency of existential *there* is no doubt that it agrees with the looser syntactic organization of conversation:

**16** **There's a girl at work**, *and [she]'s a top qualified chef.* (CONV †)
cf. *A girl at work is a top qualified chef.*

**17** **There's the unemployment**, *he ain't mastered [that one].* (CONV)
cf. *He hasn't mastered the unemployment.*

These constructions are reminiscent of dislocation patterns, with prefaces (11.5.3). The use of the existential clause makes it possible to present one unit of information at a time.

The density of existential *there* in conversation is sometimes quite extreme:

**18** A: *Are you going to do any washing?*
B: *Well,* **there is** *some there to do, yeah.*
A: *Put the fire on in here for a little while.*
B: *Well,* **there's** *only not a great deal, I mean* **there's** *a load in there*
*already done, I think, is it done? – Yeah, that's done.*
A: **There's** *the stuff on the floor.*
B: *And* **there's** *that on the floor,* **there's** *a couple of loads there.*
A: *Loads?*
B: *Yeah,* **there's** *the blacks under there.*
A: *Oh,* **is there***? **There's** *black upstairs.*
B: *And* **there's** *black upstairs, that have to be put in.* (CONV)

Here existential *there* comes in handy as a device for bringing attention to things which are to be done.

In contrast, the lower frequency of existential *there* in the written registers (especially news) is the result of planned language production, so that the writer can pack more information into a single clause. We have seen evidence elsewhere of the tight information packaging in news, e.g. high lexical density (2.2.9) and a high degree of noun phrase complexity (8.1.1). A lower frequency of existential *there* is in agreement with this. On the other hand, fiction and academic prose contain types of writing which seem to favour the use of existential *there*, in particular description (**7, 11**) and argumentation (**12**).

## 11.4.8 Existential clause v. locative inversion

Where there is an opening place adverbial, existential clauses appear to be closely related to constructions with locative subject-verb inversion (11.2.3.1B):

> **Behind the sundial there were a few trees, some of them in flower**: *a small path led into their deceptive shallow depths, and [there, in a hollow a few yards from a high brick wall that bordered the garden, stood a sculpture].* (FICT)

In this passage, we find existential *there* and locative inversion (in *[]*) in the same orthographic sentence. Note that the opening of the last main clause contains locative *there*: unlike existential *there* it must be spoken with stress, and is in initial focus position in its clause. Its locative meaning is made explicit by the following more precise specification of position.

Although existential clauses and locative inversion appear to be identical in use, the choice is by no means indiscriminate.

### 11.4.8.1 Existential clause v. locative inversion: distribution

This section is based on an analysis of all sentences beginning with three prepositions having a locative core meaning: *behind*, *beside*, or *between*. The sample represents only a selection of the relevant constructions.

**CORPUS FINDINGS [1]**

➤ The majority of instances of both types were found in fiction: 44% for existential *there* and 77% for locative inversion.

➤ Existential clauses are overwhelmingly marked by the verb *be* and indefinite notional subjects.
> ➤ Over 95% of all existential clauses occur with the verb *be*.
> ➤ c. 90% of all existential clauses occur with indefinite notional subjects.

➤ In contrast, locative inversion occurs about half the time with verbs other than *be*. In addition, locative inversion occurs with definite inverted subjects about 35% of the time.

➤ Locative inversion is far more common than existential *there* in the material included in the survey.

**DISCUSSION OF FINDINGS**

While existential clauses place focus on something whose existence or occurrence is being asserted (11.4.7) and often lack an adverbial expansion (11.4.6), constructions with locative inversion place focus on the particular place where something is found or happens. We find a variety of verbs:

> 1 *Round her **burned** iron-spiked circles of tapering candles, yellow-bright in the dark. Before her **lay** heaps of flowers.* (FICT†)
> 2 *Behind her **trailed** a gaggle of over-age girls-about-town all with their eyes open for the main chance.* (FICT)
> 3 *Behind him **can be seen** a picture of the Tibetan director.* (NEWS)

Other verbs found with locative inversion include: *hang, march, run, sit, stoop, stretch, stride, swell, swim, walk*. These are all verbs which describe position or movement.

As the focus is less on existence with locative inversion, we also find a higher number of definite noun phrases than in existential clauses:

4 *Beside Zella sat **Arnie himself**.* (FICT†)

5 *Behind, walked **Sgt Forth's widow Gill, and their son Christopher**.* (NEWS†)

6 *Key divisions along the palate are represented in Figure 1. Behind the upper teeth is **the alveolar ridge**, a source of some confusion in articulatory descriptions.* (ACAD)

These noun phrases have none of the meaning of 'bringing something back to mind', which is often characteristic of existential clauses with definite notional subjects (11.4.7). The bulk of the subject noun phrases are indefinite, however, as they serve to introduce new information (as in **1–3** above). This brings us to the core meaning of clauses with locative inversion.

Clauses with locative inversion present a situation before our eyes, from the initial starting-point (typically a location defined in relation to something given in the context), through the type of position or movement specified by the verb, to the person or thing in focus. Note particularly example **5** above, which describes a procession, and example **6**, which refers to a figure in the text.

Locative inversion is relatively common in fiction (see also 11.2.3.1B), where it is natural to include descriptions of settings. Although existential *there* can also occur in such contexts, its area of use is wider than locative inversion. It is easy to find examples of existential *there* where locative inversion would be inappropriate or less felicitous:

7 *Between the sisters **there was love of a singularly pure kind, proof against many trials**.* (FICT)

8 *Between the two of them **there was no pretence**.* (FICT)

9 *At that moment a rifle cracked. The bullet pinged against the railings, and whirred off on a ricochet. The leader checked suddenly, undecided. Behind him **there was an outbreak of curses, and a scream or two**.* (FICT)

10 *He was sitting behind his desk. Beside him **there was a calendar with a square red frame around yesterday's date**. He moved [the red frame] and felt [its] magnetic base gripping the surface again.* (FICT)

Examples **7** and **8** describe relationships, but not in physical terms. In **9** the focus is on the occurrence of events, which cannot be located visually. Straightforward location is described in **10**, but here the existential clause is used as a springboard in the further development of the text, so the existential choice is more appropriate.

To conclude, locative inversion is restricted in use compared with existential *there* and is particularly associated with fiction. After an opening place adverbial, however, it is far more common than existential *there*.

## 11.4.9 Existential constructions with *there* v. *have*

Clauses with existential *there* are often compared with structures containing a noun-phrase subject preceding the verb *have*:

1 *Att'y <= Attorney>: then I advise you to get a taco burger, try that one. Duke: ... the taco **has** meat in it. I'll try that one.* (FICT)
   cf. **There** *is meat in the taco.*

2 *The door **has** a fairly big opening in it at eye-level through which some daylight filters, and the wall on either side of it is furnished with hooks.* (FICT)
   cf. **There** *is a fairly big opening in the door.*

Although the two constructions overlap, they differ both in meaning and function even in instances where both are possible.

In *have*-existentials a predication is made of the noun phrase in subject position, so the clause in effect tells 'This is what the taco/door is like'. Focus falls on the new information (e.g. *meat* in **1**), which follows the substantive piece of given information (*the taco*), even though *in it* provides a further lightweight and unfocused reference to it at the end of the clause. In the *there*-clause, on the other hand, the attention is drawn to the existence of something in some location, and new information precedes old. Consequently the *have*-existential in **1** has a more natural starting point than the corresponding *there*-construction for picking up a referent introduced in the preceding sentence, thus making for cohesion. The use of the *have*-existential in **2** provides similar starting points for the two coordinate clauses (saying something about the door and the wall, respectively). Furthermore, the lightness of *in it* in the *have*-existential in **2** makes it easier to add a postponed postmodifying relative clause to *opening*, whereas the relative clause would be less appropriate in the corresponding *there*-existential, where the more substantial phrase *in the door* intervenes:

*?There is a fairly big opening in the door at eye-level through which some daylight filters, and the wall on either side of it is furnished with hooks.*

*There*-existentials are by far the more common option, and were therefore the focus of attention in this section.

# 11.5   Dislocation

**Dislocation** has to do with the distribution of information, but it is not a simple word-order option. There are two major types of dislocation: **prefaces** (3.4.3) and **noun phrase tags** (3.4.4A). Both types involve a definite noun phrase occurring in a peripheral position, with a co-referent pronoun in the core of the clause. Prefaces occur in initial position:

***This girl** this morning **she** threw a wobbly.* (CONV)

In contrast, noun phrase tags occur in final position:

*I think **he**'s getting hooked on the taste of Vaseline, **that dog**.* (CONV)

The discourse functions of dislocation (see 11.5.3) may be seen as primarily concerned with:

• information flow
• emphasis.

## 11.5.1 Prefaces

Prefaces may precede both declarative and interrogative clauses. The relationship between the preface and the clause it is attached to may vary. In many cases, the preface is co-referent with a subject pronoun; for example (with co-referential pronoun in *[]*):

1 ***Sharon** [she] plays bingo on Sunday night.* (CONV)
2 ***All that money**, I mean, in the end is [it] worth rescuing?* (CONV)
3 ***That picture of a frog**, where is [it]?* (CONV)
4 *"**That crazy Siberian, what's his name**, [he] got one of the best houses in town."* (FICT†)
5 *"**The guy who opened the new boutique**, you know, **the little guy with the turban**, [he] said he might be hiring."* (FICT)

However, a preface can also be co-referent with an object pronoun:

6 *Well **Bryony** it seemed to be a heavy cold that was making [her] feel miserable.* (CONV)
7 *"But **Anna-Luise**—what could have attracted [her] to a man in his fifties?"* (FICT)

The pronoun may be embedded in a dependent clause, as in **6**.

The preface and the pronoun may be adjacent, as in **1**, **4**, and **5**, or separated, as in the other examples. This implies that the option is not chosen primarily for the purposes of re-ordering the information presented.

## 11.5.2 Noun phrase tags

Noun phrase tags may follow both declarative and interrogative clauses. The tag is normally co-referent with the subject of the preceding clause:

*Has [it] got double doors **that shop**?* (CONV)
*Did [they] have any, **the kids**?* (CONV)

The tags here serve as clarifications, establishing beyond doubt the reference of the preceding pronoun.

## 11.5.3 Prefaces and noun phrase tags: distribution

**CORPUS FINDINGS** [2]

➤ Prefaces and noun phrase tags are almost exclusively conversational features:
  ➤ Both types of dislocation occur over 200 times per million words in conversation and occasionally in fictional dialogue, but very rarely in written prose.

**DISCUSSION OF FINDINGS**

Prefaces and noun phrase tags are well suited to the needs of conversation. Rather than integrating all the information in the core of the clause, the speaker separates out crucial bits of information which are then attached more loosely to the clause, at the same time as a co-referent pronoun in the core of the clause indicates how the preface or the tag is related to the main proposition.

Prefaces serve to establish a topic. The same work can be done by separate clauses:

1 A: *When I went to the hospital today,* **there was this girl**, *right*
   B: *Yes*
   A: *[She] took an overdose.* (CONV†)

2 **What about your secondary school**? *Did you still go [there]?* (CONV)

3 **Do you know the woman at the end of our road**? *Takes me to – school every day. – [She]'s got a D reg Sierra – with a, a locking petrol cap – something went wrong with this other one.* (CONV)

In **1** the topic is new information established through an existential clause; in **2** and **3** it is information that is known to the hearers, but which might not be uppermost in their minds, so is primed by interrogative constructions.

Prefaces are a sign of the evolving nature of conversation. Note how the first speaker in **1** appeals to the addressee by adding the discourse marker *right*. The addressee responds and the original speaker goes on to the main point. In **4**, the addressee picks up the topic before the first speaker gets to the proposition:

4 A: **That woman on** **Terminator**
   B: *[She]'s ugly.*
   A: *[She]'s not.* (CONV)

The discourse functions of noun phrase tags are more difficult to pin down. Frequently they have a clarifying function (see the examples in 11.5.2, 14.3.2.4D). As they are co-referent with the subject, they can perhaps be regarded as retrospective topic markers: a speaker has treated something as given information by referring to it with a pronoun, but then realizes that it may be unknown or the reference unclear. Sometimes they may serve the principle of end-weight:

"*[It] must have come as a bit of a shock,* **the idea of**, *er,* **Rhiannon coming and settling down here after everything**." (FICT)

Unlike prefaces, however, which are regularly realized by full noun phrases, tags may consist of a demonstrative pronoun:

5 *[It] was a good book* **this**. (CONV)

6 *[That]'s marvellous* **that**, *isn't it yes?* (CONV)

The noun phrase tag in such examples serves to emphasize the proposition, in much the same way as declarative tags (3.4.4C).

The use of noun phrase tags fits in with the general characteristics of conversation: the clarifying function with the evolving nature of conversation, the emphasizing function with the prevalence of emotive expressions.

# 11.6 Clefting

Clefting is similar to dislocation in the sense that information that could be given in a single clause is broken up, in this case into two clauses, each with its own verb (cf. 3.6.5). There are two major types of cleft constructions: *it*-clefts and *wh*-clefts.

*it*-cleft:

**It's a man I want**. *Just a man. That's all.* (FICT†)
*cf. I want a man.*

*wh*-cleft:

**What I want is something to eat**, *now!* (CONV)
*cf. I want something to eat.*

Both cleft types (and the reversed variant of *wh*-cleft; 11.6.3) are used to bring particular elements into additional focus, which may be contrastive. The extra focused element normally appears early in *it*-clefts and late in *wh*-clefts, a property which means that these structures are also connected with information distribution and cohesion (11.6.4).

## 11.6.1   *It*-clefts

*It*-clefts consist of:

- the pronoun *it*
- a form of the verb *be*, optionally accompanied by the negator *not* or an adverb such as *only*
- the specially focused element, which may be of the following types: a noun phrase, a prepositional phrase, an adverb phrase, or an adverbial clause
- a relative-like dependent clause introduced by *that*, *who/which*, or zero, whose last element receives normal end-focus.

The specially focused element is in bold in the examples below and the dependent clause placed in *[]*; a variety of focused elements is illustrated, corresponding to various grammatical roles in the dependent clause:

1   *His eyes were clear and brown and filled with an appropriate country slyness. It was **his voice** [that held me].* (FICT) <noun phrase; subject>

2   *It was only **for the carrot** [that they put up with his abominable parties].* (FICT†) <prepositional phrase; reason adverbial>

3   *It is **to this discussion** [that we now turn].* (ACAD) <preposition of prepositional verb plus object noun phrase>

4   *It is **here** [that the finite element analysis comes into its own].* (ACAD) <adverb; place adverbial>

5   *It was **because they were frightened**, he thought, [that they had grown so small].* (FICT) <clause; reason adverbial>

In a rare variant of *it*-clefts, the focused element is placed in initial position:

6   *The ceremony was in the hands of Mr Alexander Dubcek, who <...> **He** it was [who ushered in the new head of state to the dais in Prague Castle where the oath was sworn].* (NEWS†)

The combination of fronting and the *it*-cleft construction has a restricting effect: 'it was he and no one else'.

## 11.6.2   *Wh*-clefts

*Wh*-clefts consist of:

- a clause introduced by a *wh*-word, usually *what*, with its own point of focus, typically at its end
- a form of the verb *be*
- the specially focused element: a noun phrase, an infinitive clause, or a finite nominal clause.

The specially focused element is in bold in the examples below, and the dependent *wh*-clause placed in *[]*:

1   *[What I really need] is **another credit card**.* (CONV) <noun phrase; direct object>

2 *"[What I do object to] is **violence on TV**."* (NEWS) <noun phrase; object of prepositional verb>

3 *[What you should do] is **tag them when they come in**.* (CONV) <bare infinitive clause; predicate>

4 *[What he did] was **to go to Holy Trinity Church**.* (FICT†) <*to*-infinitive clause; predicate>

5 *"[What they will be hoping for] is **that they can get to a few months before the next election, take the brakes off and try to deceive people once again things are back on course**."* (NEWS) <*that*-clause; complement of verb *hope*>

*Wh*-clefts are less flexible than *it*-clefts in that they cannot be used to focus on a prepositional phrase, an adverb phrase, or an adverbial clause. Compare:

6 *[What she admires in him] is **the unwounded boy of twenty years ago**. It is **to that boy** [that she has remained faithful]. The other boy, who is drinking his tea, is watching her.* (FICT)

While an *it*-cleft is possible as an alternative to the *wh*-cleft in the first sentence here (i.e. *It is the unwounded boy that she admires*), there is no alternative to the *it*-cleft in the second sentence. *Wh*-clefts, on the other hand, permit focus on a nominal clause and on the verb plus accompanying elements in the predicate (as in **3**, **4**, and **5** above); this possibility is excluded with *it*-clefts.

## 11.6.3    Reversed *wh*-clefts

Some **reversed *wh*-clefts** look exactly like ordinary *wh*-clefts, apart from the position of the *wh*-clause in relation to the focused element. The focused element is in bold in the examples below, and the *wh*-clause placed in *[]*:

1 *A: And you can fly on a Sunday – from Birmingham.*
  *B: Yeah. It's a lot.*
  *A: to there.*
  *C: Yeah?*
  *A: You see **a weekend flight** is [what you want].* (CONV) <noun phrase; direct object>

2 *To all appearances he was drifting. In actuality he was drifting. **Drifting** is [what one does when looking at lateral truth].* (FICT) <*ing*-participle; verb phrase>

3 *"There's a lot more darkness in this second TV series compared with the last one but **darkness** is [what comedy is all about]."* (NEWS†) <noun phrase; complement of preposition>

4 *"Poor Albert," Carrie said <...> He heard what she said and shouted down to her. "**Help** is [what I want], not your pity."* (FICT†) <noun phrase; direct object>

5 *Suppose we believe that **snow** is [what is muffling the sound of traffic], or that flipping the switch made the windscreen wipers start to work, or that it is **the position of the car's heater** [that accounts for the driver's left knee being warm].* (ACAD) <noun phrases; subjects>

In examples **1** to **3** the focused element is picked up from the preceding text, which accounts for the early placement. The initial placement in **4** seems to be used for rhetorical effect; the order underlines the contrast between *help* in initial position and *your pity* at the end. Example **5** illustrates how reversed *wh*-clefts and *it*-clefts can be used in the same context, with much the same effect.

A very common type of structure contains a demonstrative pronoun (usually *that*) followed by a form of *be* plus a dependent clause introduced by a *wh*-word:

  **6** ***That's what*** *I thought.* (CONV†)

  **7** ***That's how*** *I spent my summer vacation.* (FICT)

  **8** ***That's why*** *we asked.* (NEWS†)

  **9** ***This is what*** *it means to say such systems are effective mixing devices.* (ACAD)

Although these structures are not normally reversible (cf. *\*What I thought was that*, *\*How I spent my summer was that*, etc.), they are structurally related to reversed *wh*-clefts. Moreover, like **1** to **3** above, they open with a reference to the preceding text. In the discussion below they will be referred to as **demonstrative *wh*-clefts**.

## 11.6.4  Cleft constructions: distribution

Four major types of cleft constructions are distinguished for distributional analysis:

- *It*-clefts (11.6.1)
- Ordinary *wh*-clefts (11.6.2), including occasional related constructions: *all I did was ...*, *all it takes is ...*, etc.
- Reversed *wh*-clefts (11.6.3), including occasional related constructions: *I'm the one who ...*, *they're the ones who ...*, etc.
- Demonstrative *wh*-clefts (11.6.3), including occasional related constructions: *that was the reason why ...*, *here is where*, etc.

> **CORPUS FINDINGS** [2]

➤ *It*-clefts are relatively common in all registers but most frequent in academic prose.
➤ Ordinary *wh*-clefts are most frequent in conversation.
➤ Reversed *wh*-clefts are infrequent in all registers.
➤ The distribution of demonstrative *wh*-clefts is sharply stratified by register: common in conversation and rare in academic prose.

**Table 11.17**  **Distribution of cleft constructions across registers; occurrences per million words**

each ■ represents 100    ▢ represents less than 50

|  | CONV | FICT | NEWS | ACAD |
|---|---|---|---|---|
| *it*-cleft | ■■■■ | ■■■■ | ■■ | ■■■■■■ |
| ordinary *wh*-cleft | ■■■ | ■■ | ■ | ■ |
| reversed *wh*-cleft | ■ | ■ | ▢ | ▢ |
| demonstrative *wh*-cleft | ■■■■■■■■■ | ■■■ | ■ | ▢ |

➤ In conversation, demonstrative *wh*-clefts are particularly common with the patterns *that is/was/etc. what ...* and *that is/was/etc. why ...* (occurring c. 500 and 200 times per million words respectively).[1]

➤ The patterns *that is/was/etc. how/where/when* each occur around 50 times per million words in conversation.

➤ Demonstrative *wh*-clefts with *this* (*this is/was/etc. what/why/where*) are considerably less common.

### DISCUSSION OF FINDINGS

Although all cleft constructions give prominence, there are important differences between the types. Some of these differences have to do with the form of the elements that can be highlighted (11.6.1–3). Others have to do with the type of prominence expressed.

*It*-clefts are typically contrastive; the contrast is often quite explicit:

1 *But it wasn't **the colour of his eyes** that was peculiar to him, it was the way he walked.* (FICT)

The focused element in an *it*-cleft is not infrequently a pronoun or some other form which expresses given information:

2 *I think it was **me** that was being a bit, got a bit het up.* (CONV†)

3 *It was **then** that she and the three other women who formed a team for one section of the building did the room.* (FICT†)

4 *These are the faculties which make clerks into merchants, and merchants into millionaires. It is **these** which enable the discontented clerk to earn more than eighty pounds a year.* (ACAD)

The early position of the focused element makes it suitable both for expressing a connection with the preceding text and for expressing contrast.

With ordinary *wh*-clefts, the focused element is at the end, in agreement with the information principle (11.1.1). The purpose of the construction is to signal explicitly what is taken as background and what is the main communicative point:

5 *There was an enormous expansion of credit to finance cumulative budget deficits of $1,400 billion. What was worrying about this phenomenon was **its accompaniment by financial hooligans**.* (NEWS)

6 *No that's Nescafé. What we usually have is **Maxwell House from work**.* (CONV)

The *wh*-clause in **5** carries an explicit reference to the preceding text: *this phenomenon*. Example **6** occurs in a context where different sorts of coffee are discussed. In both cases, the main communicative point is given at the end.

While the focused element of ordinary *wh*-clefts expresses new information, it is typically context-dependent in reversed *wh*-clefts and demonstrative *wh*-clefts (see the examples in 11.6.3). Indeed, the main purpose of demonstrative *wh*-clefts is to underline or sum up what has been said or written in the preceding text. Compare the use of three types of cleft in this example:

7 ***It is motherhood not man-eating that is now uppermost in the 46-year-old Oscar-winner's mind**. "I would love another child but I have to be aware of the possibility that I'm not going to be able to have one of my own," she says. "**That's why adoption appeals. What I would like is a multi-racial child**."* (NEWS)

The example opens with an *it*-cleft expressing an explicit contrast and ends with a *wh*-cleft which moves from given to new information. In between there is a demonstrative *wh*-cleft which expresses a conclusion based on what the speaker has just said.

The register distribution of cleft constructions is somewhat surprising, since they are found in both conversation and the formal written registers. Notice, first of all, that cleft constructions are syntactically integrated, making use of function words to build a close-knit structure. This is the probable reason why clefting, unlike dislocation, is common both in conversation and in the written registers.

*It*-clefts are especially common in academic prose, because they allow very precise statements to be made. They are also useful in other ways:

> It is in fact the case that whereas not all the early investigators even tried to validate their reasoning, several, including Cauchy, Servois and Boole, certainly did. And *[it was in this connection that Servois, in 1815, introduced the notions of functions which are 'distributive' and 'commutative', terms still used today (see Section 1.2)]. [It was in this atmosphere that Peacock, his friends Babbage and Herschel having worked in the calculus of operations, introduced (1830, 1833, 1842) his two concepts of algebra: arithmetic algebra and symbolic algebra].* (ACAD)

The information in the subordinate clauses is here presented as known, as something which is not at issue. It has been pointed out that such clefts are characteristic of written texts where the writer does not wish to take responsibility for the truth or originality of the statement.

The association between *wh*-clefts and conversation has probably to do with the low information content that we frequently find in the *wh*-clause. A speaker may use a *wh*-clause as a springboard in starting an utterance: *what I think ...*, *what I want to say ...*, *what we need ...*, *what this means ....* Reversed *wh*-clefts have the properties of fronted elements and are infrequent, like fronted elements in general.

The most striking differences have to do with demonstrative *wh*-clefts. The register distribution, with conversation and academic prose at opposite ends, suggests that the difference is one of formality. This is supported by the behaviour of constructions opening with *this* and *that*; the more formal *this* is, in fact, the preferred form in academic prose (although rare compared to other devices). The very common use of *that's what*, *that's why*, etc. in conversation is probably also connected with the high degree of repetitiveness in this register (2.2.1, 13.2 and 14.2.2), since demonstrative *wh*-clefts typically sum up what has been said or written in the preceding discourse.

## 11.7 Syntactic choices in conversation v. academic prose

With the exception of passives and existential clauses, the choices dealt with in this chapter are relatively rare. This does not mean that these choices are unimportant. When they are used, they are significant and contribute to the building of a coherent text. Moreover, the use of these devices varies by register.

The relationship between syntactic choices and register is clearly seen if we contrast some features of conversation and academic prose, i.e. the registers which tend to differ most. In the following, + and − indicate a higher v. lower relative frequency in the two registers:

|                              | CONV | ACAD |
|------------------------------|:----:|:----:|
| marked word order            |  −   |  +   |
| passive constructions        |  −   |  +   |
| existential *there*          |  +   |  −   |
| prefaces and noun phrase tags |  +   |  −   |
| demonstrative *wh*-clefts    |  +   |  −   |

Word-order variation and passive constructions are compatible with the complex structures of academic prose, which in turn reflect the complexity of content and the opportunity to edit and re-write.

Conversation, on the other hand, is produced on the spur of the moment. The online production is eased by the use of prefaces and tags and, in general, by shorter and simpler clauses, including minimal existential clauses. The language of conversation is also less varied (cf. 2.2.1 and 14.1.2.7), and relies on demonstrative *wh*-clefts and other more-or-less fixed expressions (cf. 13.2).

# 12

# The grammatical marking of stance

*See page xiii for contents in detail*

## 12.1 Overview

In addition to communicating propositional content, speakers and writers commonly express personal feelings, attitudes, value judgments, or assessments; that is, they express a 'stance'. The present chapter surveys the major linguistic devices used to express stance, describing the range of meanings associated with these forms, and the ways in which speakers and writers exploit those resources. In doing so, we connect a number of topics discussed separately in other chapters (especially Chapters 6–10).

Stance meanings can be expressed in many ways, including **grammatical** devices, word choice, and **paralinguistic** devices. To some extent, personal stance can be conveyed through paralinguistic devices such as loudness, pitch, and duration, as well as non-linguistic devices such as body position and gestures. Such expression of stance is not linguistically explicit, and as a result it can be unclear just what attitudes or feelings a speaker is intending to convey. Further, in writing there are few non-linguistic or paralinguistic devices available for the expression of stance. For example, there is nothing in the way the present paragraph is printed that conveys the author's personal stance—whether it was written 'angrily' or 'happily', or whether the author thought the content was 'boring' or 'amazing'.

For these reasons, both speakers and writers commonly express stance meanings overtly, using either grammatical or lexical means. With grammatical marking, some grammatical device is used to express a stance relative to another proposition. Two common devices are **adverbials** (Chapter 10) and **complement clauses** with verbs and adjectives (Chapter 9). Stance adverbials express the attitude or assessment of the speaker/writer with respect to the proposition contained in the main clause:

> *Obviously your parents don't care what you do.* (CONV)

> *Unfortunately it's true.* (CONV)

In contrast, with complement clauses the main clause verb or adjectival predicate can express speaker stance with respect to the proposition in the complement clause (in *[ ]*):

> *I really doubt [that the check is there].* (CONV)

> *To me it's just amazing [that people <...> are upset about making eight million dollars a year].* (CONV†)

Stance meanings can also be conveyed through lexical choice alone, as in:

> *I hate my job and I hate the BS that I go through.* (CONV)

> *They're very nice, cats are.* (CONV)

Such value-laden words differ from grammatical stance devices in that they do not provide an attitudinal or evaluative frame for some other proposition.

In many cases, an expression of stance is overtly attributed to some third person rather than to the speaker/writer, as in:

> *Susie really will be surprised when she sees him.* (CONV)

> *She thinks that Pam's just acting like a spoiled brat.* (CONV)

Further, many expressions of stance are not directly attributed to any specific person, as in:

*It would be possible to suppose, for instance, that the true Schrodinger-like equation involves non-linearities.* (ACAD†)

The analysis of stance in fiction is especially problematic in that there are multiple 'voices' to consider. From one point of view, most modern fiction might be considered 'stanceless' because the author rarely expresses his or her own personal attitudes or evaluations. However, it is very common for fictional characters to express stance. In addition, we are often told the private thoughts and attitudes of fictional characters even when they are not expressed in dialog:

*I **hoped** it might calm my juddering nerves.* (FICT)

*How I **wished** I could buy him a record-player for all those useless records.* (FICT)

*I **wondered** suddenly whether her unexpected visit could have anything to do with my phone call.* (FICT)

In our discussion of fiction below, we focus on the stance of fictional characters rather than of the author.

The present chapter focuses primarily on grammatical stance devices. While value-laden word choice and paralinguistic devices can reflect underlying attitudes or feelings, they do not overtly express an evaluative frame for some other proposition. However, these are important mechanisms used to express stance, and thus we present a brief overview of their use in the following two subsections. In 12.2–5, then, we provide a more detailed survey of the use of grammatical stance devices in English.

## 12.1.1  Paralinguistic and non-linguistic devices

In conversation, emotive and attitudinal stance meanings can be conveyed through a number of non-linguistic means (such as body posture, facial expressions, and gestures) and paralinguistic devices (such as pitch, intensity, and duration). As a result, it might be argued that speakers in conversation express a kind of linguistically covert stance with every utterance, even when the speaker does not directly articulate a stance. To understand the implied stance in these cases, we must be able to infer the feelings and attitudes from the speaker's intonation, facial expressions, etc.

Analysis of extra-linguistic devices is beyond the scope of the present grammar. However, our knowledge of such devices is sometimes invoked by speakers and writers who describe the way in which participants speak. In particular, manner adverbs following a speech-act verb are commonly reported in fiction to reflect an underlying attitude, as in:

*'He's really upset,' Irmgard said **nervously**.* (FICT)

*'I don't see how you can know that', she said, **severely** again.* (FICT)

*'Do you?' Helen spoke **angrily**.* (FICT)

Similar devices are also occasionally found in news:

*'I will kill you if you don't behave,' he said **flatly**.* (NEWS)

*To test my own four-year-old's reaction, I asked her, 'If your sister is a girl, what is your brother?' A long pause followed, and then she said **tartly**: 'a mouse'.*

*I said rather **disappointedly**, 'Why did you say that?' The prompt reply was, 'ask a silly question, and you get a silly answer'.* (NEWS)

Note that there is nothing in the quoted speech of these characters that overtly conveys the attributed stances of nervousness, severity, anger, flatness, disappointment, etc. However, as readers we have no difficulty imagining the tone of voice and body gestures that could accompany these attitudes or feelings.

Fiction writers are especially fond of these devices, using an extremely wide array of adverbs to convey the stance of fictional characters when they speak. Such manner-of-speaking adverbs modifying speech-act verbs occur over 500 times per million words in fiction. The following list includes only a small sample:

> *bitterly, bullishly, casually, despairingly, desperately, dismissively, earnestly, eagerly, emotionally, happily, impishly, incredulously, ominously, optimistically, proudly, waggishly, wistfully, wryly.*

## 12.1.2    Lexical marking of stance

Affective or evaluative word choice differs from grammatical stance marking in that it involves only a single proposition, rather than a stance relative to some other proposition. With such value-laden words, the existence of a stance is inferred from the use of an evaluative lexical item, usually an adjective, main verb, or noun. In many instances, such expressions are used to directly attribute an emotional or attitudinal state to the speaker, such as:

> *I'm not **happy**!* (CONV)    *Yeah, I **love** that film.* (CONV)

In other cases, lexical stance expressions simply assert that an evaluative property is true of some person or object, as in:

> *The nurses are **wonderful** there.* (CONV)    *This cake is **lovely**.* (CONV)
>
> *He's a **jerk**.* (FICT)

Many of the most common words in English are evaluative and used for the lexical expression of stance. In conversation, the most common predicative adjectives include *good, lovely, nice,* and *right* (all occurring more than 100 times per million words; 7.5.1). These forms are typically used to express positive feelings attributed to a pronoun, which often refers to the general situation, as in:

> *Oh, that's **nice**.* (CONV)    *That was **good**.* (CONV)

Several of the most common attributive adjectives in conversation are also evaluative, including *bad, good, nice,* and *right*:

> *We all thought it was a really **good** value.* (CONV)
>
> *You could probably buy a **nice** little two-bedroom bungalow.* (CONV)

Verbs in simple declarative sentences are also used in conversation for lexical expressions of stance. For example, the most common verbs in conversation include *like, love, need,* and *want,* which express an emotion or attitude towards whatever is referred to by the direct object (cf. 5.2.2.2):

> *I **love** the color of the rice.* (CONV)
>
> *I **need** another coat-hanger.* (CONV)

Such lexical expressions of stance are not restricted to conversation. For example, in academic prose the most common predicative adjectives include *difficult, important, likely, necessary, possible, true* (7.5.1). Although these forms usually control a following complement clause, they can also be used as direct lexical expressions of stance:

> *These experiments are **difficult**.* (ACAD†)
>
> *The abnormality may be very minor or it may be vitally **important**.* (ACAD)

Similarly, several of the most common attributive adjectives in academic prose are also evaluative (7.4.2), including *appropriate, good/best, important, practical, useful*:

> To produce the **best** results the plant should be supplied with water that contains no contamination. (ACAD†)

> The division of economic functions has temporarily outstripped the development of **appropriate** moral regulation. (ACAD†)

As all the above examples illustrate, purely lexical expressions of stance depend on the context and shared background for their interpretation. There is nothing in the grammatical structure of these expressions to show that they mark stance: they are simple declarative structures that give the appearance of presenting stanceless 'facts'. Stance is in a sense embedded in these structures, dependent on the addressee's ability to recognize the use of value-laden words.

# 12.2   Major grammatical devices used to express stance

Grammatical stance devices—the focus of the present chapter—include two distinct linguistic components, one presenting the stance and the other presenting a proposition that is framed by that stance. In the following sections, we survey the structure, meanings, and register distribution of the major grammatical devices used to mark stance. The nature of the two components in relation to each device type is explained in the discussion following A to E below.

**A   Stance adverbials (cf. 10.3)**

- single adverbs and adverb phrases
  > **Unfortunately**, we cannot do anything about it. (NEWS)
- hedges (a sub-class of adverbs)
  > He's **kind of** talked himself into it. (CONV)
- prepositional phrases
  > **In actual fact** only a fraction of this number actually occurs. (ACAD)
- adverbial clauses
  > **As one might expect**, Gauss didn't collaborate much with others. (ACAD)
- comment clauses (a sub-class of finite adverbial clauses)
  > You just have to try and accept it, **I guess**. (CONV)

**B   Stance complement clauses**

- controlled by a verb (cf. 9.2.2, 9.4.2)
  > I just **hope** that I've plugged it in properly. (CONV)
- controlled by an adjective (9.2.5.1, 9.4.5.2)
  > I'm **very happy** that we're going to Sarah's. (CONV)
- extraposed structures (9.2.3, 9.2.5.2, 9.4.3, 9.4.5.3)
  > It's **amazing** that judges can get away with outrageous statements. (NEWS)
- controlled by a noun (8.12–14)
  > **The fact** that he will get away with attacking my daughter is obscene. (NEWS)

C   **Modals and semi-modals (6.6)**

> I *might* be up before you go. (CONV)
>
> She *has to* go to a special school. (CONV)

D   **Stance noun + prepositional phrase**

> They deny *the possibility* of a death wish lurking amidst the gardens of lust. (ACAD)

E   **Premodifying stance adverb (stance adverb + adjective or noun phrase) (cf. 7.13.1, 7.14.2.4, 7.14.2.6)**

> I'm *so* happy for you. Honestly, I'm *really* happy for you. (CONV)
>
> Orogenies and accompanying metamorphism of *about* this age (that is, *about* 478 million years B.P.) have been recognised. (ACAD†)

These major construction types form a cline in the extent to which they represent grammatical marking of stance. The clearest cases are stance adverbials and complement clause constructions. In these cases, there are two distinct structural components: one expressing the stance, while the other is a clause that presents the proposition framed by the stance expression.

The use of modal verbs is less clearly grammatical marking of stance, because the modal verb (as stance marker) is incorporated into the main clause (expressing the framed proposition). Stance noun + prepositional phrase constructions have two distinct components, but it is not always clear that the prepositional phrase actually presents a 'proposition'. Finally, adverb premodifiers are incorporated into a phrase and have local scope only within that phrase, rather than reporting a stance towards an entire proposition.

Stance nouns taking a prepositional phrase complement have not been discussed as a class elsewhere in the grammar. However, these nouns include many of the same nouns that can control noun complement clauses (8.14), such as *fact, hope,* and *fear*:

> If the second prevails, **the fact** [of the defendant's fault] is decisive against him. (ACAD)
>
> There's **no hope** [for their future]. (FICT)
>
> **My fear** [of dentists] dates back to my earliest experiences in the twenties. (FICT)

In addition, many stance adjectives and verbs that can control *that-* or *to-* complement clauses have abstract noun counterparts that take prepositional phrase complements. Such nominalizations, some of which can also take noun complement clauses (8.14), include *possibility, probability, likelihood, importance, need, necessity, requirement, certainty*:

> Many of those who were interested in investing were still not aware of **the importance** [of pre-registering]. (NEWS)
>
> There is also **a need** [for joint detailed pre-planning for disasters]. (NEWS)
>
> On the other hand, the greater the branching in the alkane, the less is **the likelihood** [of the appearance of the molecular ion ]. (ACAD)

## 12.2.1 Variability in the structural characteristics of stance devices

The grammatical devices used to mark stance differ structurally in many important ways. First, they come from many structural levels: words (e.g. adverbs such as *unfortunately*), phrases (e.g. prepositional phrases functioning as adverbials, such as *in actual fact*), and clauses (e.g. adverbial clauses, like *as one might expect*).

Second, single-word stance markers can come from a wide range of word classes, including adverb (e.g. *surprisingly*), lexical verb (e.g. *love*), modal verb (e.g. *might*), predicative adjective (e.g. *essential*), and noun (e.g. *importance*).

Third, the structural relation between the constituent presenting the personal stance and the constituent presenting the qualified proposition can vary. In many cases, the proposition is given in the main clause, with the stance marker occurring in some peripheral or embedded structure. This relationship holds clearly for stance marked with adverbials. Thus, in the sentence:

**Sadly**, *[the troubles ended all that]*. (NEWS)

the propositional information (shown in *[]*) is given in the core of the main clause, while the personal stance (in bold) is expressed by a more loosely attached clause element (3.2.8.2, 10.3).

Constructions with modal verbs are similar to adverbials in that the propositional information is given by the main clause. In this case, the modal verb is incorporated into the main clause, as part of the verb phrase, although it is understood semantically as providing a stance frame for the entire clause.

In other cases, this structural relationship is reversed, with the propositional information being presented in some embedded structure. In particular, the stance marker occurs in the main clause when the propositional information is expressed by a complement clause:

**I was getting a bit upset** *[that my voice was going a bit]*. (CONV)

Similarly, prepositional phrase complements presenting the primary propositional information are subordinate relative to a controlling stance noun, such as:

*Ultimately students will recognize* **the logic and necessity** *[of the scheme]*. (NEWS)

Regardless of the structural relationship, in most cases the stance marker precedes the structure expressing the informational proposition. This ordering relationship holds for stance markers with complement clauses, stance noun + prepositional phrase structures, and premodifying stance adverbs. Adverbials are much more flexible in their ordering, but the large majority of stance adverbials occur in initial or medial positions (10.3.4).

Similarly, modal and semi-modal verbs occur before the main lexical verb and thus typically before the presentation of new information in the clause. This ordering of constituents reflects the primary function of stance markers as a frame for the interpretation of the propositional information. In most cases, speakers and authors first identify their personal perspective—their attitude towards the proposition, the perspective that it is true from, or the extent to which the information is reliable—thereby encouraging listeners and readers to process the following propositional information from the same perspective.

The one notable exception to this ordering of information occurs with comment clauses, which typically occur in final position. Comment clauses are primarily a spoken feature, being especially common in conversation (10.3.2.1, 10.3.4, 12.5):

> [*Well I have to wait a couple of more seasons*] **I guess.** (CONV)

These structures suit the difficulties speakers face in online production. After presenting a proposition, speakers may subsequently realize that it needs qualification, and so add a hedging comment clause such as *I think* or *I guess*.

## 12.3 Major semantic distinctions conveyed by stance markers

Stance markers can be used to present a wide range of personal meanings. Further, the meaning of a stance marker can be ambiguous in some cases. For example, the main clause verb *hope* in the following sentence conveys both a personal attitude and an epistemic stance (lack of complete certainty):

> I **hope** *there's enough there.* (CONV)

Despite these difficulties, it is useful to group stance markers into three major semantic categories: **epistemic**, **attitudinal**, and **style of speaking**.

### 12.3.1 Epistemic stance

Epistemic stance markers are used to present speaker comments on the status of information in a proposition. They can mark certainty (or doubt), actuality, precision, or limitation; or they can indicate the source of knowledge or the perspective from which the information is given. Many individual stance markers convey only a single stance meaning; for example, the adverb *probably* provides an assessment of certainty or doubt, as in:

> He has **probably** *been with his company for 13 years and in his present job for four.* (NEWS)

However, some stance markers do not fit neatly into one of these semantic categories. For example, the verb *think* controlling a *that*-complement clause not only marks the degree of certainty (being less certain than verbs like *know* but more certain than verbs like *suspect*), but also indicates the source of knowledge:

> *Since last year* I **think** *they have improved.* (NEWS†)

All types of grammatical stance devices can be used to mark epistemic stance:

### Marking certainty (or doubt), actuality, precision, or limitation
**A   Adverbial**

Single adverb:

> *It was* **definitely** *a case of exploiting child labour.* (NEWS)
>
> *In the tropics, hsemonchosis must be considered,* **possibly** *originating from hypobiotic larvae.* (ACAD)
>
> **Typically,** *the Urgonian limestones are thought of as rudist reef deposits.* (ACAD)

Prepositional phrase:

> *In fact it's actually quite nice.* (CONV)
>
> *The camel is **without doubt** one of the natural world's most remarkable forms of transport.* (NEWS)

Hedge:

> *Then we realized that you had to [**sort of**] [**like**] turn it off.* (CONV)

Comment clause:

> *Well, I'm going to feel lucky if my car isn't towed, **I think**.* (CONV)

**B   Verb/adjective/noun + complement clause**

Verb + complement clause:

> *I **know** I can get off the bus.* (CONV)
>
> *I **doubt** whether we would have played in the cold and soaking conditions we had here today.* (NEWS)
>
> *The great moment **seems** to be slipping away.* (NEWS)
>
> *Sheaths at the base **tend** to exceed the length of the internodes.* (ACAD†)

Adjective + complement clause:

> *In fact I'm not **sure** that they did very much at all.* (CONV)
>
> *We can be **certain** that the differentiation of the division of labour inevitably produces a decline.* (ACAD†)

Verb/adjective + extraposed complement clause:

> *So it was **possible** that he had taken the letter home.* (NEWS)
>
> *Indeed it **seems** that girls very quickly replaced boys at this task.* (ACAD)

Noun + complement clause:

> *There was also a **suggestion** that the bidder may be a financial buyer.* (NEWS)
>
> *This results from the **fact** that it is so difficult to distinguish deterministic chaos from highly random behaviour.* (ACAD)

**C   Stance noun + prepositional phrase**

> *But there is a **real possibility** of a split within the Lithuanian party.* (NEWS)

**D   Modal verb in extrinsic sense (6.6)**

> *I think you **might** be wrong.* (CONV)
>
> *He **must** have been really frightened when he died.* (NEWS)
>
> *Without international collaboration there **could** be interference and general chaos.* (NEWS)
>
> *Legumes **may** have smaller conversion efficiencies than cereals.* (ACAD†)

## Marking the source or perspective of knowledge

Adverbial:

> ***According to a Swedish magazine, Veckans Affaerer,** the two have been engaged in secret talks for several weeks.* (NEWS)
>
> ***From the interactional perspective outlined above,** this is what would be expected.* (ACAD)

Verb + complement clause:

> *Up to 400 Cuban military advisors **are reported** to be at fortified bases in northern Panama.* (NEWS)

> ***Mitscherlich claimed** to show that the proportionality factor, C, was a constant for each fertilizer.* (ACAD†)

Noun + prepositional phrase:

> *He found himself menaced by **the rumor** of another mission to Bologna.* (FICT†)

## 12.3.2 Attitudinal stance

Stance markers in the second major semantic category report personal attitudes or feelings. Some stance forms in this category seem clearly attitudinal (e.g. adverbials such as *ironically* and *fortunately*), while others seem to mark personal feelings or emotions (e.g. verbs such as *fear* and *love*, or adjectives, such as *happy* and *angry*, controlling complement clauses).

Marking attitudes or evaluations:

> ***Fortunately** this did not stop the women from trying.* (NEWS)

> ***Interestingly** sudden electrical death is more likely following right coronary artery occlusion.* (ACAD)

Marking personal feelings or emotions:

> *I was **happy** to see them again.* (FICT)

> *I **love** to have them around me all the time.* (NEWS)

However, the distinction between attitudes and emotions is often fuzzy, with many forms seeming to convey both meanings:

> *I **hope** you told him we swear a lot here.* (CONV)

> *We **expect** it to contribute 4.5 per cent of profits.* (NEWS)

> *Therefore, **as anticipated**, hyperparathyroidism is regularly associated with hypophosphatemia.* (ACAD†)

Overall, attitudinal stance markers are less common than epistemic markers, and they are also more limited grammatically. In particular, some adverbial categories, such as comment clauses and hedges, are not used to mark attitudinal stance. However, attitudinal stance can be marked by the other adverbial categories as well as most types of complement clause constructions:

### A Adverbial

> ***Amazingly**, the ghost disappeared after the exorcism.* (NEWS)

> ***Sadly** it is still not known if there are infinitely many regular primes.* (ACAD†)

### B Verb/adjective/noun + complement clause

Verb + complement clause:

> *I **wish** it was Friday though.* (CONV)

> *I **prefer** to have fruit really.* (CONV)

Adjective + complement clause:

> *I was **curious** to see why it had happened.* (FICT)

*I'm so **angry** our little boy is dead because someone wanted to drive fast.* (NEWS)

Verb/adjective + extraposed complement clause:

*It's **amazing** what they're doing with them.* (CONV)

*It's **tragic** that the Health Service is taking second place to a holiday camp.* (NEWS)

*It is **essential** that the blade angles match the air angles closely at all radii.* (ACAD†)

Noun + complement clause:

*These figures lead to **an expectation** that the main application area would be in the office environments.* (ACAD)

*Our reason for driving on the right in America and on the left in Britain is just **our expectation** that this is what others will do.* (ACAD)

**C  Stance noun + prepositional phrase**

*The attack left them with **a fear** of going out at night.* (NEWS)

**D  Modal verbs**

Some modal verbs used with intrinsic meanings can be regarded as attitudinal (6.6):

*Well he **ought to** talk to Nicola about that.* (CONV)

## 12.3.3  Style of speaking stance

The third major semantic domain for stance devices is style of speaking, presenting speaker/writer comments on the communication itself. Stance adverbials are the primary grammatical device, although some complement clause constructions also present this stance. The remaining stance devices are rarely, if ever, used.

**A  Adverbial**

Single adverb and adverb phrase:

***Honestly,** I've got no patience whatsoever.* (CONV)

***Quite frankly,** we are having a bad year.* (NEWS)

Prepositional phrase:

*Then, **with all due respect,** I must tell you that whether my daughter leaves home or not is none of your business.* (FICT)

Adverbial clause:

*I don't think it was her mother, **to tell you the truth.*** (CONV)

***To put it bluntly,** they have uncontrollable passions.* (FICT)

*'**Strictly speaking,**' he says, 'this isn't my beat'.* (FICT)

*I was quietly confident and, **to be honest,** I deserved to win.* (NEWS)

**B  Verb + complement clause**

*I **swear** there was a moon – I **swear** there was a moon earlier.* (CONV)

*I shall **argue** that a state that accepts integrity as a political ideal has a better case for legitimacy than one that does not.* (ACAD)

## 12.4  Attribution of stance to the speaker or writer

Stance markers differ in the extent to which they can be attributed to the speaker/writer. Many are overtly attributed (12.4.1). Others express stance without overtly identifying the speaker/writer (12.4.2). Finally, some stance markers are ambiguous as to whether they are reporting the stance of the speaker/writer or of some third person (12.4.3). Such ambiguity can be compounded when a sequence of stance markers is used. However, in examples such as the following, it will be assumed by default that the writer's stance is being expressed:

> It **would certainly** be **unwise** to **claim** any great statistical value for such findings as there are. (ACAD)

## 12.4.1  Explicit attribution of stance

There are systematic relations between the grammatical form chosen for stance markers and the extent to which stance is attributed to the speaker/writer. Several forms with first person pronouns make the attribution overt:

- Comment clause

  > I got lots of them, **I think**. (CONV)

- I/we + verb + complement clause

  > **I know** you've just started. (CONV)
  >
  > **I hope** it's in the other room. (CONV)

- I/we + be + adjective + complement clause

  > **I am sure** this is completely untrue. (NEWS)

- It + verb/adjective + me/us + extraposed complement clause

  > **It amazes me** that they can just stand on the street. (FICT)
  >
  > But **it seemed odd to me** that Ted should. (FICT†)
  >
  > **It seems to me** that the same is true of the much older history of Europe. (ACAD)

- My/our + noun + complement clause

  > **My impression that** I had been hurled into a coarser world was heightened at the beginning of each day. (FICT)
  >
  > Mr Beregovoy said that the French government's decision showed "**our desire to** accelerate economic and monetary union". (NEWS)
  >
  > A few years ago, I wrote expressing **my concern that** the village of West Linton, Peeblesshire, had 'moved'. (NEWS†)

All the above structures can also be used with third person pronouns or full noun phrases to show that the expressions of attitude or emotion are attributed to a third person rather than to the speaker/writer. This use is especially common in news and fiction:

> **She hoped** he would not bang his books on the floor above their heads. (FICT)
>
> **They loved** to work. (FICT)
>
> **Triplex hopes** to start work on the site early next year. (NEWS)

## 12.4.2  Implicit attribution of stance to the speaker/writer

More commonly, the attribution of stance is not overt but can be easily inferred as that of the speaker/writer. Modal verbs regularly have this characteristic, as do most stance adverbials and many complement clause constructions:

- Modal verb

  *Without international collaboration there **could** be interference and general chaos.* (NEWS†)

  *It **might** be that it only affected the absorption and emission processes of black bodies.* (ACAD)

  *Even now it **might** be too late: imports are rushing in to replace the shortfall.* (NEWS)

- Adverbial

  *That's **probably** what they're going to think anyway.* (CONV)

  *I haven't thought about it yet anyway, **to be honest with you**.* (CONV)

  ***Typically**, the exit Mach number from the turbine of a jet engine will be about 0–5.* (ACAD)

- Probability verb + complement clause

  *But the market **seems** to have been generating some big increases for certain quite junior City people.* (NEWS)

  *The existence of such conflict **tends** to generate complementary specialisation.* (ACAD)

- *It* + verb/adjective + extraposed complement clause

  *It **seems strange** that her career has been made up entirely of films that really haven't been all that good.* (NEWS)

  *It is perhaps **more likely** that they were associated with locomotion from the beginning.* (ACAD)

  *It **seems probable** that the damage to the paddy is mainly due to free iron and aluminum ions.* (ACAD)

## 12.4.3  Ambiguous attribution of stance

Finally, as has already been noted, many stance markers are ambiguous as to whether they mark the stance of the speaker/writer or that of some third party:

### A  Passive verb + complement clause

*The allegations **are believed** to involve several teenagers aged from 12 to 18. At least some of the abuse **is claimed** to have taken place last year. The complaint to gardai **is believed** to involve only one teenager.[1]* (NEWS)

The use of the short passive (3.6.2) avoids the need to mention the subject or agent of the stance verb. In news, this seems to be a deliberate strategy to avoid direct responsibility for the reported stance.

Passive verbs controlling a complement clause also occur in extraposed constructions:

*It **was expected** that they would interview him later today.* (NEWS)

*It **has been suggested** that at least five alleles are concerned.* (ACAD†)

**B   Adverbial *ed*-clause**

Adverbial clauses with an *ed*-participle can be ambiguous in a similar way to the passives discussed above:

> *As expected, the volume of retail sales rose 0.5 per cent in August.* (NEWS)
>
> *Therefore, as anticipated, hyperparathyroidism is regularly associated with hypophosphatemia.* (ACAD†)

**C   Noun + complement clause**

Ambiguous stance marking also arises with nouns controlling a complement clause (when they are not accompanied by a genitive or possessive pronoun):

> *This is **the claim** that industrialism had lightened the intensity of human productive activity.* (ACAD)

In some cases, though, it is clear from the context to whom the stance should be attributed:

> *The loyalty of the group to the European denominations reflects a deepseated preference for foreign religious institutions and **a strong belief** that African Christianity did not suit the elite.* (ACAD) <i.e. 'the group' believes that African Christianity did not suit the elite>
>
> *The campaign was pragmatic rather than moralizing in tone, in **the expectation** that that would be more likely to be effective.* (ACAD) <i.e. the campaigners expect that that would be more likely to be effective>

**D   Noun + prepositional phrase**

> *The reason for choosing the last phrase first is that there is **less likelihood** of the intonation being distorted.* (ACAD)

Here the 'likelihood' is presented as universal, so belief in it can be attributed to the writer as well as third parties.

## 12.5   Register differences in the marking of stance

Nearly all the grammatical features discussed in this chapter have functions besides stance marking. For example, adverbials are commonly used to mark circumstance (e.g. place, time, process) in addition to stance (10.2). Complement clause constructions are commonly controlled by a wide range of verbs and adjectives (e.g. speech act verbs, verbs of effort) in addition to verbs and adjectives marking stance (9.2, 9.4). A wide range of nouns can control complement clauses (8.14), and modal verbs can have non-stance meanings (e.g. personal ability; 6.6).

Previous chapters have discussed the register distribution of these grammatical constructions, but they have not distinguished stance markers as a distinct subclass (except for the discussions of the relevant semantic domains of verbs and adjectives controlling complement clauses in 9.2 and 9.4, and stance adverbials in 10.3). In contrast, the present section describes the distribution of only those forms that function as stance markers. The grammatical devices used to mark stance are considered overall in 12.5.1, while the following two sections (12.5.2–3) present more detailed discussions of adverbials and complement clauses.

## 12.5.1    Major stance devices across registers

In the following Corpus Findings, all modal verbs are included except *can* and *could* occurring with personal ability meanings. Modal verbs are problematic, since they have many meanings and are often ambiguous. However, most occurrences of modal verbs can be considered as indicating either epistemic or attitudinal stance (with the exception of the personal ability meanings for *can* and *could*). The modal *will* and the semi-modal *be going to* with future meaning are included in the frequency counts, since they can be interpreted as marking a kind of epistemic stance (6.6.4.3). That is, they are used to predict that a proposition will be true at some future time—a departure from a simple assertion of the proposition.

**CORPUS FINDINGS** [2,3,4]

➤ Overall, stance markers are common in all four registers (see Figure 12.1).
  ➤ Stance markers are considerably more common in conversation than in the written registers.
  ➤ At the same time, stance markers are surprisingly common in the written registers.
➤ Modals (including semi-modals) and verb/adjective/noun complement constructions are the most common grammatical categories of stance marker.
  ➤ Modals are by far most common in conversation.
  ➤ Complement constructions are more common in fiction and news than in the other registers, but they are also common in conversation.
➤ Overall, adverbial stance markers are considerably less frequent than the other grammatical categories.
  ➤ Adverbial stance markers are most common in conversation, but also relatively common in academic prose.

**Figure 12.1**

**Distribution of stance markers by major grammatical category**

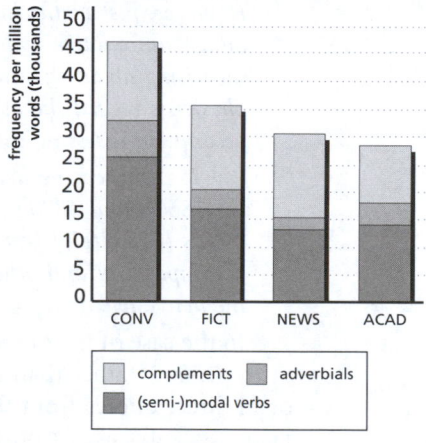

**DISCUSSION OF FINDINGS**

Given the high personal involvement of conversation, where it is always topical to talk about oneself, it is not surprising that stance markers are used most frequently in this register. As illustrated in the following conversation excerpts, multiple grammatical stance devices are often used in close proximity to one another:

A: It is **amazing** though how fast you **can** –
B: Yeah
A: <unclear> because *[I mean]* *[I'm already thinking]* <unclear>
B: You're *[probably]* *[going to]* have rain going up to Bay City. (CONV)

> A: *Well, I had a great time with Aunt Margaret. I'm **glad** I got to stay with her.*
>
> B: *Oh yeah. I **imagine** she was <unclear> too.*
>
> A: *Yeah, I **think** she's really lonely.* (CONV)

These excerpts also illustrate how personal feelings and attitudes are commonly expressed in conversation through evaluative lexical choice (e.g. *how fast, a great time, really lonely*). Although these forms are not grammatical stance devices, they do contribute to the overall emphasis on personal expression typical of conversation.

It is more surprising that stance markers are prevalent in academic writing, especially given the general lack of first person involvement in that register. That is, authors of academic articles and books rarely refer to themselves overtly. However, it is not at all uncommon to find personal attitudes and estimates of likelihood expressed in academic writing through impersonal stance devices such as modal verbs, adverbials, and extraposed complement clauses. For example, consider the following extracts from academic books:

> *However, just as the latter **[might] [be thought]** to have an intuitive grasp of affairs automotive which **ought to** be taken into account by anyone prone to theorising about the motor car, so it is **conceivable** that the way theoretical physicists regard the objects of their study **might** be a factor to be taken into account in assessing their significance.* (ACAD)

> *It then became **necessary** to discover the cause of nitrification. During the 1860's and 1870's great advances were being made in bacteriology, and it was **[definitely] [established]** that bacteria bring about putrefaction, decomposition and other changes; it was therefore **conceivable** that they were the active agents in the soil <...>* (ACAD†)

In the case of fiction and news, stance devices often report the stance of some third person (rather than the author or the narrator), either in descriptive prose or in direct quotes from that person.

Descriptive reports of third person stance:

> *She **felt** that she **should** somehow have escaped it, that she **should** have been changed.* (FICT)

> *Some observers then **thought** he **might** not even survive that long.* (NEWS)

Direct quotes:

> *"But **actually** I **think** I saw him."* (FICT)

> *"I never **[really] [thought]** I **would** go there," he said.* (NEWS)

Further, fictional prose commonly reports the private thoughts of characters, which often include multiple stance markers:

> *She **[must] [think]** she's human, he **decided**. **Obviously** she doesn't know.* (FICT)

> *Then I **realized** how absurd I was being. **Obviously** he **would** have gone out for cigarettes.* (FICT)

Overall, modals (including semi-modals) are the most common grammatical device used to mark stance. The relative distribution of modal and semi-modal verbs, as well as the distribution and use of individual modal verbs, is discussed in 6.6. Modal verbs are especially common in conversation, where they often occur together in the same turn or interaction:

A: I **had to** be there at four o'clock in the morning to open that place, I was responsible for the existence of bread. If I didn't get there by four, it **would** not be ready that day, right? It probably **wouldn't** be on the shelf until two in the afternoon or something, that's a lot of responsibility and, you know, I felt like he **should** be paying me for it. (CONV)

A: The only thing she **[might]** **[have to]** pay for is having it put in a box with styrofoam.
B: Yeah, she probably **will** at one of those mailbox places.
A: Maybe I **should** give her another fifty for that. (CONV)

In addition to being the most frequent, modals are also probably the least informative type of stance marker. First, the stance reported by modal verbs is not directly attributed to the speaker/writer, regardless of the grammatical subject of the clause. For example, in both of the following sentences from the above excerpt, the speaker is presumed to be expressing her own assessment of obligation:

I **had to** be there at four o'clock. (CONV)

He **should** be paying me for it. (CONV)

With modal verbs, there is no way to overtly associate the expressed stance with the speaker/writer. Rather, unless the modal occurs in a report of the speech or thought of some third person, the attitudes or assessments expressed are assumed to be the personal stance of the speaker/writer.

Further, there are a limited number of modal verbs, and thus they can be used to express only a limited range of meanings. At the same time, each individual modal verb is polysemous (6.6). For example, the modal *can* is used to express permission, logical possibility, or personal ability, and in many cases the intended meaning is not clear. Finally, modal verbs are relatively simple grammatically, involving only a modification to the verb phrase, in contrast to the grammatical dependencies that occur with adverbials and complement clauses. All of these factors probably contribute to the extremely frequent use of modal verbs, especially in conversation.

The other two major grammatical categories used for stance devices—adverbials and complement clauses—are made up of several different grammatical constructions (e.g. single adverbs, prepositional phrases, and adverbial clauses within the general class of stance adverbials). It turns out that the different types of stance adverbials and stance complement constructions are used in quite different ways across registers. Thus, these categories are dealt with in more detail below.

## 12.5.2   Stance adverbials across registers

The expressions *I mean* and *you know* (which are very common in conversation; see also 12.5.3) are excluded from this analysis, since they behave more like discourse markers than stance comment clauses (10.3.1.4C).[5]

**CORPUS FINDINGS** [2,3]

➤ Single adverbs are the most common category of stance adverbial in all registers.
➤ In conversation, over 65% of all stance adverbials are single adverbs.

➤ Prepositional phrases as stance markers are most common by far in academic prose, while they are notably rare in conversation.

> ➤ Proportionally, almost 30% of the stance adverbials in academic prose are prepositional phrases.

➤ Conversely, adverbial clauses as stance markers are most frequent by far in conversation, while they occur with moderate frequencies in the other three registers.

> ➤ Proportionally, about 20% of the stance adverbials in conversation are adverbial clauses.

> ➤ Although adverbial clauses are less frequent in fiction, they are more important proportionally, comprising almost 30% of all stance adverbials.

➤ Comment clauses are generally rare as stance markers: they are used with moderate frequency only in conversation.

➤ Only a few lexical expressions are common as comment clauses.

> ➤ There are interesting differences in the use of these expressions between AmE and BrE (see Table 12.1).

**Figure 12.2**
**Breakdown of stance markers within the adverbial category**

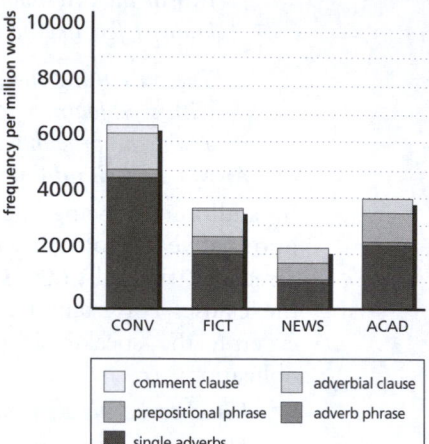

**Table 12.1**   **Distribution of comment clauses as stance markers across dialects and registers; occurrences per million words**

each ● represents 10

|  | AmE CONV | BrE CONV | FICT | NEWS | ACAD |
|---|---|---|---|---|---|
| *I think* | ●●●●●●●●● ●●●●●●●●● | ●●●●●●●●● ●●●●●●●●●● ●●●●●●●● | ●●● |  |  |
| *I suppose* | ●● | ●●●●●● | ●●● |  |  |
| *I guess* | ●●●●●●●●● ●●●● |  | ● |  |  |
| *I believe* | ● |  | ● |  |  |
| *it seems* |  |  |  | ● | ● |

---

**DISCUSSION OF FINDINGS**

Stance adverbials are most plentiful in conversation, especially single adverbs and, to a lesser extent, adverbial clauses (cf. 10.3.2.1). The large majority of single adverbs are epistemic, with the forms *actually*, *really*, and *probably* being particularly frequent:

> *I like this area, I **really** do. **Actually** if I could afford to live here I would.* (CONV)

> ***Probably** I don't know **actually**.* (CONV)

Adverbial clauses in conversation commonly mark a proposition as shared background or indicate the manner of speaking:

*As you say, it was part of the holiday.* (CONV)

*I mean you can't, **as I've said before**, you can't exactly expect them to be super models.* (CONV)

*I had endless trouble, **as you know**, with Shirley.* (CONV)

***To be honest**, I haven't got that much time.* (CONV)

*I don't think there'll be enough nuts, **to tell you the truth**.* (CONV)

Academic prose is similar to conversation in showing a heavy reliance on single adverbs as stance devices, especially those indicating epistemic stance. However, it also shows a very common use of prepositional phrases as stance adverbials for similar purposes.

Single adverbs in academic prose:

***Generally**, two types of tests are employed in laboratory surveys.* (ACAD)

*The opposing attitude was **perhaps** best expressed by the great French naturalist, the Comte de Buffon.* (ACAD)

Prepositional phrases in academic prose:

***In fact**, more often than not, it will be found that the work of mass selection must be repeated annually.* (ACAD)

*[**In fact**], [**in some respects**] at first they did so better than Copernicus's calculations.* (ACAD)

As already observed, comment clauses are generally rare compared to other types of stance adverbials. However, a few particular expressions are notably common as comment clauses in conversation. The comment clauses *I think* and *I suppose* are somewhat more common in BrE than AmE, while *I guess* is almost exclusively an AmE expression. In conversation these expressions typically occur in turn-final position:

*It means the sod hasn't paid **I think*** (BrE CONV)

*I'm going to get a new one for the basement **I think*** (AmE CONV)

*She's all right **I suppose*** (BrE CONV)

*You'll probably see her Saturday **I suppose*** (AmE CONV)

*His dad had to go out and earn extra money **I guess*** (AmE CONV)

*She doesn't want me to go **I guess*** (AmE CONV)

Although comment clauses are primarily a conversational feature, the expression *it seems* (and occasionally *it appears*) is used as a comment clause in the expository written registers. Unlike comment clauses in conversation, this expression usually occurs in medial position:

*Neither, **it seems**, does it believe in newfangled technology.* (NEWS)

*The conclusion, **it seems**, is intolerable.* (ACAD)

However, *it seems* sometimes also occurs as a final comment clause:

*But they do happen, **it seems**.* (NEWS)

## 12.5.3    Stance complement constructions across registers

### CORPUS FINDINGS [2,3]

➤ Conversation, fiction, and news use stance complement constructions to nearly the same extent; these devices are less common in academic prose.

➤ However, the specific grammatical devices preferred in conversation and academic prose are nearly opposites:

  ➤ Verb + complement clause: extremely common in conversation (verb + *that*-clause is especially common); relatively rare in academic prose.

  ➤ Extraposed complement clause: rare in conversation; common in academic prose (extraposed *to*-clause is especially common).

  ➤ Noun + complement clause: extremely rare in conversation; moderately common in academic prose.

➤ Fiction is similar to conversation in its preferred stance complement clause types.

➤ News, on the other hand, is somewhat similar to academic prose in this respect.

  ➤ The notable exception to this generalization is that news shows a greater reliance on verb/adjective + complement clause constructions (especially adjective + *to*-clauses).

➤ Stance noun + prepositional phrase constructions are moderately common only in academic prose.

  ➤ Nine stance nouns are relatively common controlling *of*-prepositional phrase complements in academic prose (see Table 12.2).

### DISCUSSION OF FINDINGS

In conversation, there is a very heavy reliance on *that*-complement clauses to mark stance (typically with the complementizer *that* omitted). These constructions are especially common when controlled by the verbs *think, know,* and *suppose*:

**Figure 12.3**
**Breakdown of stance markers within the complement category**

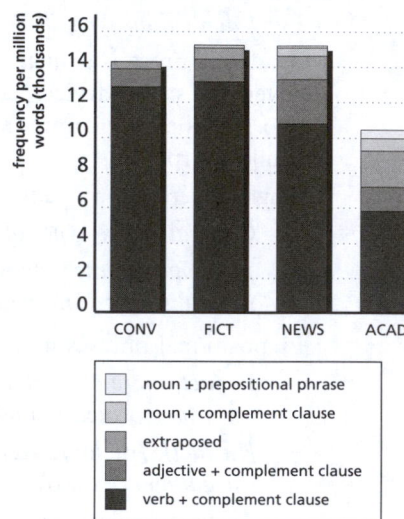

- noun + prepositional phrase
- noun + complement clause
- extraposed
- adjective + complement clause
- verb + complement clause

**Figure 12.4**
**Breakdown of stance markers for *that*-clauses and *to*-clauses**

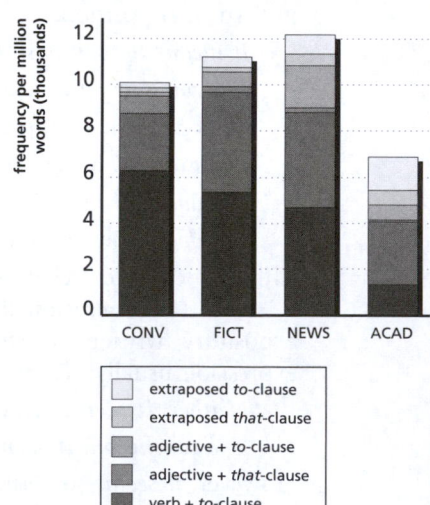

- extraposed *to*-clause
- extraposed *that*-clause
- adjective + *to*-clause
- adjective + *that*-clause
- verb + *to*-clause
- verb + *that*-clause

**Table 12.2** **Most common stance nouns occurring with an *of* prepositional phrase; occurrences per million words**

| ▰ over 50 | ▪ over 20 | ▮ over 10 | | |
|---|---|---|---|---|
| | **CONV** | **FICT** | **NEWS** | **ACAD** |
| *possibility* | | ▮ | ▪ | ▰ |
| *value* | | | ▪ | ▰ |
| *evidence* | | ▮ | ▪ | ▮ |
| *importance* | | | ▮ | ▰ |
| *problem* | | | ▮ | ▰ |
| *understanding* | | | ▮ | ▰ |
| *significance* | | | | ▪ |
| *validity* | | | | ▪ |
| *risk* | | | | ▪ |

> *I **think** I'll go to bed early tonight.* (CONV)
>
> *Yes but heavens you **know** you'll never climb with that.* (CONV)
>
> *I **suppose** it's pretty difficult really.* (CONV)

These same grammatical devices are also extremely frequent in fiction, with a wider range of stance verbs commonly controlling the *that*-clauses (including *think, know, believe, feel, suppose, realize, hope*). In this register the *that*-clauses typically report the thoughts and feelings of fictional characters, rather than the personal stance of the author:

> *I **knew** she would be busy, and I **hoped** she wouldn't be able to check up on me.* (FICT†)
>
> *I **realized** it hadn't turned out very well.* (FICT)

In contrast, academic prose shows a strong preference for extraposed *to*-clauses, especially those controlled by adjectival predicates marking possibility, necessity/importance, or personal evaluations.

Extraposed *to*-clauses with adjectives expressing possibility, necessity, or importance (9.4.5.3):

> *It may be **possible** to obtain more reliable breakage figures at a later stage in the selection programme.* (ACAD)
>
> *It is **essential** to conserve water on the land owing to uncertain future supplies.* (ACAD†)
>
> *It is **vitally important** to develop skills at least partially independent of a single notation.* (ACAD)

Extraposed *to*-clauses with adjectives expressing other evaluations:

> *It is **convenient** to discuss these processes in two parts.* (ACAD)
>
> *Here it is **useful** to consider the degree of reaction.* (ACAD)
>
> *It is **clearly inappropriate** to involve Julie in a prolonged conversation as soon as she arrives on the ward.* (ACAD)

In news, other adjectives marking likelihood, evaluation, or other feelings are commonly used as stance markers, but in this case they often control a simple post-predicate *to*-clause rather than an extraposed construction (9.4.5).

Post-predicate *to*-clauses with adjectives expressing likelihood:

> *Some parts of the industry are **likely** to be very profitable.* (NEWS †)

> *He is **certain** to become a leading force in South African politics.* (NEWS)

Post-predicate *to*-clauses with adjectives expressing evaluations:

> *The judge was **wrong** to treat the proceedings as properly constituted representative proceedings.* (NEWS †)

> *If you can't make a straightforward decision you'd be **wise** to put things off and wait.* (NEWS †)

Post-predicate *to*-clauses with adjectives expressing other feelings:

> *But Tatum is not **afraid** to take a few knocks.* (NEWS)

> *I am not **ashamed** to say it brought me close to tears.* (NEWS)

> *I am **proud** to be with him now.* (NEWS)

Finally, stance nouns controlling complements are relatively common in academic prose and, to a lesser extent, in news, predominantly with epistemic meanings. *That*-clauses, *to*-clauses, and *of*-prepositional phrases (especially with an *ing*-clause as complement) can occur with stance nouns like *fact, hope, possibility, doubt, suggestion, belief, assumption, chance, desire, tendency, hope*, and *problem* (see also 8.14).

Stance noun + *that*-complement clause:

> *The **fact** that the two results are different shows that this order matters.* (ACAD)

> *The surgeon had already informed Mr and Mrs Reynolds of the **possibility** that an abdomino-perineal resection of rectum may be required.* (ACAD)

Stance noun + *to*-complement clause:

> *Similarly, the element potassium has a strong **tendency** to lose an electron and form a cation.* (ACAD †)

Stance noun + *of* + *ing*-complement clause:

> *Her lower legs were so badly crushed there was no **hope** of saving them.* (NEWS)

> *Moreover, there is no **possibility** of capitalism developing while the majority of the labouring population consists of independent peasantry.* (ACAD)

In addition, stance noun + *of* + noun phrase constructions serve similar functions, especially in academic prose:

> *This states precisely the practical **importance** of conventionalism for adjudication.* (ACAD)

> *The **value** of a decent novel cannot be captured from a single perspective.* (ACAD †)

# 13

# Lexical expressions in speech and writing

*See page xiii for contents in detail*

# 13.1 Overview

In English, there are many multi-word expressions that function as a structural or semantic unit. The most common of these are phrasal verbs and prepositional verbs, such as *get up, carry* NP *out, look at, talk about, get out of, look forward to.* These are verb + particle and verb + preposition combinations that comprise a single entity with respect to both their meaning and structure (5.3).

Different kinds of multi-word expressions can be distinguished according to their idiomaticity and invariability. At one extreme are **idioms**, which are relatively invariable expressions with meanings that cannot be predicted from the meanings of the parts. That is, idioms are expressions which have to be learned as a whole, even if we know the meanings of the individual words composing them. In many cases, an entire idiom can be replaced by a single word with similar meaning. Most phrasal verbs and many phrasal-prepositional verbs are idiomatic and can be paraphrased in this way (5.3):

| | |
|---|---|
| *crop up* → *occur* | *look forward to* → *anticipate* |
| *get up* → *rise* | *put up with* → *tolerate* |
| *carry out* → *undertake, perform* | *get away from* → *escape* |
| *put off* → *postpone* | |

In addition, there are a number of longer expressions that function as idioms. Many of these are complete predicates (e.g. verb + object): phrases that can be replaced by a single lexical verb, such as

| | |
|---|---|
| *kick the bucket* → *die* | *beat about/around the bush* |
| *bear in mind* → *remember* | → *prevaricate* |

Note that idiomatic expressions are not completely invariable. For example, the verb in all of the above expressions can vary for tense, number, and aspect. However, these expressions are relatively fixed in that they must include the specified content words to give the idiomatic meaning. For example, the expressions *kick the pail* and *hit the bucket with your foot* are nearly equivalent to *kick the bucket* in terms of their literal meaning, but they would not work as idiomatic expressions for 'die'.

**Collocations**, on the other hand, are associations between lexical words, so that the words co-occur more frequently than expected by chance. For example, in academic prose, the adjective *obvious* has a number of **collocates**: *difference, difficulty, challenge, example(s), fact, problem(s), question(s), reason(s), way.* Unlike idioms, collocations are statistical associations rather than relatively fixed expressions. Moreover, the individual words in a collocation retain their own meaning. However, part of the extended meaning of a word is the fact that it tends to co-occur with a specific set of collocates.

In fact, words with similar meaning are often distinguished by their preferred collocations. For example, when considered out of context, the adjectives *little* and *small* are similar in meaning and might even be cited as synonyms. However, these two adjectives in fact co-occur with quite different sets of following nouns. Some preferred collocates of *little* in conversation:

| | | | |
|---|---|---|---|
| *baby* | *devil* | *kitten(s)* | |
| *bag* | *dog* | *kid(s)* | *thing* |
| *bit(s)* | *girl(s)* | *lad* | *while* |
| *boy(s)* | *duck(s)* | *man* | |

Some preferred collocates of *small* in conversation:

| | | | |
|---|---|---|---|
| *amount(s)* | *piece* | *quantities* | *world* |
| *letters* | *print* | *sum* | |
| *part* | *proportion* | *size* | |

Words can also have strong associations with different grammatical structures; such co-occurrence patterns are called **lexico-grammatical associations**. For example, Chapter 9 shows that verbs such as *think* and *know* are strongly associated with *that*-complement clauses, while verbs such as *like*, *want*, and *need* are strongly associated with *to*-complement clauses. The verbs *wish* and *expect* are grammatical with both *that*-clauses and *to*-clauses, but they have a stronger lexico-grammatical association with *to*-clauses (being about ten times more common controlling that type of complement clause).

As a second example, consider the way that valency patterns are differentially associated with particular verbs, as described in 5.2.4. For example, the verbs *stand*, *change*, and *begin* are similar in that all three have the potential to occur with both intransitive and monotransitive valency patterns. However, these verbs have different lexico-grammatical associations: *stand* usually occurs as an intransitive verb with an optional adverbial of place; *change* usually occurs as a monotransitive verb with a noun phrase functioning as direct object; and *begin* usually occurs as a monotransitive verb followed by a complement clause functioning as direct object.

The primary focus of the present chapter is on lexical patterns in a slightly different sense: it considers the way in which word forms often co-occur in longer sequences, called **lexical bundles**. Lexical bundles can be regarded as extended collocations: bundles of words that show a statistical tendency to co-occur. In conversation, common lexical bundles include sequences such as:

| | |
|---|---|
| *do you want me to* | *I said to him* |
| *going to be a* | *I don't know what* |

Quite different lexical bundles are common in academic prose, including sequences such as:

| | |
|---|---|
| *in the case of the* | *there was no significant* |
| *it should be noted that* | |

It is important to emphasize the difference between idioms and lexical bundles. Idioms are relatively invariable expressions with a meaning not derivable from the parts, but they are not necessarily common expressions at all. In contrast, lexical bundles are the sequences of words that most commonly co-occur in a register. Usually they are not fixed expressions, and it is not possible to substitute a single word for the sequence; in fact, most lexical bundles are not structurally complete at all (as in the above examples).

At the same time, lexical bundles are much more common than idioms. For example, all of the bundles listed above occur at least 20 times per million words, and many of them are considerably more common. In contrast, stereotypical idioms such as *kick the bucket* (meaning 'die') and *a slap in the face* (meaning 'an affront') are used occasionally in fiction (less than five per million words), but they are very rarely attested in the other registers (including conversation).

This chapter deals with the lexical end of grammar, describing systematic patterns of use that can only be identified through large-scale corpus studies. This approach can open our eyes to an aspect of language we often ignore: grammar is not just a study of abstract classes and structures, but of particular words and their particular functions within those classes and functions. Such information is also important for the learner of English as a foreign language: producing natural, idiomatic English is not just a matter of constructing well-formed sentences, but of using well-tried lexical expressions in appropriate places.

As already noted, the primary focus of the chapter is on lexical bundles. However, to limit the scope of this description, we focus only on the two registers in the LSWE Corpus that show the most striking differences in language use: conversation and academic prose. Further, the description of lexical bundles in conversation is based primarily on analysis of BrE, although we also note selected bundles that are particularly common in AmE conversation.

Section 13.2 describes the most common lexical bundles in conversation and academic prose, discussing the different grammatical correlates of these lexical sequences in the two registers. Then 13.3 further discusses the use of idiomatic expressions. Finally, 13.4 and 13.5 describe other major systematic lexical associations in English: free combinations of verb + adverbial particle in 13.4, and binomial phrases in 13.5.

## 13.2 Lexical bundles

Lexical bundles are recurrent expressions, regardless of their idiomaticity, and regardless of their structural status. That is, lexical bundles are simply sequences of word forms that commonly go together in natural discourse.

To make the scope of our investigation more manageable, a lexical bundle is defined here as a recurring sequence of three or more words. Shorter bundles are often incorporated into more than one longer lexical bundle. For example, the three-word lexical bundle *I don't think* is used in many four-word bundles, such as *but I don't think, well I don't think, I don't think so*, and *I don't think I*.

In identifying lexical bundles, we have relied on orthographic word units, even though these sometimes rather arbitrarily combine separate words. For example, compare the following:

| | |
|---|---|
| *into* v. *on to* | *cannot* v. *could not* |
| *place-name* v. *place name* | |

Two-word contracted combinations might be considered a type of lexical bundle, since they are composed of three lexical units (e.g. *I don't* → *I do not*). However, in most analyses here, we have treated contracted forms as a single word.

A combination of words must recur frequently in order to be considered a lexical bundle. In most cases, these bundles are not structural units, and they are not expressions that speakers would recognize as idioms or other fixed lexical expressions.

For the analysis of four-word sequences in the present chapter, we set a minimal cut-off of at least ten times per million words in order for a sequence to be considered a recurrent lexical bundle. However, we also identify those bundles that recur with much higher frequencies. Five-word and six-word lexical bundles are much less common than four-word bundles, and we therefore use a lower cut-off for their analysis (see below).

Other combinations of words are often repeated within the span of a single discourse. In many cases, though, these combinations do not represent lexical bundles in our sense, because they are not widely used across texts. In addition, locally repeated combinations can show some variation in form (e.g. with a word omitted or an additional word inserted), while a lexical bundle represents a specific recurrent word combination. Local repetitions typically reflect the immediate topical concerns of the discourse. In contrast, lexical bundles can be regarded as lexical building blocks that tend to be used frequently by different speakers in different situations. The following conversational excerpt illustrates this difference; local repeated combinations are given in *[]*, while lexical bundles are marked by bold italics (including three-word, four-word, and two-word contracted bundles).

A: *His girlfriend had a heart transplant.*
D: **I know** *I read that.*
C: **Did you see that** *thing on* <unclear>
D: **You shouldn't** *believe that though.*
B: *Who's Vinnie Jones?*
   <...>
C: *You like Vinnie Jones,* **don't you**?
A: *No.*
C: **Yes you do**.
A: *Vinnie Jones,* **he's such** *a hard bloke.*
C: *Yeah.*
B: **It's really** *funny, that man.*
A: *[I reckon he] er well, – probably [could] –*
   *[I don't reckon] Eric [Cantona could].*
B: *[Don't reckon Cantona could] what?*
A: *[I don't reckon Cantona could] beat him up.*
C: *yeah.*
B: *nor do I.*
A: <unclear> *couldn't, but Mark Hughes might.*
   **But I don't know why we're talking** *about this.* (CONV)

As illustrated by the above excerpt, lexical bundles usually do not represent a complete structural unit. It turns out, though, that these bundles fall into several basic structural types. In conversation, for example, a large number of lexical bundles are constructed from a pronominal subject followed by a verb phrase plus the start of a complement clause, such as *I don't know why* and *I thought that was*. In academic prose, on the other hand, lexical bundles are more commonly parts of noun phrases and prepositional phrases, such as *the nature of the* and *as a result of*.

In the majority of cases, lexical bundles extend across structural units. Thus many bundles in conversation contain the beginning of a main clause, followed by the beginning of an embedded complement clause. These lexical bundles form recurrent discourse building blocks, with the following slot being used to express the content specific to each individual situation.

Conversational examples building on *I don't know why*:

*I don't know why* he didn't play much at the end of the season. (CONV)
*I don't know why* Catherine finds that sort of thing funny. (CONV)

*I don't know why* Colin came. (CONV)

*I don't know why* I did it. (CONV)

Conversational examples building on *I thought that was*:

But *I thought that was* Friday. (CONV)

*I thought that was* Drop Dead Fred. (CONV)

*I thought that was* going to happen. (CONV)

Oh *I thought that was* quite good. (CONV)

Most lexical bundles in academic prose are also incomplete structural units, and these are similarly used as discourse building blocks. However, those building blocks tend to be nominal rather than clausal chunks. For example, the lexical bundle *the nature of the* consists of an incomplete noun phrase containing the beginning of an embedded *of*-phrase (including the beginning of a definite noun phrase). The lexical bundle *as a result of* consists of an incomplete prepositional phrase: a preposition plus noun phrase, followed by the beginning of an embedded *of*-phrase.

Academic noun phrases completing the lexical bundle *the nature of the*:

*physical world, soil, work, country, moral obligation,*

*issues involved, the social processes which underlie them*

Academic noun phrases completing the lexical bundle *as a result of*:

*his work, this change, abnormally high rainfall, centuries of*

*experience, trials over a period of three years*

These examples illustrate a fundamental difference between the lexical bundles found in conversation and those found in academic prose: most lexical bundles in conversation are building blocks for verbal and clausal structural units, while most lexical bundles in academic prose are building blocks for extended noun phrases or prepositional phrases. (Compare the differing distributions of verbal and nominal structures between these registers; 2.3.5.)

## 13.2.1 Operational definition of lexical bundles

Lexical bundles are identified empirically, as the combinations of words that in fact recur most commonly in a given register. Three-word bundles can be considered as a kind of extended collocational association, and they are thus extremely common. On the other hand, four-word, five-word, and six-word bundles are more phrasal in nature and correspondingly less common. In conversation, there are also recurrent two-word contracted bundles, which are composed of three grammatical word forms (e.g. *she didn't* → *she did not*). In typical written prose, these would be expressed as three separate words; thus, these two-word contracted sequences in conversation might also be compared to three-word bundles in academic prose.

The general distribution of each type of bundle is considered below, and 13.2.3 and 13.2.4 provide detailed lists of the four-word, five-word, and six-word lexical bundles found in conversation and academic prose.

To qualify as a lexical bundle, a word combination must frequently recur in a register. In the following findings, lexical sequences are counted as 'recurrent' lexical bundles only if they occur at least ten times per million words in a register. These occurrences must be spread across at least five different texts in the register (to exclude individual speaker/writer idiosyncrasies). Because five-word and six-word bundles are generally less common, a lower cut-off of at least five times per million words is used for those types.

Only uninterrupted combinations of words have been treated as potential lexical bundles. Thus, lexical combinations that span a turn boundary or a punctuation mark are not considered.

Longer lexical bundles are usually formed through an extension or combination of one or more shorter bundles:

*do you want; you want me; want me to; me to do* →

*do you want me; you want me to; want me to do* →

*do you want me to; you want me to do* →

*do you want me to do*

In the lists in 13.2.3 and 13.2.4, shorter bundles that are extended to form longer recurrent bundles are marked with a '+'.

## 13.2.1.1 Lexical bundles in conversation and academic prose

**CORPUS FINDINGS** [3]

➤ Both conversation and academic prose use a large stock of different lexical bundles (i.e. bundle types).

   ➤ Conversation contains a larger stock of lexical bundles than academic prose; in addition, conversation uses over 1,000 recurrent two-word contracted bundles (e.g. *I don't*).

➤ There are almost ten times as many three-word lexical bundles as four-word lexical bundles, in both conversation and academic prose.

   ➤ Similarly, there are about ten times as many four-word lexical bundles as five-word lexical bundles.

Figure 13.1
**Number of lexical bundles in conversation and academic prose**

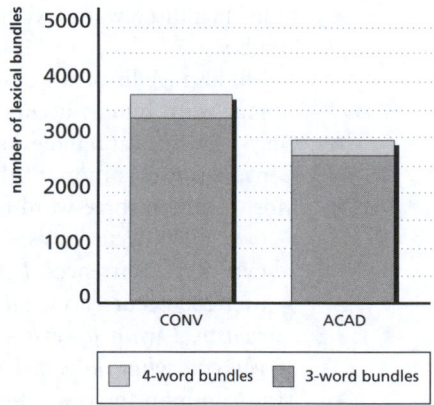

Figure 13.2 **Percentage of words in recurrent v. non-recurrent expressions—conversation**

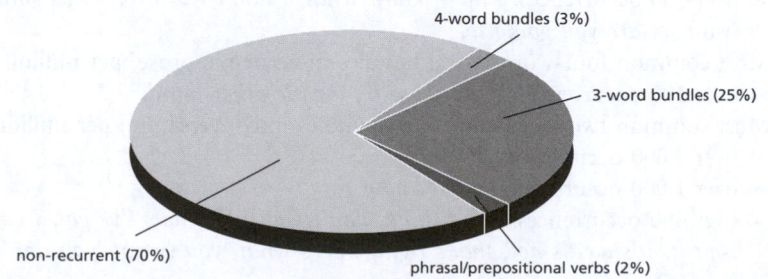

**Figure 13.3** **Percentage of words in recurrent v. non-recurrent expressions—academic prose**

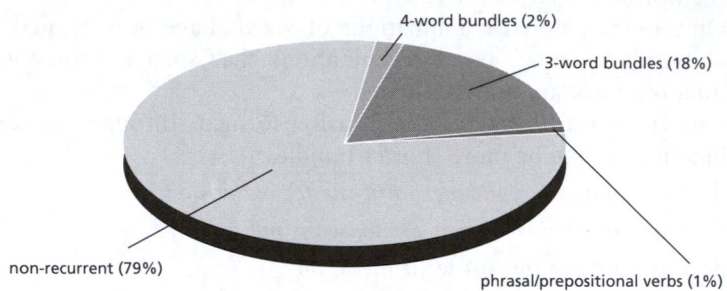

4-word bundles (2%)

3-word bundles (18%)

non-recurrent (79%)

phrasal/prepositional verbs (1%)

➤ Lexical bundles (as tokens or instances) are extremely common in both conversation and academic prose:
  ➤ Three-word bundles occur over 80,000 times per million words in conversation; over 60,000 times per million words in academic prose.
  ➤ Four-word bundles occur over 8,500 times per million words in conversation; over 5,000 times per million words in academic prose.
➤ On average, individual lexical bundles in conversation and academic prose occur with about the same frequency.
➤ Individual three-word lexical bundles are slightly more frequent than four-word lexical bundles.
  ➤ The average three-word bundle occurs 25 times per million words, while the average four-word bundle occurs about 20 times per million words.
➤ Only a few lexical bundles occur with very high frequencies.
➤ Conversation has more of these very common lexical bundles than academic prose.
➤ Most common three-word lexical bundles in conversation, per million words:
  ➤ over 1,000 occurrences: *I don't know*
  ➤ over 400 occurrences: *I don't think, do you want*
  ➤ over 200 occurrences: *I don't want, don't want to, don't know what, and I said, I said to, I want to, you want to, you have to, do you know, you know what, have you got, what do you, I mean I, have a look.*
➤ Most common three-word lexical bundles in academic prose, per million words:
  ➤ over 200 occurrences: *in order to, one of the, part of the, the number of, the presence of, the use of, the fact that, there is a, there is no.*
➤ Most common four-word lexical bundles in conversation, per million words:
  ➤ over 100 occurrences: *I don't know what, I don't want to, I was going to, do you want to, are you going to.*
➤ Most common four-word lexical bundles in academic prose, per million words:
  ➤ over 100 occurrences: *in the case of, on the other hand.*
➤ Most common two-word contracted bundles in conversation, per million words:
  ➤ over 2,000 occurrences: *I don't*
  ➤ over 1,000 occurrences: *don't know*
  ➤ over 400 occurrences: *don't think, don't want, I'm not, I've got, I can't, I didn't, isn't it, it's a, it's not, that's right, that's what, you've got, you don't.*

➤ In both conversation and academic prose, an important proportion of discourse is made up of recurrent lexical bundles.

 ➤ In conversation, about 30% of the words occur in a recurrent lexical bundle; if two-word contracted bundles are also considered, almost 45% of the words in conversation occur in a recurrent lexical bundle.

 ➤ In academic prose, about 21% of the words occur in a recurrent lexical bundle.

➤ However, the majority of words in both conversation and academic prose occur in non-recurrent expressions (i.e. text that is not part of a recurrent expression, as we have defined it):

 ➤ 70% of the words in conversation (c. 55% considering two-word contracted bundles);

 ➤ 79% of the words in academic prose.

➤ Similar patterns are found for the use of local repeated lexical bundles (based on analysis of all four-word bundles in the first 1,000 words of each text):

 ➤ In conversation: 77% of the lexical bundles are not repeated; 15% of the lexical bundles are repeated once; 6% of the lexical bundles occur three to four times; 2% of the lexical bundles occur five to nine times; less than 1% of the lexical bundles occur over ten times.

 ➤ In academic prose: 83% of the lexical bundles are not repeated; 11% of the lexical bundles are repeated once; 4% of the lexical bundles occur three to four times; 2% of the lexical bundles occur five to nine times; less than 1% of the lexical bundles occur over ten times.

➤ Most lexical bundles are not complete structural units:

 ➤ In conversation, only 15% of the lexical bundles can be regarded as complete structural units.

 ➤ In academic prose, less than 5% of the lexical bundles represent complete structural units.

➤ The structural correlates of lexical bundles are quite different in conversation and academic prose (see Tables 13.1–2).

 ➤ In conversation, most lexical bundles are parts of declarative clauses or questions; about 90% of all lexical bundles include part of a verb phrase.

 ➤ In academic prose, over 60% of all lexical bundles are parts of noun phrases or prepositional phrases.

➤ Most lexical bundles bridge two structural units; in many cases, the last word of the bundle is the first element of the second structure (see Table 13.3).

 ➤ In conversation, verbs and function words are equally common as the ending word of four-word lexical bundles.

 ➤ In academic prose, function words are by far most common as the ending word of four-word lexical bundles.

 ➤ The most common function words in this role are articles, prepositions, and complementizers.

## DISCUSSION OF FINDINGS

As Figure 13.1 shows, there are many more three-word lexical bundles than four-word lexical bundles. The most common three-word bundles can be extended to form numerous four-word lexical bundles. For example, the three-word bundle *I don't know* is used in 15 common four-word lexical bundles (such as *I don't know what* and *I don't know why*). *I don't think* is used in 13 common four-word lexical bundles (such as *I don't think so, I don't think he*); the bundle *do you want* is used

**Table 13.1**  **Proportional distribution of four-word lexical bundles across the major structural patterns in each register**

| | CONV | ACAD | example |
|---|---|---|---|
| **patterns more widely used in conversation** | | | |
| personal pronoun + lexical verb phrase (+ complement clause) | 44% | — | *I don't know what* |
| pronoun/NP (+ auxiliary) + copula *be* (+) | 8% | 2% | *it was in the* |
| (auxiliary +) active verb (+) | 13% | — | *have a look at* |
| *yes-no* and *wh*-question fragment | 12% | — | *can I have a* |
| (verb +) *wh*-clause fragment | 4% | — | *know what I mean* |
| **patterns more widely used in academic prose** | | | |
| noun phrase with post-modifier fragment | 4% | 30% | *the nature of the* |
| preposition + noun phrase fragment | 3% | 33% | *as a result of* |
| anticipatory *it* + VP/adjectiveP (+ complement-clause) | — | 9% | *it is possible to* |
| passive verb + PP fragment | — | 6% | *is based on the* |
| (verb +) *that*-clause fragment | 1% | 5% | *should be noted that* |
| **patterns used in both registers** | | | |
| (verb/adjective +) *to*-clause fragment | 5% | 9% | *are likely to be* |
| other expressions | 6% | 6% | |
| **total** | **100%** | **100%** | |

in eight common four-word lexical bundles (such as *do you want to, do you want a*).

Of course, using a different operational definition of 'recurrent lexical bundles' could greatly influence the overall proportions of conversation and academic prose regarded as recurrent language. For example, including two-word sequences would result in much higher proportions of recurrent language in both registers. Further, setting a higher or lower cut-off for 'recurrent' would also obviously influence these statistics. Even with these caveats, though, there are many interesting points of comparison in the use of lexical bundles between conversation and academic prose.

Overall, conversation makes use of a larger stock of lexical bundles than academic prose, and lexical bundles make up a somewhat greater proportion of the total discourse in conversation (especially if two-word contracted sequences are included). Conversation is often regarded as extremely formulaic, and some scholars have suggested that most conversational utterances are composed of relatively fixed lexical bundles. However, it turns out that the perception of repetition and formulaic language in conversation actually has several different sources.

The majority of words produced in conversation do not occur in three-word and four-word lexical bundles, as they are defined in this chapter. At the same time, conversation does use a large number of lexical bundles, and an important proportion of any conversational exchange incorporates recurrent lexical bundles.

**Table 13.2**  **Number of different four-word lexical bundles across the major structural patterns in each register**

| | CONV | ACAD |
|---|---|---|
| **patterns more widely used in conversation** | | |
| personal pronoun + lexical verb phrase (+ complement clause) | 187 | — |
| pronoun/NP (+ auxiliary) + copula *be* (+) | 33 | 5 |
| (auxiliary +) active verb (+) | 56 | — |
| *yes-no* and *wh*-question fragment | 49 | — |
| (verb +) *wh*-clause fragment | 17 | — |
| (*and* +) NP | 9 | — |
| quantifier expressions | 4 | — |
| adverbial clause fragment | 10 | 4 |
| meaningless sound bundles | 4 | — |
| **patterns more widely used in academic prose** | | |
| noun phrase with *of*-phrase fragment | 16 | 69 |
| noun phrase with other post-modifier fragment | — | 15 |
| prepositional phrase with embedded *of*-phrase fragment | 6 | 56 |
| other prepositional phrase fragment | 7 | 35 |
| anticipatory *it* + VP/adjectiveP (+ complement clause) | — | 24 |
| passive verb + PP fragment | — | 16 |
| copula *be* + NP/adjectiveP | — | 11 |
| (NP +) (verb +) *that*-clause fragment | 3 | 13 |
| **patterns used in both registers** | | |
| (verb/adjective +) *to*-clause fragment | 20 | 24 |
| other expressions | 3 | 5 |
| **total** | 424 | 277 |

In addition, conversation uses a considerable amount of local repetition, repeating expressions from the immediate context. In many cases, these locally repeated expressions are not lexical bundles as we have defined them. Further, it is common to find speakers repeating elements from previous utterances, without repeating complete lexical sequences.

**Table 13.3**  **Grammatical category of the ending word in four-word lexical bundles (approximate proportional distribution)**

| | CONV | ACAD | example |
|---|---|---|---|
| verb | 40% | 5% | *I want to know* (CONV) |
| pronoun | 15% | — | *well that's what I* (CONV) |
| other function word | 40% | 85% | *I went to the* (CONV) *in the case of* (ACAD) |
| noun | — | 10% | *at the same time* (ACAD) |

In the following conversational excerpt, lexical bundles (including three-word, four-word, and two-word contracted bundles) are marked in bold, while local repeated combinations are given in SMALL CAPS:

Text sample 1: CONVERSATION

A: **I'M NOT SURE** *if* THEY'RE GOING *away this weekend,* **I'M NOT SURE** *when* THEY'RE GOING –

B: *Oh,* **well they're not** *going tomorrow* \<laugh\>

A: *Oh, must be Friday then, I knew they were going away for the week, weekend*

C: **That's very** *nice too.*

A: *The first time* \<unclear\> *were saying this* –

B: *It's tricky* **to have to get** *here*

A: *I know* \<laugh\> *– the evil look, I shall move* **in a minute** \<laugh\>

C: *Bite back*

A: *Funny old tramp, the leaves fall off him without those, they get stalkier and stalkier* **as time goes on**

C: *Yeah,* **yeah well** I'VE GOT AN ORDINARY \<unclear\>

A: *pot, it came from* \<unclear\>

C: I'VE GOT AN ORDINARY \<unclear\>

C: *just keep peeling the bottom ones off it, just get* \<unclear\>

A: *My yucca's dying*

B: *Oh dear*

C: *That could well be the compost, poor leaves and things*

B: *Maybe*

A: **Well I think I've** *overwatered it* (CONV)

This excerpt illustrates the dense use of recurrent lexical bundles and repeated local expressions in conversation, while at the same time showing the typical pattern of using non-recurrent expressions to a greater extent than recurrent ones. Many lexical bundles are repeated locally, in addition to their being recurrent across texts. For example, the sequences *I'm not sure* and *they're going* are of this type in the above interaction. Other sequences are repeated locally but are not commonly recurrent across texts, such as the expression *I've got an ordinary* in the above excerpt. In addition, some expressions above include several repeated elements even though they are not exact repetitions, as in:

*I'm not sure if they're going away*

*I'm not sure when they're going . . .*

*well they're not going*

*I knew they were going away*

For the most part, such repeated sequences are localized to particular contexts, rather than representing a general use of recurrent lexical bundles or idioms across texts.

It is worth noting that recognizably trite or idiomatic expressions are typically not frequent. For example, the expression *that's very nice* occurs only about once in a typical 40-hour sample of conversation (less than five times per million words), even though the expression seems common and over-used. (The shorter contracted sequence *that's nice* is much more common, occurring over 60 times per million words.)

Other expressions represent common lexico-grammatical combinations, even though the specific lexical bundle is not common. Thus in Text sample 1, Speaker C's utterance *That could well be the compost ...* contains the frequently used frame: possibility modal + *well be*. This sequence is relatively common in both conversation and fiction, with the combinations *might/may/can/could + well be* all being attested. However, none of these individual modal verbs is used frequently enough in this frame to form a common lexical bundle.

While the extent to which conversation uses recurrent language might be as expected, it is likely to be more surprising that recurrent lexical bundles occur so frequently in academic prose. The following sentence illustrates the relatively dense use of lexical bundles in an academic book:

> *An isolation area* **is used to** *house the foster mothers and re-derived litters until* **it can be** *confirmed that their health status* **has not been** *compromised* **as a result of the** *procedure.* (ACAD)

In both conversation and academic prose, lexical bundles can be strung together in a series. For example, in Text sample 1, the expression *I'm not sure if they're going* actually represents three different lexical bundles occurring in sequence:

> **I'm not sure** + **if they're** + **they're going**

Similar overlapping sequences commonly occur in academic prose. In the following example, each lexical bundle is enclosed in numbered brackets:

> *Very little is known about the control of the timing of these events [₁* **but** *[₂* **it** *[₃* **is₁** *] clear₂] [₄* **that₃** *] there are₄] [₅* **at least two₅** *] underlying clocks.* (ACAD)

As illustrated by all the above examples, most lexical bundles are not complete structural units. In conversation, a few bundles can be used as complete utterances, such as:

> *I don't like it*          *That's a good idea*

However, other bundles that could stand alone are in fact usually completed with a complement clause, for example:

> *well I don't know*          *I didn't know that*
>
> *I think I might*          *I don't want to*

In academic prose, there are almost no lexical bundles representing complete structural units. Instead, most bundles span two structural units, such as a noun phrase + beginning of a prepositional phrase. As a result, most of these lexical bundles end in a function word, usually either an article or a preposition; for example:

> *the end of the*          *as a result of*
>
> *in addition to the*          *in the case of*
>
> *the presence of a*          *the point of view of*

When a lexical bundle is structurally complete in academic prose, it is typically a prepositional phrase that functions as a discourse signalling device; for example:

> *for the first time*          *in the first place*
>
> *in the same way*          *on the other hand*
>
> *in the present study*          *in the next chapter*

Although both conversation and academic prose make frequent use of recurrent lexical bundles, the structural correlates of those bundles are notably different in the two registers. In conversation, the large majority of lexical bundles are clause segments: either declarative structures with a subject pronoun followed by an extended verb phrase, or interrogative structures.

Declarative clause segments as lexical bundles in conversation:

| | |
|---|---|
| *I don't know what* | *I said to him* |
| *I don't know how* | *I would like to* |
| *I don't think I* | *well you'll have to* |
| *I thought it was* | *you might as well* |
| *I don't want to* | |

Interrogative clause segments as lexical bundles in conversation:

| | |
|---|---|
| *can I have a* | *what are you doing* |
| *have you got any* | *what did she say* |
| *do you know what* | *what's the matter with* |
| *do you want to* | *how do you know* |
| *are you talking about* | |

In some cases, there is a grouping of lexical bundles composed of interchangeable elements. For example, most of the sequences made up of the following elements occur as recurrent lexical bundles in conversation:

**I/you + don't/didn't + know/think/want + complement-clause**

In other cases, the grouping of bundles can be summarized as a frame with a single more variable slot, such as:

**I want to *[do/get/go/see/be/know]***

**do you want *[to/a/me/some/any/it/the]***

In contrast to the dependence on clausal elements in conversation, most lexical bundles in academic prose are composed of nominal or prepositional elements:

| | |
|---|---|
| *the end of the* | *the relationship between the* |
| *one of the most* | *an increase in the* |
| *the results of the* | *as a result of* |
| *the way in which* | *in the case of* |
| *the extent to which* | *on the basis of* |
| *the fact that the* | |

Some of these elements co-occur in extremely productive frames, such as '*the __ of the __* '. Many words, e.g. *end* and *base*, can fill the slot within the frame and make a lexical bundle:

**the *[end/base/position/size/structure/purpose/nature ...]* of the**
  (used for 43 different lexical bundles)
**in the *[case/absence/form/presence/number/process/study ...]* of**
  (used for 17 different lexical bundles)
**as a *[result/function/consequence/matter/means]* of**
**it is *[(im)possible/(un)likely/important/necessary ...]* that/to**

## 13.2.2  Key to lists of lexical bundles

The following sections present organized lists of the common four-word, five-word, and six-word lexical bundles found in conversation (13.2.3) and academic prose (13.2.4). Three-word lexical bundles are too numerous to list in a work of this scope; however, the most common three-word bundles are listed in Corpus Findings above.

For four-word lexical bundles, any sequence that does not recur at least ten times per million words is excluded. Because five-word and six-word lexical bundles are considerably less common than four-word, bundles recurring more than five times per million words are included for those categories.

The lists in the following sections are annotated for four major frequency benchmarks, showing occurrences per million words as follows:

| | | | |
|---|---|---|---|
| over 100 | *** | over 20 | * |
| over 40 | ** | over 10 | (not marked) |

For five-word and six-word lexical bundles, the symbol $^\wedge$ means at least five occurrences per million words.

Some lexical bundles of a given length are incorporated into longer lexical bundles, and these are marked with a '+' either before or after. For example, in conversation the four-word bundle *I don't know what+* is incorporated into two different five-word bundles: *I don't know what to+* and *I don't know what it+*. These five-word bundles are in turn incorporated into six-word bundles: *I don't know what to do* and *I don't know what it is*.

Similar extensions occur in academic prose. For example, the four-word bundle *it should be noted+* is incorporated into the five-word bundle *it should be noted that +*, which is in turn incorporated into the six-word bundle *it should be noted that the*.

Lexical bundles are grouped according to their structural correlates, and each lexical bundle is listed in only one category. However, these categories are not always mutually exclusive. For example, in conversation some lexical bundles in the category 'personal pronoun + verb phrase' include fragments of *wh*-clauses (e.g. *I don't know why, I can't remember what*); these bundles could have been listed in the category 'Lexical bundles with *wh*-clauses'. In academic prose, some four-word lexical bundles consisting of a noun phrase are incorporated into longer lexical bundles consisting of a prepositional phrase (e.g. + *the end of the* → *at the end of the*). Each lexical bundle is listed in the appropriate category for a given length, without consideration of corresponding longer lexical bundles.

## 13.2.3   Lexical bundles in conversation

Although most lexical bundles do not represent complete structural units, they can be grouped into categories according to their structural correlates. In conversation, 14 major categories can be distinguished:

- personal pronoun + lexical verb phrase
- pronoun/noun phrase + *be* +
- verb phrase with active verb
- *yes-no* question fragments
- *wh*-question fragments
- lexical bundles with *wh*-clauses
- lexical bundles with *to*-clauses
- verb + *that*-clause fragments
- adverbial clause fragments
- noun phrase expressions

- prepositional phrase expressions
- quantifier expressions
- other expressions
- meaningless sound bundles

## 13.2.3.1 Personal pronoun + lexical verb phrase (+ complement-clause fragment)

**CORPUS FINDINGS** [3]

The lists in this section are organized according to the different subject pronouns (*I*, *you*, other), and according to the main verb (*know*, *think*, *want*, *said/tell*, *like*, *mean*, modal/semi-modal verbs, and other verbs).

➤ By far the most prevalent type of lexical bundle in conversation is a clause fragment, consisting of a subject pronoun followed by a verb phrase. In many cases, the verb phrase is extended by the beginning of a following complement clause.

➤ **Four-word bundles:**

➤ **Expressions with *I* + *know***: ***\*\*\*I don't know what+*, *\*\*well I don't know*, *\*\*I don't know how+*, *\*\*I don't know if+*, *\*\*I don't know whether+*, *\*\*I don't know why*, *\*\*oh I don't know*, *\*but I don't know*, *\*I don't know where+*, *I didn't know that*, *I didn't know what*, *and I don't know*, *so I don't know*, *I don't know about*, *I don't know I*, *I don't know who*, *I don't really know*, *yeah I know but*, *I know what you+*, *I mean I know*.

➤ **Expressions with *I* + *think***: *\*\*+I don't think so*, *\*but I don't think*, *\*I don't think he*, *\*I don't think I+*, *\*I don't think it+*, *\*I don't think it's*, *\*I don't think you+*, *\*no I don't think+*, *well I don't think*, *I don't think she*, *I don't think that*, *I don't think they*, *I don't think we*; *\*\*I thought it was+*, *\*I thought I would*, *\*I thought that was*, *\*I thought you were*, *\*I would have thought*, *and I thought oh*, *and I thought well*, *so I thought well*, *I thought he was*, *I thought they were*, *I thought to myself*, *I thought you said*; *\*\*I think it was*, *I think I might*, *I think I would*, *I think it's a*, *I think it is*, *I think you should*, *I was thinking of*.

➤ **Expressions with *I* + *want***: *\*\*\*I don't want to+*, *I didn't want to*, *but I don't want+*, *I don't want it*, *no I don't want+*; *\*+I want to do*, *\*I want to get*, *\*I want to go+*, *\*I want to see*, *and I want to*, *I just want to*, *I want to be*, *I want to know*, *I want you to*.

➤ **Expressions with *I* + *said/tell***: *\*\*+I said to him*, *\*and I said to+*, *\*so I said well*, *\*+I said to her*, *\*I said well I*, *and I said I*, *and I said oh*, *and I said well*, *so I said to*, *I said I don't*, *I said I would*; *\*\*I tell you what+*, *\*I'll tell you what*.

➤ **Expressions with *I* + *like***: *\*\*I would like to+*; *I don't like it*, *I don't like that*, *I don't like the*, *I don't like them*.

➤ **Expressions with *I* + *mean***: *\*I mean I don't+*, *but I mean I*, *yeah but I mean*, *I mean if you*, *I mean it's not*, *I mean it was*, *I mean you know*.

➤ **Expressions with *I* + modal/semi-modal verb**: *\*\*\*I was going to+*, *\*\*I'm not going to*, *\*I'm going to do*, *\*I'm going to get*, *\*I'm going to go*, *\*I'm going to have+*, *I'm going to get*, *I'm going to put*, *I'm just going to*, *well I'm going to*; *I would have to*, *I would love to*, *I would rather have*, *I would have been*; *I'll give you a*, *I'll go and get*, *I'll have a look*, *I'll have to go*, *I'll have to get*; *I shall have to*; *I don't have to*, *I had to go*, *I have to go*; *\*I've got to go*, *I've got to do*, *I've got to* get; I can't be bothered, I can't do it, I can't remember what, I couldn't believe it; I might as well; I used to go.

➤ **Other expressions with I + verb phrase:** *I haven't got a, *I haven't got any, I see what you+, I went to the, I was talking to, I was trying to.

➤ **Expressions with you + know:** **+you know what I+, you don't know what, you know when I, you know when you, you know where the, you know I mean.

➤ **Expressions with you + want:** **+you don't want to, **+you want me to+, **+you want to go, *+you want to do, you want to be, +you want to come, you want to get, you want to see.

➤ **Expressions with you + modal/semi-modal verb:** **you don't have to, *you have to do, and you have to, you have to go, you have to have, you have to pay, well you'll have to; *you're going to have, *you're not going to, *you were going to, you're not going to, if you're going to, you're going to get; *you can have a, and then you can, you can do it, you can get a, you can have it; you've got to be, you've got to do, you've got to go, you've got to have; you have to be; *you might as well; you'll be able to, you're not supposed to, you don't need to.

➤ **Other expressions with you + verb phrase:** you see what I+, +you think about it, you haven't got a.

➤ **Expressions with he/she + said:** he said to me, and she said oh, she said to me.

➤ **Other pronoun + verb phrase expressions:** *he was going to, he's not going to, she was going to; *we're going to have, we were going to, we're not going to, we used to have; *+us have a look+; they're not going to, they were going to, they don't want to; it's not going to, it was going to.

➤ **Five-word bundles:** I don't know what it+, I don't know what to+, I don't know how many; I don't know how much^, I don't know how you^, I don't know if I^, I don't know if it's^, I don't know if you^, I don't know what I^, I don't know what the^, I don't know what they^, I don't know where it^, I don't know whether I^, I don't know whether it's^, I don't know whether you^; I know what you mean, I know what it is^; No, I don't think so^, I don't think I would^, I don't think it is^, I don't think you can^; I thought it was a, I think it might be^; I don't want to be, I don't want to go, but I don't want to^, I don't want to do^, I don't want to see^, no I don't want to^; I want to go to^; and I said to her^, and I said to him^; I tell you what I^; I would like to go, I would like to see^; I mean I don't know^; **+I was going to say, I'm going to have to, I won't be able to^, I see what you mean; **+you know what I mean, you know what it is^; +you want me to do, you want to go to, +you want a cup of+^; you're going to have to, you won't be able to, you see what I mean.

➤ **Six-word bundles:** I don't know what it is, I don't know what to do, you want a cup of tea^.

**DISCUSSION OF FINDINGS**

The majority of the lexical bundles in this category have a first person pronoun as subject together with a stative main verb. Further, most of these bundles are used to begin an utterance, and they end with the beginning of a complement clause: either a *that*-clause (usually with the complementizer *that* omitted), a *to*-clause, or a *wh*-clause. For the most part, the main clause verbs in these sequences mark personal stance, reporting personal feelings, thoughts, or desires (9.2.2.2, 9.3.2.2, 9.4.2.7, 12.3). These recurrent lexical bundles thus seem to function as **utterance launchers**, presenting a personal stance relative to the information in the following complement clause.

A large number of these bundles report negative personal states in the first person; for example, *I don't know, I don't think, I don't want, I don't like*:

> **I don't think** *I could handle it.* (CONV)
>
> **I don't think** *it's very good.* (CONV)
>
> **I don't know what** *she's got.* (CONV)
>
> **I don't know why** *he does it.* (CONV)
>
> *Oh* **I don't want to** *hear this.* (CONV)
>
> **I don't like it** *when they're horrid to each other.* (CONV)

In addition, the verbs *think* (especially past tense *thought*) and *want* are used in many affirmative lexical bundles to report first person states:

> **I thought he was** *going for three weeks.* (CONV)
>
> **I thought I would** *warn you, though.* (CONV)

The expression *I want* is usually followed by a *to*-clause:

> *Yeah* **I want to go** *and see that.* (CONV)
>
> *Oh I don't know what* **I want to do** *tonight.* (CONV)

There are fewer lexical bundles with *you* as subject pronoun. Several of these occur with the main verb *want*. However, these are mostly part of larger interrogative or conditional clauses:

> *Do* **you want me to** *send them today?* (CONV)
>
> *Craig do* **you want to do** *something?* (CONV)
>
> *If* **you want to come** *along.* (CONV)

The verb *say* (especially past tense *said*) is one of the few dynamic verbs used in these lexical bundles. These expressions most commonly report the speech of the first person:

> **I said to him**, *you need it.* (CONV)
>
> *Anyway,* **I said I would** *make inquiries.* (CONV†)
>
> **And I said well** *why don't we call it that.* (CONV)

In addition, *said* is the only verb to be used in multiple expressions reporting the actions of a third person:

> *Because* **she said to me**, *is your brother called Anthony?* (CONV)
>
> **And she said oh** *I didn't know what to do.* (CONV)

The subject pronoun *you* is also used in several lexical bundles with modal or semi-modal verbs; many of these expressions are used as directives:

> *Oh* **you have to go** *back down there.* (CONV)
>
> **You've got to have** *one for a change.* (CONV)
>
> *Well if you're not working* **you might as well** *go.* (CONV)

Finally, two expressions that can function as discourse markers also combine with clause fragments to form lexical bundles: *I mean* and *you know*. *I mean* almost always functions as a discourse marker in these bundles:

> *Well I –* **I mean I don't** *know, but I just –* (CONV)
>
> **I mean it's not** *as if it would be that difficult.* (CONV†)
>
> **But I mean I** *suppose it's true.* (CONV)
>
> **Yeah but I mean** *that's – that's not the thing.* (CONV)

*You know* more commonly takes a following *wh*-clause as complement, especially in the five-word lexical bundle *you know what I mean*:

> *I got this brain problem,* **you know what I mean?** (CONV)

> *But my mum's pretty good,* **you know what I mean,** *she – as long as I can arrange it around her she'll arrange her arrangements around me sort of thing.* (CONV)

However, *you know* also functions as discourse marker in some of these bundles:

> *My first year at Grange Hill, right,* **you know when I** *used to wear boxer shorts with no knickers on underneath.* (CONV)

In addition, these two discourse markers commonly co-occur with each other to form lexical bundles *I mean you know* and *you know I mean*:

> **I mean you know** *you say all these people are coming.* (CONV†)

> *But what I thought I would do – is like for Ellie and Linda – for Christmas presents – say –* **I mean you know** *it won't be a lot but – that'll be it.* (CONV)

> **You know I mean** *I didn't think anything of it.* (CONV)

These expressions are associated with personal speech habits, with some individuals making an extremely frequent use of them:

> A: *Yeah, well* **you know what I mean,** *for no reason – and you're not really – you feel guilty for being snappy, but then you er –* **know what I mean?**

> B: *Mm. Don't say* **do you know what I mean** *– Carole says it all the time.* (CONV)

> A: **You know I mean** *some people are so, sort of, un – untrustworthy and –*
> B: *Yes.*
> A: *Well they're just not honest, are they?*
> B: *No, no – they're not.*
> A: **You know I mean** *alright y– you want to sell your house and everything, but I mean for goodness sake, I mean –*
> B: *You've got to live with yourself.*
> A: *That's right, I mean.* (CONV)

## 13.2.3.2 Pronoun/noun phrase + *be* +

**CORPUS FINDINGS** [3]

The lists in this section are organized according to the different subjects: impersonal pronouns (*it, that, there*) and other noun phrases. Notice that for this purpose existential *there* (3.6.3, 11.4.1) is grouped with impersonal pronoun subjects.

➤ The following lexical bundles are all clause fragments, mostly consisting of an impersonal or demonstrative subject pronoun followed by the copula *be*, which is often contracted onto the pronoun (e.g. *it's, that's*). In some cases, the copula is followed by the beginning of a complement clause or noun phrase subject predicative.

➤ **Four-word bundles:**
  ➤ **Expressions with *it* (+ auxiliary) + copula *be* (+ ...):** \*\**it's going to be, it's got to be, it must have been, it used to be, it's a bit of+, it's a lot of+*, and *it was a, it was a bit, it was in the, it's not too bad, it's up to you.*
  ➤ **Expressions with *that* (+ auxiliary) + copula *be* (+ ...):** \**that's what I mean,* \**that's what I said+, that's what I'm saying, that's what I thought, that's what I was, that's what it is, well that's what I, that's a good idea, that's going to be.*
  ➤ **Expressions with *there* (+ auxiliary) + copula *be* (+ ...):** \**there's a lot of,* and *there was a, there's going to be.*
  ➤ **Expressions with personal pronoun + copula *be* (+ ...):** \**I'm going to be, you're going to be, he's going to be, I was in the.*
  ➤ **Expressions with other noun phrase (+ auxiliary) + copula *be*:** *but the thing is, the only thing is, some of them are.*
➤ **Five-word bundles:** *it's a bit of a^, it's a lot of money^, it's nothing to do with^, that's what I said to^.*

The majority of these lexical bundles have impersonal pronouns as subject, with the main content following the copula. The pronoun *it* and existential *there* are often only vaguely referential, if at all (11.4.1):

> *So ok, let's hope **it's going to be** nice.* (CONV)

> *Well I don't know, **it's up to you**.* (CONV)

> *I don't think **there's going to be** a lot left there.* (CONV)

The demonstrative pronoun *that* in these bundles is usually followed by a *wh-*clause referring to the content of previous discourse:

> ***That's what I said** to Dave.* (CONV)

> A: *Just because we've got a fair idea of who's going to fill the post doesn't mean to say that they will fill, does it? I mean –*
> B: *Exactly*
> C: ***That's what I'm saying**, yeah.* (CONV)

> A: *She spoils him boy.*
> &lt;...&gt;
> A: *Yes she licked him half way through a bad one.*
> B: *Yeah but –*
> A: *Well **that's what I mean**.* (CONV)

## 13.2.3.3 Verb phrase with active verb

The lists in this section are organized according to the different main verbs: *have, go, get/got, put, see, want*, modal/semi-modal verbs, and other verbs.

➤ The following lexical bundles are all verb phrases plus a part of a following complement phrase or clause.
➤ **Four-word bundles:**
  ➤ **Expressions with *have*:** \*\*+*have a look at,* \*\**let's have a look+,* \**go and have a+,* \*+*and have a look+,* \**have to have a, going to have a, got to have a, had a bit*

*of, have a bit of, have a cup of*+, *have a go at, have a look in, have a lot of, have a word with.* (*Have a look* rarely occurs in AmE conversation; 13.3.2.1.)

➤ **Expressions with *go*:** +*go to the toilet*, \**go to the bathroom* (AmE), *got to go to, have to go and, have to go to.*

➤ **Expressions with *get/got*:** *get on with it, get rid of it, got a bit of, got one of them, haven't got a clue.*

➤ **Expressions with *put*:** \**put it in the*, \**put it on the*, *put the kettle on, put them in the.*

➤ **Expressions with *see*:** *see if I can*+, *see if we can, see if you can.*

➤ **Expressions with *want*:** +*want a cup of*+, +*want me to do.*

➤ **Other modal or semi-modal expressions:** \*\**going to be a*, \*\*+*going to have to*, \*\**going to have a*, \**going to do it*, \**going to get a*, *going to go and, going to go to, going to try and*; \*\*+*was going to say, was going to be, was going to do*; \**not going to be, not going to get*; \**have to do it, have to pay for; used to be a, used to have a.*

➤ **Other verb phrase expressions:** \*\**thank you very much*, \**don't worry about it*, \**got a lot of, give it to you, hang on a minute, oh look at that*, +*tell you what I.*

➤ **Five-word bundles:** *go and have a look, and have a look at, have a look at it, have a look at the, have a cup of tea*, +*want a cup of tea, let's have a look at*^, *let me have a look*^, *got nothing to do with*^, *see if I can get*^.

### DISCUSSION OF FINDINGS

This category of extended verb phrase expressions is unlike the other categories of lexical bundles, in that a large number are relatively idiomatic (13.1, 13.3). In general, lexical bundles are not idiomatic, even though they are the most frequent lexical combinations. However, this category includes many expressions that are both frequent and relatively idiomatic, with the entire lexical bundle having a meaning that cannot be easily derived from the individual parts:

> *Yeah, I'll* **have a cup of tea**. (CONV)
>
> *Oh well,* **let's have a look. Let's have a look at** *this.* (CONV)
>
> **Hang on a minute**, *you can have some of mine.* (CONV)
>
> *You might as well* **get on with it** *Neil.* (CONV)
>
> *I* **haven't got a clue** *where I'm going.* (CONV)
>
> *Oh I think I may have to* **go to the toilet** *before I go home.* (CONV)
>
> *Well that ain't* **got nothing to do with** *his kidney problems.* (CONV)

## 13.2.3.4   *Yes-no* question fragments

### CORPUS FINDINGS [3]

The lists in this section are organized according to the different main verbs used in the question: *have, got, know, want, talk/tell*, modal verbs, and other verbs.

➤ The lexical bundles in this category all begin with either an auxiliary verb or a modal verb, followed by a subject pronoun. This type of bundle is the beginning portion of a yes/no question.

➤ **Four-word *yes-no* question bundles:**

➤ ***Yes-no* question with *have*:** \**can I have a*+, *can I have some, did you have a.*

➤ ***Yes-no* question with *got*:** \**have you got a*, \**have you got any, have you got the.*

> ➤ **Yes-no question with *know*:** \*\**do you know what+*, *do you know how*, *do you know that*.

> ➤ **Yes-no question with *want*:** \*\*\*+*do you want to+*, \*\**do you want a+*, \*\**do you want me+*, \**do you want some+*, *do you want any*, *do you want it*, *do you want the*.

> ➤ **Yes-no question with *talk* or *tell*:** +*are you talking about*, *did I tell you*.

> ➤ **Yes-no question with modal/semi-modal verb:** \*\*\*+*are you going to+*, \*\**are we going to*, *am I going to*; \**do you have to*, *have you got to*.

> ➤ **Yes-no question with other verbs:** \**would you like to*, *did you see that*, *do you think I*, *is that the one*.

➤ **Five-word yes-no question bundles:** \**do you want me to+*, \**do you want to go*, +*do you want to do*, *do you want a bit*^, *do you want a cup+*^, *do you want some more*^, *do you want to come*^, *do you want to take*^; \*+*are you going to do*; \**do you know what I+*; *can I have a look*^.

➤ **Six-word yes-no question bundles**: \**do you know what I mean*, *do you want me to do*, *do you want a cup of*^.

*Yes-no* questions with the verb *want*, asking about the needs or desires of the addressee, are the most common type of lexical bundle in this category:

> **Do you want a bit** more? (CONV)

> **Do you want me to** send them today? (CONV)

Other relatively common interrogative lexical bundles are formed with *can I have* and *have you got*. Both of these expressions are used to form expressions functioning as indirect requests:

> **Can I have a** little bit please? (CONV)

> **Have you got any** money with you today? (CONV)

Finally, the relatively fixed expression *Do you know what I mean?* is included in this category. In many contexts, this expression functions more like an extended discourse marker (14.3.3.3) than a genuine *yes-no* question:

> Probably just glad that someone's doing their job. **Do you know what I mean?** (CONV)

## 13.2.3.5 *Wh*-question fragments

The lists in this section are organized according to the different *wh*-question words (*what*, *where*, *how*), and by the most common main verbs occurring with *what* (i.e. *do* and *say*).

➤ The lexical bundles in this category typically begin with a *wh*-question word, followed by a modal or other auxiliary verb, which in turn is followed by a subject pronoun. This type of bundle is the beginning portion of a *wh*-question.

➤ **Four-word *wh*-question bundles:**

> ➤ **Wh-question with *what* ... *do*:** \*\**what are you doing*, \**what did you do*, *what do you do*, *what have you done*.

> ➤ **Wh-question with *what* ... *say*:** \**what did you say*, \**what did he say*, *what do you say*, *what did she say*.

➤ Other **wh-question with what:** ***what do you mean**, ***what do you think+**, ***what do you want+**, ***what do you call+**, **what have you got**, and **what have you, what time is it, what's the matter with, what are you going+.**

➤ **Wh-question with where:** **where are you going; where did you get.**

➤ **Wh-question with how:** ***how do you know; how do you spell; how much do you+.**

➤ **Five-word wh-question bundles:** ***what are you going to+**, **what are you talking about^, what do you call it, what do you think of, what do you want to+, how much do you want^.**

➤ **Six-word wh-questions:** **what are you going to do, what was I going to say^, what do you want to do^.**

**DISCUSSION OF FINDINGS**

*Wh*-questions with *do* as main verb, asking about present or past actions, are the most common lexical bundles in this category:

> **What are you doing** here? (CONV)

> **What did you do** on Tuesday night? (CONV)

*Wh*-questions with *say* are also included in this category; these request reports of past speech events:

> And **what did she say**? (CONV)

In addition, there are a few lexical bundles formed with *where* and *how*:

> **Where did you get** all the beads from? (CONV)

> **How do you know**? (CONV)

## 13.2.3.6 Lexical bundles with *wh*-clause fragments

**CORPUS FINDINGS** [3]

➤ The lexical bundles in this category are of two types: verb phrases followed by a *wh*-clause, or bundles that represent the beginning of a *wh*-clause.

➤ **Four-word bundles with wh-clauses:**

➤ **Expressions with know + wh-clause:** *+*don't know what it+*, *+*don't know what to+*, +*don't know what the*; **+*know what I mean*, *+*know what to do*, *+*know what it is*, +*know what you mean*, *know where it is.*

➤ **Expressions with see + wh-clause:** +*see what I mean*, +*see what you mean.*

➤ **Other expressions with wh-clauses:** what I'm going to, what you're going to, what I want to+, what you want to+, +what I said to, when I went to, when we went to.

➤ **Five-word bundles with wh-clauses:** +*don't know what it is*, +*don't know what to do, what you want to do, what I want to do^.*

➤ **Six-word bundles with wh-clauses:** what I was going to say^.

**DISCUSSION OF FINDINGS**

Most of the lexical bundles included in this category are used in larger clausal expressions with a pronominal subject (13.2.3.1–2). Other examples of this type are:

> I **don't know what to get**. (CONV)

> He wouldn't **know what to do**. (CONV)

> Yeah, I **see what you mean**. (CONV)

**13.2.3.7** **Lexical bundles with *to*-clause fragments**

For verb phrases followed by a *to*-clause, the lists in this section are organized according to the main clause verb or predicative adjective (*want, be able, like*). For bundles beginning a *to*-clause, the lists are organized according to the verb of the *to*-clause (*go, do,* other).

➤ The lexical bundles in this category are of two types: verb phrases followed by a *to*-clause, or bundles that represent the beginning of a *to*-clause.

➤ **Four-word *to*-clause bundles:**
  ➤ ***Want* + to-clause:** *\*+don't want to go, +don't want to be, +don't want to do; \*want to do it, \*want to go to, want to go and.*
  ➤ ***Able* + to-clause:** *\*be able to get, be able to do, might be able to.*
  ➤ ***Like* + to-clause:** *+would like to go.*
  ➤ ***To*-clause with *go*:** *\*+to go to the+, to go and get, to go and see, to go in the, to go out with.*
  ➤ ***To*-clause with *do*:** *to do with it, to do with the.*
  ➤ ***To*-clause with other verb or adjective:** *to be able to, to get rid of, to have a look+.*

➤ **Five-word *to*-clause bundles:** *to go to the toilet^, to have a look at^.*

The most common bundles in this category occur with *want* as the main clause verb, followed by a *to*-clause. Many of these bundles are included in larger clausal lexical bundles with a pronominal subject (13.2.3.1):

> But I **don't want to go** home. (CONV)

> I didn't really **want to do it** very well. (CONV)

Other common lexical bundles in this category use the verb *go* in the *to*-clause:

> You want me **to go and get** it for you? (CONV)

> Anna-Marie is quite prepared **to go out with** other men if she wants to. (CONV)

**13.2.3.8** **Verb + *that*-clause fragments**

➤ Only a few lexical bundles in conversation are composed of a main verb followed by a *that*-clause (with the complementizer *that* omitted). However, as we showed in 13.2.3.1, there are a large number of lexical bundles that follow the pattern: personal pronoun + lexical verb phrase + *that*-clause.

➤ **Four-word bundles:** *think I'm going to, \*thought it was a, said I don't know.*

*That*-clauses are extremely common in conversation (9.2.6), where they typically occur with a few selected main clause verbs (e.g. *think, say, know*) and a personal pronoun as subject of the main clause. As a result, most lexical bundles that incorporate *that*-clauses include both the main clause subject pronoun as well as the main clause verb (e.g. *I don't think he, I said I would*; 13.2.3.1). Although the lexical bundles in the present section begin with the main clause verb, they also commonly co-occur with personal pronouns as subject of the main clause:

> Well, I **thought it was a** good film. (CONV)

> She **said I don't know.** (CONV)

## 13.2.3.9 Adverbial clause fragments

**CORPUS FINDINGS** [3]

➤ Relatively few lexical bundles initiate an adverbial clause, which usually has a contingency meaning. These fall into two main groups: lexical bundles beginning an *if*-clause, and lexical bundles beginning with a complex subordinator, which have the structure *as* + adverb + *as* + pronoun:

➤ **Four-word adverbial clause bundles:**

> ➤ **If-clauses:** \*\**if you want to, if you don't want*+, \**if you've got a, if you can get,* +*if I can get.*

> ➤ **Adverbial clauses with complex subordinators *as* + adverb + *as* + pronoun:** \**as long as you*+, *as far as I*+, *as soon as I, as soon as you.*

> ➤ **Other adverbial clause fragments:** *because/cause/cos I want to.*

➤ **Five-word adverbial clause bundles:** *if you don't want to^, if you know what I*+^, *if you think about it^, as far as I'm concerned^, as far as I know^, as long as you don't^.*

➤ **Six-word adverbial clause bundles:** *if you know what I mean^.*

**DISCUSSION OF FINDINGS**

Several of the lexical bundles initiating adverbial clauses are *if*-clauses, with *you* as subject and the main verbs *want* or *got/get*:

> **If you want to** come, get five pounds to me with your name and number. (CONV)

> But like it's different **if you've got a** really bad cold. (CONV)

In addition, this category includes several adverbial clauses beginning with complex subordinators of the form *as far/long/soon as*:

> Because they couldn't have any children of their own, **as far as I know.** (CONV)

> You know, you can go and do things like that, **as long as you don't** get caught. (CONV)

> Oh **as soon as you** find your thing, it's ok, you can stop looking then. (CONV)

Finally, the relatively fixed response *because/cause/cos I want to* is also included in this category:

> A: Can I go now?
> B: Why?
> A: **Cause I want to.** (CONV)

## 13.2.3.10 Noun phrase expressions

**CORPUS FINDINGS [3]**

➤ The lexical bundles in this category are of two types: the beginning of a noun phrase including *of*, and other noun phrases and noun phrase fragments.

➤ **Four-word noun phrase bundles:**

    ➤ **Noun phrase (fragment) including *of*:** \*\*+*the end of the*+, \*+*the back of the*, \*+*the middle of the*, \**the other side of*+, +*other side of the, the side of the, the top of the, the bottom of the,* +*end of the day,* +*the end of it;* \*+*the rest of the,* +*the rest of it;* \**that sort of thing; the name of the; most of the time; quite a lot of.*

    ➤ **Other noun phrase or noun phrase fragment:** \*\**or something like that,* \**and things like that,* \*+*nothing to do with, something to do with, and the other one, the other day and, the one with the, the last time I, o'clock in the morning.*

➤ **Five-word noun phrase bundles:** +*the end of the day, the other side of the, three quarters of an hour*^.

**DISCUSSION OF FINDINGS**

Most of the lexical bundles in this category consist of an incomplete noun phrase containing an *of*-phrase, usually identifying a physical location: the head noun specifies some position (the *back, middle, top, bottom, other side,* etc.) with respect to the complement of *of*:

> *Don't sit on **the back of the** bike.* (CONV)
>
> *Jimmy kicked it right into **the middle of the** field.* (CONV)
>
> *It's more likely to be at **the top of the** pile.* (CONV)

Several of the other noun phrases in this category are more idiomatic. Some of these are coordination tags (2.9.2) used for hedging functions or generally vague reference:

> *I think he means people who are regarded by others as sort of experts and psychics and wise men **and things like that**.* (CONV)
>
> *Before I go to bed I have baked beans on toast **or something like that**, you know.* (CONV)
>
> *Here is the moon – Now if we can sort of simplify the whole thing, forget about the continents **and that sort of thing**.* (CONV)

Other expressions are used with a quantification meaning and emphatic effect:

> *It's **quite a lot of** work to do on this cataloging.* (CONV)
>
> *Cause I want **nothing to do with** her.* (CONV)

## 13.2.3.11 Prepositional phrase expressions

**CORPUS FINDINGS [3]**

➤ The lexical bundles in this category begin with a preposition, and are of two types: prepositional phrases or prepositional phrase fragments with an *of* following the noun, and other prepositional phrases or prepositional phrase fragments.

➤ **Four-word prepositional phrase bundles:**

    ➤ **Preposition + noun phrase fragment containing *of*:** \*\**at the end of*+, \**in the middle of*+, *at the back of, on top of the, for a couple of, for the rest of.*

> ➤ **Other prepositional phrase or prepositional phrase fragment:** *at the same time, *for a long time, by the time I, in the morning and, up in the morning, on the other side, in the first place.*
➤ **Five-word prepositional phrase bundles:** ***at the end of the+, at the end of it^, *in the middle of the.*
➤ **Six-word prepositional phrase bundles:** *at the end of the day.*

**DISCUSSION OF FINDINGS**

Lexical bundles incorporating prepositional phrases in conversation are used primarily as time or place adverbials.

Temporal references:

> *I get paid **at the end of the** week.* (CONV)
>
> *The only time we got chips was **in the middle of the** week.* (CONV)
>
> *So you can also phone him **at the same time**.* (CONV)
>
> *Well I haven't had fish **for a long time**.* (CONV)

Spatial references:

> *Oh look **at the back of** the door window.* (CONV)
>
> *Or if we're not there, go **on the other side** of the park.* (CONV)

In addition, this category includes the relatively fixed expression *at the end of the day*, which also has temporal connotations:

> *And I end up with nothing **at the end of the day**.* (CONV)

## 13.2.3.12 Quantifier expressions

**CORPUS FINDINGS** [3]

➤ The few lexical bundles included in this category all begin with the quantifier *all.*
➤ **Four-word quantifier bundles:** **all of a sudden, all over the place, +all the rest of+, all the way round.*
➤ **Five-word quantifier bundles:** *+all the rest of it^, and all the rest of+ ^.*
➤ **Six-word quantifier bundles:** *and all the rest of it^.*

**DISCUSSION OF FINDINGS**

These are all relatively fixed expressions, for the most part used for generally emphatic functions:

> *Why is the car **all of a sudden** making that noise.* (CONV)
>
> ***All of a sudden** my little cousin screams.* (CONV†)
>
> *Yeah it's just like all sticking out **all over the place**.* (CONV)

In contrast, the six-word lexical bundle *and all the rest of it* is used as a coordination tag hedge (2.9.2) for vague reference:

> *He does manpower forecasts every year – er – and he comes up with – x equals yz **and all the rest of it**.* (CONV)

### 13.2.3.13 Other expressions

➤ A few lexical bundles do not fit neatly into any of the other categories.
➤ **Four-word bundles:** *\*no no no no, \*two and a half, three and a half.*
➤ **Five-word bundles:** *on and on and on^.*

**DISCUSSION OF FINDINGS**

A few extended numeric phrases, such as *two and a half* and *three and a half*, are used fairly commonly in conversation. In addition, two recurrent iterative bundles are included: *no no no no* marking emphatic negation (while often providing processing time), and *on and on and on* marking continuation of some process:

> A: *Is that your mother's father?*
> B: **No no no no** *– no it's my father erm – no – and she lives in this flat*
> *<...>* (CONV)

> *Well it's just – it just goes* **on and on and on**, *doesn't it?* (CONV)

### 13.2.3.14 Meaningless sound bundles

➤ Finally, a few meaningless sound bundles are used commonly in conversation.
➤ **Four-word bundles:** *\*\*da da da da, \*doo doo doo doo, \*la la la la, \*\*mm mm mm mm.*

**DISCUSSION OF FINDINGS**

Meaningless sound bundles occur in conversation for two main reasons. First, the repetition of *mm* (14.3.3.6) is used as a 'backchannel' to mark agreement or affirmation:

> A: *And they keep giving her a courtesy car – so I should think so after spending twenty-one grand.*
> B: **mm mm mm mm mm mm mm** *I should think it would.* (CONV)

In addition, a few repetitive sound bundles are used for musical purposes, to hum a song without the words:

> *Oh oh she comes – da na na na na na – doo da da – oh oh here she comes –* **da da da da da**, *oh yeah – oh oh here she comes.* (CONV)

Although such sound repetitions are 'meaningless' in the sense of having no referential meaning, it is clear that they can be used for various communicative purposes, including emphasis in the first example above.

## 13.2.4 Lexical bundles in academic prose

Lexical bundles in academic prose can also be grouped into categories according to their structural correlates; 12 major structural categories can be distinguished:

- noun phrase with *of*-phrase fragment
- noun phrase with other post-modifier fragment

- prepositional phrase with embedded *of*-phrase fragment
- other prepositional phrase fragment
- anticipatory *it* + verb phrase/adjective phrase
- passive verb + prepositional phrase fragment
- copula *be* + noun phrase/adjective phrase
- (verb phrase +) *that*-clause fragment
- (verb/adjective +) *to*-clause fragment
- adverbial clause fragment
- pronoun/noun phrase + *be* (+ ...)
- other expressions.

Following the practice in 13.2.3, the following sections present lists of the four-word, five-word, and six-word lexical bundles in each of these categories.

## 13.2.4.1  Noun phrase with *of*-phrase fragment

**CORPUS FINDINGS** [3]

➤ There are a large number of lexical bundles in academic prose consisting of a noun phrase followed by a post-modifying *of*-phrase.

➤ **Four-word bundles:** \*\*+*the end of the*, \*+*the beginning of the*, \*+*the base of the*, \**the position of the*, \**the shape of the*, \**the size of the*, \**the structure of the*, \*+*the surface of the*, *the top of the*, +*the start of the*, +*the form of a*, *the form of the*, *the length of the*, *the magnitude of the*, *the edge of the*, *the composition of the*, *both sides of the*, *the centre of the*, *the temperature of the*, +*the level of the*, +*the context of the*, +*different parts of the*, *other parts of the*, *part of the body*, *parts of the body*, *parts of the world*, +*the part of the*, \**the rest of the*, *the total number of*, *the first of these*, *and the number of*, *the sum of the*, \*\*+*one of the most*+, *one of the main*, \*+*the case of the*, +*the case of a*, \*\*+*the nature of the*, \*+*the use of the*, \**the value of the*, \**the role of the*, \*+*the basis of the*, *the purpose of the*, *the use of a*, *the importance of the*, \**the results of the*, *the effect of the*, *the effects of the*, \**the development of the*, \*+*the time of the*, *and the development of*, *the development of a*, *the formation of the*, *the history of the*, +*the course of the*, +*the early stages of*, *the origin of the*, \**the presence of a*, *the presence of the*, +*presence or absence of*, *the absence of a*, *the existence of a*, +*point of view of*, +*the point of view*+, *the ability of the*, *the needs of the*, *the work of the*, \*\**per cent of the*, \*+*the division of labour*, \**the secretary of state*.

➤ **Five-word bundles:** +*the point of view of*, *the aim of this study*+^, *the presence or absence of*, *the first part of the*^, *the other end of the*^, *the rate of change of*^, *one of the most important*^.

**DISCUSSION OF FINDINGS**

The lexical bundles in this category cover a wide range of meanings. A few functions, however, are especially important. First, a number of these lexical bundles are used for physical description, including identification of place, size, and amount:

> The plant, therefore, draws its nutrients from near **the surface of the** soil.
> (ACAD)

*Usually the passages formed by the vanes are of constant depth, the width diverging in accordance with* **the shape of the** *vanes.* (ACAD†)

*The heads of insects are broadly divisible into three types (Fig. 6), depending on the inclination of the long axis and* **the position of the** *mouthparts.* (ACAD)

*Rotating stall may lead to aerodynamically induced vibrations resulting in fatigue failures in* **other parts of the** *gas turbine.* (ACAD)

**The size of the** *sample varies with the objective and the method chosen.* (ACAD†)

*He asks what each legislator might do to reduce* **the total number of** *incidents of injustice or unfairness.* (ACAD†)

A second group of lexical bundles in this category marks simple existence or presence:

*A reheat system incurs some penalty in pressure loss due to* **the presence of the** *burners and flame stabilizing devices.* (ACAD†)

*Principles (1) and (2) lead us to interpret this regular correlation as an indication of* **the existence of a** *local reality.* (ACAD)

Other lexical bundles identify a variety of abstract qualities:

*The amount of rainfall considered necessary has therefore but local significance, for it depends on* **the nature of the** *country.* (ACAD†)

*The labour time socially necessary to produce the necessities of life of the worker is* **the value of the** *worker's labour power.* (ACAD)

**The use of a** *constant inner diameter is often found in industrial units.* (ACAD†)

Finally, a fourth group of lexical bundles describes processes or events lasting over a period of time:

*They contributed only very slowly to* **the development of an** *additional depletion zone.* (ACAD†)

*An appropriate design should be developed so that the results do not vary beyond acceptable limits during* **the course of the** *program.* (ACAD†)

## 13.2.4.2 Noun phrase with other post-modifier fragments

**CORPUS FINDINGS 3**

➤ Relatively few recurrent expressions are composed of a noun phrase followed by a post-modifier other than an *of*-phrase.

➤ These fall into two major types: a noun phrase with a post-nominal clause fragment, and a noun phrase with a prepositional phrase fragment.

➤ **Four-word bundles:**
  ➤ **Noun phrase with post-nominal clause fragment:** \*\*+*the way in which+,* \**the ways in which,* +*way in which the,* +*such a way that;* \*\*+*the extent to which+,* +*extent to which the;* \*\**the fact that the, the fact that it; the degree to which.*
  ➤ **Noun phrase with prepositional phrase fragment:** \**the relationship between the, the difference between the, an important part in, an important role in,* \**an increase in the,* +*the same way as.*

➤ **Five-word bundles:** *the way in which the,* +*such a way as to^, the extent to which the, and the extent to which^.*

**DISCUSSION OF FINDINGS**

Several of the lexical bundles in this category describe how a process occurs, especially using *the way(s) in which* and *the extent to which*:

> *This concerned **the way in which** electrons were ejected from metals by an incident beam of light.* (ACAD)

> ***The extent to which** sodium enters the melilite structures is not precisely known.* (ACAD)

Other lexical bundles are used to identify relationships among entities:

> *They also varied with respect to the loci of changes envisaged, and **the relationship between the** project initiatives and the past, current and proposed developments.* (ACAD†)

> ***The difference between the** two weights is equivalent to the weight of the equal volume of water.* (ACAD)

Finally, this category includes the only noun + complement clause combination to recur frequently, *the fact that the* (8.14.1, 9.2.7):

> ***The fact that the** pressure gradient is acting against the flow direction is always a danger to the stability of the flow.* (ACAD)

## 13.2.4.3 Prepositional phrase with embedded *of*-phrase fragment

**CORPUS FINDINGS** [3]

The lists in this section are organized alphabetically by preposition.

➤ A large number of lexical bundles consist of a prepositional phrase with an embedded *of*-phrase fragment functioning as post-modifier of the noun.

➤ **Four-word bundles:** *about the nature of, \*\*as a result of+, \*as a function of, \*as part of the, as a consequence of, as a matter of, as a means of, as part of a, \*\*at the end of+, \*\*at the time of+, \*at the beginning of+, \*at the level of+, at the expense of, at the start of+, by the end of+, by the presence of, by the use of, for the development of, for the purpose of, for the purposes of, from the point of+, \*\*\*in the case of+, \*\*in the absence of, \*\*in the form of+, \*\*in the presence of, \*in a number of+, \*in terms of the, \*in the context of+, \*in the course of+, \*in the development of, \*in the number of, \*in the process of, in a variety of+, in the area of, in the direction of, in the face of, in the formation of, in the pathogenesis of, in the study of, in the treatment of, in the use of+, in view of the, of a number of, of some of the, of the effects of, of the nature of+, of the use of, \*\*on the basis of+, on the part of+, on the surface of+, over a period of, \*to the development of, +to that of the, to the presence of, to the use of, with the exception of.*

➤ **Five-word bundles:** *\*as a result of the, as in the case of, \*\*at the end of the, at the beginning of the, at the time of the, at the base of the^, at the end of a^, at the end of this^, at the level of the^, at the start of the^, at the time of writing^, by the end of the, from the point of view+, \*in the case of the, in the case of a, in the context of the, in the division of labour, in the form of a, in a number of ways^, in a variety of ways^, in different parts of the^, in the course of the^, in the early stages of^, in the use of the^, of the nature of the^, on the basis of the, on the basis of their^, on the part of the^, on the surface of the^, similar to that of the^, similar to those of the^.*

➤ **Six-word bundles:** *from the point of view of.*

**DISCUSSION OF FINDINGS**

Most of the lexical bundles included in this category mark abstract, logical relations. A large number of these are formed with the prepositions *as* and *in*:

> **As a result of** *these two factors, molecules of both A and B have a greater tendency to escape.* (ACAD†)

> *Maturation-events within the respondents produce changes* **as a function of** *the passage of time per se.* (ACAD†)

> **In the absence of** *coupling, the signal is the single line shown in (1).* (ACAD)

> **In the case of** *helium, however, an octet is impossible.* (ACAD)

The expression *on the basis of* is also relatively common with this function:

> *It is risky to make a final selection* **on the basis of** *a single year's trial.* (ACAD)

In contrast, lexical bundles of this type beginning with the preposition *at* are used mostly to mark temporal relations:

> **At the end of** *this period the land may again be ploughed.* (ACAD†)

> *Active Rules are all those Rules contained in the Activity state* **at the time of** *evaluation.* (ACAD)

Finally, a number of the bundles beginning with *in* have a specialized function identifying time periods or processes:

> *About 20 calories of heat is emitted by 1 cubic centimeter of granite* **in the course of** *a million years.* (ACAD)

> *The specific goals of an individual institution or enterprise are very important* **in the process of** *defining particular regulations.* (ACAD†)

> *The existence of this concept is implicit* **in the development of** *all mathematical analysis.* (ACAD)

## 13.2.4.4 Other prepositional phrase (fragment)

**CORPUS FINDINGS** [3]

The lists in this section are organized alphabetically by preposition.

➤ There are also many lexical bundles beginning with a prepositional phrase without an embedded *of*-phrase.

➤ **Four-word bundles:** *as in the case+, \*\*+at the same time+, between the two groups, \*by the fact that, \*for the first time, from the fact that, \*in such a way+, \*in the same way+, \*in the present study, in a way that, in addition to the, in an attempt to, in contrast to the, in relation to the, in the early stages+, in the first place, in the next chapter, in the next section, in the nineteenth century, in the sense that, in this case the, \*in the United States, in England and Wales, in the United Kingdom, of the fact that, +of the most important, of the nineteenth century, \*\*\*on the other hand, \*on the one hand+, on the grounds that, +similar to that of+, similar to those of+, to the extent that, to the fact that, with respect to the.*

➤ **Five-word bundles:** *and at the same time^, at the same time as^, in the same way as, in such a way that, in such a way as+^, of the way in which^, on the one hand and^.*

➤ **Six-word bundles:** *in such a way as to^.*

**DISCUSSION OF FINDINGS**

Lexical bundles beginning with the preposition *in* are especially common in this category. Several of these are used to identify a particular location or time period (e.g. *in the United States, in the nineteenth century*). Others are used to specify a particular discourse context:

> However **in the present study** *accident drivers refer to all drivers reporting accidents irrespective of original samples.* (ACAD)

> **In the next chapter** *we shall discuss the concept of a limit in more detail.* (ACAD)

Two specific lexical bundles are especially common in this category: *at the same time* and *on the other hand*. Both of these have relatively idiomatic meanings, and both are used as linking adverbials (10.4.1) to compare two propositions or events. *At the same time* is used to contrast two propositions or events which are considered compatible (or both considered true):

> *In this way, Marx's work reunited, in a coherent fashion, the intellectual consciousness of the diverse experience of Britain, France and Germany, and yet* **at the same time** *offered a basis for the theoretical interpretation of these differences in social, economic, and political structure.* (ACAD)

*On the other hand* is used for contrasting two arguments or events which are presented as mutually exclusive:

> *'Concentration' refers to the process whereby, as capital accumulates, individual capitalists succeed in expanding the amount of capital under their control. Centralisation,* **on the other hand**, *refers to the merging of existing capitals* <...> (ACAD)

## 13.2.4.5  Anticipatory *it* + verb phrase/adjective phrase

**CORPUS FINDINGS [3]**

➤ Lexical bundles that initiate extraposed structures (beginning with anticipatory *it*; 3.6.4) are of two types: those controlled by an adjective phrase, and a fewer number controlled by a verb phrase (usually in the passive voice).

➤ **Four-word bundles:**
  ➤ **Anticipatory *it* + adjective phrase:** ***it is possible to, *it is possible that+, it is not possible+, it is impossible to, it is likely that, it is unlikely that, *it is important to, it is important that+, **it is necessary to, it is interesting to+, *it is clear that+, it is not clear, *it is difficult to, it is easy to, it is not surprising+, it is true that.*
  ➤ **Anticipatory *it* + verb phrase (usually passive):** *it can be seen+, *it should be noted+, *it has been shown+, *it has been suggested+, it has also been, it is to be, it may be that, it was found that.*

➤ **Five-word bundles:**
  ➤ **Anticipatory *it* + adjective phrase:** *it is not possible to, it may be possible to, it should be possible to^, it is also possible to^, it is possible that the^, it may be necessary to, it is not necessary to^, it is interesting to note+^, it is clear that the^, it is important that the^, it is not surprising that^.*

➤ **Anticipatory *it* + verb phrase (usually passive):** *\*it should be noted that+, it may be noted that^, \*it has been suggested that, it has been shown that, it can be shown that^, it can be seen that, it has been argued that^, it has been found that^.*

➤ **Six-word bundles:** *it is interesting to note that^, it should be noted that the^.*

**DISCUSSION OF FINDINGS**

The majority of lexical bundles initiating an extraposed structure have predicative adjectives controlling a complement clause, which is usually a *to*-clause (9.4.5.3). These report the stance of the writer; for example, possibility/likelihood, importance, necessity:

> With experience **it is possible to** recognize regularities in the patterns of soil distribution. (ACAD)

> **It is important to** distinguish between the processes of growth and development. (ACAD†)

> **It is necessary to** remember, however, how divergent were the experiences of the various countries in western Europe. (ACAD†)

In contrast, most of the extraposed lexical bundles with verb predicates are passive constructions that take *that*-clauses. The main verb in these structures similarly presents a kind of stance, in most cases identifying the information in the *that*-clause as beyond dispute:

> **It should be noted that** selection within a pure line offers little scope for further improvement in yield. (ACAD†)

> Furthermore, **it can be seen that** the best efficiency is achieved with the heat-exchanger by-passed. (ACAD)

> **It has been shown that** in concentrated sulphuric acid, hydrocarbons containing a tertiary hydrogen atom undergo hydrogen exchange. (ACAD)

## 13.2.4.6  Passive verb + prepositional phrase fragment

**CORPUS FINDINGS [3]**

➤ **Four-word bundles:** *\*is shown in figure/fig., are shown in table, \*is based on the, +be found in the, can be found in, is referred to as, referred to as the, be related to the, is related to the, +be taken into account, be thought of as, be used as a, can be seen as, is given by the, is known as the, was approved by the.*

➤ **Five-word bundles:** *is to be found in^.*

**DISCUSSION OF FINDINGS**

Only a few lexical bundles in academic prose are built around a verb phrase, and the majority of these lexical bundles incorporate a passive voice verb followed by a prepositional phrase. Mostly the prepositional phrase marks a locative or logical relation, rather than identifying the agent in a *by*-phrase.

Two expressions are moderately common in this category. The first identifies tabular/graphic displays of data:

> Examples **are shown in table** 3.7. (ACAD)

> A diagram of an apparatus used for steam distillation **is shown in figure** 6.24. (ACAD)

The second identifies the basis of some finding or assertion:

> *The explanation of this **is based on the** fact that the radial distribution of axial velocity is not constant across the annulus.* (ACAD)

## 13.2.4.7   Copula *be* + noun phrase/adjective phrase

**CORPUS FINDINGS** [3]

➤ The lexical bundles in this category all begin with the copula *be* (or *may be*). There are two main sub-groups here, depending on whether the subject predicative is a noun phrase or adjective phrase.

➤ **Four-word bundles:**
  ➤ **Copula *be* + noun phrase:** \*+*is one of the*+, +*are a number of*, *is part of the*, *be the result of*, *is a matter of*, *is the same as*, +*was no significant difference*.
  ➤ **Copula *be* + adjective phrase:** *is due to the*, *may be due to*, *is equal to the*, *is similar to that*+.

➤ **Five-word bundles:** *is one of the most*, +*was no significant difference between*, *is similar to that of*^, *may or may not be*^.

**DISCUSSION OF FINDINGS**

There is some overlap between this category and the other lexical bundles that include a noun phrase with an embedded *of*-phrase (13.2.4.1 and 13.2.4.3). That is, expressions with *one of*, *number of*, *part of*, *result of*, and *matter of* all occur in other categories. In this category, these bundles occur as subject predicative to the copula *be*:

> *The recently completed Muda River project in Malaysia **is one of the** most sophisticated irrigation schemes in the world.* (ACAD)
>
> *Cosmos **is part of the** UK Alvey Programme.* (ACAD†)
>
> *That is, one explanation sees the right ear advantage to **be the result of** stimulating a particular ear.* (ACAD†)

Lexical bundles with adjectival subject predicatives are used to identify causative relations (*is/be due to*) or comparative relations (*is equal/similar to*):

> *Chemical constraints **may be due to** shortages of nutrients.* (ACAD†)
>
> *The integral **is equal to the** area under this curve between the limits $P_0$ and P.* (ACAD)

## 13.2.4.8   (Verb phrase +) *that*-clause fragment

**CORPUS FINDINGS** [3]

➤ Lexical bundles incorporating a *that*-clause are of two main types: those that include the main clause verb, and those comprising only the *that*-clause.

➤ **Four-word bundles:**
  ➤ **Verb phrase + *that*-clause:** \*+*should be noted that*+, +*be noted that the*, +*has been shown that*, \*+*has been suggested that*, +*can be seen that*, +*does not mean that*, *is that it is*.
  ➤ ***That*-clause:** \**that there is a*, \**that there is no*, *that it is a*, *that it is not*, *that it is the*.
  ➤ **Noun + verb phrase + *that*-clause:** *studies have shown that*.

➤ **Five-word bundles:** +*should be noted that the*^.

Most lexical bundles including a main clause verb followed by a *that*-clause are part of a larger extraposition structure; these overlapping expressions are dealt with in 13.2.4.5. For example:

> It **should be noted that** the police can insist on entering the premises even against the wishes of the organisers. (ACAD†)

In contrast, those lexical bundles comprising only a *that*-clause often occur as complement clause in unmarked declarative structures. These recurrent *that*-clause structures are of two types. One has existential *there* as subject, with the present tense copula *is* as verb:

> Japanese scientists have found, as might be expected, **that there is a** positive correlation between transpiration rate and crop yield. (ACAD)

The second type has an extraposed clause embedded in the *that*-clause, with *it* as subject and the copula *is* as verb:

> This means **that it is not** necessary to require that the wavefunction is unchanged by the interchange of two identical particles. (ACAD)

## 13.2.4.9 **(Verb/adjective +)** *to*-clause fragment

**CORPUS FINDINGS [3]**

➤ A relatively large number of lexical bundles incorporate *to*-clauses. These fall into three main types: (1) predicative adjective + *to*-clause; (2) (passive) verb phrase + *to*-clause; (3) simple *to*-clause.

➤ **Four-word bundles:**
> ➤ **Predicative adjective + *to*-clause:** *are likely to be, *is likely to be, more likely to be, are more likely to, may be able to, should be able to, will be able to, +is not possible to.
>
> ➤ **(Passive) verb phrase + *to*-clause:** *has been shown to+, +been shown to be, have been shown to, *can be used to, may be used to, *is said to be, does not seem to+, was found to be, would have to be.
>
> ➤ **To-clause:** *to be able to, *to ensure that the, +to be found in+, to be the most, to deal with the, to do with the, to say that the.

➤ **Five-word bundles:** +is not to say that, +is interesting to note that^, can also be used to^, has been shown to be^, does not seem to be^, to be found in the^, to be taken into account^.

**DISCUSSION OF FINDINGS**

Lexical bundles with predicative adjectives controlling a *to*-clause are all used to indicate possibility/ability:

> Nevertheless, such work **is likely to be** amply rewarding. (ACAD)
>
> Thus, it **is not possible to** speak of absolute strengths of acids and bases. (ACAD)
>
> Within a few years we **should be able to** measure the spreading rate accurately and directly. (ACAD†)

In contrast, several of the lexical bundles with verb predicates controlling a *to-clause* are used to identify previous findings or known information. In most of these cases, the controlling verb is in the passive voice:

> The free-radical mechanism, however, **has been shown to** operate in some cases. (ACAD)

> The amount of combined nitrogen brought down by the rain **was found to be** far too small to account for the result. (ACAD)

> Glutinous rice **is said to be** similar to the mochi gomi rice produced in small quantities in the United States. (ACAD†)

## 13.2.4.10 Adverbial clause fragment

**CORPUS FINDINGS** [3]

➤ Only four lexical bundles begin with an adverbial clause; three of those are introduced by the subordinator *as*.

➤ **Four-word bundles:** *\*as shown in figure/fig., \*as we have seen, as we shall see, if there is a.*

**DISCUSSION OF FINDINGS**

Lexical bundles beginning with the subordinator *as* are used for deictic reference to other discourse segments:

> A curve of s.f.c. against specific thrust may be plotted **as shown in Fig.** 3.16. (ACAD)

> Each individual value is, **as we have seen**, the bond dissociation energy of that particular bond. (ACAD)

> The distinction between easy and hard cases at law is neither so clear nor so important as this critic assumes, **as we shall see** in Chapter 9. (ACAD)

## 13.2.4.11 Pronoun/noun phrase + *be* (+ ...)

**CORPUS FINDINGS** [3]

➤ In contrast to the many clause-initiating bundles in conversation (13.2.3.1–2), only a few lexical bundles begin clauses in academic prose. These all have copula *be* as the main verb, and either the demonstrative pronoun *this*, or existential *there*, as subject.

➤ This category includes a larger number of five- and six-word lexical bundles, although most of these are relatively infrequent.

➤ **Four-word bundles:**
> ➤ **This + be (+ ...):** *this is not the, this is not to+.*
> ➤ **There + be (+ ...):** *\*there was no significant+, there are a number+, there has been a.*

➤ **Five-word bundles:** *this does not mean that^, this is not to say+^, there was no significant difference+, there were no significant differences^, there was no correlation between^, there are a number of, there is no doubt that^, +aim of this study was^, it is one of the^.*

➤ **Six-word bundles:** *this is not to say that^, there was no significant difference between, the aim of this study was^.*

**DISCUSSION OF FINDINGS**

Unlike the clause-initiating bundles in conversation (13.2.3.1–2), those in academic prose all have impersonal subjects.

Lexical bundles with *this* as subject are used to link the information that follows to the preceding discourse:

> *Because of the wide diversity of outlook on sexual matters between the generations, the necessity may be particularly marked where sexual considerations exist.* **This is not to say that** *the child or young person is always right <...>* (ACAD)

Phrases beginning with existential *there* are used for informational packaging purposes (11.4.7). Phrases about statistical significance or correlation are particularly common in academic prose (especially in research articles):

> *Investigations in the Philippines showed that* **there was no significant difference between** *submergence depths 0 to 25 cm (Bulanadi et al. 1959).* (ACAD)

## 13.2.4.12  Other expressions

**CORPUS FINDINGS [3]**

➤ Finally, there are a few lexical bundles in academic prose that do not fit neatly into any of the other categories.

➤ **Four-word bundles:** *\*as well as the, as well as in, than that of the, may or may not+, the presence or absence+.*

# 13.3  Idiomatic phrases

Idiomatic phrases—expressions with a meaning not entirely derivable from the meaning of their parts (13.1)—can represent many different kinds of structural units. Some idioms are *wh*-questions, such as:

> *how do you do?*               *what on earth ...?*
> *what's up?*                       *what in the world ...?*

Other idioms are complete noun phrases, and a relatively large number of idioms are complete prepositional phrases.

Noun phrase idioms:

> *a piece of cake*               *nothing/anything/something the matter*
> *a slap in the face*

Prepositional phrase idioms:

> *as a matter of fact*          *not on your life*
> *for the time being*           *out of order*
> *in a nutshell*                    *up to date*
> *at/on the double*

A larger number of idioms are verb-based. Phrasal and prepositional verbs, discussed in 5.3, are used commonly in all registers. In addition, there are a number of verb phrase + complement combinations that function as idioms (e.g.

*bear in mind* and *have a look*). Structurally, these expressions fall into two main categories: verb + prepositional phrase idioms, and verb + noun phrase idioms.

Selected verb + prepositional phrase idioms:

| | |
|---|---|
| *bear in mind* | *get into the swing of* |
| *beat around the bush* | *gets on my nerves* |
| *be out of the question* | *go off the deep end* |
| *be up for grabs* | *step on the gas* |
| *come as a surprise* | *go through a rough time* |
| *fall in love* | *take into account* |

Selected verb + noun phrase idioms:

| | |
|---|---|
| *change [one's] mind* | *make up [one's] mind* |
| *do a snow job* | *miss the boat* |
| *drive me ...* | *rain cats and dogs* |
| *give me/us a break* | *serve [one] right* |
| *hold your horses* | *stand a chance* |
| *keep an eye on X* | *take the bull by the horns* |
| *kick the bucket* | *throw the book at* |
| *kick a/the habit* | *waste [one's] breath* |
| *lose [one's] head* | |

Many of these expressions illustrate how there can be a certain amount of variability in the use of an idiom. Some idioms have a slot that can take a fairly wide range of fillers, although these are usually constrained semantically. For example, the slot in the idiom *drives me __* can be filled by any of a range of adjectives meaning 'mentally unstable', including *mad, nuts, crazy, insane, batty*, as well as the phrase *up the wall*.

> *This phone **drives me nuts**.* (CONV)

> *She **drives me batty**.* (CONV)

In most idioms, while the key content words are usually invariable, there is often considerable variation in the morphological form of verbs and in the choice of determiners for noun phrases:

> *The cabinet has already **changed its mind**.* (NEWS)

> *Maybe she'll **change her mind**.* (FICT)

> *Once you've seen it, you'll want to **change your mind**.* (FICT)

Idioms also differ in the extent to which their meaning can be derived from the component parts. For example, the literal meaning of the expression *change [one's] mind* is closely related to the intended meaning of re-thinking a decision. In contrast, the literal meaning of expressions like *kick the bucket* have almost no relation to the intended meaning of dying.

## 13.3.1 Idiomatic phrases across registers

For the most part, idioms are not common. While most *wh*-question, noun phrase, and prepositional phrase expressions (such as *what on earth, how do you do, a piece of cake, a slap in the face, on the double, not on your life*) are used occasionally as idioms in fiction (generally less than five per million words), they are rarely attested in the other registers. Surprisingly, such expressions are generally rare in conversation. That is, these idioms are used more commonly to represent stereotyped dialogue in fiction than in actual conversation:

> *How do you do*, Mr. Mason. (FICT)
>
> *Carrying Elfie can't be any* **piece of cake** *when she's got an arm like that!* (FICT)
>
> *And Leroy shouted back: '***not on your life***'.* (FICT)

Although they are greater in number than other types, verbal idioms are in general rarely used. Even common expressions, such as *change (one's) mind*, occur fewer than ten times per million words in the LSWE Corpus. Other expressions, such as *do a snow job* and *kick the bucket* are rarely attested.

Most verbal idioms are relatively colloquial. They are used primarily in fiction, with less frequent use in conversation:

> *Escape* **was out of the question**. (FICT)
>
> *On the other hand, Pinkie seemed to have* **lost his head** *to a certain extent.* (FICT)
>
> *And then my old woman* **kicked the bucket**. (FICT†)
>
> *When are you going to do it?* **Take the bull by the horns**. (CONV)

However, a few of these expressions are used primarily in academic prose or other kinds of expository writing:

> *We should* **bear in mind** *three by now well-established points* <...> (ACAD†)
>
> *It is important for children to learn to* **take into account** *their potential audience when they are producing written work.* (ACAD†)

Interestingly, many colloquial idioms are used occasionally in news reportage, lending an informal, vivid color to otherwise serious discussion:

> *Now I'm not saying Ian Rush* **missed the boat** *entirely, but he might find it pretty interesting when Gullitt and Van Basten discuss their life and work.* (NEWS†)
>
> *He immediately* **got into the swing of it** *and was quickly given authority by his colleagues.* (NEWS†)
>
> *The triumph* **came as a surprise** *to many.* (NEWS)
>
> *After lunch, India* **stepped on the gas** *and Gooch turned, not before time, to the off-spin of Eddie Hemmings.* (NEWS†)
>
> *But it is important for parents to be aware and* **keep an eye on** *their children.* (NEWS)

Despite the general rarity of most idioms, a few verbs are especially productive in combining with noun phrases to form idioms. The three verbs *have*, *take*, and *make*, which are particularly noteworthy in this regard, are dealt with in the following section.

## 13.3.2 Verb + noun phrase combinations with *have, make,* and *take*

Three verbs are particularly productive in combining with a following noun phrase to form relatively idiomatic expressions: *have*, *take*, and *make*. The resultant expressions form a cline of idiomaticity. At one extreme there are clearly idiomatic expressions, such as *have a look*, *make a killing*, and *take time*:

*Michael can I* **have a look** *please.* (CONV)

*When we go public, you'll* **make a killing**. (FICT†)

*Do you think you can* **take time out** *to have a cup of tea?* (CONV)

At the other extreme, there are expressions that retain the core meaning of these verbs:

*Well, we* **have** *an extra one.* (CONV)

*He* **made** *a sandwich.* (FICT)

*You can* **take** *a snack in your pocket.* (FICT)

In between are a number of relatively idiomatic expressions, such as *have a chance, have a bath, make a deal, make a statement, take a walk*. In these expressions, the meanings of individual words are retained to some extent, but the entire expression also takes on a more idiomatic meaning. Further, many of these expressions could be replaced by a single verb:

*have dinner* → *dine*

*make provision (for)* → *provide (for)*

*take part* → *participate*

### CORPUS FINDINGS [1,2]

➤ All three of these verbs combine with a large number of different noun phrases to form relatively idiomatic expressions.

➤ Selected noun phrases combining with *have* in conversation or fiction: *a baby, a bath, a care, a/no/the chance (to), children, no choice, a clue, dinner, a drink, a fit, a go (at), a heart, an/no idea, a look (at), lunch, a mind (to), no intention, reason, a rest, a/no/the right, a talk (about/with), a taste (for), tea, time, trouble, a word (with)*.

➤ Selected noun phrases combining with *have* in news and academic prose: *access, an/ the advantage, control, (no/some/any) difficulty, no doubt, an/no/the effect, implications, influence, the opportunity, no plans, the potential, problems, a role, sex*.

➤ Selected noun phrases combining with *make* in conversation or fiction: *an appointment, arrangements, a bargain, a/the bed, a (clean) break, a (telephone) call, contact, a deal, a decision, a/any/no difference, an/every effort, eyes, a fool of one(self), fun, a fortune, a fuss, a bad/good impression, a joke, a killing, a living, love, matters (worse), a mistake, money, a move, a noise, a nuisance, a pest of oneself, plans, a point, a profit, sense, a sound, a speech, a statement, a (fresh) start, time, work*.

➤ Selected noun phrases combining with *make* in news and academic prose: *amends, assumptions, choices, comparisons, demands, headlines, her/his appearance, her/his comeback, her/his debut, history, judgements, predictions, progress, provision, recommendations, reference, use (of)*.

➤ Selected noun phrases combining with *take* in conversation or fiction: *advantage, ages, aim, a bath, a break, a (deep) breath, a breather, a cab, a call, care, a chance, charge, command, control, a course (in), a degree (in), drugs, effect, a (quick) glance, a hike, an hour/hours, an interest, a joke, a leak, a (good/quick/closer) look, a message, a minute, a nap, (any/no) note, (any/no) notice, the opportunity, pains, (any/no) part, a pay cut, a pee, a peep, a picture/photo, a/the piss, pity, place, pleasure, possession, refuge, revenge, a risk, a seat, shape, shelter, a shower, sides, (a long) time, a train, a trip, the trouble, turns, a walk, a (long) while*.

➤ Selected noun phrases combining with *take* in news and academic prose: *account (of), (any/no) action, advantage (of), a/the decision, effect, exception (to), (the) form (of), heart, hold, the lead, her/his life, months, office, the plunge, precedence, responsibility, root, (a/the) step/steps, the title, their toll, the view, years.*

➤ A few of these combinations are notably common (see Table 13.4).

**Table 13.4** **Common idiomatic expressions with *have, make,* or *take* + noun phrase; occurrences per million words**

▧ over 40    ▪ over 20    ▎ over 10

|  | CONV | FICT | NEWS | ACAD |
|---|---|---|---|---|
| have (no/the) time | ▪ | ▪ | ▎ | ▎ |
| have a look (at) | ▪ | ▪ |  |  |
| have an/no/any idea |  | ▪ | ▎ |  |
| have an/no/the effect |  |  |  | ▪ |
| make (any/no) sense |  | ▪ | ▎ | ▪ |
| make use of |  |  |  | ▪ |
| take place |  | ▪ | ▪ | ▧ |
| take part |  |  | ▪ | ▎ |
| take advantage (of) |  |  | ▪ | ▎ |
| take a (good) look |  | ▪ |  |  |
| take care |  | ▪ |  |  |
| take (any/no) action |  |  | ▪ |  |
| take (the) form (of) |  |  |  | ▪ |

➤ Although conversation has few common idiomatic phrases formed with these verbs, the phrase *have a look* is particularly common in BrE conversation, occurring about 200 times per million words.

  ➤ This phrase rarely occurs in AmE conversation, although the related expression *take a look* occurs about 20 times per million words.

### DISCUSSION OF FINDINGS

Although earlier studies have claimed that formulaic language is dominant in conversation, idiomatic phrases with the verbs *have, make,* and *take* are by far more common in the written registers. In fact, several of these phrases are notably common only in news reportage and/or academic prose.

In particular, idiomatic phrases formed with *make* and *take* tend to be used commonly in written exposition:

*This did not merely contradict experiment; it **made no sense** at all.* (ACAD)

*Alternatively, in our laboratory we have **made good use** of carbol fuchsin stain.* (ACAD)

*The hearing will **take place** in Ipswich on April 6.* (NEWS)

*Their negotiators have refused to **take part** in further talks with departmental heads.* (NEWS†)

*She wants the government to **take advantage** of EC environmental funds to maintain Essex sea defences.* (NEWS)

*Chester City Council may **take action** against British Rail over its failure to remove a portable ticket office.* (NEWS†)

> *Communist writings typically **take the form** of fictional utopias.* (ACAD)

Fiction writers commonly use a few of these same expressions:

> *The question **made no sense**.* (FICT)

> *At some point a negotiation would **take place**.* (FICT)

In addition, two expressions formed with *take* are common in fiction but not the expository registers:

> *Here; **take a look** at his schedule.* (FICT)

> *I **take care** to keep out of their way.* (FICT)

Common phrases formed with *have* tend to be more colloquial. The phrase *have time* (often in a negative context) is found in all four registers, although it is less common in news and academic prose:

> *I don't **have time** to play.* (CONV)

> *One never **had time** to think about it.* (FICT)

> *They themselves **had insufficient time** to offer this kind of support.* (ACAD†)

*Have a look* is found commonly in conversation and fiction. It is particularly common in BrE conversation:

> *But I'll **have a look** through these leaflets.* (BrE CONV)

> *Do you want to **have a look**?* (BrE CONV)

The expressions *have a look* and *take a look* are used with nearly equivalent meaning, but they have very different distributions. Both expressions occur with moderate frequencies in fiction:

> *We'll go up and **have a look**.* (FICT)

> *Step out and **take a look**.* (FICT)

However, in conversation the two expressions are distributed differently across dialects. In BrE, *have a look* is extremely common, while *take a look* is relatively rare; in contrast, *take a look* is moderately common in AmE, while *have a look* is rare:

> *Well, I'll **take a look** and see how it is then.* (AmE CONV)

The phrase *have no idea* is used commonly in fiction and occasionally in news with colloquial, emphatic overtones:

> *He **has no idea** what we will do next.* (FICT)

> *Mr. Brown's remarks reveal he **has no idea** what he is talking about.* (NEWS)

Finally, the expression *to have some/little effect* is used commonly in written exposition to describe the influence of various factors:

> *Small variations in form are found to **have little effect** on the final performance of the compressor.* (ACAD†)

## 13.4   Free combinations of verb + particle

Many verbs combine with an adverbial particle or a preposition to make a relatively fixed or idiomatic phrasal verb (*look up*) or prepositional verb (*look at*); these are described fully in 5.3. In contrast, free combinations of verb + particle, such as *go in*, do not have idiomatic status and should not be regarded as a structural unit. However, many of these verb + particle free combinations have strong collocational associations.

**CORPUS FINDINGS [1,2]**

➤ A number of verb + particle/preposition free combinations are common in the LSWE Corpus.

   ➤ Over 40 times per million words: *come back, come down, come in, come out, come to, come up, do* NP *with, go back, go down, go in, go out, go to, go up, live in, put* NP *in, put* NP *on, return to.*

   ➤ Over ten times per million words: *appear in, arrived in, born in, come into, come round, come with, contain* NP *in, describe* NP *as, describe* NP *in, died in, discuss* NP *in, do* NP *at, do* NP *to, dress* NP *in, find* NP *in, be given in, go away, go over, go round, happen in, have* NP *in, know* NP *for, leave* NP *in, look back, look in, looked out, lost in, make* NP *in, make* NP *to, move to, pass through, place* NP *in, play in, put* NP *into, reflect in, remain in, say in, see in, set in, sit in, stand in, stay in, transfer* (NP) *to, went off, work in.*

➤ Many of the common free combinations are particularly frequent in conversation (and to a lesser extent fiction). For example, the following combinations all occur over 100 times per million words in conversation: *come back, come down, come in, come to, go back, go down, go in, go to, go round, go up, put* NP *in, put* NP *on.*

**DISCUSSION OF FINDINGS**

Certain free combinations of verb + particle recur frequently because some verbs have particular adverbial relations that they commonly co-occur with. In particular, the verbs *come* and *go* very commonly co-occur with directional particles such as *back, down, in, to, up.* These free combinations are especially common in conversation:

> They said **come back** next weekend. (CONV)

> You say that every time you **come in** this door. (CONV)

> I'll **go down** and get it. (CONV)

> Oh I **went to** the doctor's last night. (CONV)

The verb *put* is also notably common with the directional particles *in* and *on*:

> I'll **put it on** the table. (CONV)

> You're supposed to **put tomato puree in** it, aren't you? (CONV)

Free combinations are less common in academic prose, and those combinations that do recur tend to occur in the passive, and to mark textual/logical rather than directional/spatial relations:

> If you are a person of fastidious intellectual taste you will not much care for the comic-strip account **given in** the preceding paragraph. (ACAD)

> As **described in** the previous chapter, higher plants synthesize their tissues from simple substances. (ACAD†)

> Compressibility effects will be **discussed in** the next sub-section. (ACAD)

# 13.5 Coordinated binomial phrases

Binomial phrases consist of two words from the same grammatical category, coordinated by *and* or *or*. Although the most common kind of binomial phrase comprises two coordinated nouns, words from all four major grammatical categories can be combined:

**Noun *and* noun**

> *fish and chips   mum and dad   night and day   health and safety*

**Verb *and* verb**

> *go and get   come and sit   wait and see*

**Adjective *and* adjective**

> *black and white   nice and warm*

**Adverb *and* adverb**

> *back and forth   in and out*

Most binomial phrases occur too infrequently to be considered part of recurrent lexical bundles. For example, the following binomial phrases occur only once in the LSWE Corpus:

**Noun *and* noun**

> *bread and potatoes   activities and programs   confidence and flexibility*

**Verb *and* verb**

> *come and examine   go and rebuild   read and absorb*

**Adjective *and* adjective**

> *beautiful and ripe   big and powerful   bright and bouncy*

**Adverb *and* adverb**

> *back and up   down and sideways   slowly and inexorably*

However, there are a number of binomial phrases that are recurrent and can be regarded as a special category of lexical bundle. Although most recurrent binomial phrases are not very common, a few are used frequently.

## 13.5.1   Key to lists of binomial phrases

The lists in the following sections are annotated for three frequency benchmarks showing occurrences per million words as follows:

|          |       |          |              |
|----------|-------|----------|--------------|
| over 40  | **    | over 5   | (not marked) |
| over 20  | *     | other    | ^            |

## 13.5.2   Verb *and/or* verb

**CORPUS FINDINGS** [1,2]

➤ Although verb *and* verb binomial phrases are most common in fiction, relatively few of these phrases are recurrent in that register.

➤ Verb *and* verb binomial phrases are relatively rare in news and academic prose.

➤ In contrast, conversation has a large number of recurrent verb *and* verb binomial phrases.

> ➤ Binomial phrases with *go and* verb are most common, especially: ***go and see,* **go and get,* *go and have,* *go and do.*

> ➤ Other verbs in recurrent binomial phrases with *go and*: *make, buy, tell, ask, sit, find, put, take, look, watch, say, give, collect, pick, went and had*^, *went and got*^.

➤ In AmE conversation, many of these verb combinations commonly occur without the coordinator *and*:

➤ Especially common bi-verbal phrases with *go* in AmE: \*\**go see*, \*\**go get*, \**go look*, \**go do*.

➤ Binomial phrases with *come and* verb are also common:
  ➤ Verbs in recurrent binomial phrases with *come and*: *get, see, sit, say, have, help, stay, tell, pick, look, do, came and said*^.

➤ The verb *try* is also used in several recurrent binomial phrases in conversation:
  ➤ \**Try and get* is relatively common (9.14.13).
  ➤ Other verbs in recurrent binomial phrases with *try and*: *find, remember, do, make, put*.

➤ Finally, the two expressions *sit and watch* and *wait and see* recur in conversation.

➤ Relatively few binomial expressions connecting verbs with *or* recur in the LSWE Corpus. The following expressions recur with relatively low frequencies (slightly less than five per million words): *say or do, said or did, seen or heard, confirm or deny*.

## DISCUSSION OF FINDINGS

The most common recurrent binomial phrases with the form verb *and* verb build on the verbs *go* and *come*. In these expressions, the first verb serves primarily to mark the direction of the action, while the second verb expresses the consequent action to be accomplished:

> *My dad wants to **go and see** a film.* (CONV)

> *I've got to **go and get** a drink.* (CONV)

> *Shall I **come and help** you?* (CONV)

> *I'm slightly starting to regret inviting my girlfriend to **come and stay** with me for three weeks in France.* (CONV)

With these two verbs (*go* and *come*), the coordinator *and* is occasionally omitted, making the relationship between the verbs even closer:

> *I should **go do** some filing.* (CONV)

> *Charlotte, **come sit** on your potty, quickly.* (CONV)

The combinations *go get* and *go see* are especially common in AmE conversation:

> *We'll **go get** some coffee or something, okay?* (AmE CONV)

> *I'm going to **go see** what that thing on the roof is like.* (AmE CONV)

The expressions *sit and watch* and *wait and see* both combine the meaning of stationary action with that of visual perception:

> *It's the sort of film you can **sit and watch** a few times.* (CONV)

The verb *see* often has a metaphorical sense in this expression:

> *I'm just going to **wait and see** what he says.* (CONV)

The verb *try* is also relatively common as the first member in recurrent binomial phrases. In this case, the second verb functions like an infinitival complement to *try*, which can be connected by either *and* or *to* (see 9.4.11):

> *I'm going to **try and put** them up today.* (CONV)

> ***Try to put** some on.* (CONV)

Finally, the few recurrent binomial verb expressions connected with *or* are used to connect complementary acts:

> *She didn't seem to mind what she **said or did**.* (FICT)

> *They hadn't **seen or heard** anything.* (FICT)

### 13.5.3 Noun *and*/*or* noun

**CORPUS FINDINGS** [1,2]

➤ Noun *and* noun binomial phrases are by far most common in academic prose, and to a lesser extent in news.

➤ Many nouns are extremely productive in combining with a large number of other nouns to form binomial phrases.

➤ The following nouns occur as the first member in over 40 different binomial phrases in academic prose: *activity/activities, age, cells, content, control, development, disease, education, experience, groups, growth, ideas, information, interests, knowledge, nature, needs, power, problems, production, research, size, skills, status, structure, time, values, water, work.*

➤ The majority of binomial phrases in news and academic prose are not recurrent.

  ➤ For example 22 of the 29 highly productive nouns in the above list do not occur in any recurrent binomial expression.

➤ There are a number of recurrent noun *and* noun binomial phrases in news and academic prose: *accident and emergency, age and sex, aims and objectives, bed and breakfast, boys and girls, business and city, east and west, education and training, family and friends, gas and coal, goods and services, growth and development, health and safety, heat and work, individuals and groups, information and education, input and output, justice and fairness, knowledge and skills, law and order, males and females, materials and methods, men and women, north and south, oil and gas, patients and methods, policy and resources, pressure and temperature, prince and princess, research and development, rights and duties, science and technology, size and shape, space and time, speech and writing, strengths and weaknesses, stress and strain, temperature and pressure, theory and practice, time and place, time and effort, trade and industry, training and enterprise, trial and error.*

➤ In contrast, noun *and* noun binomial phrases are generally rare in conversation, and they are also relatively rare in fiction compared to written exposition.

  ➤ For example, there are no nouns in conversation that are productive even to the extent that they occur as the first member in 20 different binomial phrases.

➤ Despite the general rarity of these expressions, conversation and fiction have some recurrent noun *and* noun binomial phrases; these fall into a few major semantic categories:

  ➤ **Relational expressions** (mostly female/male): *\*mum and dad, \*men and women, mother and father, mummy and daddy, husband and wife, Mr and Mrs, ladies and gentlemen, women and children, father and son.*

  ➤ **Food combinations:** *bread and butter, fish and chips, salt and vinegar, food and drink.*

  ➤ **Time expressions:** *years and years, day and night, days and nights, night and day, Saturday and Sunday.*

  ➤ **Other:** *hands and knees, flesh and blood, bits and pieces, loads and loads, name and address, life and death.*

➤ Relatively few binomial expressions connecting nouns with *or* recur in the LSWE Corpus. The following expressions recur with relatively low frequencies (around five per million words): *tea or coffee, day or night, man or woman, parent or guardian, increase or decrease, presence or absence, success or failure.*

Most noun *and* noun binomial phrases in written exposition are not recurrent expressions. However, certain nouns are very commonly paired up with a second noun to form such phrases. For example, the noun *research* combines with the following second-member nouns in binomial phrases: *development, teaching, practice, consensus, education, experimentation, statistics, planning, observation, study, design, experience, treatment, training, theory, information, innovation, industry, developments, pedagogy.* Of these combinations, only the phrase *research and development* recurs frequently in academic prose.

Most of the recurrent binomial phrases in academic prose have complementary referents, providing a more exhaustive coverage of a referential domain:

> The **size and shape** of grain may vary widely between varieties. (ACAD†)

> Only by the union of **theory and practice** can social change be effected. (ACAD†)

> We shall need to know the way in which ambient **pressure and temperature** vary with height above sea level. (ACAD†)

In conversation, most noun *and* noun binomial phrases are recurrent expressions, usually referring to physical entities that commonly go together in people's experience. The majority of these expressions are from one of three semantic domains.

**Relational expressions** (mostly female/male):

> My **mum and dad** went out the other day. (CONV)

> They got **men and women** in the same dormitory. (CONV)

**Food combinations**:

> Did they put **salt and vinegar** on them? (CONV)

> Can I have two plates of **bread and butter**? (CONV)

**Time expressions**:

> She's been sick continuously, **day and night**. (CONV)

> Little trick I learnt **years and years and years** ago. (CONV)

Only a few recurrent expressions connect binomial nouns with *or*. In written exposition, these expressions usually combine referents with opposite meaning, suggesting that the proposition is true under all circumstances:

> In other words, certain expenditures may **increase or decrease** as the program progresses, and others remain fixed. (ACAD)

> The type of fuel-wood available in an area is determined by the vegetation, that is, the **presence or absence** of plants, their distribution and their frequency. (ACAD)

## 13.5.4 Adjective *and/or* adjective

➤ Adjective *and* adjective binomial phrases are by far most common in fiction (and to a lesser extent in academic prose).

➤ Many adjectives are extremely productive in combining with a large number of adjectives to form binomial phrases.

➤ The following adjectives occur as the first member in over 40 different binomial phrases in fiction: *black, bright, cold, dark, hard, hot, large, long, old, pale, small, soft, strange, tall, thin, warm, white, young.*

➤ The majority of binomial phrases in fiction are not recurrent.

➤ Except for the phrase *black and white*, none of the highly productive adjectives in the above list occur in a recurrent binomial expression.

➤ However, there are a number of recurrent adjective *and* adjective binomial phrases in news and academic prose:

➤ **Demographic/institutional attributes:** *economic and monetary, economic and political, economic and social, political and economic, political and social, social and political, social and economic, social and cultural, social and psychological, social and emotional, personal and social, mental and physical, physical and mental.*

➤ **Opposite or complementary attributes:** *formal and informal, initial and final, male and female, old and new, positive and negative, primary and secondary, small and large, strong and weak, upper and lower.*

➤ **Other attributes:** *national and international, safe and effective, rich and famous.*

➤ In conversation, adjective *and* adjective binomial phrases are generally rare, and only a few of these expressions are recurrent: *black and white, lovely and warm, nice and warm.*

➤ Binomial adjective phrases with *or* are generally rare in all registers. The only recurrent adjective *or* adjective expression in the LSWE Corpus is the phrase *positive or negative* in academic prose.

### DISCUSSION OF FINDINGS

While adjective *and* adjective binomial phrases are very common in fiction, almost none of these phrases occur as recurrent expressions. However, a number of adjectives in fiction are very productive as first member in combining with a wide range of other adjectives to form binomial expressions. For example, the adjective *cold* combines with the following second-member adjectives to form binomial phrases in fiction:

> *aloof, blue, blustery, bright, brittle, calculating, clean, clear, cutting, damp, distant, dreadful, dry, dusty, gloomy, gritty, hot, hungry, idle, impassive, lifeless, miserable, misty, peaceful, pervasive, precise, shivering, shrewd, sick, silent, soft, stiff, terrible, tired, unemotional, unhappy, violent, wailing, wet*

For example:

> *It was **cold and wet** inside.* (FICT)

> *Michael Lee realized how **cold and calculating**, how vicious and cunning she was.* (FICT†)

In contrast, news and academic prose have fewer adjective *and* adjective binomial phrases overall but a greater number of recurrent expressions of this type. A large number of these phrases refer to complementary demographic or institutional attributes:

> *Second, it defines the basic attributes of **social and cultural** similarity which constitute the criteria of becoming a member of these sets or collectivities.* (ACAD)

> *Relatively little inequality existed, although the Olofin and Idejo commanded greater **economic and political** power than commoners.* (ACAD)

Other recurrent adjective *and* adjective phrases in news and academic prose are used to list opposite attributes, for the purposes of all-inclusive description (cf. a similar use of noun *and/or* noun binomials in 13.5.2):

> **Old and new** members are welcome. (NEWS)
>
> Folds and faults are the details of the patterns of deformation, **strong and weak**, that geologists map in the field. (ACAD†)
>
> These signs arise from the fact that a wave function can have **positive and negative** regions. (ACAD†)

## 13.5.5  Adverb *and/or* adverb

**CORPUS FINDINGS** [1,2]

➤ Adverb *and* adverb phrases are considerably less common than the other types of binomial phrase.

> ➤ Such phrases are very rare in academic prose and news.
>
> ➤ In conversation and fiction, there are a number of recurrent expressions combining binomial adverbs: *again and again, back and forth, here and there, here and now, in and out, now and then, now and again, on and off, so and so, there and then, up and down.*

➤ Few adverb *or* adverb phrases are used in the LSWE Corpus.

> ➤ The following expressions recur in conversation and fiction: *once or twice, sooner or later.*

**DISCUSSION OF FINDINGS**

Recurrent adverb *and* adverb phrases are used in conversation and fiction, primarily to convey complex directional or temporal information:

**Adverb *and* adverb phrases with directional meaning:**

> Shall we count how many times Alex has been **in and out** of here saying he's going home? (CONV)
>
> He passed pages rapidly **back and forth** before his eye. (FICT)
>
> Chano laughed kindly, and her stomach heaved **up and down**. (FICT)

**Adverb *and* adverb phrases with temporal meaning:**

> They could have mended it **there and then**. (CONV)
>
> Every **now and then** when they feel like it, they take a handful of films and get them developed. (CONV)

# 14

# The grammar of conversation

# 14.1 Introduction

In earlier chapters, the grammar of conversation has been explored in relation to the contrasting three written registers of fiction, newspaper journalism, and academic prose. In this chapter, we focus on conversation as a variety of language deserving particular attention in its own right. This is not only because it represents the spoken language in contrast to the other three registers, but also because the grammar of conversation has been little researched until recently, when the advent of sizeable computer corpora have made such research feasible for the first time.

The Greek origin of the word *grammar* itself (from *gramma* 'a letter', 'a piece of writing') reminds us that the Western grammatical tradition is founded almost exclusively on the study of written language, a bias which still exists today. However, conversation is certainly not a 'special' or 'unusual' register. In fact, conversation is the most commonplace, everyday variety of language, from which, if anything, the written variety, acquired through painstaking and largely institutional processes of education, is to be regarded as a departure. Hence there is a compelling interest in using the resources of the LSWE Corpus of spoken language transcriptions to study what is characteristic of the grammar of conversation. The fact that this Corpus material consists of transcriptions—speech rendered in written form—means that even here, the reliance on the written form of the language cannot be escaped (see also 14.1.2.1). Nevertheless, the existence of such a large body of transcribed speech makes it feasible to seek an answer to the following question, which has recently excited considerable interest: is there a distinctive grammar of spoken language, operating by laws different from those of the written language? If so, what are these laws, and what are the functional or other principles underlying them?

In fact, the main answer to this question provided by this book is already clear: the evidence of the analyses presented in earlier chapters is that the same 'grammar of English' can be applied to both the spoken and the written language. Throughout earlier chapters we have followed the method of comparing the four registers, including conversation, on the basis of a shared set of categories, such as adjective, noun phrase, relative clause, and linking adverbial. We would argue that the absence of a particular grammatical feature in one of the subcorpora is not proof that such a feature never occurs in that register. For example, there is no occurrence of the sequence *those which* … in the AmE conversation subcorpus of the LSWE Corpus, and there is only one occurrence in the BrE conversation subcorpus (each of these subcorpora consists of about four million words). However, that does not mean that such a form could not occur in AmE conversation. A wiser conclusion would be to say that such a feature occurs so infrequently in that variety—is so uncharacteristic of conversation—that the Corpus provides no instance of it.

Hence investigating the grammar of conversation, in this light, becomes a matter of investigating the grammatical features that are especially characteristic of conversational language, as compared with other registers, using the 'general English' set of categories or features employed for written as well as spoken English. Even features which are felt to belong exclusively to speech—such as the occurrence of false starts and hesitation pauses—are found from time to time in written registers. This is especially the case in fiction, where speech is being simulated:

> '*I er that is to say we er feel that we well, that we can't go on like this.*'
> (FICT)

To characterize the grammar of conversation, then, one of the first tasks of this chapter (14.1.2) will be to bring together the more striking quantitative findings of earlier chapters, as to what is special about conversational grammar. Further, we interpret this synthesis in terms of the situational and functional determinants of conversation.[1]

In 14.2, we turn to an aspect of spontaneous spoken language which has led some people to see the grammar of speech as degenerate or inchoate. We examine performance phenomena of dysfluency and error—such as hesitations and repairs—which in their more extreme form seem to threaten the whole idea that conversation has a 'grammar'.

The next part of the chapter (14.3) will address an important problem for the description of the grammar of spoken language. Whereas the **sentence** has been treated, traditionally and in modern theory, as the fundamental structural unit of grammar, such a unit does not realistically exist in conversational language. Although orthographic transcriptions, such as are used in our conversational subcorpus, conventionally contain sentence-final punctuation marks (periods, question marks, and exclamation marks), the places where these are inserted by the transcriber can be somewhat inconsistent, although no doubt reflecting cues such as falling intonation and pause in the stream of speech. In reality, conversation has no generally recognizable sentence-delimiting marks such as the initial capital and final period of written language.

Further, there are no reliable methods for defining sentences in terms of their syntactic form or semantic content in conversation. We may wonder what (if anything) should replace the sentence as a basis for dividing a spoken discourse into maximal grammatically analysable (parsable) units? In practical terms, it is possible to segment conversation grammatically in terms of independently analysable **clausal** and **non-clausal** units (cf. 3.1), which we will subsume in this chapter under **C-units** (14.3.1.3). More generally, 14.3 will analyse conversation from a combined functional and constructional point of view. In doing this, it will examine different structural phenomena (such as elliptical and non-clausal material) which are typical of spoken dialogue, and which characterize it as very different from all three written registers, with the possible exception of the simulated dialogue found in fiction.

Finally, 14.4 will examine a number of special topics in the area of conversational grammar: the use of vocatives, the use of questions with assertive words like *some*, the use of independent clauses beginning with *let's*, the grammar of direct speech quotation, and vernacular (or non-standard) grammar in conversation. This grouping of topics reflects the way that the chapter is necessarily selective. One reason for this is that many aspects of conversational grammar have already been dealt with, at varying degrees of detail, in earlier chapters. Another reason is simply the immense scope of the subject of conversational grammar, which could not by any means be described exhaustively in a single chapter. In spite of the limitations on what can be attempted, however, this final chapter aims to provide a broad conspectus of English conversational grammar from both a formal and a functional point of view.

## 14.1.1   An example of conversation

Before going further, we present a conversational extract (labelled 'Damn chilli') which illustrates many typical grammatical features of conversation. It will be used as a sample from which to exemplify such features in the functional survey which follows (14.1.2). From the transcription, it is not always clear what is occurring among the interlocutors, in spite of the relatively straightforward syntax and vocabulary of this extract. It will help to know something of the setting: a family of four is sitting down to dinner; *P* is the mother, *J* the father, and David (*D*) and Michael (*M*) are their 20-year-old and 17-year-old sons.

**Damn chilli**

D1:  *Mom, I, give me a rest, give it a rest. I didn't think about you. I mean, I would rather do it. <unclear> some other instance in my mind.*

P1:  *Yeah, well I can understand you know, I mean [unclear] Hi I'm David's mother, try to ignore me.*

D2:  *I went with a girl like you once. Let's serve this damn chilli.*

M1:  *Okay, let's serve the chilli. Are you serving or not dad?*

J1:  *Doesn't matter.*

P2:  *Would you get those chips in there. Michael, could you put them with the crackers*

J2:  *Here, I'll come and serve it honey if you want me to.*

P3:  *Oh wait, we still have quite a few.*

D3:  *I don't see any others.*

P4:  *I know you don't.*

D4:  *We don't have any others.*

P5:  *Yes, I got you the big bag I think it will be a help to you.*

J3:  *Here's mom's.*

M2:  *Now this isn't according to grandpa now.*

P6:  *Okay.*

M3:  *The same man who told me it's okay <unclear>*

P7:  *Are you going to put water in our cups? Whose bowl is that.*

M4:  *Mine.*

P8:  *Mike put all the water in here. Well, here we are*

J4:  *What.*

P9:  *Will y'all turn off the TV*

J5:  *Pie, I'll kill you, I said I'd take you to the bathroom.*

P10:  *Man, get your tail out of the soup – Oh, sorry – Did you hear I saw Sarah's sister's baby?*

M5:  *How is it?*

P11:  *She's cute, pretty really.* (AmE CONV)

This dinner table interaction touches on several seemingly unrelated topics. Reference is made not only to the dinner and its accompaniments (e.g. water, chilli, crackers, cups, bowl) and to other people (grandpa, Sarah's sister's baby) and apparently to a household pet named Pie, but also to an imaginary situation in which *P* speaks (in *P1*), to switching off the television, to past meetings, etc.). Some lines are opaque out of context (e.g. *No this isn't according to grandpa now*; *Oh sorry*; and *Man, get your tail out of the soup*). Even the interpretation of *J's What* (*J4*) can only be guessed at. The shared background information and the shared physical and temporal space required to fully understand this excerpt are considerable. In this respect, although the difficulty of making sense of it on the page may be an unfamiliar and disorienting experience for many readers, the extract is typical of conversation.

## 14.1.2    A functional survey of conversation

In the following subsections (14.1.2.1–8), we identify a spectrum of 'external' (social, psychological, and physical) determinants of conversation, and use these to identify and explain many of the striking grammatical characteristics of conversation noted in earlier chapters.

Unlike most other registers, conversation cannot be easily characterized in terms of communicative goals or social functions. The most that can be claimed is that it is a pervasive activity among human beings, and that its primary function appears to be to establish and maintain social cohesion through the sharing of experience, although secondarily it may promote other goals such as entertainment (e.g. through jokes and narratives), exchange of information and control of others' behaviour. Our operational definition of conversation is inclusive enough to subsume many more specific types of verbal behaviour, such as instructing, counselling, insulting, swapping anecdotes or conducting a business telephone call.

### 14.1.2.1    Conversation takes place in the spoken medium

Conversation takes place in speech—by use of an oral-auditory channel. Perhaps this point is so obvious that it does not need labouring.

Unfortunately, the Corpus data we are using lacks some important evidence on the nature of spoken grammar. The LSWE conversational subcorpus has only orthographic transcriptions, lacking phonetic and prosodic information, to represent the complex auditory events of spoken discourse. Other features which could be included in an ideal transcription include:

- Tone units; nuclear tones; varying degrees of stress
- Varying lengths of pause
- Paralinguistic features such as tempo and loudness
- Voice qualities such as whisper and breathy voice.

Of these, the prosodic and pausal phenomena in the first two lines are the most important for conveying grammatically relevant distinctions. The use of orthographic devices such as the question mark (?) cannot compensate for the absence of indicators of intonation and stress. Let us examine two fragments of transcribed speech where these types of information could be important:

   *One of my friends is bisexual,* **Sam.** (BrE)

The function of the final noun *Sam* is unclear: is it a vocative, or a noun in apposition to *one of my friends*? Almost certainly, pause and intonation would have resolved the ambiguity of the transcription. On the other hand, a glance at the header information for the text in question will let us know that the person addressed in this case was not called 'Sam', and therefore for all practical purposes resolve the ambiguity.

   *I told you what she said* **didn't I**? (BrE)

In English, question tags have a somewhat different meaning, according to whether they have a rising or falling nucleus. The transcription does not disambiguate this, although the use of the question mark makes a rising tone more likely.

On the other hand, for many purposes of grammatical research, the absence of prosodic information may make comparatively little difference, since the context generally resolves ambiguities left by lack of intonation. Even in cases where the context sometimes does not help very much, as in the case of the question tag, it can be reasonably argued that we are not dealing with a grammatical distinction here, but with a semantic or pragmatic distinction realized directly through intonation. In other words, the difference between falling and rising tones in a question tag does not need to be treated in grammar, although it is relevant to other aspects of linguistic description.

Nevertheless, our description here lacks important layers of information which would be retrievable from the sound recording of a conversation, or, even more, from a video recording. This lack requires us to be careful in not attributing too much certainty to the conclusions we reach and the interpretations we make on the basis of written evidence only. Despite careful training of the transcribers, the written form of the transcription is likely to reflect individual styles of transcribers: for example, in the placing of commas or periods, in the choice between conventional and non-standard spelling (e.g. in *gotta* and *got to*), and in the use of contractions. At the same time, the choice made by the transcriber is likely to reflect the realities of the spoken recording, when measured in broad quantitative terms.

It also needs to be emphasized that transcription is a highly conventionalized practice, adopting virtually wholesale the rigid orthographic habits (e.g. in the spelling of words, and the marking of spaces between them) which have grown up for the written language. This remark even applies to cases where the standard orthography has been avoided, in order to represent something approximating to the spoken pronunciation, as in abbreviated forms such as *gotta*, *gonna*, and *cos*. These semi-standardized 'informal spellings' are themselves governed by convention. For example, the familiar spellings *ain't* and *eh?* represent words whose actual pronunciation can be more similar to /ɪnt/ and /eɪ/ respectively.

## 14.1.2.2   Conversation takes place in shared context

Conversation is typically carried out in face-to-face interaction with others, e.g. family members or friends, with whom we share a great deal of contextual background. Face-to-face interaction means that we share not just an immediate physical context of time and space, but a large amount of specific social, cultural, and institutional knowledge.

In keeping with this shared knowledge, conversation is marked grammatically by a very high frequency of pronouns, as contrasted with a very low frequency of nouns (2.3.5; 2.14.4). The user of personal pronouns (by far the most common class of pronouns) normally assumes that we share knowledge of the intended reference of *you, she, it*, etc. This sharing of situational knowledge is most obvious in the case of first and second person pronouns (especially *I* and *you*) which, referring directly to participants in the conversation, are the most common in this variety. (They account for 29 of the 47 personal pronouns in 'Damn chilli'.) Pronoun reference, however, represents only the most common variety of **grammatical reduction** that characterizes conversation, others being the use of ellipsis and of substitute proforms (e.g. *one/ones* substituting for a nominal—

4.15.2—and *do it/that* substituting for a verb or verb phrase—5.4.3.2). In the extract 'Damn chilli', substitution is illustrated by:

> *I mean, I would rather* **do it**. *(D1)*

and both substitution and ellipsis (signalled by <–>) are illustrated in this sequence of turns:

> *Here, I'll come and serve it honey if you want me to* <–>. *(J2)*
> *Oh wait, we still have quite* **a few**. *(P3)*
> *I don't see any* **others**. *(D3)*
> *I know you don't* <–>. *(P4)*

Obviously such structure-erasing devices signal dependence of communication on contextual clues—which may, or may not, have been overtly signalled in the preceding discourse. The frequency of ellipsis in conversation (see also 14.3.5) shows up especially in situational ellipsis (3.7.5; e.g. *Doesn't matter* in 'Damn chilli' *[J1]*), in ellipsis across turns (as seen in turn *P4* above), and also commonly in answers to questions (3.7.3–4). Reduction means the simplification of grammatical structure, hence the reduction of the number of words uttered, by reliance on implicit meaning or reference, as supplied by mutual knowledge. Often this implicit meaning is retrieved anaphorically, by a previous verbal reference (as in *she* in 'Damn chilli', co-referring to *Sarah's sister's baby* in (*P10*)), but frequently it is retrieved from the situation outside language. Another type of reliance on situational reference is through the use of deictic items (*this, that, these, those, there, then, now,* etc.), most of which again are particularly common in conversation (4.4.3.1). In 'Damn chilli', we note particularly the use of deictics in *D2* (*this damn chilli*), *P2* (*those chips in there*), *J3* (*Here's mom's*), *M2* (*Now this isn't according to grandpa*), and *P7* (*Whose bowl is that?*). The more private the conversation, the more the understanding of it tends to rely on such deictic identification of reference.

As the 'Damn chilli' example shows, another factor which contributes to the difficulty of making sense of a transcription is the use of **non-clausal** or grammatically fragmentary components in speech (3.15.2; see also 14.3.2–4). Although such material can be found in written language (e.g. in headlines and lists), it is far more pervasive and varied in speech. The word-class of **inserts** (2.2.3.3, 2.5), including grammatical isolates such as *yeah* (*P1*), *okay* (*M1*), and *sorry* (*P10*), is the clearest case of material which cannot be fitted into canonical grammatical structures such as clauses and phrases. These 'stand-alone' words rely heavily for their interpretation on situational factors, which may be expressed through language but also through other means. For example, *thanks* or *sorry* may be a follow-up to a non-verbal action, as well as to a verbal one (as the example *Oh, sorry* in *P10* shows).

To the extent that conversation is dependent for its meanings on the immediate context, it is less dependent on the articulation of overt grammatical structure. The occurrence of inserts at the word level is matched by the occurrence of disjunctive elements such as **prefaces** and **noun phrase tags** (3.4.3–4) at the phrase level: a further realization of the context-bound nature of conversation (see also 14.3.2). Yet a further manifestation of this is the not-infrequent occurrence in conversation of **unembedded dependent clauses** (3.14) such as *When you're ready* or *If you don't mind* as complete grammatical units. In our analysis, these are counted as examples of non-clausal rather than clausal units, since they lack the normally expected main clause structure.

### 14.1.2.3 Conversation avoids elaboration or specification of meaning

The characteristic of 'non-elaboration' arises from the reliance on context just discussed. In drawing heavily on implicit meaning, conversation forgoes the need for the lexical and syntactic elaboration commonly found in written expository registers. It was observed in 2.2.9 that conversation has a strikingly low **lexical density** in comparison with the three written registers. Similarly, it was seen in 2.10 that conversation has a remarkably low degree of grammatical elaboration, as is shown by a mean phrase length much lower than that of news and academic writing. This variability of syntactic elaboration, in practice, is strongly associated with the noun phrase.

In particular, participants in conversation make the most use of pronouns, characteristically reducing the noun phrase to a simple monosyllable; at the other extreme, they find little call for the more elaborated forms of noun phrase structures, containing noun heads with various forms of modification. Such elaborated phrases are frequently found, however, in the decontextualized medium of written texts, where the author needs to be more explicit about what is referred to. In the implicit milieu of conversation, not only are nouns far less common than in written registers (2.3.5), but there is a notable absence of complexity of pre-modification and post-modification (8.1.1).

Attributive adjectives, noun modifiers, and relative clauses (8.2.1, 8.6.1), for instance, are markedly rare in comparison with the other registers. Also, attributive adjectives in conversation are largely simple and monosyllabic (7.4.2), as contrasted with the polysyllabic adjectives (with suffixes such as -ful, -ous, -ent, -less) which often occur in the expository written registers (7.9.2.1). A powerful illustration of this avoidance of noun phrase elaboration in conversation is seen in 4.1.1, where nominal elements were found to make up only 55 per cent of a specimen passage of conversation, while such elements comprised about 80 per cent of a specimen passage of newspaper language of comparable length.

The figures for genitives and possessives are also telling, in showing the contrary claims of implicitness and elaborative explicitness in these categories. The genitive, as an elaborative noun-headed, noun-modifying construction, is predictably rare in conversation (4.6.11), and here 'Damn chilli', as a short extract containing four genitives (*David's, mom's, Sarah's* and *sister's*), is highly atypical. In contrast, possessive determiners such as *your, her* (4.4.2.1), being pronominal, are particularly frequent. However, within these categories, independent (non-modifying) genitives (such as *mom's* in J3 of 'Damn chilli') are about twice as frequent in conversation as in the written registers (4.6.11), and possessive pronouns such as *mine* (see M4 of 'Damn chilli'), which occur independently as heads, again occur much more frequently in conversation (4.11.2). Presumably these forms are more frequent in conversation because they are typically elliptical and reliant on context.

Turning to other word-classes, we observe (2.3.5, 2.4.14) that conversation has a higher frequency than the other registers of verbs (especially primary and modal verbs), adverbs, particles, and inserts. These word-classes perhaps reflect a tendency for conversation to be concerned with actions and attitudes. However, the most important thing they have in common is a negative one: they are all word-classes which have little or no association with the noun phrase. In a register where the noun phrase is stripped down to bare essentials, other elements of the sentence such as verbs and adverbs benefit from a comparative gain in frequency.

Since syntactic elaboration goes hand in hand with the detailing of semantic specification, we can make a further negative association, in conversation, between the avoidance of elaboration and the avoidance of specification of meaning. Without context, *she* as a noun phrase, for example, tells us little, except that the person referred to is female. This strongly contrasts with a noun phrase such as the following from 'Damn chilli', which provides a considerable amount of explicit information about the referent:

> *The same man who told me it's okay (M3)*

This example is again rather exceptional for conversational language. Just as speakers in conversation usually avoid referential specificity such as this, so they also tend to avoid being specific about quantity and quality, as is shown by speakers' tendency towards vagueness which has been noted, and often condemned, by critics of the 'slovenliness' of conversation. The frequent, apparently compulsive, use of general conversational hedges such as *kind of*, *sort of*, and *like* (10.3.3; Table 10.15) is one conspicuous example of this. Others are the use of quantifying hedges such as the *odd* of *forty odd*, and the *-ish* of *eightish* (2.7.7.3), vacuous nouns like *thingy* (4.1.1.3), and vague coordination tags (2.9.2.1) such as *or something*, *or something like that*, *and stuff*, and *and things like that*.

Seen from the vantage point of written language, with its emphasis on specificity, such vagueness appears to be a culpable lack of precision. But, from the viewpoint of conversational partners, greater precision would not only be superfluous, but it would also need more processing and delay the ongoing dynamic of the conversation (14.3). Being inexact about values and opinions, like being unspecific in reference, is a strategy which relies on an implied sharing of knowledge and experience.

## 14.1.2.4 Conversation is interactive

Conversation is co-constructed by two or more interlocutors, dynamically adapting their expression to the ongoing exchange. Most obviously, the to-and-fro movement of conversation between speaker and hearer is evident in the occurrence of utterances which by their nature either form a response, or elicit a response. In conversational analysis, these utterance-response sequences, known as **adjacency pairs**, may be either symmetric, as in the case of one greeting echoing another, or asymmetric, such as a sequence of question followed by answer. Here is one of the examples from 'Damn chilli':

> P3: *Whose bowl is that.*
> M4: *Mine.*

It is not at all surprising that questions and imperatives, the sentence types that typically elicit a response, are more frequent in conversation than in written language. Questions are three to four times more common (3.13.2.5) and imperatives are more than five times as common (3.13.4.2) in conversation as in any of the other registers. Many response forms (minimally such monosyllables as *yeah*, *no*, and *mm*) lack the full syntactic articulation of the clause, which is understandable, since they rely on the context created by the preceding turn. These inserts often have a stereotyped initiating or responding function within an adjacency-pair framework: e.g. greetings such as *hi*, farewells such as *bye*, backchannels such as *uh huh*, response elicitors such as *okay* (2.5; see also 14.3.3). What is more surprising is the high frequency of questions which are not full clauses: nearly half the questions in conversation take the form of non-clausal fragments or tags such as *Really?* and *What for?* (3.13.2.6). It is clear that often the pervasive non-clausal forms already mentioned in 14.1.2.2 have a cohesive, communication-sharing function as well as a context-invoking function.

Among the types of interrogative structure in conversation, about one in four questions are question tags (added to declarative clauses), whereas this proportion drops dramatically to one in 15 in fiction, and one in 100 in academic prose (3.13.2.6). The important point about question tags, here, is that they add an interrogative force to a declarative one, combining assertion with a request for confirmation, thus illustrating the characteristic 'negotiation' or **co-construction** of meaning between interlocutors. Whereas standard *wh-* and *yes-no* interrogatives enjoy well-established (though limited) conventions of use in written language and spoken monologue (e.g. in rhetorical and self-addressed questions), the same is not true of question tags, whose function is more closely bound up with the mutuality of conversation.

Already noted in 14.1.2.2 is the common routine use in conversation of discourse markers and other elements on the periphery of clause structure (see also 14.3.3). They are typically used to signal the pragmatic or discoursal role of the speaker's utterance, dynamically shaping it to the ongoing exchange. 'Damn chilli' provides an example where the overuse of such forms suggests irony:

> P1: **Yeah, well,** I can understand **you know, I mean** <...>

The peripheral adverbs dealt with in 10.3–4, i.e. **stance adverbials** and **linking adverbials**, similarly have a discoursal function, being markers respectively of the speaker's attitude to what is said, and of a link or transition between neighbouring parts of the discourse.

Stance adverbials are exceptionally frequent in conversation (10.3.1.5, 10.3.2.1) and so too are linking adverbials (10.4.1.8, 10.4.2.1), although they are slightly more frequent in the contrasting register of academic prose. What is striking, however, is that the linking adverbials frequently used in academic prose (such as *therefore* and *however*) are quite different from those used in conversation (such as *anyway* and *so*). Whereas the former are used to signpost the logical and argumentative links between one part of the discourse and another, the latter are used more dynamically and interpersonally, to signal transitions in the interactive development of discourse.

These interaction signals shade into **discourse markers** (see also 14.3.2.2 and 14.3.3.3), the term used in 3.4.5 for items 'loosely attached to the clause and connected with ongoing interaction'. These include some single word **inserts,** like *well* and *now* as utterance introducers, as well as formulaic clausal forms such as the inevitable *I mean* and *you know*. Other interactive conversational inserts are interjections and response forms such as *oh*, *right*, *yeah*, and *okay*, which, like discourse markers, can either stand alone or attach themselves to larger discoursal units (14.3.3). As an example, in 'Damn chilli' we find:

> D2: *Let's serve this damn chilli.*
> M1: **Okay,** *let's serve the chilli.*

and later:

> M2: *Now this isn't according to grandpa now.*
> P6: **Okay**.

In conversation, discourse markers can be said to have a 'discourse management' function, which they share broadly with **vocatives** (3.4.6; see also 14.4.1) or address forms. Like discourse markers, vocatives are generally loosely attached to the beginning or end of a clausal or non-clausal unit. They typically identify, by a name or some other appellation, whoever is being addressed by a particular remark. 'Damn chilli' has seven examples: *Mom* (in *D1*), *dad* (*M1*), *Michael* (*P2*), *honey* (*J2*), *Mike* (*P8*), *Pie* and *Man*—this last appellation, surprisingly, appears to be addressed to the dog. But as is evident from these examples, vocatives have not only an identifying but also an attitudinal function, which leads on to the theme of the next section.

It has also been suggested in 3.8.4.1 that there is an interactive explanation for the high frequency in conversation of **negation** and of the adversative conjunction *but*. These are both devices to deny or counteract the expectations of those involved in dialogue: negation and contradiction imply interaction between opposing points of view.

## 14.1.2.5 Conversation is expressive of politeness, emotion, and attitude

The interactive nature of conversation just discussed extends to the use of polite or respectful language in exchanges such as requests, greetings, offers, and apologies. Here certain inserts have a stereotypical role in marking polite speech acts: *thanks* and *thank you*, *please*, *bye*, and *sorry*, for example. Such conversational routines are historically derived by ellipsis from more elaborated, clausal expressions, but for the purposes of present-day English grammar they are best regarded as unanalysed formulae (14.3.3.8). Vocatives such as *sir* and *madam* also have a respectful role, although such honorific forms are rare in English compared with many other languages. More typical of English is the use of stereotypic polite openings such as the interrogative forms *would you* and *could you*, functioning as requests in 'Damn chilli':

> P2: **Would you** get those chips in there. Michael, **could you** put them with the crackers.

As we see, such polite directives are found even in the speech of a mother to her children in the privacy of a family meal.

In other cases, the collective first person imperative *let's* (14.4.4.3) is used as a somewhat less face-threatening alternative to the second person imperative:

> M1: Okay, **let's** serve the chilli. Are you serving or not dad?

Notice also here the way a question follows up the directive *let's*. The preference for questions, as being less confrontational in many situations than other sentence types, is also suggested by the fact that questions are at least twice as common as imperatives (3.13.2.5, 3.13.4.2) in conversation.

However, it must not be supposed that conversation preserves polite norms all (or even most) of the time. The second person imperative also occurs in 'Damn chilli' as a balder form of directive, addressed in one case by a son to his mother (*give it a rest*, *D1*) and in another case, it seems, to the dog (*get your tail out of the soup*, *P10*). Vocatives are remarkably versatile, too, in conveying a varied and highly coloured range of speaker-hearer attitudes. Endearments (e.g. *honey*, J2) and laconically familiar appellatives we will call **familiarizers** (e.g. *man*, P10) are far more characteristic of conversation than honorific forms such as *sir* and *madam* (see also 14.4.1).

At the less restrained end of the emotional spectrum are frequently occurring interjections such as *oh, ah*, and *wow* (2.5; see also 14.3.3.1) and, much less commonly, exclamatives such as *what a rip-off!* (3.13.3, 14.3.4.2). As a more positive indicator of speaker attitude, the common predicative adjectives in conversation (7.5.1) are mostly evaluative (*good, lovely, nice*, etc.), and various types of evaluative intensifier can also be added, including the characteristically conversational use of intensifying coordination: e.g. *nice and strong, good and fresh* (7.10.2).

### 14.1.2.6  Conversation takes place in real time

Many conversational traits arise from the fact that conversation is typically spontaneous, so that speakers are continually faced with the need both to plan and to execute their utterances in real time, 'online' or 'on the fly'. Consequently, conversation is characterized by what has been called 'normal dysfluency': for example, it is quite natural for a speaker's flow to be impaired by pauses, hesitators (*er, um*), and repetitions such as *I – I – I* at points where the need to keep talking (14.3.1) threatens to run ahead of mental planning, and the planning needs to catch up (see also 14.2).

However, we should also note the importance of a phenomenon the opposite of that above: where the speaker knows pretty well what to say, and indeed the hearer may to some extent share that knowledge. Here planning runs ahead of speech production. To save time and energy, speakers aim to reduce the length of what they have to say. Speed of repartee, making an opportune remark, getting 'a word in edgeways' in a lively dialogue, or reaching the point quickly, may all add urgency to the spoken word. In fact, in conversation speed of communication can vary a great deal according to the needs of encoding and decoding.

In a familiar context, where many of the words to be uttered are largely predictable, devices for reducing the length of utterances are likely to be routinely employed. In phonological terms, fast, informal speech is often marked by effort-reducing features such as elision and assimilation. Although such features are not directly visible in our orthographic transcriptions, a reduction of length may also be readily observed on the levels of morphology and syntax, through contractions and other morphologically reduced forms, and the types of ellipsis already mentioned in 14.1.2.2 (see also 14.3.5).

One common effort-saving device in conversation (and in spoken language generally) is the use of **contractions**: reduced enclitic forms of the verb (e.g. *it's, we'll*) and of the negative particle (e.g. *isn't, can't*) (see the Appendix). Another is **situational ellipsis** (3.7.5; see also 14.3.5.1), taking the form of the omission of words of low information value (e.g. *Doesn't matter*, J1). This type of ellipsis is termed 'situational' because the missing elements are retrievable through situational knowledge, rather than through anaphoric reference to a previous mention. However, it is often a condition of this type of ellipsis that the elements omitted are so stereotyped as to be predictable in any situation. Situational ellipsis gives rise to sentences which fail to conform to the ideal of sentence grammar—where every sentence has a finite verb and every finite verb has a subject: *Got a* *pen? Didn't know it was yours.* In fact, very often the omission of subject and operator result in an utterance or clause lacking any verb at all, e.g.: *No problem* (cf. *There's no problem*—14.3.4.1–2).

Quite apart from this, the syntax of conversation differs from the 'sentence grammar' typical of planned writing in ways which bear the marks of online planning pressure. In 'Damn chilli', the last turn (*P11*) has a structure scarcely paralleled in written English, where the last two words *pretty really* are tagged on to the simple clause *She's cute*, elaborating and modifying retrospectively the intended meaning of *cute*. Prefaces and tags, noted elsewhere (3.4.3–4, 11.5, 14.3.2) as characteristic of spoken English, can take the form of stand-alone phrases placed respectively before and after a clause, elaborating part of the meaning:

> Cos **Brenda whose horse I ride up at Bridley** – *I was telling her* (BrE†)

The effect of such devices is to eliminate complex phrases from the body of the clause, where they could cause processing hold-ups both for the speaker and the hearer. This type of functional explanation can be given for many non-clausal phenomena in conversational grammar, where the tendency to avoid detailed nominal reference (14.1.2.2) works hand in hand with the principle of economy of effort to produce various kinds of elision and reduction (see also 14.3.1.3–4).

### 14.1.2.7 Conversation has a restricted and repetitive repertoire

As shown in 13.2.1.1, conversation is appreciably more repetitive than the three written registers. Speakers often repeat partially or exactly what has just been said in the conversation, thus relieving online planning pressure by a device which may be called **local repetition**. Here is an example from 'Damn chilli':

> D2:  <...> *Let's serve this damn chilli.*
> M1: *Okay, let's serve the chilli.*

However, conversation is repetitive in a more global sense, in that it relies more on stereotyped, prefabricated sequences of words, which in Chapter 13 were called **lexical bundles**. Take, for example, four-word bundles such as *Can I have a, Do you know what:* in Table 13.2 (p. 997), it was seen that in equivalent samples, conversation has 424 of such bundles, whereas academic prose has only 277.

This stronger tendency to repeat the same repertoire is no doubt explained in part by the constraint of online processing in speech. Time pressure makes it more difficult for speakers to exploit the full innovative power of grammar and lexicon: instead, they rely heavily on well-worn, prefabricated word sequences, readily accessible from memory.

Another piece of evidence for stereotyped verbal repertoire in conversation is the low **type-token ratio** (2.2.1) of conversation compared with written registers. This tendency also shows up in our grammatical analyses in the steepness of rank-frequency curves for vocabulary filling particular syntactic roles. For example, the particularly high frequency of modal auxiliaries in conversation is largely due to the extremely common use of the modals *will, can, would,* and *could* (this frequency declines quickly with other modals such as *must, might, shall,* and *may* which are many times less frequent than *will*—cf. Table 6.6). Likewise in the list of verbs taking *that*-clauses as complements, a very small number of such verbs, particularly *think, say,* and *know,* are massively more common than the other verbs in conversation (9.2.2.3), and make up a larger percentage of the occurrences than in the written registers.

In contrast, written registers tend to have a larger number of common verbs, which have less dramatically high frequencies. Something similar is observed for verbs taking an infinitive complement (9.4.2.9), where *want* is far ahead of the field, in comparison both with other such verbs in conversation, and with the highest-frequency verbs in written registers. Other instances of the dominance of high frequency items are found in the area of adverbials. They include single-adverb circumstance adverbs (10.2.5), stance adverbs (10.3.3), and linking adverbs (10.4.3.1), where again a large percentage of occurrences is due to a small number of very common words: adverbs such as *there, just, so, then, anyway, though,* and *now.* Similarly, the higher frequency of adverbial clauses in conversation than in written registers (10.2.8.9) is largely due to the very high frequency of clauses introduced by *if, when,* and *because* (the last often reduced to the monosyllable spelt *'cause* or *cos*).

The extract 'Damn chilli' also illustrates how in conversation we tend to use the same common words and expressions over and over again. For example, although verbs are frequent in the passage, they are almost all of the simplest and most frequent types. In the following list, the main verb lexemes occurring more than once in the passage have the number of occurrences appended: *give* 2, *think* 2, *mean* 2, *be* 10, *serve* 4, *get* 3, *put* 3, *have* 2, and *see* 2 (5.2.2.2). Turning to auxiliary verbs, it is also noticeable that the four most common modals in general English are the only modals which occur in this extract: *will* 4, *would* 3, *can* 1, *could* 1 (6.6.2).

### 14.1.2.8    Conversation employs a vernacular range of expression

Conversation typically takes place privately between people who know one another, perhaps intimately: it is remote from and little influenced by the traditions of prestige and correctness often associated with publicly available written texts, where the English language is 'on its best behaviour'. Hence the style of conversation is overwhelmingly informal. This shows in 'Damn chilli' in lexical choice (e.g. of *get, damn,* and *cute*), but also grammatically in the use of verb and negative contractions (such as the repeated use of *it's* and *don't*). Such contractions are informal in style, while also contributing to the economy of online speech processing (14.1.2.6). Another aspect of vernacular grammar is the occurrence of regional dialect forms: thus in 'Damn chilli', turn *P9* contains the second person pronoun *y'all*, associated with the southern states of the USA.

Moreover, in some conversational material we find morphological forms which tend to be regarded as outside the citadel of standard English, such as *ain't,* or *aren't* in the combination *aren't I* (3.8.2.6). Similarly, most conversational speakers show little or no inhibition about using the non-standard *me and Ann* construction (4.10.6.3) in place of the more polite and more prestigious construction *Ann and I.* Turning to the oblique case form of interrogative pronouns, *whom* is extremely rare in the conversational Corpus: even for the oblique-case functions of object and prepositional complement, the officially stigmatized form *who* is almost always preferred (3.13.2.7, 8.7.1.2).

Stigmatized or non-standard features also occur at the syntactic level. Thus in the transcriptions of conversation, coordinators at the beginning of an orthographic sentence or utterance are in general much more frequent than in other registers (2.4.7.4)—another feature often frowned on in the written language. Subject-verb 'discord' between singular and plural, yet another aspect of grammar which tends to attract censure, does not suffer from this inhibition to the same extent in conversation. For example, the construction with *there is/was* followed by a plural noun phrase is more common in conversation than the corresponding 'concordant' version *there are/were* (3.9.1.5). On vernacular grammar in conversation, see also 14.4.5.

## 14.1.2.9  Lack of functional explanation

Before reaching the end of this functional survey of the language of conversation, it should be acknowledged that not every feature of a register has a readily available functional explanation. In some cases of grammatical divergence, written registers and spoken conversation may have simply developed along different paths: the independent development of one from the other need not have been driven by functional considerations.

Consider, for example, the case of the genitive v. the *of*-phrase (4.6.12). Historically, these have been competing constructions for more than a millennium, and the *of*-phrase increased notably in the Middle English period under the influence of French. However, the *of*-phrase is still rare in spoken English, as contrasted with its heavy use in the written language. Over the centuries the grammar of written English has been more under the influence of foreign languages carrying prestige, notably French and Latin, whereas the grammar of spoken English has maintained its development more independently of these external scholarly influences. Another reflection of this is the rather high frequency in conversation of phrasal verbs (5.3.2.2) such as *turn off* in turn *P9* of 'Damn chilli'.

Another case of historically competing constructions is the choice between *not*-negation and *no*-negation, the former again being more favoured by spoken language and the latter by the written language. In 3.8.4.2 it was seen that *not*-negation was chosen in about 90 per cent of instances in conversation, compared with about 70 per cent of instances in newspaper language. Although a functional explanation of the preference was suggested there, this remains very much a matter for speculation.

A final area where functional explanations do not tell the whole story is in the syntax of the English verb, where again we can see a long-term historical development of grammaticalization taking place. Semi-modals such as *be going to*, *have got to*, and *had better*, particularly frequent in conversation (6.6.2), comprise a historically transitional category, and are becoming progressively grammaticalized, in that they are losing their association with the grammatical constructions they exemplify in their written form. For example, *be going to*, historically containing the progressive aspect of the verb *go*, no longer has the meaning associated with that form. Instead, it conveys futurity, typically associated with intention. A similar observation can be made about *have got to*, a semi-auxiliary historically evolving from the perfect aspect of *get*. A further sign of grammaticalization is that, in speech, these semi-modals are given a much reduced pronunciation orthographically represented by the spellings *gonna*, *gotta*, and *better* (with loss of *had*).[2]

In an earlier wave of grammaticalization, largely completed in the sixteenth century, the English class of modal auxiliary verbs evolved from full lexical verbs. We see a relic of the full verb from which *will* developed in instances such as:

> *I just willed him with all my mind to believe me* (FICT).

This grammaticalization tendency has gone so far as to reduce the central modals to little more than invariable verbal 'particles' in present-day English. But for some time now a fresh wave of auxiliary creation has been under way, most clearly seen in the phonological reduction and semantic specialization of *be going to, have got to, had better,* and *want to*. Regarding the pronunciation of any particular semi-modal token, we cannot draw any conclusions from its spelling in transcription. However, the fact that transcribers often find it more appropriate to render semi-modals in conventionalized non-standard written forms such as *gonna* is a sign that, for present-day English speakers, the standard written form, which preserves the historical syntactic origin of these forms, is often no longer felt to be appropriate. Occasionally, as the examples just discussed suggest, a functional perspective on the characteristics of spoken grammar can be helpfully complemented by a historical perspective.

---

**Special conventions for representing transcribed dialogue in this chapter**

In the remainder of this chapter, the abbreviations AmE and BrE will be used, for simplicity, for examples from American conversation and British conversation respectively, omitting the abbreviation CONV. Parts of conversational turns in { } represents speech which overlaps with the speech of another speaker. The symbol / is occasionally used to signal the location of overlapping speech where this has no relevance to the example being presented. (For other conventions, see the 'Symbols and notational conventions' section at the front of the book.)

---

## 14.2 Performance phenomena: dysfluency and error

The reasons why dysfluency is a normal accompaniment of spontaneous speech have been mentioned in 14.1.2.6. It remains to discuss the grammatical relevance and incidence of dysfluency.

It is sometimes supposed that dysfluency is so pervasive a feature of ordinary speech that, by the standards of written language, spoken language is grammatically inchoate. It is true that dysfluency sometimes reaches pathological extremes—as in the following example:

> 1 *No. Do you know erm you know where the erm go over to er go over erm where the fire station is not the one that white white* (BrE)

But in extreme cases like this we can usually point to factors leading to unusual pressure on the online planning capability of the speaker. Here the speaker is trying to explain how to reach a local shopping amenity. The online problems here are cognitive more than syntactic: how to (a) retrieve and interpret her own map of the locality, (b) calculate the best route to take, (c) estimate the hearer's geographical knowledge of the locality, and (d) explain the route to take, in the light of (a), (b), and (c). This is not an easy task, and it is not totally surprising that the speaker has to make four or five different attempts to begin her utterance, and finally fails to complete it.

While it is rare for speakers to become as inarticulate as in **1**, it is completely normal for speakers to produce utterances with minor dysfluencies. In most cases, these minor performance problems do not interfere with understanding at all. The following extract is fairly long and grammatically complex (the speaker is describing his dog's behaviour):

> 2 *The trouble is {if you're} if you're the only one in the house he follows you and you're looking for him and every time you're moving around he's moving around behind you* <laughter> *so you can't find him. I thought I wonder where the hell he's gone* <laughter> *I mean he was immediately behind me.* (BrE)

Here the only dysfluency is the initial repetition of *if you're*, which, as the parentheses indicate, is occasioned by overlapping speech from another participant. The utterance consists of a sequence of clause-like units, such that if we wanted to analyse it in terms of traditional complex and compound sentences there would be little difficulty in doing so.

In 14.2.1–5 below, we survey different kinds of dysfluency: silent and filled pauses, repeats, retrace-and-repair sequences, types of incompleteness, and syntactic blends.

## 14.2.1 Hesitations: silent and filled pauses

The most obvious form of dysfluency is a hold-up in delivery, i.e. a hesitation pause: a period of silence where the speaker appears to plan what to say next. It is only identifiable as a **hesitation pause** in the transcription where a pause is marked by a dash ( – ) in the middle of a turn. Sometimes this occurs in the middle of a grammatical unit (a clausal unit or a non-clausal unit; 14.3.1.3), as in **1** below, while in other cases it occurs at the beginning or end of a grammatical unit, where the dysfluency is less marked, as in **2** and **3**:

> 1 *So, – boy they've got a nice system over there hooked up.* (AmE †)
> 2 *That's probably what I'll do. – That's, that's a good idea.* (AmE)
> 3 *Do we have a couple of dice about? – Or shall we just guess.* (AmE)

Often the pause is accompanied by some other form of dysfluency:

> 4 *That's a very good – er very good precaution to take, yes.* (BrE)

Example **4** combines a pause (after *good*) with two other forms of dysfluency, a hesitator (*er*) and a repeat (of *very good*).

A **filled pause** is occupied not by silence, but by a vowel sound, with or without accompanying nasalization. Such **hesitators** are usually transcribed in the AmE transcriptions *uh* and *um*, and in the BrE transcriptions *er* and *erm*. (No difference in pronunciation is implied by these different transcription practices.)

### 14.2.1.1 Frequency of filled and unfilled pauses

**CORPUS FINDINGS**

Since the marking of pauses in the transcriptions is impressionistic, and in many transcriptions no distinction is made between different lengths of pauses, we cannot rely on consistency of practice. Notwithstanding, Table 14.1 gives, from the

**Table 14.1** **Frequency of unfilled and filled hesitation pauses, averaged across AmE and BrE conversational subcorpora; occurrences per million words**

● = over 1000

| unfilled pause ( – ) | filled pause (*uh*, *er*) | filled pause (*um*, *erm*) |
|---|---|---|
| ●●●●●●●●●●●●●●●●●●●●●●●● | ●●●●●●●●● | ●●●●● |

evidence of transcriptions, the frequency of filled and unfilled pauses, and also gives the frequency of the nasalized and oral variants of the filled hesitation pause.[3] The choice between unfilled and filled pauses is conditioned by syntactic position:

➤ Unfilled pauses tend to occur at major boundaries between syntactic units.

➤ Filled pauses occur at lesser or medial syntactic boundaries (in addition to major boundaries), such as before the beginning of dependent clauses and coordinate constructions.

➤ In this respect, the filled pauses (*uh*, *um*, etc.) are intermediate between unfilled pauses and repeat phenomena (14.2.1–2 and Table 14.5) in marking a hold-up in the production process.

### DISCUSSION OF FINDINGS

The different grammatical distributions of filled and unfilled pauses relate to their typical functions. Filled pauses are devices for signalling that the speaker has not yet finished his or her turn, and for discouraging another speaker from taking the floor. Hence, a filled pause is most useful at a point of grammatical incompletion which is nevertheless a major planning point, such as the beginning of a dependent or coordinate clause. For example, the pronoun *she*, as a nominative personal pronoun, almost invariably marks the onset of a new clause structure, which might be expected to be a fairly major forward-planning site in the course of syntactic composition. In AmE conversation, the details for this pronoun are as follows: only one *she* in more than 500 instances is preceded by an unfilled pause; one *she* in 65 instances is preceded by the hesitator *uh* or *um*; and one *she* in 77 is preceded by another *she*—the hesitator and repeat phenomena being quite common in this context. Further details are given in Table 14.5.

The unfilled pause, on the other hand, tends to occur at more major points of transition, points where an **utterance launcher** (such as *oh*, *well*, *okay*; 14.3.2.1) is likely to occur. In contrast to *she* above, take, for example, the insert *okay*: approximately one *okay* in ten is preceded by an unfilled pause, whereas one *okay* in 113 is preceded by a filled pause (*uh* or *um*). This marked difference is presumably because *okay* is very typically used as an insert coming at the beginning or end of a major grammatical unit. The contrast between *she* and *okay* is shown in Table 14.2, where the figures are expressed as percentages of all occurrences of the word in question.

**Table 14.2** **Percentage unfilled and filled pauses preceding the two words *she* and *okay* in the AmE conversation subcorpus**

each ■ represents c. 1%     ▫ represents less than 1%

| | unfilled pause ( – ) | filled pause (*uh* and *um*) |
|---|---|---|
| *she* | ▫ | ■■ |
| *okay* | ■■■■■■■■■ | ■ |

## 14.2.2 Repeats

In addition to using a filled hesitation pause, another strategy a speaker may use to gain time is to begin and then re-begin the same piece of speech. The same bit of language can be repeated until the speaker is able to continue. Such dysfluencies may be termed **repeats** (the term 'repetition' being reserved for the more general phenomenon of verbal repetition, whether deliberate or involuntary):

> 1 *I hope that, uh, Audrey sent in that article to the News Press* **to**, **to** *get back with them* (AmE)
>
> 2 *Hopefully,* **he'll**, *er,* **he'll** *see the error of his ways.* (AmE)

Sometimes the repeated dysfluency reaches an almost pathological extreme, as in the following example, which illustrates how overlapping speech is particularly likely to give rise to such repetition:

> 3 *A: Yeah it {does <unclear>}.*
> *B: {Yeah,* **it**, **it**, **it** *is}* **it's** **it's** **it's** **it's** *good*
> *A: Yeah.*
> *B: I'd recommend that book to anybody.* (AmE)

In the simplest and most common cases, one word or even less than one word (half a syllable, say) is repeated, producing a momentary 'stutter' effect:

> *The problem is that* **i–** **it's** *not just a straightforward correlation.* (AmE †)
>
> *Ah but it's silly because the thing is,* **th– the– they're**, *well* **the, th– those,**
> **th– those** *two rooms look as if a bloody tip has hit it!* (BrE)

(Note that in these examples the '–' indicates the end of a word-fragment, i.e. a word which is incompletely articulated.)

### 14.2.2.1 Multiple consecutive repeats

**CORPUS FINDINGS**

➤ The likelihood of the repetition decreases sharply with the number of words repeated, so that the overwhelming majority of examples are of a single repeat (e.g. *the the*).

➤ There are extremely few instances of three or more repeats (e.g. *the the the the* …).

Table 14.3 **Examples of one-word (dysfluent) repeats in AmE conversation; occurrences per million words**

each ■ represents c. 25     ❙ represents less than 12

|  | doubles (e.g. *I I*) | triples (e.g. *I I I*) | quadruples (e.g. *I I I I*) |
|---|---|---|---|
| *I* | ■■■■■■■■■■■■■<br>■■■■■■■■■■■ | ■■ | ❙ |
| *the* | ■■■■■■■■ | ■ | ❙ |
| *and* | ■■■■■■ | ■ | ❙ |
| *it* | ■■■ | ❙ | ❙ |
| *you* | ■■■ | ❙ | ❙ |

➤ There is a predictably sharp decline in the number of instances as one increases the number of consecutive words repeated; Table 14.5 gives examples of unplanned repeats of some of the most common words in the Corpus.

**Table 14.4** **Examples of two-word and three-word sequences in repeats; occurrences per million words**

each ■ represents c. 5     □ represents less than 2

|  | doubles (e.g. *I'll I'll*) | triples (e.g. *I'll I'll I'll*) |
|---|---|---|
| *I'll* | ■■■■■■■■■ | □ |
| *it was* | ■■■ | □ |

### DISCUSSION OF FINDINGS

Repeats, as a form of dysfluency, are presumed to be unplanned or involuntary. Since repetitions of words and phrases can also occur deliberately, there is sometimes a difficulty in deciding whether a given instance is a case of dysfluency or not. Of the following examples, **4–6** show clear cases of deliberate repetition for intensifying or attention-getting purposes, whereas **7** is less clear:

4  *Oh **wait, wait, wait**, you forgot this.* (AmE)

5  ***Hey, hey, hey, hey, hey*** (AmE)

6  *I **cried and cried and cried and cried**.* (AmE)

7  *But not, **it's suspended, it's suspended** but it's not disallowed.* (BrE)

In fact, if we examine the context of **7**, it is seen to belong to a training session in which the speaker is instructing a group of addressees about official regulations. In such a context, deliberate repetition, for clarity and emphasis, is common:

7a  *A: And that is about **what happens when someone leaves a job of their own accord**. – So **what happens when someone leaves a job of their own accord, what happens** to their unemployment benefit.*

    *B: {**Suspended**.}*

    *C: {**Suspended** pending} enquiries.*

    *D: Yeah.*

    *A: But not, **it's suspended, it's suspended** but it's not disallowed.* (BrE)

In the above passage, several repetitions (shown in italics) seem to be deliberate rather than dysfluent. In this context, the balance of the evidence tips in favour of the last utterance also containing deliberate repetition.

## 14.2.2.2 Frequency of repeats

### CORPUS FINDINGS

The likelihood of repeats varies with grammatical factors, in addition to the overall frequency of the repeated word. In Table 14.5, we present the frequency of single repeats (i.e. of 'doubles' as in Table 14.3) as a percentage of the total number of occurrences of a word. Understandably,[4] the percentage of word tokens that are repeated seldom reaches higher than 1 per cent, which is to say that in every hundred occurrences of a word, it is exceptional for more than one repeat to occur. The words are chosen to represent more commonly repeated words—mainly function words—which are grouped into word classes, to show varying tendencies towards dysfluent repetition. For contrast, we also present one or two word classes which rarely feature in repeats.

The figures in Table 14.5 are taken from the 4.1-million-word AmE conversation section of the LSWE Corpus. (The comparable BrE conversation section of 3.9 million words was used, alongside the AmE corpus, in most other counts in this chapter.) The right-hand column shows, for comparison, the proportional occurrence of filled pauses (14.2.1), represented by just the one hesitator *uh* for the purposes of this comparison.

**Table 14.5** **Percentage frequency of involuntary repeats for some common English words in particular word classes: AmE conversation**

each ● represents approximately 0.1%

| word | tokens in a repeat | tokens with filled pause (*uh*) |
|---|---|---|
| **personal pronouns—nominative** | | |
| *I* | ●●●●●●●●●●●●●●●●●●● | ●●●●●●● |
| *they* | ●●●●●●●●●●●●●●●●● | ●●●●●●●●● |
| *he* | ●●●●●●●●●●●●●●●● | ●●●●●●●●●●● |
| *she* | ●●●●●●●●●●●●●● | ●●●●●●●●● |
| *we* | ●●●●●●●●●● | ●●●●●●●●●● |
| **personal pronouns—nominative and accusative** | | |
| *it* | ●●●●●●●●● | ●●● |
| *you* | ●●●●● | ●●●●● |
| **personal pronouns—accusative** | | |
| *him* | ●● | – |
| *me* | ● | – |
| *them* | – | – |
| *us* | – | – |
| **possessive determiners** | | |
| *our* | ●●●●●●●●●●●●● | ●●●● |
| *their* | ●●●●●●●●●● | ●●●●● |
| *my* | ●●●●●●●● | ●●●●●● |
| *your* | ●●●●●●● | ●●● |
| **articles** | | |
| *the* | ●●●●●●● | ●●●●●●● |
| *a* | ●●●●●● | ●●●● |
| *an* | ● | ●●●●●● |
| **conjunctions** | | |
| *if* | ●●●●●●●●●●●●●●●● | ●●●●●●● |
| *and* | ●●●●●●●●●●●● | ●●●●●● |
| *when*[5] | ●●●●●●●●●● | ●●●●●●●●● |
| *because* | ●● | ●●●● |
| **prepositions** | | |
| *with* | ●●●●● | ●●● |
| *at* | ●●●● | ●●●● |
| *for* | ●●●● | ●●● |
| *of* | ●●● | ● |

Table 14.5    **continued**

| word | tokens in a repeat | tokens with filled pause (*uh*) |
|------|--------------------|----------------------------------|
| **verbs** | | |
| *is* | ● ● ● ● ● ● ● ● ● | ● ● ● |
| *was* | ● | ● |
| *were* | ● | ● |
| *would* | ● | ● |
| *can* | ● | ● |
| *says* | ● | – |
| *said* | – | – |

➤ Among personal pronouns, nominative pronouns such as *I* show the strongest tendency to recur in repeats, whereas accusative pronouns almost never recur.
➤ Possessive determiners resemble the definite article *the* in showing a fairly strong tendency to be repeated. These words all introduce definite noun phrases.
➤ Conjunctions vary, but on the whole they show a strong tendency to form repeats.
➤ Prepositions, on the other hand, show a weaker tendency to be repeated.
➤ Apart from *is*, the verbs investigated show an extremely weak tendency to be repeated.
➤ Repeats and filled pauses, as hesitation phenomena, show parallel tendencies to co-occur with certain word classes.

### DISCUSSION OF FINDINGS

Perhaps the most remarkable contrast in our results is between nominative and accusative personal pronouns. Nominative pronouns such as *I*, *she*, and *we* occur almost invariably at the beginning of a clause—often at the beginning of a turn—where the build-up of planning pressure on the speaker is likely to be great:

> And so, **she she** wanted to do some research someplace else I think (AmE †)

> Except of course, **I er, I, I** couldn't read my road map there in, in Brussels. (BrE)

Repeats are a way of relieving that planning pressure.

In strong contrast, accusative pronouns such as *me* and *him* almost always occur towards the end of a major syntactic unit, and therefore are extremely unlikely to be the locus of a repeat. *It* and *you* were included in the table as pronouns which can be either nominative and accusative—and, predictably, their use as repeats is intermediate between the two categories. We examined 300 occurrences of *you you* and discovered no plausible instance of *you you* being a dysfluent repeat in object or prepositional complement position (although there was a sprinkling of *you you* instances as false starts; 14.2.3). The overwhelming majority of *you you* repeats were in subject position preceding a predicate. Similar observations apply to *it it*:

> Yeah **you, you** call that maths! (BrE)

> Basically **it, it** sucks to have four bathrooms when it comes to cleaning. (AmE)

Alongside the personal pronouns we should consider the related possessive determiners *my*, *your*, etc., which resemble *the* and *a* in invariably introducing a noun phrase. Like *the*, these forms have a fairly high repeat index, suggesting that the beginning of a full noun phrase (containing a noun head, a preceding determiner, and optional modifiers) is also a major point of planning pressure. Compare:

> Aye, **the the – the** summer house is Victorian. (BrE)
>
> Or just **a, a** basket of muffins, you know, different, different muffins? (AmE)
>
> Now you can sell us **our, our** tickets back as well. (BrE)
>
> No, and then they put on **their, their** fake accent. (AmE)

Full noun phrases, of course, contain at least one lexical word—an item that may cost the speaker effort to retrieve from memory. It is noticeable that the repeats in the above examples are immediately followed by lexical words, viz. *summer*, *tickets*, and *fake*.

The evidence of repeats confirms that speakers have to plan hardest when embarking on major syntactic units, including finite clauses and full noun phrases.

The reason why the indefinite article is less prone to repeats than the definite article is not clear. One possible reason is lower frequency: perhaps, all things being equal, the higher a word's frequency, the more likely it is to form repeats. That is, it is plausible that the more frequent a word is, the more readily retrievable it is from a speaker's memory. No hard searching has to be undertaken to select the most highly predictable words from the speaker's vocabulary at a given point in the conversation. Rather, it is easy for the speaker to utter a very frequent word, without having a clear plan for what words will follow it. Hence, such a word precedes a natural hesitation point in the utterance, and becomes natural locus for a repeat.

Particularly intriguing is the very low repeat index for the pre-vocalic indefinite article *an*. A plausible hypothesis is that the use of *an* is the opposite case from the use of a very common word such as *the*. Before choosing *an*, the speaker must at least have selected the word which is to follow it—a word beginning with a vowel sound—otherwise the speaker would choose the much more frequent indefinite article variant *a*. Hence there is no propensity to hesitate over the word *an*.

If this explanation is accepted, then it has an interesting consequence: the repeat phenomenon is not motivated by the need to 'buy time' in a general sense, but by a logjam in planning the very next word precisely at that point in the utterance in which the repeat occurs. Anticipating the next section, another observation of interest is that (with one exception)[6] the quasi-repeat sequence *an a* never occurs in the AmE conversation data under study, whereas *a an* does occur about ten times per million words:[7]

> I would like **a, an** egg and a whole wheat English muffin. (AmE)
>
> Yes. And that would make it **a, an** even cooler outfit, wouldn't it? (BrE)

This appears to confirm the above assumption that, as the more frequent form, *a* is the 'default' choice of indefinite article, made when speakers have as yet no clear idea of what word follows.

Turning to conjunctions, the high frequency of repeats with common clause-introducing words like *and*, *if* and *when* is explicable in terms of the earlier finding that words occurring at or towards the beginning of a clause or turn are likely to be points of online planning pressure:

*I'm pretty confident that, um, we can take care of it **if, if,** I mean if your guys are behind me* (AmE†)

*Can I give you this tomorrow **when when** you've got change?* (BrE)

*She used to be my beautician **and and** that's how I knew her / you know* (AmE)

This is, however, in very marked contrast with the low frequency of repeats for *because* and its aphetic form *cos* (also spelt *cause*): a finding which is difficult to explain.

The reason why prepositions trigger fewer repeats than, for instance, conjunctions and possessive determiners is also not immediately obvious. After all, prepositions are high-frequency words which introduce a major syntactic unit, the prepositional phrase, where a major planning effort might be expected. One counterbalancing factor, however, is that prepositions are often lexically predictable after a preceding noun, adjective, or verb. Thus, a sequence such as *a lot of, play with,* or *good at* is likely to form a single locution in the lexical memory of an English speaker, who will therefore hit a planning problem only after the preposition has been enunciated.

The last major category in Table 14.5 is that of verbs. With the exception of the form *is*, the high frequency verbs illustrated—forms of the copula and auxiliaries—have a comparatively low incidence of repetition. It thus appears that these verbs do not coincide with a particularly demanding planning pressure point, although they typically begin a verb phrase, which, by implication, brings with it the planning of the complements of the verb. One reason why they do not trigger repeats may be that subjects, in conversation, tend to be very simple (4.1.5), and may therefore constitute the main planning point for the whole of the subsequent clause including the verb phrase. An example of an *is is* repeat is:

*Now the problem **is is** that he couldn't pass our level four.* (AmE)

The repeat of *is* appears to be particularly prevalent when the subject preceding *is* is a full noun phrase, particularly an utterance-launching fixed expression (or lexical bundle) such as *the problem is*, and the predicative following it is a fairly heavy constituent.

Without discussing filled pause phenomena in detail here (see also 14.3.3.7), we will point out that in Table 14.5 the pattern of frequency for filled pauses (with *uh*) is very similar to that of repeats, suggesting that the functions of these two mechanisms of hesitation are similar. The figures for filled pauses strengthen the claim that the beginning of a clause and the beginning of a noun phrase, in that order, are the two major loci of online planning pressure.

On the other hand, unfilled pauses, although generally much more frequent than filled pauses, are much less frequent in these grammatical positions. This suggests that their function is somewhat different, and in particular that they have very little role in the introduction of full noun phrases. This fits in with the argument presented above (see Table 14.2) that unfilled pauses are more adapted to hesitation points associated with the most major grammatical transition points.

### 14.2.2.3 Repeats of forms with verb contractions

There are many other aspects of repeats which we do not have space to consider: notably partial repeats such as *they they've* (combining a pronoun with a pronoun accompanied by its verb contraction) and *a an* (combining the two forms of the definite article).

However, before concluding this section we present a table of repeats of personal pronouns + enclitic verb contractions, such as *I'm* and *we've* (see the Appendix). Repeats of these contraction forms are among the most frequent— indeed, *it's, it'll* and *they're* are proportionally more common in repeats than any of the single words in Table 14.5. It is likely that such contractions are processed by the speaker and hearer as single words, and therefore, for the purposes of studying dysfluency phenomena, that they should be treated as such. In fact, considered as single words, some of them are among the most frequent items in the spoken language, and their position at the beginning of a clause gives them an exceptionally high repeat index.

In Table 14.6, contractions have been divided into four groups, according to the verb contraction used. Group A includes all contractions of the verb *be* (including *'s*, which can also be a contraction of the verb *have*). Group B includes all forms with *'ll* (=*will*), group C includes all forms with *'ve* (=*have*), and group D includes all forms with *'d* (=*had* or *would*).

**Table 14.6** **Frequency of involuntary repeats for some subject + verb contractions: AmE conversation**

each • represents approximately 0.1%

| word | tokens in a repeat |
|------|--------------------|
| **A) pronoun + 's/'re/'m** | |
| *it's* | •••••••••••••••••••• |
| *they're* | ••••••••••••••••••• |
| *he's* | •••••••••••••••• |
| *she's* | •••••••••••••• |
| *I'm* | •••••••••••• |
| *you're* | ••••••••• |
| *we're* | •••••••• |
| **B) pronoun + 'll** | |
| *it'll* | •••••••••••••••••• |
| *I'll* | ••••••••••••••••• |
| *they'll* | ••••••••••••••• |
| *we'll* | ••••••••••••• |
| *you'll* | •••••••••••••••• |
| *he'll* | ••••••••••••• |
| *she'll* | •••••••••• |
| **C) pronoun + 've** | |
| *they've* | ••••••••••••••••••• |
| *I've* | ••••••••• |
| *we've* | •••••• |
| *you've* | ••• |

Table 14.6    **continued**

| word | tokens in a repeat |
|---|---|
| **D) pronoun + 'd** | |
| I'd | ●●●●●● |
| she'd | ●●●●● |
| he'd | ●●●● |
| you'd | ●●● |
| we'd | ●● |
| they'd | – |

**CORPUS FINDINGS**

➤   Contractions with *'s/'re/'m* and *'ll* are repeated more often than those with *'ve* and *'d*, the last being rarely repeated.

**DISCUSSION OF FINDINGS**

There is a strong association between the overall frequency of a contraction group and the extent to which the forms in the group are repeated. Contractions with *'s/ 're/'m* occur over 20,000 times per million words, contractions with *'ll* and *'ve* occur around 5,000 times per million words, while contractions with *'d* are much less common (around 1,000 per million words). These overall frequencies correspond to the general decrease in the proportional occurrence of repetitions across the four groups. What this seems to show is that there is indeed a positive association between frequencies of forms and their tendency to occur in repeats.

## 14.2.3    Retrace-and-repair sequences: reformulations

The unplanned repeats discussed in the preceding section are sometimes termed **false starts**; this is indeed what they are, because the speaker says something, then goes back to the beginning of the piece and repeats what has already been said. There is, however, another set of cases that can more appropriately be called 'false starts', or even more precisely **retrace-and-repair sequences**. These occur when the speaker retraces (or notionally 'erases') what has just been said, and starts again, this time with a different word or sequence of words. In the following examples showing some typical features of retrace-and-repairs, the retrace is in bold, whereas the repair is enclosed in *[...]*:

1   *Your face was down instead of up and so that's why **the**, [all my] labor was in my back 'cos you were pushing the wrong way **and**, uh, [but] luckily at the very end, just before I went into delivery, you flipped around somehow <...>* (AmE†)

2   *So **before we issue** – [before we hand over] the B one what do we do?* (BrE)

3   *Dad, **I don't think you sh–**, [I think you should] leave Chris home Saturday.* (AmE)

Repeat-and-repairs are often accompanied by other dysfluencies. For example, **1** contains two instances of a single-word false start, in the second case followed by another dysfluency in the form of a hesitator *uh*. It is notable that all three examples above show a repair that involves backtracking to the initial part of a clause. A retrace-and-repair sequence leads to a repair procedure like that of a writer who erases what has already been written, and writes some new words over the top.

## 14.2.4    Utterances left grammatically incomplete

Leaving an utterance uncompleted is not always an unplanned dysfluency, but it usually is. There are four main situations where the speaker starts to utter a grammatical unit and fails to finish it: A self-repair, B interruption, C repair by another interlocutor (cooperative completion), and D abandonment of the utterance.

### A    Incompletion where the speaker abandons and 'repairs' by starting anew

> *We did, we did try to pu– well, as I say, with the trouble we had upstairs, we just thought it just wasn't worth our while to sort of mess around and try to do any more.* (BrE†)

> *That's such a neat, it's so nice to know the history behind it.* (AmE)

This type of performance error is no different, in principle, from the repeat-and-repair sequence mentioned above in 14.2.3. The motive for both types is the same: abandoning some piece of discourse, in order to attempt a reformulation. The only difference in practice is that in the incompletion case now being considered, the whole utterance or turn up to that point is abandoned: the speaker discards it all and starts afresh.

### B    Incompletion where the speaker is interrupted by another speaker, or (sometimes) by another event

In these cases, the incompletion is caused by something extraneous to the speaker's own speech processes.

> **1** A: *There's a whole bunch of Saturdays.* **If you just put your**
> B: *This is a Sunday.*
> A: *No, no, no.* (AmE)

> **2** A: *<...> So, uh, I saw him, I took him to lunch and, I, I, I'm* **surprised at how [old]**
> B: *{Mature he is?}*
> A: *Yeah, he really {has}*
> B: *{Yeah, he seemed} to be that way.* (AmE)

Example **1** shows a simple case of one speaker (*B*) interrupting another—*A*. Example **2** is more complex: it shows two examples of interruption, both by speaker *B*. In both cases, too, there is a stretch of overlap (marked by curly brackets) before *A* gives up trying to complete her utterance.

### C    Incompletion where the hearer rather than the speaker 'repairs' the utterance—by finishing it

In transcription, this may be difficult to distinguish from interruption. However, it is clear in the following cases that speaker *B* is collaborating with speaker *A*, to co-construct a clause spanning the two turns:

> **3** A: *I played,* **I played against erm**
> B: **Southend.** (BrE)

> 4  A: *She pays a certain amount,* **but erm – you get erm**
>    B: **Subsidised**.
>    A: *That's right. Yeah.* (BrE)
>
> 5  A: **My favorite is not to put a red sauce on but just a slice up cherry**
>       **tomatoes and just put that on and put, that, not just mozzarella,**
>       **but the cheese that has a really heavy flavor, like, um**
>    B: **Cheddar?**
>    A: *That or like feta, or goat cheese or something that has a real strong*
>       *flavor but not too much.* (AmE)

In these examples, the co-construction by A and B is signalled by the preceding hesitation by speaker A, who is clearly having difficulty finding the missing word. It is also signalled in examples **4** and **5** by A's subsequent turn, accepting B's completion as appropriate. Notice that B's repair utterance in **5** is marked as interrogative: more like a tentative suggestion than a definite completion.

In another variant of this co-construction phenomenon, speaker B repeats the function word with which speaker A's incomplete turn ended:

> 6  A: *It's just* **a**
>    B: **a** *hunch* (AmE)
>
> 7  A: *And also my explanation is if I'm making somebody really blonde, I*
>       *like to do it with foils because I* <unclear> *the cap –* **is**
>    B: **Is** *gonna show.*
>    A: **is** *gonna show.* (AmE)

Note in the last example how speaker A confirms speaker B's addition by repeating it. A significant point about these examples is that speaker B backtracks to the beginning of the phrase in which speaker A finished speaking (a noun phrase in **6** and a verb phrase in **7**). This suggests that the phrase is the operational syntactic unit of production here (cf. 14.2.2.2 on hesitation at the beginning of noun phrases).

**D  Incompletion where none of the conditions above holds**

This is the case where a speaker simply abandons an utterance, with no interruption or attempt at repair. The motive for incompletion in this case may not be clear. It could be that the speaker loses the thread of what he or she is saying, or decides to abandon a remark that no one is listening to, or breaks off by design to avoid embarrassment or some other unpleasant consequence:

> 8  A: **So it was just, you know**.
>    B: *Yeah.* (AmE)
>
> 9  A: *That's the way I'm reading it.* **I'm –**
>    B: *Ignore it cos the man might – just leave him in there renting it until*
>       *or when forever it goes up.* (BrE)
>
> 10  *Well, we went to, we went to San Francisco* **because I remember,** *uh,*
>        *uh, oh, what the heck's the name of that hotel we stayed? Big hotel.*
>        *Mm. Oh, anyway, uh, but we just stayed there a couple nights and*
>        *that's all, and then we took the bus back, of course.* (AmE)

## 14.2.5   Syntactic blends

The term **syntactic blend** (or **anacoluthon**) is applied to a sentence or clause which finishes up in a way that is syntactically inconsistent with the way it began.

The speaker 'switches horses in mid-stream', so to speak. This is another type of performance error which appears to be caused by working memory limitations. The clauses concerned tend to be fairly long, i.e. considerably longer than the seven-word average (14.3.1), which suggests that the speaker suffered from a kind of syntactic memory loss in the course of production. Syntactic blends tend to make good sense: we feel that we know what the speaker wanted to say, and that, given a second opportunity, he or she would no doubt have rendered the message in a different syntactic form.

The following examples erroneously contain two main verbs. After each example, we add two likely reconstructions of the two competing syntactic models the speaker appears to have confused:

1  *About a hundred, two hundred years ago **we had** ninety-five per cent of people – i– in this country **were employed** in farming.* (BrE)
   cf. *Ninety-five per cent of people in this country **were employed** in farming.*
   cf. ***We had** ninety-five per cent of people in this country **employed** in farming.*

2  *In fact **that's** one of the things that there is a shortage of in this play, **is** people who actually care er, erm – about what happens to erm each, each other.* (BrE)
   cf. *One of the things that there is a shortage of in this play **is** people who actually care.*
   cf. ***That's** one of the things that there is a shortage of in this play: people who actually care.*

It is worth noting the syntactic complexity of the two examples above, particularly in the length of the non-final noun phrases they contain. These are among the chief obstacles to syntactic processing in speech, as has been seen in 14.1.2.6 (cf. also 11.1.3 on the principle of end-weight).

One of the problems in recognizing syntactic blends is unclarity about what makes a well-formed grammatical construction in speech. Some types of apparent blend are relatively systematic, and it could be argued that they are not performance errors: that in speech, the language tolerates a freedom of syntactic structure that would generally be regarded as unacceptable in writing. Examples are:

3  *So if you **were** – in receipt of income support then you **don't** have to pay very much.* (BrE)

4  *The smallest room they have is for twenty-five to thirty people **which** I mean even **that** may be too big for what we want.* (BrE †)

5  ***You**'re talking about a week and a half or something aren't **we**?* (BrE †)

Example **3** illustrates a mismatch of verbs in the independent and dependent clauses of a conditional construction: it would normally be expected that a hypothetical past form in the *if*-clause would be matched by a hypothetical modal (especially *would*) in the independent clause. Example **4** exemplifies a relative clause with a redundant 'resumptive' pronoun (in this case *that*) duplicating the function of the relativizer (*which*). Example **5** has a question tag (*aren't we*) whose subject (*we*) does not match the subject (*you*) of the preceding declarative clause. These anacolutha suggest that a change of perspective has taken place in the course of the construction—something speakers will scarcely notice in the ongoing dynamic of conversation. Further examples of anacolutha are:

> *We have all these twentieth century uh devices that we have eighteenth*
> *century people running them* <...> (AmE†)
> *Uh he's a closet yuppie is what he is* (AmE†)
> *You know who else is like that is Jan.* (AmE)

### 14.2.5.1 Syntactic blends v. semantic gap-filling clauses

Syntactic blends should be distinguished from a special syntactic phenomenon
found in conversation, whereby the speaker uses a clause intrusively in a position
where only a single word or a phrase would be appropriate in written language:

> *I've seen Star Wars **God knows how many times**.* (AmE)
> *She's socially just like **I don't even know what**.* (AmE)
> *The birds and the deer and **who knows what else**.* (AmE)

The pattern here is relatively predictable, and usually seems to contain the verb
*know* and a following *wh*-word. Functionally the clause is the linguistic equivalent
of hand-waving, indicating that the amount or degree defies the speaker's ability
to express it. Thus, although anomalous from the standpoint of normative
grammar, this construction should be included in the grammar of spoken English.
It is not a case of anacoluthon.

## 14.3 The constructional principles of spoken grammar

Focusing now on how the grammar of conversational English is constructed, it
may be useful to see the grammar of conversation as to some extent a different
system with different rules from the grammar of written English. For example, we
might want to address the issue of 'sentencehood' for spoken grammar: can we
define some major syntactically independent unit of spoken grammar comparable
to the sentence in written English? (See also 14.3.1.3.)

The crucial difference here is the one identified in 14.1.2.6: that spoken
language takes place in real time, and is subject to the limitations of working
memory, so that its principles of linear construction are adapted to that purpose.
A writer can retract a sentence—and it can be as if it never existed for the reader.
Reformulating for a speaker, however, means adding utterances—but there is no
possibility of making previous utterances disappear. We may refer to the grammar
of speech as 'dynamic', in the sense that it is constructed and interpreted under
real-time pressure, and correction or reformulation is possible only through
hesitations, false starts, and other dysfluencies.

In contrast, the grammar of writing is more architectural, in the sense that a
written sentence has a static existence: its author can construct it over an extended
period of time, rethinking and revising according to need. The writer and reader
may contemplate the end result as an enduring object, backtracking and re-
reading if necessary to ensure fuller comprehension.

### 14.3.1 Principles of online production

Three principles of online production for spoken English grammar can be stated
briefly in dynamic terms as follows:

- keep talking
- limited planning ahead
- qualification of what has been said.

The first principle '**keep talking**' makes us aware of the obvious need to keep the conversation moving forward. A conversationalist cannot simply stop, since the result can amount to a communicative breakdown: a unilateral suspension of conversational activity. As we have seen, whenever planning reaches a dead-end, there are three main repair strategies to retrieve the situation. One is to hesitate (14.2.1), to give yourself more time to plan. Another is to backtrack and re-start, leaving your rejected piece of discourse dangling and incomplete (14.2.2–3). A third strategy is to yield the floor to another person, leaving your utterance unfinished, without attempting to complete it (14.2.4).

However, all these strategies have their drawbacks: dysfluency can bring risk of misunderstanding, loss of communicative effectiveness, even loss of face. In general it is to be assumed that human speakers have the goal of achieving an 'ideal' verbal performance that does not suffer from these disadvantages.

The second principle '**limited planning ahead**' follows naturally from the first, together with human memory limitations. It makes us aware of the fact that speakers (and hearers) suffer from limited planning time: it is often claimed that the working memory with which we operate in speech processing has a span of about seven words. There is a severe limit to the amount of incomplete syntactic structure we can hold in the working memory at one time—and there is also a similar limit to the amount of planned structure we can hold in readiness for future completion. One result of this is that the spoken medium, more strikingly than the written medium, discourages the elaboration of structure (and hence meaning) at the beginning or in the middle of a clause. Subjects, for example, are typically very simple compared with objects (4.1.2), and this **end-weight** effect (11.1.13), although also observed in written English, is much more extreme in spoken English, where subjects typically consist of a single word.

The third principle '**qualification of what has been said**' follows from the first and the second. If (in accordance with the first two principles), we have little chance to plan or elaborate structure as we proceed, there may be a need to elaborate and modify the message retrospectively, that is, to 'tag on' as an afterthought some elements which, in a logically structured and integrated sentence, would have been placed earlier.

The following sub-sections (14.3.1.1–4) survey several syntactic phenomena associated with planning considerations in conversation.

### 14.3.1.1 Parenthetical structures

One syntactic phenomenon which is inimical to the 'limited planning ahead' principle is a **parenthetical**, or interpolated structure, particularly if it is lengthy. By this is meant a digressive structure (often a clause) which is inserted in the middle of another structure, and which is unintegrated in the sense that it could be omitted without affecting the rest of that structure or its meaning. Parenthetical clauses put a particular kind of pressure on the temporary memory: it is necessary for the speaker or hearer to hold suspended in memory the part of the utterance leading up to the parenthesis, in order to be able to pick this up again when the parenthesis is finished:

1 *[We cannot all,] as it already been emphasised – by the last speaker –
we may not all be able to do the same things.* (BrE)

2 *And it would seem to me – that [unless this morning's exercise] – which
has been so rewarding and so profitable – unless this morning's exercise
is to dissipate – into another piece of feeling – and er – pleasurable
discussion – then we ought to take quite seriously – the, the words of
Jesus. – Go and do!* (BrE)

As 1 and 2 show, it is quite likely that the speaker will not be able to resume the
main structure after the interpolation without backtracking and repeating part of
the preceding main structure. Significantly, the preceding parts of the above
examples marked by *[ ]* are abandoned as false starts, when the speaker resumes
the main thread after the parenthesis. Examples 1 and 2 also illustrate how such
parentheses are liable to occur in less conversational styles of speech, when the
speaker is closer to the written medium: for example in public speaking.

## 14.3.1.2  The 'add-on' strategy

Although dysfluency is endemic to speech, it rarely reaches such a degenerate level
as example 1 in 14.2 above, and indeed there are many quite complex utterances
which contain little or no sign of planning difficulty. This appears to be because
speakers are skilled at adapting their language to the constraints of the principle
'Limited planning ahead'. Returning to example 2 in 14.2 (and omitting the
overlap *if you're*), we could represent relations of embedding and coordination by
bracketing as follows (bearing in mind that a certain amount of structural
ambiguity arises in such analyses):

2a *[The trouble is [[if you're the only one in the house] [he follows you] [and
you're looking for him] [so you can't find him.]]] [I thought [I wonder
[where the hell he's gone]]] [I mean [he was immediately behind me.]]*
(BrE)

The structural embedding in this example is far from simple, showing a
combination of ten clauses, with seven examples of embedding and coordination.
(The full-stops—an artifact of the transcription—are disregarded.) But if we
divide it in a more basic way, simply using vertical lines for clause boundaries, we
notice that the utterance neatly divides into a linear sequence of finite clause-like
units, which follow in line without overlap or interruption, illustrating what we
may call the **add-on** strategy:

2b *The trouble is | if you're the only one in the house | he follows you | and
you're looking for him | so you can't find him. | I thought | I wonder |
where the hell he's gone | I mean | he was immediately behind me.*

The semantic relations between the clause-like chunks themselves are important to
the overall interpretation, but each chunk expresses what can be considered a single
idea, and within each chunk, the syntactic processing required is simple: for
example, each unit except the first has a single-word pronoun subject. Although the
transcription does not allow us to map syntax on to prosody, there is likely to be a
fairly close correlation between these clause-like chunks and the units of intonation.

This analysis of speech into clause-like chunks can be contrasted with an
attempt to apply such an analysis to expository writing:

*Despite the abnormal morphogenesis observed in such grafts, the range of
differentiated tissues formed in such an 'experimental teratoma' can be used*

*to provide an estimate of the developmental potential of the transferred tissue.*
(ACAD)

In this example there are no vertical lines demarcating finite clause-like chunks, because there is only one finite clause (viz. the independent clause) in the whole sentence. Virtually all the complexity is at phrase level.

### 14.3.1.3 Clausal and non-clausal units (C-units)

In the above section, we took example **2** of 14.2 and analysed it in two ways: (a) in terms of conventional sentence structure (embedding and coordination of clauses), and (b) in terms of individual clause segments, seen as a linear sequence. Now we consider a third way of analysing the example, this time in terms of units which are independent or self-standing, in that they have no structural connection with what precedes or follows in the conversation. These units may be regarded, for the purposes of segmenting dialogue into grammatical units, as **maximal** (or independent) **units** of conversational syntax.

The most important kind of maximal unit will be called the **clausal unit** (this corresponds closely to the 'T-unit' which has been used in reference to written language). A clausal unit is a structure consisting of an independent clause together with any dependent clauses embedded within it.[8] (Dysfluency phenomena in the form of incomplete clauses can be discarded when dividing a speech sequence into clausal units.) The above example therefore consists of three clausal units, numbered *(a)–(c)*, whose boundaries are marked here by ||. In **2c** below we mark these maximal-unit boundaries, as well as the clause boundaries marked in **2b** above:

> **2c** || *(a) The trouble is | if you're the only one in the house | he follows you | and you're looking for him | and every time you're moving around | he's moving around behind you | so you can't find him.* || *(b) I thought | I wonder | where the hell he's gone* || *(c) I mean | he was immediately behind me.* ||[9]

As **2c** shows, clausal units can easily reach considerable length, chiefly by means of the 'add-on' strategy already illustrated in 14.3.1.2. The following shorter example shows that a clausal unit can be quite complex in terms of embedding (this one contains two complement clauses), while raising few problems of processing for the speaker or hearer, because its 'add-on' structure minimizes the pressure on the working memory.

> || *I think [you'll find [it counts towards your income]].* || (BrE)

We might try to analyse the syntax of speech by segmenting a conversation into clausal units, as above. However, we would not progress very far without coming across segments which are not clausal units nor part of clausal units: segments consisting entirely or partly of non-clausal material (3.15.2), and which will be referred to as **non-clausal units**. (cf. 14.3.3–4).

In contrast to **2** above, the following example shows how a conversation can consist mainly or entirely of non-clausal units (*A* is a woman aged 30, and *B* is a woman aged 85; the non-clausal units are in bold):

> A: || **No,** || *I would even give you that chair in there* ||
> B: || **Mm.** ||
> A: || *It came from Boston, by covered wagon.* ||
> B: || *That's such a neat,*[10] || *it's so nice to know the history behind it.* ||

> A: || *Yeah,* || *yeah.* ||
> B: || *So this was your mother's?* ||
> A: || *No,* || *my father's.* ||
> B: || *Your father's mother?* ||
> A: || *Yeah.* || *Her name was Martha* <name> ||
> B: || *Uh huh.* ||
> A: || *And then she married Alfred P* <name>, *my grandfather.* ||
> B: || *Your grandfather.* || (AmE)

As this example suggests, it is possible to segment a conversation exhaustively into a sequence of clausal units and non-clausal units. The interest of such an exercise lies partly in studying the extent to which spoken grammar departs from the model of canonical written prose in which clause structure predominates 100 per cent over non-clausal phenomena. It should be remembered, however, that this 'ideal' rarely exists even in writing: there are many non-clausal phenomena in written texts, found for example in newspaper headlines, in headings, and lists that occur in expository texts, and in the simulated dialogues of fiction writing. Nevertheless, the use of non-clausal material in conversation is particularly extensive and varied, and will be studied further in 14.3.1.4 and 14.3.3–4.

Clausal and non-clausal units are maximal grammatical units in the sense that they cannot be *syntactically* integrated with the elements which precede or follow them. (The highlighting of the word 'syntactically' here is important: of course there are many interconnections between units on the semantic and discoursal levels.) We will use the umbrella term **C-unit**[11] *for both clausal and non-clausal units: i.e. for syntactically independent pieces of speech.*

A 'compound sentence' has traditionally been taken to be a composite of two or more coordinated main clauses. Here, on the other hand, we separate the two or more coordinated independent clauses and treat them as separate units.[12] There are two good reasons for this separation. One is that coordinated units need not be of the same type: a clausal unit can be coordinated with a non-clausal unit, as in:

> *One shower of rain **and** you've lost it anyway.* (BrE)

Another reason is: just as a written sentence (despite prescriptive disapproval) can begin with a coordinator, so can a turn in spoken English. In fact, *but* (2.4.7.4) is one of the more common turn-openers in English dialogue:

> A: *Whenever you're ready to take me shopping.*
> B: ***But** where – are we going shopping?* (BrE)

Compound C-units are thus eliminated from our analysis for practical reasons. This does not mean, however, that a coordinator cannot occur in the middle of a C-unit: at a lower level in the grammatical hierarchy (for example, at the level of phrase or dependent clause) a C-unit may, of course, contain coordinate constituents (2.9).

## 14.3.1.4 Distribution of clausal and non-clausal units

To illustrate how this C-unit model can be applied to spoken grammar, it seems worthwhile to provide an estimate of the relative distribution of clausal and non-clausal material in the spoken Corpus. For this, we have counted clausal units and non-clausal units in 20 sequences of 50 C-units from 20 samples of conversation (ten of AmE and ten of BrE conversation). Since the length of each unit (particularly non-clausal units) is often very small – one or two words – we also made a count of words comprising the clausal units and non-clausal units. The brief excerpt below shows a specimen of how the analysis was done: C-unit boundaries are marked || and are followed (except at the beginning of the passage) by Cl (clausal) or NCl (non-clausal) to indicate the kind of unit that precedes.

> A: || *So do you think an alligator would like salt water?* <Cl> ||
> B: || *It would probably kill him wouldn't it?* <Cl> ||
> A: || *That one on the news has been out in the ocean for a while.* <Cl> ||
> B: || *Really?* <NCl> ||
> C: || *What are you talking about?* <Cl> *I didn't hear.* <Cl> ||
> A: || *That alligator in the ocean.* <NCl> || *I was asking him how he thought it liked salt water.* <Cl> ||
> C: || *Oh.* <NCl> (AmE) ||

Table 14.7 shows the results of the count.

**Table 14.7** **Distribution of clausal units and non-clausal units in a sample of AmE and BrE conversation**

|  | clausal units | non-clausal units | total |
|---|---|---|---|
| unit count | 614  (61.4%) | 386  (38.6%) | 1000  (100%) |
| word count | 4615  (86.0%) | 754  (14.0%) | 5369  (100%) |
| words per unit | 7.52 | 1.95 | 5.37 |

### CORPUS FINDINGS

➤ Non-clausal units account for over one-third of the units in conversation.
➤ However, their average length is only two words.

### DISCUSSION OF FINDINGS

Table 14.7 shows the proportion of non-clausal material in conversation from two perspectives. Although the frequency of non-clausal units is high (more than a third of all units), their length on average is less than two words. This is largely because nearly a half of all non-clausal units consists of single-word inserts—that is, stand-alone words such as interjections. These inserts (14.3.3) have been treated as grammatically independent in cases where punctuation marks, pauses, or turn-boundaries in the transcription separate them from the preceding and following units (e.g. *Hi* in the following exchange is a separate non-clausal unit):

> A: **Hi**
> B: *I like your outfit.* (AmE)

However, in cases where they are separated from the preceding or following word sequence by nothing other than a space in the transcription, they are counted as part of that unit:

> **Hi** *Lisa, what a pretty shirt, is it silk?* (AmE)
> **Hey** *thanks for the note, Tom. I'll follow up on that.* (AmE)

In these instances, *Hi* is considered part of the larger non-clausal unit *Hi Lisa,* and *Hey* is considered part of the larger clausal unit *Hey thanks for the note.*

It will be noticed that the average length of clausal units is close to that often mentioned as the approximate allowance for storage in working memory (seven words). In other words, clausal units typically lie within the range of what can be planned at one time in the word-chain. Non-clausal units also contribute to this relief of pressure on working memory, in that they themselves rarely consist of more than a few words.

## 14.3.2 Prefaces, bodies, and tags

The three principles presented in 14.3.1 conspire on the one hand to simplify the propositional information structure of conversational grammar. On the other hand, at a higher level they interface with discourse structure to form composites in which one or more clausal units, constituting the **body** of the speaker's message, are preceded or followed by outlying elements which may be called **prefaces** and **tags** (3.4.3–4). We will call these **composite** utterances. Using them, a speaker is able to cope with planning pressure, and at the same time to convey some fairly complex messages. In their dynamic structure, the resulting composites are structurally unlike the architecturally integrated sentences typical of written prose, and yet have something of a similar complexity of communicative function. Table 14.8 shows how it is possible to combine preface, body, and tag to form a more complex whole.

**Table 14.8** **Composite utterance structure**

| preface(s) | *North and south London* | |
|---|---|---|
| body | | *they're two different worlds* | |
| tags | | | *aren't they? in a way* |

However, it would be misleading to suggest that such composite utterances are a regular or dominant feature of conversational grammar. As will be shown in 14.3.4, there is much more to account for, for example, when we consider the varied functions of C-units.

The term **utterance,** which has so far been avoided in this book, refers here to a pragmatic rather than a grammatical unit. Utterances are associated with particular pragmatic (illocutionary) functions, such as expressing an opinion, seeking advice, or requesting information. It is possible, however, to define the composition of an utterance in terms of grammatical units, viz. clausal units and non-clausal units. At one extreme, a composite utterance may consist of preface(s), a body, and tag(s), as indicated in Table 14.8. At the other extreme, a **simple** utterance can consist merely of a one-word non-clausal unit, such as *Okay,* fulfilling the pragmatic function, in this case, of assent. Figure 14.1 represents the varying structures of utterances in terms of grammatical units forming prefaces, bodies, and tags:

- Elements in parentheses are optional
- Links between preface and body, or body and tag, are established by: (a) co-reference, (b) coordination, or (c) prosodic connection.

We take it for granted that an utterance is contained within a single turn. In some instances, an utterance appears to straddle more than one turn, i.e. where one

**Figure 14.1** **Structure of utterances**

| (preface(s)) | + body | + (tag(s)) |
|---|---|---|
| typically consisting of one or more NCl-units (Cl-units can also occur instead of NCl-units) | typically consisting of one or more Cl-units (NCl-units can also occur instead of Cl-units) | typically consisting of one or more NCl-units (Cl-units also occur instead of NCl-units) |

> A: *It's just **a***
> B: ***a** hunch* (AmE) <repeated from example **6**, 14.2.4>

We have also seen how the co-constructive reply can independently vary its force between assertive and interrogative. The interrogative reply was illustrated in:

> *the cheese that has a really heavy flavor, like, um*
> B: ***Cheddar?*** (AmE †) <repeated from example **5**, 14.2.4>

In the following sub-sections, we consider in more detail each of the three main components of composite utterances.

## 14.3.2.1 Prefaces and other utterance launchers

**Utterance launchers** is a term we can use for expressions which have a special function of beginning a turn or an utterance. They include **prefaces** (3.4.3) in addition to other locutions which are integrated into the syntactic structure of the utterance they introduce. In fact, their grammatical status is sometimes ambiguous, as will be seen in 14.3.2.2. In general, they have a role not only in propelling the conversation in a new direction but also in providing the speaker with a planning respite, during which the rest of the utterance can be prepared for execution. These conversational launching-devices include **fronting**, **noun phrase prefaces**, **discourse markers**, and **overtures**.

### A Fronting

The grammatical shape of clausal units is overwhelmingly conformant to the dominant SVO/P/A word order of English (where O or P or A is a complement of the verb), and the exceptions to this order (disregarding ellipsis) are rarely found in conversation. The variant word order O/P/A SV known as **topicalization** or **fronting** (11.2.2) is found only under highly restricted conditions, illustrated in the following examples (the fronted object is boldfaced):

1 A: *You always remember numbers. Don't you? Car numbers and telephone numbers and –*
   B: ***Car numbers** I remember more by the letters than the numbers* (BrE)

2 *and the letters with the car go together. And then the numbers, **the numbers** I don't remember well. **Some of them** I do.* (BrE)

Fronting is a device for information management: it capitalizes on word order flexibility to give thematic prominence to one element in the immediate context. However, such flexibility is very limited in present-day English.

**B   Noun phrase prefaces co-referential to pronouns**

Noun phrase prefaces have already been discussed in 11.5: they are more common in conversation than fronting is, combining a topicalizing function with the division of a clause frame into two more easily managed chunks. The following examples illustrate the device of noun phrase prefaces co-referential to a pronoun in the following clause:

> 3  *This little shop – **it**'s lovely* (BrE)
> 4  ***Those Marks and Sparks bags**, can you see **them** all?* (BrE)
> 5  *you know, **the vase**, did you see **it**?* (AmE)

The preface plus body could be replaced, in more orthodox sentence grammar, by a single clause in which the prefatory noun phrase replaces the co-referential pronoun in the clausal unit: e.g. example **3** corresponds to *This little shop is lovely*. In practice, the device of co-referential non-clausal units can occasionally be extended to more than one element of the clause:

> *Oh **Nathan in the bathroom**, is **that** where **he** is?* (AmE)

Here *that* stands proxy for the adverbial *in the bathroom*, and *he* for the subject noun phrase *Nathan*, so that the whole is broadly equivalent in meaning to the clausal unit *Is Nathan in the bathroom?*

**C   Discourse markers and other prefatory expressions**

Commonly an utterance opens with a single prefatory word, which has the function of orienting the listener to the following utterance, especially in relation to what has preceded. Such prefatory words can be of various types: they may be inserts (**discourse markers** such as *well* and *right*, **interjections** such as *oh*, and **response forms** such as *yeah* and *okay*) or they may be classed as adverbs (**stance adverbs** such as *anyway* or **linking adverbs** such as *so* and *then*). (See also 14.3.3.)

In fact, the boundaries between these categories are far from clear-cut in conversation (cf. 10.3.1.4, 10.4.3), and many words are multi-functional in their discourse role. Some examples are:

> A: *I've never seen such a clean garage*
> B: ***Well**, there's nothing in the garage.* (AmE)
> A: *erm, that was immediately after the war, you know, the first war*
> B: ***Right**—did your wife come from the same area?*
> A: ***Well**, in a way, although her parents were Scotch* (BrE)
> ***Oh,** I should have let you read the paper, I never thought of it.* (AmE)
> A: *I got to hang onto the railing.*
> B: ***Okay**, do you want to switch sides with me, or?* (AmE)
> A: ***Okay**, I'll meet you over there. / Alright.*
> B: ***So** I'll see you at the house.* (AmE)

Sometimes such particles are used in combination:

> ***Yeah, so** it's mostly I'm going to be fighting with the seniors.* (AmE†)
> ***Yeah. So anyway** it's supposed to be more aerodynamic I guess.* (AmE)
> ***Okay well then**, shoot, shoot, it's not going to be Star Wars.* (AmE)

We use the term 'discourse marker' also for a further category of utterance launchers consisting of more than one orthographic word. Usually these are similar in form to comment clauses (3.11.6). Common examples are (see also 14.3.3.3):

> *I mean, look (here), mind (you), see, you know, you see*

For example:

> A: **You know** *I never did get to spin. But I / was like*
> B: *That was cool.* (AmE)

> A: **I mean** *are these the same, these are the same?*
> B: *Uh huh. Those are kind of further back.* (AmE)

## D   Overtures (longer expressions)

On other occasions, the speaker uses a longer expression from a stock of ready-made utterance openers available in the language:

> 1   *But **the trouble is** a lot of engineering, a lot of engineering is now making into that.* (AmE)
> 2   *I'll tell you what I've just had a thought.* (AmE)

Such multi-word expressions are a more explicit way of signalling a new direction in the conversation; the list is more open-ended than that of discourse markers. Further examples, with a rough indication of the pragmatic force they signal, are:

| | |
|---|---|
| *I would have thought* | (politely putting a point of disagreement) |
| *Like I say* | (repeating a point the speaker made earlier) |
| *The question is* | (presenting an issue in an explicit, forceful way) |
| *There again* | (adding a contrasting point to an argument) |
| *What we can do is* | (proposing a joint course of action) |
| *You mean to say* | (asking for confirmation of a point the speaker finds difficult to believe) |
| *Going back to ...* | (returning to an earlier topic) |

Other overtures are: *No wonder, For one thing, The (only) thing is, As a matter of fact*. Here are a few examples:

> A: *And uh you have to have your water tested and that's it*
> B: *Geez*
> A: **I would have thought** *there was a lot more* (AmE†)

> *But **like I say** I know they both smoked pot and I don't like it.* (AmE)

> *Hm. **The question is** how many people are willing to spend a lot of money for this CD-ROM.* (AmE)

> *I have a room, I could do that, I could go upstairs but **there again**, you're shut off from everything aren't you?* (BrE†)

> *Not to worry. Not to worry. Erm – **what we can do is** er – use something here.* (BrE)

> **you mean to say**, *we're paying two and half thousand pounds worth of repairs, I says, and they're not done?* (BrE†)

> **Going back to** *the subject of their parents thinking about it. How did you find you know having someone living in your house and things like that?* (BrE)

> *Because people don't want to buy a repossessed house. **For one thing**  they think it's unlucky.* (BrE)

> *I don't mind driving it <= the car> down there, but* **the thing is** *how am I gonna get back if I drive it down.* (BrE†)

## 14.3.2.2 The ambivalent grammatical status of utterance launchers

There are several problems regarding the grammatical status of utterance launchers in relation to what follows them.

One difficulty arises over the separation or non-separation of inserts (such as interjections and discourse markers) from a following unit. A criterion for recognizing inserts as a separate word class is that they are peripheral to and separable from other (core) grammatical structures. Words such as *oh*, *okay*, and *right* can stand on their own as non-clausal units. However, they can also join with a following C-unit to form a larger structure. Note the varied uses of *oh* in the following:

> A: *Hey Tina, so how was camping?*
> B: *I haven't gone yet.*
> A: **Oh** *yeah? Well how was your trip?*
> B: *I went up to,* **oh**, *I went up to* <unclear> *yesterday. I took a ride up there to uh*
> A: **Oh**, *yeah that's pretty.*
> B: *Lobster Hut.*
> A: **Oh**.
> B: *Ate some nice fish. I went up there to get fish.*
> A: **Oh** *yeah? Was it too tasty?*
> B: **Oh**, *it was awesome.* (AmE†)

The only criterion which helps segmentation here is whether the insert is separated prosodically (in terms of intonation) from the following unit. Given that we do not have prosodic information for the LSWE Corpus, we have to rely on punctuation in the transcriptions (chiefly pause dashes, commas and periods) as a way of deciding whether to mark a boundary after an insert. Because the use of punctuation presumably coincides largely with important prosodic breaks, it can generally be assumed to signal grammatical independence.

A further difficulty of grammatical status arises with certain discourse markers. Some of the expressions listed above, such as *I mean* and *you know*, are capable of functioning as a main clause, with the following clause functioning as a complement clause. At the same time, because many of these constructions can also be comment clauses or discourse markers occurring in medial and final positions in the clause, there is often no clear way of choosing between the main clause analysis and the comment clause analysis for constructions in initial position. Intonation evidence, if available, would help to determine this. Other criteria which recommend analysis as an initial discourse marker are discussed in A to C below.

### A Supplying *that* as complementizer after the verb

This criterion is difficult to apply because *that* is extremely rare in conversation as a complementizer following the most common verbs (like *know*). Instead, omission of the complementizer is normal in this context (9.2.8.1–3). However, it is possible, though unusual, in conversation for *you know* to occur declaratively with a *that* complementizer:

  **1** *I don't know –* **you know that** *there are lots of Navajos living in Utah.*
  (AmE)

Because of this structural ambiguity, it is often necessary to appeal to discourse considerations. Thus, in examples such as the following, *you know* has the interactive and cohesive meaning associated with its discourse marker function. Here *you know* signals something like the following: the speaker is imparting new information to the hearer, but is also appealing to the hearer's shared knowledge or experience for the acceptance of this information:

  **2** *the woman said not to wear sandals and so I ended up having to wear these things.* **You know**, *they have no heel and are completely flat.* (AmE †)

In **2**, if the complementizer *that* was added, the discoursal function of *you know* would clearly be different.

B  **Followed by a non-declarative clause, such as an interrogative**

The following examples illustrate another situation where *you know*, although placed initially, could not be followed by the complementizer *that*. This is because the constructions which follow are not declarative clauses and are therefore incompatible with *that*-clause complementation:

  **You know** *let's talk to them too.* (AmE)

  **You know** *like American Indians.* (AmE)

  *But* **you know** / *d'you remember me going round the corner and seeing that erm –* (BrE)

Whereas in some cases the grammatical function of *you know* is unclear, in the majority of cases where it is initial and is not followed by something which definitely has to be a complement, it takes on the role of a discourse marker.

  The criteria which apply to *you know* above also apply to *I mean*, *you see*, and *see* as utterance launchers, thereby confirming their status, in the majority of instances, as discourse markers:

  **I mean**, *if you wanted you can use the big screen.* **You see** *cos, we put it that position cos er, the only dead part of the club is just – literally / in the corner.* (BrE)

  **See** *they have a little plate there so it's not on the cord.* (AmE)

The complementizer *that* could not be appropriately inserted in any of these instances.

C  **The same expressions used in medial and final positions**

When functioning as discourse markers, all these expressions are interactive and cohesive: *I mean* signals that a clarification is going to follow, whereas *you see* and *see* signal that what follows is an explanation of what has preceded. In the following examples, their function as discourse markers is exemplified in non-initial as well as initial positions.

Non-initial use as discourse markers:

  *Don said to come up early today if you want sandwiches. Just to order* **I mean**. (BrE)

> A: *And they spend hundreds of dollars on those dogs **you know**.*
> B: *Yeah I know.* (AmE)
>
> *Oh I've locked the door again, I've gotta keep the door locked **you see*** (BrE)

Initial use as discourse markers:

> *There's this panda – and he's really bored with, **I mean** he's getting no sex so he breaks out of erm – London Zoo to go off and find a partner.* (BrE)
>
> A: ***You know** she went all the way up to calculus in high school.*
> B: *Well that ought to be able to help you out.* (AmE)
>
> A: *And, **you see**, they use instead of one-quarter or a cup of pureed*
> \<unclear\> *sweet potatoes, they just use a little*
> B: *Oh, I see.*
> A: *small jar of baby's it's near as good as fresh.* (AmE)

These expressions typically retain the same interactive function when they occur initially, finally, or medially. Hence, when they initiate an utterance, they can usually be regarded as discourse markers, behaving as unanalysable wholes. They contrast, interestingly, with expressions composed of the verbs *know*, *see*, and *mean* with a different subject (e.g. *I know*, *I see*, *you mean*), which keep the same meaning whether as main clauses or as comment clauses. There are, however, conversational expressions such as *I guess* (especially in AmE) on the boundary between the two categories above:

> *I think he did a superb job for his first try but um it was kind of surreal **I guess**.* (AmE)

We have classified *I guess* as a stance adverbial in 10.3.2.1C when it occurs medially or finally in a clause. Initially, it is treated as a main clause with a *that*-clause complement:

> ***I guess** I did leave the door open.* (AmE)

Hence, *I guess* is not considered to be a discourse marker.

## 14.3.2.3 Extending the body

The body of an utterance can be a single C-unit, which can be elaborated through the 'add-on' strategy (14.3.1.2). It should be noted, too, that the 'add-on' strategy can be used to add one clausal unit to another, thus extending the body in another way. This can happen by **coordination**:

> A: *It was pretty cool, it was pretty chill. **And** uh the food was hell it was good.*
> B: *Oh yeah?*
> A: *Yeah. **And** we had some beers **and** then Jeff had to take pictures of the place and stuff like that.* (AmE)
>
> *Yeah. I don't, I didn't have his number **but** I was going to get it through this other guy.* (AmE)
>
> *Yeah I mean y'all can come with us to go get um wine or alcohol or whatever **or** you can stay.* (AmE)

Also relevant here are the conjunctions *so* (2.4.7.2) and *because* (3.14)—the latter frequently occurring in conversation transcriptions in its aphetic form *cos* or *'cause*. These behave in some ways like coordinators in conversational discourse: *because* almost always follows rather than precedes the main clause, and *so* (unless accompanied by *that*) does so invariably. Hence, although technically these items are not coordinators (2.4.7, 10.4.1.4), they may be placed alongside *and* and *but* in their exemplification of the 'add-on' strategy:

> *She doesn't like people smoking in her house –* **Because** *she says I don't want my bedroom smelling of smoke, her sheets and – everything else.* (BrE)

> *I couldn't find them.* **So** *I went to the manager's. He said what's wrong now?* **So** *I told him that I liked those so well.* (AmE)

One clausal unit can also be added to another by simple juxtaposition (in this and the following examples, ‖ marks clausal unit boundaries):

> *Don't know where the hell she'll sleep,* ‖ *she got to sleep in the living room.* (BrE)

> *You should go see it,* ‖ *it's so funny.* (AmE)

The comma here marks a transition between two independent clauses; i.e. two clausal units. Although, again, the punctuation cannot be relied on for consistency, we may take it as a signal that the two clauses are not distinctly separated by a major intonation break or a pause, so that it is reasonable to take them to be part of the same utterance. In other cases, the running together of clausal units is even more obvious, since no punctuation separates the independent clauses:

> *It's up that way* ‖ *it's in Lagoona* ‖ *that's it.* (AmE†)

The following extended example shows how coordination and juxtaposition can build up an extremely elaborate conversational turn, especially a turn with a narrative function. In this example, ‖ = a C-unit boundary; | = a boundary which could be a C-unit boundary on an alternative analysis; / = a marker of speaker overlap (although the actual overlapping speech is not represented); and () enclose a false start not considered to be a C-unit:

> *Sure we got there um at seven actually around six fifteen* ‖ **and** *class starts at seven* ‖ **and** *I went up in this building that was about five or six stories high* ‖ **and** *I was the only one there* ‖ **and** *I was the only one there* ‖ *I was the / only there. /* ‖ **And** *I yeah I was thinking* | *gosh you know is this the right place* | *or maybe everyone's inside waiting for to come in* ‖ *there's nothing said* | *you know come on in* | *knock on the door* | *and come in or anything like that (so I finally)* ‖ *right around seven o'clock people started showing up* ‖ **and** *I won't mention how* ‖ **and** *I jumped around their phone a few times* ‖ **and** *she's very –* ‖ *how should I say* ‖ *she's just so easy to talk to* ‖ *she's* ‖ *it's like she's totally frank* ‖ *she's very personal, very personable* ‖ **and** *she just comes right out with whatever she needs to say* ‖ **and** *she's real easy to deal with* ‖ **and** *in fact I mentioned to her right off* ‖ *you know her name is <unclear>* ‖ *I said <unclear>* ‖ *I saw you featured in the Los Angeles magazine* ‖ *it's a* | *it's a magazine of the Los Angeles Times and comes out every Sunday with the magazine* ‖ **and** *so they did a big old article on voiceover about a month and a half ago –* ‖ **and** *so apparently it's really getting a lot of attention as being a good career as far as paying well* ‖ *she was saying that introductory night that it pays better than an actor for the time you put in.* (AmE)

Although there are some aspects of this segmentation which are debatable, the overall linear, incremental style of syntax demonstrates the 'add-on' strategy in a particularly striking way.

## 14.3.2.4  Tags

We turn now to the third principle in 14.3.1: 'Qualification of what has been said'. The tendency to add elements as an afterthought to a grammatical unit, especially a clausal unit, can be illustrated by a number of different strategies which can be characterized as the adding of **tags** (3.4.4), or retrospective qualifications loosely attached to the preceding clausal material. Seven kinds of tag are noted:

### A  Retrospective comment clauses (3.11.6)

> *And then they're open seven days a week **you say**.* (BrE)
>
> *Mm I wouldn't go into Amanda Close **I don't think*** (BrE)

The speaker here adds a comment clause which in effect modifies the stance of the preceding clause: it is a kind of propositional hedge (12.3.1).

### B  Retrospective vagueness hedges

> *And it was her second car that she'd ever had **sort of thing**.* (BrE)
>
> *North and south London they're two different worlds aren't they? **in a way**.* (BrE)

Final hedges such as these indicate that the speaker would like the hearer to take the preceding message 'with a pinch of salt', i.e. not to understand it as absolutely or literally true. In 10.3.1.1, such locutions are classified as stance adverbials of **imprecision**.

### C  Question tags

As we have seen (3.13.2.4), question tags have an interactive function of eliciting the hearer's agreement or confirmation. They can also be seen as having a role of retrospective qualification:

> *Well, that little girl's cute **isn't she**?* (AmE)
>
> *You get more done that way **huh**?* (AmE)
>
> *You had a nice trip though **yeah**?* (AmE)

Here the qualification is pragmatic. The speaker begins by making an assertion, then retrospectively turns its force into that of a question.

### D  Noun phrase tags (11.5.2)

A further type of tag takes the form of repeating a noun phrase with further elaboration, presumably to clarify a reference that might otherwise be unclear:

> *He's had **a blind** put up – **a special blind that that leads straight across the fanlight**.* (BrE)
>
> *You always remember **numbers**. Don't you? **Car numbers and telephone numbers and** –* (BrE)

As the opposite of noun phrase prefaces (11.5.1), noun phrase tags frequently take the form of an appended noun phrase co-referentially linked to a pronoun in the body of the clause:

> *I mean **it** was the only one with its own kitchen, **the one I was gonna have**.* (BrE)
>
> *I just give **it** all away didn't I Rudy **my knitting**?* (BrE)
>
> *Oh I reckon **they**'re lovely. I really do **whippets**.* (BrE)

The major motivation for this device seems to be the need to clarify reference retrospectively. It appears that the use of a personal pronoun is the first resort of the speaker, who at the end of the clausal unit may suspect (perhaps through a non-verbal signal from the addressee) that its reference is unclear to the addressee. Hence the appending of a clarificatory noun phrase.

### E Other non-clausal units retrospectively added

Tags sometimes take the form of non-clausal units which repeat some of the form and/or content of the preceding clausal unit:

> 1 *I don't care about work and them being in a muddle,* **no not at all.**
> (BrE)
>
> 2 *I mean she never liked that car.* **Ever.** (BrE)

Here the tag achieves the reinforcement, or emotive strengthening, of a negative in the preceding clausal unit. It is interesting that this reinforcement can be achieved either by using further negatives, as in **1**, or by using a non-assertive form such as *ever*, as in **2**.

### F Self-supplied answers

Yet a further case of retrospective qualification is shown by a tendency for speakers to suggest answers to their own questions (3.13.2.1):

> *What time are they supposed to be due back –* **early?** (BrE)
>
> *What are you going to get –* **some wine?** (AmE)

In effect, these merged adjacency pairs convert a *wh*-question into a *yes-no* question. They resemble conducive *yes-no* questions (14.4.2) in biasing the question towards an answer which the speaker considers to be likely. Although they vary in their effects from hedging to reinforcing and biasing, these self-supplied answers resemble other tag types in enabling the speaker to qualify the force of a preceding message.

### G Vocatives

A final vocative can be regarded as an additional tag type (3.4.6): it is a retrospective qualification of a message in the sense that it often signals an attitude to the addressee:

> *Hey thanks for the note,* **Tom.** *I'll follow up on that.* (AmE)
>
> *I just give it all away didn't I* **Rudy** *my knitting?* (BrE)

The attitudinal use of vocatives will be further discussed in 14.4.1.

### H More than one tag

Tags often occur in combination. It is noteworthy that in **1** and **2** below, the question tag does not occur in final position, but is followed by another tag:

> 1 *North and south London they're two different worlds* **aren't they?** *in a*
> **way.** (BrE)
>
> 2 *Depends on what you want most* **don't it I suppose.** (BrE)

(On the non-standard verb form *don't* in **2**, see 14.4.5.3.) The last example in G, repeated below, contains three tags: *didn't I, Rudy,* and *my knitting.*

> *I just give it all away* **didn't I Rudy my knitting?**

Note that these could in principle occur in any order:

- *didn't I + my knitting + Rudy*

- *Rudy* + *didn't I* + *my knitting*
- *my knitting* + *didn't I* + *Rudy*
- etc.

In general, tags seem to be fairly free in their ordering, and this underlines their character as items which are peripheral to syntax and positionally relatively unconstrained.

## 14.3.3    More on non-clausal units: inserts

Non-clausal units can be broadly divided into two categories: (a) single words (like *Hi*) known as **inserts** (sometimes occurring with added modifiers, as in *Hi there*) and (b) **syntactic non-clausal units**, such as *My turn?*. These are called syntactic because they may be characterized in terms of units which *are capable of entering into syntactic relations with others* for forming larger units such as clausal units. However, by calling a phrase like *My turn?* a non-clausal unit, we indicate that it is not, in this occurrence, a part of a larger unit, but a detached noun phrase. Syntactic non-clausal units can be single words, phrases, or unembedded dependent clauses, such as:

> *If only it was a little shadier.* (AmE)

or combinations of these. Syntactic non-clausal units are discussed in detail in 14.3.4.

**Inserts**, on the other hand, are defined (2.5) as a class of words: they are **stand-alone words** which are characterized in general by their inability to enter into syntactic relations with other structures. However, inserts have a tendency to attach themselves prosodically to a larger structure (14.3.3), and as such may be counted as part of that structure. They comprise a class of words that is peripheral, both in the grammar and in the lexicon of the language. In fact it may be questioned whether some inserts are words at all: this applies to interjections (such as *ugh*, *ooh*), response forms (such as *uh huh*, *mhm*) and hesitators (such as *mm*, *uh*). Such vocables as these often have uncharacteristic features of pronunciation (e.g. un-English consonants such as the velar fricative /x/; medial /h/; lack of an oral vowel sound—e.g. /mhm/).

In practice, however, the boundary between inserts and syntactic non-clausal units is a gradual one. Looking at the insert category more generally, it may be likened to a set of three or more concentric circles, representing central and progressively more peripheral members. There are six defining features that apply to its more central members:

(1) They may appear on their own, i.e. not as part of a larger grammatical structure.

(2) On the other hand, they may appear attached (prosodically, or, in the transcription, by absence of punctuation) to a larger structure, which may be a clausal unit or a non-clausal unit.

(3) They rarely occur *medially* in a syntactic structure.

(4) They are morphologically simple.

(5) They are not homonyms of words in other word classes.

(6) Semantically, they have no denotative meaning: their use is defined rather by their pragmatic function.

It is the first criterion which makes inserts form a very common type of non-clausal unit: words like *Oh*, *Yeah*, and *Uh huh*, for example, frequently occur alone as a response turn, forming non-clausal units of minimal length and complexity. The second criterion accounts for the resemblance of inserts to peripheral adverbials (10.1.1, 10.3–4). The other criteria provide a convenient means of defining the core of the insert category.

However, we also apply the term 'insert' to other words which occur in a stand-alone way, for example, *God* and *sorry* when used in exclamatory isolation, even though lexically (and in meaning) these forms derive from another word class (*God* is a noun, *sorry* an adjective). Some items such as these are subject to phonological modification in their insert function: e.g. *gawd* and *gosh* are euphemistic variants of the expletive *God*. In this they resemble not only interjections but also response forms such as *yes* and *no*, which can similarly undergo phonetic modifications reflected in spellings like *yeah*, *yep*, and *nope*.

Extending the class of inserts one stage further, we include in it items which consist of more than one orthographic word, but behave pragmatically and lexically as unanalysable formulae. Examples are *thank you*, *excuse me*, and *good God* (as an expletive). Expressions of these kinds have various restrictions and peculiarities which make them behave like atomic wholes. For example, they have pragmatically specialized functions, such as thanking and apologizing; they are sometimes grammatically anomalous (the verb of *thank you*, for example, has the outward appearance of an imperative, but clearly is not one, since it is followed by *you* rather than *yourself*). They also cannot be easily varied: consider, for example, non-existent variations such as ?\**thank me*, \**thank you a lot* (contrast *thanks a lot*), ?\**excuse me a little* (non-occurring as an apology), ?\**almighty God* (non-occurring as an expletive, as contrasted with the irregular *God almighty*).

Inserts can be grouped into several major functional types (cf. 2.5). However, it should be noted that different functions shade into one another, and that individual inserts can be versatile in taking on different conversational roles. For example, *oh*, as by far the most common of the **interjections** (A), shares also in the functions of **discourse markers** (C) and **response forms** (F). *Okay* can act as discourse marker, response elicitor, and response form. In the following sub-sections, we describe the major functions of inserts, examining their role both as separate non-clausal units and as peripheral parts of other units.

## 14.3.3.1 Interjections

The term **interjection** is applied here to inserts which have an exclamatory function, expressive of the speaker's emotion. In what follows, we illustrate interjections in approximate order of frequency, while grouping together interjections of similar function. (The frequency distribution of interjections, as well as other inserts, is presented in Tables 14.9 and 14.10.) We also comment briefly on their meaning—that is, their pragmatic function.

*Oh* is by far the most common interjection. Its routine use to introduce utterances or to respond to the utterances of others often gives it the character of a discourse marker. *Oh* also frequently combines with other inserts; some of the most common combinations are: *Oh yeah*, *Oh yes*, *Oh no*, *Oh aye* (regional BrE), *Oh well*, *Oh God*, *Oh I see*, *Oh right*. Although the use of *oh* is highly conventionalized, its core function appears to be to convey some degree of surprise, unexpectedness, or emotive arousal. Hence it is suitable for introducing or responding to a remark treated as 'news', indicating something the speaker has just found out or noticed:

> A: *I think it's a mosaic.*
> B: **Oh**, *it is a mosaic.* (AmE)
>
> **Oh**, *I should have let you read the paper, I never thought of it.* (AmE)
>
> **Oh** *how awful! How absolutely how naff!* (BrE)
>
> A: *Nicky got that for him.*
> B: **Oh**, *did she?*
> A: *Yeah. I think so.* (AmE)
>
> *Your birthday's in May – third week in May.* **Oh** *that reminds me, remind, Aunty Margaret, it's her anniversary.* (BrE)

**Ah** (in its core use)[13] and **wow** are less 'routine' expressions of emotional involvement than *oh*. They are considerably less common and tend to convey greater intensity of feeling. *Wow* typically indicates that the speaker is surprised and impressed—perhaps even delighted. A third interjection of emotive involvement is **ooh**, which is like *ah* in being capable of expressing both pleasant and unpleasant feelings:

> *Seriously!* **Ah!** *It's people like him / really bug me* (AmE)
>
> A: *They're chocolates.*
> B: **Ah** *isn't that nice.* (BrE)
>
> A: **Oh wow**, *they really did that tree nice.* **Wow.**
> B: *Very pretty.* (AmE) <admiring decorations>
>
> A: *In Hudson Bay, they have a whole floor, huge floor, the size of a city block, on men's clothing.*
> B: **Wow.**
> A: *It's just incredible.* (AmE†)
>
> A: *How big was it?*
> B: *Four pounds.*
> A: **Ooh**, *that's little.*
> B: *It's tiny.* (AmE) <talking of a premature birth>

Two less common interjections of more restricted use are **Cor** and **Aha**. The former (in BrE) expresses some degree of amazement, whereas the latter carries the meaning of sudden recognition:

> **Cor** *he had a lovely physique, cor.* (BrE)
>
> *It's really high sound quality. Let's see,* **aha**, *this one is yours.* (AmE)
> <discussing sound equipment>

**Oops** and **Whoops** can be seen as variants of the same interjection: they are used at the moment when a minor mishap occurs—for example, when the speaker spills something. It is often difficult to infer the nature of the mishap from the transcription.

> A: *Can we get out this way?*
> B: *Yeah you can go right thro–* **oops** *maybe you can't that guy's parked in the alley ha.* (AmE) <driving a car>
>
> **Ooh!** *I've got too many.* **Oops oops.** (BrE) <dealing during a card game>
>
> A: *I don't think I can do this with a knife and fork*
> B: *It picks up good, but it's a little messy*
> A: *Oh yeah, it's* <unclear> *messy –* **oops**, *sorry.* (AmE) <while eating>

> *Yeah, we have to go down to the road see that corn we got,* **whoops** *sorry, sorry, I knocked some stuff over.* (AmE)

> **Whoops,** *easy Chester. Chester down. Thank you.* (AmE) <talking to a dog>

The next group of interjections is associated with unpleasant emotions. Although they can cover a range of emotions, it is possible to characterize their central meanings as follows: **ugh** typically expresses a degree of disgust, and **ow** and **ouch** give voice to (typically physical) pain, whereas **aargh** and **urgh** seem more generalized in expressing pain and displeasure. **Tt** (an alveolar click, which is often repeated) registers some degree of regret or disapproval, whereas **hm** appears to convey doubt or lack of enthusiasm.

> A: *She burnt popcorn back there.*
> B: **Ugh** *it reeks.* (AmE)

> A: *Oh that's the most terrible figure. Look at her feet!* <unclear>
> B: *Yeah.*
> A: **Ugh.**
> B: *But I don't like his face.* (BrE)

> **Ow!** *I've got a stomachache. I ate too much I think.* (BrE)

> **Tt** *ooh!* **Ouch** *my neck hurts. Mm.* (BrE†)

> *I don't like that, diet food,* **aargh***! I gave it to her without telling her what it was. Mm this is good.* (AmE)

> A: *So when do you eat?*
> B: *Um,* **tt***, I guess I tend to snack a lot.* (AmE)

Other interjections of miscellaneous effect are illustrated below. **Ha** is not to be associated with the transcription of laughter, since a separate tag (<laugh> or <laughing>) is used for that purpose. *Ha* appears to have a range of functions, including the familiar one of a 'mirthless laugh', and it often occurs in series. **Yippee** is a rather rare interjection expressing delight (the example below is ironic):

> *I find that so funny, oh* **ha ha ha ha***.* (BrE)

> A: *Kay's birthday is Friday.*
> B: **Yippee***, I won't be there.* (AmE)

The class of interjections also includes occasional and rarer forms such as *whoopee* (delight), *wowee* (astonishment), and *yuck* (revulsion). It is, indeed, to some extent an open-ended class.

### 14.3.3.2 Greetings and farewells

Greetings are typically reciprocated in a 'symmetrical' exchange, as illustrated below:

> A: **Hi** *Margaret.*
> B: **Hi.** (AmE)

> A: **Hello,** *Joyce.*
> B: **Good morning,** *Bob.* (BrE)

As these examples show, a vocative commonly follows the greeting word, which can also introduce a more extended utterance:

> *Hello is that Cindy Jones?* (BrE)
>
> *Hello, can I have a three pound fifty car wash please.* (BrE)

In general, the briefer the greeting, the more informal it is (thus *hi* is more informal than *hello*, which is in turn less formal than the 'good forms' *good morning, good afternoon,* and *good evening.* However, these 'good' forms can be abbreviated by the omission of the word *good* itself:

> A: *Come on, Charles.* **Morning**.
> B: **Morning**. (AmE)

There are also rarer dialectally restricted forms such as *hiya* and *wotcha* in BrE, and *hey, howdy,* and *how (are) you doing* in AmE. *Good day* (commonly associated with Australian English) is rare as a greeting in both AmE and BrE.

Farewells, or leave-takings, follow the same principles as greetings in being typically reciprocated, also in the preference for short forms in more informal contexts:

> A: *Okay.* **Bye** *Butch.*
> B: **Bye** *Butch,* **bye** *Marc.* (AmE)
>
> A: **See you**.
> B: **Bye bye**.
> C: **Bye bye**. (AmE)
>
> A: *Oh.* **Goodbye** *Robin.*
> B: **See you later**. *Thank you for a lift. Love you lots.* (BrE)

*Good night* is restricted to leave-taking at night-time, especially before going to bed:

> A: *Well <yawning> nine o'clock, time for bed*
> B: **Good night**. *Aqua.* (AmE)

Other restrictions apply to *ta ta, cheers,* and *cheerio,* which are dialect leave-takings, largely restricted to certain British speakers: as in *Ta ta David. Cheerio* (BrE†).

### 14.3.3.3 Discourse markers

Discourse markers (14.3.2.1C, 14.3.2.2) are inserts which tend to occur at the beginning of a turn or utterance, and to combine two roles: (a) to signal a transition in the evolving progress of the conversation, and (b) to signal an interactive relationship between speaker, hearer, and message. Words and phrases which are discourse markers are often ambiguous, sharing the discourse marker function with an adverbial function. (For example, *now* and *well* are both circumstance adverbs—see 10.2.1—as well as discourse markers.)

The items included as 'discourse markers' are open to debate. For our purposes the category includes interactive uses of *well, right,* and *now,* as well as of the finite verb formulae *I mean, you know,* and *you see.* Many other less frequent forms, such as *mind you* and *now then,* might also be regarded as discourse markers, as could some inserts primarily considered under other headings, such as *oh* in 14.3.3.1 above, and *okay* in 14.3.3.6 below.

*Well* is a versatile discourse marker, but appears to have the general function of a 'deliberation signal', indicating the speaker's need to give (brief) thought or consideration to the point at issue. It is a very common turn initiator with a variety of functions, usually serving to relate a speaker's response to the ongoing conversation. This responsive role of *well* is clearly illustrated in **1** below. Sometimes, as in **2**, the response follows an agreement marker such as *yeah*. More often, however, *well* marks continuation but with something of a contrast, as in **3** and **4**. This same theme of continuation with contrast explains the use of *well* in contexts of disagreement and in prevaricating answers to questions, as in **5**.

> **1** *He said,* **well,** *I'd like to read a little bit about it first—I said,* **well,** *can you read my first volume, you'll see for yourself, you know, but he said,* **well,** *what about this,* **well,** *you know,* **well,** *you know, and he hems and haws and he won't come out and say yes or no* (AmE)
>
> **2** *A: we were talking about walking last night.*
> *B: Yeah,* **well,** *I used to walk a lot, but I, er, I <...> now all I do is eat.* (AmE†)
>
> **3** *A: You are always hungry.*
> *B:* **Well** *I'm not now.* (BrE)
>
> **4** *A: How much rice are you supposed to have for one person?*
> *B:* **Well,** *I don't know.*
> *A: Half a cup or –* **well** *I'm asking you!* (BrE)
>
> **5** *A: You never say what Stafford is, why is he going before the <unclear> parole board? You never say.*
> *B:* **Well,** *I don't know why.*
> *A:* **Well,** *it's a badly written story.* (AmE)

*Well* can also occur in the middle of an utterance as a signal of self-correction or deliberation over the choice of expression:

> *The boss and the secretary work late all night,* **well,** *not all night but late into the night* (AmE)
>
> *I don't know. It's funny that him and Gloria have never gotten married and yet they've stayed together for –* **well** *Julian's seven, at least eight years.* (AmE)

**Right** is another common discourse marker often used at the beginning of a turn, and conveying 'decisiveness'. It signals that the speaker is initiating a new phase of the conversation, especially one where some kind of action will be required:

> *A: No, but it all adds up – I was sitting there the other day adding up your things*
> *B:* **Right** *now you can discuss with Wayne about the sheds.* (BrE)
>
> *A:* **Right.** *Matthew, have you, have you anything else? –* **Right,** *are we ready? What am I standing on? Will you prop it up please? – Oh I forgot it's bin day I'll have to hurry back from school –* **Right,** *troops forward march! Put the key in me pocket.*
> *B: Rebecca's the colonel.*
> *A: Rebecca's the colonel?*
> *B: Yes*
> *A:* **Right** *colonel! Open the door please.* (BrE)

*Right* also resembles *okay* and *alright* (14.3.3.6) in their use as response forms indicating understanding and compliance:

> *A: It's just an excuse! Get on the phone and phone them up!*
> *B:* **Right** *Claire, I will.* (BrE)

In addition, especially in AmE, *right* is used as a response form indicating agreement:

> A: *And so I know that had to have to been service.* {*It was*}
> B: {**Right.**}
> A: *not*
> B: **Right**
> A: *that she was being talked to too much.*
> B: **Right**
> A: *Um – I don't know. She's just like – you don't need to be here. Well when you have fifty sixty thousand dollars invested in a business I think that you need to be there. And I just don't throw money away like that – nonchalantly.*
> B: **Right. Right.** (AmE)

Here *right* takes on the character of a backchannel (14.3.3.6).

Elsewhere *right* functions as a response elicitor (cf. 14.3.3.5), as in *You know who Stan is, right?.*

**Now** as an utterance launcher seems to have the function of clearing 'a bit of conversational space' ahead. It often marks a return to a related subject, and at the same time a new departure. In the following examples it serves to seek or provide additional background information while at the same time continuing the current topic of the conversation:

> A: *Alan doesn't want anybody doing a sort of flaky job so you know they haven't gotten the students who would do it.*
> B: **Now** *who is he, I don't know.* (AmE)
> A: *He won. Of course, Willy and Ted didn't get a single point, I got a few, Michael got everything.*
> B: **Now** *see that's what blew my mind about Michael, too, I realized that he was a closet brainiac.* (AmE)

On the discourse markers *you know, I mean,* etc. see 14.3.2.2B above.

### 14.3.3.4   Attention signals

Attention signals have the main function of attracting the attention of addressees—for example, when speakers want to make clear that they are addressing a particular person:

> *Oh you're not,* **hey** *you're not supposed to say that.* (AmE)

> **Hey** *Rob do you want to lend me fifty p?* (BrE)

> A: *Is she on the phone – she kind of quiet over there*
> B: *She needs it*
> A: **Yo** *Tonia*
> B: *She's okay*
> A: *Tonia – are you going to answer us.* (AmE)

> <shouting> **Hey,** *Raymond,* **yo,** / *what's happening?* (AmE)

> **Say,** *Mom, have you got any paint rollers.* (AmE)

Such attention grabbers are familiar and often impolite in their effect—especially where followed by a directive (e.g. *Hey stop bitching* (BrE)), or in combination with the vocative *you*:

> **Hey you,** *I buttered that bread for you and you didn't eat it.* (BrE)

Attention signals also acquire more general exclamatory functions: for example, *hey* in the following simply adds an emotive 'punch' to the speaker's remark:

> **Hey** *let's read a story.* (BrE)

### 14.3.3.5 Response elicitors

Response elicitors can be characterized as generalized question tags, such as *huh?* (especially AmE), *eh?* (BrE; usually pronounced /eɪ/), *alright?*, and *okay?*. *Right* and *see* can also occur in this function, although as inserts, they are more likely to act as discourse markers (14.3.3.3). Whereas clausal question tags, such as *isn't it*, have a role of inviting agreement or confirmation from the hearer, these one-word response elicitors often have a more speaker-centred role, seeking a signal that the message has been understood and accepted. An exception is the question tag *right?*, which normally requires a verbal response:

> *A: You know who Stan is, **right?***
> *B: I've heard his name.* (AmE)

The other response elicitors illustrated below are somewhat peremptory: they are typically used in familiar, casual exchanges, and would seem rude if they occurred in a formal situation. They can follow statements, questions, or directives:

> *Oh hi, you're Brent's, you're Brent's older sister, **huh?** Your brother's so cool* (AmE)
>
> *Jordan what's the matter? What's the matter **eh?*** (BrE)
>
> *Might as well get rid of it **eh?*** (BrE)
>
> *I will leave her the message, **okay?*** (AmE)
>
> *Just leave out the smutty stuff, **okay?*** (AmE)
>
> *It's like a magnet obviously **see?*** (BrE)

### 14.3.3.6 Response forms

Response forms are inserts used as brief and routinized responses to a previous remark by a different speaker. These include responses to questions (typically *yes*, *no*, and their variants), responses to directives (e.g. *okay*), and responses to assertions (e.g. **backchannels** such as *uh huh*, *mhm*).

The first set of examples below shows the canonical positive **yeah** (or *yes*, *yep*) and negative **no** (or *nope*, *unh unh*) in answers to questions. Note that the positive response form without a final consonant, *yeah* (/jɛə/), is appropriately treated as canonical in conversational English, where it is considerably more frequent than *yes* (see Table 14.9).

Positive responses:

> *A: Does somebody have a pencil?*
> *B: **Yeah**, here.*
> *A: Thank you.* (AmE)
> *A: Did you have a good time when you went up to King's Lynn?*
> *B: **Yes**. It was very pleasant.* (BrE)
> *A: Hi Annie, enjoyed your days off?*
> *B: **Yep**, lovely thank you.* (AmE)

Negative responses:

> A: *You don't need it wrapped?*
> B: **No**, *I'm going to stick it in an envelope with a little card and just mail it in a padded envelope.* (AmE)

> A: *Want a sip of this, Cooper?*
> B: **Nope**, *I got tea.* (AmE)

> A: *With a cherry on the top?*
> B: **Unh unh**.
> A: *Oh, I forgot you don't like cherries. Whipped cream?* (AmE)

The spellings **yep** and **nope** represent variants of *yeah* and *no* with a stop consonant—in effect, an abrupt lip closure—at the end. They sound more abrupt and peremptory than the more common variants with a final vowel. Somewhat more casual and routine, as positive and negative answers to a question, are **uh huh** (= *yeah*) and **huh uh** (= *no*), which will be discussed further, with *unh unh* (= *no*), below:

> A: *That girl – she had a bad year like I did, too, remember she started last year?*
> B: **Uh huh**. <= yeah>
> A: *She didn't start this year*
> B: *At all?*
> A: **Huh uh** <= no> (AmE)

**Yeah** and **no** and their variants are also used in responding to directives, although in these contexts politeness encourages the use of stronger positive responses such as *sure* and *certainly*, and of weakened or indirect negative responses:

> A: *Can you reach me three of those small tins – at the top – the processed ones.*
> B: **Yeah**. (BrE)

> A: *Why don't we just sign them now.*
> B: **Sure**. (AmE)

> A: *Can I put the water on?*
> B: *You don't need it on!* (BrE)

Notice the avoidance of a bleak 'no' in the last example: the questioner is left to infer from the indirect answer that permission is refused.

An offer can also be gently refused by *no thanks* or something similar:

> A: *Have you had some / cake?*
> B: *Er* **no** *I'll give it a – miss right now* **thank you**. (BrE)

**Okay** serves as a routine compliant response not only to directives but to a range of other speech acts relating to future actions, such as suggestions, offers, advice, and permission-giving. Note the repeated use of *okay* in the following extract:

> A: *Can I help today?*
> B: *No we just wanted to stop to see what beads you have.*
> A: **Okay**.
> C: <unclear> *in stock.*
> A: **Okay**. *What we need to do is uh – go to the studio.*
> C: *Oh,* **okay**.
> A: *Yeah, out of a catalogue. And look it up for the*
> C: **Okay**.

> A: *There {will be}*
> B: *{Is there a} public restroom in this mall?*
> A: *Well, I have one. I have one here. Go over against the door and the door*
>    *right there <unclear>*
> B: *Uh huh. Oh, **okay**, thank you.* (AmE)

*Yeah* also frequently serves as a response to a statement. It might be supposed that, in general, statements (which impart rather than elicit information) do not need a response from the hearer. However, in practice responses to statements are very frequent. Functionally, these inserts can be classified as **backchannels** because of their role in signalling feedback to the speaker that the message is being understood and accepted. Given the interactive nature of conversation, backchannels are important in indicating that speaker and hearer are keeping in touch with one another, and that communication is still in progress.

Other common 'affirmative markers', apart from *yeah* and its variants, have a more casual, routine quality, and are therefore more likely to take a backchannel function: **mm**, **uh huh**, and **mhm** (the last also rendered *mm hmm* in some transcriptions):

> 1 A: *and their lawn is high up, up the road, [you know]*
>    B: **Mm**
>    C: **Yeah**
>    A: *so he dug up the lawn and put a little garage in* (BrE)
>
> 2 A: *And then we stopped in Arizona to see Aunt Marie, [see], on the way.*
>    B: **Mhm**. (AmE)
>
> 3 A: *Her name was Martha <name>*
>    B: **Uh huh**.
>    A: *And then she married Alfred P <name>, my grandfather.* (AmE)

The spellings of *mhm* and *uh huh* imperfectly show their close correspondence. Their pronunciations are /mhm/ and /əhə/, the former being the nasal variant, and the latter the oral variant of the same basic form.

*Uh huh* and *mhm* also have negative counterparts normally spelt *huh uh* and *unh unh*. Both are often spoken with a rising tone. The reverse spelling *huh uh* is assumed to be a rendering of the AmE response form /mʔm/ (with a medial glottal stop), which has a negative function similar to that of *no*:

> 4 A: *Yeah. Let me see your top but [see] this one wasn't ready to come*
>    *out.*
>    B: **Huh uh**
>    A: *and I really don't think that one was ready to come out either.* (AmE)
>    <talking about teeth>

As the above example shows, this negative form *huh uh* can also occur as a backchannel; we have already noted its nasal equivalent /nʔn/ or /ŋʔŋ/, represented in the transcriptions as *unh unh*:

> 5 A: *People don't like to sit in banquets for a long time.*
>    B: **Unh unh**. (AmE)

Whereas these reduplicative forms all have a casual, non-committal air, towards the other end of the scale there are backchannels such as *really* and *I see* which are stronger in indicating a high degree of interest in what the previous speaker had to say:

> 6 A: *She's real good, the people like her real well over at the hospital.*
> B: **Really?** (AmE)

> 7 A: *And, [you see], they use instead of one-quarter or a cup of the pureed*
> *<unclear> sweet potatoes, they just use a little*
> B: *Oh,* **I see.**
> A: *a small jar of baby's it's near as good as fresh.* (AmE)

Before leaving the topic of backchannels, we draw attention to the expressions *you know*, *you see*, and *see* which are indicated by *[]* in examples **1**, **2**, **4**, and **7** above. These were discussed in 14.3.3.3 as discourse markers, but functionally, it can now be observed that they tend to occur in declarative utterances preceding backchannels. This is not accidental: these discourse markers can act as monitoring devices, whereby the person who holds the conversational floor can check that other participants are still 'tuned in' to what is being said. They help to elicit backchannels.

A more negative type of feedback is supplied by question forms such as *huh?* and *eh?* (as well as the question word *what?*), which can act as (somewhat impolite) response forms as well as response elicitors (cf. 14.3.3.5 above). As response forms, they signal lack of understanding and a wish to have the message repeated. In this respect they are the opposite of backchannels:

> A: *And then what brought them here, I wonder.*
> B: **Huh?**
> A: *What brought them here?* (AmE)

> A: *Where are we at?*
> B: **Eh?**
> A: *Where are we going?* (BrE)

> A: *Do you do these, too?*
> B: **What?**
> A: *Do you do crossword puzzles?* (AmE)

More polite repetition elicitors are mildly apologetic formulae such as *sorry?*, *(I) beg your pardon* (BrE), and *excuse me* (AmE); 14.3.3.8.

### 14.3.3.7 Hesitators

These have already been discussed in 14.2.1: they are pause fillers, whose main function is to enable the speaker to hesitate, i.e. to pause in the middle of a message, while signalling the wish to continue speaking:

> *You know this is, this is* **uh** *pretty heavy stuff.* (AmE)

> A: *How much was it?*
> B: **Er er,** *ninety pound I think, I can't remember.* (BrE)

> A: *How am I gonna get it back to you?*
> B: **Um,** *I'll come over to your house.* (AmE)

> *My* **erm** *hairdresser brought, you know those* **erm,** *kiddies' chairs we were selling* (BrE†)

*Uh* and *er* are best regarded as variant spellings of the same form, favoured respectively in the AmE and BrE transcriptions. The same applies to the nasalized variants *um* and *erm*.

### 14.3.3.8   Various polite speech-act formulae

Under this heading we place inserts or formulae used in conventional speech acts, such as thanking, apologizing, requesting, and congratulating. Such formulae also frequently elicit a polite reply. For example, in the case of thanks, an appropriately polite reply is a **minimizer** such as *No problem* or *You're welcome*. In the following examples, explanatory notes are added in <> to indicate the speech-act function:

> A: *Would you like another drink Adam?*
> B: *Yes* **please** *– .* (BrE) <**please** *is a request 'propitiator'*>

> *Can I have a – another two Diet Cokes* **please**? **Thank you**. (BrE)
>     <requesting; thanking>

> A: **Thanks** *Carl, I appreciate it.* <thanking>
> B: **You're welcome** *and* **good luck** *huh.* (AmE) <acknowledging thanks; good wishes>

> A: *That helps, that helps.* **Thank you**.
> B: **No problem**, *I just had to brown-nose with Greg for a little while.* (AmE) <acknowledging thanks and 'minimizing' the debt>

> A: **Sorry**, *I didn't mean to scare you.* <apologizing>
> B: **That's okay**. (AmE) <acknowledging the apology>

> A: *Get off.*
> B: *Shut up!*

> A: *Ah!* **Beg your pardon!** <apologizing>
> B: **Sorry**. (BrE) <apologizing>

> <belch> *–* **Pardon me**. (AmE)
> <apologizing for a minor social transgression, e.g. coughing, sneezing>

> A: *now this is the famous budgie is it?*
> B: **Pardon**? <requesting a repetition (14.3.3.6)>
> A: *That's your famous budgie?* (BrE)

> A: *I'm getting my lip pierced.*
> B: **Excuse me**, *you are not getting your lip pierced.* (AmE) <a mock-apology, here prefacing a refusal>

> A: *Tell Teresa I said* **good luck** <sending good wishes>
> B: *I will.*

> A: *or else* **congratulations**, *whichever* <congratulating>
> B: *whichever* (AmE)

The final example shows how these polite expressions can be incorporated into direct speech quotation.

These formulae behave as invariable items, in effect as inserts, but they can also combine with grammatical constructions such as prepositional phrases and complement clauses:

> **Thank you** *both for having us.* (BrE)

> **Thank you** *very, very, very, very much.* (BrE)

> **Sorry** *to keep bothering you.* (AmE)

In such constructions we do not consider them to be inserts, since they take part in free constructions (see also 14.3.4.2H).

The apology forms *pardon?*, *sorry?*, *(I) beg your pardon?*, *pardon me?*, and *excuse me?* are used as more polite equivalents of *what?* (14.3.3.6), seeking repetition of a previous speaker's message. *Excuse me* can also be used as a polite, apologetic attention signal (14.3.3.4), used for example in approaching a stranger. Like most of the examples of this use in the LSWE Corpus, the following example of *excuse me* takes place in direct speech quotation:

> *He goes up to the, he goes up to the bartender. He says **excuse me**, why is there a bear sitting over there?* (BrE)

### 14.3.3.9 Expletives

The term **expletive** is used here for taboo expressions (swearwords) or semi-taboo expressions used as exclamations, especially in reaction to some strongly negative experience. Like other inserts, expletives are relatively detached elements, although they can be linked prosodically to a larger syntactic unit. Their most common positions are (a) stand-alone occurrence, often as a complete turn, and (b) initial occurrence within a clause, utterance, or turn. They also occasionally occur in final position in a clause. Medial position is very rare, except in the special case of introducing direct speech quotation:

> *You're supposed to [say], **golly**, thanks Baloo.* (BrE)

A verb of thinking, as well as a verb of saying, may precede the expletive in such contexts:

> *She just [thought] **my God** I only have six months.* (AmE †)

Since we are here considering expletives as a class of inserts, we do not include multi-word expressions which have a fairly variable syntactic structure; many expletives are capable of internal syntactic and lexical variations, as in 14.3.4.2G. However, we do include purely formulaic multi-word expressions, such as *my God* or *bloody hell*. Expletives also very often co-occur with other inserts, especially interjections like *Oh hell*. However, in such cases we do not count the interjection as part of the expletive.

Expletives can be usefully subdivided into **taboo** expletives, which make reference to one of the taboo domains of religion, sex, or bodily excretion, and **moderated** (or euphemistic) expletives, which camouflage their taboo origin by various phonetic modifications (e.g. *gosh* for *God*) or by substitution of different but related words (e.g. *goodness* for *God*). Obviously the moderated expletives are socially acceptable in many situations where some taboo expressions are ruled out. On the other hand, the taboo expressions, where they are used at all, tend to be used frequently: their use can be dense in particular conversations, and completely absent from others.

We do not include under expletives non-exclamatory taboo expressions ('swearwords'), such as the adjectives or adverbs *bloody* (especially BrE) and *fucking*, unless these are habitually combined with words otherwise classed as expletives, as in *bloody hell*. Such words are not themselves inserts, and can combine with other words in the normal clausal syntax of English, as in *It cost me ten bucks just to get the bloody picture taken* (AmE). We also exclude taboo insults such as *you bastard!* (14.3.4.2G), which are abusive exclamations, and refer to people, whereas true expletives have a vaguer situational application.

The following are examples of expletives:

A **Taboo expletives**

> This is, **God**, a bloody afternoon wasted! (BrE)
>
> oh **Jesus**, I didn't know it was that cold. (AmE)
>
> A: I know what I forgot to get in town. **Damn!**
> B: What?
> A: A comb. (BrE)
>
> **Shit**, play a fucking domino **goddammit**. (AmE)
>
> **Bloody hell!** He's gone mad. (BrE)
>
> In Tunisia in hospital? Oh! **Shit!** That's pretty good (BrE)
>
> **Goddamn assholes**, even though we make more fucking money than anyone in the restaurant. (AmE)
>
> **Fuck**, I feel fucking sweaty, I can feel it already. (AmE)

Clearly there is wide variation in the degree of force an expletive carries, and in the degree of offence it can cause. For example, *damn*, classed above as a taboo expletive because of its taboo religious associations, is a much milder term than most of the other terms illustrated in that class.

B **Moderated expletives**

> **My gosh**, what a great idea. (AmE)
>
> A: Nineteen dollars.
> B: **Geez**, that is expensive. (AmE)
>
> Oh boy, **gee** you've got some nice pictures. (AmE)
>
> A: I think, Maureen, I remember when we were about fifteen, at the last count she had forty-nine first cousins!
> B: Wha–
> C: Really?
> A: Let alone second cousins, but first cousins, she had
> B: **Heavens!**
> A: forty-nine!
> B: **Good grief!** (BrE)
>
> A: Er sorry, Liz McColgan's just knocked ten seconds off the world record.
> B: Yeah! **Good Lord!** (BrE)
>
> Oh **heck** well you'll have to go on the bus. (BrE)

As with taboo expletives, there is variation in the force and applicability of moderated expletives. It will be noted in the above examples that some expletives in this class (e.g. *gosh* and *gee*) can easily associate with pleasant, as well as unpleasant, experiences. Such moderated expletives are similar in function to interjections such as *oh* and *wow*, in that they may express a generalized reaction of surprise or emotional involvement.

## 14.3.3.10 Distribution of inserts

**CORPUS FINDINGS**

Since inserts tend to differ in BrE and AmE, the frequency figures in Tables 14.9–10 distinguish the two regional varieties. Because the same word is sometimes used in a number of overlapping functions, we do not attempt to distinguish the multiple functions of a single word in the frequency counts. Instead, we group inserts according to their major function, and give their total frequency under that heading. Where the word acting as an insert also has a non-insert function, we do of course restrict the frequency count to its insert use.

**Table 14.9** **Frequency of the most common inserts in AmE and BrE conversation; occurrences per million words (inserts are listed under the category to which they most commonly belong)**

each ■ represents c. 500     ▢ represents less than 250

| | AmE | BrE |
|---|---|---|
| **primarily interjections (14.3.3.1)** | | |
| *oh* | ■■■■■■■■■■■■■■■■■ | ■■■■■■■■■■■■■■■■■ |
| **primarily discourse markers (14.3.3.3)** | | |
| *well* | ■■■■■■■■■■■■ | ■■■■■■■■■■ |
| *you know* | ■■■■■■■■■ | ■■■■ |
| *I mean* | ■■■■ | ■■■ |
| **primarily response forms (14.3.3.6)** | | |
| *yes* | ■■■ | ■■■■■ |
| *yeah* | ■■■■■■■■■■■■■■ ■■■■■■■ | ■■■■■■■■■■■■■ ■■■■■ |
| *no* | ■■■■■■■■■■■■■■ | ■■■■■■■■■■■■■■■■ |
| *mm* | ■■ | ■■■■■■■■ |
| *uh huh*[14] | ■■■ | ▢ |
| *okay*[15] | ■■■■■■■■■■■ | ■ |
| **hesitators (14.3.3.7)** | | |
| *uh/er* | ■■■■■■■■■■■■■ | ■■■■■■■■ |
| *um/erm* | ■■■■■■ | ■■■■■■ |

## DISCUSSION OF FINDINGS

The most noticeable finding is that although the same functions are performed by inserts in AmE and BrE conversation, many inserts are strikingly more common in one variety than the other. For example, among backchanneling response forms, the nasalized variants *mm*, *mhm* are more common in BrE than in AmE, and the oral variants *uh*, *uh huh* are more common in AmE. Again, the attention signal *hey* is more frequent in AmE, as is the response elicitor *huh?*, as contrasted with the British forms *oi* and *eh?* The response form *okay* is also vastly more frequent in AmE than in BrE.

A further observation is that informal, phonologically reduced forms tend to predominate. Among response forms, *yes* (the 'careful' form, with a final sibilant) is far less frequent, especially in AmE, than *yeah*, and casual forms with a final lip-closure (*yep*, *nope*) also have some currency. Among greetings, the informal *hi* is much more common that *hello* in AmE, and among leavetakings, the canonical form *good(-)bye* is surprising rare alongside *bye* and *bye bye*. In fact, the 'good' formulae (*good morning, good afternoon, good evening, good night, good day*) are rare as an entire group, even including abbreviated forms such as *morning*.

**Table 14.10** **Frequency of selected less common inserts in AmE and BrE conversation; occurrences per million words (inserts are listed under the category to which they most commonly belong)**

each ■ represents c. 50     □ represents less than 25

| | AmE | BrE |
|---|---|---|
| **primarily interjections (14.3.3.1)** | | |
| *ah* | ■■■■■■ | ■■■■■■■■■■■■■■ ■■■■■ |
| *ooh* | ■■■■ | ■■■■■■■■■■■■■ |
| *ha* | ■■ | ■■■■■■■■ |
| *wow* | ■■■■■■■■ | ■ |
| *aargh* | ■■■■■■ | ■ |
| *aha* | □ | ■■■■ |
| *tt* | □ | ■ |
| *whoa* | □ | ■ |
| *cor* | □ | ■ |
| *oops* | ■ | □ |
| *whoops* | ■ | □ |

less frequent forms include *ugh, aw* (AmE), *coo, och* (BrE, especially Scots), *whoopee, wowee, yippee, yuck*

| | AmE | BrE |
|---|---|---|
| **primarily greetings, farewells (14.3.3.2)** | | |
| *hi* | ■■■■■■■■ | ■ |
| *hello* | ■■■■ | ■■■■■ |
| *bye* | ■■ | ■■ |
| *bye bye*[16] | ■■ | ■ |

less frequent forms include *good-bye, (good) morning, (good) afternoon, (good) evening, good night, cheerio* (BrE), *hiya* (BrE), *howdy* (AmE), *tata* or *tara* (= 'good-bye'; BrE), *see you (later), take care* (AmE)

| | AmE | BrE |
|---|---|---|
| **primarily discourse markers (14.3.3.3)** | | |
| *now* | ■■■■■ | ■■■■■■■■■■■ |
| *you see* | ■ | ■■■■■■■■ |

less frequent forms include *see, look, mind (you)*

| | AmE | BrE |
|---|---|---|
| **primarily attention seekers (14.3.3.4)** | | |
| *hey* | ■■■■■■■■■■■■ | ■■ |
| *oi* | □ | ■ |

less frequent forms include *say, yo*

| | AmE | BrE |
|---|---|---|
| **primarily response elicitors (14.3.3.5)** | | |
| *huh* | ■■■■■■■■■■ | ■ |
| *eh* | □ | ■■■■■■ |

Table 14.10 **continued**

| | AmE | BrE |
|---|---|---|
| **primarily response forms** (14.3.3.6) | | |
| *yep* | ▪▪▪▪ | ▪▪ |
| *aye* | ▫ | ▪▪▪▪▪▪▪▪ |
| *nope* | ▪▪ | ▫ |
| *mhm* | ▪▪▪▪▪▪▪▪▪▪▪▪▪ ▪▪▪▪▪▪▪▪ | ▪▪▪▪ |
| *unh unh*[17] | ▪▪ | ▫ |
| *alright*[18] | ▪▪▪▪▪▪▪▪▪▪▪▪▪ | ▪▪▪▪▪▪▪▪▪▪▪ |
| *huh uh* | ▪▪ | ▫ |

infrequent forms include *aye, okie-dokie, okie doke*

| | AmE | BrE |
|---|---|---|
| **primarily polite speech-act formulae** (as inserts) (14.3.3.8) | | |
| *thank you* | ▪▪▪▪▪▪▪ | ▪▪▪▪ |
| *thank you very much* | ▪ | ▪ |
| *thanks* | ▪▪▪▪ | ▪▪ |
| *sorry* | ▪ | ▪▪▪▪ |
| *pardon* | ▫ | ▪▪ |
| *excuse me* | ▪ | ▪ |
| *please* | ▪▪▪▪ | ▪▪▪▪▪▪▪ |

infrequent forms include *thanks a lot, ta* (= 'thank you'; BrE), *congratulations, pardon me, (I) beg your pardon*

| | AmE | BrE |
|---|---|---|
| **primarily expletives** (as inserts) | | |
| *God* | ▪▪ | ▪▪▪▪ |
| *my God* | ▪▪ | ▪ |
| *Christ* | ▫ | ▪ |
| *damn* | ▪ | ▫ |
| *hell* | ▪ | ▫ |
| *fuck* | ▪ | ▫ |
| *shit* | ▪ | ▪ |
| *gosh* | ▪ | ▪ |
| *my gosh* | ▪▪ | ▫ |
| *geez/gees* | ▪ | ▫ |
| *gee* | ▪ | ▫ |
| *my goodness* | ▪ | ▫ |

less frequent forms include *Jesus, Jesus Christ, blimey* (BrE), *bullshit, balls* (BrE), *bugger* (BrE), *crumbs* (BrE), *crikey* (BrE), *(God) dang (it)* (AmE), *(gosh) darn (it)* (AmE), *goddammit* (variously spelt), *golly, (good) heavens, (good) Lord, heck, blimey* (BrE), *goodness (me)*

*Note*: Taboo or semi-taboo terms like *fuck, shit, hell,* and *heck* are often more frequent in non-expletive uses, which are not counted here. For example, with such uses these forms function as verbs or nouns: *Fuck off, What the hell* ... (14.3.4.2G).

The tendency towards informality and phonological reduction is generally stronger in AmE. To a considerable extent, the informality reflects the familiar, private nature of most conversation. It may also reflect, however, a general drift towards the casualization of everyday speech in both AmE and BrE (cf. the use of first-name terms among vocatives; 14.4.1).

It is tempting to see cultural differences behind the AmE speakers' greater use of expressions of thanks (*thank you* especially), and BrE speakers' greater use of 'negative' or redressive politeness in the use of *sorry* and *please*.

## 14.3.4    Syntactic non-clausal units

**Syntactic non-clausal units** differ from inserts in that they can be given a syntactic description in terms of the structures and categories of sentence grammar. These units are often classifiable according to standard phrase categories, such as noun phrases (*poor kids, no sweat*), adjective phrases (*perfect, good for you*), adverb phrases (*not really, absolutely!*) or prepositional phrases (*for goodness' sake!*). On the other hand, they are often phrases augmented by inserts or other syntactically peripheral elements, such as vocatives (*oh shame! ah you cunt, this way please, good play there, dude*) which help to underline their discourse roles, e.g. as exclamations or as directives. Others have the form of unembedded dependent clauses (e.g. *not to worry* is a negative infinitive clause).

Looking at syntactic non-clausal units more carefully, it is useful to note the varied functions they perform. In most cases, the 'fragmentary' nature of these units, i.e. the absence of a clausal unit structure, reflects a dependence of the message on context, explicable in general terms either by anaphoric or situational ellipsis. For example, *perfect* could in principle be elaborated into *that's perfect*, or *absolutely* into *I agree with you absolutely*, but many such 'reconstructions' have dubious linguistic motivation: indeed, in the above cases alternative verbalizations could be proposed (e.g. *this is perfect; that's absolutely true*).

A number of functional categories can be usefully distinguished: the most important is that of elliptic replies.

### 14.3.4.1    Elliptic replies

In the to-and-fro of conversation, it is natural for one speaker to build on the content of what a previous speaker has said, and to avoid unnecessary repetition. Thus ellipsis is a pervasive feature of conversational dialogue. In the present section we discuss only cases of anaphoric ellipsis, where the missing content is directly recoverable from the preceding utterance(s) (cf. the discussion of ellipsis in 3.7). The paradigm case is an elliptic reply to a *wh*-question:

> 1  A: *Where did you guys park?*
>     B: **Right over here**. (AmE) <i.e. **We parked** right over there.>

Less typically, the roles of question and assertion may be reversed, the assertion eliciting a question in reply:

> 2  A: *Well I personally think it's too cold to snow tonight.*
>     B: **Too cold**? (BrE) <i.e. *Is it too cold to snow tonight?*>

An assertion may also elicit another assertion in reply, particularly in the case of co-construction (14.2.4C).

> 3  A: *It takes about – well*
>     B: **About two ticks**, *ya. Alright.* (AmE)

Alternatively, a question may elicit another question which is elliptic:

> 4 A: *Did you have a good weekend?*
>   B: *Yeah. / **Yourself?*** (AmE)

Example **5** combines two kinds of ellipsis pattern: *A*'s assertion elicits from B an elliptic question, consisting just of a *wh*-word, which in turn elicits an elliptic answer, in the form of a *because*-clause, from *A*:

> 5 A: *This is what gets me, this is what gets me about people, you know periodically there's this effort to, to ban Tarzan from the school somewhere.*
>   B: ***Why?*** *<is there this effort ... somewhere  omitted>*
>   A: ***Because he and Jane aren't married.*** (AmE †)

In example **6**, there is a yet more complex case of continuing ellipsis, where *B*'s first turn sparks off a disagreement from *A*, which is in turn queried by *B*, and confirmed further by *A*. The same syntactic frame underlies turns *A2*, *B2*, and *A3*, but in each case the subject and verb—*they started*—are elliptated:

> 6 A1: *and one, one is from the Hotel <unclear> in Paris which is one of the oldest hospitals in the, in the world.*
>   B1: *<unclear> where they started in fourteen hundred, fifteen <unclear>*
>   A2: *No,* ***earlier than that***
>   B2: ***Earlier even?***
>   A3: ***Probably the tenth, eleventh century.*** (AmE)

This example also illustrates how analysis of syntactic non-clausal units requires more than the grammar of single phrases. Turn *B2* has two separate adverbials: a time adverbial (*earlier*) and a focus adverbial (*even*). Similarly, turn *A3* contains an adverbial (*probably*) followed by the noun phrase (*the tenth, eleventh century*). These units with two clause elements (either adverbial + adverbial or adverbial + noun phrase), even though they lack a finite verb, more closely approximate to full clauses than those consisting of just one phrase.

## 14.3.4.2  Other types of syntactic non-clausal unit

### A  Condensed questions

From questions such as those in **2**, **5**, and **6** above, we turn here to questions for which situational ellipsis is the best explanation:

> *More sauce?* (BrE) <i.e. 'Would you like more sauce?'>
>
> *Any luck?* (AmE) <i.e. 'Did you have any luck?'>
>
> *Any more questions for me?* (AmE) <i.e. 'Do you have any more questions for me?'>
>
> *You should go to the Salsa Club.* ***Not your thing?*** (AmE)

Two conventionalized types of condensed questions are ones which begin *How about* and *What about*, and normally lack a main verb structure:

> ***How about*** *your wife?* (BrE)
>
> *Now* ***what about*** *a concert this Friday?* (BrE)

In all these cases there is no sure way of adding to an elliptated structure to complete a regular clausal question, yet the interpretation of the question depends heavily on context.[19]

## B Echo questions

Additional categories of condensed structure to consider are echo questions (3.13.2)—questions which request confirmation of what has already been said, by repeating part of its content. Some echo questions repeat the structure of what was said earlier, using interrogative intonation, or else make the purpose of the echo question clear by the use of the words *did you say*:

> A: *I don't see nothing in San Francisco.*
> B: *Oh,* **did you say San Francisco?** (AmE)

> A: *Yeah, could I please have some Percoset?*
> B: **Can you have Percoset, did you say?** (AmE)

On the other hand, often the echo question simply reiterates part of the nearby utterance which needs to be repeated or clarified:

> A: *The weather was really crappy.*
> B: *Oh yeah?*
> A: *Yeah, we ended up coming home Saturday?*
> B: *Are you serious?*
> A: *Yes.*
> B: **Saturday?** (AmE †)

> A: *They have white chocolate. They have it for one of their mocha drinks or something, but you can get white chocolate hot cocoa.*
> B: **White chocolate hot cocoa?** (AmE)

As is often the case, here the reason for seeking a repetition is not so much that the questioner failed to decode the previous remark, as that he or she found it difficult to believe.

## C Elliptic question-and-answer sequences

We have noted (in 14.3.2.4F) the tendency of speakers to answer their own questions, or rather to proffer an answer to their own questions, in the form of another interrogative. In some cases the initial question is elliptic; e.g. *Why* and *Why not* in the following examples:

> A: *Did you talk to <unclear>?*
> B: *No.* **Why,** *did she call?* (AmE)

> A: *Oh, I don't want to go on tour trip I mean uh a boat.*
> B: **Why not,** *do you get sea sick?* (AmE)

In other cases, the second interrogative, the proffered answer, is elliptic:

> *Where can I get parchment paper?* **An art store?** (AmE)

> *Where was that now?* **In California?** (AmE)

## D Condensed directives

Condensed or elliptical directives are a fairly rare but diverse group. The following have the force of commands (addressed to children or pets) or else, in the case of the last example, a piece of advice:

> **No crying.** (AmE)

> **Head down!** *Come on,* **head down.** (BrE) <talking to a dog>

> **Up the stairs, now.** (BrE) <to a child>

> **Careful when you pick that up**, *it's ever so slippery.* (BrE)

In the following examples, the directive force of the utterance is marked, and somewhat softened, by the use of the politeness insert *please*:

> *Down! Down the stairs please!* (BrE) <to a child>
>
> *Hands off the jug please.* (BrE)
>
> *Thirty pence please.* (BrE) <asking for payment>

### E  Condensed assertions

Non-clausal units with assertive force often consist of a noun phrase or an adjective phrase:

> A: *Why does he just hang it – you know – put in the tumble dryer or hang it in the garage?*
>
> B: *Too lazy! – Easier to do it that way!* (BrE)
>
> *Very special. Prawns in it and all sort* (BrE) <in a restaurant>
>
> *No wonder this house i– is full of dirt!* (AmE)

### F  Elliptic exclamatives

Reduced exclamative clauses (3.13.3) typically have ellipsis of a pronoun subject and a form of the verb *be*: e.g. *What a sweet child* can be analysed as an elliptical form of *What a sweet child he/she is*, the actual choice of subject being determined only by context. Further examples:

> *How cool!* (AmE)
>
> *How wonderful. Good for you.* (AmE)
>
> *What an unfortunate first experience.* (AmE)
>
> *What a joker, eh?* (BrE)
>
> *Oh this is lovely isn't it? What a nice wide street.* (BrE)

### G  Other exclamations (including insults)

> *The bloody key! – The key to the bloody boiler!* (BrE)
>
> *Ah! That boy! This is the one who said – I think we should be allowed to hit girls.* (BrE)
>
> *Timmy! Sit down! Good boy!* (BrE †) <addressing a pet>

Particularly characteristic are disparaging or abusive exclamations, often containing expletives and used with varying degrees of playfulness. One type (referring to the addressee) contains *you* either at the beginning or the end or both:

> *How did you get two of those phones, **you little devil**?* (AmE)
>
> *Come on **you silly cow*** (BrE)
>
> *Oh come on, **lazy lot of buggers you**, come on –* (BrE)

These exclamatory noun phrases superficially resemble vocatives, and can combine, like vocatives, with an imperative or other clausal unit, as the examples show. Another type is directed to third persons, and can be introduced by the definite article: e.g. *the dirty bugger* (BrE).

Yet another group shows how expletives (14.3.3.9) can be extended in the direction of becoming free expressions: *damn you, bugger me* (BrE), *fuck that, sod the choir* (BrE). These have the appearance of imperatives, but are clearly not—in the first example, an imperative would contain *yourself*, not *you*. Historically, they are subjunctive clauses, but in the present context we treat them simply as formulae with phrasal elaborations. Expletives can also be crafted into ornate noun phrases:

> *Fucking hell's bells – Hell's bells and little fishes you* (BrE)

For contrast, we turn finally to a small group of genteel exclamatory words and phrases which function like expletives, except that they have no taboo associations:

> **Boy,** *there's a lot of rocks, huh?* (AmE)
>
> \<laughing> **My word!** *I've never heard of anybody starting to jimmy a car without the people standing there and saying which car.* (AmE)
>
> A: *No, I have, I'll try pie next time. I had all the cake last night.*
> B: *Oh,* **my.**
> C: **My, my, my.** (AmE)
>
> *Oh* **dear** *the phone is ringing.* (AmE)
>
> *Have you been swearing!* **Oh dear me!** *That's naughty!* (BrE)

*Dear* and *dear me* express sad emotions such as regret or disapproval.

### H  Various polite speech acts

Polite formulaic expressions were discussed in 14.3.3.8. However, as we noted with impolite expressions in G above, the boundary between formulae and free expressions is a gradual one, and there is need to acknowledge the range of non-clausal variations on the basic formulae which are possible, for good wishes, thanks, apologies, and other polite speech acts. As the following examples show, these may be elaborated according to need (the formulaic elements are in bold italic):

> **Happy** *birthday to you.* (AmE, BrE)
>
> *Okay one more here. Okay* **happy** *birthday from Marla.* **Happy** *birthday to a person with style, grace and dignity.* (AmE) \<reading out birthday messages>
>
> *Oh,* **Happy** *Saint Patrick's Day, everyone.* (AmE)
>
> **Congratulations** *to you my dear brother on all your fine accomplishments in school.* (AmE) \<reading from a letter>
>
> **Glad** *you could make it.* (AmE)
>
> **Thanks** *a lot,* **sorry** *about that.* (BrE)
>
> **Sorry** *about cutting the top of your head off – but never mind, you know!* (BrE) \<referring to a photograph>
>
> **Sorry** *I've been a while, I went into mum's to take her shopping and Uncle Philip was there.* (BrE)

### I  Vocatives

Vocatives can constitute a 'lone' non-clausal unit, with or without accompanying inserts: *Darling! Hey Martin.* On the other hand, they more frequently act as prefaces or tags to a larger construction, such as an imperative (3.13.4.1) or a declarative clause:

> *Yes I'm coming in a moment* **darling.** (BrE)

They will be discussed further in 14.4.1.

**J    Other phrases as prefaces and tails**

These categories of non-clausal unit have already been discussed in 14.3.2.1 and 14.3.2.4.

### 14.3.4.3    Elliptic phrasal non-clausal units in their context

The dependence of non-clausal units on context for their interpretation is most obvious in the case of elliptical replies to questions, where the words ellipted can often be directly retrieved from the preceding question, as was seen in 14.3.4.1.

In many other cases, the 'meaning gap' left by the absence of a clausal unit is supplied by convention (e.g. *Good luck* and *Thanks for* ... are ritualized speech acts of good wishes and gratitude). In yet further instances (e.g. many of the examples in 14.3.4.2D–G), what is omitted by ellipsis is unclear from the transcription, and may stem from some aspects of context not evident from the verbal record. Here is an example of indirect anaphoric ellipsis:

> A: *Have we got any Red Stripe?*
> B: **Not a lot.** (BrE)

The interpretation of the elliptical reply here seems to be: 'We have some Red Stripe, but not a lot'.

Apart from the relatively 'well-behaved' types of ellipsis illustrated above, there are many other types of ellipsis which arise in dialogue, and for which it is difficult to specify rules:

> A: *Can I have a drink?*
> B: *Yeah, what would you like?*
> A: *I would like strawberry.*
> B: <–> **With or without ice?**
> A: <–> **With** <–> . (AmE)

However, it can be misleading even to think in terms of a 'meaning gap' when no propositional message is conveyed. Interjections and expletives, for example, generally operate at an emotive level of communication where nothing in the form of a proposition need be implied. The same goes for many exclamatory phrases such as the insults illustrated in 14.3.4.2G.

## 14.3.5    Ellipsis in clausal units

It is only a small step from the non-clausal units described in 14.3.4 to another common phenomenon of conversation: clausal units with ellipsis of one or more of their semantically essential components (on ellipsis generally, see 3.7). These are considered to be clausal units, because they can still be analysed in terms of the elements: subject, verb, object, predicative, or adverbial, even though some of these clausal elements will have been ellipted. In most cases, ellipsis in conversation can be classified as **initial ellipsis** and **final ellipsis**. There is also a less-frequent phenomenon of **medial ellipsis**.

### 14.3.5.1    Initial (situational) ellipsis

Initial ellipsis has already been illustrated in 3.7.5 under the heading of **situational ellipsis.** This is the dropping of words with contextually low information value, when these occur at the beginning of a turn, a clause, or (occasionally) a non-clausal unit. The main types have been introduced already (the position of omitted material is indicated by <–>):

**A   Ellipsis of subject**

This takes place when the subject of a declarative clause is omitted, normally at the start of a turn:

> <–> *Must be some narky bastards in the rugby club!* (BrE) <*There* is omitted>

> A: *Are your parents well off?* –
> B: <–> *Depends what you call well off really.* (BrE) <*It* is omitted>

> A: *What's concubine?*
> B: <–> *Don't know, get a dictionary.* (BrE) <*I* is omitted>

*Don't know* with initial ellipsis of *I* is often represented orthographically in the reduced form *dunno*:

> A: *And what do you think she'll say?*
> B: <–> *Dunno.* (BrE)

**B   Ellipsis of operator** (i.e. ellipsis of auxiliary or *be*)

This occurs in *yes-no* interrogatives:

> *Oh.* <–> *You serious?* (BrE) <*Are* is omitted>

> <–> *That too early for you?* (BrE) <*Is* is omitted>

> <–> *Your Granny Iris get here?* (BrE) <*Did* is omitted>

**C   Ellipsis of subject and operator**

This type of initial ellipsis can occur at the beginning of a declarative or an interrogative clause.

Declarative clauses:

> A: *I love French beaches.*
> B: *Yeah* <–> *telling me.* (BrE) <*You're* is omitted>

> A: *Do you want me go hire a video camera while I'm at it?*
> B: *Yeah* <–> *be great.* (BrE) <*That/it would* is omitted>

Interrogative clauses:

> <–> *Know what I mean?* <*Do you* omitted>

> *Why aren't you working?* <–> *Got a day off?* <*Have you* omitted>

**14.3.5.2   Initial ellipsis**

**CORPUS FINDINGS**

> ➤  There is more initial ellipsis of all types in BrE than AmE.
> ➤  These types are shown in Table 14.11 in order of frequency.

**DISCUSSION OF FINDINGS**

The findings here have to be treated with caution, since it is possible that transcribers varied in the extent to which they were sensitive to the observing and recording of these omissions. But the evidence strongly suggests that BrE speakers are more inclined to use initial (situational) ellipsis than AmE speakers.

**Table 14.11**  **Frequency of initial ellipsis in AmE and BrE conversation; occurrences per million words**

each ▮ represents 1000     □ represents less than 1000

| ellipsis of | AmE | BrE | overall |
|---|---|---|---|
| subject | ▮ | ▮▮▮ | ▮▮ |
| subject + operator [20] | □ | ▮ | ▮ |
| auxiliary | □ | □ | □ |
| part of noun phrase | □ | □ | □ |

One example of this trend is the occurrence of *Depends* ... (with ellipsis) as contrasted with *It depends* .... In the BrE conversational subcorpus, almost 60 per cent of these constructions had ellipsis of the subject, compared to only about 30 per cent with ellipsis in the AmE subcorpus. This also shows, perhaps surprisingly, that there are contexts in BrE where the occurrence of subject ellipsis in declarative clauses is more common than the occurrence of an overt subject.

### 14.3.5.3   Final (post-operator) ellipsis

Final ellipsis in a clause usually takes the form of the omission of any words following the operator: i.e. the finite auxiliary or copula.

> A: *I suppose Kathy is still living in that same place.*
> B: *Yeah, she is <–>.* (AmE) *<living in that same place* omitted>
> A: *Do you have a couple of dollars in cash?*
> B: *Uh, no I don't <–>.* (AmE) *<have a couple of dollars* ... omitted>
> A: *But, can't they treat it in this country?*
> B: *Yeah, they probably can <–>.* (BrE) *<treat it in this country* omitted>
> A: *Who's coming tomorrow Vicki?*
> B: *Di <'s coming* omitted>
> A: *Is she <–>? Is Di coming? No I don't think so. <coming* omitted>
> B: *Nanny.*
> A: *No, nanny's not <–>.* (BrE) *<coming* omitted>

Most examples of final ellipsis are in replies to questions. However, the last example illustrates a different pattern: where a speaker expresses agreement or disagreement with a preceding assertion. Three other variants of final ellipsis are shown in the following example:

> A1: *I'm not going out with her at the moment.*
> B1: *Ah!*
> A2: **But I should be** *<–> by around Tuesday night. <going out with her* is omitted>
> B2: *You said by Monday last time.*
> A3: **Did I** *<–>? Well I lied. <say by Monday last time* is omitted>
> B3: *Yeah, **you did** <–>.* (BrE †) *<say by Monday last time* is omitted>

The first case of ellipsis, in turn *A2*, is superficially medial rather than final ellipsis. However, it contains the omission of the main verb and complement, which is the key characteristic of final ellipsis (an optional adverbial is retained). Such examples are treated as variants of final ellipsis. The second example is in turn *A3*, in a question responding to the interlocutors's statement, and asking for verification. The third example (turn *B3*) provides that verification, in the form of an assertion. This extract illustrates further the density of ellipsis that can arise in dialogue, because of the repeated carrying over of contextually understood content from one turn to the next.

In the main, the evidence is that AmE conversation is less prone to the use of final ellipsis than BrE conversation (see Table 14.12 on p. 1108).

There are other kinds of final ellipsis, such as ellipsis after an infinitive *to* and after a *wh*-word:

> A: *Oh dear! – Take me home!*
> B: ***I'd love to*** <–>. (BrE) <*take you home* omitted>
> A: *Yeah, I think stealing is the biggest thing.*
> B: *Cos that's what Jeff's* <unclear> *was doing. Either that or drugs. I'm not sure **which*** <–>. (AmE) <*is the biggest thing* (?) omitted>
> *But she completely lost it. I and I still don't really know **why or how*** <–>. (AmE) <*she lost it* omitted>

Compare also 14.3.4.1 and 14.3.4.2C on elliptic direct questions such as *Why?*.

## 14.3.5.4  Medial (operator) ellipsis

Medial ellipsis occurs where the operator (i.e. the finite auxiliary or copula) is omitted: e.g. *You better* (instead of *You'd better*); *I gotta go* (instead of *I've gotta go*). It is particularly common in the semi-modals *had better*, *have got to* (often transcribed with the spelling *gotta*) and *be going to* (often rendered *gonna*), and is probably a sign of the continuing grammaticalization of these constructions (14.1.2.9).

> *Oh. Nobody would marry you. You're, **you*** <–> ***better** keep the one you've got* <laugh>. *You're in the same boat as I am sir.* (AmE)
> *Yeah dude, **I*** <–> ***gotta** start working.* (AmE)
> *Uh huh Kayla Ann Marie* <name> *and **we*** <–> ***gonna** call it Kam* (AmE)

The formulaic AmE greeting *How are you doing* (often spelt *How ya doing*) is another more or less conventionalized context favouring medial ellipsis:

> ***How*** <–> ***ya** doing Ms.* <name>*?* (AmE)

Apart from its somewhat limited occurrence in declarative clauses, medial auxiliary verb ellipsis occurs in *wh*-interrogatives, between the question word and the subject:

> *What* <–> *she say?* (AmE)
> *When* <–> *you coming back?* (AmE)
> *When* <–> *you gonna do that then?* (BrE)
> *When* <–> *you doing the shop like, next week?* (BrE)
> *How* <–> *we doing Kevin?* (BrE)

This omission of this pivotal element of clause structure is on the borderline between the grammatical omission process of ellipsis and the phonological omission process known as **elision**. Unlike initial and final ellipsis, it does not rely on contextually retrieved information. In any case, it shows a trend evident from the transcriptions, particularly in AmE, and in the casual style of speech used among younger speakers. Unlike initial and final ellipsis, it is somewhat more common in AmE than in BrE speech.

**14.3.5.5** **Distribution of initial, medial, and end ellipsis**

Table 14.12 **Initial, end, and medial ellipsis in AmE and BrE; occurrences per million words[21]**

each ▌ represents 1000    ▯ represents less than 1000

|                  | AmE | BrE   | overall |
|------------------|-----|-------|---------|
| initial ellipsis | ▌▌  | ▌▌▌▌▌ | ▌▌▌     |
| medial ellipsis  | ▌   | ▯     | ▌       |
| final ellipsis   | ▌▌  | ▌▌▌▌  | ▌▌▌     |

➤ Initial ellipsis is somewhat more frequent than final ellipsis, which in turn is more frequent than medial ellipsis.
➤ This tendency is more marked in BrE than in AmE.
➤ In general, BrE conversation contains more clause-level ellipsis than AmE conversation.

Provided the findings do not simply represent a more 'reconstructive' attitude on the part of the transcribers of the American data, it appears that AmE conversation adheres closer to the norms of written grammar in respect of most kinds of ellipsis. This contrasts with the popular view of AmE speakers as more laid-back than.BrE speakers.

# 14.4 Selected topics in conversational grammar

Inevitably this chapter cannot cover all significant areas of interest in the grammar of conversation. In this final section of the chapter we examine five areas of specific interest which have not been dealt with in depth elsewhere, and which relate to the social, interactive functions of conversation: vocatives, conducive questions, first person imperatives, direct speech reporting, and vernacular grammar.

## 14.4.1 A closer look at vocatives

Vocatives are important in defining and maintaining social relationships between participants in conversation. The following categories represent an approximate scale from the most familiar or intimate relationship to the most distant and respectful one.

A  Endearments: e.g. *baby, (my) darling, (my) dear, honey, hon, love, sweetie (pie)*

   1  *Is that you **darling** come here **sweetie pie**.* (AmE)

   2  ***Honey**, can I use that ashtray please?* (AmE)

   3  *Ah, daddy what on earth did you let him do that for **dear**?* (BrE)

B  Family terms: e.g. *mummy, mum, mommy, mom, ma, daddy, dad, pop, pa, da, grandma, granddad, grandpa, granny)*

4 *Thanks* **Mom** *– okay – talk to you later – see you soon – bye.* (AmE)
<on the telephone>

5 *I said no, no come on* **Grandpa**, *I'm not tired.* (AmE)

6 *Anyway she's shouting away,* **Dad dad dad**. *So I says, what?* (BrE)

7 **Mum**, *have you ever seen a duck with a bow-tie on?* (BrE)

C Familiarizers: e.g. *guys, bud, man, dude, buddy, mate, folks, bro.* All these forms are chiefly AmE, except *mate*, which is BrE.

8 *Hey,* **man**. *I'll make this real short. What's happening,* **man**? (AmE)

9 *It's time to light the candles* **guys**. (AmE)

10 *Got a ticket* **mate**? (BrE)

11 *Howdy* **folks**! *Whatcha doing John?* (AmE)

D Familiarized first names (shortened and/or with the pet suffix *-y/-ie*): e.g. *Marj, Paulie, Jackie, Tom*

12 *Hey,* **Mike**, *grab your dominoes!* (AmE)

13 *What I'm gonna do* **Jenny** *is I'm going to switch to this other printer.*
(AmE†)

14 *Look here* **Paulie**, *you come and have a look at this.* (BrE)

15 **Chris, Chris**, *if you hate the guy just say fuck off.* (BrE)

E First names in full: e.g. *Marjorie, Paul, Jennifer, Thomas*

16 *Huh, you get to do this next year,* **Jason**. (AmE)

17 *A: Morning* **Diane**.
*B: Hi,* **Joyce**, *how are you?* (AmE)

18 *Just come round this way* **Muhammad**. (BrE)

F Title and surname: e.g. *Mrs Johns, Mr Graham, Ms Morrissey.*

In the AmE conversational Corpus data, surnames have often been deleted for reasons of confidentiality, and replaced by the empty tag <name>.

19 *How ya doing* **Ms.** <name>? (AmE)

20 *Hello* **Dr. Denton**. *How do you do?* (AmE)

21 *I'll let you know as soon as I know. Alright* **Mr Jones**? *Thanks. Bye.*
(BrE)

G Honorifics: e.g. *sir, madam*

22 CUSTOMER: **Madam**! **Madam**! *May we have two glasses of water please? Thank you.* (BrE) <from a restaurant meal>
CUSTOMER: *Tell me what you've got here will you?*
WAITER: *Okay yes* **sir**. *Stuffed mushrooms.* (BrE) <from a restaurant meal>

23 *Oh. Nobody would marry you. You're, you better keep the one you've got* <laugh>. *You're in the same boat as I am* **sir**. (AmE)

H Others (including nicknames): e.g. *boy, red dog, lazy!, everyone, you, Uncle Joe.*

24 *Hello* **lazy**! (BrE)

25 *Oh, make your bloody mind up* **boy**! (BrE)

26 *Hi,* **Aunt Margaret**? (AmE)

27 *Come on* **you reds**, *come on* **you reds**, *come on* **you reds** *–* (BrE)

Group H covers a wide range of nominal structures which can act as vocatives, including some quite complex noun phrases:

> **28** ***Those of you who want to bring your pets along,*** *please sit in the back of the space ship.* (BrE)

On closer examination, it is clear that there are other distinguishing factors among these types in addition to differences of familiarity. One difference, for example, is that **familiarizers** and **honorifics** do not require knowledge of the name of the person, or cognizance of that person as an individual. Unlike most of the other categories, they can be used in addressing strangers (however, familiarizers like *buddy* (AmE) and *mate* (BrE) may not be welcome to the addressee in this case). Familiarizers are the opposite of honorifics, in that they mark the relationship between speaker and addressee as a familiar one (often a friendly relationship between equals) rather than a more distant and respectful one.

However, in general vocatives maintain and reinforce an existing relationship. Endearments clearly have a special role in this respect, usually marking a bond of closeness and affection between close family members, sexual partners, and other 'favourite' people. Also obviously special in marking close relationships are kin terms such as *mum* (BrE) or *mom* (AmE) and *dad*. Kin terms are almost always used to address more senior family members (parents, grandparents, etc.) rather than those of the same or lower generation. They are also generally **hypocoristic** ('pet') forms, rather than regular common nouns such as *mother* and *father*.

Since **first-name terms** are normal nowadays between not only friends but colleagues and even casual acquaintances, first-name vocatives also have an important social role in showing the recognition of individuality among participants in conversation. Often a familiarizing form—either a short form such as *Chris* (for *Christine* or *Christopher*) or a hypocoristic form in *-y/-ie* such as *Chrissy* or *Hughie*—is preferred as the main option of personal address. In contrast, the title + surname option is increasingly relegated to marking a more distant and respectful relationship towards an acquaintance.

Type G above, 'honorifics', is an uncommon category: the relationship of respect towards an addressee is rarely marked by such vocatives in present-day English, as contrasted with many other languages. There are exceptional cases: for example in formal service encounters, as in our restaurant examples in **22** above. Here a curious feature is that the respect vocative is not only used by the waiter to the customer, but by the customer to the waiter—perhaps a new development in the democratic avoidance of asymmetry in personal relations. It is also significant, as seen in example **23** above, that honorifics are often used in conversation jokingly, rather than as a serious mark of respect.

The final category 'H. Others' is a miscellany of varied types of vocative which are too rare to merit a category in themselves. They include some disparaging or belittling forms of address, such as *lazy* or *boy*; but these vocatives are distinguished from insulting exclamations such as *you bastard* and *you silly sod* (14.3.4.2G). Interestingly, both types of noun phrase can occur in the same utterance, with the vocative modifying the insult—a juxtaposition which highlights their different functions:

> *You bastard, Peter!* (BrE)

Occupational or status vocatives, such as *doctor, nurse, Mr President, soldier* are extremely rare in normal conversation. Other relatively rare vocatives are the personal pronoun *you* and third person pronouns like *somebody* and *everyone* (4.13.4.1).

## 14.4.1.1 The distribution of vocatives

Here we take further the issue of the position and distribution of vocatives, already touched on in 3.13.4.1.

**CORPUS FINDINGS** [23]

**Table 14.13** **Proportional use of vocative types in a combined sample of AmE and BrE conversation**[22]

each ■ represents c. 5%     □ represents less than 2.5%

| A | endearments | ■ |
|---|---|---|
| B | kinship terms | ■■ |
| C | familiarizers | ■■■ |
| D | first names (shortened or with -*y* (*ie* suffix)) | ■■■■■■ |
| E | first names (in full) | ■■■■■■■ |
| F | titles + surnames | □ |
| G | honorifics (e.g. *madam*, *sir*) | □ |
| H | other | ■ |

➤ First names are used as vocatives much more commonly than the other major vocative categories.

➤ There are also major differences in the preferred positions of vocatives:
  ➤ final c. 70%—where the vocative follows the C-unit to which it is most closely attached, e.g. *Come on*, **Sam**;
  ➤ initial c. 10%—where the vocative precedes the C-unit to which it is most closely attached, e.g. **Mike**, *come on*;
  ➤ stand alone c. 10%—where the vocative is not attached to any other unit, e.g. **Mom!**;
  ➤ medial c. 10%—(a) where the vocative occurs in the middle of a clausal unit or non-clausal unit, e.g. *What have we lost at home*, **Paulie**, *this season?*, or (b) where the vocative occurs between two C-units, and there is no indication of closer attachment to one unit or the other, e.g. *I'm sorry* **Asia** *that's just not my identity*.

➤ The choice among grammatical positions for vocatives is strongly influenced by the length of the C-unit to which it is attached:

**Table 14.14** **Proportional use of initial v. final vocatives, as a function of length of the associated C-unit**[23]

each ■ represents c. 5%     □ represents less than 2.5%

| position | length of the unit (in words) containing a vocative | | | | |
|---|---|---|---|---|---|
| | 1–3 | 4–6 | 7–9 | 10–12 | 13– |
| initial | ■ | ■ | ■ | □ | □ |
| final | ■■■■■■■■■ | ■■■■■ | ■■ | ■ | □ |

## DISCUSSION OF FINDINGS

The most significant fact to emerge from Table 14.13 is that first-name address predominates: Types D and E amount to c. 60 per cent of all vocatives used, with a roughly equal split between familiarized first names (Type D) and full, unshortened first names (Type E). In any case, the distinction between Types D and E is of doubtful significance nowadays, because many short forms are being treated as 'standard' names in their own right—a trend which in itself illustrates the progressive familiarization of naming habits in the English-speaking world. Of the other categories, those which have a familiarizing effect (Types A–C) are more than twice as frequent as those which have a distancing or deferential function (Types F–G). Hence the overall picture emerges of a norm of first-name address, with vocatives being used vastly more as markers of familiarity than as markers of respect.

Vocatives occurring in **final** position are much more common than those in **initial** position. In addition, there is a noticeable difference between the lengths of units associated with a final vocative and an initial vocative. Initial vocatives tend to be associated with longer units, whereas final vocatives are associated with shorter units.

Why is a final position chosen in some instances, and an initial position in others? Three functions of vocatives should be distinguished:

(1) getting someone's attention
(2) identifying someone as an addressee
(3) maintaining and reinforcing social relationships.

The suggestion is that an initial vocative combines (1) an attention-getting function with (2) the function of singling out the appropriate addressee(s). On the other hand, a final vocative is more likely to combine function (2) with function (3), that of adjusting or reinforcing the social relationship between the speaker and the addressee. Familiarizing vocatives, including use of first-name terms, typically signal a relationship of acquaintance or friendship. Failure to use first-name address may signal a number of things, not least that the speaker has forgotten the addressee's name! Familiarizers, too, are used recurrently for the maintenance of relationships, as is suggested in the following extended examples:

1 *A: Good morning* **Ben.** *You're on your own for two weeks.*
  *B: Yeah, can you believe that* **man.** *How do you get out of that?*
  *C: So what's up* **Ben?** *There's no hot water at my house. I'm going nuts.*
  *A: <unclear>*
  *B: Did they? Oh my gosh. <laugh> Good morning* **Betty.** *Good morning*
     **Mr** *<name>*
  *D: Hey* **Ben** *how are you?* (AmE)

2 *From Dusk till Dawn, yeah. That one* **dude,** *it was nuts.* **Dude** *there*
  *was so many vampires every, I've never seen that many scary people in*
  *like the special effects. It was like, it was crazy* **dude.** *It was a crazy*
  *movie. Have you seen it? Have you heard about it?* (AmE) *<discussing a*
  *movie>*

On the other hand, vocatives are not used among close associates where neither their addressee-identifying role nor their relationship-maintenance role is felt to be necessary—often, presumably, because the participants in a conversation are totally sure of their mutual relationship. In the samples analysed, there are long conversations where no vocatives occur (e.g. in discussion between mother and daughter, or between wife and husband); and there are other conversations—especially multi-party dialogues—where vocatives are extremely frequent.

Certain of these vocative functions are more or less likely to be associated with units of differing lengths. For example, an initial vocative can serve as an attention-getter and can also have the function of clearing space for a lengthy turn. The final vocative, on the other hand, is more likely to occur after a short remark, where attracting attention is not a problem, and where the social role of the vocative can combine with that of singling out the addressee. Many vocatives occur after a single-word insert, which may itself be a preface to a lengthier unit—see **4, 8, 11, 12, 17, 20, 24** and **26** in 14.4.1. In such cases, the period of less than a second between the beginning of the utterance and the use of the vocative means that the addressee-identifying function can still be prominent—supremely so in the case of the attention-getter *Hey*, as in example **12** in 14.4.1, repeated here:

> **12** *Hey,* **Mike,** *grab your dominoes!* (AmE)

The final vocative is somewhat more frequent in AmE conversation than in BrE. This suggests that the function of reinforcing the relationship (especially its familiarizing function) through use of vocatives is stronger among AmE speakers than among BrE speakers. More research is needed on this.

## 14.4.2 Conducive *yes-no* interrogatives

**Conducive questions** are *yes-no* questions which have a built-in bias towards one answer rather than another. Certain question types discussed in 3.13.2 have this element of bias: question tags, which typically seek confirmation of the speaker's point of view (3.13.2.4), are the most frequent category of such questions in conversation. Other types are rhetorical questions (3.13.2.1) and questions in declarative form (3.13.1). This section, however, addresses itself to two types of conducive question which have interesting functions in conversation: those which contain a negative word (normally the **negative** particle *not* or *-n't*) and those which contain an **assertive** word belonging to the series *some, somebody, someone, sometime(s), something, somewhere, already* (as contrasted with the non-assertive forms *anybody, anyone, ever, anything, anywhere, yet*).[24]

Negative interrogative:

> **Won't** *you come back?* (AmE)

Assertive interrogative:

> *Do you want* **some** *food?* (AmE)

Both these question types have the normal form of a *yes-no* question with inversion, but contrast with another form of interrogative, which is regarded as more neutral. Thus the negative interrogative above contrasts with *Will you come back* (the same question without negation) and the assertive interrogative above contrasts with *Do you want any food* (the same question with a non-assertive form *any* substituted for *some*).

Since the majority of questions have neither assertive nor non-assertive forms, these two categories have to be considered independently. There is also the possibility of the positive/negative distinction intersecting with the assertive/non-assertive distinction, as in:

Negative assertive:

> *Oh can't you / can't you leave **some** of it until tomorrow morning?* (BrE)
>
> *And didn't they move up north **someplace**?* (AmE)

Negative non-assertive:

> *Aren't you wearing **any**?* (AmE) <referring to underwear>

However, these combined types are rare and are ignored in the following discussion.

It is also possible for more than one assertive or non-assertive form to occur in the same question:

> *Have you done **any** downhill skiing **yet**, Willy?* (AmE)
>
> *Was **someone** growing **something**?* (AmE)

## 14.4.2.1 Negative *yes-no* interrogatives

In spite of their grammatical form, positive and negative interrogatives do not bias a question respectively towards a positive and negative answer. Positive interrogatives, in fact, are the neutral 'open-minded' kind of interrogatives which are not biased either positively or negatively. Negative interrogatives have a more complex effect: they challenge a negative expectation that has been assumed to exist in the context, and thus indicate the speaker's inclination towards a positive answer. Consider these examples:

1   *A: One's Peter's and one's ours. Yet get a* <unclear>
    *B: **Can't** I take them both?* <talking apparently of keys> (BrE)

2   PARENT: *Say thank you to granddad.*
    GRANDDAD: ***Don't** I get a kiss for them sweeties?* (BrE)

3   *A: Don't mention her name please.*
    *B: Why? **Don't** you like her?* (BrE)

In **1**, *A*'s utterance indicates that one key should be assigned to each person. *B*'s negative question challenges this, indicating a preference for taking both keys. In **2**, the scene is obviously one where Granddad has given sweets (candy) to his grandchild, and is soliciting his reward. The child's behaviour suggests that no kiss is forthcoming; Granddad's negative question challenges this disappointing outcome. In **3**, *A*'s turn implies displeasure at the unnamed woman referred to; *B*'s negative question indicates surprise at this implication: its force is 'I would have expected you to like her; now it appears you don't.' Negative questions disown a negative expectation and embrace a positive one.

## 14.4.2.2 Negative v. positive *yes-no* interrogatives

**CORPUS FINDINGS**

To compare the use of positive and negative questions, we analysed the frequency of questions beginning with a selection of operators (*can, am/is/are, does/do, had*) followed by personal pronouns, compared with their negative counterparts *can't, isn't/aren't, doesn't/don't* and *hadn't*.[25]

**Table 14.15 Proportional use of negative *yes-no* v. positive *yes-no* interrogatives**

each ● represents c. 5% of all *yes-no* interrogatives

|  | negative interrogatives | positive interrogatives |
|---|---|---|
| AmE | ● | ●●●●●●●●●●●●●●●●●●●● |
| BrE | ●● | ●●●●●●●●●●●●●●●●●● |

### DISCUSSION OF FINDINGS

The finding that negative *yes-no* interrogatives are much less frequent than their positive counterparts is predictable, considering that they tend to presuppose a more constrained situation. For example, the question:

> *Will you be home on Sunday morning?* (AmE)

is a straightforward request for information, whereas:

> *Won't you be home on Sunday morning?*

evokes a more specific context (e.g. a sudden change of travelling plans) in which the speaker had expected the hearer to be home on Sunday morning, and then discovered that the contrary was being assumed.

## 14.4.2.3  Assertive *yes-no* questions

Assertive questions, as their name suggests, have a bias towards an underlying positive proposition, in which an assertive form such as *somebody* or *already* would appear:

> *So have you **already** turned in the application?* (AmE)
>
> *Have we **already** gotten your contract?* (AmE)

Here the assertive word is the adverb *already*, and its use (rather than the non-assertive form *yet*) suggests that the speaker is already inclined to assume the truth of the assertions 'You have already turned in the application' and 'We have already gotten your contract'. If *yet* had been used, as in:

> *Have we gotten your contract **yet**?*

the question would have been more open to either a 'yes' or 'no' answer; in fact, some bias towards 'no' might be suspected.

> *Ever* is a non-assertive adverb which commonly occurs in questions referring to the past. It has no assertive counterpart: although in principle the adverb *sometime* or *sometimes* could replace it, in practice this hardly ever occurs:

> *Have you **ever** seen that commercial for Showtime on Saturday night?* (AmE)
>
> *?Have you **sometimes** seen that commercial for Showtime on Saturday night?*

## 14.4.2.4  Assertive v. non-assertive *yes-no* questions

### CORPUS FINDINGS

➤ With *some* and words beginning with *some* (*someone*, *something*, etc.) the choice between *some-* and *any-*forms is more or less even.

> ➤ In fact, in AmE there is a slight preference for *some-*forms (c. 52% of all forms).
>
> ➤ In BrE there is a stronger preference for *any-*forms (c. 60% of all forms).

➤ In contrast, both AmE and BrE strongly favour interrogatives with *yet* over interrogatives with *already*.

**DISCUSSION OF FINDINGS**

The relative frequency of these interrogatives depends a great deal on the specific assertive and non-assertive forms concerned. Disregarding *already* and *yet*, the relatively high frequency of *some*-forms (*some*, *somebody* etc.) v. *any*-forms (*any*, *anybody*, etc.) is due to two special kinds of use of these assertive questions.

## A Offers, invitations, etc.

A large proportion of *some*-questions tend to occur as **commissive** speech acts such as offers and invitations:

> *Do you want **some** bread and butter with jam Charlotte?* (BrE)
>
> *Liam do you want **some** dinner?* (BrE)
>
> *Would you like **some** tea or **some**, **something**?* (AmE)
>
> *Can I take **some** things in for you?* (AmE)
>
> *Want **some** more tea Dave?* (BrE)
>
> *Is there **something** else we can show you?* (AmE)

In all these the speaker is offering something for the (assumed) benefit of the hearer, and the use of the assertive form can be explained as a politeness strategy to encourage acceptance. By using *some*, the speaker is politely anticipating a 'yes' answer.

In other cases the assumption of a 'yes' answer is less obviously motivated, although it makes sense in context:

> 1 *Should we go down and get **something** to eat?* (AmE)
>
> 2 *Did you guys want to order **something** to drink?* (AmE)
>
> 3 *Does **somebody** have a question on that?* (AmE)

Although not offers, these questions make suggestions for future action, where the speaker can be expected to encourage a positive outcome. Other examples are requests:

> 4 *Could **someone** dictate this to me?* (AmE)
>
> 5 *Can I borrow **some** tape?* (AmE)
>
> 6 *Can I have **some** beans now?* (BrE)

In **5** and **6**, the future action is to the benefit of the speaker, and the assertive request suggests that the speaker regards the action as possible, and is in fact making a bid for that positive outcome. Contrast **4** with *Could anyone dictate this to me?*, which suggests that the speaker doubts whether anyone could perform the task.

## B The *or something* construction

The second special case favouring *some*-words in assertive interrogatives is the use of the coordination tag (2.9.2) *or something*, which makes the question more imprecise, in a 'hand-waving' way that is often convenient in conversation:

> *Were you by the highway **or something**?* (AmE)
>
> *Do you have a, a calculator or **something** we can use?* (AmE)
>
> *Shall we go in there and help find a jigsaw **or something**?* (BrE)

*Or anything* is grammatically possible but scarcely appropriate here.

## 14.4.3 First person imperatives with *let's*

Although *let's* is by origin a second person imperative (= *let us*; 3.13.4),[26] in present-day English conversation it is for practical purposes an invariant pragmatic particle introducing independent clauses in which the speaker makes a proposal for action by the speaker and hearer. In this special sense, it may be described as a marker of a first person plural imperative, in which the 'we' that is the implied subject of the main verb is interpreted as including the hearer: *Let's eat breakfast*; *Let's go honey.*

In meaning, the *let's* construction is quite flexible. Although typically used to propose a joint action by speaker and hearer(s), it sometimes veers towards second person quasi-imperative meaning, in proposing action which is clearly intended to be carried out by the hearer. Note the telltale use of *please*, a clear indicator of directive force, in the following example. This style of crypto-directive (camouflaging an authoritative speech act as a collaborative one) is used especially by adults addressing children. The following is said by a classroom teacher to students:

> *You all have something to do for Ms. <name>?* **Let's** *do it please.* (AmE)

The following examples, all from a single (one-sided) conversation between mother and infant, show the opposite tendency of veering towards first person singular (exclusive) meaning. In effect, the meaning is equivalent to 'Let me ...':

> *Ian, Ian, Ian, it's all right,* **let's** *wash your hands –*
>
> *There we go,* **let's** *wipe your teeth off, come on* **let's** *wipe the front teeth off. Okay, okay,* **let's** *take your bib off <...>* (AmE)

The same tendency, this time by a medical specialist addressing an adult, is shown in:

> **Let's** *have a look at your tongue.* (AmE)

### 14.4.3.1 Common accompaniments of *let's*

*Let's* clauses occur with rather few variations or embellishments. The question tag *shall we* (3.13.2.4D) occurs very rarely (especially in AmE), and other question tags, such as *okay?*, are similarly infrequent:

> *Okay well* **let's** *keep that on* **shall we?** (BrE)
>
> **Let's** *take turns* **okay?** (AmE)

Negatives are also infrequent. Two variants, *let's not* and *don't let's*, occur, but the latter is particularly rare and of doubtful acceptability:

> 1 **Let's not** *talk about her any more, please?* (AmE)
>
> 2 *Oh, well then* **don't let's** *put a five hundred dollar stipend in.* (AmE)

The *let's* construction occurs infrequently with question tags (less than ten per million words in AmE conversation), or with other peripheral elements, such as vocatives (in AmE about ten per million words in final position, and slightly more frequently in initial position; less than this in BrE). The vocatives are sometimes 'familiarizing' in tone (14.4.1): they add a marker of personal relationship to the proposal. Endearments like *honey* or familiarizers like *man* occur as well as personal names. Also jocular nicknames like *chatterboxes* appear:

> *Okay* **chatterboxes,** *let's have it – How was your day then* **love?** (BrE)

One reason for the sparseness of vocatives with *let's* may be that *let's* implies some previously identified addressee(s) sharing in a scenario, so that there is no need for one major function of vocatives: that of singling out the addressee from other possible candidates.

In one regard, the addition of peripheral elements is much more frequent: this is in the occurrence of inserts and other utterance launchers before *let's*. In AmE, the most common utterance launchers are: *well*, *okay*, *yeah* in that order:

> **Well let's** *see what they are playing here at the Cinema.* (AmE)
>
> **Okay**, *so* **let's** *take a left here and see where it goes.* (AmE)
>
> **Yeah let's** *have some ice please.* (AmE)

In BrE, the utterance launchers *come on* and *right* have a higher frequency than *okay* and *yeah*:

> 3 **Come on let's** *get back to the classroom.* (BrE)
>
> 4 **Right**, *let's stop and* **have** *a sandwich,* **shall we?** (BrE)

Among main verbs following *let's*, *see* is by far the most common verb in AmE. In fact, *let's see* has an idiomatic status as an overture (14.3.2.1D); its typical function seems to be that of signalling that the speaker is searching for information, for example trying to retrieve some fact from memory:

> *Um,* **let's see**, *I'll have to give you some more.* (AmE)
>
> **Let's see**. *Are you working now?* (AmE)

In BrE, the main verb *have* is more common than *see*, being used in reference to actions (e.g. *have a look*) in a way which is uncharacteristic of AmE. It can be seen in retrospect that the BrE example **4** has three typically unAmerican features for a *let's* construction, viz. the initial discourse marker *right*, the final question tag *shall we*, and the main verb *have*.

Another important verb, second in frequency in both AmE and BrE conversation, is *go*:

> *Man,* **let's go** *to Yellowstone National Park.* (AmE)
>
> *Come on Dad /* **let's** *go.* (BrE)

Overall, the *let's* construction is more than twice as frequent in AmE than in BrE conversation. There is no obvious explanation for this very substantial difference, but very tentatively we may suggest that AmE speakers are using the construction more flexibly, in a way which emphasizes the egalitarian, cooperative aspects of human relations. *Let's* involves both speakers and addressees in an apparently equal task.

## 14.4.4 Direct speech reporting (quoted speech)

Direct speech reporting (where the speaker gives an apparently verbatim report of what someone said) is an important and recurrent feature of conversation.

### 14.4.4.1 Using utterance-launchers to open quoted speech

Interestingly, the absence of auditory quotation marks seems not to cause an interpretative problem in spoken narration: this is partly because speakers employ a range of devices to show that they are moving into direct speech mode. In the middle of a turn, speakers tend to rely on utterance-openers such as *oh*, *well*, *look* and *okay* to signal that they are embarking on direct speech quotation. In the following examples, we insert quotation marks, for illustrative purposes, at the points where quoted speech is assumed to begin and end:

> *And seeing I haven't got an account with them I don't think they'll say "**well** you can – have some anyway."* (BrE)

> *and, uh, and a teacher comes up to me and she says, "**Oh**, you've got a stain on your pants!"* (AmE)

> *Dagmar said "**Oh**, I sort of sense that a couple of times when I stayed at your parents' house that I didn't feel very welcome" and I said "**Well, see**, I told you."* (AmE)

> *Anyway erm I said to him "**look**. A woman needs a man to support her."* (BrE)

The same phenomenon can be observed with verbs of thinking. Note the use of *hey* to introduce direct speech in the following example:

> *You look at yourself and think "**hey** I didn't have any food today"* (BrE†)

### 14.4.4.2 Repetition of reporting clauses

Another ploy speakers use to clarify the fact that they are reporting quoted speech is the repetition of two or more reporting clauses (*I said* or something similar) in quick succession:

> *Well, **she said** "Three-thirty" and then **she said** "Well, you'd better make it four."* (BrE)

> *So **I told him** the other day, **I said**, "Tony, you can't tell me that I'm too attentive to you."* (AmE†)

> *He, he sat here this morning **he said** all serious **he said** "I'm cutting out potatoes, bread, biscuits and all sweet things."* (BrE)

### 14.4.4.3 Reporting clauses with *go*

A further major point of interest about direct speech quotation is the use of various substitutes for *said* or *says*. The above examples illustrate the use of *say* as the standard expected verb in this construction. On the other hand, the verb *go* is becoming widely used as a speech reporting verb, especially among younger speakers:

> *Yeah, **he went** "Oh!" **He goes**, "Who put that there?" And the bit where **he goes he goes** "Urgh, cobwebs," and **she goes** "Piss off!" **She goes** "Mum, come and sit here," **she goes** "Piss off!" like that and **the mother goes** "You talking to me?"* (BrE)

> *And **I was going**, "Well, I need a lot of help." **She goes**, "Well just get anyone in."* (BrE)

> *Well of course they're losing money, I've left, **she goes** "Oh I never thought about that, you think they'll hold that against us?" **I go** "Well they offered me the position man. You're not very popular down here," **she goes** "But let's go tomorrow" and **she says** "Okay."* (AmE)

As these examples show, *go* as a verb of speech reporting can occur in various forms (*go, goes, went, going*) according to normal variations of tense, person, and aspect. But the predominant form is the third person singular present tense *goes*, used in reporting past speech events. The same choice (*says*) is also very frequent with *say*, suggesting that in reporting previous conversations, speakers like to dramatize the dialogue by the use of the historic present (6.2.1.1).

### 14.4.4.4 Opening quoted speech with *be* + *like, all*

Some conversationalists, commonly younger ones, mark quoted speech using the highly versatile particle *like*, typically preceded by forms of *be*. Less commonly, direct quotation is marked by *all*, typically preceded by a past tense form of *be*, as illustrated by:

> He goes, "Some day I might have a kid and <laugh>." *I'm **like*** "No!" (AmE)
>
> Okay cool well anyway my mom**'s *like*** "I was thinking of getting them something from Hickory farms" <laugh> *I **was all*** "Mom!" (AmE)
>
> And I'm like, "You were there, why didn't you help" <unclear>. He **was all** "Well I wanted to stay out of it." (AmE)

Notice the switch between present tense and past tense in the reporting clauses of the last two examples. The transition between historic present and narrative past is apparently made in speech with great ease, and with little regard for consistency in sequence of tenses.

### 14.4.4.5 The past progressive with reporting verbs

Although the non-progressive form of the reporting verb (e.g. *says, said*) is normal in reporting quoted speech, there is a special 'evidential' function of the past progressive (e.g. *was/were saying*) in conversation, as illustrated in the examples below. The non-progressive or simple aspect is used for dramatically reporting the words of a speaker in narrative, as has already been amply exemplified 14.4.4.1–4. The emphasis with simple aspect falls on the act of speaking, rather than on the nature of what was said. With the past progressive, on the other hand, the focus tends to be on the reported message itself, e.g. the degree of authority it carries for the reporting speaker, and the evidence it provides:

> but Yvonne **was saying** on my wages I wouldn't get a mortgage! (BrE)
>
> Now I don't know what they were worth and she **was saying** – they must have been worth quite a bit cos they're big detached solid houses aren't they? (BrE)

(The distinction between direct and indirect speech reporting is blurred with structures of this type, and so quotation marks are not used in the examples of this section.)

The past progressive is frequently used with the subject *I*, where naturally the speaker vouches for the authority of her own message:

> I **was** just **saying** to Yvonne er I'm rapidly running out of my physio allowance (BrE)
>
> I **was saying** to dad in bed last night Karen's twenty-three this year (BrE)

As the following examples show, the past progressive is also associated with indirect speech reporting, as opposed to the direct quotation typically associated with *said*:

> I had a little chat with an old man today about his flowers – So he smiled at me. Yeah, so he was cutting his like flowers off, so I **said** oh they're really nice. He **was telling** me that they'd died of the frost or something. (BrE)

> *Cos I **was telling** her that you bought one she **said** oh why didn't you tell her, she could have had mine.* (BrE)

One implication of the non-progressive is that the speech event took place at a specific time, often in a sequence of narrative events:

> *He **said** may I speak to Ellen, I **said** just a minute, I **said**, he **said** this is Matt and I **said** / Oh, just a minute* (AmE†)

In contrast, there in no such implication with the past progressive, which may refer somewhat vaguely to a recent time in the past, and also may give the general gist of what was said, rather than a word-by-word account:

> *Because you **were telling** me about that on the phone the other day.* (AmE)

> *This morning I **was asking**, um, Rita and Carol about Randy and his, his AWOL status and what they were doing.* (AmE)

> *and I **was** just **talking** to her downstairs and **was asking** her like the differences between here and the States, you know the boar– cos she was in a boarding school before, and she **was saying** erm how you know just generally the people are nicer and the blokes talk to you –* (BrE†)

> *and, uh, Mary **was** like **saying**, yeah, let's be friends and stuff and then like five minutes later she won't talk to him, you know?—Okay, when we're in private we can be friends, but you know when we're not, and I **was telling** Jacob it's the same thing Ed does to me – Ed's like yeah, / let's be friends* (AmE)

## 14.4.5    Vernacular or non-standard grammar

The term **vernacular**, referring to the popular, untaught variety of a language found in colloquial speech, will serve to cover a range of phenomena in popular speech which may to a greater or lesser extent be felt to lack prestige and to be inappropriate for serious public communication, especially written communication. Similarly, it is often felt that such forms of language are signs of 'ill-educated' usage and should not act as a model for foreign learners of the language. On the other hand, vernacular features of grammar can be highly prized because of their role in establishing and maintaining social solidarity among the speakers in selected groups, and in bringing vigour and colour into speech style. This is especially true of ethnic and regional dialect forms. Some vernacular features are wide-ranging, being found, for example, on both sides of the Atlantic. Others are restricted to certain regional dialects.

The terms **vernacular** and **non-standard** can be used more or less interchangeably, except that 'non-standard' is more negative and perhaps misleading in suggesting a clear-cut dichotomy between two varieties of language: one which matches up to the 'standard' and one which does not. The notion of 'standard English' is, in fact, itself problematic in talking of the spoken language. In practice, there is a continuous range of acceptability. At one extreme we find widely used and widely accepted colloquialisms like *aren't I* (3.8.2.6) and *they* as a gender-neutral pronoun (4.10.1.3); at the opposite extreme there are stigmatized forms, such as the multiple negation of *She ain't never given me no problems* (3.8.7.1).

In this final section, we survey and illustrate the main vernacular features of conversation with examples from AmE and BrE conversation. (The treatment is not exhaustive; in particular, we ignore here forms such as gender-neutral *they*, and *who* as object, which are widely accepted in speech, and may be regarded as habitual features of spoken English.) The phenomena described below are:

A **Morphophonemic features** e.g. *me* /mɪ/ as a variant of *my*. This shows up in our data simply at the level of spelling, reflecting a different pronunciation from the standard one. It is marginal to grammar.

B **Morphological features** e.g. *yous* as a plural second person pronoun, instead of the standard form *you*. Another example is the use of *throwed* rather than *threw* as the past tense of *throw*. Morphological features also show up as spellings not found in the standard language. However, they are characterized on the level of morphology (rather than phonetics/phonology).

C **Morphosyntactic features** e.g. the use of the base form of the verb *give* as a past tense. There is no spelling evidence here: rather, two or more morphological forms which exist in standard English have a distribution different from that in the standard language: *she give* etc.

D **Syntactic features** e.g. multiple negation—*I don't want no more chips*. In this case, the rule which differs from standard English can be stated in purely syntactic terms. That is, after *not*, one of the negative series *no*, *nobody*, *nothing*, *never*, etc. substitutes for one of the non-assertive series *any*, *anybody*, *anything*, *ever*, etc. (cf. 14.4.2).[27]

## 14.4.5.1 Morphophonemic variants

A brief illustration of these will suffice:

1 The reduced pronoun **me** /mɪ/ instead of **my** /maɪ/:
   *That's what **me** Mum always said <...>* (BrE)

2 The reduced pronoun **'em** /əm/ instead of **them**:
   *Ah but you won't see **'em**. But they're there.* (BrE)

3 The reduced pronoun /jə/ (sometimes spelt **ya**) instead of **you**:
   *Nice seeing **ya**.* (AmE)

Another morphophonemic feature, usually not represented in the transcriptions, is /ɪn/ (spelt *in'*) as a pronunciation of the *-ing* verb suffix.

## 14.4.5.2 Morphological variants

A *Ain't* is a common negative contraction, with a range of pronunciations including /ɛnt/, /ɪnt/, /ɛn/. It corresponds to the standard informal contractions *isn't*, *aren't*, *hasn't*, *haven't*, *'m not* (3.8.2):

   *He's left now, **ain't** he?* (BrE) <= *isn't*>
   *They probably **ain't** at home.* (AmE) <= *aren't*>
   *Morgan **ain't** got no food.* (AmE) <= *hasn't*>
   ***Ain't** you lot ever heard of tea bags?* (BrE) <= *haven't*>
   *I **ain't** gonna get my bonus anyway.* (AmE) <= *'m not*>

B *Innit* (3.13.2.4B) commonly occurs as the spelling of a reduced question tag /ɪnɪt/ in BrE. It is a reduced form of *isn't it*, and may also be regarded as a further reduction of *ain't it*:

   *That's alright then, **innit**?* (BrE)

There is a tendency for *innit?* to be generalized to other contexts, apart from those where *isn't it* would be appropriate, and therefore to develop a role as a universal question tag, along the lines of *huh?* or *eh?* (14.3.3.5):

> *Teachers are very unfair in this school **innit?*** (BrE)

**C** Second person plural personal pronoun forms *y'all* (also spelt *you all*) and *yous* have currency in particular dialect areas (4.10.1.2):

> *For once in your lives can **yous** not be nice in this house* (BrE; especially Northern Ireland)

> *Come back up here, right now. All of **yous**.* (AmE; especially north-east)

> *Okay, I think that got it, well thank **y'all**, **y'all** have a nice day.* (AmE; especially southern states)

> There is no issue of prestige here: *y'all*, in particular, tends to be held in high regard by speakers of southern AmE.

**D** Irregular past tense forms of regular verbs, or regularized past tense forms of irregular verbs (5.2.6):

> *My brother **drug** me out to run* (AmE) <cf. standard *dragged*>

## 14.4.5.3   Morphosyntactic variants

Irregular verbs are one area in which there are many vernacular variants. However, morphological spelling and pronunciation variants which are non-standard, such as *throwed*, *blowed*, and *writ*, rarely occur in adult speech. Instead, forms which occur in standard English are employed for different syntactic and semantic functions. This places them under the **morphosyntactic** heading.

**A** The *-s* form of the verb is used with plural, first person and second person subjects. The combination *I says* (3.9.4) is particularly current:

> ***I says** no, Andrea, you're not adopted.* (AmE)

> *Oh yeah. Whatever they want **they gets**.* (BrE)

In the past tense of *be*, *was* is similarly used instead of *were*:

> *My **legs was** hurting* (BrE)

> *The time **you was** doing that **we was** on the coast just out of Portland at our friend's store.* (AmE)

> *I know last Tuesday when I worked **they was** in bed on time or whatever but **they** still **was** not asleep.* (AmE)

**B** The opposite pattern shows up in the invariant use of the base form of the present tense, where the *-s* form occurs in standard English. The form *don't* instead of *doesn't* is especially current:

> ***He don't** have no manners* (AmE)

> *Well **she don't** know much about him **do she**?* (BrE†)

Also the past plural *were* can be used after a singular subject some areas of the UK. Vacillation between *was* and *were* is common:

> *But it w– it **was** thick, **it were** bloody rank, it **was**.* (BrE)

> *Football **was** good yesterday **weren't it** Data?* (BrE)

**C** With certain common verbs, the past tense form is generalized to the past participle function:

we got a mirror at the back there what was **took** off one the dressing tables (BrE†) <cf. standard *taken*>

They've **froze** his bank account! (BrE) <cf. standard *frozen*>

So that's it. The booze has got **hid**. (BrE) <cf. standard *hidden*>

Oh I've **forgot** someone's hat (BrE) <cf. standard *forgotten*>

**D** With some very common verbs, the converse pattern occurs, with the past participle form being generalized to the past tense function:

I **seen** it before that one. The Marathon Man. (BrE)

You **done** it last year didn't you? (BrE)

**E** A further type of vernacular variant, with irregular verbs, is the generalization of the base form to the past tense:

Well she **give** me that one the other night. (BrE)

I just **come** up here to see uh somebody called Dora. (AmE)

Most of the remaining examples of vernacular morphosyntactic variants concern the noun phrase:

**F** The zero plural of a noun of measurement occurs at the end of a noun phrase after a numerical expression—*two pound*, etc. (4.5.4B):

The most you're spending for that is ten **pound**. (BrE)

They're twelve **foot**, I know that one in the front room is twelve **foot** wide. (BrE)

He got under there, he was about eight **foot**. (AmE†) <talking of an alligator>

He says if he doesn't stop drinking he'll be dead in five **year**. (BrE)

The next three examples of vernacular morphosyntactic variants involve pronouns; the first has been mentioned, with respect to coordination, in 4.10.6.3:

**G** The use of noun phrase constructions in which the accusative personal pronoun is distanced from the finite verb in subject position:

Well **us lot** must walk about half a mile a day you know. (BrE)

**Me and Jody** had a contest for the ugliest pictures. (AmE) <**Jody and I** would normally be considered standard>

**H** *Them* as demonstrative determiner and pronoun, corresponding to standard English *those* (cf. 4.4.3, 4.14):

Did I post all **them** letters on Monday? (BrE)

**Them** on the bottom they're bound to get their feet wet aren't they? (BrE)

**I** The use of *what* as a relative pronoun (see 8.7.1.1):

Gotta make sure she's got the book **what** I had last week. (BrE)

and I was getting some of them **what** must have been a monthly thing. (BrE)

(This last example also shows *them* used as in H above.)

**J** Intrusive *what* introducing a comparative clause (cf. 3.11.4, 7.8):

It's harder than **what** you think it is this (BrE)

Orange flavours that's about as much as **what** we'd ever get in here! (BrE)

Finally, in Type K we have a morphosyntactic variant concerning adverbs and adjectives.

**K** The use of the adjectival form (without -*ly*) in an adverbial role (cf. 7.12.2):

> *Yeah, but then I wanted to go back so* **bad** (AmE†)
>
> *Oh you're* **awful** *warm.* (AmE)
>
> *And the watermelon is very sweet and so maybe, I'll bet it'll sit there* **fine** *until after the ritual and keep* **good**. (AmE)

Such forms are more prevalent and acceptable in AmE. Of course, some cases of adjective-adverb homonymy are part of the standard: e.g. *long, hard*. Other cases are widely accepted and used in AmE speech, such as *real* as a premodifying adverb (e.g. *real good*).

## 14.4.5.4 Syntactic variants

Turning to syntactic variants, we list only two types, which have both been discussed elsewhere.

**A** The multiple negative construction (3.8.7.1), e.g.:

> *Don't say I* **never** *gave you* **nothing**.[28] (AmE)

**B** The double comparative construction (7.7.5):

> *Sometimes, that is so, so much* **more easier** *to follow.* (AmE)

## 14.4.5.5 Conclusion

It is worth noting that vernacular features of grammar are not always used consistently by the same speaker in the same conversation. Even within the same sentence, the choice between standard and non-standard forms can vary:

> *By the way* **you was** *going unh unh dude,* **you were** *setting 'em up.* (AmE)

Morphosyntax is the area where most differences occur between standard and vernacular grammar. Almost all differences involve morphological forms, and most may be traced historically to the tendency for English morphology to be progressively simplified through generalization across different choices in grammatical categories such as person and case. Certain generalizations have been enshrined in standard usage, while others have remained in popular speech only. The two areas of English morphology which contain most irregularity—the personal pronouns and the irregular verbs—also account for most of the vernacular features noted in this final section.

# Contractions

# Appendix: Contractions

There are two major classes of contraction in English: verb contraction (e.g. *she's going*) and *not*-contraction (e.g. *couldn't go*). In addition, there are a large number of structural reductions common in speech but not normally represented in writing (e.g. *Djeet yet?* for *Did you eat yet?*). In this appendix, we briefly survey the structural options for the two major types of contraction found in both spoken and written registers, and then present corpus findings describing their grammatical distributions (see also 3.8.2.5).

## A.1 Verb contraction

Verb contraction occurs with the primary verbs **be** and **have** as well as with the modal verbs *will* and *would*:

**Table A.1: Contracted forms of primary verbs (main verb or auxiliary)**

| | present tense | | | past tense |
|---|---|---|---|---|
| | 1st person | 2nd person + 3rd person plural | 3rd person singular | |
| **be** | am ~ *'m* | are ~ *'re* | is ~ *'s* | |
| **have** | have ~ *'ve* | have ~ *'ve* | has ~ *'s* | had ~ *'d* |
| **modal verbs** | | will ~ *'ll* | would ~ *'d* | |

Past tense forms of **be** (i.e. *was*, *were*) cannot be contracted, probably because they would be easily confused with the present tense forms (*'s* and *'re*). *Have* is rarely contracted when it is a main verb (as in *I've no idea*), while the contraction of third person *has* and past tense *had* when they occur as a main verb is extremely rare.

The contractions *'s* and *'d* are ambiguous (with *'s* representing *is* or *has*, and *'d* representing *had* or *would*). In addition, *'s* has two other uses: representing the object pronoun *us* in the contracted form *let's*, and representing *does* following *wh* question words (e.g. *What's he want?*). Because contracted *has* and *had* are almost always followed by a past participle form (i.e. they function as perfect aspect markers), the intended meaning of these ambiguous forms is usually transparent in context. For example:

> *That's* not true. (CONV) <*That is*>
> *It's* got a sticker on it. (CONV) <*It has*>
> *Let's* see what happens. (CONV) <*Let us*>
> *What's* it matter? (FICT) <*What does*>
> *We'd* been there for like two hours. (CONV) <*We had*>
> No, I don't think *he'd* do it. (CONV) <*he would*>

Verb contraction requires a preceding 'host' in the sentence. In most cases, that host is a pronoun (e.g. *I'm, you'd, she'll, that's*). However, many other forms preceding a primary verb can serve as host, including full nouns, *wh*-words, and *there*:

> *Gerry'll* phone you during the show. (FICT)
> *Where'd* you get that haircut? (FICT)
> *How's* it going? (CONV)
> *There's* no doubt that's going to lead to dumping. (NEWS)
> *Now's* the time to go on a seed hunting expedition in your garden. (NEWS)

If there is no preceding host, as when subject-auxiliary inversion occurs with *yes-no* questions, then there is no possibility of contraction. For example:

> *Is* that on the sea? (FICT)

but not:

> * *'s* that on the sea?

In addition, primary verbs in clause-final position cannot be contracted; for example:

> I don't know what it *is*, so no wonder I can't talk about it. (FICT)

but not:

> * I don't know what it*'s*, ...

Further, when the noun phrase preceding a primary verb contains a postmodifier, it rarely serves as host to contraction. For example, it would be extremely unusual to find the copula *is* contracted in examples like the following:

> [The impression given by the marketing campaign] *is* that you are being invited to invest in a single entity. (NEWS)

## A.2 Negative contraction compared with verb contraction

*Not*-contraction occurs when *not* is reduced and attached to a preceding primary verb (as main verb or auxiliary verb) or modal verb. The resulting negative auxiliary verb is spelled with a final *n't*, as in: *aren't, isn't, haven't, didn't, can't, couldn't*, etc. The *am* form of **be** does not occur with contracted *n't* in standard usage, although the non-standard form *ain't* can be used with this meaning. The modals *will* and *shall* have coalesced forms with *not*-contraction: *won't, shan't*. The form *mayn't* does not occur at all in the LSWE Corpus, except for six examples in older BrE fiction.

Both types of contraction are possible with the primary verbs **be** and **have**, as well as the modal verbs *will* and *would*, when followed by *not*:

| verb contraction | not contraction |
|---|---|
| it's not | it isn't |
| I've not | I haven't |
| you'll not | you won't |
| I'd actually not | I actually wouldn't |

In practice, verb contraction is rarely found with *would* + *not*.

The following tables summarize a series of corpus analyses of the use and distribution of contractions. All tables present the percentage of forms that are contracted (rather than frequency counts). For verb contraction, questions are excluded from the total counts, since the contracted option is not possible in that case.

Table A.2 gives the overall proportional rate of contraction for each verb form in each register. Tables A.3–A.5, then, show the influence of a range of contextual factors in favoring or disfavoring contracted forms. For example, pronoun subjects generally favor the occurrence of contractions, while full noun phrase subjects generally do not. The patterns of use for *be* contraction are given in Table A.3; *have* contraction in Table A.4; and modal contraction in Table A.5.

The remaining tables document the patterns of use for negative contraction. Tables A.6–A.7 focus on *not* contraction, while Tables A.8–A.9 investigate cases where either the verb or *not* could be contracted.

The influence of contextual factors is described relative to the overall rates of contraction found in each register, presented in Table A.2 and Table A.6. For example, *be* is contracted about 50 percent of the time in conversation when it co-occurs with a full noun phrase as subject. Because the overall rate of *be*-contraction in conversation is about 75 percent, this represents a 25 percent lower-than-expected proportional rate (i.e. relative to the theoretical potential of 100 percent contracted). In contrast, *be* is contracted only about 30 percent of the time when it occurs with a pronoun subject in news. However, because the overall rate of *be*-contraction in news is only about 10 percent, we can see that this factor of pronoun subject strongly favors contraction in that register. Similar patterns can be observed for each of the major types of contraction described in the following tables.

(The reported findings for conversation are based on the transcription practices of the corpus transcribers. Certain forms are especially difficult to decipher in speech, such as the difference between *we're* and *we are*. In most cases, though, there is little uncertainty for transcribers in choosing between contracted and non-contracted forms.)

## A.3 Corpus distribution: verb contraction

In general, contractions are strongly associated with the spoken language. As Table A.2 indicates, verb contractions are most likely to occur in conversation, but also occur frequently in written registers with a large admixture of spoken style, such as fiction writing. The common occurrence of contractions in fiction and (to a lesser extent) in news can be largely explained by the direct reporting of spoken discourse in those registers.

Tables A.3–A.5 show how other factors tend to favor the use of contractions. Verb contractions occur predominantly after pronoun subjects, rather than after full noun phrases. They also have a stronger tendency to occur before common verbs such as *give*, *go*, and *get* than before other main verbs.

Contractions of *be* are more strongly associated with the copula and progressive constructions than with the passive (Table A.3). Of these contractions, the contraction of *am* to *'m* after *I* shows the strongest tendency of all, while *are* is comparatively more inclined towards retention of the full form.

**Table A.2: Proportional use of target verb as a contraction**

each ■ represents 5%  □ represents less than 2.5%

| *be* | | |
|---|---|---|
| CONV | ■■■■■■■■■■■■■■■ | (c. 75%) |
| FICT | ■■■■■■■■■ | (c. 45%) |
| NEWS | ■■ | (c. 10%) |
| ACAD | □ | (less than 2%) |

| *have* (for main verb and auxiliary functions combined) | | |
|---|---|---|
| CONV | ■■■■■■■■■■■ | (c. 55%) |
| FICT | ■■ | (c. 10%) |
| NEWS | ■ | (c. 5%) |
| ACAD | □ | (less than 2%) |

| *will/would* | | |
|---|---|---|
| **CONV** | | |
| will | ■■■■■■■■■■■■■■■ | (c. 75%) |
| would | ■■■ | (c. 15%) |
| **FICT** | | |
| will | ■■■■■■■■■■ | (c. 50%) |
| would | ■ | (c. 5%) |
| **NEWS** | | |
| will | ■ | (c. 5%) |
| would | □ | (less than 2%) |
| **ACAD** | | |
| will | □ | (less than 2%) |
| would | □ | (less than 2%) |

As Table A.4 shows, *have* contractions are far more likely to occur with the auxiliary **have** than with the main verb **have**. In addition, there is a particularly strong tendency to contract *have* to *'ve* after *I*, *you* and *we*. The likelihood of contraction after third-person pronouns is lower.

*Will* and *would* are the only two modal auxiliaries which can be contracted. Table A.2 shows that *will* is contracted to *'ll* more frequently than *would* is contracted to *'d*. Table A.5 looks in more detail at the patterns of contraction with *will*. Its contracted form *'ll* shows major distributional tendencies already noted with other verb contractions:

- highest frequency with conversation and next highest with fiction;
- strong predilection for pronoun subjects;
- tendency to occur more readily before common verbs.

## A.4 Corpus distribution: negative contractions

As Table A.6 shows, the overall pattern of register distribution for verb contraction is repeated for negative contraction, in that the order of frequency conversation > fiction > news > academic writing is strongly maintained. The slightly higher proportion of contraction following **do** than the modals is not surprising, given that three negative modals (*mayn't*, *mightn't* and *shan't*) are absent or virtually absent from the conversational LSWE Corpus.

## A.5 Corpus distribution: negative contractions v. verb contractions

In the remaining two tables, we examine the factors which influence the choice between verb contraction and *not* contraction, where the possibility of either is available. It turns out that when the verb is *be*, there is a strong weighting in favor of verb contraction, whereas

**Table A.3: Departure from the register norms for contraction of *be*, depending on contextual factors**

(reporting only the factors that are influential in a register; academic prose is omitted because there are too few tokens of *be*-contraction)
each < or > represents 5% departure from the register norm
< marks proportionally greater use of *be* with FULL FORM
> marks proportionally greater use of *be* CONTRACTION
= marks a pattern of use equal to the register norm

```
              <·············· | ··············>
        greater proportion | greater proportion
          of FULL FORM  |  of be CONTRACTION
     than the register norm | than the register norm
```

**CONV** (norm c.75%)
**form of *be***

| | |
|---|---|
| am | &#124; >>>> |
| is | = |
| are | < &#124; |

**subject noun phrase**

| | |
|---|---|
| pronoun | &#124; >> |
| non-pronominal subject | <<<<< &#124; |

**function of *be***

| | |
|---|---|
| copula | &#124; >> |
| progressive aspect | &#124; >> |
| passive voice | <<< &#124; |

**main verb occurring with progressives and passives**

| | |
|---|---|
| 11 most common verbs | &#124; >> |
| other verbs | <<<< &#124; |

```
              <·············· | ··············>
        greater proportion | greater proportion
          of FULL FORM  |  of be CONTRACTION
     than the register norm | than the register norm
```

**FICT** (norm c. 45%)
**form of *be***

| | |
|---|---|
| am | &#124; >>>>>> |
| is | = |
| are | < &#124; |

**subject noun phrase**

| | |
|---|---|
| pronoun | &#124; >>>> |
| non-pronominal subject | <<<<<< &#124; |

**function of *be***

| | |
|---|---|
| copula | &#124; >> |
| progressive aspect | &#124; >> |
| passive voice | <<<< &#124; |

**main verb occurring with progressives and passives**

| | |
|---|---|
| 11 most common verbs | &#124; > |
| other verbs | << &#124; |

```
              <·············· | ··············>
        greater proportion | greater proportion
          of FULL FORM  |  of be CONTRACTION
     than the register norm | than the register norm
```

**NEWS** (norm c. 10%)
**form of *be***

| | |
|---|---|
| am | &#124; >>>>>>> |
| is | = |
| are | < &#124; |

**subject noun phrase**

| | |
|---|---|
| pronoun | &#124; >>>> |
| non-pronominal subject | < &#124; |

**function of *be***

| | |
|---|---|
| copula | &#124; > |
| progressive aspect | = |
| passive voice | < &#124; |

**main verb occurring with progressives and passives**

| | |
|---|---|
| 11 most common verbs | &#124; > |
| other verbs | = |

**Table A.4: Departure from the register norms for contraction of *have* (main verb and auxiliary functions), depending on contextual factors**

(reporting only the factors that are influential in a register; academic prose is omitted because it contains too few tokens of *have* contraction)
each < or > represents 5% departure from the register norm
< marks proportionally greater use of *have* with FULL FORM
> marks proportionally greater use of *have* CONTRACTION
= marks a pattern of use equal to the register norm

```
              <·············· | ··············>
        greater proportion | greater proportion
          of FULL FORM  |  of have CONTRACTION
     than the register norm | than the register norm
```

**CONV** (norm c. 55%)
**form of *have***

| | |
|---|---|
| have | &#124; >>> |
| has | <<<<<<<<< &#124; |
| had | <<<<<<<< &#124; |

**subject noun phrase**

| | |
|---|---|
| 1st or 2nd person pronoun | &#124; >>> |
| other pronouns | <<<<<<< &#124; |
| non-pronominal subject | <<<<<<<<< &#124; |

**function of *have***

| | |
|---|---|
| main verb | <<<<<<<<< &#124; |
| perfect aspect | &#124; >> |

**main verb occurring with perfect aspect**

| | |
|---|---|
| 11 most common verbs | &#124; >>>> |
| other verbs | < &#124; |

```
              <·············· | ··············>
        greater proportion | greater proportion
          of FULL FORM  |  of have CONTRACTION
     than the register norm | than the register norm
```

**FICT** (norm c. 10%)
**form of *have***

| | |
|---|---|
| have | &#124; >>>>>>> |
| has | << &#124; |
| had | << &#124; |

**subject noun phrase**

| | |
|---|---|
| 1st or 2nd person pronoun | &#124; >>>>>> |
| other pronouns | << &#124; |
| non-pronominal subject | << &#124; |

**function of *have***

| | |
|---|---|
| main verb | << &#124; |
| perfect aspect | &#124; > |

**main verb occurring with perfect aspect**

| | |
|---|---|
| 11 most common verbs | &#124; >> |
| other verbs | = |

```
              <·············· | ··············>
        greater proportion | greater proportion
          of FULL FORM  |  of be CONTRACTION
     than the register norm | than the register norm
```

**NEWS** (norm c. 10%)
**form of *have***

| | |
|---|---|
| have | &#124; > |
| has | < &#124; |
| had | < &#124; |

**subject noun phrase**

| | |
|---|---|
| 1st or 2nd person pronoun | &#124; >>>>>> |
| other pronouns | < &#124; |
| non-pronominal subject | < &#124; |

**function of *have***

| | |
|---|---|
| main verb | < &#124; |
| perfect aspect | = |

**main verb occurring with perfect aspect**

| | |
|---|---|
| 11 most common verbs | &#124; > |
| other verbs | < &#124; |

**Table A.5: Departure from the register norms for contraction of modal *will*, depending on contextual factors**

(reporting only the factors that are influential in a register; academic prose is omitted because there are too few tokens of *will* contraction)

each < or > represents 5% departure from the register norm
< marks proportionally greater use of *will* with FULL FORM
> marks proportionally greater use of *will* CONTRACTION
= marks a pattern of use equal to the register norm

|  | <·············· \| ··············> |
|---|---|
|  | greater proportion \| greater proportion |
|  | of FULL FORM \| of *be* CONTRACTION |
|  | than the register norm \| than the register norm |
| **CONV (norm c. 75%)** | |
| **subject noun phrase** | |
| pronoun | \| >> |
| non-pronominal subject | <<<<<<<<<<< \| |
| **main verb** | |
| 11 most common verbs | \| >> |
| other verbs | < \| |
| **FICT (norm c. 50%)** | |
| **subject noun phrase** | |
| pronoun | \| >>> |
| non-pronominal subject | <<<<<<<< \| |
| **main verb** | |
| 11 most common verbs | \| >> |
| other verbs | < \| |
| **NEWS (norm c. 5%)** | |
| **subject noun phrase** | |
| pronoun | \| >>>>>>> |
| non-pronominal subject | < \| |
| **main verb** | |
| 11 most common verbs | \| > |
| other verbs | = |

**Table A.6: Proportional use of *not* as a contraction following *do* or a modal verb** (excluding cases where the modal verb is contracted, as in: *But we'll not hold our breath.* (NEWS))
each ■ represents 5%

| CONV | | |
|---|---|---|
| *do* + *not* | ■■■■■■■■■■■■■■■■■■■■ | (nearly 100%) |
| modal + *not* | ■■■■■■■■■■■■■■■■■■■ | (c. 95%) |
| **FICT** | | |
| *do* + *not* | ■■■■■■■■■■■■■■■ | (c. 75%) |
| modal + *not* | ■■■■■■■■■■■■■ | (c. 65%) |
| **NEWS** | | |
| *do* + *not* | ■■■■■■■■■■■■ | (c. 60%) |
| modal + *not* | ■■■■■■■■ | (c. 40%) |
| **ACAD** | | |
| *do* + *not* | ■ | (c. 5%) |
| modal + *not* | ■ | (c. 5%) |

with other contractible verbs, the tendency is in the opposite direction, favoring *not* contraction.

As Table A.8 shows, with the verbs **have**, **will**, and **would**, *not*-contraction is overwhelmingly the preferred choice. Table A.9, therefore, concentrates only on factors influencing the choice of contraction type with **be** + **not**. Academic prose is omitted because of the small number of contractions it contains.

**Table A.7: Departure from the register norms for contraction of *not* following a modal verb, depending on contextual factors**

(reporting only the factors that are influential in a register; academic prose is omitted because it contains too few tokens of *not* contraction)

each < or > represents 5% departure from the register norm
< marks proportionally greater use of *not* with FULL FORM
> marks proportionally greater use of *not* CONTRACTION
= marks a pattern of use equal to the register norm

|  | <·············· \| ··············> |
|---|---|
|  | greater proportion \| greater proportion |
|  | of FULL FORM \| of *not* CONTRACTION |
|  | than the register norm \| than the register norm |
| **CONV (norm c. 95%)** | |
| **co-occurring modal verb** | |
| *can* + *not* | \| > |
| *could* + *not* | \| > |
| *might* + *not* | <<<<<<<<<<<<<<<<< \| |
| *may* + *not* | <<<<<<<<<<<<<<<<< \| |
| *must* + *not* | << \| |
| *should* + *not* | \| > |
| *will* + *not* | \| > |
| *would* + *not* | \| > |
| *shall* + *not* | = |
| **subject noun phrase** | |
| pronoun | = |
| non-pronominal subject | = |
| **clause type** | |
| declarative | = |
| interrogative | = |
| **FICT (norm c. 65%)** | |
| **co-occurring modal verb** | |
| *can* + *not* | \| >>> |
| *could* + *not* | << \| |
| *might* + *not* | <<<<<<<<<<< \| |
| *may* + *not* | <<<<<<<<<<< \| |
| *must* + *not* | < \| |
| *should* + *not* | = |
| *will* + *not* | \| >>> |
| *would* + *not* | = |
| *shall* + *not* | \| > |
| **subject noun phrase** | |
| pronoun | \| >>> |
| non-pronominal subject | <<< \| |
| **clause type** | |
| declarative | = |
| interrogative | \| >>>>> |
| **NEWS (norm c. 40%)** | |
| **co-occurring modal verb** | |
| *can* + *not* | \| >> |
| *could* + *not* | \| > |
| *might* + *not* | <<<<<<<< \| |
| *may* + *not* | <<<<<<<< \| |
| *must* + *not* | <<<<< \| |
| *should* + *not* | <<<< \| |
| *will* + *not* | \| > |
| *would* + *not* | < \| |
| *shall* + *not* | <<<<< \| |
| **subject noun phrase** | |
| pronoun | \| >>>>>>> |
| non-pronominal subject | <<< \| |
| **clause type** | |
| declarative | = |
| interrogative | \| >>>>>>>> |

Table A.9 shows that the tendency for **be** to be contracted in preference to the following negative is especially strong with first- and second-person pronouns (as in *I'm not, you're not, we're not*). Indeed, with *I'm not* the alternative of negative contraction does not really exist. The tendency is, however, very much in the

**Table A.8: Proportional use of verb contraction v. *not* contraction – *be* / *have* / *will* / *would* + *not***

each ■ represents 5%    □ represents less than 2.5%

| | verb contracted | not contracted | *ain't* | uncontracted |
|---|---|---|---|---|
| **CONV** | | | | |
| ***be* + *not*** | ■■■■■■■■■■■■■■ | ■■ | ■■ | ■ |
| ***have* + *not*** | ■ | ■■■■■■■■■■■■■ | | □ |
| ***will* + *not*** | ■ | ■■■■■■■■■■■■■■ | | □ |
| ***would* + *not*** | □ | ■■■■■■■■■■■■■ | | □ |
| **FICT** | | | | |
| ***be* + *not*** | ■■■■■■■■■ | ■■■■■ | ■ | ■■■■■ |
| ***have* + *not*** | □ | ■■■■■■■■■ | | ■■■■■■■■ |
| ***will* + *not*** | ■ | ■■■■■■■■■■■■ | | ■■■ |
| ***would* + *not*** | □ | ■■■■■■■■■■■ | | ■■■■■■■■ |
| **NEWS** | | | | |
| ***be* + *not*** | ■■■■ | ■■ | □ | ■■■■■■■■■■■■■■ |
| ***have* + *not*** | □ | ■■■■■■ | | ■■■■■■■■■■■■■■ |
| ***will* + *not*** | ■ | ■■■■■■■■ | | ■■■■■■■■■■■■ |
| ***would* + *not*** | □ | ■■■■■■ | | ■■■■■■■■■■■■■■■ |
| **ACAD** | | | | |
| ***be* + *not*** | □ | □ | □ | ■■■■■■■■■■■■■■■■■■ |
| ***have* + *not*** | □ | ■ | | ■■■■■■■■■■■■■■■■■■ |
| ***will* + *not*** | □ | ■ | | ■■■■■■■■■■■■■■■■■ |
| ***would* + *not*** | □ | ■ | | ■■■■■■■■■■■■■■■■■■ |

opposite direction with non-pronominal subjects (i.e. mainly full noun phrases). These, as already observed, do not easily accept verb contraction, and so *not* contraction, or no contraction at all, is the favored option.

**Table A.9: Departure from the register norms for verb contraction v. *not* contraction with *be* + *not*, depending on contextual factors**

each < or > represents 5% departure from the register norm
< marks proportionally less use of the stated option
> marks proportionally greater use of the stated option
= marks a pattern of use equal to the register norm

```
        <··············· | ················· >
        smaller proportion | greater proportion
      than the register norm | than the register norm
```

**CONV**
(compare to the baselines of c. 70% *be* contracted, c. 10% NOT contracted, c. 10% *ain't*, c. 5% uncontracted)

| subject noun phrase | | example |
|---|---|---|
| 1st person pronoun (*we are not sure*) | | |
| *be* contracted | &#124; >> | we're not sure |
| not contracted | << &#124; | we aren't sure |
| *ain't* | = | we ain't sure |
| uncontracted | = | we are not sure |
| 2nd person pronoun (*you are not angry*) | | |
| *be* contracted | &#124; >>> | you're not angry |
| not contracted | << &#124; | you aren't angry |
| *ain't* | = | you ain't angry |
| uncontracted | < &#124; | you are not angry |
| other pronouns (*he is not prepared; that is not all*) | | |
| *be* contracted | = | that's not all |
| not contracted | = | that isn't all |
| *ain't* | &#124; > | that ain't all |
| uncontracted | < &#124; | that is not all |
| non-pronominal subject (*unemployment is not enough*) | | |
| *be* contracted <<<<<<<<< &#124; | | unemployment's not enough |
| not contracted | &#124; >>>>>>>> | unemployment isn't enough |
| *ain't* | &#124; > | unemployment ain't enough |
| uncontracted | = | unemployment is not enough |

**FICT**
(compare to the baselines of c. 50% *be* contracted, c. 25% *not* contracted, c. 5% *ain't*, c. 20% uncontracted)

| subject noun phrase | |
|---|---|
| 1st person pronoun (*I am not sure*) | |
| *be* contracted | &#124; >>>>>> |
| not contracted | <<<<< &#124; |
| *ain't* = | |
| uncontracted | < &#124; |
| 2nd person pronoun (*you are not angry*) | |
| *be* contracted | &#124; >>>> |
| not contracted | <<< &#124; |
| *ain't* | = |
| uncontracted | < &#124; |
| other pronouns (*he is not prepared; that is not all*) | |
| *be* contracted | < &#124; |
| not contracted | = |
| *ain't* | = |
| uncontracted | = |
| non-pronominal subject (*unemployment is not enough*) | |
| *be* contracted | <<<<<<<<< &#124; |
| not contracted | &#124; >>>>> |
| *ain't* | = |
| uncontracted | &#124; >>>> |

**NEWS**
(compare to the baselines of c. 20% *be* contracted, c. 10% *not* contracted, < 1% *ain't*, c. 70% uncontracted)

| subject noun phrase | |
|---|---|
| 1st person pronoun (*I am not sure*) | |
| *be* contracted | &#124; >>>>>>>> |
| not contracted | << &#124; |
| *ain't* | = |
| uncontracted | <<<<<< &#124; |
| 2nd person pronoun (*you are not angry*) | |
| *be* contracted | &#124; >>> |
| not contracted | < &#124; |
| *ain't* | = |
| uncontracted | <<<<< &#124; |
| other pronouns (*he is not prepared; that is not all*) | |
| *be* contracted | &#124; >>> |
| not contracted | = |
| *ain't* | = |
| uncontracted | <<<<< &#124; |
| non-pronominal subject (*unemployment is not enough*) | |
| *be* contracted | <<<< &#124; |
| not contracted | &#124; > |
| *ain't* | = |
| uncontracted | &#124; >>> |

# Endnotes

## Chapter 1

1 Another corpus project, the International Corpus of English (ICE), has begun undertaking the grammatical analysis of national varieties on a worldwide scale (see S. Greenbaum (ed.), *Comparing English Worldwide*, Oxford: Clarendon Press, 1996). The ICE contains national subcorpora which are much smaller than those of the LSWE Corpus (one million words each), but which represent a wide range of national dialectal varieties.

2 The ambiguity concerning the number of participants is especially noticeable in the BrE subcorpus, where each interaction is separated as a distinct 'conversation'. In contrast, there are many fewer 'conversations' in the AmE corpus, where the tape recorder was left running without interruption, and thus it is easier to determine the total number of different participants. In both cases, we have taken a conservative approach in counting the number of participants.

   As a result of this difference in data collection, individual 'conversations' in the AmE subcorpus are much longer than in the BrE subcorpus. Thus, in AmE a single 'conversation' often contains speech recorded in multiple situations, such as the interactions at breakfast followed by going out to shop; the interactions that occurred during a day at the office; and a series of interactions at home, in the car, at the country club, and then back at home again.

3 The distribution across topics in the AmE news text subcorpus was estimated from analysis of 1,570 texts sampled randomly from the three news sources.

## Chapter 2

1 Based on computer analysis of the entire corpus.

2 Based on a 15-million-word subset of the LSWE Corpus. Approximate number of words in the registers: conversation (BrE only) 3.4 million, fiction 4.8 million, news 4.5 million, academic prose 2.7 million.

3 Based on a five-million-word subset of the LSWE Corpus. Approximate number of words in the registers: conversation (BrE only) 0.7 million, fiction 1.9 million, news 1.1 million, academic prose 1.1 million.

4 Based on interactive coding of 200 occurrences from each register, selected at random.

5 Based on samples extracted from all texts of sufficient length in the LSWE Corpus:

| text length | number of samples |
|---|---|
| 100 words | 644 |
| 1,000 words | 644 |
| 10,000 words | 409 |

TTR results based on the average TTR across text samples from each register.

6 In conversation, findings are based on coordinators initiating a new speaker turn (either at the start of the turn or preceded only by a response word, a hesitator, or some other insert).

7 Based on all phrases occurring in two text samples from each register:

| CONV | 1,107 phrases |
|---|---|
| FICT | 507 phrases |
| NEWS | 320 phrases |
| ACAD | 255 phrases |

8 In calculating lexical density we have treated all occurrences of *be*, *do*, and *have* as function words, since these are the predominant uses of the forms. Inserts which are identical in form to a lexical word have been included among the lexical word tokens. The component parts of multi-word lexemes have been counted separately. These simplifications should be kept in mind in evaluating the register comparison.

9 Based on analysis of the subset of the Corpus specified in note 2 to this chapter. Study of occurrence as stranded prepositions: all prepositions followed by a question mark. The material for Table 2.9 included (1) all independent *wh*-questions ending in one of the following prepositions, and (2) all cases where these prepositions were found before a *wh*-word and followed by a question mark within a span of 12 words: *at*, *by*, *for*, *from*, *in*, *of*, *on*, *to*, *with*. Approximate number of occurrences analysed for Table 2.9: conversation 1,200, fiction 600, news 40, academic prose 50.

## Chapter 3

1 Based on analysis of a 15-million-word subset of the LSWE Corpus. Approximate number of words in each register: conversation (BrE only) 3.4 million, fiction 4.8 million, news 4.5 million, academic prose 2.7 million.

2 Based on analysis of a five-million-word subset of the LSWE Corpus. Approximate number of words in each register: conversation (BrE only) 0.7 million, fiction 1.9 million, news 1.1 million, academic prose 1.1 million.

3 Based on the subset of the LSWE Corpus specified in note 1 to this chapter plus approximately a million words of American conversation.

4 Based on the fiction and conversation material specified in notes 1 and 3 of this chapter.

5 Frequency of negation with lexical *have* in each register (normed per million words):

| | AmE CONV | BrE CONV | FICT | NEWS | ACAD |
|---|---|---|---|---|---|
| negated ***have*** + *a/any* | 225 | 420 | 360 | 250 | 170 |
| negated ***have*** + *the* | 55 | 50 | 25 | 20 | 15 |

6 Based on analysis of 200 tokens for each contraction variant (800 tokens total), selected at random from conversation.

7 Based on analysis of 400 tokens randomly selected from the LSWE Corpus (100 occurrences from each register). All contexts are included, not just ones where *not* and *no* could both occur.

8 *Based on analysis of 400 tokens randomly selected from each register (1,600 occurrences total).

9 Based on analysis of 25 text samples of 2,000 words randomly selected from each register (c. 50,000 words from each register; 200,000 words total).

10 The study includes both independent and dependent interrogative clauses.

## Chapter 4

1 Based on analysis of a 15-million-word subset of the LSWE Corpus. Approximate number of words in the registers: conversation (BrE only) 3.4 million, fiction 4.8 million, news 4.5 million, academic prose 2.7 million.

2 Based on computer analysis of a 15-million-word subset of the LSWE Corpus (see note 1 to this chapter), confirmed from concordance listings.

3 Based on computer analysis of a five-million-word subset of the LSWE Corpus, confirmed from concordance listings. Approximate number of words in the registers: conversation (BrE only) 1 million, fiction 1.9 million, news 1.1 million, academic prose 1 million.

4 Based on computer analysis of all texts from fiction in a 15-million-word subset of the LSWE Corpus (see note 1 to this chapter), comparing BrE and AmE texts.

5 Based on interactive coding and computer analysis of a random sample from the registers in the LSWE Corpus.

6 Based on analysis of the following number of noun phrases from each register:

| | | | |
|---|---|---|---|
| CONV | 684 | NEWS | 489 |
| FICT | 869 | ACAD | 436 |

7 The findings reported in 4.8.1.4 are based on analysis of a 5.33-million-word sample of academic prose. All derived nouns were confirmed by hand. The findings reported in 4.8.2.1 are based on subcorpora of just over four million words of AmE conversation and just over two million words of AmE newswire reports. All noun compounds spelt as single words (i.e. with no intervening hyphen or space) were manually picked out from computer-generated lists of words with frequencies over five words per million.

8 Based on analysis of the following number of noun phrases from each register:

| | | | |
|---|---|---|---|
| CONV | 2756 | NEWS | 1556 |
| FICT | 2734 | ACAD | 1616 |

9 Based on analysis of 50,000 words of text from each register (25 text samples; 2,000 words each). The total frequencies were confirmed from analysis of a 15-million-word subset of the LSWE Corpus (see note 1 to this chapter).

10 All occurrences of the selected head nouns with *s*-genitives or *of*-phrases were analysed: 643 constructions for the phrase length analysis, and 605 constructions for the information status analysis.

11 All occurrences of *it* + *be* + *I/he* v. *me/him* were analysed:

| | | | |
|---|---|---|---|
| CONV | 94 | NEWS | 16 |
| FICT | 131 | ACAD | too few for reliable analysis |

12 All occurrences of *as/than* + *I/he* v. *me/him* were analysed:

| | |
|---|---|
| CONV | 38 |
| FICT | 16 |
| NEWS and ACAD | too few for reliable analysis |

13 All occurrences of coordinated noun phrases with *I/me* or *he/him* were analysed:

| | | | |
|---|---|---|---|
| CONV | 364 | NEWS | 327 |
| FICT | 897 | ACAD | too few for reliable analysis |

14 Based on analysis of 200 tokens of *himself* selected randomly from each register.

15 Based on analysis of 400 tokens selected randomly from each register.

16 Because conversation is interactive and produced under real-time constraints, syntactic role is sometimes indeterminate. For this reason, the analysis of syntactic role is based on only the written registers.

17 The material for -*tion* was restricted to words ending in -*ation*.

## Chapter 5

1 Based on computer analysis of the entire LSWE Corpus. Results were confirmed from concordance listings.

2 Based on computer analysis of all texts from the four core registers in the LSWE Corpus (conversation, fiction, news, and academic prose). Results were confirmed from concordance listings.

3 Based on interactive coding and computer analysis of a random sample of 200 occurrences for each verb from each of the four core registers in the LSWE Corpus.

4 Based on computer analysis of all texts from fiction and news in the LSWE Corpus, comparing AmE and BrE patterns of use. Results were confirmed from concordance listings.

5 Based on computer analysis of an eight-million word sample from the four core registers in the LSWE Corpus (two million words from each register). Results were confirmed from hand analysis.

6 Based on hand analysis of the LSWE Corpus four-million word sample of AmE conversation (for *have got*) and a computer analysis of the same sample (for *have gotten*).

7 The frequencies reported in Figures 5.9–5.12 are based on the distribution of the most common verbs, that is, all verbs occurring more than 300 times per million words in at least one register.

8 Based on a count of active verbs occurring with a pronoun as subject only. The larger percentages on the right in Table 5.3 represent an estimate of the proportion of full noun phrase subjects which are inanimate, from a random sample of 200 tokens with full noun phrase subjects. The figures on the right are larger, because a large proportion of pronominal subjects—e.g. *they*, *this*—give no indication of animacy.

9 These verb valency classifications exclude rare usages. Some of the intransitive verbs can occasionally be used in transitive patterns. For example, *go* can be used as a reporting verb that takes direct speech as an object:

> And I just **went** 'oh God'. (CONV)

Again, some of the transitive verbs can occasionally be used in intransitive patterns:

> This is an area where the Organisation for Economic Co-operation and Development needs to **give** generously. (NEWS†)

In addition, the verb *mean* is used intransitively in the fixed phrase *I mean*:

> You know, **I mean**, I miss them. (AmE CONV)

## Chapter 6

All lexical verb counts include occurrences of the relevant verb forms as part of multi-word lexical verbs as well as of one-word verbs, unless the text differentiates them.

1 Based on computer analysis of the entire LSWE Corpus. Results were confirmed from concordance listings.
2 Based on computer analysis of all texts from the four core registers in the LSWE Corpus. Results were confirmed from concordance listings.
3 Based on interactive coding and computer analysis of a sample from the four core registers in the LSWE Corpus.
4 Based on analysis of all verbs that have an overall frequency greater than ten per million words, considering finite clauses only. Non-passive verbs include active voice transitive verbs as well as all intransitive verbs.
5 Based on analysis of all verbs that have a frequency greater than four per million words in a register.
6 Based on all tensed verb phrases with these verbs as the main verb, including phrases marked for perfect aspect, progressive aspect, and/or passive voice.
7 These counts exclude complex aspectual verbs that are marked for both perfect aspect and progressive aspect: a combination extremely rare in all registers (see further discussion in 6.5).
8 Counts include both non-contracted and contracted forms (such as *'ll* and *can't*).
9 Percentages are computed from interactive analysis of a random sample of 100 tokens for each modal verb. These percentages were then applied to register counts from the full LSWE Corpus.
10 The distinction between volition and prediction is often ambiguous. The relative frequencies reported here are based on an assessment of the most likely meaning associated with each instance.

## Chapter 7

Unless otherwise stated, counts in this chapter are of the specific word form cited, not including any inflectional variants, e.g. a count of *young* does not include *younger* and *youngest*.

1 Based on computer analysis of the entire LSWE Corpus. Results were confirmed from concordance listings.

2 Based on computer analysis of all texts from the four core registers in the LSWE Corpus. Results were confirmed from concordance listings.
3 Based on analysis of a random sample of 200 tokens for each of these adjective or adverb forms, selected from across the LSWE Corpus. Results were confirmed from concordance listings.
4 This account excludes the use of *good* and *really* as responses in conversation.

## Chapter 8

Counts of postmodifiers in this chapter do not include complement clauses, which are treated separately.

1 Based on computer analysis of the entire LSWE Corpus. Results were confirmed from concordance listings.
2 Based on computer analysis of all texts from the four core registers in the LSWE Corpus. Results were confirmed from concordance listings.
3 Based on interactive coding and computer analysis of a random sample from the four core registers in the LSWE Corpus.
4 Based on interactive coding and computer analysis of all tokens of these words in the LSWE Corpus.
5 Based on analysis of the referential chains in the first few paragraphs from 44 academic prose texts. To be included, the same referent had to be referred to at least three times in those paragraphs. In all, 300 noun phrases were analyzed, i.e. three noun phrases referring to each of 100 different referents.

## Chapter 9

Some verbs are classified differently in this chapter and Chapter 5. This happens where their meanings, when accompanied by complements, differ from their core meanings. For example, *show* with a *that*-clause falls in the domain of communication, while its core meanings, with direct and indirect object noun phrases, falls in the domain of activity. For the same reason, some verbs are classified differently in different sections of this chapter.

1 Based on computer analysis of the entire LSWE Corpus. Results were confirmed from concordance listings.
2 Based on computer analysis of all texts from the four core registers in the LSWE Corpus. Results were confirmed from concordance listings.
3 Based on interactive coding and computer analysis of a sample from the four core registers in the LSWE Corpus.

## Chapter 10

1 Based on interactive coding and computer analysis of a 100,000 word sample from four registers in the Corpus: conversation, fiction, news, and academic prose. Prepositional phrases associated with prepositional verbs and adverbials embedded within other adverbials are included in the counts. Coordinated adverbials are counted as two adverbials, as in:

> The officers **abruptly** and **inexplicably** left the hotel. (NEWS†)

Adverbial prepositional phrases with coordinated objects of the preposition, however, are counted as only one adverbial:

**In Glasgow and Edinburgh**, they have established two of the country's first delicatessens. (NEWS†)

2 The category of single adverbs includes fixed phrases, such as *of course* and *sort of*, because these function as a unit and have idiomatic meanings. Other items that preserve the meaning of the individual words (such as *in contrast*) or which occur in other forms (such as *in fact*, which also occurs as *in actual fact*) are not analyzed as single adverbs.

3 Frequencies are slightly below the total count for adverbials, and percentages are slightly below 100%, because the positions of some adverbials are indeterminate.

4 Based on computer analysis and editing of all texts in the LSWE Corpus.

5 Based on computer analysis and editing of all texts in four registers of the LSWE Corpus. Analyses were hand edited to ensure accuracy. Conditionals with other forms of the verb *be* can be realized with *should* and subject-operator inversion. For example, *If this is so, they are not alone* (FICT) could be rewritten as *Should this be so, they are not alone*. However, such structures are not covered in the analysis here.

## Chapter 11

1 Based on a 15-million-word subset of the LSWE Corpus. Approximate number of words in the registers: conversation (BrE only) 3.4 million, fiction 4.8 million, news 4.5 million, academic prose 2.7 million.

2 Based on a sample of 200,000 words from the LSWE Corpus: 25 texts of 2,000 words each from conversation (BrE only), fiction, news, and academic prose.

3 Based on a sample of 100,000 words from the LSWE Corpus: 25 texts of 2,000 words each from fiction and news.

4 Based on a sample of 200 tokens of the verbs *give*, *offer*, and *sell* selected at random from each register. (Only 140 tokens of *offer* occurred in academic prose.) In all, 2,340 occurrences of these verbs were analysed, yielding 544 instances of the two word-order patterns under consideration here:

| | |
|---|---|
| verb with indirect object + direct object | 431 tokens |
| verb with direct object + *to*-phrase | 113 tokens |

5 Based on all long passives in the 200,000-word sub-sample described in note 2 to this chapter, a total of 242 long passives.

6 Based on a sample of 100 existential clauses selected at random from each register.

7 The sequence *carry up* was too infrequent to be included here. In eight cases out of nine, the object was placed in mid-position, which is consistent with the literal meaning of the particle.

## Chapter 12

1 The gardai are the police in the Republic of Ireland.

2 Based on computer analysis of all texts from the four core registers in the LSWE Corpus. Results were confirmed from concordance listings.

3 Based on interactive coding and computer analysis of a sample from the four core registers in the LSWE Corpus.

4 Counts include all occurrences of modal verbs, but only those adverbials and complement clauses that have meanings related to stance.

5 The expression *you know* is extremely common in conversation (occurring well over 1,000 times per million words), but it is best regarded as a discourse marker (14.2.2.3B) rather than a comment clause. Its function is interactive rather than stance-marking, and it is much more flexible in its grammatical distribution than comment clauses like *I think* and *I suppose*. One reflection of this greater flexibility is the fact that *you know* commonly co-occurs with other discourse markers, as in:

*And I thought* **well, okay, you know,** *I did it because I was wondering* <...> (CONV)

In final position, *you know* is more similar in function to the other comment clauses:

*We didn't think to take down all the different places we went to* **you know**. (CONV)

*I've never seen that yet* **you know**. (CONV)

However, unlike stance-marking comment clauses, *you know* does not have the meaning it would have as a matrix clause preceding a complement clause. The last sentence above, for example, does not correspond to the sentence *You know (that) I've never seen that yet*. In many cases, moreover, final *you know* seems to function like a question tag and often occurs with a question intonation:

*But none of them seemed to know what they were doing,* **you know**? (CONV)

Similar considerations apply to the omission of *I mean* (14.3.3.3) from the list of stance-marking comment clauses.

## Chapter 13

1 Based on computer analysis of the entire LSWE Corpus. Results were confirmed from concordance listings.

2 Based on computer analysis of all texts from the four core registers in the LSWE Corpus. Results were confirmed from concordance listings.

3 Based on computer analysis of all texts from conversation and academic prose in the LSWE Corpus. Results were confirmed from concordance listings.

Lexical bundles were identified using two criteria: (1) a minimum cut-off frequency of at least ten occurrences per million words (or over 50 occurrences in a five million sub-corpus for a register); and (2) a distribution across at least six different texts in the sub-corpus (to avoid identification of lexical bundles characteristic of personal styles rather than the register).

## Chapter 14

1 In this chapter, as elsewhere in this book, we are using the term 'conversation' operationally, to characterize a subcorpus which was collected by lending tape recorders to a cross-section of adult native speakers (American and British), and transcribing all the day-by-day interactions that they recorded over a sample period (see 1.5.1). The samples so obtained correspond fairly closely to the common interpretation of the term 'conversation': they largely consist of private everyday spoken dialogue conducted between people of comparable social status, who are relatively well-known to one another.

2 Note also occasional occurrences in which *gotta* is preceded by the dummy auxiliary do: *I guess don't gotta tell you* (BrE CONV).

3 These findings are tentative, and are based on an analysis of hesitation phenomena occurring before very common words selected according to their word class.

4 Note that the count of singles comprises all tokens of the word concerned, including those that occur in doubles. Similarly, every triple or higher n-tuple is decomposed into doubles for the purposes of the count: a treble, for example, represents two doubles, and a quadruple three.

5 The figures are calculated for all occurrences of *when*, including cases where it is an adverb instead of a conjunction. However, in both these functions, *when* is a clause-introducing word.

6 The one exception itself is interestingly unusual:
> *Get an attic to my room to, get **an**, **a** ladder from my room to the attic* <...> (AmE CONV)

The speaker has already embarked on a false start in the words *get an attic to my room* (substituting *attic* for *ladder)* and then begins a second false start (*an*) before retracing to *a ladder*. So in this atypical case the less usual form *an* becomes the 'default', having already been used in a preceding false start.

7 A similar tendency, though less extreme, occurs in the British conversational data, where repeat sequences *a an* outnumber repeat sequences *an a* by nearly five to one.

8 Non-clausal material, particularly single-word inserts, may also be part of a clausal unit, if integrated with it prosodically, or (in the transcriptions) not separated by punctuation (see 14.3.1.4).

9 In the first clausal unit of **2c**, *The trouble is* is assumed to be the matrix clause, and all the other clauses which follow are assumed to be dependent clauses either directly or indirectly embedded in *The trouble is* .... Other possible analyses would treat *and you're looking* ... or *and every time* ... as the beginning of a new clausal unit, but these would not fit easily with the meaning of the extract.

10 Although incomplete (see 14.2.4), *That's such a neat* is counted as a clausal unit. For the purposes of segmentation, we have to make a somewhat arbitrary decision over how to count incomplete transcription phenomena resulting from dysfluency or unclarity. The practice has been to count an

incomplete structure as a clausal unit only where it contains a finite verb as part of its main (i.e. highest level) structure.

11 The term C-unit derives from educational research and research on second-language acquisition, where it is often seen as the spoken counterpart of the T-unit of Hunt (1965), which applies to the written language, and is equivalent to a clausal unit as defined in this chapter. See for example C. Chaudron (1988) *Second Language Classrooms: Research on Teaching and Learning*, Cambridge University Press, p. 45.

12 However, we do not count as separate clausal units coordinated predicates which share the same subject (or subject and auxiliary): e.g. *Oh we'll eat dinner there and then go to the club* (AmE) is just one C-unit.

13 *Ah* also occurs in the transcriptions as an equivalent of *uh* and *er*, i.e. as a hesitator.

14 The hyphenated variant spelling *uh-huh* also occurs.

15 In the transcriptions *okay* is occasionally spelt *OK*. Both spellings are included in the frequency count.

16 The hyphenated variant spelling *Bye-bye* also occurs.

17 The hyphenated variant spelling *unh-unh* also occurs. This form is used as a negative response form in AmE.

18 In the transcriptions, *alright* and *all right* are alternative spellings for the same adverb; both are included in the frequency count.

19 Note that the *about* in *how/what about* does not always function as a preposition. It can be followed by clauses which cannot act as prepositional complement, e.g.:
> *What about if we just put the standing fan in the hallway?* (AmE CONV)
> *How about **we put the beer back**.* (AmE CONV)

20 When the finite copula *be* is omitted, leaving a verbless main clause construction, this is not included in the present table, but is counted as a non-clausal unit, e.g. *Oh, no problem*; *Bit rich you know*.

21 The counts for final ellipsis do not include total ellipsis of a dependent clause: e.g. *I see* ..., *Are you sure* ... ?

22 The position and category of vocatives has been studied in a sample of c. 100,000 words, selected from both AmE and BrE conversations.

23 Where grammatical criteria are unclear, use is made of the criteria of (1) position in the turn or (2) position in an orthographically defined unit in the transcription. Turns are clear-cut: a vocative which is initial in a turn will always be regarded as initial in the relevant unit; whereas a vocative which is final in a turn will always be regarded as final. As regards orthographic units in the transcription, a vocative which is separated from a preceding unit by a full stop and from the following unit by a comma is regarded as most closely attached to the following unit – and vice versa if the positions of the comma and full stop are reversed. A vocative not separated by any punctuation mark from one contiguous unit, but separated from the other contiguous unit by a comma or other separation marker, is deemed to be

more closely related to the unit which is not separated from it by punctuation. (See 14.1.2.1 on the use of transcription evidence.) The length of units is measured in grammatical word forms, counted so as to exclude the vocative itself.

24 This study is confined to words for which there is a clear equivalence between the assertive and non-assertive forms. *Already* and its non-assertive equivalent *yet* are exceptional in that neither of them belongs to the class of words beginning with *some-* or *any-*. Other assertive or non-assertive forms are disregarded either (1) because they have no equivalent form, or (2) because they do not characteristically occur in assertive/non-assertive interrogatives: e.g. *at all, anyhow, somehow. Any-place* and *someplace* are infrequent alternatives to *anywhere* and *somewhere* in AmE conversation.

25 We had to take into account the occurrence of interrogatives with uncontracted negatives, where *not* invariably follows the subject, e.g.:

**Do we not** have the squirt bottle of ketchup anymore? (AmE CONV)

However, this variant of negative questions was rare, especially in AmE, where less than ten examples occurred per million words. The figure for BrE was c. 20 examples per million words.

26 The full form *let us* occurs occasionally, even in the conversational subcorpora, in special contexts such as calls to prayer: *Let us pray.*

27 There is an argument, however, that multiple negation is a semantic-level rather than a syntactic-level phenomenon. Thus a sentence such as *I don't want no sugar on them today* could be grammatical in standard English, but only if it were to be interpreted as a logical double negative meaning *It is not the case that I want no sugar on them today.*

28 Notice that this example has a third negative, *Don't*, which is not italicized, because it is not part of the multiple negation construction. In the standard English 'translation' of this example, *Don't* would remain unaffected: *Don't say I never gave you anything.* This is a reminder that more than one negative can occur in the same sentence or clausal unit in standard English, each negative expressing a logical negation. An example: *you can't just not have speed limits* (AmE CONV †).

# Bibliography

## A. Corpus-based studies of present-day English: general

Aarts, J. & W. Meijs (eds) (1984) *Corpus Linguistics: Recent Developments in the Use of Computer Corpora in English Language Research*, Amsterdam: Rodopi

Aarts, J. & W. Meijs (eds) (1986) *Corpus Linguistics II. New Studies in the Analysis and Exploitation of Computer Corpora*, Amsterdam: Rodopi

Aarts, J. & W. Meijs. (eds) (1990) *Theory and Practice in Corpus Linguistics*, Amsterdam: Rodopi

Aarts, J., P. de Haan, & N. Oostdijk (eds) (1993) *English Language Corpora: Design, Analysis and Exploitation*, Amsterdam: Rodopi

Aijmer, K. & B. Altenberg (eds) (1991) *English Corpus Linguistics. Studies in Honour of Jan Svartvik*, London: Longman

Allwood, J. & M. Ljung (eds) (1980) *ALVAR: A Linguistically Varied Assortment of Readings. Studies Presented to Alvar Ellegård on the Occasion of his 60th Birthday*, Stockholm Papers in English Language and Literature 1, Department of English, University of Stockholm

Altenberg, B. (1996) *ICAME Bibliography 3 (1990–4)*. Available on line from ICAME Bergen: Norwegian Computing Centre for the Humanities

Aston, G. & L. Burnard (1998) *The BNC Handbook: Exploring the British National Corpus with SARA*, Edinburgh: Edinburgh University Press

Barnbrook, G. (1996) *Language and Computers. A Practical Introduction to the Computer Analysis of Language*, Edinburgh: Edinburgh University Press

Biber, D. (1993) 'An analytical framework for register studies', in Biber & Finegan (eds) 1993: 31–56

Biber, D. (1993) 'Representativeness in corpus design', *Literary and Linguistic Computing* 8: 1–15

Biber, D. (1996) 'Investigating language use through corpus-based analyses of association patterns', *International Journal of Corpus Linguistics* 1: 171–197

Biber, D., S. Conrad & R. Reppen (1994) 'Corpus-based approaches to language issues in applied linguistics', *Applied Linguistics* 15: 169–189

Biber, D., S. Conrad & R. Reppen (1998) *Corpus Linguistics: Investigating Language Structure and Use*, Cambridge: Cambridge University Press

Biber, D. & E. Finegan (1991) 'On the exploration of computerized corpora in variation studies', in Aijmer & Altenberg (eds) 1991: 204–220

Black, E., R. Garside & G. Leech (eds) (1993) *Statistically-driven Computer Grammars of English. The IBM/Lancaster Approach*, Amsterdam: Rodopi

Chafe, W.L. (1992) 'The importance of corpus linguistics to understanding the nature of language', in Svartvik (ed) 1992: 79–97

Fillmore, C. J. (1992) 'Corpus linguistics' or 'Computer-aided armchair linguistics', in Svartvik (ed) 1992: 35–60

Francis, W. N. (1979) 'Problems of assembling and computerizing large corpora', in Bergenholtz & Schaeder (eds) 1979: 110–123

Francis, W. N. (1980) 'A tagged corpus: problems and prospects', in Greenbaum, Leech & Svartvik (eds) 1980: 192–209, London: Longman

Francis, W. N. & H. Kučera (1982) *Frequency Analysis of English Usage. Lexicon and Grammar*, Boston: Houghton Mifflin

Fries, U., G. Tottie & P. Schneider (eds) (1994) *Creating and Using English Language Corpora: Papers from the 14th International Conference on English Language Research on Computerized Corpora*, Zurich 1993, Amsterdam: Rodopi

Garside, R., G. Leech & T. McEnery (1997) *Corpus Annotation. Linguistic Information from Computer Text Corpora*, London: Longman

Garside, R., G. Leech & G. Sampson (eds) (1987) *The Computational Analysis of English*, London: Longman

Granger, S. (ed) (1998) *Learner English on Computer*, London: Longman

Greenbaum, S. (ed) (1996) *Comparing English Worldwide: the International Corpus of English*, Oxford: Oxford University Press

Greenbaum, S., G. Leech & J. Svartvik (eds) (1980) *Studies in English Linguistics for Randolph Quirk*, London: Longman

Hofland, K. & S. Johansson (1982) *Word Frequencies in British and American English*, Bergen: Norwegian Computing Centre for the Humanities / London: Longman

Johansson, S. (ed) (1982) *Computer Corpora in English Language Research*, Bergen: Norwegian Computing Centre for the Humanities

Johansson, S., in collaboration with E. Atwell, R. Garside & G. Leech (1986) *The Tagged LOB Corpus. Users' Manual*, Bergen: Norwegian Computing Centre for the Humanities

Johansson, S. & K. Hofland (1989) *Frequency Analysis of English Vocabulary and Grammar*, vols 1–2, Oxford: Clarendon Press

Johansson, S. & A.-B. Stenström (eds) (1991) *English Computer Corpora: Selected Papers and Research Guide*, Berlin & New York: Mouton de Gruyter

Kennedy, G. (1998) *An Introduction to Corpus Linguistics*, London: Longman

Klegraf, J. & Nehls, D. (eds) (1988) *Essays on the English Language and Applied Linguistics on the Occasion of Gerhard Nickel's 60th Birthday*, Heidelberg: Julius Groos

Kučera, H. & W. N. Francis (1967) *Computational Analysis of Present-day American English*, Providence, R.I.: Brown University Press

Leech, G. & A. Beale (1984) 'Computers in English language research', *Language Teaching and Linguistics: Abstracts* 17: 216–229

Leech, G., G. Myers & J. Thomas (eds) (1995) *Spoken English on Computer: Transcription, Mark-up and Application*, London: Longman

McEnery, T. & A. Wilson (1996) *Corpus Linguistics*, Edinburgh: Edinburgh University Press

Partington, A. (1998) *Patterns and Meanings: Using Corpora for English Language Research and Teaching*, Amsterdam: John Benjamins

Pearson, J. (1998) *Terms in Context*, Amsterdam: John Benjamins

Sampson, G. (1995) *English for the Computer: the SUSANNE Corpus and Analytic Scheme*, Oxford: Oxford University Press

Sinclair, J. McH. (1982) 'Reflections on computer corpora in English language research', in Johansson (ed) 1982: 1–6

Sinclair, J. (1991) *Corpus, Concordance, Collocation*, Oxford: Oxford University Press

Stubbs, M. (1996) *Text and Corpus Analysis*, Oxford: Blackwell

Svartvik, J. (ed) (1992) *Directions in Corpus Linguistics*, Proceedings of Nobel Symposium 82, Stockholm, 4–8 August 1991, Berlin & New York: Mouton de Gruyter

Svartvik, J. (ed) (1990) *The London-Lund Corpus of Spoken English: Description and Research*, Lund Studies in English 82, Lund: Lund University Press

Svartvik, J. & R. Quirk (eds) (1980) *A Corpus of English Conversation*, Lund Studies in English 56, Lund: Lund University Press

Thomas, J. & M. Short (eds) (1996) *Using Corpora for Language Research. Studies in the Honour of Geoffrey Leech*, London: Longman

Tottie, G. & I. Bäcklund (eds) (1986) *English in Speech and Writing: A Symposium*, Studia Anglistica Upsaliensia 60, Stockholm: Almqvist & Wiksell

Wichmann, A., S. Fligelstone, T. McEnery & G. Knowles (eds) (1997) *Teaching and Language Corpora*, London: Longman

## B. Corpus-informed grammars of present-day English

Greenbaum, S. (1996) *The Oxford English Grammar*, Oxford: Oxford University Press

Greenbaum, S. & R. Quirk (1990) *A Student's Grammar of the English Language*, London: Longman

Leech, G. & J. Svartvik (1994) *A Communicative Grammar of English*, London: Longman (2nd edn)

Quirk, R., S. Greenbaum, G. Leech & J. Svartvik (1972) *A Grammar of Contemporary English*, London: Longman

Quirk, R., S. Greenbaum, G. Leech & J. Svartvik (1985) *A Comprehensive Grammar of the English Language*, London: Longman

Sinclair, J. (ed-in-chief) (1990) *Collins COBUILD English Grammar*, London & Glasgow: HarperCollins

## C. Corpus-informed studies of specific areas of present-day English grammar

Aarts, B. (1992) *Small Clauses in English: the Nonverbal Types*, Berlin & New York: Mouton de Gruyter

Aarts, B. & C. F. Meyer (eds) (1995) *The Verb in Contemporary English. Theory and Description*, Cambridge: Cambridge University Press

Aarts, F. (1971) 'On the distribution of noun-phrase types in English clause structure', *Lingua* 26: 281–293

Aarts, F. (1993) '*Who, whom, that* and *Ø* in two corpora of spoken English', *English Today* 9: 19–21

Aarts, F. (1994) 'Imperative sentences in a corpus of English conversation', *Leuvense Bijdragen (Leuven Contributions in Linguistics and Philology)* 83: 145–155

Aarts, J. & F. Aarts (eds) (1995) '*Find* and *want*. A corpus-based case study in verb complementation', in Aarts & Meyer 1995: 159–182

Abberton, E. (1977) 'Nominal group premodification structures', in Bald & Ilson (eds) 1977: 29–72

Aijmer, K. (1984) '*Go to* and *will* in spoken English', in Ringbom & Rissanen (eds) 1984: 141–157

Aijmer, K. (1984) 'Sort of and kind of in English conversation', *Studia Linguistica* 38: 118–128

Aijmer, K. (1985) 'What happens at the end of our utterances? The use of utterance-final tags introduced by *and* and *or*', in *Papers from the 8th Scandinavian Conference of Linguistics*, O. Togeby (ed), 117–127, Institut for Nordisk Filologi, University of Copenhagen

Aijmer. K. (1986) 'Discourse variation and hedging', in Aarts & Meijs (eds) 1986: 1–18

Aijmer. K. (1986a) 'Why is *actually* so frequent in spoken English?' in Tottie & Bäcklund (eds) 1986: 119–129

Aijmer, K. (1986b) 'Speaking with many voices: direct and indirect speech in English conversation', in *Papers from the 9th Scandinavian Conference of Linguistics*, Ö. Dahl (ed), 1–14, Department of Linguistics, Stockholm University

Aijmer, K. (1988) '"Now may we have a word on this": The use of *now* as a discourse particle', in Kytö et al. (eds) 1988: 15–34

Aijmer, K. (1989) 'Themes and tails: The discourse functions of dislocated elements', *Nordic Journal of Linguistics* 12: 137–154

Aijmer, K. (1996) *Conversational Routines in English: Convention and Creativity*, London: Longman

Algeo, J. (1988) 'British and American grammatical differences', *International Journal of Lexicography* 1: 1–31

Altenberg, B. (1984) 'Causal linking in spoken and written English', *Studia Linguistica* 38: 20–69

Altenberg, B. (1986) 'Contrastive linking in spoken and written English', in Tottie & Bäcklund (eds) 1986: 13–40

Altenberg, B. (1987) 'Causal ordering strategies in English conversation', in *Grammar in the Construction of Texts*, J. Monaghan (ed), 50–64, London: Frances Pinter

Altenberg, B. (1993) 'Recurrent verb-complement constructions in the London-Lund corpus', in Aarts et al. (eds) 1993: 227–245

Altenberg, B. & M. Eeg-Olofsson (1990) 'Phraseology in spoken English', in Aarts & Meijs (eds) 1990: 1–26

Andersson, E. (1985) *On Verb Complementation in Written English*, Lund Studies in English 71, Lund: Gleerup/Liber

Axelsson, M. W. (1998) *Contraction in British Newspapers in the Late 20th Century*, Studia Anglistica Upsaliensia 102, Uppsala: Acta Universitatis Upsaliensis

Bache, C. (1985) *Verbal Aspect. A General Theory and Its Application to Present-day British English*, Odense: Odense University Press

Bäcklund, I. (1984) *Conjunction-headed Abbreviated Clauses in English*. Studia Anglistica Upsalienia 50, Stockholm: Almqvist & Wiksell

Bäcklund, I. (1986) '"Beat until stiff." Conjunction-headed abbreviated clauses in spoken and written English', in Tottie & Bäcklund (eds) 1986: 41–55

Bäcklund, I. (1988) 'Grounds for prominence. On hierarchies and grounding in English expository text', *Studia Neophilologica* 60: 37–61

Bäcklund, I. (1988) 'To begin with, this is the problem, for example. On some reader-oriented structural markers in English expository text', *Studia Linguistica* 42: 60–68

Bäcklund, I. (1989) 'Cues to the audience. On some structural markers in English monologue', in Odenstedt & Persson (eds) 1989: 29–39

Bald, W.-D. (1972) *Studien zu den Kopulativen Verben des Englischen*, Munich: Hueber

Bald, W.-D. and R. Ilson (eds) (1977) *Studies in English Usage: The resources of a present-day English Corpus for Linguistic Analysis*, Frankfurt am Main: Peter Lang

Bald, W.-D. (1987) 'Reduced structures in English grammar', in W. Lörscher & R. Schulze (eds) *Perspectives on Language in Performance. Studies in Linguistics, Literary Criticism, and Language Teaching and Learning. To Honour Werner Hüllen*, Tübingen: G. Narr. 69–87

Bald, W.-D. (1988a) 'A note on the textual distribution of *one*', in Klegraf & Nehls (eds) 1988: 156–160

Bald, W.-D. (1988b) *Kernprobleme der Englischen Grammatik. Sprachliche Fakten und Ihre Vermittlung*, Berlin & Munich: Langenscheidt-Longman

Bald, W.-D. (1988c) '*If*-Sätze im Englischen', in Bald 1988b: 38–50

Barkema, H. (1993) 'Idiomaticity in English NPs', in Aarts et al. (eds) 1993: 257–278

Berglund, Y. (1997) 'Future in present-day English: corpus-based evidence on the rivalry of expressions', *ICAME Journal* 21: 7–19

Biber, D. (1985) 'Investigating macroscopic textual variation through multi-feature/multi-dimensional analyses', *Linguistics* 23: 155–178

Biber, D. (1986) 'On the investigation of spoken/written differences', *Studia Linguistica* 40: 1–21

Biber, D. (1986) 'Spoken and written textual dimensions in English: resolving the contradictory findings', *Language* 62: 384–414

Biber, D. (1988) 'A textual comparison of British and American writing', *American Speech* 62: 99–119

Biber, D. (1988) *Variation across Speech and Writing*, Cambridge: Cambridge University Press

Biber, D. (1989) 'A typology of English texts', *Linguistics* 27: 3–43

Biber, D. (1992a) 'On the complexity of discourse complexity: a multidimensional analysis', *Discourse Processes* 15: 133–163

Biber, D. (1992b) 'Using computer-based text corpora to analyze the referential strategies of spoken and written texts', in Svartvik (ed.) 1992: 213–252

Biber, D. & E. Finegan (1988) 'Adverbial stance types in English', *Discourse Processes* 11: 1–34

Biber, D. & E. Finegan (1989) 'Styles of stance in English. Lexical and grammatical marking of evidentiality and affect', *Text* 9: 93–124

Black, M. (1977) 'An investigation into factors influencing the choice between the syllabic and contracted form of *is*', in Bald & Ilson (eds) 1977: 171–189

Breivik, L. E. (1981) 'On the interpretation of existential there', *Language* 57: 1–25

Breivik, L. E. (1990 [1983]) *Existential 'there'. A Synchronic and Diachronic Study*. Studia Anglistica Norvegica 2, Oslo: Novus

Bublitz, W. (1988) *Supportive Fellow-speakers and Cooperative Conversations*, Amsterdam: John Benjamins

Bublitz, W. (1989) 'Ausdrücke des Kenntnisnehmens (Hörersignale) oder des Stellungsnehmens (Redebeitrage): *yes* und verwandte Formen', *Folia Linguistica* 23: 67–104

Buysschaert, B. (1982) *Criteria for the Classification of English Adverbials*, Brussels: AWLsK

Bybee, J. L. & D. L. Slobin (1982) 'Rules and schemes in the development and use of the English past tense', *Language* 58: 165–189

Caie, G., K. Haastrup, A. L. Jakobsen, J. E. Nielsen, J. Sevaldsen, H. Specht & A. Zettersten (eds) (1990) *Proceedings from the 4th Nordic Conference for English Studies* (Helsingør, 11–13 May 1989), 2 vols, Department of English, University of Copenhagen

Carter, R., & M. McCarthy (1995) 'Grammar and the spoken language', *Applied Linguistics* 16: 141–158

Channell, J. 1994. *Vague Language*, Oxford: Oxford University Press

Close, R. (1980) '*Will* in *if*-clauses', in Greenbaum, Leech, & Svartvik 1980: 100–109

Coates, J. (1977) 'A corpus study of modifiers in sequence', in Bald & Ilson (eds) 1977: 9–27

Coates, J. (1980) 'On the non-equivalence of *may* and *can*', *Lingua* 50: 209–220

Coates, J. (1983) *The Semantics of the Modal Auxiliaries*, London: Croom Helm

Coates, J. (1987) 'Epistemic modality and spoken discourse', *Transactions of the Philological Society* 110–131

Coates, J. (1995) 'The expression of root and epistemic possibility in English', in Aarts & Meyer 1995: 145–156

Coates, J. & G. N. Leech (1980) 'The meanings of the modals in modern British and American English', *York Papers in Linguistics* 8: 23–34

*Collins COBUILD Grammar Patterns 1: Verbs* (1996) London: HarperCollins

Collins, P. (1985) '*Th*-clefts and *all*-clefts' *Beiträge zur Phonetik und Linguistik* 48: 45–53

Collins. P. (1988) 'The semantics of some modals in contemporary Australian English', *Australian Journal of Linguistics* 8: 261–286

Collins, P. (1991) *Cleft and Pseudo-cleft Constructions in English*, London & New York: Routledge

Collins, P. (1994) 'The structure of English comparative clauses', *English Studies* 75: 157–165

Collins, P. (1996) '*Get*-passives in English', *World Englishes* 15: 43–56

Conrad, S. (1996) 'Investigating academic texts with corpus-based techniques: an example from biology', *Linguistics and Education* 8: 299–326

Conrad, S., & D. Biber (forthcoming) 'Adverbial marking of stance in speech and writing', *Evaluation in Discourse*, ed. by S. Hunston, London: HarperCollins

Crystal, D. (1980) 'Neglected grammatical factors in conversational English', in Greenbaum, Leech, & Svartvik (eds) 1980: 153–166

Dubois, B. L. (1972) 'Meaning and distribution of the perfect in present-day American English prose', unpublished Ph.D. dissertation, DAI 33/ 12–A, 6892f, University of New Mexico

Dušková, L. (1971a) 'Some quantitative aspects of continuous forms in present-day English', *Prague Studies in English* 14: 7–39

Dušková, L. (1971b) 'On some functional and stylistic aspects of the passive voice in present-day English', *Philologica Pragensia* 14: 117–144

Ehrman, M. (1966) *The Meanings of the Modals in Present-day American English*, The Hague: Mouton

Ellegård, A. (1978) *The syntactic structure of English texts*, Gothenburg Studies in English 43, Gothenburg: Acta Universitatis Gothoburgensis

Elsness, J. (1981) 'On the syntactic and semantic functions of *that*-clauses', in Johansson & Tysdahl (eds) 1981: 281–303, Department of English, Oslo University

Elsness, J. (1982) '*That* v. zero connective in English nominal clauses', *ICAME News* 6: 1–45

Elsness, J. (1984) '*That* or zero? A look at the choice of object clause connective in a corpus of American English', *English Studies* 65: 519–533

Elsness, J. (1997) *The Perfect and the Preterite in Contemporary and Earlier English*, Berlin & New York: Mouton de Gruyter

Enkvist, N. E. (ed.) (1982) *Impromptu Speech: A Symposium*. Publications of the Research Institute of the Åbo Akademi Foundation 78, Åbo: Åbo Akademi

Erman, B. (1986) 'Some pragmatic expressions in English conversation', in Tottie & Bäcklund (eds) 1986: 131–147

Erman, B. (1987) *Pragmatic Expressions in English. A Study of 'you know', 'you see' and 'I mean' in Face-to-face Conversation*, Stockholm Studies in English 69, Stockholm: Almqvist & Wiksell

Fletcher, P. & M. Garman (1995) 'Transcription, segmentation and analysis: corpora for the language impaired', in Leech et al. (eds) 1995: 116–127

Fox, B. A., & S. A. Thompson (1990) 'A discourse explanation of the grammar of relative clauses in English conversation', *Language* 66: 297–316

Francis, G. (1991) 'Nominal groups and clause structure', *Word* 42: 145–156

Francis, W. N. (1992) 'A versatile suffix: English -*en*', *Om språk og utdanning, Festskrift til Eva Sivertsen*, ed. by A.-M. Langvall Olsen & A. M. Simensen, 45–54, Oslo: Universitetsforlaget

Fries, U. (1993) 'The comparison of monosyllabic adjectives', in *The Noun Phrase in English: Its Structure and Variability. Anglistik & Englischunterricht*: 49. Heidelberg: C. Winter, pp. 25–44

Geisler, C. (1992) 'Relative Infinitives in spoken and written English', in Leitner (ed.) 1992: 213–230

Geisler, C. (1995) *Relative Infinitives in English*, Stockholm: Almqvist & Wiksell

Geluykens, R. (1984) 'Focus phenomena in English. An empirical investigation into cleft and pseudoleft sentences', *Antwerp Papers in Linguistics* 36, University of Antwerp

Geluykens, R. (1987) 'Tails (right-dislocations) as a repair mechanism in English conversation', in *Getting One's Words into Line: On Word Order and Functional Grammar*, J. Nuyts & G. de Schutter (eds), 119–129, Dordrecht: Foris

Geluykens, R. (1988) 'Five types of clefting in English discourse', *Linguistics* 26: 823–841

Geluykens, R. (1991) 'Information flow in English conversation: a new approach to the given-new distinction', in *Functional and Systemic Linguistics: Approaches and Uses*, E. Ventola (ed), 141–167, Berlin: Mouton de Gruyter

Geluykens, R. (1992) *From Discourse Process to Grammatical Construction: On Left-dislocation in English*, Amsterdam: John Benjamins

Gnutzmann, C., R. Ilson & J. Webster (1973) 'Comparative constructions in contemporary English', *English Studies* 54: 417–438

Granger, S. (1983) *The 'be' + past participle Construction in Spoken English with Special Emphasis on the Passive*, Amsterdam: North-Holland

Greenbaum, S. (1969) *Studies in English Adverbial usage*, London: Longman

Greenbaum, S. (1984) 'Corpus analysis and elicitation tests', in Aarts & Meijs (eds) 1984: 193–201

Greenbaum, S. (1988) 'Syntactic devices for compression in English', in Klegraf & Nehls (eds) 1988: 3–10

Greenbaum, S. & G. Nelson (1995a) 'Nuclear and peripheral clauses in speech and writing', in G. Melchers and B. Warren, *Studies in Anglistics*, 181–190, Stockholm: Almqvist & Wiksell

Greenbaum, S. & G. Nelson (1995b) 'Clause relationships in spoken and written English', *Functions of Language* 2.1: 1–21

Greenbaum, S. & G. Nelson (1996) 'Positions of adverbial clauses in British English', *World Englishes* 15: 69–81

Greenbaum, S., G. Nelson & M. Weitzman (1996) 'Complement clauses in English', in Thomas & Short (eds) 1996: 76–92

Gustafsson, M. (1982) 'Textual aspects of topicalization in a corpus of English', *ICAME News* 6: 46–76

Gustafsson, M. (1983) 'Fronting of adverbials in four genres of English', in Jacobson (ed.) 1983: 7–17

Haan, P. de (1984) 'Relative clauses compared', *ICAME News* 8: 47–59

Haan, P. de (1987) 'Relative clauses in indefinite noun phrases', *English Studies* 68: 171–190

Haan, P. de (1988) 'A corpus investigation into the behaviour of prepositional verbs', in Kytö et al. (eds) 1988: 121–135

Haan, P. de (1989) *Postmodifying Clauses in the English Noun Phrase. A Corpus-based Study*, Amsterdam: Rodopi

Haan, P. de (1990) 'Structure frequency counts of modern English: the set-up of a quantitative study', *Dutch Working Papers in English Language and Linguistics* 13: 1–15

Haase, I. (1988) 'Temporafolge und Bedingungstyp im Konditionalen Satzgefuge', in Mindt (ed.) 1988: 69–76

Haegeman, L. (1983) *The Semantics of 'will' in Present-day British English: a Unified Account*, Brussels: AWLsK

Haegeman, L. (1984) 'Pragmatic conditionals in English', *Folia Linguistica* 13: 485–502

Hardy, D., & A. Leuchtmann (1996) 'Topic versus cohesion in the prediction of causal ordering in English conversation', *Discourse Processes* 21: 237–254

Hasselgård, H. (1991) 'Sequences of temporal and spatial adverbials in spoken English: some pragmatic considerations', *ICAME Journal* 15: 3–17

Hasselgård, H. (1992) 'Sequences of spatial and temporal adverbials in spoken and written English', in Leitner (ed.) 1992: 319–328

Hasselgård, H. (1993) 'Sequences of time and space adverbials in clause-initial position: a survey of ordering principles', in *Proceedings from the 5th Nordic Association of English Studies Conference*, Reykjavik 1992, 45–57, J. D'Arcy (ed), Reykjavik: University of Iceland Publishing Co.

Hasselgård, H. (1996) *Where and when? Positional and Functional Conventions for Sequences of Time and Space Adverbials in Present-day English*, Acta Humaniora 3, Oslo: Universitetsforlaget

Helt, M. E. (1997) 'Discourse marker and stance adverbial variation in spoken American English: a corpus-based analysis', unpublished Ph.D. dissertation, Northern Arizona University

Hermerén, L. (1978) *On Modality in English: A Study of the Semantics of the Modals*, Lund Studies in English 53, Lund: Lund University Press

Hermerén, L. (1978) 'Testing the meanings of modals', *Studia Anglica Posnaniensia* 10: 137–140

Hermerén, L. (1986) 'Modalities in spoken and written English. An inventory of forms', in Tottie & Bäcklund (eds) 1986: 57–91

Huddleston, R. (1971) *The Sentence in Written English: A Syntactic Study Based on an Analysis of Scientific Texts*, Cambridge: Cambridge University Press

Hudson, J. (1990) 'A computerized study of multi-word fixed-phrase adverbials', in Caie et al. (eds) 1990: 335–341

Hunt, K.W. (1965) 'Grammatical structures written at three grade levels', NCTE Research Report No. 3, Champaign, Illinois: National Council of Teachers of English

Hurk, I. van den, L. Kager, L. Kemp & M. Masereeuw (1984) 'To strand or not to', *ICAME News* 8: 71–83

Hüllen, W. (1987) 'On denoting time in discourse', in *Grammar in the Construction of Texts*, J. Monaghan (ed), 50–64, London: Frances Pinter

Ikegami, Y. (1989) 'Have + object + past participle' and 'get + object + past participle' in the SEU Corpus', in *Meaning and Beyond*, U. Fries & M. Heusser (eds), Tübingen: Gunter Narr Verlag

Jacobson, S. (ed.) (1980) *Papers from the Scandinavian Symposium on Syntactic Variation* (Stockholm, 18–19 May 1979), Stockholm Studies in English 52, Stockholm: Almqvist & Wiksell

Jacobson, S. (1982) 'Modality nouns and the choice between *to* + infinitive and *of* + *ing*', *Studia Anglica Posnaniensia* 15: 61–71

Jacobson, S. (ed) (1983) *Papers from the Scandinavian Symposium on Syntactic Variation* (Stockholm, 15–16 May, 1982), Stockholm Studies in English 57, Stockholm: Almqvist & Wiksell

Jacobson, S. (1985) 'Form vs. meaning in noun phrases with an *of*-construction', in *Papers from the 8th Scandinavian Conference of Linguistics*, O. Togeby (ed), 426–436, Institut for Nordisk Filologi, University of Copenhagen

Jacobson, S. (ed) (1986) *Papers from the 3rd Scandinavian Symposium on Syntactic Variation* (Stockholm, 11–12 May 1985), Stockholm Studies in English 65, Stockholm: Almqvist & Wiksell

Jacobson, S. (1989) 'Some observations on article variation in English', in Odenstedt & Persson (eds) 1989: 99–108

Jahr, M-C. (1981) 'The s-genitive with non-personal nouns in present-day British and American English', *ICAME News* 5: 14–31

Johannesson, N.-L. (1982) 'On the use of post-modification in English noun phrases', in *The 8th LACUS Forum 1981*, W. Gutwinski & G. Jolly (eds), 187–195, Columbia, S.C.: Hornbeam Press

Johansson, C. (1993) 'Whose and of which with nonpersonal antecedents in written and spoken English', in Souter & Atwell (eds) 1993: 97–116

Johansson, C. (1995) *The Relativizers whose and of which in Present-day English. Description and Theory*, Stockholm: Almqvist & Wiksell

Johansson, S. (1980) *Plural Attributive Nouns in Present-day English*, Lund Studies in English 59, Lund: Lund University Press

Johansson, S. & B. Tysdahl (eds) (1981) *Papers from the 1st Nordic Conference for English Studies (Oslo, 17–19 September 1980)*, Department of English, University of Oslo

Johansson, S. (1986) 'Some observations on the order of adverbial particles and objects in the LOB Corpus', in Jacobson (ed.) 1986: 51–62

Johansson, S. (1995) 'Some aspects of verb-adverb combinations', in Aarts & Meyer (eds) 1995: 219–240

Johansson, S. & E. H. Norheim (1988) 'The subjunctive in British and American English', *ICAME Journal* 12: 27–36

Johansson, S. & S. Oksefjell (1996) 'Towards a unified account of the syntax and semantics of GET', in Thomas & Short (eds) 1996: 57–75

Kennedy, G. (1987) 'Expressing temporal frequency in academic English', *TESOL Quarterly* 21: 69–86

Kennedy, G. (1987) 'Quantification and the use of English: a case study of one aspect of the learner's task', *Applied Linguistics* 8: 264–286

Kirk, J. M. (1988) 'Inter-corpus comparisons. The primary verb BE', in *Proceedings of the XIII ALLC Conference*, Norwich, 1986, J. Hamesse (ed), 123–133

Kjellmer, G. (1979) 'On clause-introductory *nor* and *neither*', *English Studies* 60: 280–295

Kjellmer, G. (1980) '*Accustomed to swim*: *accustomed to swimming*. On verbal forms after *to*', in Allwood & Ljung (eds) 1980: 75–99

Kjellmer, G. (1980) '"There is no hiding you in the house": on a modal use of the English gerund', *English Studies* 61: 47–60

Kjellmer, G. (1982) '*Each other* and *one another*. On the use of the English reciprocal pronouns', *English Studies* 63: 231–254

Kjellmer, G. (1982) 'What to do? On non-finite direct questions in English', *English Studies* 63: 446454

Kjellmer, G. (1983) '"He is one of the few men in history who plays jazz on a violin". On number concord in certain relative clauses', *Anglia* 101: 299–314

Kjellmer, G. (1984) 'On the grammatical number of relative *what*', *English Studies* 65: 256–273

Kjellmer, G. (1985) '*Help to/help* revisited', *English Studies* 66: 156–161

Kjellmer, G. (1986) '"Us Anglos are a cut above the field": On objective pronouns in nominative contexts', *English Studies* 67: 445–449

Kjellmer, G. (1988) '"What a night on which to die!" On symmetry in English relative clauses', *English Studies* 69: 559–568

Kjellmer, G. (1989) '*Even if* and *even though*', *English Studies* 70: 256–269

Kjellmer, G. (1992) '*Old as he was*: a note on concessiveness and causality', *English Studies* 73: 337–350

Krogvig, I. & S. Johansson (1984) '*Shall* and *will* in British and American English: a frequency study', *Studia Linguistica* 38: 70–87

Krug, M. (1994) 'Contractions in spoken and written English: a corpus-based study of brachychronic language change', unpublished M.A. thesis, University of Exeter

Kussmaul, P. (1978) '*In fact, actually, anyway*: Indikatoren von Sprechakten in Informellen Gesprochenen Englisch', *Die Neueren Sprachen* 27: 357–369

Lange, D. (1988) 'Tempusrelationen und Verben im Zusammenhang mit *that*-clauses', in Mindt (ed) 1988: 84–93

Leech, G. & J. Coates (1980) 'Semantic indeterminacy and the modals', in Greenbaum, Leech & Svartvik (eds) 1980: 79–90

Leech G. & J. Culpeper (1997) 'The comparison of adjectives in recent British English', in T. Nevalai-

nen & L. Kahlas-Tarkka (eds) *To Explain the Present: Studies in the Changing English Language in Honour of Matti Rissanen*, 353–374, Helsinki: Société Néophilologique

Leech, G. & Li, L. (1995) 'Indeterminacy between noun phrases and adjective phrases as complements of the English verb', in Aarts & Meyer 1995: 183–202

Leech, G., B. Francis & X. Xu (1994) 'The use of computer corpora in the textual demonstrability of gradience in linguistic categories', in *Continuity in Linguistic Semantics*, C. Fuchs & B. Victorri (eds) 57–76, Amsterdam: John Benjamins

Leitner, G. (ed.) (1992) *New Directions in English Language Corpora. Methodology, Results, Software Developments*, Berlin: Mouton de Gruyter

Leitzke, E. (1989) *(De)nominale Adjektive im heutigen Englisch. Untersuchungen zur Morphologie, Syntax, Semantik und Pragmatik von Adjektiv-Nomen-Kombinationen der Typen 'atomic energy' und 'criminal lawyer'*, Tübingen: Max Niemeyer

Lindblad, I. & M. Ljung (eds) (1987) *Proceedings from the 3rd Nordic Conference for English Studies (Hässelby, 25–27 September 1986)*, 2 vols. Stockholm Studies in English 73, Stockholm: Almqvist & Wiksell

Magnusson, U. (1989) 'The verb *do* in the LOB Corpus', in Odenstedt & Persson (eds) 1989: 131–145

Mair, C. (1987) '*For/to*-infinitival clauses in contemporary British English. A study based on the material collected in the Survey of English Usage, University College London', *English Studies* 68: 545–559

Mair, C. (1987) 'Tough-movement in present-day British English. A corpus-based study', *Studia Linguistica* 41: 59–71

Mair, C. (1987) 'Instabile Infinitivkonstruktionen im heutigen Englisch', *Linguistische Berichte* 3: 381–397

Mair, C. (1988) 'Extraposed gerundial subject clauses in present-day British English. An investigation of the corpus of the Survey of English Usage, University College London', *Arbeiten aus Anglistik und Amerikanistik* 13: 51–63

Mair, C. (1990) *Infinitival Complement Clauses in English: A Study in Discourse*, Cambridge: Cambridge University Press

Mair, C. (1994) 'Is *see* becoming a conjunction? The study of grammaticalisation as a meeting ground for corpus linguistics and grammatical theory', in Fries et al. (eds) 1994: 127–137

Mair, C. (1995) 'Changing patterns of complementation, and concomitant grammaticalisation, of the verb *help* in present-day British English', in Aarts & Meyer (eds) 1995: 258–272

McCarthy, M. J. and Carter, R. A. (1997) 'Grammar, tails and affect: constructing expressive choices in discourse', *Text* 17 (3), 405–429

Meijs, W. (1984) '"You can do so if you want to"—some elliptic structures in Brown and LOB and their syntactic description', in Aarts & Meijs (eds) 1984: 141–162

Meijs, W (ed.) (1987) *Corpus Linguistics and Beyond. Proceedings of the 7th International Conference on*

*English Language Research on Computerized Corpora*, Amsterdam: Rodopi

Meyer, C. F. (1987) *A Linguistic Study of American Punctuation*, Frankfurt am Main: Peter Lang

Meyer, C. F. (1987) 'Apposition in English', *Journal of English Linguistics* 20: 101–121

Meyer, C. F. (1989) 'Restrictive apposition: an intermediate category', *English Studies* 70: 147–166

Meyer, C. F. (1991) 'A corpus-based study of apposition in English', in Aijmer & Altenberg (eds) 1991: 166–181

Meyer, C. F. (1991) *Apposition in Contemporary English*, Cambridge: Cambridge University Press

Meyer, C. F. (1995) 'Coordination ellipsis in spoken and written American English', *Language Sciences* 17: 241–269

Meyer, C. F. (1996) 'Coordinate structures in English', *World Englishes* 15: 29–41

Mindt, D. (1987) *Sprache. Grammatik, Unterrichtsgrammatik: Futurischer Zeitbezug im Englischen I*, Frankfurt am Main: Diesterweg (Schule und Forschung, Schrifenreihe für Studium und Praxis)

Mindt, D. (1988) *EDV in der angewandten Linguistik. Ziele—Methode Ergebnisse*, Frankfurt am Main: Diesterweg

Mindt, D. (1995) *An Empirical Grammar of the English Verb: Modal Verbs*, Berlin: Cornelsen Verlag

Myhill, J. (1995) 'Change and continuity in the functions of the American English modals', *Linguistics* 33: 157–211

Myhill, J. (1997) '*Should* and *ought*: the rise of individually oriented modality in American English', *English Language and Linguistics* 1: 3–23

Nakamura, J. (1991) 'The relationships among genres in the LOB corpus based upon the distribution of grammatical tags', *JACET* (The Japan Association of College English Teachers) *Bulletin* 22: 55–74

Nakamura, J. (1992) 'The comparison of the Brown and the LOB corpora based upon the distribution of grammatical tags', *Journal of Foreign Languages and Literature* 3: 43–58, College of General Education, University of Tokushima

Nakamura, J. (1993) 'Quantitative comparison of modals in the Brown and LOB corpora', *ICAME Journal* 17: 29–48

Nässlin, S. (1984) *The English Tag Question: A Study of Sentences Containing Tags of the Type 'isn't it?' and 'is it?'* Stockholm Studies in English 60, Stockholm: Almqvist & Wiksell

Nattinger, J. R. & J. S. DeCarrico (1992) *Lexical Phrases and Language Teaching*, Oxford: Oxford University Press

Nehls, D. (1988) 'Der englische Verbalaspekt', in Bald 1988b: 192–208

Nevalainen, T. & M. Rissanen (1986) ' "Do you support the do-support?" Emphatic and non-emphatic DO in affirmative statements in present-day spoken English', in Jacobson (ed.) 1986: 35–50

Noël, J. (1993) 'Adjectives and nouns with reported clauses' *ICAME Journal* 17: 49–71

Odenstedt, B. & G. Persson (eds) (1989) *Instead of Flowers. Papers in Honour of Mats Rydén on the Occasion of his 60th Birthday*, Umeå Studies in the Humanities 90, Stockholm: Almqvist & Wiksell

Olofsson, A. (1981) *Relative Junctions in Written American English*, Gothenburg studies in English 50, Gothenburg: Acta Universitatis Gothoburgensis

Olofsson, A. (1990) 'A participle caught in the act. On the prepositional use of *following*', *Studia Neophilologica* 62: 23–35

Oostdijk, N. (1984) 'An extended affix grammar for the English noun phrase', in Aarts & Meijs (eds) 1984: 95–122

Oostdijk, N. (1986) 'Coordination and gapping in corpus analysis', in Aarts & Meijs (eds) 1986: 177–201

Oostdijk, N. (1988) 'A corpus linguistic approach to linguistic variation', *Literary and Linguistic Computing* 3: 12–25

Oostdijk, N & P. de Haan (1994) 'Clause patterns in Modern British English: a corpus-based (quantitative) study', *ICAME Journal* 18: 41–79

Opdahl, L. (1990) '*Close* or *closely* as verb modifier? In search of explanatory parameters', in Caie et al. (eds) 1990: 201–212

Opdahl, L. (1991) '*-ly* as adverbial suffix: corpus and elicited material compared', *ICAME Journal* 15: 19–35

Övergaard, G. (1987) 'Duration, progression, and the progressive form in temporal *as*-clauses', in Lindblad & Ljung (eds) 1987: 265–280

Övergaard, G. (1992) 'On the use of the mandative subjunctive in English language the time machine', in *Papers in Honour of Bengt Odenstedt*, L.-E. Edlund & G. Persson (eds), 203–227, Stockholm: Almqvist & Wiksell

Palmer, F.R. (1988) *The English Verb*, 2nd edn, London: Longman

Paradis, C. (1997) *Degree Modifiers of Adjectives in Spoken British English*, Lund: Lund University Press

Persson. G. (1974) *Repetition in English. Part 1: Sequential Repetition*, Stockholm: Almqvist & Wiksell

Persson. G. (1989) 'On the semantics of collective nouns in English', in Odenstedt & Persson (eds) 1989: 179–188

Prince, E. F. (1978) 'A comparison of *wh*-clefts and *it*-clefts in discourse', *Language* 54: 883–906

Quirk, R. (1960) 'Towards a description of English usage', *Transactions of the Philological Society*, 40–61

Quirk, R. (1965) 'Descriptive statement and serial relationship', *Language* 41: 205–217

Quirk, R. (1970) 'Aspect and variant inflexion in English verbs', *Language* 46: 300–311

Quirk, R. (1984) 'Recent work on adverbial realisation and position', in Aarts & Meijs (eds) 1984: 185–192

Quirk, R., A. Duckworth, J. Rusiecki, J. Svartvik & A. Colin (1964) 'Studies in the correspondence of prosodic to grammatical features in English', in *Proceedings of the 9th International Congress of Linguists*, 679–691, The Hague: Mouton

Randow, E. Von. (1986) *Valente Substantive des Englischen*. Tübinger Beiträge zur Linguistik 294, Tübingen: Gunter Narr Verlag

Ringbom, H. & M. Rissanen (eds) (1984) *Proceedings from the 2nd Nordic Conference for English Studies* (Hanasaari/Hanaholmen, 19–21 May 1983). Publications of the Research Institute of the Åbo Akademi Foundation 92. Åbo: Åbo Akademi

Rissanen, M. (1980) 'On the position of *only* in present day written English', in Jacobson (ed) 1980: 63–76

Rudanko, J. (1991) 'On verbs governing *-ing* in present-day English', *English Studies* 72: 55–72

Rudanko, J. (1992) '*Resorting to* and *turning to*: on verbs governing *-ing to* in present-day English', *English Studies* 73: 68–79

Rudanko, J. (1995) '*Balking at* and *working at*: on verbs governing *-ing at* in present-day English', *English Studies* 76: 264–281

Rusiecki, J. (1985) *Adjectives and Comparison in English. A semantic study*. London: Longman

Rycker, T. De. (1984) *Imperative Structures: Form and Function in Conversational English*. Antwerp Papers in Linguistics 38, Department of Linguistics, University of Antwerp

Sahlin, E. (1979) "*Some*" *and* "*any*" *in spoken and written English*, Studia Anglistica Upsaliensia 38, Stockholm: Almqvist & Wiksell

Schiffrin, D. (1981) 'Tense variation in narrative', *Language* 57: 45–62

Schiffrin, D. (1985a) Multiple constraints on discourse options: a quantitative analysis of causal sequences', *Discourse Processes* 8: 281–303

Schiffrin, D. (1985b) 'Conversational coherence: the role of *well*', *Language* 61: 640–667

Schneider, E. W. (1992) '*Who(m)*? Case marking of *wh*-pronouns in written British and American English', in Leitner (ed.) 1992: 231–245

Souter, C. & E. Atwell (eds) (1993) *Corpus-based Computational Linguistics*. Amsterdam: Rodopi

Stein, G. (1979) *Studies in the Function of the Passive*, Tübingen: Narr

Stein, G. & R. Quirk (1991) 'On having a look in a corpus', in Aijmer & Altenberg (eds) 1991: 197–203

Stenström, A.-B. (1982) 'Feedback', in Enkvist (ed.) 1982: 319–340

Stenström, A.-B. (1983) 'Questioning strategies in English and Swedish conversation', in *Cross-language Analysis and Second Language Acquisition 2*, K. Sajavaara (ed), 67–78, Jyväskylä Cross Language Studies 10, Jyväskylä: University of Jyväskylä

Stenström, A.-B. (1984a) 'Discourse tags', in Aarts & Meijs (eds) 1984: 65–81

Stenström, A.-B. (1984b) *Questions and Responses in English Conversation*, Lund Studies in English 68, Lund: Lund University Press

Stenström, A.-B. (1986) 'What does *really* really do? Strategies in speech and writing', in Tottie & Bäcklund (eds) 1986: 149–163, reprinted in *Grammar in the Construction of Texts*, J. Monaghan (ed.), 65–79, London: Frances Pinter, 1987

Stenström, A.-B. (1986) 'A study of pauses as demarcators in discourse and syntax', in Aarts & Meijs (eds) 1986: 203–218

Stenström, A.-B. (1987) 'Carry-on signals in English conversation', in Meijs (ed.) 1987: 87–119

Stenström, A.-B. (1990) 'What is the role of discourse signals in sentence grammar?', in Aarts & Meijs (eds) 1990: 213–229

Stenström, A.-B. (1995) 'Some remarks on comment clauses', in Aarts & Meyer (eds) 1995: 290–301

Stenström, A.-B. & J. Svartvik (1993) 'Imparsable speech: repeats and other nonfluencies in spoken English', in Oostdijk & de Haan (eds) 1993: 241–254

Svartvik, J. (1966) *On Voice in the English Verb*, The Hague: Mouton

Svartvik, J. (1968) 'Plotting divided usage with *dare* and *need*', *Studia Neophilologica* 40: 130–140

Svartvik, J. (1980) '*Well* in conversation', in Greenbaum, Leech, & Svartvik (eds) 1980: 167–177

Svartvik, J. (1982) 'The segmentation of impromptu speech', in Enkvist (ed.) 1982: 131–145

Svartvik, J. & O. Ekedahl (1995) 'Verbs in public and private speaking', in Aarts & Meyer (eds) 1995: 273–289

Sørheim, M-C.J. (1981) 'The genitive in a functional sentence perspective', in Johansson & Tysdahl (eds) 1981: 405–423

Taglicht, J. (1977) 'Relative clauses as postmodifiers: meaning, syntax and intonation', in Bald & Ilson (eds) 1977: 73–107

Taglicht, J. (1983) *Message and Emphasis*, London: Longman

Taglicht, J. (1988) 'Relative clauses in English', in Bald 1988b: 244–253

Tesch, F. (1988) '*Some* und *any* in affirmativen und negativen Kontexten', in Mindt (ed.) 1988: 59–68

Tesch, F. (1990) *Die Indefinitpronomina 'some' und 'any' im Autentischen Englischen Sprachgebrauch und in Lehrwerken*, Tübingen: Gunter Narr

Thavenius, C. (1983) *Referential Pronouns in English Conversation*, Lund Studies in English 64, Lund: Lund University Press

Thavenius, C. (1984) 'Pronominal chains in English conversation', in Ringbom & Rissanen (eds) 1984: 209–219

Thompson, S. A. (1983) 'Grammar and discourse: the English detached participial clause', in *Discourse Perspectives on Syntax*, F. Klein-Andreu (ed), 43–65, New York: Academic Press

Thompson, S. A. (1985) 'Grammar and written discourse: initial versus final purpose clauses in English', *Text* 5: 55–84

Thompson, S. A. & A. Mulac (1991a) 'The discourse conditions for the use of the complementizer *that* in conversational English', *Journal of Pragmatics* 15: 237–251

Thompson, S. A. & A. Mulac (1991a) 'A quantitative perspective on the grammaticization of epistemic parentheticals in English', in *Approaches to Grammaticalization: Volume II*, E.C. Traugott and B. Heine (eds), Amsterdam: John Benjamins

Tottie, G. (1980) 'Affixal and non-affixal negation. Two systems in (almost) complementary distribution', *Studia Linguistica* 34: 101–123

Tottie, G. (1981) 'Negation and discourse strategy in spoken and written English', in *Variation Omnibus*,

H. Cedergren & D. Sankoff (eds), 271–284, Edmonton, Alberta: Linguistic Research

Tottie, G. (1982) 'Where do negative sentences come from?' *Studia Linguistica* 36: 88–105

Tottie, G. (1983) *Much about 'not' and 'nothing': A Study of the Variation between Analytic and Synthetic Negation in Contemporary American English*, Lund: CWK Gleerup

Tottie, G. (1983) 'The missing link? or, Why is there twice as much negation in spoken English as in written English?' in Jacobson (ed) 1983: 67–74

Tottie, G. (1984) 'Is there an adverbial in this text? (And if so, what is it doing there?)', in Ringbom & Rissanen (eds) 1984: 299–315

Tottie, G. (1986) 'The importance of being adverbial. Adverbials of focusing and contingency in spoken and written English', in Tottie & Bäcklund (eds) 1986: 93–118

Tottie, G. (1988) 'No-negation and not-negation in spoken and written English', in Kytö et al. (eds) 1988: 245–265

Tottie, G. (1991) *Negation in English Speech and Writing. A Study in Variation*, San Diego: Academic Press

Tottie, G. & G. Övergaard (1984) 'The author's would. A feature of American English?' *Studia Linguistica* 38: 148–165

Tottie, G. & C. Paradis (1982) 'From function to structure. Some pragmatic determinants of syntactic frequencies in impromptu speech', in Enkvist (ed.) 1982: 307–317

Vandepitte, S. (1993) *A Pragmatic Study of the Expression and the Interpretation of Causality Conjuncts and Conjunctions in Modern Spoken British English*, Verhandelingen van de Koninklijke Academie voor Wetenschappen, Letteren en Schone Kunsten van België, Turnhout (Belgium): Brepols Publishers

Varantola, K. (1984) *On Noun Phrase Structures in Engineering English*, Turku: University of Turku

Viitanen, O. (1986) 'On the position of *only* in English conversation', in Tottie & Bäcklund (eds) 1986: 165–175

Virtanen, T. (1992a) 'Temporal adverbials in text structuring: on temporal text strategy', in *Nordic Research on Text and Discourse, NORDTEXT Symposium 1990*, A.-C. Lindeberg, N. E. Enkvist & K. Wikberg (eds), 185–197. Åbo: Åbo Academy Press

Virtanen, T. (1992b) *Discourse Functions of Adverbial Placement in English*, Åbo: Åbo Akademy Press

Wales, K. (1996) *Personal Pronouns in Present-day English*, Cambridge: Cambridge University Press

Warren, B. (1978) *Semantic Patterns of Noun-noun Compounds*, Gothenburg Studies in English 41, Gothenburg: Acta Universitatis Gothoburgensis

Warren, B. (1984) *Classifying Adjectives*, Gothenburg Studies in English 56, Gothenburg: Acta Universitatis Gothoburgensis

Warren, B. (1987) 'A certain misclassification', in Lindblad & Ljung (eds) 1987: 363–377

Wekker, H. (1976) *The Expression of Future Time in Contemporary British English*, Amsterdam: North-Holland

Westney, P. (1986) 'How to be more or less certain in English: scalarity in epistemic modality', *IRAL* 24: 311–320

Wikberg, K. (1989) 'On the role of the lexical verb in discourse', in *Essays on English Language in Honour of Bertil Sundby*, L. E. Breivik, A. Hille & S. Johansson (eds), 375–388. Studia Anglistica Norvegica 4, Oslo: Novus Forlag

Wikberg, K. (1993) 'Verbs as indicators of text type and/or style: some observations on the LOB Corpus', in Souter & Atwell (eds) 1993: 127–145

# Lexical index

# W

wager 666
wages 594
wages council 594
waggishly 968
wait 367, 382–3, 472, 474, 694, 703
wait for 416, 694
wait for/with 481
waiter 314
waitress 314
wake up 408
walk 367, 382, 471, 474, 955
wanna 707
want 159, 174, 343, 362–3, 368, 371, 373–4, 382, 434, 454, 459, 464, 472–4, 481, 659, 696–7, 702, 705, 707, 709–12, 740–1, 743–4, 750, 752, 755, 968, 989, 993–5, 999–1000, 1002–4, 1007–11, 1050
want to 484, 751, 994, 1009
want(s) 711
war 593
-wards 540
warm 441, 445
warn 370, 665, 693, 696, 700, 710
warn (NP about) 742, 755
  be warned about 742
warning 68
was 1007, 1058, 1123
was based 474
was saying/thinking 472
wash 593
wash out 148
washed 148
watch 367, 382, 472–3, 481, 686, 701, 706, 742
water 592–3
water authorities 593
water balloon 593
wave 459, 464
way 626, 628ff., 633–4, 654–5, 988, 1016–18
  the way 448
ways 1016
we 328–9, 331, 334ff., 939, 1002, 1057
we all 329
we'd 1062
we'll 1061
we're 1061
we've 1061
we—us 335ff.
weak 445
weaker 537
wealthy 522

wear 367, 382, 472
wed 396–7
wedded 397
weekend 593
weekly 60
weirdos 285
welcome 370, 718, 743, 745
welfare 593
well 140, 148, 442, 539, 542, 547–8, 561, 563, 1000, 1002, 1024, 1046, 1054, 1074, 1086–7, 1096, 1118
well be 999
well-known 673
went 358, 1031
went to 1009
were 851, 919ff., 1058, 1123
wet 444
wh- 612
*wh*-clause 563, 602, 646ff., 909, 996, 1001, 1003, 1005, 1009
wh-cleft 958ff.
*wh*-question 405, 996, 1001 1008–9, 1024–5, 1081ff., 1107
*wh*-word 204–5, 405, 899–900, 909ff., 920, 1066ff., 1100
wharf—wharfs/wharves 286
what 87, 205, 406, 609ff., 683, 687, 994–5, 1000, 1002–3, 1005–6, 1008–9, 1011, 1024, 1124
what for 108
what on earth 1025
what's 1024
what? 1092
whatever 920
when 87, 194–5, 406, 608–9, 612, 624–5, 626ff., 823, 841–3, 998, 1003, 1050, 1057, 1059
whenever 844
where 87, 406, 608–9, 611–12, 624–30, 844, 1002–3, 1008–9
where's 186
whereas 844
wherever 844
whether 85, 646, 683, 690–2, 844, 901, 920, 1003
whether/if 690
which 87, 180, 195, 223, 584, 608ff., 615–17, 627, 629–30, 1000, 1016–18
while 77, 85, 839, 842–6, 849ff.
whilst 844
whisper 370, 459, 665
whistle 460
whit of 251

white 445, 508, 512, 514
who 87, 180, 195, 214, 336, 406, 608–9, 611ff., 1050
who knows 865
whoa 1097
whole 512–13
whom 87, 214, 608ff., 612, 614–15, 1050
whoopee 1085, 1097
whoops 1084, 1097
whose 87, 608–9, 611–12, 617–19
why 87, 204, 608ff., 612, 624–5, 627–9, 991, 995
wickedest 523
wide 59, 509
wider 524
wife—wives 286
wild 444
will 73, 165, 452, 455–6, 483–9, 495–6, 499, 502, 734, 979, 981, 1049–50, 1052
will go 501
willing 484, 530, 718–19
willingness 652–3
win 368, 382
wind up 436, 445ff.
window(s) 303
wine 244
wink 460
wire 662, 666
-wise 56, 540
wise 718, 720, 986
wisely 856
wish 370, 481, 652, 661, 663, 693, 696, 702, 706, 709, 755, 974, 989
wished 967
wistfully 968
witch 315
with 74–5, 106, 137, 415, 423, 634–6, 844, 1018, 1057
with all due respect 975
with reference to 75
with regard to 75
with respect to 75
with the exception of 75
with you 449
withdrawal 304–5
within 74
without 74
without doubt 973
withstand 490, 743
witness 463
wizard 315
wolf—wolves 286
-women 312
woman/women 594, 613–14
woman—women 286
women candidates 594

# Conceptual Index

*Note:* Headwords in **bold** type indicate major topics; page references in **bold** type indicate main reference to a particular topic; page references in *italics* indicate tables.

Compiled by Meg Davies, Registered Indexer (Society of Indexers)